Nikephoros II Phokas, 912–969

A copper *follis*
of Nikêforos II Fôkas
according to Schlumberger

Dedicated to the memory of the great Byzantinists G. Schlumberger, A. Dain and G.T. Dennis, and to the memory of the capital of the second Rome, the city of Constantinople.

Theofanô at Drizion. Nikêforos leaving for a campaign. (*Skylitzes, public domain*)

Nikephoros II Phokas, 912–969

The White Death of the Saracens

Ilkka Syvänne

Pen & Sword
MILITARY

First published in Great Britain in 2025 by
Pen & Sword Military
An imprint of Pen & Sword Books Limited
Yorkshire – Philadelphia

Copyright © Ilkka Syvänne 2025

ISBN 978 1 39900 528 9

The right of Ilkka Syvänne to be identified as
Author of this Work has been asserted by him in accordance
with the Copyright, Designs and Patents Act 1988.

A CIP catalogue record for this book is
available from the British Library.

All rights reserved. No part of this book may be reproduced,
transmitted, downloaded, decompiled or reverse engineered in
any form or by any means, electronic or mechanical including
photocopying, recording or by any information storage and retrieval
system, without permission from the Publisher in writing. No part of
this book may be used or reproduced in any manner for the purpose of
training artificial intelligence technologies or systems.

Typeset by Mac Style
Printed in the UK by CPI Group (UK) Ltd, Croydon, CR0 4YY.

The Publisher's authorised representative in the EU for product
safety is Authorised Rep Compliance Ltd., Ground Floor,
71 Lower Baggot Street, Dublin D02 P593, Ireland.
www.arccompliance.com

For a complete list of Pen & Sword titles please contact

PEN & SWORD BOOKS LIMITED
47 Church Street, Barnsley, South Yorkshire, S70 2AS, England
E-mail: enquiries@pen-and-sword.co.uk
Website: www.pen-and-sword.co.uk
or
PEN AND SWORD BOOKS
1950 Lawrence Road, Havertown, PA 19083, USA
E-mail: uspen-and-sword@casematepublishers.com
Website: www.penandswordbooks.com

'He who once sliced men more sharply than the sword
Is victim of a woman and a sabre.
He who once held the whole world in his power
Now small, is housed in but a yard of earth.'
John Bishop of Melitene,

>   tr. by Wortley in Skylitzes p.270 with small changes

'... and so he brought together eighty thousand men under
pretence of a military expedition...
And what forces! ... Nikêforos did not look for quality in them,
but only for quantity...'

>   Liudprand, *Legatio*, tr. by Wright

'... [Nikephoros Phokas the victorious = *Nikêforos Fôkas o nikêtês*]... He was neither accessible to flattery, nor inclined to anything but the truth, nor did he admit expansion of his administration towards vulgar luxury nor dissipate the imperial treasures, but always took the middle and imperial course. His appearance was also full of grace and seriousness; he was cheerful of character, but introvert where reflexion on his imperial task was concerned; always sober, showing a grave aspect on his brow; capable of both absolute earnest and subtle joking; formidable to check an enemy. It was fated, however, that even he would become a plaything of fortune and of the sway of the irrational.'

>   Psellos *Historia syntomos*, 105, pp.99, 101, tr. by W.J. Aerts

Roman and Saracen battle tactics
according to Leôn, Taktika 18.22-3, 18.108-149 (esp. 18.129)

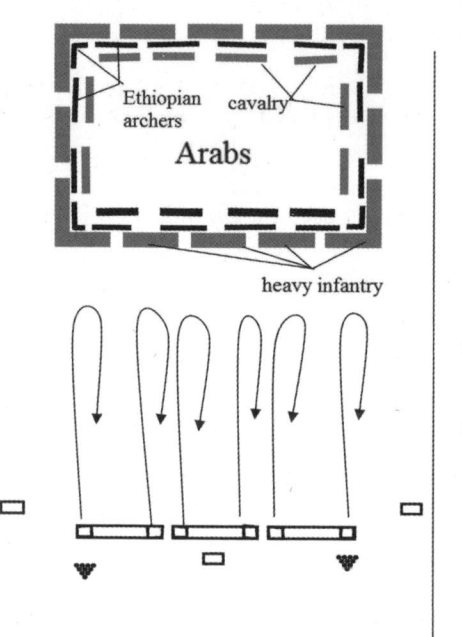

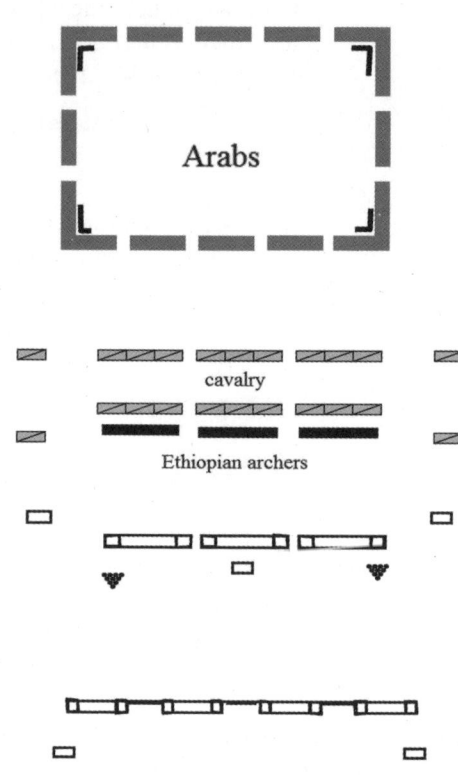

Phase 1: Roman promachoi / proklastai / koursôres skirmish to draw out the Arab cavalry and "Ethiopians".

The Arabs employed Ethiopian archers as mounted infantry accompanying their cavalry for the purpose of providing protection against the effective Roman mounted archery.

Phase 2: Arab cavalry charge out of the hollow oblong with Ethiopian mounted infantry accompanying and pursue the Roman promachoi up to the Roman promachos taxis. Once within the range of bows, the Ethiopians dismount and move in front of their cavalry and the Arab line shoots a volley of arrows which the Roman first line answers with a volley of arrows. Leôn expected that the Romans would be able to withstand this while the Arabs would be forced into flight. The Romans were expected to possess superiority in archery duels (see also PM 4.17).

Contents

Acknowledgements	ix
List of Plates	x
List of Maps	xii
Introduction	xiv
Abbreviations	xvi
Maps	xvii

Chapter 1	The Introduction	1
Chapter 2	Enemies, Neighbours and Roman Response in the 950s	58
Chapter 3	The Fôkas Family (Fôkades) (see also Appendix VI)	96
Chapter 4	The Last Years of Rômanos I Lakapênos and the Rise of the Fôkades in 941–5	103
Chapter 5	The Sole Reign of Kônstantinos VII in 945–56, Bardas Fôkas domestikos	122
Chapter 6	Nikêforos Fôkas the Younger as *domestikos tôn scholôn*: The Last Years of Kônstantinos VII in 956/7–9	186
Chapter 7	Nikêforos Fôkas the Younger as *domestikos tôn scholôn tês Anatolês* and *megas domestikos* under Rômanos II (9 November 959–15 March 963)	209
Chapter 8	The Reign of Nikêforos II Fôkas (16 August 963–11 December 969)	269
Chapter 9	Nikêforos II Fôkas: The Saint and Bearer of Victory	348

Appendix I: New Battle Formations in the Sylloge Tacticorum	353
Appendix II: De velitatione *of emperor Nikêforos Fôkas*	379
Appendix III: Nikêforos Fôkas' Military Reform and Praecepta Militaria *in ca. 957*	405
Appendix IV: The anonymous De re militari *and Fighting in the Mountains*	429

Appendix V: The Gotha Ms. and the Muslim Art of War 451
Appendix VI: Genealogical Table of the Fôkas Family 469
Notes 470
Select Bibliography 514
Index 527

St. Theodoros Tyron (Têron / Tiron)
Patmos Monastery, ca. 1200.

Note the height of the kite-shield which corresponds with the requirement to possess shields at least 140 cm in height.

Acknowledgements

First of all, I would like to thank the Commissioning Editor Phil Sidnell for accepting the proposal for a book which had been waiting on my 'bookshelf' for two decades. He also deserves a big thanks for his patience. Special thanks are also due to Matt Jones, Marketing and other staff of Pen and Sword Publishing for their stellar work and for the outstanding support they give for the author. I would also like to thank many of my friends and family for their support and patience. If there are any mistakes left, those are the sole responsibility of the author.

List of Plates

Nikêforos Fôkas leading a cavalry charge. The equipment drawn after Skylitzes. (*Author's drawing*)

Nikêforos II Fôkas in the sixteenth-century manuscript Marciana, Venice. (*Author's painting after the original*)

Imperial guardsman, Menologion of Basil II. (*Author's painting after the original*)

Nikêforos II Fôkas in Zonaras. (*Author's drawing*)

Roman cavalry AD 883. Homily of Gregory the Theologian. (*Author's painting after the original*)

Histamenon nomisma of Nikêforos II Fôkas. Constantinople mint; struck 967–9; Christ Pantokrator and Theotokos with Nikêforos. (*CNG Coins*)

Histamenon nomisma of Nikêforos II Fôkas. Constantinople mint; Struck 967–9; Christ Pantokrator and Theotokos with Nikêforos. (*CNG Coins*)

Nomisma of Nikêforos II Fôkas. Constantinople mint; struck 967–9; Christ Pantokrator and Theotokos with Nikêforos. (*CNG Coins*)

Histamenon nomisma of Iôannês Tzimiskês. Constantinople mint; struck ca.973–6; Christ Pantokrator and Tzimiskês being crowned by the Theotokos. (*CNG Coins*)

Kônstantinos VII. (*Public domain*)

Kônstantinos VII. (*Public domain*)

Roman soldiers in a tenth-century work of art. (*Public domain*)

Basileios B. Boulgaroktonos (Basil II the Bulgarslayer) depicted in a painting. This painting shows nicely how the emperors would have dressed during military campaigns. (*Public domain*)

The terrain of the landing beach as seen towards Chandax in Crete on 13 July 960. (*Author's photograph*)

The landing beach of the Roman fleet near Chandax on 13 July 960 as seen from the Castle Kules. (*Author's photograph*)

Harbaville Triptych c.950. Left: Saint Theodorus Tyro (soldier); Right: Saint Theodorus Stratelates (general). (*Public domain, Marie-Lan Nguyen*)

Harbaville Triptych c.950. Left: Saint George; Right: Saint Eustace. (*Public Domain, Marie-Lan Nguyen*)

Saint Theodore the Stratelate, Menologion of Basil II. (*Author's painting after the original*)

Marine, Menologion of Basil II. (*Author's painting after the original*)

St George (tenth century). (*Public domain*); St Demetrios (eleventh or twelfth century). (*Source: Schlumberger*)

St Theodore and St George, tenth- or eleventh-century; St Demetrios and St George, tenth- or eleventh-century. (*Source: Schlumberger*)

A stone medallion depicting an unknown emperor located in Venice. It was originally located in Constantinople. The emperor in the medallion is sometimes identified as Alexios I Komnenos, but this is by no means certain. It could depict almost any emperor from the tenth- and eleventh-centuries and Nikêforos II Fôkas is certainly a plausible candidate, because the medallion depicts an elderly short emperor with a broad chest. Unfortunately, the damage to the nose makes this identification only tentative. (*Source: Schlumberger*)

Nikêforos II with mace in Skylitzes. (*Public domain*)

Saint Demetrius, eleventh century. (*Author's drawing/painting after the original*)

Turkish *ghulam*. (*Author's drawing*)

Combat scene in the Manasses manuscript. (*Source: Schlumberger*)

Three *katafraktoi* and a mounted archer. (*Author's drawings*)

Leôn Fôkas (brother of Nikêforos) with his son Bardas. (*Vinkhuijzen Collection, New York Public Library/public domain*)

A soldier in the tenth-century enamel (*Source: Schlumberger*)

Psilos equipped with an arrow-guide. (*Author's drawing*)

A hoplite in ersatz armour after Nikëforos' reform. (*Author's drawing*)
   A *menavlos* (one version). (*Author's drawing*)
   A hoplite variant before Nikêforos. (*Author's drawing*)
   A peltast in the *Sylloge tacticorum*. (*Author's drawing*)

Roman footmen in a miniature painting (tenth- or eleventh-century). (*Public domain*)

Icon of Saint Demetrios (early-fourteenth century). (*Public domain, Marie-Lan Nguyen*)

Prophet Muhammad at the Battle of Bakr (thirteenth-century manuscript). The painting represents well the typical Bedouin cavalry employed by the Hamdanids and Tarsiotes in the tenth century. (*Public domain*)

Saracens on a campaign. (*Source: Schlumberger*)

Kaisar Bardas Fôkas, father of Nikêforos, with two Saracens. (*Vinkhuijzen Collection, New York Public Library/public domain*)

Nikêforos Fôkas meeting Liudprand. (*Vinkhuijzen Collection, New York Public Library/public domain*)

An equestrian statue depicting Otto I the Great; A painting of Saint Athanasios of Athos (date 1290); Frankish soldiers in the Gall manuscript ca. 890. (*Public domain*)

An icon of Saint George and the youth of Mytilene. British Museum. Mid-thirteenth century. (*Author's photograph*)

List of Maps

Imperial Palace	xviii
Constantinople	xx
Roman Empire in 949–70	xxi
Kappadokia, Charsianon, Sebeasteia and Lykandos	xxii
Fortifications and Roads in tenth-Century Syria	xxiv
The themes of Seleukeia with portions of Kibyraiôtai (west), Anatolikon (north) and surrounding regions	xxvi
Major fortified centres and routes (Asia Minor)	xxvii
Road network leading to Tarsus, Adana, Sision, Germanikeia, Adata and Melitênê	xxviii
Road network leading to Tarsus, Adana, Mopsuestia, Nikopolis, Germanikeia, Seleukeia and Antiocheia	xxviii
Saracen Frontier Zone	xxix
Upper Mesopotamia	xxx
The Principal Muslim States in the Roman Sphere ca. 950 Shown with the Crescent Symbol	xxxi
The permanent conquests of the Cretan Arabs until ca.961 according to Vassilios Chrisitides (1984, 165–6, 192), and the city of Bari	xxxii
Armenia in ca. 936	xxxiii
Temenos, Bagras	xxxiv
Tripoli, Amida and Thessalonika	xxxv
Antardos (Tortosa, Tartus), Laodicea ad mare (Laodikeia, Latakia, Syria), Martyropolis (Mayyafariqin)	xxxvi
Antioch	xxxvii
Russia	xxxviii
Bulgaria in ca. 950	xxxix
Italy Topography	xl
Political Map of Italy in c. 950	xli
Fraxinetum (Fraxinet)	xlii
Military Themata and Tagmata in about 930	7
Siege of Germanikeia in 949	135
Siege of Tarsus in 949	138
Siege of Karin in 949	140
Bardas Fôkas and his sons Nikêforos and Leôn against Sayf ad-Dawla in 950	146

Batte of the Lykos Valley in October 950 with the likely stages of the battle	148
The Battle of the Pass of al-Kankarun	151
The Battle of the Passes of Germanikeia and Adata in 950	154
Roman operations against the Hamdanids in 952	158
The Battle of Adata / al-Hadath on 30 October 954: The Initial Deployment of the Armies after Skirmishing	172
The Main Stages of the Battle of Adata on 30 October 954	173
The Spring Campaign in the East in 956	179
The Probable Route of the Fleet to Crete in 960	217
The Landing on Crete on 13 July 960	220
The route of Sayf ad-Dawla to the Roman ambush	235
Battle of Adrassos on 8 November 960	236
Anazarbos and Roman Siege Lines (12 December 961–10 January 962)	243
Anazarbos (walls) with a photo	244
The Military operations from December 961 until September 962	249
The Siege of Sis in 962	251
The Aleppo Campaign in December 962	255
The Battle of Aleppo on 20 December 962	256
The Siege of Aleppo (20–31 December 962)	259
Nikêforos' campaign against the Emirate of Tarsus in 964	277
Nikêforos' campaign in the east in 965	283
The Battle of Tarsus in the spring 965	286
Edessa	303
The campaign of Nikêforos Fôkas in the autumn 966	305
The campaign of Nikêforos Fôkas against the Muslims in 968	334

Introduction

This book has been long in the making. It began as a project to understand the development of the Roman army and its cavalry forces at a time when I wrote my doctoral dissertation in 2002–2003, after which I started further preparations for the topic by obtaining all the primary sources, by writing a number of studies dealing with Roman armed forces after 641, and by visiting, for example, Crete in 2006. It is thanks to the encouragement of my wife and children that the unfinished book was taken out of the old files and finishing touches added.

In this monograph the 'East Romans' are called Romans and not Byzantines (this is a later and incorrect term), while I have adopted a dual practice when transliterating names and titles. I use the Greek versions of the personal names of the emperors (Nikêforos Fôkas instead of Nikephoros Phokas or Nicephorus Phocas; Iôannês/Johannes Tzimiskês instead of John Tzimiskes; Kônstantinos instead of Constantine, etc.). Similarly, I employ Greek names for the other period Romans, while I have purposefully retained the commonly-used names for the narrative sources (i.e. Constantine instead of Kônstantinos) and for foreigners (non-Romans). The sole exceptions to this rule are the emperors and other individuals who also wrote some of the extant sources, for example Leo VI Wise and Constantine VII Porphyrogennetos. In their case I have used the Greek version of the name in the text so that Leo is called Leôn and Constantine is called Kônstantinos – except in the bibliography, where I have retained their English versions to enable the readers to find the sources more easily. I have also usually retained the Greek letters as written rather than transliterated them as pronounced, hence *bigla* rather than *vigla* or *Basileios* (in English Basil) rather than *Vasilios*, or *etaireiai* instead of *hetaireiai*, or *oplitai* instead of *hoplitai*. I have adopted a dual practice concerning place names, so that some of those have retained their usual English forms (e.g. Tarsus rather than Tarsos, or Cilicia rather than Kilikia) while others have been changed. The different forms of the names are given in the index. I have prepared the maps at different times so these may have different versions of the place names.

The inhabitants of the territory of the Rus'/Rhos are in this book called Russians and their land Russia (*Ruscia*) because that was their name already when for example Saxo Grammaticus (turn of the thirteenth-century) wrote his histories. The name Russia and Russians derive from *Rus'*, *Rhos*, *Roslagen*, *Ruotsi*, *Root'si* and *Ruscia*. The original *Rus'/Rhos* came mainly from the territory of modern-day Sweden (henceforth Swedes), who then intermingled with the local Finnish-Karelian, Estonian, Slavic tribes and others, and so became the ancestors and creators of the later countries of Belarus, Ukraine and Russia. In short, the origin of the states of Russia, Ukraine and Belarus is the same; the Russia/Ruscia of the Rurikid Princes with a capital located in Novgorod or Kyiv/Kiev, the latter of which is today the capital of Ukraine. No insult is therefore meant towards anyone who might take offence from the use of the words Russia and Russians in this context. I also call the Bulgars with the name of Bulgarians just for the sake of ease, because the Bulgars inhabited the first Bulgarian Empire. In this study the various Black groupings and Sudanese/Nubians/Ethiopians in the service of the different Muslim states are collectively called blacks or black Africans to separate these from the other ethnicities in their armies. Older research literature used to refer to black Africans as 'negroes' until the 1980s or, in some cases, until the 1990s to separate them from other ethnic groupings, but since this is no longer the norm I have opted to use the term 'blacks' instead of this while still meaning the above. It should be noted however that the word negro (from Latin *niger*) means black so there is no real change in the meaning. No insult is meant by this and I apologize if this causes any kind of hurt feelings.

I have usually drawn the maps on the basis of *Tabula Imperii Byzantini* or *Barrington Atlas* or *Google Maps* or *Open Street Map* or a combination except when stated otherwise.

Abbreviations

BA	*Barrington Atlas*
BELA 1	*Byzance et les Arabes 2.1* (reconstruction based on BELA 2)
BELA 2	*Byzance et les Arabes 2.2* (Arabic sources in translation)
DAI	*De Administrando Imperio* by Kônstantinos VII
DC	*De Ceremoniis* by Kônstantinos VII
DOS	*Dumbarton Oaks Seals*
DRB	*De rebus bellicis* (fourth-century military treatise)
DRM	*De re militari* = PKA = *On Campaign Organization and Tactics* in Dennis (1985, 246ff.)
DV	*De velitatione, De velitatione bellica, Peri paradromês, On Skirmishing*
DV D	*De velitatione* Dennis edition
DV DM	*De velitatione* Dagron & Mihaescu edition
GM	Georgius Monachus and its Continuation (Pseudo-Symeon), Bekker ed., see also GM (PG) and PSs
GM (PG)	Georgius Monachus and its Continuation (Pseudo-Symeon), *Patrologia Graeca* ed. see also PSs
HI	heavy infantry
LA	*Life of Athanasios of Athos, Version B*
LD	Leo the Deacon
LG	Leo Grammaticus (Leôn Grammatikos)
LI	light infantry
MS	Maurikios' *Strategikon*, Maurice's *Strategikon*
ND	*Notitia Dignitatum*
ODB	*Oxford Dictionary of Byzantium*
OT	*Taktika* of Nikêforos Ouranos
PKA	*Peri katastaseôs aplektoû* = DRM
PMBZ	*Prosopographie der mittelbyzantinischen Zeit Online*
PSs	*Pseudo-Symeon*, ed. Sullivan in RFNF Text 3
RFNF	*The Rise and Fall of Nikephoros II Phokas*
SAC	*Salerno Chronicle, Chronicon Salernitatum*
SAQ	*Syntaxis armatorum quadrata in the Byzantine Interpolation of Aelian*
SC	*Synopsis Chronike*, see *Constantine Manasses*
SCC	*Science and Civilization in China*
SLs	Symeon the Logothete, revised text, ed. Sullivan in RFNF Text 2
SLw	Symeon the Logothete, Wahlgren ed. and tr
ST	*Sylloge tacticorum* of Leôn VI
TC	Theophanes Continuatus
TIB	*Tabula Imperii Byzantini*

Maps

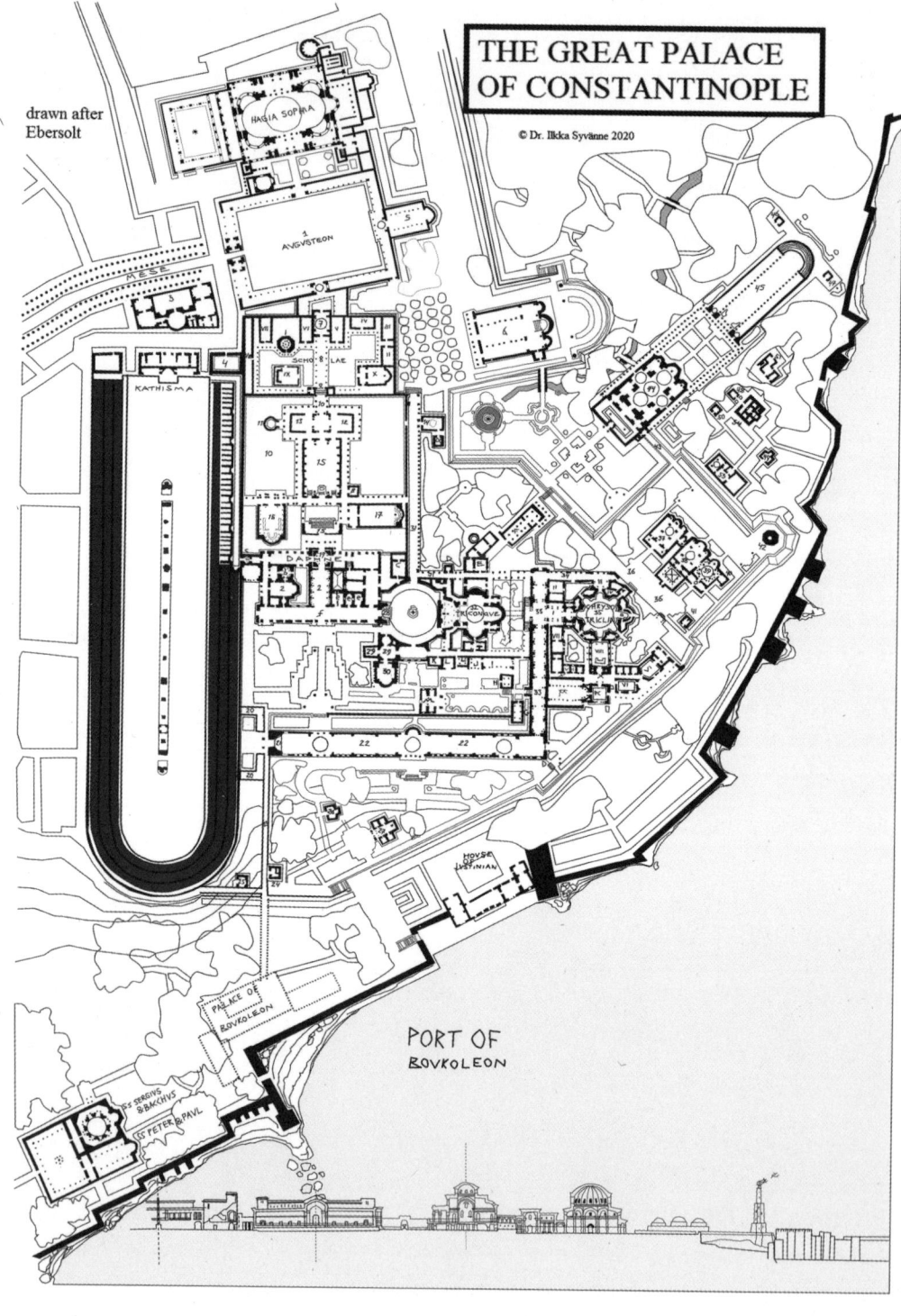

Maps xix

THE KEY TO THE MAP OF THE PALACE

1. Augusteon.
2. Milion.
3. Thermae of Zeuxippos.
4. Noumera.
5. Senate.
6. Magnaura.
7. Chalke.
8. Scholae.
   I-VII. 1-7 Scholae.
   VIII. Stables of mules.
   IX. Triklinos of the Scholae.
   X. Church of the Saints-Apostles.
9. Gate of the Excubitae or courtiers.
10. Tribunal.
11. Lychni.
12. Triklinos of the Excubitores.
13. Triklinos of the Candidati.
14. Oaton / Troullos / Tholoton (domed hall).
    α Sakelle.
15. Consistory.
    β Small Consistory.
16. Triklinos of the 19 Beds.
17. Church of the Lord.
18. Onopodion (a reception room).
19. Daphne.
    a. Augusteos.
    b. Octagon.
    c. Spiral staircase.
    d. Church of St. Stephen.
    f. Oratory.
    g. Gallery.
20. Stables.
21. Skyla ('bitch', female dog = Trophy Room).
22. Justinianos.
23. Gallery of Markianos.
24. Church of St. Peter and Oratory of the Archistrategos.
25. Church of the Virgin.
26. Oratory of St. Paul and St. Barbara.
27. Pentacubiculum of St. Paul.
28. Abside.
29. Baths built by Theoktistos.
30. Thermastra ('furnace room').
31. Passageway of the Lord.
32. Triconque built by Theophilos.
    A. Sigma.
    B. Phiale.
    C. Pyxitis and Triklinos.
    D. Eros.
    E. Karianos.
    F. Margaritis.
    G. Camilas.
    H. 2nd. Cubiculum.
    I. Mousikos.
    J. 4th Cubiculum.
    K. Chamber of the Empress.
    LL. Dressing room.
    M. Triklinos and 4 chambers.
33. Lausiakos.
34. Passages of the 40 Saints.
35. Chrysotriklinos.
    I Tripeton (vestibule).
    II. Dietarikion.
    III. Pantheon.
    IV. Phylax.
    V. Oratory of St. Theodoros.
    VI. Apartments of the Empress.
    VII. Apartments of the Emperor.
    VIII. Dining Room.
    IX. Kenourgion.
    X. Great Gallery.
36. Terrace.
37. Church of St. Demetrios.
38. Church of the Virgin of Pharos.
39. Church of Aelian.
40. Oratory of St. Clement.
41. Oratory of the Saviour.
42. Pharos.
43. Gallery of the Terrace of Pharos and New Church.
44. New Church.
45. Tzykanisterion.
46. Treasury of the New Church.
47. Financial offices of the New Church.
48. Treasury.
49. Vestiarion (Public Treasury).
50. Oratory of St. John the Baptist.
51. Aetos and Oratory of the Virgin.
52. Apartments in the form of pyramid and oratory of the Virgin.
53. Baths.

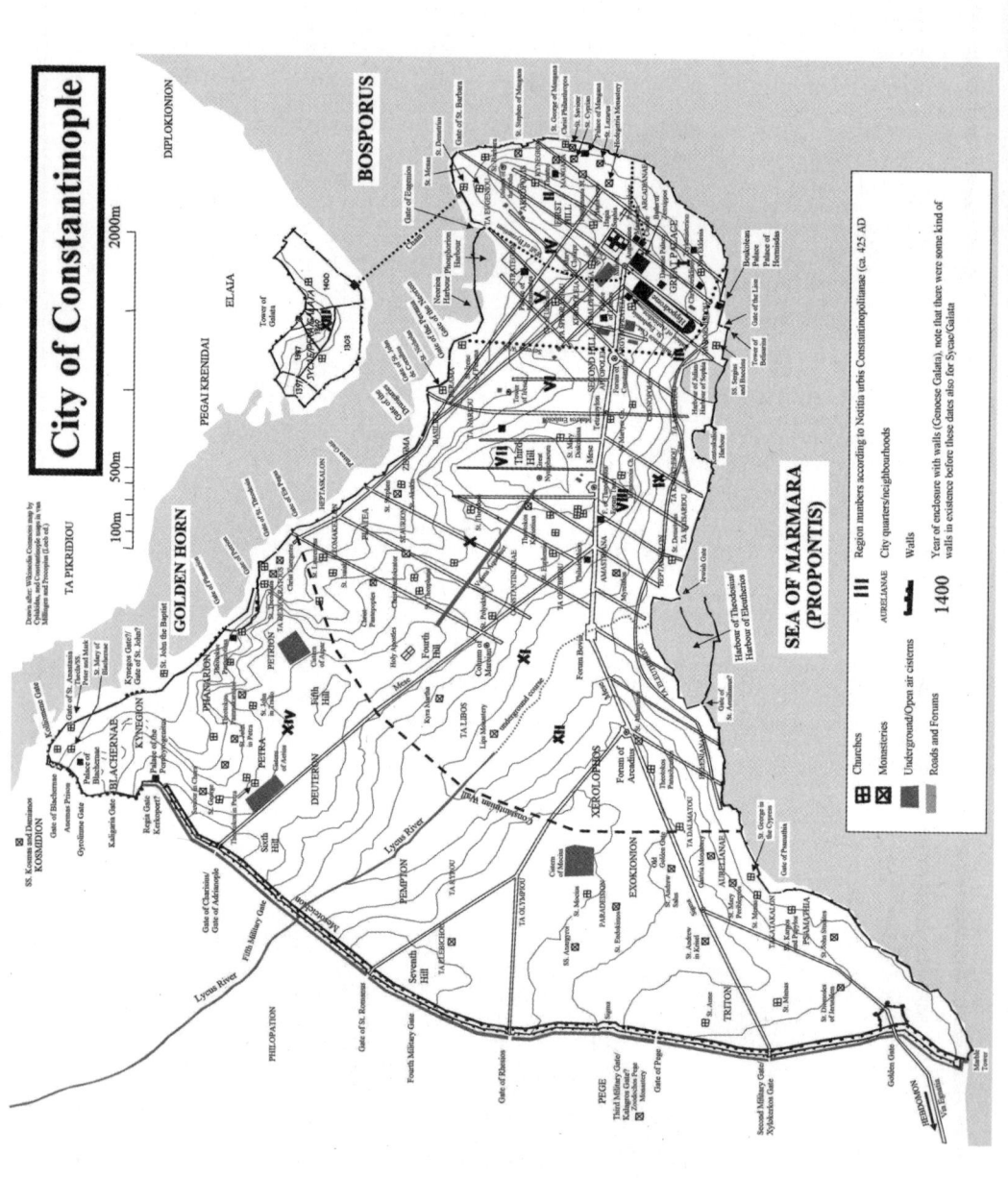

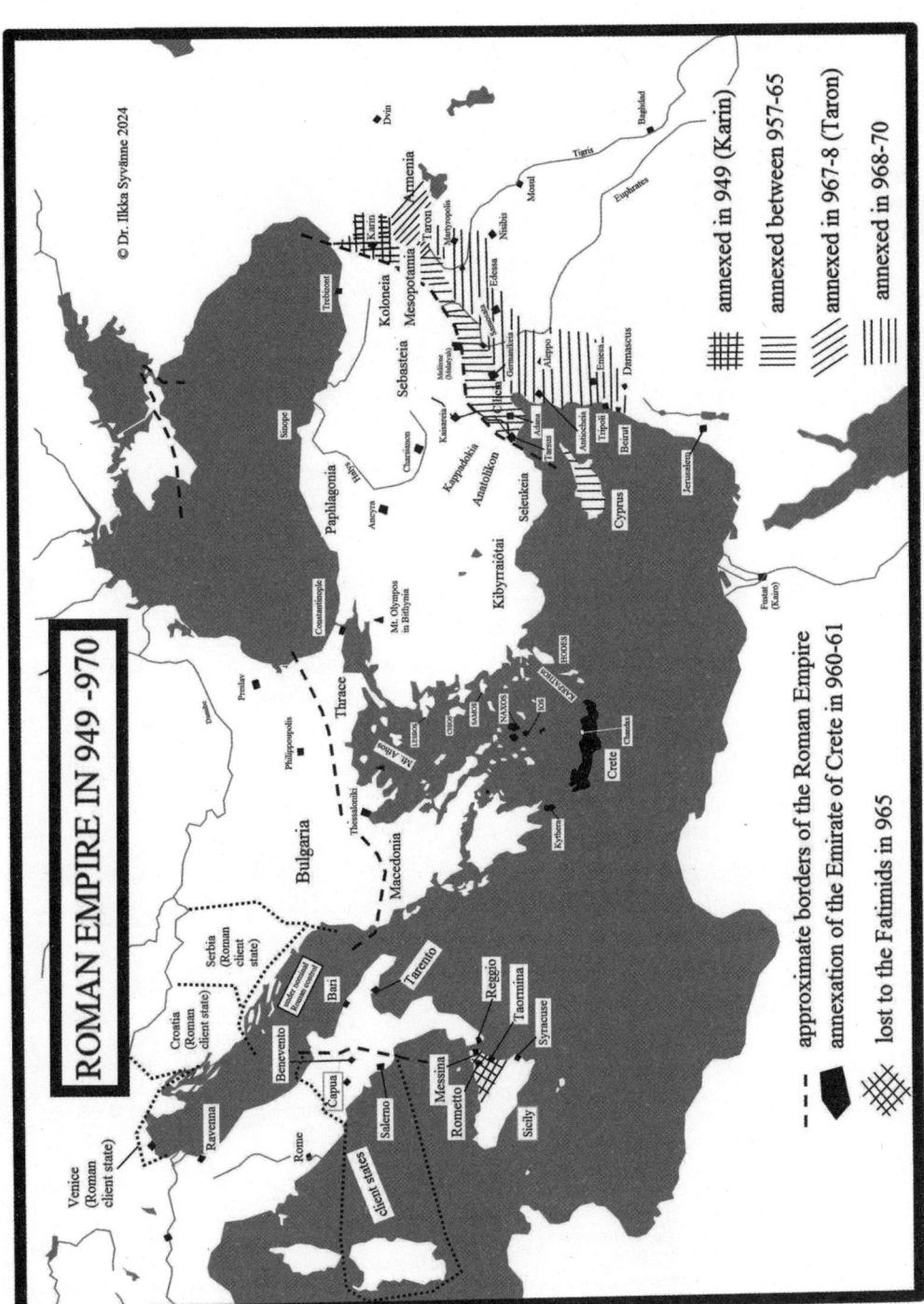

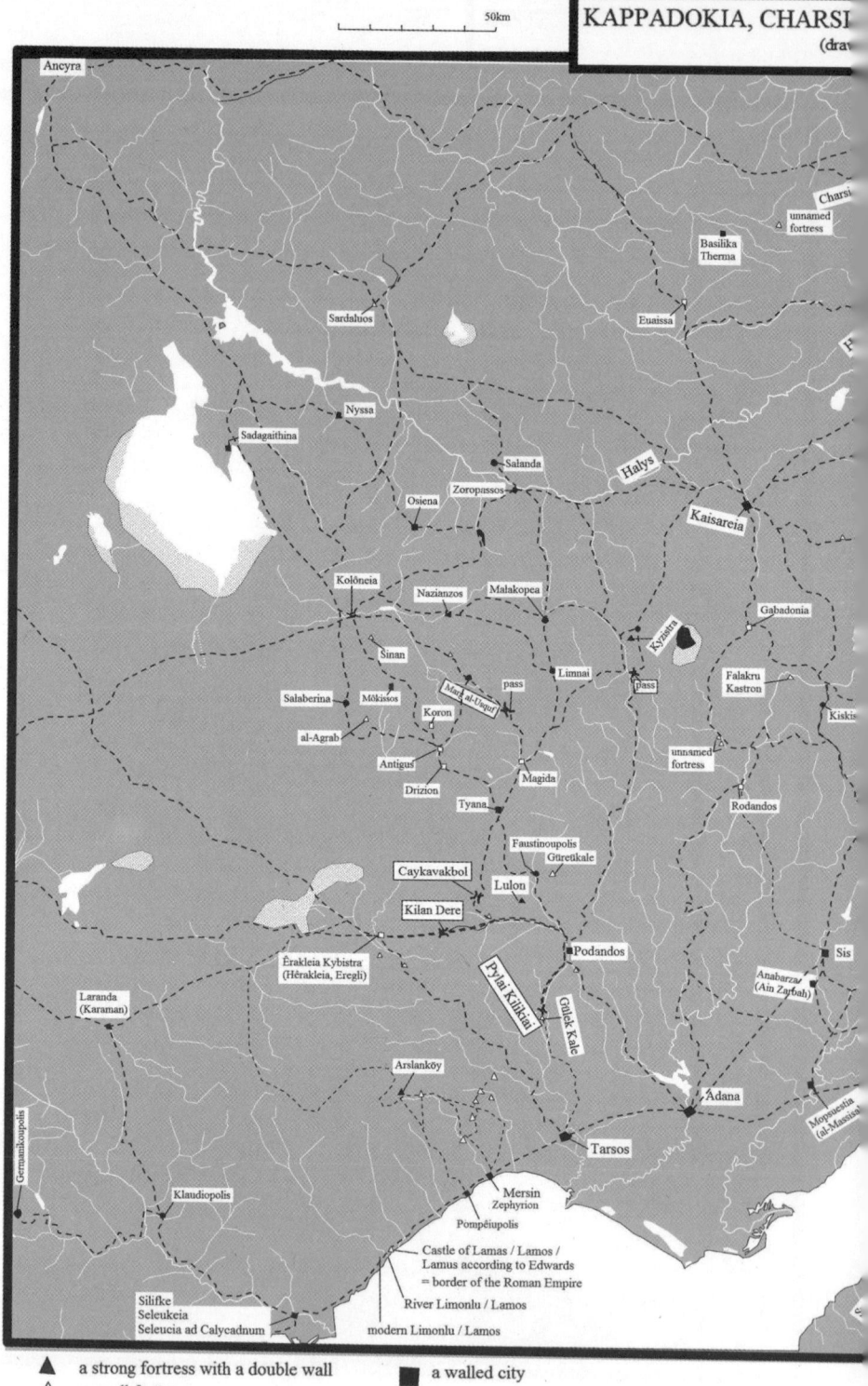

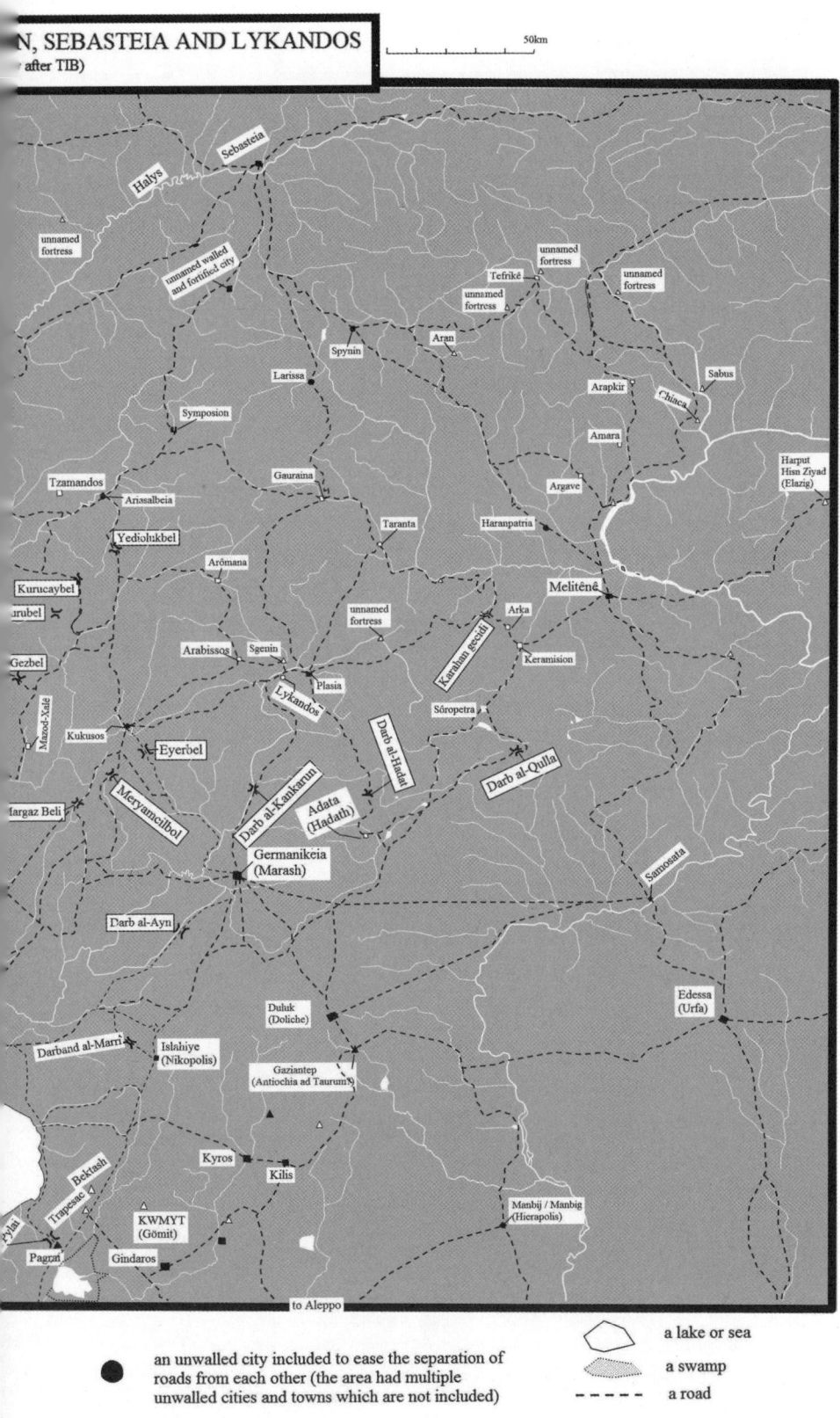

FORTIFICATION

ROADS IN THE 10th CENTURY SYRIA

50km

c. 30 km to Martyropolis

Heliopolis
Hagios Barsumas
Gaktay
Karkarou
Samosata
Hisn ar-Ran (Chesara / Chasanara)
Amida (Diyarbakir)
Constantia (Tella)
Mardin
Edessa (Urfa)
Resaina (Ras al-Ain)
Raqqa (Kallinikos)
Sura
Sergiopolis (Rusafa)
Cholle
Zenobia
Deir ez-Zor
al-Mayadin ar-Rahba
Dura-Europos

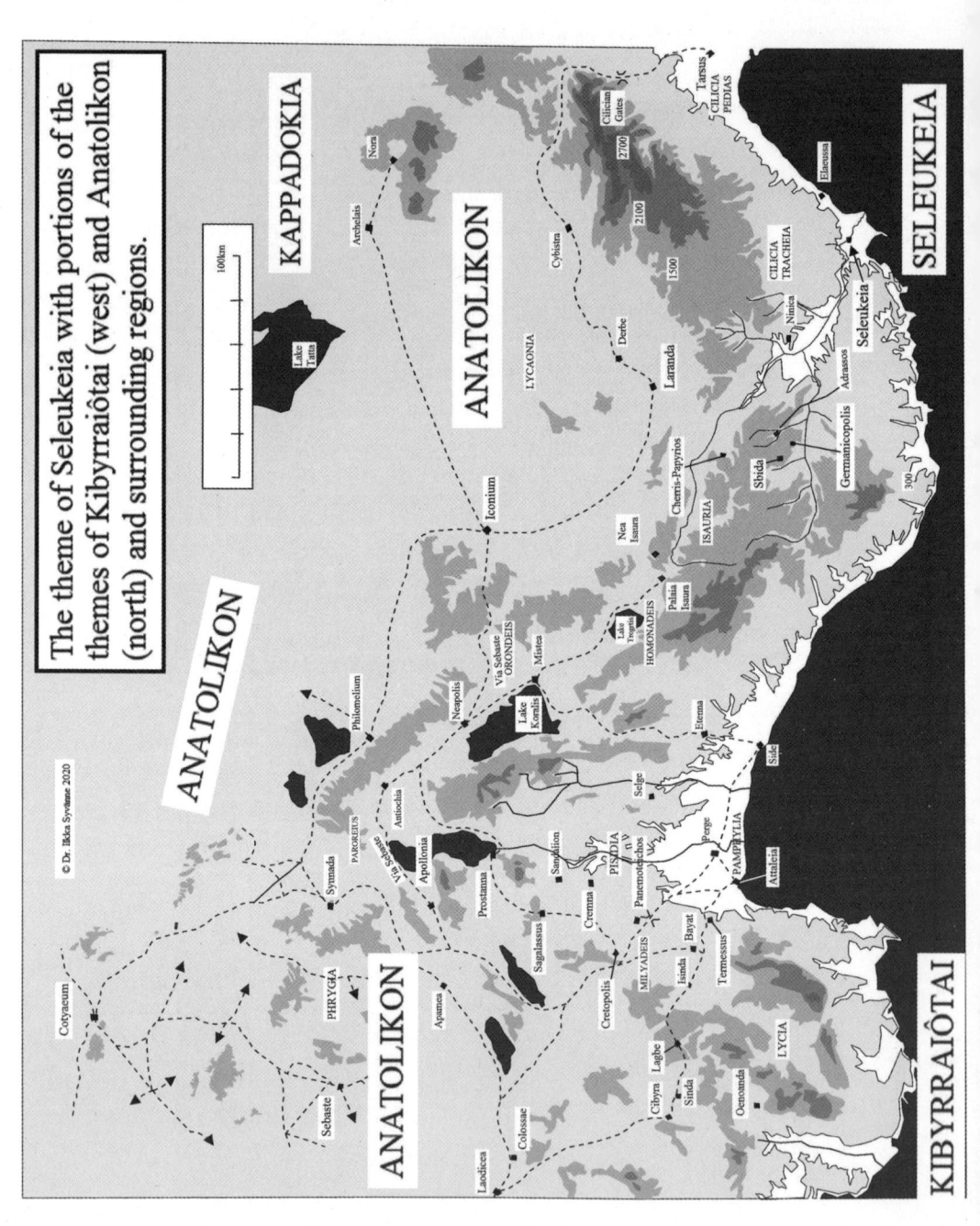

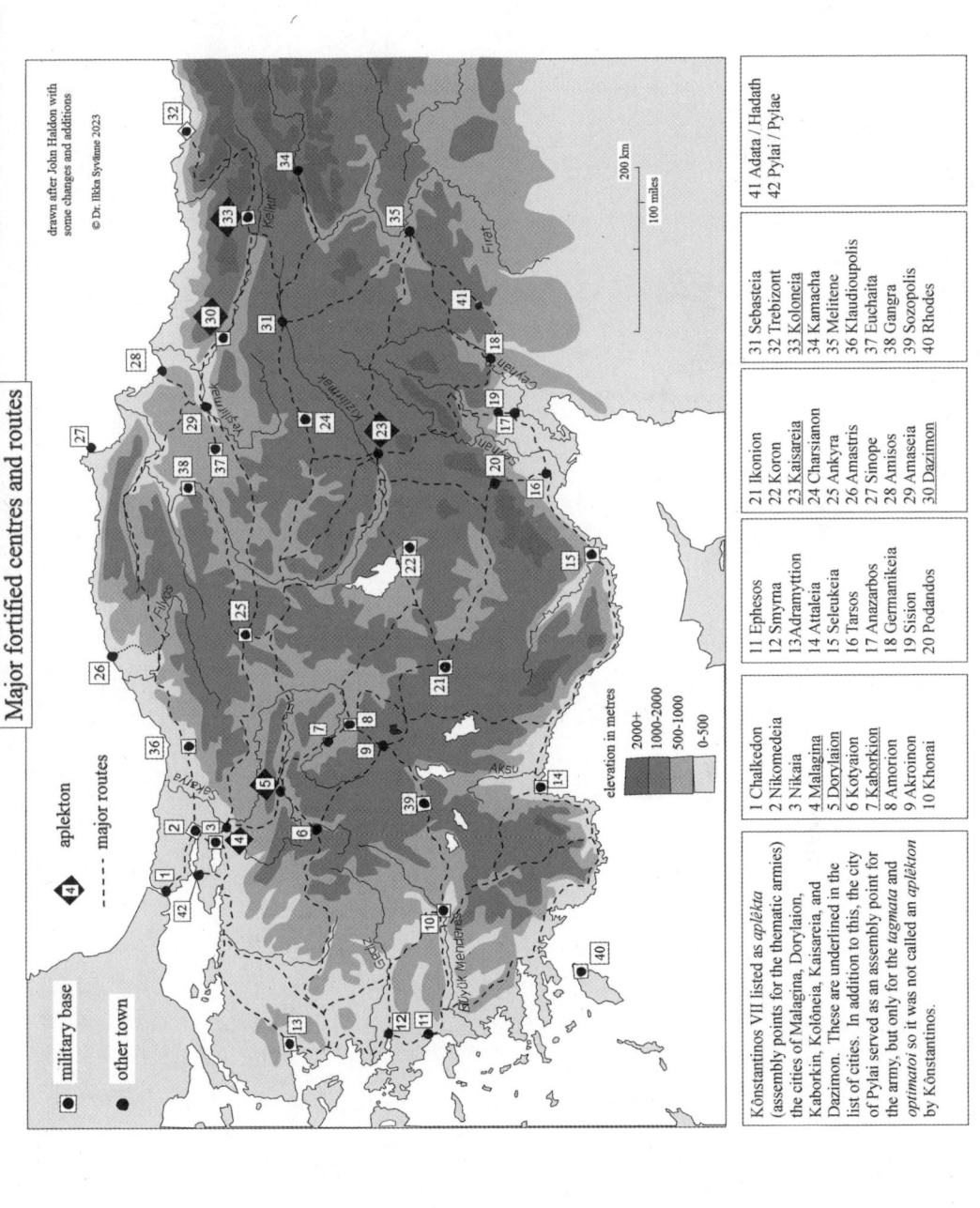

xxviii Nikephoros II Phokas, 912–969

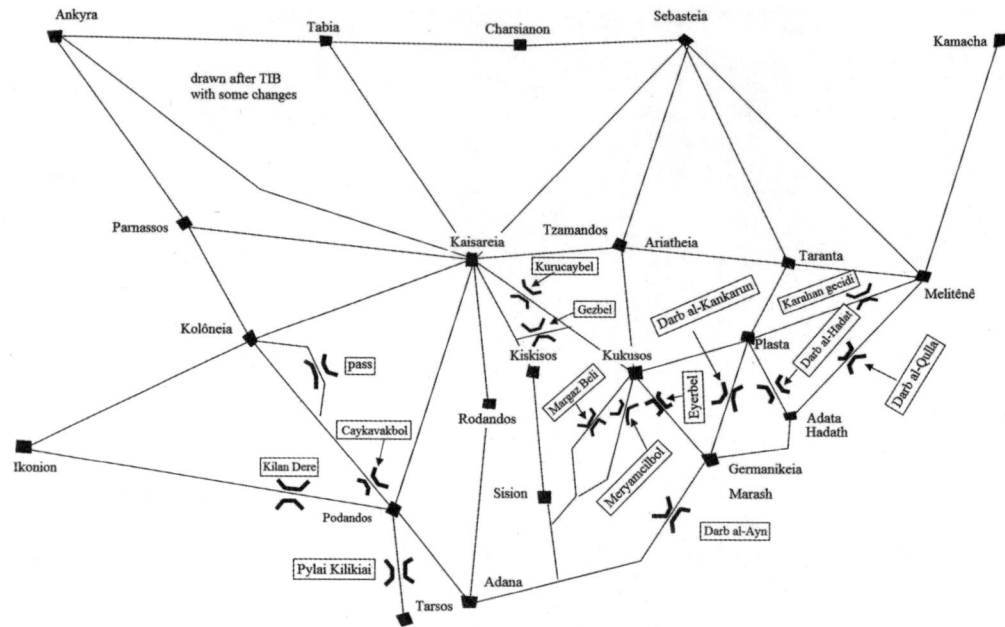

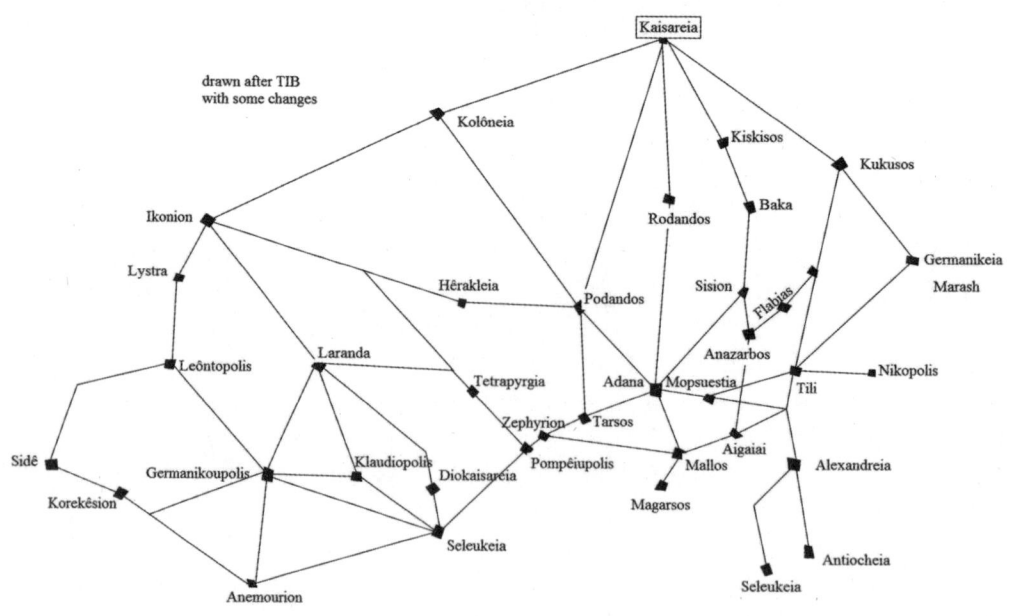

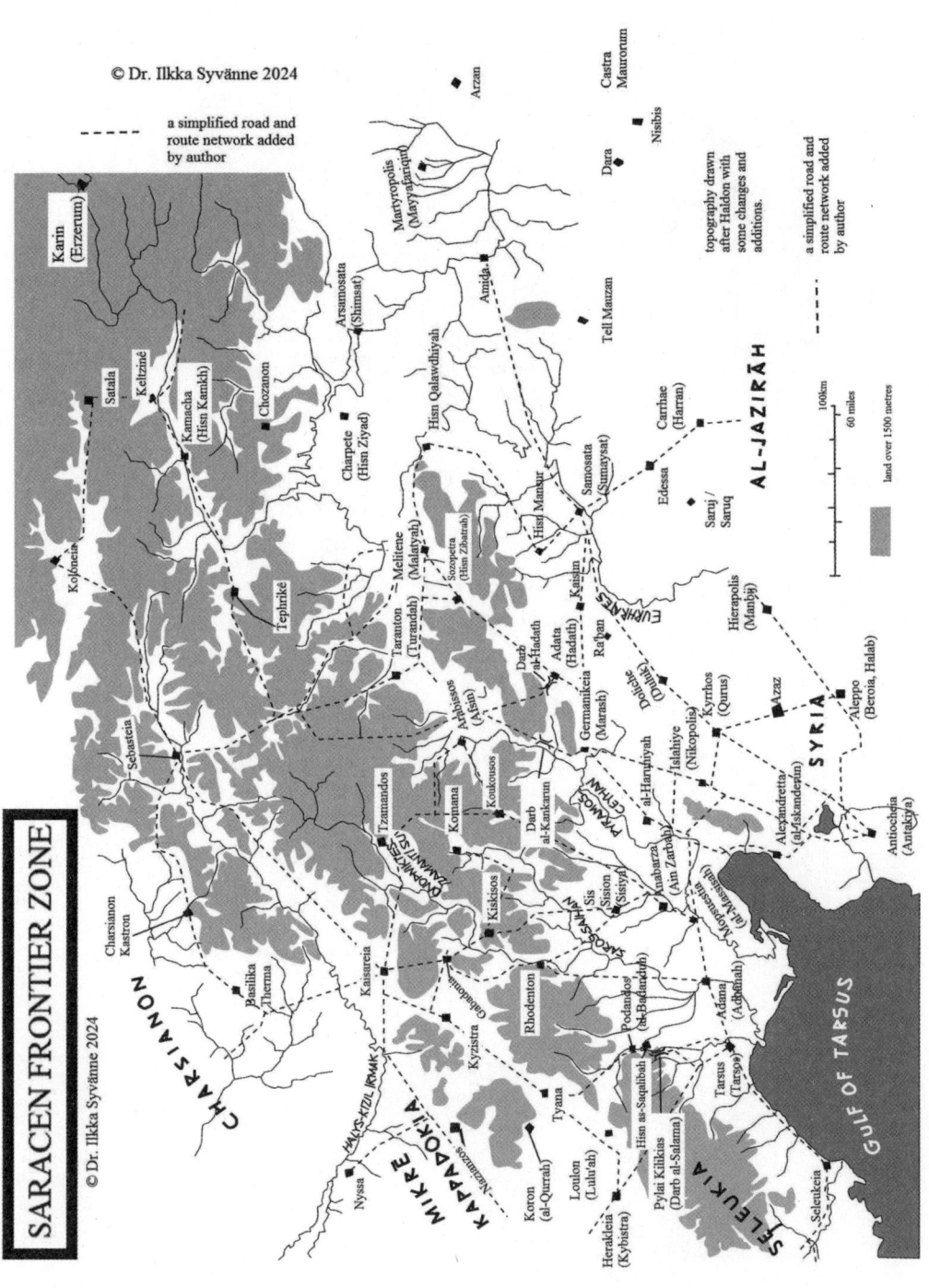

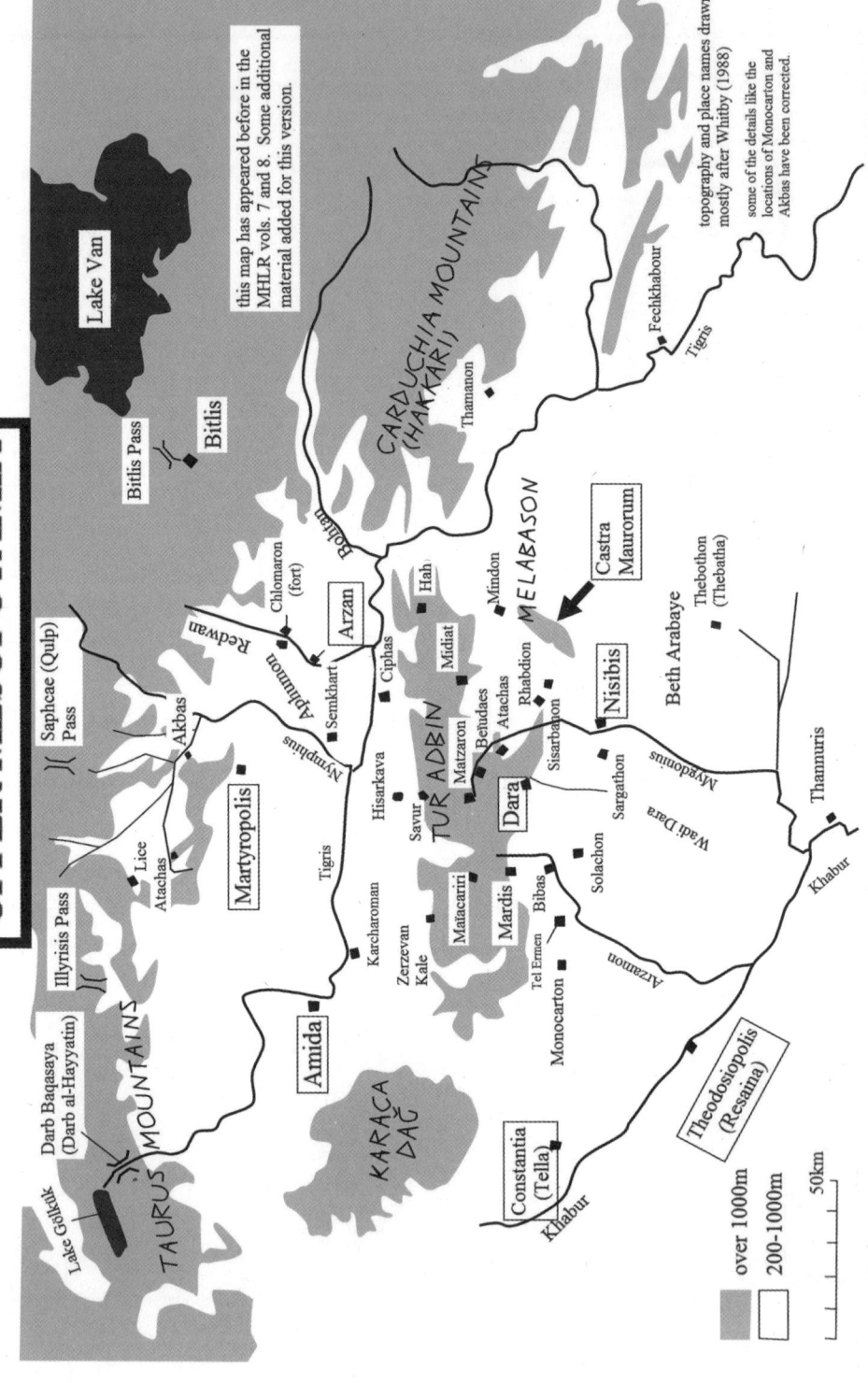

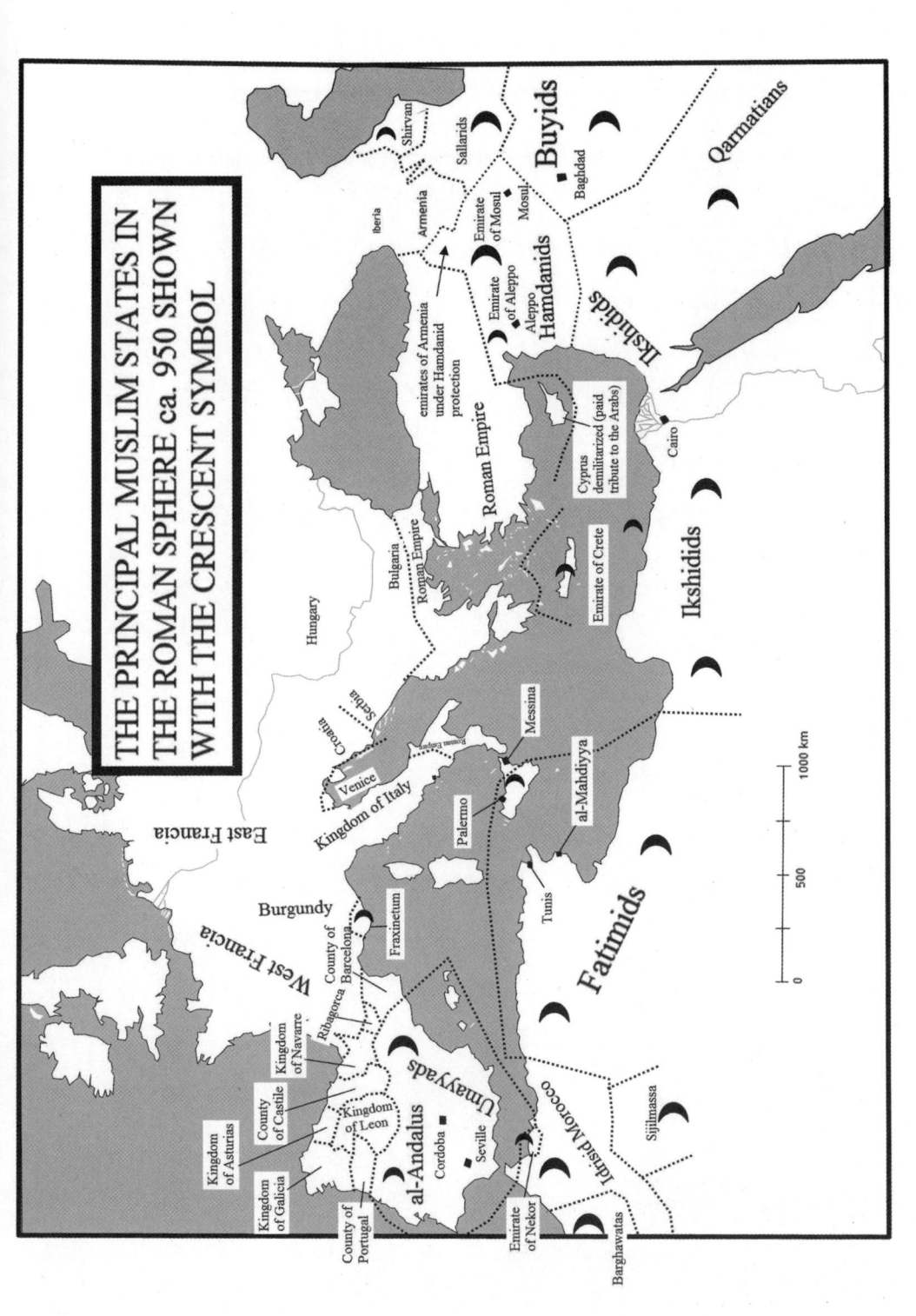

xxxii Nikephoros II Phokas, 912–969

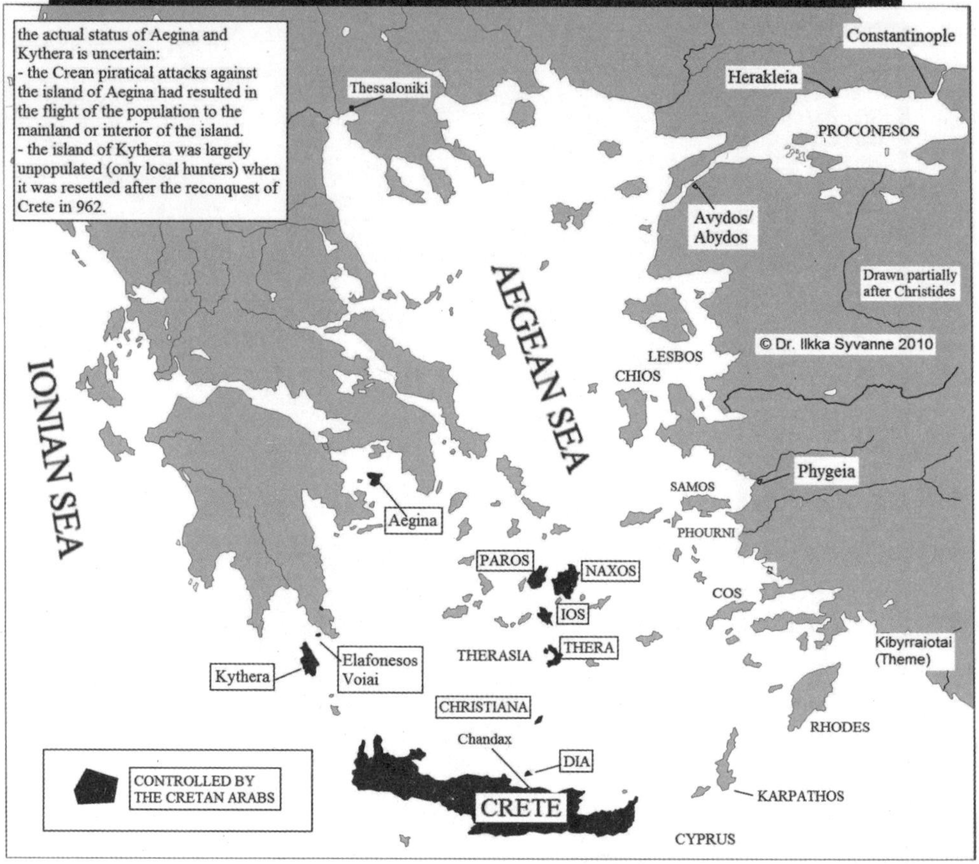

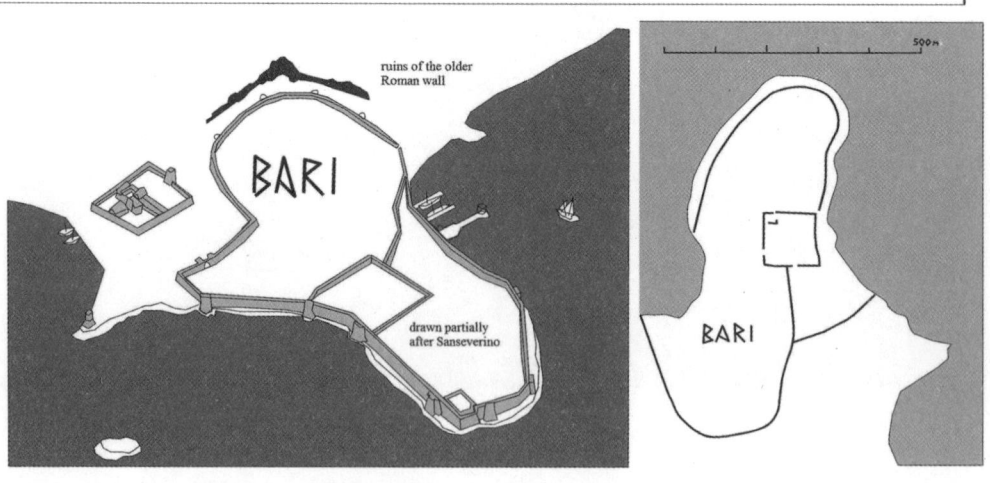

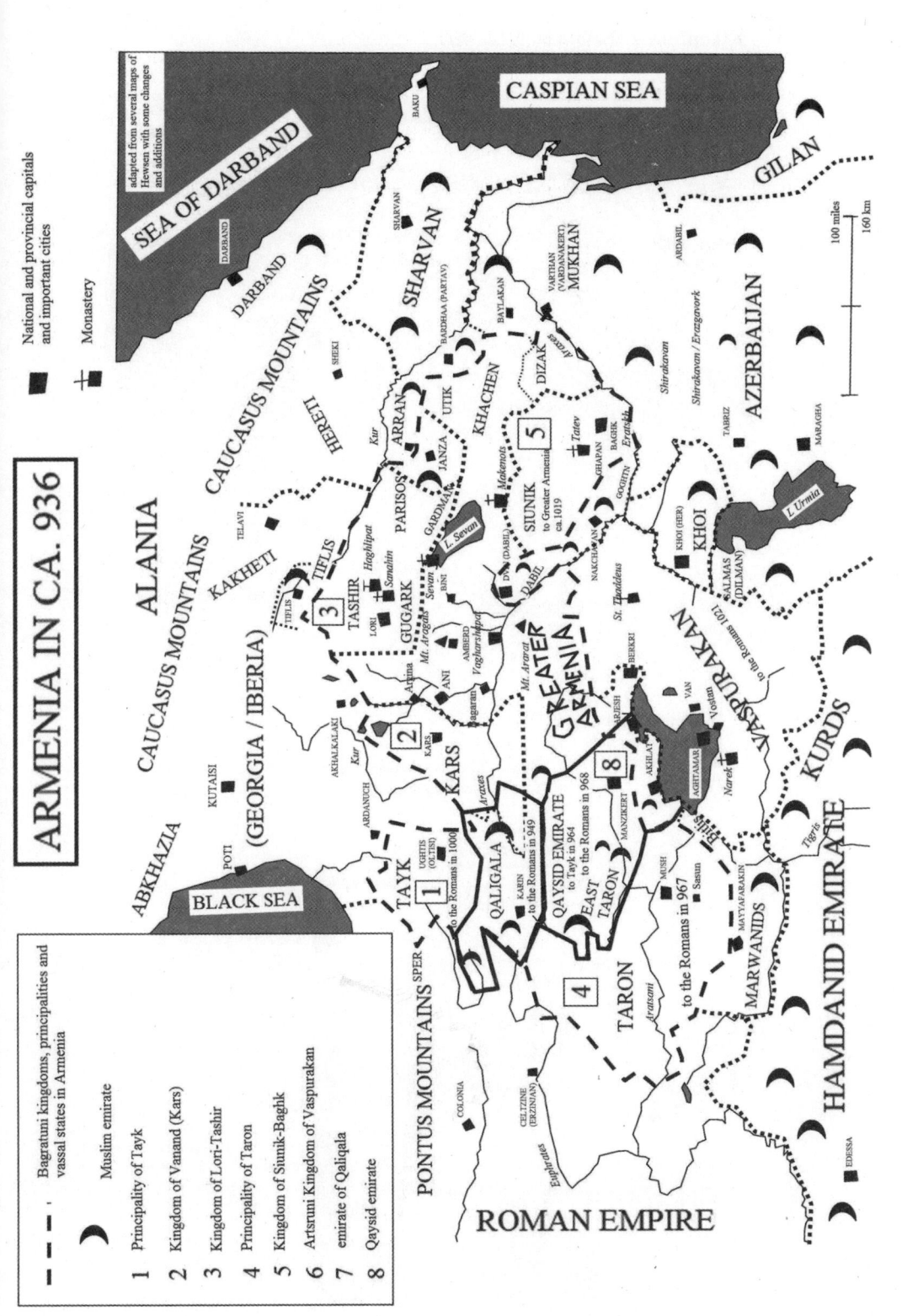

xxxiv Nikephoros II Phokas, 912–969

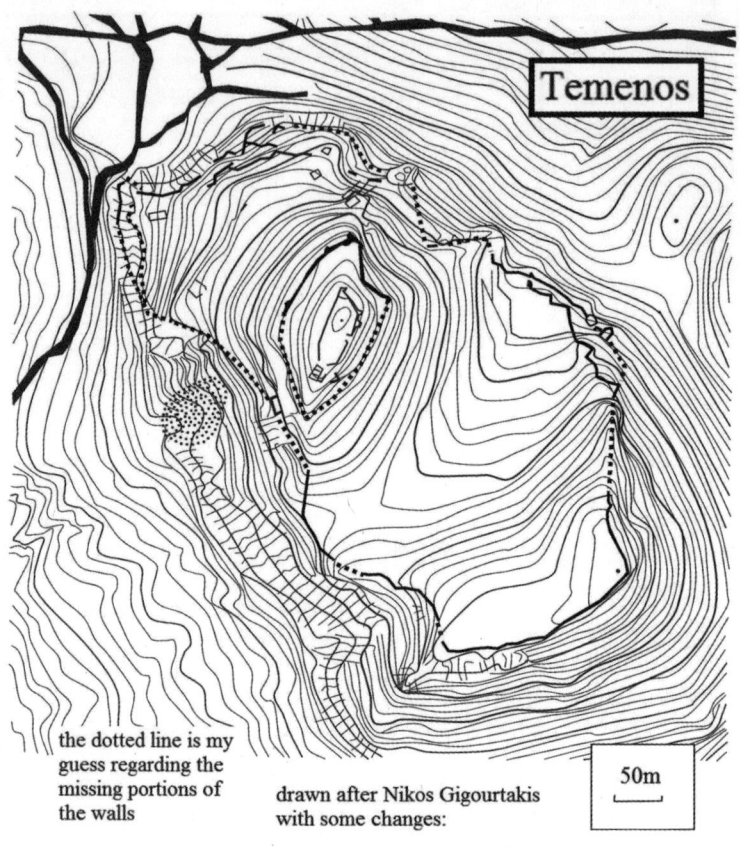

Temenos

the dotted line is my guess regarding the missing portions of the walls

drawn after Nikos Gigourtakis with some changes:

50m

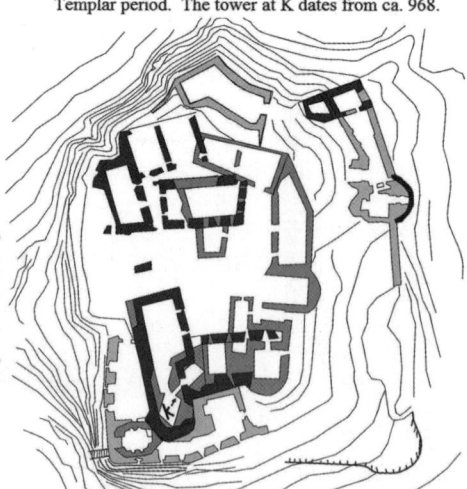

Bagras / Pagrai

All walls except the tower at K date from the Templar period. The tower at K dates from ca. 968.

post Crusade era (Armenian?)
upper level
middle level
lower level (outer wall)

30m

it is probable that the original fortress built by Nikeforos was at least as large as the remaining fortress, because the outer walls in the remaining fortress, it was meant to house 1,000 infantry and 500 cavalry

none of the remains of walls has been dated to the period before 968, which means that it is possible that the Arab fortress of Bagras was located elsewhere.

drawn and commented after Sinclair (esp. 308, 315-20, 330)

Maps xxxv

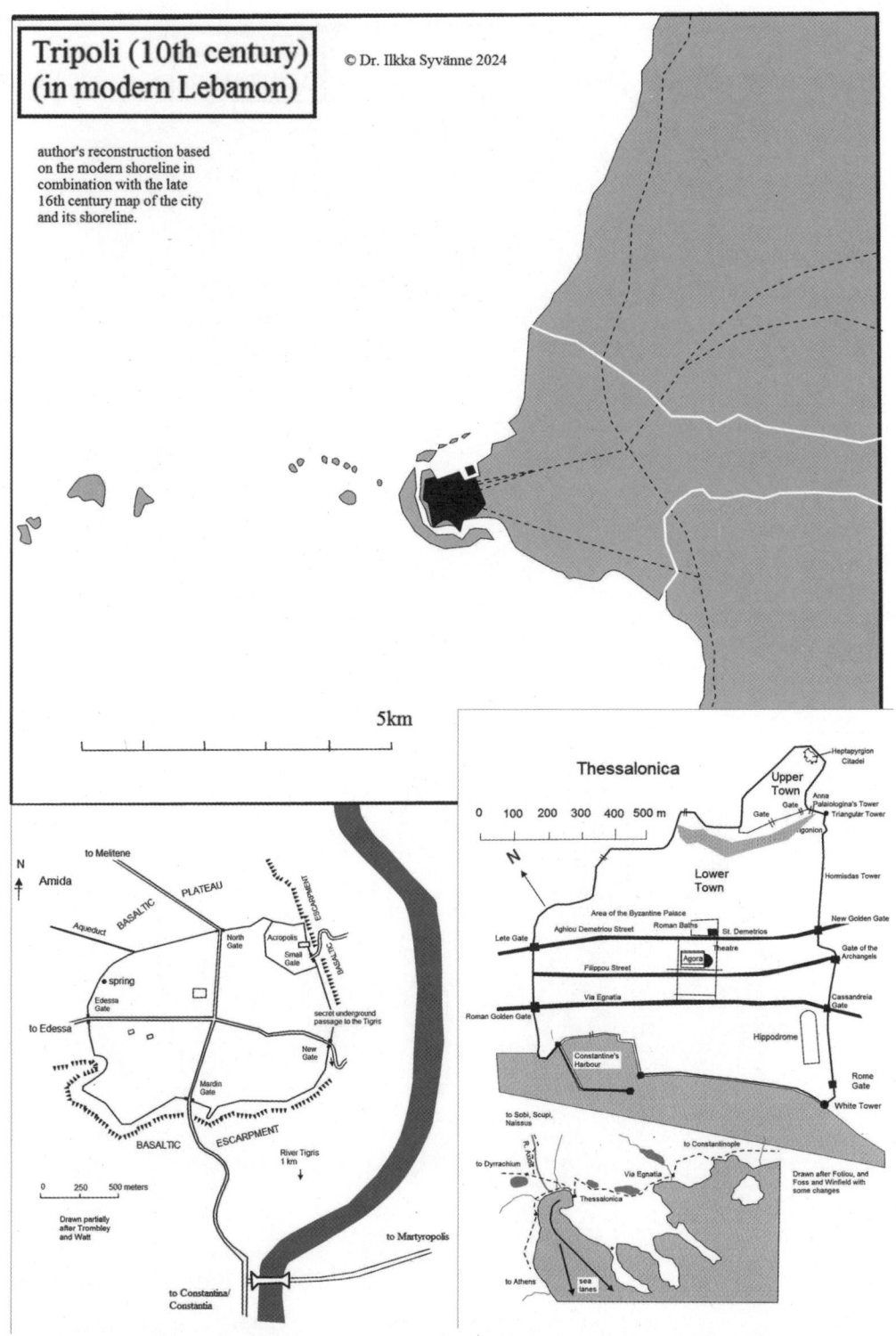

xxxvi Nikephoros II Phokas, 912–969

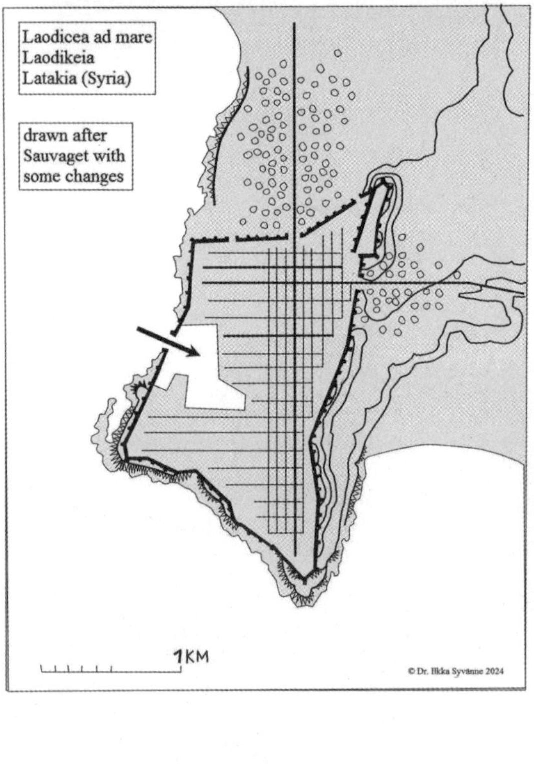

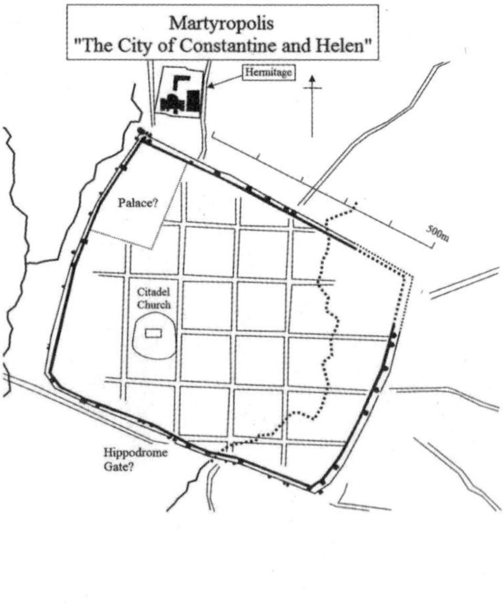

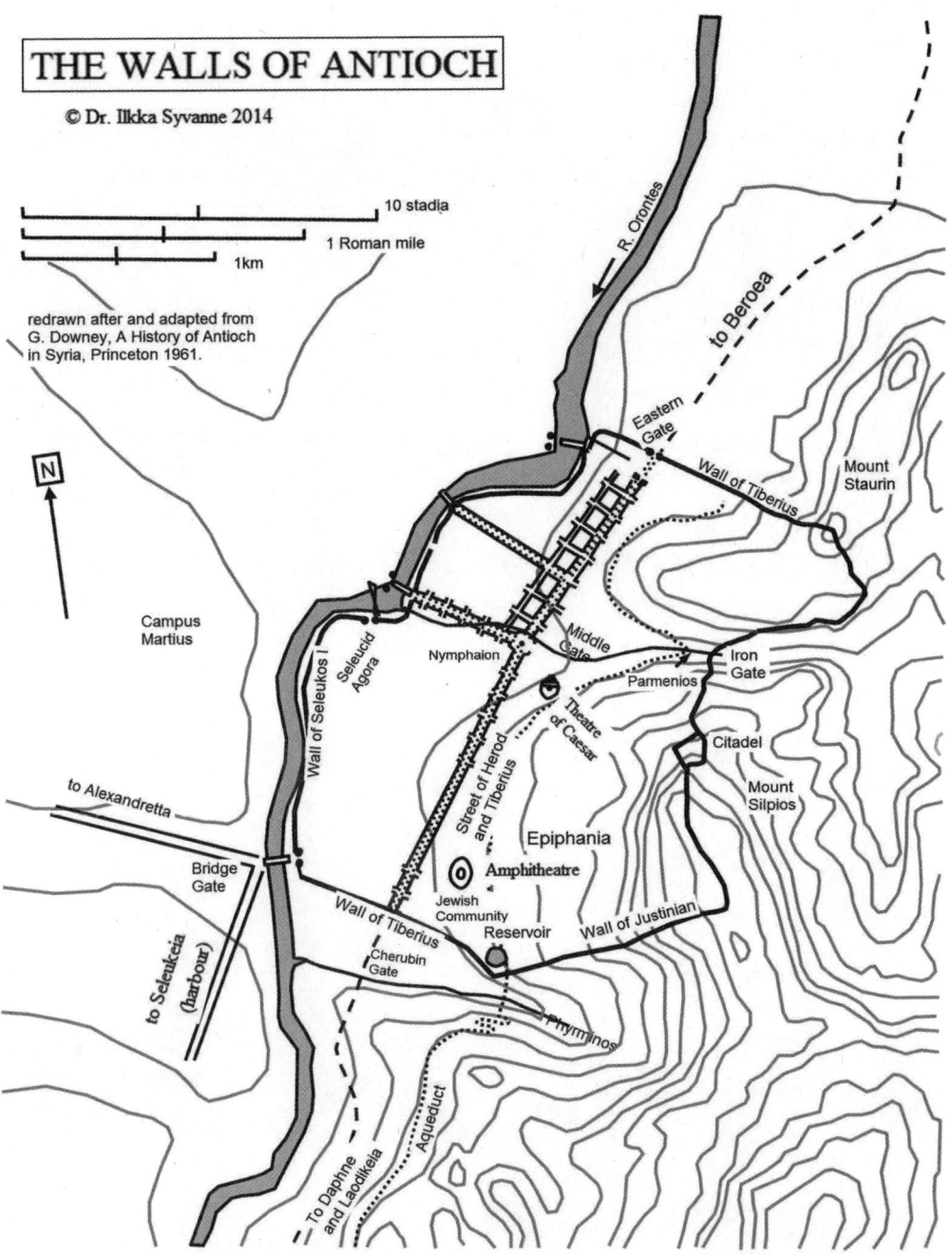

xxxviii Nikephoros II Phokas, 912–969

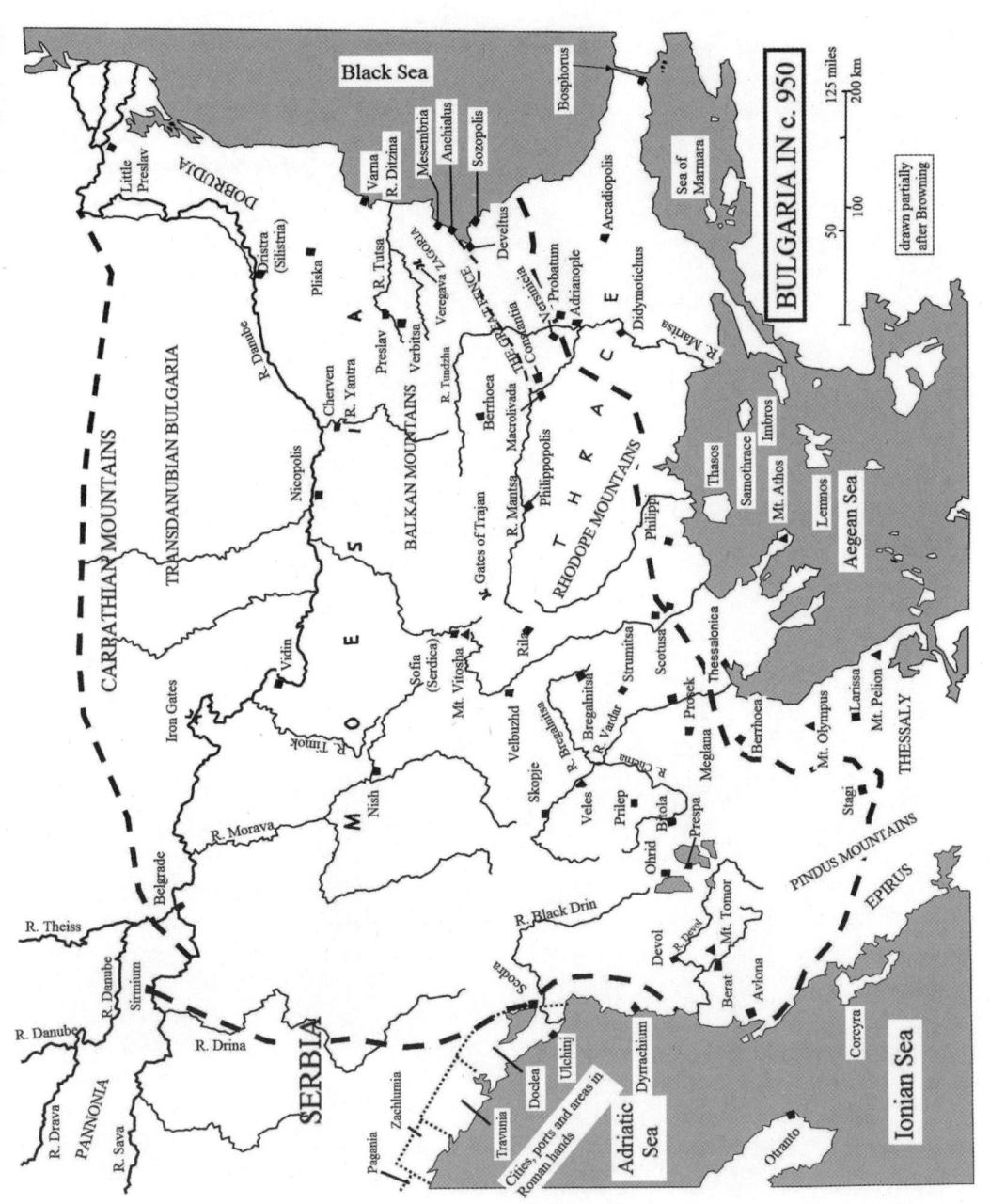

Nikephoros II Phokas, 912–969

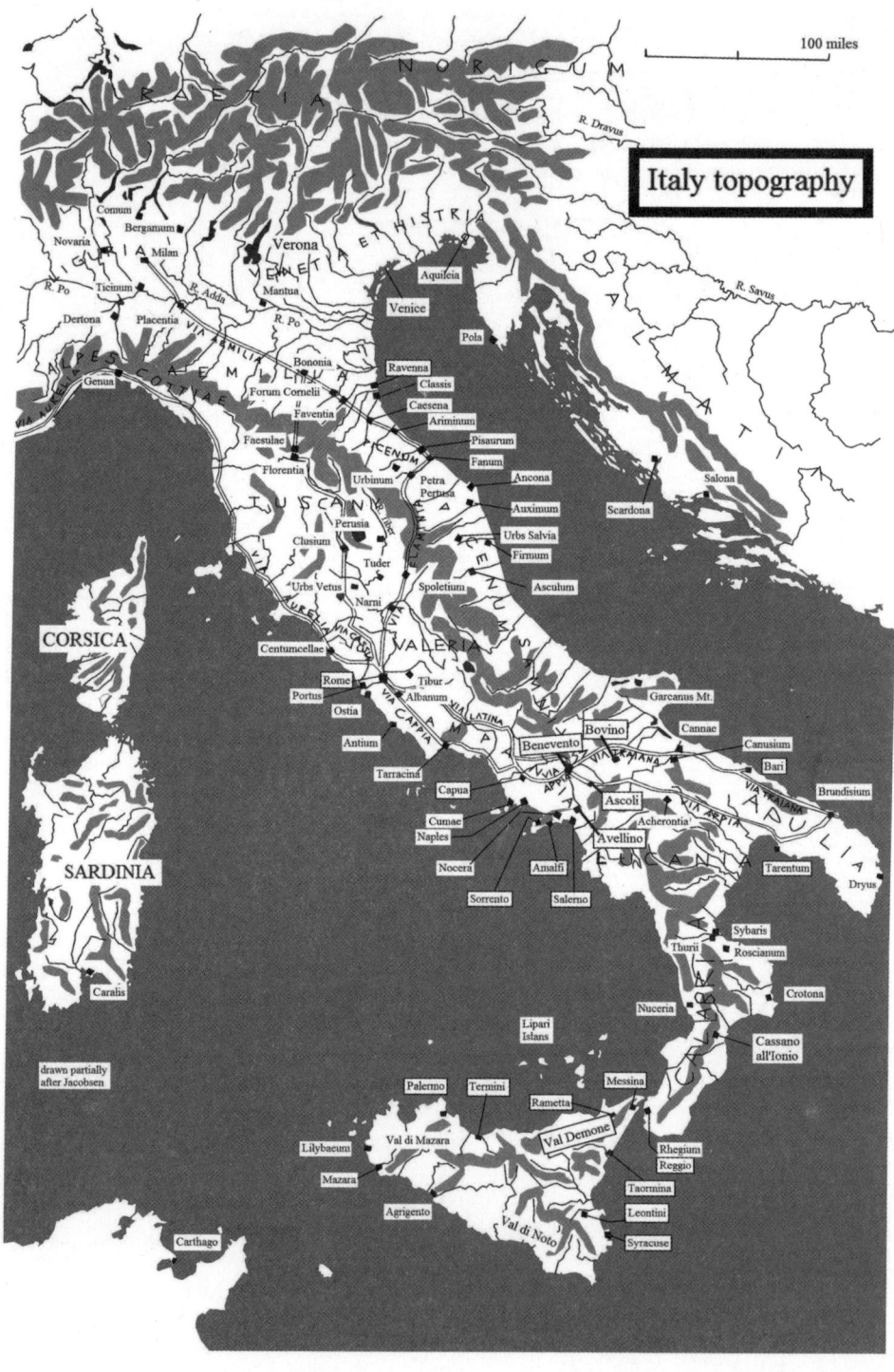

Maps xli

Fraxinetum (Fraxinet)

The site of a Muslim fortress in Provence in about 887/9 - 972, which consisted of the forces dispatched from al-Andalus. The fortress was located at the top of the hill Mont des Maures above the modern day village La Garde-Freinet. At its height Fraxinetum controlled the passes of the western Alps. The end of this Muslim enclave came as a result of their capture of Abbot Maiolus of Cluny in 972. When Maiolus was ransomed, he organized a revenge. The forces of Provence, Piedmont and Septimania defeated the Muslims at the battle of Tourtour in the summer of 972 and the fortress fell after a short siege.

Abbaye de Saint-Gall (939)

Grand Saint-Bernard (?)

Grenoble (930?)

Drawn after Ballan (2015) with some changes and additions.

Grenoble settled by Andalusian troops in 942 and abandoned in 970.

Novalaise (906)
Suse (919)

Asti (919)

Acqui (919-35)

Embrun (916)

Sisteron (911)
Apt (923)

Nice (Andalusi occupy Nice in 942)

Arles (934)
Aix (923)

Antibes (?)

Marseilles (923)

Frejus (destroyed in 940)

Toulon (940)

Fraxinetum / Fraxinet

The Muslims from Fraxinetum joined the Fatimid attack on Genoa in 935 and destroyed the port of Frejus in 940. This provoked Hugh, King of Italy, to seek an alliance with the emperor Rōmanos I.

The Roman Imperial Fleet destroys the Muslim fleet with liquid fire in 941

Hugh of Italy besieges Fraxinetum in 941, but abandons the siege when he hears that his rival for the Italian throne Berengar of Ivrea intended to invade Italy. Hugh makes a deal with the Muslims and uses these to block the Alpine passes against his foe.

Chapter One

The Introduction

1.1. The Literary Sources

The literary sources for the era of Nikeforos II Fôkas can be classed into Greek, Slavonic, Latin, Armenian-Caucasus, and Arabic sources.

The principal Greek sources are the narrative works of history (e.g. Theophanes Continuatus, Skylitzes, Leo the Deacon), the compilations of Kônstantinos VII Porfyrogennêtos (*De Thematibus, De Ceremoniis, De Administrando Imperio*) and the military manuals (Leôn's *Taktika* and *Sylloge tacticorum/Syllogê taktikôn, Praecepta militaria, De velitatione,* Ouranos' *Taktika* with *Peri thalassomachias, De obsidione toleranda, Memoranda inèdit sur la défense de places*, Heron of Byzantium's *Parangelmata Poliorcetica and Geodesia*; Syrianus Magister's treatise; anon. *Naumachica* produced for *parakoimômenos* Basileios and new 'editions' of the older treatises). The most important of these are the histories of Skylitzes and Leo the Deacon, and the military treatises attributed either to Nikêforos himself (*Praecepta militaria*) or to his inner circle (*De velitatione, De re militari*). The most important Slavonic source is the so-called *Chronicle of Nestor* also known as the *Russian Primary Chronicle*. The Latin sources consist mainly of the Italian chronicles. The most important Latin source is Liudprand the Bishop of Cremona. The most important Armenian-Caucasian sources are Matthew of Edessa and Stephen of Taron, while the most important Arabic sources are Mutanabbi, Miskawayh, Yahya of Antioch and Bar Hebraeus.[1]

For further information regarding these sources, the reader is advised to consult the works mentioned in the bibliography. Here it suffices to note that we are particularly well-served by literary and narrative sources, because this was a period during which Byzantine-Rome flourished both culturally and militarily, with the result that a lot of literary works were produced.

1.2. Roman Society

Tenth-century Roman society had retained its Roman character throughout the centuries. At the top of the society were still the emperor (*Augustus, augoustos*) now called *basileus* (king), with possible co-emperors, empress (*Augusta, augousta, basilissa*) and the imperial family. There still remained the Senate, but it was the emperor who had the final say in everything. The emperor was the head of the civil government, army, navy, and of the Church. He was the deputy of the God on

The imperial administration, ca. 700-1050

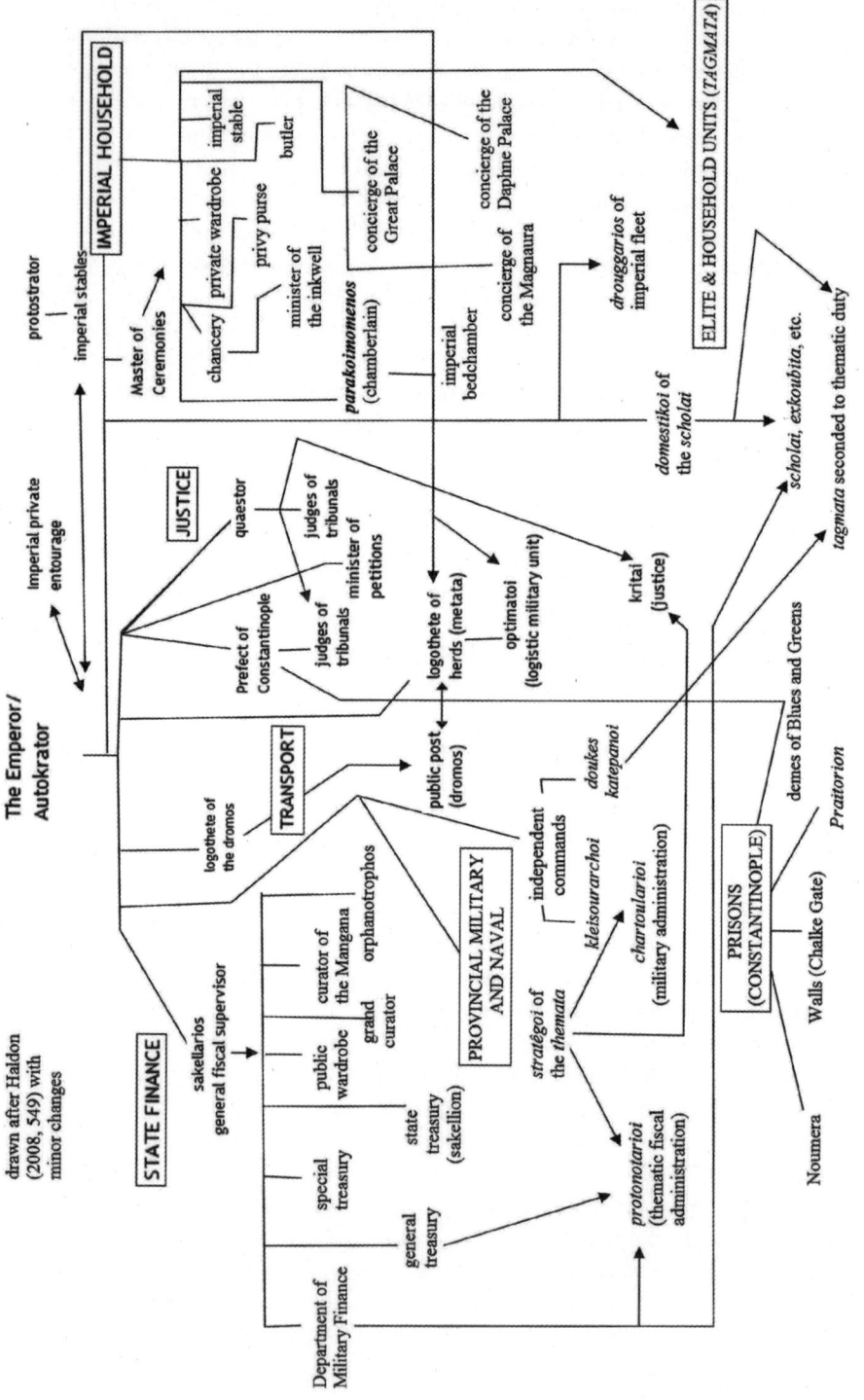

earth. The emperor could appoint and dismiss at his whim all the key personnel in the civilian and military administration and even Church patriarchs with the risk of raising opposition among the Church. The key problem for the Romans remained the fact that they had never solved adequately the problem of succession of the emperors. Any ambitious general with access to large-enough military forces could try to usurp power. The emperors tried to solve this question by dividing the forces into smaller armies; by using their ability to promote the careers of individuals; by using eunuchs (as they could not become emperors) both as civil servants and as generals; and through legislation. None of these provided a permanent solution to the problem of succession. The diagram on the opposite page shows the administrative structure of the Empire.

Roman society was a class society which consisted of the *dynatoi* (powerful) and the 'poor'. The *dynatoi* consisted of those who had high position in the civil, military or ecclesiastical hierarchies. The aristocracy consisted primarily of the landed aristocrats of the provinces who held military positions in the thematic forces. The 'poor' consisted of everyone else, with the result that 'poor' does not necessarily mean economic position, but rather position within the society. The emperors sought to limit the abuse of the poor by the powerful with a variety of measures consisting of the use of patronage and laws.

Like all medieval economies, the Roman economy was based on agriculture, but the merchants, traders and manufacturers of arts and crafts and luxury goods had an important role in it. The state controlled the way commerce was conducted, so it had granted monopolies to a number of merchant houses and merchant guilds. The state also set up the wages, prices and hours of work for the workers. The importance of commerce meant that the bankers and moneylenders also had an important role in society.

The state derived most of its taxes from the 'poor', but the imperial estates, mines and monopolies had an important role too. The largest monopoly of the Empire was the Imperial court, which had a monopoly in ore and a de facto monopoly on the silk industry. The privileged class of the *dynatoi* had tax privileges, so most of the taxes came from the so-called poor or from the imperial domains. However, the class of the *dynatoi* was not closed. It was possible to rise to a position of importance through achievement and/or patronage both in the civil and military services. The level of learning had an important role in this. The expectation was that the members of the civilian and military services would be literate and well-educated. The principal means for the emperor to control the *dynatoi* was his power to either promote or destroy the career of anyone.

East Roman society appreciated literacy, education, art and culture highly and they used knives and forks when eating. The women had a better position in Byzantine-Rome than in the rest of Europe. The women were considered the intellectual equals of men, so the daughters of the wealthy also received an education, but in wealthy households the women were still separated into their own women's quarters, guarded by eunuchs just like the women were separated into their own balcony in the churches. Similarly, despite their education, it was still very difficult for women to have a career of their own except as prostitutes (considered as a special class) or as nuns and abbesses. It is because of this that we do not know of any women generals in the Roman armed forces. Certain professions were not open for women.

Most of the East Romans were highly religious and sometimes also superstitious. The Church had a very important role in society – it was present everywhere and its high ranking members were considered to belong to the class of the *dynatoi*. Its monasteries were present in every corner of the Empire and were among the greatest land owners in the land, hence the imperial land legislation to restrict their influence. The monasteries consisted of several classes. These were either free or autodespotic (founded by a special imperial charter or by a private individual). The monasteries therefore consisted of the following: imperial monasteries founded on imperial domains under direct imperial control; monasteries controlled by the Patriarch, metropolitans, and bishops; daughter-houses of an earlier monastery; and monasteries founded by individuals, who owed their allegiance to the founder. In addition to these there were so-called *lauras* in which the monks lived separated from each other as hermits, and then there were actual hermits who lived completely alone. Superstition had an important role in the society in the form of astrology, soothsayers, omens and even cultists and heretics of various kinds – the last-mentioned were obviously considered as heretics or as Satan worshippers.

1.3. The Organization of the Roman Army and Military Lands[2]

The early-tenth century military structure of the Roman Empire consisted of the land forces and naval forces. The land forces were divided into the salaried professional soldiers making up the so-called *tagmata* (all collectively called *scholarioi*); imperial bodyguards; thematic forces (*themata*, the soldiers of which were all collectively called *stratiôtai*); *foideratoi* distributed to the provinces but serving collectively under *komês tôn foideratôn*; private retinues of the *dynatoi* in general and in particular of the retinues of the landed aristocrats; mercenaries; foreign allies; and paramilitary civilian forces. The naval forces consisted of the Imperial fleet based at Constantinople; of the naval *themata* Aegean Sea, Samos and Kibyrraiôtai;[3] of the provincial fleets equipped by the state, but which were detached to serve in the non-naval *themata*; of the naval forces of the *archôntoi-abydykoi*;[4] and of the corvéed civilian ships. On the basis of Kônstantinos Porfyrogennêtos' *De Ceremoniis* (44.37–8, 45.17–34), the *themata* of Hellas, Peloponnesos, Nikopolis and Kephallenia should also be considered naval *themata*, but it is clear that all of the coastal and riverine *themata* had at least some naval units of which we know next to nothing, just like we know very little of the naval forces of the *archôntoi-abydykoi* who were placed in control of important port cities. The regular part of the armed forces therefore consisted of the *tagmata*, imperial bodyguards, Imperial Fleet and *themata* (both naval and land).

The *tagmata* and imperial bodyguards were recruited, equipped and paid by the state. The members of the Imperial Fleet were recruited and paid by the state, but in addition to this they possessed military lands (*strateia*), just like the thematic naval forces, to support them.[5] Similarly, the naval detachments posted in the non-naval *themata* were paid and equipped by the state, even if these in normal times served under the *stratêgoi* of the *themata*[6] – one may assume that they could also possess military lands to support them if they did not consist of foreign mercenaries. The members of the land-based *tagmata* did not possess military lands to support them, but this does not mean that they could not have owned land and property as individuals. They certainly did!

The *themata* (both naval and land) were stationed in the *themata* (military districts/provinces). Each *thema* had a *stratêgos* (general) who was in charge of the recruitment and maintenance of the thematic forces in his own *thema*. The *stratêgos* was also the commander-in-chief of the thematic forces stationed in his own *thema*. The *stratiôtai*, the soldiers of the *themata* settled on military lands (*stratiôtika ktêmata*), either campaigned themselves or supported a salaried *stratiôtês* (a soldier). The *stratiôtai* of the *themata* were required to bring their own horses and equipment for campaign. They received a small salary and cash allowances in return for military service (*strateia*) and a share of the spoils of war, but the income from the military lands formed the principal source of revenue needed for the financing of their equipment and horse.

The exact origins of the thematic system are not known and it was regulated by custom and by the terms found in the tax registers until 947 when Kônstantinos VII Porfyrogennêtos (McGeer, 2000, E.1, pp. 17, 71) enacted the first actual novel to regulate the system. The requirement to serve as a *stratiôtês* (soldier) in return for military lands was originally personal and hereditary, so that the duty to serve together with the military lands passed from father to son, but so that the actual military service could still be performed by a replacement *stratiôtês* funded by the *stratiôtês* himself or by several *stratiôtai* jointly – this could happen for example because the *stratiôtês* was too old or young or infirm to serve in person. In other words, the *stratiôtês* who actually performed the military service could have several contributors (*syndotai*) to enable him to serve. In addition to this, especially in the tenth century, the military service (*strateia*) could also be commuted into a cash payment, which could then be used by the state for the hiring of full-time soldiers or foreign mercenaries. The military lands were partially exempted from taxation to enable the owners to perform their military service, and the terms concerning this were registered in the tax registers. As will be made clear later, this has misled the previous generations of researchers into the false assumption that the East Roman thematic forces consisted solely of *stratiôtai* who performed their military service as mounted cavalry.[7] In truth, we should count the entire registered force of *stratiôtai* (including the *syndotai*) as thematic forces because (excluding those who could not serve due to old age or other infirmity) the *stratiôtai* not on campaign duty were still used as garrison forces or as infantry. For further details, see the discussion concerning the numbers below.

The map opposite, drawn after Haldon (2021, 72–3) shows the *themata* and *tagmata* in about 930.

Eric McGeer summarises (2000, 17) the reasons for the introduction of the legislation to regulate the military service and military lands in the tenth century as follows: 1) to prevent the alienation of the soldiers' properties; 2) to enable the soldiers or their heirs to recover their lost military lands; 3) to make certain that those who had acquired military lands continued to provide the military service required by the terms registered in the tax records for the lands in question; 4) to prevent the *dynatoi* (powerful persons called *prosopa*, military officials, magnates, church lands, monasteries) from exploiting their position to obtain military lands so that they could bring at least some of these into their personal service. The reason for the sudden need for land legislation resulted from the accumulation of problems after the severe famine of the years 927–8, which had thrown the countryside into turmoil. The *dynatoi* had exploited the situation by obtaining military lands and other agricultural lands, thereby diminishing the tax yield and number of men performing military service.[8]

Therefore, the land legislation not only concerned the military lands proper, but also the village communes in which these were located. The village was a territorial, social, economic, and a fiscal unit which also included the military lands and religious or charitable foundations (church property, monasteries etc.). The village had joint tax obligations so that each villager was required to pay his share. When the *dynatoi* used their influence to obtain lands, both military and regular, the remaining villagers (the 'poor') had to bear the extra tax burden (which impoverished them making them easier pickings for the *dynatoi* later) while the tax yield still dropped in practice, because even when the *dynatoi* paid the land tax (*demosion*), they were immune from the other forms of taxation. This means that there were then fewer persons performing the *corvées* (unpaid labour) for the state, while the number of men performing military service also diminished. The lands of the *dynatoi* were considered separate tax units so that they did not share the duties of the village commune, not to mention their illegal means of avoiding taxation through their influence and patronage. The land legislation was meant to correct all of these abuses.

The Military Themata and Tagmata in about 930 : The Key

1. Tagmata and Imperial Fleet	11. Dalmatia	22. Chaldia	**Created in 935:**
2. Thrakê	12. Laggobardia	23. Koloneia	A) Melitene
3. Makedonia	13. Aegaios Pelagos (Aegean Sea, naval)	24. Kharsianon	B) Kaloudia
4. Strymôn	14. Samos (naval)	25. Sebasteia	C) Hanzit
5. Thessaloniki	15. Kherson (Klimata)	26. Anatolikon	
6. Hellas	16. Optimaton	27. Kappadokia	
7. Nikopolis	17. Opsikion	28. Kibyrraiôtai (naval)	
8. Peloponnêsos	18. Boukellarion	29. Seleukeia	
9. Kephallênia	19. Thrakêsion	30. Lykandos	
10. Dyrrachion	20. Paphlagonia	31. Mesopotamia	
	21. Armeniakon		

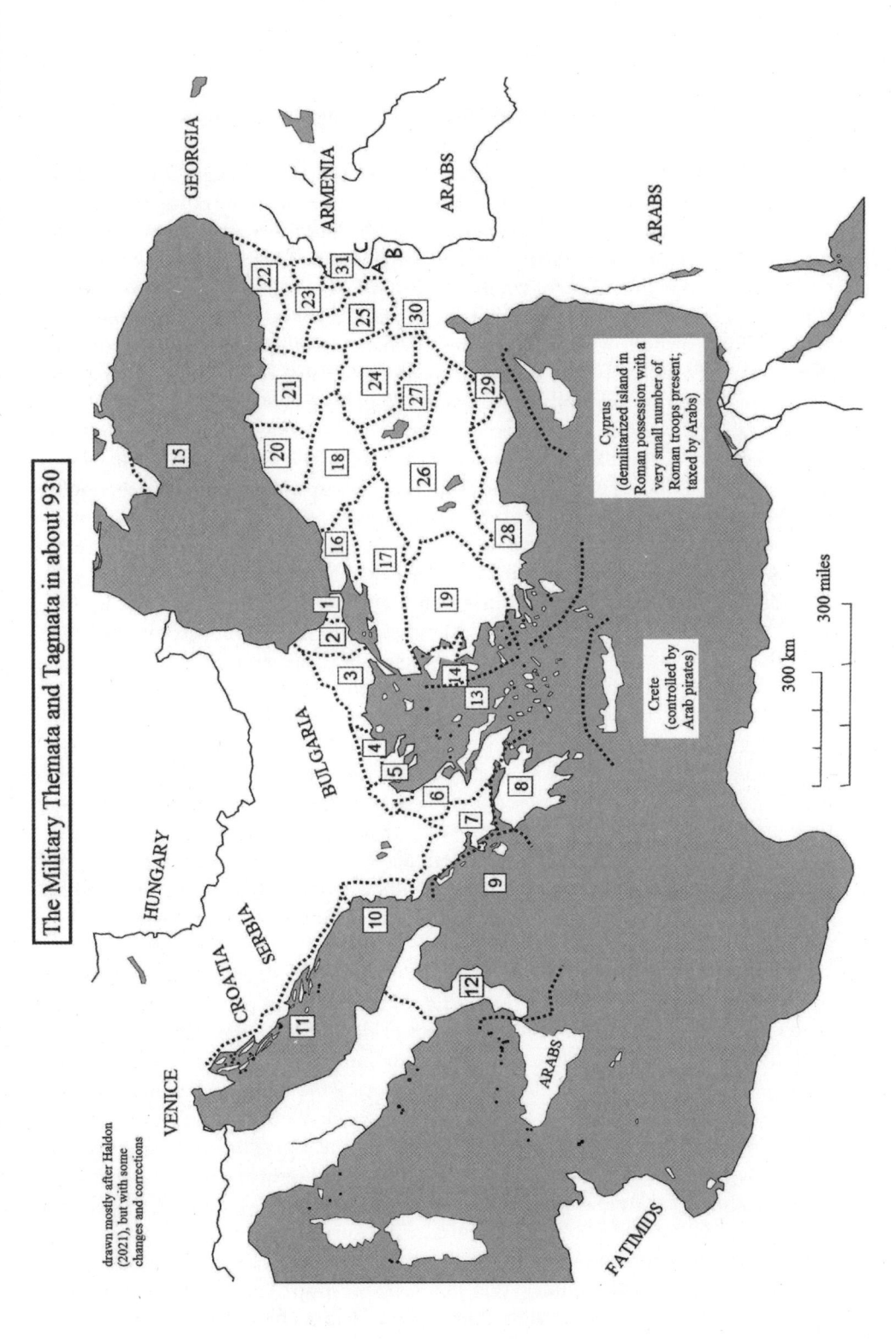

8   Nikephoros II Phokas, 912–969

Under Rômanos I and Kônstantinos VII Porfyrogennêtos, the state aimed to prevent the alienation of the farms and military lands, or the state sought to restore these to their rightful owners, or the state imposed the same military duties for the new owners. It was because of this that Kônstantinos set the value of the inalienable *strateia* at four pounds of gold (288 *nomismata*) for the cavalryman and two pounds for a sailor/rower. In other words, the cavalryman needed 288 *nomismata* of land to equip himself as a horseman for combat duties, which equalled two *zeugaria* of land (i.e. two typical households). Additionally, he enacted laws to restore the properties to the original owners or required the new owners to perform the military service. Nikêforos II Fôkas raised the minimum inalienable value of the military lands of the *klibanoforoi* from four to twelve pounds of gold, which prevented the sale of military lands altogether. His primary goal was to prevent the selling of the lands in order to ensure the availability of thematic soldiers or at least the converting of the personal military service into a contribution of money and supplies which would then be used for the upkeep of a professional army.[9]

One of the reasons for the enacting of the land laws was the need for the state to deal with the emergence of the landed aristocracy that had resulted from the militarization of society between the seventh and ninth centuries, so that by the tenth century the regional military administration (the administration of the thematic lands) was in the hands of the local magnate families. Eric McGeer (2000, 28–31) divides the landed aristocracy into three categories: innermost circle consisting of the courtiers and members of the imperial entourage; outer circle consisting of the high-ranking military and civil officials; outermost circle consisting of the military magnates of the thematic lands. It was the outermost circle of landed magnates in the *themata* that posed a challenge to the state and emperor because these magnates, the *stratêgoi* of their *themata*, had significant personal wealth and prestige together with sizeable private retinues, not to mention the fact that they could influence the decisions of the imperial officials who were eager to please these powerful individuals. The combination of military command with personal wealth was a potentially dangerous combination.

The state aimed to preserve the viability of the tax system while preventing the magnates from becoming too powerful. However, at no point in time did the state remove the tax exemptions or privileges of the *dynatoi* – the state only sought to limit their oppression of the poor and their interference with the tax yield of the state. The obvious reason for this was that everyone in power belonged to the *dynatoi*-class and in order to survive each power block needed the support from at least a section of the *dynatoi* to succeed. The aim of the Macedonian dynasty was to prevent any one of the magnates from becoming too powerful and able to overthrow them. In this, they were obviously only partially successful, because Rômanos I, Nikeforos II Fôkas and Iôannês I Tzimiskês all usurped power while keeping the members of the imperial family in their positions as figureheads. Regardless, it is still clear, as Eric McGeer notes, that the Roman Empire remained a centralized monarchical state governed from the Imperial Palace of Constantinople. Eric

McGeer also notes that the majority of the great military aristocratic families were located in the *themata* of Anatolikon, Cappadocia and Paphlagonia which shared a similar topography of hills and plains that supported a pastoral economy in which wealth was concentrated in the hands of a few. These areas were sparsely populated, with few towns and cities, and the control of the state was very limited in these areas to begin with. In contrast the coastal areas with their immediate hinterlands were densely populated agricultural lands with many towns and cities. It was in this area that the imperial government was in full control, so able to prevent the magnates from gaining control of these territories through the land legislation that the emperors enacted for this purpose.

The imperial government was similarly able to prevent the magnates from acquiring control of the newly-conquered territories in Cilicia and Syria with the establishments of crown-owned estates and domains under Nikêforos Fôkas and Iôannês Tzimiskês. In fact, Nikêforos Fôkas (McGeer, 2000, H) actually cancelled all land acquisitions by the *dynatoi* in the frontier districts without any compensation. This demonstrates the power of the emperor over the landed aristocrats in no uncertain terms. It is therefore with good reason that Eric McGeer (2000, 31) considers the land legislation of the Macedonian emperors as a success. It constrained the *dynatoi* in the territories they already held. In short, when land legislation was used in conjunction with imperial patronage and promotion, it enabled the emperors to assert or reassert their authority in such areas where the landed aristocrats were not as numerous and dominant as they were in the central plateau of Anatolia/Asia Minor.

1.4. The Roman Armed Forces: The Size in about 930–59[10]

The evidence for the size of the Roman armed forces during this era is based on three sources: Roman military treatises, the most important of which is Leôn's *Taktika*; Arab geographers; and numbers in narrative sources. The following discussion deals separately with the numbers in the land and naval forces in the same way as the period sources.

The Size of the Thematic Armies from Arabic Geographers ca. 840
We are fortunate to possess numerical evidence for the size of the Roman armies in the texts of the Arabic geographers. The most important of these are Ibn al-Faqih, Qudama/Kudama and Ibn Khurdadhbih/Khurradadhbih. Some historians are of the opinion that all three derive their accounts from a single source, al-Djarmi/Jarmi (e.g. Treadgold), while others are of the opinion that the evidence for this is not conclusive (e.g. Haldon). The following list of soldiers in the *themata* is based on the translation of al-Faqih/Fakih in Brooks (1901, 72–7), Ibn Khurdadhbih (pp. 76–84), Qudama (pp. 195–9) and Haldon (2000, 314). The information in it is datable to the middle of the ninth century. In my opinion, it gives us a rough estimate of the

actual combat-ready cavalry forces of the Roman Empire at this time. The reasoning for this conclusion is based on Leôn's *Taktika* and the narrative sources, and an explanation will be provided below. In other words, I do not accept John Haldon's conclusion that the Arab geographers would have given the paper strengths kept in the registers and that the actual campaign armies would have been smaller. It is the other way around, the Arab geographers give us the select campaign forces, in addition to which came the regular thematic soldiers kept in the registers and which were not considered campaign-ready select (*epilektoi*) soldiers.

	Ibn al-Faqih	Qudama
West of Khalig (European provinces, i.e. west of the Straits of Bosporus and Dardanelles)		
1. Talaya/Tafla district of Constantinople up to the Makron Teichos (Long Walls)		
2. Thrace (Europe)	5,000	5,000
3. Macedonia	5,000	lacuna
East of Khalig (Asian provinces)		
4. Paphlagonia	5,000	lacuna
5. Optimaton (at this date served as baggage handlers for the imperial *tagmata*)	4,000	4,000
6. Opsikion	6,000	6,000
7. Thrakesion	10,000	6,000
8. Anatolikon	15,000	15,000
9. Seleukeia (*kleisoura* under *kleisourarchês*)	no figure	5,000
10. Kappadokia (*kleisoura* under *kleisourarchês*)	4,000	4,000
11. Charsianon	4,000	4,000
12. Boukellarion	8,000	8,000
13. Armeniakon	9,000	4,000
14. Chaldia	10,000	4,000

According to Qudama (p.199), the eleven Asiatic *themata* had 70,000 men in total, while the figures of al-Faqih add up to 75,000 men plus the unknown number (4,000?) for the *kleisoura* of Seleukeia.[11] It is therefore clear that both sources give roughly the same number of men for the eastern *themata*. This may result from careless copying of their source(s) or from slight variations in the size of the Roman armed forces. According to Ibn Khurdadhbih (p.84), the Romans had 120,000 soldiers in total. This means that the *themata*, *tagmata* and other forces in Europe consisted of 50,000 men in total if we deduct from the total the 70,000 men mentioned by Qudama, and 41,000 men if we deduct from the figure the likely strength of the eastern *themata* (79,000 men) in al-Faqih.

Neither Ibn al-Faqih nor Qudama mention the following *themata* which we know to have existed in about 840 (the probable date for the information): Aigaion Pelagos

(Aegean Sea, naval), Dyrrachion (Dyrrachium), Hellas, Kephallênia (Cephalonia/ Kephalonia), Cherson/Kherson (Climata/Klimata), Kibyrraiôtai (naval *thema*), Peloponnêsos, Sikelia (Sicily/Calabria until 902), Thessalonikê. If each of the seven land-based *themata* had 4,000 picked horsemen, as expected by Leôn o Sofos for the *themata* of the east (see below), then these had in total 28,000 horsemen, which leaves either 22,000 horsemen (Qudama) or 13,000 horsemen (al-Faqih) for the four *tagmata* (*scholai; exkoubitoi; bigla / arithmos / arithmoi; hikanatoi*). One can therefore conclude the garrison at Constantinople consisted of 13–22,000 horsemen, which is still relatively imprecise.

Fortunately, we can obtain further clarity to the numbers because we possess numerical evidence for the size of the *tagmata* also in the Arabic sources.[12] According to Qudama (pp.196–7) the garrison at Constantinople consisted of 24,000 men in total, with 16,000 horsemen and 8,000 footmen. The cavalry was divided into four divisions. The *scholarioi* under the *megas domestikos* consisted of 4,000 horsemen. The *megas domestikos* served simultaneously as an overall commander of all armed forces of the Roman Empire and was in charge of ordering the levying of troops. In 960, to enable the offensive against Crete, the emperor Rômanos II (959–963) divided the office into *domestikos anatolês/ domestikos tês anatolês* (Domestic of the the East) and *domestikos dyseôs/ domestikos tês dyseôs* (Domestic of the West), with the former commanding the armies of the East while still being the supreme commander of all forces, while the latter commanded the armies of the west. The second of the units was the *taxis* (means the *bigla / arithmoi*) and it also consisted of 4,000 horsemen. The third unit was the *exkoubites / exkoubitoi* and it also had 4,000 horsemen. Their commander was the *drouggarios* – this is a mistake because the commander of the *exkoubitoi* was the *domestikos* while the commander of the *bigla* was the *drouggarios*. Depending on the reading of the Arabic text, the fourth was called *fidaratiyyīn* (means clearly the *foideratoi*)[13] or *qanātiyyīn* (means clearly the *ikanatoi* from the spellings of *oi kanatoi, i kanati*) and it similarly had 4,000 men.[14] It accompanied the emperor during his campaigns, just like the *tagma* of *etaireia* was to do later. I prefer the reading *ikanatoi* because the *ikanatoi* are known to have belonged to the *tagmata* while the *foederatoi* were separate thematic combat units regularly organized under the *komês tôn foideratôn* (*comes foederatorum*), under whom served the *tourmarchai*.[15] Ibn Khurdadhbih (p.76, 81)[16] in his turn states that the garrison of Constantinople consisted of 4,000 cavalry and 4,000 infantry. In my opinion, it is easy to see that the original meaning was that each infantry and cavalry *tagmata* consisted of 4,000 men. However, in practice the size varied from one period to another.

By combining the information provided by Ibn Khurdadhbih and Qudama regarding the Roman armed forces with the treatise of Philotheus in 899, Warren Treadgold (1980, 274–7; 1992, 88–9) has reconstructed the command structure of the 4,000-strong cavalry *tagmata* based in Constantinople as follows (overall commander added to the reconstruction):

1 *domestikos/drouggarios*
2 *topotêrêtai*
1 *chartoularios*
20 *komêtes* or *skribones*
100 *kentarchoi* (*domestikoi, drakonarioi*); the Arab geographers confirm this figure – see later!
1 *prôtomandatôr* (*proximos, akolouthos*)
40 *bandofori* (*protiktores, eutychoforoi, skeptroforoi, axiomatikoi, drakonarioi, skeuoforoi, signoforoi, sinatoroi, labouresioi, semioforoi, doukinatoroi*)
40 *mandatoroi* (*thuroroi, diatrechontes*)
204 officers and 1 *domestikos/drouggarios*

According to Qudama, the infantry garrison of Constantinople consisted of two 4,000-strong divisions, the *optimatoi* and *noumera*. The inclusion of the *optimatoi* among the garrison is in my opinion a mistake, because Qudama includes (197–8) the *optimatoi* also among the *themata*, which means that the second of the infantry units stationed at Constantinople was the *teichos* (Walls, *teichistai*) under the *teicheiotes* or *komês tôn teicheôn* (Count of the Walls), which we know to have existed in the city of Constantinople ever since the *Makron Teichos* (Great Walls) were built under Anastasius I. However, Qudama was not entirely mistaken in the inclusion of the *optimatoi* among the infantry *tagmata*, because the *optimatoi* of the *thema Optimaton* were used as baggage handlers for the *tagmata*.[17]

In fact, we can confirm the figures of Qadama by combining those with the information regarding imperial expeditions given by Kônstantinos VII in his *De Ceremoniis*. John Haldon (1990) has edited and translated these as three treatises on imperial expeditions. The key piece of evidence is the information that states that each *optimates* was assigned one pack-animal. When one remembers that each group of four horsemen were required to have one squire with a pack-animal to carry their gear, this results in a simple computation of 4,000 *optimatoi* x 4 horsemen, which equals 16,000 tagmatic horsemen, the figure given by Qudama for the *scholai, exkoubitoi, bigla* and *ikanatoi*.[18] It should be noted, however, that in practice the *tagmata* almost never campaigned with their full mobilization. This is also noted by Kônstantinos in the very same treatise. He states that some of the *tagmata* always remained behind to protect the walls of the capital, while also noting that 100 *optimatoi* with their pack-animals were assigned to serve in the imperial entourage as their baggage-handlers. However, it is clear that the *tagmata* that remained behind in Constantinople consisted of the infantry *teichistai* and *noumeroi* used on the walls and that the expectation was that the four cavalry *tagmata* would accompany the emperor in their entirety, hence the fact that only 100 *optimatoi* were assigned for the imperial entourage. The best evidence for this is that Kônstantinos required the entire force of the *optimatoi* to be present at Pylai, so that each one of them would be given a single pack-animal to attend. When one deducts from this number the 100 *optimatoi* assigned to the imperial service, one gets a total of

15,600 horsemen for the *tagmata* accompanying the expeditionary army led by the emperor in person, while the imperial bodyguards (300 *etaireiai* and 100 *basilikoi*) add the missing numbers so that the total number of elite cavalry accompanying the emperor was still 16,000 cavalrymen.[19] In short, the numerical information of Qudama is more than confirmed by Kônstantinos VII.

Therefore, it is clear that the cavalry component of the garrison of Constantinople was 16,000 horsemen in about 808–40. It is a mistake to think that Qudama's numbers would be too large on the basis of the information concerning the presence of the detachments drawn from the *tagmata* or from the Imperial bodyguard units (e.g. *basilikoi* and *magklabitai*) for the various campaigns mentioned by the military treatises such as Kônstantinos Porfyrogennêtos' texts or the *De re militari* (*Campaign Organization and Tactics* in Dennis).[20] It was a very rare event in history for the imperial bodyguard units to march out for campaigns in their entirety – a good example of this is the small numbers given for the Praetorian Guard in earlier times (e.g. Pseudo-Hyginus 30: four praetorian cohorts with 400 praetorian horsemen). This means that during the first half of the tenth century the central reserve in Constantinople is likely to have consisted on average of about 16,000 cavalry and 8,000 infantry, in addition to which came the Imperial Bodyguards (e.g. the *etaireia*, *basilikoi*, and *magklabitai*), the Imperial Fleet, the soldiers of the *eparch* of Constantinople, the demes and other civilian paramilitary forces including civilian ships, and whatever soldiers or sailors were on leave in the city.

Information in Leôn's *Taktika* (4.1–3, 18.136–50)
By far the most important piece of evidence for the size of the Roman army is Leôn's *Taktika* and in particular its sections dealing with how to fight against the Hagarenes (Muslims). According to Leôn, when the *stratêgos* faced Arabs and these had a small army, he was to choose about 4,000 picked men (*epilektoi* = chosen picked elite force) who were to be deployed in the standard manner into three lines and ambushers: the first line was to consist of the three *mere* with outflankers on the right and flank guards on the left; the second line of four *mere* with fill-up men between those to make the intervals equal in proportion with the first line; the third line of rear guards placed behind the flanks of the second line; and lastly the commander was to post ambushers either in ambush on both sides if this was possible, or hidden behind the first line in a *drouggos*-array (irregular order) to surprise the enemy with a sudden outflanking. The *stratêgos* was to have under him a *tourmarchês* (formerly *hypostratêgos*) who had under him *drouggarioi*. They had under them the *komêtes* and other officers. During the sixth century, this array was reserved only for large cavalry armies, which means that the preference had changed.

If the Arabs outnumbered the army of the *stratêgos*, he was to double the size of his force to 8,000 men by strengthening it with detachments drawn from fellow *stratêgoi*. This means that each of the neighbouring *stratêgoi* dispatched only a detachment and not his entire picked elite force (*epilektoi*) that averaged about 4,000 men to assist the *stratêgos* in need. This was obviously a wise precaution because it would have been foolish to dispatch the entire picked forces so that the defence of their own *thema* would have been left entirely in the hands of the common thematic soldiers. The larger cavalry army was distributed into battle formation exactly as the smaller version. If even this was not enough, then the size of the army was to be tripled to 12,000 men so that two other *stratêgoi* joined him with their entire picked (*epilektoi*) force. This array was deployed in a similar manner, as three lines (in truth two lines and rear guards) with ambushers.

If the enemy had invaded with a really large army, Leôn instructed all *stratêgoi* of the east to unite their forces so that each chose a picked body of about 4,000 horsemen by separating the useless men from the good quality fighters. The total so achieved consisted of more than 30,000 horsemen. According to Leôn, the separating of the useful men from the useless was necessary because a lack of adequate training and carelessness had diminished the numbers of useful men. This shows in no uncertain terms that the thematic registers included far more men than 4,000 horsemen per *thema* in the east, which means that the large army sizes given by the narrative sources are entirely plausible.

It is also important to note that Leôn's figures confirm that each of the eastern *themata* was expected to be able to raise 4,000 first-rate horsemen for any campaign. This confirms the numbers given by the Arab geographers, all of whom give the eastern *themata* a minimum of 4,000 men. Leôn's numbers confirm that these mean the elite cavalry component of each *thema*. This in its turn means that each of the *themata* had also an unknown number of second-rate horsemen, either because they lacked training, equipment or a horse, which are not included in the figures.

We know on the basis of the extant legislation that the registers of the thematic cavalry included impoverished *stratiôtai* (thematic soldiers) who were unable to equip horsemen for service. It was because of this that such impoverished *stratiôtai* could be grouped together as contributors (*syndotai*) to provide a single *strateia* (military service denoting the service of a single cavalryman); or they could be transferred to irregular forces (part time soldier-farmers); or placed on garrison duty; or temporarily exempted from the *strateia* until their economic situation improved. This means that the thematic registers of *stratiôtai* with *stratiôtika ktêmata* (military lands) included far more cavalrymen than Leôn and the Arabic geographers include in their figures. In addition to this, there were at least three other classes of soldiers that belonged to the thematic system: the infantry of the interior, Armenian infantry, and the sailors, but these were not included in the categories given by Leôn or the Arabic geographers and should be added to their figures.[21]

In sum, it is clear that we should at least double the cavalry figures given for the *themata* by Leôn and the Arabic geographers to take into account the useless category together with the useful fighters – it is in fact quite probable that there were more useless men than useful men, because several of these could be needed for the support of one man who could fight. However, since it is probable that at least some of the useless men were incorporated into the thematic infantry and garrison forces because they lacked a horse, I have still estimated that the number of useless men add to the total number of thematic cavalry only about a third (i.e. each of these men had a horse, but were not otherwise up to regular combat because of lack of equipment or training). If we therefore remove the 16,000 cavalry *tagmata* from the 120,000 horsemen given by the Arabic sources, we get in total 104,000 horsemen for the first rate thematic forces, which means that the total number of thematic horsemen, both useless and useful, was about 140,000 horsemen. It should be remembered that this is not the total number of horsemen in the thematic armies, because the *dynatoi* possessed their own private armies.

One may estimate that the thematic infantry forces, which were used for both campaigning and for the guarding of the strongholds and places of habitation, consisted at least double the cavalry total so that there were at least 280,000 thematic footmen (including the cavalrymen without horses) in total, meaning that the potential military strength of the thematic armies, which was never achieved in practise, consisted of a minimum of 280,000 footmen and 140,000 horsemen plus the private retinues of the *dynatoi*. Their numbers could be bolstered further with the *tagmata* and foreign mercenaries.

It is therefore easy to see that when the sources give the imperial armies the size of 80,000 or 100,000 that this is entirely plausible and should be accepted at face value. Such forces clearly included infantry and signified a major effort by the emperor – even much smaller numbers often meant a major effort in situations in which the Empire faced multiple threats. We should not forget that according to Kônstantinos Porfyrogennêtos (DAI 31.71ff.) even so small a nation as the Croats was able to field an army of 60,000 cavalry and 100,000 foot, with their fleet consisting of 80 *sagenai* (small galleys) and 100 *kondourai* (boats, cutters). Why should we doubt the figures of a far larger nation? It is clear that the information presented by Kônstantinos is relatively accurate because it is clear that it was based on the information given to Kônstantinos by his military intelligence services, and we should not forget Kônstantinos' purpose in writing, which was to instruct his son in the conduct of foreign policy. Why should we therefore not accept what is in the sources? My answer is that we should.

The Size of the Navy
According to John Haldon's estimate, in 949 the Imperial Fleet consisted of 150 *ousiai*-crews.[22] The *ousia* had a single crew of 108–110 rowers, who could also be expected to serve as fighters when needed. This gives us the total strength of 16,200 to 16,500 rowers, in addition to which we should calculate the sailors, mariners, marines, officers, and support personnel such as sail makers, carpenters, clerks,

secretaries and so forth. In 949 the Imperial Fleet included at least 100 *ousiaka chelandia* (warships with a single *ousia*), 8 *pamphyloi* and 20 *dromônes* (each with a double *ousia*) for a total 128 galleys. Of these, 7 *pamphyloi*, 33 *ousiaka chelandia* and 20 *dromônes* (each with a double *ousia*) were dispatched against the Arabs of Crete in 949; while 1 *pamfylos* and 24 *ousiai* (Kônstantinos does not state if these had ships) were left behind to guard Constantinople; 7 *ousiai* were stationed at Dyrrachion and Dalmatia; 3 had been sent to Spain; and 3 were based in Calabria. Kônstantinos fails to state where the remaining ten *ousiai* were stationed. In addition to this, there were two imperial *dromônia* constructed under Leôn VI, which were stationed at Constantinople, each with an *ousia* so that the total number of *ousiai* was 150.[23] It is of note that at any given point in time, the Imperial Fleet had dispatched detachments around the Mediterranean, with the implication that these were used for the protection of Roman merchant ships and harbours and for maritime raiding and other piratical activities, as well as escorts for diplomats.

The size of the Imperial Fleet (Const. *De Cer.* 44.19–20, 45.6–11) had diminished from the year 911, and its ships were now also smaller than in 911, but with the difference that both the *pamfyloi* and *dromônes* were equipped with three *sifones* to shoot liquid fire (Greek fire).[24] The idea behind the change was clearly to use smaller, more manoeuvrable ships as firing platforms in naval combat. It is possible that this was a response to the appearance of the Rus' (the ancestors of both Russia/ Ukraine) as a maritime threat. The Russians possessed smaller, swift Viking-style vessels, which required the use of smaller vessels against them so that the Romans could reach these vessels in shallower waters. However, the Rus'-ships were no match against a real naval encounter because their *monoxyles* were too small and very vulnerable to Greek fire.

The size of the Imperial Fleet was obviously a conscious decision. The authorities in charge (mainly the emperor and *drouggarios tou ploimou*) considered this to be adequate to the demands, but the campaign of 960 shows that it was not the entire naval potential of the Imperial Fleet.

In my opinion, the marines of the Imperial Fleet were the 4,000 *noumera*, which would mean that each of the 128 ships of the Imperial Fleet could possess ca. 31 men (if each ship had the same number of men) from the *noumera* as their complementary force of marines. In practise, the number of marines drawn from the *noumera* for this duty would have varied according to the size of the vessel and the number of men drawn from the land forces to serve on board.

We can also use the same document to calculate the thematic naval forces of Hellas (911 campaign), Aegean Sea/Aegaios Pelagos (911 and 949 campaigns), Samos (911 and 949 campaigns), Kibyrraiôtai (911 and 949 campaigns), Peloponnesus (very rough estimate based on 949 campaign), Nikopolis (very rough estimate based on 949 campaign), and Kephallenia (very rough estimate based on 949 campaign).[25]

In 949, the *thema* of the Aegean Sea had at least 6 *pamfylia chelandia* (120 men per ship) and 4 *ousiaka chelandia* (manned by 108 men) and an extra *ousia* of rowers. We should add to these figures also the sailors, mariners, marines and officers. The size of the *thema* appears to have diminished after the campaign of 911, which presumably reflects the problems resulting from the severe famine of 927–8 and decisions made at the imperial level regarding the demands made of the naval *themata* regarding their required contribution of forces. The next major naval operation against the island of Crete in 960 demonstrates that when necessary the numbers could be bolstered significantly.

In 949, the *thema* of Samos had a minimum of 4 *dromônes* (each manned by 220 men), 6 *pamfylia chelandia* (each manned by 150 men), and 9 *ousiaka cheleandia* (108 men each). The same comments about the situation in 911 and 960 apply also for this *thema*.

In 949, the fleet of the *thema* of Kibyrraiôtai consisted of a minimum of 4 *dromônes* (each with a crew of 220 men), 8 *pamfylia chelandia* (crews of 150 men), 10 *ousiaka chelandia* (110-man crews), 18 *galeai*, and 3 *ousiai* of rowers elsewhere. In contrast to the *themata* of the Aegean Sea and Samos, the size of the *thema* of Kibyrraiôtai had remained basically the same as in 911.

My estimated size for the *thema* of Peloponnessus is that it had 34 *chelandia* with 16 *ousiai* (ca. 1,760 rowers) of regular rowers and 18 *ousiai* of Mardaites (ca. 2,000 rowers), and I estimate that Kephallenia and Nikopolis both had 18 *chelandia* (each with an *ousia* of rowers) for a total of 2,000 Mardaite rowers for each of the *themata*. In 911, the *thema* of Hellas contributed 10 *dromônes* for a campaign against Crete so that each *dromôn* carried 230 oarsmen and 70 soldiers for a total of 3,000 men. One may make the educated guess that at least 1,000 men remained behind, so the total would have been 4,000 men. It is possible that the strength diminished slightly, as it did with the *themata* of Samos and the Aegean Sea, so that there were only 3,000 men in the *thema* by 949. Similarly, it is also probable that the ship type was now the smaller *chelandia*, because the Imperial Fleet had increased the number of smaller vessels (*chelandia* and *pamfyloi*) at the expense of the largest *dromônes*. As already discussed, each of the *themata* possessed reserves of men that contributed to the overall effort by providing upkeep for the men who actually served. Similarly, the number of ships could be increased by adding civilian ships to the numbers or by building new ones. For example, according to the *De Ceremoniis* (45.6–7), the Imperial Fleet had six recently-constructed ships. The requirement in the *Taktika of Leôn VI* (5.9) was simply that the *stratêgos* assigned to combat duties at sea was required to prepare ships, some for fighting at sea and others for the transport of horses, and still others for the transport of arms and other equipment.

According to Hélène Ahrweiler, the non-naval *themata* appear to have possessed separate provincial fleets equipped and paid by the state. These fleets consisted of the lighter vessels (*chelandia* and *galeai*) and were usually crewed by natives recruited from all regions of the Empire and not only from the province/*thema* where they served. In the normal manner, these were placed under the control of a *tourmarchês tou ploimou* (*tourmarchês* of the fleet), who was a subordinate of the *stratêgos* of the *thema*. However, during great naval expeditions these ships were united with the Imperial Fleet so that the ships served under the *drouggarios tou ploimou*. It is because of this that I would suggest that the provincial fleets were actually only detachments of the Imperial Fleet, dispatched to serve under the *stratêgoi* of the *themata*. We do not know how many ships these provincial fleets had and which of the provinces had these detachments, which complicates the calculation of the totals. What is clear is that the size of these fleets were modest, because for example the *tourmarchês* of the *thema* of Peloponnêsos had a fleet of only four *chelandia* under him, with the implication that there cannot have been more than a couple of dozen *chelandia* that could be used to bolster the size of the fleet dispatched for some major operation. In addition to this, it is also known that the naval *themata* also dispatched detachments of ships to serve under army commanders or to the city of Constantinople when the Imperial Fleet was campaigning elsewhere.[26]

The standard crews for the fighting galleys were: 1) *chelandion, ousiakon chelandion* (pl. *chelandia*), a galley with an *ousia* (108 or 110 men) of rowers who seconded as fighters, but in addition to which was an unknown numbers of sailors; 2) *pamfyla, pamfylos, pamfylon, ousiaka pamfyla*, (pl. *pamfylia, pamfyloi*), a galley with a crew of 120, 130, 150, or 160 men (note, however, it has been conjectured that *pamfylos* actually meant the crew and not a special type of ship); 3) *dromôn, dromôn trieres* with two *ousiai* (220 or 230) of rowers plus the sailors, mariners and marines for a total of about 300 men. However, there is evidence for even larger crews. Cosentino notes that a Sicilian inscription documents a *pemptokentarchos*, which implies he served as a commander of 500 men. This means that there were not only smaller vessels than the *chelandion*, such as the fifty-oared *galea*, but also larger galleys or galleys loaded with additional crew. This means that one cannot use the number of ships to count the maximum numbers on board.[27]

In addition to this, there were also the ships of the so-called *komêtes-archôntoi-abydykoi* of the Imperial Fleet, each in charge of sections of the coast, each with his own detachment of ships and soldiers to control the commercial activity and movement of people, merchandize and ships in the area assigned under his control.[28] It is impossible to estimate the size of these contingents. One may only imagine that these ships were usually not used in actual naval operations against enemy fleets except in great emergencies.

The number of ships corvéed from the civilians is even more difficult to establish than the totals for the formal establishments. Their numbers must have depended on the situation and location of corvéeing.

1.5. The organization of the *themata* and *tagmata*

1.5.1. The *themata*

As the above has made clear, the provincial armies, the *themata*, consisted of the *stratiôtai* who held military lands (*stratiôtika ktêmata*), so that these were divided into land and naval *themata* called *o thematikos stolos* (under a *stratêgos tôn Kibyrraiôtôn, stratêgos tês Samou, stratêgos tou Aigaiou Pelagous*; the commander of the Imperial

Fleet, the *drouggarios tôn ploimôn*, ranked below them in hierarchy but was still their commander in practice).[29]

The *stratiôtai* of the *themata* also included special types of soldiers. In the category of infantry, there were the Armenian infantry of the small *kleisoura* of the Taurus range, which I assume to have been created after the writing of the *Taktika* of Leôn (18.128) because in that treatise the light infantry was placed on the heights while the thematic cavalry engaged the retreating Saracens in the pass. In contrast to this, in the *De velitatione* (3.3) we find the pass blocked by heavy infantry.

In addition to this, there were also special light cavalry categories both in the western and eastern *themata*. In the eastern half of the Empire, the irregular light-cavalry was called *apelatai* (or *trapezites*, or *tasanarioi* or *tasinakia*, or in the widest sense *akritai* when the source meant the inhabitants and soldiers of a border region). In the western portion of the Empire they were known as *chonsarioi/ chôsarioi* ('Hussars') from the Bulgarian word for robber. The *apelatai* were used for the raiding of the enemy territory and as scouts and guides for the expeditionary armies. They were recruited both from the foreigners and from the *stratiôtai* of the *themata* who were unable to serve in the line cavalry. In the east, the foreign element consisted mainly of Armenians (Armenians called them *tasanarioi*), while in the west the foreign element consisted mainly of Bulgarians. The *apelatai* of the *themata* were included in the muster lists, but it is not known if they possessed military lands or were paid to serve.[30]

The fact that the tenth-century expeditionary armies usually included also infantry forces means that the *stratiôtai* of the *themata* who were unable to serve even as light cavalry *apelatai* were used as heavy and light infantry according to their means.

The land *themata* were further divided into the regular *themata* each under *stratêgos* and smaller units called *kleisourai* (passes), each of which was placed under a *kleisourarchês*. The *stratiôtai* of the *themata* were mostly part time soldiers or their replacements, paid by the *stratiôtai-syndotai* who owned the military lands. The regular replacements continued to belong to the *themata*, but when the state had opted to commute military service for gold and supplies, so that the state then recruited professional soldiers and foreign mercenaries, these replacements belonged to the professional army called the *tagmata*. For the command structure of the thematic *stratiôtai*, see the attached diagram showing both the thematic and tagmatic officers. The size and number of the *themata* varied according to their strategic importance (see above), so new *themata* were added in the course of the tenth century as the Romans re-conquered lands lost.

The thematic forces also appear to have included remnants of the late Roman *foideratoi* (*foederati*, Federate forces), units which now served under the *archôn tôn foideratôn* who is clearly the successor of the Late-Roman era *comes foederatorum* (*komês tôn foideratôn*). As already noted, it has been speculated that the *foideratoi* served as one of the units of the *tagmata* in the early-ninth century, but the case for this is uncertain. It is actually far likelier that the *foideratoi* remained as a special unit category among the thematic forces which had one supreme commander, regardless of their place of service, just as was the case during the Late-Roman era. In other words, it is probable that the *foideratoi* were equipped, organized and paid through the office of *archôn tôn foideratôn*, even when these were stationed in the *themata* that had *stratêgoi* as their supreme commanders. It is also clear that the position the *archôn tôn foideratôn* was an important one, because the title *archôn tôn foideratôn* (*phoideratoi*) occurs five times in Theophanes Continuatus and it was granted to persons of great importance. The subordinates of the *archôn tôn foideratôn/ komês tôn foideratôn* consisted of the *tourmarchai* and other officers typically belonging to the *stratiôtai* of the *themata*.

For the military hierarchy of the officers of the *themata*, see the diagram on page 29 together with the Index.

1.5.2. The *Tagmata*, Imperial Fleet, Imperial Bodyguards, Demes and Constantinople

The fully professional portion of the Roman armed forces consisted of the *tagmata*. The *tagmata* consisted of full-time soldiers paid and equipped by the state. The majority of these forces were stationed around the capital, but detachments drawn from these forces were also stationed in the *themata* to bolster their numbers in strategically-important locales. During this era the *tagmata* consisted of the cavalry *tagmata scholai, exkoubitoi, bigla/artithmoi, ikanatoi, basilikê etaireia,* and of the infantry *tagmata noumera* and *teichistai* (Walls) and of the baggage handlers of the *tagmata* called *optimatoi*. The case for the *foideratoi* is uncertain, but as far as can be gauged from the extant evidence these appear to have formed separate mercenary forces usually posted in the *themata*. The *athanatoi* (Immortals) and the famous Varangian Guard did not yet exist. The former was created by Iôannês I Tzimiskês and the latter by Basileios II Boulgaroktonos (Basil II the Bulgar Slayer). The case of the Imperial Fleet (*to Basilikoploimon, Basilikou ploimou*) is actually complicated because its sailors were given military lands in return for service (inalienable land value assessed at two pounds of gold), while they were still considered to belong to the *tagmata* recruited, paid and equipped by the state.

For the military hierarchy of the officers of the *tagmata*, see the diagram on page 29 together with the Index.

The question of who were the Imperial Bodyguards is complicated because we possess information about very specific small units of bodyguards which may have been independent small units or units belonging to the larger bodies of Imperial Bodyguards. The following list is based on D'Amato's list (2012, 30–39) and Bury (1911, 106ff.) but it should be understood that there remains a lot of room for further speculation, not least because some of the historians consider the *basilikê etaireia* to be part of the *tagmata* rather than of the imperial bodyguards. I agree with this view, because the DRM (1.158–68) clearly implies that the *etaireiai* belonged to the *tagmata*. In short, I consider the following units to belong to the imperial bodyguards proper: *basilikodromônion, maglavitai, basilikoi anthrôpoi, archôntogennematai, sardoi* and *stratôres* while the *etaireiai* still served bodyguards in practice.

Scholai, Scholae

The *scholai* were the direct successors of the *scholae palatinae* units (originally known as *aulici, corporis in aula, protectores, domestici*[31]) created either in the late-second or early-third century and which became famous only during the fourth century under Constantine the Great.[32] The original *scholai* were elite cavalry units accompanying the emperors, which appear to have consisted mainly of foreigners. The *scholae palatinae* became parade-ground units by the sixth century, but in the mid-eighth century Kônstantinos V restored their combat effectiveness as an elite cavalry unit by reorganizing them together with the *exkoubitoi*. Kônstantinos V used the enlarged and reorganized *tagmata* as a counter-balance against the thematic forces. The commander of the newly-organized *scholai* was the *domestikos tôn scholôn*, also known as the *megas domestikos*, who usually also served as supreme commander of all Roman forces. As already noted, the office was divided into western and eastern commands during the reign of Rômanos II in 960, but the *domestikos anatolês/ domestikos tês anatolês/domestikos tôn scholôn tês anatolês* (Domestic of the Schools of the East) was the *megas domestikos* and the *domestikos duseôs/domestikos tês duseôs/ domestikos tôn scholôn tês duseôs* (Domestic of the Schools of the West) his subordinate. In the ninth century the unit consisted of 4,000 elite cavalry (see above), but its size may have been increased subsequently because there were altogether fifteen units of *scholai* in the mid-tenth century, each under a *komês*, which may imply the size of 7,500 horsemen.[33]

Exkoubitoi, Excubitores

The *exkoubitoi* were the direct descendants of the Late-Roman *excubitores* which had been created by Zeno I to serve as a counter-balance against the other units of bodyguards (*scholae, protectores-domestici*). The original size of the *excubitores* was only 300 men, so it was mainly used for its primary purpose of being personal bodyguards of the emperor, while in the latter-half of the sixth century their commander, the *comes excubitorum*, became de-facto supreme commander of all-armed forces and the designated successor of the emperor. The officers of the *excubitores*, the *scribones* (*skribônes*), were similarly used as commanders and special operatives of the emperor.[34] The unit was reorganized and strengthened by Kônstantinos V as a full-sized cavalry combat unit for the same purpose as the *scholai*. The overall commander of the reorganized *exkoubitoi* was also called *domestikos tôn exkoubitôn*. The unit consisted of 4,000 elite horsemen (see above).

Arithmoi/Arithmos/Vigla/Bigla[35] (the Watch)

The *tagma* of *arithmoi/arithmos/bigla* appears to have been established by the empress Irene/Eirene for her personal protection in about 786/7. The *tagma* was built mainly from older, pre-existing cavalry units drawn from the Thrakesion *thema*. Most of these units appear to have existed already during the Late-Roman period. In my opinion. it is likely that at least some of the cavalry units in question had the word *scutarii* as part of their title because the troopers of the *bigla* were called *skoutarioi*.[36] The name *arithmoi* comes from the fact that the cavalry units of the new bodyguard unit *bigla* were collectively called in the plural the *arithmoi*, but were also called *arithmos* in the singular because it was considered as one unit. The reason why these units received the name *bigla* is that their principal mission was to guard the empress. The overall commander of the *tagma* of *bigla* was *drouggarios tês biglas*, because the *tagma* was irregular in size and consisted of several *arithmoi*. This unit is not to be confused with the *noumera/numeri*, which, as will be made clear below, consisted of infantry. The unit of *bigla* consisted of 4,000 elite cavalrymen.

Ikanatoi[37]

The *ikanatoi* were created by Nikêforos I in 809. We know this on the basis of the *Life of Patriarch Ignatius* by Nikêtas David (3.25–8, p.6). According to David, it was Nikêforos I who created the corps in 809. It was originally a small bodyguard unit that protected Nikêforos' son which also served simultaneously as a cadet corps, but it was soon transformed into a real fighting unit consisting of 4,000 elite horsemen under their supreme commander the *domestikos tôn ikanatôn*.

Basilikê etaireia[38]

The consensus opinion among the historians is that the so-called *basilikê etaireia* (Companions of the *Basileus*) was created in the mid-ninth century. Treagold (1995, 110) dates the addition of the *etaireia tagma* to a period very soon after 840. This means that the size of the garrison at Constantinople and the size of the central reserve available for the emperor to use were increased from the size given by the Arab geographers (see above), but by how much we do not know. Raffaele D'Amato suggests on the basis of *Campaign Organization* (*De re militari* 8) that the size of the unit was 1,000 horsemen, but this is an incorrect assumption. This is the size of the cavalry *parataxis* accompanying the emperor in that treatise, which included besides the *etaireiai* also the *athanatoi*. In fact, most of the *etaireiai* were included in the cavalry totals. See Appendix 4. Furthermore, on the basis of Kônstantinos VII's three treatises on *Imperial Expeditions* (Haldon, 1990 C text 420ff.), we know that on other occasions the emperor could be accompanied by as few Companions as 300 horsemen (Kônstantinos gives only 200 natives and 100 foreigners). And we should not forget that the unit included also footmen (see below) and that some of the *etaireiai* definitely remained behind in Constantinople to protect the empress and the city. In short, it is clear that the numbers given by the military treatises cannot be taken as evidence for the size of the entire unit. My own educated guess is therefore that the size varied according to the availability of foreign mercenaries and prisoners, but that on average, before the introduction of the Varangian Guard, this *tagma* probably consisted of between 2,000 and 4,000 horsemen and footmen.

The Companions served as personal bodyguards of the emperor, and the unit consisted of four divisions: the *megas* (Great), *mese* (Middle) and *mikro* (Small) *etaireia*, and of the *pezetairoi* (Foot Companions commanded by the *etaireiarchês tôn pezôn*). The *megas etaireia* consisted of the Macedonians; the *mese etaireia* consisted of the Farganoi and Khazars; the *mikro/trithe etaireia* consisted of foreigners like the Turks, Khazars, Hungarians/Magyars, Saracens (*Agarenoi*), Christianized Moors, ex-Muslim 'blacks' (known as Indians) and Franks. The Macedonians of the Great Companions were the most loyal element among all bodyguards towards the Macedonian dynasty.

The overall commander of the *etaireiai* was called the *etaireiarchês*, also known as *megas etaireiarchês*. This office was among the most important in the Empire. Each of the four divisions had their own *etaireiarchês* (pl. *etaireiarchoi*) and these were commanded by the *megas etaireiarchês*. At some point in time in the tenth century the number of foreigners increased so much that a separate *tagma* of *ethnikoi* was formed under an *ethnarchôs*, but it is possible that this was just a new name for an already existing division (e.g. for the *mikro etaireia* which disappeared from the sources at some unknown point in time). The *etaireiai* were therefore composed mainly of foreigners and included also units composed of foreign prisoners. These included for example Khazars, Farganoi, Hungarians and the Rus'/Russians/Varangians. The members of this unit were obviously also used as marines and rowers.

Noumeroi, Noumera, Numeri

My educated guess since 2011 has been that the *noumeroi/noumera* were actually originally the marines of the Imperial Fleet posted in the city of Constantinople (Syvänne, *MHLR1*, 233, 276, 337) because the various infantry *numeri/arithmoi* are the only known units to be based in the city of Constantinople that could be thought to be the marine component of the Imperial Fleet. For example, the *arithmoi/numeri* are attested to have been present in the city of Constantinople in 358/9, from which these were then sent to Paphlagonia. Further support for this conclusion comes from the fact that the *noumera* are known to have been used for the defence of the Walls of the Imperial Palace in Constantinople, the Hippodrome area and the imperial prison called *ta noumera* (the former baths of Zeuxippus).[39] The commander of the *noumera* was the *domestikos tou noumerôn*. My educated suggestion is that as marines the *noumera* also guarded the Theodosian Sea Walls close to the Imperial Palace and the ships of the Imperial Fleet. The strength of the unit was 4,000 marines/footsoldiers.

Teichistai, Teichos (the Walls)

As already discussed, the *teichos/teichistai* were originally created under Anastasius/Anastasios I to man the *Makron Teichos* (Great Walls). It was the second of the infantry units stationed at Constantinople. In my opinion it appears to have retained its primary function, which was the defence of the Great Walls, also during this era because it was grouped together with the peratic demes and *exkoubitoi* under the *domestikos tôn exkoubitôn* (see below), with the implication that they continued to protect the area between the city of Constantinople and Great Walls by being posted on the walls when it was considered feasible to defend those. The commander of the *teichistai* was called *komês tôn teicheôn, teichôn*, or *tou teichous* (Count of the Walls).[40]

Optimatoi, Optimates

The *optimatoi/optimates* were originally a Late-Roman elite cavalry unit apparently consisting of barbarian 'knights' (*optimates*, the best) of Germanic origins. We find these as separate elite cavalry divisions in the *Strategikon*, and then in the seventh century in the *thema* of the *opsikion*, with the implication that the *optimates* had served under the *praesental magistri militum* during the Late-Roman period. It was probably after the revolt of the *opsikion thema* under Artavasdus in 743 that Kônstantinos V broke the original *thema* of the *opsikion* into three parts to diminish its threat as a military power: the *boukellarion* (*bucellarii*) and *opsikion* remained as *themata*, but the third, the *optimatoi*, became one of the imperial *tagmata*, but the *optimatoi* were still punished for their role in the revolt. Their new status was to serve as baggage handlers for the fighting *tagmata*, as each *optimates* was assigned one pack-animal to attend. The *optimatoi* numbered 4,000 baggage handlers/ footmen under the *domestikos tôn optimatôn*.[41] As already noted, this suggests that there were at least 16,000 horsemen in the *tagmata* of the *scholai, exkoubitoi, bigla* and *ikanatoi*.

The Imperial Fleet (*to basilikoploimon, basilikou ploimou*)[42]

The city of Constantinople had possessed an Imperial Fleet from the day Constantine the Great chose the city of Byzantion as his capital. During the Late-Roman period, the *praesental magister* served as its overall commander, but other *magistri* could also be placed in command of the Fleet. In addition to this, the Imperial Fleet still had its own separate naval commander (admiral) who was called either *nauarchos* (and *archegos*?) or *stratêgos*, and under him served *merarchai* in charge of the divisions of ships. At some unknown point in time, probably already in the seventh century, the commander of the Imperial Fleet received a new title, *o drouggarios tou ploimou* or *drouggarios tôn ploimôn* (Drungary of the Fleet), but in the seventh century he appears to have usually served as a subordinate of the *stratêgos tôn Karabisianôn* (General of the Karabisian theme) which was abolished and subdivided under Leôn III. The office became the most important naval command under Basileos I, so the *drouggarios tou ploimou* usually served as the supreme commander for all fleets; the tagmatic and thematic fleets, provincial fleets and corvéed civilian ships.

The principal duty of the Imperial Fleet was the protection of the capital and the sea routes leading to it (ten *chelandia* were posted at Stenon to protect the Bosporus and one may make the guess that another ten *chelandia* may also have been posted, for example, in Abydos to protect the Hellespont) together with the offensive operations, but at any given point in time there were also detachments of ships of the Imperial Fleet serving throughout the Mediterranean. These ships protected the Roman merchant ships and port cities, carried ambassadors and envoys, and conducted piratical raiding and other small-scale military operations. And, as noted above, in my opinion it is also probable that the ships of the provincial fleets were actually detachments of the Imperial Fleet sent to serve under local leadership.

The *drouggarios tou ploimou* also appears to have been placed in control of the defence of the coastal areas and commercial activity passing through sea (or other water) lanes, so that it was his department that oversaw officials (variously called *komêtes-archôntoi-abydykoi*[43]) that had been dispatched to the provinces. Each of these officials was stationed in control of a port city and was also in charge of the section of the coast designated to him. Their duty was to control the commercial activity and movement of people, merchandize and ships in the area assigned to them. Each of the *komêtes-archôntoi-abydykoi* had their own detachment of ships and soldiers to control the commercial activity and movement of people, merchandize and ships in the area assigned under his control. The extant sources mention the existence of the *kometes-abydykoi* at least for the following cities and regions: **Black Sea**: Sinope, Amisos, Rôsia, Cherson, Lykostomion, Debeltos; **Propontis**: Nikomedia, Panion, Abydos; **Aegean Sea**: Christopoulis (Kavalla), Thessalonica, Skyros, Chrepou, Thebes, Athens, Chios (ninth century), Strobylos, Rhodes, Smyrna, Ephesos, Nauplia-Argos, Cyprus (first-half of tenth century); **West**: Corinth, Patras, Bageneria, Palermo, Cagliari (Sardinia). Hélène Ahrweiler notes that the list is incomplete and that it is therefore possible that Prespa and Niceae may also have been controlled by such *archôntoi*.[44]

Basilikoi anthrôpoi/basilikoi ('imperial men')[45]
In addition to the above, the emperor also had his own personal bodyguard of officers called *basilikoi* or *basilikoi anthrôpoi* under the *prôtospatharios tôn basilikôn* (*prôtospatharios* of the *basilikoi*) who could also be called *katepanô tôn basilikôn*.

The subordinates of the *prôtospatharios* were, in descending order of importance; the *domestikos tôn basilikôn*,[46] *spatharioi*, *kandidatoi* and imperial *mandatôres*. At some unknown point in time (my educated guess is that this division existed from the start), the *spatharioi* (sword-bearers) appear to have been divided into two separate classes, so that there were bearded non-eunuch *spatharioi* and eunuch *spatharokoubikoularioi*.[47] My own educated guess is simply that the bearded *spatharioi* were bodyguards of the emperor, while the *spatharokoubikoularioi* were bodyguards of the empress. This means that the *basilikoi* were all considered to be officers, hence D'Amato's statement that the *basilikoi* were guard officers of the Palace. The *basilikoi* were used as guards in the throne room (Khrysotriklinos), the Imperial Palace (Magnaura), the Hippodrome, as messengers (*mandatôres*), and as imperial squires/grooms (*stratôres* under the *prôtostratôr*). The imperial grooms are not to be confused with the *stratôres* serving under the *komês tou stablou*, whose responsibilities were far more wide-ranging. The imperial grooms were specifically in charge only of the horses of the imperial entourage and of the *basilikoi* accompanying it. The *basilikoi* were used as personal armed escort and attendants for the emperor at court and during military campaigns, and acted as an actual combat unit on several campaigns. The extant seals also prove that the *basilikoi* were used as relatively low-ranking civil officers.

The strength of the *basilikoi anthrôpoi* is not known. Treadgold (1995, 109–10) suggests on the basis of Ibn Khurdadhbih's (p.81) referral to the 400 guardsmen at the Hippodrome that the size of the *basilikoi* contingent consisted of two *banda*, each 200 men strong. This is quite possible because their main duty was to guard the emperor.

oi magklabitai/magglabites/magglabitai (mace-bearers)

The *magklabitai/magklabites* (mace-bearers) were a detachment of the imperial bodyguards who were armed with a *mag(g)labion* (cudgel) and sword. The earliest known reference to the unit dates from the ninth-century *vita* of Filateros the Merciful, whose son Iôannês was a *spatharios* and *magglabites*. It is probable that the *rabdouchoi* (bludgeon-carriers, mace-bearers) were a synonym for *magglabitai*. Their commander was called *epi tou magglabiou* or *prôtomagglabitai* or *magglabites*. According to D'Amato, the *prôtomagglabitai* held the rank of *komês tês kortês* (officer in charge of the Imperial Tent) during imperial campaigns. In the tenth century this was a very high-ranking position, but the individual rank-and-file *magglabitai* could still be illiterate. The subordinates of the *prôtomagglabitai* consisted of the *dekanoi* (commanders of ten) called *koleatoi* (sheath-bearers), also armed with clubs/maces. The *prôtomagglabitai* had his own grooms/squires (*stratôres*), just like all other high-ranking officers.[48]

The *magklabitai* had multiple duties. They preceded the emperor at ceremonies; they opened up certain gates of the Imperial Palace every morning; they performed special operations such as assassination, execution and capture of enemies of the emperor; diplomatic missions; and accompanied the emperor on campaigns. As close personal bodyguards of the emperor they would have had to protect him against the many conspiracies against his life.[49]

The origin of the *magklabitai* is not known with certainty, and many theories have been presented as a result. For example, Raffaele D'Amato suggests that the mace-bearers may have been created by Irene before the *bigla*, but also suggests on the basis of their duties and clothing that they may have been successors of the Roman *lictores*.[50]

We find mace-bearers doing the same as early as 602, when the personal bodyguards (*sômatofylakes*) of the emperor Maurikios (Maurice) restored order among the populace of Constantinople with iron maces (sing. *distrion*, pl. *distria*). In other words, it is clear that the mace-bearing special unit of personal bodyguards accompanying the emperor was already in existence by the end of the sixth century. It is therefore possible that these personal bodyguards of the emperor were indeed successors of the *lictores* as suggested by D'Amato, but not conclusively so. It is also not known with certainty if the mace-bearers of the Late-Roman era were a separate unit of personal bodyguards or if these were attached to the *excubitores*, who are known to have served as personal bodyguards of the emperor. The latter option, however, is likelier because Theofylaktos Simokattes used the term *sômatofylakes* when he meant the *excubitores*.[51] The size of the unit is not known, but it cannot have been very large: a few dozen or 200 at most.

Archôntogennematai (the sons of the officers)[52]
Raffaele D'Amato includes the *archôntogennematai* (the sons of the officers) among the Imperial Bodyguards, and in his opinion these formed a special corps of guardsmen. Its members were selected from the most illustrious families of Rome whose fathers had served or were still serving among the *tagmata*. They performed the duties of pages in public ceremonies. The practice of having the sons of important commanders as hostages in the Imperial Court was an ancient one, so it is impossible to date the origin of this institution. The sons of the officers were obviously schooled to become officers, while also serving as hostages.

Sardoi (Sardinians)[53]
According to Raffaele D'Amato, we should also list the *sardoi* (Sardinians) as a separate special unit of bodyguards. The Sardinians were known as fearless fighters, so their inclusion among the bodyguards is understandable. However, in my opinion it is uncertain if the Sardinians were actually a separate unit of bodyguards. It is actually quite possible that they belonged to the *etaireia*.

Stratôres tou stablou/staulou[54]
The *stratôres* formed a *schola* at the Imperial Court and in the staff of high-ranking provincial administrators. These *stratôres* are not to be confused with the imperial *stratôres* serving under the *prôtostratôr* in the *basilikoi*. Their overall commander was the *komês tou stablou/komês tôn basilikôn stablôn*, who was later also called *domestikos* of the *stratôres*. The *komês tou stablou* was a high-ranking official whose duty it was to obtain horses and mules for the army. In addition to this, he was in charge of the horses in Constantinople and in the imperial estates of Malagina. The *komês* had several ranks of subordinates serving under him, which included at least the following high-ranking officials (*archôntes tou stablou*); *chartoularioi* (*chartoularios tou stablou* and *chartoularios tôn Malaginôn*), *komêtes tôn Malaginôn* and many others (*epeiktês, saframentarios, syntrofoi tôn sakellariôn, kellarios, apothetês*), the functions of which are not elaborated by the sources.

Basilika dromônia, basilikodromônion, basilikon dromônion, basilika agraria (the emperor's two *dromônia* and the two *agraria* of the empress)[55]
The Roman emperors (*augoustoi*) and empresses (*augoustai*) had always possessed two imperial barges each so that each possessed both the red and the black barges (*agraria tôn rousiôn kai maurôn*). The emperor travelled in the red barge (*agrarion,*

agrarion tôn rousiôn tou basilikou) together with the *drouggarios tês biglês, drouggarios tou ploimou, logothetês tou dromou, etaireiarchês, mystikos, deêseos, domestikos tôn scholôn, parakoimômenos, prôtobestiarios*, and chosen personnel from the bedchamber. The rest of the nobility were placed on the black barge which followed behind the red barge. The red and black barges (*agraria*) of the *basileus* and their rowers and the other crew were under the command of the *prôtospatharios tês fialês* (*Prôtospatharios* of the Basin/Harbour), who also acted as a judge on issues concerning their crews. The red and black barges of the empress (*basilissa*) were originally under the *epi tês trapezes tês augoustês* (Master of the Table of the *Augusta*). The reign of Leôn VI saw a change in the practices, in that he built two *dromönia* for himself to replace his barges. The second of these *dromônia*, the one which followed after the emperor's *dromônion*, was called *akolouthos* (follower, attaché). Rômanos I Lakapênos placed both the *dromônia* and the *agraria* of the empress under the *prôtospatharios tês fialês*, who also served simultaneously as *prôtokarabos* (pilot, steersman) of the *dromônion* of the *basileus*. Each of the *dromônia* had two *prôtokaraboi*, each of whom commanded a single *ousia* of rowers. The senior of these was called *prôtos prôtokarabos*. After the reign of Rômanos I Lakapênos, the *prôtos prôtokarabos* of the *dromônion* of the emperor was simultaneously the *prôtospatharios tês fialês*. The subordinates of the *prôtokaraboi* consisted of the *prôtoelatai* (first-rowers) and *deuteroelatai* (second-rowers).

The approximate strength of the crews of the two *dromônia* can be calculated on the basis of Kônstantinos VII's *De Administrando*. He stated that when the emperor made a short trip, he left an *ousia* of soldiers/rowers at the Hippodrome to replace the *tagma* of *bigla* that left the Hippodrome to accompany the *domestikos tôn scholôn* as required by custom. This means that the imperial *dromônion* had at least two *ousiai* of rowers with the implication that the total crew of the *dromônion* was 300 men. This means that the two *dromônia* had at least 600 men, in addition to which we need to calculate the crews of the two *agraria* of the empress for a total of ca. 1,200 men. Raffaele D'Amato (2012, 32) estimates that the size of the bodyguard unit (means the crews of the two *dromônia* of the emperor) was 1,000 men in total. This is indeed a realistic estimate when one also adds to the figures the supporting personnel. During times of war the crews of these two *dromônia* were actually equipped with combat gear and dispatched to serve in the Imperial Fleet, while the ten *chelandia* of the Imperial Fleet that were permanently posted at the Bosporus (Stenon) provided replacement crews for the two *dromônia*. The crews of the barges of the empress were apparently not used as combat troops in like manner.

The *Demes* (Circus Factions): Blues with Whites and Greens with Reds[56]

One of the principal pastimes for the Romans was following their favourite charioteer teams. The fans of the charioteer teams had formed four groupings: the Green, Red, Blue and White teams/*demes*, but the principal fan groups were the Greens and Blues. The Reds were considered a subunit of the Greens and the Whites were considered a subunit of the Blues. The *demes* had also an important

Officers of the themata and tagmata (after Treadgold and D'Amato)

Themata	scholai	exkoubitoi/ evkoubitores	vigla / arithmoi	ikanatoi	noumeroi	teichistai	optimatoi	Basilikou ploimou
strategos	domestikos	domestikos	drouggarios	domestikos	domestikos	komes	domestikos	drouggarios
tourmarches	topoteretes	topoteretes	topoteretes	topoteretes	topoteretes	topoteretes	topoteretes	topoteretes
chartoularios	chartoularios	chartoularios	chartoularios	chartoularios	chartoularios	chartoularios	chartoularios	chartoularios
								protonotarios
komes	komes	skribon	komes	komes	tribounos	tribounos	komes	komes
kentarches	domestikos	drakonarios	kentarches	kentarches	bikarios	bikarios	kentarches	kentarches
komes of the etaireiai								komes of the etaireiai
protokankellarios							protokankellarios	
protomandator	proximos	protomandator	akolouthos	protomandator	protomandator	protomandator		protomandator
bandoforos	protiktor	drakonarios	bandoforos	bandoforos				
.	eytychoforors	skeuoforors	labouresios	semeioforos				
.	skeptroforrs	signoforos	semeiforors	semeioforos				
.	axiomatikos	sinator	doukinator	doukinator				
mandator	mandator	mandator	mandator	mandator	legatorios	legatorios		mandator
.	.	legatarios	legatarios	legatarios	mandator	mandator		
.			thuroros					

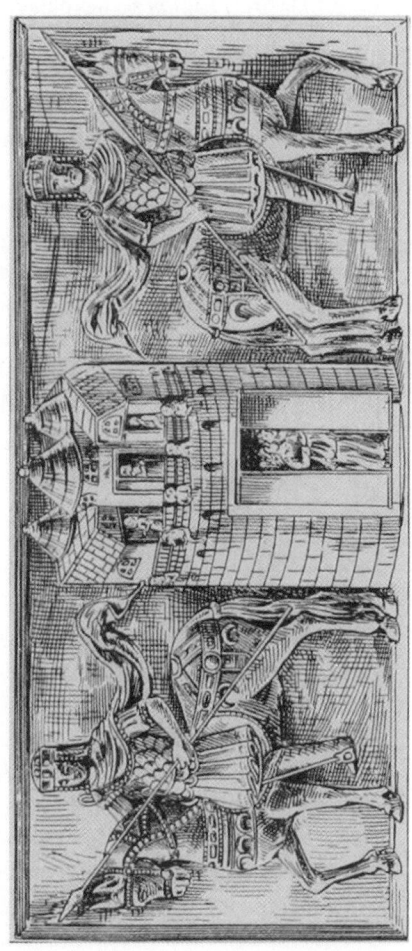

Troyes Casket (11th century)
Source: Schlumberger

role in the crowning of new emperors as symbolic representatives of the people (*populus*) so that the different circus factions were also seen as representatives of the seasons of the year in the following manner: Greens (spring), Reds (summer), Blues (autumn), and Whites (winter). There were supporters of these *demes* throughout the Empire. However, from the military point of view the two principal groupings were the *demes* of the city of Constantinople and its suburbs up to the Great Walls, both of which appear to have been under the *demarchoi* of the Blues and Greens of the city of Constantinople. When assigned for military duty, each of the *demarchoi* of the Blues (*o demarchos tôn Benetôn*) and Greens (*o demarchos tôn Prasinôn*) appear to have had the additional title of *demokratês*, because this was the title carried also by the *domestikoi* of the Schools and *Excubitores* when they commanded the Greens and Blues. The factions were hierarchically organized so that below each *demarchos* served several ranks of officials and officers, the titles and functions of which are not fully understood. The members of the factions could be called collectively either *dêmôtai* or *faktionarioi*. For military purposes, the factions appear to have been divided so that the suburban factions protected the Great Walls together with the military and other paramilitary forces assigned for this duty, while the factions of the city protected the Theodosian Walls together with the military and paramilitary forces assigned for this duty. For further details, see below.

The Defensive Arrangements of the City of Constantinople

The capital Constantinople and its surroundings also appear to have had a special defensive arrangement which involved both the *tagmata* and the *demes* of the area so that: 1) the peratic Green (*oi peratikoi Brasinoi*) and Blue (*oi peratikoi Benetikoi*) *demes* (the Greens and Blues located between the Great Walls and Theodosian Walls), *teichistai* (the Walls), and the *exkoubitoi* appear to have all been subjected to the authority of the *domestikos tôn exkoubitôn*; 2) while the Blue (*oi politikoi Benetikoi*) and Green (*oi politikoi Brasinoi*) *demes* of the city of Constantinople, the *noumera*, and the *scholai* appear to have been subjected to the authority of the *domestikos tôn scholôn*. When the *domestikoi* of the Schools and *Excubitores* acted as commanders of the *demes*, they used the title of *demokratês* (pl. *demokratai*), which was otherwise used by the *demarchoi* of the *demes*.[57] The reason for this is not known, but my educated guess is that this referred to the defensive organization of the city of Constantinople so that the *domestikos tôn exkoubitôn* with the peratic Greens and Blues, *teichistai* and *exkoubitoi* was responsible for the defence of the Great Walls and the area between it and the city of Constantinople, while the *domestikos tôn scholôn* (presumably the *domestikos duseôs*, the Domestic of the Schools of the West after its creation) with the *demes* of the city, *noumera* and *scholai* was responsible for the defence of the Theodosian Walls.

The Prefect of the City, *eparchos tês poleôs*, appears to have been in charge of the defence of the city and its seashore, so he commanded the paramilitary forces consisting of the guilds of craftsmen and merchants (*systemata*) and of the *demes*, in addition to which he commanded his own detachment of soldiers, the Urban Police and City Guard (*pedatoura* or *kerketon*). The soldiers (*stratiôtai*) of the *eparchos* were commanded by *kenturiôn*.[58] However, it is clear that in practice the command of the defence of the city could be assigned to the Domestic of the Schools or anyone that the emperor thought suitable for the task. This was definitely the case when the emperor campaigned in person with the *domestikoi* of the *scholai* and *exkoubitoi*, because in that case the emperor appointed an overall commander for the city under whom served the soldiers of the *tagmata* and *eparchos*.[59] It is similarly clear that the defensive strength of the city was always bolstered by whatever other military forces were present in the city or close by (e.g. by the *themata*, mercenaries, retinues of the *dynatoi* and wealthy, imperial bodyguards etc.) and available for this purpose.

The defence of the maritime frontier of the city of Constantinople was obviously primarily the duty of the Imperial Fleet and its *drouggarios*, but when the Imperial Fleet and *drouggarios* were absent on campaigning the duty fell to the designated commander of the naval detachments left for the defence of the city. It is obvious that neither the *drouggarios* nor the temporary commander of the ships posted in Constantinople had the authority to act on their own. Both had to take into account the decisions made by the person in charge of the defence of the entire city, whether this was the emperor or someone he assigned in charge.

The command structure of the thematic and tagmatic armies

By comparing the information with the Roman sources we can also use the Arab geographers as the basis for the reconstruction of the command structure of campaigning forces.

Both Ibn Khurdadhbih (p.84) and Qudama (p.196) offer the following hierarchy for the Roman army (with my comments inside parentheses in Italics). According to both, each *patrikios* commanded 10,000 men. Each *patrikios* had under him two *tourmarchai* [*also called merarchai in Roman sources*] both of whom commanded 5,000 men. Each *tourmarchês* had under him five *drouggarioi*, each of whom commanded 1,000 men. Each of the *drouggarioi* in their turn had five *komêtes*, each in command of 200 men. Each *komês* had under him five *kentarchoi* [*also called in Roman sources (h)ekatontarchoi ekatontarchai*] each in command of 40 men [*on the surface it would seem that the Arab sources have confused the kentarchos and pentêkontarchês with each other, but Philotheos' text confirms that each kentarchos commanded 40 men, for which see the above list of 204 officers in a tagma; the implication is that the number of men under the kentarchoi varied according to the unit and situation*]. Each *kentarchos* in his turn had under them four *dekarchoi* each in charge of ten men. On the basis of the Roman sources, it is clear that the above is an idealized paper version of the command structure and that it also omits some ranks of officers (*pentêkontarchês* and *pentarchês*), which were probably used only when the situation required.

Leôn VI's *Taktika* (18.136–149) suggested the following scheme for the 4,000 picked horsemen of a *thema*: 800 *pentarchai* (*pentarchês* = first among five); 400 *dekarchai* (*dekarchês* = first among ten); 80 *pentêkontarchai* (*pentêkontarchês* = commander of 50) or *tribounoi* (*tribounos* = tribune); 40 *kentarchoi* (*kentarchos* =

centurion) or *ekatontarchai* (*ekatontarchês* = commander of hundred); 20 *komêtes* (*komês* = count); 4 *drouggarioi* (*drouggarios* = commander of a throng) or *chiliarchoi* (*chiliarchos* = commander of a thousand); 2 *tourmarchai* (*tourmarchês* = commander of a *tourma*); 1 *stratêgos*. Leôn defines the maximum sizes of the units at *Taktika* (4.43–9), stating that the *bandon* was to consist of 200–400 men, but actually allows also a smaller size (18.144), *drouggos* not more than 3,000 men, and *tourma* not more than 6,000 men, which shows that the above figures were changed accordingly for the higher ranking officers when the *stratêgos* commanded a larger force.

The *Sylloge tacticorum* of Leôn VI (35) gives us the following command structure: *a stratêgos, tourmarchai/merarchai, drouggarioi, komêtes, kentarchoi/ekatontarchoi, lochagoi, dekarchoi, pentarchoi, tetrachoi* (commander of four), which appears to be the command structure of the cavalry. The *Sylloge tacticorum* (35.10) also includes the rank of *taxiarchos*, who is a commander of a *taxis* (formation/unit) and the equivalent of a *tagmatarchês* (commander of a *tagma*), so the minimum number of men commanded by the *tagmatarchês* and *taxiarchos* was 200 men. It is uncertain whether this was an official or unofficial title and whether the *taxiarchos* could also be commander of a cavalry unit and not only of infantry, as he did later in the century. Whatever the case, during the early-tenth century to the latter part of the tenth century, the *taxiarchos/taxiarchês* was definitely an official title for an infantry officer who commanded a *taxiarchia* of infantry (1,000 infantry = 400 *oplitai*, 300 *psiloi*, 200 *akontistai* and *sfendobolistai*, 100 *menavlatoi*), and was considered to be the equivalent of a *chiliarchos/chiliarchês*, the commander of a *chiliarchia*. It was also in the latter-half of the tenth century that the rank of *archêgetês/oplitarchês* is mentioned as commander of the entire infantry contingent by the *De re militari*.[60]

It would be very strange if the infantry would not have had a separate commander, because it is clear that it must have had in situations in which the *stratêgos* and cavalry were not present. Therefore, it is clear that it existed even when not mentioned. We find a similar omission in the sixth-century *Strategikon*, and yet we know from Theophylact's text that the armies of Maurikios had separate infantry commanders who usually appear to have been *hypostratêgoi*.[61] In sum, I would suggest that there was always a separate infantry commander in existence, but whether he was already officially called *archêgetes/oplitarchês* before the late-tenth century is uncertain.

In the *Sylloge tacticorum* the *stratêgos* had under him an unspecified number of *tourmarchai*, which clearly took into account the fact that the size of the force serving under him varied in size, so that there could be more *tourmarchai* than either the Arab geographers or Leôn VI's *Taktika* give in their examples. Also in variance with the above sources, each of the *tourmarchai* commanded between 3,000 and 9,000 men, so that each of them had exactly three *drouggarioi* under their command, while the size of the *drouggos* varied between 1,000 and 3,000 men. If the force consisted only of 4,000 men, as Leôn VI relates in the *Taktika*, then the size was obviously adjusted to take this into account. In contrast to the above treatises, the size of the *bandon* is also redefined as follows: in the infantry *tagmata*, the *bandon* was to consist of 200–400 men; in the cavalry the size varied from 50–350 or 400 men, but so that it was identical with the *allagion* (number). The *allagion* is defined as follows: the regular *allagion* consisted of 50–150 men; the royal *allagia* could possess up to 320, 350 or even 400 men, because the *allagia* of Thrakesion had 320 men, Charsianon 350 men and some of the western *tagmata* up to 400 men. The interesting point here is that the different types of units were expected to have different paper sizes for their *allagia*. Chatzelis and Harris (126, n.151) suggest, in my opinion correctly, that the royal *allagia* meant the professional soldiers of the *tagmata*, while the regular *allagia* meant the soldiers of the *themata*. This means that when the *tagmata* were posted in the *themata* as detachments (*peratika tagmata*), these units (e.g. Thrakesion, Charsianon, west) continued to use the royal *allagion*, even when the thematic units in the same provinces were organized according to the regular *allagion*.

In the *Sylloge tacticorum* Leôn also states that the commander of the *bandon* was the *komês* and that the *ekatontarchos* was also known as *kentarchos* or *kentarion*, while the *pentêkontarchos* commanded 50 men. The *lochagos* was usually the file-leader (means actually only the infantry formations) when there were 32 or 16 ranks, while the *dekarchos* was the file-leader if there were ten or fewer men in the file. The *pentarchos* was the first among five and the *tetrarchos* was the first among four.

It is possible that this tidy organization was already in the process of changing during the turn of the tenth century when the treatise was written, according to its preface. The *De Ceremoniis* and *Kletorologion* of Philotheos suggest that the *drouggarios* and *komês* had the same number of men under their command during the early-tenth century, so that by the middle of the century the two titles became fused into *drouggarokomês*.[62] One possible answer to this phenomenon is that the size of the contingent that a *drouggarios* could bring to the scene of operations apparently varied greatly, as even the title implied, with the implication that the two titles could be identical.

1.6. Military Unit Orders: Open, Close, Interlocked and Irregular

The unit orders for both cavalry and infantry had basically remained the same ever since those were first recorded in Hellenistic Greece. We find exact figures for these in the tenth-century *Sylloge Tacticorum* (43.6–7), the figures which are also confirmed by earlier numbers in Leôn's *Taktika* (17.72) and Maurikios' *Strategikon*.[63] Both cavalry and infantry had four basic unit orders: open (*araiôsis*), close (*pyknosis*), shields interlocked (*synaspismos/chelônê/syskouton*) and irregular (*drouggos, drouggisti*). Each footman and horseman occupied in width an *orguia* in open order (*araiôsis*) during march (4 *pêcheis* = 187.38 = ca.187.4cm), half an *orguia* in close order when battle was expected (*puknôsis* = 3 *podes* = 3 x 31.23 cm = 93.69cm = ca. 94 cm; shields brought rim-to-rim so that the actual width varied) and a third of an *orguia* during battle in the shield-interlocking order (*synaspismos/chelônê/syskouton* = 2 *podes* = 2 x 31.23cm = 62.46 cm). The irregular-*drouggos* order did not have any specific width or depth for the horseman or footman because it was irregular non-rank-and-file order, while the other orders were rank-and-file orders.

The infantry version of the *synaspismos* order had three basic variants: 1) shield-interlocking in width without shield roof; 2) shield-interlocking both in width and depth so that it had a shield roof, which the soldiers used when kneeling to receive enemy missiles and when fighting upright; 3) shield-interlocking only in depth to receive cavalry charge so that the four front ranks interlocked their shields; 4) shield-interlocking in width and depth with a shield roof which was used when storming fortifications, so that the rear rankers could kneel to help those behind to climb on top of the shield roof. As is obvious, the depth of the rank-and-file order also varied according to the type of unit and equipment. One may assume that in the infantry open order the depth was the same as width, but in the case of the close order (shields rim-to-rim) and shield-interlocked orders it is clear that the size of the shield and the type of spear used influenced the depth of the formation.

In the case of the cavalry, the open order obviously meant also greater depth between ranks of horses, so that one may expect that the interval between the ranks was the same as in width. In the case of the cavalry close order *puknôsis*, we actually have exact figures also for the depth of the array from the *Strategikon*, which states that in close order the cavalry files were three feet (93.69cm = ca. 94cm) wide, while the depth of each rank was eight feet (249.84cm = ca. 2.5m). This means that in close order the horses were in nose-to-tail order. The cavalry *synaspismos* appears to have been equally as wide as the infantry version, while it is probable that the depth of the array was the same as with the *puknôsis*-order. This order appears to have been used by stationary cavalry units to receive a volley of enemy arrows or javelins. The *Peri strategikes*, which was recommended reading for the emperor during campaigns, includes also the interjection of the first and second rank horses so that they lined up the heads of the horses of the second rank with the shoulders or flanks of the horses of the first rank. In light of the recommendation, it is possible that this method was used by some period commanders.

In addition to this, the tenth-century Romans also employed a large rank-and-file triangle/wedge of *katafraktoi* mainly for the breaking of enemy infantry formations, which appears to have been reintroduced into the Roman armies as a result of Leôn's *Sylloge tacticorum* (904). See Appendix I.

The irregular order for both cavalry and infantry meant unit orders which were not organized according to rank-and-file structure and which could take many shapes and sizes.

1.7. The Cavalry[64]

At the beginning of the tenth century, Roman combat methods were largely the same as those we find in the *Strategikon*, so Leôn reproduced large portions of Maurikios' text both in the *Problemata* (questions answered with quotes from the *Strategikon*) and in the *Taktika*. However, Leôn appears to have known that he needed to reform this system for the Romans to be able to crush the Saracen infantry formations. His solution was to write the *Sylloge tacticorum* in 904, which reintroduced the large triangle/wedge of *katafraktoi* for the purpose of breaking up enemy infantry formations together with the use of the hollow infantry square and oblong. This system was put into good use by Iôannês Kourkouas.[65] Regardless, the information provided by the *Strategikon* and which was retained in Leôn's *Taktika* still retained its relevance because the combat systems described in those can also be found in the *De velitatione* (written after 969 on the basis of Nikêforos Fôkas' instructions) and later in Nikêforos Ouranos' *Taktika* (Chapters 1–55 reproduce Leôn's *Taktika*; treatise datable to the first decade of the eleventh century) as alternatives for the use of hollow infantry square and cavalry formation based on the use of the *katafraktoi* wedge.

It was because of this that we find Roman cavalry equipped and operating as it was during the Late-Roman period. There were some modifications, though, which will be analyzed in their proper places. The key difference was obviously the composition of the cavalry forces, which were now made up of the *tagmata* and *themata*, so that the quality of the latter varied from one *thema* to another. The *stratêgos* of a *thema* was required to select men at the prime of their life with enough wealth to provide a fully equipped horseman, so that there were others who did all the farm work and provided the necessary equipment and horse for service. The horsemen were obviously required to possess a mount together with the saddle, saddle cloth, stirrups, lasso and so forth. Each was required to have a coat of mail reaching their ankles; an iron helmet with a small plume; a shield; a bow with a bowcase; spare bow strings; two quivers each holding 30 or 40 arrows; two short cavalry *kontaria*-lances (*kontarion* 3.74m in length) that could be used either as thrown weapons or for thrusting; a *spathion*-sword; a *tzikourion* (double-sided axe with a blade on one side and a sharp spear on the other); and a loose mantle. Those recruits who were unskilled with the bow were to carry *kontaria* with a full-size shield (*skoutarion*). If possible the troopers were also to wear a thorax-breastplate, which was now called *klibanion* (pl. *klibania*), greaves (*podopsella*) and surcoats. If possible the troopers were also to carry two javelins (*akontia*) or thrown weapons (*riktaria*). The *Strategikon* did not require this, but these were used also by Late-Roman cavalry. The heads and breasts of the horses of the officers were to be armoured with iron or padding (e.g. cowhide) and additionally, if possible, their abdomens were to be protected by small pieces of quilting hanging from the saddles. The horses stationed in the front rank were required to be armoured in this manner. The horses were also to be decorated so there were four tassels on the haunch strap, one on the horse's brow and another under the chin.

The individuals and cavalry units (*bandon/tagma, moira/drouggos, meros/tourma*) were trained in the use of weapons (long range with bows, short range with spears, javelins and swords) and drilled in combat manoeuvres so that the units were able to assume the required unit order, countermarch, about turn, wheel and so forth.

The Roman combat doctrine with both cavalry and infantry called for the use of ambushes, surprise attacks, night attacks, guerrilla warfare and stratagems, rather than the fighting of pitched battles. See Appendix 2. It was only when these had failed to achieve the desired outcome that the general was expected to fight an open pitched battle if the situation allowed it, and even then he was expected to attempt to ambush the enemy with ambushers attached to the battle formation.

The largest cavalry battle formation with three lines was meant for armies that had more than 10,000–15,000 men, but during this era this version was also used by armies as small as 3,000–4,000 horsemen.[66] The first line consisted of three divisions (*mere, tourmai*), each of which was divided into three *moirai/drouggoi* so that the flank *drouggoi* consisted of the *koursôres*-runners (usually about one-third of the division, also known as the first fighters: *promachoi, proklastai*), while the middle *moira* consisted of the *difensôres*-defenders (usually two-thirds of the division, also known as *ekdikoi*). The *koursôres* were always used as pursuers, but their use in combat varied in that they either skirmished first as *promachoi* (the usual pattern during this era) or joined the *difensôres* in a mutual charge. The *koursôres* used the irregular order *drouggos* and gallop in skirmishing and pursuing, while the *difensôres* used always the close order *pyknosis* and canter both in attack and when acting as defenders/reserves for the *koursôres*. On the left side of the first line were three *banda* of flank guards (*plagiofylakes*) and on the right side were one or two *banda* of outflankers (*yperkerastai*). The flank guards and outflankers were positioned either even with the line, or hidden behind the flank as *drouggoi*, or in front of the first line.[67] The alternative posting of these units in front of the first line was a new development and is not to be found in the *Strategikon*. Their names betray their principal purposes, but both could obviously be used for the outflanking and defending, the former happened when the Romans outflanked the enemy on both sides while the latter happened when the enemy outflanked the Romans on both sides. The outflanking was done by having the wing units encircle the enemy formation in crescent order (a concave column advancing with the sides first) while any hidden *drouggoi* burst forth from behind these.

The second line consisted of four divisions (*mere/tourmai*) similarly divided into *moirai* of *koursôres* and *difensôres*. It was posted three or four bowshots (990–1,320m) behind the first. The purpose of the distance was to allow the divisions of the first line one or two attempts at regrouping against their pursuers before they reached their reserves. In the *Strategikon* the principal purpose of the second line was to act as a reserve force for the first line, so that the flank divisions protected the flank divisions of the first line while the two divisions in the middle protected the centre division of the first line. This system had been modified after the sixth century, so that now the flank divisions of the second line could also be used offensively for the outflanking of the enemy formation. Between the divisions of the second line were three fill-up *banda* that kept the distance between the divisions proportionate to the front line. Their second purpose was to retreat backwards to open a route for the retreating divisions of the first line, meaning that they actually halted its retreat by being in front of them. The third line, the rear guard, consisted of a *bandon* posted on both flanks. As the name implies, its primary purpose was to protect the rear in conjunction with the fill-up *banda* of the second line, while its secondary purpose was to act as last reserves for the entire force. In addition to this, the expectation was that the commander would detail three or four *banda* as ambushers (*enedroi*). If the terrain allowed, they were used properly as ambushers, but if this was not possible then these *banda* were to be hidden behind the flanks of the first line in irregular formation to outflank the enemy. If there were more than could be incorporated into the *meros/tourma* structure the extra horsemen were to be posted either on the flanks to outflank the enemy and/or behind the second line as a third line and/or ambushers. The best units were posted in the centre of the formation, both in front (the centre division of the first line) and behind (the middle divisions of the second line), while the depth of the cavalry *banda* varied from eight to ten ranks.

The second major variant of the above formation was the medium-sized cavalry army (5,000–10,000/12,000 men), which had only two reserve divisions (*mere*) with a fill-up *bandon* between. The third and smallest version that had less than 5,000 men and had only one *meros* in its second line, but as noted, during the tenth century this was no longer the norm: even armies as small as 3,000–4,000 horsemen could have four divisions in the second line and a third line behind it. In fact, there were even more variants in use than this, probably resulting from use of the hollow infantry square and oblong as a battle formation. When the Romans used the hollow square/oblong with cavalry, the cavalry formation charging out of this formation depended on the number of cavalry inside and number of intervals in the infantry formation. This could result in a cavalry formation that had, for example, three divisions in front and three behind, three in front two behind, three in front one behind and all of these without flank guards, outflankers, fill-up *banda* and a third line, unless of course the commander detatched some *banda* from the wings of the first line to act as flank guards and outflankers for his first line.

The following diagrams show the traditional versions of the cavalry formation which also remained in use after the reintroduction of the cavalry *katafraktoi* as a method of breaking through the enemy formations. The first diagram shows the large cavalry array and is taken from the *Strategikon*. As already discussed, this was the principal cavalry formation also for the smaller cavalry armies during this era. The other main variants before the reforms in the *Sylloge tacticorum* are given after that.

Leôn was apparently acutely aware of the fact that these cavalry formations were not particularly effective against the hollow infantry squares, oblongs, and bearers of *menavlia* employed by the Arabs, because in his *Taktika* the Roman cavalry depended mainly on their mounted archery to break up the Saracen infantry. The Roman cavalry lacked a specialized cavalry hammer that could be used to crush the enemy infantry formation. His solution in the *Sylloge tacticorum* was to reintroduce the specialized *katafraktoi* cavalry, deployed as a massive triangle/wedge for this purpose. The standard version of the new cavalry formation consisted of: the

STRATEGIKON 3.8

Large Cavalry Army ca. 10,000 up to ca. 42-49,000 horsemen

used also by small to medium sized cavalry armies during the 10th century

Promachos taxis

| Plagiofylakes, 1-3 banda | Meros of Bixellationes up to 5,000 men | Meros of Foideratoi up to 5,000 men | Meros of Illyrikianoi up to 5,000 men | Hyperkerastai, 1-2 banda |

Taxis deutera, boêthos taxis

| Meros | Tagma | Meros of Optimatoi | Tagma | Meros | Tagma | Meros |

Notofylax — Touldon — Reserve horses 1 — Reserve horses 2 — Notofylax

⚔	Stratêgos (general)
Φ	Hypostratêgos (lieutenant general)
N̄	Taxiarchos of the Optimates
ε̃	Merarchês
ℳ̊	Moirarchês
†	Bandon of the defensores
†	Bandon of the koursores
♂	Deputatoi (medical corpsmen)
λ	Reserve horses, if present
T	Touldon (baggage train)
ς	Bandon of the baggage train guard, if present

The Introduction 39

Diagrams of the small and medium sized cavalry in the *Strategikon* which Leon's *Taktika* gives as alternatives for similarly sized armies. One should add to these the flank guards, outflankers, ambushers and other missing units. Note, however, that there were also variants which did not have these just as there was a variant which had three divisions in the second line.

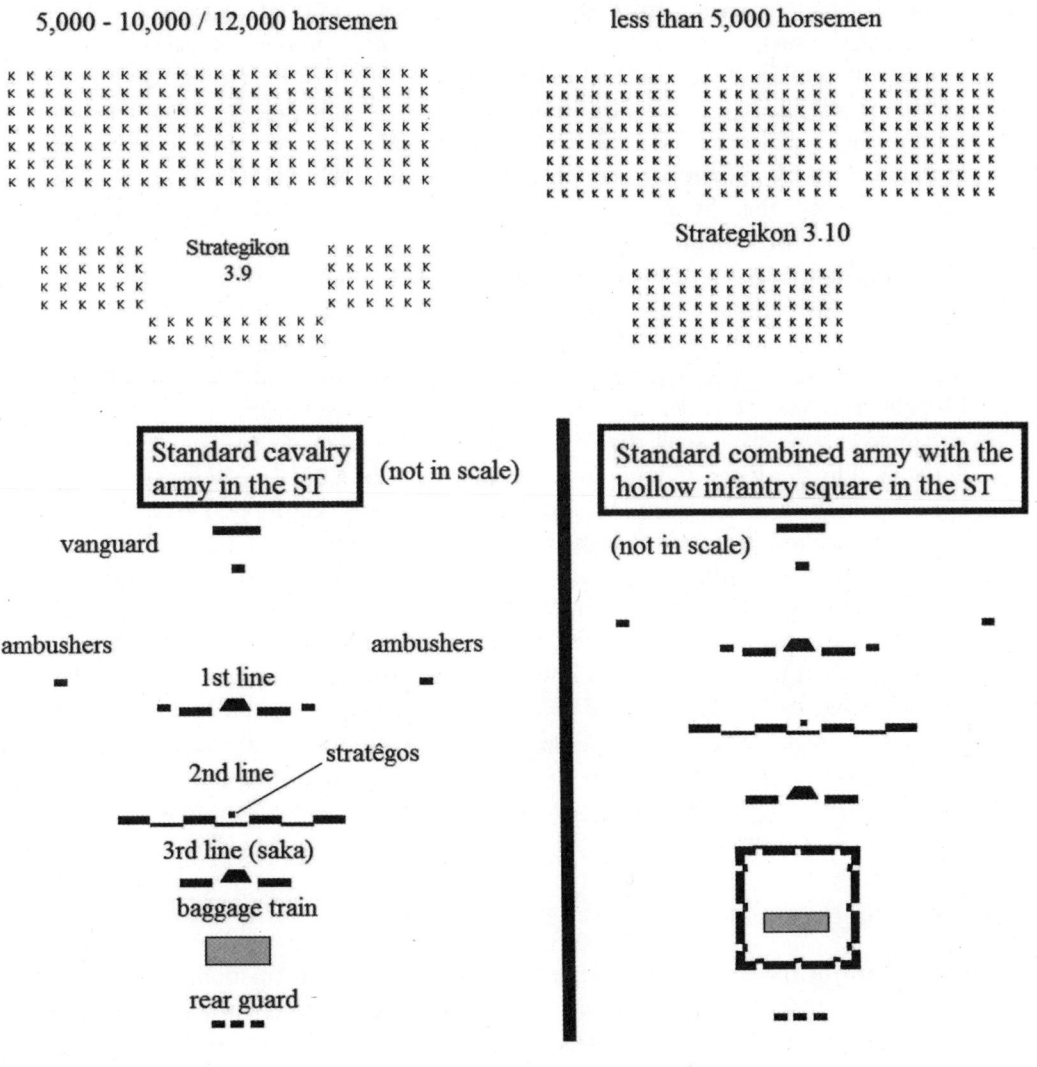

vanguard (*prokoursatôres* and their *difensôres*); first line with three divisions (left divisions, middle-division wedge, right division), flanking units (flank guards and outflankers), and ambushers; a second line of four divisions with the fill-up *banda* placed behind the intervals and the general's flag guard; a third line similar to the first if possible; the baggage train for the pure cavalry army or hollow infantry square if infantry accompanied the army; and three units of rear guards. The second of the major reforms in the *Sylloge tacticorum* was that the cavalry army was usually combined with the hollow infantry square so that the typical ideal army included both infantry and cavalry. In the *Sylloge tacticorum*, there were also smaller variants for cavalry armies that had less than ca. 3,000 horsemen, which were later abandoned. Just like their Arab variant, these appear to have been used when there existed a danger that the enemy could outflank the army. See the above diagrams (not in scale) with Appendices 1 and 5.

It was apparently up to the commander to decide which of the cavalry combat tactics and formations to use in different situations because it is clear from the appearance of the new edition of Maurikios' *Strategikon* (Ambrosian version), from the inclusion of Leôn's *Taktika* in the *Taktika* of Ouranos, and from the texts of *De velitatione* and *De re militari*, that the cavalry formation with two battle lines remained in use even after the writing of the *Sylloge tacticorum* and *Praecepta militaria*. On the basis of Ouranos' *Taktika* (63, esp. 63.3: *katafraktoi* left with the infantry when the rest of the cavalry raided enemy territory), *De velitatione*, and *De re militari*, it is clear that the *katafraktoi* were typically not used alongside other cavalry forces when the cavalry conducted guerrilla operations or raids, or when the enemy did not use effective infantry forces (in the DRM the *katafraktoi* were not used against the Bulgarians, Hungarians or Pechenegs; see Appendix 4). However, when the enemy fielded effective close-order infantry, as did the Arabs and Russians, the *katafraktoi* could be very effective indeed. Even if the *katafraktoi* were also used against cavalry forces, especially as a counter measure against enemy *katafraktoi*, their principal use on the battlefield was against enemy infantry. In sum, the principal use of the *katafraktoi* in combat remained the same as it had been during the Late-Roman period.[68]

1.8. The Infantry[69]

At the turn of the tenth century, the infantry equipment, formations and tactics were the same as they had been in the sixth century as described by Syrianos Magistros and Maurikios. The tactics were still based on the use of the infantry phalanx and its variations. It is because of this that we find Leôn VI repeating the *Strategikon* and Kônstantinos VII recommending the military treatise of Syrianos Magistros for campaign reading.

According to Leôn's *Taktika* (6.20ff.), the period infantry was divided into two classes: the *oplitai/skoutatoi* (heavy shield-bearing infantry) and *psiloi* (light infantry), because the Romans classed the *peltastai* (medium infantry) among the *psiloi*, but he appears to have changed his mind in the *Sylloge tacticorum* (38.6) by including this category, possibly for the sake of completeness. Each of the Roman *skoutatoi* was to be equipped with a *spathion*-sword; a *kontarion* (3.74m spear/lance); a large rectangular oblong shield called *thyreos*; a helmet with a small plume; a sling; a double-bladed axe *tzikourion* (one side bladed, the other with a spike/spear); an axe for cutting; another type of double-bladed axe. In the *Sylloge tacticorum* (38), Leôn adds to the list of shields other shield variants (teardrop, kite and round shields), *menavlion* spears 3–4m in length and allows longer length for the *dory*-spear (*kontarion*) with a length of 3.74–4.7m.

The picked men in the battle array, all the men if possible but at least the first two in each file, were to wear the *zaba* (pl. *zabai*, usually chain mail reaching the ankles) or *lôrikion* (pl. *lôrikia*, chain mail armour in general or a lamellar jacket).[70] The men were also to attach at the plates or shoulders of the *zaba* small pennons. In addition to this, they were also required to wear greaves (*periknêmides, podopsella, chalkotouba*) made of iron or wood so that at least the men in front and rear had these.

On the basis of the *Taktika* (7.3, 7.53–5), we know that the *skoutatoi* could also be equipped with darts (sing. *martzybarboulon*, pl. *martzybarboula*, now called *saliba* – presumably the same as *matzoukion, matzoukia*) and short javelins (*riktaria*). The heavy infantry in close *pyknôsis* order was expected to throw the darts or javelins or *tzikouria*-axes (sing. *tzikourion*; this resembled the Frankish tactics with their *francisca*-axes) when the enemy advanced close enough. The *skoutatoi* did this under the covering fire of the light-infantry archery. After this, the *skoutatoi* were still expected to wait for the enemy to continue their attack and then throw their *kontaria*, after which they engaged the enemy with their swords. This represented two changes in preference after the *Strategikon*. Firstly, the *tzikouria*-axes had been added to the repertoire, and secondly Maurikios had expected that his *skoutatoi* would attack the enemy rather than wait for the enemy to attack. This represents the same kind of difference in the attitude to infantry combat as were the contrasting tactics between Julius Caesar and Pompey. The former preferred attack, because it made the men bolder, while the latter preferred waiting in place, because this retained the cohesion of the formation.

In Leôn's *Taktika* (6.27, 9.71, 11.22, 19.14, 19.16, 19.69), the short thick spear called *menavlon/menavlia* (*pl. menavla/menavlia*) appears to have been used at least by the *akontistai* (javelin throwers) and marines/rowers, and by the Saracen heavy infantry, so one may expect that it was also one of the alternative weapons for the *oplitai* (*hoplitai*) when the *Taktika* was written, even if Leôn specifically classifies it as one of the weapons used by the *oplitai* only in the *Sylloge tacticorum* (38.3). As noted, Leôn's instructions in the *Sylloge tacticorum* (38) add some missing details, but are still by and large similar in content. For these, see in particular Appendix 1.

In Leôn's *Taktika*, the light infantry foot archers were equipped with bows; quivers holding 30 or 40 arrows; arrow-guides with corresponding darts carried in small quivers; small round shields; slings; and axes. Those who were inexperienced in archery carried short javelins (*riktaria*), round shields, slings, and axes. In ancient times these javelineers could also be called *peltastai*, even if the term could also be used to cover any 'medium infantry' type of troop between the *oplitai* and *psiloi*. Hence it is not surprising to learn that in his *Sylloge tacticorum* Leôn reintroduced the *peltastai*-type of troops armed with swords, spears ca. 5m in length, and 'javelins' (*akontia, riptaria*) with a length of ca. 2.5–8m. They had slightly smaller shields and were less heavily-armoured than the *oplitai*. See Appendix 1. What is interesting, however, is the lengthening of the spears of both *oplitai* and *peltastai* in conjunction with the use of the *menavlatoi* and hollow infantry square, apparently in response to enemy cavalry. There was a clear tendency to lengthen the spears into pike length in the tenth century, quite clearly as a response to the introduction of the *katafraktoi*-wedges in combat. See Appendices I.2 and III.4.

The infantry were trained to fight both as individuals and as units, so they were taught for example: how to assume different unit orders; face left and right; about face; turn; wheel; countermarch; how to open up the array; divide and double the ranks and files; how to form up a double phalanx, or double-front, and so forth. The same material can be found both in the *Taktika* and the *Sylloge tacticorum*, but the latter includes also Hellenistic material left out of the former. The standard combat formations were based on the phalanx tactics, but so that the principal battle formations were the single phalanx with reserves; double phalanx with reserves; hollow square/oblong; and marching formation in difficult terrain. The favourite tactics in infantry warfare was the use of ambushes, surprise attacks, night attacks, guerrilla warfare and stratagems, rather than the fighting of pitched battles, because this always entailed the risk of defeat.

The standard depth of the *skoutatoi* phalanx was 16 ranks, which could easily be divided into eight- or four-rank formations. When the army was organized in a lateral phalanx and when it had over 24,000 footmen, it was organized as four divisions (*mere*) side-by-side, and if the army had fewer men it was organized as three divisions. Leôn's description of the infantry phalanx was entirely based on the *Strategikon* (see the diagram opposite, which includes some emendations based on the sixth-century sources[71]). If there were more than 24,000 men, half of their number was required to be light-armed *psiloi* and if there were less than 24,000 men then a third of the force was to consist of light-armed. The *psiloi* were deployed either on the flanks, or behind, or wherever required. The cavalry was deployed on the flanks. If there were more than 12,000 horsemen, these were deployed ten deep, and if less five deep. If the baggage train with its ballistae-wagons and trebuchet wagons followed behind, the Romans used the single phalanx with the cavalry and infantry reserves posted on the flanks of the baggage train and in the middle of it, but if the baggage train did not follow, the Romans typically used the double phalanx. The baggage train with its artillery pieces, drivers and accompanying soldiers, was used against any attacks from the rear so that its absence required the posting of the second phalanx behind. If the Romans used the hollow square/oblong, this array obviously provided an all-round protection, with the cavalry and infantry forces posted inside providing reserves.

THE LATERAL PHALANX OVER 24,000 FOOTMEN IN THE *STRATEGIKON*

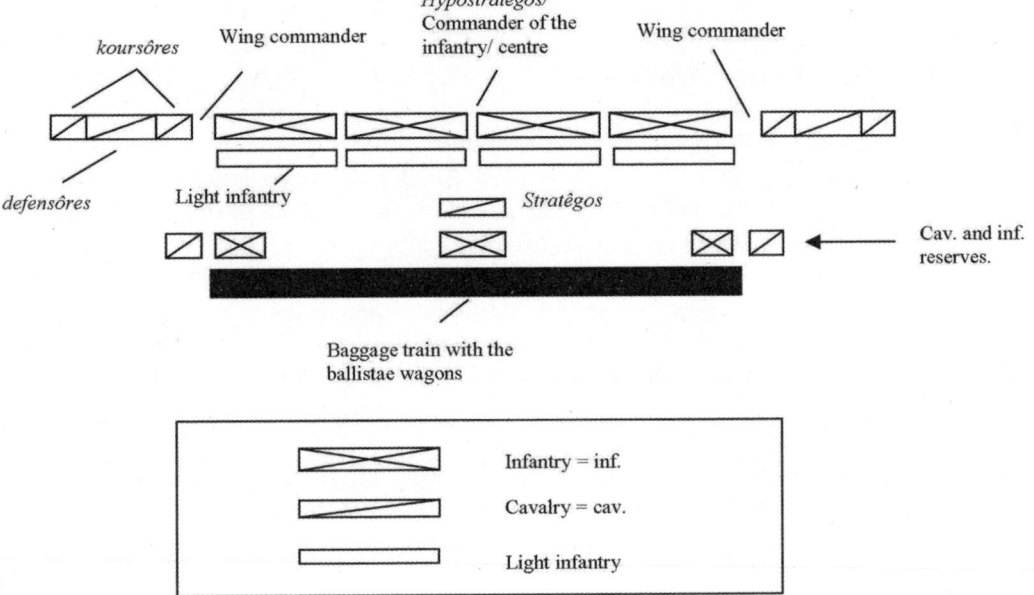

The basic formation for use in difficult terrain called for the use of lighter equipment by the *skoutatoi*, so that these were deployed in shallow, two-to-four man deep columns, with the posting of groups of four-five light infantry around it in irregular order, with possible cavalry detachments to serve as protective cover for the two-to-four columns. Most of the foot archers, however, were left with the *skoutatoi* columns. The light infantry were expected to attempt to outflank the enemy if possible, and if the terrain allowed the columns were to be wheeled into a phalanx.[72]

This basic structure was reformed in the early tenth century by none other than Leôn VI himself in the *Sylloge tacticorum*, in which he elaborated the use of the hollow infantry square as a battle formation, not just its standard use as a marching formation, while also adding a variation of the pure infantry formation without any cavalry to the repertoire. The *Strategikon* had already noted that there could be infantry armies operating on their own without cavalry support in the context of fighting in difficult terrain,[73] but the pure infantry formation presented by the *Sylloge tacticorum* is still a new development not to be found in any of the previous extant treatises. See Appendix 1 for further details.

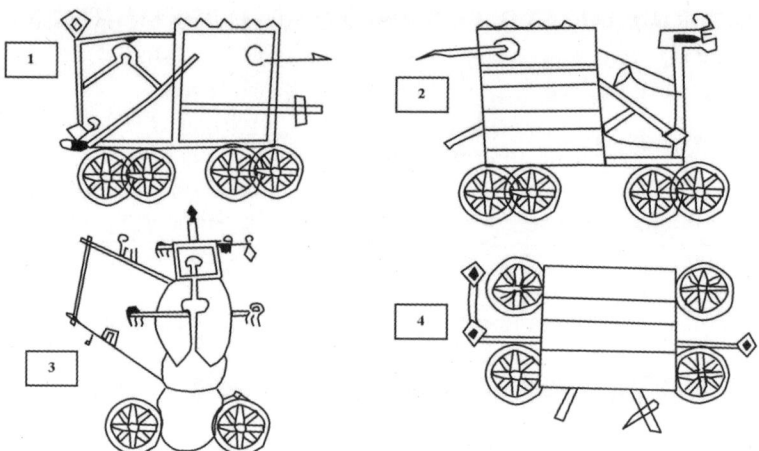

Ballistae wagons/carts and a possible 10th century *"tichodifrus"*

Source: DRM, Vatican Library, Cod.Gr.1164, f.238v, Rome (Dennis, 1985, *"Campaign Tactics"*, 261).

The childlike drawings of military machines from the anonymous tenth century *DRM* demonstrate the remarkable continuity of the Roman military methods throughout the centuries. The figures one and two are clearly wagon-mounted ballistae and the figure three a cart-mounted ballista, but the fourth figure is less easy to explain. However, since the fourth figure was to be used in the field together with the ballistae wagons and carts and because it bears some resemblance to the *tichodifrus* of the fourth century *De rebus bellicis*, it is in my opinion likely to be the tenth century equivalent of the *tichodifrus*, a device used to protect the ballistae wagons and men operating these.

1.9. Marching and Encamping (LT 9–11; ST 21–2)

The Roman army, regardless of its composition, was always expected to use spies, scouts and patrols around it so that the enemy could not surprise it during marching or in its encampment, while it was also expected that the army built a fortified camp for each night with outposts of pickets, guards and patrols around it so that the enemy could not surprise it during the night. In enemy territory and in the vicinity of enemy forces, the army was expected to march in combat formation if the terrain allowed this. The composition of the army (proportion of infantry vis-à-vis cavalry) and its formation and equipment were expected to be suited to the terrain where the army campaigned. Likewise, it was expected that the Romans carried with them adequate amounts of provisions, while the surveyors were to ensure that the army also had access to water. The general was also expected to make certain that the merchants were treated fairly, so that they would continue to transport supplies for the army (LT 11.7). This shows that the Roman logistical network was based on purchases made from these merchants. This ideal was not always achieved.

Leôn's *Taktika* (LT 11) demonstrates that the Roman marching camp had remained largely the same ever since the Late-Roman period, because his text is mostly based on the *Strategikon*. It was expected that the camp always had some form of fortifications in enemy territory, and that it was pitched on open level terrain so that there were no heights close by that the enemy could use for missile attacks against the Romans. The defences of the marching camp consisted of the ditches and palisades, or of the trench (*fossa*), and/or of the caltrops (used in particular on rocky terrain where it was impossible to dig a trench/ditch), or of some other kind of wall made of wood, stone or other material. Additionally, the general could build a wagon fort called *karagos* when these accompanied the army, or he could order the building of a wall of pointed stakes called *stabarosai*, consisting of lumber or trees felled on the spot (*abatis*). Leôn (LT 11.22) also includes a new invention among the possible defences of the marching camp. This had been invented by Nikêforos Fôkas (grandfather of the likenamed emperor) during the Bulgarian campaign in about 894. Nikêforos had protected his marching camp with an improvised wall which consisted of two pieces of wood (each about three *spithamai* long) joined together like the letter lambda into which he had then joined another piece of wood (a *menaulon* five or six *spithamai* long) so that it became three-legged. On the tip of the *menaulon* he had fixed a large broadsword blade about two *spithamai* in length. In addition to this, Nikêforos had used wooden ersatz caltrops. Additionally, during the raid against the Saracens in about 900, this very same person had fooled the enemy by lighting many fires in his encampment during the night when he in reality withdrew from enemy territory with all of the captured loot. These were basically the only additions that Leôn made to the information provided by the *Strategikon*.

The marching camp in the *Taktika* had only two broad roads, crossing each other in the middle of the camp, so that there were only four main gates with a large number of small postern gates. The infantry was posted along the edges of the camp, after which there was a clear space of 300 to 400 feet where the rest of the tents (cavalry, baggage animals and non-combatants) were pitched, the interval providing protection against enemy missiles. The *stratêgos* had his tent close to the crossroads at the centre, but so that it was placed off to one side, the idea being that the traffic would not bother the *stratêgos*. This had been an addition to Roman combat doctrine made by the emperor Maurikios himself, for which see Syvänne

6th Century Roman Marching Camp.
Source: *Strategikon* 12.C after the so-called "short treatise on marching camps".

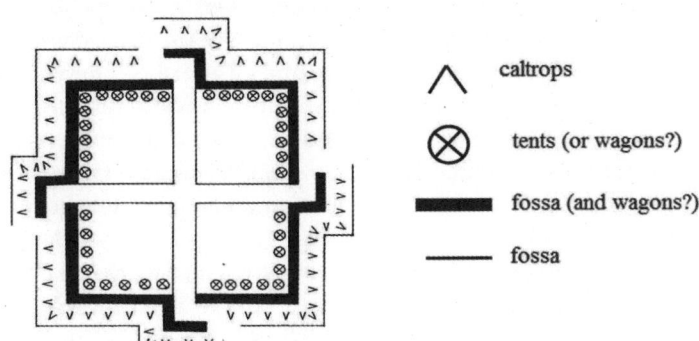

According to Corippus (*Iohannidos* 8.324-9), the general's tents as well as a large altar for sermons were placed in the centre of the camp. This implies that the placing of the general's tent to one of the quarters and not in the crossroads was probably added to the genre by the Emperor Maurikios who did not like being bothered by outside noises.

(LRCT). The *tourmarchai* pitched their camps in the middle of their own forces, so that they kept messengers in attendance at the tent of of the commander.

Leôn VI reformed this basic marching camp structure in the *Syllyge tacticorum* so that its inner structure was changed to take into account the basic infantry combat formation, the hollow square. The principal change concerned the number of large gates and roads. In the new system the marching camp had four main roads and eight main gates. However, since Leôn was still working on the basis of what he had been taught he retained one of the features from the *Strategikon* which was no longer relevant after the change in the camp structure, and which created a separate space in the middle of the marching camp for the commander and his entourage. Leôn VI (ST 22.7) states that the tent of the general was to be separated from the multitude and roads so that it would be free from noise. The new camp structure meant that this was always the case when the tent was pitched in the centre of the camp, so the instruction was basically unnecessary. However, on the basis of the fact that Nikêforos Ouranos retained the text of Leôn's *Taktika*, while versions of the Late-Roman marching camp were also included among the illustrations of the *De re militari*, it is likely that the Late-Roman version presented in the *Strategikon* remained in use as one possible alternative structure for the Roman marching camp. For example, it is possible that the Roman commander could choose to use the marching camp with fewer main gates and roads when he wanted to make his camp more secure against attack or when it consisted of a smaller number of men.

As noted, the probable idea behind the change in the numbers of main gates and roads was to make the camp structure closer to the actual combat formation, but here is where the problem lay. If the gates and roads followed the actual combat formation with eight intervals, the resulting quarters in the marching camp were disproportionate. Therefore, just as others before me, I have made the assumption in the diagram opposite that the main gates of the marching camp were not in the same place as the intervals in the hollow square combat formation. It is far likelier that the marching camp was divided into equal sized quarters. It was presumably because of this that the number of gates and main roads was changed in the *De re militari/Campaign Organization* (e.g. 1.128ff.; Appendix 4.4) to follow the actual combat formation, so there were twelve gates with six roads and in the standard combat formation there were sixteen *taxiarchiai* instead of twelve, because this made each section equal in proportion. See the diagrams on pages 45, 47 and 435–6 together with my biography of Iôannês Tzimiskês. However, it should be noted that the eight main gates/four roads structure was still retained in Ouranos' *Taktika* (62, esp. 62.4). This suggests that this same camp structure remained in use even after the reforms presented in the *De re militari* because Ouranos wrote his *Taktika* after this treatise. It was up to the commander to decide which to use according to the terrain and situation.

On the basis of this one may actually speculate that: 1) the camp structure of the *De re militari* was also used at least from the 960s onwards, as the treatise appears to have been written at the instigation of none other than Nikêforos Fôkas himself,[74]

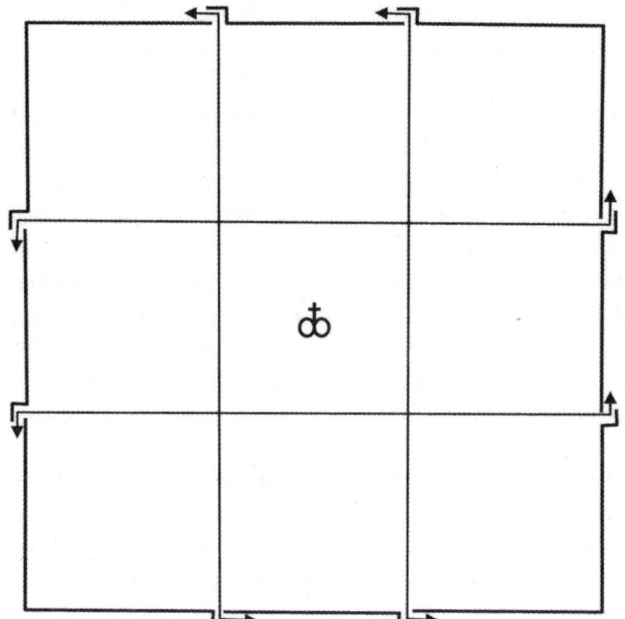

The new 10th century marching camp with four roads and eight major gates.

I have made the assumption that the marching camp was divided into equal quarters so that the stratêgos was positioned in the central quarter.

but it is possible that it was in use before this (e.g. it is quite probable that Leôn Fôkas had used this system in difficult terrain); 2) the camp structure presented by the *De re militari* represented a return to one of the alternative marching camp structures that had been used in the past because its structure followed the same structure that we find in use in the *Syntaxis armatorum quadrata* (sixteen *taxiarchiai*), which was based on the texts of Ailianos and Polybios (see Appendix 1); and 3) the camp structure was the personal recommendation of the unknown author (Leôn Fôkas?) for Basileios II. It is because of this that I also include the marching camp meant for sixteen *taxiarchiai* as reconstructed on the basis of the *De re militari* by R. Grosse and G.T. Dennis. It is added to Appendix 4. The diagram is also valuable for another reason. It shows where the different imperial bodyguard units were located when the emperor campaigned in person. Note, however, that the *athanatoi* (Immortals) *tagma* was created by the emperor Iôannês Tzimiskês, so before his reign their place would have been occupied by some other imperial *tagma*.

1.10. Siege warfare

Tenth-century siege tactics were highly sophisticated and based on Greco-Roman traditions. It was because of this that the Romans reproduced copies of ancient siege treatises (e.g. Biton, Filon of Byzantium, Athenaos, Heron of Alexandria, Apollodoros of Damascus, *De constructione helepoleos* and works of stratagems (e.g. Polyaenos with its excerpts), and it was because of this that new treatises were compiled on the basis of these in the tenth century. The tenth-century treatises include Heron of

Byzantium and *De obsidione toleranda*, the former being entirely based on the earlier works (Athenaeos, Biton, Heron of Alexandria, Apollodoros), while the latter also appears to have used earlier treatises as its sources. The so-called *Mémorandum sur la défense des places* also belongs to the category of treatises that used earlier treatises as its basis, so its text is very close to the *De obsidione toleranda*.[75] In addition to this, the *Taktika* (15) and *Sylloge tacticorum* (53–4) of Leôn VI, and Nikêforos Ouranos' *Taktika* (65) contain chapters devoted to siege tactics, just as the reproduced earlier treatises like those of Syrianos Magistros and Maurikios.

These extant treatises and the narrative sources prove that the Romans either retained knowledge of how to build or continued to use the various kinds of stone throwers and artillery pieces of antiquity. The principal artillery pieces were the various types and sizes of traction trebuchets and ballistae, but the knowledge of how to build the onager, double-shooting ballista and repeating ballista was clearly retained. The types of munitions for these obviously included stones, arrows, fire-arrows, and firebombs. In addition to this, the Romans also had siphons to shoot liquid fire, the newest invention being the hand-held version of the flame-thrower reputedly invented by the emperor Leôn VI the Wise himself. The Romans also continued to use the other traditional types of siege techniques, which included the use of mounds, tunnelling, 'hand grenades', siege towers, battering rams, borers, drills, various types of sheds, a fire hose to spread fire, and so forth, all of which could be learnt and copied from the ancient treatises. However, the fact that the

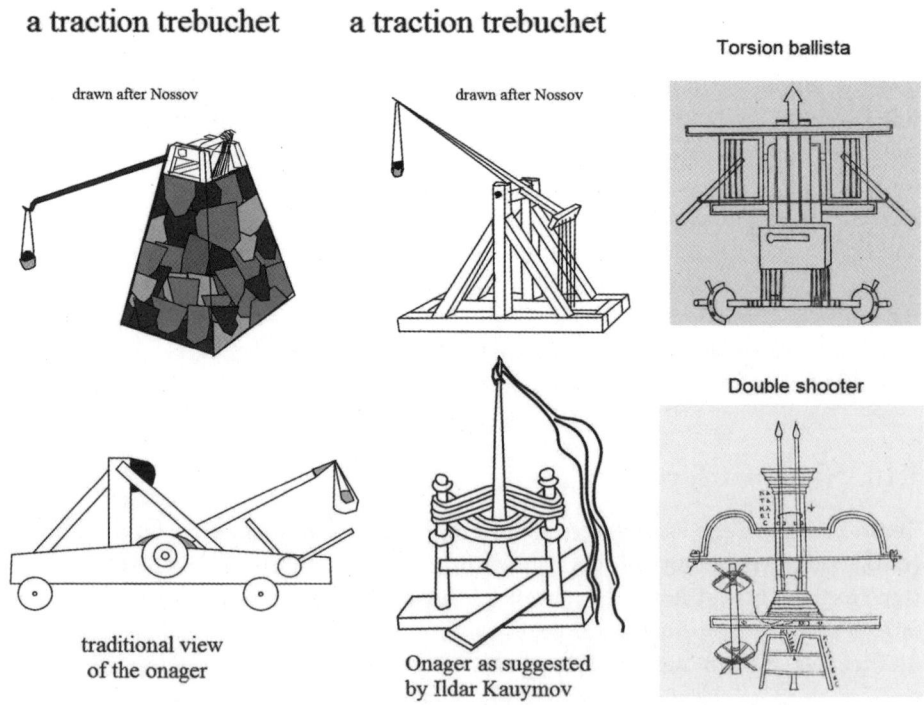

Heron of Byzantium siege tower

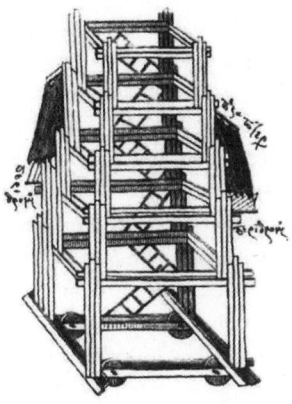

Heron of Byzantium: One version of the battering ram.

Heron of Byzantium flame-thrower

Heron of Byzantium (after Apollodoros): early Greek and Roman version of the flame-thrower used against city walls.

Ballista quadrirotis in the fourth century *De rebus bellicis*. It is very likely that some of the cart-mounted artillery pieces used in the tenth century bore resemblance to.

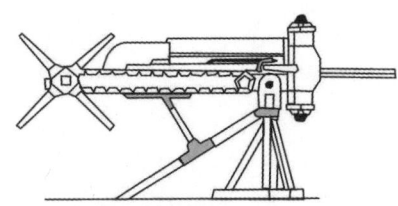

Philon's Repeater
(Drawn after Diehl and Schramm, 1918, Tafel 7)

period Romans continued to employ the ancient siege equipment treatises and all of their siege engines does not mean that all of the period commanders would have used those in the field or would have even considered the ancient texts and their engines as useful. The best evidence for this is that, whereas the unknown author of the DRM (27) referred his readers to the 'outstanding and very practical' ancient siege treatises, Nikêforos Ouranos (OT 65.22) noted that his generation had tried all of these (mentions e.g. siege towers, rams, scaling ladders, tortoises etc.) but had found out that only the undermining of the walls (i.e. tunnelling/mining) and use of *laisai* (easily-portable protective sheds) were actually useful. This demonstrates nicely how the different commanders could have very different views of the practicability of the ancient texts and how this was likely to influence their conduct of war.

Siege warfare can be divided into two broad categories: the defensive and offensive siege techniques. The standard features in offensive sieges were: 1) the continuous progressive ravaging of the territory in the proximity of the place that one intended to besiege in order to diminish the availability of provisions and help from these areas; 2) the building of forts in strategic locations for the purpose of isolating the object of attack; 3) the offering of the terms of surrender to the enemy at first to avoid the costly siege; 4) the use of surprise attacks if possible; 5) the use of a traitor to bring about the conquest of the city; 6) if the enemy had refused to surrender the possible use of assault in tortoise formation with ladders possibly with some sheds; 7) if the first assault had failed or was considered too costly to attempt, the building of siege engines and use of mounds and mines against the enemy; 8) if the place was considered too costly to take by other means, the starving of the defenders to surrender; 9) the acceptance of a ransom payment for not besieging or continuing to besiege the location; and 10) the Romans could also attempt to offer new terms of surrender to the enemy if the siege had lasted for a long time.

The standard defensive siege techniques consisted of: 1) the use of a scorched-earth strategy to make the attack difficult if there was prior information of the enemy invasions; 2) the building of sophisticated fortifications with enough provisions and defenders placed inside to withstand a siege; 3) the exploitation of defensive features like walls and towers and the use of siege engines and other tactics like mattresses to negate the effects of the attack; 4) the sending of a relief army against the besiegers; 5) the use of a diversionary invasion either on land or sea; 6) the employment of guerrilla warfare against the besiegers in an effort to force them to leave; and 7) if the situation appeared hopeless, then the Romans usually offered a ransom in return for the city/fortress, or the Romans attempted to negotiate favourable terms of surrender if the enemy did not accept the ransom.

1.11. Naval warfare

The naval forces consisted of the mariners/sailors, rowers/marines, naval soldiers, craftsmen and artisans, bureaucrats and so forth. The workhorse of the Roman navy was the swift *dromôn* (runner), which was used as a general term to describe all galley warships. However, the *dromôn* was still divided into special types of vessels, of which only the largest variant was called *dromôn* or *dromôn trieres*. The Romans used their naval forces for intelligence gathering; protection of the sea lanes, merchant ships, coasts and coastal cities and towns; raiding of enemy ships and towns; piracy; transporting of messages and embassies; transporting of soldiers and supplies; amphibious operations; sieges; and destruction of enemy fleets when necessary.

Ships[76]
1) Galea (LT 19.10, 19.81), a small and fast single-banked (*monoreme*) galley which probably had 25 oars on both sides (i.e. it probably resembled the old *pêntekontoros*). As a monoreme, it was essentially a smaller variant of the *pamfylos* (see below). The *galeai* and *pamfyloi* were developed further in the western Mediterranean, so that it had both monoreme and bireme variants, with the size of the ship made bigger. It is uncertain if these ships were ever equipped with flame-throwers to shoot liquid fire, but obviously one should not preclude the possibility that this was occasionally done, for example by using the simple hand-held versions invented by Leôn o Sofos. The attached drawing shows one possible reconstruction of a monoreme type *dromôn*.

2) Ousiaka chelandion, a single-masted or double-masted bireme war galley with a single *ousia* of 108 or 110 crew acting as rowers/fighters, plus the other crew (sailors, captain, artillerymen etc.) manning the galley. The *ousiaka chelandia* was a bireme with one rower per oar and 25 oars per row, with eight to ten spare rowers. These ships could also be equipped with flame-throwers and artillery pieces (traction trebuchets and ballistae). The mast could be equipped with a ram, which could then be dropped on the enemy vessel. The ships could receive additional protection from protective screens made of leather or other fabric. The image overleaf shows one possible reconstruction of a bireme *dromôn*. Note, however, that such a vessel could also have a spur/spike/ram in the bow which is not included in the drawing.

3) Pamfylos/chelandion pamfylos (this latter term presumably referred to a converted version of the *pamfylos*) was a monoreme (when built as *pamfylos*) or bireme (when a *dromôn* had been modified as such) galley with a crew of 120, 130, 150, or 160 men.[77] When the ship was originally built as a *pamfylos*, the rowers were all placed on the deck, meaning that the largest version for crews of 150 or 160 men would probably have had 25 oars on both sides, each manned by three rowers (ten men in reserve when the crew consisted of the 160 men), while the smaller variant for crews of 120 or 130 men would have had 20 oars per side, each manned by three rowers (ten men in reserve when the crew consisted of 130 men). When a bireme *dromôn* was converted into a *pamfylos*, the rowers were removed from the lower deck/hold to free it for other use (transport of horses, baggage, commander's quarters etc.). According to Leôn (LT 19.42), the *dromôn* that the *stratêgos* was to prepare as his

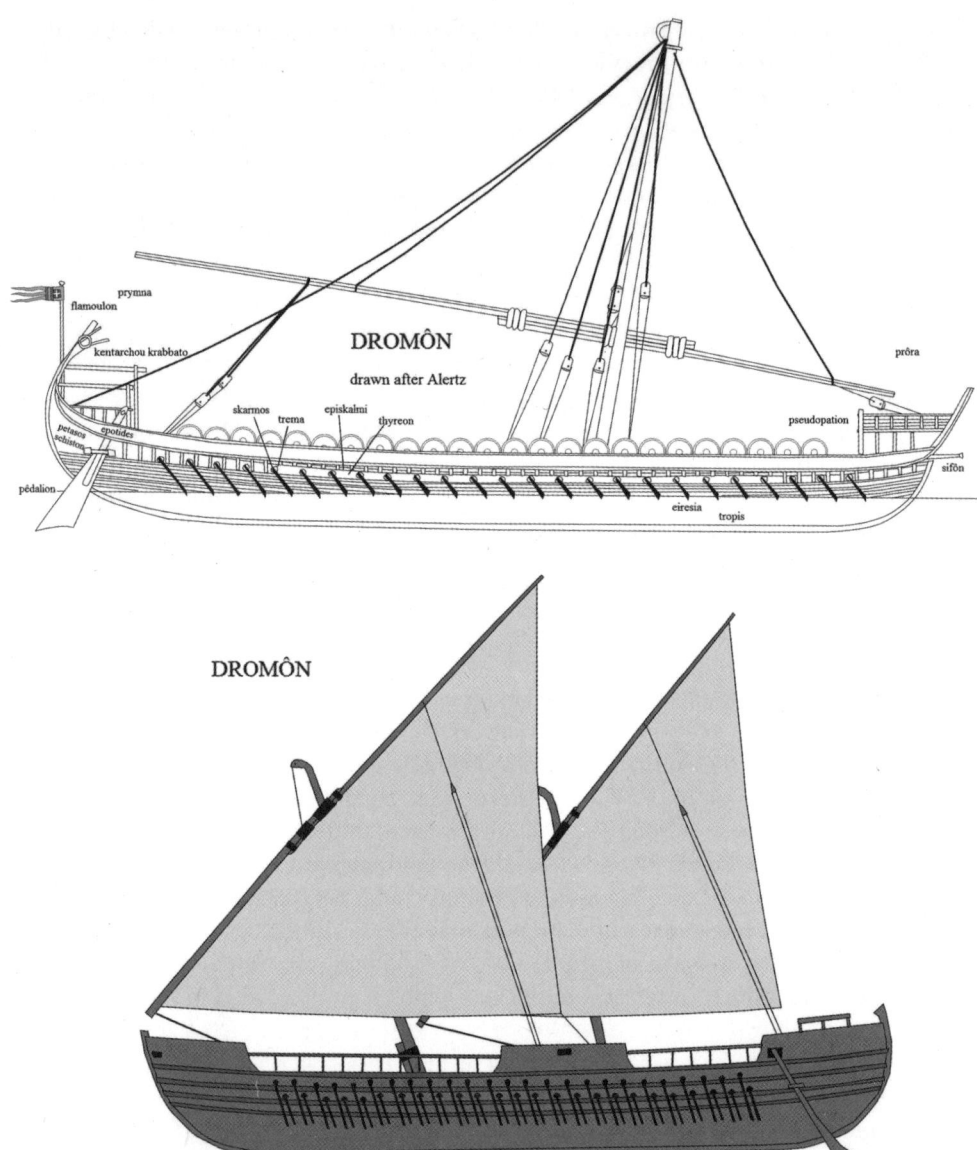

The *dromôn* drawn after Hocker with some small changes. Hocker suggests that the Arab heavy warship would have looked similar while Konstam suggests that this type of ship was actually the Arab *shalandī musattah* so that he reconstructs the Roman *dromôn* to be different in design. According to Konstam's interpetation, the sides of the *shalandī* were made higher than in the Roman warships. On the other hand, according to Agius, the *shalandī* was actually a copy of the Roman *dromôn* so that the Arab galleys that differed in design bore other names.

flagship was to be superior in size and speed to other ships and this ship was known as *pamfylos*. The soldiers on board were to consist of the chosen elite with better equipment than the rest. This suggests that the flagship of the *stratêgos* was actually larger than the typical *pamfylos* and *dromôn*, but how much larger is anyone's guess.

These ships could also be equipped with flame-throwers to shoot liquid fire and artillery pieces (traction trebuchets and ballistae). The mast could also be used as a sort of battering ram by placing a ram on it, which could then be dropped on the enemy vessel. The ships could receive additional protection from protective screens made of leather or other fabrics. When used as horse transports, the *pamfyloi* could transport three horses side-by-side and these could be landed on a beach with a ramp, for example in a column of three-by-twelve as shown in my reconstruction on page 54. The attached drawings of the *pamfyloi* show how I envisage the basic structure of the larger version of the *pamfylos* when it was used as a landing craft. When the cavalry was landed directly on the beach the *pamfyloi* obviously also carried the cavalrymen and their servants, which in the example means 36 horsemen and nine servants. The reader is advised to consult these drawings in the context of the landing of the Roman cavalry on Crete in 960.

In my opinion the likely sources of inspiration for the *pamfyloi* type of ships were the ancient *hippagus* (horse transport) and *actuaria* (transport ship), both of which had rowers on the deck and cargo in the hold.[78] One may also speculate if the Imperial Barges (*agraria*) had a similar single-bank structure with a hold below left for imperial usage.

4) *Dromôn, dromôn trieres*, a double-masted bireme galley with a double *ousia* of men (216 or 220/230 men) acting as rowers/fighters, plus 70 marines (or soldiers from the *themata, tagmata*, imperial bodyguards) and other sailors, mariners, artillerymen, captain etc. The size of the actual *dromôn* (and not the actual when the word is used in the general sense to describe warships) appears to have varied slightly, but there were always three rowers per oar on the upper deck (hence the term *dromôn trieres* that was sometimes used for these). The standard *dromôn* appears to have had 25 oars per side on each deck, so with three rowers per oar on the upper deck (for a total of 150 rowers, as required also by the conversion into *pamfylos*) and one rower per oar on the lower deck/hold (50 rowers), so there were a total of 200 rowers and 16 or 20 or 30 extra men.

Leôn (LT 19.9–10) notes that the *stratêgos* of a *thema* was to construct both smaller *dromônes* like the *galeai* and *monêreis*, and also larger *dromônes*, so that their size reflected what was needed. This obviously suggests that the Romans did indeed possess some extra large *dromônes* too, if the *stratêgos* of a naval *thema* considered this necessary.[79] These are likely to have had three masts and possibly even three men per oar on both decks, so the ship would have been the equivalent of the ancient 'sixes'. Note also the already-mentioned referral to *dromônes* with crews of 500 men.[80] The *dromônes* were always equipped with flame-thrower *sifônes* to shoot Greek Fire (LT 19.8), and there could be three of these per ship (Kônstantinos, *De Cerimoniis*[81]). Naturally the *dromônes* could also include artillery pieces such as traditional traction trebuchets/mangonels (shot stones or firebombs) and ballistae (shot fire-arrows, or arrows, or stones), together with *cheirotoxobolistrai* (crossbows). The mast could be used as a sort of battering ram by placing a ram on it, which

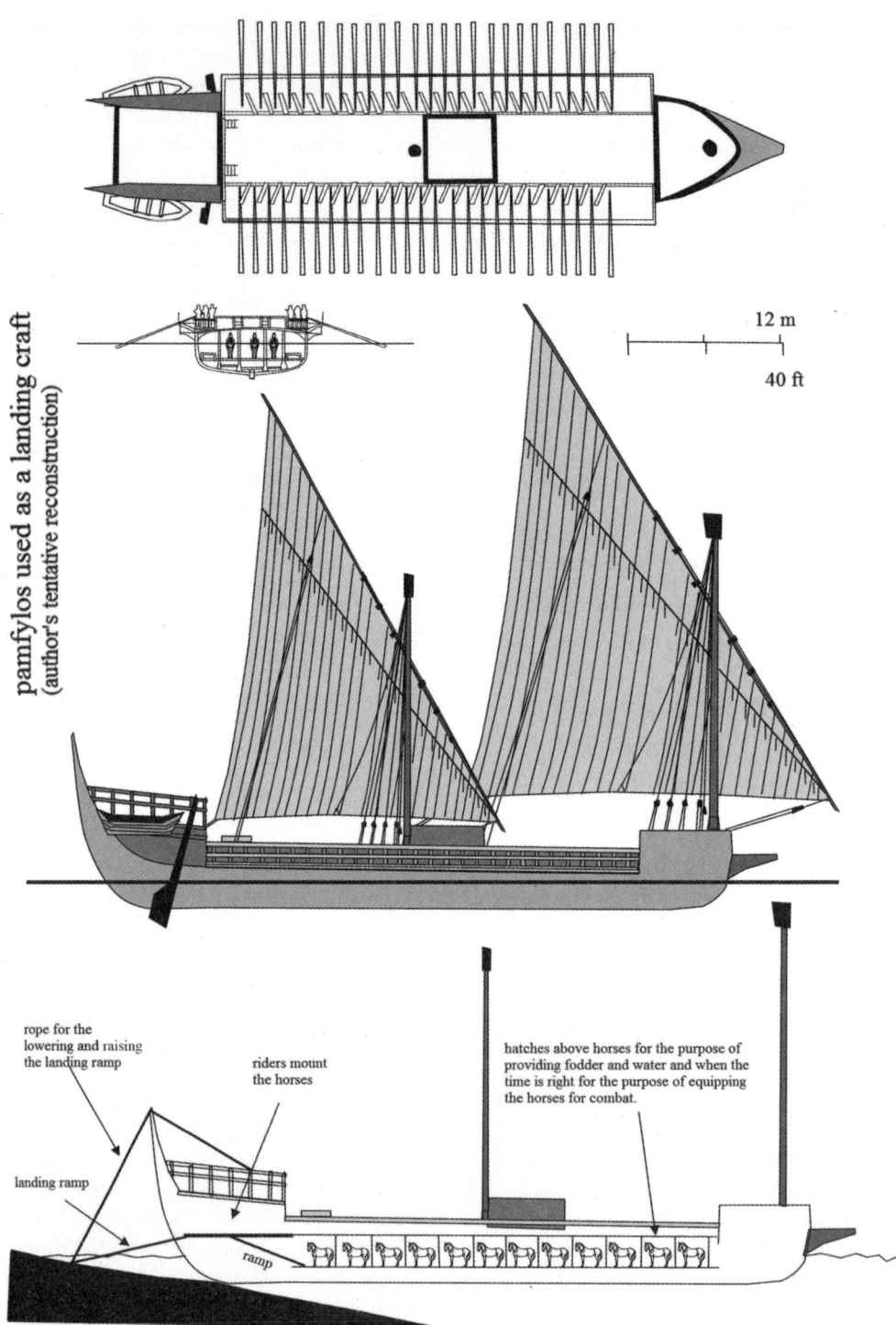

pamfylos used as a landing craft (author's tentative reconstruction)

12 m
40 ft

rope for the lowering and raising the landing ramp

riders mount the horses

hatches above horses for the purpose of providing fodder and water and when the time is right for the purpose of equipping the horses for combat.

landing ramp

ramp

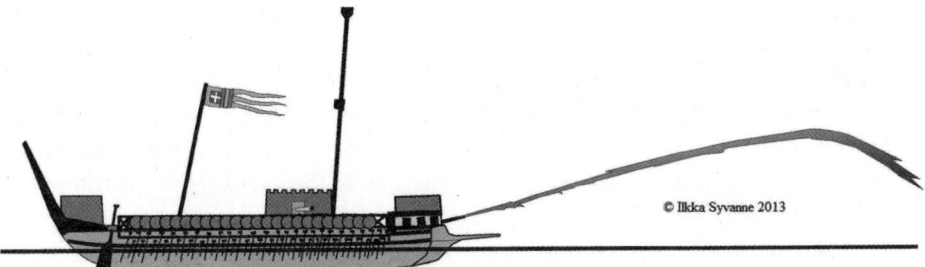
Fire-bearing trireme dromon in combat readiness firing its prow flamethrower

could then be dropped on the enemy vessel. The ships could receive additional protection from protective screens made of leather or other fabric.

As regards the rowing arrangements, we can make some educated guesses on the basis of the paintings of the galleys in the *Skylitzes Matritensis*. These images show the rowers either pulling or pushing the oars (i.e. the rowers had their backs towards the movement or they faced it). This suggests that, depending on the situation, the rowers could row either backwards or forwards, and also the possibility that in some cases the rowers did both at the same time depending on their location on the oar.

The Romans and Muslims both appear to have also employed ships that had single rudders for steering, or alternatively two steering oars and one rudder.[82] The use of a single rudder was not a new invention, even if its use had caught on slowly, because it was used by the Romans already at the turn of the fourth century as I have noted in a paper presented at Norfolk in 2014. The use of the single rudder may have given those ships that had it a slight advantage in manoeuvrability.

In addition to the above ship types, the Romans had merchant, transport and cargo ships – which could also be used as landing craft for the cavalry – small river vessels, boats, barges and other special types of ships employed by civilians.

Naval Tactics[83]

Roman naval tactics resembled their land tactics, with the difference that on the seas they had to pay more attention to the wind, current, time of year, weather, and the location of the coast and reefs. Just like on land, the Romans still preferred to win their wars with surprise attacks or ambushes against careless enemies rather than fight naval battles. Their battle arrays were almost always preceded by three- to-four scouting ships, that could also be left in front to break up the cohesion of the enemy formation. If the navy sailed along the coast, there were also scouts and patrols on land. The naval battle formation was basically a phalanx, which was usually divided into three divisions, the left, centre, and right. The naval phalanx had different variations for different situations: the basic line abreast; two lines abreast; crescent (used for outflanking); crescent with two lines; convex with one line (used for breaking through the enemy middle); convex with two lines; and the defensive circle. In addition to this, it was recommended to possess separate small reserve detachments for the left and right wing and for the centre that could be used to outflank the enemy or prevent outflanking, or act as emergency reserves against enemy breakthroughs. The merchant and transport ships accompanying the fleet were kept out of harm's way by placing them behind the battle line.

Roman naval tactics were based on the use of the war galley, so it is not a great surprise to find them using the ancient Greek galley tactics, which were adapted to the use of spurs/spikes instead of the true rams and to the use of the flame throwers.

1) The *diekplous* manoeuvre was now performed so that: a) a *dromôn* from the centre would rush forward into the interval between two enemy galleys, followed by another; the first would shear the oars while using flame-throwers and missiles, and the second would either ram the immobile ship with a spike and board it if the first one had not set it on fire or engage the stationary enemy vessel with flame-throwers and missiles; b) the rest of the *dromônes* near the resulting opening would rush to the gap and then attack the enemy line from behind); and c) other *dromônes* on the other places of the battle line could attempt a similar manoeuvre.
2) In the *periplous*, the *dromônes* on the wings would try extend the line to outflank the enemy line while using flame-throwers and missiles.
3) The *dromônes* could attempt to board the enemy vessel, but the preferred tactic at this time was the use of flame-throwers and missiles at distance to overcome the enemy.
4) The ramming with the spur-spike or bow of the galley, which was not the preferred tactic with the spur or bow, but was still used.

Regardless of the tactics adopted, open sea naval battles began at long range with the trebuchets, ballistae, crossbows, bows, slings and staff-slings, and when the enemy was close enough the Romans then engaged the foe with their flame-throwers that shot liquid fire. The *stratêgos* undoubtedly decided in advance the general tactics to be adopted. In other words, he must have decided in advance whether he wanted his captains to engage the enemy primarily with the flame-throwers and missiles or whether he wanted his captains to capture some enemy ships, but it is still clear that the captains were also forced to make their own decisions on the spur of the moment, and in truth it is clear that the quality of the captains and their crews actually decided the battles when both sides (refers to the Arabs, the principal enemy at sea) used similar ships and tactics. The role of the *stratêgos* was limited to the situation before the battle, in that he decided when and where and how to engage the enemy, but once battle formations were formed he could influence the outcome only through the use of reserves and by his personal example.

The battles along rivers differed from the above in that the battle formation consisted of two to three lines of small- or medium-sized *dromônes* deployed from bank to bank, behind which were the transport ships. The preferred way to disembark forces on the beaches both on the seas and along the rivers was to do this unopposed, but if the Romans faced a contested landing zone, then they used artillery, flame-throwers and missiles to clear the beachhead so that their forces could disembark. As already noted, the Romans possessed specialized ships for landing operations, so they could disembark even cavalry in fighting formation. See the events of the year 960. The navy was naturally also used in sieges, either to convey provisons and reinforcements into a besieged city, or used to protect the city against an enemy fleet, or offensively in sieges of enemy cities to subject the location to a blockade.

Above: Naval combat (Oppian ms. 11th cent.). Note the use of the diver /swimmer. Public domain.
Below left: two ships united to attack enemy walls from the sea (Heron Byzantinus ca. 950). Public domain.
Below right: Greek fire used in a naval battle (Skylitzes ms. 12th cent.). Public domain.

Chapter Two

Enemies, Neighbours and Roman Response in the 950s

2.1. The Light-Haired Peoples: the Franks and Lombards in Italy[1]

In the tenth century the Lombards and Franks were no longer considered as enemies because they were co-religionists and for most of the period at peace and in alliance with Rome. The small Lombard principalities were no longer even fully independent, but under Roman or Frankish influence. This, however, does not mean that the Romans would not have faced the Lombards as enemies, because the Lombards rebelled against both the Romans and Franks. There was actually sporadic fighting between the Romans and Lombards at least in 936, 940 and 955. In the former instances, the Romans in Italy did not have any particular trouble, but in 955 they had to dispatch reinforcements from Constantinople. Italy was divided into three parts: 1) the Kingdom of Italy in the north (Kingdom of Lombardy; the principalities of Tuscany, Verona, Romagna and Pentapolis; Duchy of Spoleto; and Papal State) which was under the Frankish rulers; 2) the small independent principalities of the south of Italy (independent Italian duchies of Gaeta, Naples, Sorrento and Amalfi; the Lombard double Duchy of Capua and Benevento; the Lombard Duchy of Salerno); 3) the Roman territories in the south (the *themata* of Calabria, Lucania and Loggobardia). Kônstantinos VII (DAI 27.63–4) claims that Naples, Amalfi and Sorrento had always been subjects of the Roman emperor, but this was not true in practice. These duchies just like Capua/Benevento and Salerno were Roman subjects only in name.

The Romans were able to enforce their rule over the independent small states of the south only sporadically. The small Italian duchies of Campania had far greater influence on the regional politics than would be apparent from their size. On top of this, at this time the Duchy of Amalfi held far greater importance in the trade networks of the Mediterranean than the city of Venice, so the Amalfitan traders formed an important element even within the city of Constantinople. The navy of the city of Amalfi was actually powerful enough even to fend off the Sicilian Arabs, but the Amalfitans and the other Campanian small duchies were equally prepared to ally themselves with the Arabs if this served their interests. The Romans were able to enforce their rule on these small Italian duchies only when they were able to dispatch an expeditionary force from the Balkans and/or had Franks as their allies. The main reason for this was that the Romans did not possess an adequate number of soldiers in the south of Italy to keep the territories that their expeditionary forces from the Balkans had been able to conquer during their campaigns. The Roman forces were thin on the ground and were scattered in small garrisons. This forced them to rely on the support of the local elites, which included even the employment of the local Lombard nobility as feudal vassals in the western manner. Therefore, excluding the periods when the Romans were able to send expeditionary forces and/or use Frankish allies, the strategy was purely defensive.[2]

Most of Italy was in Frankish hands, but after the death of Charles the Fat in 888 the Carolingian Empire had been divided into East Francia (Germany), West Francia (France), Lower Burgundy, Upper Burgundy, and the Kingdom of Italy, each of which had a king of its own. In addition to this, each of the kingdoms in question was further divided into territories held by various feudal nobles who often acted independently of each other. A good example of these divisions was Italy, which consisted of numerous independent principalities even if it had a single king. From the year 926 onwards the King of Italy was Hugh of Provence (Hugues D'Arles or Hugues de Provence) who preferred peaceful relations with the Romans because he needed their support against his rival feudal lords in Italy. Hugh in his turn provided military help to the Romans which enabled them to crush the Lombard lords of Salerno and Capua-Benevento in about 934, who were then forced to abandon their conquests in Lucania and northern Calabria. The alliance was also mutually beneficial against the Arabs. Berengar of Ivrea conspired against Hugh in 940, but was forced to flee to the court of Otto in 941. Berengar returned back to Italy in 945 and inflicted a defeat on Hugh with the result that Hugh fled to Arles while Berengar used Hugh's son as a titular king. Berengar took the throne himself in 950.

The Kingdom of Italy was a scene of continuous fighting between different contenders for the throne, and in 951–2 drew the King of East Francia (Germany) Otto I the Great to the scene, with the result that the King of Italy Berengar II recognized Otto as his overlord. Berengar II revolted in 958, which drew Otto I back into Italy in 961 with the result that he was crowned Emperor by Pope John XII on 3 February 962. This meant the uniting of East Francia (Germany) and the Kingdom of Italy into what was later given the name Holy Roman Empire. In short, it was not only the common enemy and common religion which prevented conflict between the Romans of Constantinople and Kingdom of Italy, but also the internal feuds within the Kingdom of Italy.

The subjects of the Kingdom of Italy consisted of local nobility, independent cities, the Papal domains, and Lombard duchies. Their armed forces consisted of the citizen levies, mercenaries, and retinues of the wealthy. In the case of the Lombard duchies, the core of the army consisted of the feudal levies/retinues of professional cavalry and local levies. The forces of East Francia proper consisted of: 1) the general levy of all men able to bear arms, who both maintained and defended the local fortifications; 2) a select levy of wealthier individuals who could serve abroad as infantry forces; 3) substitute professional soldiers paid by the wealthier persons assigned to the category of select levy; 4) professional heavy cavalry (mounted *loricati*, the 'knights') of the nobility and ecclesiastical institutions; 5) the royal household troops; and 6) royal garrisons. The infantry fought in phalanx formation, where the forces of the general levy were of lesser quality than other forces because of their poorer training and equipment. The light cavalry and heavy cavalry could be used for both cavalry charges and feigned flights. The Ottonian forces included foot archers and mounted archers, but their numbers were too small to be of significance against enemies such as the Magyars/Hungarians or Romans. As we shall also see from the comments of Leôn the Wise, the main strength of the Ottonian infantry and cavalry lay in close quarter combat.[3]

The Romans faced the Lombard duchies, the independent duchies of Campania (nominally under Roman rule), the Kingdom of Italy and Muslims of Sicily as neighbours in Italy. In the northern Balkans the neighbouring areas were the client states of Venice and Croatia (both nominally under Roman rule), while in the west it was the client island of Sardinia.

According to Leôn's estimate, the Franks and Lombards still formed a similar potential threat as they had when Maurikios wrote his *Strategikon*. In fact, Leôn's text follows closely the *Strategikon*, but now with the difference that Leôn not only advised how the *stratêgos* could oppose them, but also how to emulate their tactics if the situation for that was favourable – the latter was obviously the case when the *stratêgos* faced an enemy using large numbers of mounted archers on a level unobstructed terrain. The Lombards and Franks were still considered – and rightly so – bold, audacious and impetuous in combat, who regarded even a short retreat as a humiliation and so they preferred to fight in hand-to-hand combat both on horseback and on foot. This is obviously only partially true, because the narrative sources prove that the Ottonian forces were just as prepared to attempt to fool the enemy with feigned flight as the sixth-century 'Light-Haired' peoples were.[4] Regardless, it is still clear that the most obvious quality of the 'Light-Haired' peoples was their determination to hold their ground and fight. It was because of this that their cavalry was ready to dismount and fight as infantry if battle went against them. This made them dangerous foes to face.

According to Leôn, the typical armament of the Lombards and Franks consisted of shields, lances (*kontarioi*) and swords carried on straps from shoulders or around the waist. Their battle-line was well-drawn and closely packed and consisted of men grouped together on the basis of kinship, or some common bond or feudal oath. Their attack was considered impetuous and fearless, both on foot and on horseback. The Franks in particular were also considered to be disobedient towards their leaders. In combat, both the Lombards and Franks tended to avoid anything complicated so they often fought without order, and this was particularly true of their cavalry. The principal reason for this was that the levy in particular lacked adequate training for complicated manoeuvres. The principal weakness of the 'Light-Haired peoples' was that they fought willingly only as long as had been determined in advance and if the time limit was passed they accepted this only with great resentment, with the result that the entire army could melt away when the men returned to their homes. Additionally their leaders were easily bribed (Leôn stated this from personal experience); both nations were also considered pampered and soft by Roman standards, so their men were easily overcome by physical labour, fatigue, heat, cold, rain, lack of provisions (in particular lack of wine) and by the postponement of battle. In other words, the delaying of combat hurt the Ottonian armies in two ways: the soldiers were prepared to serve only as long as agreed; and the soldiers became easily demoralized when they faced difficult conditions.

The use of difficult and wooded terrain was an effective countermeasure against the lancer-cavalry fielded by the Lombards and Franks, because both types of terrain broke the cohesion of their cavalry formation. Ambushes against the rear and flanks were also effective, because both nations did not pay adequate attention to security. They were easily fooled by feigned flight and ambush so that they pursued without order and their poorly-organized marching camps were vulnerable against night attacks with archers. If the *stratêgos* decided to engage them in combat, he was to use the basic cavalry formation with two lines and rear guards, or the infantry phalanx with cavalry posted either on the wings and/or behind (the single infantry phalanx if the baggage train followed to protect the rear and the double phalanx if it did not follow).

The good relationship between East Francia and Rome was doubly beneficial to the Romans, because not only did the two share a common enemy in Italy, the Muslims, but East Francia also fought against the Hungarians who sometimes posed a threat to the Romans. Therefore, it is not surprising to learn that East Francia and Rome both saw it advantageous to maintain cordial relationships with each other.

2.2. The Hungarians/Magyars ('Turks'), Bulgarians and other 'Scythians'[5]

The principal potential enemies in the Balkans consisted of the Hungarians, Bulgarians, Slavs and of the Russians. The last two are treated separately, because these formed a different type of military threat. This chapter deals with the nomadic cavalry type of enemies, which included not only the Hungarians and Bulgarians but also any tribal grouping that employed nomadic cavalry tactics (e.g. the Pechenegs, Khazars, Volga Bulgars) or these as auxiliaries.

As noted by Leôn VI the Wise in his *Taktika*, the Hungarians and Bulgarians did not pose any immediate threat to the Romans in the early-tenth century, because the Bulgarians had become Christians and the Hungarians were separated from the Romans by the Bulgarians. This was obviously true only as long as the rulers had no other ideas. Leôn's successor Alexandros launched a disastrous war against Bulgaria in 913 which ended only in 927. Just like other nomadic rulers, the ruler of Bulgaria was originally called *chaganus/khagan/khan*, but from the year 913 the Bulgarian ruler was called 'Tsar' (emperor), derived from Caesar. In the peace treaty of 927 the Romans recognized Peter I (927–69) as Tsar of Bulgaria and the independence of the Bulgarian Church, while Rômanos I gave his granddaughter in marriage to Peter and agreed to pay an annual tribute to the Bulgarians. The peace lasted for the next forty years, partially because the Hungarians launched a series of invasions of Bulgarian territory – it is quite possible that they did at least some of these raids on behalf of the Romans, just as they had done in the instance mentioned by Leôn. The fact that Leôn mentions this shows that the bribery of the Hungarians against the Bulgarians was one of the methods of diplomacy that the Romans could be expected to employ. In 965 Nikêforos II ended the yearly payments and launched a new series of open hostilities between the countries.

According to Kônstantinos VII Turkey (i.e. Hungary, Magyar) consisted of the following eight tribes/clans: the ruling tribe, *Kabaroi*, which had split off from the Khazars and which was ruled by the Arpad dynasty; and the seven Hungarian tribes/clans proper (second tribe *Nekis*; third *Megeris*; fourth *Kourtougermatos*; fifth *Tarianos*; sixth *Genach*; seventh *Kari*; and eighth *Kasi*). The *Khagan* of the Khazars had raised the Kabaroi under the rule of Arpad as the ruling tribe, and the Kabaroi in their turn had taught the Khazar language to the Turks (Hungarians) who also retained their other 'Turkish language' (this would be Hungarian).[6] All of the tribes/clans had their own princes/rulers (*archônta/archoi*), but these did not act independently during wars. The tribes had a mutual agreement to fight together under a hierachial leadership, and the '*megas archôn*' (Grand Prince) of all of the tribes was a member of the Arpad-family, under whom served *gylas/gyula* (apparently the war leader) and *karchas* (the judge who acted also as war leader). The military leaders of the Kabaroi and seven Magyar tribes served under their leadership. However, in spite of this hierachial leadership structure, in practice the various military leaders of the tribes conducted wide-ranging separate raids throughout Europe, reaching even the south of France, Italy and Roman territory. One of the possible reasons for this raiding was that the area conquered by the Hungarians offered insufficient pasturage for the entire Hungarian nation, but it is equally possible that the sole reason for the raiding was just a lust for booty. What is certain, however, is that eventually the Hungarians started to settle in permanent villages and started to merge with the local population (including, for example, remnants of various nomadic groupings and Slavs).[7]

The Roman territories (Dalmatia and areas south of Bulgaria even as far as Constantinople) and client states (Croatia and Serbia) were potentially vulnerable to Hungarian raids in the right circumstances. The principal strategic means of dealing with the Hungarian threat consisted of their distraction with bribery to act as Roman proxies, for example against Bulgarians (Leôn, *Taktika* 18.40), of the use of the Pechenegs as Roman proxies against the Hungarians and vice versa (Kônstantinos, DAI 3–4), and obviously the presence of Bulgaria between Rome and Hungary. Leôn VI the Wise had indeed employed the Magyars against the Bulgarians in 895–6, but he abandoned his allies after he had concluded peace with Bulgaria in 896. The standard operating procedure was obviously to use any corruptible neighbour or close-by tribe/nation (during this time the borders were permeable so that a large force of soldiers could pass through the territory of another tribe/nation) for the creation of distraction and we shall see Nikêforos employing this concept during his reign.

Leôn states that of the Scythian nations only the 'Turks' (Hungarians) and Bulgarians organized their armies well and were ready to engage the enemy in close combat under a single commander. According to him (*Taktika* 18.41), the differences between these two were so small that it sufficed for him to discuss only the tactics of the 'Turks' (Hungarians). Both had a monarchical form of government and both peoples were held in obedience towards their ruler with cruel oppressive punishments.

According to Leôn, the Turks were also hardy, greedy and treacherous, and sought to gain riches through duplicity, surprise attacks, ambushes and scorched-earth warfare. However, after their adoption of Christianity and other Roman customs, the Bulgarians were no longer considered treacherous. The military equipment of both nations consisted of swords, *lorikion*-armour, bows and lances/spears (*kontarioi*). They carried the spear on their shoulders while they wielded the bow with both hands and used either as the situation required, but all of them were superb archers. They took a huge number of horses, ponies and mares on campaign to provide them with food and milk and also to make their army look more numerous than it was. They did not fortify their encampments and were spread out in several encampments according to their tribes and clans until the day of the battle, and it was only then that they united their forces. They always posted sentries far away from their encampments so that they would not be surprised by the enemy. Their battle formation consisted of several *moirai drouggisti* (*moirai* of irregular size) that were separated from each other only by a short distance so that their battle formation looked like a single long line. In addition to this, they posted a separate force behind to act as ambushers or reserve. The baggage train together with a small guard was placed a mile or two behind either on the left or right. They could also post extra horses behind their array for the protection of the rear. Their favourite tactics were the use of bows at long range, ambushes, encirclements, feigned flights with ambushes, and the use of scattered formation for harassment (i.e. the initial array spread out to harass and encircle the enemy). They conducted pursuit recklessly and ruthlessly. Both nations suffered greatly from a shortage of pasturage, and were vulnerable when the Romans used well-ordered infantry formations, hand-to-hand combat, and night attacks. The use of lancers on level and unbroken terrain and the use of dense well-ordered cavalry formations against them was also advantageous. It was also possible to bribe some of their greedy commanders to desert to the Romans. If the Roman army had infantry present, the cavalry was to be posted behind it, but if the Romans had only cavalry present then it was to be deployed regularly. The pursuits were to be cautious because the 'Turks' used feigned flights and ambushes. It was also preferable to have some obstacle like a river, marsh or a lake behind to protect the rear and it was also necessary to make certain that there were adequate supplies, forage and water available.

We learn further details of their fighting methods from the comments added to the original text of Aelian's *Taktika* in the tenth-century *Byzantine Interpolation of Aelian*. According to this text (Devine ed. 38.3; Dain ed. C3), the Bulgarians, Turks (Hungarians) and Patzinakians (Pechenegues) employed *amfippoi* cavalry where each rider had two horses so that they could transfer from one horse to another. This is not explained by any of the sources and therefore leaves open the following options: 1) the likelier alternative is that each rider had two horses so that one was used for travel and the other for combat and that the horse that had been used for transport was then left behind the battle line; 2) the second option is that the spare horses were retained in the battle formation between the files of the mounted men. Even if the first alternative is likelier, the second version would explain better the term *amfippoi*, because all nomadic cavalry had spare horses that they could use for travel without the term *amfippoi*.

2.3. The Slavs[8]

The Slavic nations and tribes in the Balkans consisted of Croatia, Serbia, various tribes in Roman territory and of the subjects of the Bulgarians. At this time Croatia and Serbia were allied client states, while the Slavic tribes that lived in the Roman territory had become Hellenized and Christian during the reign of Basileos I. According to Leôn, thanks to the actions of his father the Slavs no longer posed a threat so that he included a description of their fighting methods only for the sake of completeness. According to Leôn's description, each of the Slavs was formerly equipped with two short javelins (*akontia mikra*) and other throwing weapons, and large rectangular shields similar to the *thureoi* used by the Romans. The Slavs also used wooden bows and poisoned arrows, which required the taking of antidotes. The Slavs typically placed their homes in wooded difficult terrain which served as their places of refuge. Leôn's recommended way of fighting against the Slavs was to use ambushes and surprise attacks against them.

In the earlier *Strategikon*, we find a far more detailed description of the Slavic tactics. The *Strategikon* retained its relevance also in the tenth century so that a copy of it was produced in the scriptorium of none other than Kônstantinos Porfyrogennêtos, not to mention the fact that other copies of the text were produced before and after him, also in the tenth century.[9] According to the *Strategikon*, the Slavic peoples specialized in the use of difficult terrain, ambushes, sudden attacks, and raids, because they were aware of their relative weakness in pitched battles against the Romans. If the Slavs could not avoid pitched battle, they had their own peculiar style of fighting. To quote my *Military History of Late Rome Volume 8*: 'At first they all shouted together possibly howling like wolves and moved forward a short distance to see if their opponents would lose their nerve. If this happened, the Slavs attacked without remorse. The Slavic leaders and kings advanced in front of their men. If the enemy did not show any signs of nervousness, the Slavs turned around and ran to the woods. This flight could be authentic but more often than not it was a feigned flight meant to induce the enemy to follow them into the woods.' The Roman counter tactics were to try to avoid fighting close to the woods or to try to draw the enemy into pursuit with a feigned flight, or surprise attacks against their settlements when they did not expect this.

The narrative accounts prove that the independent/semi-independent nations of the Slavs, namely Croatia and Serbia, both continued to employ their forces in the same manner as described by the *Strategikon* of Maurikios. In other words, both the Croats and Serbs still possessed relatively-lightly equipped forces which they employed in like manner for fighting among the mountains and forests, just as they had during earlier periods, the only difference being the increased importance of cavalry. They also possessed naval forces which employed relatively light craft, just as the Slavs of the earlier centuries. According to Kônstantinos (DAI 31), at the height of their power the Croats had 60,000 horse and 100,000 infantry, while their fleet consisted of 80 *sagenai* (small galleys) and 100 *kondourai* (boats, cutters). However, at the time when Kônstantinos wrote their strength had diminished significantly thanks to civil war, so there were then only 30 *sagenai* left. The rest of the figures are missing thanks to a lacuna in the text, but if the proportions for the other forces are the same then the rest of the forces available to the ruler of Croatia consisted of 22,500 cavalry, 37,500 infantry and 38 *kondourai* (rounded up from 37.5). These forces, however, were not enemies of Rome, but the forces of their client king and ally. The Serbs and other Slavic nations of the area (mostly descendants of the unbaptized Serbs) inhabiting the coastal areas (Zachlumi, Terbounites, Kanalites, Pagani/Arentani) were similarly subjects of Rome, even if the inhabitants of the coastal areas engaged in piracy. The Serb nation had been seriously weakened by their previous subjection by the Bulgarians. It had been only very recently that they had regained their independence from Bulgaria with Roman assistance.

2.4. Russia/Ruscia (Rôsia, Rhosia)

The ruling and dominant element in early Russia (the land of the Rus'/Rhos, Ruotsi, Ruscia) came from the region of Roslagen located in modern-day Sweden. As is well-known from the *Russian Primary Chronicle*, also known as the *Chronicle of Nestor*, in 862 the Slavs of Novgorod invited Rurik to become their ruler and that later the Russians also took control of Kyiv/Kiev[10] and many other regions around. Most of the Russian fighters were in fact Swedes, but their numbers were bolstered by other Scandinavian adventurers; Finns, Karelians, Estonians and in particular by the Slavic tribes and then later by members of various nomadic groupings (e.g. Hungarians, Pechenegs, Bulgars, Khazars etc.) who were employed as cavalry.[11]

The cities of the area became strongholds of the Rurikid princes, who then assumed the title *chaganus* (*chagan/khagan*) from the Turkish Khazars. The *chaganus* of the *chagani/chagans* (prince of princes) was located in Kiev, and the other *chagans* recognized him as their superior. The elite part of the armed forces consisted of the retinues of the *chaganus* and nobles called *druzhina/varjazi*. The majority of their members consisted of the Scandinavians, but the retinues were open to all expert fighters from any corners of the earth (included therefore e.g. Balts, Finns). The Russian military organization and combat methods were entirely based on Viking tactics, so their principal fighting force on land consisted of the infantry (equipped with spears, javelins, axes, swords, armour, helmets, shields and to a lesser extent with bows and thrown stones) that fought by using a phalanx/shield wall, while their naval strength consisted of the Viking-style ships, but these were usually smaller than the Viking ships used in the North Sea theatre because the Russians needed to transport them on land in the rapids of the Dnieper. The smallness of the ships made them very vulnerable in naval combat with the much larger Roman galleys. This, however, was a minor matter in comparison with the threat posed by Roman liquid fire. The use of liquid fire (Greek Fire) gave the Romans an absolute naval superiority over the Russians. The Russians possessed some cavalry forces which fought as spear-armed cavalry, together with some Hungarian, nomadic and Slavic auxiliary cavalry forces, but neither the Viking-style infantry nor the cavalry were a match against the Roman heavy cavalry cataphracts of this era.[12]

However, it was not the military superiority of the Roman *katafraktoi* or liquid fire that were the principal means of keeping the Russians at peace. It was diplomacy. The fleet transported the Roman envoys bearing gifts for this purpose every year. The Romans were to make certain that the Pechenegs were on their side, because they could prevent the Russians from sailing through the cataracts of the Dnieper. The Pechenegs could also be needed against the Hungarians. It was also similarly important to retain peace with them because they could threaten Cherson (Roman Crimea). The Uzes in their turn could be used against the Pechenegs while the Khazars could be checked with the help of Alans (Ossetians), Uzes and Volga Bulgars. The Roman *modus operandi* was always to employ others as their proxies if at all possible.[13]

According to Kônstantinos Porfyrogennêtos (DAI. 9),[14] the standard Russian maritime trading mission (the terms of trading guaranteed in the treaty between the two made in 911), or military campaign against the Romans consisted of the following elements. Firstly, the Russians gathered their forces in the northern parts of their realm in Novgorod, Smolensk, Chernikov and Vyshegrad, after which they all sailed down the Dnieper in their *monoxyla* (small Viking-style vessels) into Kyiv/Sambatas. It should be noted that on the basis of Kônstantinos' account it is clear that Kyiv/Kiev was not yet the permanent residence of the ruler of Russia (in this case Igor), but merely the assembly point for the Russians who either intended to trade or raid Rome, even if it is clear that Kiev was already in the process of becoming such. According to Kônstantinos, Novgorod was the capital of Sviatoslav/Svyatoslav, '*o archôn Rôsias*', and was still the largest of the Russian cities in the tenth century. At the time Kônstantinos wrote the original text in ca. 944, Svyatoslav was still a child and his father Igor's deputy-ruler as Prince of Novogorod. It was only in 945 when Igor died that Svyatoslav actually became the '*o archôn Rôsias*' (prince of Kiev). His mother Olga (945–69) was the acting regent until 969. Svyatoslav ruled as sovereign from 969 until 972. This implies that Kônstantinos completed his text on Russians only after Igor had died in 945.

The Kievan Russians obtained their *monoxyla* from their Slavic subjects (Krivichians, Lenzanenes, and others). While the Kievan Russians wintered in the Slavic lands (Vervichians, Drugovichians, Krivichians, Severians and others), the Slavs built the bottom halves of the *monoxyla* during the winter and then in the spring they transported these to the lakes that flowed into the Dnieper, after which they took the *monoxyla* to Kiev. In the month of April, the Kievan Russians returned to Kiev, where they bought the *monoxyla* from the Slavs. The Russians outfitted the unfinished boats/ships with oars, rowlocks and tackle from their old *monoxyla*, which were at the same time dismantled. After this they started their travel along the Dnieper towards the Black Sea. The travel along the Dnieper was hindered by seven rapids. The Pechenegs typically attacked the Russians at the fourth rapids, where the ships had to be transported on land for six miles, and then again at the seventh rapids. When the Russians reached the island of St. Gregory in the middle of the Dnieper, they no longer needed to fear the Pechenegs because the river was from then onwards too wide. At the island of St. Aitherios in the estuary of the Dnieper, the Russians fitted their *monoxyla* with tackle, masts, sails and rudders. The distance from Kiev to the mouth of the Dnieper was 953 km. After this, the Russians sailed along the western coastline of the Black Sea and the Pechenegs shadowed them along the shore up to the river Selinas, which was a tributary of the Danube. It was there that the Russians entered Bulgarian territory, where they had to fear the Bulgarians. When they reached the district of Mesembria, their troubles ended if they were conducting a trading mission, because it was there that the Russians reached Roman territory. As noted above, if the Romans were at war with the Russians and had adequate forces present near their capital, they had nothing to fear from the Russians thanks to their tactical superiority on land brought by their *katafraktoi* cavalry and on their tactical superiority at sea thanks to their liquid fire.

2.5. Caucasus, Armenian Highlands and Arab Emirates

In the tenth century the area of Armenia, Iberia, Azerbaijan and the Caucasus consisted of multiple different principalities. In Anatolia the eastern neighbours of Rome or states close to Rome consisted of the Christian kingdoms of the Bagratuni dynasty of Armenia, the Bagrationi (an offshoot of the Armenian Bagratuni) dynasty of the Principality of Iberia (modern north-eastern Turkey and south-western Georgia),[15] Georgian Abkhazia (modern western Georgia),[16] and Arcrunid

Vaspurakan. In addition to these, there were local Christian and Muslim dynasties in each of these that acted independently when this suited their interests. Depending on the conflict in question, all of these were either allies or at least neutral countries during this period.

After the great massacre of the Armenian nobility by the Arabs at Naxchawan in 705, Ashot IV Bagratuni fled to his feudal domains in Sper, while his cousin Adarnase fled to Iberia (K'art'li). The silver mines of Sper helped the Bagratuni in their efforts to increase their domains, while their cousins now known as Bagrationi became the most important princeply house in Iberia. Eventually in about 884/5 both Constantinople and Baghdad recognized Ashot V Bagratuni as King of Armenia, so the Armenian Kingdom, extinct ever since 428, was reborn. In Iberia the Georgian Kingdom was revived by Adarnase Bagrationi in 888, with the result that both Georgia and Armenia were ruled by the same Bagratid dynasty, but the Armenian king held the superior position. The principalities of Tarawn, Tayk (Tao) and K'larjhet'i-Ardanujhi, Kars and Tashir-Joraget (or Lori-Tashir) were ruled by members of the Bagratid family. The Georgian kingdom of Abxazet'i (Abasgia) was under a separate dynasty, which from 978 onwards also claimed to be rulers of Iberia. The eastern neighbours of Iberia were the kingdom of Kaxet'i (in Arabic Sanariya), the Duchy of Heret'i, and the Arab emirates of Tiflis, Janza, Sharwan (under Sharwanshahs) and Darband. During this era the Arab emirates facing the Caspian Sea were not involved in any major operations against Rome. In fact, they had problems of their own. They were targeted by the Russian naval raids which required the intervention of the Buyids of Bahgdad. South of Iberia (north-east Armenia) were the Armenian principalities of Parisos, Xach'en, and K't'ish. South of the former were the Armenian Siwnik/Siunik principalities consisting of Siwnik/Siunia, Gelark'uni and Vayoc'jor. Their neighbours were the Arab emirates of Dabil (Duin, Dwin, Dvin) and Golt'n that were fighting against each other for the possession of Naxchawan. South of Golt was located the Arab emirates of Khoy (Her) and Salmast.

Southern Armenia consisted of four independent states, the most important of which was the Arcrunid principality of Vaspurakan. The other three were Tarawn west of Vaspurakan and the principalities Anjewac'ik and Mokk east of Vaspurakan. Anjewac'ik belonged to the Arcrunids, so in practice it formed a part of the principality of Vaspurakan, but the Arcrunids were able to acquire Mokk only later, after 976, which means that at this time it formed a separate independent Armenian kingdom. The Kurdish dynasty of Marwanids ruled the territory south of Tarawn.

During this era there were several Arab emirates in the Caucasus-Armenia area facing the Romans. The emirates of Dabil (Duin, Dvin, Dubios), Nashawa (Naxdawan), Qaliqala (Karin, Erzerum, Theodosioupolis), Arjilsh (Arcei), Barghiri (Berkri), Dat al-J'auz (Arcke), Khilat (Xiat) and Minasrjird (Manzikert, Manazkert) were officially part of Bagratid Armenia, while the emirates of Mayyafariqin, Bitlis (Balalesh), Salamas (Salamast) and Huy (Her) were fully independent Muslim emirates. The most important of these was the medium-sized Qaysid Emirate of Minasjird (Manzikert), which was in practice independent from the Bagratid dynasty. The Qaysid Emirate, located north of Lake Van, consisted of Manzikert, districts of Apahunik, Kori, Varainunik, Aliovit, Bznunik and Hark, and of the cities Akhlat (Xlat), Adiljevas (Arcke) and Arjish (Ardesh).

The following discussion of the Armenian and Georgian armed forces concentrates on the Christian principalities of this area. For the military forces employed by the Arab, Daylami and Kurdish emirates, see Chapter 2.7. Armenian society proper was a feudal society in which the upper echelons of the society consisted of the royal family, magnates and lesser lords. The feudal nature of the society meant that Armenia was a house divided. The different feudal lords often promoted their own position at the expense of others, and also at the expense of their mutual interests as a nation.

Armenian society was divided into the royal family (Bagratuni), magnate families called *nakharars* and lesser nobility called *azats*, priests, and the non-noble (*an-azat*) *ramik* (which included people of the towns, traders and the peasants *shinakan*). The nobility (magnates and lesser nobility) had their own retinues of soldiers, so their sizeable retinues of heavy-cavalry 'knights' formed the elite of the armed forces. These 'knights' were fully armoured and equipped with lances, swords, maces, shields and bows. In addition to this, the Armenians also possessed light cavalry (mounted archers and javelineers) and high-quality infantry (both light and heavy). The cavalry was equally well-suited for long range and melee combat, just as was their infantry, which fought in phalanx formations. The same was true of the Armenians living inside the Roman Empire. It was therefore not surprising that the Romans also employed Armenians (both native and allied Armenians) in their armed forces. The Armenians recruited from Roman territory and from free Armenia and from among the refugees of Muslim-held Armenia were found particularly useful as infantry forces in the *kleisourai* of the border regions.

Georgian society, both in 'Iberia' and in Abkhazia, resembled that of Armenia in that it was feudal by nature, with the royal family (Bagrationi) followed by the nobles (*aznaurni*) who served as feudal mounted 'knightly' warriors, priests, common folk who served as foot soldiers, and semi-dependent peasants with no military obligations. Most of the fighting was performed by the cavalry forces provided by the nobility.[17] The cavalry forces were fully equipped (spear, sword, mace, bow, shield) and armoured multipurpose troopers. The infantry forces consisted of both light and heavy infantry which fought in phalanxes.

2.6. The Persians and Persian Tactics of Leôn's *Taktika*[18] (see also Appendix 5)

On the surface, Leôn appears to have included Persian tactics and Roman counter tactics against them only for the sake of completeness of information, but his description is not entirely without value because the Muslim cavalry, especially the

Ghulam elite cavalry, operated like the Persians of old times. The best evidence for this is the continued reproduction of Sasanian cavalry formation in the Arabic military treatises, together with Sasanian texts on archery and other aspects of warfare.[19] See Appendix 5. On top of which, the Romans also continued to see the former lands of Persia in Muslim hands still as Persia. As if this would not have been enough of a reason to include information about the formation in question, Leôn (*Taktika* 18.26) actually instructed the Roman commander to use this array against enemy cavalry lancers, and in fact we also have evidence for its use in the *De velitatione* (DM 16.6; D 16.61–3), which lists two different cavalry formations, one with three divisions in front and four behind (possibly the standard formation described in detail by both Maurice and Leôn), and another which had three divisions in front and behind – and the latter is the Persian array described by Leôn and also the cavalry array that was sometimes used in conjunction with the infantry hollow square.

Leôn instructed the general to array the first line of the cavalry formation into three equal divisions so that the centre had 400 to 500 extra elite soldiers. The 400 – 500 extra elite soldiers in the centre are clearly the same as we find the Romans and Arabs using as cavalry wedges/triangles of *katafraktoi/ghilman*. Each *tagma* was divided into first and second line, which means that the second line consisted also of three divisions.[20] The extant Muslim military treatises based on Persian sources also include outer wings for this array, which can be considered to have been the equivalents of the Roman outflankers and flank guards. The baggage train and equipment were placed behind the array. If the enemy consisted of cavalry lancers, the Roman commander was instructed to place his battle formation in difficult or rough terrain so that he could employ archery effectively against the lancers, whose array would be broken by the terrain. It was unlikely that the lancer charge would succeed in such conditions.

If the Roman general faced such a warlike enemy, he was expected to delay combat and post his camp on difficult terrain and fight against the enemy when it suffered from the summer heat in the afternoon. These were the Persian tactics against the Romans during the Late-Roman period, and the tactics that the Romans employed successfully against the Germanic peoples then and also during the so-called Byzantine era. If the Romans faced a 'Persian' array, they were instructed to use infantry or dismounted cavalry in difficult terrain or cavalry lancers on level and unobstructed terrain, and hand-to-hand combat in general. The array was also considered vulnerable on the flanks and rear because it did not have adequate numbers of flank guards – and indeed it was very vulnerable if the array did not possess extra flank units.

In short, Leôn advised the Roman *stratêgos* to use the Persian array, with mounted archers and terrain against enemies like the Franks and Lombards who employed cavalry lancers.

2.7. The Arabs/Saracens (Agarenoi) and other Muslims (see also Appendix 5)

The principal Muslim states consisted of Sunni Umayyad Spain; the Shia/Shiite Fatimids of North Africa and Sicily; the Sunni Ikhshidids of Egypt; the Shiite Hamdanids of Syria-Cilicia, with some territory in the Upper Mesopotamia (the Hamdanids did not actively promote the Shiite sect); the Emirate of Melitene until 934; the Sunni pirate Emirate of Crete;[21] the Sunni Abbasid Caliphate under the Buyid sultans; the Persian Sunni-dynasty of Samanids in Khorasan and Transoxiana (claimed descent from the Mihran Bahram Chobin); the Daylamite Shiite Buyids in Iraq and central and southern Iran; the remnants of the Iranian Saffarids in Sistan; the competing Ziyadids in Yemen; and the Yuririds in Sana'a.

After the conquest of Melitene by the Romans led by Iôannês Kourkouas in 934, the principal enemies for the Romans were the pirate Emirate of Crete and the Hamdanids of Cilicia-Syria, with the former posing primarily a piratical threat, while the latter posed a threat to the Romans both on land and sea. The political situation vis-à-vis the various Arabic enemies was favourable for the Romans from the 930s until the 970s. The peaceful relationship with East Francia and Bulgaria and the crushing of the Rhôs/Rus fleet in 941 with the subsequent conclusion of the peace with Russia in 944, enabled the Romans to concentrate their efforts against the Arabs. Furthermore, after the collapse of the authority of the Abbasid Caliphs in Baghdad the Muslims no longer posed a unified threat, even if most of the Muslim emirates recognized the Caliph as their official head of state. As if that would not have been enough, many of the Muslim states were at a state of war with each other.

The Arabs of Crete originated in Spain, but their relationship with the Umayyad Caliphate was anything but good because they recognized the Abbasid Caliph as their sovereign. The principal allies of the Cretan pirates were the Egyptians, who not only provided them with Jihadist fleets but also built ships for them in their own shipyards. The Cretan fleet as such was a typical Muslim fleet, with *koumbaria*, *shalandi* and *shini* ships (see the discussion later) which the Cretans could also build in Crete thanks to its abundant forests. Besides Arabs, the crews appear to have included black troops provided by the Ikhshidids of Egypt. According to Vassilios Christides, the Cretan Arabs had permanently conquered the islands of Dia, Christiana, Ios, Thera, Paros, Naxos, Elafonesos (Voia), Aegina, Neon and possibly Kythera. I consider the conquest of Aegina to be an overstatement, because the interior was held by Romans. Similarly, the island of Neon near Constantinople was not really in Arab hands. It was only a stopping place for the pirates. Likewise, the island of Kythera was not really occupied by the Cretan corsairs because its only inhabitants in 962 were local hunters, not to mention the fact that all of the Roman fleets could easily bypass it when going either to Italy or back. In short, the corsairs occupied these only in name and presumably used them only as places of anchorage.[22] However, on the basis of Theodosios the Deacon's description, we know that the Cretans were highly effective as pirates, so many of the Roman islands and coastal areas were either completely unoccupied or the inhabitants had retreated to the interior in fear of the corsairs.

The statement 'an enemy of my enemy is my friend' held true for the Romans. Therefore, the Romans maintained a friendly relationship with the Umayyad Caliphs of Spain. The Fatimids had overthrown the Aghlabids of North Africa and Sicily, which had resulted in fighting between the Romans and Fatimids in Sicily and Italy (and also between the Fatimids and the forces of East Francia) during this era. The Fatimids possessed a sizeable fleet together with a well-organized army, so they posed a formidable threat, but the Romans had three major advantages in this situation. In Italy they had the forces of East Francia on their side, while the Umayyads of al-Andalus and the Ikhshidids of Egypt threatened the Fatimids from east and west. The friendly relations with the Umayyads paid dividends in this theatre too. It took until 969 for the Fatimids to deal with the double threat of the Umayyads and Ikhshidids – in fact it was in 969 that the Fatimids launched their final invasion of Egypt, followed by advance into Syria which brought their land forces into conflict with the Roman land forces already in the 970s. In fact, the problems that the Fatimids faced enabled the Romans to regain control of a vast area of the island of Sicily, known as Val Demone in the 930s, so fighting on the island still continued even into the 960s, and the Arabs were able to capture the cities of Taormina and Rometta only after long sieges in 962–4.[23] On the basis of the existence of Sardinians among the imperial bodyguards, it is probable that the island of Sardinia still officially recognized the Roman emperors as their overlords, even if the inhabitants were fully independent in practice.[24] The continued resistance of the Sicilians therefore enabled the Sardinians to keep their island free from the Muslims.

The threat that the Fatimids posed to the Ikhshidids of Egypt also helped the Romans in their operations against the Cretan Emirate and Hamdanids: 1) The Ikhshidids could not effectively help the Cretan Arabs with their fleet because it was needed against the powerful Fatimid fleet; 2) the threat of the Fatimid land army limited the numbers of volunteers that could join the yearly invasion of Roman territory that began every September. The Muslim naval assets in the Eastern Mediterranean consisted of the fleets of Crete, Tarsus/Tarsos, the Syrian coastal towns (mainly Tripoli and Tyre) and the Egyptian fleet of the Ikhshinids. It was also beneficial for the Romans that the island of Cyprus was demilitarized – it was officially still part of the Roman Empire, while it paid taxes and tribute to both the Caliph of Baghdad and Emperor of Constantinople. However, the demilitarization also had its downside, which was that when the Egyptians supported the Tughur/Thughur (area of conflict with the infidels), they sometimes dispatched a fleet and not only land forces, and when this happened the fleets of Egypt, Tarsus, Tripoli and Tyre were usually assembled at Cyprus before invading Roman territory proper.[25]

The military organization, tactics and numbers of the two principal Muslim enemies, the Fatimids and Hamdanids, will be discussed in greater detail at the end of this chapter. The analysis of the threat posed by the Muslims begins with the information provided by the Roman sources themselves.

The principal forms of warfare against the Muslims were: 1) defensive guerrilla warfare; 2) creation of a no-man's land between the Romans and Muslims with raiding and pillaging; and 3) the gradual re-conquest of territory from the Muslims. The principal methods of re-conquest were the devastation of the border region for the purpose of capturing key cities and fortresses through siege. The devastation made it more expensive for the Muslims to upkeep the garrisons in these places, while also diminishing the availability of defenders and supplies. When the Romans conquered the border region, they typically either killed and enslaved the population or forced them to convert to Christianity and replaced the ethnically-cleansed population with new Armenian settlers so that the re-conquered areas were organized as small 'Armenian' themes for defensive purposes.[26] However, as we shall see in the context of the events of the year 952, on rare occasions the Romans could also retain the local Muslim emir with his forces in their service.

2.7.1. The Saracens in Leôn's *Taktika* (see also Appendix 5)

On the basis of the narrative sources, Leôn's *Taktika* (18.103ff), and *De velitatione*, we know that the threat from Cilicia-Syria towards Roman-held territories had several elements. There were the massive invasions of Muslim volunteers from Egypt, Palestine and Syria which joined the Arab forces in August and then invaded together in September. The Arabs maintained their own land forces which they used for raiding of the Roman territory also at other times of the year. Firstly, they could embark their forces on ships to raid the Roman coastline and, secondly, they could raid across the Taurus range on their own. However, since the Arabs of the 'Tughur' lacked the numbers for simultaneous land and naval operations with their *koumbaria*-ships (they used the same men for both), they could not launch combined land and naval operations. This gave the Romans a significant advantage over them when their forces did not include volunteers from other regions. If the scouts reported that the Arabs were planning a land campaign, the Romans could send the *dromônes* of the Kibyrraiôtai fleet against the coastal regions of Tarsus and Adana to create a diversion, and if the Arabs campaigned by sea, the Romans were to invade their territory with land forces for the same purpose. However, the combined simultaneous attack with both naval and land forces against the Arabs was still considered the best option. Leôn advised the *stratêgos* to attack the Arabs during winter in particular because during that period they had access only to their own forces. The commander was to hide his troops so that he could then wipe the enemy out with a surprise attack while the enemy was in marching formation. Leôn also advised taking the offensive when the Romans had assembled a large army for this purpose.

If the Arabs invaded through the Taurus range, Leôn instructed the Roman commander to engage the enemy forces in the narrow passes only when they were returning and exhausted and possibly carrying booty. The *stratêgos* was instructed to post the archers and slingers on the heights while the Roman cavalry attacked, or alternatively the commander was to use ambushes or barricades of trees and rolling rocks. This is basically the same approach that we find the Late Romans using, and which we find also in the texts of Vegetius and Maurikios,[27] and which were further elaborated into perfection in the late tenth century *De velitatione* (e.g. 20–3). As my short summary of the *De velitatione* in Appendix 2 shows, the key difference in the text of Leôn and *De velitatione* is that in the latter the passes could also be blocked by a heavy infantry phalanx. However, since we know that many of the examples of the *De velitatione* date from the reign of Leôn, we know that the infantry could also be used in this manner even during his reign even if he fails to mention this. Regardless, it is still clear that the creation of the smaller infantry *themata*, the so-called Armenian *themata*, along the border region during the reign of Kônstantinos VII (912–59, sole reign in 945–59) is likely to have resulted from the need to possess some high-quality infantry forces in full combat readiness close to the passes to block them from the returning Arab forces. The use of the light infantry and cavalry for this in the text of Leôn is likely to reflect the earlier dearth of such forces close to the passes, so the commander was forced to use the cavalry or obstacles for the blocking of the passes.

According to Leôn, the Arabs were motivated by Jihad and formed a dangerous enemy in pitched battles. The Arabs did not transport their baggage in wagons and pack animals, but on camels, asses and mules, and they brought vast numbers of these to create an impression of a huge army, as they raised a dense array of pennants above the pack animals to make their army look larger than it was. They used drums and cymbals in combat both to direct their forces and to scare the enemy. The Saracens also used camels for the purpose of scaring enemy horses unaccustomed to them. It was because of this that the Romans had to familiarize their horses with camels and the loud cacophony of the drums and cymbals.

The Arabs had copied many of their combat methods from the Romans, so they employed the hollow square and oblong as their marching and combat formation. Both of these formations were difficult to break. The Arabs were also not frightened by impetuous enemy charges, nor could they be fooled into incaution with delaying tactics. When attacked with missiles, the Muslim infantry knelt and protected themselves with their wall of shields. When the Saracens then noted that their enemy had become tired, they rose up and attacked to close quarters. On land this usually meant that the cavalry and the light infantry 'Ethiopians' (see below) advanced through the intervals of the hollow square/oblong to attack the Romans. It is also probable that the Saracen mounted archers were deployed as 128 horsemen in the rank-and-file rhomboids known as *karadis* (sing. *kurdus*) which were perfectly suited to the use of archers because these could easily retreat through the intervals.[28] The Saracen infantry/marines followed the same approach also when fighting at sea, so that their marines first received the enemy missiles with their wall of shields after which they rose up and advanced to fight hand-to-hand.

According to Leôn, the Saracen infantry did not break their ranks and usually withstood two to three attacks, after which they usually became either so emboldened that they attacked, or panicked and fled. This means that the Romans typically sent their *koursôres/promachoi/proklastai* forward to skirmish with bow in the irregular *drouggoi*-order, which they then repeated two to three times. According to Leôn, the Arabs were always bold when they expected to win, but if they suffered a setback they saw it as the will of God (Allah) and fled in complete panic. According to Leôn, the Arabs were also hot-headed by temperament because they dwelt in a hot climate, which may have given cool-headed Roman commanders an advantage in certain situations.

In the Roman manner, the Saracen cavalry was equipped with bows, swords, lances (*kontarioi*), shields and axes, and they also wore a full set of armour for the body, arms, and legs, with a helmet for the head, but notably not for the horse – which made these vulnerable. This pattern was changed by the mid-tenth century, because we find the Hamdanids using triangles/wedges of *katafraktoi* in the 950s. It is once again probable that the Saracens had copied this practice from the Romans, because we find the use of the *katafraktoi* wedges being promoted in the *Sylloge tacticorum* of Leôn VI (dated 904) before this.[29]

The Saracens also typically posted Ethiopian (meaning the Black Africans) light infantry in front of their cavalry. These were unarmoured bowmen feared for their archery skills. The Ethiopian infantry was transported on their own horses, or behind the horses of the cavalrymen if the fighting took place near their own territory, while the regular shield-bearing infantry marched and fought in the hollow square and oblong formations.

Roman counter measures against the Saracens were well-developed by this date. The Roman commander was advised to exploit the cold winter weather and heavy rain, because the former bothered the Arabs and the latter loosened their bow strings. The preferred time for attack was therefore wet weather, with the implication that the Romans had an advantage at close quarters fighting. The commander (Leôn, *Taktika* 18.22–4, 18.125ff.) was also required to ensure that the army had a large number of bows and arrows when the Romans were fighting against the Saracens and Kurds. The reason for this was that both nations valued their horses highly, so when their horses were targeted by archers they often lost their morale. Leôn therefore advised that once the Saracens in their hollow square/oblong had withstood the two or three Roman attacks with bows and had then become bold enough to attack, that the Romans were to receive this charge by archery, so that the men in front and the men a little behind them shot a barrage of arrows at the enemy. The Romans were also advised to use poisoned arrows for this. The Saracens were very vulnerable to this tactic because they valued very highly their expensive horses, the so-called *faria*, on top of which their unarmoured Ethiopian archers and other foot archers were defenceless against this barrage of arrows. According to Leôn, this usually led to the flight of the enemy.

According to Leôn, the Roman commander was to employ the standard cavalry formation against the Saracens, so its size varied according to the situation from 4,000 to 8,000 to 12,000 all the way up to over 30,000 horsemen. As an example, he gives the deployment pattern of the selected cavalry force of 4,000 horsemen provided by a single *thema*, which was proportionally increased as the size of the army was increased. The first line (*promachos*) consisted of 1,500 horsemen divided into three divisions (*mere*) of 500 horsemen each. A third of each *meros* was to consist of the *koursôres* (posted on the flanks) while two-thirds were to consist of the *difensôres* (in the centre of the *meros*). The *koursôres* were to open the battle by charging at gallop from the formation in irregular order (*drouggos/drouggisti*) while the *difensôres* retained their close order and advanced at the required speed, which was in the attack/support-phase the canter. On the left of the first line were the 100 flank guards (*plagiofylakes*) and on the right the 100 outflankers (*yperkerastai*). In the example given, Leôn (*LT* 18.136, 18.713–6) places these slightly in front of the first line in readiness to encircle the enemy. These also used the gallop in irregular order. Initially the *stratêgos* commanded the entire line from the front (ahead of the

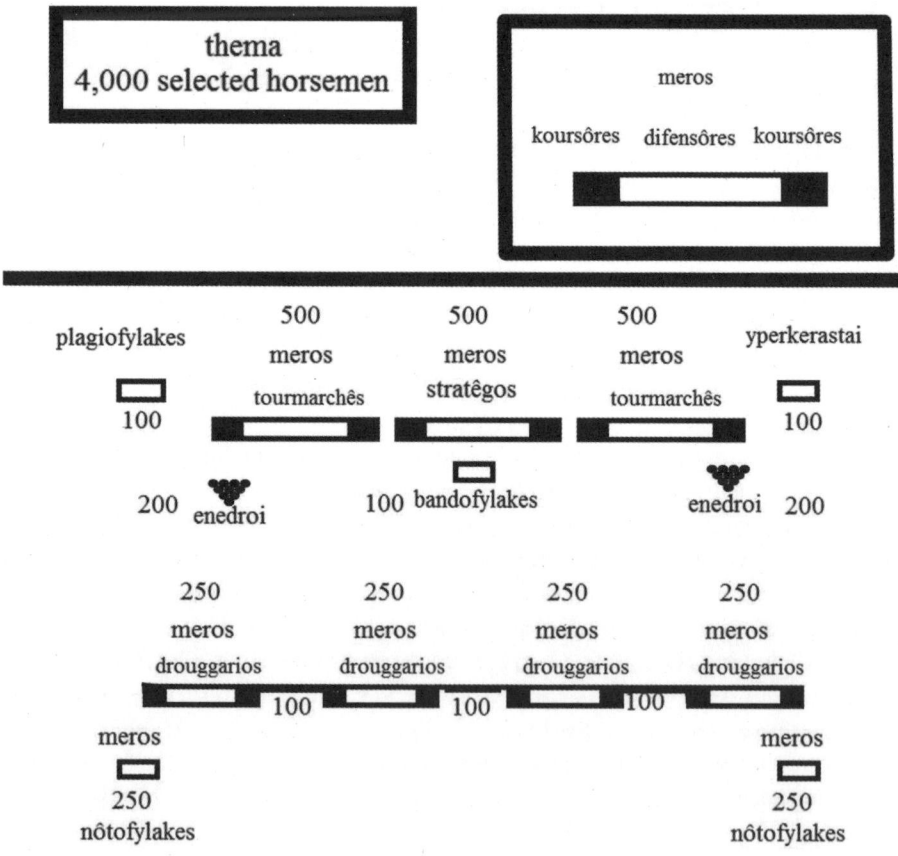

centre *meros*) and apparently assumed a position just behind it when the enemy was close, because Leôn expected the *stratêgos* to use his personal retinue of 100 horsemen (*ST* calls these *bandofylakes* and I have used the same name for these in the accompanying diagram) as reserves. The location of the *stratêgos* means a significant change after the sixth century, because Maurikios expected the overall commander to be always in the centre of the second line after the attack started, while it was the *ypostratêgos* (highest ranking *merarchês* who acted as second-in-command) who commanded the centre of the first line. The other two *mere* of the first line appear to have been under *tourmarchai* because there were two in this cavalry army.

The second (*deuteros*) reserve line consisted of 1,000 horsemen divided into four *mere* of 250 horsemen, each of which was probably deployed into *koursôres* and *difensôres*. Since the army had four *drouggarioi*, it is probable that these were placed in command of each. There were three fill-up *banda* between the *mere*, each consisting of 100 horsemen. The third (*tritos*) line consisted of the 500 *nôtofylakes* (rear guards), which were divided into two *mere* of 250 horsemen each. In addition to this, the commander was to post two *tagmata* of ambushers (*enedroi*), each consisting of 200 horsemen, in hidden locations to ambush the enemy if the terrain allowed this. If this was not possible, then the *enedroi* were to be stationed behind the battle line in irregular order (*drouggoi*) so that they could then surprise the enemy by suddenly charging from behind the formation. In such a situation, the *enedroi* were normally hidden behind the outflankers and flank guards, but since in this case these two units consisted only of 100 men each and were also posted in advance of the first line, I have assumed that the ambushers were in this case posted behind the flank *mere* of the first line.

The cavalry array was used regularly, so after the *promachoi koursôres* had skirmished in irregular order at gallop, the first line with its outflankers and flank guards and ambushers attempted to outflank the enemy or alternative at least sought to prevent outflanking by the enemy while still engaging the enemy frontally, and if the divisions of the first line were forced to retreat the divisions of the second line were to defend them. However, Leôn's instructions (*LT* 18.148) also show that some significant changes had taken place after the sixth century when the *Strategikon* was written. This not only means the location of the *stratêgos* in the array, but also real tactical changes. According to Leôn, the first line either charged against the enemy or it received the enemy's charge. In the *Strategikon*, the Romans always charged against the enemy and did not receive the enemy attack. If the enemy fled, the pursuit was to be cautious. This is common for both Maurikios and Leôn. If the enemy resisted, the second line was to charge so that its flanks outflanked the enemy and attacked the enemy's rear. This suggests that the second line was divided in two (or at least its flank divisions) and were used to outflank the enemy. This is something that Maurikios had opposed vehemently in the sixth century, for which see my *Late Roman Combat Tactics*. Leôn instructed further that the third line could also be used for the outflanking of the enemy formation in conjunction with the first and second lines, targeting the enemy's flank or rear. In short, there is a clear change in the use of the reserves between the sixth and tenth centuries, with Leôn's instructions for the use of reserves being closer to what we find in the *De velitatione bellica* and *Praecepta Militaria*. Maurikios had opposed this, because the progressive sending of the second and third lines to the flanks created a single line formation.

2.7.2. Imperial Mounted Campaigns against the Arabs of *Tughur* in ca. 717–959 (see also Appendix 5)

The typical size for the army on a campaign can be reconstructed from multiple sources: narrative histories, information provided by Arab geographers and military treatises. Let us begin with the information provided by the Arab geographers. According to Ibn Khurdadhbih (81–2), when the emperor went on a military campaign he was accompanied by *patrikioi*, each of whom had 12,000 cavalry consisting of 6,000 soldiers and 6,000 servants. This gives us a total of 48,000 horsemen for the imperial campaigns. This is actually very close to the maximum number of horsemen that the cavalry army depicted by Maurikios and Leôn could hold without making changes to its battle formation. For additional information, see Syvänne, *LRCT*. Ibn Khurdadhbih goes on to claim that when the emperor campaigned against the Arabs he marched to Dorylaeum (Dorylaion), which was a four days' march from Constantinople. The figure of 48,000 horsemen is indeed a quite plausible figure in light of what Leôn states (over 30,000 horsemen used in major campaigns) and in light of what is stated in the narrative sources. On the basis of Ibn Khurdadhbih (p84), we also know that the combat-ready portion of the Roman cavalry consisted of 120,000 men in total, which shows that the figure of 48,000 horsemen was achievable even without resorting to the use of second rate soldiers.

We also possess evidence for the large imperial cavalry campaigns in the east in the works of Kônstantinos Porfyrogennêtos, who extracted material from earlier military treatises into the *De Ceremoniis*. The most important of the authors used by Kônstantinos was Leôn Katakylas, who wrote in the reign of Leôn VI and who drew his material from the experiences of the previous emperors, the most important of whom were the Isaurian emperors, Theofilos, Michaêl III and Basileios I the Macedonian. Kônstantinos' text consists of three parts, which have been edited, translated and commented on by John Haldon as Texts A, B, and C in 1990. I will summarise this material while demonstrating that it contains very valuable information regarding both the size of the major campaigning cavalry army under an emperor and about the battle formation used in such circumstances. As will be shown later, both of these are of the greatest importance for the analysis of the Roman campaigns in late 959.

Kontantinos' text A provides us with the major *aplêkta* (thematic marching camps, depots/dumps and assembly points for the armies) that the Roman armies used when marching towards Arab enemies. The *aplêkta* consisted of Malagina, Dorylaion, Kaborkin, Kolôneia, Kaisareia, and Dazimon in the *thema* of the

Armeniakoi. The city of Pylai also served as an assembly point for the army, but only for the *tagmata* and *optimatoi*, so it was not called an *aplêkton*. The *stratêgoi* of the *Thrakêsioi* and *Anatolikoi* were to join the emperor at Malagina. The general instruction was that each of the *themata* was to join the emperor at the nearest *aplêkton* along his marching route, but the *domestikos tôn scholôn* and the *stratêgoi* of *Anatolikoi* and *Seleukeia* were to meet the emperor at Kaborkin/Kaborkion. When the campaign was against Tarsus, the remaining *themata* were to assemble at Kolôneia, from which they presumably marched to meet the emperor at Kaisareia. If the campaign was against 'eastern regions', the *stratêgoi* of Kappadokia, Charsianon and Boukellarioi were to meet the emperor at Kolôneia, while the *stratêgoi* of the Armeniakoi, Paphlagonia and Sebasteia were to meet the emperor at Kaisareia. If the expedition was towards Tephrikê, located on the border of the *thema* of Kolôneia (i.e. against free Armenia), then the Armenian *themata* (Armeniakon, Chaldia, Kolôneia and Charsianon; these had a minimum of 16,000 cavalry) were to assemble at Bathyx Ryax (presumably somewhere close to the scene).

Kônstantinos gives us two different schemes for the imperial campaign: the taking of the offensive against the Arabs, and defence against the Arabs of Cilicia. He gives us the defensive alternative almost as an afterthought in the C Text (618ff.) by noting to his son that, when the Saracens of Tarsus (i.e. Cilicia-Syria) invaded, the Romans had a system of beacons located at fortresses at Loulon, Mt. Argeas, Mt. Samos, Aigilon, Mt. Olympos, Mt. Kyrizos, Mt. Mokilos above Pylai, and then on the hill of St. Auxentios, which was seen in the Imperial palace. With this system the emperor learnt of the invasion within one hour so that preparations against it could begin immediately. This system was abandoned during the reign of Michaêl III because it could distress the citizens in the capital. However, since Kônstantinos included this piece of information for his son, it is possible that the system was not entirely abandoned – only its final portions were, so that the message could still be conveyed privately with a small delay (e.g. by ship from Pylai) to the emperor without panicking the population. The other fact that bespeaks for the continued existence of some system of warning based on beacons is that we never find Sayf ad-Dawla (al-Dawla/ad-Dawlah/al-Dawlah) using the route which had had beacons in the ninth century.

Texts B-C deal primarily with the procedures that were followed when the emperor planned to conduct an offensive campaign with cavalry. The emperor was expected to make inquiries about various possible offensive actions so that only he and those closest to him knew what his real plans were. After this, the emperor was expected to order the *stratêgoi* to secure fortresses, evacuate populations where needed, prepare weapons and horses, send scouts to reconnoitre, prepare bridging equipment, and order the authorities to observe the mustering of the forces. In the meanwhile, the emperor ordered the central administration to assemble baggage and pack-animals, horses and anything else needed for the campaign. After this, the emperor nominated a person to be in charge of the defence of Constantinople, in command of the *tagmata* in the city (*teichistai* and *noumera*) and the forces of the *eparchos* of the City. Then the emperor dispatched most of the *tagmata* to Pylai, while he performed religious rituals in the city.

Text C, which is based mainly on the treatise of Leôn Katakylas, gives us a very detailed list of things carried by the imperial entourage and of the various different sets of protocol that the emperor was to follow in each situation, with particular attention being paid to the campaigning in Syria. Besides the necessities like water, wine, food, antidotes, medicine, tents, 'Turkish baths' (i.e. Hungarian baths),[30] clothes etc., the most notable feature of the imperial baggage train was the reading material that the emperor was expected to take with him: books of Church liturgy; military treatises, books on mechanics and siege machinery and production of missiles, books of history, especially those by Polyainos (a very comprehensive list of stratagems) and Syrianos Magistros (contained e.g. descriptions of the building of cities and marching camps, siege techniques, marching procedures, use of the infantry phalanx, ambushes, a naval treatise, public speaking to the troops); an oneirocritical book; a book of chances and occurrences: a book dealing with weather and other similar books used by sailors. The books on sleep interpretation and chances may have been needed for the calming of the soldiers' nerves or these were included because Kônstantinos or his source believed in such.[31] From the point of view of military campaigns, it is important to note that the reading list included books on siege techniques, naval warfare and on the use of the infantry phalanx in combat. This means that the imperial campaigns sometimes included also naval and infantry forces and not only cavalry as the rest of the description of the procedures imply.

When the emperor together with the *magistroi* and *patrikioi* sailed on warships from Constantinople to Pylai, he was met by all those that had been gathered there in advance, who included the *basilikoi*-bodyguards, the tagmatic troops, and by the *optimatoi* baggage handlers and their officers. As already noted, the entire corps of 4,000 *optimatoi* was assembled at Pylai to join the expedition, so that 3,900 *optimatoi* were assigned to the baggage train of the *tagmata* and 100 to the imperial baggage train, meaning that there were in total 15,600 regular horsemen in the *tagmata* and 400 imperial bodyguards (300 *etaireiai* and 100 *basilikoi*) accompanying the emperor. This entourage then travelled to the first *aplêkton* to meet the first batch of thematic forces, and from there to the other *aplêkta* as required by the campaign plan.[32] When the emperor then met the assembled forces in each of the *aplêkta*, he reviewed the troops and distributed money and other goods to them in order to ensure their eagerness to fight. All of the thematic troops to be reviewed were to remain mounted, while their officers dismounted and fell upon the ground to show their subservience to the emperor. The fact that all troops remained mounted means that we are here dealing with the traditional assembly of thematic forces which consisted solely of mounted men. The distribution of money and other valuables to the thematic soldiers, the *tagmata*, imperial bodyguards and all officers was to be repeated, for example, every week or every other week or as often as needed to maintain morale.

According to Text B (107–21), when the Roman army marched safely on Roman territory, in front at a distance of a mile from the emperor were horses with purple brocades, after them the *basilikoi archôntes*, then the *stratôres* with saddled horses and the emperor's retinue, and then the emperor himself. It is probable that the emperor was similarly protected by the *basilikoi*, *stratôres* and others as discussed below on the basis of Text C. Behind the emperor at a distance of three bowshots (ca. 990 m) followed the cavalry of the *tagmata* and *themata* deployed as a single well-ordered *strateumata* (i.e. as an army deployed in battle formation). The *tagmata* were deployed in the centre, and on both sides of the *tagmata* were the *themata* so that the best units were deployed closest to the *tagmata*.

When one combines this information with the order of march by the tagmatic forces (see the diagram below) we can reconstruct the cavalry battle formation. The *scholai* and *exkoubitoi* formed the centre *tourma/meros* of the front line, so that it had 8,000 horsemen in total (*Sylloge tacticorum* 35.2 gives 9,000 as the maximum size for the *tourma*). The two other *tagmata*, the *arithmoi* and the *ikanatoi*, each 4,000 strong (*ST* 35.2 gives the *tourma* the minimum size of 3,000 men) were deployed in the second line as two *tourmai/mere* to protect the centre.[33] The flanks that consisted of the *themata* must have been formed in the same manner, with each of the front divisions (*tourmai/mere*) consisting of at least 8,000 horsemen (two standard chosen-4,000-cavalrymen detachments), while their rear was protected by

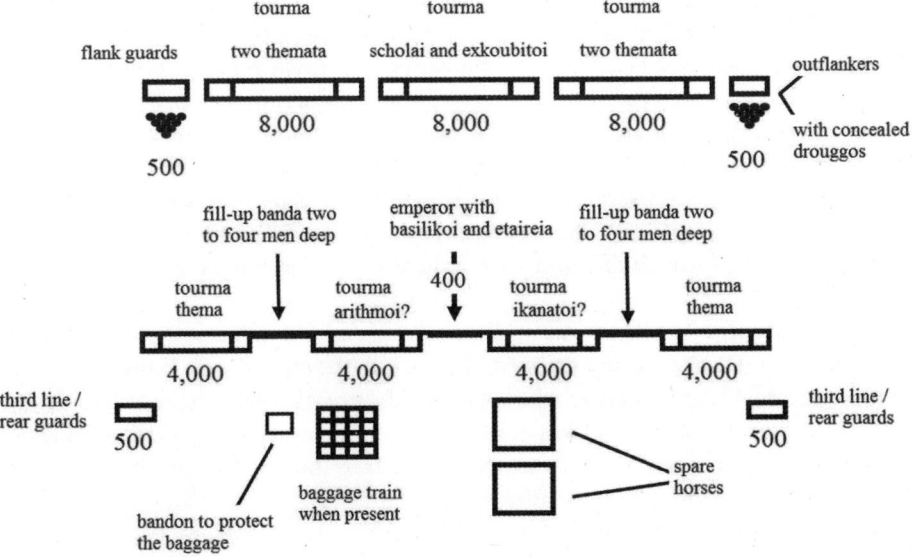

two *themata* of 4,000 horsemen, one per flank. This gives us a minimum size of 40,000 horsemen for the imperial cavalry army. However, as we shall see, there were also smaller *themata* from the border regions present, which implies that these were used to add flank guards and outflankers for the first line, and the fill-up *banda* for the second and third lines. On the basis of Text C, in hostile territory the vanguard consisted of 500 *akritai*, while the two outlying flanks had 500 horsemen each and the rear 1,000 horsemen. These would have enabled the commander to post, for example, 1,000 horsemen as flank guards and outflankers for the front line, 1,000 horsemen as third line rear guards and the remaining 500 men as fill-up *banda* (250 horsemen for each flank interval) while the imperial bodyguards would have filled the interval between the two centre *tourmai* of the second line. This would give us a minimum size of 42,500 horsemen for the imperial cavalry army, which is very close to the size of 48,000 horsemen given by Ibn Khurdadhbih (81–2), and I would suggest that Ibn Khurdadhbih's figure reflects the typical size for the imperial cavalry army because the above reconstruction of mine added only the vanguard, flank guards and rear guards of the army to the figure of 40,000 horsemen.

According to Text B, during marching the formation was also always surrounded by chosen thematic detachments that were on all four sides (front, flanks and rear) so that the enemy could not surprise the Romans. The vanguard was to consist of the men of the *thema* which bordered the enemy country targeted. The army was to pitch a fortified camp with a defensive ditch every night. When the army reached the border-lands, there were to be at least two picket lines around the perimeter. In the marching camp, the personal safety of the emperor was in the hands of the *drouggarious tês biglas* and *etaireiarchês*, but the *drouggarios* was the man whose duty it was to ensure the security of the entire army. In the evenings the *drouggarios* together with 100 *scholarioi*[34] stood at the outer perimeter of the imperial tenting area, while the *etaireia* under *etaireiarchês* guarded the inner perimeter near to and just outside the pavilion. When the emperor was joined by the thematic forces, a third layer of guards was added, another layer of *etaireia* was posted between the *scholarioi* and *etaireai* posted near the pavilion. The reason for this was clearly to secure the emperor against a possible assassination attempt by a thematic *stratêgos*. The *drouggarios tês biglas* also assigned the *komêtes tês kortês* (counts of the tent) from the *themata* to attend the emperor when the army encamped. When the *drouggarios* wanted to patrol the thematic forces during the night, he took with him these *komêtes* and *mandatôres* and then inspected the perimeter guards and outer pickets.

When the entire force was assembled at Dazimon, Kaisareia or at another place, the *tagmata* and bodyguards were posted closest to the emperor, so if the army came across a narrow pass or bridge, the *tagmata* advanced in the following order: first the *scholai*, second the *exkoubitoi*, third the *arithmoi*, fourth the *ikanatoi*, followed by the *themata*. During the march the emperor was accompanied by those that he summoned to his side, and these included *magistroi*, *patrikioi* and imperial eunuchs. In front of the emperor were the *praipositoi*; the *koubikoularios* with the

Life-Giving Wood of the Cross; and in front of the *koubikoularios* were the *basilikoi*, together with the *signoforos* (carrying the golden-bejewelled cross). Two shield-bearing *kandidatoi* or *spatharioi* (these belonged to the *basilikoi*), left and right of the emperor, rode alongside the emperor so that they received and guided anyone who wanted to approach the emperor. When the army was in hostile territory in Syria, the *prôtostratôr tou Basileôs* together with three *stratôres*, *komês tou stablou* and three saddled horses were placed behind the emperor. The obvious purpose of this was to enable the emperor to flee on those saddled horses while the *basilikoi*, *stratôres*, *prôtostratôr* and *komês* protected his flight. One may assume that commanders-in-chief of the armies (e.g. the *domestikoi*) had similar security systems in place for their own security.

When the emperor was about to cross into Syria, the baggage-train and all superfluous tents and luxurious equipment and all poor and lame beasts were left behind, and these were handed over to the *prôtonotarios* of the *thema* through which the emperor intended to return to Roman territory. In other words, the campaign plan was to conduct a large scale chevauchée. When the army entered Syria, the *basilikoi, etaireia, scholarioi* guarding the imperial tenting area, the tent attendants and other imperial staff were bribed with an extra sum of money. The officers accompanying the emperor were also bribed with sizeable handouts. When the army entered Syria, the *drouggarios tês biglas* was in charge of the overall security of the army, so when the emperor gave the order to do so, the *drouggarios* sent 500 *akritai* (i.e. *apelatai, trapezites,* or *tasanarioi* known in the western portions as *chonsarioi/chôsarioi*) to serve as a vanguard at a distance of two miles in front of the emperor (i.e., in front of the army in battle formation). Since Kônstantinos calls this group of 500 *akritai* a single *thema*, it is probable that we are dealing with the force provided by a small border *kleisura/thema* (which often meant the so-called Armenian *themata*) closest to the enemy, which Kônstantinos also mentions in the context of imperial campaigns. The *drouggarios* was also to dispatch a *thema* (presumably also consisting of 500 horsemen) to each side of the emperor (i.e., the army) at a distance of two miles to serve as flank guards, while two *themata* (probably 1,000 horsemen) were dispatched behind as rear guards.

The Text C gives us also the procedure of what to do once the imperial expedition returned from Syria, but this does not need to concern us here because it consists merely of protocol and ceremony meant to impress in particular the inhabitants of the city of Constantinople.

2.7.3. The Hamdanids of Mosul and Aleppo[35] (see also Appendix 5)

The capture of Melitene by the forces led by the *domestikos* Iôannês Kourkouas in 934 was a pivotal moment, which he followed by capturing areas belonging to the district of Samosata. The buying of peace from the Hungarian invaders in the same year was just a distraction. The Romans appear to have spent most of the year 935 in consolidating their gains. In my opinion, it was probably at this time that the Romans organized three new border *themata* in the region conquered, which are later mentioned in the *Taktikon of Escurial*. The first of these was the *thema* of Melitene itself, the second was Hanzit which was located east of Melitene between the rivers Euphrates and Arsanias/Murat Su, and the third was called Kaloudia after the city of Kaloudia (south-east of Melitene).[36] The area around Arsamosata/ Shimshat also appears to have been formed into the theme of Arsamosata in about 935/6 or after 970.[37] This was not the only success the Romans had at this time, because the Bedouin Arab tribe of Banu Habib emigrated onto Roman soil and converted to Christianity in 936. The deserters consisted of 12,000 cavalry, armed and equipped from head to foot, and their families, clients and their slaves. Prior to this the Banu Habib had inhabited the area around Nisibis and Mesopotamia (Jazira/Gazira) and had terrorized the Romans living in the border region. The Banu Habib belonged to the Taglibite tribal confederacy, which was also the parent tribe of the Hamdanids. The reason for the desertion of the tribe was that their chieftain/sheik had fought unsuccessfully against al-Hasan ibn Hamdan (Nasir ad-Dawla). When the sheik was defeated and killed by Nasir's forces in November 935, his tribe sought a place of refuge on Roman soil. This was a major success for Roman diplomacy. They had now both gained a fully equipped cavalry army while weakening the enemy's defences in Mesopotamia/Jazira.[38] However, the forces of the victorious side of the Muslim civil war, the Hamdanids, were to become the principal menace for the Romans.

In 904 or 905 the Caliph Muktaff had appointed Abu'l-hayga (Abdallah b. Hamdan) as governor of Mosul, which marks the beginning of the Hamdanid dynasty. His eldest son al-Hasan ibn Hamdan, better-known as Nasir ad-Dawla ('Defender of the Dynasty'), was appointed as his successor in Mosul in December 935, so he served as governor of the provinces Jazira/Gazira, Diyar Rabi'a, Diyar Modar and Diyar Bekr. However, his former ally, the Daylamite Ali b. Ga'far, sought independence in Diyar Bekr. In response to this, Nasir ad-Dawla dispatched his younger brother Ali ibn Hamdan, better-known as Sayf ad-Dawla ('Sword of the Dynasty'), against Ga'far. Sayf achieved success and followed this by securing also Diyar Modar and Mesopotamia for his brother. Unlike many other period dynasties, the Hamdanids were pure-blooded Arabs and proud of it. Sayf saw himself as a holy warrior whose duty it was to fight against the Romans, and he had participated in at least the 931 campaign against them under the leadership of his uncle Sa'id b. Hamdan. Sayf ad-Dawla was also a cultured figure, who not only protected poets but was also an accomplished amateur poet himself – a figure of romances. In November 935–November 936 Sayf was transferred to serve under the command of his brother Nasir ad-Dawla, and in this capacity he achieved the already-mentioned successes, as a result of which he became quasi-autonomous ruler of Diyar Bekr himself. The Arabs also appear to have invaded Armenia in 936, but with little success.[39]

The Roman government recognized the danger posed by the consolidation of the position of Hamdanid dynasty under Nasir and Sayf and sought to isolate them. Rômanos had already dispatched envoys to Mohammed ibn Tugdji, the

Ikhshidid governor of Egypt, in 937 and to the Caliph in Baghdad in 938. The negotiations continued until 938 and resulted in a truce between Rome and the Caliph and Ikhshidids. The exchange of prisoners took place at Lamus in October 938. There were 800 extra Muslim prisoners, with the result that the Muslims had to seek additional Roman prisoners for the exchange. The process took an additional six months to accomplish, so the Roman prisoners were finally released at Podanus in 939. The truce between the caliph (which included also Tugdji of Egypt) and the emperor appears to have come into existence only when the two sides exchanged prisoners, even if the expectation obviously was that no fighting would take place during the negotiations. This gave Sayf a chance to break these negotiations without actually crossing the will of the caliph. Consequently, Sayf began his operations against the Romans in September 938 (in other words before the truce and exchange of prisoners by the Romans and Caliph) by launching an invasion of Anzitene. Sayf advanced towards Dadim, while his subordinate Hasan b. Ali al-Qawwas marched towards Hisn at-Tell. The results of these two attacks are not known, but it is known that Sayf continued his march to Hisn Ziyad (Harput/Hartabirt; Ziata of Ammianus Marcellinus?) which is located north of Dadim. Sayf captured Hisn Ziyad and stayed there for seven days, until the *domestikos* Iôannês Kourkouas arrived at the head of an army of 200,000 men – according to Ibn Zafir. The figure is clearly an exaggeration, but still indicative that the Romans probably had numerical advantage. One may make the educated guess that this was a typical large cavalry army of the period, namely an army of 30,000 to 48,000 horsemen while the Roman infantry was probably marched to block the likely routes of retreat towards the south (see Appendix 2). However, Sayf retreated eastward towards Simsat/Shimsat/Arsamosata with the Roman cavalry in pursuit. Sayf stopped at al-Muqaddamiyya (an unknown village between Hisn Ziyad/Harput and Shimsat) to face the pursuers, but abandoned the plan – presumably because the Romans had not yet scattered to pillage – and retreated to the area between two fortresses, Salam (unknown) and Ziyad (i.e. towards the south/south-west?) which he reached on 8 October 938. Now Sayf felt that the time was right. As the Roman forces had spread out in search of booty, this meant that Iôannês Kourkouas was accompanied only by about 20,000 horsemen. In other words, Sayf had conducted a feigned flight in the course of which the Romans had dispersed. It was a grave mistake for such an experienced commander as Iôannês to allow this to happen. The resulting battle lasted until nightfall and the Romans suffered a crushing defeat. The Saracens captured 70 patricians and a large number of ordinary prisoners. The booty included the throne of the *domestikos* and his other belongings. After this, hostilities ceased because the caliph and emperor had by now concluded the truce.[40]

It is clear from the details (see Appendix 2) that the battle between Iôannês and Sayf was a cavalry battle, but we unfortunately do not know if Iôannês used the cavalry formation of Maurikios or if he used the reformed cavalry formation of Leôn the Wise with the *katafraktoi* wedge. In other words, we do not know if this was one of the battles that influeced Nikêforos Fôkas later when he reformed the latter cavalry formation. Furthermore, we do not know if any of the members of the Fôkades family participated in this campaign. On balance it is unlikely they did, because the likeliest office held by Bardas Fôkas at this time was the *stratêgos* of the *Anatolikon* theme (see later). It would have been there that Bardas schooled his sons in the arts of guerrilla warfare which are analysed and explained in Appendix II.

The truce appears to have omitted the territories formally belonging to a third party. Therefore Sayf ad-Dawla continued his offensive in the autumn of 939 and invaded the independent portion of Armenia and Iberia. The Romans had been building a fortress at the village of Hafgig opposite Theodosioupolis (Karin) and this was his first objective. The village appears to have been on Armenian soil,[41] so the Romans were not breaking the truce. They had advanced into territory officially controlled by Abas Bagratuni, the ruler of Armenia (and Iberia). Abas Bagratuni clearly did not want to protect the Muslim emir of Qaliqala (Karin) and may even have cooperated with the Romans in secret, which drew Sayf to the scene. Sayf marched through Nisibis and Mayyafariqin past Muslim-held Lake Van and Manzikert, and then turned north-west towards Karin. The Romans destroyed hastily what thay had built and fled, after which Sayf retired to Arzen where he spent the winter. Sayf resumed operations in spring 940. The Arabic sources give us conflicting accounts of what happened after this. According to al-Azraq, Sayf called all Armenian lords to do obeisance at Tadvan by Lake Van. The Arab-Armenian emirs Ahmed al-Rahman Abu'l-Mu'izz (Lord of Hilat and, Adelgivaz, Argish, Perkri), and Abd al-Hamid (Lord of Manzikert, Dasht al-Warak, the steppe of Varak probably at Kore, and al-Hark/Bulanyq) responded to the call. The same was true of the Armenian lords Asot b. Gargur (Grigorik) who was Prince of Taron, and Ibn Gagik b. ad-Dirani, the King of Vaspurakan, and of the Prince of Princes Bagratuni Abas (929–53). However, according to Ibn Zafir, Sayf called only the Bagratuni, the King of Armenia and Georgia, to Hilat/Khilat in 940. Abas Bagratuni submitted and obtained peace by seceding several fortresses to Sayf. The ruler of Vaspurakan also handed over two localities which modern research has not been able to put on the map. According to the same source, with the exception of the Prince of Taron the other Armenian princes submitted, with the result that Sayf pillaged Taron. The refusal to obey is not surprising, because the relatives of Taron, the Taronites/Tornikioi, held high positions in Rome. According to Abu Firas, an Armenian Prince named Abu'l-Yaqzan al-Ala b. Maslama al-Sulami (of the family of the Gahhafides) fled to Roman territory and then returned with a Roman army of 20,000 men commanded by a patrician, but only with the result that Sayf defeated him after which the Prince in question submitted to the Hamdanids. One wonders if this referred to the Prince of Taron and his Roman relatives the Tornikioi? It was after this that Sayf marched against Abu'l-Mu'izz al-Sulami (clearly the same person as Ahmed al-Rahman Abu'l-Mu'izz) and Abu Salim and subdued both. After having secured Armenia, Sayf advanced into Roman territory and invaded Chaldia. The emperor wrote an angry letter in response, because there was supposed to be peace between Constantinople and Baghdad. Sayf responded by putting the city of

Koloneia under siege. The local *stratêgos* was Theofilos Kourkouas, the brother of Iôannês Kourkouas, so it is not surprising to find Iôannês Kourkouas cooperating with his brother.[42]

Iôannês sought to block Sayf's route of retreat by positioning his army south of the Muslims, but Sayf reacted to the threat quickly and abandoned the siege and started a retreat with the *domestikos* in pursuit. The end result was the same. Sayf defeated Iôannês again and was able to retreat safely to his own territory. Once again it is obvious that the battle between Iôannês and Sayf was a cavalry battle,[43] but we are again ignorant of the array used by Iôannês. This means that we do not know if this was one of the battles that influenced Nikêforos Fôkas to reform the battle formation in the *Praecepta militaria*. However, I would suggest that in this case the information concerning the Roman cavalry formation is meaningless, because the defeat during pursuit suggest that Sayf ambushed Iôannês because he was following without adequate safety measures roughly in the same manner as described by the *De velitatione* (D 16.28ff.; DM 16.3). This treatise mentions that the people of Tarsus ambushed an unnamed Roman *stratêgos*, with the Arabs dispatching a fake force to raid while they posted their main force in ambush. When the *stratêgos* then witnessed the clouds of dust over the horizon, he started pursuit with the *tourmarchos*, with his men placed in front as *prokoursatôres* (vanguard), and when the vanguard performed the reconnaissance poorly the entire force fell into an ambush. In this case, Sayf would have dispatched a chosen force to feign retreat while he posted his force in the ambuscade. After this, Sayf appears to have abandoned the frontier zone and marched further south in preparation for the power struggle within the caliphate. The caliph ar-Radi died in December 940, but his health appears to have been precarious before this. This is the likeliest explanation for the absence of Sayf when Iôannês Kourkouas launched a punishing expedition in Mesopotamia. The Romans reached Kafartouta not far from Dara and Resaina in November 940 and massacred those whom they did not take captive. The death of the caliph and the power struggle preoccupied Sayf and his brother Nasir from the following year until late 944, so the situation was very opportune for the Romans to renew their operations in 941.[44]

It is once again very unlikely that any of the Fôkades would have been involved in the above campaigns of Iôannês Kourkouas for the very same reasons as were mentioned previously, but one cannot preclude this possibility in its entirety.

In light of the initial absence of Iôannês Kourkouas during the Russian invasion in 941, it is very likely that he continued his operations in Mesopotamia in the spring and early summer of 941. See Chapter 4. The sources do not explain why Iôannês Kourkouas, a man so successful previously, suddenly lost two major cavalry battles against Sayf ad-Dawla. In my opinion the likeliest reason is that, as a *dynatos*, he had exploited his position by using coercion and force when he extended his domains at the expense of the thematic *stratiôtai*. This was precisely one of the reasons stated in his dismissal from office later, and notably it is claimed to have been the reason why Bardas Fôkas was later unsuccessful. It is easy to see that the thematic soldiers were not willing to fight under such a commander.[45]

In sum, we do not know what role, if any, the Fôkades played in the wars described above, but given the fact that Bardas Fôkas' sons Nikêforos the Younger, Leôn and Kônstantinos were all experienced commanders by 945, and given the fact that we find Bardas Fôkas in command of a significant army in 941, it is very likely that all Fôkades saw at least some action during the years described above. It is probable that the head of the family, Bardas Fôkas, was in charge of the defence of the southern frontier facing the themes of the Anatolikon and Kappadokia, while his superior Kourkouas conducted his operations further east and north. The reasoning behind this conclusion will be discussed in Chapters 3 and 4. The above account has also provided an important background for the events of the year 941, because the defeats suffered by Iôannês Kourkouas and his brother Theofilos in 939–40 in conjunction with the events of the year 941 formed the background to their fall from grace and for the rise of the Fôkades back into favour, which previous research has failed to note.

After Sayf ad-Dawla had managed to secure his position by late 944, the Hamdanids of Aleppo had become once again the principal enemy of the Roman Empire. Their campaign pattern in the following years followed the one described by Leôn and *De velitatione*. The main invasion took place in September after the arrival of the Jihadist reinforcements from Egypt, Palestine, Phoenicia and Syria. Jihadists from other areas could also join their numbers, but their numbers were always very few in comparison with the above. At other times of the year the Hamdanids had access only to their own forces, which made them particularly vulnerable against diversionary operations as stated by Leôn VI.

The frontier zone facing the Romans was created by the Abbasids. It ran from the Cilician plain up to Armenia, so the area called *al-Sham* consisted of Cilicia and northern Syria, while *al-Jazira* encompassed all the territory northeast of it. See pages xxix, xxxi and xxxiii. The area facing the Roman border was called *al-thughur* (clefts) while the interior behind it was called *al-awasim* (protectors). The towns, cities and fortresses of *al-thughur* formed the protective layer for the Euphrates-Mediterranean trade route which passed through Aleppo to Antioch, and had staging posts for raids and invasions into Roman territory, while the populations of *al-awasim* formed the reserves in depth for the forces posted in *al-thughur*. The entire population of *al-thughur* was expected to train in military arts and be ready to fight. Each of the towns in the *al-thughur* had also a garrison of soldiers reinforced by volunteers called *ghazis* (fighters of faith) that were maintained through donations coming from their provinces. The elite corps of the army, the *ghilman* (slave soldiers, sing. *ghulam*), were maintained by the donations of the caliphal family.[46]

Therefore, the bulk of the Hamdanid military forces consisted of the soldiers and volunteers from the towns and fortresses of *al-thughur* and of foreign mercenaries and *ghilman*, which would then be reinforced by volunteers and professional soldiers from other places in August–September. The Hamdanid armies were therefore multiethnic. The sources mention the Arabs, Bedouins, Daylamites, Turks, Kurds, Armenians, Slavs and even Greeks among the Hamdanid armies, but it is clear that the vast majority of the foreigners consisted of the Daylami, Turks, Kurds and Bedouins.[47]

The Dailamites/Dilemnites/Daylami were tribesmen from the shores of the Caspian Sea and Elburz mountains who had already served as elite infantry forces and palace guards under the Sasanians and Abbasids. The Daylami mercenaries used swords, dirks, pikes, brightly painted shields, battleaxes, bows and arrows, but most used the famous *zhupins* (a two-pronged short spear used either for thrusting or for throwing) to deadly effect against their enemies. When attacking they advanced by using the phalanx formation. In defence they linked their shields together to give the appearance of a solid formation (shields interlocked in the *synaspismos* order rim-to-boss in width), which any enemy charge (in all likelihood a cavalry charge) would find hard to penetrate. They were equally skilled in the use of open and irregular formations and their particular speciality was fighting in mountaineous terrain (they were mountaineers) so they were exceptionally well-suited to fighting in the passes and mountains of the Taurus range.[48]

The Turkish *ghilman* were elite slave-soldiers who were particularly famous for their mounted archery skills. On the basis of the extant Arabic archery treatises,[49] the *ghilman* appear to have been trained in the Persian way of archery which stressed in particular 'shower archery' in mounted combat even if it did not forget the more powerful slower techniques. This made them particularly dangerous foes to face when the cavalry horses were not protected by cataphract armour. However, the Turkish *ghilman* were not only famous for their archery but also for their readiness to face the enemy at close quarters and it was because of this that the *ghilman* were usually the most heavily armoured cataphract corps in the army. Their only weaknesses were the high cost and their quarrels with the Daylami. Regardless, their services were so highly appreciated that all Muslim rulers were ready to buy and maintain this slave corps. The emirs of Mosul and Aleppo both hired and employed Daylami infantry and *ghilman* cavalry, but it is possible that Sayf ad-Dawla stopped using Turkish slave forces after their mutiny in 957, which had been instigated by the Romans.[50]

The Kurds are attested to have served throughout the Islamic world as cavalry forces, and the Hamdanids are no exception. Sayf ad-Dawla typically used the Kurdish horsemen either on their own or together with the Bedouins as light cavalry in raids, ambushes and scouting. The Kurds had strong tribal loyalty and took pride in their ancestry. Later sources also suggest that some of the Kurds may have fought as infantry or as cataphract cavalry.[51]

Thanks to the swiftness of their Arab horses, the Bedouin forces (the *Arabitai*) formed the best light cavalry of their era. The bulk of the Bedouin forces employed by Sayf ad-Dawla consisted of the Banu Kilab and Banu Numair and they wore very little or no armour at all and fought primarily by using the lance. The Arab horses enabled them to outrun any Roman cavalry unit, with the result that Nikêforos Fôkas (see the year 955) forbade his cavalry forces from pursuing them. All the Romans could do against them was to use archery, while maintaining order and reserves behind to counter their attacks against the Roman baggage train. The typical Bedouin tactics were the use of surprise attacks and ambushes and the shadowing of the enemy army so that they could exploit any opportunities that might present themselves for pillage. The Bedouins had a number of weaknesses too. One of these was their greed. They could be expected to pillage even their own allies if the situation allowed this, but this proclivity for plunder was usually overlooked by their employers thanks to their valuable services at other times. Michaêl Attaleiatês also claims that the Arab horses had one weakness over the Roman ones, which was that while the Arab horses were faster on short distances they had less stamina over long distances, so that it was possible to catch them if one just persisted long enough. On the basis of the *Praecepta militaria*, this was either not known to Nikêforos or alternatively he thought such a long pursuit to be too dangerous to perform in the middle of a battle, which he was, after all, describing. I would suggest that the latter alternative is true, namely that Nikêforos did not want to separate a part of his army in a pursuit while the battle was unresolved. It would be very strange if he would not have known the differences between the different horse breeds if Michaêl Attaleiatês knew them. The Bedouin were also otherwise unreliable as allies because they decided for themselves for how long they wanted to campaign, which often meant the fact that they refused to fight during winters.[52]

On the basis of the *Praecepta militaria*, the Hamdanid battle formations and tactics were the mirror images of the Roman ones, in that they employed fortified marching camps, pike phalanxes, hollow infantry square, *katafraktoi* wedge and regular cavalry, the only real difference being the employment of the Arabitai cavalry, which enabled the Hamdanids to harass the Romans with relative impunity. On the basis of the extant Arabic military treatises,[53] we also know that there was a slight difference in the cavalry formation employed because the Muslim military manuals suggest that the Arabs employed the old Persian cavalry formation with two lines (both lines consisting of the outer left, left, centre, right and outer right), behind which were the infantry, marching camp and cavalry guard units. The Roman answers to this were to stress the fighting spirit of their forces so that they could defeat the enemy through better morale while also increasing the numbers of men through the thematic system. The principal weakness of the Hamdanid military system was that the *al-thughur* lacked the fiscal revenues necessary for the maintenance of the armed forces stationed there. According to one Arabic source, the tax revenues covered only half of the costs. This proved problematic when the central treasury at Baghdad was not interested in providing the missing sums of money. It was thanks to this that the Hamdanids had to find a way to finance the upkeep of their soldiers, which was possible only through successful raiding of Roman territory. This they achieved initially. The heroic and successful leadership of Sayf ad-Dawla also inspired volunteers from abroad to join his expeditions, but this lasted only as long as his successes. When the Roman armies then launched successful operations of their own against the territory held by Sayf ad-Dawla and destroyed everything in their path, the revenues available for Sayf ad-Dawla diminished even further. When Sayf ad-Dawla suffered a series of defeats, resulting in the loss of prestige while also losing sources of revenue, he faced a series of internal rebellions and troubles from which the Hamdanids never recovered.[54] War is always also economic activity.

2.7.4. The Fatimids vs. Sicily and Italy[55] (see also Appendix 5)

In 909 the Fatimids overthrew the Aghlabid dynasty in Tunisia. The Fatimids claimed to be descendants of Ali, the fourth Caliph, and Fatima, Muhammad's daughter. The Fatimids perceived themselves to be infallible and divinely guided rulers known as Imāms. They saw both the Umayyads of Spain and Abbasids of Baghdad as usurpers, so their first objective was to overthrow both after which they would establish themselves as rulers of the whole world. When 'Ubayd Allāh Sa'īd (22.8.909–4.3.934) entered the former capital of the Aghlabids, Raqqāda, on 15 January 910, he became the first ruling Fatimid Imām and when he did so he assumed the titles *al-Mahdi* ('the one who will appear at the end of the world to restore justice'), or *al-Mahdi Billah*, ('The Rightly Guided by God') and *al-Mu'mimīn* (Commander of the Faithful). At the same time the Fatimids also became masters of the Arabs in Sicily.

The Romans and Fatimids fought with varying success in the waters and coasts of Sicily and Italy, but from the year 938 onwards the Romans had the upper hand against the Fatimids and also against the Arabs of Fraxinetum who were subjects of al-Andalus, the rivals of the Fatimids. In about 938 the Sicilians rose in revolt against the Arabs which enabled the Romans to launch an offensive. Rômanos dispatched some ships with provisions which forced the local Muslim commander to ask help from Africa, which was dispatched. Initially, the Romans appear to have regained control of most of Sicily because even the city of Agrigento (Girgenti) was in their hands. However, with the arrival of the reinforcements the Arabs were able to crush the revolt, and they placed the city of Agrigento under siege for a second time, which lasted for eleven months. It was only November 940 or in 941 that the city surrendered, and even then the Arabs were forced to allow most of the inhabitants to flee to Calabria, but most of the area known as Val Demone remained in Roman hands until the 960s. The fact that the Sicilians continued their guerrilla warfare against the Muslim Arabs helped the Romans immensely.[56]

The army that had captured Tunisia consisted mainly of Berbers/Moors, so the Kutāma/Kītama formed the dominant element among these. According to the Persian traveller Nāṣir-I Khusraw, the Kutāma numbered 20,000 horsemen in Egypt in 1047. One may assume that their numbers were far greater when the Kutāma formed the main strength of the Fatimid armies in North Africa. Their principal weapon was still the javelin. The Fatimids had also other major Berber groupings in their service, but it is not known with certainty when they recruited the Maṣāmida, Baṭilīs, and Barqiya. The Barqiya (Berbers of Barqa/Cyrenaica) were included in the army of Jawhar[57] that conquered Egypt in 969 so they were recruited earlier than this, but their numbers are not known. The Baṭilīs who also arrived with Jawhar numbered 15,000 horsemen in 1047 and were settled in Cairo. The other Berber groupings included at least the Zuwayla and Zenata. The Maṣāmida are claimed to have been introduced by al-Aziz (18.12.975–13.10.996), but this is not known with certainty. In 1047 they numbered 20,000 footmen armed with spears and swords. It is probable that the Fatimids already had some mercenaries and slave forces in their service before the conquest of Tunisia.

The Fatimids inherited from the Aghlabids slave Black African troops and *Saqaliba/Saqāliba* slave troops (Slavs and other European slaves)[58] both of which they were eager to include in their regular army. In 1047 in Egypt the Zanj (Ethiopian Blacks) numbered 30,000 swordsmen and they were also in the majority among the 30,000 mercenaries. The numbers of the Ṣaqāliba slave troops remained relatively modest, but they were still the elite force of the army. The slave soldiers, regardless of origin, were always the best drilled soldiers in the army. The Fatimid army that entered Egypt under Jawhar in 969 consisted of the Berbers (the Kutāma being dominant among them), Arabs, Ṣaqāliba (Slave soldiers), Rūm (Romans) and Blacks. The 'Romans' were obviously slave troops too. The initial force entering Egypt is claimed to have consisted of 100,000 men, which was later reinforced by 200,000 men. The latter force consisted of 100,000 Kutāma, 40,000 other Berbers, and 60,000 Black slave soldiers. These numbers have not been accepted by modern authorities, but I do not see any reason to doubt them because the numbers are in agreement with what we know from the ancient sources for the sizes of the Berber/Moor armies.[59] There exists a clear consistency as far as the numbers are concerned for the Berber armies of different eras. It was only after the Fatimids entered Egypt and Syria that they introduced the Turkish slave soldiers (*ghilman*), Daylami and other forces (e.g. Armenians, Kurds, Bedouins etc.) employed by Middle-Eastern Muslim principalities. Similarly, it was only after the Fatimids had entered Egypt and Syria that they started equipping their forces with heavier armour to counter the Roman heavily armoured forces. In other words, they copied the combat methods of their enemies.

Fatimid military doctrine resembled closely the description of Leôn regarding the enemies of his own day, before the Saracens of Cilicia introduced the *katafraktoi* into their armies. According to Qadi al-Numan (summary in Beshir, 51–2), the Fatimids employed spies, guerrillas and vanguards in front of the army and fortified marching camps. They also used flags, standards and emblems to separate the different units and tribes from each other. They chose a battle-cry in advance, so one of Allah's names was the recommendation. The commander was expected to encourage the men with a speech before battle. The different tribes were arrayed separately for combat and the commander was expected to make certain that the *karādis* (128-horseman rank-and-file rhomboids) and lines were correctly formed. The battle formation was divided into two wings and a centre, each under a separate commander. Messengers were used to convey orders. Single combat with the enemy was permitted. The battle started with the advance of the infantry and foot archers (presumably mostly Black Sudanese slaves known for their archery skills) while the cavalry on the wings protected their flanks. The footmen were not allowed to break ranks under any condition so that the enemy's feigned flight would not cause the formation to break up. If the enemy retreated, the pursuit was to be performed by cavalry and foot archers, just as in the text of Leôn. In other words, the Fatimids were vulnerable to the same tactics as the Saracens of Cilicia and Syria were before the Hamdanids. The pursuers included a separate vanguard that was expected to find out if the enemy had placed ambushes in thickets or other places. This is the type of enemy force that the Romans would then have faced on land in Sicily and Italy.

When the Fatimids entered Tunisia they also inherited a navy from the Aghlabids. This force consisted of the naval officers in Aghlabid service, people of Sicily commandeered into service, and people of the coastal towns of Barqa and Tripoli in Libya. The ships were therefore manned by the former enemies of the Fatimids, so the Berber forces (Kutāma ad Zuwayla) of the Fatimids came to serve as marines on board those ships. The ship types employed by the Fatimids consisted of the *āsātil* (sing. *uṣtūl*, a large warship), *shīnī* (war galley), and generic warships (*markab harbī*). The principal fighting tactics were the use of naptha or other types of fire weapons and the boarding of enemy vessels. The Fatimid fleets varied in size from modest forces counted at most in dozens to fleets of 100 ships or more. According to extant sources, al-Mahdi (909–34) constructed 900 ships in al-Mahdiyya while al-Mu'izz (953–75) built 600 ships. These figures are usually doubted by modern historians (e.g. Lev), but their credibility is in my opinion confirmed by the problems that the Fatimids had in finding enough wood for them. It was because of this that al-Mu'izz had to obtain wood from Sicily and from the private stores of Jawhar. The command structure of the fleet is not known with certainty, but something can still be said about this. The port of al-Mahdiyya was the principal naval base during the North African period, so its governor was in charge of obtaining provisions for the navy. Below him served an officer called *ṣāḥib al-baḥr* or *mutawallī al-baḥr*, which is translated by Canard to be Chief of the Navy or Director of the Navy, but this is contested by Yaacov Lev because the fleets always appear to have been commanded by the governor of Sicily. He suggests that one of the duties of this officer was the building of the ships, but notes that his exact duties are not known with certainty. This is the naval force and its marines that the Romans faced in Sicily and Italy. It was a match for the Romans so sometimes the Romans defeated them while at other times the Fatimids defeated the Romans.[60]

According to D. A. Agius,[61] the *shīnī* used by the Fatimids could be absolutely huge by the standards of the day, because on one occasion ten Fatimid *shīnīs* carried 10,000 men, with the implication that each ship carried on average about 1,000 men. This suggests that *shīnī* had a capacity of roughly 2,000 tons. The Romans had larger versions of the *dromônes*, but these were not even close to this size. The combat record, however, demonstrates that these huge ships did not make the Fatimid navies superior to the Roman ones, even if it is clear that several smaller Roman *dromônes* were needed to face a single behemoth like this. However, the average size of the *shīnī* was far more modest, so that the typical vessel appears to have carried only 150 footsoldiers, with the implication that these had a 300-ton capacity. What is notable is that even this vessel was bigger than the biggest Roman *dromônes*, the triremes. Still another type of *shīnī* is said to have had 140 oars, which is once again slightly bigger than the Roman *dromônes*. It is therefore clear that the Romans preferred speed and manoeuvrability over size while the Fatimids and other Muslim principalities preferred size over speed. This indicates that the bigger ships were primarily intended for boarding actions, even when they carried fire-weapons (naptha). Leôn (LT 19-15-6) confirms this by stating that the Saracens (*Sarakenoi*) usually sought to withstand the Roman missile attack with a tortoise formation (shields interlocked, men kneeling), after which they rose up and fought with swords and *menavlia*.

The second of the major war galley types was the *shalandī*, which appears to have been derived from the Roman (Greek) word *chelandion*, so it was a copy and in fact the Roman sources also call this type of ship in Arab service with the name of *dromôn*. According to Agius, one should not equate *shalandī* and *shīnī* with each other. *Shīnī* was a distinctly separate type of vessel. Agius does not give a description of the *uṣṭūl* (large warship), but I would assume that it was either *shīnī* or *ghurāb*, the latter of which one Muslim source claims to have been the largest warship in use. However, the evidence for this is conflicting, because some twelfth-fourteenth-century sources claim that the *ghurāb* was undecked and had 140 or 180 oars, while a sixteenth-century Muslim source equates the *ghurāb* with the western *galea* of the same era. On the basis of this I would suggest that *ghurāb* (which was already in use during the tenth century) may indeed have been an undecked monoreme which was extraordinarily large so that it already resembled the later western *galea*. Who was the first to invent this type of ship is difficult to know.

In addition to this, the Fatimid fleet just like the other Muslim fleets in the Mediterranean region possessed other galley variants, which included horse tranports and cargo ships. The evidence also suggests that the Muslim fleets carried flame-throwers to shoot Greek Fire, which were called *ḥarrāqa*, and also mangonels/trebuchets to throw fire bombs. In short, it is clear that the Fatimid Fleet and the Muslim fleets in general were a match against the Roman fleets when led by able admirals.

Roman soldiers (source: Oman)

Chapter Three

The Fôkas Family (Fôkades)[1]
(see also Appendix 6)

Family Origins

The origins of the Fôkas family are not known with definite certainty, because none of the contemporary Roman sources refer to them. In about 1070 the historian Michaêl Attaleiatês states that the Fôkades descended from the Roman Fabii. His account is marred by the fact that Michaêl Attaleiatês was a fervent supporter of emperor Nikêforos Botaneiatês, who descended from the Fôkades on his mother's side. This, however, is in my opinion not conclusive evidence against the origins of the family, because aristocratic families often married far and wide while their male members were also in the habit of siring bastards. There were undoubtedly tens of thousands of descendants of the Fabii in existence at the time and it is quite probable that the story of the origins of the family was transferred from one generation to another thanks to its attractiveness. On the other hand, the Arab historian Ibn al-Athir claims that Nikêforos Fôkas was a descendant of an Arab from Tarsus, so the family of Fôkades would have been typical border-region *akritai* noblemen/bandits. I consider this to be plausible as well. It would not have been impossible for the border region aristocratic military families to have had very mixed origins. In fact, it is very likely that their blood lines were very mixed. This is basically all that we know of the earlier origins of the family, which has left the field open for modern theories. On the basis of the common use of the name Bardas among the Fôkades Ivan Djurić has suggested that the family origins rested in Georgian Iberia.[2] I would suggest that all three versions are correct, and the Fôkades were descendants of the Fabii family, Arabs and Georgians, but I would also suggest that this is only a partial picture because it is clear that the Fôkades were descendants of all sorts of different nationalities that inhabited that corner of the Roman world, but noting that the Greek, Arab, Georgian (probably Armenian as well) and local Cappadocian (included significant numbers of Italian settlers[3]) elements would have been dominant.

Nikêforos the Elder[4]

The Fôkades appear prominently in the sources for the first time only in 872, when a Cappadocian/Kappadokian soldier was presented to the emperor Basileios I the Macedonian. Basileios appointed this man as *tourmarchês* – probably of Cappadocia/Kappadokia – so that both the *tourmarchês* and his son Nikêforos (grandfather of the emperor) participated in the campaign against the Hagarenes (Saracens), probably in 873. It is not known if the newly-appointed *tourmarchês* was a simple soldier or regional notable before his appointment. Jean-Claude Cheynet notes that several Fôkades are known before the seventh century, but excepting some ecclesiastical figures, thereafter the usage of the family name Fôkas drops from sight. In my opinion the likely reason for this was the notoriety and infamy of the usurper Fôkas I.[5]

The first Fôkas to rival the *akritai* families of the Argyroi,[6] Doukai,[7] and other heroes of the border wars was Nikêforos the Elder, the grandfather of the similarly-named emperor. He was born in about 855 because in about 872/3 he was nominated as a *magklavitês* among the *maglavitai* (imperial bodyguards) of the emperor Basileios. He accompanied the emperor during the campaign against Samosata in 873. He caught the eye of the emperor, who promoted him to the position of *prôtostratôr*. He was also given a palace (*oikos*) located close to the Church of Saint Thekla in Constantinople. At some point in time after this, but before 885, Nikêforos was appointed as a *stratêgos* of Charsianon. Nikêforos was then promoted to the position of an overall commander of all Roman forces in the south of Italy at some point in time between June 885 and June 886. He replaced Maxentios the Kappadokian, who had commanded the Roman forces in Italy together with the elite forces of Kappadokia, the last-mentioned of which he had probable brought with him from his *thema*. Nikêforos in his turn appears to have brought with him the elite forces of his own *thema* so that the thematic forces of Charsianon and Kappadokia fought together in South of Italy.

At some unknown point in time after this, Nikêforos was recalled from Italy by the new emperor Leôn VI and promoted to the position of *domestikos tôn scholôn*. The office had been left open by the death of Andreas the *Stratêlatês*/Andreas the Scythian, whose date of the death is not known. In this capacity Nikêforos spent several years fighting against the Saracens. In 894 Leôn declared war against Symeon of Bulgaria so that the *tagmata* (*etaireiai* under Kourtikios the Armenian) and western *themata* served under Prokopios Krinitês. This army was completely defeated by Symeon in Macedonia while Nikêforos was serving in the east. After the armistice had been concluded with the Arabs, Nikêforos was transferred to the west. Nikêforos marched on land against Bulgaria while *patrikios* Eustathios led a fleet to the Danube where they shipped the Hungarian allies across the river against the Bulgarians in 895. Symeon opted to negotiate and the *domestikos tôn scholôn* and *drouggarios tou ploimou* were both recalled.

In 896 Leôn Katakalon Abidelas replaced Nikêforos, but was defeated by the Bulgarians. We do not know if Nikêforos had died, or was then dispatched to the east, or whether he now fell from imperial favour. That depends solely on the dating of Nikêforos' successes against the Tarsiote Arabs mentioned by Leôn's *Taktika* and *De velitatione*. If these are dated to the period before Nikêforos' war against

Bulgaria in 895, then Nikêforos either died or fell into imperial disfavour. If these successes are dated to the period after 896, then Nikêforos probably conducted the successful campaign against Adana in about 900/901. Jean-Claude Cheynet suggests that Nikêforos the Elder died in about 895/6, so the successful raid against Adana took place between 886 and 895.

The sons of Nikêforos the Elder: Leôn and Bardas[8]

Leôn Fôkas was born in about 875/880 and achieved the same position, *domestikos tôn scholôn*, as his father by 917. Bardas Fôkas, the father of Nikêforos the Younger, the topic of this biography, was born in 879 and appears to have attained the position of *stratêgos* first in his native Kappadokia, followed by a promotion to the position of *stratêgos* of Anatolia. In this capacity Bardas appears to have participated the campaign against Symeon/Simeon of Bulgaria led by his brother Leôn.

Bardas Fôkas was married with a member of the powerful Maleinoi family whose power base was also located in Kappadokia, as was the case with the Fôkades. The union between these two powerful houses secured the province to the Fôkades in the future power struggles. The marriage proved fruitful. The pair had at least five children, three boys and two daughters. The eldest of the boys was Nikêforos, the future emperor, who was born in 912. His first brother Leôn was born in about 915. The third of the sons, named Kônstantinos, was presumably born very soon after this (ca. 917–8?), because he was old enough to become *stratêgos* of Seleucia in 945. The date of the birth of the two daughters Fôkaina (first names unknown) is not known, but it is known that one of the daughters was married to the father of Iôannês Tzimiskês, the future emperor. Since it is known that the first mentioned daughter was old enough to give birth to Iôannês Tzimiskês in about 925, it is clear that she must have been born at the latest in about 907–910 – meaning that she was actually the eldest of the children. Iôannês Tzimiskês' father belonged to the Kourkouas family, which had its powerbases in the Anatolikon and Armeniakon themes and in the Khozan region of the theme of Mesopotamia. Tzimiskês family and Kourkouai both appear to have had Armenian roots or at least some Armenian ancestors. The family name of Tzimiskês appears to derive from the name of a village/town Tchimishgezek in Armenia, which belonged to the theme of Mesopotamia or Hanzit after it had been created. A fuller discussion of the origins of the Tzimiskês family will be offered in the biography of Iôannês Tzimiskês. This marriage united the Fôkades with the Kourkouai and its Tzimiskês branch. The second daughter was probably married to Theodoulos Parsakoutênos, with whom she sired three sons; Theodôros, Bardas and Nikêforos. This united the Fôkades with the Parsakoutênoi, who, unlike the other families mentioned, appear not to have been a major military house because the first known member of this family was Theodoulos. In my opinion this suggests that the marriage between these two families took place after the Fôkades had fallen temporarily away from imperial favour, in other words after 919.

In 917 the brothers Leôn and Bardas Fôkas marched against the Bulgarians under the leadership of Leôn, the *domestikos tôn scholôn*. The Romans were severely defeated at the Battle of Acheloos/Achelaus on 20 August 917 and then again at the Battle of Katasyrtai close to the city of Constantinople, also in the same year. The Romans had adopted the same strategy as Nikêforos the Elder in 895 but with the difference that instead of the Hungarians the intended allies against the Bulgarians were the Pechenegs. The plan did not come to fruition because the *drouggarios tou ploimou*, Rômanos Lakapênos, and Iôannês Bogas, the Roman envoy to the Pechenegs, quarrelled and when the Pechenegs saw the Roman commanders quarrelling they abandoned the campaign – in my opinion the likeliest reason for the change of heart was that by then the Pechenegs had actually learnt of the Roman defeat at Acheloos and that the Roman land army and fleet had failed to cooperate their movements effectively, with the result that the Pechenegs arrived too late. On top of that, Rômanos failed to pick up the fugitives from the Battle of Acheloos. Rômanos was placed under investigation for his conduct and would have been punished had he not been saved by *magistros* Stefanos, one of the regents at the time.

The ruling emperor Kônstantinos VII was still underage so the actual rulers were the regents, of whom the most important at this time was his mother Zôê and her collaborators. This gave both Leôn Fôkas and Rômanos Lakapênos the chance of attempting to usurp power leaving Kônstantinos as their puppet ruler. Leôn was the first to try this openly. Leôn had married the sister of Kônstantinos the *parakoimômenos*, the most powerful eunuch in the court, so he was confident that he would win the power struggle. Leôn did not hide his intentions and acted like the throne would belong to him thanks to his family background (Skyl. 9.10). This does indeed suggest that the Fôkades believed themselves to have descended from some important Roman family which may have held the throne at some point of time in the past. It is therefore not surprising that Leôn's plans reached the ear of Theodôros, the tutor of Kônstantinos VII. He contacted Rômanos Lakapênos and managed to convince him to take the lead against the Fôkades. Rômanos acted after he received a sealed letter from Kônstantinos which secured his position. Kônstantinos the *parakoimômenos* attempted to force Rômanos to take the Imperial Fleet away from Constantinople, but Rômanos countered this with the statement that it was impossible to force the men to sail unless they had their salaries paid. When Kônstantinos the *parakoimômenos* then went to pay the salaries, Rômanos signalled his men to capture the *parakoimômenos* so that he was imprisoned in the trireme flagship. When the news of this was brought to Zôê and other senior officials, they summoned the patriarch Nikolaos and the leading senators to discuss what to do next. It was decided to send an embassy to Rômanos to ask why he had acted like he had. The men of the fleet drove them away with thrown stones. Next morning Zôê came in person to Boukoleon where she summoned her son and his entourage. It was only then that she learnt of the plan of Theodôros the tutor from the tutor himself. He stated that the plan had been instigated because Leôn had destroyed the army, while Kônstantinos the *parakoimômenos* had destroyed the Imperial Palace.

Then the emperor Kônstantinos VII wrested power from his mother, undoubtedly as instructed by Theodôros, and brought back to the palace the Patriach Nikolaos and *magistros* Stefanos. At the same time as this happened Leôn was removed from office and replaced by the *magistros* Iôannês Garidas. At the instigation of Iôannes Garidas, the emperor then appointed Iôannês' son Symeon and his wife's brother Theodôros Zoulfinezer (*stratêgos* of the Aegean Sea[9]) as commanders of the *etaireiai*. The *etaireiai* appear to have been the most important unit of bodyguards and actually were so effective that they together with the armed oarsmen of the Imperial Fleet had been able to defeat the *tagmata* serving under the *domestikos tôn scholôn* Iôannes Doukas when he had attempted to usurp power after the death of Alexandros in 913.[10] The emperor swore that Leôn had nothing to fear, with the result that he returned to his home. When this happened, the relatives of Leôn were immediately kicked out of the palace. When the relatives then arrived at the city home, Leôn rode to meet Rômanos in an attempt to form an alliance. Rômanos acted as if he would agree only to prevent Leôn from starting a revolt. After this, Leôn appears to have continued his journey to Kappadokia in order to raise the flag of revolt among his loyal supporters. On 24 March 918 Rômanos informed his supporters in the palace that Leôn was planning to attack the palace which he had forestalled with promises. Theodôros the tutor duly asked Rômanos to bring his fleet to the palace harbour of Boukoleon to protect the emperor, which Rômanos did on 25 March 918. The *magistros* Stefanos fled from the palace, while the Patriarch Nikolaos was expelled from there by the supporters of Rômanos. Now the Imperial Palace was in the hands of Rômanos and his supporters and Rômanos was in his turn duly appointed as *magistros* and *megas etaireiarchês* (commander of the *etaireiai*). Rômanos and Kônstantinos the *parakoimômenos*, the latter under duress, both sent a letter to Leôn not to be alarmed by the recent developments, with the result that Leôn remained quietly at his home in Kappadokia.

On 9 May 919 Kônstantinos VII was married to Elenê (Helen), the daughter of Rômanos, and Rômanos was proclaimed as *basileopator* (Father of the Emperor) while Rômanos' son Christoforos was appointed as *megas etaireiarchês* in his place. It was as a result of this that, according to Skylitzes, the relatives of Leôn Fokas convinced him to revolt. According to Symeon the Logothete (136.4), the relatives in question were commanders in the *themata* and *tagmata*. Leôn summoned to his side Kônstantinos the *parakoimômenos*, the brothers Kônstantinos and Anastasios Goggylios and Kônstantinos Malelia (*prôtoasekretis*). According to the *Nikonian Chronicle* (912, p.47), Leôn's forces were drawn from Lycia, Thrace (presumably the Thrakesion theme), Colchis, Iberia, Pamphylia and from many regiments. This list omits Kappadokia and Anatolikon. One wonders if this implies that Bardas Fôkas was not among the rebels because that would certainly explain why he was retained in service? According to the same text, the army consisted of brave soldiers equipped with lances, shining helmets and shields and javelins. Some of the soldiers had gold-encrusted shields, and there were men with quivers, experienced horsemen and armoured men (presumably *katafraktoi*).

Leôn claimed to be fighting on behalf of Kônstantinos VII against the usurper Rômanos. Rômanos countered by sending imperial letters carried by two couriers. One of these, the cleric Michaêl was captured and punished, but the other, the prostitute Anna (later honoured with the title *Basilikê*), managed to deliver the message, with the result that Kônstantinos, the son of Michaêl Barys and commander of the *ikanatoi*, deserted to Rômanos. His example was soon followed up by Balantês and Atzmoros, both *tourmarchai* by rank. When Leôn's army then reached Chrysopolis opposite Constantinople, Rômanos dispatched Symeon (prefect of the inkpot) in a *dromôn* with a sealed imperial chrysobull addressed to the rebel and his army. Leôn attempted to prevent the reading of the letter, but in vain, and when its contents were read the entire army deserted to Rômanos whose cause appeared to have imperial backing. Leôn fled to the fortress of Areo, but he continued his flight to a village called Oe-Leo when he was denied entry. It was there that he was captured by Michaêl Barys and others sent in pursuit. He was taken to the capital and blinded en route.

All Fôkades and men closely associated with them naturally lost their offices at this time, and this also meant Bardas Fôkas, the father of Nikêforos. It has been suggested that Leôn's brother Bardas was not among the active participants of the revolt because he is not mentioned in the context of this revolt and was only dismissed from office after it.[11] In my opinion this is not conclusive. It is quite possible that Bardas joined his brother in revolt, and survived as a result of being married to the Malenoi, while his daughter was married to a member of the Kourkouai family. We should remember that Iôannês Kourkouas, the *drouggarios tês biglas*, was the trusted henchman of Rômanos and definitely in a position to save Bardas. It is therefore quite possible that Bardas was allowed to retire at the request of Iôannês Kourkouas, only to be recalled back into service later, but on balance it is likelier that Bardas was not among the active participants of the revolt.

After this followed yet another conspiracy against Rômanos by others in which the Fôkades did not participate, but the plot was discovered. The key figures of this plot were blinded and then paraded together with Leôn on a mule through the city centre. Rômanos accused the empress Zôê of having conspired against him, so she was expelled from the palace and sent to a monastery. The emperor's tutor Theodôros and other important figures were also expelled from the palace and ordered to remain in the Opsikion. Iôannês Kourkouas, the *drouggarios tês biglas*, was placed in charge of the purge. He is the man who became famous as the conqueror of the Emirate of Melitene. On 14 December 920 Rômanos was enthroned as *Kaisar*. The Fôkades were naturally excluded from all important positions and commands in and around the capital. This, however, does not mean that the Fôkades would not have had a powerbase of their own. They were still one of the most important military families of the border regions, with their own military forces in the province of Kappadokia, and in this capacity they acted as *akritai*, who can be described as feudal lords and bandits fighting their own wars in the border region with the Muslims. However, as will be made clear below, in the context of the events of the year 941, it is very likely that Bardas was reappointed as a *stratêgos* of a theme (probably either of Anatolikon or Kappadokia) very soon after his short-lived disgrace.

The Education of Nikêforos Fôkas

The sources do not describe the education that Nikêforos received in his youth, but several things can be guessed on the basis of his background and later skills. As noted by Charles Personnaz, it is clear that as an upper class person Nikêforos received an education in the classics, so he studied the ancient classical texts. It is also clear that he received spiritual education, which included the learning of Christian calendar, visits to monasteries, knowledge of the Bible and Lives of the Saints, and participation in religious ceremonies. It is very likely that Nikêforos received his spiritual education mainly from his uncle Michaêl Maleinos. It is similarly clear that Nikêforos received a thorough training in all military skills, which included riding, swordplay, use of spears and javelins, and archery. In addition to this, he would have received a basic military training in military campaigning and formations.[12] As a member of the military elite it is also probable that he had already read military manuals in his youth. These must have included at least Maurikios' *Stratêgikon*, the *Taktika* of Leôn VI, Ailianos (Aelian), and possibly also other treatises dealing with naval and siege warfare for which, see Syvänne (2013b) with some of these listed also in the bibliography.

Roman infantry (10th or 11th cent.). Source: Schlumberger

Chapter Four

The Last Years of Rômanos I Lakapênos and the Rise of the Fôkades in 941–5

4.1. The Background to the Events of 941

Rômanos had not respected his promises towards the tutor of Kônstantinos and had promoted himself to supreme emperor while naming his wife *augousta*, followed by the promotion of his sons Christoforos (the eldest of the sons and intended successor), Stefanos and Kônstantinos as emperors, so that all of these stood above Kônstantinos VII in the order of succession. It was presumably because of this that Rômanos thought it acceptable to marry Kônstantinos' son Rômanos with the illegitimate daughter of Hugh, rather than with a daughter born from wedlock. Christoforos died in 931, but Rômanos did not change the order of succession. The emperor Rômanos sought to secure the position of Stefanos by marrying him to Anna, who belonged to the family of Katakylas. The other children of Rômanos were also married to strategically well-chosen individuals.

The reign of Rômanos Lakapênos was highly successful in the east, so the new *domestikos tôn scholôn* Iôannês Kourkouas, his brother Theofilos Kourkouas, and his son Rômanos all achieved remarkable successes in the east against the Muslims, the most important of which was the conquest of the Emirate of Melitene by Iôannês Kourkouas in 934. Rômanos was also able to negotiate peace with the Bulgarians, with concessions that included marriage between Tsar Peter, the son of Symeon, and Rômanos' granddaughter Maria (daughter of Rômanos' son Christoforos and Sofia, daughter of Nikêtas the patrician) on 8 October 927. Further, Rômanos had opted to buy peace from the Hungarians twice, and he was also eager to grasp the opportunity for an alliance and pact of marriage when Hugh, King of Italy (Hugues de Provence), proposed an alliance against Fraxinetum, the Muslim enclave in Provence consisting of al-Andalusian soldiers. In return for the alliance Rômanus suggested marriage between Hugh's daughter and Rômanos, son of Kônstantinos VII and Elenê (Helen daughter of Rômanos I Lakapênos).

4.2. The Russian invasion and Bardas Fôkas in 941

The Muslims of Fraxinetum/Fraxinet were a pain in the butt for both Burgundy and Italy, but it was the destruction of the port of Frejus by the Muslims of Fraxinetum that finally convinced Hugh of Provence, the King of Italy, to seek an alliance with the Romans. He needed a fleet to engage the enemy and only the Romans could provide him with such. There were potentially three Muslim fleets to deal with: the fleet of al-Andalus; the local fleet of Fraxinetum; and en route the Fatimid fleet of Sicily – the last of which the Romans needed to neutralize too if they wanted to sail to Fraxinetum. Therefore, in 941 Hugh dispatched envoys to Constantinople to seek an alliance. The first embassy of Hugh appears to have reached the city of Constantinople either just before the Russians attacked or as they began their invasion, because the second embassy of Hugh was in Constantinople in September 941. Rômanos dispatched the first embassy together with his own envoys back to Hugh with the answer that he would provide a navy if Hugh would marry his daughter to Rômanos, son of Kônstantinos VII. The next set of envoys from Hugh suggested a marriage with an illegitimate daughter of his, which suited Rômanos I Lakapênos. The marriage ceremonies were finally performed in Constantinople between Rômanos and Bertha of Provence, the illegitimate daughter of Hugh, in September 944. However, the military aspects of the alliance had already been put into effect before this, probably in 942.[1] The key piece of evidence in this text for the dating of the events in Constantinople is the fact that Rômanos I Lakapênos had already suggested the marriage pact when the Romans were still fighting against the Russians.

The Russian attack caught the Romans at a bad time. The Imperial Fleet had been dispatched to protect the Greek islands against the Saracens. The Roman capital was therefore vulnerable from the sea. As if this was not enough, the main Roman army under Iôannês Kourkouas was fighting against the Saracens in the east.[2] This was either exploited by the Russians under Igor, or his invasion of Roman territory was just an unlucky coincidence. Constantin Zuckerman suggests that the leaders of the Russian expedition were actually Igor and Oleg, which is possible.[3] We do not know why Igor invaded. One of the possible reasons for the sudden surprising invasion by the Russians was that Rômanos had discontinued the payments agreed in the aftermath of the peace with Bulgaria, or that Igor just sought to increase those payments, as he was in the habit doing with the other neighbouring nations. The latter alternative is likelier. Unfortunately, we do not have solid evidence for the size of the invading force because none of the sources bothers to give us exact figures excepting the number of ships.

According to Skylitzes, Theophanes Continuator, Pseudo-Symeon (Continuator of Georgius Monachus) and Nestor, the Russians collected 10,000 ships, while according to Zonaras the Russians collected as many as 15,000 ships. However, the figure is put at 1,000+ vessels by Liudprand of Cremona. Theophanes Continuatus calls the Russian ships *dromitai* which he likens to the vessels used by the Franks. It is possible that this has influenced the text of Liudprand to equate the Russian ships with the western *galeai*, so he has not accepted the larger figures. Notably Liudprand equates the Russians with Nordmen/Normans (Nordmannos), which clearly supports the view that most of the Russians consisted of the Scandinavian Vikings. The principal problem with these figures is that we do not know the typical size of the vessel (*monoxyla*) used by the Russians beyond the fact that these were typically smaller than the Viking ships because the rapids required smaller ships and because most of these were also built by the Slavic subject tribes. The Russians of the fifteenth- and sixteenth-centuries were still using these kinds of ships, according to Olaus Magnus' *History of the Northern Peoples* (ca. 1555). According to Olaus Magnus, period-Russians employed 20- or 25- man boats that the Russians were in the habit of carrying into the forests and woods if needed. We actually find the Derevlian Slavs using precisely the same-sized boats in 945 (Nestor AM 6453).

On the basis of this, I am making the educated guess that the average boat size was indeed 20 to 25 men, so that only the flagship and vessels of other important individuals may have been larger, carrying a maximum of 60 to 100 men. We know that the size of the Russian force was immense because the Romans had difficulty in dealing with it, but it is still clear that the size was not anywhere close to 200,000 to 250,000 men or 300,000 to 375,000 men that the 10,000 or 15,000 ships would imply – unless, of course, some of these would have been barges drawn by the other ships. The figure of 1,000+ ships is also too small a figure, because that would give us only about 20,000 men, which would have been too small a force to ravage the entire area that the Russians ravaged in 941. In 1043 the Russians assembled a huge force from all subject and allied peoples 'inhabiting the northern islands' so that the total size of the force was claimed by Skylitzes (21.6) to be 100,000 men. This figure is too large for this occasion, because it was only in 944 that Igor assembled a similarly-massive army for a campaign against the Romans. However, it would still have to have been large enough to cause problems for the main Roman army that consisted of over 40,000 men according to the *Chronicle of Nestor*. I would therefore suggest that the original size of the invading force was about 70,000 men, so there were roughly 3,000 to 3,500 boats and ships in the Russian force. This would take into account the cumulative number of casualties that the Russians appear to have suffered in the course of the campaign while still being able to make their retreat.

According to Nestor, the Bulgarians informed Rômanos I of the approach of the Russian fleet. This would have happened when the Russian fleet reached the mouth of the Danube where they entered the Bulgarian territory. If it indeed were the Bulgarians who first informed Rômanos, it would explain the haste and panic that followed and it would also mean that the Russians had managed to negotiate a deal with the Pechenegs/Patsinakians, while also surprising the inhabitants of Cherson in such a manner that they would not have been able to dispatch a swift vessel to Constantinople to warn of the impending invasion. Whatever the truth, the delay in the receipt of information between Cherson and the Bulgarian border would not have been more than a couple of days at most. However, according to *The Life of St. Basil the Younger*, the saint actually prophesised that the Russians would invade, which, if true, would probably imply that Basil had heard about the preparations from representatives of the Church in the north. If Basil really made such predictions, these were not heeded by imperial authorities, who made no preparations on the basis of these.

According to Liudprand, the principal reason for the sleepless nights that Rômanos I Lakapênos had after he had received news of the impending invasion was that he had dispatched the entire Imperial Fleet against the infidel Saracens. The other reason for the troubled nights was that the Roman field army under Iôannês Kourkouas was fighting against the Arabs in the east. Iôannês was clearly seeking to exploit the chaos in the aftermath of the death of the caliph and so continued the campaign he had begun in late 940 because this is the only logical explanation for the fact that he arrived so late on the scene. The city of Constantinople therefore lacked a fleet and a field army. According to Liudprand of Cremona, the problem concerning the fleet was solved when someone found out that there were 15 half-sunk *chelandia* at the harbour. When Rômanos I heard this, his mood lifted up and he ordered the shipwrights to repair the *chelandia* and equip them with flame-throwers at the bow, the stern, and on both sides of the ship. From the Greek sources we learn that, in addition to these, he had some triremes, but unfortunately we are not told from which source these came. My educated guess is that two of these were probably the Imperial *dromônia*, in addition to which there may also have been some other *dromônes* present, or alternatively the Imperial barges were converted into triremes. In addition to this, even if the sources fail to note their presence, it is probable that the emperor would have had at his disposal the ten *chelandia* of the Imperial Fleet that were permanently posted at the straits and mouth of the Bosporus (Stenon), because these usually remained behind when the rest of the Imperial Fleet campaigned elsewhere. As noted above, it was these that provided replacement crews for the two Imperial *dromônia* when these had sent their crews to serve in the naval campaign. This would have given Rômanos a fleet of 25 *chelandia* and an unknown number of trireme *dromônes/dromônia*. The fleet was placed under the command of Theofanês, the *prôtobestiarios*. He took a defensive position at the Hieron while the Russians moored off the Lighthouse (Faros) and the adjacent shore, which means the mouth of the Bosporus. The Russians had pillaged everything possible en route from Mesembria (where the Roman territory began) up to the mouth of the Bosporus, which had obviously given the Romans time to make their defensive preparations.

The defensive preparations also included the assembly of land forces from every quarter possible for the defence of the capital. The Roman field army that was campaigning against the Saracens under Iôannês Kourkouas in Asia was immediately recalled to protect the capital, but since he was apparently too far away to assist immediately, Rômanos I gave command of the forces patrolling the Asian side of the Bosporus to Bardas Fôkas, while Theofanês with the fleet blocked the Straits of Bosporus.

The extant sources state that by 944 Bardas Fôkas had served for a long time and well when under others, while Theophanes Continuatus (p.424.16) states in the context of the events of 941 that Bardas Fôkas was *patrikios* and ex-*stratêgos* (the usual translation for the *apo stratêgôn*) when he was placed in command of the cavalry and chosen men. Cheynet, Sullivan, Wortley and Runciman all interpret on the basis of Theophanes Continuates that the referrals to 'long and distinguished' meant only the period before 919.[4] Whether this was the case depends on the translation of '*Bardas patrikios apo stratêgon o Fôkas dia gês meta ippeôn kai ekkritôn andrôn tou paratrechein autous*' in Theophanes Continuatus. One could perhaps rather interpret this so that Bardas Fôkas was appointed to command as a *patrikios* from the position of a *stratêgos* having previously been a *stratêgos*. This would reconcile the sources, while also explaining the referral to the chosen men (*ekkritôn andrôn*) in both Theophanes Continuatus and Skylitzes (these were the chosen horsemen of a theme that Bardas had brought with him) and also the presence of Macedonians in Bardas' force, as stated by Nestor and *The Life of St. Basil the Younger*, and it is the interpretation that I adopt here. The following discussion of the composition of the force serving under Bardas Fôkas provides additional argumentation in favour of this view.

This also means that it is very likely that the sons of Bardas, Nikêforos the Younger (the topic of this biography), Leôn and Kônstantinos had served under their father when he was *stratêgos* of some unnamed province or several provinces in succession. We know the names of only two themes/provinces in which Bardas had served, the themes of Anatolikon and Kappadokia, but it is quite probable that he had also served in other provinces before being promoted to the command of those. These other possible candidates include the themes of Boukellarion, Paphlagonia and Armeniakon. I would suggest that when Rômanos decided to reinstate Bardas Fôkas into a command position after 919, he probably did that by giving him one of the less dangerous provinces such as, for example, the province of Paphlagonia or Armeniakon, because the first wife of Nikêforos the Younger belonged to the Pleustai who originated in the Pontos region. It is in fact possible that he was in command of one of these when the Russians attacked, because these locations would explain why Bardas was close to the scene and patrolling the coastline which the Russians attacked, but it is actually far likelier that he was the *stratêgos* of Anatolikon at this time because that was the senior ranking among the *stratêgoi* and the highest position he held before becoming *etaireiarchês* and then *domestikos*, and we know that he schooled many of the future commanders, including his sons (DV D Preface 42ff.; DM Preface 7–8), in the art of guerrilla warfare while being the *stratêgos* of either Kappadokia or Anatolikon. His likely career path after 919 would have been to progress from one of the lesser *themata* to the theme of Kappadokia and from there to the Anatolikon. The reason for his absence from the campaign led by Iôannês Kourkouas in 941 would have been the fact that the Anatolikon protected the section of the frontier facing Tarsus, which was not the target of the Roman invasion. It is probable that his sons received their basic schooling in military arts from their father and learnt the basic military theory from the books of history and military treatises, but it is probable that at some point in time (perhaps in about 927–33?) during their early military careers they would have served in the *archôntogennematai* (the sons of the officers). As already noted, the *archôntogennematai* were an imperial bodyguard unit where the sons of important military officers were schooled in military arts while also serving as hostages. Given the fact that Nikêforos was born in 912 and his brothers Leôn and Kônstantinos soon after, and all of them and also the editor of the *De velitatione* (possibly Leôn) were schooled in the arts of skirmishing and guerrilla warfare by Bardas, it is clear that Bardas Fôkas served as a *stratêgos* of the themes of Kappadokia and Anatolikon at some point in time during the period 919 to 941, because his children were too young to be schooled in the military arts before 919. One may assume that Nikêforos would have moved to serve under his father at some point in time after ca. 932/3. It was then that Bardas Fôkas fought continually with the Saracens, most of which conflicts have not found their way into the narrative histories because fighting was endemic and small scale, usually involving only the emir of Tarsus and his men. The Preface of *De velitatione* also makes it clear that once Bardas had been promoted as *stratêgos* of the Anatolikon, his successor in Kappadokia was Kônstantinos Maleinos, brother of his wife. For the tactics that Bardas Fôkas brought to the state of perfection, see Appendix 2.

In 941 Nikêforos would have been about 29-years-old, while his brother Leôn would have been about 26-years-old and Kônstantinos 23–24-years-old. Nikêforos can therefore be considered to have been a veteran commander by this stage of his life, and particularly well-versed in the kind of skirmishing and guerrilla warfare that was practised along the border facing the Arabs. The same was obviously true of his brothers Leôn and Kônstantinos, both of whom were appointed *strategoi* of *themata* at the same time as Nikêforos was appointed as *stratêgos* of Anatolikon in 945. These appointments suggest that the men had had some military experience before and their father had clearly been their principal tutor. It is very likely that at least Nikêforos and Leôn accompanied their father in this campaign against the Russians, because they are later mentioned to have been present in the capital when Kônstantinos VII retook the reins of power from the Lakapênoi, but the whereabouts of Kônstantinos Fôkas during this campaign is less certain. It is possible that he was left behind.

It is possible or even probable that it was very soon after this that Nikêforos married his first wife from the family of Pleustai (from the Pontos region), with whom he sired a son named Bardas, but it is also possible that the marriage took place later. According to Skylitzes (14.2) and Leo the Deacon (3.4), the son was accidentally killed by the son's cousin Pleustes when the two were jousting on horseback, the exact date of which is not known, except that it took place a few years before 963, which once again suggests that the marriage took place in about 941–6. The death of the son was a hard blow to Nikêforos, who abstained from eating meat from that date onwards until 20 September 963. As regards the dating of the death, Skylitzes merely states that it was not known if Nikêforos really abstained from meat or if he merely wanted to deceive those in power. The last statement fits the period when Kônstantinos VII and his son Rômanos were jointly emperors. Since this happened a few years before 963, one may perhaps put the date of the death to the period 958–9, but once again this is not conclusive because 'those in power' can also be taken to mean the imperial favourites.

According to Nestor and *The Life of St. Basil the Younger* (3.23–8), the Roman commanders facing the Russians were the *domestikos* Pantherios with 40,000 men, Fôkas the Patrician with the Macedonians, and Theodôros the *Stratêgos/Stratêlatês* (also known as Theodôros Spoggarios) with the Thracians, meaning that their forces were supported by other illustrious nobles. The Roman fleet was commanded by Theofanês. The Greek/Roman sources (e.g. TC 6.39–41, pp.423–9; SL 136.73–6; Skyl. 10.31–2; GM p.915) claim that the Roman main army was under Iôannês Kourkouas and that Iôannês was removed from office and replaced by Rômanos' relative Pantherios (probably Sklêros[5]) only after the return of Theofanês to the capital. It is actually probable that Nestor and his source, *The Life of St. Basil the Younger*, are correct here and that Iôannês Kourkouas had already been removed from office before the decisive battle with the Russians in September 941, the likely reason for such being that he had been too slow to bring help to the scene, which would have made his position untenable in the aftermath of the previous defeats he had suffered in the east in 939–40. I am assuming that Theodôros the *Stratêgos* with the Thracians was originally patrolling the European side of the Straits of Bosporus because we find Bardas Fôkas patrolling the opposite shore.

According to the Roman sources, Bardas Fôkas brought with him a force consisting of cavalry (*ippeôn*) and chosen men (*ekkritôn andrôn*).[6] The 'chosen men' clearly means the chosen cavalrymen of a *thema*, which according to Leôn the Wise consisted of about 4,000 horsemen on average. In fact, Pseudo-Symeon (GM p.915) even calls the forces of Bardas' chosen cavalry (*meta ippeôn ekkritôn*). Nestor states that Bardas led Macedonians, which I interpret to mean the *megas etaireia* (which consisted of the Macedonians) rather than the men of the *thema* of Macedonia, which would have served under Theodôros the *Stratêgos* during this campaign. Bardas was now clearly appointed as *etaireiarchês* having previously been a *stratêgos*. In fact, it is probable that he was actually made *megas etaireiarchês*, because he was the commander of the *megas etaireia*. In the absence of the Roman main army under Iôannes Kourkouas, Rômanos I Lakapênos clearly needed an experienced commander for his land forces. The appointment as *etaireiarchês* also explains why Bardas and his sons were to have an instrumental role in the overthrow of Rômanos I and his sons. They were present in the capital and in command at least of the *megas etaireia* and possibly in command of all *etaireiai*. It is of note that the *megas etaireia* consisted mainly of Macedonians who felt particular loyalty towards the Macedonian dynasty and therefore towards Kônstantinos VII. This was to have a decisive role in the events that unfolded.[7] Rômanos I Lakapênos had made a serious miscalculation when he had given his enemy control over the key unit of the imperial bodyguards.

According to the account of Symeon the Logothete, the Roman fleet under Theofanês engaged the Russians at Hieron. This took place in June. According to Liudprand, the timing was perfect. The winds suddenly died so the Romans could use their flame-throwers without any fear. As locals, the Romans would obviously have known this in advance from the visible signs (winds, clouds, etc.). Liudprand adds that Igor gave the order for his fleet not to kill the enemy but to take them alive. If true, this would have eased the task for the Roman fleet greatly. The *dromôn* of Theofanês spearheaded the attack, so his ship was the first to be rowed through the enemy lines, in the process of which he incinerated vast numbers of enemy ships while putting others to flight. Even without Greek fire the encounter would have had the same result. The Roman ships were massive by comparison, so their galleys would have sunk the small Russian vessels even by using ramming tactics. Symeon adds that the remaining *dromônes* and triremes of the Roman fleet followed the example of their admiral and completed the rout. The Romans had so few ships that the flame-throwers in the bow, stern and sides worked to perfection when the small *dromitai/monoxyla* surrounded them. It is probable that Symeon's *dromônes* are the *chelandia* of Liudprand, while the triremes of Symeon means the largest class of Roman war-galleys, the *dromônes trieres*. Some of the Russians who attempted to save themselves by jumping off their boats were drowned because of their armour, while those who managed to stay afloat were usually burned. Only those ships who had been far enough from the Roman fleet were able to flee to the eastern shore where the large Roman ships could not reach them because of their deep keels. By staying in shallow waters, the surviving Russians managed to reach a spot called Sgora in Bithynia where they made a landing. The Roman fleet appears to have shadowed them without attempting to engage the enemy in the shallow waters.

According to the *Chronicle of Nestor* and *The Life of St. Basil the Younger*, the surviving Russians who had landed in Bithynia then proceeded to pillage the coastline of the Black Sea up to Heraclea and Paphlagonia and south of it up to Nicomedia, where the Russians pillaged the lands along the gulf. The Russian raid lasted from June to September 941, so it is clear that the Russian force was very sizeable and that the Romans were initially forced to rely on guerrilla warfare. The Russians captured, killed and tortured the Romans. Some of the prisoners were crucified, others put to the stake, others had iron nails driven through skulls, and still others were used for target practice with bows and arrows. Churches, monasteries and villages were burned and booty gathered. This proves nicely how large a force the Russians had – even after their naval defeat they possessed enough men to pillage most of Bithynia. According to the Roman sources, Bardas Fôkas with his cavalry and chosen men (the cavalry of his theme) wiped out one large force of Russians that had been sent to forage. This is a schoolbook tactic from the *De velitatione* (see Appendix 2). Bardas clearly lacked a large enough force to engage the entire Russian force or even its main force, so he opted to engage one of the columns that the Russians had dispatched to pillage. His scouts and patrols would have informed him of the leaving of the enemy force from its camp, after which the scouts would have directed his force to the location where it was favourable to engage the enemy.

According to the Roman sources, Iôannês Kourkouas arrived immediately after this and defeated the Russians because they were scattered about here and there. However, Nestor and *The Life of St. Basil the Younger* give us a different version.

The Last Years of Rômanos I Lakapênos and the Rise of the Fôkades 111

According to these sources, the Russians were surrounded when the Roman army from the east arrived. The Russians were caught between the 40,000 men of the *domestikos* Pantherios, the Macedonians of Fôkas and the Thracians of Theodôros. To me this suggests that the forces under Theodôros had been shipped across to Asia so that his 'Thracians' approached the Russians from the west while Bardas' forces came upon the Russians from the south and the Roman main army from the east, with the result that all three Roman forces were then united for the decisive battle. I would suggest that Nestor and *The Life of St. Basil the Younger* have indeed preserved for us the details of the last decisive battle on land which is missing from the Roman sources. Pantherios replaced Iôannês Kourkouas before the decisive battle because he had not arrived fast enough and because he was suspected of having imperial aspirations.[8]

However, we can reconcile the Roman sources and Nestor if one assumes that Iôannês arrived when the Russians were spread out to pillage and had inflicted similar defeats on their scattered forces as Bardas had, but failed to achieve a decisive victory with the result that the Russians were to assemble their surviving forces somewhere along the Black Sea coast (possibly near Heraclea). It would have been then that Rômanos removed Iôannês Kourkouas from office and replaced him with Pantherios (Skleros?). According to Skylitzes and Symeon the Logothete, Iôannês Kourkouas was removed from office only after the war because the other emperors felt envy towards him in a situation in which the ruling emperor Rômanos I wanted to marry Iôannês' daughter Eufrosynê to his grandson Rômanos. This sounds like a whitewash and not the real reason for the dismissal and can be proven to be so by the fact that Rômanos I Lakapênos had already decided to marry Rômanos, the son of Kônstantinos VII, to the daughter of Hugh well before the end of the Russian war because the second embassy of Hugh was present when it ended in September 941.

I would suggest that Theophanes Continuatus (p.429) has preserved the real reason for the dismissal of Iôannês Kourkouas from office when he claims that Iôannês was accused of seeking the throne at the head of his army, and of illegal acquisition of villages and lands. This sounds like the real reason. Iôannês had not returned quickly to defend the capital, so it is easy to see why the emperors, including Rômanos I Lakapênos, would have started to think that Iôannês was seeking the throne, and on the basis of the timinng of the embassies of Hugh of Provence it is clear that this decision was taken earlier than September 941, which times the removal of Iôannês from office to the period before September too. The emperors could think that Iôannês was using the Russians for the weakening of the position of the Lakapênoi in the capital, so Iôannês would have arrived at the scene as a saviour of the Roman Empire. Iôannês' standing would also have been weakened in imperial eyes by the two years of defeats he had suffered previously and by the massive corruption (acquisition of villages and land) that he had practised, the last of which could also have been interpreted as an attempt to weaken imperial authority. The presence of the forces under Bardas Fôkas, Theodôros and the fleet of Theofanês, plus the presence of the enemy forces on Roman soil, together with the diminished prestige of Iôannês Kourkouas thanks to his corruption and two defeats in 939–40, would certainly have made it easier for the Lakapênoi to get rid off Iôannês – which they indeed appear to have managed to do without trouble.

In short, by omitting the major pitched battle fought between the Romans and Russians mentioned only by Nestor and *The Life of St. Basil the Younger*, the Roman sources purposefully give us the wrong picture of the timing of events – it is even possible that Iôannês was removed from office in such a manner that he did not engage the Russian forces in any form or manner. Regardless, it is still clear that the Roman sources have left us with adequate pieces of evidence to correct the received image that their incomplete account give us. For example, the Roman chronicles place the dismissal of Iôannês Kourkouas immediately after the return of Theofanês to the capital after his naval victory. It is easy to see that this means the first return of Theofanes to the capital, which would have taken place after his first naval victory, after which followed the dismissal of Iôannês from office.

According to Nestor and *The Life of St. Basil the Younger*, when the Russians noted that the Romans under Pantherios, Fôkas and Theodôros had surrounded them, they opted to attack and it was only with great difficulty that the Romans prevailed, with the result that the Russians fled back to their ships at night and then fled away. In this case it is likely that the entire Roman force consisted of cavalry for two reasons: 1) the Romans were unable to defeat the Russians decisively, which is easy to understand if the Romans had cavalry and faced a disciplined infantry shieldwall; and 2) the Romans had previously been conducting a guerrilla war against the spreadout Russians. It is possible that Nikêforos the Younger and his father had previously participated in some of the campaigns of Iôannês Kourkouas or some other general, meaning that this was not Nikêforos' first large scale battle, even if it's clear that it was his first large scale battle involving Russian infantry. Regardless, it is still clear that the experience gained from this campaign would have been good schooling for the future emeperor. After their defeat the Russians in their ships attempted to flee towards the west, but Theofanês was expecting this so he once again inflicted a crushing defeat on the enemy and pursued the fleeing Russians with his flame-throwers incinerating every vessel caught in their path. This last battle between the Romans and Russians took place in September. The surviving Russians fled during the night. According to Nestor (AM 6449, 6452–4), when Igor then reached Kiev/Kyiv after his defeat, he started assembling a new great army to exact revenge on the Romans.

Rômanos I Lakapênos rewarded Theofanês with the title *parakoimômenos* and the Russian captives were executed to satisfy the bloodlust of the ruler and populace. After this, the Roman main army returned to the east under its new commander Pantherios,[9] a relative of Rômanos I.

Constantin Zuckerman (1995, 265) has suggested that the surviving Russian vessels fled towards the east because their route to the west was blocked by the Roman fleet and the Russian vessels were too small for the crossing of the Black Sea. This is indeed possible, even if I would not preclude the possibility that the

Russian boats would have fled to the open sea once this was possible (i.e. during the night) because in emergencies humans are prone to take even desperate measures in order to be able to flee from danger. On the basis of his interpretation of the *Genizah Letter* and various Russian chronicles, Zuckerman further suggests that it was because of the flight of his ships through the lands occupied by the Khazars that Oleg (the 'senior' ruler) was forced to negotiate with the Khazars so that the Russian vessels could be allowed to return unharmed. The letter further claimed that it was thanks to two defeats in a row[10] that Oleg now felt too ashamed to remain in Kiev/Kyiv and left the city in Igor's possession. Zuckerman further suggests that Oleg retained control of his own retainers and decided to invade Bardh'a in Persia (in modern Azerbaijan) in 943/4 where his forces suffered from diarrhoea caused by local food and water. The invasion could only have been made with Khazar approval, which lends further support for the reconstruction of Zuckerman, and in fact the Khazars and Alans appear to have joined this expedition. The diarrhoea was not enough to subdue the Russians who were besieging Bardh'a, but in the end the Muslims prevailed when they managed to ambush Oleg, so that he and 700 of his men died in the winter of 944/5. This reconstruction of Oleg's end by Zuckerman is quite plausible but ultimately uncertain.

4.3. The Roman Military Operations in 942

The defeat of the Russians in September 941, peace with Bulgaria, alliance with Hugh of Provence, the civil war within the Caliphate and the ongoing guerrilla warfare by the local Sicilians against their Arab oppressors ensured freedom of operation for the Romans in late-941 and in 942.

The Romans appear to have dispatched their fleet to Fraxinetum in 941 or 942. The two Christian rulers united their forces against the Saracens of Fraxinetum and their masters in al-Andalus. Rômanos I Lakapênos dispatched the Imperial Fleet, or a portion of it, with its fire-bearing *chelandia* to the scene, while Hugh advanced on land with his army. See the map of Fraxinetum in the Maps Section. The Roman fleet burned the local Muslim fleet (with its possible reinforcements) into cinders and Hugh proceeded to besiege Fraxinetum. Hugh was on the point of capturing the fortress, but then arrived the news that his rival for the Italian throne, Berengar of Ivrea, was assembling forces from Francia and Swabia with the intention of crossing the Alps. Therefore, Hugh decided to send the Roman fleet back to their own country, while he made an agreement with the Saracens, his aim being to block the Alpine passes with these Saracens of al-Andalus. This he did at the expense of Christian blood, as was noted by Liudprand of Cremona.[11]

The Romans launched an invasion of Sayf's territory between 24 December 941 and 21 January 942 and advanced up to Hamus, which was at a distance of six parasangs from Aleppo. They destroyed, massacred and pillaged everything along the route, and took 15,000 captives (women and children). The emir Nasr al-Tamali exacted revenge in the same year by advancing from Tarsus into Roman territory which he then proceeded to pillage. He brought back a large number of prisoners, together with a large number of distinguished Roman patricians.[12] This means that the local Roman *stratêgoi* of the *themata* close to Tarsus (possibly Kappadokia, Seleukeia, Kharsianon and Anatolikon?) had united their forces but only with the result that they had been defeated by the army of Tarsus. It is unlikely that any of the Bardas Fôkas family would have been involved in the defence against al-Tamali, because it is very probable that Bardas Fôkas and his sons Nikêforos and Leôn were now in Constantinople.

4.4. The Roman Empire from late 942 until 945

The Romans continued their offensive against Hamdanid territory in October or November 942, with the *domestikos* Pantherios[13] now in charge of the operations. The situation was very opportune, because the civil war within the caliphate still preoccupied Sayf's time, while the Fatimids were also preoccupied with a civil war of their own. Abu Yazid revolted against the Fatimids in 943 and his revolt lasted until 947, so that the Fatimid navy did not pose any serious threat to the Romans in Sicily or Italy during those years. The Romans played a double game with the Fatimids during that era. They dispatched an embassy to negotiate with the Fatimids while actively supporting the uprising in Sicily. The revolt in the Valley of the Demon in Sicily lasted at least until the 960s, even if the Fatimids had managed to limit its scope significantly by about 947. Krinitês, the Roman *stratêgos* of Calabria, also played a double game of his own. He overtaxed his subjects so that he could sell provisions to the starving Fatimids during their civil war in return for exorbitant prices. When Kônstantinos later learnt of this, he relieved Krinitês from office. He was allowed to retire in infamy, which he fully deserved because it was thanks to his help that the Fatimids survived and were in a position to demand that the Romans resume their tribute payments and send back the refugees from their realm. When the Romans refused, the Fatimids began their counter-offensive against the Romans of Sicily under the new governor al-Hasan b. Ali b. Abi'l-Husayn the Kalbite after he had arrived in Sicily in 336 (23 July 947–10 July 948).[14]

According to the Arabic sources, the Roman invasion force against the Hamdanids consisted of 80,000 men, which is well within the capabilities of the Roman Empire when one adds the thematic infantry to the major cavalry army (30–48,000 horsemen). The objective of the Roman invasion appears to have been to obtain the Mandylion of Edessa, the Jesus image not made by human hands, which in the Greek language was called the *acheiropoietos*. In other words, Rômanos I sought to regain an important Christian relic for prestige reasons and I would suggest that his primary reason for this was a need to strengthen his own position and the position of the Lakapênoi in general on the throne in the aftermath of the feared usurpation by Iôannês Kourkouas, and that Rômanos' increasing religiosity was not as important as this, even if it too influenced the strategy adopted. Rômanos needed a symbologically-important victory in order to surpass the achievements of Iôannes Kourkouas, whose achievements were compared to those of Traianus and Belisarius by Theophanes Continuatus. In his later years Rômanos had also become increasingly religious so he had a blind faith in a number of monks, the most important of whom was Sergios, the brother of *magistros* Kosmas and grandnephew of Patriarch Fotios. This undoubtedly influenced Rômanos and his policies and played a role in the choosing of the objective of the campaign.[15]

The Romans under their *domestikos* (this would be Pantherios) marched to Diyar Bekr, where they captured a large number of captives, after which they marched to the cities of Mayyafariqin and Arzen, which they pillaged in like fashion. Following this, the Romans captured Amida (north of Edessa), Dara and Nisibis (both east of Edessa) in quick succession. Dara was captured on 18 May 943, after which the Romans besieged Nisibis which fell quickly. Following this the Romans marched to Edessa and dispatched a message to the inhabitants of Edessa that they would not only spare the place but would also release a number of Muslim captives if they would deliver the Edessan Mandylion to the Romans.[16]

By approaching Edessa from the direction of Dara and Nisibis, the Romans cut off possible relief coming from the direction of Mosul. The Edessans dispatched the message to Baghdad, where the new caliph Muttaqi assembled his jurists who came to the conclusion that the saving of Muslim lives was the priority, which meant that it was permissible to hand over the Mandylion in return for Muslim captives. While the negotiations lasted the Romans continued their operations in Mesopotamia by sacking the city of Ras al-Ain south-east of Edessa in about November 943 and took thousands of captives, but were soon forced to evacuate the area thanks to harassment by Bedouins. It is not known if Nikêforos Fôkas or his relatives participated in this campaign, but as we shall see the lessons learnt here found their way into Nikêforos' treatise *Praecepta militaria*. This obviously suggests that he or his relatives or close associates were present during this campaign. In the end the two sides agreed on terms according to which the Edessans would hand over the Mandylion while the Romans released 200 Muslim captives, gave 12,000 silver pieces and promised not to attack Edessa and its neighbouring cities Harran (Carrhae), Saruq, and Samosata. On 15 August 944, the Mandylion was brought inside the city of Constantinople through the Golden Gate. The Patriarch, and the senior emperor Rômanos I and his sons Kônstantinos and Stefanos together with Kônstantinos VII, received the holy relic with great rejoicing. The ceremony in the Imperial Palace was held on 16 August, after which the Mandylion was carried to its resting place in the church of Hagia Sofia. This was the high point of the reign of Rômanos I, but little did he realize that it would be followed by his fall soon after this. Rômanos I Lakapênos failed to foresee the direction of the threat facing him (his sons). However, before this took place there was still hard fighting for the Roman armies in the east.[17]

According to the treaty conducted between Tuzun, the leader of the Turkish *ghilman* and de facto ruler in Baghdad, and Nasir ad-Dawla in 943, Nasir was in charge of Jazira/Gazira, while Syria was to be governed by Ikhshid, who had in his turn also managed to obtain from the caliph (before Tuzun arrested him in September 944) the land of Egypt for 30 years. Ikhshid left his brother Tugg b. Shabib at Damascus with orders to guard the territory while he returned to Egypt. Tugg departed Damascus in 332 (4 Sept. 943–23 Aug. 944) and marched to Tarsus and then invaded Roman territory, where he captured the village of Maluriya not far from Burgut and the defile of Darb al-Rahib. The location is unknown but clearly close to Tarsus and the Cilician Gates. It is probable that Tugg's invasion of Roman territory was meant as a diversionary operation at a time when they were ravaging Mesopotamia. The exact date is unknown. Ikshid left Syria and retired to Egypt after Tuzun had imprisoned the caliph in September 944, which gave Sayf ad-Dawla the opportunity he had been seeking and he occupied Aleppo while the forces of his brother Nasir under the command of Husayn b. Sa'id advanced into Azerbaijan where they raised the Daylamite family of Musafirides as their client rulers. In the summer of 944 the Daylamite dynasty of Buyids/Buwayhids attempted to capture Baghdad from the Turks of Tuzun but were severely defeated.[18]

The Roman preoccupation with the eastern campaign and with the capture of the Mandylion had left its western flank vulnerable. There were not enough soldiers present in the Balkans to protect it from enemies, but in defence of Rômanos one can state that the Balkans should have been safe from enemy invasions in a situation in which the Romans and Bulgarians were at peace. Consequently, the Turkish (Hungarian) invasion in April 943 took the Romans once again completely by surprise. After the death of Symeon the Bulgarian, his realm had weakened so much that it no longer possessed adequate strength to prevent the Hungarian raids. Therefore, the Hungarians had been able to pass through Bulgaria in 934, and now again in 943, so that on both occasions Rômanos I dispatched *patrikios* Theofanês to negotiate with them and on both occasions Theofanês bought the peace with money and valuables. The Roman prisoners were also ransomed with money. The Hungarian raiders appear to have consisted of the southern Hungarian tribes and not of the royal tribe, so that the leaders of the two raids were the Gyula (*gyla* in DAI) and Horka (*karchas* in DAI). However, on the basis of *The Life of St. Basil the Younger* and Skylitzes, there are also strong indications that smaller, lesser raids took place more frequently, so the invasions of 934 and 943 were only the best-known thanks to the size of the invading force. It is because of this that we find Kônstantinos VII negotiating with both *gyla* and *karchas* when he became the sole ruler. Some of the Hungarian raiders appear to have penetrated even as far as Attica and Boeotia. For example, in Boeotia there is a village known as Ungria and a lake called Ungro-limne.[19]

According to the *Chronicle of Nestor* (AM 6452/AD 944),[20] Igor of Kiev's preparations for a war of vengeance against the Romans were finally finished in 944. Igor had collected a huge army consisting of the Varangians (Northmen),

Russes/Russians (these would be the Northmen already living in Russia, or Swedish Northmen from Ruotsi/Sweden/Sverige), Polyanians (Slavs of the Kiev/Kyiv region), Slavs (presumably other Slavic groupings from modern day Poland, Slovakia, Bohemia/Chechia and elsewhere), Krivichians (Slavs of the Smolensk, Vitebsk and Polotsk regions), Tivercians (Tyversy, Slavs from the Dniester), and Pechenegs, meaning that Igor had also received hostages from them as a guarantee of their alliance. This was a huge force assembled from the entire region between the Black and Baltic Seas and beyond. The alliance between Russia and the Pechenegs was particularly worrisome for the Romans, as this removed the first obstacle from the invasion.

When the Khersonites learnt of the assembly of this force, they informed Rômanos immediately. The Bulgarians likewise informed the emperor that the Russians were approaching with a huge fleet and had allied themselves with the Pechenegs. Rômanos knew that he was in trouble, because his main army was fighting against the Saracens in Mesopotamia with the idea of capturing the Mandylion of Edessa. Consequently, he dispatched high ranking patricians (*boyars* in Nestor) to promise the tribute that Oleg had received and some more in return for turning around. In addition to this, Rômanos promised Igor the tribute that the Romans usually paid to the Pechenegs – this was obviously needed for the pacifying of the Pechenegs who accompanied Igor. When the Russians reached the mouth of the Danube Igor assembled his retinue to discuss the situation. The retinue advised Igor to accept the emperor's gifts, because it was risky to face the Romans at sea. Igor followed their advice and sent the Pechenegs to pillage Bulgaria while he himself, after receiving the gifts and tribute promised by the Romans, returned to Kiev. This implies that Igor kept the gifts that Pechenegs had received previously and basically betrayed his allies. When the Russians had reached Kiev, the Roman envoys arrived to finalize the actual terms of the treaty, which was concluded in 945 and is preserved in the *Chronicle of Nestor*. It was because of this that Igor turned his attention towards the Derevlians (western neighbours of Kiev) with the idea of increasing the tribute they were paying, but only with the result that he was killed thanks to the fact that he had taken with him too few men for the task. This resulted in a war between Kiev and Derevna. Kiev was now under Olga/Helga, the widow of Igor, who ruled in the name of her underage son Svyatoslav. It took until 947 for Olga to defeat the Derevlians, after which she imposed a harsher tribute on them. Two-thirds were paid to Kiev and a third to Olga in Vyshgorod, which was Olga's own city. After this she returned to Novgorod.

The pact between Hugh, the King of Italy, and Roman Empire was finalized with the marriage of Hugh's illegitimate daughter Bertha and Kônstantinos VII's son Rômanos in September 944. The marriage ceremonies were performed in Constantinople in September 944 and Bertha (still a child) took the imperial name Eudokia. According to Theophanes Continuatus and Skylitzes, Eudokia lived with Rômanos for five years and then died, still a virgin, in 949. The death of Bertha/Eudokia obviously weakened the prospects of Hugh to obtain help from

Kônstantinos VII and Rômanos II when he faced trouble with Otto I of East Francia during the 950s and 960s.[21]

In 944 Kônstantinos VII Porfyrogennêtos set in motion a plan to regain power. After all it was his birthright. He knew that this was possible only by turning the sons of Rômanos I against him. It is probable that the opportunity for this came due to the old age of Rômanos I and from his increasing reliance on the advice of the monks. The sons could also see this as a sign of weakness. Kônstantinos VII considered Kônstantinos Lakapênos to be difficult to manipulate, so he decided to try his luck with Stefanos Lakapênos. Kônstantinos VII managed to convince Basileios Peteinos from the *tagma* of *etaireiai* (*prôtospatharios* according to TC 6.53) to act as his collaborator because he had been Kônstantinos' friend from the youth. At this stage the cabal formed by Kônstantinos VII Porfyrogênnetos included also the monk Marianos, son of the former *domestikos tôn scholai* Leôn Argyros (and also brother of Rômanos, the husband of Agatha Lakapêna) and others. The known plotters included at least Manuêl Kourtikios, *stratêgos* Diogenês, someone named Kladôn, and another named Filippos. In my opinion it is likely that the plotters included also Bardas Fôkas and his sons Nikêforos and Leôn because Bardas was rewarded with the position of *domestikos* immediately after the overthrow of Rômanos I. It is probable that Bardas still served as *megas etaireiarchês*, so his support for the plot would have been instrumental. The conspirators, mainly Basileios Peteinos, managed to convince Stefanos to overthrow his father. According to Liudprand of Cremona, both Stefanos and Kônstantinos had assembled soldiers in their quarters and it was with these troops that they then apprehended their father. This means that Stefanos managed to convince his brother to join him in his endeavour to grasp power into their own hands. Theophanes Continuatus adds that Stefanos shared knowledge of the plot with the other emperors, which shows how skilfully Basileios Peteinos and Kônstantinos VII manipulated him.[22] The overthrow of Rômanos took place on 16 December 944 and he was then exiled to the island of Prote. When the rumour of this reached the ears of the populace it had already assumed two different versions. According to the first version, Rômanos had been overthrown, but according to the second version Kônstantinos VII had also been killed. The latter version roused Bishop Sigefred, the envoy of Hugh of Provence, to action. He rallied the Amalfitans, Romans from the city of Rome, and Gaetans to the support of Kônstantinos VII, and he was joined also by the populace of Constantinople. They all rushed together to the palace, with the result that the two brothers were able to calm the populace only by having Kônstantinos VII make a public appearance.[23]

The Roman sources offer conflicting information of what happened next. According to Theophanes Continuatus, Kônstantinos VII immediately held real power, while Skylitzes claims that the real power was in the hands of Stefanos, so the two Kônstantinoi held a secondary position. Theophanes Continuatus claims that it was Kônstantinos VII who now appointed Bardas Fôkas as *magistros* and *domestikos tôn scholôn*, Kônstantinos Goggylios as *drouggarios tou ploimou*, Basileios Peteinos as *patrikios* and *megas etaireiarchês*, Marianos Argyros as *komês tou stablou*, and Manuêl

Kourtikios as *patrikios* and *drouggarios tou bigla*. The list of promotions proves that these men supported the overthrow of Rômanos and were probably present in the capital when it took place. In contrast, Skylitzes claims that it was Stefanos who appointed these men to their positions. In light of the version preserved by Liudprand of Cremona, I find Skylitzes' account the more likely because he provides us with details concerning the second portion of the plot that took place after those appointments. In my opinion it is likely that Stefanos did indeed make the appointments while believing that he was promoting his supporters into high positions while in truth all of these men were supporters of Kônstantinos VII and had only pretended to be supporters of Stefanos and his brother.

Skylitzes claims that Stefanos and Kônstantinos VII quarrelled and that Kônstantinos decided to get rid of Stefanos and Kônstantinos Lakapênos only after he had learnt that Stefanos was seeking to get rid of him and his own brother. This is unlikely to be true because Skylitzes stated earlier in his text that Kônstantinos had planned this from the start. Skylitzes claims that it was only now, at the urging of his wife Elenê (the sister of the other two emperors), that Kônstantinos VII revealed his plan to get rid of the two brothers to Basileios Peteinos and that Basileios then rallied to his cause Marianos Argyros, Nikêforos and Leôn Fôkas, Nikolaos and Leôn Tornikios,[24] and others.

Nikêforos had certainly received a good education in his youth about the dangers of the Imperial Palace. Kônstantinos could no longer use Bardas Fôkas because he had been promoted to the position of *domestikos* and was campaigning against the Saracens (see below). This was not a problem, because Bardas's successor as *megas etaireiarchês* was none other than Basileios Peteinos. However, the list of persons rewarded afterwards makes it clear that Bardas with the forces under his command was firmly behind Kônstantinos VII, as were his sons. In my opinion, it is therefore quite possible that both Nikêforos and Leôn were also enrolled among the *etaireiai*. The account of Theophanes Continuatus makes it clear that the Armenian *Tornikioi* were among the Macedonians of the *megas etaireia* that committed the final overthrow. It is actually likely that the two Fôkades and two Tornikioi served as the four *etaireiarchai* of the four divisions of the *etaireiai*, so Basileios was their *megas etaireiarchês*, or alternatively that the fifth *etaireia*, the *tagma* of *ethnikoi*, had already been formed under an *ethnarchôs*, so that Basileios Peteinos served as commander of the *megas etaireia* of Macedonians, while the two Fôkades and two Tornikioi served as the *etaireiarchai* of the other four *etaireiai*. This would have given Kônstantinos VII full control over the key units after Bardas had left the capital. Whatever the truth, the stage was now set for the final curtain on the Lakapênoi.

According to Skylitzes and Theophanes Continuatus, on 27 January 945 Kônstantinos VII invited both Stefanos and Kônstantinos Lakapênos to a dinner, and when they were at the table both were arrested, removed from the palace and then put aboard a ship and exiled to the Prinkipo Islands. According to Theophanes Continuatus, the two Tournikioi and the *patrikios* Marianos and the rest of the men assigned to the task committed the act. Both brothers were tonsured as clerics and later transferred to other places.

Liudprand of Cremona provides us with a more detailed account of the actual final stage of the plot. According to him, the two Lakapênoi brothers were planning to kill Kônstantinos at their mutual dinner, and they had hidden soldiers in their quarters which would then charge to the table. Liudprand claims that this plan was betrayed to Kônstantinos VII by the commander Diavolinus, who then convinced Kônstantinos to employ Macedonians against the brothers. Liudprand claims that this Diavolinus was both the instigator of all the actions that the brothers had taken and that he was also the man who betrayed them. It would be easy to think that this person would be the Michaêl Diabolinos mentioned by Theophanes Continuatus (p.441) and Leo the Grammarian (p.330), but given the statement that the man in question both guided and betrayed Stefanos it is clear that he is actually Basileios Peteinos and that Kônstantinos VII had been playing the brothers all along. When Kônstantinos then arrived at the planned dinner and the emperors were about to be seated, the Macedonians rushed out from hiding and captured the brothers. Liudprand's account therefore provides us with further details of the events. The security measures of the two brothers were clearly compromised from the start by the fact that they relied on Basileios Peteinos and on the Macedonians loyal to Kônstantinos VII, and as already discussed it is probable that the other commanders were similarly loyal to the Macedonian House.

The overthrow of the Lakapênoi meant the rise of the Fôkades to new heights of influence within the imperial court. The witnessing and being a part of a cabal were undoubtedly valuable experiences for both Nikêforos and his brother Leôn for their future endeavours, which required keen awareness of cloak and dagger politics at the imperial court.

In the meanwhile, the new *domestikos* Bardas Fôkas[25] had continued to exploit the Muslim civil war in late December 944.[26] He passed through the Pass of al-Kankarun between Arabissos and Germanikeia, and his first target of attack was Germanikeia, which he captured. After this, Bardas Fôkas marched along the eastern side of the Amanus Mountains up to the fortress of Bagras/Bagrai just north of Antioch, which the Romans likewise captured. The energetic Jihadist *ghazi* Sayf ad-Dawla had in the meanwhile marched to Aleppo in October 944. Instead of engaging the invaders head on in territory at that time officially belonging to the Ikhshidids of Egypt, he invaded Roman territory and advanced to the region of Arabissos and 'Safsaf' in the theme of Lykandos and was able to post an ambush, presumably in the Pass of al-Kankarun, with the result that he surprised the returning Romans with a night attack in a pass that they thought to be in their own hands. As already discussed, it is likelier that Nikêforos was at the capital rather than accompanying his father, but with the caveat that this alternative cannot be ruled out entirely. It is still possible that Nikêforos accompanied his father and was not present during the final stages of the coup. The Muslims freed the prisoners and retook the booty. Sayf exploited his victory by besieging and capturing an unknown town during the

Roman soldiers (source: Oman)

winter, but he was forced to abandon his campaign in 945 because the Ikhshids dispatched an army under Kafur and Yanis al-Munid to retake Aleppo.[27]

Chapter Five

The Sole Reign of Kônstantinos VII in 945–56, Bardas Fôkas domestikos

5.1. Years 945–7: Securing the Throne and the Rise of the Fôkades[1]

After the brothers Stefanos and Kônstantinos had been exiled, Kônstantinos moved to secure his position. Michaêl the son of Christoforos was stripped of his imperial boots and made a cleric. Rômanos, son of Stefanos, was castrated. Skylitzes (11.3) also claims that Basileios, the son of Rômanos I, was castrated now, but this is a mistake because he was actually castrated in infancy at the orders of his own father Rômanos I Lakapênos, so it is no wonder that Basileios sided with Kônstantinos VII in 944–5 and became his trusted lieutenant.[2] Basileios was initially kept as *prôtobestiarios* of Kônstantinos VII, but promotion was already on the horizon. Then Kônstantinos VII enthroned his own son Rômanos II as emperor in April 945.

According to Skylitzes, Kônstantinos rewarded those who had supported him against the brothers: Bardas Fôkas was appointed *magistros* and *domestikos tôn scholôn*; Nikêforos Fôkas was appointed *stratêgos* of the Anatolikon theme; Leôn Fôkas was appointed *stratêgos* of the Kappadokian theme; Kônstantinos Fôkas was appointed *stratêgos* of the Seleukian theme; Basileios Peteinos was made *megas etaireiarchês*; Marianos Argyros was made *komês tou stablou*; and Manuêl Kourtikios was made *drouggarios tou bigla*. In other words, Kônstantinos VII kept the same men in office as before because these had supported him, while also appointing the three sons of Bardas as *stratêgoi* of *themata*. One may assume that he also retained Kônstantinos Goggylios as *drouggarios tou ploimou*, even if he is not mentioned among the conspirators or rewarded. The Fôkades now held all of the principal military positions in the Empire, while Basileios Peteinos secured the Imperial Palace.

The measures that Kônstantinos VII took to secure his throne did not prevent the forming of plots in support of the Lakapênoi against him. The first of the plots was apparently already hatched in 945[3] by Theofanês the *patrikios* and *parakoimômenos*, the hero of the war against Russia, and Patriarch Theofylaktos. Their co-conspirators included Geôrgios the *prôtospatharios* and cupbearer, and Thomas the *primikêrios*. They sought to bring Rômanos I back to the Palace, but their plot was exposed and the culprits punished, the sole exception being Patriarch Theofylaktos, who was allowed to return to his horses. This obviously referred to Theofylaktos' mania with horses, riding and horse breeding, while also meaning that he kept his position as Patriarch until his death in 956. Kônstantinos VII appointed his *prôtobestiarios* Basileios Lakapênos as *patrikios*, and *parakoimômenos*, and *paradynasteuôn* of the Senate. The last title was unofficial and meant that the person was the imperial favourite who therefore acted as a sort of prime minister/chancellor.

5.2. Kônstantinos VII as Emperor[4]

Skylizes and Theophanes Continuatus provide us with an exellent summary of the personality of Kônstantinos and his style of rule. According to Skylitzes, it was expected that Kônstantinos would be an able and vigorous emperor, but he did not live up to expectations because was too addicted to wine and easy living. This appears to be at least partially true, because he allowed his wife Elenê and Basileios the *parakoimômenos* and *paradynasteuôn* to sell offices in return for money,[5] while making military appointments to anyone who appeared to be immediately available for this, a category which obviously included eunuchs as well – obviously a perceived loyalty towards the emperor was still the most important criteria. In other words, the appointments were not based on birth or merit. Regardless of the selling of offices, Kônstantinos was still lucky in some of his appointments, which included obviously Bardas, Nikêforos and Leôn Fokas and Iôannês Tzimiskês.

Elenê and Basileios had the same father, Rômanos I, but a different mother – the mother of Basileios was a 'Scyth' slave. At some unknown point in time, Kônstantinos appointed Iôsef Briggas as *sakellarios* and after that as *drouggarios tou plôimou*, so that (TC 445) the emperor 'entrusted to him all his powers'.[6] Regardless, Theophanes Continuatus (446–9) still has a very positive view of the manner in which he ruled. According to him, Kônstantinos showed keen interest in the government of the Empire, so that he introduced improvements in the administration while engaging in diplomatic activity with foreign leaders, while also showing a keen interest in what the *stratêgoi*, *prôtonotarioi* and others wrote to him. He regarded the emperor to have been simultaneously an adviser, a mediator, a *stratêgos*, *a stratiôtês*, a *stratiarchos* and an *êgemôn*. The rise of the able Nikêforos Fôkas under the guiding eye of such an emperor is not surprising. Kônstantinos was a learned man who was interested in the fields of science and learning. He promoted all sciences, so he sought out the best scholars in each discipline and appointed these as teachers/professors. He also made the students his table companions and provided them with stipends.

The extant political and military treatises (including those by Kônstantinos himself)[7] prove that Kônstantinos sought out and collected the best military treatises of the past while also producing a policy guide for his son in the form of the *De Administrando Imperio*. At the same time as he did this, he also sought military experts and their advice – it was because of this that he later asked advice from Nikêforos Fôkas about the lack of success of his father Bardas. On the basis of Nikêforos Fôkas' *Praecepta militaria* and *De velitatione*, we know that Nikêforos was a learned man who had read the earlier military treatises and who had also participated in discussions in which such were analysed against contemporary tactics.[8] It is clear that the attention Kônstantinos paid to learning and military science benefited the Roman Empire once the right men were placed in charge in each field, and in the field of military science this meant the promotion of Nikêforos Fôkas to the highest position. In addition to this, Skylitzes and Theophanes Continuatus quite rightly note the role of Kônstantinos VII in the fields of practical arts and handificraft, and his reverent attitude towards God. Both of these were important for the maintenance of morale and loyalty of the subjects. Kônstantinos understood well the importance of being perceived as a just ruler.

5.3. Fighting and Diplomacy in 945–6

In the springtime 945 Sayf defeated the commander of the Egyptian army, the eunuch Kafur, so that he was forced to retreat to Damascus. Sayf followed and captured Damascus in April-May 945 and sent a peace offer to Ikhshids. The Ikshids answered by attacking and defeating Sayf who was forced to flee to Raqqa by the Euphrates in May-June. The Ikhshids entered Aleppo, but did not press their advantage against Sayf and concluded peace with him in October or November 945. The probable reason for Kafur's decisions to conclude peace was that he did not want the Romans to be the real winners of fighting between the Muslims. Sayf was given possession of Aleppo, Hims and Antioch. The pact was sealed with the marriage of the niece of Ikhshid with Sayf.[9] The conclusion of the pact with Ikhshids meant that Sayf ad-Dawla was once again free to resume his campaigns against the infidels in late 946.

According to Miskawayh (Vol.5, 72–3, 85ff.), the emir Tuzun, the Turkish *ghilman* leader at Baghdad, died in the year 334 that began on 13 August 945. This was exploited by the Daylamite brothers belonging to the family named Buyids/Buwayhids. The youngest of the brothers, called Ahmad ibn Buwayhid/Buyid conquered Iraq and placed the Abbasid caliph under his supervision. Ahmad received the title *Mu'izz ad-Dawla* ('Fortifier of the State') while his brother Ali (the eldest brother in Fars) received the title *Imad ad-Dawla* ('Support of the State'), and Hasan (capital at Rayy) the *Iqab Rukn ad-Dawla* ('Pillar of the State'). In these circumstances the Turkish *ghilman* joined the Hamdanid emir of Mosul, Nasir ad-Dawla. It was with their help that Nasir sought to regain the highest position in Baghdad, so he marched against Mu'izz ad-Dawlah on 2 April 946. In other words, Nasir was in no position to support his brother Sayf ad-Dawla against the Romans or Egyptians. The Turkish *ghilman* were naturally very eager to fight on behalf of Nasir against their archenemies the Daylamites. Nasir ad-Dawla actually managed to capture Bahgdad, but was then beaten back. This, however, happened only in 335 (2 Aug. 946–22 July 947). Nasir ad-Dawlah sued for peace without the approval of his Turkish mercenaries, which resulted in their mutiny and the weakening of Nasir's position to such an extent that Nasir needed help from the Buyids to crush the Turks. Thereafter, the relationship between the Buyids of Iraq and Hamdanids of Jazira (Nasir ad-Dawla) remained tense, with the Buyids launching periodical attacks to regain control of Jazira, but only with the result that Nasir ad-Dawla still managed to retain his independence for most of the time, even if he was also periodically forced to pay tribute to the Buyids. The war against the Romans was left in the hands of Sayf ad-Dawla.

The troubles of Sayf ad-Dawla had meant that Kônstantinos VII was free to pursue his own political goals while the troubles lasted. This meant the sending of envoys to Otto I and Berengar of Ivrea (he defeated Hugh of Provence in 945 and gained control of Italy) to suggest an alliance, while envoys were also sent to the emir of Tarsus and Ikshid of Egypt to discuss the exchange of prisoners. Therefore, the emperor had dispatched Iôannês Kourkouas as an envoy to the emir of Tarsus in 945. The negotiations took a while to complete and were complicated by the death of the first Ikhshidid ruler on 11 July 946. The eunuch Kafur led his army back to Egypt. En route, in Palestine Kafur handed Ibn Abd-al-Baqi 30,000 dinars for the exchange of prisoners. Sayf ad-Dawla decided to join the exchange and gave 80,000 dinars to Nasr al-Tamali for the purchase of prisoners. The two sides decided to conduct the exchange of prisoners at Lamas in October 946. The Roman envoys at the meeting were Iôannês Kourkouas and *magistros* Kosmas.[10]

5.4. Nikêforos Fôkas as *stratêgos* of the Anatolikon *thema* in 945–56

The narrative sources do not give any detailed account of the fighting between Nikêforos Fôkas and the Saracens after his appointment as *stratêgos* of the Anatolikon *thema* in 945, but we know on the basis of the *De velitatione bellica* (*Peri paradromês / Skirmishing*) that Nikêforos Fôkas used the guerrilla tactics described in that treatise and that he used the skirmishing tactics 'thousands of times' as *stratêgos* and that he repeatedly routed his foes and destroyed huge armies with these methods.[11] In practice this means – assuming at most two to three enemy raids per year on average with no enemy raids in some years[12] – that Nikêforos engaged the raiding Saracens about twenty to thirty times during his term as *stratêgos* of the Anatolikon, in addition to his participation in the major campaigns under his father. These methods are described in detail in Appendix 2, and the reader should imagine Nikêforos employing these almost yearly between the years 945 and 956. The reason why the narrative sources fail to mention this is that the fighting along the frontier of the *Anatolikon* theme was endemic and typically involved only the forces of the Anatolikon theme, with possible reinforcements from the neighbouring themes, and on the Saracen side the forces of the emir of Tarsus with possible reinforcements from the Muslim jihadist forces. During this period the Muslim and Roman sources usually pay attention only to the raids conducted by the emir of

Aleppo because these were typically the main attacks conducted by the Saracens. In fact, the best evidence of the extremely successful defence of the Anatolikon theme against the emir of Tarsus is precisely the silence of the sources, and in particular the silence of the Muslim sources. The Muslim sources tend to record only the successful operations of the emir of Tarsus, as they do for example for the years 927 and 931[13] and since no such successes are recorded for the term of Nikêforos, there are unlikely to have been any, just as the *De velitatione* states. Nikêforos defeated the emir of Tarsus with such a devastating success rate that only the forces of Sayf ad-Dawla threatened Roman interests. In the following discussion, I will therefore concentrate on an attempt to trace the other possible campaigns in which Nikêforos may have been present – for example it is clear that he accompanied his father at least in 950 and 951.

It should also be noted that as *patrikios kai stratêgos tôn Anatolikôn* Nikêforos held the highest position in the official military hierarchy, just above his father the *domestikos tôn scholôn*, even if in practice the *domestikos* acted as supreme commander. This means that it is very likely that Nikêforos participated in most of the sessions in which the emperor discussed the military strategy with his military advisors. In most cases we do not possess any direct evidence of this, but this is still obvious on the basis of Nikêforos' position and on the basis of the fact that both Psellos and Zonaras specifically note that the emperor asked Nikêforos directly why his father had been so successful as a *stratêgos*, but was so unsuccessful as *domestikos*.[14] In short, one may assume that Nikêforos was actively participating in most if not all of the important meetings in which the emperor formulated imperial diplomacy and military strategy together with Bardas. Hence there is every reason to include also a discussion of the general diplomacy and strategy of the years when Nikêforos served only as a *stratêgos* of the Anatolikon. It is clear that Nikêforos contributed to both.

The key reasons for the success of Nikêforos Fôkas as a *stratêgos* were the same that Eric McGeer (1995, 326–7) has listed for him as emperor on the basis of Leo the Deacon's depiction. Nikêforos was able to instill the discipline among his forces so necessary for his tactics to succeed thanks to the fact he was a heroic figure, much like Iôannês Tzimiskês. Nikêforos was known for his martial prowess in combat and in duels, his quick thinking and intellect, austerity, religiosity, incorruptibility, and for his physical strength. It was because of this that his soldiers adored him and were ready to follow him anywhere.

5.5. The Campaigns of Sayf ad-Dawla against the Romans in late 946 and against the Egyptians in 947

In the meanwhile, Sayf ad-Dawla exploited both the distraction caused by the negotiations and exchange of prisoners and the disorder in the Ikshidid realm. According to al-Makin (year 335, 2 Aug. 946 - 22 July 947), Sayf ad-Dawla marched against the Roman fortress Hisn Ziyad, which is another name for the fortress of Harput (Harpoot) east of Melitene. The fortress was probably the headquarters of the *thema* of Hanzit, which was located east of Melitene between the rivers Euphrates and Arsanias/Murat Su,[15] so it must have been formed after the conquest of the Emirate of Melitene in 934. Sayf's attack did not come as a surprise because the *domestikos* Bardas Fôkas engaged him there but was severely defeated, losing 20,000 killed and 2,000 captured according to al-Makin. Al-Makin does not mention the fate of the fortress, but it is quite possible that Sayf captured it thanks to his victory.[16] It is unlikely that Bardas was accompanied by his sons, because their *themata* were located in another section of the frontier, where the exchange of prisoners took place. The location was the border between Rome and Islam, the River Lamos (modern Limonlu) in Cilicia, which is located between Seleukeia and Mersin/Mersine. It is very likely that the forces of the neighbouring *themata*, Seleukeia, Anatolikon and Kappadokia, were retained in readiness here and did not accompany Bardas.

According to the *De velitatione* (D 20.50ff.; DM 20.7), every time when Ali son of Hamdan (i.e. Sayf ad-Dawla) invaded Roman territory, the *stratêgos* of Lykandos and other frontier themes invaded the territory around Aleppo and Antioch. I would suggest that this also took place now and was one of the reasons, if not the principal reason, for the fast withdrawal of Sayf ad-Dawla from Roman territory. The *stratêgos* in question would have been either the famous Armenian prince Melias (Mleh the Great), or his similarly-named son or grandson Melias who became *domestikos* under Iôannês I Tzimiskês, the latter being likelier. This Melias appears to have continued to perform similar diversionary operations against Sayf ad-Dawla every time the latter invaded Roman territory, at least until his capture by the Arabs at the Battle of Hadath in 954, if he indeed was the man who was captured there.[17] And, if he was captured at that battle by the Arabs, it is not known when he was ransomed and released from captivity. The problem is exacerbated by the fact that it is possible that the man captured was Melias the Elder, who was then succeeded by Melias the Younger, who would then have followed a similar strategy against the Arabs in the following years.

After this it was time for Sayf to march against the Egyptians. In spring 947 Sayf appears to have captured Damascus, after which he marched to Palestine. The inhabitants of Damascus appealed to Kafur, who marched against Sayf and inflicted a crushing defeat on him. Sayf evacuated Damascus and fled to Aleppo. He attacked Damascus again, but was defeated again and now had to abandon Aleppo and flee all the way to Raqqa. Kafur captured Aleppo in June–July and left Yanis al-Munisi in command. In October–November 947 Sayf attacked and recaptured Aleppo. The two sides then renegotiated new terms of peace, which this time gave Sayf ad-Dawla control of Damascus. Sayf exploited the situation by placing several members of his family in key positions, and then resumed his interrupted war against the Romans in 948.[18]

5.6. Policy of Appeasement towards Russia and Hungary in 946–7

Kônstantinos VII Porfyrogênnetos followed the standard Roman foreign policy of trying to convert the pagans to Christianity in order to bring them into the same Christian community ruled by the emperor and the Patriarch of Constantinople. Hungary and Russia were the objects of this effort. Kônstantinos sought to exploit the peace that had been concluded with Russia in 944/5 and the peace with Hungary in 943 to make certain that these would no longer invade the Roman Empire. Kônstantinos followed a policy of appeasement towards both.

After the conclusion of the peace between Rome and Russia in 945 the Western and Eastern Churches appear to have competed over influence in Russia, but the question of how this happened is contested. The dating depends on how one dates the trip or the two trips of Olga to Constantinople, and the dating depends on the information given by Kônstantinos, which fits both 946 and 957. If she visited only once in 946–7, the Orthodox Church had a head start; but if she visisted only in 957, then the Western Church was the first to seek the conversion of Russia. The reason for this conclusion is that several sources claim that Olga had been Christian for 15 years before her death in 969, which dates the conversion to the period before Olga's trip to Constantinople in September to October 957 (one of the possible dates in Kônstantinos VII's *De Ceremoniis*). On the basis of this, it has been suggested that Olga actually originally adopted the Latin rite. If true, I suspect that this was the result of the reorganization of the church structures by Otto I the Great in eastern Francia. However, if she visited Constantinople twice, first in 946–7 and then again in 957, the question remains open and depends upon which visit she was baptized, even if the latter date appears likelier for the reasons given in the discussion below.[19]

Whatever the date, Olga appears to have preferred closer relations with Constantinople, so when she visited in person the city of Constantinople, either in 946–7 or 957, she sought to be baptized. According to multiple sources, while staying in the city Olga was converted to Christianity by the Patriarch and emperor in person. According to the *Chronicle of Nestor*, the reason for this was that Kônstantinos was both amazed by the beauty and intellect of Olga, so he wanted to marry her. Being a clever woman Olga asked Kônstantinos VII to baptize her with the assistance of the Patriarch, which made Olga daughter of Kônstantinos and thereby ineligible to be the wife of Kônstantinos. Whatever the truth of this account, it is clear that Olga was now baptized into the eastern rite because so many sources attest to this event, and that the emperor Kônstantinos treated Olga in a manner that angered her. Kônstantinos, however, appears not to have understood his mistake and thought that the two sides had concluded an alliance, according to which the Romans gave money to the Russians while the Russians would send slaves, wax, furs and soldiers for Kônstantinos. The last detail proves that the Russians/Varangians were held in very high esteem as soldiers. If the conversion is dated to 946–7, then the request to include this clause was undoubtedly made by

Bardas Fôkas who had personal experience of fighting against the Russians, but if it took place in 957 it is possible that Nikêforos Fôkas was the man behind the request for Varangian mercenaries.

When Olga had then returned to Kiev, the emperor dispatched an envoy to ask for the fulfilment of the terms of the agreement, which Olga answered that she would fulfil if the emperor would spend as long a time with her in the Pochayna (stream below the heights of the old city of Kiev) as she had stayed in Constantinople. This and the following events prove that Kônstantinos had indeed insulted Olga during her stay and the marriage proposal can indeed have been such a slur on her honour. It was after this, in 959, that Olga asked Otto I of Francia to send her priests and a bishop. This implies that the conversion took place in 957 rather than in 946–7. If she visited Constantinople in 946–7 she did it for other reasons (e.g. to clarify the terms of the 945 treaty). I have included this discussion here only because Skylitzes places her visit and conversion to this year and the evidence for the dating of the conversion and trips is not secure.[20]

In the course of the years 945 and 959 Kônstantinos appears to have sent several conciliatory letters to the princes of Hungary. The fact that he addressed the letters to 'The Princes' (*De Cerimoniis* 46, p.691) means either that the power of the Arpad dynasty had weakened in relation to the other houses or that Kônstantinos sought to sow disagreement between those by favouring the native Magyar princes (*gyla* and *karchas*) over the Kabarian *megas archôn*. In 946–7 his policy appeared to have worked, because Boulosoudes (Boultzous, *karchas* of DAI 40.66–8, the third in the hierarchy) visited Constantinople to be baptized by the emperor himself. Kônstantinos therefore honoured him with the patrician rank and gifts and dispatched him back home. The news travelled fast, because next Gylas (*gyla* of DAI 40.66–8 = Gyula) came to Constantinople in 947(?) to obtain baptism and the same honours and gifts. He remained loyal to his new faith and no longer invaded the Roman Empire, while also ransoming Christians captured by others. However, Boulosoudes/Boultzous *karchas* had apparently violated his promises already in 948 and several times after that. He did the same also against the Franks, but was defeated and captured at the Battle of Lechfeld in 955 after which Otto I impaled him.[21]

5.7. The Lakapênos conspiracy in 947[22]

In 947 Leôn Kladon, Gregorios of Macedonia, Theodosios (head groom of Stefanos), and Iôannês raiktôr formed a plot to bring Stefanos from his place of exile in Mytilene back to the palace. The plan was revealed by Michaêl Diabolinos,[23] with the result that the conspirators had their noses and ears split, together with a thorough beating, followed by a parade on asses through the city. In the second year of his exile, in other words in 947, Kônstantinos Lakapênos rebelled and killed one of his guards, *prôtospatharios* Nikêtas, and was executed. It is probable that he had also been informed of the plot against Kônstantinos VII and was attempting to break free at the same time as the plotters would have launched their operation. His father Rômanos died on 16 June 948, while his brother Stefanos survived for 19 years.

5.8. Kônstantinos VII Correcting the Abuses of the *dynatoi* in 947–8

The text of Theophanes Continuatus (443–4) and the extant but undated '*Novel E*' prove that Kônstantinos VII Porfyrogênnetos was aware of the plight of the taxpayers in the *themata*.

Theophanes Continuatus claims:

> 'The emperor remembered well the injustices and injury that the miserable ill-fated poor had suffered at the hands of the *stratêgoi, prôtonotarioi, stratiôtai* and *ippotoi* in the time of his father-in-law Rômanos, and he dispatched pious and virtuous men to ease the great burden of the unwarranted requirements imposed upon the depraved poor at that time. He dispatched the *magistros* Rômanos Sarônites to the Anatolikon *thema*, the *magistros* Rômanos Mouseles to the Opsikion *thema*, *patrikios* Fôtios to the Thrakesion *thema*, Leôn Agelastos to the Armeniakon *thema*, and others to the rest of the *themata* in succession. Being instructed to do so by the emperor, they granted a small relief for the oppressed.'
>
> TC 443, translation based on the ed. and tr. of Sullivan and tr. of McGeer.

Both Denis Sullivan (RFNF, 19, 21) and Eric McGeer (2000, 68–76) date the above event and '*Novel E*' on the basis of the referral to the multitude of returning prisoners to their patrimonial soil ('*Novel E*' 3.1) to have taken place after the exchange of prisoners with the Arabs in Lamas in October 946. McGeer goes on to suggest that the Novel was drafted by Theodôros Dekapolitês, and so would have been issued either in 947 or 948 – he would therefore have succeeded Theofilos as *quaestor* either in 947 or 948. The Novel in question first set the minimum inalienable value of military lands at four pounds of gold for the *stratiôtai* (cavalry) and at two pounds for sailors. In the second portion it was stated that the owners were to pass this same amount of military lands to their natural heirs together with the military duties. The third section addressed the question of corrupt practices by the *dynatoi*. In cases in which the holders of the *stratiôtika ktêmata* had been forced to surrender their properties to the *dynatoi*, the emperor required that these were to be returned to their rightful owners. The emperor also put a stop to the practice of the *stratêgoi* demanding money from the owners of military land in return for avoiding military service.

As is clear and has been recognized for a long time, the principal aim in the sending of the officials to the *themata* were twofold: the tax relief to the poor who had been oppressed by the military, and the restoration of military lands to their rightful owners with the duties involved. If Bardas Fôkas had served as a *stratêgos* of the Anatolikon just before 941, it is clear that he was one of the persons who had caused such problems for the taxpayers before his appointment to the higher offices. However, I would suggest that there may also have been another source of motivation for the sending of the officials and legislation when one notes the first place where the officials were sent. Nikêforos Fôkas had been appointed as *stratêgos* of the *thema* of the *Anatolikon* and it was his *thema* that was among the first visited. If he was already following the policy for which he became famous as a *stratêgos*, namely the exaction of military service from greater numbers of people with fewer resources, it is possible that his *thema* was among the first to be targeted because his policies would have caused an inordinate amount of suffering. The setting of the value of inalienable military land for the cavalry *stratiôtai* at four pounds of gold by Kônstantinos VII may also have had the secondary intention of making it clear to the *stratêgoi* that they could not demand cavalry service or money from men who had less land than this – and as we shall see, when Nikêforos became emperor he did that and demanded cavalry service from those who were required to perform only infantry service. I would indeed suggest that Nikêforos was already seeking to increase the size of the army under his command with the measure mentioned, and that Kônstantinos' Novel prevented this. Whatever the truth, on the basis of the outstanding combat performance of the forces serving under the *stratêgos* Nikêforos, it is clear that his *stratiôtai* did not see themselves oppressed, even if the inspectors visited his *thema* among the first. The *De velitatione* of Nikêforos Fôkas (see Appendix 2) specifically noted that the *stratiôtai* of the *themata* were not to be fleeced, oppressed or ill-treated, while the unknown editor of the same text notes that the *stratiôtai* of Nikêforos fought well under him. It is therefore probable that while Nikêforos probably required the thematic soldiers under him to perform service at the higher pay grade, he also allowed them to do so with less expensive gear. This, however, is just my educated guess based on the *Praecepta militaria* of Nikêforos Fôkas, which allowed the use of ersatz armour by the *stratiôtai*, while also limiting the number of horsemen required to be equipped as *katafraktoi*. One can actually think that this was seen favourably by the former footsoldiers who were now allowed to fight as cavalry, which was possible because they were not required to carry the full panoply of gear still demanded in the *Sylloge tacticorum* of Leôn the Wise (see Chapter 6 with Appendix 1).

5.9. Sayf ad-Dawla and Romans Resume their Hostilities in 948

In spring 948 the Romans launched yet another strike against Sayf ad-Dawla in Syria at a time when he appears to have faced a revolt by the Kurds under Abu Taglib al-Kurdi in the fortress of Barzuyah (north of Apamea in the valley of Orontes in the mountain chain between Tripoli and Antioch). One wonders if the

Romans had had a role in the revolt or if they knew of it. Whatever the truth, the timing of the Roman raid was perfect, even if the execution left a lot to be desired, as we shall see. The Romans managed to capture booty in the form of men and women, after which they turned around. Sayf, who was in Aleppo, reacted quickly and gave pursuit and killed most of the Romans, so managing to release all of the Muslim captives. After this, Sayf marched against the Kurdish rebels and put the fortress of Barzuyah under siege, which lasted until either late-948 or into the first half of 949. This is unfortunately all that we know of the Roman raid on the basis of Dahabi and al-Mahasin.[24]

The details suggest that the campaign was launched by a *stratêgos* of a theme facing Syria, and not by the *domestikos* Bardas Fôkas. In light of the fact that the emir of Tarsus did not engage the invaders, it is very unlikely that the *stratêgoi* of Seleukeia (Kônstantinos Fôkas), Anatolikon (Nikêforos Fôkas), or Kappadokia (Leôn Fôkas) would have been involved,[25] which means that the possible candidates for the invading *stratêgos* are the *stratêgoi* of Lykandos, Kharsianon, Sebasteia and Mesopotamia. Indeed, it is probable that this was one of the campaigns launched by Melias, the Armenian *stratêgos* of Lykandos (DV 20.7).

Later in the same year the *stratêgos* of Kappadokia, Leôn Fokas, took advantage of the absence of Sayf, who was still besieging Barzuyah, and marched against al-Hadat/Hadath/Adata, which was a strategically important fortress at ca. 1,000 m altitude on the southern feet of the Taurus-Antitaurus range. It was located at the southwest end of the Pass of Hadath/Adata and at the crossroads between Marash/Germanikeia and Malatya/Melitene. The exact location, however, is not known, but the accompanying maps in the maps section show the likely location. The population of Hadath pleaded for help from Sayf, but the latter was unable to come to their assistance because the siege of Barzuyah required his full attention. Consequently, Hadath surrendered to Leôn, who then levelled its walls. The fortress of Barzuyah in its turn surrendered to Sayf at some point in time between 11 July 948 and 30 June 949.[26]

Even if the extant sources fail to mention any activity for Nikêforos for this year, the circumstantial evidence (Romans launching an offensive against Tarsus in 949) suggests that while Leôn was besieging Hadath, Nikêforos was fighting defensive guerrilla warfare very successfully against Saracen raiders which the *De velitatione* (D Preface 42ff.) claimed him to have done against the invaders 'thousands of times'. The enemy he faced would have consisted of the forces of the emir of Tarsus and the results of the success of this year would be visible in 949 (see below).

5.10. The Roman Offensive in the East in 949

The Romans appear to have envisaged a massive and resolute offensive against the Muslims in the eastern half of the Mediterranean for the year 949. The main objective of the offensive was the recapture of the island of Crete from the Saracens, with three other invasions launched against the cities of Tarsus, Germanikeia (Marash) and Karin (Theodosioupolis, Erzurum, Qaliqala). It is probable that the planning process for the offensives against Crete and the 'Cilician' Arabs was started early during the sole reign of Kônstantinos VII Porfyrogennêtos. However, it is still likely that the simultaneous triple offensive by the Fôkades against the Hamdanids exploited their troubles with the Buyids.

Mu'izz ad-Dawla, the Buyid emir of emirs (sultan) in Baghdad, had decided to annex the territory of Nasir ad-Dawla. He started his campaign between 4 March and 2 April 949 and marched towards Mosul. Nasir fled to Nisibis while calling for his brother Sayf ad-Dawla to help him. Sayf acted as asked and departed Aleppo between 2 May and 31 May 949, but then turned back before reaching Raqqa when he was informed that Nasir and Mu'izz ad-Dawla had reached an agreement, according to which Nasir would pay tribute to Mu'izz. The reason for the change of heart was that the brother of Mu'izz was facing troubles in Khorasan, Gurgan and Azerbaijan and had pleaded for help from Mu'izz.[27] It was then because of this that Sayf ad-Dawla was able to turn his army against Leôn Fôkas, who was besieging Germanikeia.

The attack against Tarsus would have been the duty of Nikêforos Fôkas, who was the *stratêgos* of the neighbouring Roman province Anatolikon, even if this is not mentioned by either Bar Hebraeus or Miskawayh. On the basis of the *De velitatione*, it is very likely that the ability of Nikêforos to launch this offensive resulted from the very successful defence of his own province against the emir of Tarsus in 948. Leôn Fôkas in his turn would have exploited the successful destruction of the fortress of Hadath in 948, which opened up the route from the Pass of Hadath to Germanikeia while allowing him to block the supply route to the city of Germanikeia from the south. The previous ravaging of the territory also eased the siege of Germanikeia in another way, by diminishing the availability of supplies and men. The name of the commander who led the army against Karin is not known with certainty, because the Muslim sources do not name him, while Stephen of Taron states only that the commander of the Karin army was *domestikos Č'mškik* (this would be Tzimiskês, who was not yet the *domestikos*) and that his young grandson *Kiwr̀-Žan* [*Kur(ios) Iôannês*] carried out many feats of daring in the course of the campaign. The latest translator of Stephen of Taron, Tim Greenwood (pp.203–1), suggests that the commander was Theofilos Kourkouas,[28] the grandfather of Iôannês Tzimiskês, or that Stephen of Taron has misidentified the commander. It is indeed possible that Stephen of Taron has mixed up his sources and names, but I would still suggest that the overall commander was actually the *domestikos* Bardas Fôkas, because the mother of Iôannês Tzimiskês was the daughter of Bardas Fôkas (and the sister of Nikêforos Fôkas), so he was also the grandson of Bardas Fôkas and not only of Theofilos, and that the young Iôannes Tzimiskês served under Bardas. However, I would also suggest that Theofilos Kourkouas accompanied them, because he was nominated *stratêgos* of Karin (DAI 43–6) after the campaign.[29] These three Roman invasions of Saracen Cilicia and Armenia were undoubtedly meant to tie up the resources of the Muslim emirs of Tarsus, Aleppo and Karin so that they would not be able to provide any assistance for the Saracen defenders of Crete.[30]

It is certain that Bardas Fôkas and his sons Nikêforos and Leôn were all present at the court when the emperor and his advisors laid out their campaign plans for the year 949, because such a process definitely included the *domestikos* Bardas, and the *stratêgoi* Nikêforos and Leôn who were put in charge of the land operations in the east, and Kônstantinos Goggylês in charge of the amphibious landing on Crete. It is clear that Nikêforos would have had a chance of influencing the overall strategy while also learning more about the imperial strategy in the Mediterranean region, including its naval aspects. This experience would come in handy later when Nikêforos was himself put in charge of the invasion of the island of Crete in 960.

This was also one of the instances in which Kônstantinos VII Porfyrogennêtos made military appointments solely on the basis of the person's closeness to the emperor, the other possibility being that the emperor did not trust anyone with naval experience to take charge of the operations because he feared that these might be loyal towards the Lakapênoi. Whatever the reason, he appointed an effeminate eunuch of the bedchamber from Paphlagonia called Kônstantinos Goggylios (Goggylês) in charge of the naval expedition. He held the dignity of *patrikios* as a sign of his position.

The first to invade enemy territory in spring 949 appears to have been Leôn Fôkas. His target was the city of Germanikeia (Marash). There were three routes that he could have taken to the city. He could have used the two roads from the north, either by using the road from Kukusos to Germanikeia or the road from Plasta/Lykandos to Germanikeia, but I would suggest that he used the more easterly route leading through the Pass of Hadath that he had opened in the previous year. By using this route, he would have made it difficult for the defenders of Germanikeia to detect his approach while he would have also blocked the enemy's supply route from the south-east. We can calculate the approximate size of the army led by Leôn Fôkas against the city of Germanikeia/Marash on the basis of the length of the siege works which were located at a minimum distance of two bowshots (660 m) away from the walls. See the accompanying map of the siege. The length of the inner siege wall was circa 9,500 metres, which means that there were a minimum of 9,500 hoplites and 9,500 light infantry for a total of 19,000 infantry (assuming two men per metre: DRM 1, 21; see the discussion below) manning the walls, in addition to which came the reserves, servants and cavalry. This figure corresponds almost exactly with the figures given by the *Sylloge tacticorum* (see Appendix 1: 4) for the largest combined cavalry and infantry army given by that treatise, which encompassed 26,184 men in total, of whom 19,414 were infantry and 6,770 cavalry. One may therefore make the educated guess that this was indeed the army fielded by Leôn Fôkas, even if it is still possible that he had a larger force because the city of Germanikeia definitely had a sizeable population, even after its pillage by the forces of Bardas Fôkas in 945.

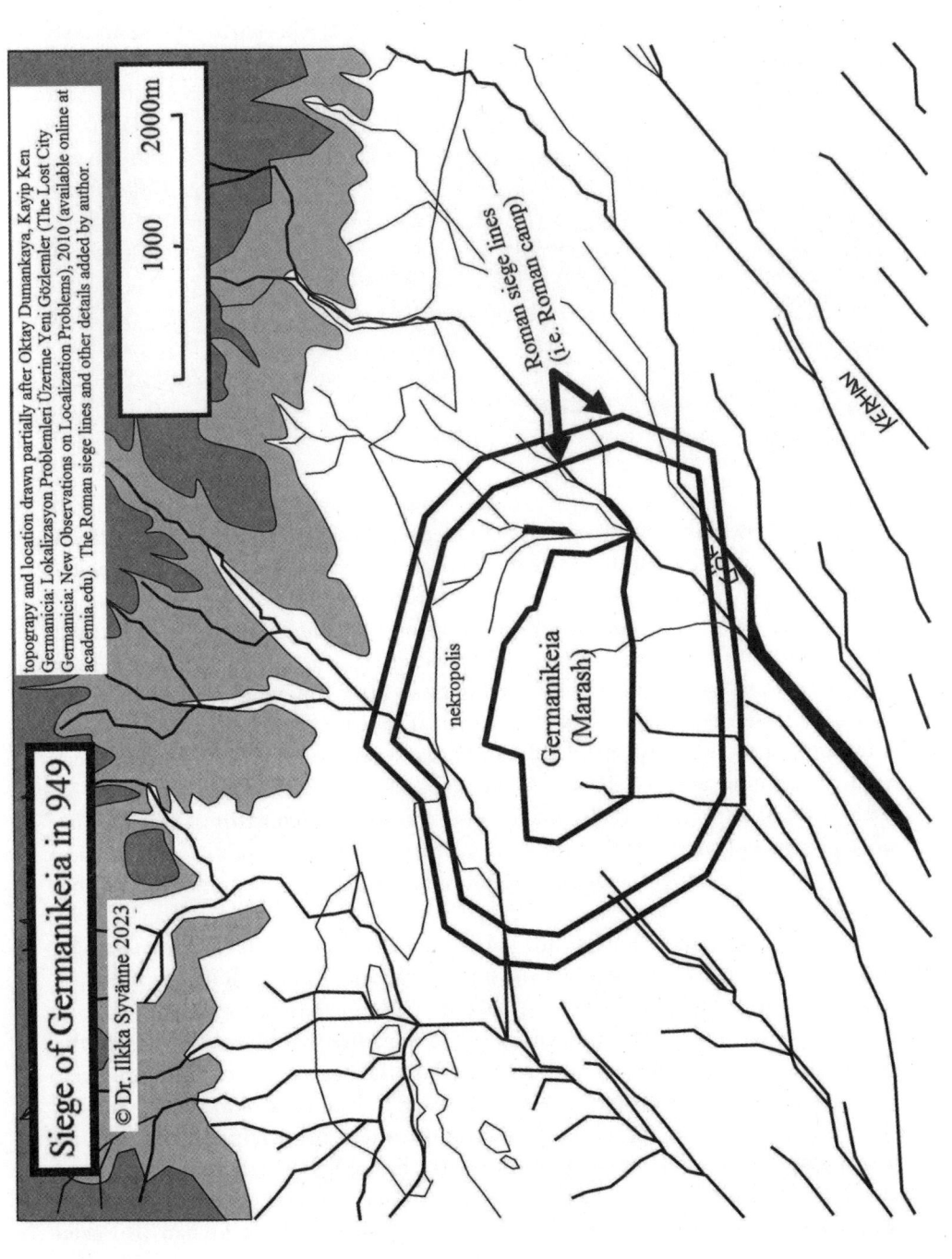

19th century drawing of Marash / Germanikeia (public domain)

Sayf ad-Dawla's response was to march against Leôn, but the latter inflicted a crushing defeat on Sayf at the Battle of Marash (Germanikeia) at some point in time in late-May to early-June, so that Sayf was forced to retreat all the way to Aleppo. I would suggest that in this case Sayf had probably brought with him a sizeable force in order to relieve the city, so Leôn was actually forced to abandon the siege temporarily and build a new camp further away, after which he fought a battle by using the tactics described in the ST or the DV and LT.[31] According to Kamal ad-Din, the victory over Sayf enabled Leôn Fôkas to capture the city of Germanikeia, while Nikêforos captured Tarsus.[32] The walls of Germanikeia were demolished. The defeat of Sayf ad-Dawla by the forces of Leôn Fôkas (consisting probably only of the Kappadokian *stratiôtai* with reinforcements from the neighbouring themes) was a major achievement and an excellent example of the outstanding generalship of Leôn.

Since this was an offensive into Muslim Cilicia in which the purpose was to capture a heavily fortified city, it is probable that Nikêforos Fôkas used the marching and combat methods described in the *Sylloge tacticorum* (Appendix I). or in his *Praecepta militaria* (see later), but it is likelier that he was now using the former which he would then have reformed on the basis of his own experiences. In other words, it is probable that once past the Cilician Gates in Roman hands, the army assumed the marching formation in which the infantry was deployed as a hollow square and cavalry in depth with the wedge of *katafraktoi* posted in the first line. In light of the fact that Nikêforos had detailed instructions for the way this kind of army was to be used in battle, it is likely that he had also used the battle formation in practice. Therefore, it is also probable that he fought a battle on this occasion, as implied for example by Ibn al-Athir's account (BELA 2, 159), before putting the city of Tarsus under siege.

There are two different ways for estimating the size of the army that Nikêforos led against Tarsus. The first is to assume that he led an army similar to the one he described in the PM, and the other is to estimate the necessary size on the basis of the force needed to besiege the city of Tarsus if it was done by the book as described in the DRM (see Appendix 4). If the size of the army that Nikêforos led was as in his model army in the PM, then he had about 5,568–6,008 horsemen plus the bodyguards, and an infantry force of 11,200 *oplitai*, and 4,800 *psiloi/toxotai*, plus unknown numbers of specialist units like Russians, bodyguards, artillerymen and siege engineers. For the details, see Appendix 3. The key pieces of information in the DRM (1, 21) are: 1) in the marching camp there were to be two hoplites for each *orguia* (1.87 m), behind whom were equal numbers of javelineers and archers; 2) the shape of the siege camp was a circle around the enemy fortifications, so the inner wall (contravallation) was placed two bowshots or more from the enemy wall. In the context of the siege of Tarsus this means that the inner wall (circumference ca. 7,226.6 m) was to possess a minimum of 7,200 (rounded down) hoplites (assumption being one hoplite per metre) and 7,200 javelineers, slingers and archers for a total of 14,400 footmen, while the outer wall (circumvallation) would have required 16,338 men so that the entire length of the siege works would have required almost 31,000 footmen. However, even if the DRM fails to state this, I am assuming that when the Romans employed the double wall during a siege that they did not necessarily use the regular system for both walls, but rather a reduced version of it (e.g. one soldier per *orguia*), who could then be reinforced from the unattached soldiers, cavalry, servants and bodyguards, or from the soldiers posted to protect the other wall, if subjected to an attack. In short, it is quite possible or even likely that the army that Nikêforos Fôkas describes in the PM was roughly of the same size as the forces that he led as a *stratêgos* of the Anatolian theme against Tarsus. The same would be true of the armies that marched against the cities of Germanikeia and Karin.

The siege procedures followed by Nikêforos during his siege of Tarsus would have followed the standard tactics of posting the Roman force as a circle around the city with a double wall, so the Romans would have employed all of the siege techniques at their disposal. See the map on the next page. We do not know how the siege ended (assault, or surrender, or negotiated surrender?) and whether it involved negotiations, but it is clear that it involved the demolishing of its defences. This question receives further attention in the context of the events of the next year, 950.

After his retreat to Aleppo, Sayf appears to have learnt of the Roman advance under Bardas Fôkas against the city of Karin (Qaliqala) because he left Muhammad b. Nasir ad-Dawla in charge of Aleppo while he marched to Mayyafariqin. The Romans captured the city of Karin on 1 *Rabi* (28 August–27 September 949) and demolished its walls. We can calculate the approximate minimum size of the Roman force required to besiege Karin also on the basis of the information provided by the

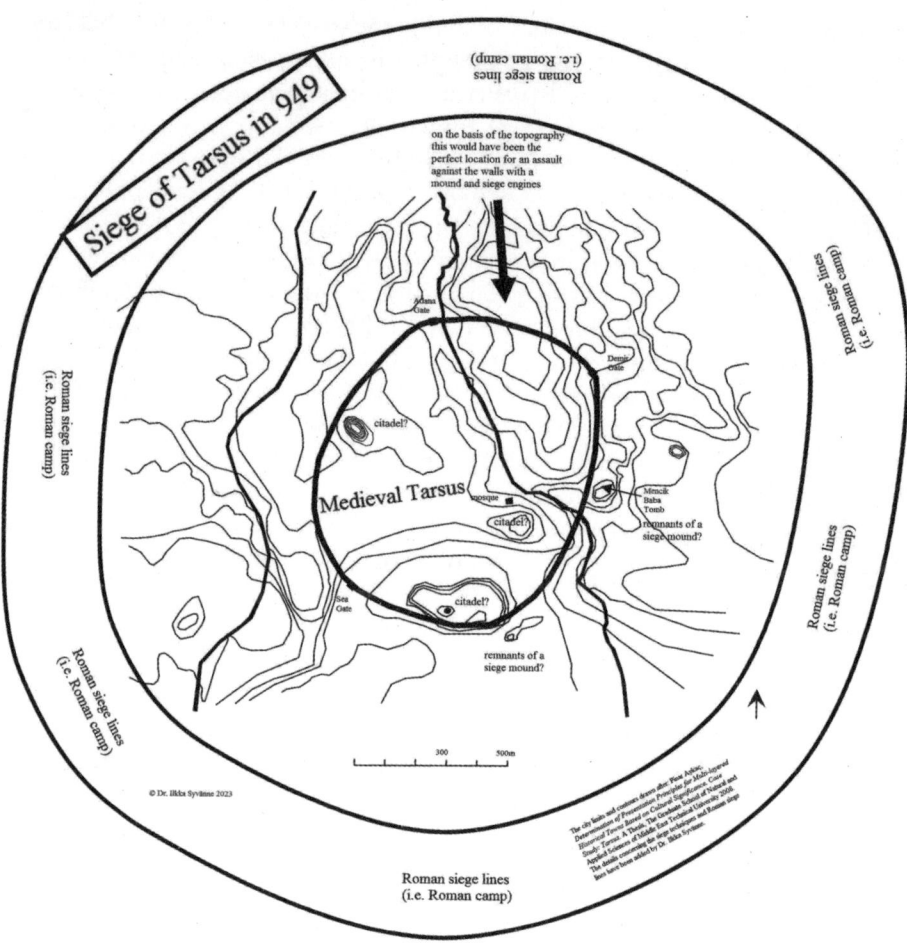

DRM. When the circumference of the inner wall was approximately 6,284 metres, there would have been at least approximately 6,284 hoplites and 6,284 light-armed for a total of 12,586 infantry, plus the reserves, servants, artillerymen and cavalry. See the map on page 140 of the siege of Karin. It is possible that Sayf arrived too late to relieve the city, or that he did not think it possible to do so in the aftermath of his defeat at Germanikeia/Marash. Sayf clearly settled on the defence of the Emirate of Mayyafariqin (Martyropolis) and did not seek to protect the other Arab emirates that were officially part of Armenia. This meant the end of the Arab Emirate of Qaliqala, which was now annexed into the Roman Empire.

The absence of Sayf was exploited by Leôn Fôkas, who besieged Bouqa/Buqa/Baqa, a fortified city/town close to the city of Antioch. Muhammad b. Nasir ad-Dawla, the emir of Antioch, marched against him, but was defeated with heavy losses in 338 (1 July 949–19 June 950), with the implication that this took place

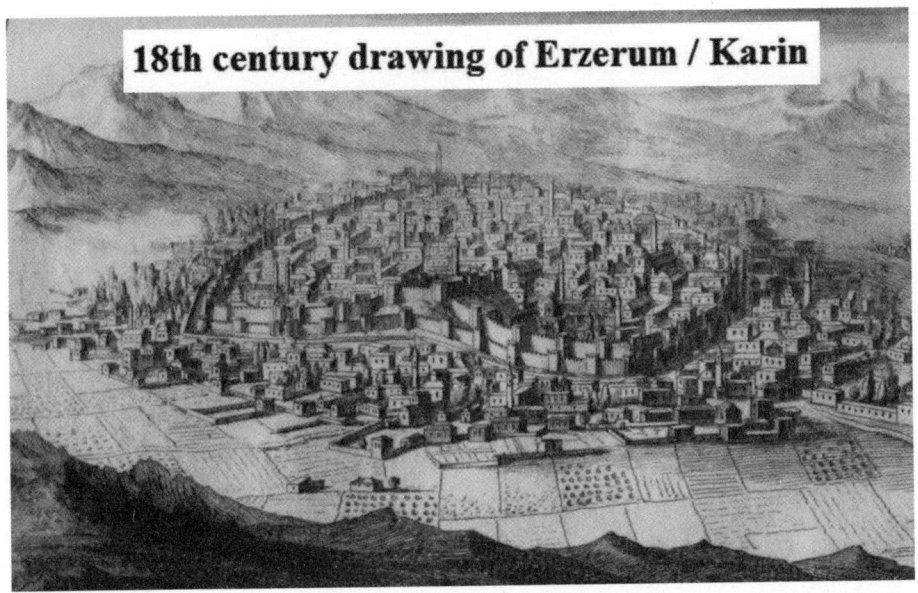

18th century drawing of Erzerum / Karin

probably in late summer or early fall 949, rather than in early 950. Even if Kamal al-Din implies that Tarsus fell simultaneously with Germanikeia, it is probable that the siege of Tarsus lasted longer, until late summer, because it was Leôn alone who advanced against Bouqa.

The brothers Leôn and Nikêforos and the unknown commander in charge of the siege of Karin had humiliated Sayf ad-Dawla, who spent winter 949–50 preparing a major invasion of Roman territory to exact vengeance for the series of defeats he had suffered in 949.

In the meanwhile, the Romans had also launched their operation to retake the island of Crete. The Romans understood the strategic importance of the island of Crete very well, so they had launched their first attempts to recapture Crete immediately after its conquest by the Andalusian Arabs in 824 or 827, launching three naval unsuccessful expeditions in the course of the years 827–9. The island was and is strategically extremely important, as it is located between Greece, Asia Minor, Cyprus, Syria, Egypt and North Africa. This enabled its new Muslim rulers to raid Roman territories from their centrally-located position. Therefore, the Romans repeated their efforts by launching a new, more determined effort in 842–3. This invasion was already a partial success, as parts of the island were recovered. It was only thanks to the political intrigues that this effort came to naught. The same was true of the attempt to retake the island in 866, which did not even reach the island thanks to the political chaos in the capital. The Romans repeated their effort under the admiral Himerios in 911, but with just as little success as before, on top of which Himerios' fleet was destroyed by the Muslims when he was returning home.

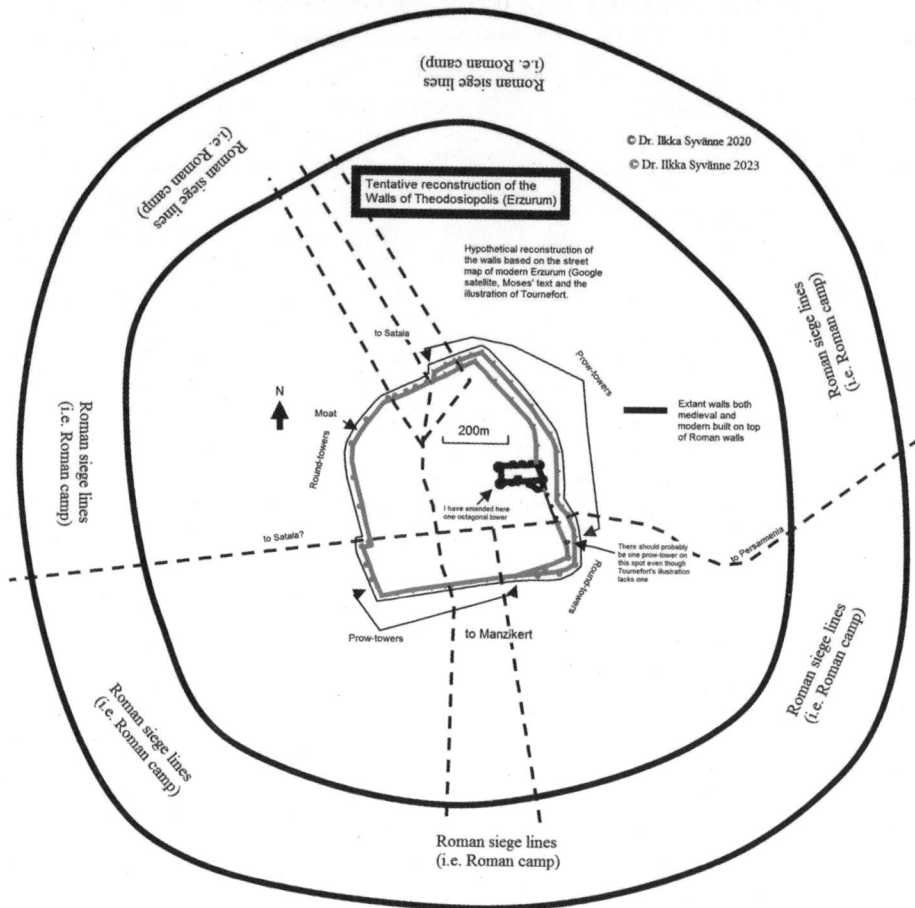

SIEGE OF KARIN IN 949

Kônstantinos VII Porfyrogennêtos was not going to let these setbacks deter him. He appears to have started to make plans and preparations for the campaign immediately after he became sole ruler.[33] Kônstantinos appears to have dispatched an envoy to Cordoba immediately, in that he had arrived there already between 17 August 945–1 August 946. The initial goal appears to have been forming an alliance against the Fatimids in Sicily, but it is still probable that the negotiations included other elements, like the question of Crete, which was in the hands of the enemies of al-Andalus. This did not produce immediate results, so a further exchange of envoys followed during the years 947–9.[34] In 947 the eunuch and chamberlain Solomon visited the court of Cordoba with the purpose of forming an alliance, but only with the result that the negotiations continued. He then travelled to the court of Otto I, possibly at the same time as the envoy of the caliph Abd ar-Rahman travelled there. The idea was to form an alliance with Otto I against their mutual enemies in Italy and the Balkans. In response, Otto I dispatched the famous historian Liudprand as his envoy to Constantinople, while the envoys of Berengar of Italy also travelled to Constantinople to present their case before the emperor. The Spanish envoys were received by the emperor on 28 October 948 and then dispatched back in 949, together with Roman envoys. It is probable that some sort of agreement was reached, even if it is possible (as suggested by Vasiliev, BELA, 331) that in 949 the mission of the Roman envoys was to observe how the caliph reacted to the invasion of Crete and that the warships (see below) which were posted in Spain were there to reconnoitre. Whatever the truth about the role of the envoys and ships in 949, it is still clear that some sort of alliance had been concluded, because the caliph did not resume hostilities against the Romans when they invaded Crete. It is also possible that the ships posted in Spain that were mentioned in the *De Ceremoniis* (see below) were actually ships that carried the envoys to Spain.

We are fortunate to possess exact troop strengths and the strategic positions of the Roman fleet for the campaign to retake the island of Crete because Kônstantinos preserved these in his *De Ceremoniis* (44–5). In 949 the operational plan for the reconquest of Crete divided the Imperial Fleet and other fleets into units that were used for the attack and into units that were left either to guard Constantinople and other key locations, while other units were sent to keep an eye on the potential enemies in Sicily, Spain and North Africa.[35]

The Imperial Fleet dispatched 20 *dromônes* (each with a double *ousia*), 7 *chelandia pamphyla/pamfyloi*, 33 *ousiaka chelandia*, 9 Russian *karabia* and 2 prisoners' monoremes against the Arabs of Crete, while 1 *pamfylos* and 24 *ousiai* (Kônstantinos does not state if these had ships, but it is very likely that they did) were left behind to guard Constantinople. Additionally, 7 *ousiai* were stationed at Dyrrachion and Dalmatia for their protection, while 3 *ousiai* (clearly *ousiaka chelandia*) were sent to Spain (it is possible that these carried the envoys) and another 3 to Calabria.[36] The ships that were sent to Spain and Calabria were undoubtedly used primarily for intelligence gathering duties to make certain that the fleets of al-Andalus and Sicily would not be able to surprise the Romans. As noted earlier, Kônstantinos fails to state where the remaining ten *ousiai* of the Imperial Fleet were stationed. The city of Constantinople was additionally protected by 6 *chelandia pamfyla* and 4 *chelandia ousiaka* commanded by the *stratêgos* of the Aegean Sea (*Aigaion Pelagos*), while the *stratêgos* left an *ousia* behind to cut timber in his own theme.

The *stratêgos* of Samos and *prôtospatharios* and *asêkrêtis* Iôannês were dispatched to Africa with 4 *dromônes*, 6 *chelandia pamfyla* and 9 *chelandia ousiaka*. Their principal mission was clearly to monitor the activities of the Fatimid navy and possibly also to engage the fleets if necessary, as this was already a force that could engage and defeat medium-sized enemy fleets in the right circumstances.

The *stratêgos* of the Kibyrraiôtai together with 6 *chelandia pamfyla* and 6 *chelandia ousiaka* guarded his theme, so there was also another detachment of 2 *pamfyloi* and 4 *ousiaka chelandia* present, while 2 *ousiai* cut wood. Rhodes was guarded by Stefanos, the brother-in-law of the emperor and son of Rômanos I, with one *ousia* (*ousiaka chelandia*), 4 *dromônes*, 9 *galeai* of Antalya, while 6 *galeai* had been left behind to guard the theme. The two *galeai* of Antioch in Cilicia were posted to protect the same theme. The *De Ceremoniis* does not specify how many *galeai* of Karpathos there were, except that one of these was left to guard the island of Karpathos. One may make the educated guess that, whatever the number of the rest, these joined the invasion fleet. The *De Ceremoniis* states that from the theme of Pelopennesos the *tourmarchês* of the coast with four *chelandia* did something that is not named thanks to a lacuna, but one can make the guess that he either stayed behind to protect the coast or joined the invasion fleet.

The cavalry force on board consisted of 4,643 horsemen in total, and included both *scholarioi* and *stratiôtai*. The entire fighting force consisted of 12,628 men, which means that the infantry force (i.e. of the regular infantry, marines, oarsmen, sailors, prisoners and mercenaries) consisted of 7,985 men if the men belonging to the fleet participated in the landing. This was significantly less than was the case in 911, when the invasion force consisted of 37,140 men in total, but still enough for the Romans to be able to land their forces on the island without serious opposition. The probable reason for the small size of the fleet and for the appointment of the inexperienced eunuch as commander was that the emperor did not fully trust the fleet and its experienced commanders. However, the principal reason for the failure of the campaign was the commander Kônstantinos Goggylês and not the size of fleet and army accompanying him. When he landed his army on the island, presumably close to the city of Chandax, he did not build a fortified camp for the night. When the islanders noted this, they launched a surprise attack against the invaders and killed or captured large numbers of Romans. However, the attendants of Kônstantinos Goggylês rallied around him, took him on board a ship and saved him.[37] Thus ended this attempt to retake the island. It was the only setback suffered by the Romans in 949.

5.11. Year 950: Wars Continue

The Roman strategy for the year 950 was to begin peace negotiations with Sayf ad-Dawla (which for the Muslims always meant a truce) for the purpose of exchanging prisoners, which the Romans now had in plenty thanks to the victories of the previous year. The probable reason for this is that the Fatimids had crushed the revolt of Abu Yazid, so they were once again free to turn their attention against the Romans in revenge. It also enabled them to represent themselves as champions of Jihad against the infidels. In this situation it was probably preferable to negotiate rather than to fight.

The Cilician Theatre of Operations: Diplomacy Fails[38]
Meanwhile, in spring 950 the emperor had dispatched an embassy, probably under the leadership of Nikêtas Chalkoutzês, to negotiate with Sayf ad-Dawla. Therefore

Sayf, who was at the time in Mayyafariqin (Martyropolis), travelled via Amida to Aleppo to meet the Romans. The negotiations initially progressed well, but then a subordinate of the emir killed one of the members of the Roman embassy. Sayf promised recompensation but refused to hand over the culprit, with the result that the negotiations broke up. However, it is quite probable that Sayf had intended this from the start, so the murder was not necessarily even accidental. The reason for this suspicion is that Sayf had made preparations for an offensive well before this by asking permission from the caliph, and he launched an offensive against Roman territory in August or September 950 – with the implication that Jihadists had been called for this all the way from Egypt. Furthermore, 4,000 men from Tarsus under *cadi* (Islamic judge) Abu'l Husayn were already waiting for his arrival in the neighbourhood of Marash/Germanikeia. This force was clearly used as a vanguard for the main army.[39] The presence of the Tarsiote army under the *cadi* Husayn may suggest that Nikêforos Fôkas had allowed the Tarsiote soldiers to leave the city of Tarsus in 949 in return for the surrender of the city, but not conclusively, because it is quite plausible that the 4,000 men were drawn from the ranks of those who had remained outside the city during its siege. Furthermore, the fact that the leader of the Tarsiotes was a *cadi* and not an *emir* can be seen as an indication that the *emir* had died during the siege of 949 and a new emir had not yet been appointed by Sayf ad-Dawla.

The Cilician Theatre of Operations: Sayf ad-Dawla Invades in August-September 950[40]
Sayf took with him the Roman envoys as hostages and marched his army of 30,000 men to the neighbourhood of Germanikeia where he met the 4,000 men (probably cavalry) from Tarsus, so that he had in total 34,000 men under his command. The Arabic sources do not give us any breakdown of the units, but on the basis of the sizes given in the DV (Appendix 2: 5.3) one may assume that the cavalry units had ca.13,600 horsemen while the infantry consisted of about 20,400 footmen. The details of his campaign suggest that Sayf's principal aim during this campaign was the destruction of the Roman field army.

Sayf invaded Roman territory along the road that passed along the River Gayhan through the Pass of al-Kankarun to Lykandos at some point in time during the period from 18 August to 16 September. Sayf's first targets of attack were two villages that were located along the River Gayhan called Hisn al-Uyun and as-Safsaf, both of which he captured. It is possible that these villages were actually two small fortresses that protected and blocked the road from Germanikeia to Lykandos possibly somewhere close to the Pass of al-Kankarun. The next places mentioned in the itinerary of Sayf are al-Funduq (located between Germanikeia and Tzamandos-Samandu), Sanabus (located on the road from Arabissos via Tzamandos to Kaisareia close to Tzamandos-Samandu), Tzamandos, and Kaisareia (Caesarea).[41] The itinerary of Sayf led him through the theme of Lykandos, past its capital Lykandos, to the theme of Kappadokia (Kaisareia). This obviously means that the Romans had allowed Sayf purposefully through the mountain passes so that they could then engage him with a guerrilla campaign that would then force him into a retreat and the Romans could then annihilate his army at a pass when he was returning, as this was the preferred tactic in the DV. It is also possible that it was then that Melias, the *stratêgos* of Lykandos, conducted one of his trademark diversionary operations against the territory of Aleppo and Antioch (DV D 20.50ff., DM 20.7), because both of these were vulnerable. In the course of this shadowing warfare the Romans attempted to ambush enemy vanguards, detachments, foragers, pillagers and baggage animals (see Appendix 2). The first to engage the invaders would have been the forces of the *stratêgos* of Lykandos, who may have followed this with the diversionary operation already mentioned, after whom the responsibility would have fallen on the *stratêgos* of Kappadokia, Leôn Fôkas.

When the Muslim army reached a location known as al-Sanabus (close to Tzamandos), Sayf arrayed his forces in formation to march to Tzamandos (a city in the theme of Lykandos) so that Mutanabbi was himself located in the vanguard. When Mutanabbi then returned back to the main army, he saw Sayf ad-Dawla on his horse advancing in front of the ranks while brandishing his lance, at which point Mutanabbi recited a poem to him in which he promised victory for the Muslims while also stating that they would be able to reach Tzamandos before the *domestikos* (Bardas Fôkas), and that if the *domestikos* continued his retreat he would have to retreat all the way to the Bosporus. This means that Sayf was closer to Tzamandos than Bardas Fôkas. Sayf, however, appears not to have attempted to capture Tzamandos, because Mutanabbi states that he bypassed it and marched to the Halys River, and from there to Sariha, where Sayf encamped to besiege the city. On the basis of Dahabi's account we know that Sayf had marched past Kaisareia to the Halys River and from there to Sariha and Charsianon.

The fact that Bardas did not engage Sayf's forces at this stage suggests that he considered his forces too small for such an operation. It is likely that he had been assembling his forces at Kaisareia (one of the *aplekta*-assembly points for the thematic forces), where he would have been joined by the forces of his son Leôn (the *stratêgos* of the theme where Kaisareia was located). It is probable that Bardas and Leôn retreated from Kaisareia to protect it from the outside if Sayf decided to besiege it. Sayf in his turn bypassed Kaisareia because it was clearly too well defended and advanced to besiege Sariha. Since Bardas had not deployed his army for combat when Sayf was near Kaisareia or crossing the River Halys, it is clear that he lacked adequate forces. It is therefore probable that the forces of his son Nikêforos Fôkas had not yet joined him. Therefore, the likely reason for the choice of invasion route by the Tarsiote force was that Nikêforos was blocking the Cilician Gates (see Appendix 2: 4). It was only later, when Nikêforos had joined forces with his father and brother, probably somewhere close to Charsianon, that the route back to Tarsus was opened, with the result that the Tarsiote forces used it for the retreat (see the discussion below). It is therefore probable that Bardas, Leôn and a detachment of cavalry sent by the unknown *stratêgos* of Lykandos continued shadowing warfare after Sayf had bypassed Kaisareia. The route which the Muslims adopted after the crossing of the Halys is not known with certainty (the two possible routes are given in the map on page 146; the westernmost route is the likelier one), but it is clear that when they reached the city of Sarinha and abandoned their attempts to besiege it they turned east towards the fortress city of Charsianon after they reached the road leading there, and once they reached that area they pillaged and burned everything in the neighbourhood while the Romans attempted to ambush them.

Siege and Battle of Sariha/Charsianon (beginning of October 950?)
When Sayf had encamped his army before Sariha to besiege it, Bardas Fôkas appears to have decided to harass him, because it was then according to Dahabi (BELA 2, 242) that Sayf's vanguard encountered the forces of the *domestikos* and defeated them, so that the *domestikos* was forced to seek shelter from behind the walls of a fortress (see Appendix 2: 5.6 Version 2). The fortress in question must have been Charsianon with its garrison of infantry. It was then that Sayf appears to have abandoned the siege of Sariha with the idea of pursuing the defeated foe, because according to Mutanabbi the Muslims ended up burning only the suburbs, churches and surrounding regions of both Sariha and Charsianon.[42] In other words, Sayf had marched past Kaisareia (the HQ of the theme of Kappadokia) to Charsianon (the HQ of the theme of Charsianon) in an effort to annihilate the main enemy army under the *domestikos*. The Roman commander, Bardas Fôkas, and presumably also both of his sons Nikêforos and Leôn[43] were too fast for him, so they had already retreated from Charsianon when Sayf's forces reached it. The probable route taken by Nikêforos from his own theme to join the forces of his father and brother at Charsianon would have taken him from the Gates of Cilicia to Kaisareia (a route open after the Muslims had crossed the Halys) and from there to Sebasteia and Charsianon. This defeat was not of great significance for the Romans because they had been able to retreat to the safety of the Roman fortress.

After this, Sayf returned back to the River Halys, crossed it, and marched along it towards the south, after which he built a fortified marching camp where he left most of his forces and baggage, and then led the cavalry force out in the middle of the night to surprise the Romans, with the result that the two armies fought a battle at Batn al-Luqan, which has been identified as the Valley of the River Lykos. When one places this account on the map, it is clear that Sayf first marched past Sebasteia, the HQ of the *thema* of Sebasteia, to the River Halys, crossed it and then marched along it southwards with the idea of retreating home – or rather with the idea of making it appear as if he was retreating. He had clearly learnt from his spies and scouts that the *domestikos* had been reassembling his shattered army. The likely location for this is the *aplekton* Dazimon in the Armeniakon *thema* which is located just south of the Valley of Lykos. It would have been there that the forces of the theme of Armeniakon were added to the numbers. When Sayf learnt of this he left his infantry and baggage train behind and made a night march against the enemy. The distance between the armies would have been approximately 80 km so

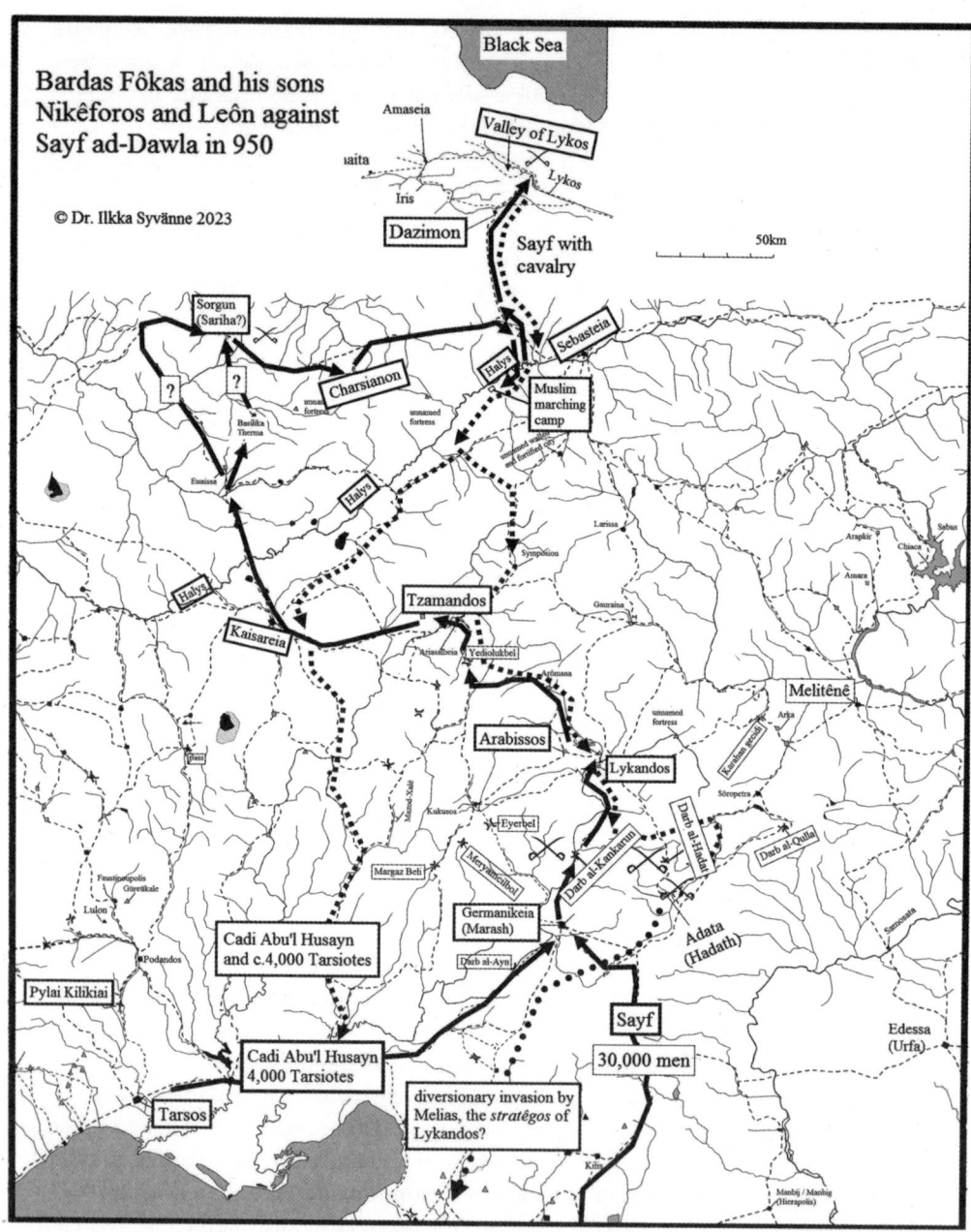

the Romans were within night attack distance when one used cavalry. On the basis of the fact that the battle was fought in the Valley of Lykos and not near Dazimon, there are two possibilities. Firstly, it is possible that the Romans were aware of the move made by Sayf and withdrew their cavalry force from Dazimon to the Valley.

The DV (Appendix 2: 5.3) expected that the *stratêgos* would be able to change his camp even in the middle of the night, so this would have been just a standard move in such situations if one wanted to avoid the danger of an attack against the encampment. The other alternative is that the Romans had been assembling their forces in the Valley from the start so that they would not be within easy striking distance of the enemy.

The Battle of the Valley of Lykos/Lycus River in about October
On the basis of several sources we know that the Romans had assembled an army large enough (Appendix 2: 5.3) to engage Sayf. This Roman army was clearly a cavalry force (it is so in the DV). According to Mutanabbi, Firas, DV and other sources, this army included not only the *domestikos* Bardas Fôkas but also his sons, which must mean Nikêforos and Leôn and possibly also Kônstantinos.[44] It is also probable that their forces had been reinforced by the elite cavalry detachments of other nearby *stratêgoi*, which must have included the forces of Sebasteia and Armeniakon. Bardas Fôkas had also posted his forces in a location in the Valley of Lykos that had several fortifications nearby that provided places of refuge plus infantry forces to protect cavalry fugitives if the battle ended badly for the Romans (see Appendix 2: 5.6 Version 2). See the maps on pages 146 and 148.

Our main problem is that we do not know the size of the Roman cavalry force, while we know the approximate maximum size of the Muslim cavalry force when the army consisted of about 34,000 men. According to Mutanabbi (BELA 2, 308), the *domestikos* led thousands of cavalrymen (i.e. less than a myriad). Ibn Zafir (BELA 2, 124) states that the Muslims defeated the Romans and captured 120 patricians; this would imply that the Romans had more than 6,000 horsemen (if each commanded 50 men). Al-Makin (BELA 2, 190) claims that the Romans lost 30,000 men and that 2,000 patricians were taken captive. This is clearly a gross exaggeration and not backed by the version given by the eyewitness Mutanabbi. It is probable that al-Makin confuses the size of the Muslim army with that of the Roman force, and the number of captives with the estimated casualty figures among the Romans. Dahabi (BELA 2, 242) states that the Roman prisoners included 400 notables, but it is difficult to estimate the size of the force merely on the basis of this. On the positive side is the fact that the information given by Mutanabbi is in full agreement with the *De velitatione* (Appendix 2: 5.6), according to which Bardas Fôkas, Nikêforos and Leôn all considered a cavalry force of about 5–6,000 sufficient to engage any enemy force. Therefore, the likeliest size for the Roman cavalry force in this case is indeed the 5–6,000 cavalrymen (DV) or at most 9,000 (several thousands of Mutanabbi), even if it would be very strange for Bardas not to have assembled a larger army from the combined tagmatic and thematic forces (Lykandos, Kappadokia, Anatolikon, Charsianon, Armeniakon and Sebasteia). However, given the fact that Mutanabbi was himself present and his information is in agreement with the information provided by the DV, it is far likelier that we are here dealing with a force of approximately 5–6,000 horsemen.[45]

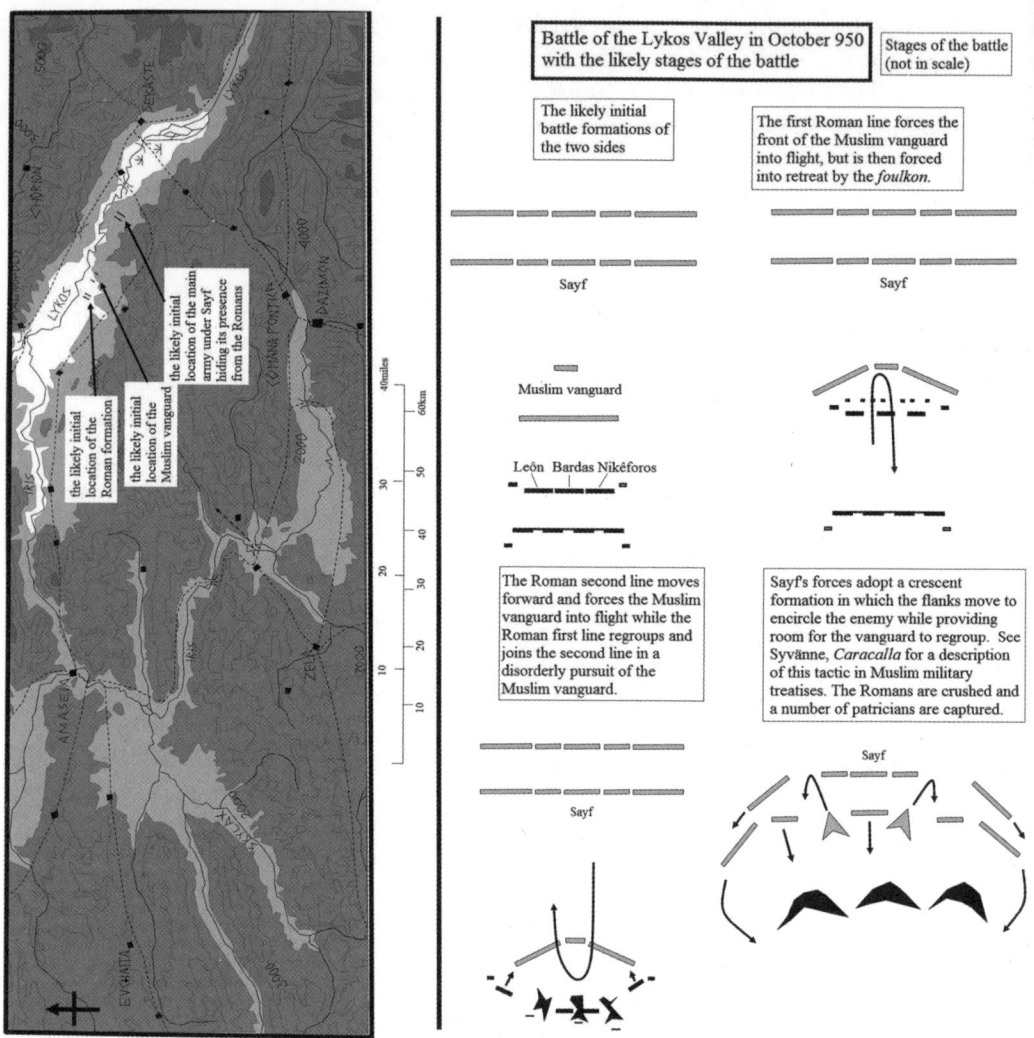

According to Mutanabbi, the reason for the Roman defeat was that the *domestikos* attacked and then pursued with abandon the Muslim vanguard because he believed it to be the entire enemy force. When the main force under Sayf ad-Dawla arrived, the Romans were routed, with a large number of Roman horsemen being killed and more than 80 patricians, *zirwar* and principal officers being captured. This suggests the use of a simple tactic of feigned flight by the Muslims so that the pursuing forces under Bardas Fôkas and his sons were then surprised by the actual Muslim army in full combat formation. It is unlikely that we would here be dealing with an ambush, because the battle took place in a wide river valley. The topographical map above shows the likely location for the battle and for the mistake made by Bardas. The location depicted would have given Bardas a view of the approaching Muslim force, so he would have been able to see the reserve descending from the higher ground while the presence of the main army under Sayf ad-Dawla remained hidden further away.

The likely course of events is that Bardas, Nikêforos and Leôn had arrayed their forces opposite the Muslim cavalry vanguard consisting of the frontline and their *foulkon/defensôres*. Bardas had previously been defeated in Charsianon/Sariha by the Muslim cavalry vanguard/raiders, so it is easy to see why he believed that he faced the entire Muslim cavalry detachment. We can also reconstruct the likely sequence of combat on the basis of these details. Bardas would have deployed his cavalry in the standard two-line formation with small rear guards as depicted in the DV and LT, while his enemies would have deployed a single battle line with *defensôres/foulkon* as depicted in the DV. See Appendix 2. The first Roman line would have pushed the first Muslim line back to their *foulkon*, which would have then tilted the balance in favour of the Muslims, with the result that the first Roman line retreated to the second line. The Roman second line (flanking units outflanking the enemy on both sides, with the two centre units advancing in close order against the enemy while the retreating first line used the intervals for regrouping) then tilted the balance so that the entire Muslim vanguard fled towards their main army under Sayf. Only this sequence explains why the entire Roman force pursued without reserves, with the result that the entire Roman force lost its formation and had become a *drouggos*. When this irregular mass of men then came face-to-face with the main Muslim force under Sayf which was in perfect order, it lost its moral ascendancy and was simultaneously outflanked by a numerically superior enemy force. We do not know the Muslim formation, but it is very likely that it had also two battle lines so that the flanks of both lines were sent to encircle the Romans with a crescent formation, which would also have simultaneously given room for the vanguard between the wings for regrouping. This is one of the ancient Persian battle formations preserved in the Muslim military tradition, as depicted in the military treatise known as the *Gotha Manuscript* (*Goth ms*), for which see Appendix 5 together with Syvänne (*Caracalla*, 239).

It should be noted that the Muslim sources make too much of this defeat. In truth, the defeat in such an encounter was not considered a major disaster in the DV (e.g. 17.123ff; Appendix 2: 5.4, 5.6) because this still caused damage to the enemy, which was the purpose of such attacks. The best evidence for this is that the defeat did not hinder the Roman ability to destroy the invading Muslim force. On the contrary, it was now the turn of the Muslims to retreat hastily towards their own territory while the Romans harassed them.

The Muslims Retreat into Roman Ambushes: The Battle of the Passes of Germanikeia and Adata

With the defeat of the *domestikos*, Sayf ad-Dawla had achieved the principal goal of his campaign so he was ready to start the retreat. When he reached the baggage train and his infantry forces on the southern side of the Halys River, the Tarsiote forces decided to separate from the main army and retreat back into Tarsus (Dahabi in BELA 2,242), presumably through the route that led past Sis and Anazarbos. As noted above, the probable reason for this decision is that the route lay open after Nikêforos Fôkas had joined his father's army. It is not known what Nikêforos did after the defeat of the Valley of Lykos, but it is very likely that he accompanied his father and brother when they shadowed Sayf, because Bardas certainly needed all of the cavalry for this.

Sayf ad-Dawla intended to retreat through the Pass of al-Kankarun, but, thanks to information provided by the Roman envoy Nikêtas Chalkoutzês through bribed Arabs, the Romans had blocked this pass and the nearby passes with felled trees (abatis) and infantry forces, while the Roman cavalry harassed the Muslim rear. This followed the instructions of the DV (Appendix 2: 6) to the letter, which is not surprising because it was based on the experiences of Bardas, Nikêforos and Leôn Fôkas. According to Dahabi (BELA 2, 242), the Roman force that attacked the rear of the Muslim force was under the *domestikos*, but it has been suggested by a number of modern scholars that it was actually Leôn Fôkas. The reason for this suggestion is a misunderstanding of the text of Skylitzes/Cedrenus and the referral in the DV (Preface 19–24) to a situation in which the entire Roman army was unable to resist Hamdan and the Cilicians, which 'one of the best *stratêgoi*' readdressed with the forces of his own theme alone.[46] The evidence for the commander being Bardas Fôkas is much stronger because the commander is claimed to be the *domestikos*. Skylitzes (11.9.25ff.) also states that it was thanks to the information secretly provided by Nikêtas Chalkoutzês that Bardas Fôkas was able to ambush Sayf in the narrow passage.

In sum, it is clear that it was Bardas Fôkas, the man who had perfected the tactics of guerrilla warfare (DV Preface 31–2), who once again demonstrated his unsurpassed skills as a guerrilla leader during the endgame of this campaign. His sons Nikêforos and Leôn were schooled by an unsurpassed expert practitioner of shadowing warfare. It is clear that the Roman forces under Bardas Fôkas that were attacking the *saka* of Sayf consisted of both infantry and cavalry, because this was the expectation in the DV (see Appendix 2: 6). We do not know the size of the force under Bardas, but one may make the educated guess that he would have already replaced the cavalry losses easily from the nearby fortresses when in the *themata* of Armeniakon and Charsianon, while it is probable that he now had more infantry than cavalry with him because he was now entering difficult terrain where the principal fighting force of the army was expected to be its infantry. Fortunately, Nikêforos Fôkas gives us in his PM (see later) the expected size of the infantry force when its cavalry component consisted of 5–6,000 cavalry (the large cavalry army in the DV). The cavalry force of this size would have been accompanied by at least 11,200 *oplitai*, and 4,800 *psiloi*. When one takes into account the forces at the passes, Bardas had at his disposal a numerically superior force facing a tired foe.

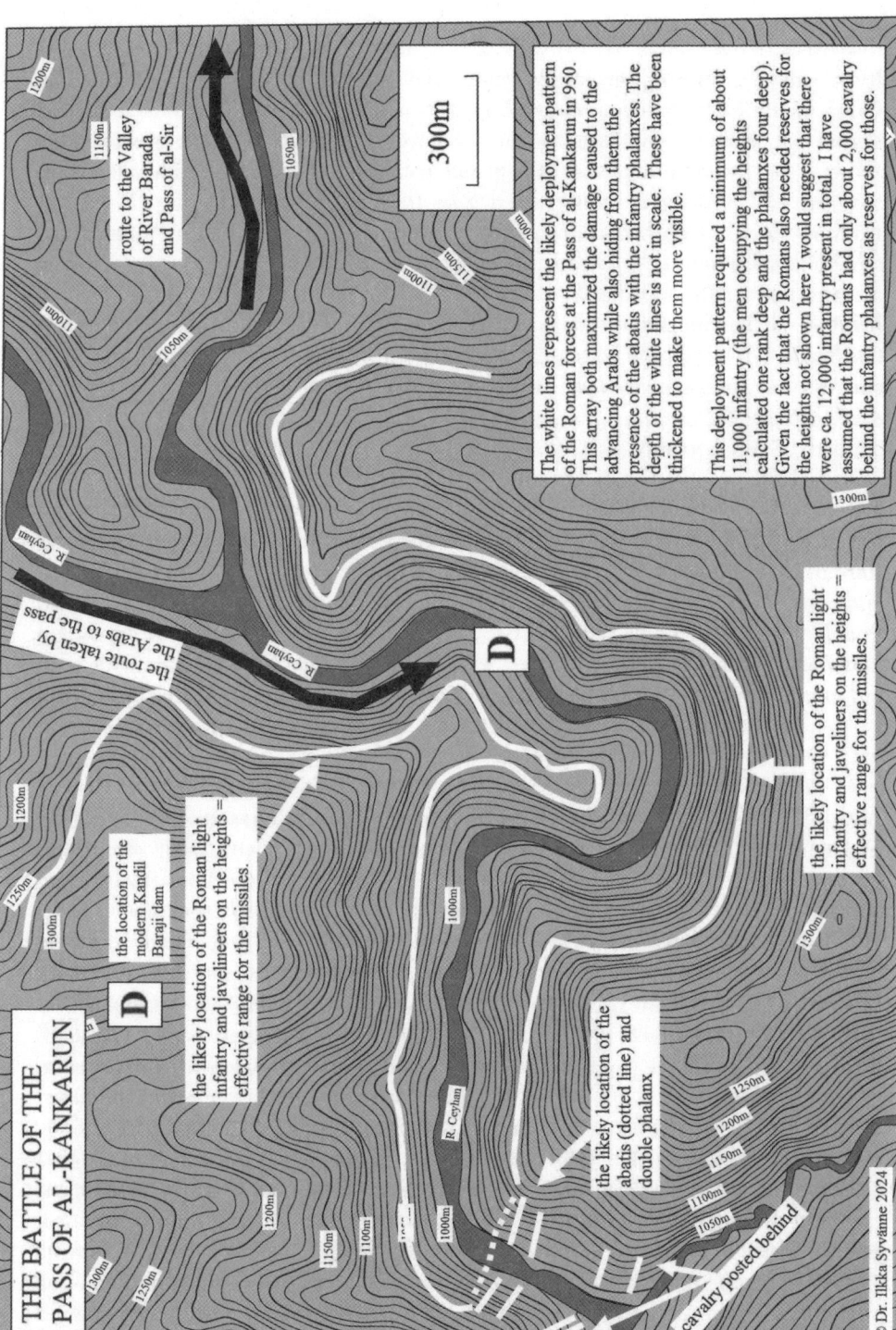

Bardas Fôkas would have deployed his infantry in the manner described in the DV, so the hoplites formed the front ranks and the light infantry the rear. The depth of the infantry formation and its marching formation would have reflected the terrain, so in difficult terrain it would have been two or four ranks of hoplites followed by the light-armed, while in open terrain it would probably have been four or eight ranks of hoplites followed by the light infantry. In difficult terrain there would also have been light infantry and javelineer groups both on the flanks of the infantry phalanxes and in front of it. The infantry formation would also have been adapted to the width of the terrain. The cavalry would have been posted behind, on the flanks and in advance depending on the terrain, but so that when the Romans attacked the Muslim *saka*, the infantry would have spearheaded it as described in the *De velitatione* while the cavalry was used either as reserve or for pursuit of the foe.

In the DV (Appendix 2: 6), the expectation was that the *stratêgos* would have bypassed the enemy emir and occupied the pass with a combined force of infantry and cavalry, leaving one of his best commanders to lead the shadowing force behind the enemy. Since we know that in this case the shadowing force was under Bardas himself, it is probable that he dispatched his best commander to the Pass of al-Kankarun to block it. It is very likely that this best commander was his eldest son Nikêforos, who we know to have been present earlier during the same campaign, while it is very likely that the commander of the force blocking the next pass at al-Sir (see below) was his other son Leôn. Therefore, in the following account I will call the commander of the forces occupying the Pass of al-Kankarun Nikêforos, even if the Arabic sources do not state this anywhere.

Consequently, when the Muslim army reached the Pass of Kankarun they were in deep trouble when they found it blocked by felled trees and infantry, with the Roman light infantry occupying the heights from which they rolled stones and rocks and shot or threw all kinds of missiles. The fact that the Arabs marched into the pass suggests that they did not immediately see that the pass was blocked by an abatis, hence the fact that they were subjected to the Roman attack by rolled stones and rocks and missiles before coming to grips with the abatis and infantry behind it. The accompanying map shows the likeliest location for this, as it perfectly hides the presence of the abatis from the approaching enemy, so they would face serious punishment before reaching the site. The location shows the superb skills of Nikêforos as a commander. He placed his forces in a perfect position to exploit the terrain. The Roman envoy Nikêtas Chalkoutzês, who had bribed some of the Saracens, was able to exploit the resulting confusion and escape. It is probable that the Roman infantry behind the abatis was deployed two deep as in fortified camps (first line consisting of hoplites and the second of archers, slingers and javelineers), or a two-to-four deep hoplite phalanx with light infantry behind, which was the suggested depth for difficult terrain, with a second phalanx posted behind (see Appendix 2: 4, 6) because the territory behind them was in enemy hands. It is probable that a single line of light infantry sufficed for the heights in most locations, while also remembering that there were also places where it was impossible to place any fighters and there would also have been locations where the Romans would have placed several lines of infantry for safety reasons. The cavalry force that would have accompanied the *stratêgos* posted at the pass (i.e. Nikêforos) would have been placed behind his two infantry phalanxes.

Once it was recognized that it would be impossible to fight their way through, Sayf decided to use a pass which was next to a mountain called al-Sir which would enable him to reach Adata/Hadath. The route passed along a river valley which then rose to a ridge, after which followed another river valley (see the attached map). Sayf took control of the cavalry rearguard to protect his infantry and baggage train against the shadowing forces led by Bardas Fôkas. The fact that the Muslims had to ascend a ridge before descending into the valley of the River Barada divided the Muslim force in such a manner that Bardas was able to destroy a portion of Sayf's rear guard. When the Muslims then halted at the River Barada they saw that the Romans had also occupied the Mountain of al-Sir and blocked the pass. This means that the Romans (probably under Leôn) had placed their blocking forces at the mouth of the pass and not deeper into it as Nikêforos had done at the Pass of al-Kankarun.

The Muslims were in a terrible predicament, but with the help of a guide Sayf was able to send his army towards the left, to another side path which had not been occupied by the Romans, while Sayf once again took command of the cavalry rear guard. In other words, this route would not be the well-known Roman path/road leading to the north-east corner of the Valley of the Lake Adata, which is likely to have been blocked by the Romans (under Kônstantinos Fôkas?),[47] but the side path/pass shown in the map on the next page. The Roman forces under Bardas attacked the Muslims incessantly throughout the day, so the fighting stopped only when night fell. When this happened the followers of Sayf abandoned him on the battlefield and fled to their baggage train. Sayf, who had been deserted, followed in their footsteps and found the baggage train and his men at the foot of a mountain close to Lake Adata/al-Hadath. However, this was a trap that the Romans had prepared for them because they had occupied all the mountains around. In other words, the Muslim marching camp had been surrounded from all sides in the same manner as described in the DV (Appendix 2: 6), but in this case the Romans did not need to surround it from the side of Lake Adata/marshy terrain. It is obvious that the force blocking the route of retreat from the Arabs was the same force that had previously blocked the Pass of al-Kankarun, because this force would have been the only force that was available for this after the Arab attempt to force their way through the pass had failed. In short, it is probable that it was thanks to the personal initiative of Nikêforos Fôkas that the Romans achieved such an outstanding victory over the enemy as they did, unless it had been his father Bardas who had ordered him to do that through a courier. By now the Romans would in all probability have had a minimum of about 36,000 infantry and 10–15,000 cavalry surrounding the demoralized Arabs, but it is quite possible that there were even more Roman forces

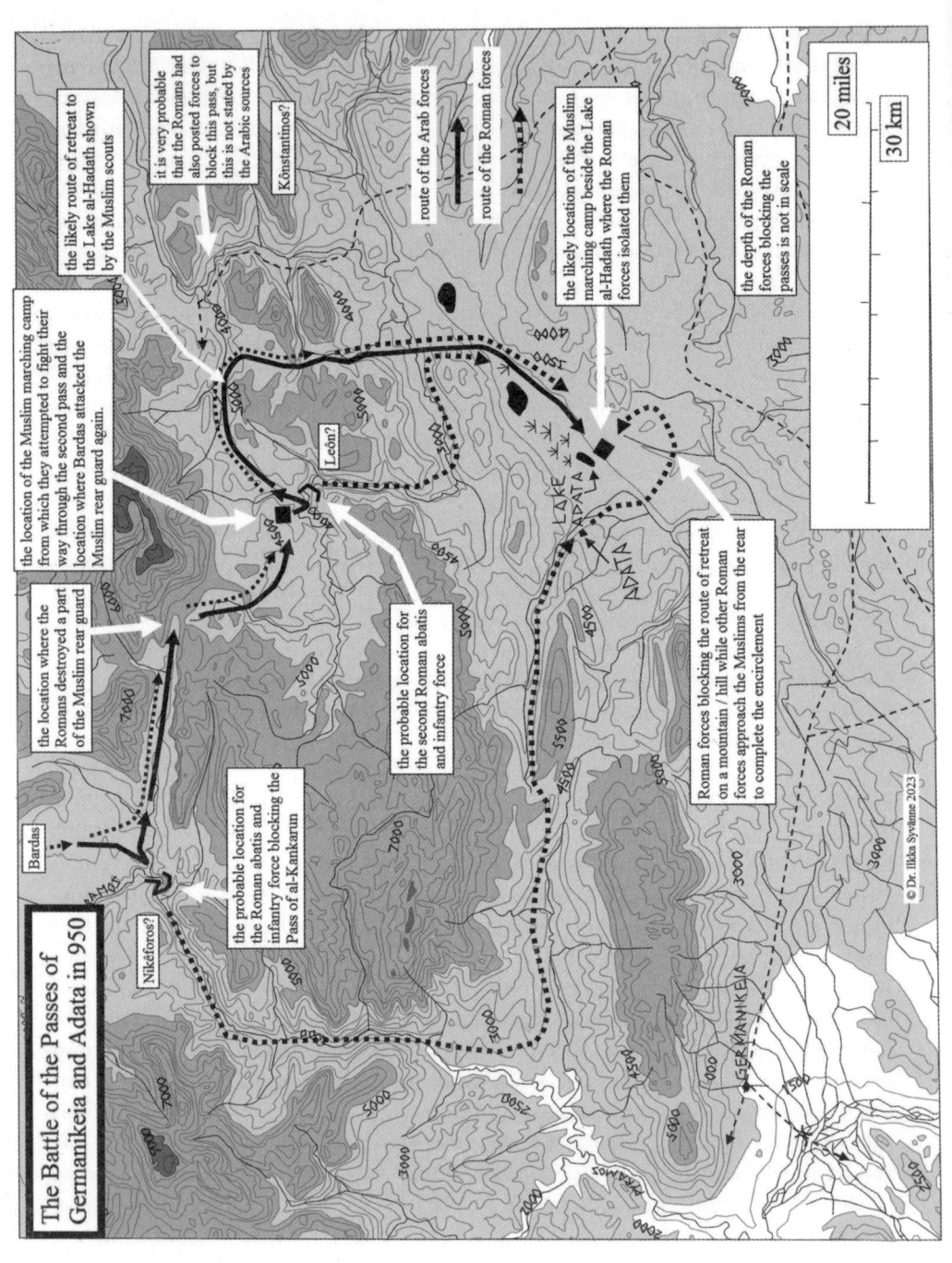

present if the Romans had also occupied the pass leading to the northern portion of the Valley and if they had assembled more cavalry from the *themata*, which they certainly could do easily if Bardas so decided.

Sayf tried to assemble his men for one more attempt, but nobody paid any heed to his pleas. The forced march, night march and fighting had tired and demoralized his army to such an extent that it had stopped being a viable fighting force. Sayf ordered all 400 Roman prisoners killed and the baggage train torched during the night of 25 and 26 October[48] to encourage the Muslims to fight but to no avail, after which he and a few of his loyal companions fought their way through the cordon.

The Romans abandoned the pursuit of Sayf to kill and take prisoners. This time the Romans did not have to engage in any heavy fighting when attacking the enemy camp because its defenders were too tired and demoralized to resist the attack effectively. The Muslim sources give us different figures for the casualties suffered. Some of these state that Sayf had lost almost his entire army, which would mean that he lost almost 30,000 men plus servants, some of whom were killed while others were captured. The prisoners included both *emirs* and *cadis*. Others claim that Sayf lost only 5,000 killed and 3,000 captured.[49] This last figure appears too small in light of the fact that Sayf had lost control of his army, and so was only able to fight his way through the Roman cordon with a small number of men. Therefore, it is clear that he lost at least 25,000 men, plus an unknown number of servants and beasts of burden.

This was a major victory for the Roman arms, but it did not deter the Muslims in the least in the following year. The call for Jihad and revenge was just too powerful in their minds. The only way to put a stop to that would be the annihilation of the Muslim armies, ethnic and/or religious cleansing of the conquered territory, and the annexation of their lands – as the policies of conquest by Nikêforos Fôkas and Iônnês Tzimiskês show.

5.12. Year 951: Sayf ad-Dawla's War of Revenge

In 951 the Romans appear to have sought to concentrate their war efforts against the Fatimids, who had launched an invasion against their territories in Italy, because the *domestikos* Bardas Fôkas sent envoys to Sayf ad-Dawla suggesting an armistice and exchange of prisoners. Sayf was in no mood for negotiations and launched a triple invasion in the spring. Sayf concentrated his forces at Harran (Carrhae) and then advanced via Amida and invaded Roman territory in Anzitene, while the Tarsiotes invaded Roman territory simultaneously by land and sea. The obvious reason for Sayf's choice of invasion route was that it offered the Romans less chances of blocking his route of retreat.[50]

On the basis of Leôn's *Taktika* it is clear that the Tarsiote forces had been reinforced by Jihadists from the Levant and Egypt, which means that this was a major invasion. It was only when these had been added to the numbers that the

Tarsiotes were able to conduct a simultaneous attack by land and sea. Since the Muslim sources fail to mention any successes for the Tarsiotes, it is clear that the fleet of the Kibyrraiôtai, possibly with help from Samos, defended the coastline and islands successfully, while Kônstantinos Fôkas, the *stratêgos* of Seleukeia, defended his coastal theme equally well. It is possible that Nikêforos Fôkas and his brother Leôn (see Appendix 2: 1) performed simultaneously their trademark successful defences of their themes against Saracen raiders, but it is likelier that the main invasion by the Tarsiotes followed the coastline, so that both both the naval and land forces could support each other. The invasion of enemy territory by Kônstantinos Fôkas next year is also suggestive of this. He was clearly exploiting the successful defence of his domains in 951, which would have left the forces of the emir of Tarsus seriously depleted.

In the meanwhile, Sayf had led his army from Harran via Amida to pillage Anzitene. In response the Romans launched a diversionary campaign against Sayf's rear that included a ruse. The Romans had convinced one Christian in Amida to betray the city. This person had informed the Romans that there was an underground conduit through which the city could be entered, but the locals uncovered the plot in time to prevent this. Consequently, Sayf was able to return to his territory with all the booty the soldiers had managed to gather while not losing a city to the Romans. The idea of this raid was clearly to revive the morale of the Muslim forces after the massive defeats suffered in 949–50.[51]

After this, Sayf assembled all the forces available in Syria, Gazira/Jazira and Mosul for a major invasion of Roman territory. He launched his invasion in October with the idea of repeating the invasion of the previous year, but this time he left a force behind to guard the Pass of al-Kankarun so that the Romans would not be able to block it as they had in 950. This corresponds roughly with one of the possible invasion tactics described in the DV (Appendix 2: 5.4), but with the difference that in this case Sayf led the raiding cavalry force in person against the Romans. Sayf halted his force close to Arabissos and then dispatched raiding parties to pillage the surrounding areas. Then he ordered his army to continue its march to Tzamandos with the idea of continuing his invasion all the way up to Charsianon. It was then that his scouts brought the information that the Romans had assembled an army of 40,000 men at Tzamandos to block his route. Sayf would have wanted to engage the Romans but his soldiers refused, which shows that morale had not yet recovered from the previous losses. Therefore, Sayf used the arrival of winter as an excuse to withdraw from Roman territory. This time the Romans did not control the passes so he was able to bring his entire force together with the booty and prisoners back to Aleppo. There was only one major setback that Sayf suffered this year, which was that his territory was hit by a major earthquake which demolished the fortresses of Ra'ban, Duluk (Doliche), and Tull Hamid. Duluk was hit worst, as it also lost three towers. The Muslims needed to rebuild these and many other fortifications in the following year.[52]

On the basis of the size of the Roman army assembled at Tzamandos it is likely that it also included the forces of Nikêforos and Leôn Fôkas and that it was commanded by their father Bardas. The Muslim sources unfortunately fail to give us the composition of the army, which means that we do not know if the army consisted of combined forces or of cavalry alone. Both are possible. As we have already seen, the Romans could collect cavalry armies of over 40,000 horsemen. If the army consisted of cavalry, it could have used either the *Sylloge tacticorum* formation with the *katafraktoi* wedge, or the more traditional double-line described by Leôn the Wise in his *Taktika*, Kônstantinos VII in *De Ceremoniis* and Nikêforos Fôkas in *De velitatione*. There is no way of knowing what the battle plan of Bardas was. If the army was a combined force, then it is possible that it was expected to use the tactics described in the *Sylloge tacticorum*.

Italian Theatre of Operations in 951
As already noted, the war between the Fatimids and Romans was inevitable after 947 because Kônstantinos refused to pay tribute. It was because of this that the Romans dispatched a sizeable army to Otranto under Malakênos to join forces with the *stratêgos* of Calabria, Paschalios, while the fleet was placed under Makroiannês. Once disembarked, the soldiers treated the local population high-handedly, which the Fatimids were able to exploit when they launched their counter offensive. On Wednesday 2 July 951 'a slave' called Farag Muhallad embarked an army of 7,000 horsemen and 3,500 footmen in transport ships and sailed from Africa to Sicily. The emir Hasan united these Africans with his Sicilian forces and on Saturday 12 July 951 led the combined force againt Regium/Reggio, which had been abandoned by its inhabitants. Consequently, Hasan dispatched raiding parties to the theme of Calabria, after which he besieged Gerace (Garaga), but had to abandon the siege when he learnt that the Roman army that had landed at Otranto was approaching. Consequently, Hasan concluded a truce in return for hostages and payment of tribute. After this, Hasan led his force against the Roman field army, but these decided to retreat rather than fight – so that they even abandoned Otranto. It is probable that they actually sailed to Sicily to threaten the base of the enemy because it is there that we find them in 952. Consequently, Hasan advanced to besiege Cassano with the same result, so he accepted a truce in return for hostages and tribute probably because he needed to return to Sicily. This ended the campaign season, so Hasan returned to Sicily with the idea of renewing the offensive next year.[53]

5.13. Year 952: Roman Offensives against the Fatimids and Hamdanids

The Roman strategy for the year 952 was to be on the offensive both in Sicily against the Fatimids and in the east against the Hamdanids. The failed peace negotiations of the previous year proved that it was futile to attempt to negotiate with Sayf ad-Dawla before further aggression could convince him to adopt a more conciliatory attitude. Sayf ad-Dawla appears to have been preoccupied with the reconstruction and rebuilding of the fortresses and cities destroyed by the Romans or demolished by the earthquake of the previous year. The list of fortifications to be rebuild was long: Germanikeia (Marash), Hadath, Awasim, Thughur, Duluk, Ra'ban, and Tell Hamid (or Tell Khalid)[54].

The Roman Offensive against the Hamdanids[55]

Consequently, the Romans were the first to resume hostilities in the spring of 952 by launching a triple offensive which is likely to have been cavalry raids. The first of these invasions was directed against the Muslims attempting to rebuild the fortifications of Ra'ban. The second was directed against Diyar Modar. The third was directed against the area controlled by the city of Amida.

The force that attacked the Muslims at Ra'ban was under Kônstantinos Fôkas, which implies that he or Nikêforos had effectively destroyed the Tarsiote forces in the previous year and so was now able to advance as far as Ra'ban, which was ca.17 miles (27.2 km) from the River Euphrates as the crow flies. The Muslims under their emir Abu Firas, or Sayf ad-Dawla himself as claimed by ibn-Shaddad (BELA 2, 197), were now victorious and Kônstantinos could not prevent the rebuilding of the walls.

The second of the Roman forces advanced into Mesopotamia, crossed the Euphrates, and then marched on the east side of the Euphrates. The route taken by this force was so close to the city of Ra'ban that it is clear that the commander of this force must have cooperated with Kônstantinos somehow. In fact, it is possible that

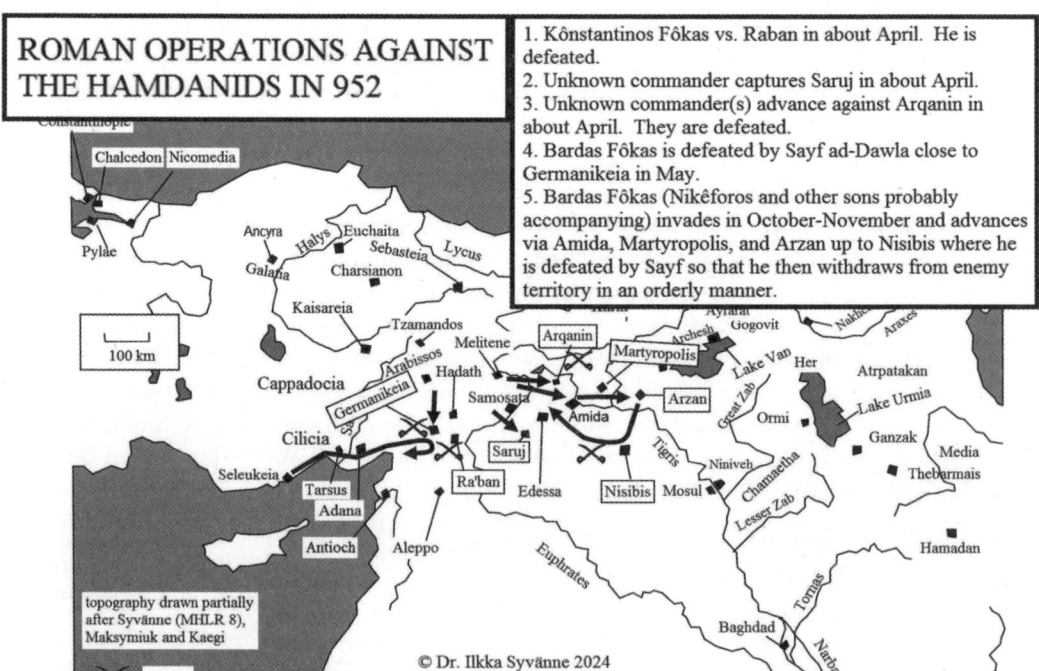

they had invaded together, with Kônstantinos being tasked with the destruction of the Muslims forces rebuilding Ra'ban while the rest of the force marched to Diyar Modar. Whoever the commander was he was more successful than Kônstantinos, because the Romans captured the village of Sarug/Saruj, burned its mosques and took its inhabitants into captivity. It is very unfortunate that we do not know who the commander of this expedition was, or the size of the force, or its composition. It is possible that it was a fast cavalry raid by a *stratêgos* (the likeliest candidate being Melias from Lykandos, but one cannot entirely rule out Nikêforos Fôkas or Leôn Fôkas if this invasion force cooperated with Kônstantinos), or alternatively that it was a major invasion led by the *domestikos*, but the former is likelier because we find Bardas operating against Sayf at Germanikeia very soon after this, in about May 952. It is therefore probable that this invasion was a diversionary operation led by Melias or Nikêforos or Leôn.

The third of the Roman invasions was directed against Amida. This invading force definitely consisted of cavalry because al-Fariqi (BELA 2, 116–7) states so, which means that it was definitely a cavalry raid conducted by a *stratêgos* or *stratêgoi*. Their numbers were bolstered by the forces of Ubayd Allah al-Ahwal, the emir of Melitene. They advanced together against the fortresses of the territory of Amida, where they besieged the fortress of Arqanin (mod. Ergani/Arghana, south of Arghana Maden) located north-west of Amida. This proves that the Romans had retained the Muslim emir of Melitene in their service after the conquest of that city in 934. Taksin, the governor of Mayyafariqin (Martyropolis), and al-Hasan b. Ahmad, the governor of Amida, united their forces and advanced against the Romans. They managed to surprise the Romans, with the result that the Roman force was destroyed. One wonders if they had been betrayed by the emir of Melitene. My educated guess is that they were.

In the meanwhile, Sayf had continued the reconstruction of the destroyed defences of his domains, and his priority was the rebuilding of the walls of Germanikeia during the *muharram* 341 (May 951–27 June 952 in Mutanabbi)/341 (29 May 952–17 May 953 in al-Din), which implies that the following battle took place in about May 952. The Romans could not allow this, so Bardas Fôkas marched against him in person with the result that the two fought a major battle somewhere close to Germanikeia. The poem of Mutanabbi (BELA 2, 317–9) implies that Sayf achieved his victory over Bardas with a cavalry attack that was carried to close quarters with spears and sabres, and that this attack was directed against the Roman flank with the result that Bardas abandoned the battlefield and his army, which in turn caused its defeat. In other words, it is likely that Sayf used a cavalry ambush or outflanking attack with a crescent formation (see Appendix 5). We do not know what type of army Bardas had brought to the scene or its composition, but one may make the educated guess that it was either the cavalry army of the ST or its combined army, because there had to be several major battles that had ended in Roman defeat for Nikêforos Fôkas to reform these tactics in his PM. Considering the location where the battle took place, it is probable that all of the sons of Bardas were present in the defeat. It is similarly probable that Iôannes Tzimiskês was present, as Bardas would still have been schooling him in military arts.

On the basis of Aini's account (BELA 2 a.341, 268), we know that Sayf exploited his victory over the Romans by advancing with a small cavalry force through the Pass of al-Kankarun up to Charsianon. According to Aini, this campaign took place in summer, which places it in the immediate aftermath of Sayf's victory over Bardas at Germanikeia in May. Sayf then went on to defeat both Iôannês Tzimiskês and Nikêforos Fôkas in a battle near Charsianon. One may make the educated guess that the Romans shadowed the advancing enemy force in the manner described in the DV (see Appendix 2) while reinforcements were brought to the scene. When there were then enough men for a battle, Nikêforos (clearly as a *stratêgos*), and Iôannês (undoubtedly as a second-in-command), decided to engage Sayf's force somewhere close to Charsianon with the result that they both suffered a humiliating defeat. The result, however, was not a complete disaster because the Romans were able to flee to Charsianon while the Arabs were still forced to begin their retreat. In short, the defeat was still a defensive victory for the Romans as it stopped the enemy raid.

In the *gumada* 341 (24 Oct.–21 Nov. 952) Bardas Fôkas attempted to wrest the initiative by leading his army against al-H.r.š (unknown), which belonged to the domains of Amida. He advanced as far as Amida, Mayyfaraqin, Arzan and Nisibis (BELA 2, 116). In the meanwhile, Sayf had assembled his forces to engage the invaders. According to Aini (BELA 2, 268), Sayf's army had been reinforced by Egyptian forces under ibn al-Ziyada. These reinforcements were undoubtedly needed because Sayf had lost such large numbers of his frontier Tughur forces in 950. This time Sayf appears to have surprised the Romans somewhere close to Nisibis, with the result that he captured large numbers of Romans together with a sizeable booty. This means that Sayf had once again surprised Bardas, which implies that Bardas had either advanced carelessly or that his scouts had performed their job poorly. It should be noted, however, that this was not a major defeat for the Romans because the Muslim sources nowhere claim to have destroyed the entire invading army, which must have retreated back to Roman territory after this in an orderly manner. On the basis of this, it is very likely Sayf had just ambushed one of the Roman raiding parties in the same manner as the Romans ambushed Muslim raiding parties when they invaded, the procedures of which are described in the DV (see Appendix 2). The rest of the Roman army would have withdrawn under the protection of the hollow infantry square to their own territory. It is once again likely that most of Bardas' sons, Nikêforos definitely included, accompanied their father, together with Iôannês Tzimiskês, so Nikêforos was in a position to observe what had caused the defeat.

War against the Fatimids in Sicily and Italy in 952

As already noted, in 951 the Romans had chosen not to fight in Sicily and Italy, but the situation changed in 952. They had strengthened this force with the local

Sicilians and were ready to engage the Fatimids in a decisive battle. The Fatimid governor of Sicily, al-Hasan the Kalbite, had to defeat this army if he wanted to reconquer the territory the Fatimids had lost to the Romans in Sicily. Both were now ready to accept battle on 8 May 952. The Romans were defeated and routed after a violent battle, with the result that the Muslims were able to massacre and capture Romans until nightfall brought an end. The Romans abandoned their baggage train, valuables and beasts of burden as booty for the Faithful. Al-Hasan dispatched the severed heads of the enemy to the different villages in Sicily and Africa as signs of his victory over the infidel. After this, al-Hasan repeated his failed attack against the city of Gerace and put it under siege, but could not capture it this time either, being forced to accept the payment of tribute. After this, he dispatched a detachment against the village of Petracucca, which his forces captured and pillaged. Al-Hasan returned to Sicily, where he stayed the entire year 341 (29 May 952–17 May 953), which presumably means that he stayed there during winter 952–3. The caliph al-Mansur (17.5.946–18.3.953), however, was not happy with the progress of the campaign. After all the only real result of the war so far was the defeat of the Roman field army, pillaging of patches of countryside and some payments of money, while there was no real progress either in Sicily or in Italy. Therefore, al-Mansur openly expressed his unhappiness with the progress at the same time as the Roman embassy under Iôannês Pilatos arrived to negotiate in 952. The Romans wanted a long truce, but the Fatimids granted only a short truce in return for Roman tribute payments. The truce lasted until 955. Both sides had clearly suffered enough casualties so that the Roman readiness to buy the peace was found acceptable by the Fatimid caliph. The caliph al-Mansur died on 19 Mars 953 and was succeeded by Mu'izz. When this happened, al-Hasan left his son Abu l'Husayn Ahmad in charge of Sicily and travelled to Africa to show obeisance to the new caliph.[56]

The Romans definitely needed to adopt a conciliatory tone towards the Fatimids in a situation in which they had suffered two minor (at Ra'ban and Arqanin) and three major defeats (at Germanikeia, Nisibis and in Sicily) all in the same year of 952. They needed all of their available forces in the east when they faced major invasions both on land and sea. As *stratêgos* of the Anatolikon and son of Bardas Fôkas, Nikêforos would have been aware of the grand tactical situation and of the diplomatic negotiations, so he may have participated in the strategy discussions at court during the winter breaks in hostilities.

5.14. Year 953: The Ruse and Invasion of Sayf and Roman Guerrilla Warfare[57]

According to Mutanabbi (BELA 320–1), a Roman envoy (probably Basileios of Rhodes) arrived on 20 March–18 April 953 to discuss the exchange of prisoners, but Sayf only humiliated him. The emperor had not listened to the advice of Saint Paul of Latrus, who had told him that it would be futile to send any envoys to Sayf ad-Dawla.[58] It is clear that Saint Paul of Latrus understood better the character of Sayf than either the emperor or *domestikos*. Sayf was a Jihadist, with whom it was ultimately impossible to negotiate because he saw it as his mission to wage Jihad against the infidels. It was impossible to conclude any permanent peace with him. The only viable option available to the Romans was to annihilate him and his armies. The Romans were to have a similarly deeply religious paladin in the form of Nikêforos Fôkas once he became emperor.

However, al-Fariqi (BELA 2, 116–7) gives us a different version of what happened immediately after the campaigns of the year 952. According to him, it was after these successes that Sayf ad-Dawla agreed to a truce when the envoys of the *domestikos* arrived in 342 (18 May 953–6 May 954), with the implication that Sayf played a ruse against the Romans because he invaded Roman territory again in 953. The unfortunate detail in his account is the date, because it does not correspond exactly with the date given by Mutanabbi and also allows the dating of Sayf's ruse to the year 954. However, when one remembers the fact that Sayf ad-Dawla faced a revolt of Bedouin tribes of Jazira in the region of Harran (Carrhae) in spring 953 (see the next subchapter), the likelihood for the conclusion of a truce with the Romans increases. The probable reason for the rebellion of the Bedouins is that the Romans had just ravaged their lands, both close to Saruj and Nisibis, while Sayf had failed to provide them with adequate protection. I would suggest that Sayf ad-Dawla did indeed conclude a truce with Basileios of Rhodes in early May, just before he launched his offensive against the rebel tribes in early June.

If my speculation about the dating of Sayf ad-Dawla's truce with the Romans is correct, then the reason for Roman inaction during the revolt of the Bedouin tribes of Jazira against Sayf is that the Romans were under the false impression that the two sides would exchange prisoners during the truce. This, however, proved a mistake. When Sayf had advanced from Aleppo to Harran in the summer he crushed the rebellious Bedouins, the Uqail, Qushair and Aglan, and took hostages from them. Following this, Sayf immediately continued his offensive against the Romans. The army that Sayf led against the Romans is stated to have been exceptionally large ('innumerable'). Therefore, it is not surprising to learn that the Romans did not attempt to face Sayf in pitched battle and rather resorted to a guerrilla campaign and use of a diversionary invasion (see Appendix 2: 5.7).

Sayf led his army to Duluk and then across the Euphrates and its associated rivers at the bridge of Sanga. Following this, Sayf probably led his forces past the city of Adata through the Pass of Darb al-Qulla to a region called Zibatra and then heavily ravaged the suburbs of Arqa/Arka and Melitene. According to Ibn Zafir and Abu Firas (BELA 2, 126–7, 362–3), Sayf captured both Arka and Melitene and torched them. After these major successes Sayf decided that it was time to retreat to his own territory, but the route which he planned to take, the Pass of Darb al-Manzar, was blocked by the forces of Kônstantinos Fôkas. The exact location of this pass is not known, but it must have been either south or south-east of Melitene as modern reseachers like Canard and Vasiliev have suggested. We do not know the whereabouts of Nikêforos, but it is likely that he was initially sent to block one of the passes leading away from Roman territory, after which he joined his father Bardas and brother Leôn when they started their diversionary invasion of enemy territory.[59] When Sayf learnt that the Romans were blocking his route of retreat he dispatched his elite Daylami infantry into the pass, but they were defeated in heavy fighting by the Armenian infantry holding the pass. Sayf abandoned the attack and decided to retreat by using the longer route. As noted by Vasiliev (BELA 1, 349), the likely reason for this decision was that the Romans also blocked the other passes leading to Syria, so Sayf opted to use the longer route via Anzitene/Armenia.[60] It is very likely that Nikêforos would have been posted in one of those passes at least initially. According to Mutanabbi and Abu Firas (BELA 2, 323, 362), Sayf then returned towards Melitene with the Romans in hot pursuit, allowing Sayf to ambush the pursuers so that large numbers of Armenians were killed. It is therefore clear that the scouts had performed their duties poorly and Sayf was able to ambush the pursuing forces of Kônstantinos Fôkas. Nikêforos Fôkas warned against this possibility in his *De velitatione* 9.46–56 (see Appendix 2: 5.3 with 6). The problem we have here is that we do not know how seriously the Roman pursuers were defeated on this occasion because it is possible or even probable that Sayf ambushed only the Roman vanguard with the other forces escaping unscathed. After this Kônstantinos abandoned the pursuit and joined forces with his father and brothers. Kônstantinos was clearly operating quite far away from his province, which demonstrates the flexibility of the Roman command structures.

This time Sayf bypassed the ruined Melitene while pillaging whatever there was left and crossed the Qabaqib (River Tochma Su) and then the Euphrates close to the fortress of Hisn al-Minshar (unknown)[61] so that he then arrived at a region known as Batn Hinzit and Sumnin (Simsat, Arsamosata).[62] According to Ibn Zafir (BELA 2, 127), the inhabitants of Batn Hinzit had not been expecting to be attacked, so the Muslims were able to obtain vast amounts of booty. The Romans had clearly overlooked this possibility.

Sayf then turned towards Lake Gölkak and marched to the fortress of Arqanin. There he learnt that the *domestikos* had invaded Syria and was ravaging the region of Aleppo (Ibn Zafir in BELA 2, 127), the capital of Sayf. The news of this spurred Sayf into action, so he marched first to Amida and then past the fortress of Hisn ar-Rum (east of Amida) before crossing the Euphrates at Samosata. When Sayf reached Duluk, he learnt that the Romans had already retreated from Syria. He started a hot pursuit with his cavalry forces and caught the Romans 'behind Marash' at the River Saihan/Gayhan/Jaihan near Germanikeia on 25 July 953. He had only 600 Jihadist elite horsemen, while the Romans had a sizeable army.[63] I would suggest that the 'behind Marash' (Germanikeia) at the River Jaihan means in this case the valley of the ancient Pyramos, which ran along the route leading north through the Pass of al-Kankarun. The elite 600 cavalry are likely to have consisted of the *ghulam/ ghilman* (Turkish 'slave' soldiers), just like the 500 horsemen accompanying Sayf in the battle of Hadath/Adata in the following year. It is also clear that these were equipped as *katafraktoi*.

Considering the distances between the different Roman commanders, who would have occupied different passes leading out of Roman territory, and the time needed to unite those forces with each other, then the time needed for the Romans to raid the territory around Aleppo and then return to the border, it is very likely that the Roman raiding force consisted only of cavalry, so the commanders had left their infantry behind in the passes to protect those against the enemy while also securing their own route of retreat from enemy territory.[64] It is quite probable that the passes blocked by the Romans consisted of the following, starting from the easternmost controlled by the forces of Kônstantinos: the Pass of Darb al-Manzar (location unknown, but probably south or south-east of Melitene); the Darb al-Qulla; the Darb al-Hadath; and the Darb al-Kankarun. It is easy to see that the remaining three passes were held by the forces of Leôn, Nikêforos and Bardas Fôkas, who would then have united their cavalry with the cavalry forces of Kônstantinos. The presence of Nikêforos in the raiding force is confirmed by Muslim sources (e.g. BELA 2, 196) – he was therefore in a position to observe the disgustingly avaricious behaviour of his father in person, which he later criticized openly to the emperor (see Chapter 6) – but it is easy to make the educated guess that Leôn would also have accompanied his relatives, because the events took place so close to his theme and because Skylitzes (11.9.1–40) names him in the context of this battle. One may make the educated guess that the combined cavalry force consisted of at least 15,000 horsemen if one assumes that Nikêforos, Leôn and Bardas all brought 4,000 to the scene and Kônstantinos only 3,000 (his forces had suffered casualties), but it may have been significantly stronger than this if Bardas had brought more tagmatic forces while assembling horsemen from the themes of the interior.

According to Mutanabbi (BELA 2, 325, 327), Sayf travelled from Amida to the River Gaihan/Jaihan in just three nights, so he was able to catch up with the retreating Roman force only by using a night march during the last night. In other words, Sayf covered a distance of about 300km in three nights, meaning that he was left with a force of 600 horsemen when he reached Jaihan/Gaihan with the night march. By using spare horses and by exchanging horses, for example at Samosata and Duluk, the *katafraktoi ghilman* could easily reach the scene of battle in full combat condition. Typically the use of a night attack would mean that Sayf's idea would have been to surprise the Romans by attacking them in their encampment at the crack of dawn, but this is contrasted by the account given by Skylitzes 11.9.1–40 (the same account in Kedrenos/Cedrenus).[65] Skylitzes claims that the Roman defeat was the result of Bardas' insatiable greed, with the implication that the Roman army had already been deployed for marching or combat when the forces of Sayf suddenly emerged from behind. This conclusion receives additional support from the location ('behind Marash' at Jaihan), which suggests that at least some of the Roman units had entered the valley of Pyramos leading to the Pass of al-Kankarun, so Sayf did not face the entire Roman force, but only its rear guard. In short, it is possible that Sayf purposefully and quite wisely delayed his attack to take place only when the Roman army had already entered the valley so that his numerically-small elite cavalry force could attack the Romans from behind without the fear of being outflanked. This would have enabled him to instill panic in the Roman marching column starting at their rear. According to the Muslim sources, Sayf launched an immediate cavalry attack while wielding lances of Hatt (clearly indicating very high quality) and sabres (probably Indian steel sabres as in the previous year BELA 2, 318) with the result that the Romans were utterly routed, Bardas wounded in the face, Leôn son of Maleinos killed, and Kônstantinos Fôkas and many others taken captive. The wounding in the face proves that Bardas Fôkas was an exceptionally active man for his age, because he was already approximately 73-years-old. If Bardas had decided to take command of the rear guard as Sayf had done repeatedly to protect the retreat of his own men, and which many other commanders had done in the past and would do later, then it was his son who attempted to come to his rescue, but if it was Kônstantinos who commanded the rear guard (his men would have been demoralized by the previous defeat), then it was Bardas who attempted to rescue his son.

In short, Skylitzes claims that the reason for the exceptionally poor performance of the Roman army was not the surprise but the ravenous greed and avarice of Bardas which bordered on insanity. It was because of this that when the forces of Sayf suddenly appeared everyone deserted Bardas, so he would have been captured by the enemy had not his attendants rescued him while protecting him with their interlocked shields, which implies the presence of infantry, but not conclusively so because this same formation was also employed by cavalry.[66] However, the fact that Bardas was saved by attendants who adopted the *synaspismos* formation for the protection of their employer could be used as evidence for the employment of the night attack tactic by Sayf against the Roman encampment, so his forces would have charged inside the Roman encampment up to the centre where the Roman commander was located, with the result that everyone inside the Roman marching camp panicked and fled. It is impossible to be absolutely certain which of these alternatives is correct, but since Skylitzes (and later Nikêforos also) stated that the reason for the poor performance of the Roman soldiers under Bardas was his avarice, it is far likelier that the Roman army was not surprised in their encampment and had already been deployed for marching.[67] The Roman soldiers would have just not been willing to fight for their greedy commander when the latter had stolen from them their hard-earned booty. It is probable that the forces of Nikêforos and Leôn fought well and did not scatter and flee, because Skylitzes contrasted the behaviour of Bardas with the behaviour of his sons Nikêforos and Leôn, both whom were above stealing booty from their soldiers.

Whatever the exact details, this battle was a major defeat for the Romans and a source of great joy and glory for Sayf and his men, who entered Aleppo in triumph in August. Bardas Fôkas was grief-stricken by the capture of his son, so it is no surprise that he and the emperor dispatched Paulos Monomachos as an envoy to

Sayf to negotiate the exchange of prisoners. The Romans had good reasons to be optimistic about the outcome, because they also held Sayf's relatives as captives. Bardas Fôkas offered a ransom of 800,000 dinars and 3,000 Arab prisoners in exchange, but Sayf refused this offer. The Roman and Arab sources offer differing accounts of what happened next. According to Ibn Saddad, when Bardas learnt of the refusal of Sayf, he bribed a Christian perfumer at Aleppo to poison his son, which was then duly accomplished, but according to the usual version among the Muslim sources Kônstantinos actually caught an illness from which he then died, after which Sayf sent his personal condolences to the father. Still another Arabic version claims that Kônstantinos actually died in combat a year later, but it is easy to see that this not true. According to the version preserved by Skylitzes and Yahya, Sayf attempted to convert Kônstantinos to Islam, and when he refused, Sayf had him poisoned with the result that the Roman envoy had to return empty-handed. When Bardas then learnt of the death of his son, presumably in spring 954, he clearly believed that he had been murdered (if the account of the parfumer is incorrect) and executed all of the relatives of Sayf ad-Dawla in Roman hands. This ended all negotiations between the two parties.[68] Both men who had lost their relatives were undoubtedly teething with anger.

5.15. Year 954: The Battle of al-Hadath/Adata, October 954

Modern Reconstruction

In 954 Sayf ad-Dawla marched towards a location called al-Hadath, because he had learnt that its inhabitants had written to the *domestikos tôn scholôn* Bardas Fôkas ('Ibn al-Fuqas') with the idea of asking him to rebuild its walls. The reason for their unhappiness towards Sayf was that the defences of the city had not been rebuilt. As the events of the previous two years demonstrate, the strategy of Sayf at this time was the refortification of the frontier. Consequently, he reacted immediately to the news to ensure that the Romans would not be able to push their frontier into Muslim territory. Sayf reached al-Hadath on Wednesday 18 October 954 and started constructing trenches and foundations around the place immediately. The Domestic of the Schools had under him 50,000 cavalry and infantry, consisting of 'Greeks' (i.e. Romans), Armenians, Russians, Slavs, Bulgarians and Khazars. The Romans reached the scene on Friday 20 October 954. A stalemate ensued. On Monday 30 October 954 Sayf ad-Dawla launched an attack at the head of his 500-strong corps of *ghilman* with the other forces following. The battle lasted from the morning until just after midday. Sayf directed his 500-man force of *ghilman* directly at the bodyguards of the Domestic and defeated the Romans, killing 3,000 Romans in the process. He also captured large numbers of *scholarioi* and their *archôntes*, most of whom he executed. Sayf stayed in the area to complete the reconstruction of the defences of the city of Adata. The construction of the walls and towers lasted until 12 November, after which Sayf returned to Aleppo in triumph.[69]

The Foundation for My Reconstruction of the Battle of al-Hadath

The above summary represents the results of the previous research, but we can go further than this by combining the information in the sources with the information provided by the military treatises and terrain. The key pieces of evidence which allow us to reconstruct the battle are:

1) The Romans brought with them 50,000 cavalry and infantry, consisting of Romans (Greeks), Armenians, Russians, Slavs, Bulgarians and Khazars (Mutanabbi, BELA 2, 331; v.14).
2) The Roman forces included *katafraktoi* and *scholarioi* (Mutanabbi, BELA 2, 332, v.16–9).
3) Sayf arrived at al-Hadath on Wednesday 18 October 954. The Romans arrived opposite him on Friday 20 October. This means that the Romans had been assembling their forces for the purpose of marching to Adata but were forestalled by Sayf thanks to the timely intelligence he got of the Roman aims. The battle was fought on Monday 30 October. See Mutanabbi, BELA 2, 331 (in truth a commentary by some unknown hand preceding the actual poem). The dates mean that both sides encamped on the location, so it is clear that the Romans did not use a hollow infantry square as a place of refuge but a fortified marching camp. The subsequent details also make it clear that the Romans did not build their marching camp close to the city of al-Hadath because it did not serve as a place of refuge for the entire cavalry force, most of whom fled to the mountain behind the city. The large size of the Roman infantry force and the fact that it it did not play any role in the combat means that the Roman marching camp (at least 2.5 km by 2.5 km) was located somewhere east or north-east of Lake Adata and the marshy terrain north and north-east of it.
4) Abu Firas (BELA 2, 364) states that at the beginning of the battle the city of al-Hadath was between Sayf and the *domestikos*, which means that Bardas had approached from the east while Sayf had retreated to the hill behind the city (this would be the Mount Uhaydib/al-Uhaibid, which dominated al-Hadath). The likely reasons for the abandonment of the recently-built defences by Sayf are that the inhabitants of Adata were not loyal to the Arabs and the walls were not yet defensible. However, it is probable that this withdrawal did not take place immediately, but only after a prolonged period of fighting and skirmishing around the city.
5) According to Mutanabbi (BELA 2, 331), who was present at the battle (v.42–3), the battle lasted from morning until after midday, which means that there was a prolonged period of skirmishing with missiles before the next events took place. Even if Roman combat doctrine expected that the cavalry would fight alone against the enemy cavalry when it had been deployed for this purpose, it is still clear that the Roman marching camp

must have been at a distance of several miles to the east or north-east for its infantry forces to remain inactive during these hours. The marshy terrain and Lake Adata between the site of battle and marching camp would have prevented any active role from the infantry. The readiness of the Roman cavalry to fight it out without any attempt by the high command to bring infantry forces to the scene would have resulted from their theoretically-advantageous position (they had the high ground) against the Arab forces.

6) The final phase of the battle began with the Roman *katafraktoi* driving the Muslim first line towards the second line commanded by Sayf in person (Mutanabbi v.21–3).

7) Sayf launched a counter attack at the head of his 500 *ghilman* who were supported by other forces, so he abandoned his Rudayni-spear and used his Masrafi-sword (Mutanabbi, BELA 2, 331; v.23–8, 37). This means that Sayf favoured the tactic of forcing the men to advance to close quarters. Nikêforos clearly copied this approach from Sayf when he demanded that the front rankers in the *katafraktoi* wedge use maces rather than spears.

8) Sayf's cavalry attack crushed the Roman wings and forced them towards the centre (Mutanabbi, BELA 2, 333, v.25). In other words, Sayf would have used the crescent formation (wings advancing in column formation around the Roman wings while the retreating first line regrouped between the wings and centre) while he led his 500 cataphracted *ghilman* straight at the enemy centre, which would have been disordered by the previous contact with the first Muslim cavalry line and by the pursuit at the gallop. It is probable that the instructions in the ST for the use of the *katafraktoi* both in charge and pursuit contributed to the defeat. The ST (46.6, 46.9) instructed the *katafraktoi* wedge to use spears and gallop in the attack, which increased the chances of breaking the cohesion of the formation. In addition to this, the ST expected that the *katafraktoi* wedge would perform the pursuit of the enemy, which would naturally disorder the array even more, while the flanking units followed it as its defenders. This tactic obviously broke the contact between the units too. For further details, see Appendix 1. It is unlikely to be a coincidence that soon after this Nikêforos Fôkas felt it necessary to reform the system so that the *katafraktoi* were required to use the trot/canter during the charge and ordered the pursuit of the enemy to be performed by the flank divisions of the first line together with the *prokoursatôres*, while the *katafraktoi* reformed themselves and followed at a slower pace. See Appendix 1 with Appendix 3.4–7. In the PM Nikêforos also did away with the fill-up *banda* between the second cavalry line, which we still find in the ST. In my opinion, the likely reason for this reform can be found in the instructions in the PM for the use of the third line. The PM stated that when the enemy had *katafraktoi* of its own and fought on equal terms with the first cavalry line (see Appendix 3.8), the general was advised to dispatch the

three divisions of the third line through the intervals of the second line to outflank the enemy. In other words, it is probable that when Sayf's cavalry encircled the Roman first line, Bardas was expected to dispatch the third line *saka* to the flanks to oppose this move, but only with the result that these became tangled with the fill-up *banda* posted between the divisions of the second line.[70] In sum, this battle certainly stands as one possible source of inspiration for the reforms in the PM because Nikêforos was himself present and could witness in person the problems associated with the tactics of the ST.

9) The defeated Romans were dispersed on Mount Uhaybid, so Sayf and his horsemen pursued them up to the mountaintop while the cowardly *domestikos* fled and Nikêforos Fôkas hid himself in the sewer or water conduit below ground (Mutanabbi BELA 2, 333–4, v.29–37; Yahya 343/ BELA 2, 96–7. This would be the move to the Mount Uhaydib/al-Uhaibid mentioned by Abu Firas (BELA 2, 364), which took place after the initial situation in which the city of al-Hadath was between the two armies. The flight of the Romans uphill to the top of Mount Uhaybid and the location where Nikêforos hid himself means that Sayf had manoeuvred his army during the previous night so that he had turned the tables against the Romans. Now Sayf's army had its back towards the south, which provided a safe route of retreat for his army if the battle ended badly. This position forced the Romans to array their cavalry for combat so that the city of al-Hadath and Mount Uhaybid were behind them.[71] There are two possible reasons for the location of the Roman battle formation so that it had the city of Adata/al-Hadath behind it. Firstly, it is possible that they were surprised by Sayf's move (which must have been a night march with fires left alight on Mt. Uhaybid to fool the Romans), so that when the Romans had deployed their army towards the city of al-Hadath and Mount Uhaybid on the morning, their scouts suddenly informed them that the Arabs were actually behind them, with the result that the Romans had to turn their formation against the new threat. Secondly, it is possible that, when the Romans learnt of the new location of Sayf's force, they purposefully positioned themselves between the city and Arabs with the idea of blocking the route there. The former is likelier, because it is difficult to see why the Romans would have deployed their army purposefully so that they had no safe route of retreat to their marching camp. Considering Nikêforos Fôkas' location after the battle (sewer or water conduit), it is probable that he commanded the Roman right wing from the front.

10) The Romans lost about 3,000 soldiers, both cavalry and infantry, while large numbers of *scholarioi*, commanders and patricians were captured (Mutanabbi BELA 2, 331–2; Ibn Zafir, BELA 2, 125). The small number of cavalry and infantry casualties means that this was a cavalry battle and

that the Roman marching camp was not affected by the flight and provided a place of refuge for Bardas. The inclusion of infantry among the casualty figures means that Bardas had reinforced his cavalry line with light infantry archers and slingers. This tactic had undoubtedly been copied from the Arabs. We find Nikêforos Fôkas employing the same tactic at the battle of Tarsus in 965.[72] In fact, the DRM (19.27–35) advised the inclusion of infantry archers behind the first cavalry line to keep at bay the Arabs and Turks (in the DRM these would be the Hungarians), both of whom were primarily light cavalry mounted archers. The infantry archers had longer range than the mounted archers so this was an advantageous thing to do, at least for the beginning of the battle. In short, Bardas Fôkas had adopted the same tactic of posting infantry archers and slingers just behind his first cavalry line with the idea of breaking up the enemy's cavalry charge with missiles before his cavalry would make contact with them. In fact, this seems to have worked, but obviously with the result that the light infantry became separated from the first cavalry line when it started its pursuit. The fact that the Romans posted infantry archers and slingers just behind their front line suggests that the Arabs employed primarily light cavalry archers in front, with the implication that Sayf was using the crescent cavalry formation in which the front consisted of these (see Appendix 5: 5.1–2). The version with the extra flank guards is likelier in this case because the Romans were deployed in depth. At the beginning of the battle the Arab formation would have been square, so the crescent shape was adopted when the cavalry started advancing towards the enemy. The Arab cavalry line was wider than the Roman one, which was to have its consequences when the Romans failed to prevent the outflanking while their centre also collapsed.

The Numbers and Composition of the Armies

We can also estimate the proportions of the combined Roman army on the basis of three military treatises, the *Sylloge tacticorum* (46), *Praecepta militaria* (1–4),[73] and *De re militari* (1, 3, 5–8, 10, 13, 15, 17, 21). In the PM (4.4), Nikêforos Fôkas specifically noted that the same proportions for each arm of service and unit were to be followed, whether the cavalry force was larger or smaller, with the implication that the same was true for the infantry force. This means that when the Romans had 50,000 men: the ST divided this force into 37,000 infantry (74 per cent) and 13,000 cavalry (26 per cent); while the PM divided this same force into 36,500 infantry and 13,500 cavalry. It is obvious that the proportions are quite similar in the ST and PM, but in the DRM the proportion of the cavalry has been increased, so when the Romans had 50,000 men they would have had 34,000 infantry (68 per cent) and 16,000 cavalry (32 per cent). The figures in the DRM represented the need for increasing the size of the cavalry force when the emperor led the army in person, which was not the case in this battle. Therefore, considering the fact that the ST is likely to be representative of combat doctrine prior to the writing of the PM by Nikêforos Fôkas, one may make the educated guess that the Roman cavalry force in this battle consisted of approximately 13,000 horsemen and their infantry force of 37,000 footmen.

We can calculate the approximate sizes of each of the divisions in the roughly 13,000 cavalry army by comparing it with the 6,770 model army in the ST. The former is about 1.92 times greater in size than the 6,770 horsemen force, which means the following: 1) the vanguard consisted of approximately 960 horsemen (roughly 640 in front and 320 behind); the flank guard with the ambushers placed behind it (their presence could not be hidden by terrain in this case) consisted of 384 cavalry; the outflankers with the ambushers placed behind 384 cavalry; all three divisions of the first line consisted of 960 horsemen,[74] for a total of 2,880 cavalrymen; the second line of four divisions of 960 horsemen each, for a total of 3,840 cavalry plus 50 *bandofylakes* of the *stratêgos* (*domestikos*)[75] and three 192 cavalrymen fill-up *banda* (fill-up *banda*, total 576); the *saka* consisted of three divisions each 960 cavalry for a total of 2,880 cavalry; the rear guards of the marching formation consisted of three divisions of 192 cavalry for a total of 576 cavalry. This gives us approximately 12,530 horsemen. In other words, the figures should be seen only as approximations, which they are. The extra men would have been posted as supernumeraries.

It is probable that the force fielded by Sayf ad-Dawla in this battle belonged to the category of a large army as described by the *De velitatione* (see Appendix 2: 5.3), so it consisted of approximately 12,000 cavalry and 24,000 infantry, meaning that Sayf had roughly the same number of horsemen as the Romans – which is nicely proven by the results of this battle.

My Reconstruction of the Battle of Adata on 30 October 954 (see also the maps on the following pages)
In sum, the Arabs were first to arrive on the scene on 18 October, but it did not take long for the Romans to appear on 20 October. The Romans started to harass the Arabs, with the result that they retreated to Mount Uhaybid behind the city of Adata. The location up the mountain was untenable to the Arabs, with the result that Sayf performed a night march during the night of 29–30 October which the Romans failed to notice immediately, probably because Sayf had kept lights up the mountain. Consequently, when the Romans deployed for combat on the morning of 30 October they were opposite Adata when their scouts informed them that the enemy was now behind them. Bardas had been outmanoeuvred by his wily foe, so he could not seek help from his infantry that lay behind a lake and a marsh. The Romans still deployed for combat, confident in their victory as they held the higher ground. After the initial period of skirmishing with vanguards had ended, the Romans waited for the enemy to attack because they had posted infantry slingers and archers behind their first line. When the Arabs then attacked by using the crescent array, the Roman cavalry and infantry broke this attack with a barrage of missiles, after which the wedge charged and then began the pursuit of

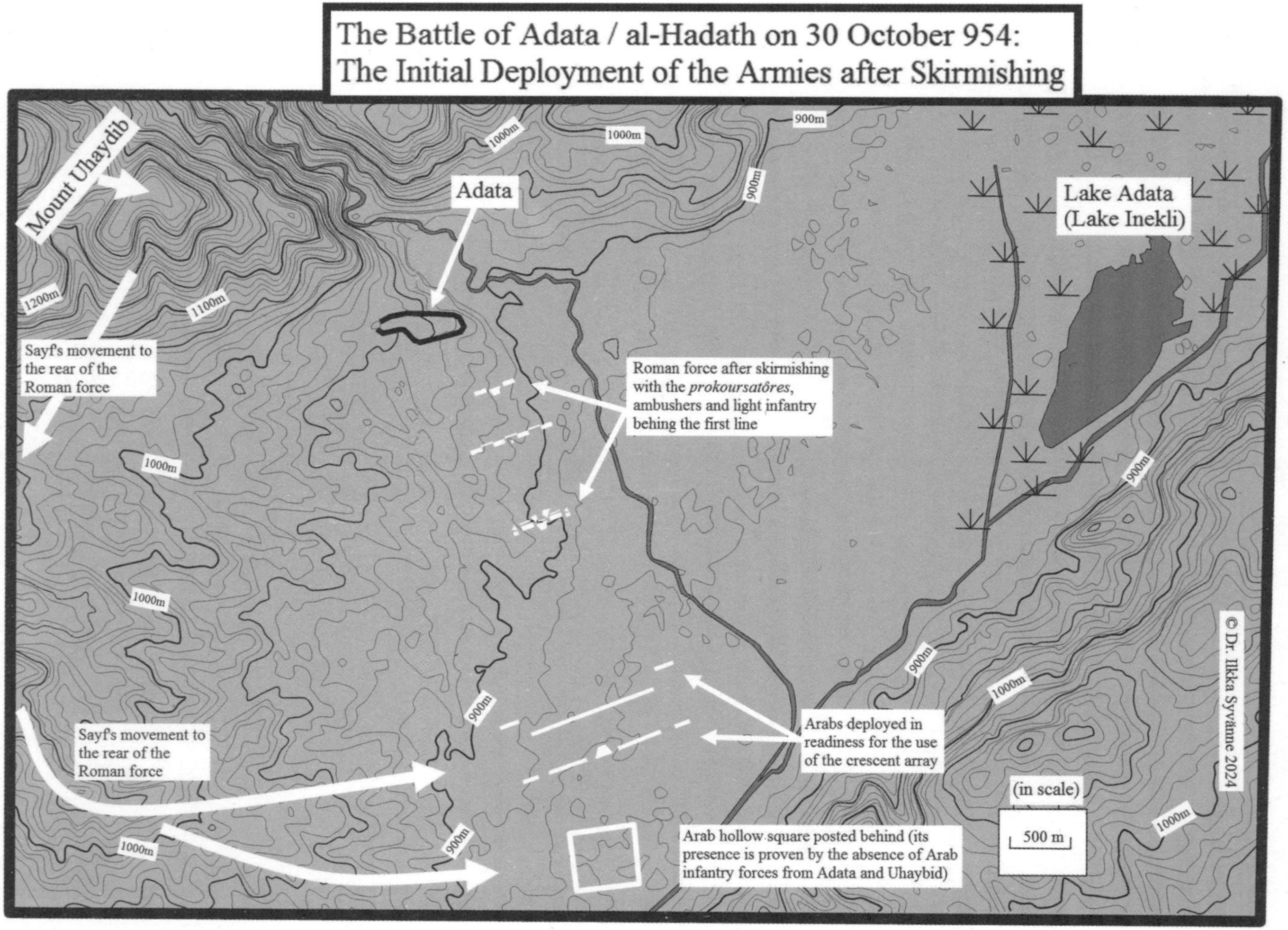

The Battle of Adata / al-Hadath on 30 October 954: The Initial Deployment of the Armies after Skirmishing

Lake Adata (Lake Inekli)

Adata

Mount Uhaydib

Roman force after skirmishing with the *prokoursatores*, ambushers and light infantry behind the first line

Arabs deployed in readiness for the use of the crescent array

Arab hollow square posted behind (its presence is proven by the absence of Arab infantry forces from Adata and Uhaybid)

Sayf's movement to the rear of the Roman force

Sayf's movement to the rear of the Roman force

500 m (in scale)

© Dr. Ilkka Syvänne 2024

| 1 | The initial battle formations after the cavalry skirmishing had ended. The Romans waited for the enemy to attack because they had infantry archers and slingers behind the first line. | # THE MAIN STAGES OF THE BATTLE OF ADATA ON 30 OCTOBER 954 |

© Dr. Ilkka Syvänne 2024

Bardas

infantry slingers and archers — the *prokoursatôres* behind the first line

the ambushers behind the outer wings

Nikêforos?

| 2 | the Arabs start to encircle the Romans |

Roman infantry slingers and archers deploy to block the encirclement so that they and the units posted in the wings force the outflanking Arab wings into retreat with a barrage of missiles while the Roman centre does the same.

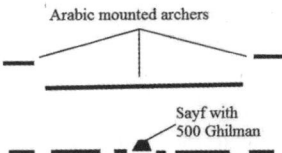
Arabic mounted archers

Sayf with 500 Ghilman

| 3 | Sayf's counter attack with the 500 *ghilman* forces the Romans into flight while his wings encircle the Roman first line. It is possible that the wings of Sayf's centre disordered the Roman wedge further by attacking its flanks. |

the Roman wedge pursues at gallop and becomes disordered while the *prokouratôres* fail to protect its flanks

the first Arab line regroups between the centre and wings

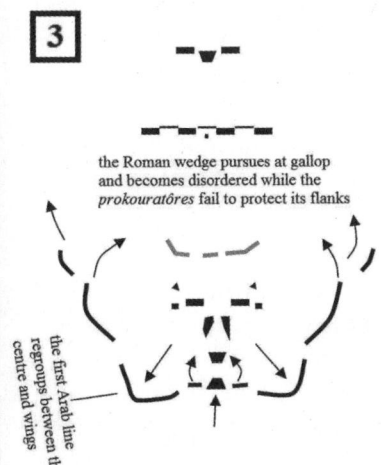

| 4 | The Roman *saka* is unable to move through the second line while the Roman first line is in full flight. Bardas decides to flee and the entire Roman army joins him. Nikêforos hides himself in the sewer of Adata while the Arabs pursue the fleeing Romans uphill to the top of the mountain Uhaybid. |

the fill-up *banda* fail to move out of the way and disorder both the second line and *saka*

the fleeing first line runs into infantry and disorders it

the regrouped first line joins Sayf in pursuit

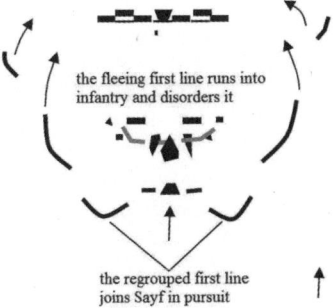

the fleeing foes. The pursuit at gallop disordered the wedge, while the supporting units (the cavalry wings and *prokoursatôres*) failed to provide adequate support. This enabled Sayf to crush the Roman wedge with his *ghilman* and force them and their supporting units into disorderly flight, which also disordered the light infantry posted behind. It is possible that the wings of Sayf's centre attacked and disordered the flanks of the Roman wedge while his own wedge charged it frontally, because Nikêforos (PM 4.12) later required that the *prokoursatôres* would deploy 50 horsemen on both flanks of the wedge to protect its charge. When the entire first line was in flight, Bardas attempted to save the day by sending the *saka* forward against the enemy's wings, but the fill-up *banda* between the intervals of the second line failed to move out in a timely manner, with the result that the entire Roman line became disordered. When this happened Bardas fled and with him the entire army. Bardas managed to make his way to safety, but his son Nikêforos was not so lucky because the wings of the Arab crescent bypassed him so that he was forced to hide himself underground in Adata until the night covered his flight to his father. The Arabs pursued the defeated Romans up to Mount Uhaybid, while the entire Roman cavalry force scattered in flight.

The Romans lost 3,000 cavalry and infantry killed. The losses also included large numbers of captives from the ranks of the *scholarioi* and their *archôntes*, most of whom Sayf executed. This proves nicely that most of the casualties were suffered by the cavalry, and in particular by its elite units posted in the middle, because these were the forces that the Arabs could encircle most easily when the Roman flanks fled. The captured notables included Theodôros the One-Eyed, the *stratêgos* of Lykandos, who was related to Bardas (his son-in-law?), and Bardas' grandson (Mutanabbi BELA 2, 331–2, v.35). Theodôros the One-Eyed would be the *T.m.d.s* (Theodoulos Parsakountênos/Parsakoutênos) of J.C. Cheynet (see his Appendix 5).

This was a humiliating defeat for Bardas Fôkas, but it had one positive outcome for the Roman Empire afterwards, because Nikêforos had been in a position to observe what went wrong with the result that he eliminated the tactical problems in the PM.

5.16. Year 955: Roman Offensives and Diplomacy

Diplomacy and operations against the Hamdanids

Despite the setbacks of the previous years the Romans had not yet given up hope of negotiating an exchange of prisoners and the conclusion of a truce. Consequently, Kônstantinos VII Porfyrogennêtos dispatched yet another envoy to Sayf who arrived at Aleppo on 13 May 955. The envoy was escorted by the horsemen from Tarsus, Adana and Massisa, which shows that he had passed through the Cilician Gates to Muslim-held territory. It is fairly likely that the initiative for the exchange of prisoners was also supported by Bardas, because his relatives were among the captives taken by Sayf in 954, but we do not know what the attitude of Nikêforos was to these negotiations. The results, however, were the same as before. Sayf humiliated the Roman envoy and dispatched him back empty handed.[76]

Therefore, the Romans besieged the newly-refortified city of Adata/al-Hadath on 26 August 955. The Romans considered the situation opportune because its inhabitants were still ready to betray the city to the Romans because they did not consider the walls provided by Sayf ad-Dawla to be sound (Mutanabbi, BELA 2, 337) – the reason being that the mortar had not yet set. One wonders if the real reason was actually dissatisfaction with Muslim rule which Mutanabbi just covers under the claim that the inhabitants were not satisfied with the walls that had been built? The Romans had reinforced their army with Slavs, Bulgarians, Russians and others as in the previous year. After all, most of the Roman army had survived the defeat at Adata, so that it was relatively easy to repeat the offensive. It is therefore clear that the Romans once again fielded a large army, which is likely to have consisted of the same number of men as in 954. According to Yahya (p.772, Chapter 74 / 113), the commander of the Roman army was once again the *domestikos* Bardas Fôkas, but this is not accepted by most modern historians, all of whom place the dismissal of Bardas from office to the period between late 954 and early 955.[77] I see no reason to doubt the text of Yahya, because the evidence used to counter this is not really relevant. See the discussion in the context of the events of the next year, 956. It is not known if Nikêforos Fôkas was accompanying his father on this campaign, but this is very likely, just as it is probable that both Leôn Fôkas and Iônnês Tzimiskês were among the commanders.

Sayf ad-Dawla learnt of the siege on 28 August. He reacted quickly and had already begun his march towards Adata on 29 August with the idea of relieving the besieged city immediately. This was indeed necessary, as the mortar had not yet set properly, with the result that the Romans were able to breach the outer walls before he could reach it. When Sayf reached Ra'ban, he learnt that the Romans had blocked all routes to the besieged city so that it was impossible to obtain any information about the situation, which obviously means that Bardas had blocked not only the most direct route to the Valley of Adata, but also the other possible side paths. This did not deter Sayf, who continued his march. When this happened, the Romans retreated in confusion from the hills blocking the route, with the result that the garrison of Adata was able to make a sortie in which they destroyed the abandoned siege engines. This appears to have taken place on 2 September.[78] Unlike the inhabitants, the garrison had remained loyal to the Muslim cause.

The disorderly retreat of the Roman army is not surprising, because the commander of the army was once again Bardas Fôkas, who had demoralized his army with his avarice, which had resulted in a series of defeats, which had demoralized the army even further.

The Sicilian and Italian theatres of war in 955–6
In 955–6 the Fatimids were at war with the Umayyads of Spain. The reason for the war was the capture of the Fatimid ship carrying diplomatic messages from

Sicily by a commercial vessel which belonged to the Umayyad Caliph Abd al-Rahman III. This event took place in 955–6. The response was swift. The new Fatimid Caliph, Imam al-Mu'izz (19.3.953–21.12.975), ordered the governor of Sicily to raid Almeria, which the latter conducted with great success because the Umayyads were completely surprised. The Umayyads responded by sending 70 ships against the Fatimid port of al-Kharaz (la Calle) and the environs of Susa. The Fatimid sources claim that it was the Umayyads who proposed an alliance to the Romans so that they could combine their fleets against the Fatimids. The timing was perfect, because the truce between the Fatimids and Romans ended in that very same year. The same sources claim that the Romans then dispatched a fleet to join the Umayyad fleet while they at the same time sent an embassy to negotiate a truce with the Fatimids. The Fatimids refused to accept the proposal of the truce and on 9 August dispatched a sizeable fleet, together with a large force under Ammar b. Ali b. al-Husayn, to Palermo to join forces with his brother al-Hasan b. Ali b. al-Husayn, the governor of Sicily. The problem we have here is the dating of the events, because the Muslim sources offer different dating schemes. The *Cambridge Chronicle* dates the arrival of Ammar in Palermo on 9 August 464 (955–6), while the *Kitab al-Uyun* and al-Numan date it to the year 345 (15 April 956–3 April 957). This discrepancy allows the dating of the events to different years. Since al-Numan (d. 974) was himself a participant on the Fatimid side and the official historian, I am assuming that his dating is correct, so the exchange of diplomatic messages and envoys between the Umayyads and Romans on the one side and then between the Romans and Fatimids on the other took until late-spring or early-summer 956 to accomplish. It was then after this that the Romans and Umayyads decided to join forces in earnest, while the Fatimids decided to dispatch reinforcements to Sicily, presumably under Ammar the brother of Hasan.[79]

Diplomacy with East Francia in 955–6
The Italian and Balkan theatres of war also required diplomatic activities elsewhere. The Romans were acutely aware of the Hungarian threat in the Balkans and also of the Fatimid threat in Italy. East Francia, the First German Reich, held the key position in both theatres. Consequently, when the emperor learnt that Otto I the Great had inflicted a crushing defeat on the Hungarians at the Battle of Lechfeld in August 955, he dispatched an envoy to Otto to congratulate him on his victory and presumably to discuss other urgent business – which undoubtedly included a suggestion to form an alliance against the Hungarians, and possibly also against the Fatimids in Italy. This alliance appears not to have materialized, and we find the Hungarians invading Thrace again in 958.[80]

It is not known with certainty if Nikêforos participated in the discussions regarding diplomacy prior to his participation in the campaign in Adata with his father, or if the emperor took the diplomatic initiative without hearing the opinions of either Bardas or Nikêforos. However, on balance it is far likelier that both father and son were present when the diplomatic initiative was taken because Otto I defeated the Hungarians in August and both the son and father abandoned the siege of Adata on about 2 September. This means that it is very likely that Bardas and Nikêforos were both advising the emperor at this time. It is in fact quite probable that it was during one of these policy discussions during the years 955–6 that Kônstantinos asked Nikêforos the famous question as to why his father had been so successful when serving under others while he was so unsuccessful when he held the highest command.

5.17. Year 956: The Romans on the Defensive in Italy and East

The defence against the Saracens of Tarsus and Aleppo: the spring 956

The Roman strategy for the year 956 was to conduct an active defence against the Arabs on multiple fronts. The defeats of the previous years and the old age of Bardas had diminished his eagerness for conquests. The Romans had dispatched a fleet to Italy with the task of engaging the Fatimid fleet, while they had put their eastern armies in combat readiness. Iôannês Tzimiskês was already actively raiding Diyar Bekr in early spring (see below), while Leôn Fôkas was in full readiness to launch similar raids into enemy territory. One may make the educated guess that Nikêforos Fôkas was in similar readiness at his theme, unless he was accompanying his father at the assembly point of the main forces, wherever that was located in this year. In fact, it is quite possible that Nikêforos was accompanying his elderly father at least initially, because Bardas was already suffering from the effects of old age (TC 6.41, 459) so that there would have been a need for the participation of someone younger and more active. The Saracens of the east were planning to conduct a double offensive by both a fleet and land army, but this was to take place in late-summer – early-autumn as every year, which in its turn means that these forces were reinforced by the Jihadists from Syria, Phoenicia and Egypt. The Saracen fleet was to consist of the Tarsiotes and was to include Jihadists, while Sayf ad-Dawla would lead the land army which would also be strengthened in like manner with Jihadists. However, there was to be a lot of fighting to be done before the Jihadists arrived.

The core of the following account comes from the poems of Mutanabbi and in particular from his commentators, one of whom was unknown while the other was Yazigi. In the following account I call them collectively Mutanabbi. Their accounts are complemented by bits and pieces of information provided by other sources.[81] According to Mutanabbi, Iôannês Tzimiskês had been conducting a series of raids against Diyar Bekr in spring 956. He appears to have been exploiting the revolt of the tribe of Banu Numair. When the news of this was brought to Sayf ad-Dawla at Aleppo he assembled his forces and departed on 28 Aptil 956. He left his cousin Abu'l Asha'ir Husayn b. Ali b. Husayn b. Hamdan in charge of the defence of the rear, assigned to reconstruct the fortress of Arandas (unknown) which was located between Duluk (Doliche) and Germanikeia. When Sayf reached Harran (Carrhae) he was met by the sheiks of the Banu Numair who begged for forgiveness. Sayf granted this and continued his journey via Hisn al-Ran to Hisn al-Hamma and from there to Hisn Arqanin, all of which were located in territory controlled by him. It was then on Saturday 10 May that Sayf advanced into enemy territory. At the same time as this happened, the Romans were advancing into Muslim territory with the purpose of attacking Amida. This force was commanded by a patrician (Iôannês Tzimiskês) below whom served other patricians. They had reached the pass leading into enemy territory when they learnt of the approach of Sayf, presumably from their scouts. The Romans chose to flee. The obvious reasons for the flight were twofold: the Romans force consisted solely of cavalry, which was unsuited to fighting in the pass, while the enemy also outnumbered them.

After getting through the pass, Sayf encamped his army at Lake Shimsat (Arsamosata), which implies that he pitched his camp either north or north-east of Lake Gölkük, because the normal Arabic term for the lake was Lake Sumnin. The difference in names is likely a reflection of from which side the lake was looked at. This served as a base camp for the raiding cavalry forces, which were dispatched to raid the surrounding regions. On Sunday 11 May Sayf dispatched two *ghilman* with a detachment to scout the route to the River Arshanas and fortress Ashwan, while he followed in their footsteps. Sayf encamped his army at a village called *.n.h.y.* beside the fortress of Ziyad (Harpoot/Harput) where he received the cavalry vanguard he had dispatched to reconnoitre. On the following morning Sayf marched to the River Arshanas, where he encamped his army beside the fortress of Ashwan. Aswhan was opposite the village/town of al-Ashkuniyya (Arshkeni), the residence of the patrician Iôannês Tzimiskês.[82] Sayf had boats and rafts built for the crossing, after which on Monday 12 May he ordered a part of his cavalry to swim across the Arshanas with orders to attack the enemy forces at Arshkeni from behind. The Romans were surprised and defeated, probably because they mistakenly believed that the infantry forces on the opposite shore were the entire enemy force opposing them. This victory enabled Sayf to transport his infantry across on boats and barges on Thursday 15 May. Howard-Johnston is correct to point out that the river crossing was a very bold move right in front of the enemy castles. After this Sayf marched against Tell Bitriq (the City of the Patrician, which would be Ashkuniyya/Arshkeni) and *a.s.f.wan* (interpreted as Usfuwan by Canard) – both unknown locations close to Arshkeni according to the prevailing modern interpretation.[83] I would suggest that Tell Bitriq and Arshkeni are actually the same place, because the accounts state that the Arab cavalry defeated the Romans there after they had swum across the river and after which the town was torched. I would also suggest that it is probable that *a.s.f.wan* is actually the fortress Ashwan, because Mutanabbi states that after having torched Arshkeni/Tell Bitriq (likely to mean the HQ of the patrician), he turned against another town (i.e. turned around), which was also burned in like manner, after which there is no account of any recrossing of the River Arshanas. Regardless, even if my interpretation above is correct, I have

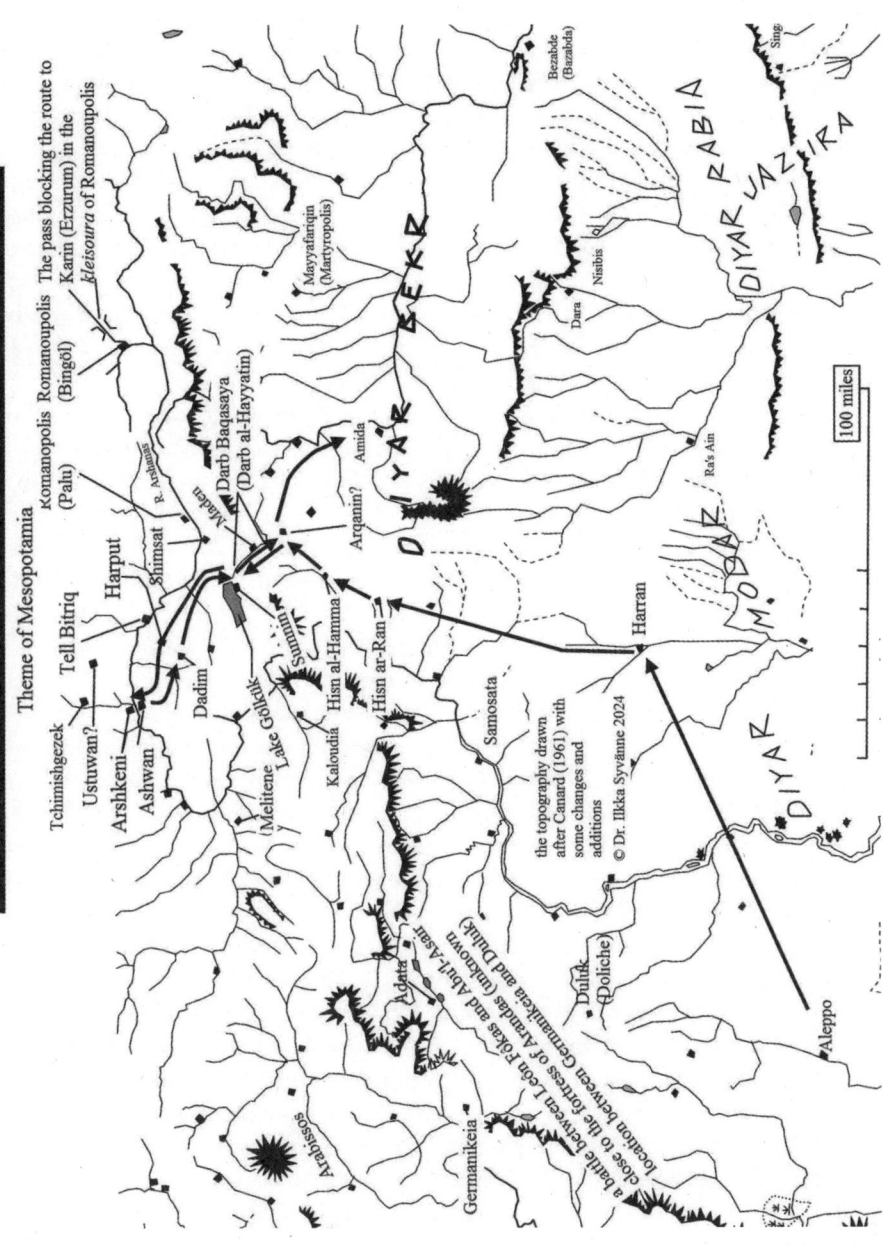

still included in the map on the previous page the locations which Howard-Johnston suggests for the Tell Bitriq and *a.s.f.wan* (Usfuwan).

It was then after the torching of *a.s.f.wan* (which I would identify as Ashwan) that Sayf dispatched his cavalry detachments against the surrounding regions from his base camp, which caused considerable damage to the Romans. On Saturday 17 May Sayf broke camp and marched against a village/town known as Huri (unknown), which he torched along with other villages while taking captives. On 18 May Sayf proceeded to besiege the fortress known as Dadim, which he found occupied by a Roman garrison on Tuesday (20 May) or Thursday (22 May). This sequence suggests that Sayf was on the southern side of the River Arshanas when he torched *a.s.f.wan*, hence my suggestion that it was Ashwan. Sayf was close to capturing the location on Friday 23 May, but then according to Mutanabbi he received the news that the Romans under the son of Shumshqiq (BELA 2, 347: i.e. Iôannês Tzimiskês) had collected a sizeable army with the intention of blocking his route of retreat through the defile called Baqsaya or Darb al-Hayyatin, Pass of Tailors or Lady's Suit (Kamal ad-Din, BELA 2, 182; Yahya 345, BELA 2, 97).

In contrast to Mutanabbi, Yahya (pp.772–3, Chapter 74 / 114 also in BELA 2, 97) claims that the Roman force at the pass was commanded by the *domestikos* and Iôannês Tzimiskês, while Kamal ad-Din (BELA 2, 182–3) claims that the commander was *K.du/Kadhu*, the son of the *domestikos*. It should be noted that the *Kadhu* or *K.du* (= *Ni k.du s/Ni kadhu s*) may hide the name Nikêforos, because Leôn was definitely not present at the pass. He was operating against the cousin of Sayf close to the town of Duluk at the same time. As son of the *domestikos*, Nikêforos (*Ni k.du s*) would definitely be a suitable candidate for the position, but there remains the problem that it was only after the campaigns of this year that Nikêforos replaced his father as *domestikos*, not to mention the fact that it would be strange to see him promoted over his more successful brother Leôn if he had just lost a major battle.[84] This, however, is not conclusive because he may have remained in the area and was the person who led the very successful raid against Martyropolis later in the year. This would have restored his reputation. See below. Nevertheless, on balance it is unlikely that either of these alternatives could be correct because Mutanabbi was himself present at the battle and it would be very odd if he failed to mention the presence of the *domestikos* or his son Nikêforos, because that would have added to the prestige of Sayf. On the other hand, one cannot entirely rule out this possibility because it was after this campaign that the relationship between Sayf and Mutanabbi turned sour, so that Mutanabbi was actually forced to flee from the court of Sayf in 957. The evidence is therefore inconclusive, but the likeliest version is that Iôannês Tzimiskês was the man in charge. Consequently, I will offer a more detailed analysis of the battle at the pass in the biography of Tzimiskês rather than in the biography of Nikêforos Fôkas.

When Sayf learnt of the Roman plan he abandoned the siege and marched at the double past a mountain called Hamutah into the Valley of Sumnin, where he pitched his camp. On Saturday morning 24 May Sayf led his army into the pass until he reached the place which was occupied by the enemy under the patrician, where he ordered an attack but the enemy fought back with great determination. The likeliest location for the Roman army is north of the village of Madan, because this is the only place which the enemy approaching from the north could not bypass by using a path. It was then that Sayf ordered his forces to attack the enemy where these thought themselves to be safe thanks to their advantageous position (BELA 2, 341). It was presumably because of this that it was occupied by only 300 archers (BELA 2, 345). At that moment the Muslims got very lucky because it started to rain, which made the Roman composite bows useless. It was then thanks to this that the Arabs were able to outflank and defeat the Romans. The Arab cavalry pursued the defeated Romans up to a location known as *T.h.ras*. The pursuit lasted until the afternoon. The battle and pursuit turned into a massacre, the Romans losing 4,000 killed, which included the *patrician* 'Rumanus ibn al-Balantas' (Rômanos Balantios/Balantas, brother-in-law of Iôannês Tzimiskês), 'Ibn F.sir' (the 'best' of the Christian cavalry), '*zirwar*' of Keltzene and Erzindjan, and large numbers of others, while 'ibn Qalmut' was captured. The booty included mules, oxen, fabric and brocades. After this Sayf continued his march, reaching Amida on Sunday 25 May 956.

In the meanwhile, the Romans had not been idle. The energetic Leôn Fôkas had exploited the absence of Sayf by advancing against Sayf's cousin Abou-l-Achair-ibn-al-Hasan-ibn-al-Housein-ibn-Hamdan (Abu'l Asha'ir Husayn b. Ali b. Husayn b. Hamdan) who had been left in charge of Delouk/Duluk with orders to refortify the fortress of *Ar.m.da* (Arandas). Leôn, the son of the *domestikos* (this establishes Bardas in this office for this year), attacked, defeated and captured Abou-l-Achair/ Abu'l Asha'ir and took him to Constantinople, where he later died. The key piece of information in the dating of the offices and the whereabouts of Nikêforos and Bardas is the statement that it was Leôn, the son of the *domestikos* who carried out the successful attack. This key piece of information is included both in the text of Yahya and of Kamal ad-Din, which means that the earliest possible dates for the appointment of Nikêforos as the new *domestikos* are either at the very end of 956 or at the very beginning of 957.[85]

The defence against the Saracens of Tarsus and Aleppo: the autumn 956[86]

In the autumn (on *gumada* 11 = 10 Sept.–8 Oct.) Sayf ad-Dawla launched yet another invasion of Roman territory, as was the habit among the Arabs. As was also typical for the autumn invasions, the army included Jihadists and was conducted by land and sea. The absence of Egyptian Jihadists was exploited by the Christian king of Nubia who invaded Egypt (Yahya 75–6, pp.773–4) and pillaged the area until the Egyptian army inflicted a defeat on them. The countries that dispatched Jihadists against the Romans also had borders with enemies, both Christian and non-Christian, who might exploit this.

The Romans used a three-fold response to this: 1) Bardas Fôkas together with the commanders *al-R.s.t* (the son of the deceased al-Balantos), *stratêgos* Leôn, 'ibn Gudal/Guzul' (patrician of the theme of Macedonia), *B.r.kil* (patrician of the theme of Chaldia), and probably others that Kamal ad-Din just fails to mention, conducted a guerrilla campaign against the invading Sayf; 2) while another Roman army conducted a diversionary campaign against Martyropolis under an unknown commander (Tzimiskês?); and 3) the fleet of the Kibyraiôtai/Kibyrraiôtai theme defended the coast against the Tarsiote fleet while Nikêforos would have protected his theme against the Tarsiote land forces. It is probable that we should unite *al-R.s.t* (the son of al-Balantos) with the *stratêgos* Leôn into the *stratêgos* Leôn Balantios, the son of the deceased Rômanos Balantios. The patricians Gudal of Macedonia and *B.r.kil* of Chaldia were likely to be the *stratêgoi* of these provinces rather than *tourmarchoi*.[87] If we assume that each of the commanders mentioned meant a *stratêgos* and that each of these, the *domestikos* included, brought with them about 3,000–4,000 horsemen, the size of the Roman army would have been approximately 12–16,000 strong. On the basis of the *De velitatione* it is clear that this force consisted only of cavalry. See Appendix 2.

The army under Bardas conducted a shadowing campaign until the Arabs reached the region of Charsianon '*Sariha*'. Since the target of the attack was Charsianon, it is probable that Sayf would have used either the Pass of al-Kankarun or of Adata when entering enemy territory. It was there that Bardas decided to engage the invaders, presumably with the idea of preventing the siege of Charsianon. The battle tactics would have followed the schemes described in the DV (see Appendix 2), so Bardas would have used cavalry for the combat with his rear protected by the fortress of Charsianon and the infantry. This battle ended just as the previous ones in which Bardas had decided to engage Sayf's forces with cavalry. The Romans were utterly defeated. It is unfortunate that the sources do not give us any details of the battle, but it is probable that the victory was once again achieved primarily by the Turkish *ghilman* under the personal leadership of Sayf. The Arabs took as captives Leôn Balantios and Gudat, while the *domestikos* and *B.r.kil* of Chaldia were put to flight. It is once again very likely that the poor reputation of Bardas among the soldiers contributed to the defeat. The Arabs pillaged '*Sariha*' and the region around Charsianon, but failed to capture the key fortresss Charsianon – presumably because the remnants of Bardas' force had retreated there. After this, Sayf began his retreat. We do not know the reason why he did so, but there are two likely reasons. Firstly, it is clear that the Arab invaders must have been tired by the time they reached Charsianon thanks to the fact that the Romans had harassed them constantly, which suggested that it was now time to retreat. Secondly, it is possible that it was at Charsianon that Sayf learnt for the first time of the Roman invasion of the region of Tarsus, so he decided to march there on the double. What is certain is that Sayf did indeed march close to Tarsus, because it is at Adana that he met the emir of Tarsus who had just been defeated by the Romans. The location of Adana suggests that Sayf had retreated through one of the routes that were located between the Cilician Gates and the passes of Eyerbel/al-Kankarun. If these had been blocked by Roman soldiers, then this campaign would have been one of the instances in which Sayf fought his way through. Even if Sayf was not returning to Adana to help the emir of Tarsus against the Romans, the choice of one of these routes was undoubtedly wise because it is probable that the Romans had blocked the other passes mentioned as they had done in the past, so Sayf wisely chose to use one of the routes between those.

In contrast to Bardas, the Roman army that conducted the diversionary raid against Martyropolis (Maiperkat) was remarkably successful. The Romans pillaged Martyropolis and took all its inhabitants as captives. In addition to this, the Romans burned all of the surrounding villages before departing. It is unfortunately impossible to know for certain who conducted this diversionary operation against Martyropolis because the sources fail to mention him. It is possible that it was done on the personal initiative of the *stratêgos* of Hanzit (this would be Iôannês Tzimiskês) or that he had been ordered to do so. On the other hand, we know that the sources do not mention the presence of Nikêforos in the army of his father, while it is known that he succeeded his father in the office of *domestikos* immediately after this. This suggests that Nikêforos may have been in charge of this diversionary operation, so Iôannês Tzimiskês served as his second-in-command, but not conclusively so because his whereabouts are rarely stated in the Muslim sources. However, if Nikêforos was indeed in charge of this campaign, he would have been a celebrated figure at the very same time as his father was forced to resign in disgrace. If Nikêforos had been in charge of the defence of the pass of Baqsaya or Darb al-Hayyatin mentioned above, this outstanding success would have exculpated his reputation just in time for him to succeed his father in office. However, on balance it is still likelier that the man in charge was Iôannês Tzimiskês.

In 956, at the same time as Sayf ad-Dawla conducted operations on land up to Charsianon and the Romans launched their diversionary raid against Martyropolis, the Saracen fleet of Tarsus raided the Roman coastal areas. They appear to have exploited the absence of a part of the Roman Imperial Fleet which had been dispatched to join forces with the Umayyad fleet off the shore of Sicily. The Romans had clearly retained the rest of the Imperial Fleet in the city of Constantinople for its defence, because its presence is not attested among those who defended the coast against the Tarsiotes.

The man opposing the Fleet of Tarsus, Basileios Examilitês (Hexamilitês), *patrikios* and *stratêgos* of the Kibyraiôtai/Kibyrraiôtai (Kibyrrhaiotai) *thema*, was still a young man but highly intelligent and very experienced for his age.[88] Consequently, he launched a surprise attack at a time when the Hagarene fleet was seeking to make a landing (proven by the outcome) somewhere close to the coast of Lycia. Basileios arrayed his numerically inferior fleet in a counter-formation (*antiparataxis*) against the numerically superior foe, which means that he deployed the fleet in the convex formation (centre advanced and flanks refused). This formation was used when the admiral[89] knew that the enemy had a numerical advantage so it was certain that they would outflank the Roman formation. The idea was therefore to win the battle with the centre alone, where the admiral would post his best ships with the flagship spearheading the attack.⁹⁰

The battle progressed as Basileios had envisaged, so after some shouting and shoving his flagship was the first to penetrate the enemy formation, apparently in such a manner that his galley used its spur to ride over the oars of one of the enemy vessels. When this happened, the Roman flagship started using its siphons to shoot liquid fire into the enemy vessels around it, which were torched. This enabled the rest of the ships of the centre to follow the example of their flagship, so they also penetrated the enemy formation while using siphons to shoot liquid fire around. The enemy vessels were engulfed in flames. The battle ended in complete victory. The Hagarenes were either slaughtered or taken prisoner. Most importantly, all of the enemy leaders/admirals (*êgemonoi*), chiefs/captains (*archontoi*) and steersmen/commanders (*kaitoi* = *qa'ids*) were captured alive. The fact that the entire Saracen fleet was either destroyed or captured means that it was fighting with its back against the shoreline of Lycia. The prisoners were dispatched to Constantinople, where Kônstantinos VII paraded them in the Hippodrome.⁹¹

This major naval victory weakened the threat posed by the fleet of Tarsus to such an extent that the Romans were able to dispatch a sizeable fleet under Basileios *prôtokarabos* to Italy in 957.⁹² I identify this Basileios *prôtokarabos* with the victorious *stratêgos* of the Kibyraiôtai/Kibyrraiôtai theme. However, before this took place, it was time for Basileios to exploit his naval victory by raiding the coastline of Tarsus, in the process of which the Romans torched many villages while killing 1,800 Arab soldiers. Bar Herbaeus claims that it was only after this that Sayf conducted the above-mentioned invasion of Roman territory around Charsianon, but it is easy to see that this invasion was actually simultaneous with the Tarsiote campaign against the Romans because, according to Bar Herbraeus and the other sources, the emir of Tarsus went to meet Sayf after he had conducted his campaign and was resting in Adana for a few days. It was then that Sayf encouraged the emir and said that he should not be afraid of the Romans, after which Sayf continued his journey to Aleppo.

In sum, Sayf had defeated Tzimiskês and had burned his headquarters, but the Romans had captured his cousin while destroying the army accompanying him; Sayf had inflicted a defeat on Bardas near Charsianon while capturing several smaller fortresses and villages, but the Romans had captured the city of Martyropolis with its inhabitants while the Kibyraiôtai/Kibyrraiôtai Fleet had defeated the Tarsiote fleet and torched the surrounding areas of the city of Tarsus. It is therefore clear that the Romans had inflicted at least the same amount of damage to their enemies as they were receiving at their hands. Regardless, it had now become apparent that while other Roman commanders were achieving a string of successes, the *domestikos* Bardas was not. It was then as a result of this that Kônstantinos was to ask Nikêforos the momentuous question of why Bardas had been so successful when serving under others but so unsuccessful when placed in charge. The results of this question will be discussed in the next chapter.

However, the quid pro quo was not the only achievement of the year for the Romans, because it was also in the same year that they obtained a new religious relic from Arab-held territory thanks to the personal heroism of the Antiochene deacon Job, who took the hand of Saint John the Baptist from its sanctuary in the city of Antioch in the middle of the night and carried it to Constantinople. The arrival of this important religious relic was used as a publicity stunt by the emperor to raise the morale of the Roman population.

Operations against the Fatimids in 956–7
As already discussed in the context of the events of the year 955, the Umayyads of Spain and Fatimids of North Africa and Sicily were at war with each other and as a result the Umayyads had proposed an alliance with the Romans. The Romans had responded to this with duplicity, by agreeing to the alliance while proposing truce to the Fatimids. The Fatimids, however, had refused to conlude the truce. The negotiations appear to have lasted until late-spring or early-summer, because it was only in August 956 that the Fatimids dispatched their fleet under Ammar to Palermo to join forces with his brother Hasan, the governor of Sicily, which was decimated by a storm close to Palermo on 9 August 956. It was thanks to this disaster that the Fatimids delayed their operations and wintered in Palermo, before launching their operations against Calabria only in the following spring of 957. The Romans had not been idle either. As we shall, see they had dispatched a fleet of their own, possibly already under Basileios *prôtokarabos*, to Italy to join forces with the Umayyad fleet.[93] It is clear that Nikêforos participated in the sessions in which the Roman strategy was formulated, because the sending of the fleet to Italy to join forces with the Umayyads was a major decision in a situation in which the Romans still had to face the resurgent Hamdanids in the east.

Below: Roman cavalry attacking a fortress (10th cent.)

source: Schlumberger

Chapter Six

Nikêforos Fôkas the Younger as *domestikos tôn scholôn*: The Last Years of Kônstantinos VII in 956/7–9

'Romanos, the child of Constantine [*in truth this person would be Kônstantinos*] ... When the barbarian, however, overrunning all of Roman territory freely destroyed everything and especially, when the Cretan commander had bungled the works [*i.e. the emperor is Kônstantinos and not Rômanos*], he did not know what to do further and resorted to his only and final hope, <I mean Nikephoros Phokas>, a man such as nature had never before created, brave of hand, extremely clever of mind. His father Bardas had already been in charge of the eastern part, second, it is true to his son, but not much inferior to him in bravery and strategical insight. Now, when the emperor had started his conference with Nikephoros, he asked: 'how can Roman power be ruined like this?' and Nikephoros is said to have answered without any diffidence: 'You are the emperor, my father is a commander [*stratêgos*] and you neglect the empire, while he loves only money. [*i.e. Bardas was a dynatos who had exploited his position at the expense of the thematic stratiôtai, while also stealing their booty so that these were not motivated to fight under his command. The referral to the absence of the emperor from the battlefield could be thought of as criticism of the fact that Kônstantinos was not leading the armies in person, as had for example Basileios I. It is in fact possible to think that it was after this that Kônstantinos wrote the treatise on Imperial Expeditions to the* De Ceremoniis *in about 957–8 and prepared to lead the army in person into Syria in 959, which Skylitzes 11.17 claims to have been his plan for that year.*]. But if you wish to achieve a change in the affairs, do not expect an immediate improvement of the collapsed power [*the restoration of the morale and the raising and training of the new soldiers would take some time to accomplish*]. I am ready to create the necessary resources of virtue for later military actions and under these conditions to resume warfare against the barbarians'. The emperor was only too glad to offer him the opportunity to do as he proposed, and Phokas immediately took care of the affairs [*Nikêforos replaced his father as* domestikos tôn scholôn], analysed the situation and restored the quota, partly from foreign forces [*i.e. Nikêforos hired foreign mercenaries*] and partly by his own activity to arm the agrarians and to transform the clodcutters into swordsmen [*i.e. Nikêforos required the themata contribute more men, but most of the reinforcements would have been drawn from the themata of the interior as required in the DRM 28. The DRM specifically notes the contrast between the* stratiôtai *of the interior and the borders, the latter of which were brave and warlike thanks to the constant warfare, while the former were not. If the soldiers were not drilled constantly and sent into action yearly, they were in danger of becoming mere farmers and merchants. In short, it is clear that Nikêforos drew most of his new recruits from the themata of the interior, and that he drilled these to the standard required. Unlike his father Bardas, Nikêforos would also show proper respect to the soldiers that served under him, ensuring that they were paid regularly and were not subjected to any abuse. This is what he also required in his DV 19, for which see Appendix 2 (2)].* He trained their arms for shooting the bow, for throwing the spear [*akontion, the javelin*], and for holding the lance [*makron doru, a long lance*] in a tight grip, and taught them to shoot on horse-back and to hit the mark when fleeing [*according to Manasses 5663ff., Nikêforos was a master equestrian trainer*], and further to fight on the battle-field, to attack and defend walls, to lay a siege to a city. [*The newly raised men needed to go through the entire training scheme, but it is also clear that the veterans were now re-trained to follow the methods described in the PM. This treatise represents a simplified version of the ST, so Nikêforos phased out combat methods that he considered harmful. For the differences, see Appendices 1 and 3*]. Then, after he had sufficiently finished his preparations, he confronted the barbarians and achieved the results spoke by everyone.'

Psellos (*Istoria syntomos, Historia Syntomos*, 103; *CFHB 30*, pp.94, 96, tr. p.95, 97 by W. J. Aerts with my comments inside parentheses in Italics. We have a similar account in Zonaras 16.23, which has been translated by Eric McGeer (1995, 179–80).

When Nikêforos Fôkas was appointed *domestikos tôn scholôn*, his brother Leôn succeeded him in the position of *stratêgos* of the Anatolikon *thema* [TC 462; PSs 7, 755], while Leôn's successor as *stratêgos* of the *thema* of Kappadokia was Kônstantinos Maleinos. The mother of Nikêforos belonged to the family of Maleinos, so Kônstantinos Maleinos was a maternal uncle of Nikêforos. The Fôkades kept the most important military commands in their own hands or in the hands of their close relatives. It is clear that the above frank exchange of opinions took place during the winter break in hostilities, which dates the promotion of Nikêforos Fôkas to the position of *domestikos* to the winter 956–7.

According to the *De velitatione* (Preface), when Kônstantinos Maleinos was the *stratêgos* of Kappadokia, he regularly used guerrilla tactics and achieved great successes with them, the details of which have not been preserved for us excepting the occasion when he accompanied Leôn Fôkas in his campaign against Sayf ad-Dawla in 960,[1] which gives us a perfect example of the successful use of skirmishing tactics. As noted by Canard and Dennis, it is also possible that he was the ibn al-Mala'ini defeated by the Tarsiotes in 962.[2] This is all that we know of him, which means that his successes as *stratêgos* of Kappadokia are not known in any detail

– all that we know is the above. He employed guerrilla tactics regularly with great success, which obviously means that the emir of Tarsus or the other emirs were unable to achieve any major successes in his territory before 962.

The above quotation, information in the PM (see Appendix 3), and the referrals to the fair treatment of the soldiers by Nikêforos Fôkas and the demands for these in the DV (see Appendix 2) and DRM (esp.28–9), suggest that the key elements in Nikêforos' military policies and successes were the following: 1) increased numbers of *stratiôtai* (Nikêforos increased their numbers even more when he became emperor) and mercenaries; 2) very thorough training and drilling of the soldiers and officers; 3) the writing of military treatises for the officers to ensure that they had all the necessary information also in writing (the PM and the memoranda of Nikêforos, which became the DV in the hands of the editor); 4) the respectful treatment of the *stratiôtai*; 5) the regular and prompt payment of salaries; 5) the fair distribution of the spoils of war; 6) the instillment of religious fervour in the soldiers (e.g. PM 6.2–3) prior to combat to make them fight more eagerly; and 7) the inspiring leadership of Nikêforos and his relatives (Leôn Fôkas, Iôannês Tzimiskês, and Kônstantinos Maleinos).

The year 956 saw an important event in the imperial family, when the heir apparent Rômanos chose to remarry against the wishes of his father Kônstantinos VII. Rômanos had fallen in love with a beautiful Greek woman from the region of Lakonia named Anastasia/Anastasô. Anastasia was the daughter of a tavern keeper, so she had very humble origins. The son was so smitten by her beauty that he would not listen to any opposing views and married her. Anastasia took the imperial name Theofanô. She was to play an important role in the life of Nikêforos Fôkas, both good and bad.

6.1. 957: The Year When Nikêforos Fôkas Made His Mark on the Strategy of the Empire

As agreed with the emperor Kônstantinos VII Porfyrogennêtos, the new *domestikos* Nikêforos set out to reform the army and strategy. The cornerstones of the strategy adopted jointly by the emperor and *domestikos* for the year 957 were the following: 1) the recruitment and training of new thematic recruits; 2) the recruitment of new foreign mercenaries, which entailed the conversion of the Russians into the Orthodox faith and the recruitment of significant numbers of Russians into the Roman army; 3) the reform of combat methods (PM and draft versions of the DV), which were distributed as memoranda to the officers; 4) the undermining of the loyalty of the enemy *ghilman*; 5) the dispatch of a fleet to join the Umayyad fleet with the aim of destroying the Fatimid fleet so that favourable terms of peace could be negotiated; and 6) the destruction of the rebuilt fortifications at Adata by using the Roman field army under the personal command of Nikêforos.[3]

The fact that the *domestikos* Nikêforos wrote letters secretly to the *ghilman* of Sayf ad-Dawla and managed to bribe them to change sides means that Nikêforos had come to the conclusion that the principal reason for the battlefield successes of Sayf were his cataphracted elite *ghilman* of Turkish descent.[4] On the basis of the above accounts, where it is stated that Sayf achieved his victories with either 500 or 600 horsemen accompanying him, it is clear that this analysis was accurate. The undermining of the loyalty of these *ghilman* therefore became the cornerstone of the strategy of Nikêforos, and the results of his unorthodox methods became visible immediately. As will be made clear in the forthcoming biography of Tzimiskês, the Romans also managed to convert to their side some of the highest ranking Turks in the Buyid court, which sabotaged their operations against the Romans at every opportunity. These traitors included Alptakin. For example it is quite possible that when Alptakin destroyed the Khurasani forces in 962 mentioned by Miskawayh (191–2, 5.p.208) that he was not doing that only as a representative of the Buyids but also as a secret operative of the Romans.

According to Yahya and Nikêforos himself (BELA 2, 375), in 957 the *domestikos* (i.e. Nikêforos) besieged the fortress of al-Hadath (Adata), with the result that it surrendered on 2 June–1 July 957. Its defenders were allowed to depart the fortress and go to Aleppo. Soon after this Adata was formed into a new theme, later named as such in the *Taktikon* of Escurial. This begs the question of why Sayf ad-Dawla failed to come to its rescue, because Kamal ad-Din claims that it was only on 31 July–29 August 957 that the *domestikos* dispatched the letters to the *ghilman* that undermined their loyalty. It is clear that the two historians have made a mistake regarding the dating, so the rebellion of the *ghilman* in truth took place simultaneously with the siege of Adata. This is actually obvious from the fact that the plot was exposed when Sayf had left Aleppo and was on his way to engage the Romans. In short, Nikêforos was able to render his enemy incapable of defending the recently rebuilt city with a well-placed bribe. Nikêforos was acting with far greater insight than his father had done. It was wiser to undermine the enemy's ability to fight with a sweetener than fight it on equal terms on the battlefield. According to Kamal ad-Din, when Sayf had just left the city of Aleppo to fight against the Romans the plot of the *ghilman* to betray Sayf ad-Dawla to the Romans was exposed by his chamberlains, and it was the *ghilman*'s officer ibn Kaygalag/Kaigalag, also of Turkish origins, who informed Sayf of the plot. Sayf assembled the Arabs and the Daylami, the latter being vehement enemies of the Turks, and gave them the order to kill all the *ghilman* when he gave the signal for this. This they did, killing 180 *ghilman* and capturing approximately 200 more. Sayf had their hands, feet and tongues cut off. The surviving *ghilman* fled Aleppo with Sayf in pursuit. When Sayf reached Aleppo, he ordered the killing of 400 Roman prisoners as a revenge for undermining the loyalty of the *ghilman*. In addition to this, Sayf ordered the son of the *domestikos* to be put in chains in the basement of his palace. This son of a *domestikos* would not be the son of Nikêforos or Bardas, but the grandson of Bardas captured at the Battle of Adata in 954. In other words, he would have been the son of Theodôros the One-Eyed, who is called *T.w.d.s* (Theodoulos Parsakountênos/Parsakoutênos) by J.C. Cheynet (see Appendix 6). Sayf rewarded ibn Kaygalag/Kaigalag with high offices, while all the privileges of the Turkish *ghilman* were removed.

The problem with the *ghilman* was not restricted to Sayf, because in the following year of 958 the Turkish and Daylamite *ghilman* both revolted against his brother Nasir ad-Dawlah in Mosul, with the result that Nasir engaged and defeated both groups with the help of his personal retainers and the populace of Mosul. The surviving *ghilman* fled to Baghdad to the safety provided by the Buyid sultan Mu'izz ad-Dawlah, the official overlord of Nasir and Sayf ad-Dawla.[5] One wonders if Nikêforos' diplomacy and bribes were also behind this revolt, or if the revolt had been instigated by the Buyid Mu'izz ad-Dawlah, or if Nasir had similarly removed the privileges from his *ghilman* as a safety measure so these then revolted, or if all of the above are true. The likeliest of these, however, is that the mutiny had been instigated with the bribes of Mu'izz.

The Romans were also lucky in 957 because the domains of Sayf ad-Dawla and his neighbours up to the Persian Gulf were hit by multiple natural disasters. First came locusts in huge numbers which destroyed the crops so badly that Sayf did not have even enough provisions to campaign in the autumn of 957. After this followed a pestilence among the population weakened by famine. Then, in winter 957–8, followed torrential rains in some places while other places had no rain at all. The Great Sea (either the Persian Gulf or the Caspian Sea, probably the latter) also saw a drop in the level of water so that new hills and islands appeared. This is to be connected with the earthquake which struck the mountains in the region of Rayy in Persia in 958. In other words, the sea level lowered permanently as a result of this earthquake, which proves it to have been a very significant event.[6] These natural disasters obviously weakened both Sayf and his potential Muslim supporters in the east.

Diplomacy with Russia

As noted in the context of the events of the year 946–7, it is possible that the Russian queen Olga visited Constantinople in 957 rather than in 946–7 and that it was in 957 that she was baptized, after which she concluded a treaty with the Roman emperor which she did not keep because Kônstantinos had treated her badly. The treaty had stipulated that she was to send Russian/Varangian mercenaries for the Romans, which shows that these were held in high esteem in Roman territory as soldiers.[7]

If this event took place in 957, it is probable that this request had been made by the *domestikos* Nikêforos Fôkas. It is this fact in particular that bespeaks for the date 957. As we have seen, Nikêforos Fôkas set out to increase the size of the Roman army with both foreign mercenaries and native recruits. The value of Russians as steady infantry was recognized and the reforms that Nikêforos made to the structure of the infantry hollow square required more Russians to serve in the intervals of the formation than was the case previously. The Russians were useful both as line infantry able to withstand an enemy cavalry attack, and as a highly mobile force which could also serve as mounted infantry alongside cavalry for the purpose of providing them with steady infantry if there was a need for this. See Appendices 1 and 3. Whatever the case, these mercenaries were never sent.

The western sources inform us that it was in 959 that Olga asked Otto I of Francia to send her priests and a bishop. This suggests that the souring of the relationship had taken place just before this, which in its turn implies that the baptism had taken place in 957. Adalbert of Trier (the later Archbishop of Magdeburg) was consecrated as Bishop of Russia, but his mission failed because the Russians were vehemently pagan, so he returned to Francia in 962. Olga also tried to convert her son Svyatoslav, but with no result because he knew that his pagan subjects despised Christians.[8]

Despite the fact that the Romans were unable to obtain mercenaries from Russia, the situation was beneficial to the Romans as it allowed them to continue their campaigns against the Arabs during those years. The man who was in charge of these operations was Nikêforos Fôkas. However, the situation was to change when Svyatoslav reached adulthood because he needed to demonstrate his merits as a warlord and he chose to do so at the expense of Roman interests.

The Romans and their Umayyad allies vs. the Fatimids in 957–8

As noted above, the Romans and Sunni Umayyads had concluded an alliance against the Shiite Fatimids in 956 with the result that the Fatimids had dispatched a fleet under Ammar to Palermo. Ammar's fleet had been hit by a storm close to Palermo on 9 August 956 with the result that he had to delay his operations against Calabria until spring 957, which then enabled the Romans and Umayyads join forces in the same year.

According to al-Numan, Ammar defeated the Romans under an unknown commander in the spring 957 and then returned to Mahdiyya, the Fatimid capital in North Africa. The caliph then dispatched a new fleet under Gawhar/Jawhar and Hasan, the brother of Ammar and governor of Sicily, to Sicily. The fleet under Hasan duly defeated the allied fleet composed of both Romans and Umayyads. According to al-Numan, Ammar had no role in this battle. The Umayyad fleet fled south-west towards the coast of North Africa, where the locals defeated it on land, and from there to Spain, while the Roman fleet under an unknown commander fled towards the Straits of Messina to defend Calabria. The Fatimid fleet defeated the Romans again, which enabled the Fatimids to disembark their army in Calabria where they torched many villages and churches.[9] In my opinion, it is likely that it was this success of the Fatimid navy against the Romans and their ravaging operations in Calabria that encouraged the discontented Neapolitans and Lombards into revolt and alliance with the Fatimids, a revolt which is mentioned by Theophanes Continuatus (6.30–2, 453–6) as the reason for the sending of Marianos Argyros with an army and fleet to Italy, which took place in 958.

The problem with this is that the Sunni sources offer an entirely different version of events. According to the *Cambridge Chronicle*, the Fatimid fleet under Ammar was dispersed by a storm off Sicily on 9 August 956, so they were only able to launch their offensive against Roman Calabria with diminished numbers in the first days of spring 957. It was in the same year that the Roman naval commander, Basileios *prôtokarabos*, landed at Rhegium/Reggio and then proceeded to capture Termini in Sicily and the island of Rhib, while also destroying a mosque in some unknown place. It is probable that Basileios *prôtokarabos* was actually Basileios Examilitês from the Kibyraiôtai/Kibyrraiôtai theme. The *Cambridge Chronicle* then claims that Basileios engaged and defeated the Fatimid fleet under Hasan at Mazara off the coast of Sicily, sinking twelve Muslim ships in the process while taking large numbers of captives. The *Kitab al-Uyun* states that the fleet of Hasan was dispersed by a storm, so the Romans defeated them close to the Island of Rahib (Rhib) in the straits of Messina with the Muslims losing twelve ships. Similarly, Ibn al-Hatib claims that the storm destroyed the first fleet of Hasan, with the result that the Romans were able to capture a fortress in Sicily (this would be Termini).[10]

If one were to try to reconcile these sources, then it might be possible to think that Ammar was initially successful in spring 957, but was then forced to abandon the campaign when the Romans and Umayyads joined forces. When Ammar then brought the news of this to Mahdiyya, the Fatimid caliph dispatched a new fleet under Hasan and Dawhar against the allies, with the result that both enemy fleets were utterly defeated, the Romans actually twice. Hasan then disembarked his forces in Calabria and pillaged the area, but this was cut short by the arrival of the Roman fleet under Basileios *prôtokarabos*/Examilitês. The sending of naval reinforcements under Basileios in 957 was possible thanks to the destruction of the Tarsiote fleet in 956 and the sending of these reinforcements to the scene would have reflected the strategy that the new *domestikos* Nikêforos and emperor Kônstantinos formed jointly to meet the crisis. Their first plan, the joint operation with the Umayyad fleet, had failed, so they had to dispatch a new fleet to the scene. The surprised Hasan then attempted to retreat with his booty towards Sicily, but with the result that his fleet was dispersed by a storm, which in its turn enabled Basileios to inflict a defeat on Hasan near the Island of Rhib and/or possibly again at Mazara. It is probable that the defeat of Hasan took place in the autumn, because storms were/are more typical for that time of the year, and secondly because it would have taken a while for the Romans to respond to the defeat of the allied fleet. Basileios exploited his victory by capturing the island of Rhib and the fortress of Termini in Sicily, while Hasan fled to Mahdiyya to collect a new fleet for the next year. This, however, was not the end of the Roman troubles. The previous success of the forces of Hasan had encouraged the discontented Neapolitans and Lombards to revolt, which required the sending of far larger forces to crush. The Roman response was to dispatch a fleet and army under Marianos Argyros in 958 on the basis of the timing of the events in the Arabic sources.[11] It is clear that as the new *domestikos* Nikêforos Fôkas was closely involved in important strategic decisions such as the sending of Basileios *prôtokarabos* and Marianos Argyros to Italy.

6.2. Year 958: The Romans vs. Hamdanids, Italian Rebels, Fatimids and Hungarians[12]

In spring 958 the Romans were clearly planning to continue their offensives against Sayf ad-Dawla and Italian rebels, because the circumstances for this were very favourable. The Hamdanids had been weakened by defeats, famine and pestilence and by the revolt of the *ghilman*, while the Fatimid fleet had suffered a defeat in the previous year, so both Nikêforos and Kônstantinos thought that it would be possible to limit the number of enemies by buying a truce from the Fatimids, but in this they were mistaken, so the Roman reinforcements dispatched to Italy under Marianos Argyros were also forced to fight against the Fatimids as well. Nikêforos and Kônstantinos both considered the Balkan frontier secure, because they were at peace with Bulgaria, so they could dispatch an army from the Balkans together with a fleet under Marianos Argyros to Italy to crush the Neapolitan and Lombard rebels. In this they were also mistaken. The Bulgarians failed to protect the frontier against the Hungarians.

However, the key elements of the strategy adopted by Kônstantinos and Nikêforos remained the same. They sought to conclude peace treaties or treaties of alliance with all other parties than the Hamdanids and Arabs of Crete. In fact, we can time all of the other campaigns, wars and treaties on the basis of information provided by Abu Firas regarding the dates of the treaties concluded between the Romans and their neighbours. According to emir Abu Firas (BELA 2, 368–40), a subordinate of Sayf ad-Dawla, the emperor Kônstantinos VII had concluded a truce with the entire west, meaning that the Romans had concluded peace with the Bulgarians, Russians, Turks (Hungarians), Franks and other peoples of the west (includes undoubtedly the Fatimids) before he dispatched *parakoimômenos* Basileios, the son of Rômanos I and brother of the empress, against Sayf ad-Dawla. This means that all of the campaigns against other nations had been concluded by the time Basileios campaigned against the Arabs, which dates these to the previous period.

The course of the war between the Romans and Fatimids in the spring to summer 958
In 958 the Roman strategy against the Fatimids was initially to seek a truce with promises of tribute, but this came to naught initially. The Romans appear to have taken this step at the same time as they prepared to send a fleet and army under Marianos to Italy to crush the revolt. One may therefore speculate that the second portion of the Roman strategy was to convince the Fatimids to sign a long truce with a demonstration of military strength under Marianos Argyros. The fact that the leader of this naval expedition was one of the most important men of the Roman Empire proves that it was a major effort, which is also confirmed by the account of Theophanes Continuatus, who states that the land forces consisted of the Thracian and Macedonian armies. Marianos held the title of *stratêgos* of Calabria and Lombardy, while the commanders of the fleet were Krambeas and Moroleôn.[13] The

peace with Bulgaria was thought to secure the Balkans, so that it was safe to send land forces to Italy as well. It is clear that the new *domestikos tôn scholôn* Nikêforos Fôkas contributed heavily to the adoption of this approach, but it should be noted that this was not a new strategy. The Romans had already adopted the same strategy in 955. The Romans sought to pacify the Fatimids with a combination of force and diplomacy so that they could concentrate their forces against Crete. As usual, the Romans sought to avoid simultaneous wars on multiple fronts. It is therefore clear that Nikêforos shared the same perception of the strategic situation as the other persons in high positions.

The forces of Marianos Argyros had probably reached Italy in about April 958, because his forces were not present when the Hungarians invaded Roman territory in April. The Romans landed at Otranto and proceeded to besiege Naples by land and sea. The land army surrounded the city while the fleet took control of all sea routes. The encirclement was so tight that no supplies were able to reach the city and the famine-stricken defenders were forced to surrender. Theophanes Continuatus and Sunni sources offer us differing accounts of how the war at sea progressed, but which are possible to reconcile if one makes the assumption that the Sunni sources and Skylizes have left out the naval battle mentioned by Theophanes Continuatus. According to Skylitzes, when Marianos arrived the Saracens simply fled on their ships, which were then destroyed in a storm close to Palermo, with the result that the two sides agreed to continue their previous agreement. However, according to the Sunni sources this time the brothers Ammar and Hasan joined their forces and advanced against Marianos Argyros, presumably with the idea of relieving the city of Naples. According to these same sources, Marianos decided to flee, but this did not bring victory to the Muslims because they actually lost one ship to the Romans in the process. I would suggest that it was then that the battle between the fleets mentioned by Theophanes Continuates took place, so the flight of the Roman fleet was actually a feigned flight. According to Theophanes, the two fleets engaged each other with the Roman fleet using liquid fire while the galleys were intermingled with each other. It was then that the strong wind started blowing against the Muslim fleet, which helped the Romans to sink the enemy ships with their crews. I would suggest that the Romans knew that the direction of the wind would typically blow against the enemy if they would face them at a spot of their own choosing at the right time. Both Leôn o Sofos (*Taktika* 19.57) and Syrianos Magistros (*Naumachica* 12) recommended the exploitation of weather against the enemy, so this is not surprising.[14]

We can then add the information from the Sunni sources to explain what happened next. According to these Muslim sources and Skylitzes, the fleet of Ammar was utterly destroyed in a storm somewhere close to Palermo. The location Palermo suggests that the Muslim fleet was in the process of retreating after the defeat described by Theophanes. The corpse of Ammar was found among the debris of the ships on the following morning. The funeral proceedings were performed by his brother Hasan. The Romans were once again very lucky. The timing of the truce before the campaign of Basileios and the subdual of the Neapolitans by famine suggest that the naval encounters between the Fatimid and Roman fleets took place in late spring.[15]

Theophanes claims that it was the Fatimid emir (caliph al-Mu'izz) who begged for peace, while the Fatimid sources claim that the Romans begged for peace. Qadi al-Numan claims that the reason for the Roman readiness to negotiate and agree to pay a tribute was that the Fatimids had successfully raided Calabria where their forces had laid waste many towns, but this was not the real reason, because the Romans had by then reconquered the rebel areas and had defeated the Fatimid fleet twice, while the Fatimid fleet had also been further decimated by two storms. The Romans agreed to pay the Fatimids a yearly tribute in return for the truce because they wanted to concentrate their efforts against Crete and Aleppo. The Fatimids in their turn were also ready to conclude the truce because they had already lost two fleets to storms while suffering other setbacks, while also being at war with the Umayyads of al-Andalus.[16]

I would suggest that both Theophanes and al-Numan have preserved for us partial evidence, so both have omitted some of the details. The Shiite/Sh'ia al-Numan has left out all of the defeats suffered by the Fatimids which have been preserved only by Theophanes and Sunni Muslim sources, while Theophanes has left out the Roman defeats and the fact that the Romans still bought the peace with money. The probable reasons for the Roman readiness to buy the peace would have resulted from two facts: the Hungarian invasion had proved that the Bulgarians would not protect the Balkan frontier, so the Romans needed to return the Thracian and Macedonian armies back to their regular staging areas; and the Romans wanted to avoid war on several fronts when they aimed to engage the Hamdanids and retake Crete. It is probable that the Fatimid caliph did indeed dispatch envoys to Constantinople in early summer 958, because the Muslims of Fraxinetum also dispatched envoys of their own to Constantinople and begged for peace, which was granted to them, which would have been a very strange thing to do if the Fatimids had been as successful as al-Numan claims. In short, it is likely that the Fatimids dispatched envoys in summer 958, with the result that the two sides concluded the truce in about June–July 958.[17]

The Umayyads must have been aware of the Roman intentions, because they also proposed a truce to the Fatimids at the same time in 958, but this was rejected by the Fatimids. However, there is still no evidence of further clashes between these two, so we do not know what happened after the initial refusal. The truce between the Fatimids and Romans lasted until the Romans began their campaign to retake Crete in 960.[18]

According to Theophanes Continuatus (6.32, 455–6), when the emir of Egypt (Kafur the Eunuch?) heard of the great Roman naval victory, he dispatched envoys to Constantinople to conclude peace, which the emperor agreed to. It was because of this that Kafur the Eunuch felt strong enough to disregard Mu'izz ad-Dawla's demands for tribute, and it was because of this that Jihadists were not available from

Egypt at the time when the Romans renewed their offensive against the Hamdanids in about September. Theophanes also claims that the emir of Persia who had fought against the Romans and had suffered numerous defeats sought peace with the emperor. The emperor agreed to this, which presumably means that Nikêforos Fôkas had also advised this. The emir dispatched hostages to Constantinople. The identity of the emir of Persia is not known with certainty. Sullivan (RFNF, 37) notes that this could mean Muizz ad-Dawla of the Buyid-dynasty (controlled Persia) or Sayf ad-Dawla of the Hamdanid dynasty. On the basis of the events of the year 958, one can rule out any treaty between the Romans and Sayf, so the likeliest candidate would be Mu'izz ad-Dawla of Baghdad whom we find operating against the Hamdanids as early as 2 September 958, with the implication that the Romans must have defeated the Fatimids already in early summer. The numerous defeats suffered by the emir of Persia must mean the defeats that the Arabs had suffered in general over the years, because the caliph of Baghdad was officially their ruler. The use of the Buyids against the immediate neighbours of Rome would have followed the age-old diplomatic traditions in which the Romans incited someone else against their immediate neighbours. It is clear that, as *domestikos*, Nikêforos once again had a role in these diplomatic manoeuvres. The forceful response in Italy and Sicily had brought about significant advantages also on other fronts.

In short, Nikêforos' strategy was working, but it would cause him problems in the future, because the successful Italian campaign increased the reputation of Marianos Argyros among the soldiers to such an extent that he could be seen as a contender for the throne in 963 (see e.g. LD 3.2). His reputation would improve even further as a result of his successful defence of the capital against the Hungarians in 961.

The 'Turkish' (Hungarian/Magyar) Invasion in April 958

On the basis of Theophanes Continuatus (6.47, 462–3) we know that the Hungarians invaded Roman territory in March–April and that they reached the gates of Constantinople on 11 April 958. It was presumably thanks to the crushing defeat at Lechfeld in 955 that the Hungarians/Magyars started to look for other, easier places to pillage, and on the basis of their previous major campaigns in 934 and 943 and numerous lesser raids, the Roman Empire appeared a possible target. The absence of the Thracian and Macedonian armies gave the ravenous Magyars a golden opportunity which they could not resist. According to Simone de Kéza, the leader of the expedition was Taksony (Taxis of DAI), the grandson of Arpad, which would mean that this was a major expedition led by the king of Hungary (ca. 947–ca.972), while the *Illuminated Chronicle* (62) claims that the leader was *capitaneus* Opous (Apor) chosen by common will. In light of the success and lack of resistance, it is likelier that Kéza's version is the correct one. Both Simone de Kéza and *Illuminated Chronicle* state that the Hungarians first entered Bulgaria, and when nobody came against them they advanced all the way up to Adrianople, which they stormed and captured, after which they advanced to the walls of Constantinople. It is clear that the Bulgarians had willingly allowed the Hungarians passage through their territory, and in fact it is possible that their ruler Peter had even bought peace from the Hungarians by giving them gifts, just as he had done previously when the Hungarians wanted to march through his territory against Serbia (anon. notary, 42). If the latter is true, then the Bulgarians had made a grave mistake – as will be shown below.

When the massive Hungarian army then encamped before the gates of Constantinople, the emperor Kônstantinos suggested that the Hungarians send two champions to fight against his giant duellist. If the Hungarians were able to defeat the giant in a wrestling match, then the Romans would start to pay tribute to them. According to the version preserved by Kèza, the Hungarians were initially unwilling to accept this but when the Romans continued to harass them a Hungarian called Botond was chosen as their champion, but according to the *Illuminated Chronicle* the leader Apor ordered Botond to accept the challenge. Botond then acted as ordered and advanced alone before the Golden Gate and struck it with a battle-axe (*dolabra*) so hard that a crack appeared. The striking of the gate signalled the symbolic capture of the city, which the Romans answered by sending their champion through the gate. The wrestling match/duel had a large audience. The Roman emperor and empress watched from the walls, together with the other Romans, while the Hungarians watched the event from their horses. Botond broke the arm of the Roman, who later died of this injury. The Hungarians then demanded that the Romans respect their promise and start paying tribute, which the emperor answered with a laugh. The host that the enemy had brought before the gates of Constantinople was huge. According to the Hungarian sources, the Magyars then held a council, as a result of which they abandoned the siege, pillaged Greece and Bulgaria and returned to Pannonia. If the Bulgarians had paid the Hungarians to leave them at peace they were certainly disappointed in their hopes.[19]

According to Theophanes Continuatus (6.47, 462–3) and Pseudo-Symeon (PSs 755–6), the Hungarian invaders had reached the gates of Constantinople on 11 April 959, after which they pillaged Thrace and took much booty. It was then that the emperor dispatched: the *patrikios* and *domestikos* of the *exkoubitoi* Pothos Argyros with his own *tagma*; the *stratêgos* of the *boukellarioi*; the *stratêgos* of the *Opsikion*; and the *stratêgos* of the *Thrakesion* in pursuit of the retreating enemy force. This gives us a paper strength of 24,000 horsemen (the *exkoubites/exkoubitoi* 4,000 horsemen; the *Boukellarion* 8,000; the *Opsikion* 6,000; and the *Thrakesion* 6,000) for the pursuing cavalry force, which is indeed plausible as this is the second year after the recruiting campaign of Nikêforos Fôkas. See Chapter 1.4. This strongly suggests that Nikêforos was not present in the capital, but was somewhere in the east making preparations for the spring-summer offensive against the Hamdanids. The absence of the forces from the *Optimaton* theme also indicate that Nikêforos had led the *scholai* and presumably also some other tagmatic forces such as the *ikanatoi* and *bigla* to the east. The composition of the army used against the Magyars shows nicely how the Romans could use the westernmost *themata* of Asia Minor as a strategic reserve against threats from both east and west. According to Theophanes and Pseudo-Symeon, Pothos Argyros used a night attack successfully against the invaders, slaughtered great numbers of Turks, and released captives and booty, with the result that the Magyars retreated in shame to their own territory. On the basis of the Hungarian sources, this is a slight exaggeration because after their retreat from Roman territory, the Magyars ravaged Bulgaria so that they would not return home empty-handed.

It is not known with any certainty what Nikêforos Fôkas did during the Hungarian invasion, but since he did not lead any campaign against the Arabs after the success of Tzimiskês (see below), it is likely that he returned to the capital with an army that he deemed sufficient for its defence, while leaving behind a force, probably under his brother Leôn, that he considered sufficient to deter the Hamdanids. It should be noted that it is possible that Nikêforos fell from imperial favour as a result of the Magyar invasion, because the emperor placed the eunuch Basileios in charge of the autumn campaign against the Arabs and planned to lead the next year's campaign in person.

The above account would suggest that the Magyars had not managed to force the Romans to buy peace from them, but on the basis of the information provided by Abu Firas (BELA 2, 368) it is probable that the Turks (Hungarians) and Romans did in the end conclude a peace treaty of some sort before the Romans started their campaign against the Arabs in September. On the basis of this, it is probable that in the end the Romans agreed to pay tribute to the Magyars in return for peace, probably because Nikêforos had advised this course of action to the emperor – or alternatively that the emperor simply changed his mind. The likely reason for this is that there existed the threat of a renewed invasion as long as the Hungarians tarried close by in Bulgarian territory, ravaging it instead of the better-defended Roman territory.

The Summer Campaigns against the Hamdanids in 958

According to Arabic sources it was on 23 May–21 June 958 Iôannês Tzimiskês that continued his operations against Diyar Bekr by invading the region encompassing Martyropolis, Amida and Arzan. This time he besieged the fortress of al-Yamani located close to Amida, but which is otherwise unknown. On this occasion, Sayf ad-Dawla did not advance against him in person, but dispatched his subordinate the Turkish *ghulam* Naga al-Kasaki (Tcherkesse) with 10,000 horsemen against Tzimiskês.

Canard and Vasiliev both suggest that the reason for the inactivity of Sayf was that it was at this time that the Buyid Mu'izz ad-Dawla was fighting against Sayf's brother Nasir ad-Dawla, so the latter was forced to seek a place of refuge in Aleppo.[20] This is actually unlikely to be true because the campaign of Tzimiskês took place in May-June while the campaign of Mu'izz ad-Dawla against Mosul started on Thursday, 2 September 958, and even then did not prevent Sayf from campaigning against the Romans. It was roughly at this time, around May-July, that Sayf's brother Nasir probably faced the revolt of the Turkish and Daylamite *ghilman* because Miskawayh places the event between 25 March 958 and 22 July 958. As already noted, Nasir ad-Dawlah was able to defeat both groups with the help of his personal retainers and the populace of Mosul, so the surviving *ghilman* fled to Baghdad to the safety provided by the Buyid Mu'izz ad-Dawlah. It is therefore probable that their mutiny against the Hamdanids had been incited by the Buyids.[21]

In 345 (15 April 956–2 April 957) the revolt of the Daylamite commander Ruzbahan encouraged Nasir ad-Dawla to break his peace agreement with the Buyid Mu'izz ad-Dawla, and Nasir's forces advanced against Baghdad while Mu'izz was fighting against the rebel.[22] Consequently, it is likely that the hostilities between Nasir and Buyids were initiated by the former and that it had been because of this that the Buyids had bribed the *ghilman* to revolt against Nasir. Nasir's attempt to capture the Caliphate, however, failed. After Mu'izz had crushed the rebel, he was still ready to negotiate thanks to the weakness of his own position. The two sides agreed that Nasir would continue to pay tribute, but when the latter did not make the second payment, Mu'izz started his campaign against Nasir on Thursday, 2 September 958 with the result that Nasir fled from Mosul to Nisibis and then from there to Martyropolis. The Romans were clearly no longer in the area. Yahya (78–9, 776–7) dates all of these events to the period after Sayf's defeat at Ra'ban (dated by other sources to 18 Oct.–15 Nov.), but so that Mu'izz would have already started his campaign on 4 August. It is therefore clear that his dates are not reliable, hence I follow the dating of Miskawayh who states that the operations started on 2 September. When Nasir reached Martyropolis he was deserted by his soldiers, and even by his brother Abu Zuhair, with the result that he was forced to seek a place of refuge, first at Amida and then at Aleppo, the capital of Nasir's brother Sayf. Nasir, however, had not given up the fight but continued to harass the Buyids in Mosul with the forces that had remained loyal (Bedouins and his retainers), and these prevented the arrival of any supplies to the city of Mosul while he tried to negotiate – without a result. It was then that Sayf mediated a treaty between Nasir and Mu'izz ad-Dawla. Mu'izz withdrew his army from Nisibis to Mosul in February 959. After this, Sayf negotiated by dispatching his secretary to Mosul, with the result that Mu'izz ad-Dawla agreed to give the governorship of Mosul, Diyar Rabi'ah and Rahbah to Sayf ad-Dawla instead of his brother, in return for the sum of 2,900,000 dirhems on 14 March–12 April 959 because he did not trust Nasir. The army of Mu'izz remained at Mosul until the advance payment of 1,000,000 dirhems was paid, meaning that Nasir ad-Dawla was able to enter Mosul as a subordinate of his brother on 15 June 959.[23] The probable reasons for the readiness of Mu'izz to reach a compromise was that the Egyptians under Kafur the Eunuch had not paid any tribute to Baghdad and he was facing an immediate financial crisis at a time when his problems with the *ghilman* continued.

As is clear, the problems of Sayf's brother with the Buyids were not the reason for Sayf's personal inactivity when Tzimiskês invaded. The reason must lie elsewhere. The only logical reason is that Sayf remained at Aleppo because the *domestikos* Nikêforos had assembled a large army somewhere north of Germanikeia, Adata and

Samosata, the likeliest location for this being the *aplêkton* Kaisareia. In short, Sayf remained at Aleppo to counter any attempts that Nikêforos might make against the fortresses protecting his domains. Adata had already been lost in the previous year.

According to Yahya, Iôannês Tzimiskês achieved a crushing victory against the 10,000 cavalrymen of Naga al-Kasaki. The forces of Tzimiskês routed Naga, killed approximately 5,000 and captured 3,000 captives and the entire baggage train of Naga. The sources unfortunately fail to give us any further details of this exceptionally successful battle. However, we can make some educated guesses on the basis of the very few pieces of information given. The numbers of killed and captured enemies mean that the Romans had somehow encircled the enemy cavalry formation, which could have been done only by using a cavalry formation of their own. Tzimiskês could have done that either with an ambush as described in the *De velitatione* (see Appendix 2) or by outflanking the enemy on both sides, either by using the double- (2.7.1.) or triple-line cavalry formation (see Appendix 3). The victory enabled Tzimiskês to capture the fortress of al-Yamani and return in triumph.

It is clear that Nikêforos must have remained in the east, at least until the news of the crushing defeat of Naga reached the ears of both Nikêforos and Sayf ad-Dawla, because it would have been only the complete destruction of Naga's cavalry force that would have dissuaded Sayf from attempting an immediate raid of Roman territory if Nikêforos led most of the forces under him back to the capital to protect it from the potential renewed attack of the Hungarians, and it is probable that this happened because he did not attempt to exploit the victory of Tzimiskês in July-August. The complete destruction of the 10,000-man cavalry army would have made it necessary for Sayf ad-Dawla to wait for the arrival of Jihadists from other areas, and even then the political problems of his brother (his *ghilman* probably revolted in the summer) and the natural disasters of the previous year would have lessened his eagerness for raiding in July-August. The fact that Nikêforos did not immediately exploit the victory of Iôannês Tzimiskês suggests that he must have led himself, or at least dispatched, some of the forces back to the capital to prevent the potential renewal of the Hungarian offensive in the summer. As noted above, it is also likely that Nikêforos advised Kônstantinos to sign a peace treaty with the Hungarians so that the Romans could concentrate their armies against the Hamdanids in the autumn.

The Autumn Offensive against Sayf ad-Dawla

As already noted, by about September the Romans had peace treaties or truces with the Bulgarians, Russians, Turks (Hungarians), Franks and other peoples of the west. The last-mentioned include undoubtedly the Fatimids and probably also the King of Italy and the Umayyads, with whom the Romans had been in alliance ever since ca. 955/6. The inclusion of the Franks in the list suggests that the Roman diplomats had finally been successful in their entreaties of friendship with King Otto I the Great of East Francia. After his victory over the Hungarians at Lechfeld in 955, Otto was free to concentrate his attention elsewhere and one of the things that required his attention was the situation in Italy where Berengar II had made a comeback after Otto I had returned to Germany in 952. Consequently, Otto sought and got an alliance with the Romans, which meant that they remained neutral when his son Liudolf invaded Italy in 957. On the basis of Theophanes Continuatus, we can add to the list of truces/alliances those conducted with the emir of Persia (Mu'izz ad-Dawla) and the emir of Egypt (the de facto ruler, Kafur the Eunuch). The truce with the emir of Egypt meant that Sayf's forces would not be strengthened by Egyptian Jihadists, while the truce with the emir of Persia signed before 2 September 958 meant that Sayf's brother was preoccupied with a war against the Buyids. Therefore, the Romans had completely free hands in their operations against Sayf ad-Dawla. The policies of Nikêforos and Kônstantinos ensured that they could concentrate their armies against the Hamdanids in late-958.

Consequently, it is surprising to learn that, rather than sending Nikêforos Fôkas back to the east, we find Kônstantinos Porfyrogennêtos dispatching the *patrikios* and *parakoimômenos* Basileios with a well-equipped army against Sayf ad-Dawla. The less friendly interpretation would be that Kônstantinos had lost trust in his general because the Magyars had managed to penetrate the Roman defences up to the gates of Constantinople, which would have made him suspect the strategic abilities of Nikêforos. This in its turn would have caused the placing of Basileios in charge of the campaign and the plan to campaign in person in 959. The friendlier interpretation would be that Kônstantinos preferred to retain Nikêforos in the capital just in case his services would be needed against the Hungarians, or that it was then that the son of Nikêforos died in the jousting match, with the result that the father was unable to campaign. There would also have been other good reasons for the emperor to retain Nikêforos in the capital, because after their retreat from Roman territory the Hungarians still roamed free close by in Bulgaria which they subjected to a pillage and rape. We should remember that at this time the Bulgarian border was not far from Constantinople, so the Hungarians would have remained within an easy striking distance as long as they continued raiding Bulgarian territory. According to this more favourable interpretation it would therefore have been probable that Nikêforos would also have preferred to stay in Constantinople because the defence of the capital was the principal duty of the *domestikos*, not to mention the possibility that it was then that his son had died, so Nikêforos would have been distraught and depressed. We know that he felt deep sorrow because he stopped eating meat after the death of his son, but it should be noted that Skylitzes (14.2) is sceptical about this and suggests that Nikêforos may have hidden his personal ambitions from those in power with this ploy.

The campaign can be timed to have started in about mid-September on the basis of the date of the decisive battle which took place between 18 October and 15 November. We learn from Abu Firas and from his commentator ibn Halawayh (BELA 2, 368) that Basileios brought with him so large an army that it had 12,000 servants to dig a ditch for a marching camp. We can calculate the size of the army on the basis of this figure when one remembers that there was approximately one servant per four men. In short the army consisted of approximately 48,000 soldiers and 12,000 servants for a total of 60,000 men. The second-in-command of the army was Iôannês Tzimiskês, which means that he had united his forces with the army brought to the scene by Basileios. The object of the attack was to be once again Diyar Bekr (i.e. Amida and Martyropolis), which presumably means that Basileios marched his forces through Melitene to the borders of the province of Hanzit where he would have been joined by the forces of Tzimiskês. If Basileios marched at a leisurely pace, only about 20–25 km per day, and started his march in about early-September, then he would have reached the region of Mesopotamia/Hanzit on about 20 October. However, when Basileios reached the scene, he found that Sayf had brought his *ghilman* in readiness to oppose him. This must have taken place roughly at the same time as Sayf's brother Nasir was in Martyropolis with his forces. He had been forced to flee there from Nisibis when Mu'izz ad-Dawla had brought his main army from Baghdad to the scene (Miskawayh 347, 171, p.184). It is quite possible that the Buyids and Romans were actually cooperating at this stage, because on the basis of Theophanes Continuatus they had indeed concluded a truce. If this had been the plan, it did not materialize as Basileios lacked the courage to cross the Euphrates in the presence of Sayf's *ghilman*. It is probable that Nikêforos would have acted in like manner, as it was always risky to cross a large river in the presence of enemy, so the eunuch Basileios acted wisely and in fact achieved the partial destruction of the enemy even with this move.

Consequently, Basileios changed the course of his march to Samosata. It would have taken him approximately five days for him to reach Samosata, which he would therefore have reached on about 25 October. Sayf appears to have followed on the opposite side of the river, so blocking the possibility of an advance towards Aleppo. It is probable that it was after Sayf had left Diyar Bekr that the forces of Nasir ad-Dawla deserted him at Martyropolis and joined Mu'izz ad-Dawla, with the result that Nasir was forced to flee first to Aleppo (Miskawayh 347, 171, pp.184–5). It did not take long for Basileios to capture Samosata, because, according to Abu Firas (BELA 2, 368), it took less than a day for him to capture it. According to Sibt al-Gauzi (BELA 2, 175), the Romans massacred all inhabitants of the city. After this, Basileios marched to besiege the fortress of Ra'ban, which he would have reached in about four days on 1 November (allowing two days for the stay at Samosata to complete the massacre). Sayf could not allow this, so he advanced towards the Romans. According to the Arabic sources, this took place on 18 October–15 November 958, my educated guess being that it happened in early November.

Sayf's army included cavalry, infantry, *ghilman* and his relatives, which means that it was a major army. He placed the emir Abu Firas in the vanguard and followed after him with his main army. Abu Firas encountered the Romans head on, with the result that he was utterly routed and was able to reach Sayf's forces only with difficulty. The Roman forces that had engaged Abu Firas included in its ranks

T.zi.b.q the Khazar, the chief of the Khazars. Abu had broken two lances when he fought against *T.zi.b.q* the Khazar but had not managed to kill him. Consequently the two were later able to exchange messages with each other through a prisoner that *T.zi.b.q* had captured. It is probable that Abu Firas had engaged the Roman cavalry vanguard and that the encounter had taken place in the manner described by Nikêforos Fôkas in his *Praecepta militaria*. We do not know the exact details of how the Roman vanguard vanquished the Arab vanguard beyond the fact that both fought at close quarters. One may assume that the Romans fielded altogether about 13,000 horsemen and 35,000 infantrymen which were deployed for combat as in the *Praecepta militaria* of Nikêforos. It is probable that the Romans outnumbered their enemies at this time because Sayf had just previously lost 8,000 horsemen. One may therefore assume that Sayf had only about 8,000 cavalry and perhaps 30,000 infantry, because Sayf had not suffered many casualties among his foot.

The sources do not give us any detailed description of the battle, but fortunately we can fill up the blank spots with the help of the *Praecepta militaria*. The sources only state that Sayf suffered a terrible defeat, after which Iôannês Tzimiskês gave pursuit and defeated the Arabs again so that his forces either killed or captured a large number of men, companions of Sayf and his principal *ghilman*. Sayf was able to escape the disaster in the company of very few lucky fugitives. In addition to this, the Romans captured relatives of Sayf. The captives consisted of either 1,500 or 1,700 men, who were taken to Constantinople. According to Bar Hebraeus (p.166), the Arabs lost most of their infantry; only a few were able to escape.

If one were to try to make sense of this on the basis of the *Praecepta militaria* of Nikêforos Fôkas this would result in the following conclusions. The first stage of the battle was when the Roman cavalry vanguard, which included Khazar Turks, engaged and defeated the Arab vanguard under the emir Abu Firas (see Appendix 3.5.1). Abu Firas fled to the main army under the emir Sayf. The Romans had now captured prisoners for interrogation as instructed in the PM. The Romans therefore had an accurate picture of the enemy force and its combat formation. There are two possible scenarios for what happened next.

Firstly, it is possible that the enemy did not approach the Roman hollow square, in which case the Roman commander dispatched three cavalry units on both flanks of the enemy formation (these would be the first and third lines of the regular cavalry formation) while he led the four units of the second line forward to form the centre. See Appendix 3.4. It is actually likely that in this instance the Roman cavalry was commanded by Iôannês Tzimiskês rather than by Basileios, because Tzimiskês performed the pursuit of the defeated enemy. If the Arabs had acted in this manner, the details suggest that the Roman cavalry defeated the enemy easily without any participation by infantry and then began pursuit. However, this alternative is less likely than the other version envisaged by Nikêforos, because we know that Sayf's army included *ghilman* who fought as *katafraktoi* and Bedouins (*Arabitai*), and because it was Sayf who advanced against the enemy to prevent it from besieging Ra'ban.

Secondly, it is therefore very probable that Sayf attacked one side of the Roman infantry hollow square while his *Arabitai* encircled it, so the Romans directed the *katafraktoi* wedge and its flanking divisions out of their infantry square and straight at the enemy commander and his *ghilman*. It is probable that in this case the Arabs were using similar cavalry formations as the Romans (see Appendix 5.5.5, 5.6) because the Roman cavalry outnumbered them and because the Arabs also possessed *katafraktoi* of their own. In short, the Roman *katafraktoi* wedge advanced straight at the enemy *ghilman* wedge and routed it – and with it the entire enemy cavalry force. The pursuit was performed by the flanking divisions together with the *prokoursatôres*, while the *katafraktoi* regrouped inside the hollow square. The cavalry wings of the third line, perhaps together with the other cavalry units such as the rear guards, moved outside of the hollow square and scattered the enemy *Arabitai* with arrows, but did not pursue them. The four divisions of the second line moved out of the hollow square and followed the pursuing units. The *katafraktoi* wedge of the *saka* probably followed these while the flanking divisions of the *saka* acted as its wings after they had scattered the *Arabitai*. See Appendix 3.5.5. Sayf and his cavalry would have fled into the Arabic hollow infantry square and regrouped there. When the Roman pursuers then reached the scene, Tzimiskês would have directed the *saka* with its remaining intact *katafraktoi* wedge against one of the sides of the Arab infantry square and crushed it, with the result that the enemy forces were routed and almost the entire Arabic infantry force was wiped out. The captives and booty were taken to Constantinople and paraded in the theatre and the triumph was celebrated at the Hippodrome. For a detailed reconstruction of the battle with maps, see the forthcoming biography of Iôannês Tzimiskês.

This was a major victory for the Roman arms, which also vindicated the reforms of Nikêforos Fôkas. It also enabled the Romans to capture Ra'ban, which weakened the Arabic frontier defences even further. The strategy of Nikêforos was proving its worth. As noted by Canard (1961, 797), by 959 the Romans had destroyed Sayf ad-Dawla's defensive line from Adata to Samosata, so the interior lay open for further Roman invasions. The only place still resisting was the isolated Germanikeia/Marash, and as we shall see it was this location that the Romans were preparing for siege by ravaging the surrounding regions.

6.3. The Roman Offensives under Kônstantinos VII in 959[24]

The strategy adopted by Kônstantinos VII and Nikêforos for the year 959 was to exploit the troubles of Sayf ad-Dawla to the hilt while making preparations for the reconquest of Crete. This time Kônstantinos intended to campaign in person against the Saracens of Syria.

The Arabic sources state that the Romans conducted several offensives against the Arabs in 348 (14 March 959–2 March 960), some of which took place under Kônstantinos VII and others under his son Rômanos II. In the following discussion I will divide these accordingly.

The spring offensive against the Hamdanids

The Arabic sources offer a very confused account of the campaigns of the year 959, which also confuse Leôn with his brother Nikêforos. According to Dahabi (BELA 2, 244), Abu'l –Fawaris Muhammad ibn Nasir ad-Dawla, the nephew of Sayf ad-Dawla (son of Nasir) and governor of Aleppo, invaded Roman territory but with the result that he and his entire retinue were captured by the Romans. This would obviously have taken place either in spring or early summer. The other Arabic sources offer a different version. Ibn al-Hamadani (BELA 2, 112) and Bar Hebraeus (184, p.166) both state that Muhammad the son of Nasir ad-Dawla (i.e. Abu'l-Fawaris) was captured in the neighbourhood of Aleppo. Yahya (79, 777 also in BELA 2, 98) states that the Romans launched an invasion against Qurus (Kyros, Cyrrhus) and took into captivity a great number of its inhabitants. Kyros is close to Aleppo, so this connects Yahya's account with the accounts of al-Hamadani and Bar Hebraeus. However, according to Yahya, Sayf ad-Dawla then launched a night attack against the Romans and released the prisoners. Following this, Yahya (80–1, pp.778–9) states that it was only after the death of Kônstantinos that the *domestikos* Leôn advanced through Diyar Bekr so that he forced Sayf ad-Dawla to retreat into Aleppo, after which Leôn advanced into Syria, massacred large numbers of inhabitants and demolished large numbers of fortresses while capturing Muhammad b. Nasir ad-Dawlah. As will be shown later, this account confuses the campaign conducted by Nikêforos Fôkas and Iôannês Tzimiskês which is described by Bar Hebraeus (184, p.166).

I would reconcile the above sources as follows. Firstly, Sayf dispatched Muhammad, the son of Nasir ad-Dawla, to raid Roman territory in the spring roughly at the same time as the Romans under Iôannês Tzimiskês invaded Jazira. It is possible that Sayf's intention was to launch a diversionary campaign at the same time as the Romans were invading, or, the other way around, that Tzimiskês exploited the opportunity and launched a diversionary campaign of his own when the enemy forces were preoccupied. It was then that Leôn Fôkas, the *stratêgos* of the Anatolikon, performed one of his trademark guerrilla operations against the invader and inflicted a crushing defeat on him, but Muhammad still managed to retreat into Arab held territory where he then sought a place of refuge inside the city of Kyros, which Leôn then captured together with its inhabitants and refugees. It was only now that Sayf launched his successful night attack against Leôn's siege works, with the result that the Romans suffered a defeat and were put to flight, but in such a manner that the Romans still managed to keep in custody their most important captive, Muhammad, the son of Nasir ad-Dawla, which implies an orderly retreat by most of the forces. Leôn apparently reached Roman territory without any further losses. Muhammad remained in captivity until 23 June 966 when he, the emir Abu Firas and other Arab leaders were exchanged for Roman prisoners at Samosata.[25]

As already implied, Iôannês Tzimiskês, the hero of the year 958, continued his successful campaigns in spring 959 by invading Jazira. He did this either as a continuation of his previous campaigns or as a diversionary campaign at the same time as Muhammad the son of Nasir. He would probably have advanced from his new HQ, Harput (his previous HQ Arshkeni was destroyed in 957), via Darb al-Hayyatin/Baqasaya to Amida, and from there to Martyropolis. This would have been the first time the Romans advanced against Amida and Martyropolis in this year. According to the reconstruction of Canard, Tzimiskês besieged first Amida and then Martyropolis. After their capture, Tzimiskês then marched in front of Nisibis in Diyar Rabi'a, where he rested his forces for a while. Following this, he advanced against nearby Dara and captured it. In addition to this, Tzimiskês captured and destroyed the villages of al-Hattach al-Kharakh (unknown), Bara (unknown), Funduq al-Ra's (Resaina, Ra's Ain, Theodosiopolis?) and Tell Mauzan (Constantia). From there Tzimiskês advanced to Diyar Modar, where he engaged the enemy in the neighbourhood of Edessa and Harran (Carrhae) and inflicted a serious defeat on them, capturing Abu'l-Haitam (Abulhaitham), the son of *qadi* Abu Husayn b. Abd al-Malik b Badr b. al-Haitam (Abulhucain Ali b. Abdulmalik b. al-Haitam or *qadi* ibn Hufs), with all his *ghilman*. Following this, Tzimiskês returned triumphantly to Roman territory.[26] He had been more successful than his superior Leôn Fôkas.

The planned campaign of Kônstantinos Porfyrogennêtos against the Saracens of Syria and his death[27]

According to Skylitzes (11.17), Kônstantinos VII decided to campaign in person against the Saracens of Syria, so departed from Constantinople in September 959. His first object was to visit Mount Olympos with the idea of obtaining divine support in the form of prayers from the fathers located there. This procedure had been followed ever since pagan times to encourage the soldiers to fight by claiming divine support for their campaign. His secondary object was to consult with Theodôros the Bishop of Kyzikos with the idea of discussing with him how to get rid of the Patriarch Polyeuktos who had managed to alienate some of the bishops. This was obviously bad for morale.

As already noted, it is probable that Kônstantinos was planning to conduct a similar campaign in Syria as he described in his treatise on imperial campaigns. This means that he intended to raid enemy territory at the head of a cavalry force consisting of approximately 42,500–48,000 horsemen, who were to be used in the same manner as described by Maurikios in the *Stratêgikon*, Leôn in the *Taktika* and by Leôn Katakylas in his military treatise. In other words, the cavalry was to be deployed as a double line with rear guards. See Chapter 2.7.2. This represents a change from the tactics advocated by Nikêforos Fôkas in his *Praecepta militaria* and which had brought the successes of the previous year. Therefore, it is not known with certainty if the plans of Kônstantinos were approved by Nikêforos himself – who was also required to participate in the campaign as a subordinate of the emperor (see Chapter 2.7.2.), but it is actually at least likely that the idea of increasing the size of the army had come from Nikêforos Fôkas himself, because he clearly favoured the use of large armies on every occasion that he was in charge. It is unlikely to be a coincidence that once he had been given the office of *domestikos tôn scholôn* that army sizes started to increase, the first signs of this being the armies that Basileios *parakoimômenos* and Tzimiskês led against the Arabs; the army that Kônstantinos VII planned to lead against the Saracens in 959; and the huge naval expedition against Crete in 960.

What is certain, however, is that the Hamdanids of Sayf ad-Dawla did not possess the necessary means of countering Kônstantinos VII's cavalry army with the cavalry available to them, which in its turn means that the Romans would have had operational freedom to ravage enemy territory as long as their supplies lasted. On top of that, Sayf had lost almost all of his combat-ready infantry, which means that he would not have been able to oppose the Romans even with footsoldiers. In short, the best he could have done defensively would have been to use his infantry for the protection of fortified places while his *Arabitai* and other cavalry forces attempted to harass and ambush the Romans.

According to Skylitzes, the now 21-year-old Rômanos II, the son of Kônstantinos, and his wife had formed a conspiracy to kill Kônstantinos because Rômanos was dissatisfied with the way his father handled the affairs of the state. Skylitzes claims that they had managed to convince Nikêtas the Butler to serve a poisoned purgative drink to the emperor, but the result was that Nikêtas knocked the glass so that most of it was spilled. It was then supposedly as a result of this that Kônstantinos survived, but he suffered from its results and his lungs caused him permanent pain. Unfortunately, Skylitzes does not give us an exact date for this. However, Skylitzes states that when Kônstantinos met the Bishop of Kyzikos at Mount Olympos, he fell ill either because of some physical illness or because his son poisoned him again. Theophanes Continuatus does not have any knowledge of attempted poisonings. He simply states that Kônstantinos died of illness. Whatever the truth, Kônstantinos fell ill while there, but still continued his journey towards the army and abandoned the military campaign only when it became clear that he could not lead it in person, and he returned to Constantinople, which he reached on a litter towards the end of October. He died on 9 November 959 and was succeeded by his son Rômanos.

It is impossible to know if Skylitzes had access to some secret knowledge or if he based his account solely on rumours and gossip, but it is entirely possible that there was indeed a conspiracy that included at least Rômanos and his friends. In fact, it is possible to think that there was in fact an even wider conspiracy against the emperor who had now decided to campaign in person against the enemy. One of those would definitely have been Iôsêf Briggas, the *patrikios* and *praipositos*, who became the de facto ruler under Rômanos. Furthermore, it is also possible to think that Nikêforos Fôkas and the Fôkades in general would have felt that their position was now under a threat when the emperor was about to start campaigning in person instead of relaying on their generalship. It is also possible to think that the emperor no longer had complete trust in his lieutenant Nikêforos Fôkas because the Hungarians had managed to penetrate as far as the gates of Constantinople, and because the victory over these was achieved by Pothos Argyros and not by Nikêforos. In fact, it is quite possible that the sending of the army against the Hamdanids under the *patrikios* and *parakoimômenos* Basileios, and not under the *domestikos* Nikêforos Fôkas, was a sign of this distrust, just as was Kônstantinos's plan to campaign in person in 959, but this is not conclusive – as already noted. In short, it is quite possible to speculate that Nikêforos Fôkas and the Fôkades in general were involved in a plot to kill Kônstantinos which was later suppressed by authors favourable towards the great soldier emperor. This, however, is mere speculation. None of the extant sources mention any kind of plotting by Nikêforos at this stage.

Roman cavalry attacking (11th cent.). Source: Schumberger.

Chapter Seven

Nikêforos Fôkas the Younger as *domestikos tôn scholôn tês Anatolês* and *megas domestikos* under Rômanos II (9 November 959–15 March 963)

7.1. The First Steps of Rômanos II as Emperor[1]

According to Theophanes Continuatus (469–70), the first action taken by Rômanos II was to honour the *koitônitai* (attendants of the bedchamber) and *anthrôpoi* with promotions and dignities, after which they were removed from the Imperial Palace. The *koitônitai* would presumably have been eunuch *spatharioi* and the *anthrôpoi*, the *basilikoi anthrôpoi*. This means that Rômanos did not trust these. Instead of this, he placed his personal security in the hands of Iôannês Choirinas/Choinos, who was appointed as *patrikios* and *megas etaireiarchês*. The *prôtospatharios* Sisinios was appointed as *eparchos* of the City and then later as *patrikios* and *logothetês* of the *genikon*; his successor as *eparchos* was Theodôros Dafnopatês.

The 21-year-old Rômanos also eliminated the potential threat posed by his sisters Zôê, Theodôra, Agatha and Anna. They were expelled from the palace and forced to become nuns. His mother Elenê and wife Theofanô and the one-year-old heir Basileios II were to be the sole imperial occupants of the Imperial Palace. Another heir, Kônstantinos VIII, was born to the couple in 960. Rômanos had married his wife Theofanô, of common Greek origins, in 956 against the wishes of his father because she was an outstandingly-beautiful woman, and clearly also a fertile one at that.

Rômanos promoted in particular the leading man of the Senate, Iôsêf Briggas, who already held the ranks of *patrikios, praipositos* and *drouggarios tou ploimou*. He now obtained the unofficial status of *paradynasteuôn*. Soon after this, Iôsêf was appointed to the rank of *parakoimômenos*, in which position he controlled the empire as if he was the emperor and he did this with the full support of the emperor. Therefore, the favourite of the previous emperor, Basileios the *parakoimômenos*, the eunuch son of Rômanos I, lost his position. The emperor was a pleasure-seeking young man, so he did not want to bother himself with the mundane details of administration. Rômanos II was spending most of his time in the countryside hunting wild animals while associating with young friends and flatterers, or alternatively spent his time among prostitutes, performers and clowns.

Rômanos entrusted the army into the hands of the Fôkades, and he honoured Nikêforos Fôkas, the *domestikos tôn scholôn*, with the title of *magistros* and dispatched him against the Saracens, to take control of the army assembled for Kônstantinos, while he nominated his brother Leôn first as *stratêgos* and soon afterwards as *domestikos tês dyseôs* (Domestic of the West). This means that it was Nikêforos Fôkas who now led the cavalry army that Kônstantinos had assembled in readiness for the campaign against Sayf al-Dawla. In other words, it was very soon after this in spring or early-summer 960 that the office of the *domestikos tôn scholôn* was divided, so the western armies would also be under a Fôkades when Nikêforos was campaigning elsewhere. The entire army was now placed under the two brothers, with the implication that they may indeed have been involved in the plot to kill Kônstantinos as I have speculated above. It would now be Nikêforos who led the army as *magistros* and *domestikos tôn scholôn*, and not the emperor or his trusted eunuch.

Besides the division of the duties of the Fôkas brothers and the sending of Nikêforos against the Saracens, the first acts of Rômanos as emperor were the sending of letters of friendship to every Roman military commander and the sending of similar letters to the rulers of Bulgaria, and the peoples of the West and East. In other words, the emperor secured the loyalty of his army while he confirmed the treaties of peace, alliance and truce that the Romans had concluded with foreign nations. The aim was to avoid having to fight a war on multiple fronts.

7.2. The Continuation of the Campaign against the Saracens in Autumn and Winter 959–60[2]

The Romans conducted two major offensives against the Saracens in autumn 959, one under the *stratêgos* Leôn Fôkas against the emir of Tarsus, and the other under the *magistros* and *domestikos* Nikêforos Fôkas with the *stratêgos* Iôannês Tzimiskês against Diyar Bekr. The latter campaign was the second time the Romans invaded Diyar Bakr in 959 (BELA 2, 176).

The key problem with the Roman autumn campaigns is that the sources provide conflicting information about the second invasion of Diyar Bakr. As already noted, Yahya (80–1, pp.778–9) claims that it was the *domestikos* Leôn who advanced though Diyar Bekr after the death of the emperor and forced Sayf al-Dawla to retreat into Aleppo, after which the *domestikos* advanced into Syria, massacred large numbers of inhabitants and demolished large numbers of fortresses while capturing Muhammad b. Nasir ad-Dawlah. This is impossible, because at this time Leôn was leading the campaign against the emir of Tarsus. The second campaign into Diyar Bekr was led by Nikêforos and Tzimiskês (Bar Hebraeus 184; TC 472). Yahya has himself failed to note the discrepancy of how Leôn could be in two places simultaneously, because he thinks that it was before this campaign that Nikêforos was nominated as *domestikos* of the West and Leôn *domestikos* of the East. Furthermore, it is also unlikely that Muhammad b. Nasir would have been captured by the Romans now, because Dahabi (BELA 2, 244) notes that Muhammad was captured during the same campaign that he had led against the Romans before the death of the Roman emperor. In short, it is clear that Yahya has confused his material. The problems are confounded further by the other Arabic sources which describe the same campaign. Bar Hebraeus claims that Nikêforos and Tzimiskês advanced only as far as Amida, where they killed only about 100 inhabitants while imprisoning 30 more, after which they torched the crops and retreated. On the other hand, Dahabi states that the very same raiding force advanced as far as Martyropolis, with the result that the *Hatib* (predictor) Abd al-Rahim ibn Nubata composed his verses on Jihad. Sibt ibn al-Gauzi (BELA 2, 176) also claims that the Romans invaded as far as Martyropolis. It is possible that these sources confuse the two Roman campaigns that took place in the very same area in the same year.

It is impossible to be absolutely certain, but it seems likely that all of these sources represent a partial truth, and that the Romans under Nikêforos and Tzimiskês would indeed have advanced at least against Amida and Martyropolis, where the booty gathered would have been quite modest as a result of the previous operations in the very same area, but this begs the question of how accurate the rest of the information in Yahya is when he has confused Nikêforos and Leôn with each other and the timing of the capture of Muhammad b. Nasir. I would still suggest we should assume that the other details concerning the campaign are relevant, because only these details explain why Sayf ad-Dawla failed to intervene on behalf of the emir of Tarsus. In short, it is probable that Sayf ad-Dawla initially advanced against Nikêforos and Tzimiskês, but when he learnt of the size of the enemy force he turned around and retreated to Aleppo, while the Romans pursued and attempted to catch him – to no avail. This would have been the large cavalry army of ca. 42,500–48,000 horsemen meant to perform the large-scale *chevauchée* under the emperor Kônstantinos himself, but which was now under the *domestikos tôn scholôn* Nikêforos Fôkas. Sayf lacked the numbers to engage this large cavalry force, so he settled on the defence of his capital. It was also because of the huge size of the cavalry host that the Romans were able kill very large numbers of civilians while also demolishing large numbers of smaller fortresses around Aleppo and in Syria. One may speculate if it was this experience of leading a really large cavalry army against Sayf ad-Dawla that led Nikêforos to come to the conclusion that the best policy was to invade in overwhelming numbers with armies that had a cavalry component of at least 30,000 horsemen, which gave operational freedom because none of the Arab emirates of the Thughur had enough cavalry to oppose this force. In other words, it is possible that the book of wisdom of Kônstantinos VII brought good results after his own demise, but as already noted it is at least equally plausible to think that Nikêforos, whom we found favouring large armies, was the man behind the increased numbers, so this campaign would only have vindicated his own conclusions.

It should be noted that the unknown author of the *De re militari* (probably Leôn Fôkas) opposed campaigning in Syria with an army as large as Kônstantinos VII had assembled for himself. In his opinion, Muslim territory was so badly pillaged that campaigning with a very large army like the one collected by Kônstantinos VII was dangerous for logistical reasons. The maximum size envisaged by this unknown late-tenth century author (DRM 1, 3, 5–8, 10, 13, 15, 17, 21; see Appendix 4) for imperial campaigns was approximately 30,000 soldiers (16 *taxiarchiai*, 4 *taxiarchiai* of *psilôi*, 8,200 cavalry, 1,000 horsemen of the imperial *parataxis*, plus unspecified numbers of Russians, *malartioi, bigla* and others), which he considered a large army. It is also of note that the DRM preferred the use of the combined arms approach, so the invading army would always include infantry and not only cavalry, even if the latter could also be dismounted to fight as infantry, for example in sieges. Dismounted cavalry was obviously never as effective on foot as proper footmen. However, in the same breath one should also note that this view was not shared by all military thinkers, because it is clear that Kônstantinos VII based his own treatise and plans on the texts of Leôn Katakylas and others whose treatises were based on the successful campaigns of Basileios I and his predecessors.

In the meanwhile, Leôn Fôkas had also launched his own campaign against Tarsus. He appears not to have besieged the city of Tarsus this time, so he settled on the *chevauchée* nature of his invasion. Inhabitants were both captured as booty and massacred to weaken the ability of the locals to resist further operations in the area. On 27 December 959 he captured the fortress of al-Haruniyya.[3] This suggests that he probably advanced through the Cilician Gates and then ravaged territory until he reached al-Haruniyya, after which he retreated to Roman territory.[4] The location of al-Haruniyya south-west of Germanikeia suggests that the real object was the city of Germanikeia, meaning that its surrounding fortresses and regions were demolished to weaken its defences before the actual siege. The earlier Roman operations against Ra'ban in 958 and against Kyros in spring 959 suggest a similar intent. The surrounding areas of Germanikeia were ravaged successively to weaken the ability of the garrison and inhabitants of Germanikeia to resist the Romans when the time came. One may assume that Nikêforos and Tzimiskês would have reached the neighbourhood of Aleppo approximately at the same time as Leôn captured al-Haruniyya, so it is possible that the two armies were temporarily united, after which they withdrew safely – presumably through the Adata Pass. It is also clear that the ravaging of the region around Tarsus and Adana and Syria had a similar intent as the ravaging of the regions around Germanikeia. All of these operations were preparations for the future sieges of the strategic border fortresses.

According to Skylizes (12.4), by the time Nikêforos Fôkas was dispatched against the emir of Crete he had achieved many victories over the Arabs. He claims that Nikêforos had conquered Karamnes, emir of Tarsus; Chambdan (Sayf ad-Dawla), emir of Aleppo; and Izeth, emir of Tripoli. This may mean he had defeated these in the course of his previous career, including his time as *stratêgos* of the Anatolikon when he would certainly have been forced to deal with the forces of the emir of Tarsus; or that he had defeated all of the emirs in the course of autumn 959; or the accomplishments of all of the commanders in 959 are credited to the *domestikos* alone (Tzimiskês and Nikêforos vs. the emir of Aleppo; Leôn vs. the emir of Tarsus;

the *stratêgos* of Kibyrraiôtai vs. the emir of Tripoli); or that Nikêforos conducted a spring offensive against all three emirs in 960 which is not mentioned by the Arabic sources, but for which there would definitely have been enough time before he launched his fleet from the harbours of Constantinople against Crete in early July 960; or that Skylitzes simply gives us the list of emirs that Nikêforos had defeated by 969. Given the poor quality of the sources all four alternatives are plausible, even if the last is likeliest. In this context it is important to note that when Nikêforos was still only the *stratêgos* of the Anatolikon he must have cooperated with the *stratêgos* of the Kibyrraiôtai, because the emirs of Tarsus and Tripoli also employed naval operations and amphibious landings in the rear of the Roman lines.

7.3. The Beginning of the Cretan Campaign, July 960[5]

The Initial Plans[6]

It is probable that the plans for yet another attempt at the reconquest of Crete were already completed by the emperor Kônstantinos VII before his untimely death, because he included two treatises on the subject in his *De Ceremoniis* (2.44–5): the two shortened versions of *portolan/stadiodromikon* which described the route to Crete. It is also likely that Kônstantinos VII intended to place Basileios *parakoimômenos* in charge of the Cretan campaign, because the anonymous author of the treatise known as *Naumachika syntachtheta para Basileiou patrikiou kai parakoimoumenou* mentions that Basileios had commissioned this naval treatise from him after he had defeated Sayf ad-Dawla in late-958.[7] It is clear that Basileios intended to familiarize himself with naval terminology and tactics as a form of preparation for this campaign. Basileios fell from favour when Rômanos II became the emperor. The text can therefore be dated very precisely to the period between November 958 and November 959. Pryor and Jeffreys speculate that the author of the treatise was a young member of Basileios' household, which is indeed possible, as the text has a lexicographical nature.[8]

It is also clear that Marianos Argyros had returned to Constantinople in 959, or at the latest in late-spring 960 if there had been further unrest in Italy. The sending of the fleet to Crete required that the detachment of the Imperial Fleet which had been sent to Italy would be available for this new operation. It is also clear that Marianos Argyros had brought back most of the Thracian and Macedonian expeditionary forces, so these were available for local defence and as reinforcements for the Cretan expeditionary army.

The death of Kônstantinos VII changed the plans. Now the driving force behind the invasion plans was Iôsêf Briggas, who promoted the campaign and the nomination of Nikêforos Fôkas as the commander of the expedition. The principal reason for the expedition was to put a stop to the piratical attacks of the Cretan pirates. When the Speaker of the Senate Iôsêf Briggas brought the matter to the House of the Senate, the senators and his own servants offered a number of arguments against the expedition. They reminded the emperor and the speaker that previous expeditions, in particular by Leôn VI and Kônstantinos VII, had ended in disaster with great loss of money and men. They also pointed out that the invasion might unite the neighbouring Muslims with the Umayyads of Spain and the Fatimids of North Africa, while some of them whispered that the man who could conquer Crete could desire to become the emperor. Some of them also pointed out that the long voyage across the seas would make the fleet vulnerable to storms and accidents. Iôsêf Briggas countered all of these arguments by pointing out that the Cretans were raiding coastal themes, slaughtering people, raping virgins, and destroying churches, while taking captives and slaves. It was the religious duty of Christians to fight in defence of other Christians against the deniers of Christ. God was on their side and God worked through the emperor and through his honourable and loyal servant the *domestikos tôn scholôn*. This response convinced the young emperor, who now proceeded with the plan. However, as a security measure the emperor placed in the staff of Nikêforos the *koitônitês* Michaêl the Overseer.[9] It was presumably immediately after this decision that the office of *domestikos tôn scholôn* was divided, so that Nikêforos became *megas domestikos* as *domestikos anatolês/domestikos tês anatolês* (Domestic of the East)/*domestikos tôn scholôn tês Anatolês* (Domestic of the Schools of the East), while his brother Leôn was appointed *domestikos dyseôs/domestikos tês dyseôs* (Domestic of the West)/*domestikos tôn scholôn tês dyseôs* (Domestic of the Schools of the West). According to Stephen of Taron (3.8, p.234), Iôannês Tzimiskês succeeded Leôn as *patrikios* and *stratêgos* of the Anatolikon. This was a fast-track promotion from the position of *stratêgos* of Hanzit or Mesopotamia to the highest ranking military rank, and was clearly based on the family relationship with the Fôkades plus Iôannês' outstanding combat performance. Nikêforos would take most of his forces from the eastern themes, so this was the only logical decision to make when one also needed a supreme commander for the forces that remained behind.

The new order was not approved by all persons of the previous administration, because in March 960 the informers or security apparatus denounced the *magistros* Basileios Peteinos to the emperor, with the result that Rômanos sent him into exile, where he died. Basileios was undoubtedly very unhappy with the fact that he was removed from the office of *megas etaireiarchês*. Basileios was an old associate of the Fôkades from the time Kônstantinos VII had overthrown the *Lakapênoi*, but this time they sided with the ruling emperor.

As I have noted previously, Vassilios Christides has quite correctly pointed out that the Romans feared Arab unity needlessly. The Muslim states were far too divided for them to be able to form any grand coalition against the Romans. The Umayyad Arabs were hostile to the Cretan Arabs, because these were fugitives from their realm, while they were at war with the Shiite Fatimids of North Africa. The Shiite Fatimids in their turn were hostile towards both the Umayyads and the Ikhshidids of Egypt. The principal Muslim threat consisted of the Hamdanids of Syria, but they had already been weakened by the Romans, while the island of

Cyprus was demilitarized. The Roman rear was also protected with a peace with Bulgaria, while the situation in Italy and Sicily was secure after the previous naval successes against the Fatimids. Thanks to the economic boom, the Romans could also afford to assemble a large enough navy for the expedition. In short, the timing of the invasion could not have been any better.[10]

The Ikhshidids of Egypt were already preparing to send a fleet against the Romans in spring 960, but the Egyptians had neglected the upkeep of the fleet so when the emir Kafur the Eunuch visited the arsenal he found only one large ship and another close to the river. Consequently, he demanded that the taxpayers in Cairo provide additional ships, but when the ships were launched on 10 April these were found unseaworthy, with the result that the ships sunk and about 500 persons lost their lives. The plan to launch a naval operation against the Romans indicates that the Egyptians were well-aware of the Roman plans of invading Crete in 960, as were the Fatimids and other Muslims. Plans and preparations of this size could not go undetected. It was thanks to this disaster that the Egyptians lost their will to support the Cretans. The inability of the Egyptians to support the Cretans was ensured by the domestic situation. The official head of Ikhshidid Egypt, the emir Abu'l-Qasim Unnoudjur ibn al-Ikshid, died in late-960 (7 Sept.–31 Dec. 960) and was succeeded by his brother Abu'l-Hasan Ali ibn al-Ikshid, while the emir Kafur the Eunuch remained the de facto ruler.[11] It is clear that the events taking place behind the scenes preoccupied Kafur's attention during the key moments during the latter half of 960 and early-961, so he could not pay any attention to the problems facing the Cretans.

The Military Preparations[12]

The Romans had made several attempts to retake Crete so they were in a good position to know what did not work and what route the fleet would have to take to reach the island. Furthermore, at least two treatises had been written in preparation for the campaign: the synopsis of the sea route to Crete, and the naval treatise prepared for Basileios. It is not known if Nikêforos consulted these works, but it is certain that he consulted some naval treatises to familiarize himself with the task at hand. He would definitely have been familiar with the *Taktika* of Leôn and its naval treatise, because this is mentioned in the DV (see Appendix 2) and with other standard military treatises. It is therefore clear that Nikêforos had at least a rudimentary understanding of naval warfare.

Iôsêf Briggas and Nikêforos decided to lead a significantly larger force against the Cretans than previously. Both were military men (Iôsêf Briggas was the *drouggarios tou ploimou*), so they knew the importance of numbers in combat as long as the logistical questions were solved. The final say in the planning process, however, appears to have been left in the hands of Nikêforos, because (LD 1.3) he was appointed as *stratêgos autokratôr* (meaning that he was given temporary powers of the emperor during the campaign). The situation looked good. Crete was a fertile country with abundant supplies available locally, in addition to which the large size of the fleet enabled the Romans to carry with them a large amount of provisions. The conquest, however, appears to have taken longer than planned, because Nikêforos was constantly seeking to capture Chandax through assault. According to Leo the Deacon, Nikêforos also demonstrated his military experience in amphibious operations. He fitted his horse-transport ships (*ippagogoi*) with landing ramps that enabled him to disembark his cavalry in full combat-readiness on the beach.

We have conflicting evidence regarding the size of the Roman fleet. Theophanes Continuatus claims that the Roman fleet consisted of 2,000 liquid-fire ships *(nêes)*, 1,000 *dromônes* and 307 supply ships (*karabia*). These figures are badly inflated, even if one would assume that most of these would have been smaller *galeai* that Theophanes fails to separate from the liquid-fire ships and *dromônes*. The late-Muslim source Yaqut suggests that the Romans had 700 ships, but the *Life of Athanasios Athonites* (p.11) puts the figure even lower, at 250 triremes.[13] One may assume that Theophanes' figures have inflated the numbers of warships, so that in actuality the Romans had 200 liquid-fire ships, 100 *dromônes*, and 307 transport ships. If we assume that Yaqut had the correct total, then the Romans presumably had 200 liquid-fire ships, 100 *dromônes*, 307 transport ships, and about 93 *galeai* and Russian Viking ships. If we assume that the *Life of Athanasios Athonites* is correct, then one may assume that the Romans had 200 fire-bearing triremes and 50 trireme-*dromônes*, for a total of 250 triremes, so that the rest of the force (if we assume that the Romans had a total 300 warships) would have consisted of 50 *galeai* and Russian Viking ships (these are not mentioned separately, but the sources still mention their participation), and of 307 transport ships. However, there is also another, better explanation for the figures in the *Life of Athanasios Athonites* if we assume that Yaqut's figure is slightly inflated. The initial landing on Crete (see later) appears to have been performed by about 50 horse transports (for the type of ship, see Chapter 1.5.9), so the 250 triremes of the *Life of Athanasios Athonites* were actually 200 fire-bearing triremes and 50 horse transports (*pamfyloi/ippagogoi*). If we assume the total to be 300 warships, the remaining 50 *dromônes* would have consisted of the smaller ships (*chelandia dromônes, galeai* and Russian Viking ships), in addition to which came the 307 transport ships. This is the likeliest division of the different types of ships on the basis of the numbers of horse transports.

The Roman sources fail to give us the totals for the army carried or its composition beyond the statement that it included mounted archers, well-equipped cavalry, heavy infantry, foot archers which were drawn from the Asian (at least forces from the Thrakesion and Anatolikon) and western themes (at least from Macedonia), *Sthlabêsianoi* (Slavs from the Opsikion theme), and mercenary forces (Russians). We learn from two Arabic sources (Yaqut and Ibn-Haldun) that Nikêforos had 67,000 infantry and 5,000 cavalry.[14] It is impossible to know if this figure included also the permanent units of marines accompanying the fleet, but it is clear that we should add to these figures the officers and supernumeraries, and also the sailors, craftsmen, doctors, architects, servants and other specialists who were not expected to participate in combat. The totals given by the Arabic sources are quite credible, as this was a major effort that had left the eastern themes open for enemy invasion.

In sum, Nikêforos aimed to defeat the Cretans with the following measures: 1) he aimed to achieve naval superiority with superior numbers of liquid-fire ships and other warships; 2) he aimed to clear the landing beach with the combination of artillery and liquid-fire ships, while his cavalry disembarked in full combat readiness onto the beach from his amphibious landing crafts; and 3) he aimed to defeat the enemy on land with numerically-superior forces.

The naval campaign[15]

Nikêforos Fôkas started his naval campaign in the city of Constantinople, as had all other major naval operations. The assembly point for the fleet and land forces was the harbour of Fygeia/Phygeia (the harbour of nearby Ephesus/Efesos had been abandoned because of silting). It was from there that the real campaign started and the fleet began its journey to Crete. According to Attaleiates (28.3), when Nikêforos

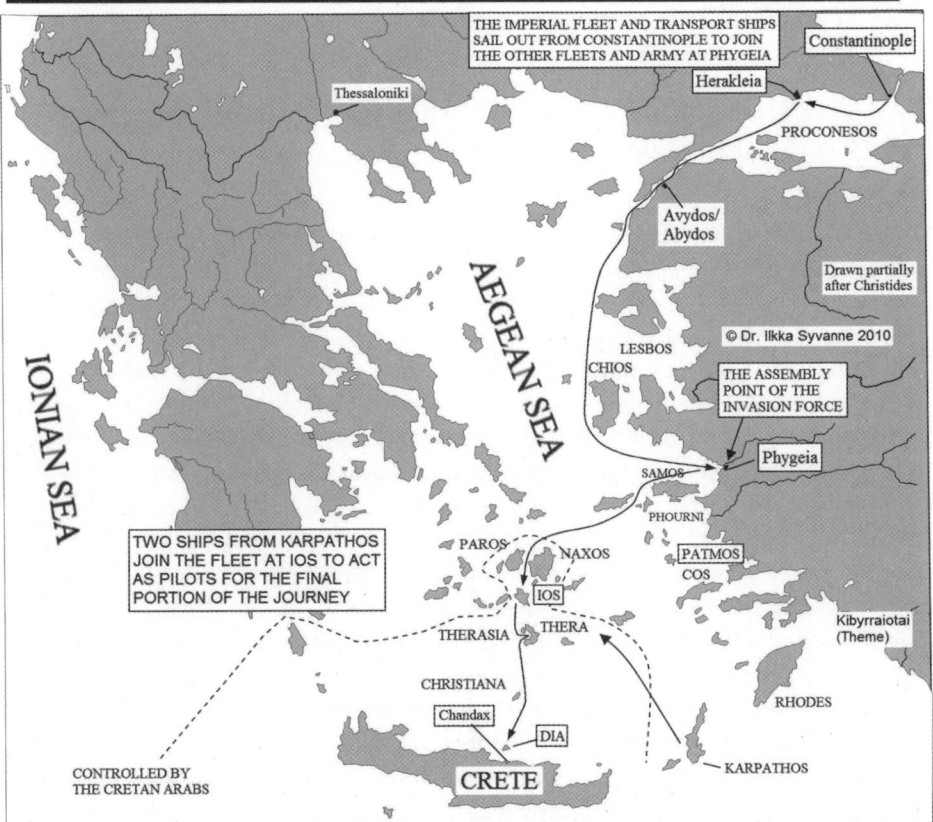

reached the island of Ios, which, as we have seen, was in Cretan hands, he faced a problem. The fleet did not have any experienced pilot to guide the fleet from Ios to Crete because the Roman ships had not sailed there in ages – which is surprising because the most recent expedition against Crete had taken place only eleven years previously. Attaleiates claims that the problem was solved when the crews of two Karpathian ships, which had sailed there by accident, promised to guide the Roman fleet to Crete. If true, this would suggest that the need for experienced pilots had not been taken into account in the planning stages, which would have been a major blunder, but I would suggest that it is far likelier that the need for pilots was taken into account and that the delay was actually caused by the fact that the two Karpathian ships had not reached the rendezvous point in time – this just would not have been known to the low-ranking officers whose account would then have found their way into the source used by Attaleiates. This, however, is merely my educated guess. It is entirely possible that the need for experienced pilots was not taken into account. Military history knows even greater blunders than this. It was after this that the fleet sailed to the island of Dia opposite Chandax, where the military operations proper began. When one takes into account the delays, the journey from Constantinople to Dia would have been accomplished in seven to ten days. The map on the previous page shows the sailing route taken.

7.4. The Landing, the Siege of Chandax, and the Conquest of Crete, 13 July 960–7 March 961[16]

The Landing

When Nikêforos had reached the island of Dia opposite Chandax, he sought to obtain intelligence of the situation facing him in Crete. According to the *Life of Athanasios Athonites* (p.11), Nikêforos dispatched three spies to Crete, who then informed him that the Cretans were very confident that they would win. Nikêforos decided to lower their confidence with a stratagem that would make his 250 triremes look like 500 triremes. Consequently, he dispatched 200 of these behind the island during the night with orders to sail back to the harbour at daybreak. The number of 200 triremes is not a mistake, because the remaining 50 triremes were the horse transports (see below). It is not known what Nikêforos did with the remaining smaller 50 warships (*chelandia, galeai* and Viking vessels). It is possible that he retained these at the mouth of the harbour to protect the horse transports and other transport ships. As I have noted previously, Nikêforos was here using a variation of an age-old stratagem, which once again proves how well-versed he was with collections of stratagems and narrative histories.

The stratagem worked. The Cretans and their fleet withdrew inside Chandax (Heraklion/Iraklion).[17] It was presumably after this that Nikêforos dispatched the fast *galeai* to capture prisoners from the shore, which is mentioned by Theophanes Continuatus (475–6). Nikêforos interrogated the captives in person and learnt from them that the emir of Crete and the leading Cretans were not at Chandax, but on their estates. I would suggest that this had been caused by the above-mentioned ruse. It had convinced the emir and his subordinates of the need to collect their land forces from their estates because they were convinced that they could not defeat the Roman fleet with the ships at their disposal. It was then as a result of this information that Nikêforos decided to make the landing immediately, which then took place on 13 July 960.

The principal source for the land operations is the *Capture of Crete* by Theodosios the Deacon,[18] who wrote its final version between 15 March and 2 July 963 on the basis of the military dispatches from the field by Nikêforos Fôkas himself.[19] It is because of this that his timing of the events is to be preferred to the one given by Leo the Deacon when it comes to the dating of the operations of Nikêforos Fôkas.

Nikêforos Fôkas made the landing in at least two stages, with the first on shore being the elite cavalry. Their mission was to clear the beach for the rest of the forces. These were disembarked on the beach in full combat readiness from the landing craft that had ramps for this purpose.[20] The disembarkation of the cavalry was undoubtedly protected by archers on board and by ships that carried naval artillery and fire-siphons.[21] According to Leo the Deacon (1.3), the Cretans had never before seen such a landing of a cavalry force, but still maintained their close *synaspismos*-array (shields interlocked).

According to Theodosios the Deacon (265–9), Nikêforos knew that he would have to initiate the battle with the enemy so he deployed his phalanxes as *oulamoi* of running towers (*pyrgodromoi*). This represents a problem, because neither of these terms was a period military term. The *oulamos* was a 32-horseman cavalry unit during Hellenistic times (Polybios, *Philopoemen*, 10.23.1–8) that were deployed as rectangles of eight files and four ranks for combat, but this is not consistent with the cavalry deployment pattern of Nikêforos himself in the PM (see Appendix 3), which required the regular cavalry to be deployed five ranks deep. However, the description would seem to fit the deployment pattern immediately after the cavalry had disembarked from the ships, and I would suggest that this is the case. Each cavalry transport disembarked its cavalry detachment of 36 horsemen straight onto the beach, so each of these formed a deep tower (see Chapter 1.5.9) three-files wide and twelve-ranks deep. Notably, the depth is consistent with the depth of the *katafraktoi* wedge, so one can think that the entire cavalry formation consisted of small columns of *katafraktoi* meant for crushing the enemy formation. According to Leo the Deacon (1.3), Nikêforos divided his phalanx into three subdivisions. This is consistent with the method of sending three divisions against the enemy from the safety of the hollow infantry square (see Appendix 3: 5.4). It is probable that landing force (the first line of three) consisted of approximately 1,700 cavalry (three divisions of 500 horsemen and two 100-horseman units on the flanks to protect these against the numerically superior enemy), which would have required circa 50 horse transports (see above) when one remembers that the extra two-to-three ships would probably have carried the supernumeraries. On the basis of Theodosios, it

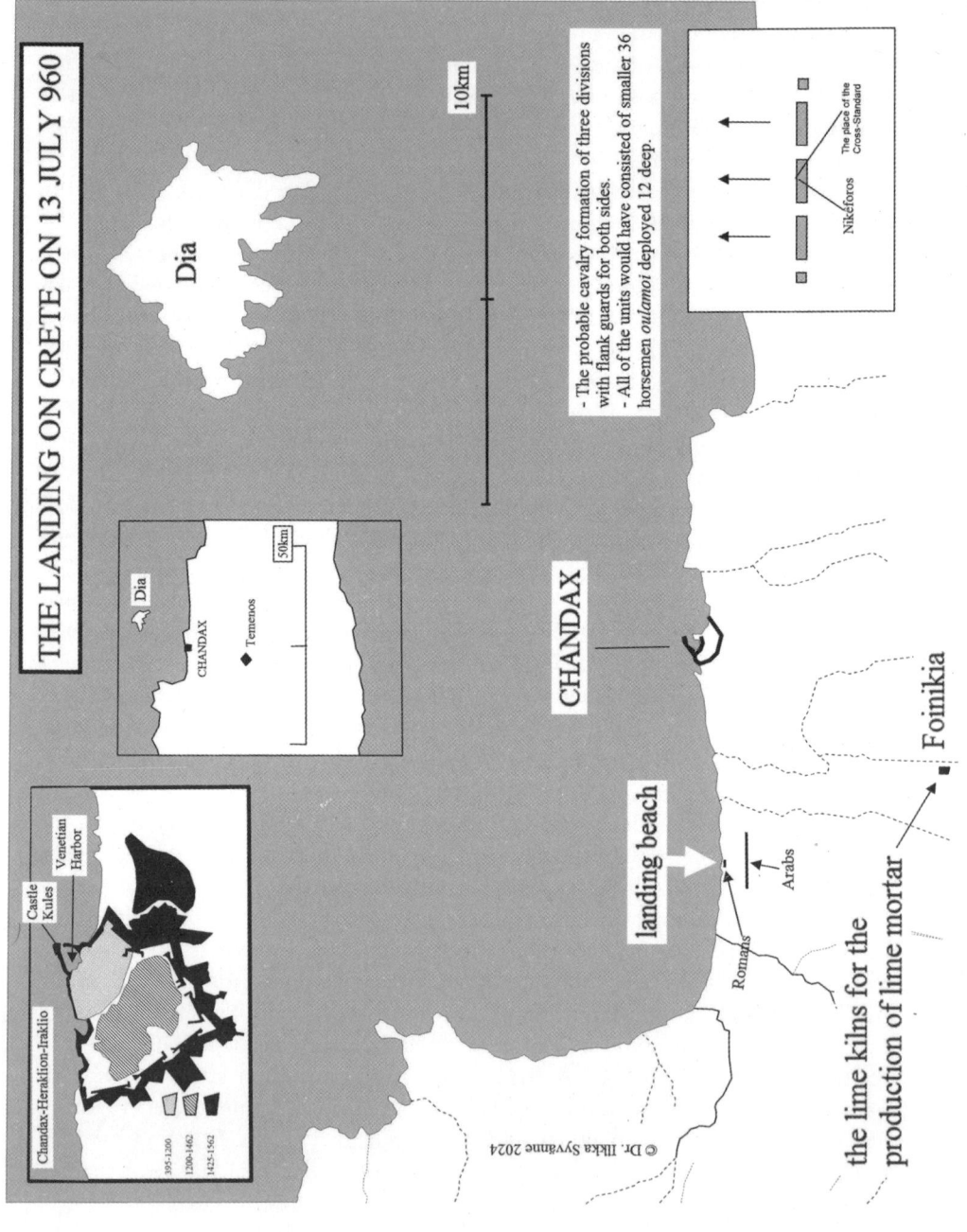

is clear that each of these subdivisions consisted of smaller units of 36-horsemen-strong *oulamoi* deployed twelve deep. According to Theodosios, the cavalry was equipped with *spatha*-type swords, *dory*-type spears, corslets of the '*thôrax*-type', and *aspis*-type shields, while according to Leo they used shields and spears. Neither specifically refers to horse-armour, but one may make the educated guess that at least the front-rankers would have had this, because the intention was to clear the beach of enemy infantry forces. It is also probable that the entire cavalry force consisted of the elite *scholarioi* under their *domestikos* Nikêforos. In light of the special deployment pattern of the cavalry forces, it is clear that these must have been trained to perform this operation well in advance of the campaign.

According to Theodosios the Deacon, Nikêforos encouraged the cavalrymen with a speech[22] before he sent them into combat, which shows nicely how the enemy was kept at a safe distance from the beach by the presence of the artillery-armed ships and by the surprise caused by the landing. After this, Nikêforos ordered the charge with trumpets, so that the frontal charge was spearheaded by the Imperial Cross-Standard (*stauros*). On the basis of this it is possible that several neighbouring *oulamoi* were united in the middle, so the centre would have been formed either into a *katafraktoi*-wedge or so that the middle of the centre of these units would have been formed with the *stauros*-bearer forming the apex of a wedge followed successively, for example, by three riders, five riders, seven riders. This interpretation, however, is not supported by the depiction of Theodosios the Deacon, who stated that the cavalry was organized as *oulamoi*, therefore I do not consider either of these versions likely. It should be kept in mind that the positioning of the *stauros*-bearer in the front rank in the navel of the centre could be interpreted to mean leading from the front.

Whatever the truth about the positioning of the *stauros*-bearer, the frontal charge itself was highly successful. The Cretan Macedonian-style pike phalanx was broken apart by the Roman cavalry attack, with everyone in desperate flight to reach the safety of Chandax. Thanks to their superior numbers the Cretans had been so overconfident that they had even taken their families to the scene of the battle to observe their heroics, only to have the result that these now became easy prey for the Roman cavalry, who killed everyone regardless of age or sex so that even babies became dinner for birds of prey. Nikêforos exploited the victory by clearing the surrounding area with swift cavalry sorties, securing the anchorage for the main portion of the fleet. Once the beach was secure the rest of the fleet beached on land and the Romans built a fortified camp for its protection. The *dromônes* were ordered to patrol the seaside, and if they saw any Arab ships, they were to incinerate them with their flame throwers. This means that at least some of the warships were kept at constant fighting readiness. It is not known if the Romans also built a siege raft opposite the enemy harbour consisting of several ships tied together, which was one of the methods used when besieging coastal cities.[23] After this, Nikêforos remained in the camp for three days, preparing the horses and riders while conducting a thorough commander's reconnaissance of the defences of the city of Chandax and its surrounding areas. The preparing of the horses and riders for three days suggests the same as has already been discussed above. The initial landing was performed only by the first cavalry line consisting of the elite *scholarioi* that had been carried in approximately 50 horse transports. The rest of the cavalry, ca. 3,300 horsemen and their riders, were carried on board the regular transport ships. The unloading and disembarkation and equipping of these took a while to perform. The horses would also have required a period of rest after the journey at sea. On the basis of his personal reconnaissance of the situation, Nikêforos found out that the city of Chandax possessed excellent defences. Its walls were built out of bricks (earth, goat and pig hair) wide enough for two wagons which had been laid out on a rocky foundation.[24]

According to the account of Attaleiates (28.4, 28.7), the seaside fortified camp was built at a distance of three *stadia* from the city of Chandax. Even with the most generous length for the *stadion/stadium* of 210 metres, this results in a total of 630 metres. This falls just short of the minimum distance of two bowshots (ca. 660m) or more in the DRM (21.81–4) so that enemy arrows and stones could not reach the inner line of Roman fortifications. It was then because of this mistake that the Arabs were able to hurl a rock in the midst of the Roman army when Nikêforos was addressing and encouraging his fellow soldiers (*synstratiôtai*), officers (*syntagmatarchai*) and admirals (*nauarchai*). This frightened the men immensely. Nikêforos calmed the uproar by lifting the rock with his hands. He then noted that the Cretan stone-thrower had launched the stone a far greater distance than any of the stone-throwing machines they had encountered previously in Kilikia (Cilicia), which demonstrated to the soldiers that they had to be more alert and braver than ever before. One may assume that the camp defences were then transferred further away from the city, so that the men would not have to fear the stone-throwers of the enemy. Nikêforos also entreated the men to put their trust in the Mother of God (Theotokos, St. Mary) and pray for Her help. It was important to lift spirits with religious indoctrination. After this, Nikêforos ordered the craftsmen from the ships, and there were thousands of them, to build a church in honour of Theotokos. The impressive domed church with columns of marble was built in just three days. After this the church was equipped with a wooden gong that was struck whenever the men were called to prayer. This not only calmed the nerves of the Roman army, but also acted as psychological warfare against the Arabs. The Romans were there to stay and they were even building churches out of marble as a sign of this. When Nikêforos learned from his brother Leôn that Saint Athanasios was at Mt. Athos, Nikêforos dispatched a boat (LA 14, 16, 19–20, 22–3) to fetch Athanasios to Crete. This is likely to have had a dual purpose. His presence would bring spiritual comfort for both Nikêforos and his troops. The other monks forced the reluctant Athanasios to obey, so he paid a visit while the war was still in progress.

It was then as a result of this intelligence gathering that Nikêforos dispatched 1,000 craftsmen to the town of Foinikia at a distance of ca. 6.3 km from the shoreline, where they fired up lime kilns to produce lime mortar for the building of a stone breakwater/jetty or breakwaters/jetties for his temporary harbour because the area lacked a harbour.[25] It is probable that these same craftsmen were also involved in the building of the above-mentioned church. The defences of Chandax suggested that Nikêforos needed a safe harbour for his ships for a longer period because the capture of the city could take a while. When the Arabs in the interior noted that the workmen in Foinikia did not have guards to protect them, they attacked the Roman workers, but contrary to their expectations the workers acted bravely and grasped their swords and launched a counter attack, with the result that the mere craftsmen defeated the bloodthirsty pirates in hand-to-hand combat so thoroughly that they even captured 250 of them. Nikêforos had clearly failed to give the workmen separate guards but this did not matter. They fought at least as well as the professional soldiers. When Nikêforos learnt of this, he had the Arabs brought to him so that these were then enslaved and used as labourers.[26]

The first battles and the first period of assaults against Chandax

It was apparently almost immediately after this that the emir arrived with his entire land army, which makes it possible that the Arabs who had attacked the workmen had been the vanguard of this army. According to Attaleiates (28.5–6), the Arabs had made a plan that they would attack the Roman encampment from two directions, one army attacking from the countryside and another from inside Chandax. This was to take place on the following morning when the prearranged signal for this would be given. The plan, however, was betrayed by two Saracen deserters. Were these in reality native Cretans or Christian captives that had converted to Islam?[27] Consequently, Nikêforos was now able to make a pre-emptive night attack (this meant marching through the night and attacking in the morning) with his army against the emir's encampment in the countryside. According to Theodosios the Deacon, the Roman cavalry phalanx coming out of the darkness consisted of 50,000 men,[28] but this figure must also include the infantry. This means that Nikêforos had left 20,000 men plus the rowers, sailors and craftsmen for the defence of his seaside camp. It is probable that Leo the Deacon (1.3–7) has confused the different night attacks conducted by Nikêforos Fôkas during this campaign, as he claims that he conducted only a single night attack against a 40,000-man relief army after the death of Nikêforos Pastilas. It is probable that the 40,000-man Arab army was actually the one led by the emir of Crete at the very beginning of the Cretan war rather than any of the later relief armies, which means that Nikêforos would have outnumbered the emir by 10,000 men.

As planned the Romans launched their attack against the Arabs at dawn with both cavalry and infantry, and the infantry phalanx (both the phalangites and archers) was so well-ordered (undoubtedly initially a hollow square during the approach march) that it moved like a well-oiled machine under its *stratêgoi*. This plan conformed to the instructions of the DRM (25) in which the location of the enemy force was known, within reach of one night's march, and smaller than the Roman army. Nikêforos surrounded the Arab marching camp from all sides, with the infantry forces being posted in front of the cavalry (see Appendix 2: 5.4, 6) and dispersed this enemy force completely, after which he returned to the siege. According to Attaleiates, the defenders of Chandax were completely unaware of what had happened so they were still planning to sortie out when those outside the walls would launch their attack. According to the version given by Theodosios, it was then that Nikêforos advanced close to the walls and brought the captured Arabs before the city where these were then decapitated in front of their fellow soldiers. According to the version given by Attaleiates, Nikêforos brought his stone throwers (*petroboloi* = probably traction trebuchets) to bear so that his engines shot rocks at the walls, to which the enemy responded in kind. It was then that Nikêforos ordered his men to hurl into the city the heads of those Arabs who had been killed previously.[29]

By combining these two accounts, it is clear that Nikêforos first attempted to lure the enemy into the making of a sortie by decapitating the captured Arabs, and when this did not work he ordered their heads to be shot inside. It was now that the enemy finally reacted as Nikêforos wished. They could not bear this sight, so they opened the gates and charged out, but only with the result that the Romans forced them back into the double moat with a frontal attack. This disaster, just like the previous ones, resulted in a very significant number of casualties among the Arab forces. This was a huge disaster for the Cretan pirates and showed to them that Nikêforos Fôkas was the master of the battlefield.

After this, Nikêforos decided to attempt to take the city with an assault, probably because he knew that his large army would consume the provisions it carried very fast. He had not yet surrounded the city with a double siege wall, so this assault was done from the seaside camp: it was thanks to this that the emir was able to get inside Chandax with the remnants of his forces. This must have taken place very soon after the sortie of the defenders of Chandax had failed, because the emir was inside the city after the Romans had assaulted it for eight days in succession. The likeliest time for this would have been the following night, so it would have been his presence that encouraged the defenders of Chandax to endure the persistent Roman assault for eight days after their failed sally. Nikêforos ordered his men to fill the moats with stones, earth and wood so that the siege sheds could be brought against the wall. The Cretans responded with showers of arrows and missiles. The Romans brought against the walls rams, tortoises, stone-throwing slings (traction trebuchets), and ladders that could be combined together. When the Roman assault had failed for eight days in succession under heavy enemy bombardment, Nikêforos attempted the same stratagem as previously, if we are to believe Theodosios, and hurled the heads of fallen enemies inside the city, with the result that the emir (who had clearly re-entered the city by then) became pale and assembled a council to discuss what to do next.[30]

The ruse of Nikêforos against defenders
The emir Kouroupas (Abd al-Aziz ibn Shu'yah) assembled the elders to discuss the available options. It was presumably then that they decided to send a fast *galeai*

to Spain and Africa (the Fatimids and Egypt) to seek aid from them, which is mentioned by Theophanes Continuatus. The Umayyads, Fatimids and Egyptians responded by dispatching envoys to investigate. They entered the city during the night, observed the situation, and all brought back to their leaders the message that the Romans had brought a massive army of multiple races and a large fleet under an able commander. The emirs took the cue and chose not to send any help.[31] The Roman invasion of Crete brought turmoil to the Islamic world. As noted, the Cretan Arabs sent an appeal for help also to the Fatimid caliph al-Mu'izz, and he acted as if he was willing to do so. Al-Mu'izz then wrote to Kafur the Eunuch and proposed the uniting of the fleets of the Fatimids and Egypt in the Barqa region of Libya at the beginning of May–June 961. At the same time, he also dispatched a threatening letter to the emperor Rômanos II in which he demanded the abandonment of the campaign. The Romans ignored the letter, while Kafur refused to cooperate with al-Mu'izz. The Ikhshids quite rightly suspected the motives of their enemy. It is very likely that al-Mu'izz's only purpose was the spreading of propaganda that stated that the Fatimids were the only true champions of Jihad against the infidels. Unsurprisingly, Crete fell without any help from any of the Muslim rulers.[32]

There were some minor piratical attacks between the Romans and Fatimids, presumably as a result of the Roman offensive in Crete, because the *Cambridge Chronicle* (6468–9) notes that in 960 the Romans captured *Ibn B.slus* who was taken to Constantinople, while in the following year the Saracens captured Sokrates. These, however, were a mere nuisance that could not prevent the fall of Crete to the Romans.

The Hamdanids may have attempted to help the Cretans with a diversionary invasion in Asia Minor in the latter half of the year 960, but it is equally possible to think that the Jihadist Sayf ad-Dawla only exploited the opportunity provided by the absence of forces that Nikêforos had taken to Crete. For these events, see the next chapter.

However, before this took place the emir and his subordinates formed a plan to make a sally out of the city. According to Theodosios, the emir had 1,050 horsemen (21 x 50 men) and 180,000 (6 x 3 x myriad) black-skinned (i.e. black-African/Ethiopian) iron-clad infantry. It is probable that we should interpret the *myrioi* as *chilioi*, so the actual number of footmen was 18,000.[33] The cavalry unit structure suggests the use of the rectangular unit formation with ten files and five ranks. The Arab plan was once again betrayed by a deserter.[34]

Nikêforos was once again able to formulate his own plans according to prior knowledge of enemy plans. He planned to lure the enemy into a sally by leading his force outside the Roman seaside camp in full view of those inside the city so they would believe that the camp had insufficient forces left.[35] Nikêforos readied his men for the battle to come with a speech which did not include a mention of the emperor. One of the accompanying *stratêgoi* criticized him for this. He was undoubtedly one of the ambitious men who sought to promote his own career by dispatching messages of incidents like this to the emperor.[36]

Nikêforos' plan conforms to the instructions of the DRM (26). The DRM advised the general to lead his cavalry force out in person while hiding most of his infantry inside the camp so that the camp looked deserted. The cavalry was then deployed into hidden places as ambushers. When the enemy then entered the camp and started to plunder, the men hidden inside the tents were to rush out and attack the enemy, while the cavalry charged out of their ambuscades and galloped to the area between the city and Roman camp with the idea of capturing the opened gates of the city. This is likely to have been the procedure that the Romans followed now, but it did not work as planned because the Arabs had another relief army in readiness outside. This begs the question of whether the Arab deserter was actually a false deserter meant to convince the Romans that they faced only the threat of an enemy sortie from the city? Whatever the truth, when the Romans who had been posted outside in ambushes were returning to their seaside camp, some of them suddenly encountered enemy cavalry forces attacking from the hills, ravines and valleys. However, the plan still worked as planned in other senses, because the Arabs who had sallied out in the darkness of the night suddenly found their way back to the city blocked by cavalry as described in the DRM. This blocking force was under the personal command of Nikêforos. In the confusion of the battle one giant Arab horseman managed to charge against him with a shield and sword in hand. Nikêforos responded by hitting the enemy close to the navel so that the man fell on the ground and died. It is probable that this is the incident mentioned by Leo the Deacon (1.5) in which Nikêforos thrust his spear with two hands through the enemy's breast so that it pierced the armour from both sides. Nikêforos stood behind the lines and steadied by his personal presence and example any portion of the cavalry line that showed any signs of flight. However, as already noted, when some of the Roman forces posted in ambush (i.e. cavalry) were returning to the camp to attack the Arabs who had sallied out, they were themselves ambushed by Arab cavalry attacking from the ravines. The *stratêgoi*[37] who led these men turned to flight and covered their necks with their shields. Their soldiers followed their example and rushed even faster to the sea and ships. According to Theodosios, it was then that the emperor Rômanos appeared in supernatural form as a cavalryman on the battlefield and brought help to the Roman cavalry in flight, with the result that the men regrouped and turned against the pursuers and engaged them at close quarters with swords and shields. This means that the situation was saved by Roman cavalry reserves. When the sun then rose the Roman cavalry completed their victory by wounding the Arab cavalry from behind. According to Theodosios, it was claimed that only four-to-ten Cretans survived the massacre. When the emir witnessed the disaster from the wall, he ordered the gates of the city closed so that the Roman cavalry would not be able to get inside the fortifications. This doomed the Arabs outside.[38]

The second period of assaults against Chandax and the change in strategy[39]

Nikêforos Fôkas thought that the time would now be ripe for yet another assault against the walls of Chandax. Battering rams, tortoises and trebuchets were once again brought to bear against the enemy defences. The aim was to attack the foundations of the wall so that it could be brought down. Nikêforos encouraged his men to do their best by going around the army. Then he resorted to yet another psychological ploy, which in this case was apparently meant to humour his own men. He ordered a living jackass shot inside the city. The men pulled the ropes of the trebuchet and the jackass flew into the air with its feet spread out. The sight put a smile on the faces of the *stratêgetês* Nikêforos and his *systratêgoi*.

It was presumably at the same time that Nikêforos came to the conclusion that it would be impossible to capture the city with a direct assault so that he settled on subduing it with famine. Consequently, he ordered the city to be surrounded with a stockade and a ditch which would have consisted of a double wall as instructed in the DRM. Nikêforos also ordered the building of new siege engines and machines for the storming of the walls. It is probable that these were built in the same manner as we find in the treatises describing siege engines but that the preference was presumably for the building of stronger and more sizeable versions.

The army was kept in fighting conditions with two measures. The men who were not manning the walls were constantly drilled, in addition to which a part of the force under Nikêforos' personal leadership was used for the clearing of Arabs from the narrow defiles, *kleisourai*, depressions, caves, marshlands and mountains. In this he was aided by the fact that deserters started to arrive in his camp daily. Nikêforos arrayed his army (*stratos*) for this guerrilla campaign in such a manner that the mounted archers (*ippotoxotai*) and Russians and the leaders (*archontoi*) of the Anatolian, Thracian, and Macedonian themes were deployed in front, while the *domestikos* (Nikêforos) followed them with the *saka*. This undoubtedly means that Nikêforos turned the typical cavalry formation upside down so that the *saka* would have had a *katafraktoi*-wedge in the middle, while the two lines posted in front would have consisted primarily of mounted archers (these would also have worn close-quarters gear) because the lighter cavalry was more effective in such terrain. The Russians would have served as mounted infantry who dismounted to fight on foot wherever infantry was needed because of the roughness of the terrain. This proved highly effective, and the Romans were able to collect all the herds of animals, together with other booty, with the result that Arabs who were hiding in the mountains and defiles were subjected to hunger by the time winter set in. The Romans also needed these provisions because they had arrived in large numbers. According to Theophanes, the Romans had actually consumed most of their provisions when winter arrived. By mid-January 961 the Romans were on the point of starvation, but it was then that the fleet carrying provisions from Constantinople arrived. However, before this took place, the Arabs who were in the mountains resorted to the desperate measure of fighting rather than being consumed alive slowly by hunger.

Nikêforos besieging Chandax (public domain)

The last desperate attack by the Arabs from the interior under the emir Karamountes[40]

The Arab refugees under their *toparchai* (regional leaders) and *falaggarchai* (infantry leaders) assembled together for a final desperate attack in a situation in which they were facing the icy cold weather of the winter outdoors without sufficient supplies. Their leader was emir Karamountes, an old rich man who had all his life sought to become the emir of Crete. In other words, he was the rival of the official emir. According to Theodosios, he had 10,000 soldiers which he intended to throw into the fight. His forces included sword-carriers, cavalry and infantry. He reorganized his forces so that new *falaggarchai* were appointed to lead the phalanxes. He also fortified his camp and promised to push the invaders into the sea.

When Nikêforos learnt of this, presumably from deserters and local Greek inhabitants, he dispatched the whole Thrakesian *tagma* (*speira* = a cohort in Leo the Deacon, i.e. 500 horsemen) under their *stratêgos* Nikêforos Pastilas against the Arabs. Nikêforos Pastilas was known as a brave man who had been wounded several times by the Arabs and who had also been captured multiple times by them only to escape from custody. Perhaps the right term for him would be 'brave to the point of being foolhardy'. This was the man who was dispatched against Karamountes by Nikêforos. Nikêforos warned Pastilas to act with caution, but his words fell on deaf ears. According to Theodosios, Pastilas attacked the enemy bravely and died fighting, but according to the less pleasant version of Leôn, Pastilas' force advanced incautiously, looting everything, with the result that the soldiers were intoxicated and then ambushed and destroyed by the Arabs.

Theodosius the Deacon (300) claims that Nikêforos responded to this by surrounding the Arabs in crags and ravines with cavalry and infantry so that the 'Cretans' became food for birds. Karamountes saved himself by hiding in a small hole cut into a rock. We get additional details from Leo the Deacon's version (1.3–7), because it is clear that he has misplaced this night attack of Nikêforos to take place at the wrong time of the campaign thanks to the fact that Leo places the campaign of Pastilas to the wrong period. According to this version, Nikêforos chose young and active soldiers and then marched out of the camp secretly with this select force. After this, he marched to the interior, where he learnt from captives that a 40,000-strong barbarian army had assembled on a hill with the aim of surprising the Romans. As noted, it is likely that Leo has here confused the sizes of the forces. The 40,000 Arabs were likely to be the force brought by the emir of Crete, while the force Nikêforos was now facing was the 10,000 men army of Karamountes. When Nikêforos learnt the whereabouts of the enemy force, he rested his men for the rest of the day and then marched through the night with native Cretans acting as guides and surprised the enemy while they were still asleep. The Romans surrounded the entire base of the hill and then launched their attack with the result that the entire enemy force was destroyed. As we have seen above, this is only partially true. The enemy leader escaped thanks to the darkness and suitable hiding place.

The fall of Chandax on 7 March 961 and the securing of the island of Crete[41]

When spring arrived in Crete in March 961 Nikêforos Fôkas thought that the time was now ripe for the final assault against the city of Chandax. He had received a shipment of supplies in about mid-January so his men were in good health – unlike the defenders. The expert craftsmen had also built the siege engines he had ordered them to build during the winter break. In addition to this, Nikêforos had secretly dug a tunnel from his siege lines into the moat. When the men doing that reached the moat, it was time to begin the assault proper. According to Leo, Nikêforos arrayed the assaulting portion of his force in a deep oblong formation (undoubtedly a hollow infantry square) in readiness at the spot where the breakthrough would take place. According to Theophanes Continuatus, this force consisted of the *tagmata*, thematic *archontoi* (presumably with their forces), Armenians, Russians, *Sthlabêsianoi* (Slavs), and Thracians. It was then that an Arab woman exposed her private parts as an insult, with the result that one of the Roman expert archers killed her with an arrow.

Nikêforos brought the stone-throwers (trebuchets) closer to the city to provide covering fire for the men using the battering ram. While this took place, men rushed into the moat and started digging through the foundations with stone cutting tools, presumably underneath the battering ram to hide their own work. The location was well-chosen, because the rock in the foundations was partly sandy so that it was easily dug. The battering ram was similarly successful and gradually increased the hole in the wall ahead. The men undermining the foundations dug through, while propping the tunnel with a wooden structure, and when the work was finished they set the wooden structure on fire and withdrew from the underground tunnel. When the wooden propping collapsed, two towers with the section of the wall between them collapsed with it. The Cretans rushed to the scene and formed a phalanx to oppose the Romans rushing inside, but to no avail. The Romans pushed and shoved their way in, with the result that the Arab line collapsed with everyone seeking to save himself. The Romans slaughtered their enemies mercilessly. When Nikêforos saw this, he spurred his horse and entered the city and restrained the killing by convincing the men to spare those who threw down their arms and surrendered. The emperor had also ordered the men not to rape any unbaptized women and girls because this would have polluted the Christian men so it is probable that very few rapes took place now. The city of Chandax fell on 7 March 961.

After the entire city was in Roman hands it was the time to divide the spoils. Nikêforos set aside the first spoils which would go to the emperor,[42] and then chose wisely only the highest ranking prisoners for the triumph and gave the rest of the booty to the soldiers. He knew full well that the soldiers would be very unhappy if he acted like his greedy father had. The first duty of the commander was to retain the loyalty of his soldiers with fair division of the booty, and there was masses of booty thanks to the piratical activities of this corsair nation. After this, Nikêforos ordered the walls of Chandax demolished in many places as a safety measure, after which he ravaged the surrounding countryside again.

When the emperor learnt of the fall of Chandax, he recalled Nikêforos immediately because Iôsêf Briggas advised him to do so. The obvious reasons were that the emperor and Iôsêf feared the prospect of usurpation, while it was also clear that the soldiers would be needed against the Hamdanids and Magyars. Nikêforos, however, ignored the order and remained on the island as long as it took for him to secure it completely. This time he met with no resistance, so the soldiers gathered booty relatively easily while taking all Arabs as captives. The entire island was now occupied. To secure it Nikêforos built a new fortress at a place called Temenos to serve as the principal garrison for the island after his departure. For the location, see the map of the landing on page 220. The garrison consisted of the Armenians, Romans (presumably soldiers from Constantinople) and soldiers of mixed races. In addition to this, Nikêforos left fire-bearing triremes behind to protect the island against Muslims. The Island of Crete was now organized as a new military theme.

The ethnic and religious cleansing of Crete[43]
The first priority for Nikêforos was the securing of the island for the Romans. According to Muslim sources, the Romans killed 200,000 Muslims, which may indeed be a relatively accurate number given the policy of killing and pillaging before Nikêforos attempted to limit the killing in the final stages of the siege of Chandax, because the captives were valuable as war booty, on top of which it was possible to convert Arabs to Christianity and use them as Roman soldiers against their former coreligionists. In fact, the son of the emir of Crete converted to Christianity and became a Roman officer. Islam, however, was to be eradicated completely as a religion from the island to secure it for Christendom. All mosques were destroyed and all Korans were burned on the orders of Nikêforos Fôkas – who was a fanatical Christian. This was not difficult to achieve because the local Greeks detested Arab rule and Islam, despite having been allowed to practise their own religion and customs as long as they paid their taxes. On top of that, the steady stream of deserters from the Arab army proves that a significant number of their soldiers were quite unhappy serving their Muslim masters[44] and changed sides at the first opportunity. It is probable that most of these consisted of the white slave troops (*Saqaliba*, white Europeans and Slavs) who now saw an opportunity to

return home or join the Christian side. It is also possible that some of the slave black troops (*Zanj*) acted in like manner and deserted to the Romans.

Just as in modern times, the destruction of the mosques and Korans caused widespread anger in Muslim countries, which then manifested itself in anti-Christian riots all over the Muslim world. For example, in Cairo the Muslim mob attacked the Melkite church of Saint Michael, plus two Nestorian churches, before one Ikhshid commander intervened and dispatched his *ghilman* to crush the riot. This demonstrates that the central authorities did not always accept such violence against their taxpaying Christian subjects.

The attack against one country by Christians and the destruction of mosques and Korans were not sufficient to unite the Muslim countries against the aggressor. In fact, as we have seen, the Muslims were entirely ready to ally themselves with the Romans against their fellow Muslims. The Muslim countries with their differing sects were just too preoccupied with their own internal quarrels for them to unite against a common religious foe – in fact, this common foe did not even exist, as Rome was quite ready to conclude alliances with Muslim countries. The most important of the divisive issues among the Muslims were: 1) the division of the Muslim countries into the Shiites and Sunnis; 2) the ethnic divisions (differing Arab groupings and Bedouin tribes, Persians, Daylami, Turks, Egyptians, Numidians, Berbers etc.); and 3) the division of these areas into various nations and principalities, each under their own ruler. These divisions persist even today.

The triumphant return of the second Belisarius to Constantinople in the summer 961

The pacification and ethnic cleansing of Crete took until the summer to accomplish, so Nikêforos Fôkas was finally able to enter Constantinople triumphantly in summer 961. According to Skylitzes and Zonaras, Iôsêf Briggas was jealous of Nikêforos' military accomplishment and convinced Rômanos II to dispatch Nikêforos to the east immediately without any triumph. However, I agree with Leo the Deacon and the consensus opinion among modern historians that this is not true, but that Nikêforos celebrated a magnificent triumph in the presence of Rômanos II in the hippodrome, just as his brother had celebrated after his victory at Adrassos/Andrassos. The key reasons for this conclusion are that Leo the Deacon wrote his text closer to the period, while it is also clear that Nikêforos started his operations against the Arabs only in December, so it is clear that he was not dispatched to the east immediately. Unsurprisingly, the vast amount of captured riches and the number and rank of captives made a great impression on the audience. The rich and powerful of the city of Constantinople were once again flooded with slaves, which they already had in abundance after Leôn Fôkas' victory at Adrassos in 960 (see the following chapter).[45]

7.5. The Defence of Roman Territory by the *domestikos tês dyseôs* Leôn Fôkas in 960[46]

The savage Magyars invade again in the summer 960[47]
In summer 960[48] the Hungarians repeated their invasion of Roman territory. They had undoubtedly learnt of the absence of Roman forces thanks to the campaign to retake Crete. The Bulgarians were just as unwilling to oppose the Magyars as before, so they allowed them to pass through their territory. The Hungarians once again invaded in massive numbers, which implies that the campaign was led either by their king as previously in 958, or by the *gyula/gylas* or *karchas*. The Hungarians outnumbered the Romans significantly, and according to Leo the Deacon Leôn Fôkas commanded only a small *ilê* of *stratiôtai*. One may assume that this meant a small cavalry army of perhaps less than half of what was available in 958, so Leôn had perhaps only about 7–8,000 horsemen available to him. However, he used these forces with his typical skill. Leôn shadowed the enemy in wooded terrain and so kept out of the enemy's sight while observing every movement the enemy made. Then, when the right opportunity presented itself, Leôn launched a night attack with his forces attacking the enemy encampment from three sides simultaneously so the Magyars would be induced to flee towards their homeland. The attack was a great success. According to Leo the Deacon, only a small number of enemies were able to escape the massacre, but it is uncertain if this is true because the Magyars repeated their invasion in the following year. Leôn apparently could not exploit this victory, because he had by then learnt of the invasion of the eastern provinces by Sayf ad-Dawla.

Both Leôn and Nikêforos Fôkas had searched for the whereabouts of Saint Athanasios after he had departed from the monastery of Mt. Kyminas (LA 14, 16, 19–20), and it was now that Leôn found him at Mount Athos when he was returning from his victorious campaign against the Magyars. Leôn greeted him happily and handed over money for the rebuilding of a church.

The Shiite Sayf ad-Dawla leads yet another Jihadist attack against the Romans[49]
Sayf ad-Dawla was well-aware of the absence of Roman forces. It was because of this that he launched a double invasion of Roman territory. The main invasion was led by Sayf in person, while the diversionary operation was led by his subordinate Naga al-Kasaki. According to ibn Fafir, it was Sayf ad-Dawla's subordinate Naga al-Kasaki (he was in charge of the defence of Diyar Bekr) who suggested to him that it might now be the right time to wrest back a fortress known as Hisn di l-Qarnayn (Fortress of Alexander the Great) located south-east of Arsamosata (Shimsat) that the Romans had recently captured. Sayf agreed to the proposition and gave Naga a large army to accomplish this. The *patrikios* Michaêl of Chanzit (Hanzit), known as Turniq (i.e. Tornik/Tornikios, of Armenian origins), marched to relieve the fortress. Michaêl, who had a sizeable numerical superiority, was defeated and

captured by Naga, but Michaêl had still achieved his main goal, which was to prevent the capture of the fortress. In other words, Naga had to retreat without having accomplished anything but a defeat of the Roman *stratêgos*.[50] The above means that Iôannês Tzimiskês' successor as *stratêgos* of Hanzit was Michaêl Tornikios, another high-ranking military commander of Armenian origins.

Leôn Fôkas acted promptly when he learnt of the enemy invasion of the eastern *themata*. He led reinforcements from the west to the east to save it from further ravaging. The first thing he did after he had crossed the straits was to learn what had happened and in what strength the enemy had invaded. He learnt that Sayf was mercilessly killing and looting everything, while destroying churches, villages and fortresses, and that he had invaded with a large army. Consequently, Leôn decided to avoid fighting in the open and so resorted to his trademark shadowing warfare so well described by the *De velitatione* (see Appendix 2).

The Arabic sources provide us with details of what happened before Leôn arrived on the scene. Sayf ad-Dawla had once again collected a large army which consisted of 30,000 soldiers[51] under his own personal command and an unknown number of men from Tarsus. If one were to make an educated guess, it would be likely that the Tarsiote contingent was once again as strong as it was in 950 (BELA 2, 241). In other words, it would have encompassed about 4,000 men, all of whom are likely to have been cavalry. We do not know what pass Sayf used when entering Roman territory, because Roman defensive doctrine recommended that the invader be allowed to enter but not allowed out (see Appendix 2). Consequently, even if the Arabs still possessed Germanikeia (Marash), it is by no means certain that they used the pass al-Kankarun north of it as an invasion route. From the Arabic sources we learn that Sayf captured many Roman towns and fortresses, while obtaining huge amounts of plunder and captives. The Romans under the new *stratêgos* of the Anatolikon Tzimiskês conducted a shadowing campaign until Sayf reached Charsianon. The presence of the fortress with its infantry forces gave Tzimiskês the chance to meet the enemy in battle. He had fought against Sayf once before in this very same location as a lieutenant general of Nikêforos Fôkas so he knew the terrain well and, just as previously, the battle ended in Roman defeat and the Romans were forced to flee inside Charsianon while the Arabs were forced to begin their retreat. This time the retreat was conducted towards the Anatolikon because it had now been emptied of soldiers.

When Sayf's route became known to the Romans, Leôn Fôkas united his forces with the forces of the *stratêgos* Kônstantinos Maleinos and other *stratêgoi* (SLs 98–9). The theme of Kappadokia was en route to Anatolikon, so it is probable that Leôn joined forces with Maleinos and the other *stratêgoi* in that province when Sayf's forces appeared there. When this happened, Leôn employed the shadowing and harassing tactics while Sayf was passing through Kappadokia and Anatolikon and which are so well described in the DV (see Appendix 2). This tactic was followed until Sayf ad-Dawla's forces reached one of the passes leading out of Roman territory.

According to Symeon the Logothete (SLs 99), Leôn Fôkas placed the ambush for Sayf at the *kleisoura* called Kylindros, close to the city of Adrassos/Andrassos (see the maps on pages 235–6), which according to Yahya (83, p.781) was called Magharah-al-Kuhl. This was an excellent learned guess based on the route that Sayf was following by Leôn, the former *stratêgos* of this precise area. However, unlike Sayf ad-Dawla, the Tarsiotes accompanying him were very familiar with the different routes and passes of the region and the Roman tactics in the region, having fought there successively against Bardas, Nikêforos and Leôn Fôkas when these had been *stratêgoi* of the Anatolikon. In fact, it is clear that Nikêforos Fôkas had already ambushed the Tarsiotes at the *kleisoura* of Kylindros at least once in precisely the same manner as we now find Leôn ambushing Sayf ad-Dawla. Unsurprisingly, the Tarsiotes did not agree with the chosen route, because they knew that it would be crowded with Roman troops. According to Miskawayh (180–1, p.196), Sayf ad-Dawla was a haughty arrogant person who was unwilling to listen to the advice of others, so when the Tarsiotes advised Sayf to abandon his planned route and follow them, he refused to listen and marched head on into the ambush prepared for him. The proud Shiite Jihadist Sayf may have also been influenced by his successful attacks through the passes held by the Romans in the past, so that he thought that he would once again be able to repeat this feat of arms. Sayf was definitely able to do that at the Pass of Baqsaya/Darb al-Hayyatin in 956, and it is quite possible or even probable that he had performed the same feat several times in such instances in which he returned safely to his own territory, even if the sources fail to mention this. If this was the reason for his arrogance, then he had clearly forgotten the massive disaster that he had suffered in quite similar conditions in 950 when the Tarsiotes had wisely chosen to use another, safer route.

Leo the Deacon claims that the army that Leôn brought to Anatolia was a small and weak army, frightened by the successes of Sayf. It was because of this that Leôn is claimed to have exhorted his soldiers not to seek an open battle and direct attack, but to seek victory through cautious planning and ambushes for the achievement of victory at minimum risk. This speech actually contradicts what he stated earlier about the mood of the army. The purpose of the speech was to squash the over-optimistic attitude among the soldiery towards the situation in the aftermath of the previous victory over the Magyars. Leo the Deacon claims that one of the arguments of Leôn was the discrepancy in the size of the armies, which the soldiers had been able to witness by observing the enemy on the plain during the shadowing warfare. Leôn was indeed warning against over-eagerness for battle when the enemy outnumbered them significantly.

According to Leo the Deacon, the location which Leôn Fôkas chose for the ambush was such that it was initially passable by horses, but then, when the terrain became difficult, it narrowed so that the enemy's marching formation would become crowded and broken. The mountains above were precipitous, while the valley and pass below was heavily wooded with ravines and brushwood. The Romans were

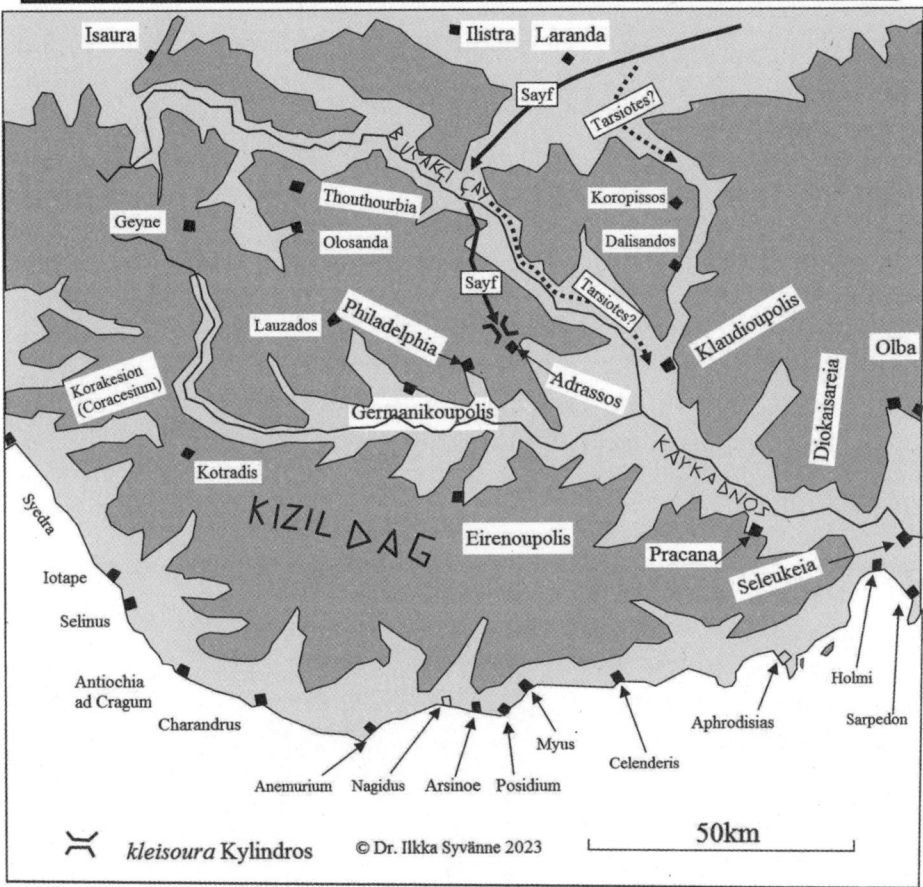

posted at intervals along the length of the ambush with orders to stay in hiding until the enemy reached the narrows and the commander sounded the trumpets. The description does indeed fit like a glove the topography just north-east of the city of Adrassos, so it is clear that the Greek sources give us the correct location.[52] The description of the ambush also fits the description of Roman tactics when the pass leading out of the Roman territory sloped downward and became very narrow and rough. See Appendix 2.6. The Arabs marched into the ambush prepared for them on 8 November 960. The location also had another advantage, which had been kindly provided by Sayf himself when he had decided to return via the theme of Seleukeia, which had not contributed men to the Cretan campaign. Lêôn was able to bring its infantry forces to the pass, which means that he had at least 10,000 infantry occupying it, in addition to which came the infantry and cavalry meant to attack the enemy from behind.

On the basis of the Roman sources, they were also very close to capturing Sayf himself. The difficult terrain ensured that flight was difficult for a mounted man. It was then presumably thanks to this that Sayf's horse faltered and he was close to being captured. It was at that moment that he was saved by the Christian renegade Iôannês, a retainer of his. Iôannês dismounted and gave his own horse to his master, with the result that the Romans captured him while his master escaped. According to Leo the Deacon, even this would not have sufficed had Sayf not resorted to the old stratagem of throwing silver and gold on his tracks to slow down the greedy pursuers. The Romans indeed captured massive amounts of booty and released all Roman captives. According to Skylitzes (12.4), the Romans captured so many Arabs that the urban and rural properties of the Constantinopolitan elite were suddenly filled with slaves. This means that most of the Arabs chose to surrender rather than fight in such a desperate situation. The surrendered high ranking Arabs included Kinanite Mungidh b. Nasr (undoubtedly related to the famous Crusader-era Usama b. Munqiddh) and Kilabite Mat'ar b. al-Baladi.[53] However, there were still those who fought in the name of Jihad rather than surrendering. These included many famous Muslim warriors. The sources mention the death of Hamid b. Nams (or Hamid Bar-Namus), Musa b. Siyakan and the *qadi* Abu Hasin/Husayn.

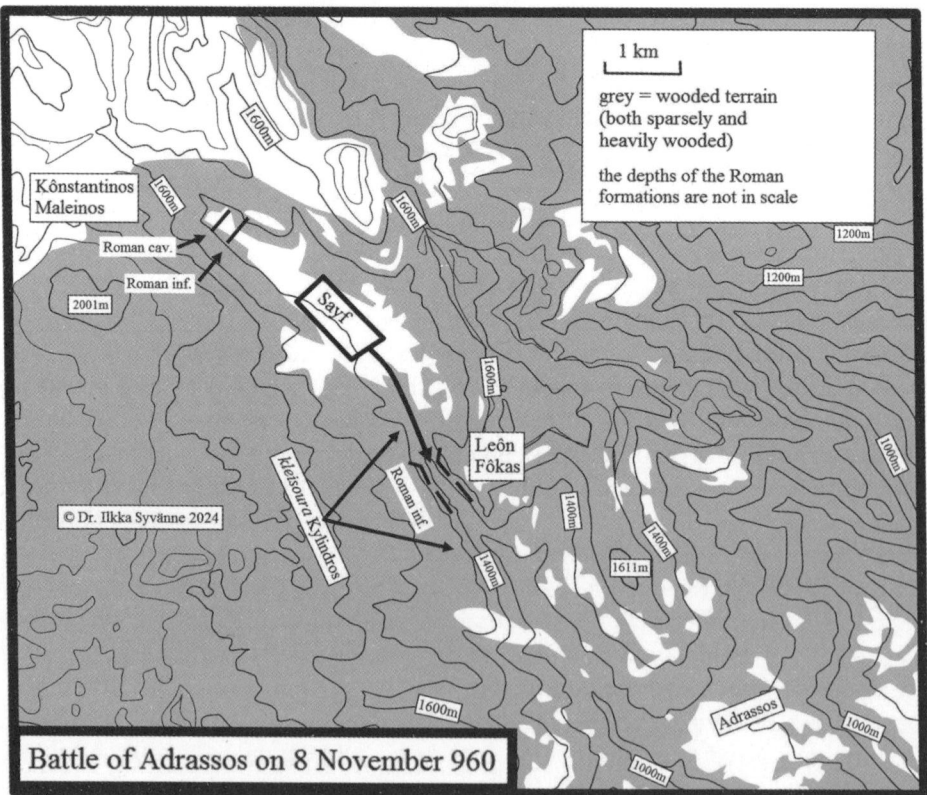

Battle of Adrassos on 8 November 960

Leôn Fôkas pursuing Sayf (slightly restored after Skylitzes)

It was thanks to this schoolbook victory over the Saracen invader by his brother Leôn that Nikêforos Fôkas would have an easier time when facing the Hamdanids in the coming years. It is clear that the brothers duplicated the tactics of each other whenever they fought in the province of Anatolikon. Later in the year Leôn celebrated a well-earned triumph in Constantinople, with the captives and spoils of war being paraded before admiring onlookers. Leôn appears to have remained in the east until late-summer 961 because he was not present in the west at the time when the Hungarians invaded once again. Even if Leôn had decimated the army of Sayf, he was still aware that he had only a small army at his disposal, so he remained on the defensive as long as his brother was campaigning in Crete.

The crushing defeat at Adrassos had another very important consequence, which has been overlooked in previous research. According to Miskawayh (198–9), Sayf ad-Dawla suffered a paralytic stroke in 961 from which he had not yet recovered even in 963. It is clear that we can connect the stroke with the stress caused by the defeat at Adrassos. Sayf ad-Dawla was clearly a man whose conscience weighed heavily on him. Sayf knew full well that the defeat and deaths of thousands of fellow Muslims had been caused by his own stubbornness The stroke in its turn would limit his ability to operate in the coming years.

7.6. Year 961: The Romans Wait for the Arrival of Nikêforos Fôkas from Crete

Overview of the Situation in 961

As already noted, the Romans remained on the defensive on other fronts as long as Nikêforos Fôkas was in Crete. This was a wise choice when resources were concentrated on that single effort. The situation persisted until the summer, when Nikêforos had finally completed his task. Leôn Fôkas did not possess any new sizeable forces with which to conduct offensive campaigns, but had to survive with the same forces that he had previously – if we assume that he had replaced the men that he had lost in the previous year. It was because of this that the Roman forces in the east conducted only raids and defensive operations.⁵⁴

The savage Magyars invade yet again either in the spring or summer 961
In 961 the Hungarian tribes once again repeated their invasion of Roman Thrace. In the absence of the *domestikos tês dyseôs* Leôn Fôkas, who was at the time in the east, the commander in chief was Marianos Argyros with the title *monostratêgos tês Macedonias* and *katepanô tês dyseôs*. This means that Leôn Fôkas was still in Asia Minor to guard it against the Arabs. It is clear that in this case the *katepanô tês dyseôs* was the acting commander for the entire Thracian front and therefore de facto second-in-command to the *domestikos tês dyseôs* in his absence. Marianos engaged and defeated the Magyars and took many captives, with the result that the barbarian invaders were forced to retreat to their own territory in a shameful manner.⁵⁵ The Hungarians were undoubtedly seeking to exploit the fact that Leôn had taken detachments from the *themata* of the Balkans to the east in 960 and that these remained there. The continuation of the Hungarian raids through the Bulgarian territory was to become one of the things that Nikêforos had to pay attention to both as *megas domestikos* and then as emperor. As a nation that followed the nomadic fighting style, the Magyars could invade quickly and retreat just as quickly. They could also raid Roman territory as small roving bands which were difficult to stop entirely thanks to their small size and scattered nature. As light cavalry, most of the Magyars were usually able to flee even when defeated in battle, except when surprised and surrounded.

Skirmishing and raiding in the East until December 961
On the basis of the extant sources, the Romans conducted only a single offensive operation during the normal campaign season in the east in 961. The forces of the theme of Kappadokia under their *stratêgos* Kônstantinos Maleinos performed a daring feat. They launched an attack against the caravan under the emir of Antioch which was bringing supplies from Antioch to Tarsus. The caravan was protected by a large army of Arabs, but even these could not save the situation because the Romans ambushed them. The Romans captured large numbers of Muslims together with the contents of the caravan, but the emir of Antioch, though wounded, still managed to flee. The emir of Antioch was obviously a subordinate of Sayf ad-Dawla, which means that it is after this that the emir of Tarsus declared himself and his subjects to be subordinates of the caliph at Baghdad (hence subjects of the Buyid emirs) and not subjects of Sayf ad-Dawla. The defeat that Sayf had suffered at Adrassos, thanks to the fact that he did not pay any heed to advice given by the Tarsiotes and his highhanded manner of treating them together with the demonstrated inability to bring supplies to the Tarsiotes, led to the irrevocable loss of face among the Tarsiotes.⁵⁶ The paralytic stroke that Sayf suffered in 961 would also have weakened his standing among the other emirs, while also weakening the

ability of the Emirate of Aleppo to recover from the defeat. This weakened the Arabs even further just before Nikêforos' arrival in Asia Minor. One wonders if the intention of the caravan had been to bring supplies and a garrison of soldiers to the city of Anazarsos/Anazarba, the target of Nikêforos Fôkas' offensive late in the same year in the territory of Tarsus.

The crushing defeat at Adrassos, the loss of the caravan, the paralytic stroke and the desertion of the emir of Tarsus meant that Sayf ad-Dawla failed to achieve a fast recovery similar to that he been able to achieve after his previous crushing defeats. Therefore, in 961 all his efforts were directed towards the recovery of his military strength to such an extent as was physically possible, while his subordinate Naga al-Kasaki conducted the only offensives of the year 961. Naga launched operations against the semi-independent Armenian-Arab emirs who were officially subjects of the Roman Empire in a territory with ill-defined borders. Naga al-Kasaki advanced first from Martyropolis (Mayyafariqin) against the emir of Melitene, Abdallah, and captured him in combat. Naga exploited his success by advancing against ibn Maslama, who appears to have been yet another Arab emir serving the Romans. The location where ibn Maslama ruled is not known, but it is probable that it was located north of the River Arsanas in Roman-held Armenia. The Romans employed their standard stratagem against Naga and posted an ambush in a defile. The desperate Naga massacred the captives and fought with great determination and actually managed to get through the ambush and reach the city of Karin, after which he returned to Aleppo where his services would be sorely needed – because Nikêforos Fôkas had by then reached the scene. Naga's operations lasted until October-November 961.[57]

Developments in Armenia[58]
According to the account of Matthew of Edessa,[59] Naga's operations against the Arab-Armenian emirs in Roman service coincided with the strengthening of the Armenian Kingdom and the weakening of the position of the Hamdanids vis-à-vis the Buyids.

According to Matthew, the military commander of the Armenians assembled and separated 45,000 men from the royal brigade and formed a new brigade called *martzpetakan*, which must be one of the necessary political manoeuvres that the King of Armenia did to secure his own position just before his enthroning ceremony, and which was clearly meant to assert his own position vis-à-vis his subjects and neighbours. It was then that Anania, the patriarch of Armenia, assembled all the Armenian princes for the anointing of the new king, because this ceremony had not yet been performed.

The ceremony was participated in by the Aghuan (Albanian) clergy and by Filippos, the King of Albania. Their participation demonstrated their position as vassals of the King of Armenia. The new king was known to be an able military commander, so the renewal of the crowning ceremony was received with great joy in all of Armenia. As a part of the ceremony the king reviewed his troops, 100,000 select soldiers known for their first-rate fighting skills. The aim was to demonstrate to the foreign participants and diplomats the military strength of the Armenian realm when it got its act together and was ready to fight as a single united nation under its own king. According to Matthew, the neighbours, the Abkhasians (including also the other Georgians because these were ruled by the same royal house), Greeks (i.e. Romans), Babylonians (the caliph under Buyids?) and Persians (the Buyids?), dispatched presents to the ruler. It is possible to think that the direct contacts between the Buyids and Armenia formed one part of the overall plan of the Buyids to weaken the position of Sayf ad-Dawla in the region, as did the desertion of the emir of Tarsus to their side. After the ceremony was over, the King of Albania returned to his own kingdom with presents.

It is probable that Naga's operations in the border region between Rome and Armenia were meant to secure a return of the Arab-Armenian emirs in Roman service to the Muslim side in a situation in which the Hamdanids could suspect possible problems in the relationship between the Romans and Armenians. The crowning ceremonies and the pompous parade of 100,000 Armenian knights were clear demonstrations of the renewed Armenian independence under the new king. According to the Armenian sources, this was to play a role in the relationship between Rome and Armenia when Nikêforos became emperor.

Developments in Baghdad[60]

In early 961 the Buyid 'Emir of Emirs' (sultan) Mu'izz ad-Dawlah fell seriously ill because he was unable to urinate. Consequently, on 24 February he handed the palace to his son Izz ad-Dawla, with vizier Muhallabi and chamberlain Sabuktakin to act as his advisors. Mu'izz was convinced that the bad air of Baghdad was the reason for his poor health and it was because of this that he ordered the building of a new palace on the highest part of Baghdad so that his health would return. Mu'izz, however, would recover his health and live until 967. Regardless, the preoccupation of Mu'izz with his health problems, the major building project, and other domestic problems, meant that the Buyids of Baghdad did not conduct any active campaigning against the Hamdanids of Mosul in 961, but this did not matter in the circumstances because the Hamdanids had been weakened already to such an extent that the Romans did not need to time their major offensives against them to coincide with Buyid offensives against Nasir ad-Dawla as they had done in 949 and 958. In other words, the Buyids would not provide any indirect military help to the Romans in 961, even if they did this in practice by accepting the declaration of the emir of Tarsus – which helped the Roman cause immensely.

7.7. The Death of the First Wife of Nikêforos Fôkas

On the basis of the fact that Patriarch Polyeuktos demanded that Nikêforos should fully perform his two year penance before marrying his second wife empress Theofanô in September 963, and because Nikêforos had looked upon the empress

Theofanô with lusty eyes before the death of her husband Rômanos II, it is clear that Nikêforos' first wife must have died during the period between October 961 and the Aleppo campaign in December 962.[61] The likeliest dates for her death would be the period after the return from Crete in summer 961 and before the Anazarbos campaign in December 961, or the period between the spring offensive in 962 and Aleppo offensive in 962, because both would explain why Nikêforos failed to lead campaigns in person during those months. The latter is probably likelier, because the period between the offensives was particularly long and the sorrow caused by the death of his wife would certainly explain why this was so, but on the basis of Skylitzes' text it did not take long for him to develop a passion for the empress, who was certainly a fertile woman whom he might have also desired for this reason after the death of his son.

7.8. December 961–March 962: Nikêforos Fôkas Launches his Grand Offensive in the East[62]

Operations against the Tarsiotes from December 961 until about March 962

When Nikêforos Fôkas returned to the eastern front he knew exactly what to do. The military success of his brother Lêon, together with the arrogance of Sayf, had ensured that the enemy would now be divided. The emir of Tarsus could not expect any immediate help from Sayf ad-Dawla thanks to the break up in relations. Nikêforos therefore led his army against the Tarsiotes at Anazarbos/Anazarba.

According to Miskawayh (191), Nikêforos Fôkas had assembled a massive army of 160,000 men (of which at least 66,000 were infantry) for the campaign against Anazarba/Anazarbos, while Bar Hebraeus (185) claims that Nikêforos led 160,000 cavalry against Anazarba. It would have been possible for the Romans to assemble a force of this size in the border region, because they could have organized supply convoys from their own territory quite easily from their operational base at Kaisareia, but it is still probable that this figure is an exaggeration, even if at the same time it is clear that Nikêforos was using an exceptionally large army, which is likely to have been significantly larger than the typical large army of 40–50,000 men that the Romans had previously employed in the east in 941, 951, 954, and 959. The reason for this is that in this case the Romans had dispatched the army that Nikêforos had assembled for the Cretan campaign immediately to the east, in order that Nikêforos could start his operations against the 'Hambdan' immediately (Skylitzes 12.10).

If we assume that Nikêforos had left about 20,000 men in Crete to garrison it, the force that had been dispatched to the east would have consisted of approximately 50,000 men, the numbers of which he could then bolster from the eastern *themata*. On the basis of the number of men needed for the inner siege line, we know that the minimum size needed for the siege of Anazarbos would have been about 12,600 footmen plus reserves of perhaps 4,000 infantry[63] and circa 6,000 cavalry, but as noted we know that he already had more men concentrated for the campaign. On the basis of the extant evidence one may make the educated guess that Nikêforos Fôkas aimed to assemble as large an infantry force as he had had in Crete, with a larger cavalry force.

This receives indirect support from the claim of Miskawayh that the infantry force that Nikêforos dispatched inside the city consisted of 66,000 footmen. The army that Nikêforos had led to Crete had consisted of 67,000 infantry and 5,000 cavalry. It would have been easy for Nikêforos to replace the infantry and cavalry forces he had left in Crete while increasing the size of the cavalry contingent significantly. If we assume that Nikêforos wanted to retain the same relative proportions for the cavalry as he did in his PM, then one may assume that his cavalry force consisted now of about 25,000 horsemen, but I would suggest that he actually fielded about 30,000 or more cavalry,[64] as this figure was the size that Leôn VI had envisaged for a cavalry army. In sum, my educated guess for the size of the Roman army is that it consisted of about 66,000 infantry and 30,000 cavalry plus servants and other support staff. The figure of 30,000 cavalry finds additional support from the number of cavalry that Nikêforos led against Aleppo in 962 (see below). It should still be remembered that this is only my best educated guess, based on the available evidence, which only suggests that Nikêforos had a significant numerical advantage over the Muslims. It is quite possible that Nikêforos led a far larger army into Cilicia, as suggested by the Arabs.

The above figures should also be compared with the size of the population in the city of Anazarbos. Miskawayh and Bar Hebraeus both claim that the city of Anazarbos contained armour, arms and other military equipment for 40,000 soldiers, with the implication that the city had either that number of soldiers or that it served as an arsenal for the armies passing through it. The figure of 40,000 fighters is actually plausible for the entire male population of the city if its population density would have followed the same density levels as ancient Roman marching camps, which would suggest a population of at least about 100–120,000 men, women and children (calculated ca. 300–350 persons per 1 ha), which may be an underestimation in light of the typical number of children at the time. Given the size of the population it is probable that Nikêforos would indeed have preferred the use of the large army for the sake of extra security, which with the servants was 160,000 strong.

On the basis of Yahya's account, the siege of Anazabos began on 12 December 961. The route from Kaisareia to get there would have used the route that bypassed either Kiskisos or Rodandas, after which the Romans would have bypassed the Tarsiote-held Sis, the defenders of which did not have the courage to bother the massive army of Nikêforos. On the basis of the accounts of Bar Hebraeus and Miskwayh, Nikêforos dispatched a detachment to capture the mountain overlooking the city, while he himself encamped opposite the city and its gate, which was located at the foot of the mountain. On the basis of the instructions of the DRM (21.66–107: Appendix 4:7.c), it is clear that Nikêforos united the camps so that in practice the entire city was surrounded with a double rampart. According

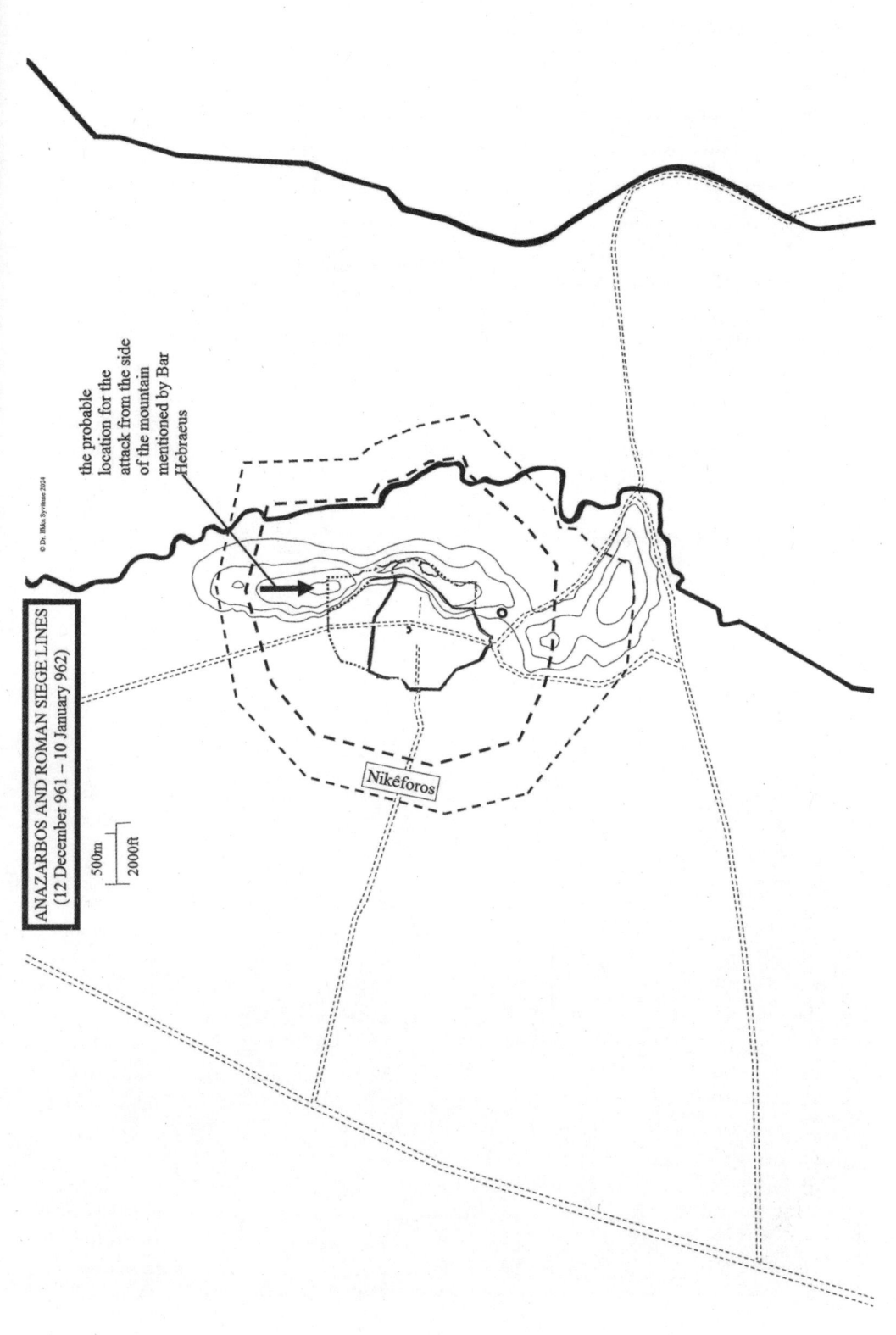

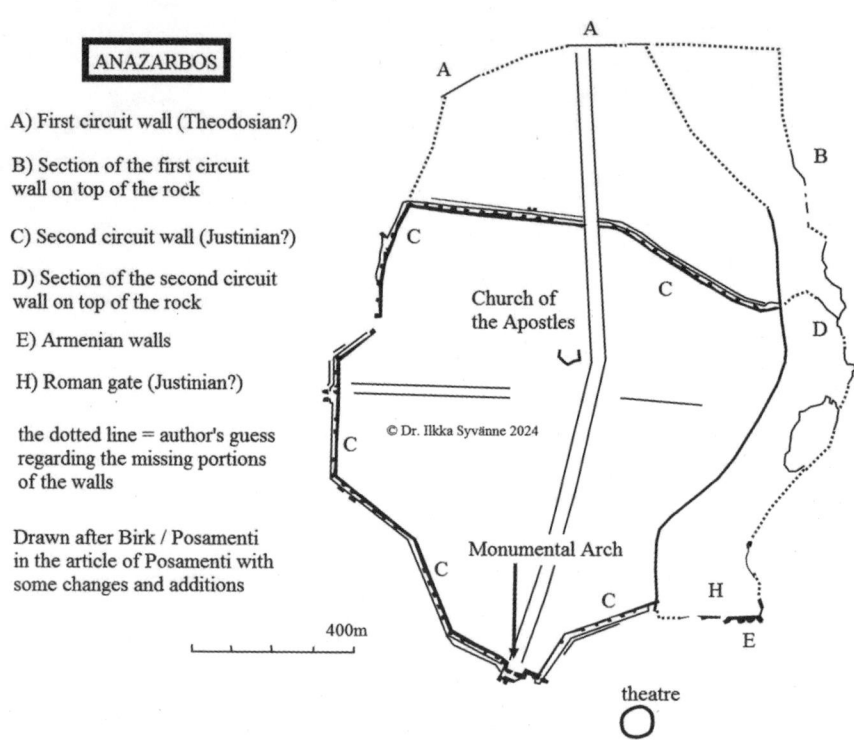

ANAZARBOS

A) First circuit wall (Theodosian?)

B) Section of the first circuit wall on top of the rock

C) Second circuit wall (Justinian?)

D) Section of the second circuit wall on top of the rock

E) Armenian walls

H) Roman gate (Justinian?)

the dotted line = author's guess regarding the missing portions of the walls

Drawn after Birk / Posamenti in the article of Posamenti with some changes and additions

Photo of Anazarbos in the 19th century. Source: Schlumberger.

to Yahya, the Tarsiotes did not stand idly by. Rashiq an-Nasimi, the *wali* of Tarsus, collected an army, which he led against the Romans. Nikêforos was not surprised and led his army against the Tarsiotes, massacred 5,000 men and captured 4,000 more, after which he returned to the siege. This sequence suggests that the Arab relief army consisted probably of cavalry which Nikêforos engaged likewise with cavalry, leaving the infantry with some cavalry behind to continue the siege. The result of the battle (a massacre with captured men) suggests that Nikêforos had superior numbers of cavalry with which he then encircled the enemy. In a situation in which the emir of Tarsus had broken relations with Sayf, the defeat of the relief force sealed the fate of Anazarbus.

The victorious Nikêforos returned to the siege, where his siege engines, which apparently included even moving siege towers probably equipped with rams, started their work. It soon became apparent to the defenders that their situation was hopeless. We have two different versions of what happened next. According to Bar Hebraeus, when the Romans on the mountain were close to breaching the walls, the Arabs dispatched envoys to negotiate terms of surrender, promising to hand over the city to Nikêforos in return for their lives and possessions. Nikêforos agreed to this with the result that the Arabs opened the gates, but when Nikêforos then entered the city he found out that he had been duped and that he would have taken the city without any promises. It was as a result of this that he ordered the inhabitants to seek safety in their mosque and that anyone who was found outside it the next day would be killed. According to the version given by Miskawayh, the Romans on the mountain had actually breached the wall (at the foot of the mountain?) with the result that their cavalrymen had entered the city and that it would then have been their presence in the city that betrayed the real situation to Nikêforos. This version actually appears likelier, as it shows why Nikêforos became aware of the Roman success. The fact that it was the cavalry that had entered the city from the mountain suggests that by then the Romans on the mountain had already taken the citadel, after which they had also breached the city wall below, followed by a cavalry charge from above into the city. The city fell on 10 January 962.

After having given his grim new instructions to the Arabs, Nikêforos appears to have retreated from the city while his soldiers occupied the entrances and gave the inhabitants a chance of finding a place of refuge inside the mosque. Even if the Arabic sources fail to mention this, it is clear that at this stage many of the inhabitants trampled each other in their effort to get into the safety of the mosque, which suited the cruel intentions of Nikêforos who undoubtedly knew that it would be impossible for all the men, women and children to get inside that building. On the following morning Nikêforos dispatched his footmen (66,000 according to Miskawayh) into the city with orders to kill every man, woman and child outside the mosque. Given the size of the population, this must have resulted in a massacre of huge proportions. Once this butchery was over Nikêforos ordered those inside the mosque to go wherever they liked before the evening, with the result that they trampled each other to death in panic when getting out, in addition to which more died en route to their homes while others lost their way. All those who had failed to make their way out of the city by evening were killed mercilessly.

According to Bar Hebraeus and Miskawayh, the Romans found as booty 40,000 suits of armour and a similar number of spears, swords and bows. In addition to this, the Romans captured everything else that the people had left behind. Nikêforos ordered the mosque destroyed, together with two walls of the city and all of its large buildings. The Romans completed the destruction with the cutting down of either 40,000 (Bar Hebraeus) or 50,000 (Miskawayh) palm trees.

Nikêforos exploited his victory by ravaging the territory of Cilicia around Anazarbos for a period of twenty-one days, in the course of which he captured fifty-four smaller fortresses, some with sword and some by capitulation. In one of the fortresses that had surrendered in return for a promise of safety there was an incident that the Arabic sources found worth mentioning because it showed the merciless nature of Nikêforos towards the Muslims. In that instance some Armenian soldiers attempted to rape some of the Arab women which led their brave husbands to grasp their swords, which Nikêforos responded to by ordering the killing of the entire throng so that 400 Arab men were killed alongside their families. Nikêforos spared only young girls and others that were suitable for slavery. The size of the garrison force, 400 soldiers, shows what the typical size for the smaller fortresses was. On 29 March 962, when Easter fasting had started,[65] Nikêforos ended his campaign and returned to Kaisareia, while stating that he would return when Easter ended. Now Kaisareia became his de facto permanent headquarters, so he could invade Muslim enemy territory in all seasons without any long breaks in between.[66]

Marius Canard (1961, 80–8) is likely to be correct in suggesting that Nikêforos would also have had other possible reasons for his retreat to Kaisareia besides the Passover. He suggests that he may have wanted to be in contact with certain persons in Constantinople (e.g. Leôn, Bardas Fökas and their clique) because by then the emperor Rômanos had already caused tumult with his wild behaviour, while leaving the actual governing in the hands of Iôsêf Briggas who had shown himself to be an enemy of the Fôkades. I agree with this suggestion. It is clear that Nikêforos was kept abreast of events at the capital. However, there is also another reason for the retreat to Kaisareia on 29 March. It is very likely that the soldiers needed a period of rest after the prolonged period of campaigning and fighting. The fact that the campaign lasted as long as it did shows that the reason was not the problems with provisions, because it is clear that Nikêforos must have organized the sending of supply columns from the Roman territory for his large army to be able to campaign over three months in enemy territory.

According to Miskawayh and Bar Hebraeus, when the Romans had started their retreat, the emir of Tarsus Ibn az-Zayyat assembled an army from the citizens of Tarsus and advanced against the Romans. According to Miskawayh, the army consisted of 40,000 citizens, while according to Bar Hebraeus the army consisted of 4,000 men. In the version of Miskawayh, Nikêforos then massacred the whole Tarsiote force together with the brother of az-Zayyat. When az-Zayyat learnt of the

Nikêforos II Fôkas in the sixteenth-century manuscript Marciana, Venice. (*Author's painting after the original*)

Nikêforos Fôkas leading a cavalry charge. The equipment drawn after Skylitzes. (*Author's drawing*)

Imperial guardsman, Menologion of Basil II. (*Author's painting after the original*)

Nikêforos Fôkas in Zonaras. (*Author's drawing*)

Roman cavalry AD 883. Homily of Gregory the Theologian. (*Author's painting after the original*)

Histamenon nomisma of Nikêforos II Fôkas. Constantinople mint; struck 967–9; Christ Pantokrator and Theotokos with Nikêforos. (*CNG Coins*)

Histamenon nomisma of Nikêforos II Fôkas. Constantinople mint; struck 967–9; Christ Pantokrator and Theotokos with Nikêforos. (*CNG Coins*)

Nomisma of Nikêforos II Fôkas. Constantinople mint; struck 967–9; Christ Pantokrator and Theotokos with Nikêforos. (*CNG Coins*)

Histamenon nomisma of Iôannês Tzimiskês. Constantinople mint; Struck ca.973–6; Christ Pantokrator and Tzimiskês being crowned by the Theotokos. (*CNG Coins*)

Kônstantinos VII. (*Public domain*)

Kônstantinos VII. (*Public domain*)

Roman soldiers in a tenth-century work of art. (*Public domain*)

Basileios B. Boulgaroktonos (Basil II the Bulgar-slayer) depicted in a painting. This painting shows nicely how the emperors would have dressed during military campaigns. (*Public domain*)

The terrain of the landing beach as seen towards Chandax in Crete on 13 July 960. (*Author's photograph*)

The landing beach of the Roman fleet near Chandax on 13 July 960 as seen from the Castle Kules. (*Author's photograph*)

Harbaville Triptych c.950. Left: Saint Theodorus Tyro (soldier); **Right:** Saint Theodorus Stratelates (general). (*Public domain, Marie-Lan Nguyen*)

Harbaville Triptych c.950. Left: Saint George; **Right:** Saint Eustace. (*Public domain, Marie-Lan Nguyen*)

Saint Theodore the Stratelate, Menologion of Basil II. (*Author's painting after the original*)

Marine, Menologion of Basil II. (*Author's painting after the original*)

St George (tenth century). (*Public domain*)

St Demetrios (eleventh or twelfth century). (*Source: Schlumberger*)

Left: St Theodore and St George, tenth- or eleventh-century. (*Source: Schlumberger*)
Right: St Demetrios and St George, tenth- or eleventh-century. (*Source: Schlumberger*)

A stone medallion depicting an unknown emperor located in Venice. It was originally located in Constantinople. The emperor in the medallion is sometimes identified as Alexios I Komnenos, but this is by no means certain. It could depict almost any emperor from the tenth- and eleventh-centuries, and Nikêforos II Fôkas is certainly a plausible candidate, because the medallion depicts an elderly short emperor with a broad chest. Unfortunately, the damage to the nose makes this identification only tentative. (*Source: Schlumberger*)

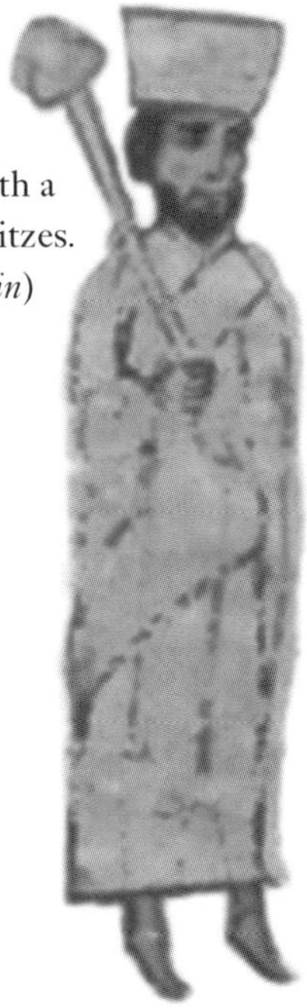

Nikêforos with a mace in Skylitzes. (*Public domain*)

Saint Demetrius, eleventh century. (*Author's drawing/painting after the original*)

Turkish *ghulam*. (*Author's drawing*)

Combat scene in the Manasses manuscript. (*Source: Schlumberger*)

Three *katafraktoi* and a mounted archer. A *spatha* and a composite bow in a holster behind the back.

On the right Leôn Fôkas (brother of Nikêforos) with his son Bardas on the left. (*Vinkhuijzen Collection, New York Public Library/public domain*)

A soldier in the tenth-century enamel. (*Source: Schlumberger*).

Psilos equipped with an arrow-guide. (*Author's drawing*)

A hoplite in ersatz armour after Nikêforos' reform. (*Author's drawing*)

A *menavlos* (one version). (*Author's drawing*)

A hoplite variant before Nikêforos. (*Author's drawing*)

A peltast in the *Sylloge tacticorum*. A helmet not covering the face, armour (here *lorikia*), a shield (here a round shield ca. 70cm), a sword, *dory*-spear (ca. 3.74m) and 'javelins' (ca. 2.5m). (*Author's drawing*)

Roman footmen in a miniature painting (tenth- or eleventh-century). (*Public domain*)

Icon of Saint Demetrios (early-fourteenth century). Note three arrows held simultaneously which indicates the use of a 'shower archery' technique in which three arrows were shot fast one after the other, after which the archer grasped the next set of three arrows for the same purpose. (*Public domain, Marie-Lan Nguyen*)

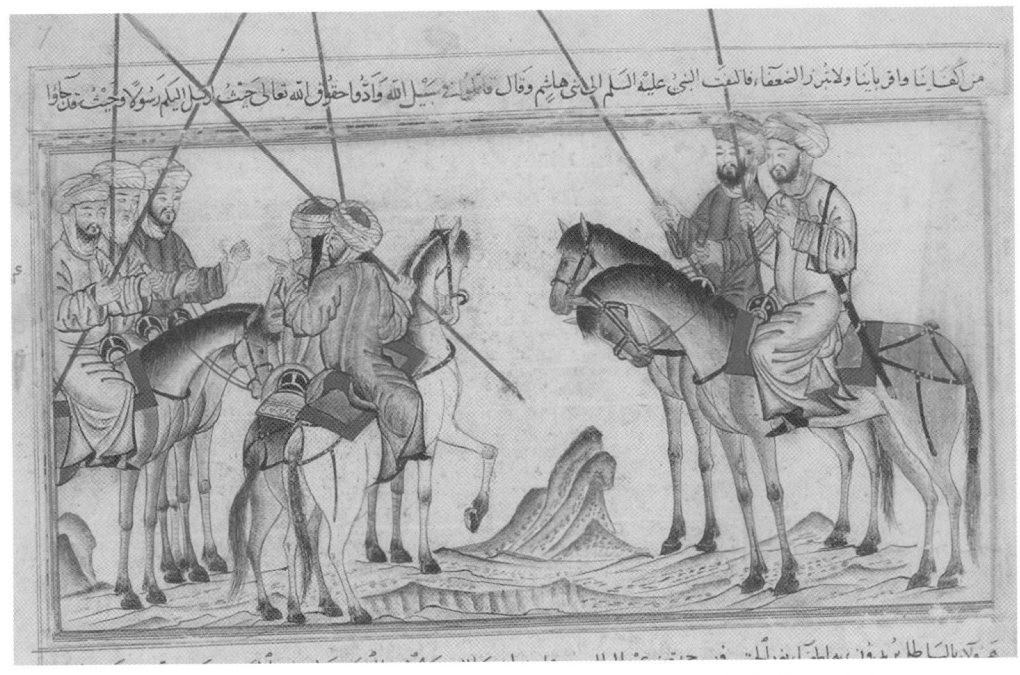

Prophet Muhammad at the Battle of Bakr (thirteenth-century manuscript). The painting represents well the typical Bedouin cavalry employed by the Hamdanids and Tarsiotes in the tenth century. (*Public domain*)

Saracens on a campaign. (*Source: Schlumberger*)

Kaisar Bardas Fôkas, father of Nikêforos, with two Saracens. (*Vinkhuijzen Collection, New York Public Library / public domain*)

Nikêforos Fôkas meeting Liudprand. The hair colouring is wrong in this image. (*Vinkhuijzen Collection, New York Public Library / public domain*)

Above left: An equestrian statue depicting Otto I the Great. (*Public domain*)

Above right: A painting of Saint Athanasios of Athos (dated 1290). (*Public domain*)

Left: Frankish soldiers in the Gall manuscript ca. 890. (*Public domain*)

An icon of Saint George and the youth of Mytilene. Mid-thirteenth century, British Museum. (*Author's photograph*)

massacre of his army together with his brother, he put on his armour and turban and threw himself off a balcony into water so that he drowned – he was clearly at Tarsus at the time. In the version given by Bar Hebraeus, the Romans killed both the emir of Tarsus and his brother Bar-Rebab at the same battle as they massacred their army.

In this case the version of Miskawayh is more likely for two reasons:[67] 1) the first Tarsiote force under the *wali* Rashiq an-Nasimi had consisted of more than 9,000 men (5,000 killed and 4,000 captured, with the rest fleeing) so it would be very strange if the next force sent against the Romans would have had fewer men in a situation in which the emir had had a longer time to assemble his men; 2) the annihilation of almost the entire available Tarsiote citizen army, which the death of 40,000 men would have meant, together with the death of his brother, would explain far better why the emir committed suicide than the mere death of his brother with a small army. This means that Nikêforos had now practically destroyed the emirate of Tarsus so it was ripe for the taking in 964, but this project was postponed to the period after the weakening of the Emirate of Aleppo so that the Tarsiotes could not hope to obtain any help from anywhere. In my opinion it is likelier that Ibn az-Zayyat was succeeded by Abu Bakr b. az-Zayyat (probably his son), attested as the emir of Tarsus in 971, rather than by the *wali* Rashiq an-Nasimi.[68]

According to Miskawayh, it had been Ibn az-Zayyat who had stopped public prayers for Sayf ad-Dawla and who had dispatched an embassy to Sayf. This may imply that before his suicide az-Zayyat had dispatched envoys to Sayf which once again pledged loyalty to him, because we find Sayf bringing help soon after this. Whatever the truth regarding the embassy of az-Zayyat given by Miskawayh, it is clear that the Tarsiotes once again started their public prayers for Sayf ad-Dawla with the result that Sayf once again started assisting them against the Romans. Yahya (86, p.784) informs us that Sayf rebuilt the walls of Anazarbos and returned the surviving inhabitants there. On the basis of other Arab sources, Canard (1961, 809) dates this to the period July–August 962. The city of Tarsus and its inhabitants would have a short breathing space before Nikêforos annexed it permanently to the Roman Empire.

7.9. Nikêforos' Spring Offensive Begins on 9 April–8 May 962[69] (see the map on page 249)

According to Yahya, the *domestikos* (i.e. Nikêforos) launched another invasion of enemy territory on 9 April–8 May 962, in the course of which he captured the fortresses of Duluk, Raban and Germanikeia. Obviously, the invasion progressed in truth via Germanikeia and Raban to Duluk (Doliche) and then back. Yahya also states that the Romans attacked the city of Manbij (Hierapolis), where they captured Abu Firas al-Harith ibn Sa'id ibn Hamdan, the governor of Manbij, who was then duly taken to Constantinople. This implies that this was a separate invasion not conducted by the *domestikos*, but on the basis of military probability it is very likely that it was not a separate invasion, but a raid conducted by a cavalry detachment at the same time as Nikêforos invaded the region. It should be noted, however, that even if Yahya does not mention the *domestikos* again in the context of the capture of Manbij, it is still possible that he also led that force because it is located so close to Duluk. However, in the accompanying reconstruction of the campaign in the text and map I am assuming that Yahya omitted the *domestikos* purposefully. Canard opposes the version given by Yahya on the grounds that both Ibn al-Athir and Miskawayh state that Nikêforos had entered Kaisareia and he would have remained there, so the first campaign would have been conducted by a *stratêgos*, similar to the campaign against Manbij. I do not accept this interpretation, but follow what Yahya states. The leaders of the campaigns were the *domestikos*, so Tzimiskês probably served as his *ypostratêgos*. The Easter ended on 6 April, so Nikêforos could have easily started his campaign on 9 April. Canard also suggests that Yahya dates the capture of Abu Firas incorrectly, because Ibn al-Athir dates it to November 962. I do not accept this version either. In late-962 the Romans were not campaigning simultaneously against Aleppo and Manbij, but only against the former. This time the city of Germanikeia was captured permanently, and became a new *thema* according to the *Taktikon* of Escurial (DV, 1986, 242). It was undoubtedly garrisoned by Armenians, just like the other new conquests along the frontier.

The probable invasion route of Nikêforos would have been from Kaisareia via Tzamandos and Arabissos to the pass of Adata/Hadath, because at this time the city of Adata was in Roman hands. The use of the Pass of al-Kankarun is less likely, because it could be controlled by the enemy. Nikêforos would therefore have approached the city of Germanikeia from the south-east, which undoubtedly surprised the enemy. It is very likely that the Roman army was approximately as large as previously, and that Iôannês Tzimiskês was accompanying Nikêforos at this stage. Once the city of Germanikeia was captured and occupied, this time permanently with a Roman garrison (probably with Armenians as usual), Nikêforos advanced together with Tzimiskês to Raban, which was captured and pillaged. It would have been here that the Roman army would have been divided so that roving cavalry columns raided the surrounding areas.

One of the raiding parties was under Theodôros Parsakoutênos, the *stratêgos* of Charsianon, the nephew of the *domestikos*. He led a separate roving column of 1,000 or 1,300 horsemen against the city of Manbij (Hierapolis), while Nikêforos captured and destroyed Duluk. In the course of the attack against Manbij, its governor, the famous historian and cousin of Sayf, Abu Firas, was captured by accident because he was hunting outside the city.[70] Abu Firas would remain a prisoner until the prisoner exchange of the year 966. During his captivity he held a discussion with Nikêforos Fôkas about the merits of the Roman and Arabs as soldiers, in the course of which the haughty Nikêforos insulted him by stating that the Arabs were mere scribes whereas Firas obviously defended the military honour of the Arabs. In fact,

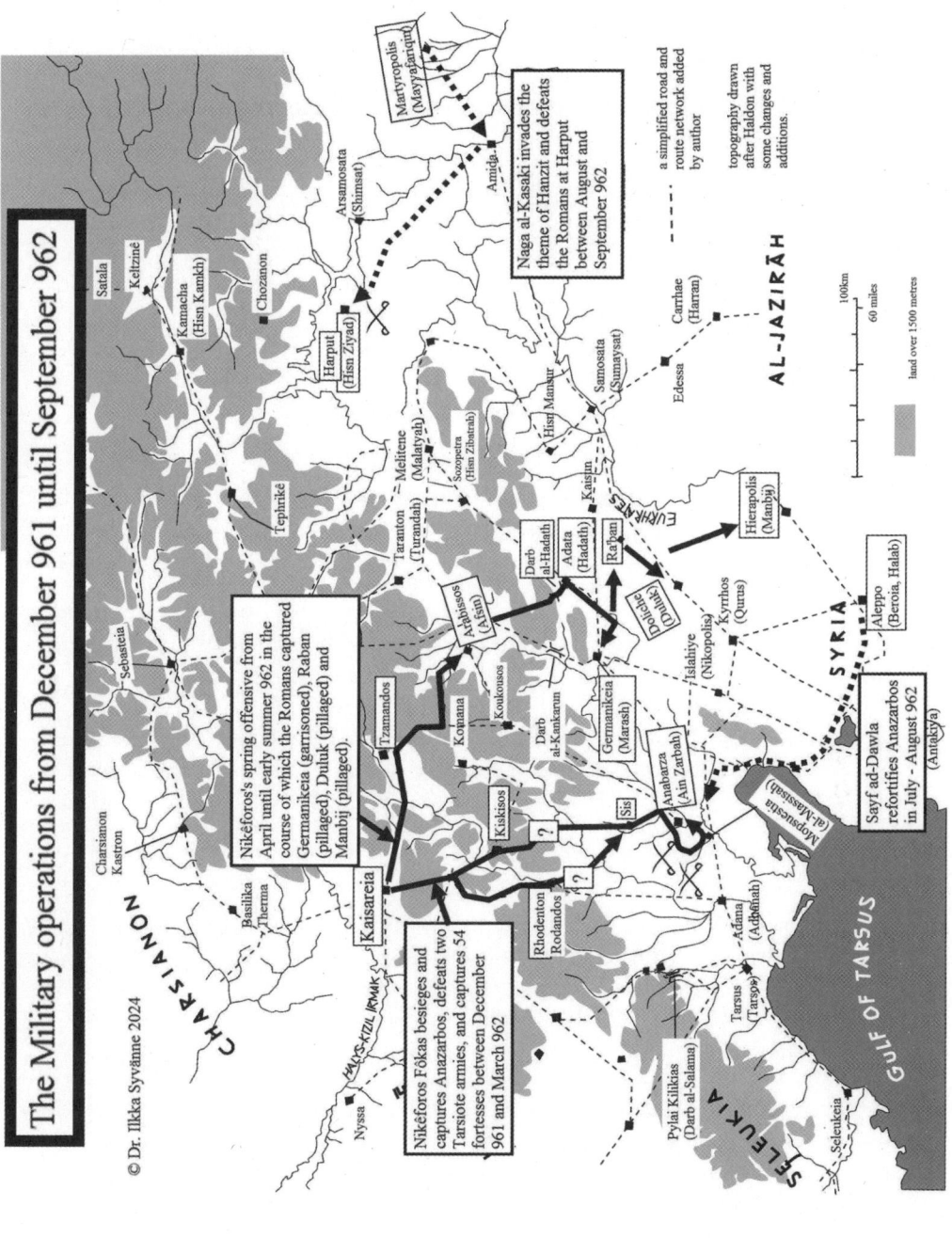

as a historian Firas went on to write a response to Nikêforos in which he extolled the merits of the Arabs as soldiers.[71]

7.10. The Hamdanid Raid against the Theme of Hanzit in Late-Summer 962

According to Canard, the Hamdanids did not sit entirely idle when all this took place. Naga al-Kasaki, the subordinate commander of Sayf, was once again active in Anzitene. On 5 August–3 September 962 he marched to Martyropolis, where ibn Nubata gave a vibrant sermon in support of the Jihad against the Christians. From there Naga marched against Hisn Ziyad (Harput, the HQ of the *stratêgos* of Hanzit). Naga won the resulting encounter and captured 500 prisoners as spoils of war.[72] Unfortunately for him and Sayf, this diversion did not take Nikêforos' eyes away from the main prize, the capital of Sayf ad-Dawla.

7.11. Nikêforos' Autumn and Winter Offensive in 962–3: the Battle and Siege of Aleppo

The Siege of Sis in Autumn 962[73] (see the map on page 251)

The first object of Nikêforos in the autumn appears to have been the city of Sis, which was located north of Anazarbos. Canard suggest that it was simultaneous with this that a separate roving column of Romans captured Abu Firas, the governor of Manbij, close to his seat of power, but as noted I agree with the dating scheme of Yahya in this case. In other words, I do not consider it probable that there would have been any separate raid towards Manbij at this time. The siege and capture of Sis by Nikêforos was probably his response to the refortification and re-population of the city of Anazarbos by Sayf ad-Dawla in July-August 962. The city of Sis had formidable defences, but as before these were no match for the Roman siege engines brought to the scene by Nikêforos. See the attached map. The city was captured, garrisoned and annexed into the Roman Empire. It was presumably then that Nikêforos marched back towards north, which may have lulled the Arabs into a false sense of security.

The Battle of Aleppo on Saturday 20 December 962[74] (see the maps on pages 255–6)

The Arabic sources provide us with conflicting information about the events that happened after this. Marius Canard classifies these into three categories, which I will try to reconcile. What is known, however, is that Nikêforos started his lightning strike against the city of Aleppo at a time when there was already snow on the ground in December 962.

According to the version provided by Shimshati, when the Romans were at the defiles entering Arab territory Sayf advanced at the head of 4,000 cavalry and

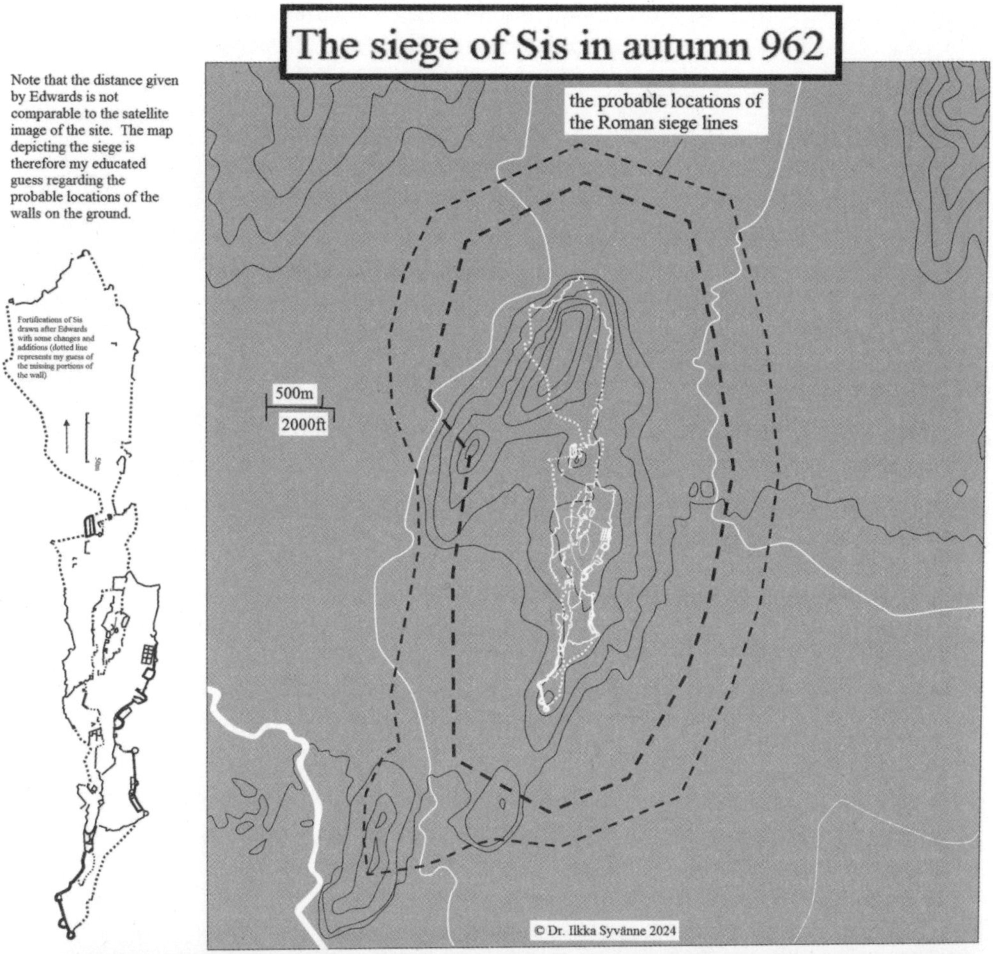

The siege of Sis in autumn 962

Note that the distance given by Edwards is not comparable to the satellite image of the site. The map depicting the siege is therefore my educated guess regarding the probable locations of the walls on the ground.

Fortifications of Sis drawn after Edwards with some changes and additions (dotted line represents my guess of the missing portions of the wall)

the probable locations of the Roman siege lines

500m / 2000ft

© Dr. Ilkka Syvänne 2024

Photo of Sis in the 19th century. Source: Schlumberger.

infantry to Azaz, but then realized that he was badly outnumbered and retreated towards Aleppo. The change of heart would have resulted from the news that the Romans had already marched through the defiles (undoubtedly through al-Kankarun and al-Hadath). According to Miskawayh (193), the Romans had 30,000 workers and craftsmen to clear the snow and to demolish buildings. It is quite clear that these now accompanied Nikêforos because he had learnt of their usefulness during the Cretan campaign. It is reasonably likely that a very significant number of the craftsmen and siege engine operators were actually drawn from the ranks of the navy, just as they had been during the Imperial and Late-Roman periods. It was then that Sayf received the news that the Romans had bypassed him and were at Amq, which is located on the plain of Antioch close to Harim (Nikêforos would build a castle there after he conquered the area as emperor). Sayf responded to this by dispatching Naga with 3,000 men towards the Romans, while Sayf himself sought to assemble an army from the inhabitants of Aleppo by promising each man a dinar for their service. When Sayf had advanced a short distance from Aleppo, the Bedouins informed him that the Romans were now at Jibrin, located thirty kilometres north of Aleppo,[75] so they would reach the city on the following morning. The likely reason for the conflicting information regarding the locations of the Roman forces is that the ones that had been seen at Amq consisted of the cavalry forces under Nikêforos Fôkas himself, while the ones that approached from the north consisted of the infantry and cavalry under Iôannês Tzimiskês. It was then that Sayf ad-Dawla deployed the citizens of Aleppo in front of the Gate of the Jews against the approaching Romans. The first to arrive were the Roman cavalry, who numbered almost 30,000. They were under the personal command of Nikêforos. The Roman combined force of infantry and cavalry (40,000 footmen armed with pikes and 20,000 cavalry used in pursuit according to Shimshati) under Iôannês Tzimiskês reached the scene in the afternoon. These figures are quite realistic and I take these at their face value. The Romans then surrounded the entire city. This would have taken place after the battle in front of the Gate of the Jews.

Miskawayh (193) claims that Nikêforos had 200,000 men of whom 30,000 were armoured (i.e. *katafraktoi*; a good indication of the results of Nikêforos' attempts to increase the number of *katafraktoi* which he continued as emperor), while 30,000 were craftsmen and artisans used to demolish buildings and to clear snow from the roads. In addition to this, the *domestikos* had 4,000 mules carrying iron caltrops which were spread around the marching camps during the nights. The figure of 200,000 men in total appears to be an exaggeration, but the other numbers are quite credible when one compares these with the figures given by Shimshati and with the figures of the Cretan campaign. It is quite clear that Nikêforos was leading a major army that was so large as to be able to overwhelm any opposition it met. On the basis of the above, the likely totals are almost 30,000 cavalry under Nikêforos; 40,000 heavy infantry with 20,000 cavalry under Tzimiskês; 30,000 craftsmen, servants, artisans and siege specialists with wagons and oxen; 4,000 mules carrying iron caltrops; plus an unknown number of spare horses. The 4,000 mules undoubtedly belonged to the baggage train of the cavalry force led by Nikêforos, while the 30,000 craftsmen etc. accompanied the mixed force under Tzimiskês. We should add to the figures the light infantry accompanying Tzimskês which on the basis of the proportions in the PM (11,200 *oplitai*, and 4,800 *psiloi/toxotai*, and unknown numbers of javelineers, Russians and slingers) would have been perhaps about 20,000 *psiloi/toxotai*. The total combat-ready force would therefore have been ca. 50,000 cavalry, 60,000 infantry and ca. 30,000 other personnel.

According to the version given by Yahya, Sayf ad-Dawla dispatched most of his men under Naga against the Romans while he stayed at Aleppo. Naga met the forces of Tzimiskês at Azaz, with the result that Tzimiskês fought against Naga in person and wounded him with a sword. Naga retreated to Sayf, who then instructed Naga to attack the Romans from behind when they arrived in front of Aleppo, but when Nikêforos arrived, Naga observed the size of the army and fled rather than attack the Romans.

The version of Kamal ad-Din is once again different. He states that Sayf dispatched Naga with the majority of his forces via Atarib (Litarbol) to Antioch; but the Romans did not advance in that direction, but rather to Duluk and from there to Tell Hamid/Khalid and Tibbil/Tubbal close to Azaz, which is located 50 km north of Aleppo. It was then that Sayf learnt of the whereabouts of the Roman army and started assembling the inhabitants of Aleppo for combat.

I would reconcile the above accounts as follows. Firstly, it is clear that Nikêforos either misled Sayf and his spies about his plans for the winter, or that Sayf and his intelligence operatives had just made the false assumption that Nikêforos would not invade during the winter because he had retreated to the north after the siege of Sis and because the passes were now blocked by snow. If the latter is true, then this was a grave failure by Sayf and his advisors, because Nikêforos had also invaded during the previous winter. It is also possible that Nikêforos had double-agents among

Sayf's spies, or that he sent a false deserter to the Arabs that misled them into a false sense of security, or that Nikêforos and his staff spoke 'openly' in the presence of some Arab captives who were then allowed to flee, or that the negotiations for the exchange of prisoners misled Sayf into a false sense of security. We know from Miskawayh (193) that Sayf had indeed prepared 700 Roman prisoners for prisoner exchange. The means to mislead the enemy are multiple and these are just my educated guesses about the ways that Nikêforos could have misled Sayf and his staff, and we know that his invasion did come as a complete surprise to Sayf because all of the sources mention this. This suggests the use of some sort of stratagem by Nikêforos. It was because of this that Sayf had only 4,000 professional soldiers with him at the time Nikêforos invaded.

When Sayf then learnt to his great surprise that the Romans were seeking to get through the snow-filled defiles, undoubtedly at al-Kankarun and/or al-Hadath, he attempted to hurry to the scene with his professional combined forces only to learn that he was too late. He would have learnt of this only when the cavalry vanguard under Naga ran into the combined infantry and cavalry force under Iôannês Tzimiskês somewhere close to Azaz, with the result that Tzimiskês wounded Naga with a sword when the two fought face-to-face on horseback. It is probable that Tzimiskês had more cavalry than Naga, despite the fact that he was commanding the infantry portion of the Roman army. When Naga then brought this news to Sayf, he decided to retreat to Aleppo, but it was then that he received the news that the Romans had been seen at Amq which indicated that they were aiming to attack Antioch. It was as a result of this that Sayf dispatched Naga with 3,000 horsemen via Atarib to Antioch with orders to engage the Romans from behind if they besieged Antioch. It is also probable that Sayf ordered Naga to also attack the Romans from behind if they did not advance against Antioch but against Aleppo. After this Sayf, who had 1,000 professional soldiers left, assembled an army from the citizens of Aleppo by arming them. He intended to lead this force to Antioch to support Naga, but was then informed by the Bedouins that the Romans were actually approaching from the north and would reach the city of Aleppo on the following morning. Consequently, Sayf deployed his citizen army in front of the Gate of the Jews. The Romans actually advanced against the city from two different directions: Nikêforos with his 30,000 cavalry advanced from the direction of Amq, while Tzimiskês with his 40,000 *oplitai*, 20,000 *psiloi* and 20,000 cavalry plus other forces advanced from the north. It was thanks to the manoeuvre of Nikêforos that Naga ended up in Antioch while Nikêforos bypassed him and advanced towards Aleppo from the west.

According to Yahya (87–8, pp.785–6), on Saturday morning, 20 December 962 Sayf had with him 100,000 citizen soldiers, which is a quite credible figure, so he could hope to be able to overcome the Romans, but this was a forlorn hope because the Roman army consisted of professional soldiers while the army of Sayf consisted primarily of hastily-armed civilians, most of whom would have been footmen. Sayf led his forces out of the Gate of the Jews and deployed to the north of the city. It is probable that in this case the Arab infantrymen were deployed in deeper than normal formation because they consisted of civilians. According to the *Revised Chronicle of Symeon the Logothete* (RFNF Text 2A, 22, pp.100–2), Sayf had assembled a great multitude consisting of Arabs, Daylamites, Kurds and people of the countryside, so the Aleppo infantry controlled the two fords of the river.

We have conflicting information about what happened next. According to the *Revised Chronicle of Symeon the Logothete,* Nikêforos observed that only one of the fords, the upper one, could be crossed by cavalry if the horses swam across it. Consequently, he led the cavalry there, the horses swam across, and attacked and crushed the enemy infantry. When Sayf saw this, he fled. After his stroke in 961 Sayf was not physically fit, so he could not attempt to restore the situation by his personal bravery. It was because of this that Nikêforos was able to capture the city

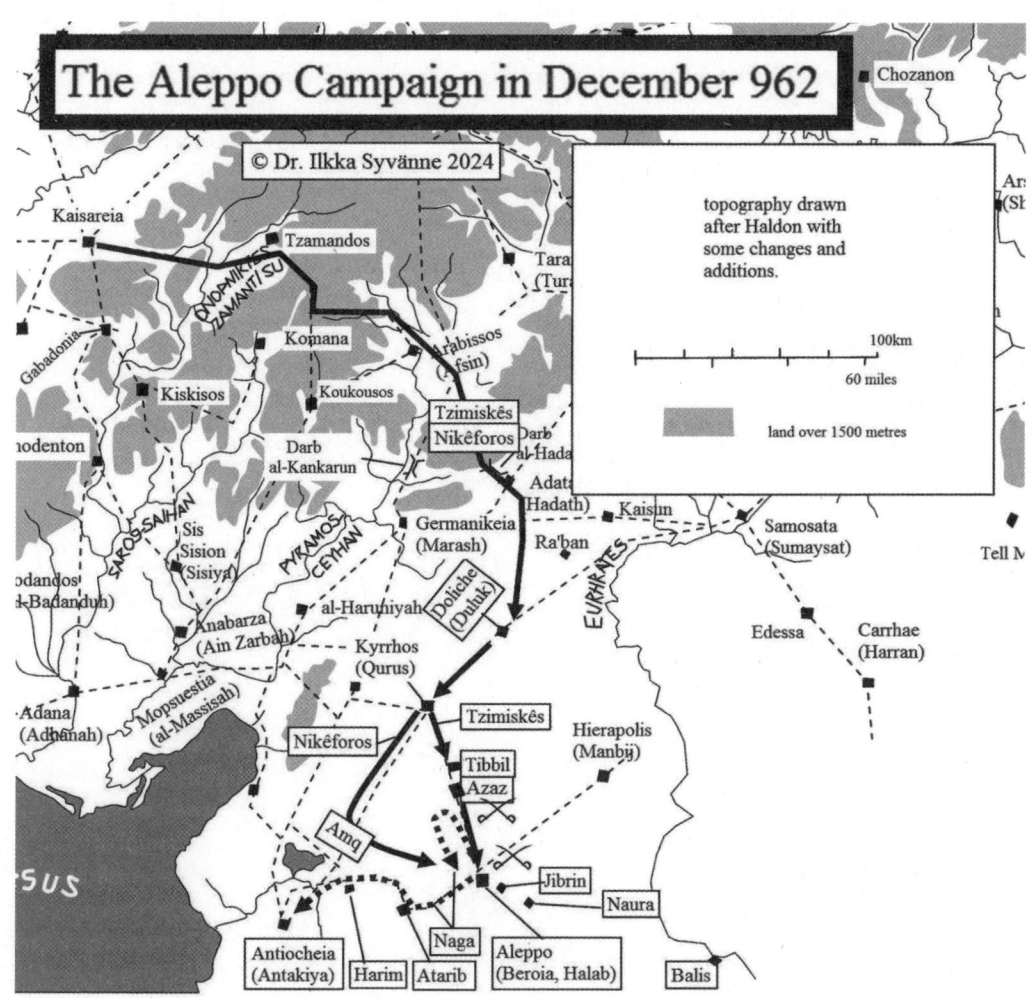

of Aleppo without a fight. The last statement considerably weakens the value of Symeon's earlier claims about the fords in the river and its crossing by swimming cavalry, but not conclusively so because there is a winding river on the west side of the city that dries up just north of the city and Nikêforos was definitely advancing with his cavalry towards the city of Aleppo from that direction. The capture of Aleppo 'without a fight' after the battle can be taken figuratively, because the opposition from within the city was definitely very weak as we shall see.

According to the account of Yahya, it was Iôannês Tzimiskês who attacked Sayf. The fight lasted for a while, after which Sayf ad-Dawla abandoned his army and fled towards Balis. Tzimiskês pursued Sayf with 20,000 horsemen up to a village called Sabin near Naura where he caught up with his prey, but Sayf was once again able to escape – presumably thanks to his extraordinarily fast horse. According to Canard, Sayf then changed the direction of his flight so that he fled south-west to Qinnasrin, where he waited for the outcome of the siege of Aleppo. Yahya claims that it was then that Tzimiskês turned and attacked the army of Sayf with the result that he massacred many of the nobles belonging to the entourage of Sayf, together with thousands of commoners when they were pressed against the Gate of the Jews in their flight. This is clearly a mistake, as it was Nikêforos who pressed the attack against the remnants of the enemy force while Tzimiskês pursued Sayf.

If one tried to reconcile the two different versions of events, it would be as follows. Nikêforos with his cavalry had advanced from the west while Tzimiskês advanced from the north, so his army was on the east side of the river once he reached it. Sayf deployed his Aleppo infantry on his left flank to block the route of Nikêforos across the river while he faced the forces of Tzimiskês with the rest.

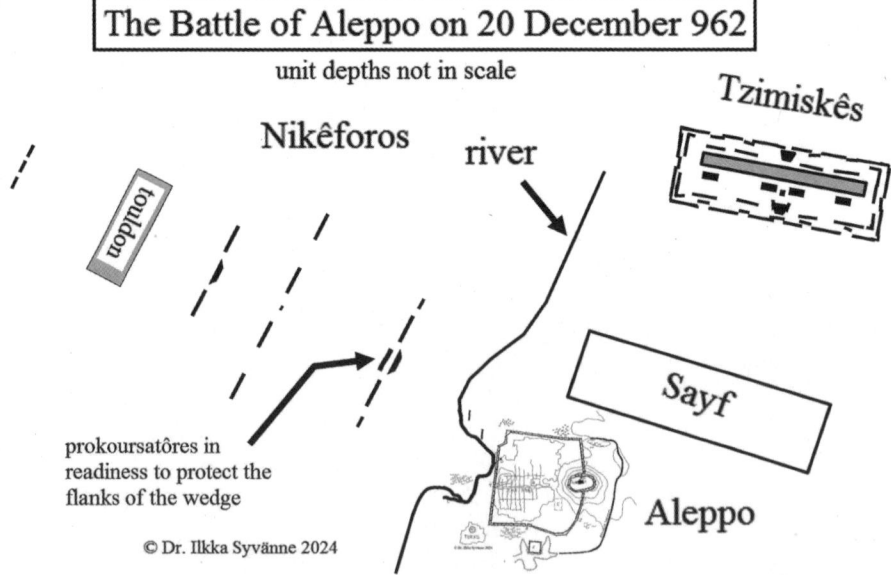

I am assuming that Sayf deployed his infantry as an oblong rather than as a single phalanx, because there existed the danger of being outflanked. This is a guess. Since it was Tzimiskês who initiated the attack, he must have attempted to break the enemy infantry formation with a cavalry charge performed at the canter by the first cavalry line with its *katafraktoi* wedge. The attack would have been directed at the point where Sayf was located. Since the battle lasted for a while, it is clear that this attack failed and that Tzimiskês' cavalry had to retreat inside the hollow infantry oblong. It is probable that while this took place the *Arabitai* of Sayf harassed the Roman hollow oblong. The decisive moment in the battle was when Nikêforos led his cavalry across the river, crushed the Aleppo infantry and then the left flank and rear of the main enemy formation. When Sayf saw this, he used the only open route of flight and fled towards the east, and then south-east towards Balis. It is clear that the crossing of the river must have taken place on the left flank of Sayf's formation because had Nikêforos crossed the river further upstream he would have approached Sayf from south by south-east, which would have blocked Sayf's route of flight towards Balis. It is unlikely that the horses of the cavalry were equipped with metal armour because they swam across the river, which means that the horses of the *katafraktoi* either wore bison hide armour as expected in the PM or had none. When the main enemy formation collapsed, Tzimiskês led his cavalry out again and began the pursuit of Sayf while Nikêforos completed the destruction of the enemy force with a pursuit up to the Gate of the Jews.

According to Miskawayh (192), most of the followers of Sayf were massacred in front of Aleppo. The casualties included many of the relatives of Sayf ad-Dawla. Bar Hebraeus goes even so far as to claim that all of the sons of Hamdan were killed, but this is an exaggeration. The day of combat ended in the siege of the city of Aleppo, which then began on the same day, 20 December 962. Shimsati claims that the Roman force that pursued the fleeing Arabs to Aleppo consisted of 80,000 cavalry and innumerable baggage, to which should be added the 20,000 cavalry that Tzimiskês used in pursuit. This figure is not reconcilable with the figures he gave earlier, so I am assuming that the 80,000 cavalry actually includes the infantry.

The siege of Aleppo from 20 December to 30/31 December[76] (see the map on page 259)

The first thing that Nikêforos did immediately after the battle was to sack the palace of Sayf, which lay outside the city. The Romans obtained massive amount of booty from the palace, which included 800 talents of silver, an innumerable amount of arms, and 1,400 mules. After this, Nikêforos set the palace on fire and occupied the suburbs of the city to begin the siege. On the basis of several Arab sources, Nikêforos was initially ready to abandon the siege in return for payments in order to avoid the need of a siege in the middle of winter that could weaken his army. This offer, which took place on Monday, 22 December, was refused by the inhabitants, with the result that Nikêforos had no other alternative than to begin siege operations proper, which included the building of the double walls around the city outside bow distance (the arrow-guides doubled the normal distance) and artillery. It is therefore clear that the trench known locally as Khandaq ar-Rum (Trench of the Romans) was not the Roman circumvallation as suggested by Canard (1961, 814). It was within easy reach of both bows and artillery, which rather suggests that it may have been the outer defensive line for the Arabs. It was located at such a distance that the Romans would have been forced to halt there to fill up the trench, which in its turn would have made them vulnerable to the bows and artillery.

The Roman siege equipment once again proved its effectiveness, with the result that the wall was already breached on 22 December, but the Roman attack against this breach was frustrated by the bravery of the inhabitants, who then repaired the breach during the following night with the result that the Romans retreated to a hill called Jabal Jaushan (unknown), which in my opinion means the hills just west of the city. This presumably means that the breach was made in the southern portion of the western wall. At that point in time, the infantry garrison of Aleppo, who must be the Daylamites, started pillaging the shops of the merchants and houses of the residents, with the result that the people abandoned their positions on the walls and hurried to their houses to protect their property. It was presumably due to this that the inhabitants reopened negotiations with Nikêforos on 23 December, who exploited this by preparing an assault for the following morning at the point between the Gate of Qinnasrin and the Hippodrome, which was detected to be vulnerable thanks to the absence of defenders. When the morning came the Romans placed their ladders against the wall and climbed to the top. It was then that the soldiers saw that the city below was in a state of civil war, with the inhabitants fighting against the Daylamites. The Romans exploited this and opened the gates and charged into the city. The city was therefore captured on 24 December. The Romans massacred everyone they found outside the citadel where the Daylamites and Arab nobility fled. Once inside the Romans found 1,200 Roman captives, 700 of whom Sayf had chosen for the prisoner exchange. All of these were now released. Nikêforos also chose 10,000 young boys and girls as slaves that he would lead back to Roman territory as spoils of war, the rest of the population being mercilessly butchered. The property of Sayf ad-Dawla, the merchants and residents were all captured, but since the Romans could not carry it all back to their own territory the rest was set on fire. One of the most important spoils of war, however, was a religious relic. The raiment of John the Baptist was found in one of the churches and was duly taken to Constantinople. The olive oil storages were also destroyed by filling the jars with water so that the oil flowed out. The mosques were likewise destroyed. The looting and destruction was completed on 28 December, after which Nikêforos announced that they would start their homeward journey.

According to the romantic Arab story, the nephew of the emperor accompanied Nikêforos and he opposed the retreat before the citadel would also be taken. Nikêforos was not willing to do this because the Romans already had more than enough booty. When the nephew still insisted, Nikêforos suggested that they would force the citadel into surrender through a proper siege, but this was not enough

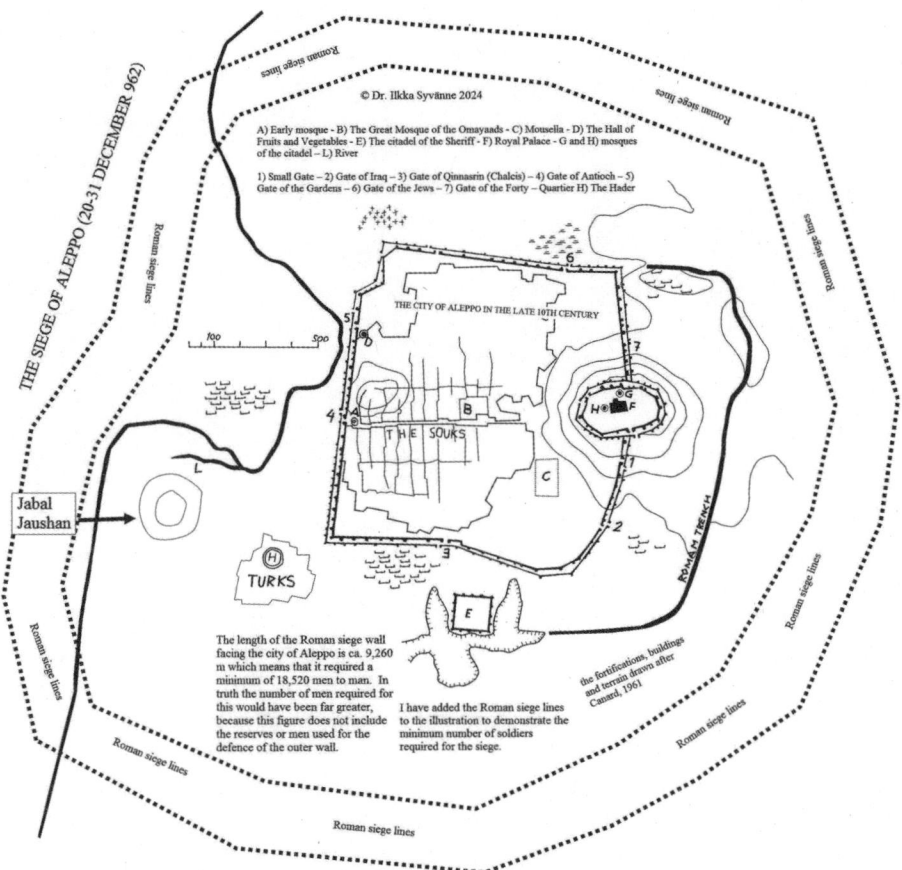

for the nephew who demanded to be allowed to assault the place. Nikêforos then stated that he was free to do as he pleased, but that he would keep the army at the city gate. The nephew then attacked with his men and was killed by one of the Daylamite soldiers because the place could be approached only in single file. When the corpse of the nephew was brought to Nikêforos, he is claimed to have ordered the killing of all Muslim prisoners as revenge. Canard suggests that the story was invented by the Arab historians to explain why Nikêforos failed to take the citadel. Canard is certainly correct in pointing out that the story includes details that cannot be true. It is clear that the nephew of the emperor cannot be the son of any of his sisters because he would have been too young to campaign, but it is possible that the 'nephew' could have been the grandson of Rômanos I, who would have been old enough by this time. Schlumberger (1890, 245–6) suggests that this man was actually the nephew of Nikêforos, which I find a very convincing explanation. I would therefore suggest that Theodôros was either the nephew of Nikêforos or an unknown grandson of Rômanos I who was accompanying the army and was killed

Aleppo in late 17th century

in action. It is probable that the truth behind the story is that when Nikêforos was already making preparations for the return journey, this 'nephew' delayed this by promising to capture the citadel by assault. Nikêforos considered this foolhardy but gave him his permission if he did this by using only his own retinue of followers. When the attempt then failed, Nikêforos led his army northwards, either on 30 or 31 December 962. Nikêforos did not pillage and ravage the surrounding fields and villages when he led the army back, and informed the locals that the territory belonged now to the Roman Empire and told them: 'You should cultivate the lands very diligently, because I will be back soon!'

Michael the Syrian/Rabo (13.4) claims that when the Romans were withdrawing from Aleppo towards the north there were some Arabs under Ibn Hamdan (Sayf ad-Dawla) who pursued them, but only with the result that the Romans turned and defeated them. Ibn Hamdan fled, but the Romans could not exploit their victory because there was some urgency in setting up Nikêforos as emperor. It is clear that there is some confusion in this account, because Rômanos II had not yet died when Nikêforos retreated, but it is still possible that Sayf ad-Dawla did indeed attempt to harass the retreating Romans with the forces at his disposal – which consisted at least of the 3,000 elite soldiers under Naga – who had by then joined Sayf at Qinnasrin, plus the survivors of the Battle of Aleppo and whatever forces Sayf could collect from the neighbourhood of Qinnasrin. Therefore, it is indeed quite possible or even plausible that the energetic Sayf attempted in vain to harass the victorious Romans, only to be defeated once again.

The fall of Aleppo caused widespread horror in north Syria, both because of the horror caused by the Roman success and because Sayf ad-Dawla deported most of the population of Qinnasrin (Chalcis) to Aleppo to repopulate it. It was presumably because of this that a portion of the population of Qinnasrin fled to Jazira, with the result that Qinnasrin was left deserted. The fall of Aleppo also caused widespread panic among the Muslim populations of Diyar Bekr, which had already been subjected to repeated Roman attacks. It was because of this that Ibn Nubata at Martyropolis composed sermons to elevate fighting spirits among the Muslim population in the hope that they would fight eagerly in Jihad against the infidels. The news of the fall of Aleppo also resulted in the rise of popular Jihadist movements in Mosul and Baghdad, while there were also recruiting efforts even as far away as Khurasan for a Jihad against the Romans. In other words, help would be forthcoming from other Muslim countries for those in the Thughur. The Fatimids exploited this in their propaganda by claiming to be the only ones who could protect Muslim lands and who could wage proper Jihad against the infidels. It was then that the Muslims would get a lucky break. The emperor Rômanos II would die on 15 March, so Nikêforos would spend the entire year embroiled in the power struggle that followed. Nothing less than his life and the lives of his relatives were at stake. Iôsêf Briggas was a personal enemy of Nikêforos who eagerly sought to use whatever means possible to overcome him.

7.12. The Fatimid Response to the Roman Reconquest of Crete in 962

The Fatimids had been unable to help Crete, but they exploited the fall of Crete in another way by demonstrating to the Muslims that they were the only rulers who could fight Jihad successfully. Consequently, they launched a determined offensive in Sicily in 962 against the territory still in Roman hands. With this in mind, they placed the city of Taormina under siege on 8 February 962. No help was forthcoming because the Romans were concentrating their efforts against the emirs of Tarsus and Aleppo. The surviving inhabitants of the city surrendered in December 962 in return for keeping their lives, which they were allowed to preserve while still becoming slaves. The city was renamed al-Mu'izziyaa in celebration of the Fatimid imam-caliph al-Mu'izz (953–75), and ethnically cleansed so that it was repopulated with Muslims.[77] After this, the Fatimids continued their efforts to push the Romans and Christians out of the island. Nikêforos would inherit this problem when he became the emperor.

7.13. The Death of Rômanos II on 15 March 963 and the Usurpation of Nikêforos Fôkas at the Beginning of July 963[78]

The death of Rômanos II and succession of Basileios II and Kônstantinos VIII as emperors

The emperor Rômanos II died on 15 March 963. This took place just two days after the birth of a daughter named Anna to him and his wife Theofanô. It is therefore possible that he celebrated the birth of his daughter too excessively. Rômanos II was succeeded by his two underage sons, Basileios II and Kônstantinos VIII, but since both were underage the empress Theofanô became the acting regent together with Iôsêf Briggas, but the real power was in the hands of the latter.

The cause of death of the emperor was (and is still) a mystery because Rômanos II was a young robust man only twenty-four years-of-age, which naturally led to rumours of foul play. The most common view of the cause of death was that it was caused by excessive debauchery, overeating and heavy drinking. The less kind version claimed that his death had been caused by his twenty-two-year-old wife, the unbelievably beautiful Theofanô. It was claimed that she poisoned him. It is usually assumed that this is only wild hostile gossip, because the death of her husband actually endangered the position of Theofanô and her two underage sons, Basileios II and Kônstantinos VIII,[79] but this is not conclusive because many people have and will act contrary to their own interests when they are being guided by their emotions, passions and feelings. It is clear that at this stage the beautiful Theofanô must have felt neglected by her husband, because the latter spent his time in the company of prostitutes and drinking buddies. Before becoming sole emperor, Rômanos had eyes only for his ravishing young wife, but when he became the sole ruler he started neglecting her because his friends urged him into an excessive luxurious style of living. It is therefore quite plausible to think that Theofanô was overwhelmed by jealousy and anger and did not think rationally. Her active participation in the assassination plot of her second husband Nikêforos actually supports this view. As will be made clear later, she was bored by the ascetic lifestyle of her second husband, with the implication that she had been looking forward to a more amorous lifestyle in the company of a man who looked like a Hercules. Furthermore, it is quite possible that she might have thought it possible to rule in the name of her sons with the aid of Iôsêf Briggas. In short, we cannot really know for certain which of the versions would be correct, because it is impossible to escape the fact that all of the extant sources characterise Theofanô as an adulteress.

According to Skylitzes (13.7), Nikêforos Fôkas had entertained imperial dreams for a long time prior to this, in addition to which he had developed a desire towards the young and beautiful empress Theofanô whom he had seen in the court. He had even frequently sent his trusted servant Michaêl to meet her – Iôsêf Briggas had noticed this and had started to labour suspicions of Nikêforos' motives. It is indeed believable that Nikêforos felt that he had greater right for the throne than inexperienced drunkards like Rômanos II or eunuchs like Iôsêf Briggas. This same sentiment appears to have been shared by other high ranking officers, if the views of Iôannês Tzimiskês in the text of Leo the Deacon reflect common views among the officer cadre, and there is no reason to doubt that they would not because it was undoubtedly difficult to take orders from persons who one despised. In addition to this, it is easy to believe that Nikêforos, who was by then a widower, could have developed sexual desires towards the young ravishing empress despite his deep religious convictions – the sinful passions of priests and pastors throughout history are well-known and repeatedly used as a source of fun in satires. It is in fact even possible that the empress reciprocated these feelings if she agreed to meet Nikêforos' trusted servant frequently. Nikêforos was known to have Herculean strength, so she might easily have developed passions towards him. It is clear that some sort of secret discussions were held for this to have happened, but we do not know what their content was. Whatever the truth about these matters, it is certain that Nikêforos had no role in the death of the emperor, because by the time he heard of it he had already disbanded his field army by sending the men back to their homes. Rather, the death of the emperor came as a nasty surprise, because Nikêforos knew that without his field army his position was weak and he feared the intentions of Iôsêf Briggas. Fortunately for Nikêforos, Briggas lacked the wisdom to act quickly.

According to Skylitzes, in April the empress Theofanô decided to summon Nikêforos into Constantinople to celebrate his well-earned triumph in the Hippodrome, with the spoils of war taken from Crete and Aleppo on display. Skylitzes claims that request was made against the wishes of Briggas, which sounds strange because this gave Briggas a chance of imprisoning his personal enemy, but it should be noted that this claim is also consistent with the statement of Leo the Deacon, who asserts that Briggas feared that once in Constantinople Nikêforos would launch his usurpation attempt because he was so popular with the army. After all, he was the *domestikos* and the capital and the surrounding areas had garrisons of *scholai* and other *tagmata*. It is also possible that Briggas feared that Nikêforos would become too popular among the masses and senatorial elite to be ousted summarily, while the empress may have wanted Nikêforos to usurp power (if she had colluded with Nikêforos via the services of Michaêl) because she, just like Briggas, did not understand that Nikêforos could not do so without his armed forces. Nikêforos was a cautious general, so he did not want to take the risk of testing on whose side the *tagmata* and imperial bodyguard units really were. He wanted to use the soldiers of the field army and its thematic soldiers on whose loyalty he could count. They were his comrades-in-arms.

According to Leo the Deacon, when Nikêforos received the summons to the capital he knew that he could not rebel immediately so he decided to bide his time until he would be able to collect a sufficient army for the usurpation. He therefore decided to go to the capital to celebrate the triumph, while hoping that the emperors would allow him to retain his command so that he could then rebel against them. Once in the capital, he was joyously received by the people and the senate and the triumph was celebrated at the hippodrome. After this, Nikêforos withdrew to his home, where he received summons from Briggas to come to the palace. Briggas aimed to apprehend Nikêforos, blind him and then exile him. Nikêforos guessed what was afoot and went to meet the Patriarch Polyeuktos at the Great Church. Nikêforos explained his predicament and convinced the Patriarch that it was unworthy of the Roman Empire to treat its best general in the way Briggas intended to do. Consequently, the two men went together to the palace, where Polyeuktos summoned the senate to hear his words. He managed to convince the senators that it would be right to dispatch Nikêforos back to the east as *stratêgos autokratôr* to lead the Roman armies against the Arabs. The senate approved the motion, and even Briggas was forced to accept it. At the same time, Nikêforos made an oath never to plot against the young emperors while the senate swore to respect the advice given by Nikêforos in public policy decisions and not to remove from office or promote anyone without the prior approval of Nikêforos. After this, Nikêforos returned home.

The list of things that required the approval of the *megas domestikôs* shows how extensive his role was in the promotion of personal careers (the *domestikos* was an important patron). He was clearly one of the key persons who formulated domestic and foreign policy, and imperial and military strategy. It is therefore clear that Nikêforos also had a role in the renewal of peace with Bulgaria which according to Skylitzes (13.5) took place now. In 963 Maria Lakapêna, the wife of Peter, the emperor of the Bulgarians, died, which endangered the peace. Peter, however, was willing to continue it and so were the Romans. Consequently, Peter dispatched two of his sons, Boris and Rômanos, as hostages.[80] The sending of hostages implies the discontinuation of tribute payments by the Romans. It was now the Bulgarians who sought peace from the Romans. Both would remain at Constantinople until their father Peter died in January 969.

If there is any truth in the claim of Skylitzes that Nikêforos paid a personal visit to Iôsêf's house in the company of only a single bodyguard, it must have taken place soon after this. As stated by Skylitzes, around supper time Nikêforos and one of his bodyguards appeared at the door of Briggas' home. When he was allowed to enter, he took Briggas with him and showed that he had a hair shirt underneath his official clothes and that he followed the monastic way of life and had every intention to become a monk as soon as possible. Briggas apologized and assured him that he would no longer entertain any doubts about him. According to Skylitzes, Briggas realized only afterwards that Nikêforos had duped him and that he had lost a golden opportunity to apprehend him.

When Nikêforos crossed into Asia, he established his HQ in Kappadokia where he drilled the men in armed Pyrrhic dance, vaulting on horses, and in the use of bow, spear and sword. According to Leo the Deacon, Nikêforos had decided to launch an attack against Sayf ad-Dawla, which means that he had postponed the usurpation to take place after that, but it is possible that this was only a ruse and that Nikêforos had already decided to launch his rebellion immediately after the army had been assembled. In the meanwhile, Briggas had started his own operations against those whom he suspected of plotting against him. These men included not only Nikêforos, but also Stefanos, the son of Rômanos I, who had been exiled. Now Briggas transferred him to Methymne and had him guarded more securely, but he did not live there for long because the empress Theofanô had him poisoned – if we are to believe Skylitzes. In this case, I am inclined to agree with Skylitzes because it would have been in the interest of her and her sons to have Stefanos killed as a safety measure.

Briggas sought to bring down Nikêforos with the help of Marianos Argyros, who was also a distinguished and successful general. Briggas promised to promote him first to the position of *domestikos tês anatolês* and then later to the position of emperor if he would help him eliminate Nikêforos. Marianos, however, suggested that Briggas should write to Iôannês Tzimiskês instead and promise him the same, because Tzimiskês was ambitious, daring and popular among the soldiers. Briggas agreed to do this. In addition to this, Briggas also wrote to Rômanos Kourkouas, a relative of Tzimiskês, with promises of rewards if he would join the plot to overthrow Nikêforos. At this time Tzimiskês was the *stratêgos* of the Anatolikon, while his relative Rômanos was probably the *stratêgos* of Armeniakon,[81] which ranked just below the Anatolikon in the hierarchy of themes. At the same time as this happened, Briggas removed all blood relatives and associates of Nikêforos from military commands and sent them into exile. In the case of Leôn and Bardas (father) Fôkas, this appears to have meant a house arrest.

Briggas promised to make Tzimiskês the *domestikos tôn scholôn tês anatolês* and Rômanos the *domestikos tôn scholôn tês dyseôs*. Neither of the recipients was prepared to betray their commander, and both went to meet Nikêforos. At the time Tzimiskês was ill, but he knew that he did not have any time to spare. When the men arrived at the tent of Nikêforos, they showed the letters and asked Nikêforos to usurp power immediately, because neither of them was prepared to take orders from an artificial woman (eunuch) from Paphlagonia. It was just not right for generals who were real men to be commanded by such creatures. According to both Skylitzes and Leo the Deacon, Nikêforos hesitated initially, so Tzimiskês and Rômanos had to push him into action. If this is not yet another story meant to hide the ambitions of Nikêforos, it is possible that he had indeed decided to fight first against Sayf and only then usurp power, but only with the result that the actions of Briggas and the demands of his subordinates forced him into revolt sooner than he intended.

It was thanks to this that Nikêforos rode immediately to his headquarters at Kaisareia, where he waited for the arrival of the rest of the field army. When the entire army was assembled in early July, the officers assembled around the commander's tent and raised their swords and proclaimed Nikêforos emperor. The 'bloodthirsty warriors' would not tolerate being ruled by infants and eunuchs. Nikêforos duly feigned reluctance and suggested that they should choose Tzimiskês instead, because he was a widower without issue as his son Bardas had died in a jousting accident. When this was responded to with a silence, Nikêforos declared that he was ready to accept the imperial burdens, after which he put on the scarlet boots. The vows given to the Patriarch Polyeuktos and the senate were thereby broken. A good general always sought to deceive the enemy and this Nikêforos had now done. After this, Nikêforos returned to his tent, and then emerged from it wearing an *akinakes* (short sword or dagger) on his belt and dory (*spear*) in his hand. Then he went before the army and exhorted it with a speech to overthrow the eunuch – a call which the army eagerly supported. Then Nikêforos visited the church of Kaisareia to obtain divine support for his cause, which was a necessary move to convince both the army and his supporters of the righteousness of his cause. Then Nikêforos made his first policy decisions in front of the army. Tzimiskês was appointed *domestikos tês anatolês*. His other supporters were also rewarded with military commands. Then the new emperor dispatched generals to the Black Sea region, which in this case meant primarily the fortress of Hieron, so when other generals were dispatched to Abydos the sea route to the city of Constantinople would be blocked both from the south and north. He had actually made preparations for this in advance, so the straits were blocked before the news of his usurpation reached the capital.

Nikêforos then arrayed his forces in a compact marching formation (a hollow square) and started his journey to Hieria. At the same time, Nikêforos dispatched the bishop Filotheos as his envoy to announce his enthroning as emperor to Polyeuktos and Briggas. He urged them to accept his nomination and in return for this he promised to protect and raise the underage sons of Rômanos II as his own. The angered Briggas had the bishop thrown into jail.

In the meanwhile, Briggas had not been idle either. He joined to his cause *patrikios* Paschalios, who had previously plotted against Rômanos II in 962, and Nikolaos and Leôn Tornikios. These were given command of the Macedonian *speira* (cohort), which obviously means the *megas etaireia* tasked with the protection of the emperor and palace. They were tasked to prevent the crossing of the straits.[82] When Nikêforos had already reached the Palace of Hieria, his father Bardas Fôkas fled to the Great Church, while Leôn Fôkas dressed himself as a common workman and escaped through the pipes in the wall before embarking on a small boat and sailed to join his brother on the opposite shore. The guards placed by Briggas had clearly performed their duties negligently. When Nikêforos led his army from Hieria past Chalcedon to Chrysopolis, Briggas apparently decided to nominate Marianos Argyros as emperor, but did not get a chance to do so thanks to the fast progress of events. The operatives of the Fôkades family and their collaborators had been active in the city. They had secured the support of Basileios *parakoimômenos*, the eunuch son of Rômanos I and a 'Scythian' woman. In addition to this, the Fôkades also had the support of the 'people on the street', which must mean the Green and Blue Factions because when the Macedonian *speira* and Saracen prisoners (*De Ceremoniis*) under the command of Marianos Argyros and Paschalios were moving through the streets of the city, they were attacked by the common people, engaging the professional soldiers in close-quarters combat. This clearly betrays the participation of the armed members of the Circus Factions. Their leaders must have been bribed in advance for this to happen. In the midst of this rioting a woman threw a ceramic pot at the head of Marianos Argyros, which hit his forehead and splattered his brains causing Marianos to die the next day. When the news of this rioting was brought to Basileios the Eunuch, he armed his more than 3,000 household members and attacked the houses of Briggas and his supporters. When their houses had been pillaged and destroyed, Basileios went to the dockyards (probably the harbour of Neorion as suggested by Sullivan/Talbot) where he apprehended the fire-bearing triremes with the full approval of the people and the senate. This means that all of the remaining members of the senate had by then joined the revolt. Then Basileios sailed these triremes across the straits.

Nikêforos and his men embarked on the ships and landed at the monastery of Abramitai, located next to the Golden Gate. Then Basileios dispatched his men to the Palace to apprehend Briggas, who had by then been abandoned by his bodyguards. Briggas fled to the Great Church, and when Bardas Fôkas saw this he left the church. Nikêforos then donned imperial garments and robe, mounted a white horse and entered the city through the Golden Gate on 16 August 963. Then he went to the Great Church, where he was crowned by the Patriarch Polyeuktos at the age of 51. The date of the crowning is also confirmed by the *Byzantine Minor Chronicle 14* (59).[83]

According to the version preserved in the *De Ceremoniis* (p.436), Briggas had actually managed to convince Bardas to return to his home before this by visiting him in person in the company of Basileios II and Kônstantinos VIII, so that the people (i.e. circus factions) then guarded the house of Bardas against the imperial authorities during the subsequent rioting. The *De Ceremoniis* (p.436–8) also states that the people defeated the Macedonians and Saracens of Marianos, destroyed the house of Briggas, captured many senators, and rioted for three days. It was during this time that Bardas Fôkas was transported from his house to the Imperial Palace by the circus faction leaders, after which on the second day Leôn Fôkas crossed into the city from the military camp located at Chrysopolis, after which Nikêforos advised Basileios, *praipositos* Iôannês and the faction leaders (*archontoi*) to meet him at the Palace of Hiereia on 15 August, and on 16 August Nikêforos then crossed the straits to be crowned on the same day.

According to Leo the Deacon: Nikêforos was closer to black than white by complexion; his hair was thick and dark; his eyes were black and piercing; his eyebrows were thick and bushy; his nose was not narrow or wide and was slightly turned up like a hook; he had a beard of moderate size with grey appearing; his stature was stooped but he had a very broad chest and shoulders, which betrayed

A bronze coin of the *basilissa* Theofanô *augusta*
It was rare for the empress to have her own coins, which is a good indication of the exceptional personal ambitions of the empress. Source: Schlumberger.

his Herculean strength. Leo the Deacon also claims that Nikêforos was the wisest and most prudent man of his generation.

However, Nikêforos was first and foremost a soldier emperor and this was in evidence from the beginning of his reign when he and his army entered the capital. According to Skylitzes (14.18), Nikêforos allowed his soldiers to loot the city, so there were thousands of illegal confiscations, and when then some of those who had suffered in their hands complained, Nikêforos simply stated that in such a large body of men there were always some bad apples and did nothing. His aim was to reward his soldiers and to retain their loyalty, so he turned a blind eye to their crimes. At the same time as this happened (LD 6.1), unscrupulous inhabitants exploited the situation and killed and looted themselves.

The crowning of Nikêforos Fôkas. (*Skylitzes, public domain*)

Chapter Eight

The Reign of Nikêforos II Fôkas (16 August 963–11 December 969)[1]

8.1. Nikêforos at Constantinople from 16 August 963 until the Spring 964[2]

When the just-crowned fifty-one-year-old Nikêforos II Fôkas reached the imperial palace he started making appointments and his first decisions as emperor. Nikêforos promoted his father Bardas to the rank of *kaisar*. Leôn Fôkas was made *kouropalatês* and *magistros*. It is possible that he was also appointed as *logothetês tou dromou*, in which office we find him in 968. In this office he was not only responsible for the state post, but also for foreign affairs and espionage. Basileios *parakoimômenos* was rewarded with the rank of *proedros*. This was a new title, meant as a special reward for the services rendered by Basileios, and probably also granted to its holder the office of *proedros* of the senate.[3] The loyal comrade-in-arms and nephew Iôannês Tzimiskes was also now reaffirmed as *domestikos tôn scholôn tês anatolês* and *magistros* and ordered to continue the interrupted campaign against the Saracens.

Nikêforos acted as if he wanted to maintain his Spartan lifestyle, which included abstinence from meat and women. It was because of this that he initially sent Antônios, a Stoudite monk, to the quarters of Theofanô to expel her from the palace and then escort her to the Petrion palace close to the Golden Horn. Iôsêf Briggas was also duly exiled. He died two years later, apparently of natural causes. Then Nikêforos feigned that it was only thanks to the demands made by the monks who accompanied him that he gave up his Spartan lifestyle and married Theofanô and restarted eating meat. In addition to this, Nikêforos started to dress in full imperial regalia to signal to everyone that he was now the emperor. As emperor, Nikêforos needed a new wife and marriage with Theofanô gave him legitimacy, but we should not forget the fact that he appears to have already developed sexual desires towards her during the lifetime of her husband. Nikêforos married Theofanô on 20 September 963.[4]

When the emperor was entering the Great Church to marry Theofanô, the Patriarch Polyeuktos took Nikêforos aside and said that he would not allow him to enter the Church before he had performed the two-year penance required from those who married for the second time. This means that it was less than two years from the death of Nikêforos' first wife, not to mention that fact that it was even less from the death of Theofanô's first husband. This did not prevent Nikêforos from carrying out his plans.⁵

On top of that Polyeuktos did not stop there, but brought forward yet another accusation to annul the marriage after it had already been consummated. Stylianos, a dean of the clergy, told Polyeuktos that Nikêforos was a godfather for one of the children of Theofanô, which made the marriage illegal. Polyeuktos demanded that Nikêforos would either divorce his wife or stay out of the church. Nikêforos chose to do the latter. Then Polyeuktos assembled the bishops and leading senators and brought before them his accusations against Nikêforos. The bishops and senators sought to endear themselves to the new emperor, so they claimed that the canonical law against the godfather was a law enacted by the inconoclast emperor Kônstantinos V Kopronymos and therefore illegal. When Polyeuktos still insisted on his claims, Bardas Fôkas swore that nothing like that had happened, after which the emperor coerced from the whistleblower Stylianos a statement that neither Bardas nor Nikêforos were godfathers of the child. At this point, Polyeuktos was forced to drop his case against the emperor. Unsurprisingly, Nikêforos never forgave Polyeuktos for what he had done.

Nikêforos bribed his newly-wed wife with fertile agricultural property which abounded in fruits and grains. Nikêforos courted the populace and circus factions who had supported his rise to power by attending chariot races in person at the hippodrome, while distributing to them the customary imperial largesse. However, Nikêforos was still a soldier by heart. He drilled the servants (*therapeutikoi*) and household retainers (*oikidioi*) in military manoeuvres and combat techniques, so that they could use the bow, draw the string and arrow to the chest (undoubtedly one of the archery techniques meant for shower archery),⁶ the use of spears and swords, and jumping on horses. In short, Nikêforos required every male member of his household to be proficient in combat techniques just in case this was needed. On the basis of Nikêforos' military training scheme for his staff, it is probable that Nikêforos began his project of turning the imperial palace into a fortress at the same time. According to Skylitzes (14.18.79ff.), Nikêforos tore down many of the beautiful palace buildings so that he could build a walled acropolis for himself which had warehouses, granaries, kitchens and bakeries for the purpose of filling the imperial citadel with provisions. According to Leo the Deacon (4.6, p.64),⁷ the wall was built towards the sea in a place where there was a slope, which clearly had a defensive purpose against attacks from the sea. Nikêforos was clearly a soldier emperor who felt secure only when protected by walls and soldiers. The project was expensive and was completed only in 969.

As a military commander Nikêforos knew the importance of numbers in warfare. If there is one constant theme in his policies, it is the constant increasing of the size of the armed forces. It was in 964 (clearly in the spring of that same year) that he issued '*Novel J*' (McGeer's designation in his book), which forbade the increasing of monastic properties at the cost of military lands. Nikêforos therefore wanted to secure the availability of soldiers in the future. He started his legislation with the religious establishment, because as a new emperor he needed the support of the military *dynatoi*. Once he had secured his own position he also curtailed their abuse of power. See Chapter 8.5.

Nikêforos spent his autumn and winter in these activities, while Tzimiskês and other generals fought on his behalf. The operations in the Emirate of Tarsus conducted by Tzimiskês were preliminary preparations for Nikêforos' own campaign that he would lead in person in the coming spring against the Emirate of Tarsus, while the invasion of the Qaysid Emirate prepared the ground for the advance into that area. Nikêforos also dispatched a sizeable fleet and army to Sicily in an obvious attempt to reconquer the entire island. However, before either of these took place, the Arabs had not remained idle.

8.2. Armenians and the Eastern Frontier[8]

After the fall of Aleppo, the first to exploit the loss of prestige of Sayf ad-Dawla were the Armenians. According to Bar Hebraeus and Miskwayh, 1,000 Armenian footsoldiers attacked Edessa and captured sheep, oxen, horses and ten Arabs as slaves. It is uncertain if the Armenian infantry consisted of mercenaries employed by the Arabs, or if they were enterprising Romans from the Armenian border themes, or Armenians from Armenia proper, or so-called Armenians who were actually Muslims in the service of the Qaysid Emirate. The likeliest of these alternatives is that the men were creative bold Armenians in Roman service from some Armenian border theme.

Bar Hebraeus also indicates that 'in these times when the Romans had gained mastery over the Arabs' they conducted a devastating invasion of Arab-controlled Armenia as far as Greater Armenia. This implies that the Romans probably invaded the Qaysid Emirate, either from Karin or from Melitene/Harput, or from both regions simultaneously. According to Bar Hebraeus, the local Armenians joined the Romans and were afraid that the Arabs would exact vengeance for their treachery. It was because of this that the Armenians fled from these regions en masse to the Roman frontier, where the Romans settled them in Sebasteia and other border fortresses that they had captured from the Arabs. Thereafter, there were large numbers of Armenian infantry accompanying the Romans, which helped them in their conquests. It is unfortunate that Bar Hebraeus fails to date the invasion more accurately, but in light of the fact that Naga exploited this only at the turn of the year 963/4, it is very likely that it took place in autumn 963, so this invasion would have been the first invasion of foreign lands when Nikêforos was already emperor. The success of the operation proves that Nikêforos was correct when he ordered the invasion to take place.

Sayf ad-Dawla had recovered his fortunes enough by summer or late-summer 963 so that he was able to launch a triple offensive against the Romans in autumn. The timing was perfect, because the Roman field army had been taken to the region of Constantinople by Nikêforos. Naga al-Kasaki invaded Roman territory close to

Melitene. It is possible that this invasion took place at the same time as the Romans invaded the Qaysid Emirate and acted as a distraction. The Tarsiotes invaded as far as Iconium (Konya). Naga was successful and returned to Martyropolis with spoils of war, and the Tarsiotes were likewise successful, but their route of retreat was blocked by the forces of Kônstantinos Maleinos. However, the Tarsiotes fought their way through successfully and reached their Emirate safely. The intention was that Sayf ad-Dawla would invade Roman territory through some other pass between those, but he did not do so because he was still suffering from the effects of his stroke. In fact, he returned to Aleppo, where he suffered yet another stroke, which everyone believed to be fatal. Sayf was clearly a man whose health suffered from his personal adversities. This was exploited by Sayf's nephew Hibat Allah (son of Nasir), who killed Ibn Danha because he believed it to be safe now.[9]

When Hibat learnt that his uncle Sayf had not died he was in trouble, because he had previously deserted his father Nasir and joined the Buyids – only to desert them as well and join Sayf's army. Consequently, Hibat fled from Aleppo with Naga in pursuit. Naga was unable to catch Hibat, but he captured his baggage and then returned and dispatched his brother Nama to Harran/Carrhae, where Hibat had found a place of refuge. Nama was unable to obtain Hibat's surrender, so the city of Harran was now a city in revolt. It was now Naga's turn to advance against Harran, with the result that Hibat fled to the safety of his father. Naga subjected the city to revenge by looting it, after which he marched to Martyropolis. When Naga did so he left the city without any government, with the result that the city fell into anarchy. Thanks to the anarchy prevailing in Diyar Mudar, no seeds were sown in the area.

When Naga reached the city of Martyropolis, he was denied an entry by Oumm-Abu-l-Ma'ali, the wife of Sayf ad-Dawla. The reason for this is not given, but it is probable that she suspected the motives of Naga and for very good reason. It was then on 2 December 963 that either 5,000 or 8,000 Khorasani Jihadists, both cavalry and infantry (the Arabic sources give two different figures), arrived to join Sayf ad-Dawla in the war against the Romans. They had marched via Azerbaijan and Armenia to Martyropolis. The leader of the Khorasanis attempted to persuade Naga to join them in their Jihad against the Romans, but Naga stated that he would attack Abu'l-Ward, the Qaysid emir in Armenia. The Qaysids would be very vulnerable after they had been defeated by the Romans earlier in the year. Naga was already contemplating an open revolt against his master, but he could not yet do so openly by attacking Martyropolis thanks to the presence of the Khorasanis. Consequently, Naga continued his march against Abu'l-Ward, the Qaysid emir in Armenia. Naga defeated the emir and captured his fortresses, and so became master of the towns of Manzikert, Khilat and Mush. Naga now possessed his own personal powerbase, so he started preparing his return to Martyropolis. In the meanwhile, the Khorasanis had continued their march to Harran and from there to Aleppo at some point in time between 18 February and 17 March 964. Their help was sorely needed, because at the time Tzimiskês was besieging Mopsuestia (Miccica, Massisah, Msis).

8.3. The Strategy of the Emperor Nikêforos Fôkas for the Year 964

The military campaigns of the year 964 prove that Nikêforos Fôkas' strategy for the year was the continuation of the series of offensives against the Saracens on the eastern frontier, while he sent a fleet under Manuêl Fôkas to Sicily with the double aim of relieving the city of Rametta while pushing the Muslims out of the island altogether. This is the only logical reason for the size of the force given to Manuêl because he not only had a sizeable fleet to support him, but also 40,000 men – some of whom were the elite *katafraktoi*. The campaigns led by Tzimiskês into the Emirate of Tarsus were preparatory campaigns for the imperial campaign led by Nikêforos himself into this very same area, while the offensive against the Qaysid Emirate in 963 had prepared the ground for the re-conquest of former Roman Armenia.

Tzimiskês versus the Tarsiotes and Sayf ad-Dawla from December 963 until spring 964[10]

Nikêforos' strategy for winter 963/4 was to prepare the ground for his own offensive in the Emirate of Tarsus later in 964. Tzimiskês' first objective was the city of Adana. This implies that Tzimiskês had either used the route from Kaisareia to Podandos, or the route from Kaisareia to Sis. Close to Adana he was confronted by enemy forces, which consisted of the select elite cavalry that had been collected from every part of 'Muslim Cilicia'. This means that the force included also the best soldiers of Sayf ad-Dawla.

According to Dhahabi, the Tarsiote force consisted of 15,000 men who put to flight the Romans opposing them, but were themselves then defeated by the Roman reserves, so 4,000 of them fled to high ground where they resisted the Romans for two days. According to the version given by Yahya,[11] the Romans killed 4,000 in the battle, with the rest fleeing to a hill close to Adana. The Romans then killed the fugitives, with the result that the people of Adana fled to Mopsuestia. Miskawayh merely states that the Romans killed 5,000 Tarsiotes in the battle, while they lost only a few casualties themselves. This was clearly a major victory. Skylitzes asserts that Tzimiskês routed the Arabs, so some of them were killed in combat while about 5,000 dismounted and found a place of refuge at the foot of a rugged mountain. Tzimiskês surrounded them, and then ordered his men to dismount, after which he led them forward on foot up the hill where the Romans proceeded to kill everyone. Nobody was able to escape the massacre because the Romans had surrounded the hill, with the result that the mountain came to be known as 'the mountain of blood'. This feat of arms increased Tzimiskês' reputation among the soldiers significantly.

If one were to combine the above information, it would yield the following conclusions. Tzimiskês had led his cavalry forces into enemy territory well in advance of his infantry who were to be used in sieges. He came across the enemy force close to Adana, and the Arabs were able to inflict a defeat on his first line,

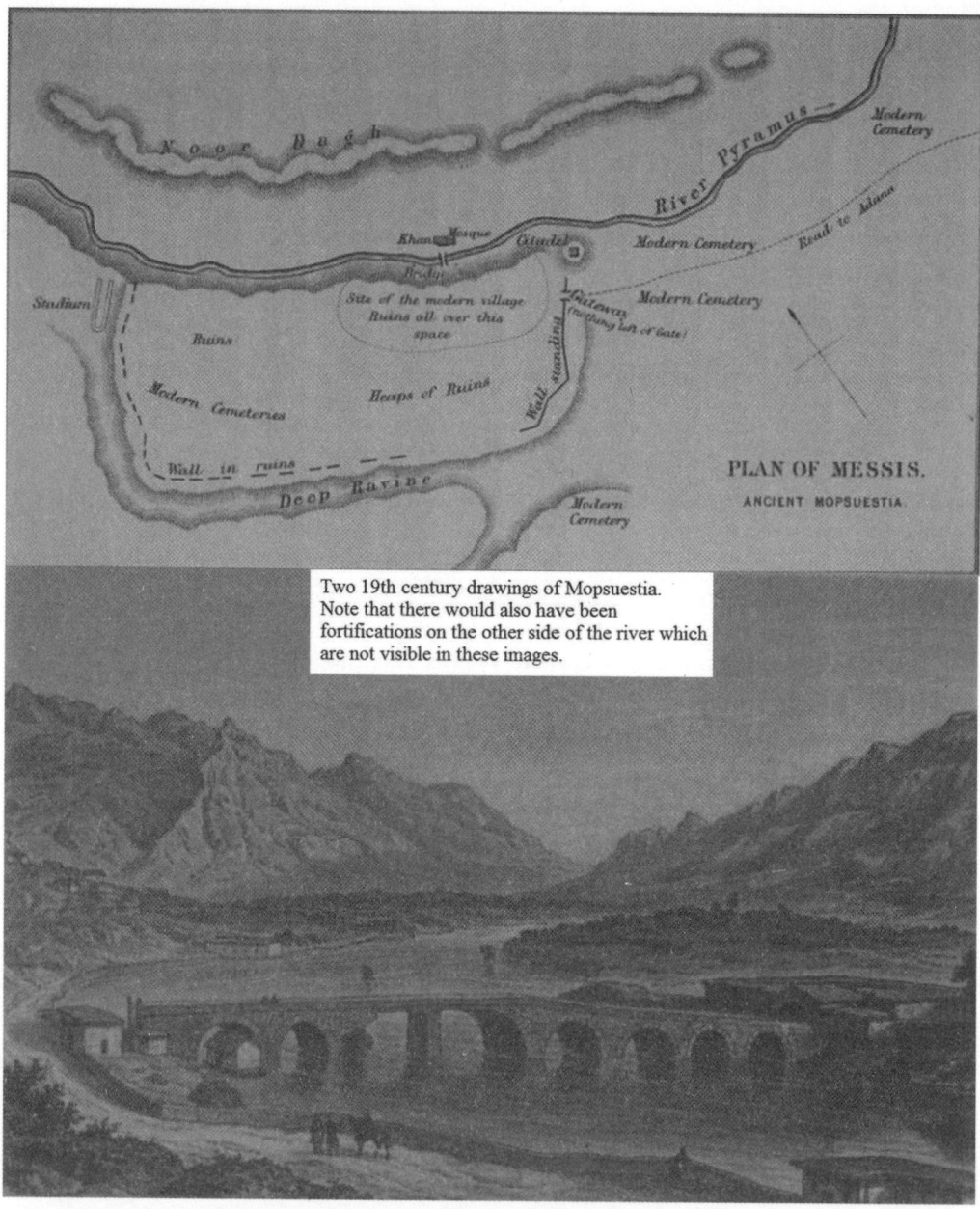

Two 19th century drawings of Mopsuestia. Note that there would also have been fortifications on the other side of the river which are not visible in these images.

but only with the result that they themselves became surrounded by the Roman reserves. The unfortunate fact here is that we do not know which of the two Roman cavalry formations Tzimiskês used, because both the version with the two main battle lines (MS, LT, DV, OT) and the version with the three main battle lines (ST, PM, OT) remained in use. Regardless, one may make the educated guess that the Roman cavalry force outnumbered the Arabs significantly. It is actually very probable that it was approximately as large as it was during the previous campaign, namely 30,000 horsemen. If Tzimiskês used two battle lines, then he outflanked the pursuing enemy with the flank divisions of his second line while the retreating first line regrouped in the intervals of the second. See Chapters 2.7.1–2. If Tzimiskês used three cavalry lines, then he would have used the divisions of the *saka* for the outflanking, while the fugitives of the first line regrouped in the intervals of the second line. See Appendix 3.8. The pursuit was clearly very effective, because the fugitives were forced to seek shelter on a hill, where two days later they were butchered by the dismounted Roman cavalry. This means that the Roman infantry followed at a distance of more than two days behind their cavalry.

After this, Tzimiskês marched against the city of Mopsuestia, which he besieged for seven days. This implies that his infantry forces had by then caught up with him. The Romans made sixty tunnels beneath the wall and breached the wall in several places, but were unable to capture the city because its inhabitants put up a determined fight. Consequently, after having spent fifteen days in Islamic territory, Tzimiskês then gave up the siege because he found the food prices too high to remain (implies the use of private entrepreneurs for the provisioning of the army) and informed the inhabitants of Mopsuestia that he would return and it would be advisable for them to leave because he would kill everyone he found there when this took place. However, the real reason may have been the imminent arrival of the relief army under Sayf (see below). After this, he burned the suburbs of Mopsuestia, Adana and Tarsus and returned to Roman soil.

It was only after Tzimiskês had retreated from Mopsuestia that Sayf ad-Dawla, who was carried on a litter, led the recently arrived Khorasani Jihadists to Mopsuestia. These were then distributed to the fortresses of Thughur, but many of them chose not to stay but travelled to Baghdad and from there to their homes. They were not encouraged to stay when most of the locals in the Thughur fled from the border region to the safety of Damascus, Ramlah and other places. On top of that, the Kurds ambushed and killed some of the returning Khorasanis somewhere north of Hulwan (Miskawayh 203). According to Yahya, the reason for the flight of the populace from Thughur was fear of the Romans, while according to Bar Hebraeus the reason was the famine caused by war. Both versions are undoubtedly true. This weakened the Thughur frontier zone even further before the main offensives led by Nikêforos in person.

However, before this could take place, Tzimiskês would make yet another attempt to take the city of Mopsuestia (Miskawayh 208; Bar Hebraeus 188), presumably in the spring. This time Tzimiskês kept the city of Mopsuestia under siege for three months and left only after having received a ransom payment from its inhabitants. The reason for the settlement was that Tzimiskês could not find enough provisions while his soldiers were suffering from a pestilence. It is probable that the agreement came about as a result of negotiations between Tzimiskês and Sayf ad-Dawla, which the two had had through their envoys.

Nikêforos' First Offensive against the Emirate of Tarsus in 964[12]

After Tzimiskês had twice failed to capture Mopsuestia, Nikêforos took command of the operations in person in spring 964. Nikêforos took with him his newly-wed wife Theofanô and her children and left them at Drizion before entering Cilicia where he assembled his forces at the *aplekton* of Kaisareia. I agree with Personnaz that it is possible that Nikêforos brought Theofanô along because he did not want to be separated from his newly-wed young wife for long, while he may also have feared in light of her reputation that it might be dangerous to leave her alone at the capital. The target of the invasion was Saracen Cilicia, because it was the gateway to Syria while its conquest would form a defensive barrier for Roman Cappadocia.[13]

Nikêforos advanced to Tarsiote territory early in spring according to the account of Leo the Deacon. Nikêforos then put the city of Tarsus under siege. The city was well fortified with a double wall and moat. In addition to this, the swift and clear River Kydnos passed through the city, so the inhabitants could block it and create a swamp when they so decided. The two halves of the city were connected by three bridges. See a simplified map of the city of Tarsus on page 138 and the siege works around it, plus Chapter 5.10. The city was also surrounded by trees, fields and meadows that hindered attacks against the city. The defenders were confident and insulted Nikêforos openly. According to Leo the Deacon, Nikêforos spent a long time in front of the city, but was at a loss of how to capture it. Consequently, he abandoned the attempt and according to Leo the Deacon and Skylitzes advanced against Adana, Rhossos, and Anazarbos, all of which he captured. Rhossos is mentioned only by Skylitzes, and it cannot be the Rhossos that is located on the Syrian coast and neither can it be the Rhossos near modern Nidge, because that was in Roman territory. Therefore, it is clear that either Skylitzes has made a mistake or this Rhossos is some unknown fortress in the neighbourhood of Adana and Anazarbos. Nikêforos captured altogether more than twenty fortresses. Leo the Deacon claims that it was after this that Nikêforos advanced against the city of Mopsuestia and captured it, but it is clear that he has made a mistake here because all of the other accounts place its capture in the following year.[14] Consequently, it is clear that Skylitzes is correct to state that after having accomplished the above, Nikêforos hesitated to attempt to capture Tarsus and Mopsuestia because winter 964/5 was approaching. Nikêforos therefore left a suitable detachment of soldiers behind in Tarsiote territory to secure the invasion route and then retreated to Kaisareia for the winter. The army was then disbanded, but ordered to assemble again at Kaisareia in the following spring, 965.

Nikêforos had definitely achieved enough military successes for a single campaign, but on the basis of the account of Leo the Deacon we know that Nikêforos was extremely annoyed and angry because as a *stratêgos* of a theme and then as a *domestikos tôn scholôn* he had captured and pillaged many cities and now that he was the emperor with 400,000 soldiers at his disposal he could not capture the medium-sized city of Tarsus. Leo the Deacon fails to mention this, but as I have already noted it is very likely that Nikêforos had captured Tarsus in 949 when he was a mere

The Reign of Nikêforos II Fôkas (16 August 963–11 December 969)

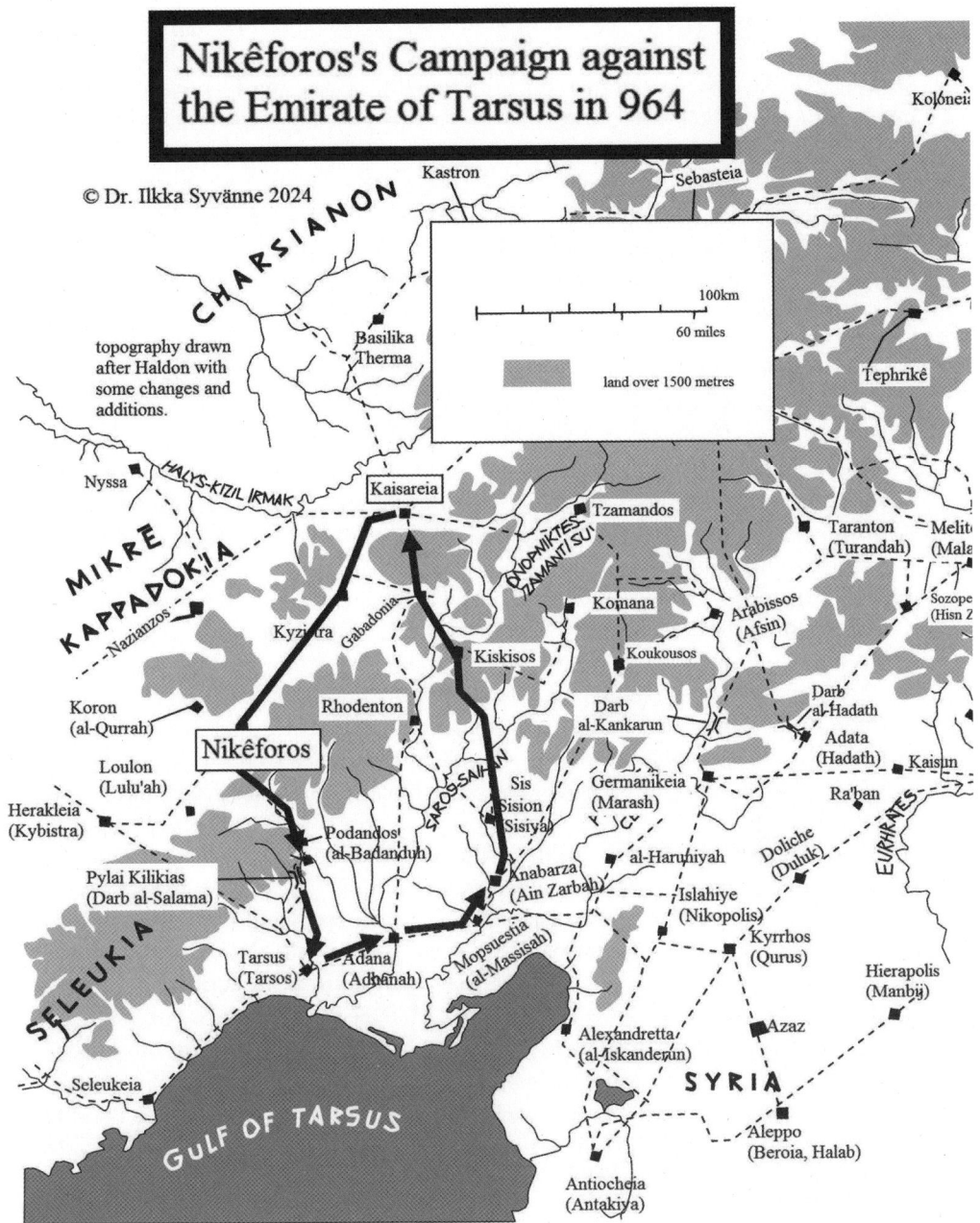

stratêgos of the Anatolikon theme, so the situation was doubly frustrating. It is clear that the 400,000 soldiers did not represent the size of the field army, but this figure is consistent with the total size of the land forces – for which see Chapter 1.4. In short, it is very likely that Leo the Deacon has preserved for us the approximate size of the thematic and tagmatic forces. Nikêforos was determined to remove this blotch from his reputation and redoubled the drilling of the soldiers for the campaign to come. The drilling of the men during the winter break was obviously standard practice, meant to keep the soldiers busy so that they would not start contemplating any plans of revolt.

The Battle of Rametta/Rometta/Rometto on Monday, 24 October 964[15]

The city of Rametta had been besieged by the Arabs in August 963 at a time when Nikêforos Fôkas was preoccupied with his revolt against Briggas. True to his character, Nikêforos Fôkas responded to this forcefully by dispatching a sizeable fleet of fire-bearing triremes, transports and merchantmen under the eunuch *patrikios* Nikêtas (brother of the *prôtobestiarios* Michaêl) and Manuêl Fôkas in spring 964. According to Leo the Deacon, Manuêl Fôkas, the commander of the expedition, was a nephew of the emperor and a rash young man.[16] As a relative, Nikêforos considered him reliable enough to be given a large army to deal with the foe, but this proved to be a mistake. According to Ibn al-Athir, the Romans had 40,000 men on board. Ahmed, the emir of Sicily, asked for help from the Fatimid caliph al-Mu'izz while he rebuilt his fleet and levied marines and soldiers for the war. Al-Mu'izz did as was asked, assembled and recruited soldiers, prepared a large war chest and placed these under al-Hasan ibn Ali, the father of Ahmed. These forces departed for Sicily in September–October 964, while another detachment reinforced those besieging Rametta. It is clear that the plea for help must have come after the Romans had already landed, which means that the initial Roman landing had taken place in summer 964, but the Muslim sources claim that the Roman fleet landed at Messina only in October–November 964 and marched immediately towards Rametta.

When one keeps in mind the fact that the plea for help must have come after the Roman landing, it is easy to reconcile the Arab sources and Leo the Deacon's account. According to Leo the Deacon, the Romans made their landing from transport ships unopposed and captured the cities of Syracuse, Himera (Termini), Leontini and Tauromenium (Taormina). This list suggests that the Romans actually made two simultaneous landings on the island, or that Manuêl dispatched a separate flying column from his landing site somewhere close to Syracuse towards Termini to isolate the Arabs in the north-east corner of the island, or that the same combined force made several landings in succession, starting with the first landing probably close to Syracuse. The likeliest alternative is that the combined forces under Manuêl would have captured first Syracuse and Leontini, which were close to each other, after which he would have marched northwards on land with the fleet sailing alongside to liberate Taormina. This would have then brought him within striking distance of the Arabs besieging Rametta, but the Romans did not yet attempt to interfere in this but sailed to Termini to isolate the Arabs in the north-eastern corner. The reinforcements from North Africa for Hasan would have arrived when the Romans were at Termini. According to Nuwayri, when Manuêl had reached Termini, he divided his army into three corps, one of which he dispatched to Palermo while he himself led two corps against Hassan. Leo the Deacon is correct to note that Manuêl would have acted more wisely if he had posted his forces into the captured cities and reduced the Arabs who had fled to the mountains through a dearth of fodder and other supplies rather than by attempting to fight them in the difficult terrain. According to Leo, Manuêl was encouraged to take the risk of battle because the previous victories encouraged him immoderately. It is in fact very likely that by doing so he acted against the instructions given by Nikêforos, because the first steps of the war clearly show that the campaign plan had been to isolate the Arabs into the north-eastern corner of the island.

When the Arabs learnt of this, Hasan, the supreme commander of the Fatimid forces, left a detachment to continue the siege while he led the rest of his forces against the Romans. The besieged Romans made a sally, but this was successfully countered by the rear guard so the Romans had to flee back into the city. The Roman main army, however, advanced, confident in its numbers and its engines of war. According to al-Athir, when the armies were locked in melee, the situation became precarious for the Muslims and it seemed as if the Romans would win, but then the Muslims showed that they were ready to die for the Jihad because the gates of paradise awaited them. On the basis of Leo the Deacon's account, it is probable that the initial setbacks of the Muslims were a purposefully feigned flight intended to draw the Roman battle formation away from its camp into difficult terrain where their ranks broke, which enabled the Arabs to launch their ambuscades. This is presumably what al-Athir means with his statement that the emir al-Hasan ibn Ammar then increased his efforts, encouraged his men and led his men forward while the Roman patricians encouraged theirs and led their men forward. The ambushing tactic is confirmed by Nuwayri who states that Hasan had posted a portion of his army in the defiles and that he completely surrounded the eight Roman units that attacked him. Just like the Romans, Hasan chose to lead his attack against the enemy commander with the idea of winning the battle with a single precision strike. The Muslim lances proved ineffective against the thick armour of the Roman general Manuêl, but when one of the Muslims directed his lance against Manuêl's horse, this unhorsed Manuêl with the result that the Muslim knight was able to hit him so hard that it finally killed him, while the Muslims also killed many other patricians.[17] The death of Manuêl demoralized the Romans who then shamefully fled.

The sequence of events suggests that despite being surrounded the Romans were still on the point of winning the battle thanks to their numerical advantage, but the situation was then saved by the Fatimid commander-in-chief al-Hasan who led a cavalry charge (his men probably consisted of cataphracted *ghilman*) against the *katafraktoi* of Manuêl Fôkas, and the Muslim cavalry won the day largely thanks to the fact that they were able to kill the Roman commander Manuêl Fôkas. It is clear that Manuêl had taken an unnecessary risk when he fought in the frontline, but in this he was following the example of his well-known relatives Bardas, Nikêforos and Tzimiskês, who had also taken personal risks when fighting against the Hamdanids.

The Muslims pursued the defeated Romans up to their marching camp where the fugitives were massacred in the trench. The Romans lost more than 10,000 men and many men of importance were captured. The battle had begun at dawn and it ended after midday. The Muslim pursuit of the scattered foes lasted until the night. The Fatimids obtained massive booty in the form of arms, horses and valuables. The most valuable of the spoils of war was apparently an Indian sword which had an inscription, which the Romans had probably captured from some Arabic knight in the east. The sword and 200 officers were dispatched to the caliph al-Mu'izz as his spoils of war. This illustrates the high appreciation of Indian steel swords at the time: these were fit for caliphs. After the crushing defeat the Romans retreated to Reggio, where they regrouped.

Following the defeat the defenders of Rametta were thoroughly demoralized. Shortly after the battle the Muslims exploited the situation by launching an incessant assault against the city which lasted throughout the day and following night with the result that the city was taken. The Roman males were all killed, while their women and children were enslaved, after which the city was repopulated with Muslims.

Hamdanids, Emirate of Mosul, the Buyids, Naga al-Kasaki and Armenians in 964–5[18]

The first Muslim ruler to exploit the troubles of Sayf ad-Dawla was the Buyid Emir of Emirs Mu'izz ad-Dawla, who advanced against Sayf's brother Nasir and invaded Jazira. This time Mu'izz ad-Dawla intended to annex it once and for all. His excuse was the fact that the tribute payments of Nasir ad-Dawla were late and so he did not pay heed to the repeated conciliatory gestures of Nasir. Mu'izz marched out of Baghdad in July 964 and what happened next followed a familiar pattern. Nasir abandoned Mosul and retreated to Nisibis. Mu'izz left a garrison of Turks and Daylamites under Abul'ala Sa'id at Mosul and ordered Subuktin to attack Nisibis. Nasir retreated from Nisibis to Martyropolis (Naga had clearly not yet captured it) on 27 August 964, with Subuktin in pursuit. Now Nasir also abandoned Martyropolis, but this was just a ploy to lure the chamberlain Subuktin there. Therefore, Subuktin returned to Nisibis. Nasir's son Abu Taglib and other sons launched an attack against Mosul, which was not successful, but at the same time they destroyed the supply fleet of Mu'izz on the Tigris. Mu'izz chased after the elusive Nasir, but in vain, which was exploited by Nasir and his sons who united their forces and captured Mosul. The Buyids faced a grave situation, and Mu'izz was forced to recall Subuktin from Nisibis, but the cat and mouse game had also tired the Hamdanids so that several of their commanders deserted to the other side, including even one of the sons of Nasir called H'amdan. The key moment was the desertion of Nasir's son Abu Taglib, who made peace with Mu'izz in return for being given control of Mosul, together with Diyar Rabia and Rahba, in return for monetary payments to the Buyids. In the difficult circumstances Mu'izz accepted this compromise.

The Reign of Nikêforos II Fôkas (16 August 963–11 December 969) 281

Now the position of Nasir was very weak, in particular vis-à-vis his son Abu Taglib. He sought to improve his own position in 965 by uniting the Hamdanid realms in common cause, when two sons of Sayf ad-Dawla, Abulmakarim and Abulma'ali, married two daughters of Nasir, while Abu Taglib married Sayf's daughter. The well-known dangers involved in the ensuing inbreeding were apparently not a subject affecting these plans.[19] Unfortunately for Nasir and the Hamdanid dynasty this did not end the differences between the different Hamdanid emirs.[20]

It was clearly only after Nasir and his enemies, the Buyids, had left Martyropolis that Naga al-Kasaki exploited the situation and marched south from Manzikert to besiege Martyropolis. The city was captured and Naga revolted openly against Sayf ad-Dawla some time in autumn 964. Naga recognized the Buyid al-Muizz as his overlord. Miskawayh places the counter offensive of Sayf ad-Dawla against Naga to the year 353, which would mean that Sayf ad-Dawla would have retaken the city of Martyropolis before 7 January 965, but as I will make clear below it is far likelier that Miskwayh has mistaken the dating, so Sayf's campaign against Naga would have taken place roughly simultaneously with Nikêforos' campaign against Tarsus in 965. The chaos caused by the fighting between Sayf and Naga enabled the Armenians to launch an offensive against the Qaysid Emirate, whose emir was now Naga al-Kasaki.[21]

According to the *Chronicle of Smbat* (a 413 = 964), in 964 the Armenians (i.e. the King of Armenia) assembled their forces together and marched to Taron, where they defeated the Arabs and captured numerous princes (emirs). Taron was now freed from the Muslims. Given the size of the Armenian field army and the weakened state of the Qaysid Emirate this is not surprising. It is easy to see that the Armenians invaded the Qaysid Emirate immediately after its new emir Naga al-Kasaki had led his forces against Martyropolis, leaving behind a power vacuum. Smbat continues his account by stating that it was then that Ghewond, the *vardapet* of the Armenian Church, visited Constantinople to discuss religious matters, after which he received gifts from the emperor and returned to Armenia. The meeting of the emperor at Constantinople places this diplomatic visit to winter 965/6. Ghewond's mission was clearly to obtain acceptance from the Roman emperor for the annexation of the former Qaysid Emirate into the Armenian Kingdom, which the Romans had already invaded in 963. According to Skylitzes (14.11), the Romans, Armenians and Iberians actually launched a coordinated attack together with a massive army against Cilicia (here clearly including the Qaysid Emirate), so it is not surprising to find that the diplomatic mission of Ghewond was a success. It is quite probable that the religious freedom given to the Jacobite Church by Nikêforos formed a part of this strategy (see Chapter 8.6). Skylitzes' text suggests that the invasion was done with the permission of Nikêforos, but since the conquest still required the sending of an envoy to Constantinople it is very likely that the annexation of the area into the Armenian Kingdom had not been accepted in advance.

8.4. Nikêforos' Strategy for the Year 965

In 965 Nikêforos launched multiple offensives against the Muslims with the aim of regaining lands lost ages ago. One of these invasion forces was led by Nikêforos in person against the Emirate of Tarsus, while a fleet was dispatched to the island of Cyprus under Nikêtas Chalkoutzês. The campaign against Tarsus was also supported by the imperial fleet. In Italy the operations against the Fatimids continued, this time under the command of *patrikios* Nikêtas.

According to Miskawayh (210–3), Nikêforos planned a triple offensive on the eastern frontier in 965, which would target Tarsus, Syria and Martyropolis. However, the account of Miskawayh telescopes the intentions of Nikêforos, because in truth Nikêforos planned a series of offensives, with the first of these being led by him in person against Tarsus while the last of these would be the attack against Martyropolis in autumn, and it is actually possible that the Martyropolis campaign was not even planned in spring, but was actually added to the objectives only after Nikêforos became aware that Sayf ad-Dawla had taken up residence there. The operations started with the main offensive of the year under Nikêforos against the Emirate of Tarsus, his subordinates including at least Tzimiskês and probably also his brother Leôn. We have no details about the Roman invasion of Syria, so one may assume that it was just a raid launched from the area of Germanikeia/Adata to Syria, either simultaneously with the Tarsus campaign, or immediately after it, or that the Syrian campaign was just a raid conducted by a flying detachment during the period when Nikêforos was besieging Mopsuestia.

The Arabs make a surprise attack against the Roman Fleet at anchor at Reggio on 6 January 965[22]

After their defeat at Rametta, the Roman fleet under Nikêtas had regrouped and anchored off the city of Reggio. The Arab emir Hasan exploited this and made a surprise attack against the Romans. The timing was perfect, as it was not typical for navies to operate in the middle of winter. Hasan achieved his surprise by using swimmers who managed to burn the Roman fleet at anchor. The swimmers clearly carried some sort of incendiary devices, which were probably fire-bombs that included naptha. This was an inventive use of swimmers/divers in warfare and a good example of the skills of Hasan as an admiral. We find somewhat similar instructions for the use of swimmers/divers also in the *Naumachica* of Syrianos Magistros (9), but his instructions referred to only the cutting of anchor cables and not the use of fire-bombs. The Arabs captured Nikêtas alive and dispatched him to Africa as a hostage. Fortunately for the Romans the Fatimids failed to exploit their victory by conquering the south of Italy, because their attention was turned towards North Africa and Egypt. It was thanks to this that *magistros* Nikêforos, the *stratêgos* of Calabria/Kalabria, was able to reorganize the defences and refortify many places, such as the city of Taranto.

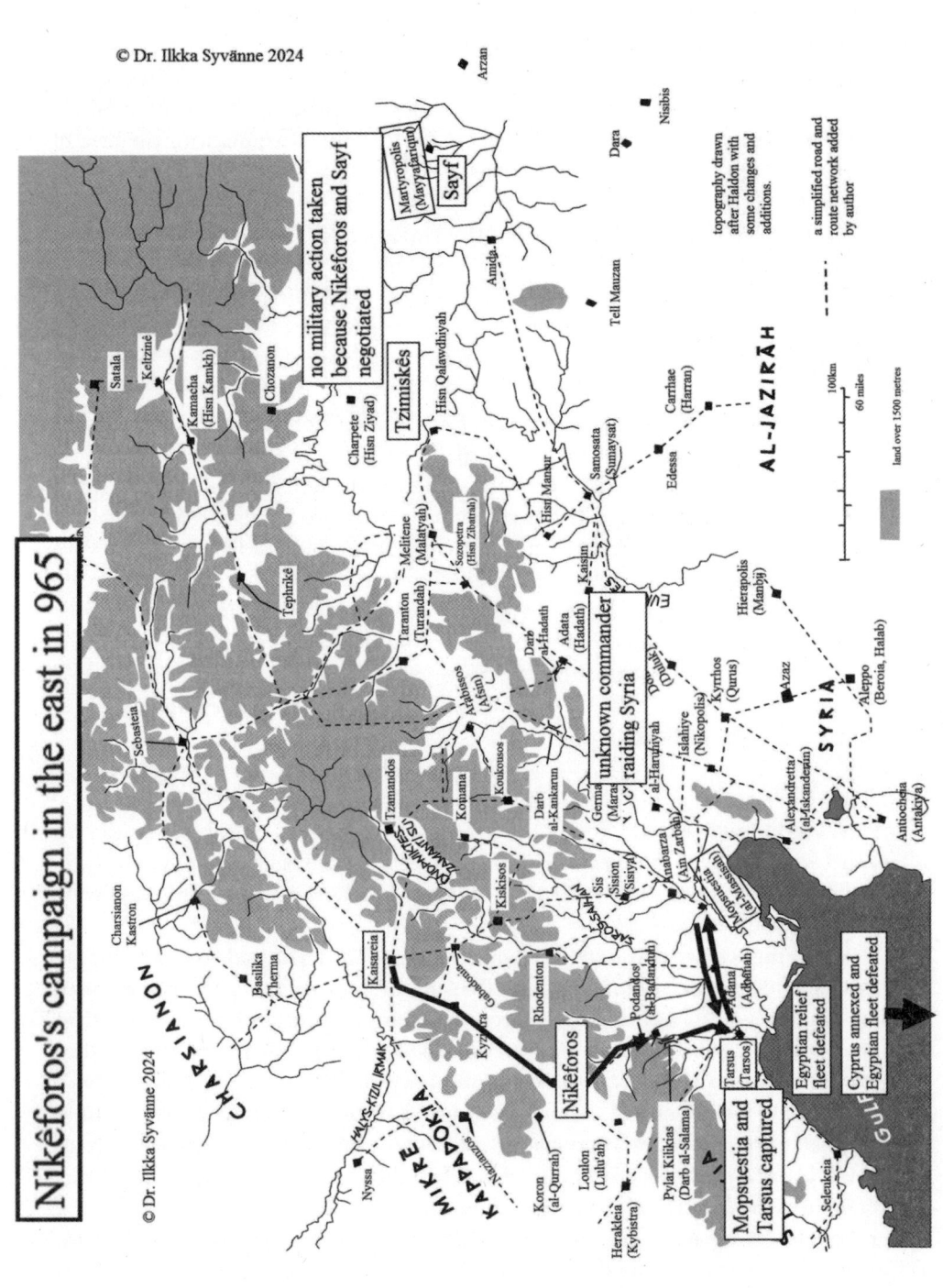

In the following year 966 Nikêforos dispatched envoys to the Fatimids to seek an armistice, which the caliph al-Mu'izz eagerly grasped later in 967/8 as he was planning to conquer Egypt. The victory enabled the Fatimids to perform ethnic cleansing while repopulating many parts of Sicily with Muslims with the idea of securing the island more firmly for Islam.

Nikêforos' second offensive against the Emirate of Tarsus in 965[23]
In 965, Nikêforos was ready to advance deeper into the Emirate of Tarsus. His aim was nothing less than the complete subjection of the Emirate under Roman rule by capturing the remaining strongholds. According to Bar Hebraeus, the Tarsiotes were well aware of the impending invasion and so dispatched envoys to Nikêforos:

> 'Nicephorus ... came and sat down in Caesarea of Cappadocia. And the sons of Tarsôs and the men of the desert (Bedouins) sent [a letter] to him saying that they would be subject unto him, and [asking] him to send some of his own to reign over them. He replied, 'Now that ye are in despair about help reaching you from the Arabs, and now that ye have eaten dead dogs because of the famine, and the pestilence also is making an end of you; ye would become subject unto me until such time as ye can become strong and rebel against me. For you, as far as I am concerned, there is but the sword.' And having burnt their letter on the head of their ambassador, he singed his beard, and drove him away. It is said that three hundred biers with dead bodies upon them went forth from Tarsôs daily.'
>
> Bar Hebraeus 189, tr. by Budge p.170.

This reaction undoubtedly reflected the angry state of mind of Nikêforos after his failure to capture the city in the previous year, but as we shall see, he did not carry out his threats in practice. In fact, he showed great clemency towards the Arabs once they had surrendered.

We do not know with certainty which route Nikêforos used to reach Tarsus, because after the garrisoning of Anazarbos and other places by the detachments left behind, now all of the passes were open to his forces, but on the basis of the text of Leo the Deacon we can make an educated guess. Furthermore, this incident provides us with an illustrative example of the type of disciplinarian Nikêforos was. In one of the defiles one of the *psiloi* was so exhausted by marching that he threw away his shield that he was carrying on his shoulder. Nikêforos saw this and ordered one of his attendants to take the shield. When the army then halted, the emperor sought out the *lochagos* of the *psilos* in question and ordered him to flog the soldier and to cut off his nose and then parade the soldier before the army as a warning example. On the following day the emperor saw that the man had not received the punishment so he ordered his superior, the *lochagos*, to suffer it instead as a warning example to others. This measure restored discipline in the army. The difficulties of the march and the target of the operation, the city of Tarsus, suggest that this time Nikêforos led his army through the Cilician Gates.

When Nikêforos reached the vicinity of Tarsus, he pitched a marching camp and surrounded it with a palisade, and then had all the meadows and trees around the city cut down in preparation for the siege. The Tarsiotes could not bear the destruction of their property and marched out and deployed their men in *synaspismos* array. This means that the citizens formed an infantry phalanx, while the professional soldiers were arrayed as cavalry. On the basis of the previous figures given for the citizen army, the Tarsiotes probably deployed about 40,000 men. One may assume that these would have been deployed as a hollow oblong rather than as a single phalanx, because the Tarsiotes under their commander Rashiq Nasimi (an appointee of Sayf ad-Dawla) advanced against an enemy force which outnumbered them.

Nikêforos responded to this by leading out of the camp a large cavalry force, which he deployed apparently as three phalanxes, with the *pansidêroi ippotai* (*katafraktoi*) posted in front. Nikêforos took command of the right wing leading forward 10,000 cavalrymen,[24] while he placed the *doux* Tzimiskês in charge of the left wing. The commanders of the centre and reserves are unknown.[25] The use of the title *doux* in this case may mean that Nikêforos had removed Tzimiskês from the office of Domestic of the East and had reappointed him as *doux* (general) in command of the units of this field army, or that he held both titles simultaneously but so that the title of *doux* was now more important as it signified a special status in the field army led by the emperor in person. Nikêforos placed archers and slingers behind the cavalry. Their presence suggests that the Tarsiotes had large numbers of Bedouin cavalry (see Appendix 4: 5c), which is also confirmed by the text of Bar Hebraeus. The deployment pattern with 10,000 horsemen so that the *katafraktoi* were posted in the centre is consistent with the instructions of how to meet the enemy from within an infantry square. If the proportions remained the same then the *katafraktoi* wedge consisted probably of ca.3,360 horsemen (beginning with the first rank: 258, 262, 266, 270, 274, 278, 282, 286, 290, 294, 298, 302) and the flanks about 3,000 horsemen, which would mean that the width of the array was close to 1,600 metres. This would have made the Roman cavalry line equal in length with the Saracen formation if it was deployed as a hollow oblong, as is likely. I have made the educated guess that Nikêforos would also have placed outflankers and flank guards on the wings and *prokoursatôres* on the flanks of *katafraktoi* for their protection, even if this is not mentioned by Leo the Deacon. Nikêforos clearly had the idea of placing the two well-known fighters and commanders, himself and Tzimiskês, in the front, so that they could lead the men forward to victory by their own personal example. This also ensured that the collapse of the wings of the first line in the manner of the battle of Adata would not be repeated.

Georgios Theotokis (p.291) has quite perceptively noted that the position on the flanks also gave Nikêforos and Tzimiskês a clear view of the *katafraktoi* so they could react immediately – for example by dispatching forces to their flanks – if this was needed. If the flanking cavalry units consisted of thematic cavalry and not of

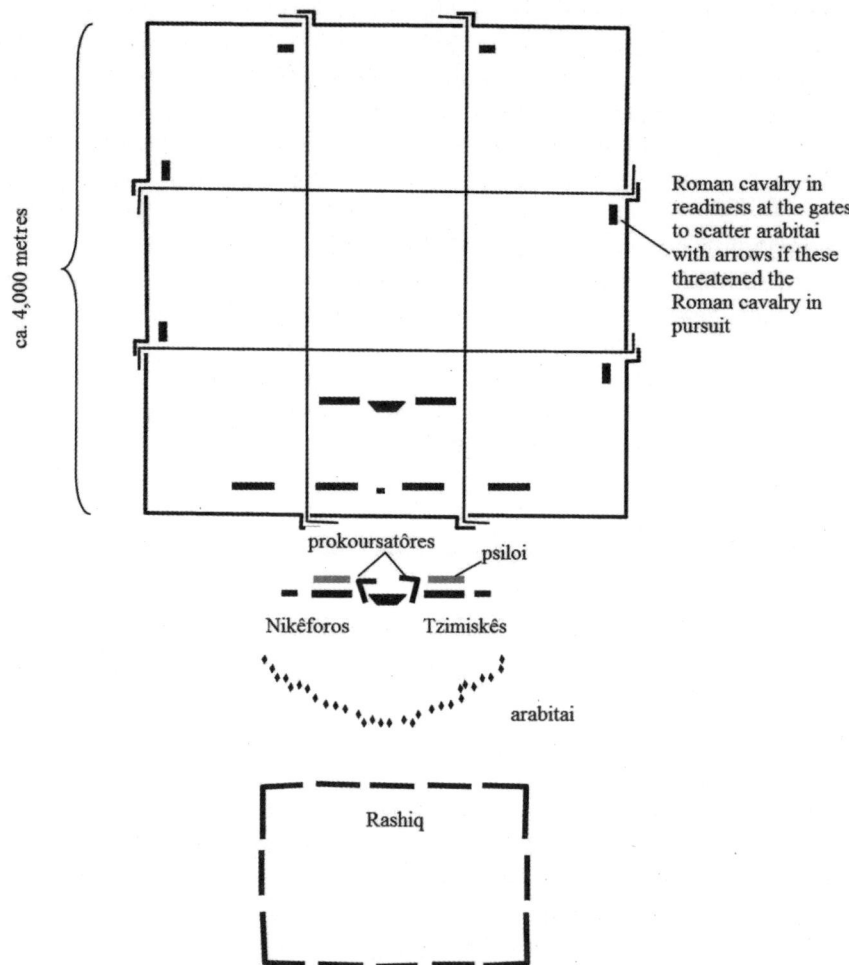

THE BATTLE OF TARSUS IN THE SPRING 965

the tagmatic elite cavalry, Theotokis (p.291) is also correct to note that Nikêforos wanted to ensure that they would also carry out their tasks by posting himself and his nephew in charge of both.[26] After all, as I have noted in the relevant chapter, it had been the collapse of the flanks that had caused the defeat at the Battle of al-Hadath/Adata on 30 October 954, where Nikêforos came so close to losing his own life.

When the enemy was close enough, the Romans in their shiny armour moved to the attack, with the archers and slingers supporting them with their missiles. It is likely that in this case the entire first line was equipped as *katafraktoi* (the two front ranks of the wing divisions), even if the wedge in the centre was the principal battering ram of the force. The spear thrusts (these would mean mainly the flank units rather than the mace- and sword-equipped centre) and the missiles shot by both cavalry and infantry forced the Tarsiotes into flight, with the result that they lost most of their men in their flight back to the city. The pursuit would have been performed as described in Appendix 3: 5.5. According to al-Athir, the left wing under Tzimiskês pursued the foes up to the walls of Tarsus where he fell on the ground and was almost captured by the Tarsiotes. I am inclined to agree with Schlumberger (1890, 496) that this incident took place now and not in 964. The pursuit was clearly carried home with utmost efficiency and this is also confirmed by other sources. The Tarsiotes lost most of their army because the Romans pursued them up to their gates. However, the Romans were still forced to besiege the city because they had been unable to enter it as a result of their pursuit.

After this, Nikêforos distributed his men and siege engines around the city. In other words, it was now that the siege lines were built around Tarsus. See Chapter 5.10 with Appendix 4.7. Nikêforos settled on starving the enemy into submission. Nikêforos placed his brother Leôn in charge of this, dispatched a vanguard under some unnamed general against Mopsuestia (Miskawayh 211), and then followed after him to the same place. Mopsuestia was now surrounded with siege lines. The defenders put up a fierce fight and shot both arrows and heavy stones so that the Romans could not approach the towers. However, this was not the first place besieged by Nikêforos. He realized that some of the towers which were located close to the river bank of the Pyramos/Saros, which ran through the city, could be undermined unnoticed as the dirt would be spread out in the river. By doing so, the Romans were able to undermine a whole section between two towers, so that the wall and towers were kept up only by the presence of the timbers supporting the structure. Then Nikêforos deployed his army in readiness for the assault and set the timbers on fire. When the supports were burned enough the two towers, the wall between, and all the men on the walls and towers fell to the ground, after which the Romans captured one portion of the town. The other portion of the town, however, remained in enemy hands as the city was divided in two by the river. The Saracens set the other half of the city on fire and fled there. This did not save them, because the Romans pursued them across the bridge and captured the other half too. The siege had lasted for fifty-five days, and in the course of it Roman cavalry detachments had raided Saracen territory as far as Antioch. The city fell on 13 - 14 July 965. The city received a garrison under a *katepanô*.[27] Nikêforos marched the captured inhabitants of Mopsuestia to Tarsus to demoralize its defenders. According to Miskawayh (211), there were altogether 200,000 captives that were now paraded before the city of Tarsus.

In the meanwhile, Leôn had suffered a minor setback during the siege of Tarsus. Leôn had dispatched a detachment of soldiers under Monastêriotês to gather forage and provisions. He had not posted a *foulkon* for the protection of his men, with the result that the Tarsiotes who remained outside the city were able to ambush them.

This, however, did not prevent the Romans from continuing their siege. It was only a minor setback. When the inhabitants of Tarsus were already in the midst of a famine and had learnt of the fall of the city of Mopsuestia thanks to the parading of its inhabitants, they begged for mercy, which Nikêforos was now ready to grant. The city fell on 16 Aug. 965. By then Nikêforos' anger had clearly diminished.

The Tarsiotes opened their gates to Nikêforos, who then entered and invited the leading men of the city, including Rashiq Nasimi, to his table for a face-to-face discussion. After the men had eaten, Nikêforos told the men to take their weapons and whatever they could carry and then travel to Antioch. Nikêforos made every effort to demonstrate his friendliness and reliability as a negotiating partner. In fact, Nikêforos even went so far as to cut off the hands and noses from some Armenians who had dared to injure the surrendered Arab men. In addition to this, three patricians were detailed to escort the Arabs while couriers were placed along the roads to guide and help the Arabs to reach Antioch. Some of the Arabs were even carried on board *chelandia* to wherever they wanted to go, which shows that the Roman fleet could operate fairly freely along the Syrian coast at this time.

The Egyptians had in the meanwhile gathered a fleet and a relief force for the city of Tarsus. These arrived on the coast three days after the city had fallen. Nikêforos had posted both men on the coast and a fleet in readiness to oppose such an attempt, and the men on land prevented the disembarkation, forcing the Egyptians to retreat. En route home, the Egyptian fleet was engaged by the pursuing Roman imperial fleet, with the result that some of their ships were sunk while others were lost at sea in the stormy weather. This bespeaks of the very high quality of the Roman ships and their crews. They appear not to have lost ships in this storm, while the Egyptians repeatedly lost ships in any stormy weather.

The emperor distributed most of the booty obtained to the soldiers to reward them and to retain their loyalty, while he took the golden cross-standards that the Tarsiotes had captured over the years. The public Mosque of Tarsus was made into a horse stable. Both places, Mopsuestia and Tarsus, were now garrisoned, refortified and turned into similarly-named themes. The city of Tarsus obtained a garrison of 5,000 horsemen, so one can make the educated guess that the city of Mopsuestia got an equal number of men. It is also clear that both cities obtained infantry forces as well to supplement their cavalry. Before leaving, Nikêforos gathered together enough provisions for both places, which lowered the food prices and lured inhabitants back into both places. The friendliness demonstrated to the surrendered Muslims now paid great dividends. The surrendered Tarsiote Arabs trusted Nikêforos. Some of the inhabitants converted to Christianity, but others were allowed to remain Muslims but on condition that all of their children were baptized. The city of Tarsus was an important city in Christianity thanks to the role of St. Paul.

According to some Arabic sources, the city of Tarsus had a tomb of the Abbasid caliph al-Ma'mun (813–33), and when the city now fell into Nikêforos' hands he had the tomb opened up and took al-Mam'un's sword as his personal spoils of war.[28]

This is indeed quite possible. The steel sword of al-Ma'mun was undoubtedly a very high quality item, well worth carrying home as a trophy.

After this, Nikêforos returned to Constantinople, which he reached in October 965. The populace and senators welcomed him with great joy. The cross-standards were now deposited ceremonially in the Great Church (Hagia Sofia). Then Nikêforos treated the populace to a series of chariot races, which cultivated his popularity among them.

After the fall of Tarsus, the Muslim response to the outstanding successes of Nikêforos Fôkas was increased fanaticism against innocent Christians, and they killed the Patriarch Iôannês of Jerusalem and torched the Church of the Holy Sepulchre in January 966, and, as already noted, Jihadist *ghazis* were streaming in from the east. According to Yahya (101–4, 799–802), the local Jews in Jerusalem also exploited this and caused even more damage than the Muslims. It also gave the Fatimids a chance to present themselves as the only true champions of Islam, because unlike the other Muslim rulers, they alone had inflicted defeats on the forces of Nikêforos in Sicily and Italy. On the Roman side, the murdering of the bishops, Christians and burning of the churches were obviously a source of anger as well, and used for inflaming hostility against the Muslims – so important when one was fighting a war against them. It is because of this that the killing of bishops and torching of churches is mentioned in the sources.

Cyprus restored to the Roman Empire in 965[29]

In 965 Nikêforos decided that it was time to end the tributary relationship with the Arabs of the province of Cyprus by dispatching an expeditionary force there under the patrician Nikêtas Chalkoutzês. The Arabs were expelled from the island. This ended the unhealthy situation in which one Roman province paid taxes to the Arabs, while also allowing its use as an assembly point for Muslim fleets for their campaigns against Roman territory. Now it became the assembly point for the Roman fleets. The Egyptians launched a counter attack and dispatched thirty-two warships to the island, but the Romans destroyed this fleet. A large number of Muslims were either massacred or taken prisoner with the rest fleeing back to Egypt. Cyprus was now once again fully Roman and reorganized as a military theme. Cyprus could no longer be used as a gathering point for the Muslim fleets heading against Roman territory.

The Hamdanid civil war and the third campaign of the year under Tzimiskês[30]

When the fleeing Tarsiotes and their commander Rashiq Nasimi reached Antioch, they brought trouble with them for Sayf ad-Dawla. There was in the city of Antioch a tax farmer, Ibn al-Ahwazi, who had amassed money from the taxpayers, and he saw an opportunity to lure Rashiq into a revolt with the claim that Sayf was not coming back from Martyropolis. It is probable that al-Ahwazi had embezzled some of the money for him to make this suggestion. It did not take long for Rashiq to be convinced, so the two men advanced against the city of Aleppo where Sayf had left Qarghuyah in charge. Qarghuyah retreated inside the citadel where he was besieged by the two rebels for three months and ten days. Sayf responded to this by dispatching a black eunuch named Bisharah with a suitable force against the besiegers. Bisharah's force consisted of Arabs, retainers and other troopers. When these approached Aleppo, Rashiq and al-Ahwazi fled. During the flight Rashiq fell from his horse, with the result that he was killed by one member of the Banu Mu'awiyah tribe who recognized him. Al-Ahwazi fled to Antioch, where he set up a Daylami named Dizbar as emir and obtained help for his cause from an Alawid of the line of Aftas. Ibn al-Ahwazi took the title *ustadh* and fleeced the population to fund the uprising. It was then that Qarghuyah led his forces against Antioch – against the wishes of Sayf. The resulting battle in front of the city was hard fought and lasted through the day and following night. At first Qarghuyah was winning, but then the battle turned in favour of al-Ahwazi because the inhabitants of Antioch came to his rescue, with the result that the forces of Sayf fled to Aleppo.

In the meanwhile, Sayf ad-Dawla had taken residence in the city of Martyropolis. It was because of this that, after the capture of Tarsus, Nikêforos had dispatched Tzimiskês with an adequate army to the east to attack Martyropolis. This implies that when the Buyids had abandoned Martyropolis in August 964 it had been reoccupied by Naga al-Kasaki, with the result that Sayf had marched there and had then convinced Naga al-Kasaki to rejoin him in return for a pardon, as mentioned by Yahya (97, 795). The timing of this reconciliation depends on the date when the Romans began planning this operation. If Sayf had marched to Martyropolis in late autumn 964 or winter 964/5, it is probable that Nikêforos had indeed been planning to launch an offensive against Martyropolis in spring 965, but if it took place roughly at the same time as Nikêforos was invading Tarsus, the attack against Martyropolis was added to the objectives only after that. The likeliest timing is that Sayf marched against Naga at Martyropolis roughly at the same time as Nikêforos launched his campaign against Tarsus, because this explains best why Sayf failed to provide any help for his subordinates at Tarsus and Mopsuestia, but this is not conclusive, even if it is likely that the targeting of Martyropolis was added to the list of objectives only after the campaign against Tarsus had ended and it was because of this that Tzimiskês was dispatched towards east where he would probably have assembled his army somewhere close to Harput in readiness to launch the attack. It is possible that the invasion of Syria mentioned earlier was actually a raid that Tzimiskês conducted when marching to the east from Cilicia. However, Nikêforos appears to have cancelled the third invasion, because in late autumn 965 Tzimiskês asked Nikêforos for permission for the attack, with the result that Nikêforos recalled him to the capital to discuss the situation.

The sources do not explain why Nikêforos forbade the invasion, but it is easy to connect this with the negotiations between Nikêforos and Sayf ad-Dawla which Yahya (96–7, 794–5) places after the recapture of Cyprus in 965. After the capture of Martyropolis, Sayf had released some of the Roman patricians (Miskawayh, 208,

211), quite likely in the hopes of obtaining a truce for an exchange of hostages and in order to gain time for a recovery from his losses. The release of the patricians was clearly a gesture of goodwill that caught the attention of Nikêforos as Sayf had wished. When Tzimiskês then asked for permission to launch an attack against Martyropolis after Nikêforos had reached Constantinople in October 965, this was opposed by Nikêforos, who recalled his *domestikos* to Constantinople to meet him (Miskawayh 213). It was presumably then that the two men had a row, as a result of which Nikêforos relieved Tzimiskês from his duties and banished him by sending him into exile on Tzimiskês' own estates. The likely reason for the quarrel would have been the subject of the attack against Martyropolis, which Tzimiskês wanted because the timing was perfect while Nikêforos opposed this because he hoped to obtain hostages and ransoms from Sayf in return for a short pause in the fighting.

Since Leo the Deacon (5.6) characterizes Tzimiskês as reckless and daring, it is very likely that he quarrelled openly with the emperor who then started suspecting his motives, while Tzimiskês naturally interpreted his exile as an ungrateful insult by a man whom he had helped into power, and it is probable that Nikêforos saw the insistence of Tzimiskês as a sign of insubordination, which was not accepted in the armed forces. As we shall see, Nikêforos always reacted harshly to instances of insubordination, even when the person had as a result of this achieved some great success. In the eyes of Nikêforos there were no good reasons for disobeying his direct orders. Nikêforos was a man who thought that only he knew what would be the best course of action to take and that he was also always right, and that nobody should be allowed to question his decisions. He was the emperor and commander-in-chief.

However, we have also other versions of the reason for this dismissal from service, the first of which is that the empress Theofanô had developed sexual desires towards Tzimiskês because Nikêforos was himself an austere, over fifty-years-old man who would rather campaign than spend time in the palace with his wife Theofanô, while Theofanô was a sexually active young woman used to having her husband in the palace. According to the same version, Nikêforos also noticed a distinct desire for the throne in Tzimiskês.[31] This is indeed possible if the story about the sexual desires of Theofanô is also true, because Nikêforos had himself been in contact with the empress before becoming emperor so he would have easily recognized any signs of sexual desire. If this is indeed the case, then Nikêforos acted with great clemency towards both the adultress and his nephew, which would probably have been caused by the fact that he knew that he owed the throne to both. We find yet another version in Psellos (Hist. 105). He claims that the reason for the exile of Tzimiskês was the innuendo spread by Leôn Fôkas against Iôannês Tzimiskês. According to him, Leôn was jealous of Tzimiskês and suspected his motives so that in the end he convinced his brother not to trust Tzimiskês. It should be remembered that Leôn was also entrusted with matters of internal security and his opinion carried weight so it is easy to see why Nikêforos exiled his nephew, who had, until then, been loyal even if clearly very ambitious.

On balance, the likeliest reasons for the dismissal of Tzimiskês from office are his disobedience of orders in the presence of other officers and suspicions of imperial aspirations. The last-mentioned appears the likeliest, because after this Nikêforos appointed only eunuchs to the position of *stratêgos autokratôr*.

The arrival of Bulgarian envoys in late-965 or early-966[32]

According to Leo the Deacon, Nikêforos Fôkas received Bulgarian envoys soon after his return from the campaign against Tarsus when Nikêforos was entertaining the populace with chariot races. This times their arrival to winter 965/6.[33] The Bulgarian ambassadors demanded the payment of the tributes that had been established under Symeon. This request angered Nikêforos to a point of rage, which Leo the Deacon describes as untypical behaviour for Nikêforos – this suggests that the anger was a premeditated reaction to an insolent demand. The fact that the Bulgarians had continually allowed the Magyars to pass through their territory into Roman lands proved the futility of such payments. According to Leo the Deacon, Nikêforos then turned towards his father Bardas and asked why he should pay a tribute to the abominable Scythians. This implies that the payments had stopped when the Tsarina Maria-Irene had died in 963 and Peter had handed over his sons as hostages. Nikêforos then ordered his retinue to slap the envoys in the face. The envoys were ordered to go home with the message to the 'leather-biting ruler' which promised that Nikêforos would lead a campaign against them in person in the coming summer. However, the actual campaign against Bulgaria was delayed by multiple other problems, so Nikêforos was finally able to launch it only in summer 967. Leo the Deacon (6.11.16ff.) mentions that prior to his appointment as *stratopedarchês* in 967 the eunuch Petros had fought bravely against the Scythians (i.e. Magyars; the Mysians in LD were Bulgarians) when they were raiding Thrace. This times his actions roughly to the year 965–6 and shows why Nikêforos was so upset by the demands made by the Bulgarians. The war, however, had ended in Roman success. According to Leo, when the two armies came face to face to fight a battle the fully armoured Hungarian commander, a man of enormous size, challenged the Romans to a duel with a lance, which Petros answered by advancing against him. Petros charged and thrust his spear with two hands straight through the enemy's chest, resulting in the enemy forces fleeing. The bravery of Petros was rewarded by Nikêforos who gave him the title *stratopedarchês* and later gave him command of the army dispatched against the Saracens.

The sudden change in the Bulgarian stance had resulted from the death of the Roman Tsaritsa Maria-Irene in 963. It had removed from the Bulgarian court the person who had had the greatest influence on Tsar Peter I. It had been immediately after her death that the peace treaty was renewed by the sending of the two sons of Peter and Maria-Irene to Constantinople, but it did not take long for Peter to fall under the influence of his more bellicose boyars. It was presumably because of their influence that Peter concluded an alliance with Otto I of Germany in 965. The principal object of the treaty was probably to join forces against the Magyars, who were not only raiding Roman territory but also Bulgarian territory, but the conclusion of this treaty also strengthened the hand of Peter vis-à-vis Nikêforos Fôkas, so he dispatched envoys to demand the payment of tributes previously agreed in 927 as a part of the treaty in which Maria-Irene had been married to Peter.[34] The Bulgarians were now ready to resume their hostilities.

8.5. The Reforming of the *Themata* and the Militarization of Society after October 965

The multiple offensives on different fronts had demonstrated that even more soldiers were needed than had been created with the measures described at the beginning of Chapter 6. The need for extra soldiers for the continuation of the conquests became acute when Nikêforos left garrisons in the cities of Tarsus and Mopsuestia. It was undoubtedly because of this that Nikêforos reformed the thematic recruiting system, together with taxation.

According to Zonaras (16.25),[35] Nikêforos II Fôkas militarized society by reforming the *themata*. Zonaras (16.25, PG 135 pp. 117–8) places the discussion of the reforms after Fôkas' second campaign against the Saracens in Cilicia, which took place in 965. On the basis of this, one may assume that Nikêforos instituted this reform on the basis of the recruiting problems that he had faced when assembling the invasion force, and because he had also lost soldiers in Italy and on other fronts. The conquered territories required garrisons, while it would also be necessary to maintain the sizeable field army in existence for the conquests to continue. The recruiting and conscription reform would have been implemented after Nikêforos had returned to the capital in October 965.

It was then that Nikêforos dispatched fiscal officials and inspectors to the *themata* to demand that those who had previously not been given military duties because of their poverty were required to serve in the public post; those who were previously required to contribute to serve the public post were henceforth required to serve in the navy; the men performing naval service were now required to serve in the infantry; the infantrymen were required to serve as cavalry; and the cavalrymen were all required to serve as *katafraktoi*. The whole society was required to be on a war footing, so each person in the military registers was required to contribute more of their personal wealth for the defence of the fatherland. It is clear that Nikêforos' principal motive was to enlarge the size and effectiveness of the army without increasing its costs to the exchequer.[36]

'Novel K' in McGeer's book on land reforms (issued between 1 September 966 and 31 August 967) which curtailed the rights of the *dynatoi*[37] to purchase military lands was probably adopted as a pre-emptive safety measure in a situation in which the crops had failed in 967 (see Chapter 8.11). The rights of compensation for the *dynatoi* for the lands confiscated from them were dealt with in 'Novel L' (McGeer's designation). 'Novel M', issued after this, prevented the purchase of military lands altogether in practice.

'*Novel M*' in McGeer's book suggests that Nikêforos' project to increase the size of the army, and in particular the number of *klibanoforoi/epilorikoforoi/katafraktoi* cavalry was not welcomed. In this Novel, Nikêforos II Fôkas notes that since the number of *klibanaforoi* cavalry had recently been increased, which clearly means the above reform in 965, he now raised the minimum inalienable value of the military lands belonging to the *klibanaoforoi/epilorikoforoi* from four- to twelve-pounds of gold. This effectively prevented the sale of military lands altogether. If a person that belonged to the *klibanoforoi/epilorikoforoi* had sold military lands to others with the maximum value of twelve pounds, he was to take back his lands with their military duties without repayment, but if the sold property was more valuable than twelve pounds then he was required to return the extra sum to the buyer. In short, the Novel forced the original owner to accept the land back and prevented the selling of such lands. The persons required to contribute a *klibanaforos* to the army were either required to serve in person or were required to pay someone to serve in his stead, or the sum was paid to the exchequer to finance the hiring of professional soldiers. Ibn Hawqal noted in particular the latter practice and how it was resented by the Romans.[38] In fact, he even claims that it was one of the reasons why Nikêforos was later assassinated, but as we shall see this was not true. The reason why Nikêforos was murdered was that he trusted his adulterous wife.

As noted, the above policies massively increased the numbers of regular Roman cavalry and *katafraktoi*, so that the *katafraktoi* were now undoubtedly posted not only in the wedge as earlier but also as the front ranks of regular cavalry units – as in the texts of Leôn VI's *Taktika* and Maurikios' *Stratêgikon*. It is clear that there were too few naval soldiers and sailors to replace all of the infantry converted into cavalry, so there were too few footmen as a result of this. Nikêforos sought to correct this discrepancy by luring more Armenians into Roman territory so that these could be used as infantry in the newly-conquered provinces – for which see Chapters 8.2 and 8.6. Nikêforos was extremely prejudiced against the Armenians as soldiers (see Appendix 2), but he understood the value of quantity and cannon fodder.

Nikêforos also knew that his power rested solely on his control over the armed forces, so he favoured them in every possible way just as the famous soldier-emperors Septimius Severus and Caracalla had done 700 years earlier.[39] According to Skylitzes (14.18), just before one of his military expeditions Nikêforos imposed additional taxes both in the form of cash payments and supplies, while also removing exceptions from taxation from the Senate and Church. Skylitzes notes that Nikêforos enacted a law which forbade the Church from increasing its real estate holdings, which clearly refers to the above-mentioned '*Novel M*' which must have been issued in about 967/8 as a response to the hostility shown by those taxed. In addition to this, Nikêforos is claimed to have enacted a novel which forbade the nomination of bishops without his permission, so whenever a bishop died, Nikêforos dispatched his own imperial agent to confiscate whatever was in excess of the regulations he had made.

The Reign of Nikêforos II Fôkas (16 August 963–11 December 969) 295

In addition to this, in order to please his soldiers Nikêforos sought to establish a law which stated that only soldiers who died in combat were to be considered martyrs. This was vehemently opposed by the patriarch and bishops, who pointed out that Canon XII of Basil the Great required the doing of two years' penance for the killing before being allowed back into communion.[40] Nikêforos imprisoned the bishops who refused to sign his bill promising martyrdom only to the soldiers, but it appears probable that Nikêforos was ultimately unable to enact the novel, yet as I have noted in my study of the Roman holy war[41] this does not mean that the soldiers would not have been promised a place in heaven when they died in combat, because they certainly were by the chaplains, monks and priests that accompanied the army on campaigns.[42]

The similarities between Nikêforos Fôkas and the great third-century soldier-emperors do not stop here,[43] because just like them he lowered the value of the gold coin, the *nomisma*, in order to finance his wars. He introduced the so-called *tetarteron*, which was smaller than the standard gold coin but with the same value. This reminds one of the so-called *Antoninianus* coin introduced by Caracalla in 215, which had the silver value of 1.5 silver *denarii*, but which had the face value of two *denarii*. Nikêforos Fôkas demanded that taxes were paid by using the heavier older gold coin, while he used the lighter gold coin for his payments. This was a wise policy decision, because it enabled him to finance his wars and building projects. The old gold coin came to be known as the *nomisma [i]stamenon* (*histamenon*). It remained in circulation alongside the new coin.[44]

At the same time as Nikêforos reformed taxation and recruitment of the thematic forces, he may also have reformed the territorial command structure of the armies by creating larger permanent territorial commands under *a doux* or *katepanô*, because their existence is recorded for the first time under his reign. This, however, is uncertain because it is possible that the reform predates his reign. The men appointed to these positions were officially generals of the tagmatic forces detached to the *themata*, so they also served as regional commanders of the thematic forces assigned under them.[45]

The grouping of territorial units of a larger area under a single commander was not a new thing in the Roman Empire, because the Romans had always done that when necessary by placing someone with temporary powers in charge of a larger area, and neither was the use of a single temporary overall commander for a large army for offensive purposes. Not even the name *doux* was new, because the Romans had used *duces* (sing. *dux*) ever since the second century, so it is easy to see that Nikêforos just revived an old Roman term. The terms *katepanô* or *stratopedarchês* for eunuch commanders (see Chapter 8) were obviously more recent, but not really that different in terms of reality. What was new about this was that these *doukes* appear to have been meant as permanent positions, in the same manner as happened during the Late-Roman period, when the *duces* had been given a permanent territorial role instead of the earlier temporary role as commanders of various detachments temporarily united for an offensive campaign or defence of territory. The combining of several territorial armies with tagmatic detachments under *doukes* stands as yet another good indication of Nikêforos' military strategy of overwhelming enemies with numerically superior forces at every point along the Roman frontier.

As already noted, Tzimiskês had the title *doux* at the Battle of Tarsus in 965, so it is likely that Nikêforos revived the title at the latest in that year. However, the first time that this title is known to have been used to designate territorial command dates from the year 969. Hans-Joachim Kühn has collected the evidence. The existence of the ducate of Chaldia is recorded for the year 969, but in my opinion it is likely that it had already been formed before that date because we find its first *doux*, Bardas Fôkas (*doux Chaldias*, son of Leôn Fôkas), leading a campaign in the area in 968. The ducate/katepanate of Thessalonike also dates from Nikêforos' reign, as does the katepanate of Italia with its capital located at Bari.[46] It is probable that the katepanate of Thessalonike was created as a response to the threat posed by the Hungarians, because they raided that territory as far as the city of Thessalonica/Thessaloniki in 967. The katepanate of Italia would have been created as a response to the threat posed by Otto I, and in my opinion the likeliest date for its creation is the year 968 when Nikêforos dispatched reinforcements there (see Chapter 8.14).

The case for the other ducates that are recorded for the year 969 are Adrianoupolis, Antiocheia and Mesopotamia, but it is not known with certainty if these actually date from the reign of Tzimiskês.[47] I would suggest that the first of these, Adrianoupolis, is likely to have been created under Nikêforos as a response to the threat of Magyars and Bulgarians, probably in about 967/8, or alternatively as a response to the Russian threat in 968/9. In my opinion, the ducates of Mesopotamia and Antiocheia were probably created under Tzimiskês thanks to the limited time that Nikêforos had for the reorganization of the east after the capture of Antioch, but this is obviously only an educated guess. The ducates could have been formed in advance.

The posting of tagmatic and other forces in the areas that became ducates and katepanates includes an interesting feature, which is that marines from the units of the *basilikoplôimou* and *mardaitai* (originally refugees from the mountains of Lebanon) were posted in these *themata*. The *mardaitai* were commanded by the *katepanô mardaitôn*.[48] The posting of the marines inland may be yet another piece of evidence for the reform of Nikêforos in which the sailors were expected to become infantry and infantry cavalry, as referred to earlier. It should be noted, however, that both the *mardaitai* and the marines of the Imperial Barges had been used in this capacity even before this. The Romans had always used detachments drawn from the navy in support of their land operations and sieges.

8.6. The Religious Convictions of Nikêforos Fôkas and his Church Policies[49]

The above has already touched on some of the religious convictions and views of Nikêforos. He was a pious Christian who lived like an ascetic, with prayers, fasting, all-night standing vigils, and sleeping on the ground – however, as we shall see (Chapter 8.15) he was still prepared to sleep in bed with his wife. In fact, according to Leo the Deacon (5.8), most of the Romans considered his religiosity and demand that everyone should follow a similar ascetic lifestyle as his principal fault. This, however, did not prevent him from acting against the Church. Rather, Nikêforos considered it his right to do so in the name of the greater good. His priority was the army and its upkeep. Consequently, he forbade the donations of real estate to the churches, while preventing the founding of new monasteries. In addition to this, he took control of the appointment of new bishops into his hands, and if any bishop opposed this he was imprisoned. Furthermore, if a bishop died, Nikêforos would always send his representative there to confiscate his property. On top of that, Nikêforos sought to give soldiers who died in combat the status of martyr, but with no success as already noted.

Nikêforos' conciliatory policy towards the Jacobite/Miaphysite/Monophysite Church was not popular among the Orthodox clergy either. He attempted to reach an agreement with them so that he could then unite the churches. It was because of this that he invited Patriarch Iôannês VIII of Sarug to Melitene while giving the Jacobites religious freedom. It is clear that the logic behind this was to make it easier for Armenians to move into the frontier themes while also securing an alliance with the King of Armenia. The second reason was that the territory to be conquered contained significant numbers of Jacobites, because when Melitene had been conquered their remaining major centres were located in Germanikeia (Marash) and Edessa. In 969 Nikêforos suddenly cancelled religious freedom for the Jacobites and called Iôannês VIII and other bishops for some sort of synod, which ended in failure when Iôannês VIII refused to acknowledge the Chalcedonian Council. As a punishment, Nikêforos had Iôannês VIII imprisoned, together with the Jacobite bishops – who were later released by Tzimiskês, undoubtedly because as an Armenian he had sympathies towards the Jacobites. It is probable that the date 969 answers why Nikêforos suddenly changed his policies. He had already conquered the main centres of Jacobite faith, so he thought that he no longer needed to conciliate them – which was not the wisest course of action to take when the border regions were inhabited by Jacobites, hence the decision of Tzimiskês to cancel it. It is therefore probable that Nikêforos' actions in this case were guided by his personal religious convictions.

According to the *Typikon* and *Life of Athanasios*, Nikêforos was very interested in monasticism, despite his actions against monasteries on behalf of his soldiers. The *Life of Athanasios* claims several times that Nikêforos repeatedly stated to Athanasios that he intended to become a monk, but was prevented from doing so by circumstances. Here I agree with the cynicism of both Athanasios (LA 34) and Skylitzes. It is clear that this is pious nonsense that Nikêforos employed to obtain the blessings of Athanasios, possibly in an effort to improve his standing among the religious establishment. He wanted to present himself in such a light to both Athanasios and the monks of Mount Athos that they would give him their blessings.

It is also clear that it was in the interest of Saint Athanasios and the monks of Mount Athos to present themselves as favourites of the emperor in order to maintain their privileges. As we have seen, in truth Nikêforos was actively seeking to become an emperor and husband of the beautiful Theofanô. He was not planning to become a hermit monk. His plan all along had been to become emperor and Athanasios realized this full-well (LA 34). On the basis of the *Life of Athanasios*, he was actually constantly trying to escape from the presence of Nikêforos, but with poor results because Nikêforos always sought him out and then used him for some publicity stunt, as he did in Crete. This brings forth the question of how ascetic and Christian Nikêforos really was? Was he just putting on a show in order to gain the support of the religious establishment, while attempting to use religion to sober the habits of his wife Theofanô and others in the imperial court? We shall never know the answer to these questions, because only Nikêforos knew what his motivations were, if even he knew. It is far likelier that Nikêforos was actually a deeply-religious person who just deceived himself with the dreams of becoming an ascetic monk, while in truth all that he really wanted was imperial power. It is this side of Nikêforos' personality that Saint Athanasios realized and which the self-delusional Nikêforos did not.

It is also clear that Nikêforos was interested in ascetism in some form (ascetism was well-suited to military life in the field) and did support the founding of some monasteries, but only those that he considered advantageous for himself and his family. Their numbers were also limited, so only the monasteries of Mount Olympos in Bithynia, Mount Kyminas and Mount Athos received donations from him. In fact, in the case of Mount Kyminas in Kappadokia, he even built monasteries, settled monks there, and provided them with annual donations for their upkeep from his own personal funds – and then from the state coffers when he became emperor. The reason why he did so was connected with his family. The first abbot of the Kyminas Monastery was his uncle Michaêl Maleinos (894–961), his spiritual father, whom he met regularly when he was the *stratêgos* of the Anatolikon in 945–56.[50] It was also there that Nikêforos was introduced to Saint Athanasios by Michaêl (LA 8, 11), so that Athanasios apparently became Nikêforos' spiritual father at about the same time as Michaêl died in 961.

As already noted, Athanasios was to play an important role in the religious thinking of Nikêforos, and Nikêforos even asked Athanasios to visit him in Crete during the campaign. In addition to this, Nikêforos asked the monasteries of Kyminas, Olympos in Bithynia and Mt Athos to pray for the success of the Cretan campaign. This obviously had a morale-boosting purpose among the soldiers as well, but it is still very probable that Nikêforos believed in the power of prayer. When Athanasios visited Nikêforos in Crete, the latter promised to found a *Laura* monastery on Mt. Athos for him and other hermits. When Chandax fell, Nikêforos fulfilled his promise, and the building of the *Laura* was partially completed by the time Nikêforos became emperor on 16 August 963. In 964 as emperor Nikêforos issued three *chrysobulla* for the benefit of the *Megale Laura*, so it was given relics and annual donations of money and wheat, with the special privilege that the

The Laura founded by Nikêforos for St. Athanasios. Source: Schlumberger.

Laura could choose its own abbot without imperial interference. Mount Athos was therefore given exceptional autonomy within the Empire. Under Nikêforos, who favoured the soldiers at the expense of religious institutions, this was a special privilege and shows how highly he appreciated the services of Saint Athanasios. Nikêforos approved of the ascetism and poverty of Athanasios and Mt. Athos and disapproved of the hoarding of material things by the other monasteries. In his mind the latter encroached on the imperial taxation and rights of soldiers. It is quite probable that it was because of this that Nikêforos favoured Mt. Athos. It was to serve as a model for the other monasteries.

8.7. The Strategy for the Year 966

The strategy that Nikêforos Fôkas adopted for the year 966 was entirely different from what it had been in the previous years. This time he did not lead any major offensives against the Muslims in the winter and spring. In 966 Nikêforos also altered his approach towards the Fatimids. The defeat of his expeditionary forces in 964–5 convinced him that the wisest policy would be to conclude a peace with the Fatimids. The second of the reasons for the negotiations with the Fatimids was the strengthening of the position of Otto I in Italy, where he was annexing areas that the Romans claimed as their own. This policy finally paid off in 967, because the Fatimids also saw this as advantageous. The Ikshidids of Egypt were in trouble. They had suffered defeats at Roman hands, and Nubians and Bedouins had inflicted them with considerable damage during the 960s, on top of which the second puppet ruler of the eunuch Kafur died in 966, which had left Kafur as de facto ruler with no suitable Ikshidid successor in sight when Kafur himself then died in 967. The rise of the Ottonian power in Italy obviously posed also a threat to the Fatimids, but even more importantly they needed a truce with Rome in order to be able to concentrate their forces against Egypt.[51]

In 966 Nikêforos had also on his hands the still unresolved question of prisoner exchange with Sayf ad-Dawla. Both had a vested interest in solving this question, because Nikêforos had relatives of Sayf in custody together with 3,000 other prisoners, while Sayf had the son of Nikêforos' sister and other important Romans in his custody. It would only be after the prisoner exchange was completed that Nikêforos planned to continue his offensive against Sayf and other Muslims. Nikêforos had also brought on himself an additional problem by refusing to resume the tribute payments to the Bulgarians. He had promised an offensive against them in 966, but he did not carry his threat out – which gave the Bulgarians a chance to invade Roman territory in the same year. It is probable that Nikêforos considered this as being relatively meaningless, because the Magyars were already raiding Roman territory through Bulgaria so this did not really increase the difficulties he faced in the Balkans. Both foes, the Magyars and Bulgars, consisted primarily of lightly-equipped cavalry raiders, so all they could do was to raid the countryside while all of the cities would be safe as long as these had adequate numbers of defenders and provisions. On the basis of the Arabic sources it is quite possible that by this time Nikêforos had already set his eyes towards the elimination of Islam in its entirety. According to these sources, at some point in time after the conquest of Tarsus but before the advance against Antioch and Damascus in 968 the emperor Nikêforos Fôkas dispatched an extremely insulting letter to the Caliph al-Muti (946–74) at Baghdad. This dates the text either to the spring or summer 966 just before the autumn offensive or alternatively to the spring/early summer 968 before the offensive, but so that the likeliest date for this is the year 966 because, as noted by Takirtakoglou (100), some of the Arab sources claim that it was in 966 that Nikêforos intended to capture the city of Jerusalem. The extant version of Nikêforos's letter is quoted in full by Schlumberger (1890, 427–30) and analyzed by Cheik-Saliba. In this letter Nikêforos bragged about his conquest of the Armenian and Mesopotamian *thughur* so that he had captured Hadath (Adata), Marash (Germanikeia), Edessa and Tarsus. He had also reached Aleppo where he had captured its women and destroyed its walls. Now Nikêforos threatened to capture Antioch and Damascus after which he promised to capture Egypt and Baghdad and from Baghdad he would advance to Shiraz and Rayy to frighten the Khurasanis of his plans. He would also conquer Mecca, Yemen and Jerusalem and conquer east and west in the name of the religion of the Cross. He ordered the Arabs, the dwellers of the sands, to return back to their lands of Sanaa and al-Tahaim.

It is therefore clear that Nikêforos planned nothing less than the elimination of Islam and the conquest of all of the territories held by them in the name of the Cross. He was a true Christian Crusader, a fanatical promoter of the Christian cause.

The letter had its intended impact on the Arabs because it is mentioned by several Arabic sources. The Muslims were extremely upset by the insults and threats and called Nikêforos the evil one. The Muslims dispatched an answer written by a master of Islamic law which refuted all of the claims and promised that the armies of the Khurasanis would march against the Romans and would conquer Constantinople so that they would then make the emperor their slave.

The Khurasanis did indeed arrive, but turned out to be completely powerless against Nikêforos Fôkas so the Muslim threats were empty words as long as the great soldier emperor Nikêforos II Fôkas, the White Death of the Saracens, was at the helm. In fact, the Khurasanis caused at least as much damage to their co-religionists at Baghdad as they did against the Romans.

The exchange of prisoners with Sayf ad-Dawla in 966

As already noted, the reason why Nikêforos refused to give permission for Tzimiskês to begin an offensive against Martyropolis were negotiations for the prisoner exchange with Sayf ad-Dawla. These negotiations were brought to a conclusion by about mid-January 966. The principal problem was that the Romans had a far greater number of important Arabs in their possession, so Sayf would have to agree to pay a ransom for their return. In the end it was decided that he would pay a sum of 240,000 Roman dinars for these. It was decided that the exchange of prisoners would be performed in two stages. On the Roman side, the first prisoner exchange involved six high-ranking Romans, which included the son of the sister of Nikêforos and the father of the son. On the Arab side, the six prisoners consisted of the relatives of Sayf, among whom was Mohammed, son of Nasir ad-Dawla. The first exchange of prisoners took place close to Hattakh, north of the city of Martyropolis, on about 28 January 966. The second exchange of prisoners, which consisted of the less important persons such as the *ghilman* of Sayf, took place at Maqila on the Euphrates close to Samosata on 24 June 966. Since Sayf was unable to pay the entire ransom, he gave the Romans two hostages as a guarantee until the entire sum would be paid. When the arrears were then paid, the hostages were released. It was then that Nikêforos was ready to launch his next offensives against the Muslims in the autumn of the same year.[52]

It was probably after the first prisoner exchange close to Martyropolis that Sayf ad-Dawla decided that it was time to resolve the revolt of Antioch.[53] Consequently, he marched at the double to Aleppo. It is very likely that Sayf's forces included also those of Naga al-Kasaki at this time, because it is clear that he was killed at the palace of Sayf and Sayf had not been there before he left Martyropolis. Sayf entered Aleppo and continued his march against Antioch immediately the following morning, presumably with the idea of surprising the enemy with his speed of march. The resulting battle ended in favour of Sayf. Dizbar was captured, but al-Ahwazi fled to the Banu Kilab. These in their turn sold him to Sayf in return for a sum of 30,000 dirhems. Dizbar was executed, but al-Ahwazi was kept imprisoned until the next Roman offensive in October 966, when he was also executed as a safety measure. It was presumably after this that Sayf ad-Dawla's retainers killed Naga with their swords in the palace at Aleppo. Sayf ad-Dawla suffered yet another stroke immediately after this, so it was his wife who then ordered the corpse of Naga to be dragged around by the foot. The location of the assassination, the Palace of Aleppo, places the murder of Naga to early-autumn 966.

The autumn offensive against Sayf ad-Dawla in 966[54]

When Nikêforos had received the ransom payments from Sayf in full, he launched an invasion against him in the autumn. The first target of his operations was the city of Amida (see the maps section). According to Yahya, the Romans killed and captured large numbers of enemies, while Bar Hebraeus states that the Romans did not capture Amida. This implies that Nikêforos settled on ravaging the surrounding areas. After this, Nikêforos marched towards Dara, after which he approached Nisibis. Since Nikêforos approached Dara first, it is clear that he had bypassed the rough and difficult terrain of Tur Abdin from the west. According to Yahya, the inhabitants of both cities were frightened by the reputation of Nikêforos and chose to flee. The Romans captured a caravan that was on its way to Martyropolis while killing large numbers of locals. According to Ibn al-Athir, Sayf ad-Dawla had been at Nisibis when the Romans approached and had chosen to flee to the Bedouins to amass them to fight the Romans, but before he accomplished his task the Romans had already marched on to Syria.[55]

Nikêforos exploited the situation further and continued his march towards Syria, while Sayf ad-Dawla marched towards him with the idea of conducting a guerrilla campaign against the Romans, but with no tangible results. It is clear that the Romans had once again invaded in such strength that Sayf could not hope to engage them in anything resembling a battle. In fact, Sayf retreated before the advancing Romans, first to Qinnasrin and then as far south as Larissa (Chaizar, Saijar) on the Orontes when the Romans approached Qinnasrin.[56] The next target on the itinerary of Nikêforos was the city of Manbij. Nikêforos could have chosen two different routes to reach it, one that went past Edessa and another that went past Resaina (Ras Ain) and Harran (Carrhae). In light of the confusion in the text of Leo the Deacon regarding the place where Nikêforos obtained the holy tile, it is probable that Nikêforos marched past Edessa. The reason for this conclusion is that Leo the Deacon states that Nikêforos obtained the tile from Edessa, after which he captured Membeze (Manbij, Hierapolis).[57] One may perhaps make the educated guess that Leo the Deacon has placed the events in the wrong order, so Nikêforos captured Edessa but left Manbij alone when its inhabitants handed over the holy tile.

Nikêforos besieged Manbij on Saturday, 7 October 966. He informed the inhabitants that he would leave them alone if they would hand over the holy brick known as *keramion*, which was claimed to have an imprint of Jesus Christ not made by human hand. When the inhabitants handed this to the Romans, Nikêforos left the city unharmed and continued his campaign to Wadi-Bouthuan (Wadi Butnan), where his forces captured large numbers of captives while one detachment captured 300 prisoners from Balis. This means that Nikêforos divided his army, so that one portion followed the road that was on the western side of the river (Wadi Butnan) while another portion (probably a cavalry detachment) advanced on the road that was east of it to Balis. The Balis detachment would have joined Nikêforos before Qinnasrin, which was Nikêforos' next object. In other words, this time Nikêforos bypassed Aleppo. We know that he also bypassed Qinnasrin, because the next location that he besieged was the fortress of Tizin, which he captured with all of its inhabitants. It is probable that Nikêforos purposefully avoided sieges of large cities when Sayf ad-Dawla was conducting skirmishing warfare against the invaders. The next target was the fortress of Artah (Artach), which was also captured. It is clear that the ravaging of territory was once again meant to ease the conquest of the larger cities of the area in the future.

Then on Tuesday 23 October 966 Nikêforos approached the city of Antioch (see the maps section), which was the largest city in the area with a population that was surpassed only by Constantinople and Thessalonica (Thessaloniki). Nikêforos dispatched a messenger to the city, who carried a promise that in return for surrender Nikêforos would allow the inhabitants to leave the city unmolested with all of their possessions. The inhabitants refused. They were confident that they would prevail thanks to the quality of its walls, the availability of provisions, and the size of the

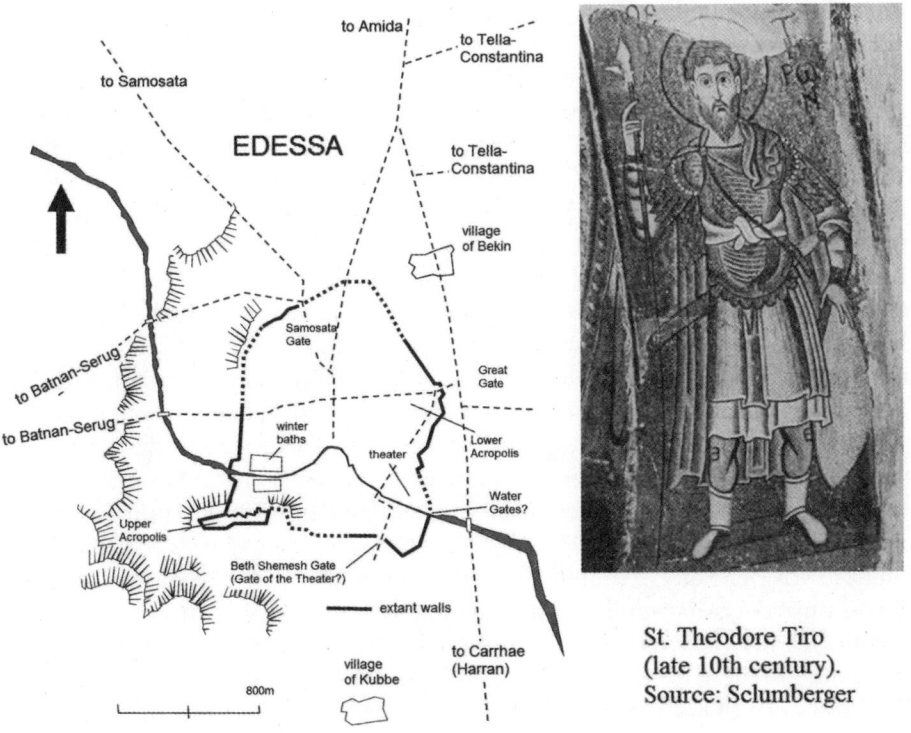

St. Theodore Tiro (late 10th century). Source: Schlumberger

population. Nikêforos set against the city his siege engines and assaulted the city for seven days, after which he gave up the attempt on the eighth day and returned to Roman territory.[58] The route which Nikêforos took is not described, but one may assume that he would have avoided the Syrian Gates and Darband al-Marri, so ensuring that Sayf ad-Dawla would not get a chance of ambushing him in either of these locations. The likeliest route would probably have taken his army to Germanikeia, which was in Roman hands, so that it would have been safe to use that road.

The Death of Sayf ad-Dawla, 8 February 967[59]
According to Yahya (108–9, 806–7), it was only after this that Sayf ad-Dawla punished the population of Antioch for their revolt under Rashiq by imposing extra tax on them: Sayf ad-Dawla had been forced to leave the punishing of the populace of Antioch half-finished by the time of the Roman invasion in October 966, so he now returned to unfinished business. This, however, was not wise in the aftermath of the successful defence of the city against the Romans. On top of this, the actions of Christoforos, the Christian Patriarch of the city of Antioch, caused further divisions within the city. He intervened successfully on behalf of his friends because Sayf held him in high regard. This caused envy among those who were not helped. The Romans were subsequently able to exploit these divisions within the city to their own advantage.

This series of setbacks was finally the one that broke the back of Sayf ad-Dawla. He suffered yet another stroke and died at the age of 54 on 8 February 967.[60] Sayf was a conscientious ruler who could not bear the responsibility that it was thanks to his failures that his subjects were dying and suffering. It was his deeply-felt sorrow at the fate of his subjects that brought his untimely demise. Sayf's servant Taqi took his corpse from Aleppo to Martyropolis where his wives and children lived. When Taqi had left the city of Aleppo, its inhabitants abandoned their allegiance to the Hamdanids and chose Alouch the Kurd as their new emir. It was at about the same time that more than 5,000 Khorasani Jihadists arrived at Aleppo under the command of Mohammed ibn Isa with the aim of attacking the Romans.[61] Consequently, he continued his march to Antioch. This was exploited by those who wanted to kill Patriarch Christoforos. The Khorasanis performed the dirty work on their behalf on 22 May 967. They accused the Patriarch of collusion with the Romans. After this, the leader of the plot, Ibn-Manik, looted the Church property.

There was actually also a continuous string of Jihadists arriving from Khorasan, some of them even bringing elephants with them. However, instead of attacking the Romans, some of these groups ended up attacking their fellow Muslims. A good example of this is provided by Miskawayh (222ff.), who states that 20,000 Khorasani raiders with elephants (with reinforcements following) raided Rayy, the capital of Buyid Ruk ad-Dawla, while he was living there. It did not stop there, because the Khorasanis went on to attack the domains of the Buyid, Rukh, again, forcing Rukh to send a plea for help to Izz ad-Dawla and the emir of Mosul, Abu Taghlib, in 967. The forces of ad-Dawla and Taghlib were obviously absent from the front facing the

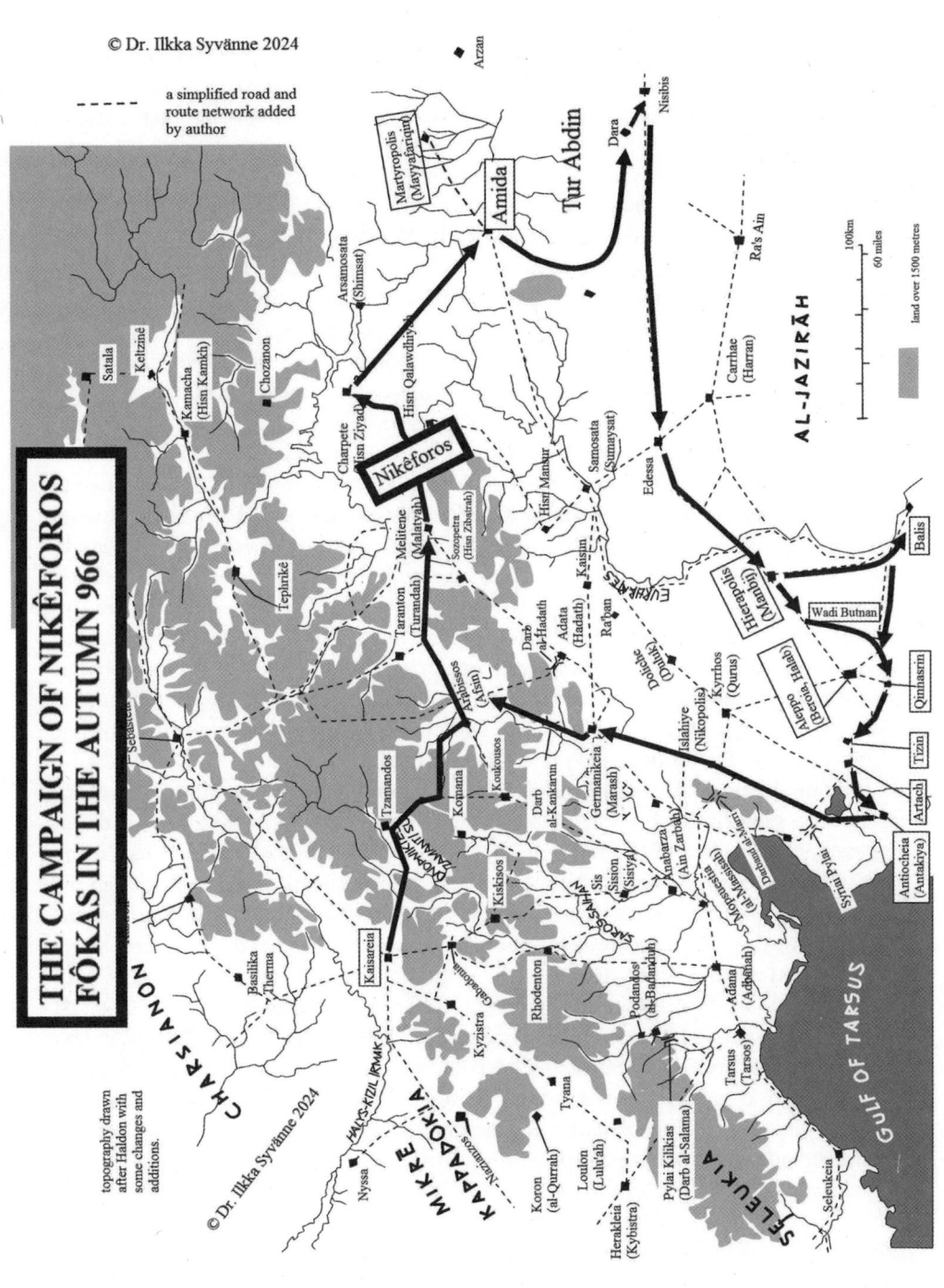

Romans, as were the Khorasani Jihadists. In other word, the horror that the military successes of Nikêforos had caused among the Muslim community, so that Jihadists started arriving from as far as Khorasan, actually resulted in further chaos among the Muslim countries.

In the meanwhile, there had been important developments taking place elsewhere. The Buyid Emir of Emirs (*emir-al-oumara*), Sultan Mu'izz ad-Dawla Ahmed ibn Boyah ad-Deilemi, had died of diarrhoea on 16 March or 31 March 967 (the sources give two dates). He was succeeded by his son Bakhtiyar Izz ad-Dawla (Izz ad-Dawla Abu Mansur ibn Bakhtiyar). The emir of Mosul, Abu Taghlib, maintained peace with him by paying his tribute in a timely manner. Taghlib's father, Nasir ad-Dawla, had advised against this because Mu'izz ad-Dawla had left only 400,000 dirhems behind thanks to his extravagant building projects. Nasir suggested that his sons should rather bribe the followers of the Buyids to desert them. The brothers Abu Taghlib and Abu'l-Bakarat and their sister disagreed and instead imprisoned their father Nasir, with the result that their brother Hamdan at Rahbah revolted. He considered himself the best rider and the bravest of the sons. He advanced from Rahbah to Raqqah, and from there to Nisibis, where he summoned all of his relatives to join his cause and assist him against Abu Taghlib, while asking Abu to release their elderly father. Abu Taghlib marched against him, but Hamdan retreated to Raqqah and then to Rafiqh. Abu besieged him there, but had to settle for a peace agreement. Nasir lived for a few months after this and died in 968. It was after this that Abu Taghlib's operatives confiscated the estates and possessions of Hamdan. Abu'l-Barakat was given command of a large army with which to subdue Hamdan. When most of Hamdan's followers deserted he fled to Baghdad.

The Buyid Izz ad-Dawla acted as a mediator, and Hamdan was allowed to return to Rahbah sometime after 25 November 968, but the civil war soon restarted and persisted for the rest of the reign of Nikêforos and beyond, so it would have been very advantageous for him to attack the Emirate of Mosul, under which was the city of Nisibis. This, however, was not in his plans. He intended to continue the conquest of the Mediterranean coastline, presumably the city of Jerusalem being his principal goal.

As regards the Emirates of Aleppo and Emesa, Sayf ad-Dawla got a successor. At the instigation of the new Buyid Emir of Emirs Izz ad-Dawla, the Abbasid caliph had appointed Sayf's son Saad ad-Dawla (Abu-l-Ma'li ibn Sayf ad-Dawla) as his successor. After his appointment, Saad/Abul-Ma'li left Martyropolis and marched to Aleppo, together with his father's chamberlain Qarghoyah, to take possession of his father's domains, which he took without trouble.

In Egypt, the eunuch ruler Kafur al-Ikhshidi had also died, on 3 May 967. He was succeeded by Abu-l-Fawaris Ahmed ibn Ali al-Ikhshid – who was still a child of eleven years old – on condition that the sons of the uncle of his father (al-Hasan ibn Abdallah ibn Thoughoudj, who was then in Syria collecting taxes) acted as regents, while the vizier Abu-l-Fadhl Dja'far ibn al-Fadhl ibn al-Fourat ibn Hinzaba administered finances. In practice, however, the vizier Abu-l-Fadhl governed the entire country alone. The country was already suffering from famine and pestilence, undoubtedly caused by the same heat wave as had destroyed the crops in Greece, which is confirmed also by the absence of water from the Nile during the years 963–8, but the vizier disorganized the realm further by arresting a large number of people who he forced to pay vast sums of money, with the result that violence and internal strife erupted in Egypt in 968, which in turn led those Egyptian notables who opposed the vizier to plead with the Fatimids to come to their rescue (e.g. Idris, 196–7).

The Bulgarian invasion of Roman territory in late-966[62]

We know from the text of Yahya that the Bulgarians exploited the fact that Nikêforos had not launched the campaign that he had promised against them, but was fighting against Sayf ad-Dawla in autumn 966. The Bulgarians proceeded to devastate the frontier provinces. In contradiction of the above, Yahya then claims that Nikêforos marched against the Bulgarians and defeated them, after which Nikêforos concluded peace with the Russians who became his allies against the Bulgarians. It is clear that Yahya has telescoped events here. The campaign of Nikêforos against the Bulgarians took place only in 967, the important point here being that the Bulgarians exploited the absence of Nikêforos by raiding Roman territory. The referral to the conclusion of a peace with the Russians will be discussed below.

8.8. The Situation in early-967

We do not know what the initial plans of Nikêforos were for the year 967, but it appears probable that he either planned a campaign against the Bulgarians, or he planned to continue his campaign against the Saracens in the east whose territory he had prepared for further operations with his grand scale chevauchée in 966 while he continued his efforts to obtain peace from the Fatimids – in the latter case his efforts met with success in 967, because the Fatimids were preparing their offensive against Egypt. At the same time, Nikêforos also sought to obtain the freedom of the admiral eunuch Nikêtas from the Fatimids, which he achieved with a gift. He had captured the sword of the Prophet Muhammad from an unknown fortress in the course of the previous campaign, and he now dispatched this as a gift to the Fatimid caliph al-Mu'izz. Could this sword be the sword of caliph al-Mamun? Leo the Deacon claims that at the same time as Nikêforos did this, he also threatened the Fatimids with full-scale war if Mu'izz failed to release Nikêtas in return for such a valuable gift. The caliph did as asked, and released Nikêtas together with all other Roman captives. Leo claims that it was because of the fear of Nikêforos, but a more likely answer is that al-Mu'izz needed a truce for his planned campaign against Egypt. Liudprand of Cremona thought that no sane person would pay such a ransom in return for a eunuch. He had a point, because the Fatimids were subsequently able to use the sword of Muhammad as a rallying point in their call for Jihad. However, it is clear that Nikêforos considered such things meaningless as long as his soldiers were battle-ready under his personal command. Nikêforos certainly knew the symbological value of religious relics for the upkeep of the morale of the populace and soldiers, because he had sought out similar Christian items, but for him the Islamic items were clearly just tools for bargaining.[63]

It is probable that the peace treaty with the Fatimids also had another unmentioned purpose. Nikêforos undoubtedly knew that the peace treaty would give the Fatimids a chance to attack Egypt with greater force, which would mean that Egypt would be unable to send Jihadists against him. It is possible that the giving of the Sword of Muhammad to the Fatimids was also intended to encourage the Shiite state to present themselves with ever greater vigour as the only true successors of Muhammad, which would naturally increase the prospect of conflict with the other Muslim states. What Nikêforos failed to foresee was that the Fatimids would actually become a greater threat than the Ikshidids had been. On the basis of Nuwayri (Year 358 = 968–9), we know that Nikêforos exploited his strengthened position vis-à-vis the Fatimids further in 968. He knew that the Fatimids were planning to invade Egypt and would not want a conflict with the strengthened Roman Empire. Consequently, he dispatched presents to al-Muizz and suggested that the latter would demolish the cities of Taormina and Rometta. The idea was clearly to demilitarize the island of Sicily so that the Fatimids would not be able to use it as a launching pad for invasions against mainland Italy. The plan was successful and al-Muizz agreed to demolish the walls of both cities. This was masterful diplomacy by Nikêforos.

Whatever Nikêforos' plans were initially, the events on the ground and the death of Ashot III, the Prince of Taron, in winter 966/7 and the ensuing flight of his sons to Constantinople in early-967 changed them.[64] The sons promised the Principality to the Romans in return for high and important positions in the Roman Empire, but the possession of the Principality of Taron was contested by the King of Armenia, so Nikêforos concentrated his armies for a campaign against a fellow Christian ruler.

The annexation of Taron in 967[65]

As already noted, Smbat mentions that the diplomatic mission of Ghewond to Constantinople in winter 965/6 was successful, but after this the relationship between the Romans and Armenians soured. He claims that the reason for this was that some eunuchs (i.e. probably Basileios *proedros*) slandered the Armenians to Nikêforos and stated that their faith was not Orthodox. Smbat claims that it was as a result of this that the emperor became angered, despite the fact that he liked the King of Armenia. He also claims that it was because of this that Nikêforos assembled a large army and prepared to march to Armenia, with the intention of destroying its population. When the King of Armenia learnt of this, he was astonished that a Christian emperor would attack fellow Christians. Consequently, he assembled the Armenian forces and prepared for war. When Nikêforos had reached Nikaia in Bithynia the patriarch of Nikaia asked why the emperor had arrived there. The patriarch corrected the misunderstanding and stated that the Armenian Church was also Orthodox in its faith. When the emperor learnt this and learnt of the bravery and military skills of the Armenian king, and also of the size of the host assembled by the Armenians, he abandoned the campaign. After this, Nikêforos ordered the patriarch to write a conciliatory letter to the Armenian king in which he explained that his behaviour had been caused by a misunderstanding and that he sought friendship with him. The letter conciliated the Armenians and both sides restored their relations.

Smbat's account clearly contains fantastical elements, but it is equally clear that it has a basis in fact. It is easy to see that the above-mentioned crisis was actually connected with the death of Ashot III, the prince of Taron, in late-966 or early-967 which then resulted in the contest of who would get possession of his lands. After the death of their father, the two sons of Ashot, Gregorios and Bagrat (Pankratios), sought a place of refuge in Constantinople. They promised to give their hereditary lands to the emperor in return for the rank of *patrikios* and large areas of revenue-yielding land. Another branch of the same family was already living in the Roman Empire, where they had served as military commanders, so it is easy to see why they chose to do so. The Roman Taronites had adopted the Greek family name Taronitai. The Armenian king clearly did not accept this initially, because both rulers assembled their forces while the Romans resorted to the use of religious propaganda to justify the war against a Christian country. However, dismissing Smbat's claims, it was not the orthodoxy of the Armenians or the size of their army that resulted in the avoidance of fighting. The King of Armenia backed away from his claims, undoubtedly because he was frightened about the prospect of having to face the emperor Nikêforos Fôkas and his massive army on the field of battle. Consequently, the Armenians accepted the annexation of Taron into the Roman Empire. It is also probable that the Romans annexed East Taron at the same time because we find them operating against the Muslims in this area in 968 after the latter had recaptured Manzikert.

An unnecessary war between two Christian powers was avoided and the Romans could concentrate their efforts against the Muslims.

Taron and Keltzene were now united and duly formed into a new theme under a *prôtospatharios*. However, from Yahya (127, 825) we learn that the Romans did not take complete control of the area at this time because the city of Manzikert was in Muslim hands in 968, requiring the Romans to conduct an offensive against it in the same year. The city of Manzikert was located close to the route that the Khorasani volunteer Jihadists were using, so one may make the educated guess that it was with their help that the Muslims were able to retake the city from the Armenians when Ashot III died.[66]

It is probable that we should also connect the skirmish between the Roman navy and the Armenians which took place during Easter (Skylitzes 14.19)[67] with the planned campaign against the King of Armenia. According to Skylitzes, the

Armenians and members of the Roman fleet fought against each other, with the result that many lives were lost and the *eparchos* of the city, Sisinnios, almost lost his life. The pacification of the city would have been the responsibility of Sisinnios, so it is not surprising that he was personally involved in the operation to quell the unrest. The probable reason for such fighting at Easter would have been the propaganda spread against the Armenian Church just before a military campaign such as that described above by Smbat. The members of the Navy and the populace obviously saw the Armenian soldiers partaking in the holy ceremonies as heretics who had to be killed. It was then as a result of this that it was rumoured that Nikêforos would want to kill those citizens who had participated in the riot against his soldiers. Skylitzes states that it was shortly afterwards that the Hippodorome incident took place (see below), which Leo the Deacon connects with the aftermath of the Bulgarian campaign in the same year. Nikêforos' unabashed favouritism for the soldiers was clearly causing him problems with the inhabitants of Constantinople, so they were always ready to assume the worst if it involved the soldiers.

The Bulgarian Campaign in the summer 967[68]

Once the Armenian threat had ended, Nikêforos was free to launch his long-promised campaign against the insolent Bulgarians. Now he had even more reasons to do so, as the Bulgarians had raided Roman territory during autumn 966 (Yahya, 115, 813). Nikêforos therefore assembled a force which he thought adequate to the task and marched against the Bulgarians in summer 967. He captured several Bulgarian border fortresses and advanced as far as the 'Great Dyke/Fence'.[69] The Great Fence was a long wall with a ditch located on the old Roman border, but which was now in Bulgarian hands. For the location, see the Bulgarian map in the Maps section. Unsurprisingly, this involved also some fighting, which was noted by Yahya who states that Nikêforos defeated the Bulgarians. The route taken by Nikêforos is not known and neither is the size of the force taken by Nikêforos, but I would suggest that it was probably about 80,000 men, because this is the size of the force that Nikêforos had assembled around the capital in 968 and which he then led east against the Arabs in August 968. In short, it is likely that Nikêforos retained the army that he had originally assembled for the Bulgarian campaign in readiness near the capital – where it consumed the supplies of the populace in 968 as claimed by Liudprand *(Legatio* 44).

When Nikêforos reached the Great Fence, he wrote a letter to Peter in which he ordered him to prevent the Hungarians from crossing the Danube, with the implication that this would be the precondition for peace. This also implies that the Magyars had continued to raid Roman territory in one form or another, even after their crushing defeats by Pothos Argyros in 958, by Leôn Fôkas in 960, and by Marianos Argyros in 961. Even the monks of Mt. Athos suffered from their attacks.[70] Peter ignored Nikêforos' demand and did the exact opposite. This means that from this date onwards the Bulgarians actually officially helped the Magyars to cross the Danube so they could raid Roman territory more easily. The ducate/

katepanate of Thessalonike was probably created as a response to this, so its *doux/katepanô* could more easily coordinate the defence efforts of several themes in the area. The Bulgarians were justifiably confident that the mountainous wooded terrain would protect them from the Romans as it had in the past, and their confidence was not ill-founded because Nikêforos also recognized the danger.

According to Leo the Deacon, Nikêforos inspected the terrain ahead and found it to be full of wooded, difficult terrain, after which it became mountainous in the region of the Haemus and Rhodope Mountains, where the terrain was further obstructed by forests, rivers and swamps. Nikêforos came to the conclusion that it would be too dangerous to lead the army into such terrain because he was acutely aware of the previous disasters that Roman armies had met there. The tactics that he had intended to employ (see Appendix 3) and the size of the army were unsuitable for the conditions prevailing in Bulgaria. In particular, the pike phalanx envisaged by Nikêforos was not well-suited to such terrain. Consequently, Nikêforos led his army back to the capital and decided to fight by proxy. It is probable that it was either now that Nikêforos created the ducate of Adrianoupolis to unite the defensive efforts against the Bulgarians, or that it was in 968/9 that Nikêforos created this larger regional command as a response to the threat posed by the Russians. The latter is probably likelier, but not conclusively so. The news of the emerging threat of Frankish invasion in Italy would also have influenced Nikêforos' decision to abandon the Bulgarian campaign (see Chapter 8.10), so he started making preparations for an offensive in Italy.

It was after this that Nikêforos chose Kalokyros, who was a son of the *archôn* of Cherson in the Crimea, as his envoy to the Russians, as asserted by the Roman sources, and concluded a peace with the Russians as stated by Yahya. Kalokyros was chosen as envoy because of his knowledge of the area and of Russian customs. Hupchick (p.230) is undoubtedly correct when he suggests that Kalokyros had arrived earlier in Constantinople to plea on behalf of the Crimeans that Nikêforos help them against the Russians. By invading Crimea, the Russians had invaded Roman territory (see below), hence there was now need for a peace treaty alongside the treaty of alliance.

Kalokyros was promoted to the rank of patrician to give him authority, with 1,500 pounds of gold to bribe the Russians to invade Bulgaria. Leo the Deacon describes Kalokyros as an impetuous, rash person, who now developed imperial aspirations of his own, so he not only asked the Russians to ally with the Romans against the Bulgarians, but asked their support for the gaining of the imperial throne for himself, in return for which he would reward them royally. The Russian ruler known in the Roman sources as *Sfendosthabos 'o archôn Rôsias'*, better known to modernity as Sviatoslav/Svyatoslav, eagerly grasped the opportunity for further glorification and started preparing a campaign. In the opinion of Leo the Deacon, this was not surprising because the Russians were an especially greedy bunch who were always ready to be bribed.

Before the year 967 Svyatoslav had been an exceptionally successful military commander who had led several lightning campaigns. He did not use any logistical train with wagons and he did not eat any boiled meat. He only cut off small strips of horsemeat, game or beef and then roasted it on coals, after which he ate it. He did not use a tent, but slept on a horse-blanket with the saddle serving as his pillow. He was a rough-riding warrior who fought in nomad style on horseback, who shaved his scalp save for a long strand of hair, and who had a moustache together with a bejewelled gold ring in one ear. These marked him as a member of the steppe nobility. Before the campaign, he also announced that he would invade an enemy's territory, which was yet another steppe practice. In 963/4 he marched to the Oka and Volga, and when he came into contact with Vyatichians he asked to whom they paid tribute. When they told him that they paid tribute to the Khazars, he marched there in the following year 965, defeated their Khagan in battle and captured the city of Sarkel (Bela Vezha) and probably destroyed *S-m-k-r-ts* at the Straits of Kerch. Then he conquered the Alans and Kasogians. The probable reason for the targeting of the Khazars was not only to obtain additional tribute-paying tribes, but also that the Crimean Goths had sought Russian help against the Khazars ever since the latter had attacked them in 963.

The advance into Crimea, however, brought Sviatoslav into conflict with the Romans as already noted above. In 966 it was the time for the Vyatichians to surrender to him. These conquests gave Sviatoslav secure, unrestricted access to the Black Sea, which could not be blocked by the Pechenegs. In addition to this, he attacked the Volga Bulgars and the Burtas, which implies an effort to establish a direct trade route to the Caspian Sea and to the tradehouses of the Samanid Dynasty.[71] Consequently, by the time Nikêforos dispatched his request for alliance, Sviatoslav was very confident that he would be able to defeat anyone.

On the basis of the Roman sources, Kalokyros intended to betray his master Nikêforos from the start, which is very believable because by promising to pay tribute to Sviatoslav in return for his help in gaining the throne he would have given the Russian ruler a greater additional incentive for this expedition. This conclusion is also backed up by Sviatoslav's habit of sending a declaration of war in advance of his invasion, which means that the Romans would have already been aware of the betrayal of Kalokyros in early 968.

As suggested by Eric McGeer, it seems very likely that the aborted Bulgarian campaign had also another consequence, which was the writing of the military treatise known variously as *De re militari* or *De castrametatione* or *Peri kastaseôs aplêktou* or *Campaign Organization and Tactics*. The treatise described how to conduct a military campaign in the difficult wooded, swampy and mountainous terrain of Bulgaria. It is very likely that this treatise was commissioned by Nikêforos II Fôkas from its unknown author because he realized that it would be potentially very dangerous to lead his 80,000-man army into such terrain if he followed the tactics that he had been using in Cilicia. It is likely that he commissioned this treatise from his brother Leôn who had experience of fighting in difficult terrain with small forces. See Appendix IV.[72]

When Nikêforos led his field army back to the capital, he decided to organize chariot races in the Hippodrome for the enjoyment of the populace. In addition to this, he thought it fit to organize a demonstration of armed combat by his soldiers for a similar purpose. Consequently, he ordered the soldiers to the stadium, where they then arrayed in units against each other and drew their swords for mock combat. The populace, however, had not been pre-warned, probably because Nikêforos was seeking a spectacle, and he got more than he desired. When the populace saw the naked swords flashing in the sun they thought that the emperor had brought the soldiers to kill the populace as revenge for their rioting in Easter. The result was chaos, in which the spectators ran to the exits and crushed each other to death before they realized that the soldiers were there only for a show. According to Leo the Deacon, who was at the time living in the capital, this incident was the beginning of the hatred towards the emperor.

Khorasani jihadists invade during summer 967[73]

The more than 5,000 Khorasani Jihadists who had arrived at Antioch under Mohammed ibn Isa exploited the absence of the Roman field army, which was campaigning against the Bulgarians during summer 967. It is probable that this operation had also been approved by Sayf ad-Dawla's successor, his son Abu'l-Ma'li, the emir of Aleppo. The Khorasanis were joined by 3,000 Muslim volunteers. According to Yahya, the Khorasani raiders were victorious and obtained both booty and prisoners, which they transported back to Antioch. This was still only a minor raid, but the Khorasanis and other Muslim volunteers repeated their invasion and in the words of Yahya this time achieved a complete victory. This means that the Muslim jihadists defeated a Roman *stratêgos* in battle – after the dismissal of Tzimiskês from office Nikêforos had left the position of *domestikos tês anatolês* unfilled – the likeliest candidates being the *stratêgos* of the Anatolikon, or the *stratêgoi* of the newly-formed *themata* of Tarsus and Mopsuestia or some *katepanô*. This is yet another example which proved the importance of numbers in combat, and in the absence of numerical superiority the importance of generalship. The Romans were not commanded by Nikêforos, Leôn or Tzimiskês and so they were now defeated. Nikêforos could not be everywhere, and he knew that he needed to solve the Bulgarian problem somehow so that he could then campaign in person against the Muslims. It is probable that the Roman raid to Serugh (Saruj/Saruq) mentioned by Bar Hebraeus was simultaneous with the Muslim raid of Roman territory, so one of the *stratêgoi* from the themes of Kharsianon, Sebasteia, and Lykandos launched a diversionary campaign after the other Roman *stratêgoi* further west had been defeated. These raiders carried home 300 Arab prisoners and plenty of cattle.

When Nikêforos returned from his Bulgarian expedition, he appointed his *o epi tês trapezês*,[74] the trusted eunuch Petros, as supreme commander of all forces in the east. While doing so, Nikêforos also made a hierarchial innovation because a eunuch could not hold the position of *domestikos tês anatolês*. Nikêforos solved the problem by appointing Petros as *stratopedarchês* and dispatched him against the Saracens. The title *stratopedarchês* was not a new term and had been repeatedly used as a synonym for the *stratêgos*, but Nikêforos now used it in a different context so that it became an official term that could mean 'commander-in-chief'.[75] Petros caught the retreating invaders close to Alexandretta, and inflicted a crushing defeat on them, in the course of which the Romans killed large numbers of Muslim nobles while capturing the commander together with large numbers of others. Petros had an army of 40,000 men, so he had a massive numerical superiority against the enemy's 8,000 men and so the overwhelming victory is not surprising. The Muslims had no chance whatsoever. It is probable that the entire Roman force consisted of cavalry in this case, because Petros was pursuing a retreating enemy, and it is also probable that he would have employed the cavalry array of Leôn VI's *Taktika*, with two main cavalry lines, because in this case his forces did not necessarily have *katafraktoi* because he was pursuing a fleeing enemy while it is also clear that his main tactic was outflanking. Just as with the Muslims (see Appendix 5.5.5), it is probable that the 'rhomboid' cavalry formation was mainly used when there was danger of being outflanked so the decisive action would be left for the Roman centre. The inhabitants of Antioch ransomed the commander with a large sum of money, clothes and Roman captives. The soldiers who had escaped the massacre were received in another manner. The inhabitants quarrelled with them and then forcibly removed from them their possessions and kicked them out of the city. This would have taken place immediately after they had fled to the city, while the ransoming of the commander would have taken place only later. The Romans exploited their victory by advancing into the neighbourhood of Antioch, which they then pillaged and took 12,000 men, women, youths and maidens as booty.

8.9. The Russians, Bulgarians and Roman Empire from late-967 until the end of 969[76]

As already noted, the bellicose ruler of Russia, Sviatoslav, did not need much convincing for the invasion of Bulgaria when the Roman envoy Kalokyros arrived with the hefty bribe of 1,500lbs of gold. The promise of Kalokyros to pay him tribute in return for military help against Nikêforos would also have stood as yet another incentive. Sviatoslav assembled his forces with the usual alacrity, but unlike on previous occasions when the campaigns were fought on land mainly with cavalry, his forces now consisted mainly of infantry that were embarked on Russian-Viking vessels which they sailed down the Dnieper to the Black Sea and then along the coast to the mouth of the Danube. The army that Svyatoslav led into Bulgarian territory was a massive Russian-Viking force that consisted of 60,000 men on board ship, in addition to which there was the logistical support unit.[77] The approach of this massive force was not a surprise. On top of that, Svyatoslav was in the habit of kindly warning his enemies of his plans so it is clear that he had once again sent a letter in advance declaring war. The Bulgarians collected an army of 30,000 men against the Russians and shadowed their fleet as it sailed along the Danube, then when the Russians finally made their landing – presumably near Pereyaslavets (Little-Preslav, Preslav on the Danube).[78] The Russians drew their swords, placed their shields in front and disembarked from their ships. The Bulgarians, not able to withstand even the first wave of attackers, fled to Dorostolon (Dristra, Silistra). Soon after this Tsar Peter had 'an attack of epilepsy' (a stroke being likelier) from which he never recovered, so he died in January 969. The Russians went on to capture eighty towns along the Danube in the course of the rest of 967 and the summer of 968, and Svyatoslav became desirous of making the city of Little-Preslav his capital, because it was centrally located between the trade routes from Greece, Russia, Hungary and Bohemia, in addition to which it gave him unobstructed access to the Black Sea – which his capital at Kiev did not.

According to *Nestor's Chronicle*, when Svyatoslav was residing at Pereyaslavets he received tribute from the Greeks. It is therefore possible that Nikêforos dispatched an additional batch of bribes at this stage,[79] but it is also possible that this referred to the sum that Kalokyros had brought. Similarly, it is possible that if Nikêforos had by now learnt of the intentions of Kalokyros, which is likely, that he now tried to bribe Svyatoslav to hand over the treacherous Roman envoy, or that Nestor has confused two different occasions in which the Romans paid tribute to Svyatoslav at Little-Preslav. In the context of the events of 970, Nestor claims that when Svyatoslav was residing for the second time at Pereyaslavets and had sent a message to the Romans that he would march against them next, the Roman envoys there replied that they

Russians pursuing fleeing Bulgarians
A Miniature in a Slavonic manuscript in Vatican according to Schlumberger. Source: Schlumberger.

would agree to pay a tribute and enquired then how many soldiers Svyatoslav had so that they could pay the right sum of tribute to him. This was a trick to find out how many soldiers Svyatoslav had. Svyatoslav realized the purpose and stated that he had 20,000 soldiers in an effort to scare the Romans, when he in reality had only 10,000 men. If this latter incident took place now, then Svyatoslav would obviously have attempted to mislead the Romans by stating a smaller figure rather than a larger figure than he had in reality in an effort to mislead the enemy before his campaign against the Romans. However, the likeliest answer to this conundrum is that we should take *Nestor's Chronicle* at its face value so we are dealing with two separate incidents and that Svyatoslav was once again true to his habits and declared in advance to the Romans that he would target them next in 968 and that Nikêforos attempted to pacify him with a new bribe while his envoys were also trying to find out the size of the enemy host.

In the meanwhile, according to Leo the Deacon, when Nikêforos had learnt of the intentions of Svyatoslav and Kalokyros, undoubtedly from the arrogantly-foolish Svyatoslav himself, he immediately started to make preparations for the defence of Constantinople while making new diplomatic moves. The first of these was the sending of a new batch of bribes to Svyatoslav, already referred to, with the aim of bribing him while also learning more about the size of the enemy host, which in this case still stood at about 60,000 men and their logistical help. Nikêforos also started equipping his infantry: arming the *lochoi*; arraying the cavalry phalanxes into deep formations; drilling his *pansidêroi ippotai* (*katafraktoi*); while posting artillery engines on the walls (*mêchanai*). In addition to this, he put in place the heavy iron chain that blocked access from the sea to the Golden Horn. These actions would have been undertaken in spring 968, so Nikêforos had prepared the field army that he had originally assembled for the Bulgarian campaign in readiness to face the Russians if these decided to advance towards the capital. This was a wise security measure, because the Russians possessed a battle-hardened 60,000-man army and a fleet. As already discussed, Nikêforos and his father Bardas had fought against the Russians in 941 so they were well aware of how to engage them. Both also knew that the *katafraktoi* were particularly effective against them.

After the attempted bribe had failed, Nikêforos knew that it was impossible to avert war with the Russians. It was clear that Kalokyros had befriended Svyatoslav. Therefore, Nikêforos opened negotiations with the Bulgarians. The emperor dispatched Nikêforos Erôtikos and Filotheos, the Bishop of Euchaita, as his envoys to the Bulgarians to remind them that both nations were Christians who should fight against the Russian pagans. They were also instructed to suggest that the alliance could be sealed with the Bulgarians handing over in marriage their royal women to the young emperors Basileios II and Kônstantinos VIII.[80] The answer to this suggestion appears to have come with the envoys that were in Constantinople at the same time as Liudprand was there in June 968 (see below). The Bulgarians agreed to the proposition and dispatched the royal women to the Roman court with the message that Nikêforos should come to their assistance immediately, which he did not do because he was planning a campaign against the Arabs. The probable reason for Nikêforos' decision to campaign in the east rather than in the Balkans was that the entire Greece and Balkans were still in the midst of famine and Nikêforos also knew that the terrain there was difficult so it was difficult to support a large army there.

Since we know that the Pechenegs invaded Russian territory in late 968 (the Russian chronicles place the invasion to this year), it is very probable that Nikêforos had resorted to the traditional use of the Pechenegs against the Russians (see Chapter 2.4).[81] This, however, did not bring instantaneous results, because Sviatoslav did not immediately rush to the rescue of his mother Olga and sons Yaropolk, Oleg and Vladimir who were besieged by the Pechenegs at Kiev/Kyiv for so long that the city was on the verge of surrender thanks to famine. This means that the siege lasted until 969. In the meanwhile, the Tsar Peter I also died in January 969, with the result that Nikêforos dispatched the sons of Peter back to Bulgaria and that Boris II now succeeded his father as Tsar of Bulgaria (Skylitzes 12.5). The idea behind the sending of the sons back immediately was to prevent the more bellicose dukes from turning against the Romans.

In late-summer or autumn 969 the Bulgarians dispatched yet another embassy to Nikêforos in which they urged him to help them. The arrival of the embassy can be dated to have taken place before 8 November 969, because when Nikêforos learnt on 8 November of the capture of Antioch (it had been captured on 28 October), he was preparing his army for a war against the Russians as promised to the previous Bulgarian embassy. Sviatoslav was therefore still in Bulgaria at least during early autumn 969.[82] This war, however, did not materialize because in the end Sviatoslav evacuated Bulgaria and marched to Kyiv to save his mother and children from the Pechenegs. Since Nikêforos did not campaign against the Russians in 969, it is likely that the withdrawal of the Russians from Bulgaria took place in autumn. At the time of the death of Nikêforos Fôkas on 11 December 969, the Roman army was concentrated in Constantinople for the launching of this campaign (LD 5.4, 6.2) against the Russians in the following year.

According to Leo the Deacon (5.4, 6.2), the combat-ready field army at Constantinople in December 969 was under the command of Leôn Fôkas, which indicates that Nikêforos had placed him in command of the campaign against the Russians, because Leôn had experience of fighting in the Balkans. When this piece of information is connected with the recommendations included in the military treatise known as *De re militari* (*Campaign Organization and Tactics*, see Appendix 4), it is clear that the first version of this treatise had quite probably already been written by Leôn Fokas when Nikêforos was still alive. It is unlikely to be a coincidence that when Tzimiskês then marched against the Russians in 971, he had approximately the same number of troops (15,000 infantry and 13,000 cavalry; see LD 8.4) as recommended by the author of the *De re militari*. It is very likely that the campaign plan and the composition of the forces for that campaign had already been prepared by Leôn Fôkas in 969. The simultaneous concentration of such a massive army at Constantinople simultaneously with the concentration of the forces in Cilicia (see below) proves that Nikêforos' efforts to increase the size of the army had been successful.

During the siege of Kyiv, the local inhabitants on the other side of the Dnieper had assembled their forces and ships in readiness but did not have the courage to engage the Pechenegs, with the result that the defenders of Kyiv were eventually in so desperate straits that they had decided to surrender to the Pechenegs on the following morning unless help arrived. It was then that a youth volunteered to take the message to the opposite shore. He went out of the city with a bridle in the hand, while asking the Pechenegs in their own language if they had seen his horse. When he reached the river, he threw off his clothes and jumped into the Dnieper. At this stage the Pechenegs realized what had happened and started shooting arrows, but the youth reached the opposite shore safely and delivered the message. The *voevoda* Pritich decided to embark his men on the ships on the following morning because he feared the revenge of Sviatoslav if he did nothing. Consequently, on the following morning the fleet approached Kyiv with trumpets sounding, which frightened the Pechenegs who thought that Sviatoslav had arrived. The Pechenegs fled from the shore. Olga and the children were now able to flee to the ships and safety. When the Pechenegs saw this they realized that Sviatoslav had not yet arrived and returned. The prince of the Pechenegs then went to meet Pritich. The prince asked who he was and Pritich answered that he was leading the vanguard of Sviatoslav. This false information convinced the Pecheneg prince to conclude a peace with Pritich, after which the Pechenegs abandoned the siege. It was only after this that Olga was able to send a message to Sviatoslav, who then duly returned and forced the Pechenegs back to the steppes. Sviatoslav wanted to continue his interrupted campaign against Bulgaria and Rome, but he was retained at Kyiv until the death of his mother, and so he was able to resume his campaign only after the death of Nikêforos in 970.

8.10. Otto I Threatens Roman Possessions in Italy in 967–8[83]

In the meanwhile there had been several important developments in the Kingdom of Italy after the year 957. As already noted, Otto I and the Romans had concluded peace in 955/6, which gave Otto a free hand in Italy against Berengar II the King of Italy. He had dispatched his son Liudolf into Italy in 957, promising the crown of Italy to his son if he could conquer it. Liudolf was highly successful and conquered most of the Kingdom, but then caught a fever and died before achieving his ultimate goal. This gave Berengar the opportunity to regain most of the lost territory. In 960 he invaded the Papal domains, with the result that the Pope renewed his plea to Otto I in summer 960, but this time with the additional bait of promising to crown him as emperor. Otto I was tempted and started making preparations. He collected his army while crowning his likewise-named son Otto II as his co-ruler at Aachen on 26 May 961. Otto also organized the administration of his domains in his absence by placing his brother in control of Lorraine and by placing his illegitimate son William of Mainz in charge of the daily administration. Then Otto I launched his invasion of Italy in August 961. Berengar's son Adelbert had an army of 60,000 men (SAC 169), but they either deserted or refused to fight and retreated to their strongholds, with the result that Otto I was able to enter Pavia unopposed in December 961 and then march to Rome where he was crowned emperor (*Caesar* and *Augustus*) by the Pope John XII on 2 February 962. The First German Reich, later known as the Holy Roman Empire, had now been born.

This was considered a grave diplomatic affront at the court in Constantinople, because in their opinion there could be only one Roman emperor, but this did not yet cause any major reactions because the Romans had their hands full elsewhere. After this, Otto returned to Pavia to continue his campaign against Berengar, but then came the news that the wily Pope had started negotiations with Adalbert the son of Berengar. Adalbert had in fact fled to Fraxinetum, and he was now allied with the Muslims. At first, Otto I did not react to this, but when he learnt that the Pope was also seeking support from Constantinople and the Hungarians he had to react. Once the malaria season was over, Otto marched to Rome to depose the ungrateful 'boy' as Pope John was called by Otto. John and Adalbert both chose to flee. Otto I now took de facto control of the Catholic Church and presided over the Synod that chose the next Pope, Leo VIII. Otto I was confident that this had settled matters in Italy and so he allowed most of his soldiers to return back north, but with the result that the population of Rome rose against him. However, the retainers of Otto crushed the populace so that they once again vowed loyalty. Otto then marched to Camerino and Spoleto because Adalbert had fled there. The inhabitants of Rome once again betrayed their oaths and deposed Leo VIII in February 964, as a result of which John XII returned to the Papal See with the help of Adalbert. According to Liudprand, when John XII was pleasuring himself with the wife of some man (John was a well-known womanizer and rapist) he was struck in the temple by the devil and so died in May 964. This is usually interpreted as 'divine' intervention, but I would suggest that John was struck in the temple by the woman's husband, or by some other husband whose wife he had seduced or raped, or that he was killed by an assassin sent by Otto. After this, the population of Rome continued their resistance against Otto I and chose Benedict V as the new Pope. Otto was forced to march back to Rome once again. He besieged the city of Rome and forced the Romans to accept his man Leo VIII (963–6) as Pope.

It was now the time for Adalbert, the son of Berengar, to launch his revolt against the rule of Otto I, to which the emperor of the German Reich responded by dispatching Burchard III of Swabia against him. Burchard defeated Adalbert at the Battle of the Po on 25 June 965, but the troubles did not end there. Pope Leo VIII had died on 1 March 965, after which the Roman religious nobility had chosen Otto's candidate, John XIII, as their new Pope, but then imprisoned him in December 965. One wonders if the invisible hand of the Constantinopolitan diplomacy and bribes were behind these repeated uprisings against the Germans? The deposed Pope dispatched a plea for help and Otto led his third expedition into

Italy. John XIII was restored on the Papal throne without opposition. The ring leaders of the opposition were hanged.

After this, Otto remained in Italy, presumably to ensure that the troubles would not renew. He even built a palace for himself at Ravenna. At the same time as this happened, Otto started enlarging his domains towards the south and the Lombard Duke Pandolf the Ironhead, the Lord of Benevento and Capua, recognized Otto as his ruler in February 967. In return for this recognition, Otto recognized Pandolf also as ruler of Spoleto and Camerino. Gisulf of Salerno and Landolf of Benevento (brother of Pandolf) followed his example soon after this and attached themselves to the German cause. This resulted in conflict with the real Roman Empire located in Constantinople. Pandolf, Landolf and Gisulf were client dukes of the Roman Empire and its emperor Nikêforos Fôkas, so with this measure Otto I was de facto intervening in the internal affairs of the Roman Empire while also annexing territory belonging to it.[84]

With these actions Otto I had essentially declared war. Nikêforos Fôkas was also personally offended by the fact that Otto was now using the title of emperor (*augustus*). The likely reason for the readiness of Otto I the Great to do so was that he had concluded an alliance with Bulgaria in 965, while also witnessing in person the weakness of the Roman position in Italy. The Romans had only very recently, in 964–5, lost a 40,000-man army and a sizeable fleet in their war with the Fatimids.

Regardless, Nikêforos Fôkas was initially prepared to negotiate because the last thing he needed was yet another major war in Italy when matters on other fronts were unfinished. Consequently, he dispatched an embassy to negotiate peace and alliance with Otto. The envoys reached Ravenna in April 967. We do not know any details of the discussions between Otto and the Roman envoys, except that the Romans were so conciliatory that it encouraged Otto to send envoys to Nikêforos.[85]

It is possible that the conciliatory tone resulted from the fact that the envoys had been dispatched to Ravenna while Nikêforos was still planning to conduct his offensive against the Armenians. Once this threat ended and Nikêforos had ended his campaign against the Bulgarians, Nikêforos was ready to assume a sterner attitude towards Otto and his demands. According to Liudprand's *Legatio* (4, 31), Nikêforos referred to this in his discussions with Liudprand. Nikêforos stated that in 967 he was preparing to launch a pre-emptive strike against Otto because he had learned that Otto was planning to invade Roman territory in southern Italy. It was then that he was met by Otto's envoy Dominicus the Venetian in Macedonia, who then tricked Nikêforos into the belief that Otto would not invade and would respect the Roman borders. Consequently, Nikêforos dispatched envoys of his own to Otto to negotiate the terms of peace.[86]

The conciliatory tone of Nikêforos encouraged Otto I to enthrone his son Otto II as his co-emperor at Rome on 25 December 967, while Otto I himself was residing in Campania within striking distance from Roman territories. When the Roman envoy arrived at Capua in January 968, Otto was emboldened to request the hand of princess (born in purple) in marriage for his son Otto II while threatening the

Romans with war in Apulia and Calabria. When the Roman envoys hesitated, Otto thought it advisable to raid Apulia and place Bari, the capital of the theme of Laggobardia, under siege in March 968. Otto saw the invasion of Roman territory as a negotiating tactic, but it had the exact opposite result when the siege of Bari failed miserably.[87]

Otto had witnessed how Nikêforos was ready to negotiate with the Fatimids after they had captured the Val Demone in Sicily and he also knew that Symeon, the Tsar of Bulgaria, had got a recognition for his title and an imperial princess for his son after he had conquered territory from the Romans, so it is easy to see why he would think that this negotiating tactic would work, but he did not take into account the analysis that Nikêforos would make of the situation as a military commander with a very long experience of guerrilla campaigns from within city walls.[88] As Liudprand was to witness in summer 968, in the eyes of Nikêforos the failure to capture Bari was a sign of weakness because it was just a tiny city. Nikêforos concluded that the army of Otto I was not to be feared. Obviously, it was impossible for Otto to besiege the city effectively because he lacked an effective navy and Nikêforos also knew this all too well. Furthermore, the rough terrain in the themes of Loggobardia and Kalabria was perfectly suited for the waging of guerrilla warfare. Liudprand (*Legatio* 7) claims that Otto abandoned the siege of Bari and retreated from Apulia only because he had advised this, but it is very unlikely that it happened because of this.[89] The walls of Bari, the rough terrain, guerrilla warfare and the lack of an Ottonian navy explain it far better. Liudprand was just attempting to bolster his credences as an envoy, while making the forces of Otto look better than they were when he was negotiating with Nikêforos in summer 968. It was after Otto I had withdrawn from Apulia that Liudprand was dispatched to the court at Constantinople to continue the negotiations. Liudprand reached Constantinople on 4 June 968. Otto I thought that he had now demonstrated his military power to his opponent so that he had strengthened his negotiating position. As noted, he was badly mistaken. The Roman response would be both religious and military. The religious side of it was the making of Otranto as a metropolis by the Patriarch Polyeuktos without any consultation with the Pope, while the military response will be discussed in Chapters 8.12 and 8.14.

8.11. Domestic troubles in 967–8[90]

The ensuing year was difficult for the Roman Empire. The powers of nature caused one calamity after another. Exceptionally hot weather in May destroyed the crops, vines and trees. In the summer there was a heavy three-hour long downpour of rain at Constantinople which flooded the streets and buildings. This was followed in September by an earthquake which levelled the city of Klaudiopolis in Galatia, but left the city of Constantinople unaffected. The rebuilding cost both money and time. The worst of the calamities was the crop failure, because it resulted in a famine which was worsened by the greed of the *kouropalatês* Leôn Fôkas. He had settled in the city as a de facto greedy entrepreneur and had bought grain at a low price for the imperial storage facilities, which he now sold to the famine-stricken Constantinopolitans at a high price and apparently pocketed the difference, with the result that the inhabitants were impoverished and still famine stricken. It was then thanks to this that the populace started spreading rumours that the brothers, Nikêforos and Leôn, were enriching themselves at the expense of the masses. The emperor appears to have been unaware of the greed of Leôn and so thought he had solved the problem.[91] Nikêforos learnt of the reality only on the Sunday of Renewal (the Sunday after Easter in 968) when he went to the Church of Great Apostles. It was then that he saw some depressed pious and decent inhabitants and asked from them what the matter was. It was only then that he learnt of the price of bread, with the result that he comforted them with gifts and hurried back to the palace where he assembled a meeting of administrators who must have also included his brother Leôn. He reproached them for not having told him of the famine and of the price that they had put on public grain, after which he ordered it to be sold at bargain prices. However, he appears not to have punished his brother, probably because he wanted to retain his loyalty.[92]

The account of Liudprand of Crèmona[93] suggests that the famine did not end in the spring, which is only to be expected when the crops had failed in the previous year. Throughout the year the populace was consuming the imperial grain, which was also needed for military campaigns. In fact, according to Liudprand, Nikêforos had himself exacerbated the situation by hoarding foodstuff for his 80,000-man army, which he then led against the Saracens in autumn 968. This will be analysed in greater detail in the chapter devoted to the embassy of Liudprand in 968. It was presumably during this preparatory period before that campaign took place that the incident with a man seeking to enter the army described by Skylitzes as an anecdote took place. He states that on one occasion when Nikêforos led the army onto the plains to drill it in combat manoeuvres, he was met by a grey-haired man who wanted to enlist in his forces. Nikêforos asked why such an old person would want to do that, to which the man responded that he was now much stronger than in his youth because then he had needed two asses to carry the grain worth one piece of gold while now he could carry on his shoulders grain worth two gold coins. Nikêforos understood the joke and did not react to it. This demonstrates nicely that Nikêforos was ready to laugh at good jokes even when he was the object of such.

In spring 968 there was yet another incident of unrest, forty days after Easter, when the emperor celebrated the Ascension of the Saviour at Pêgê, which was located outside Constantinople. It was when Nikêforos was at Pêgê that a fight broke out between the people and Armenians. The relatives of those who had died in the Hippodrome incident accused Nikêforos of being a murderer and started pelting him with dirt and stones. The Armenian soldiers responded with violence, and many people were injured. The situation persisted when Nikêforos was returning, so that it became a full-scale riot against the emperor. One woman and her daughter were foolish enough to attempt to kill the emperor by throwing stones from a roof, with the result that the praetor arrested both on the following day and had them burned to death. Leo the Deacon was present during the riot and wondered at the self-composure of Nikêforos when the people insulted and shouted at him. Nikêforos just rode slowly through the city as if nothing was taking place. Night ended the riot, and the emperor did not punish the citizens because he considered the riot to have been caused by drunkenness.

8.12. The Embassy of Liudprand to Constantinople on 4 June– 2 October 968[94]

In about April-May 968, the king of East Francia, Otto I, dispatched Liudprand, the Bishop of Cremona, as his envoy to the court at Constantinople to continue the interrupted negotiations. His official task was to obtain an imperial princess from Nikêforos for Otto I's son Otto II, but Nikêforos quite correctly judged that Liudprand's primary mission was to act as a spy, because he did not bring with him any concrete promises in return for the marriage while the previous envoys of Otto I had at least fooled him with false promises in 967. Consequently, the reception that Liudprand received now was hostile, quite unlike the reception when he had previously arrived as an ambassador of Berengar at the court of Kônstantinos VII. Liudprand and his entourage reached Constantinople on 4 June 968, and Nikêforos ordered them to dismount when entering the city. The embassy was housed in an unwelcoming stone house with guards posted around so that they were in practice imprisoned.

We learn from Liudprand's account of his embassy that Nikêforos had not been idle before his arrival. He had negotiated and concluded an alliance with Adalbert, the son of Berengar, while he had prepared a fleet and army to support him. Since Adalbert was allied with the Arabs of Fraxinetum, who had also previously concluded peace with Rome, it is possible that the alliance involved them also.

Liudprand was first received by the *logothetês tou dromou* Leôn Fokas, who in this capacity acted as de facto foreign minister and spy chief. The two had a heated discussion about Otto's title, because Leôn refused to call Otto *basileus* (here *augustus*) and kept calling him *rêga* (*rex*), which Liudprand opposed with the grammatical argument that both meant the same king. Leôn accused Liudprand of having come there to argue and not for peaceful purposes.

On 7 June Liudprand was admitted into the presence of Nikêforos in the Palace of Stefana. Liudprand, who is a very hostile source, offers us the following description of Nikêforos:

'He is a monstrocity of a man, a dwarf, fat-headed and with tiny mole's eyes [*presumably refers to Nikêforos' piercing, perceptive eyes*]; disfigured by a short, broad, thick beard half going grey [*Nikêforos was 56 so this was natural]*; disgraced by a neck scarcely an inch long [*this would be the result of his strong muscular upper body, mentioned by Leo the Deacon*]; piglike by reason of his thick abundant hair; in colour an Ethiopian and as the poet says, 'you would not like to meet him in the dark' [*i.e. he looked a ruffian*]; a big belly; lean buttocks; very long in the hip considering his short stature; small legs, fair sized heels and feet; dressed in a robe made of fine linen, but old, foul smelling, and discoloured by age [*the East Romans considered the old clothes worn by previous generations more valuable than new clothes*]; shod with Syconian slippers; bold of tongue, a fox by nature [*this view was shared by Leo the Deacon, who considered him the wisest man alive*], in perjury and falsehood a Ulysses ... At his left, not in line with him, sat the two child emperors, once his masters, now his subjects.'

Liudprand, *Legatio* 3, tr. by F.A. Wright, 236 with slight changes and comments inside parentheses.

As is obvious, the physical description by Liudprand is less flattering than Leo the Deacon's (3.8), but still in agreement with it. He basically twists the version of Leo the Deacon to make Nikêforos appear in less good light. It is worth remembering here how Leo the Deacon described Nikêforos: 'in complexion closer to black than white [*this presumably reflected his Middle-Eastern background and a life spent outdoors*]; hair thick and dark; piercing black eyes beneath thick eyebrows; medium-width nose ending in a slight upward hook; moderately sized beard with grey hair; stooped in stature; broad chested with strong shoulders; a man who looked like a Hercules; a man who was more intelligent than any other man of his generation'.

When Liudprand then appeared before Nikêforos, Nikêforos accused Otto of having captured the city of Rome illegally, while also betraying his promises of peace in 967, after which Otto had dispatched Liudprand to his court only to act as a spy. This was undoubtedly an accurate description of Liudprand's real mission. Nikêforos was certainly aware of these tricks, as he had read about them and had also written instructions about their use which we can find in the *De velitatione* (see Appendix II: Chapters 1 and 2). Nikêforos was therefore not easily fooled by the words of Liudprand. It is clear that Nikêforos was just toying with him while making certain that Liudprand would not be able to leave Constantinople too soon or send a warning to his Lord about the Roman plans.

According to his own report to Otto, Liudprand argued well on behalf of his ruler and represented his case about the imperial marriage between a Roman princess and Otto II, after which the discussion was cut short by a ceremony in which the populace (merchants and commoners) were dressed up as soldiers carrying small shields and cheap spears. See the drawings opposite of the seals to see what type of weaponry Liudprand meant. The citizen militia, consisting of the factions and guilds, was then arrayed along both sides of the street leading to Hagia Sofia so that Nikêforos rode past them while the populace shouted 'The Pale Death of the Saracens!' in his honour. After this, the emperor entered Hagia Sofia with the two young emperors following. The citizen militia clearly highly appreciated the effectiveness of Nikêforos as a war leader against the Arabs. It was well-deserved.

Nikêforos invited Liudprand to a dinner the same day. This time Nikêforos asked Liudprand to describe the army of Otto. After this, he called Liudprand a liar, because in his opinion Otto's soldiers did not know how to ride nor did they know how to fight as infantry. The reason for this was that the size of their shields, the weight of their armour, the length of their swords and the heaviness of their helmets made both impossible. With a smile he added that the Franks were also gluttonous drunkards who did not possess any real navy. According to Nikêforos, only he possessed fleets filled with stout sailors, so he would sink Otto's fleets and destroy his maritime cities and reduce to ashes the cities that are close to rivers. Nikêforos also noted that the land army of Otto was tiny in comparison, so how could Otto hope to oppose his army. This was a direct insult against the military prowess of the Frankish army, to which Liudprand responded by insulting the Romans in a very heated manner by calling all Romans greedy, promiscuous cowards. In other words, Nikêforos got the response he wished for and waved his hand to call for silence and ordered the Bishop back to his gilded prison. It was there that Liudprand pleaded with his guard and tried to bribe him to deliver his letter to Leôn Fôkas. The guard agreed to this. Liudprand pleaded to be allowed to leave.

A little later, Leôn Fôkas organized a meeting with Liudprand where Basileios the *proedros* and two teachers were also present. They noted that the Romans had never given in marriage to foreigners a princess who had been born in the purple, because the wife of Peter I had not been born in the purple. They also noted that if Otto really wanted peace in return for the princess, he should hand over Rome and Ravenna. On the other hand, if the Ottonians wanted merely peace without the princess, then they should allow the Romans a free hand against the

Left: A seal of a member of the Green Faction.
Right: A seal of a *polemarchos* of the Factions.
Source: Schlumberger.

rebelling Lombard Dukes of Capua and Benevento. Neither of these suggestions was accepted by Liudprand as a basis for further negotiation, which nicely shows that his principal mission was just to spy on what the Romans were up to. After the arguing back and forth had continued for a long time, Liudprand came up with a witticism that caused everyone except Leôn to laugh. This ended the session and everyone left. The Romans did not take the arguing seriously. They were just toying with the Ottonian envoy because they knew that he was a spy. Liudprand was then escorted back to his captivity.

On 29 June 968, Leôn invited Liudprand and the Bulgarian envoys who had arrived on the previous day to celebrate the Feast Day of the Holy Apostles at the Church of Holy Apostles. The Bulgarian envoys were seated closer to the emperor, so Liudprand rose to leave, but he was pacified by Leôn when he noted that the Bulgarians had acquired this privilege when they had concluded peace with the Romans under Tsar Symeon. Nikêforos conciliated Liudprand further by sending him food from his own table. Liudprand was once again invited to present his case, this time before the Patriarch Polyeuktos and bishops. This time the discussion concerned the religious side of diplomacy and Otto's interference in church matters in Italy, that Polyeuktos considered to belong under his thumb. No compromise was found in these discussions either. The discussion with the bishops took place eight days after the Feast Day, after the Bulgarian envoys had left. This means that the Bulgarian envoys and the emperor Nikêforos had settled their discussions concerning united action against the Russians by 7 July 968 (see pages 316–18).

In the afternoon Liudprand was rushed to the palace complex. Liudprand claims that he laughed when Nikêforos approached him on a very big unbridled horse because the contrast between the very small man and big horse was so funny. This is once again Liudprand making the best of the situation. In truth, Nikêforos was demonstrating to him how big the Roman horses were and how well the Romans rode without bridles, but Liudprand turns this upside down in his account. After this, Liudprand was once again led back to his gilded prison where he was not allowed to see anyone but his own travelling companions for a period of three weeks. During those three weeks Nikêforos was outside Constantinople at a place called Eis pêgas (At the Springs), across the Golden Horn from the Imperial Palace complex. Nikêforos ordered Liudprand to travel there, despite the fact that he was increasingly sickly thanks to his living conditions. There Nikêforos again upbraided Liudprand for the treacherous behaviour of his Lord Otto. Nikêforos noted that Otto's envoys had betrayed him with an oath, which they had also put in writing on documents. These stated that Otto would never cause a scandal in the Roman Empire, and now Otto called himself *augustus* while he also claimed themes/provinces as his own when these actually belonged to the Roman Empire. Nikêforos promised to make Liudprand a rich man if he would confirm the treaty that the envoys of Otto had made the previous year. This Liudprand refused to do, because in his opinion Nikêforos just wanted to obtain a piece of evidence of the duplicity of Otto for later use in imperial propaganda. Liudprand stated as his excuse that Otto had given him written instructions on how to proceed with the negotiations. Then Nikêforos turned to the question of the Dukes of Benevento and Capua and demanded that Otto hand them over to the Romans if he did not want a war with the Roman Empire. Nikêforos also noted that, as they spoke, his forces were invading the territories of Benevento and Capua. However, Nikêforos did not give Liudprand a chance to answer and called him to his table where his father Bardas was sitting. According to Liudprand, Bardas looked like a 150-year-old walking corpse. Indeed, Bardas was an old man by now, but still standing beside his sons. He was 89-years old. Afterwards, Liudprand was once again sent to the house of discomfort.

Liudprand was thereafter carefully guarded until 20 July so that he could not learn anything about the movements of Nikêforos. It was during that time that Grimizo, envoy of Adalbert, was brought into the presence of Nikêforos. Adalbert promised to support the Romans with 8,000 men. With this in mind Nikêforos had assembled twenty-four flame-throwing *chelandia*, two Russian ships and two Galatian (Gallic) ships (presumably *galeai*) under a eunuch to take the envoy back to Adalbert. This was the number that Liudprand was able to see himself, and he warned Otto that there could have been more – obviously Liudprand never got the chance of doing this in practice, so the text is just something that Liudprand wrote when in Roman captivity. Liudprand claimed that forty of Otto's soldiers would suffice to destroy this force – a silly claim.

According to Liudprand, the above eunuch had been given a sizeable war chest, with orders that if Adalbert brought 7,000 or more men to the scene he was to bribe them with this money, after which Adalbert's brother Cona would join the Roman army for an attack against Otto while the Romans kept Adalbert as a hostage at Bari. On the other hand, if Adalbert failed to bring that many men, the eunuch was to capture him and send him as a gift to Otto, together with the money. This fleet was dispatched on its way on 19 July 968 with Liudprand watching the spectacle from his gilded cage. My educated guess is that the katepanate of Italia was created now at the latest, so all of the forces in Italy were placed under a single commander, the *katepanô*. Only the title had changed, because Nikêforos' grandfather Nikêforos Senior had been a *monostratêgos* in Italy. The first known *katepanô* of Italia was Eugenios in 969.[95]

On the following morning, 20 July, Nikêforos once again ordered Liudprand to join him for a discussion. Nikêforos once again reminded Liudprand of the betrayal of Otto's envoy Dominic of Venice, and how Otto attacked Christians while he fought against the Muslims. Now Liudprand adopted a conciliatory tone and promised to convey the wishes of Nikêforos to Otto. On top of that, Liudprand promised that he would also be able to obtain from Otto what Nikêforos wanted. The change of tone obviously resulted from the dispatch of the fleet against Otto, and Liudprand was in a hurry to warn his master. Nikêforos knew this full-well and chucklingly asked Liudprand to join him at dinner. Nikêforos once again made fun of the military skills of the Franks and then promised to allow Liudprand to return home, but he did this only to tease Liudprand because he knew why Liudprand was so eager to return. In the following nine days Nikêforos did not send Liudprand and his companions any food, so they had to buy their own at an exorbitant price.

Nikêforos left Constantinople on the fourth day (24 July?) to begin his campaign against the Arabs, and on the following day, 25 July, Leôn Fökas summoned Liudprand to ask what he wanted. Leôn once again promised that Liudprand would be allowed to leave after Nikêforos had begun his campaign and Liudprand was once again fooled by this. On 26 July Nikêforos summoned Liudprand to the Palace of Pruas on the Asian side of the Sea of Marmara. There Nikêforos presented only one demand to Liudprand, which was that he convince his Lord to give Nikêforos a free hand against the Dukes of Benevento and Capua. Liudprand noted that, as their feudal lord, Otto was obliged to support them. This agitated Nikêforos, who then ordered Liudprand to leave. After this Nikêforos still seated Liudprand at his table, where there was the brother of the Duke of Benevento and Capua (Romuald, brother of Pandulf I of Capua-Benevento) and Byzantius of Bari. Nikêforos then ordered everyone to insult the Franks in every possible manner, but afterwards Romuald and Byzantius both sent messengers to Liudprand that stated that they had done so only under compulsion. Nikêforos was clearly planning to use the relatives of those in power as his tools in Italy to undermine their support. Afterwards, Nikêforos took Liudprand to hunt in the imperial hunting grounds to demonstrate the size of his wealth.

According to Liudprand, Nikêforos started his campaign against the Arabs in part because Greece was suffering from a famine, so it was wise to lead the army into foreign territory so that it would not consume local resources:

> 'Another reason also compelled Nikêforos to lead his army against the Assyrians [*Arabs*] at this moment. By the will of God, this year a famine had so wasted all the Greek territory that one gold piece did not purchase two of our Pavian measures of corn; and this in the very realm of plenty. Nikêforos increased this misfortune, in which field mice played their part, by himself collecting at harvest time all the available corn and paying wretched owners a very low price for it. In the Mesopotamian district, where there was an absence of mice, the crops were abundant, and the amount of corn he got from there equalled the amount of the sands of the sea. As a result of this mean transaction famine raged shamefully everywhere, <u>and so he brought together 80,000 men under pretence of a military expedition</u> [*This was not pretence. The army had been collected for the Bulgarian campaign and had then been kept in existence because of the planned campaign against Otto, which was cancelled, so the army had remained in the neighbourhood of Constantinople*], and for one whole month went on selling for two gold pieces what he had bought for one [*Nikêforos had paid with his own devalued tetarteron while he collected prices in the old coin; Roman sources, however, credit this expedient to*

The Reign of Nikêforos II Fôkas (16 August 963–11 December 969)

his brother Leôn]. These, my master [*Otto I*], are the reasons which compelled Nikêforos to lead his forces against the Assyrians just at this moment. <u>And what forces! These are not really men; they are dummies; their tongues are saucy; but 'cold are their hands in war'. Nikêforos did not look for quality in them, but only for quantity</u> [*This is a disparaging and inaccurate comment concerning both thematic and tagmatic soldiers, because even the thematic soldiers were professional soldiers. In fact, there is not much difference between the thematic soldiers and feudal knights as far as their training is concerned. Both obtained their livelihood from the land they lived in and with its help they trained and soldiered. The only real differences were that the thematic forces also included infantry and did not have a similar societal status and cultural obligations as the feudal knights. However, the important point here is that Liudprand had also realized that Nikêforos preferred to overwhelm the enemy with numerical superiority. The results bespeak for themselves. Nikêforos went from victory to victory by following this approach. As already noted, it is possible that he came to this conclusion as a result of having led the numerically-superior cavalry force against the Saracens in 959.*]. How dangerous this will be for him he will learn to his sorrow, when his unwarlike host, relying only on its size, shall be put to flight by a handful of our men who have both knowledge and appetite for figting.

When you were besieging Bari [*i.e. March–April 968*], not more than 300 Hungarians laid hands on 500 Greeks near Thessalonica and hauled them off into Hungary. [*Their presence on Roman soil would have been the result of Bulgarians raiding with them. The small numbers involved shows that this was a minor raid or a detachment sent from a base camp, which were difficult to contain when the raiding enemy forces were scattered and simultaneously raiding many locations*]. Their success induced two hundred Hungarians in Macedonia, not far from Constantinople, to attempt a similar feat; but forty of them, retiring carelessly along a narrow pass, were taken prisoner [*there were undoubtedly many similar instances which Liudprand does not mention*]. These men Nikêforos had released from prison, and dressing them in the most costly garments has made them his bodyguards and defenders [*means probably the* etaireiai; *their inclusion as bodyguards demonstrates their skills as soldiers*], to go with him against the Assyrians. What sort of an army it is you can infer from this fact: the best soldiers of them are those who come from Venice and Amalfi [*the Venetians and Amalfitans were drawn from the Latin community of Constantinople*].'

Liudprand, *Legatio* 44–5, tr. by Wright 261–2 with some changes, underlining and my comments inside parentheses.

The above account shows nicely that Nikêforos decided not to bother the local populace of Constantinople any further with the presence of his field army in a situation in which the city was already suffering from famine. It was wiser to make the army live off enemy resources. The account also shows how the Hungarians were raiding Roman territory in fast moving scattered bands in spring 968, where some of these managed to pillage with impunity while other bands met their just punishment. The account also shows that Nikêforos was quite ready to enrol Italians and captured foreigners into his army, and that he understood the importance of achieving numerical superiority over the enemy when invading. The figure given by Liudprand for his field army, 80,000 men, means only the army that had been billeted in the neighbourhood of Constantinople since summer 967, so it is possible that the actual size of the field army that Nikêforos led into enemy territory in the east was even greater, because it is probable that he would also have added some of the forces of the eastern *themata* into their numbers.

On 27 July Nikêforos gave Liudprand permission to return home, but when he reached Constantinople the eunuch and patrician Christoforos, who acted as Nikêforos' representative, told Liudprand that this could not take place because the Saracens were in possession of the sea while the Hungarians controlled the land routes, so Liudprand should wait. According to Liudprand, this was a lie used as an excuse to keep him there. This shows that the Hungarians were not quite as successful as Liudprand claimed in his comments above. Most of their raiding bands were presumably destroyed, just as they had been on previous occasions. Christoforos made certain that the situation would remain so by placing guards around the house so that nobody could leave. It was then that paupers of Latin origin attempted to approach the house to ask alms from Liudprand – which the guards threw into prison. These paupers were undoubtedly Liudprand's undercover agents who he had attempted to use as his couriers to deliver the intelligence report to Otto, but who were also recognized as such by the Roman guards and therefore thrown into prison for further interrogation. Liudprand's intelligence gathering mission proved to be a failure. Both Leôn and Nikêforos had understood its real purpose from the start. The fact that Christoforos was in charge of affairs in Constantinople means that Leôn had either accompanied Nikêforos, or was conducting operations against the Hungarians in the Balkans, or was in charge of some other portion of the eastern front. The likeliest places for him would have been to be with his brother or be in the Balkans, because Leôn's son Bardas was actually in charge of the operations against the city of Manzikert in 968 – as already noted, it is probable that it had been recaptured by the Muslims.

It was soon after this that envoys arrived from Pope John XIII which represented a hope that Nikêforos would conclude an alliance with Otto. However, since the letter called Otto Emperor of the Romans, the envoys were thrown into prison while the message itself was conveyd to Nikêforos in Mesopotamia. The answer to the letter came on 12 September, but Liudprand did not learn what was in that answer. On 17 September Liudprand was called to a meeting with Christoforos where the two debated until Christoforos finally asked if Liudprand would think it possible to conclude an alliance through the marriage. Liudprand answered that this had been his task, but that he could not answer what the situation was now because he had not been allowed to send messages. It was only then that Liudprand was given permission to return home, but before this happened Christoforos ordered

The Reign of Nikêforos II Fôkas (16 August 963–11 December 969)   331

the confiscation of many things, the most important of which were clothes made of purple silk – which were contraband. Liudpand complained that he had been allowed to buy those when Kônstantinos VII ruled, which Christoforos answered by stating that Kônstantinos was a mild man who stayed in the palace and wanted to make all people his friends, while Nikêforos was a *basileus* with quick hands [this referred also to the hand speed required from a good fencer and archer], always eager for combat. He avoided the palace like a plague. He loved arguing and strife. He did not win the friendship of foreigners with bribes, but with terror and sword. After this everything classed as contraband was taken away from Liudprand, and he was given a letter with a golden seal for Otto and a letter with a silver seal for the Pope – Leôn Fôkas sent a separate letter to the Pope through other channels. The Pope was warned against supporting the cause of Otto lest he be ruined. On 2 October Liudprand was finally allowed to depart Constantinople and he then boarded a ship, but even then it would take quite a while for him to reach the court of Otto. By that point, all of the information gathered by Liudprand would be completely worthless.

8.13. The Roman Offensives in the East in 968–9[96]

The Romans' response to the Muslim offensives in the east and re-conquest of Manzikert came in 968. This time Nikêforos would take command of the main army in order to punish the Muslims while capturing new territory from them. The task of retaking the city of Manzikert was given to Bardas, the nephew of Nikêforos, who held the rank of *doux* of Chaldia. Bardas was the son of Leôn Fôkas, the *kouropalatês*. Stephen of Taron, the source for Bardas' campaign against Manzikert, does not give us an exact date for the campaign beyond the fact that it took place in 968, but it is very likely that it took place simultaneously with the main invasion led by Nikêforos himself (possibly with the assistance of Leôn Fôkas, see above) because the first object of Nikêforos' campaign was the city of Amida. Since the targets of their invasions were so close to each other it is likely that both united their armies temporarily at Romanoupolis (Bingöl), because this city stood at the crossroads of both armies. However, one cannot entirely rule out the possibility that Bardas would have used another, more easterly route through the mountains to Manzikert, even if it was riskier thanks to the terrain. I have given both alternatives in the accompanying map on page 334. We learn from Maqrizi 8 (1824, p.21; 1895, p.634) that the Romans were also conducting naval operations against the Ikhshidids of Egypt to prepare the ground war for the ground offensive. The time was opportune because Egypt was in a state of turmoil after the death of Kafur the Eunuch. The Romans exploited this by attacking Damietta with over twenty ships and captured 150 Muslims on 10 June 968. This attack was clearly a raid conducted by the Roman fleet prior to the main campaign of Nikêforos II Fôkas in late 968. It is possible that one of its purposes would have been to draw Ikhshidid forces away from Syria for the defence of Egypt proper. In fact, it is possible that the raid against Damietta was only one of many naval raids conducted by the East Roman fleet at the time and that most of its detachments were engaged in these activities prior to the intended rendezvous with the Roman land forces under Nikêforos.

On July 27 Nikêforos started his journey from the Asian side of the Bosporus and marched to the assembly point of his army, which would have been once again the city of Kaisareia, his regular stopping point. His journey would then have gone through Melitene and Harput to Romanoupolis (Bingöl). Bardas Fôkas, the *doux* of Chaldia, assembled a large army, presumably at Koloneia, from which he then marched east to Karin and from there south-west to Romanoupolis (or he used the more eastern and riskier route through the mountains), where the two Roman armies were probably temporarily united before Bardas marched to Manzikert and Nikêforos to Amida. Both campaigns would therefore have started in August 968. The route taken by Nikêforos would have been a surprise to the Muslims, because the typical route to Amida went from Harput through the Pass of Darb Baqasaya (Darb al-Hayyatin), whereas he now used the Illyris Pass. The use of this pass is proven by the referral that Nikêforos suddenly turned towards Martyropolis instead of marching to Amida. Note that it was now possible to assemble two large armies simultaneously for the eastern front, which means that Nikêforos Fôkas' efforts to increase the size of the army had been a success.

The Siege of Manzikert ended up in Roman victory, so Bardas Junior now united the entire Taron under Roman control. In the meanwhile, Nikêforos had marched south from Bingöl towards Amida, but instead of going there he turned left towards Martyropolis and Arzen, where he marched as far as Kafartouta (Castra Maurorum, east of Nisibis) massacring and capturing en route large numbers of the inhabitants of those places. The location of Kafartouta (Castra Maurorum) shows that Nikêforos bypassed Tur Abdin this time from the eastern side and marched through Kafartouta towards Nisibis and then Syria. It is probable that this time Nikêforos adopted the more southerly route,[97] so he would have bypassed Resaina and Harran en route to Manbij. When the new emir of Aleppo, Abu-l-Ma'li, heard of his approach, he placed his chamberlain Qarghoyah in charge of the defence of Aleppo, while he himself fled to Balis. Nikêforos seems to have bypassed Aleppo this time, so on 19 October Nikêforos reached Antioch, where he stayed for two days with the idea of inducing the city to surrender, but when this did not take place, he advanced to Ma'arreh-Macrin (Maarat Misrin). Nikêforos promised to save their lives if the inhabitants surrendered. This they did and all 1,200 were transported to Roman territory. Then he captured Ma'areh al-Nouman (Maarat al-Nouman), Hamah (Hama) and Hims (Emesa), where he found the head of Saint John the Baptist.[98] Skylitzes mentions a place called Synnephion (unknown) among the places captured by Nikêforos, and it is possible that it is one of the places mentioned above or some other place not mentioned by Yahya. According to Bar Hebraeus, Emesa had been abandoned by its inhabitants so that its capture was quite easy. Consequently, Nikêforos set the city on fire and continued his journey.

The Reign of Nikêforos II Fôkas (16 August 963–11 December 969)   333

According to Yahya (127–8, 825–6), the previous campaigns and raids of Nikêforos and his subordinates had caused such widespread destruction in Syria, Diyar Modar, Diyar Rabia and Diyarbekir (Amida) that these famine-stricken regions were unable to offer any serious resistance to the advancing Romans. The previous ravaging combined with the massive numerical superiority made it possible for Nikêforos to capture almost all of the frontier cities and villages in Syria and Mesopotamia. On top of this his forces now massacred and captured men, women and children in such numbers that only 'God knew the enormity of their number'. According to Yahya, the soldiers enjoyed this immensely because they faced practically no opposition at all. Nobody had the guts to resist them. The Roman soldiers simply marched wherever they wanted and destroyed and pillaged everything at will. Yahya goes on to claim that Nikêforos then marched to Tripoli, where he arrived on 5 November 968, but on the basis of Skylizes' account (Nikêforos forced both Damascus and Tripoli to pay tribute) and Idris (p.134) it is clear that Nikêforos had actually marched from Emesa to Damascus and from there to Tripoli. The payment of tribute by the inhabitants of Damascus means that they chose to pay a ransom so Nikêforos would leave them alone, which Nikêforos gladly accepted because he was expecting to make a rendezvous with his fleet at Tripoli. Damascus belonged to Ikhshidid Egypt, which he planned to subdue in due time. The route taken by Nikêforos from Emesa to Damascus and from there to Tripoli is not known. He could have used several different routes, the likeliest of which are shown in the accompanying map on page 334. The route from Emesa to Damascus could have passed through the Bekaa Valley (between the Anti-Taurus Range and Lebanon Mountains) or alternatively east of the Anti-Taurus Range. The route from Damascus to Tripoli could have passed along the Bekaa Valley past Heliopolis, or alternatively along the coastal route past Sidon, Beirut and Byblos to Tripoli. In light of the text of al-Makin (p.241–2), the coastal route via Sidon appears to be the most likely because he confuses the campaigns of Nikêforos and Tzimiskês. He claims that the city of Antioch closed its gates from Tzimiskês after the latter had marched there from Sidon via Tripoli. It was because of this that he left Bourtzês behind to besiege it. Bourtzês then captured the city and Tzimiskês died shortly afterwards. In short, it is clear that al-Makin has preserved for us the route taken by Nikêforos.

When Nikêforos reached Tripoli, he rested the army close to the city that night and torched its suburbs. According to Leo the Deacon, Nikêforos observed that the city was well defended and more difficult to capture than the other cities. Since his fleet had not arrived thanks to adverse winds, he decided to continue his march to Arqah (Arka). The fact that Nikêforos was expecting to meet his fleet at Tripoli on 5 November 968 means that the campaign had been planned as a combined-arms operation involving the use of the Roman fleet against the coastal cities. On the basis of Skylitzes' account we know that the inhabitants of Tripoli still decided to pay a ransom before Nikêforos continued his march towards the north. On the basis of the account of Nuwayri we can actually go even further than this. According to

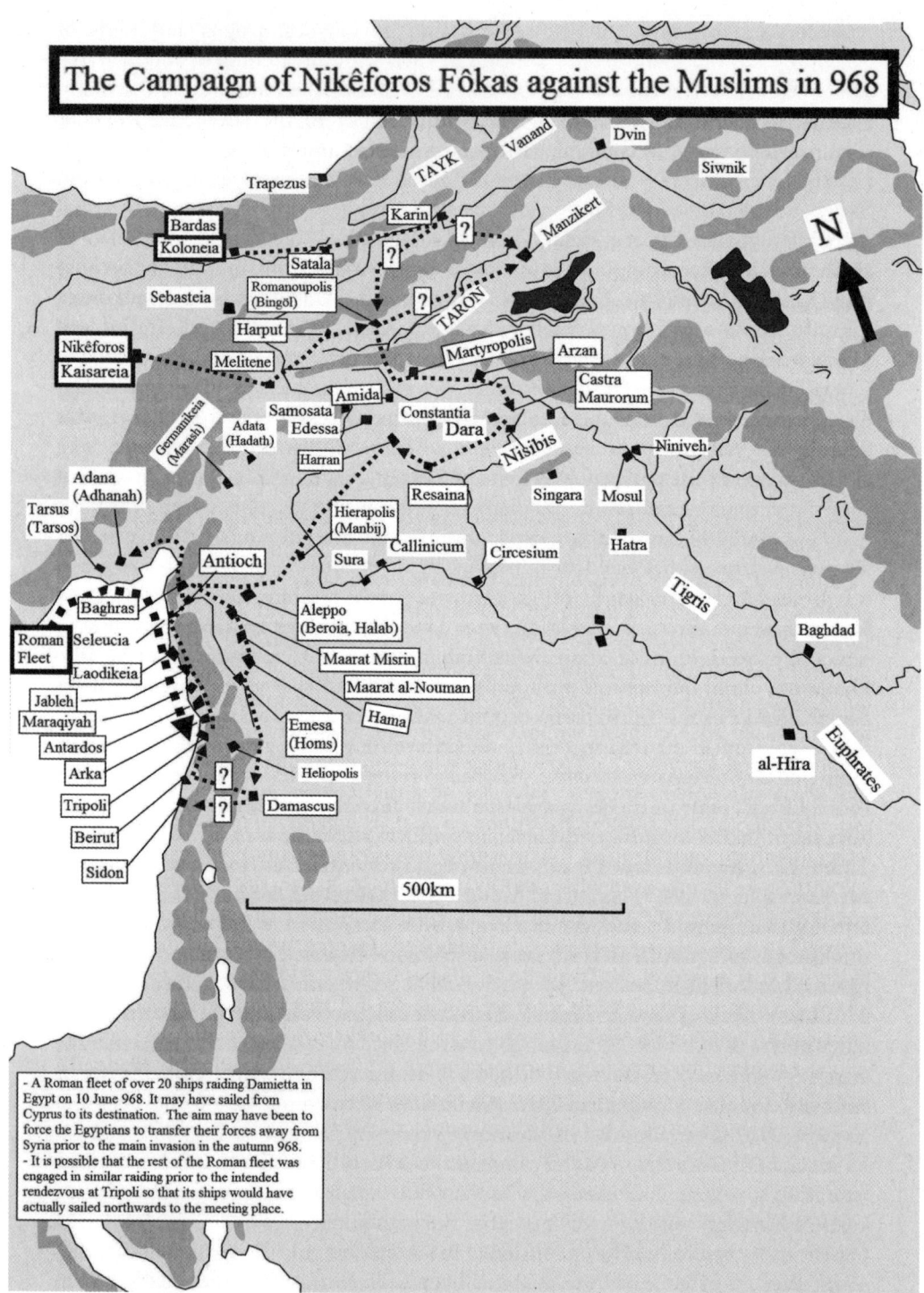

The Reign of Nikêforos II Fôkas (16 August 963–11 December 969)

Antioch in the 19th century. Note the height of the mountain. Source: Schlumberger.

Nuwayri, on the first days of the *Rabi* II in 364 (21 September 974–9 September 975) the Fatimid caliph al-Muizz dispatched Rayyan al-Khadim (eunuch of Slavic origins) against the Roman garrison at Tripoli. On the basis of this and other evidence, Sclumberger (1896, 279–80) has suggested that the city surrendered to Nikêforos II Fôkas in 968–9 and that it had received a garrison at that time. Whatever the truth regarding the exact timing of the Roman conquest of Tripoli, it is still clear that the Romans occupied it at the time of Rayyan's northern offensive in 974. In fact, the text of Psellos (*Historia syntomos*, 105) confirms the Roman capture of Tripoli for the reigns of Nikêforos Fôkas and Iôannês Tzimiskês. It is also possible that the city of Beirut had a Roman garrison at the time so that when Nasir al-Khadim al-Saqlabi (eunuch of Slavic origins) entered it either in January-February or February-March 975 he actually reoccupied it (see the forthcoming biography of Tzimiskês).

Nikêforos found out that Arka had a well-fortified citadel, but this time he besieged it, which implies that his fleet had now arrived. The fleet was obviously used to isolate the city from the sea, but it is clear that the fleet would have brought the supplies and additional siege engines that enabled Nikêforos to continue his campaign in greater security. Nikêforos surrounded the fortress with three palisades and besieged it. The Romans destroyed the towers with *(h)elepoleis* (city-takers), after which they pillaged the place for nine days (or the siege lasted nine days). The 'city-takers' were probably either battering rams or trebuchets. Nikêforos obtained an exceptionally sizeable booty. Among the captives was the emir of Tripoli, Abu-l-Hasan Ahmed ibn Nahris al-Arghali, who had been chased out by the inhabitants of Tripoli because of his tyrannical behaviour. The booty obtained from him was very significant, because Abu-l-Hasan came from a large rich family and because he had enriched himself at the expense of the Tripolitans. It is quite probable that the lure of rich booty was the reason why Nikêforos was prepared to besiege so well-defended a location.

Nikêforos then continued his journey northwards along the coast by capturing Artharthons (Antardos, Tortosa, Tartus), Maraqiyah, and Hisn-Djabalah (Djabal,

Jableh). On the basis of the text of Leo the Deacon, these were taken with the first assault. After this, Nikêforos discussed with the inhabitants of al-Laziqiah (Laodicea ad Mare/Laodikeia/Latakia) concerning the surrender of the city. Laodicea duly did so. For the location of most of the fortresses and cities mentioned, see the maps section.

Yahya then continues his account by stating that after Nikêforos had destroyed an incalculable number of villages/cities, he marched to Antioch. On the basis of the account of Bar Hebraeus, it is probable that the journey from the region of Aleppo/Antioch to Damascus and then back to Antioch had lasted for two months. According to Bar Hebraeus, in the course of the campaign Nikêforos had taken 100,000 captives; youths and maidens of the right age, because he did not capture old men or women. These were either killed or left alone. It was presumably because of this that we find in the account of Yahya the piece of information that when Nikêforos reached Antioch he divided the booty of prisoners into categories and released more than 1,000 old men and women.

On the basis of all extant sources, this time Nikêforos chose not to attempt to take the city of Antioch by force. Leo the Deacon states that after Nikêforos had pitched a marching camp in front of the city of Antioch, he made a speech to the *stratêgoi* and *lochagoi* in which he explained the reasons for his decision to use famine rather than force in this case. The words that Leo places in the mouth of Nikêforos are his own, but it is still likely that the reasons were made public and he would have had access to these. In the aftermath of the string of successful sieges, Nikêforos was aware that his officers and army were eager to capture the city with violence and subject it to pillage and rape. He did not share this view. Nikêforos called Antioch the third largest city in the world. It was also a beautiful city with impressive walls. It had a sizeable population with beautiful buildings. Nikêforos was certain that the city would fall in his hands without violence and it was because of this that in his mind it would be idiotic to destroy the city with violence. The city was in effect already their own and it was idiotic to ravage and pillage one's own land. According to the other sources, the massive amount of booty, the exhaustion of the army after a long campaign, the time of the year (winter), incessant rain, supply problems, and the outbreak of the pestilence among the soldiers also influenced his decision.

It is not surprising that Nikêforos preferred to capture Antioch through surrender, because he knew how costly it had been to repopulate the cities of Tarsus and Mopsuestia and how much money and effort this had taken in 965–6. This was particularly important when the failure of crops had led to a persistent famine in 967–8. In the case of Tarsus and Mopsuestia he had been forced to lower food prices in order to lure a population there, and then the Roman Empire (like many other places e.g. Egypt) had been ravaged by a long period of crop failures caused by heat waves, so Nikêforos did not want to repeat the same problems on an even larger scale in the city of Antioch. Nikêforos was an emperor who also knew how the economic situation looked. The lower-ranking officers, NCOs and soldiers obviously did not understand this aspect of warfare and were therefore critical of Nikêforos' very sound decision. All they thought of were the spoils of war. In addition to this, the city of Antioch was an important Christian centre with a Christian population.

Consequently, Nikêforos ravaged the neighbourhood of Antioch very thoroughly and then led his forces away to a location known as the Black Mountain, known to Yahya as Bagras (Baghras/Pagrai). This was a strategic location at the mouth of the Syriai Pylai (Syrian Gates). There he built a fortress in record time by means of his personal example. He himself carried rocks on his shoulder up the hill to the site of the fortress to encourage his men. Their emperor did not spare sweat and labour and neither should his men. The fortress was built in just three days. It may have been built on top of the older Muslim fortress which is known to have been located in Bagras. Bardas Fôkas had captured it in 944–5 (see the narrative of that year). It should be noted, however, that modern archaeology has not been able to find any traces of the walls dating from the period before 968 so it is possible that the Arab fortress was located elsewhere. See the maps section for further details. Nikêforos left Michaêl Bourtzês there as a commander with an army of 1,000 infantry (called *speira*) and 500 cavalry (called *ilê*) with orders to harass the inhabitants of Antioch constantly so that they would be unable to obtain provisions. Nikêforos left most of his men in Cilicia for the winter, where they were distributed to various locations to ease their provisioning. This army was placed under Nikêforos' trusted eunuch Petros, and he was once again given the title *stratopedarchês*. They were told to wait for the arrival of the emperor in spring, as he did not remain there, presumably because he preferred to wait for the city of Antioch to just fall into his hands before proceeding further. Nikêforos commanded that neither Michaêl Bourtzês nor Petros were to attempt to capture the city themselves. Several sources also claim that by now Nikêforos had already set his eyes on the conquest of Jerusalem.

This course of action caused the superstitious to claim that Nikêforos had left Antioch unconquered because of a prophecy that the emperor would die when the city was taken. Any sane person would have recognized the stupidity of this claim, but superstitious people were and are always ready to believe almost anything else but the rational logical explanation.

It was presumably very soon after the Romans had left the neighbourhood of Antioch and Aleppo that Qarghoyah revolted against Saad ad-Dawla, with the result that Saad fled to Martyropolis. The Muslim opposition to the Romans was even more divided and weaker. In the meanwhile, the Qarmatians had besieged and captured the city of Damascus, after which they marched to Ramlah, where they defeated the locals in a major battle on 28 October 968. This means that the Qarmatians advanced to Damascus very soon after Nikêforos had left the place. After the payment of tribute, the inhabitants of Damascus were obviously considered Roman subjects so the city had become a legitimate target from the point of view of religion. The Qarmatians were an aggressive Ishmaeli Shia (Shiite) group that dominated eastern Arabia, which means that they had exploited the inner lines of communication in the deserts to attack Damascus.

According to Yahya, after the departure of Nikêforos, a black African from Egypt arrived at Antioch. His name was az-Zoughaili, and with the fugitives that had arrived from Tarsus he raided Roman territory until he attempted to kill Alouch the Kurd, the emir of Antioch, with the result that his men were defeated while he was captured. The defenders of Antioch were clearly internally divided. It is of note that Yahya does not state that az-Zoughaili had brought with him any army. This means that he probably arrived as a refugee from the Ikhsidid realm. Therefore, he would have fled as a result of the Fatimids' conquest of Egypt. Jawhar, the eunuch commander of the Fatimid armies, entered Fustat in July 969 which can be considered to have been the end of Ikhshidid Egypt. One can therefore make the educated guess that az-Zoughalali would have arrived at Antioch at some point in time between June and August 969.

When the Romans failed to conduct any major operations during the spring and summer of 969, because they were besieging the city of Antioch from a greater distance, the emir Saad ad-Dawla saw this as an opportunity to return to his capital Aleppo. He marched from Martyropolis and halted close to Aleppo during Ramadan (19 July–17 August) and fought against Qarghonyah for three months before capturing the city, apart from the citadel where Qarghonyah (Qarghuwayh) still held out. Aleppo fell to Saad roughly simultaneously with the fall of Antioch to the Romans, meaning that neither Muslim commander was in any position to bring assistance to the besieged city of Antioch.

The plans of Nikêforos towards the city of Antioch were destroyed by the personal ambitions of Michaêl Bourtzês. Leo the Deacon claims that Michaêl was following the orders of Nikêforos, but it is clear that Skylitzes's version is correct on the basis of what happened later (see below).[99] According to Skylitzes, Michaêl did not pay any attention to the orders given and he attempted to corrupt the Antiochenes with promises, but with no result until he managed to befriend a Saracen. This man told him the height of one of the western towers known as Kalla located at the top of the mountain. Michaêl had ladders of the right height constructed, approached the tower on a moonless rainy night, placed the ladders against the wall, and led 300 men to the wall, after which they killed the guards inside the tower and the tower next to it. According to Yahya, the first on the wall were Michaêl Burtzês, Isaac (Ishaq) the son of Bahram, and a black servant of Bourtzês. After this, he dispatched a message to Petros in which he stated what he had done and pleaded for help. Petros hesitated because he knew the will of the emperor, but when Michaêl kept on sending one message after another while the Saracens attacked the Romans holding the towers, he decided to bring his army to the scene. In the meanwhile, the Saracens had surrounded the Romans and used every kind of siege engine while attempting to burn the Romans with fire. The forces of Michaêl withstood these attacks for three days and nights before help arrived.[100] On the basis of this it is clear that, after his initial hesitation, Petros must have started preparations at the latest in the morning of the second day for his army to be able to assemble and then reach Antioch on the third, while it is likelier that he had made the decision on the very same day that he got the first message. When the Antiochenes learnt of the approach of the army, they halted their attacks which gave Michaêl Bourtzês and his men the chance to come down from the walls to open up the nearest gate for the Romans.[101] It was through this gate that Petros' army entered the city and started the merciless slaughter of the populace which Nikêforos had wanted to avoid.

The city fell on 28 October 969, meaning that the siege had lasted almost a year. The length of the siege was probably one of the reasons for Bourtzês' decision to seek personal glory. The Muslims set one part of the city on fire to cover their flight though the Gate of the Sea. Those who were unable to flee through it became prey for the Romans. After the Roman soldiers had sated their bloodlust, they divided the remaining people into groups so that the old men and women and young children were ordered to leave. They dispatched as booty 20,000 fully-grown men and women plus young men to Roman territory. The relatively small numbers of slaves sent to Roman territory shows that the capture of the city had been very costly for the Roman Empire. The soldiers had either killed most of the populace, or they had been able to flee through the Gate of the Sea. It would cost a lot of money for the Romans to repopulate the city, which Nikêforos had wanted to avoid.

When Saad ad-Dawla learnt of the fall of Antioch, he fled from Aleppo to Emesa, at which point Petros exploited the Roman success by advancing there with 10,000 horsemen while the inhabitants of Aleppo sought a place of refuge under the rebel leader Qarghuyah (Qarghuwayh) in the citadel. The Romans besieged it for 27 days. The two sides then concluded a permanent truce, according to which the cities of Aleppo and Emesa and the entire province with all its cities and villages would pay tribute to the Roman emperor. The Roman emperor would place his own representative in the city of Aleppo to levy taxes on merchandise. The two sides then put the treaty in writing and the inhabitants of Aleppo gave eight hostages as a guarantee of their good faith. The treaty was signed on 14 December 969– 11 January 970, by which time the emperor Nikêforos had been assassinated.

The complete destruction of the emirates of Tarsus, Aleppo and Emesa was the true legacy of Nikêforos Fôkas. The Muslims had been pushed out of the Roman frontiers and were everywhere in flight at the time Nikêforos Fôkas was murdered. This was the result of using massive, well-drilled armies in overwhelming numbers. In addition to this, at the time of Nikêforos Fôkas' death the Romans had an absolute naval superiority on the eastern Mediterranean. This was the combined result of the capture of Crete under Rômanos II and of the naval victories against the Egyptians in Cilicia and Cyprus in 965. The Tarsiote fleet appears not to have recovered from their crushing defeat at the hands of Basileios Examilites in 956, so there had not been any need for its destruction during the reign of Nikêforos. When Nikêforos had conquered Cilicia in 965, the Tarsiote fleet had not played any role in the events.

Leo the Deacon claims that Nikêforos rejoiced when he heard of the fall of Antioch on 8 November 969, but the account of Skylitzes is here far more reliable for reasons that will be made clear. Skylitzes states that the fall of Antioch angered Nikêforos to such an extent that he levelled charges against Petros, who appears to have escaped punishments probably thanks to the fact that his hands were tied by the actions of Michaêl Bourtzês. However, Michaêl Bourtzês felt the full fury of the emperor. Nikêforos did not reward his courage and personal initiative because he had disobeyed his direct order. Bourtzês was dimissed from service, and placed under house arrest in the capital. It was thanks to this that Bourtzês subsequently joined the conspiracy against Nikêforos. It would be easy to think that Nikêforos punished the man simply because he was jealous of Bourtzês success and thought that the only person who should be gaining military glory was he alone. However, based on the reasons behind Nikêforos' refusal to capture Antioch through violence, it is clear that at the heart of the issue was Nikêforos' personal opinion of what would be best for the Roman Empire, and these he required everyone to follow blindly. In light of the facts he was right. Bourtzês had disobeyed a direct order from his superior officer and had acted against the interest of the Empire. Therefore, he had to be punished, despite his personal bravery and initiative. As noted above, Nikêforos wanted to capture the city and its inhabitants intact because these were of greater value to him and Roman Empire that way, and he was undoubtedly correct in his judgment.

8.14. Otto I Resumes His Offensive against the Romans in 968–9[102]

When Otto I had not received any message from Liudprand because Nikêforos had purposefully kept him in custody, he started moving his forces towards the south and on 2 November 968 he had reached Fermo, south of Ancona. He invaded Apulia again. The sources do not offer any details of the invasion so it is probable that it was a raid directed against undefended villages in the countryside. The only detail that we have is that Otto celebrated Christmas in Apulia.

Following this, Otto and Pandulf marched to Lucania, which belonged to the Romans as well. On the basis of the text of Liudprand (*Leg.* 56), who referred to only two themes in Italy, it is likely that Lucania had not yet been formed into an independent theme but was still a part of the theme of Apulia Loggobardia. In winter 969 the Ottonian forces ravaged and pillaged those parts of Lucania which were governed by the officers of the *basileus*, but spared the territory belonging to the Lombard duchy of Salerno, who was a client principality of the Roman Empire.

In spring 969 Otto continued his invasion into the theme of Calabria, which he proceeded to ravage in like manner. He besieged Cassano for some time, but with no result. Otto claimed suzerainty over the area, but was forced to return north after 1 May 969. He retreated to the area between Ascoli and Bovino, both of which were in Roman hands. The commanders of these two cities had cut off communications between Benevento and the coast while protecting the Roman theme of Apulia from the north. Otto's forces besieged the city of Bovino, while Pandolf continued his march to Benevento because his brother Landolf had just died. Otto returned north and placed Pandulf, the Duke of Capua, in command of the Germanic forces that he left behind, while ordering him to continue the siege of Bovino. At the same time as this happened, Otto directed Pope John XIII to give the Bishop of Benevento the right to nominate the bishops of Bovino and Ascoli, besieged by the Lombards and Germans on behalf of Otto. Otto sought to make the Lombardian clergy his own political tool, just like Nikêforos sought to do with the Orthodox cleargy in the east.

While the Germans and Lombardians were thus engaged, the Romans had completed their own preparations with the help of the reinforcements sent from Constantinople. However, they were not joined by Adalbert, despite his sworn promises. He had been trapped in the Apennines by German forces, with the result that he fled to Gaul where he died at Autun a few years later. According to the accounts of Widukind and Thietmar, this time the Romans played one of the most daring stratagems of the era. They claimed to have brought the imperial fiancée for Otto II, and so asked Otto I to send a force of soldiers to guarantee her safety. Otto I believed the lie and dispatched a part of his army together with the leading men of his realm, with the result that the Romans ambushed the Germans, killing some while taking others captives. After which the Romans exploited their victory by destroying several forts while killing and capturing even more. The prisoners were dispatched to Nikêforos at Constantinople. The Romans fled before the Germans could mount a counter-attack and then reported to the emperor what they had done.[103] It is very likely that this ruse had been pre-planned by Nikêforos and his staff, because this involved the use of an imperial princess and diplomacy in the stratagem. It was an apt revenge for the lies of Dominicus the Venetian and the surprise invasion of Roman territory by Otto I, and a brilliant example of generalship.

The Salerno Chronicle offers us a more detailed account of these events. The Siege of Bovino ended just as badly for the Ottonians. The first sally by the Roman garrison was defeated, but when the Romans repeated it, Pandulf fell from his horse twice and was taken prisoner, with the result that his forces were routed. Some of the fugitives fled towards Benevento while others fled towards Spoleto. The small force that had been dispatched by Gisulf, Duke of Salerno, to help Pandulf learnt of the defeat and immediately turned back. The Roman patrician and *katepanô* Eugenios dispatched Pandulf and other important prisoners to Constantinople, after which he invaded the Lombard Duchy of Benevento and advanced up to Avellino (south of Benevento). The terrified inhabitants surrendered. Then the victorious Roman army marched to Capua, now without its duke, which they then placed under siege while ravaging the surrounding regions. Marinus, the Duke of Naples, joined the Roman *stratêgos* to demonstrate his loyalty to the Roman *basileus*. The Neapolitans and Romans then proceeded to pillage the plain, massacre people, and burn villages. They gathered a massive amount of booty and prisoners.[104]

The *patrikios* Eugenios, together with a small retinue, visited Salerno for a few days where the local prince Gisulf treated him as befitted a representative of the *basileus*. Gisulf had now changed his allegiance back to the Roman side. The Roman army then marched through the Duchy of Benevento and captured several fortresses, but did not proceed against Benevento itself which was guarded by the sons of Pandulf and Archbishop Landolf, while the wife of Pandulf was locked inside Capua.[105]

In the meanwhile, Otto I had not stood idle, but had dispatched a large army under Gunther and Siegfrid to exact revenge. They were joined by the forces of the Duchy of Spoleto under their count Sicon. When this army reached Capua, they learnt that the Romans were no longer there but had retreated to Apulia. Therefore, the Ottonians turned their eyes there. In the meanwhile, the patrician Eugenios had been replaced by patrician Abdila. The reasons for Eugenios' dismissal were the complaints made against him. He was dismissed because of his cruelty, which I interpret to mean that he had exacted money from the populace with extremely cruel measures. The Roman army also included Romuald, the brother of Pandulf, who was in Roman service with his Lombard followers and whom we have already met when Liudprand was in Constantinople. The plan was to instal him in the Duchy of his brother, but the plan came to naught, because the Romans under Abdila suffered a crushing defeat in a major battle (this was a major battle in Italian standards, but merely a skirmish by eastern standards) which took place in front of the city of Ascoli. When the two sides arrayed their forces opposite each other, the battle was decided by the attack of the defenders of the city of Ascoli, the Alemanni and Saxons under Conon, who attacked the Romans from behind. The Romans lost 1,500 men killed and fled. Abdila had dispatched a separate *cuneus* under Romuald (clearly a cavalry wedge consisting of Lombard knights) against the Franks and Lombards of Spoleto approaching them under the *comes* Sicon. These were likewise destroyed, with the result that Romuald and many of his men were taken prisoners. None of the Franks were killed in this encounter. The only casualty on their side was one Lombard from Spoleto. This was a complete victory. The *katepanô* Abdila fled and abandoned the countryside of Apulia for the Ottonians to pillage, with the result that many of its villages decided to pay tribute to Otto I. In spring 970 the German Kaiser marched to Campania himself and attacked the Neapolitan territory in revenge for their support of *basileus* and then joined the rest of his forces, but just as before the Germans were unable to capture any of the Roman strongholds.[106]

This has taken us beyond the limits of this study. Here it suffices to note that the war between the two Christian Empires was finally solved by the change of policy by the new emperor Tzimiskês, who first decided to send Pandulf back as a gesture of his goodwill, followed by the negotiations that would eventually bring peace when the princess Theofanô was sent to Italy to be the wife of Otto II. A fuller account of the preceding wars will be offered in the forthcoming biography of Otto I the Great, while a fuller account of the changed policies under Tzimiskês will be offered in the forthcoming biography dealing with him. It should be noted, however, that it is unlikely for the more conciliatory stance of Tzimiskês to have worked without the casualties caused by Nikêforos' more bellicose stance, as had Nikêforos agreed to the propositions of Otto I after the latter had fooled him with a stratagem while invading Roman territory, it is unlikely that he could have kept the entire southern portion in Roman hands.

8.15. The Assassination of Nikêforos Fôkas on 11 December 969[107]

When Nikêforos received the news of the conquest of Antioch on 8 November 969, the cabal to assassinate him had already been formed and included at least Theofanô, the wife of Nikêforos, and Basileios the *parakoimômenos*, both of whom could plot together in secret in the palace without the interference of others. They had a common father, so it was only natural for them to communicate with each other.

There are several different versions of what really happened, as is usual when there was a conspiracy to assassinate the head of state that led to the murder of the target. The likeliest versions are those that are detailed by the Roman sources as they had better access to the news within their own realm so I will concentrate my analysis on those, beginning with the long account of Leo the Deacon, which is also included in the text of Skylitzes as one possible alternative.

When Nikêforos then publicly expressed his thanks to God for the fall of Antioch, a hermit monk gave Nikêforos a letter, which he read after the monk had departed. The letter warned the emperor that there was a plot to kill him. When Nikêforos then ordered a search for the monk, he was not found. If true, this would imply that someone privy to the plot to murder the emperor had consulted some member of the religious establishment, possibly because he or she felt anxiety about the prospect of committing such a sin. However, it should be remembered that the monkish habit could also have been a disguise. It was approximately at the same time that Nikêforos received another, even more distressing piece of news. His father Bardas died at the age of 90 years. The emperor took this blow very hard and mourned openly. The corpse of Bardas was escorted from the palace to his home, located at the Harbour of Sofia, where he was laid to rest in a coffin.

After a few days had passed and the sorrow had abated the empress Theofanô exploited this by approaching the emperor in private. She petitioned on behalf of Iôannês Tzimiskês with the pretext that it was wrong to keep in idleness a man who was a brave and skilled commander and his own nephew. As an additional excuse, Theofanô reminded Nikêforos that Iôannês' first wife Maria Sklêraina, the sister of Bardas Sklêros, had recently died so that he also needed a new wife from a noble family. If true, this statement was obviously meant to remove possible jealous thoughts from the mind of the emperor – he could have easily thought that Theofanô had sexual desires towards Iôannês, who was younger and a more vigorous man and who was also known as a womaniser and a glutton. On the basis of the sources she appears to have had far greater sexual drive than her husband who was significantly older than her and who followed a deeply religious lifestyle and who enjoyed the austere Spartan lifestyle of a soldier.[108] To her he must have appeared as a bore. To put it simply, Theofanô was only 28 years old and ravishingly beautiful, while her husband was a fifty-seven-year-old man who had developed a belly and who appears not to have had a similar sex drive to his younger spouse thanks to his austere lifestyle and age. Theofanô wanted a younger and more vigorous lover, and she thought that she had found him in the young nephew of Nikêforos Fôkas. It was because of this that all of the sources call her an adultress.

According to Leo the Deacon, Theofanô used her female wiles to convince the emperor to recall Iôannês Tzimiskês because Nikêforos was completely smitten by her beauty, so Nikêforos was always ready to grant her more favours than would have been suitable. Consequently, Nikêforos summoned Iôannês to the capital where he went to meet the emperor from whom he got the order to visit the palace every day. Once there, with the help of the empress, Iôannês was able to visit her quarters secretly and plan the assassination of the emperor. It is also obvious that the empress would have used her womanly wiles to convince Iôannês at this stage, because Iôannês was known to be suspectible to the pleasures of the flesh. It is clear that Basileios the *parakoimômenos* was present for at least some of these meetings. According to Leo the Deacon, Iôannês periodically dispatched strong and vigorous soldiers who were housed in a secret room by the empress. The men were dispatched one at a time to the secret room so that outside observers would not be alarmed by the presence of a group of armed men. On the basis of Skylitzes' text, there were three men in the room, one of whom was Atzypotheodôros, a man known to be very loyal to Tzimiskês.

On 10 December 969 Iôannês Tzimiskês convinced Michaêl Bourtzês (as noted he had a personal grudge against Nikêforos) and Leôn Pediasimos to join him. The existence of the plot, however, had been exposed. At vespers (sundown), a priest of the imperial court handed a note to the emperor, which stated that there was a plot to kill him tonight and that he should order the women's quarters searched for armed men. It is therefore clear that the priest had either heard what the empress had been discussing with others, or had seen the armed men in her quarters. When Nikêforos read the note, he ordered the eunuch chamberlain (*koitonitês*) Michaêl to make a search of women's quarters. Leo the Deacon suspects that Michaêl failed to search the room where the men were because of negligence or because of undue respect towards the empress. It is also possible that this Michaêl was also party to the plot, just like the eunuch Basileios. It was because of this that Basileios had feigned illness so that he would not be present at the palace when the murder took place. When night then fell, the empress went to see the emperor as usual and stated that she would visit the maidens recently dispatched from Bulgaria for her sons, after which she would return back to the bed of the emperor so he should leave the door unlocked. Nikêforos was fooled. The emperor then started his usual nightime routine, which involved prayers to God Almighty and reading of the Holy Bible. When his wife was late, he fell asleep on the floor upon the leopardskin and scarlet felt cloth surrounded by the holy icons of Christ, Theotokos, and of the Holy Forerunner and Herald presumably used in praying.

The Palace of the Boukoleon (source: Sclumberger)

In the meanwhile, the retainers of Iôannês had emerged from the secret room and were waiting for his arrival. They were eagerly watching for his arrival from the balcony of the second floor of the palace. On the fifth hour of the water clock (5.00 am), 11 December 969, when a vicious north wind was blowing and snow was falling heavily, the men saw Iôannês and his accomplices arriving in a small boat. The men disembarked in front of the Palace of Boukoleon (see the Imperial Palace map in the map section, with the accompanying drawing) and whistled to the retainers to lower the basket. The retainers hauled the men up to the balcony and then all together entered the imperial bedchamber through the unlocked door with their swords drawn. When the men found the bed to be empty they were petrified with horror, until a eunuch dispatched by the empress pointed out where the emperor was, after which they surrounded him – as already noted the emperor had fallen asleep and had not returned to the bed. The men woke up the emperor by kicking him. When Nikêforos then lifted his head and rested it against his elbow, the *taxiarchês* Leôn Balantês (Abalantês in Skylitzes) hit him with a sword, wounding his brow and eyelid, but without reaching his brain. Nikêforos shouted 'Help me, O Theotokos!', but to no avail as he was dragged before Iôannês who sat on the imperial bed. Lêon claims that it was because of the sword cut that Nikêforos had lost his gigantic strength, but it is at least equally plausible to think that when surprised in this manner Nikêforos lost his nerve with the result that he fell on the floor and could not even rise to his knees.

Tzimiskês is then claimed to have accused his uncle Nikêforos of being an ungrateful tyrant who owed him the throne, while claiming to be a better commander than he. Nikêforos was panicky and only kept on calling on the Mother of God for assistance when Iôannês then grasped him by the beard while his collaborators smashed his teeth with their sword handles, after which followed further mugging and torture until they became bored. It was then that Iôannês kicked Nikêforos in the chest and delivered a strong powerful cut with his sword that went right through his skull, after which Iôannês ordered the other men to use their swords too so that all of them would be equally guilty of murder. The men did as commanded and cut, slashed and hacked. One of the men thrust an *akoufion* from behind so that it went right through and emerged from Nikêforos's breast. Leo the Deacon describes the *akoufion* as a long iron weapon that resembled a heron's beak, in that it had a moderate curve that ended in a sharp point. This is clearly a description of a sabre, because Leo the Deacon previously stated that the men entered the bedchamber with their swords drawn.[109] Nikêforos had died at the age of fifty-seven.

Once the murder had been committed, Tzimiskês walked to the Chrysotriklinos where he put the scarlet boots on his feet and sat on the throne and started delivering orders to make sure that Nikêforos' other relatives would not be able to rise against him. It was at this moment that the bodyguards of Nikêforos rushed to the scene and attempted to open the iron gates to save their ruler. When Tzimiskês learnt of this, he ordered Nikêforos' head cut off and shown to the men. Atzypotheodôros cut off the head and showed it to the onlookers. When the bodyguards saw the head, they dropped their swords in despair and proclaimed Tzimiskês emperor. According to *Akolouthia* (Stichera, 62ff.), the murderers then threw Nikêforos' head under the bed and then kicked it around for sport. Nikêforos' corpse lay on the snow until late in the evening of 11 December 969, after which it was laid to rest in a wooden coffin and secretly buried in the middle of the night at the Holy Church of the Apostles in the same sarcophagus where Kônstantinos Megas (Constantine I the Great) was resting.

However, before this took place, Tzimiskês had to secure his throne with a series of measures. When the murder had been committed, Basileios *parakoimômenos* arrived at the palace bringing with him his armed corps of men, which had been 3,000 strong in 963 so it is probable that it was at least equally strong now. The purpose behind this was to secure the palace complex against possible attack by soldiers loyal to Nikêforos and his brother Leôn. Tzimiskês was then duly enthroned by Basileios at the age of 47.

When the sun rose a select corps of men, together with Basileios *parakoimômenos* and the young emperors Basileios II and Kônstantinos VIII, marched through the streets proclaiming Iôannês Tzimiskês emperor to make it clear to everyone that the power was now securely in their hands. At the same time, they appear to have declared that all signs of unrest such as looting would be punishable by death, which brought the desired result: the people did not begin rioting.

Leo the Deacon claims that while all this had been happening Leôn Fôkas had been asleep at home. Leo the Deacon accuses Leôn Fôkas of losing his wits, because he fled to Hagia Sofia. In Leo the Deacon's opinion, Leôn Fôkas had huge amounts of gold that he should have used to bribe the populace and the field army billeted in the capital, which he could then have led against Tzimiskês. In Leo the Deacon's opinion, had he acted in this manner immediately he would have succeeded because all the men in office had been appointed into these positions by Nikêforos. Leo the Deacon is undoubtedly correct in his judgement. It is because of this that Tzimiskês immediately removed from their posts the *praitor* (praetor), *drouggarios tou ploimou*, and *drouggarios tês biglas* and replaced them with his own. The relatives of Nikêforos were also exiled to their own estates. Iôannês Tzimiskês also promised safety to Leôn Fôkas and his son Nikêforos, and they came out of Hagia Sofia, after which they were exiled to Methymna in Lesbos. In addition to this, Tzimiskës removed from office all *toparchai* and replaced those with his own men, which in this case presumably means the *stratêgoi* of the *themata* and other important provincial officials. Bardas, the son of Leôn Fôkas, who had the title of *doux* of Chaldia, was dimissed and exiled to Amaseia.

Skylitzes preserves for us several other versions of the murder. According to the first version, it was Theofanô who had stopped sexual relations with her husband and that she sent one of Tzimiskês' associates to call him to the capital to meet her. She (called adultress by Skylitzes presumably for a good reason) also gave the man letters which gave Tzimiskês permission to leave his estates. When Tzimiskês had reached Chalcedon, someone asked the emperor if he would be allowed to enter Constantinople, to which the emperor answered that he should wait for a while. However, on 11 December the empress brought him to the capital and had him lifted to the palace in a basket. Tzimiskês was accompanied by Michaêl Bourtzês, Leôn Abalantês (Balantês), Atzypotheodôros and two others. They did not find the emperor in his bed but on the floor, on the mattress of scarlet-dyed felt and bearskin that his uncle Michaêl Maleinos, the monk, had slept on. The rest of the account is by and large similar to the one in Leo the Deacon. Skylitzes then notes that there were some who claimed that ten days before the murder he found a letter in his chamber which warned that Tzimiskês was plotting against him, and that in the evening that he was murdered a priest gave him a letter which warned him of the plot that was to take place the same night. Some of these sources stated that the emperor did not read the letter because he thought, wrongly, that it was a petition, while others claimed that he read it but did not react to it, or that he read it and ordered his *protobestiarios* to check out if there were reasons to worry. There were also still others that claimed that before his death Nikêforos had actually sent an order for his brother Leôn Fôkas to collect his men and rush to the palace immediately, but Leôn had not read the message immediately because he was playing dice, with the result that he read it too late. When Leôn then arrived with his men and reached the western side of the Hippodrome he heard men acclaiming Tzimiskês as emperor, at which point he lost his nerve and together with his son fled to Hagia Sofia. Skylitzes perceptively notes that he did not know which of the versions was correct. All that was certain was that Nikêforos died and that he was assassinated.[110]

Thus the life of a great Roman emperor came to an end. It was a rare occasion for an emperor to die in bed – even if Nikêforos did almost die in bed. What happened next will be told in a biography devoted to Iôannês Tzimiskês, the hammer of the Russians and Fatimids.

Chapter Nine

Nikêforos II Fôkas: The Saint and Bearer of Victory

The best way to assess the achievements of Nikêforos as emperor is to begin with the assessment of Leo the Deacon (5.8), as he was a contemporary of Nikêforos and therefore in a position to know how period Romans saw him.

According to Leo the Deacon, Nikêforos was superior to anyone of his era in bravery and physical strength. He was an experienced, tenacious, unyielding and vigorous military commander who had not been spoiled by physical pleasures and corruption. He was an impartial judge of men and a good legislator. He followed to the letter the religious ascetic lifestyle, praying regularly while also observing to the letter the demands of all-night standing vigils and the singing of religious hymns. According to Leo the Deacon, most of the people considered the last mentioned a weakness, because Nikêforos also demanded similar from those around him, and this must indeed have been a nuisance to those who did not follow a similarly religious lifestyle. It is probable that this was one of the reasons for his death, because his second wife Theofanô appears to have been one of those who were alienated by this behaviour.

The motivation behind this lifestyle is not certain. It was either because Nikêforos enjoyed it as a roughshod soldier and pretended that it was because of the demands of religion that he acted like he did and that he did this in order to instill a more sober lifestyle in others, or it was because he really believed in the power of rituals and prayers – the latter is more likely. Nikêforos was also extremely harsh towards wrongdoers and criminals, which annoyed those who wanted to follow a more corrupt and luxurious lifestyle. The sole exceptions to the impartiality of Nikêforos as judge were his soldiers, who were allowed to abuse civilians and his brother Lêon and father Bardas, because Nikêforos needed their support. Nikêforos was a soldier emperor, just like the likes of Septimius Severus had been.

The devotion to Christianity and an austere lifestyle could indeed be a weakness, and undoubtedly was, because it made Nikêforos blind to the use of the weaknesses of others for his own benefit, because all he could think of was to punish this behaviour. However, my personal view as a historian is that this devotion to Christianity and a sober lifestyle were the real secrets behind the great achievements of Nikêforos, because when these were coupled with his exceptional intellect and military ability, the combination brought unprecedented military successes. Nikêforos was an authoritarian man with an unyielding character who sought to crush the Saracens step by step until he could liberate Jerusalem from them. Leo the Deacon's judgement was that had not malevolent fortune brought an end to this man's life, the Roman Empire would have attained greater glory than ever before.[1] I agree with this view, because even though Iôannês Tzimiskês was one of the best commanders of all time, he lacked the singular drive of Nikêforos. Iôannês Tzimiskês was a man devoted to the pleasures of life, which he also demonstrated with his spendthrift habits and artistic attention to everything around him. Nikêforos had hoarded money for the purpose of increasing the size of his armed forces, which was no longer possible after Tzimiskês started wasting money while diminishing the tax revenue, both of which he did in order to secure his position as usurper. For a more detailed analysis of this, see my forthcoming biography of him.

It had also been this monastic lifestyle that had endeared Nikêforos to the soldiers. Unlike his father, he did not loot the money or lands that the soldiers considered their own. The trust and loyalty of his soldiers brought him military success. Nikêforos obviously owed his military career to his father and then the rise to the imperial position in 963 to those men like Tzimiskês who then refused to betray him, but it is still clear that without his great skills as a military commander, with the ability to retain the loyalty of his men and officers, this would not have been possible.

It was thanks to his strict Christian lifestyle, incorruptibility, Hercules-like personal strength, personal fighting skills with weapons, outstanding abilities as a commander, together with repeated demonstrations of the *coup d'oeil* so necessary for a good commander in the midst of combat that Nikêforos was able to install harsh discipline and training schemes among his forces, which in their turn enabled his soldiers to perform the orders given by him. Unlike his father, Nikêforos was universally adored by his soldiers and it was this that enabled him to achieve greatness. Nikêforos knew this and sought to retain their trust by every means possible, because his own position depended on their support.

Nikêforos had already demonstrated his great military talents as a *stratêgos* of the Anatolikon, of which we know next to nothing except that he was highly successful (see Appendix 2 with Chapter 7.5), but once in charge of the entire Roman armed forces as *domestikos tôn scholôn* he also demonstrated his skills as a skilled schemer and military reformer. Nikêforos' first action as a *domestikos* was to undermine the loyalty of the enemy's best forces, the Turkish *ghilman*, with bribes. This resulted in a serious weakening of Sayf ad-Dawla's position. Nikêforos also simplified the equipment and campaign tactics of the invading armies, while also making changes to the equipment and composition of the *katafraktoi* wedge and cavalry formation (see Appendices 1 and 3). The principal goal of Nikêforos was to increase the size of his army so that the field armies would possess a significant numerical advantage over the enemy. In short, when Nikêforos was still a mere *domestikos tôn scholôn* he also sought to increase the size of the army by enrolling landlubbers into the army while lowering the equipment demands so that it was acceptable to use ersatz equipment such as quilted armour instead of metal armour (see Appendix 3). Once he became emperor he introduced legislation (see Chapter 8.5) that demanded a greater contribution of men from the military lands, with the idea of increasing the size of his army to such an extent that it would be possible to defeat the enemy in pitched battles while also garrisoning conquered land with soldiers. This policy primarily increased the numbers of Roman regular cavalry and *katafraktoi*, because the conversion of formerly naval soldiers into infantry did not replace the numbers of infantry converted into regular cavalry. Nikêforos sought to correct this discrepancy by luring more Armenians into Roman territory so that these could be used as infantry in the newly-conquered provinces. Nikêforos was himself highly prejudiced against the Armenians (see Appendix 2), but still considered their services essential for the success of his project to enlarge the Roman Empire.

As stated by Liudprand, Nikêforos trusted more in quantity than in the quality of his forces. In other words, Nikêforos primarily sought to increase the numbers of his thematic forces rather than the number of tagmatic forces. The results speak for themselves. The use of massive armies brought results. The Muslims were pushed far away from the former border and Nikêforos was poised to continue the campaign up to Jerusalem and probably even further at the time of his death. However, thanks to his untimely death, the newly-conquered provinces in Cilicia, Phoenicia and Coelo-Syria were still not fully secured, and according to Skylitzes (15.3) were planning to revolt against Roman rule. The new ruler, Tzimiskês, had to solve this issue immediately, because in the meanwhile the Fatimids had managed to assemble a massive army of Jihadists who were moving north. For this, see my forthcoming biography of Tzimiskês.

However, on the other fronts the situation was less favourable to the Romans. As stated by Skylitzes (15.3), the risky decision to use Russians against the Bulgarians had backfired in that they had now settled on Bulgarian territory. On the plus side was the fact that now the Bulgarians were really on the same side as the Romans, with two imperial princesses at the Roman court groomed to be wives of Basileios II and Kônstantinos VIII. Furthermore, at the time of the death of Nikêforos, the Pechenegs, whose services Nikêforos had probably bought, were invading Russian territory so that the Russians had actually evacuated Bulgaria. In Italy Nikêforos had lost Sicily to the Fatimids. At the time of his death, he was also at war with the Ottonian German Reich on the Italian mainland, but it is clear that the Romans had caused at least as much damage to their enemies as had been caused to them. Furthermore, the war with the Germans was not the fault of the emperor but the fault of Otto I, who had fooled Nikêforos with conciliatory gestures only to invade Roman Italy by surprise. Nikêforos proceeded to exact a high price from the Germans for their duplicity with duplicity of his own, but his forces had been unable to deliver the killing blow to the enemy thanks to the poor combat performance of his Lombard ally Romuald. At the time of the death of the emperor, the two sides were stalemated in Italy, because the Germans were unable to capture Roman fortresses while the Romans were unable to defeat the Germans on the battlefield. To achieve that would have required the sending of a new, larger force under a competent commander to complete the mission.

In the field of domestic and religious policies, Nikêforos was a man who sought to gain complete control over both the populace and the Church so that he could tax both effectively in order to increase the size of the armed forces and reward the soldiers royally to retain their loyalty. This meant the tightening of taxation and persistent famine among the commoners thanks to the crop losses caused by heat waves in successive years. The emperor could have alleviated the distress by spending adequate amounts of money for lowering the price of corn and wheat, but Nikêforos was unwilling to do that.

Nikêforos' religious policy was harsh towards the established Church. He had his own ideas and was not prepared to tolerate any opposition. Nikêforos aimed to gain complete control over the Church and so had exiled all bishops who opposed his decisions while ensuring that all new appointments into bishoprics were made by him, while he confiscated Church property for the support of his armed forces. These policies brought money to the imperial coffers which in their turn funded Nikêforos' campaigns, but these policies were obviously opposed because Nikêforos interfered in religious matters which were not considered to belong in his sphere, while increasing famine when he refused to spend adequate amount of money for the famine relief. Both 'abuses' were corrected by Tzimiskês, who lowered taxation in

Above left: Nikêforos Fôkas entering Constantinople in 963 painted after Skylitzes.
Right: Nomisma depicting Nikêforos Fôkas with Basileios II. Source: Schlumberger.

particular for religious establishments, while from international markets he bought an adequate amount of food for the populace (Skylitzes 15.2–3). The downside of this policy was that it diminished the prospects of further conquests, because there were no longer as many soldiers available for the securing of the new conquests. Therefore, it is very likely that Nikêforos would have expanded the Roman Empire further than Tzimiskês was able to accomplish, but this would have come at the expense of the well-being of the common man, the subjects of the emperor.

Nikêforos is also considered to be a Saint in the Orthodox Church, and the monks of Mount Athos commemorate his sainthood every 11 December. This is obviously a form of thanks by the monks of Mt. Athos for the great services of Nikêforos towards that monastery.

In sum, Nikêforos Fôkas proved to be the man who opened the Muslim-held fortified border zone for Roman reconquest, and by following his uncompromisingly imperialistic policies the reconquest would have undoubtedly progressed far further than it did. Nikêforos deserves to be classed among the greatest military leaders of all ages, so we should add the epithet 'Great' to his name, as follows, *Megas Nikêforos*. Nikêforos means the Bearer of Victory and he certainly lived up to his name.

Left: a depiction of the impact of a cataphract charge on two lines of Muslim infantry. Author's drawing.

Below: Bardas Sklêros with a mace. Source: Skylitzes, Public domain.

Appendix I

New Battle Formations in the *Sylloge Tacticorum*

1. The *stratiôtai* of the *themata* (ST 36–7)[1]

Just like in the *Taktika*, Leôn's instructions in the *Sylloge tacticorum* were primarily aimed at the *stratêgoi* of the *themata*. It was because of this that we find him quoting his own words from the *Taktika* (*ST* 36 = *LT* 4.1). The descriptions of the period equipment and battle formations were therefore those that Leôn intended his thematic forces to use. The following discussion concentrates mainly on the new battle tactics introduced, so it does not deal with every matter discussed: for example, the newer version of the marching camp which was based on the use of the infantry hollow square as its basis is discussed in the introduction.

According to Leôn's *Sylloge tacticorum*, the heavy armed *stratiôtai* of the *themata* were expected to be wealthy and heavily armoured. The companions/associates of the *stratiôtês* were expected to take care of the estate and farming when the *stratiôtês* was performing his military duties. The *stratiôtai* were not yet as impoverished as they were later in the century.

2. Infantry Equipment (ST 37–8)

The *oplitai* were equipped with large shields (square with the bottom narrowing, and triangular shields 140.4 cm in height; circular 81.9cm); *dorata*-spears (sing. *dory*, 3.74–4.7 m); *menaulia* (3–4m long very thick spear);[2] 0.936m long *parameria*-swords (sing. *paramerion*, a double- or single-edged sword slung from the waistbelt). For protection they wore *lôrikia* (sing. *lôrikion*, mail or scale armour); *klibania* (sing. *klibanion*, lamellar) or *kabadia* with sleeves (sing. *kabadion*) made of cotton or coarse silk reaching the knees; arm-guards (*cheiropsella, manikellia*) made of iron, wood or leather; greaves (*podopsella, chalkotouba*) made of iron, wood or leather; plumed helmets that covered the face; and plumes attached on top of the shoulders. This was the equipment that the wealthier members of the *themata* were expected to wear when assigned for infantry duty and was undoubtedly true when service in the *skoutatoi* was still restricted to these. As we shall see, when Nikêforos Fôkas required more from each class of *stratiôtai*, the equipment requirements for the *skoutatoi/oplitai* were diminished, because he required those who had previously served as *skoutatoi* to be enrolled in the non-cataphract cavalry.

The 'medium infantry' *peltastai* of the *Sylloge tacticorum* (38.6–7) were equipped with: round shields (ca. 70cm) or oblong shields (ca. 93.6cm); armour (*lôrikia, klibania*) made from iron or horn, the *kabadia* being once again the ersatz armour; helmets not covering the face; *parameria, dorata* 3.74–4.7m in length; 'javelins' (*akontia, riptaria*) with a length of ca. 2.5–8m.

The *psiloi* were basically equipped in the same manner both in the *Sylloge tacticorum* and the *Taktika*. The *psiloi* had bows, and quivers (30 or 40 arrows per quiver) hanging from the shoulder, two bow-strings, together with arrow-guides and small bows. The *psiloi* were also equipped with javelins, very small shields, *parameria*-swords (waist-held swords) or with axes, while some had slings. Their tunics were to reach their knees and their shoes were to be moderately hobnailed.

3. Infantry formation (ST 45)

The new infantry formation in the *Sylloge tacticorum* was based on the same concepts as the traditional Greco-Roman phalanx, so the infantry force of over 24,000 footmen had four divisions of *aspidoforoi* (shield-bearers, i.e. *skoutatoi, oplitai*) and armies less than that fewer.

The largest variant in the *Sylloge tacticorum* consisted of 24,100 footmen (or more?). In front were four *tagmata* of *prokoursatôres* (4 x 1,000 light infantry *psiloi* = 4,000), deployed either as a straight line equal in length to the four *tagmata* of *aspidoforoi* following them or as triangles/wedges.

A bowshot (ca. 330 m) behind the *prokoursatôres* followed the four *tagmata* of *aspidoforoi*, each consisting of about 4,888 men, but with 22 men (*bandofylakes*-flag-guards, messengers and medical corpsmen)[3] being detailed for other duties meaning that 4,866 remained (3,650 *aspidoforoi*, 1,216 *psiloi*) for a total of 19,464 men. This array therefore had 88 supernumeraries. The intervals between the four *tagmata* were ca. 30 metres. The *stratêgos* with his fifty-man unit of *defensôres/bandofylakes* stood in the middle interval. These *tagmata* were deployed sixteen deep, and the first four and the last four ranks always consisted of the *aspidoforoi* while the men in the middle were the *psiloi* and remaining *aspidoforoi*. This made it possible for the formation to face attacks from both directions. If the enemy approached from the rear the *tagmata* were divided into a double phalanx so that the rear of the formation marched ca. 225m behind the first.[4] The baggage train was placed behind the four *tagmata* of *aspidoforoi*, while the 500 *opisthofylakes* rear guards (125 *aspidoforoi*, 375 *psiloi*) were placed a bowshot behind the four *tagmata* of the *aspidoforoi* – with the implication that the baggage train was within this same range just in front of the rear guards.

The tactical scheme envisaged was that the *prokoursatôres* would first discharge their missiles, after which they withdrew through the intervals of the *aspidoforoi tagmata* if the enemy had withstood this so that they then assumed position

New Battle Formations in the *Sylloge Tacticorum* 355

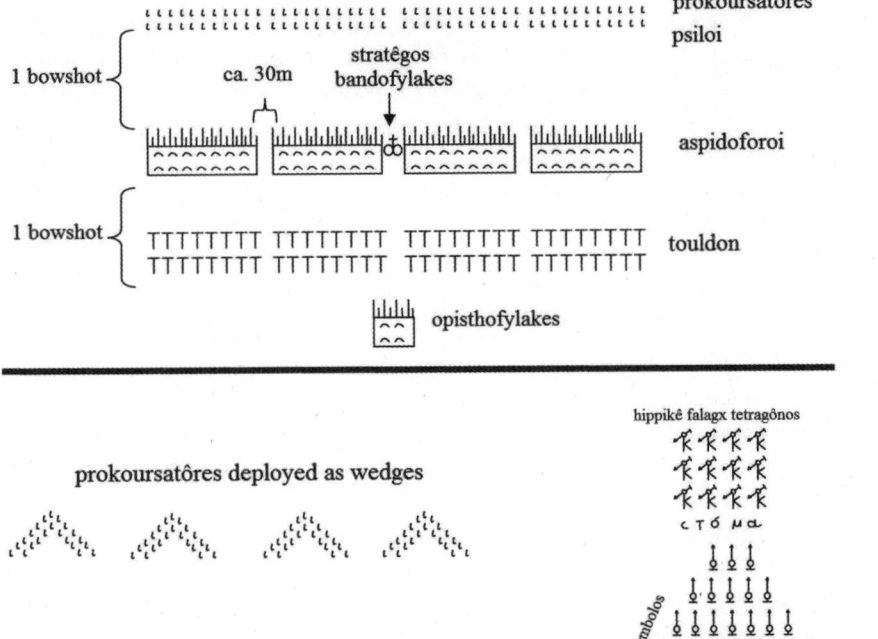

behind it. Depending on the situation, all of the infantry *tagmata*, including the *prokoursatôres* and *aspidoforoi*, could be expected to fight in irregular *drouggos* order, open order (extended width) and in the shields interlocking order (*syskouton*), using the *maza*-order (massed sphere/*drouggos*) for ambushes against the enemy. The referral to the use of the extended front and use of the massed *drouggoi* in this context means that Leôn expected the infantry to conduct outflanking attacks, especially in difficult terrain. The wedge/triangle of *psiloi* (in this case the men used the *menaulia*-spears) posted in front of the actual infantry phalanx was also used for the breaking of the enemy cavalry charge (*ST* 47.16). If the enemy attacked with great force it was expected that the infantry assumed the *syskouton* (shields interlocked) order which was also called *chêlônê* (tortoise) and assumed the round or hollow-square formation for defence.[5]

If the infantry army consisted of 10,100 (presumably from ca. 10,100 up to 24,000) infantry, then the *aspidoforoi* were divided into three *tagmata* (*mere*), each consisting of 2,162 men, for a total of 6,484 men (1,620 *psiloi*, 4,866 *aspidoforoi*) as were the *prokoursatôres* of 3,000 *psiloi*. The rearguard *opisthofylakes* consisted of 500 men (125 *aspidoforoi*, 375 *psiloi*), while the *defensôres* of the *stratêgos* consisted of 50 *bandofylakes*[6], in addition to which came 64 supernumeraries for a total of 10,098 men – plus presumably high-ranking officers.

If the army consisted of up to 6,000 infantry (presumably from ca. 6,000 up to 10,000), then the *aspidoforoi* were divided into two 1,500-man strong (375 *psiloi*, 1,125 *aspidoforoi*) *tagmata* with a depth of ten ranks (front and rear consisting of the *aspidoforoi*) for a total of 3,000 footmen, while the *prokoursatôres* consisted of three 800-strong *tagmata* of *psiloi* for a total of 2,400 for the entire vanguard. The *opisthofylakes* consisted of 400 men (100 *aspidoforoi*, 300 *psiloi*), and the *defensôres* of the *stratêgos* of 50 *oplitai*. In addition to this, there were 64 supernumeraries.

If the army consisted of 3,116 footmen, then the *aspidoforoi* were divided into two 700-strong *tagmata* (175 *psiloi*, 525 *aspidoforoi*), seven ranks deep, for a total of 1,400 men, while the *prokoursatôres* consisted of three 400-*psiloi tagmata* for a total of 1,200 men. The *opisthofylakes* consisted of 400 men (100 *aspidoforoi*, 300 *psiloi*) and the *defensôres* of the *stratêgos* consisted of 50 *oplitai*, in addition to which there were 64 supernumeraries.

4. Cavalry equipment (ST 39, 43.6–7)

The *Sylloge tacticorum* divided the Roman cavalry into *katafraktoi* (both men and horses fully armoured), *doryforoi* (spear-bearers), and *psiloi* (light-armed), consisting of the *akontistai* (javelineers) and *toxotai* (archers).

The *epanôklibana* (a surcoat worn over the *klibanion*) with tassels or plumes at the shoulders appears to have been used only when the *katafraktos* used the *klibanion*. In addition to this, the *katafraktos* was protected by an oblong shield measuring 105.3cm in height and presumably about 93.69cm in width because this was the expected file width in close order (*pyknosis*, shields rim-to-rim); arm-guards (*cheiropsella*); greaves (*podopsella*) made of iron, wood or hide; and plumed iron helmets that fully covered the face.

The *katafraktos* was armed with: a *dory*-spear (shaft eight *pêchê* in length, plus a spear head one *pêchus* or possibly more = nine *pêchê* = ca. 4.2m); a double-edged *xifos*-sword (at least 93.6cm long) hanging from the shoulder; and a single-edged *paramerion* hanging from the waist. In addition to this, they were to have a hand axe or iron mace (*siderorabdion*) hanging from the saddle; a bow

(117–125cm in length); a quiver with 30 or 40 arrows; quiver-belts with files, awls, large knives, glue and other necessary things; and two or three saddle-bags containing hardtack or flour. Their horses were armoured with face-(*chamfron*), chest and neck- (*peytral, poitrel* with *flancard, flancois, flanchard* and *crinet*) and flank/crupper- (*crupper, croupiere*) protection of either *lôrikion* or *klibanion*, consisting of either iron or horn. In this case Leôn clearly expected the horses of the *katafraktoi* to be exceptionally well-armoured because his list did not include hide and padded armour as variants.

The *doryforos* was equipped like the *katafraktos*, except that he wore lighter armour (which must have also meant that his helmet lacked a face covering) and his horse lacked armour. His equipment was said to be lighter because he needed more manoeuvrability to attack, retreat and wheel around. On the basis of later sources we can make the guess that the *doryforos* probably wore only a *klibanion* or *lôrikion* (mail or scale armour) and not the limb pieces of the *katafraktos*.[7] The *akontistai* of the cavalry *psiloi* were equipped with two or three javelins (2.8m in length), a 3.74m spear, a helmet and a shield (rectangular 93.6cm in height; round 70.2cm in width). The *psilos toxotês* was equipped with a bow, a sword hanging from the waist, a quiver; and a helmet with 'insufficient' protection. Otherwise his equipment was said to resemble that of the *katafraktos*.

The only group unable to use bows were the *akontistai* that belonged to the *psiloi* cavalry. This shows nicely that the vast majority of the cavalry – the *katafraktoi, doryforoi* and *toxotai* – were all able to use bows if necessary. The tenth-century Romans clearly recognized the importance of archery in period warfare because by the time Nikêforos Fôkas and Nikêforos Ouranos wrote their military treatises, it was recognized that all men without exception should be able to use bows.

5. Contemporary Cavalry Battle Formations (ST 46)

The *Sylloge tacticorum* is the first extant treatise that modifies the tactics that the Romans had practised ever since the sixth-century *Strategikon*. Leôn's intention was clearly to reform the tactics to meet the battlefield demands of his own day. Leôn gives us four different theoretical examples according to the size of the cavalry force, which introduce a number of changes to the cavalry array of the *Strategikon*. As the narrative makes clear, the end result included features which were impractical so Nikêforos Fôkas simplified these. This is not surprising, because Leôn was an armchair general who conceived these new formations in the imperial palace.

The *Sylloge tacticorum* (43.3–4) dictated that the depth of the cavalry formation was always ten ranks when the cavalry force consisted of at least 10,000 horsemen, and five ranks – or at least four ranks – when the army had fewer men. This resembles Maurikios' instructions in the *Strategikon* (12.B.13.5–7.) for the depth of the cavalry formation when it accompanied infantry. Maurikios instructed the cavalry to be deployed ten deep if the cavalry force accompanying infantry was large – in other words over 12,000 horsemen – and five deep if it had fewer men. This shows that similar ideas for the deployment of cavalry were already employed during the Late Roman period.

According to Leôn (*ST* 46, marginal note/*scholion*), the commander of the left was to be more illustrious than the right so that when the army marched through a defile the left wing marched through first followed by the centre and then by the right wing. However, in attack the right wing advanced first.

Leôn's largest exemplary cavalry formation (46.1–25) consisted of 18,570 men[8] (plus 220 supernumeraries) deployed as 23 divisions/*tagmata* (10 larger and 13 smaller). As we have already seen this was not the maximum achievable size, but still a major cavalry army, and even if the instructions in the *Sylloge tacticorum* are clearly meant mainly for the *stratêgoi* of the *themata*, it is still possible to think that the largest variant could also have been employed by the tagmatic forces whenever these were reinforced by some elite thematic forces.

The *tagma* of the *prokoursatôres*/frontrunners (vanguard of the array) consisted of 1,000 horsemen (250 *doryforoi* and 750 *toxotai*) deployed in irregular *drouggos*-order. They were followed by 500 *defensôres*/defenders (400 *doryforoi*, 100 *toxotai*) at a distance of four bowshots (ca. 1,200 m) deployed in close order, with the depth of the formation being five ranks (ranks 1–2 and 4–5 consisted of the *doryforoi*; rank 3 of the *toxotai*). The defenders consisted mainly of the *doryforoi*, because these were steadier in shock combat than the mounted archers. The van was placed two to three miles (one 'Byzantine' mile = 1609.9m; one Roman mile = 1480m; the former is likelier in this case) in front of the main army. The obvious purpose of the vanguard (frontrunners and defenders) was to find, engage/ambush and defeat the enemy, if possible, or at least to skirmish and harass them before retreating.

The *Sylloge tacticorum* divided the first battle line (*promachos taxis*) into three *tagmata* (divisions) of 1,500 men each (1050 *katafraktoi* and *doryforoi*; 450 *psiloi*). The two flank divisions had a frontage of 150 men and a depth of ten men, the front ranks (1–4) and the rear ranks (8–10) consisting of the *katafraktoi* and *doryforoi*, and the ranks in the middle (5–7) consisting of the *toxotai*. In short, it is clear that outer edges of both flank formations consisted of the *katafraktoi*. Just as previously, the front rank *katafraktoi* had the mission of attacking the enemy head on with a perfectly-aligned front, while the archers provided supporting fire with their bows from behind. The flank divisions were deployed in ranks and files which were no longer divided into *koursôres* and *defensôres*. The *prokoursatôres* had now taken the role of the skirmishers. This means that the *Sylloge tacticorum* fundamentally changed the basic inner structure of the cavalry divisions and the way in which these were used in combat. The flank divisions therefore acted like the *defensôres* of Maurikios' *Strategikon* and Leôn's *Taktika*, in that they always attacked using the close order, which they always employed regardless of whether they employed bows or spears. It should be kept in mind that the *katafraktoi* and *doryforoi* also carried bows, which means that both could be used as the situation required, with the implication that the entire force could be considered to have been dual-purpose forces. By stating that the middle ranks from the fifth to seventh were to consist solely of *toxotai*, the *Sylloge tacticorum* (46.4) expected that the entire first line was able to use bows. However, it is still possible that at least sometimes some of the middle ranks of the so-called *toxotai* (ranks 5–7) consisted of the *psiloi* javelin throwers (*akontistai*) rather than of the *toxotai* thanks to the fact that the *Sylloge tacticorum* (39.8–9) makes the allowance that not all of the *psiloi* were able to use the bow.

Leôn placed in the middle of the first line (*promachos taxis*) a cavalry wedge which he called *trigônos taxis* (a triangle array that in truth looked like a trapezium). At this point, the text is almost hopelessly corrupted. Leôn claims (*ST* 46.6) that the first rank of the twelve-ranks-deep wedge consisted of 122 men and the last rank of 116 men (each rank increasing the number by four), so there were in total 1504 horsemen (376 *psiloi/toxotai*, and 1128 *katafraktoi* and *doryforoi*), which is impossible! Harris and Chatzelis (*ST* p.133, n.249) suggest that the text should be emended so that the first rank had 103 men and the last 147 men (each rank increasing the number by four) for a total of 1,500 horsemen. I fully agree with this. The ranks one-to-four and nine-to-twelve consisted of the *katafraktoi*, as did the two files of both flanks, so that the mounted archers were placed in the middle. The rear rank of the wedge was placed on a level with the front rank of the flank divisions so that it formed a wedge in front of the front line. The first-to-fourth ranks consisted of *katafraktoi*, and so did the ranks from nine-to-twelve. The remaining four consisted of both lancers and archers. See the reconstruction on page 364.[9]

In combat, after skirmishing the *prokoursatôres* and their *defensôres* withdrew behind the first line through the intervals on both sides of the wedge, after which the wedge advanced at a full-out gallop against the enemy. The purpose was to crush the enemy formation before the flank divisions would even make contact with the enemy. If the wedge routed the enemy, the *Sylloge tacticorum* (46.9) instructed that the flank *tagmata* were to follow the wedge as its *defensôres*. If the wedge was unsuccessful, then the two flank *tagmata* were to join it, while the second line followed. This implies that the wedge advanced in front of the flanking *tagmata* while the flanking *tagmata* remained behind, and that the pursuit was performed by the wedge in the centre (acting as *koursôres*) in the same manner as had been the case in the ancient Illyrikian Drill of the Late Roman period (MS 6.3).

Nikêforos Fôkas was to reform this entire system in his *Praecepta militaria* (4.13–4): 1) all three units of the first line attacked simultaneously (the previous pattern had clearly allowed the enemy the opportunity of attacking the wedge when the flank *tagmata* remained behind); 2) the *prokoursatôres* formed a protective cordon for the wedge by sending 50 horsemen to its flank to prevent the enemy from harassing it (this was clearly added as an additional counter-measure as a result of the enemy counter-tactic; and 3) the pursuit of the enemy was performed by the two flank *tagmata* and not by the wedge, because in the smaller versions of the array the flank *tagmata* wore lighter equipment so they were better suited to this role. See below with the narrative.

On the right side of the *promachos taxis* were placed the so-called outflankers (*yperkerastai*) that consisted of 200 men (50 *doryforoi* and 150 *psiloi*). Their primary mission was to outflank the enemy array. On the left side of the first line were the so-called flank guards (*plagiofylakes*) that also consisted of 200 men (50 *doryforoi* and 150 *psiloi*). Their primary mission was to protect the left flank. Both were deployed in irregular order.

The *strategôs* was also to deploy two *tagmata* of hidden units (*tôn egkrymmatôn tagmata*)/ambushers (*enedroi*) in irregular order, both consisting of 100 men (15 *doryforoi* and 75 *psiloi*; depth five ranks) arrayed further out in hidden locales. According to the *Sylloge tacticorum*, these hidden units were not only used to outflank and ambush the enemy, but also as an additional protective measure against the possible use of feigned flight by the enemy. The hidden units of ambushers were a survivor from the *Strategikon*. Nikêforos Fôkas (*PM* 2.3, 4.10) removed these as an unnecessary feature, because the *prokoursatôres* and the flank guards and outflankers could already be employed in this fashion.

The *prokoursatôres, defensôres, yperkerastai, plagiofylakes* and the *enedroi* did not have *katafraktoi* amongst their ranks, because they all needed above all speed and manoeuvrability to perform their battlefield functions in the best possible way.

The second line (*taxis deutera*) or support line (*boêthos taxis*) consisted of four large *tagmata*, each 1,500 strong, placed two bowshots behind the first line. The divisions had a width of 150 men and depth of 10 men. Ranks 1–4 and 8–10 consisted of the *katafraktoi* and *doryforoi*, and ranks 5–7 of the *toxotai*. The intervals were filled up with three fill-up *tagmata*, each with a strength of 200 men (50 *doryforoi* and 150 *psiloi*). The fill-up *tagmata* were placed on a level with the last rank of the second line.[10] The *stratêgos* and his staff (*bandoforoi*/flag-bearers; *bandofylakes*/flag guards; and *salpigktai*/trumpet players) also took their place in the interval in the centre. On the basis of the *Sylloge tacticorum* 46.27 and 46.30, it is very likely that the *bandofylakes* consisted of 50 *katafraktoi oplitai* (evidently particularly well-armoured mounted bodyguards).

The principal purpose of the second line was to support the first line in combat. If any of the divisions of the first line had to flee, they were expected to flee into the intervals of the second line where the fill-up *tagmata* received and stopped their retreat while they and the divisions of the support line moved forward against the enemy. If the first line was successful, then the second line followed it to serve as its reserve, so that the *stratêgos* with the two *tagmata* of the second line followed them in an orderly manner (*ST* 46.17). This implies that the flank *tagmata* of the second line were sent forward as pursuers in such situations, or that these had already been used to outflank the enemy as Leôn instructed in the *Taktika* (18.148). The fill-up *tagmata* in the intervals was a survivor from the *Strategikon* that was later phased out by Nikêforos Fôkas, undoubtedly because their presence in the intervals hindered the effective use of the third line in combat.

One bowshot behind the second line followed the third line, called *saka*. It was arrayed exactly like the three *tagmata* of the first line, but if there were not enough

New Battle Formations in the *Sylloge Tacticorum* 361

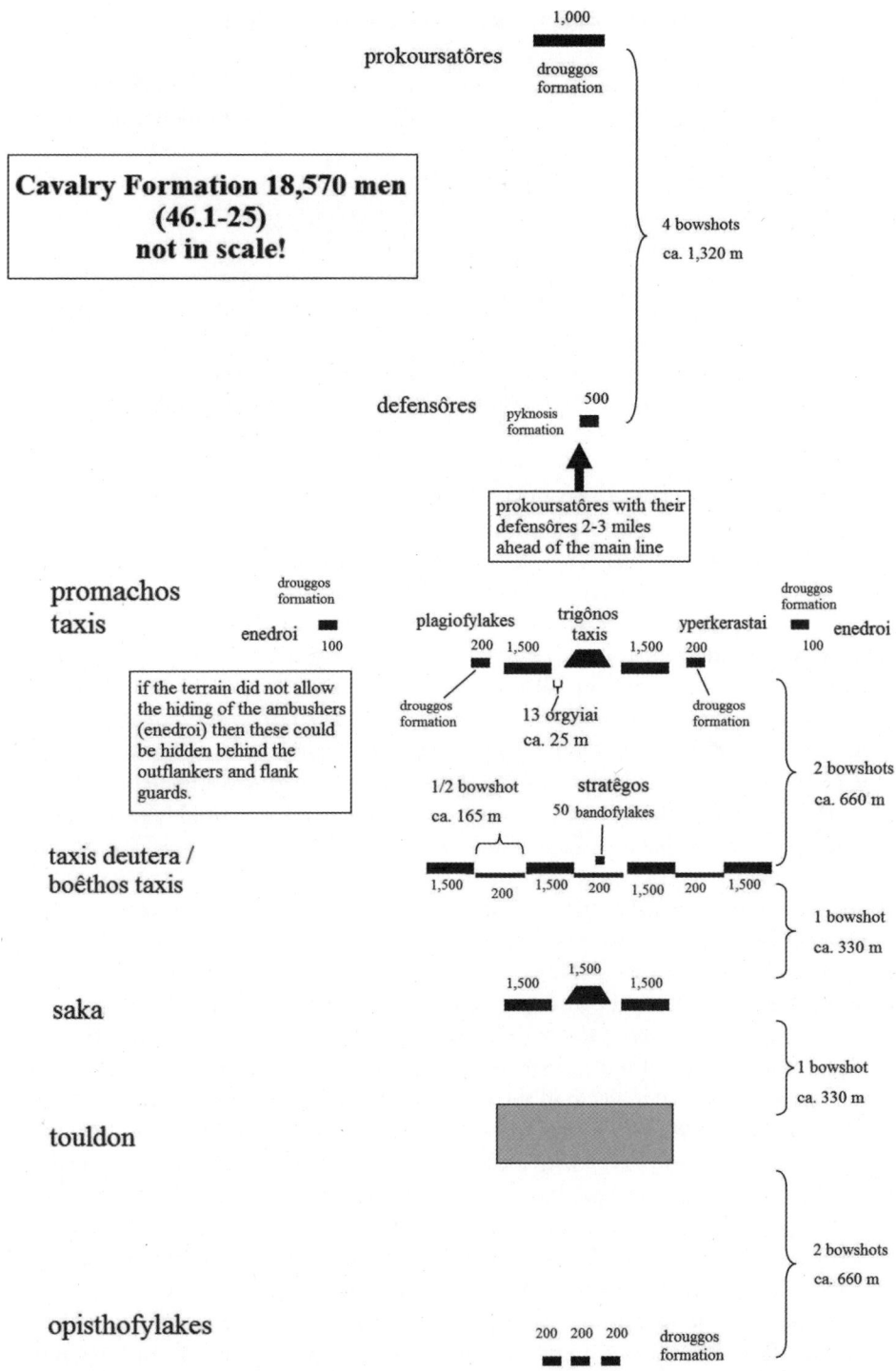

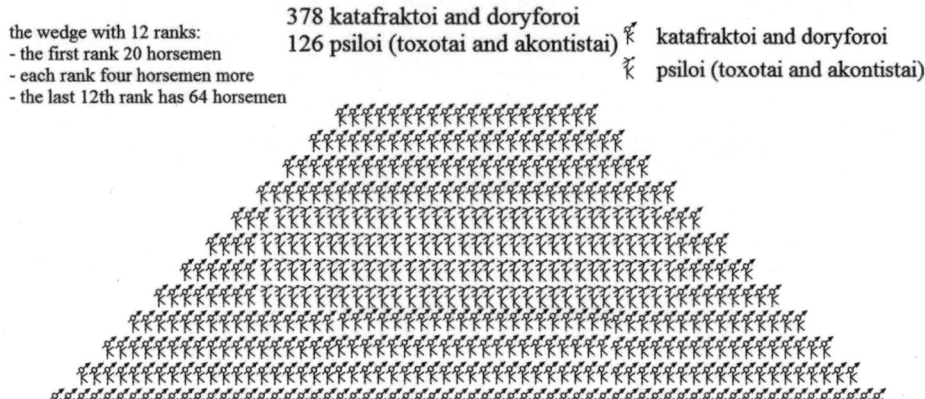

504 horseman wedge of katafraktoi (ST 46.26-9)

the wedge with 12 ranks:
- the first rank 20 horsemen
- each rank four horsemen more
- the last 12th rank has 64 horsemen

378 katafraktoi and doryforoi
126 psiloi (toxotai and akontistai)

𐰅 katafraktoi and doryforoi
𐰅 psiloi (toxotai and akontistai)

katafraktoi available then the centre division was arrayed like the flanks. The third line was called the *saka* after the Arabic *saqah*, which may mean that Leôn copied it from the Arabs, but this is not conclusive because it is possible that the Romans merely borrowed the term from them. I have also suggested that it is possible that the increased Roman use of maces originated from the Turkic peoples, so Nikêforos copied it from the *ghilman*.

The *Sylloge tacticorum* (46.17) mentions the use of the *saka* only in the context of when the enemy had already been defeated, so the *stratêgos* then dispatched the third line in pursuit of the enemy while he together with the two *tagmata* followed them, but it is clear that it acted as a true reserve force in practice that could be sent against the enemy's flanks and rear when necessary, or which could renew the fight if the first line had been defeated, or could be used against enemies approaching from the rear so that the three *tagmata* of *nôtofylakes* acted as a sort of *prokoursatôres* of the rear and retreated between its intervals if they were unable to regroup where the *touldon* (baggage train) was. The later treatises by Nikêforos Fôkas (*PM* 4.15–16) and Nikêforos Ouranos' *Taktika* (61.15–16) explain the circumstances in which the third line was used in combat. These two treatises state that if the enemy also had *katafraktoi* (i.e. the wedge in the middle), the *stratêgos* was to send the *saka* through the intervals of the support line to outflank the enemy. It was this that made the presence of fill-up *tagmata* in the intervals of the support line impractical.[11] It is clear that the *saka* with its wedge of *katafraktoi* gave the *stratêgos* another chance to try to crush the enemy array with a concentrated force of elite soldiers. In sum, the third line was a true multipurpose reserve line and not meant as a rear guard, for which purpose there were an additional three units of rear guards.

The baggage train (*touldon*) followed the *saka* at a distance of one bowshot (ca. 330m). The extreme rear was protected by the three 200-strong (50 *doryforoi* and 150 *psiloi*) *tagmata* of the *opisthofylakes* (rear guards) placed at a distance of two bowshots from the *touldon*. Leôn does not give the rear guards rank and file order, which means that they were always deployed in irregular *drouggos*-order. The guarding of the rear was the duty of the rear guards and the men belonging to the baggage train. The *saka* probably helped them only in emergencies. In addition to this there were 220 supernumeraries drawn from the ten larger *tagmata*, which included the *bandofylakes* of the *stratêgos*, and naturally the men designated to the baggage train, which are not included in the figures.

The second contemporary cavalry formation in the *Sylloge tacticorum* (46.26–31) consisted of 6,770 men arrayed in 23 *tagmata* (10 larger and 13 smaller). The *prokoursatôres* consisted of 334 men (84 *doryforoi* and 250 *psiloi*), behind which were placed their *defensôres* consisting of 166 men (123 *doryforoi* and 43 *psiloi*). The first line consisted of three larger *tagmata*. Its flank divisions, consisting of 500 men (375 *doryforoi* and 125 *psiloi*), were arrayed five ranks deep with a frontage of 100 men each. The wedge in the middle, consisting of 504 men (378 *katafraktoi* and *doryforoi*; 126 *psiloi*), was arrayed 12 ranks deep (first rank 20 men, the last 64 men). On the right were again posted the outflankers (*yperkerastai*), consisting of 100 men (25 *doryforoi* and 75 *psiloi*). On the left were likewise placed the flank guards (*plagiofylakes*), consisting of 100 men (25 *doryforoi* and 75 *psiloi*). Further out were placed the two 100-man (25 *doryforoi* and 75 *psiloi*) hidden units. The second line consisted of four larger *tagmata* that were arrayed five ranks deep with frontages of 100 men each. The three fill-up units in the intervals consisted of 100 men (25 *doryforoi* and 75 *psiloi*) each. As noted above, Nikêforos Fôkas phased these out. The *stratêgos* (general) and his *bandofylakes* (50 *katafraktoi oplitai*) took their place in the middle interval. The *saka* consisted of the two 500-man flank units (depth 5 ranks) and of the 504-man strong triangle. The *opisthofylakes* (rear guards) consisted of three 100-man units. The distances between the units were as previously mentioned. For an illustration of this array of 18,570 men, see page 364.

There are some important differences between the 6,770-man and the 18,570-man army. In the former, the number of *katafraktoi* was reduced so that only the units belonging to the wedges and *bandofylakes* included them. This is likely to be a reflection of the availability of *katafraktoi* in the *themata*. As already noted, the chosen cavalry forces of the *themata* consisted typically only of 3,000 to 4,000 horsemen, which means that an army of 6,770 consisted of the select forces of one of the larger *themata* or combined the cavalry forces of two *themata*. In fact, the small numbers of the *katafraktoi* is our best evidence for the probability that the 6,770-man force consisted solely of the thematic forces – in the case of the fully professional *tagmata* it is clear that there would also have been adequate numbers of *katafraktoi* for the other units. The second of the differences was that the units were arrayed in shallower formation in order to widen its frontage when there were fewer men available.[12] In short, it is clear that the cavalry array of 6,770 men presented the entire armed force of a single large *thema* (a military district under a *stratêgos*), or one reinforced *thema*, or the combined forces of two *themata*.

The third model cavalry formation (46.29–31) consisted of only 3,000 men (1140 *katafraktoi* and *doryforoi*, 1860 *psiloi*) arrayed as 15 *tagmata*, of which three were

364 Nikephoros II Phokas, 912–969

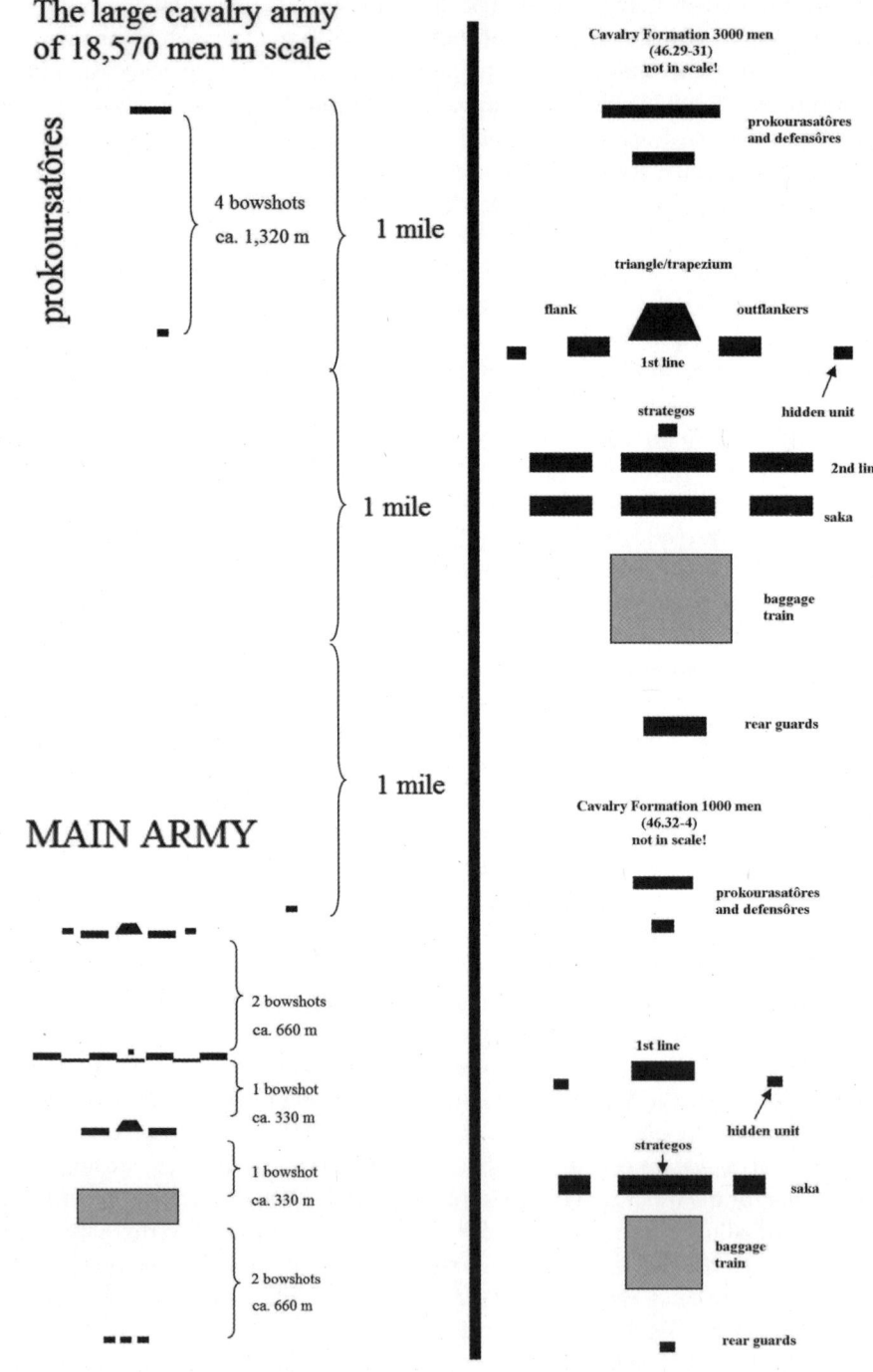

major *tagmata* (the wedge of the first line, the centre *tagma* of the second line, and the centre *tagma* of the third line). This was clearly the chosen cavalry force of a single *thema* or *tagma*. The *prokoursatôres* consisted of 200 men (50 *doryforoi* and 150 *psiloi*). The *defensôres* consisted of 100 men (75 *doryforoi* and 25 *psiloi*). The first line consisted of the wedge and of the *yperkerastai* and *plagiofylakes*. The wedge consisting of 384 men (first rank 10 men, the final twelfth rank 54 men) was arrayed in the middle. The outflankers and flank guards both consisted of 150 men (37 *doryforoi* and 113 *psiloi*). The two hidden divisions consisted of 50 men apiece (13 *doryforoi* and 37 *psiloi*). The second line consisted of two smaller flank divisions and of a larger middle division. The middle division, consisting of 370 men (91 *psiloi* and 279 *katafraktoi* and *doryforoi*) was arrayed with a depth of five ranks, each rank having 74 men. The flank divisions had 200 men (150 *doryforoi* and 50 *psiloi*) each. The *bandofylakes* of the *stratêgos* consisted of 50 *katafraktoi*. Its place is not mentioned, but was probably in the middle of the support line. The *saka* was arrayed like the second line. The rear guards consisted of 200 men (100 *doryforoi* and 100 *psiloi*). This deployment pattern places the main emphasis on the centre of the array. In other words, Leôn's aim was to achieve victory by using the select few against the chosen point in the enemy line, while the *saka* could be used to widen the frontage to outflank the enemy. This array clearly represents the select battle-ready units of a single *thema* or *tagma*.

The fourth and smallest cavalry army (*ST* 46.32–4) consisted of only 1,000 horsemen (734 *katafraktoi* and *doryforoi*, and 266 *psiloi*) arrayed as nine *tagmata* (5 larger and 4 smaller). The *prokoursatôres* consisted of 166 *psiloi*. The *defensôres* consisted of 84 *doryforoi*. The first line consisted of one 200-man-strong division of 67 *katafraktoi* and 133 *doryforoi*. The two units of ambushers consisted of 25 mixed *doryforoi* and *psiloi*. The *saka* consisted of three units, the middle one having 250 men (84 *katafraktoi* and 166 *doryforoi*). The left and right units had 100 men each, both consisting of 67 *doryforoi* and 33 *psiloi*. The rear guards consisted of one unit of 50 men (34 *doryforoi* and 16 *psiloi*). The *stratêgos* and his 50 *katafraktoi bandofylakes* (flag guard with the trumpeters) took their place in the centre of the *saka*.

It is probable that the 1,000-horseman army represented the very elite of a single *thema*, because it includes a disproportionate number of *katafraktoi* and *doryforoi*, able to use both melee and long range weapons, in relation to the number of *psiloi*. This array again shows the stress put on having the best troops in the middle of the formation. The primary intention was again to direct the attack to one chosen place, which would bring about a victory in the right circumstances, while the ambushers and the flanks of the *saka* could be used to outflank the enemy when this was possible.

6. The Combined Army (ST 47)

The largest example of the combined cavalry and infantry army in the *Sylloge tacticorum* encompassed 26,184 men in total, of whom 19,414 were infantry and 6,770 were cavalry. In addition to this, there were 264 supernumeraries (12 x 22) for the infantry and 220 (10 x 22) supernumeraries for the cavalry.

The infantry consisted of 12 large *tagmata* (the edges of the hollow square) and three minor *tagmata* (50 *bandofylakes*, 800 *psiloi* stationed at intervals, and 300 *menavlatoi*). The cavalry was deployed for combat in the same manner as depicted in the above mentioned formation for the cavalry army of 6,770 horsemen, but these were in all probability sometimes deployed in practice as in the *Syntaxis armatorum quadrata* or as in the later *De re militari* (1, 81.-21, 2.3–8, 2.11, 6, 8.24ff.), so the number cavalry units inside varied according to the size of the cavalry force, meaning that there could be four, five or six cavalry *parataxeis* (subunits) per side, which means that when these then advanced from the hollow infantry square, the end result could be: three units with one reserve unit; three units with two reserve units; or three units with three reserve units for each four sides of the hollow square.

The twelve large *tagmata*, each with 1,500 infantrymen (1,125 *aspidoforoi*, 375 *psiloi*) were usually deployed three *tagmata* per side, each *tagma* deployed with a depth of ten ranks and a width of 150 files, with the light infantry placed in the middle. This made the *tagmata* two-fronted, with *aspidoforoi* heavy infantry in front and behind, which in its turn made it possible to face threats coming from the front and rear. This was a new development from the version depicted in the *Syntaxis armatorum quadrata*, which in its turn was based on Ailianos' *Taktika*, so the so-called *Syntaxis armatorum quadrata* actually formed a part of the so-called 'Byzantine Interpolation of Aelian'. In this text the infantry formation is not double-fronted. It has heavy infantry in front and archers and other light infantry behind. Since I accept the authorship and date as recorded in the *Sylloge tacticorum*, it is clear that the information provided by the *Syntaxis armatorum quadrata* can be dated to the ninth century or before, and it is equally clear that it is fully based on the original material provided by Ailianos, as it claims to be. The improvement of the formation by Leôn can only have resulted from lessons learned. This may have resulted from some defeat caused by the penetration of the hollow square, or because it was just more sensible to protect the light infantry if the enemy had managed to penetrate the formation.

On the basis of the measurements given (*ST* 47.6), these were deployed in the *synaspismos/syskouton* order (file width 62.46cm) for combat. The hollow square had three *tagmata* per side, but the number of intervals per side varied according to situation. Leôn gives us two different figures for the intervals in the front and rear. He states (*ST* 43.8, 47.5) that the horizontal intervals were six *orguiai* (11.22m) wide, so 18 horsemen could pass through (six *orguiai* is not wide enough for this), while he states that the vertical intervals were 28 *orguiai* (52.36m). It is easy to see that both should be 28 *orguia* (ca. 52m), because this would have given the eighteen horsemen enough room to pass through the interval. According to Leôn, the twelve *tagmata* were deployed with ten or twelve intervals when the enemy force was small, but if the enemy force was stronger then the array was to have only eight intervals as instructed by Polybios (in the no-longer-extant military treatise) and Ailianos (included in the *Syntaxis armatorum quadrata / Byzantine Interpolation of Aelian*). This has led McGeer (1995, 258–9) to conclude that the diagram of the *Syntaxis armatorum quadrata* would correct the misunderstanding resulting from the texts of the *Sylloge tacticorum* and *Praecepta militaria*, and that three *tagmata* per side meant the two *tagmata* plus the corner *tagmata* as the third – as we find in the *Syntaxis armatorum quadrata*. Even if the description is accurate for the *Sylloge tacticorum* and *Praecepta militaria*, it is actually still a mistake as far as the diagram in the *Syntaxis armatorum quadrata* is concerned. In reality its diagram depicts the traditional Hellenistic sixteen *tagmata / taxiarchiai / chiliarchiai* formation in which there were 16,000 *oplitai* in the *tagmata* (each a *chiliarchia* of 1,000 men, so that each file symbol represents 100 men in the array) which we also find depicted in the *De re militari / Peri katastaseôs aplektôu* (1.1.-15). The same treatise, *De re militari* (6), includes also the twelve-*taxiarchiai* formation, which was apparently used in a similar manner as the one depicted by the *Sylloge tacticorum* and *Praecepta militaria*. The diagrams on the next two pages show the difference between the sixteen- and twelve-*taxiarchiai / tagmata* formations. The key difference was that in the sixteen-division formation the corners consisted of two divisions, while in the twelve-division formation each of the corners consisted of a single division. This means that Leôn altered the relative strength of the flank and corner units from the one that was used during the Hellenistic times (and presumably also during the Imperial and Late-Roman times) so that there were always twelve *tagmata*, even in the largest version of the hollow square formation, regardless of the size of the infantry formation. In contrast to Leôn and Nikêforos Fôkas (see the narrative), in the latter half of the tenth century the unknown author of the *De re militari* used the original Hellenistic sixteen *taxiarchiai* system of Polybios and Ailianos as the principal variant of the hollow infantry square, and the twelve *taxiarchiai* version only as an alternative for that.

It should also be noted that in practice the disposition of the forces inside the hollow square varied according to the number of cavalry. For example, if there were large numbers of those, each of the sides could have six *parataxeis* of cavalry which then advanced through the three intervals in the normal square so that the resulting battle formation for the cavalry was three units in front with three units as their reserves. This means that when the cavalry charged through the intervals the resulting battle formations per side could also have three units in front with two as reserves, three units in front with one reserve unit, and three units without reserves. It is this system that we find described in the *De re militari*.

Syntaxis armatorum quadrata
(sligthly emended version of the Parisinus graecus 2442 on the basis of Codex Burnley)

16 taxiarchiai version (16,000 hoplitai)

stratêgos with touldon

⚲	hoplititeês kontaratos (kontos-armed hopliye)
ʃ	riptaratos (slinger, javeliner)
κ	kaballarios/(cavalryman)
⊥	psilos toxotes (light archer)
ō	skoutatos (shield-bearing infantryman)
λ	touldos (baggage train)

New Battle Formations in the *Sylloge Tacticorum* 369

The 16 taxiarchiai hollow square of the Syntaxis armatorum quadrata with 8 intervals.
The rhiptaratoi and kaballarioi placed behind each interval.
The resulting extra hoplitai (two per interval) placed in the remaining intervals.

[diagram of battle formation with "stratêgos with touldon" at center]

In short, the unknown author of the *Syntaxis armatorum quadrata* in the *Byzantine Interpolation of Aelian* made a mistake when he stated (SAQ 1) that the accompanying diagram had only twelve units in total on all four sides (three per side). In the diagram on page 368 the corners consist of two divisions, which means that the unknown author interpreted the material in the same manner as Leôn. However, the rest of the instructions in the *Syntaxis armatorum quadrata* that were clearly borrowed from Polybios and Ailianos, as were the instructions of Leôn in the *Sylloge tacticorum*, were relevant to both the sixteen- and the twelve-division versions, because the number of intervals could be varied in both. In short, when the Romans had large numbers of horsemen and the enemy did not have equal numbers of infantry so there was no need to block the intervals with the

THE PRINCIPAL DEPLOYMENT PATTERNS FOR THE HOLLOW SQUARE / RECTANGLE WITH 16 OR 12 DIVISIONS

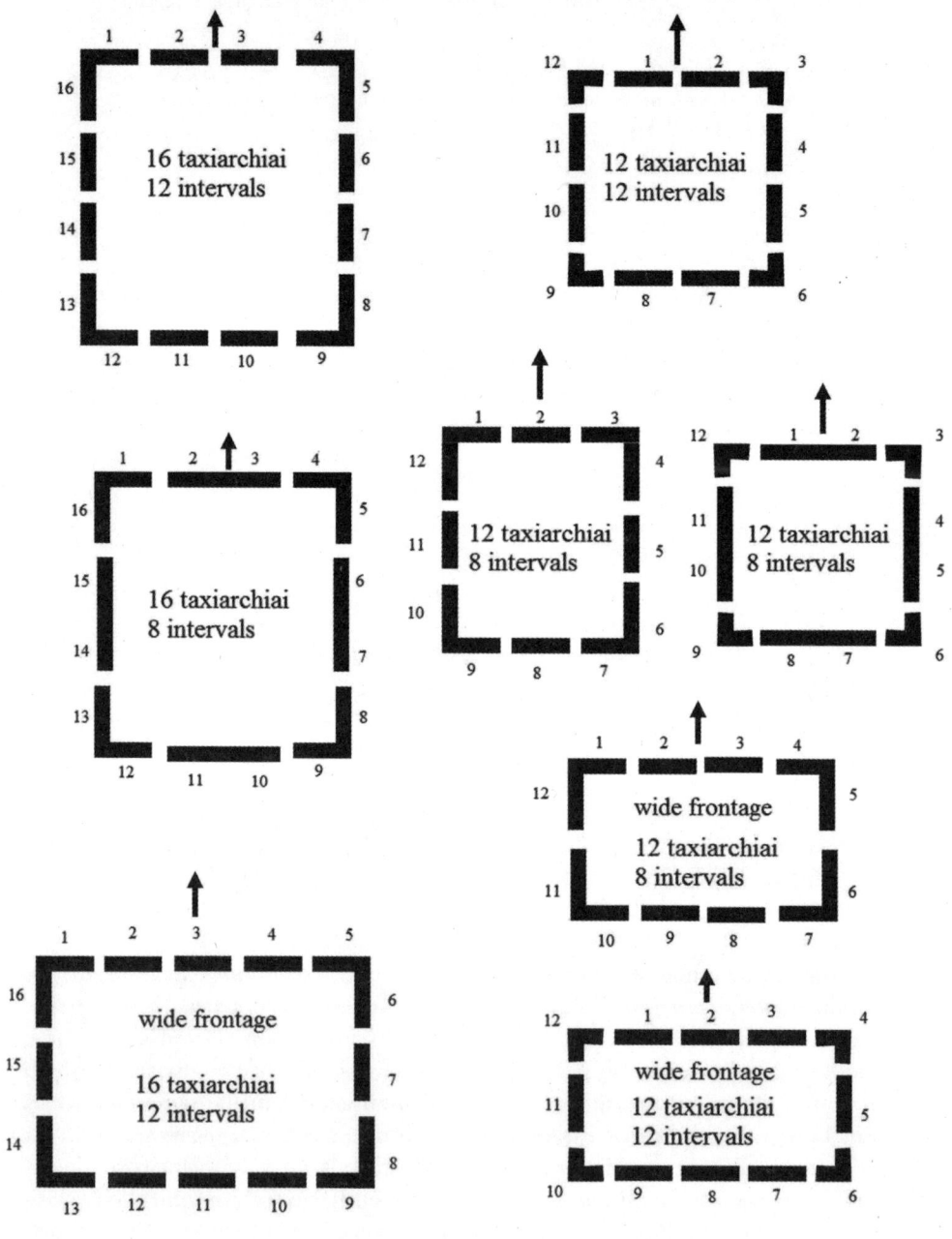

rhiptaratoi/riptaratoi, then the Romans left twelve intervals open (SAQ 3), which is the diagram that we find in the *Syntaxis armatorum quadrata* – the array with the sixteen *taxiarchiai*, but which could also be used by the twelve-*taxiarchiai* version. If the Romans had a small number of cavalry and the enemy had an equal number of infantry, then the Romans diminished the number of intervals to eight (SAQ 4). The *riptaratoi* reserve units inside the square were actually meant only for the situation in which the Romans had to diminish the number of intervals to eight.

It was because of this that the *Sylloge tacticorum* included the small *tagma* of 800 *psiloi*. These were undoubtedly deployed as eight units of 100 *riptaratoi* to block the eight intervals, and it is this number of units of *riptaratoi* that we find in the extant diagram of the *Syntaxis armarorum quadrata* (the *Codex Burnley* has preserved the correct number of eight units of *riptaratoi*, while the *Codex Parisinus* has nine). See the attached diagrams of the *Syntaxis armatorum quadrata*. The first of these is a restored version of the *Parisinus graecus* version, and I have used the *Codex Burnley* for the restoration of the number of *riptaratoi* units while I have also restored the numbers of symbols to be the same for each side of the square if there have been individual mistakes in their numbers (e.g. I have restored the number of 40 *toxotai* symbols to each flank). The diagram that has only eight intervals is my reconstruction based on the two manuscript diagrams.

The terrain varied, and so did the shape of the hollow infantry formation. It was because of this that Leôn also includes the following variants: horizontal rectangle and vertical rectangle. The horizontal hollow rectangle had four *tagmata* in front and behind and two on the flanks. The vertical hollow rectangle had four *tagmata* on the flanks and two in front and behind. Both of these obviously had eight intervals (three in front and behind, one on both flanks). Leôn unfortunately does not specify how in such instances the number of intervals was increased to ten or twelve, but one may make the educated guess that this was once again made by dividing the units as needed. On the basis of Nikêforos Fôkas' *Praecepta militaria* (2.15), we know that when the terrain was flat it was possible to adopt a wide frontage, with four or five *parataxeis* in front and back with one or two *parataxeis* per flank, leaving twelve intervals in total. This means that the commander simply varied the number of intervals by dividing or uniting the *tagmata/taxiarchiai* to enable him to use the cavalry in such a manner as seemed best, meaning that there could be, for example, four intervals in front and behind with one or two on both flanks (i.e. ten or twelve intervals). The attached diagrams show some of the ways this could be done. This obviously varied the relative and actual strengths of the different infantry units in the array. The same was obviously true for the cavalry contingents accompanying the army, because these were divided into units according to the numbers available and numbers of intervals in the hollow rectangle.

According to Leôn, the 800 *psiloi* (the *riptaratoi* of SAQ) were deployed in the intervals so that they were aligned with the last rank of the *tagmata*. As already discussed, and contrary to what Leôn states, this deployment pattern was usually used only when the array had eight intervals – there were 800 men because of this

A Large Combined Infantry and Cavalry Army
(in scale)

The reformed cavalry and infantry formation of Nikeforos Fokas

It is clear that when the stratêgos accompanied the cavalry that there remained behind a separate commander for the infantry square who may already have been called oplitarchês / archêgetes and who is likely to have been the ypostratêgos (second-in-command) of the entire army. It would have been he who had the infantry bandfylokes in attendance when the stratêgos was absent.

the stratêgos would have accompanied the cavalry

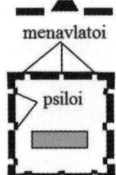

menavlatoi

psiloi

I have assumed that the cavalry rear guard remained outside the infantry square

when required the menavlatoi used as the first rank of each taxiarchia

I have assumed that the cavalry rear guard remained outside the infantry square

– but obviously this system was also used when there were twelve intervals if the situation required it, because Leôn includes 300 *menavlatoi* who could be used for blocking the remaining three intervals in the twelve-interval formation. In the *Syntaxis armatorum quadrata* all of the intervals were partially blocked by units of *oplitai*, even when there were eight units of *riptaratoi* behind. This means that Leôn or someone else before him had reformed this Hellenistic system by removing the *oplitai* from the intervals, replacing them with 300 *aspidoforoi menavlatoi*. Their mission was to initially stand along the front portion of the interval, but when the enemy *katafraktoi* approached to the distance of a bowshot the *menavlatoi* advanced 30- to 40-*orguiai* (ca. 56–75m) in front of the *oplitai* and assumed either the lateral phalanx or wedge formation. As such, the use of the infantry wedge in front of the array to break up the enemy cavalry charge was not a new idea because we find it also in *Ailianos* (Diagram in the *Codex Burnley*), but the use of the sturdy *menavlion* by the *menavlatoi* appears to be a new development, possibly copied from the Saracens who employed this type of spear. The 300 *menavlatoi* were presumably posted to the side where the Romans expected the enemy to direct their *katafraktoi*, while the 800 *psiloi* blocked the remaining intervals. Nikêforos Fôkas reformed this system, increasing the number of *menavlatoi* while also placing them as the front rank of the *oplitai* formation, which proves that there had previously been too few of these and that their position in front of the array made them too vulnerable. The increased numbers of *menavlatoi* suggest a partial return to the Hellenistic system, which had had *oplitai* in each of the intervals. For Fôkas' reform, see the narrative.

Leôn envisaged that the principal striking force of the combined formation was its cavalry, so these started the combat by advancing through the flanks of the hollow square after which they assumed their combat formation. If the cavalry defeated the enemy, they conducted the pursuit while the infantry followed behind. If the enemy defeated the cavalry, they retreated either inside the hollow square or formed up on both flanks to face the enemy. As already noted, if the enemy had a large army, then the Romans used only eight intervals. This instruction had been copied from Polybios and Ailianos. The use of twelve or ten intervals was restricted to situations in which the enemy force was smaller. If the Romans had a large force of cavalry which could not be fitted inside the hollow square, the *stratêgos* was to remove one rank from each *tagma* for the purpose of widening the formation.

The array was obviously also modified on the basis of the available number of infantry and cavalry. If the army had a total of 12,528 men of whom 9,274 were infantry and 3,244 cavalry,[13] the infantry was deployed in the same manner as in the largest variant with 12 major *tagmata* and three smaller *tagmata* (50 *bandofylakes*, 200 *menavlatoi*, 360 *psiloi*). Each of the twelve major *tagmata* was deployed 100 files wide and seven ranks deep, so that each *tagma* of 700 men (525 *aspidoforoi*, 175 *psiloi*) was again double-fronted (with the light infantry deployed in the middle). The 300 *menavlatoi* and 360 *psiloi* were deployed and used in the same manner as previously. The 3,244 cavalrymen were presumably deployed as in the third cavalry formation (3,000 men).

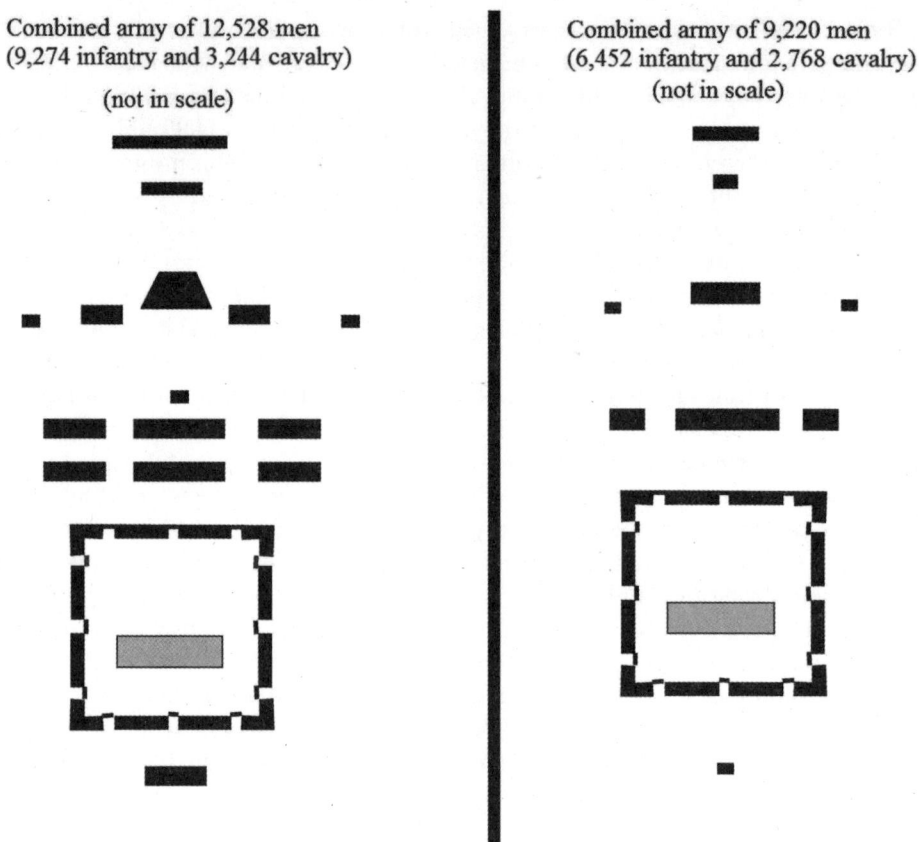

If the combined army consisted of 9,220 men divided into 6,452 infantry and 2,768 cavalry, then the infantry was once again deployed in twelve major *tagmata* and three minor *tagmata*, but now the cavalry was deployed as in the fourth cavalry formation (1,000 men). The twelve major *tagmata*, each 476 men strong (358 *aspidoforoi*, 118 *psiloi*) were deployed in a double-fronted array 7 men deep and 68 men wide. The infantry *bandofylakes* consisted once again of 50 *oplitai*, but the number of *menavlatoi* was naturally lower, 142 men, just as the *psiloi* blocking the intervals now numbered only 288 men.

If the combined army consisted only of 4,116 men (3,116 infantry, and 1,000 cavalry), then the Romans no longer used the hollow square array, but the third infantry formation with cavalry wings. The cavalry was deployed as two *tagmata* of 500 horsemen on both sides behind the infantry at a distance of a half-bowshot (165m). Each of these was divided into 166 *prokoursatôres* and 334 *defensôres*, with the latter being deployed 4-ranks deep and 83-men wide. The cavalry was needed for the protection of the flanks of the infantry because the infantry force was too small, but in such a way that the cavalry could also be used for outflanking the enemy. The expected combat sequence was as follows: 1) the cavalry *prokoursatôres*

a small combined army of 4,116 men
(3,116 infantry; 1,000 cavalry)

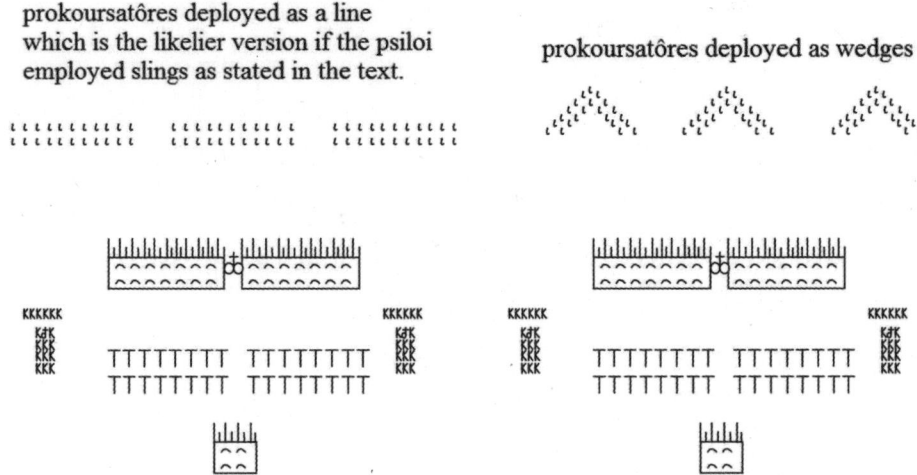

began the battle; 2) the infantry *prokoursatôres* followed them and used their slings; and 3) if the enemy forced the Romans to retreat, both returned to their original place and renewed the fight, together with the *defensôres* and *aspidoforoi*.

If the cavalry formed the majority in the combined army, then the cavalry was posted in the middle with the infantry being placed on both sides in front of the cavalry formation, because this was the basic procedure among both Romans and foreigners – only the cavalry *prokoursatôres* were in front of the infantry wings. Leôn does not specify the formation adopted by cavalry or infantry in such instances, but one may make the educated guess that the infantry flank guards were usually deployed as hollow squares (or as wedges?) according to the numbers available, as they had been in the sixth-century *Strategikon* (12.A.20–3, 12.A.89ff., 12.B.12). It is difficult to think that the infantry wings would have used the infantry formation previously described for the same reason: its outer flanks were vulnerable. In short, it is practically certain that the infantry wings were deployed as twelve-*tagmata* hollow squares on both sides, so that these preceded the cavalry deployed in the middle. It is also clear that the cavalry formation was based on the numbers of men available, but one may make the educated guess that since the cavalry was expected to be in the majority, in practice this meant only the two largest variants of the cavalry formation – which were basically the same, excepting that only the largest also had *katafraktoi* among the flank divisions of the first line. This deployment pattern suggests that the cavalry was usually used for breaking the enemy's formation, either frontally by directing the cavalry wedge into the centre of the enemy force and/or by attacking the flanks of the

A Combined Army with Cavalry in Majority
(the deployment pattern is an educated guess)
(in scale)

I have assumed that the Romans placed their baggage train inside the infantry hollow squares while the cavalry ambushers were placed behind these squares to act as hidden units.

the stratêgos would have accompanied the cavalry

I have assumed that the Romans retained the cavalry rear guards.

enemy formations (with the ambushers, flank guards, outflankers, or with the flanking units of the second line and/or with the third cavalry line) that attacked the infantry squares.

7. The Importance of Leôn's Reforms

The cavalry formations in the *Sylloge tacticorum* represent a midway point between the Late-Roman tactical system as portrayed in the *Strategikon* and the late-tenth-century system of the warrior emperors Nikêforos Fôkas, Johannes (*Iôannês*) Tzimiskês and Basilios II Boulgaroktonos. However, Leôn still retained many of the features of the larger cavalry formations of the *Strategikon*, with the result that it contained features that were not fully compatible with their intended tactical use. The fill-up *tagmata* and hidden units belong to this category. It is no wonder that Nikêforos Fôkas eliminated these features. Leôn was ready to reform Byzantine cavalry tactics. He was ready to take into account recent developments in warfare and not just be happy with what his military advisors had taught him, with the result that he adjusted the cavalry tactics he had been taught to meet the challenges of his own day. It is quite probable that it was his lack of actual military experience that made him so ready to challenge what he had been taught by his generals – after all, these were the very same men that were constantly suffering defeats at the hands of his enemies. It was these reforms of Leo VI the Wise that paved the way for the apogee of the so-called Byzantine Empire under his successors. It should be noted that it is very probable that many of the reforms were copied from earlier Greek and Roman military treatises, even if it is clear that the Saracens influenced Leôn's thinking too (e.g. the name *saka* derived from *saqah*). The Saracens were obviously using the hollow infantry square, but they had copied its used from the Romans. In this case Leôn probably employed earlier Roman sources, because the hollow square was already in use in the very same manner during the Republican to Late-

Romans fighting against Bulgarians (Manasses ms.). Source: Schlumberger

Roman periods, not to mention the fact that Leôn (*ST* 47.20) specifically mentions both Polybios and Ailianos in the context of the hollow infantry square, while we also know that the ancient Romans used *katafraktoi* in the same manner against enemy infantry. In other words, the cavalry could be posted either in front or on the flanks or inside the hollow square as needed.[14]

The probable Saracen influence on the *Sylloge tacticorum* is visible in the following: the adding of the *saka* and *opisthofylakes* to the cavalry formation; the increased use of maces by cavalry; and in the use of *menavlia*-spears by the infantry, which were standard weapons for the Saracens. It is also clear that the *menavlatoi* were included in the Roman array against the enemy *katafraktoi* because the Saracens had already used the *katafraktoi* (presumably in wedge-shaped formations, possibly copied originally from the Persians) by the time Leôn wrote the *Sylloge tacticorum*. It is therefore possible that the Saracens had actually reintroduced the *katafraktoi*-wedge into their tactics. The fact that the Saracens had copied Greco-Roman tactics so that they used the hollow infantry square/oblong with pike-armed soldiers very effectively against Roman cavalry – which was still apparently deployed in the manner described by the *Strategikon* and Leôn's *Taktika* – undoubtedly also influenced Leôn, so that he sought out, read and copied the relevant older Greco-Roman military treatises (hollow square, infantry wedge used to break the cavalry charge, *katafraktoi* etc).

Hoplite in the *Taktika* (6.21) and *Sylloge Tacticorum* (38.1-5) of Leôn o Sofos.

© Dr. Ilkka Syvänne 2024

Appendix II

De velitatione of emperor Nikêforos Fôkas

1. The author of *De velitatione*, the treatise on guerrilla warfare[1]

The title of the military treatise on skirmishing known as *De velitatione* is *Peri Paradromês tou kurou Nikêforou tou Basileôs*. Therefore, the treatise names Nikêforos Fôkas as its author. However, the preface makes it clear that the final version of the text was not Nikêforos' version, but a version that someone else had edited and compiled on the basis of the notes produced by Nikêforos himself. The task of writing down the instructions on how to conduct skirmishing warfare against a numerically superior foe by a *stratêgos* of a single *thema* was entrusted to this unknown person by Nikêforos Fôkas towards the end of his reign. The stated aim was that these methods would not be forgotten in the midst of the great successes achieved by the Romans in the 960s because the guerrilla tactics might be found useful later. It is consequently clear that the author was very close to the emperor Nikêforos and may even have been his close relative.

The unknown author had learnt the method from Bardas Fôkas when the latter had served as *stratêgos* of Kappadokia and Anatolikon. The guerrilla tactics as such were not a new invention, but according to the unknown author these methods had been forgotten and then revived by Bardas Fôkas, who then brought these methods to perfection. The same skirmishing system was then employed successfully by Kônstantinos Maleinos in Kappadokia, Nikêforos Fôkas when he was *stratêgos*, and by the unknown author himself both in the east and west. The unknown author thus stated that he wrote the *De velitatione* for the purpose of describing the guerrilla tactics for use in the east, while he promised to write a similar treatise on the methods to be followed in the west, and it has been conjectured that he may have been the author of the *De re militari* (also known as *De castrametatione Peri katastaseôs aplêktou; Campaign Organization*). Similarly, it has been conjectured that the unknown editor/compiler may have been Leôn Fôkas, the brother of Nikêforos Fôkas, who presumably did not consider it prudent to stress his authorship during the reign of Iôannês Tzimiskes or Basileios II. I consider this to be the likeliest guess, but unfortunately the final authorship remains unknown, even if we know that the text is still heavily indebted to the notes and memoranda of Nikêforos Fôkas and the exemplary use of these methods by Leôn Fôkas.[2]

The principal value of this treatise is that it gives us a list of tactics employed by Nikêforos Fôkas and other Roman commanders during this era, even when the narrative sources are silent about the details. The following analysis therefore gives a summary of the methods employed by the *stratêgoi* of the themes when the enemy force outnumbered their own force, which was usually the reality the Roman generals faced. Since it is clear that the title of the treatise credits Nikêforos with the authorship, while the preface also proves that the text was based on Nikêforos' notes and also on his own experiences, the following analysis assumes that the opinions presented in the treatise reflected those of Nikêforos himself. It was because of this that the unknown editor (as noted probably Leôn) names Nikêforos Fôkas as the author.

The treatise as such consists of at least two earlier treatises/memoranda and additions made by the editor which have not been fully edited because Book 17 contains an ending/conclusion (D 17.132–6; DM 17.13). The next Book 18 appears to be a continuation of Book 17 which implies that it was added to the text by the editor because Book 19[3] appears to be the introduction to another treatise because it discusses the training, equipment, salary and conditions of service after which follows the treatment of the actual combat methods, which includes some duplicates of the information provided by Books 1–17 (e.g. shadowing techniques and blocking the passes from retreating enemy) while also adding some material which is missing from it (e.g. diversionary invasion and sieges) so that this portion has a new ending in Book 25. Books 1–17 with the addition of Book 18 describe the guerrilla tactics in a more general manner while Books 20–25 contain more detailed information regarding the actual skirmishing. The latter portion of the text was written when there were at least two emperors (DV 19), which means that it was written either during the joint reign of Kônstantinos VII and his son Rômanos II in 955–9 or during the reign of Tzimiskês, Basileios II and Kônstantinos VIII in 969–76. If the former is the case and the referral to the emperors was not added by the editor, then the text was probably written by Nikêforos to serve as instructions to the generals at a time when he was the *domestikos*. This conclusion receives further support from the contents of Book 19, which stress the importance of the just treatment of the thematic soldiers so that: 1) they would receive their salaries (*roga*) and money for provisions regularly, in addition to which they were to receive more gifts and bonuses than they expected; 2) their households and possessions were also to be secure from the *dynatoi*; and 3) the thematic soldiers were also to be treated with proper respect and not be dishonoured and scorned. All of these questions would have been particularly relevant after the widespread corruption of Bardas Fôkas had caused the collapse of morale among the soldiers. It is therefore quite possible that the newly-appointed *domestikos* Nikêforos did indeed dispatch at least some of these instructions to the *stratêgoi* very soon after his appointment. The latter half of the text also uses as its examples events that took place before Nikêforos Fôkas became *domestikos*, so it includes referrals to Leôn's *Taktika* and the exploits of his own similarly-named grandfather during Leôn's reign. The most recent referral is to the exploits of Melias, the *stratêgos* of Lykandos who was in the habit of making diversionary operations against the area around Aleppo and Antioch when Ali the son of Hamdan (Sayf ad-Dawla) invaded Roman territory.[4]

In the following analysis the order of the books has been slightly altered in places to make the contents more logical. It should be noted that *De velitatione* was not the only treatise that contained descriptions of guerrilla tactics and stratagems. These could also be found in the *Strategikon*, the *Taktika* of Leôn, the *Sylloge tacticorum*, and many other treatises. There were also special collections of stratagems like those based on Polyainos (Polyen) or the *Kestoi* of Julius Africanus (which included germ warfare and the use of poisons) which were abridged, re-copied and compiled into other treatises. Well-read officers could also find these in the works of history. Additionally, it is probable that there were also specialized treatises dealing with chemical stratagems, the remnants of which are still visible in the extant versions of Marcus Graecus' *Liber ignium*. These included, for example (*Liber* 6, 9): the sending of messengers with the excuse of peace negotiations so they could place incendiaries in the enemy homes which would set their houses on fire at sunrise; and the placing of chemical concoctions underneath horse dung, which were then exposed by autumnal rains – with the result that the exposure of the substance to oxygen and water produced a violent burst of fire. Methods like these could easily have been employed when the Romans were invading or retreating from enemy territory in order to create chaos later, even if treatises such as the *De velitatione* do not mention their use.

2. Training and equipment: DV 19

Since the treatise consists of at least two separate treatises/memoranda, with additions made by the editor that have been combined but not been fully streamlined, the information concerning training, equipment and motivating the soldiers can only be found in Book 19, after the text had already had concluding words in Book 17.

The DV (DM 19.2) notes that the *stratêgos* of a theme could have access either to: 1) a very small number of men that were greatly inferior to the enemy; or 2) he could possess about 5–6,000 men, in which case the *stratêgos* was to draw up his army in formation and seek combat. The DV then states that the *stratêgos* was to employ stratagems, proper tactical methods, and surprise attacks, the implication being that these were more important in situations in which the *stratêgos* had a small army (i.e. less than 5,000 men). The army was to be prepared for combat by exercising and drilling so that the soldiers became accustomed to the weapons and hard labour. The thematic soldiers were to receive their salaries (*roga*) and money for provisions regularly, in addition to which they were to receive more gifts and bonuses than they expected so that they could buy the best horses and equipment. For the upkeep of morale, it was also important that their households and possessions were secure from the *dynatoi*, just as it was important that the thematic soldiers were treated with proper respect and not dishonoured and scorned.

3. Intelligence gathering: DV 1–2, 6–7[5]

The frontier zone consisted of the large border *themata* and of the *kleisourai* (mountain passes), the last of which were often so-called Armenian themes. The *stratêgoi* of the former also had control over the latter. Intelligence gathering and surveillance of the frontier consisted of several layers. Firstly, there were the observation posts in the Taurus Mountains, three- to four-miles apart from each other with the purpose of observing roads, rivers, narrows and places where the enemy could encamp. The competent sentries were to carry their own provisions and change their posts constantly so that enemy would not be able to locate them, and they were to serve only fifteen days at a time before being rotated. When they observed the enemy, they were to hurry to the next station and so forth until the message reached the cavalry posts on level terrain. The general was to pay particular attention to those who guarded the roads (*kaminobiglatores*, singular *kaminobiglatôr*), because these and the *ekspêlatores* (from Latin *expilatores*, robbers, scouts) warned the people in the countryside to take refuge.

According to Nikêforos, the Armenian themes formed a special case, because the Armenians were in the habit of carrying out their duties in a careless manner. The *stratêgos* was therefore required to select a specially-qualified group of Armenians who were to receive their salaries (*misthos*) and allowance (*annôna*) straight from the funds of the thematic army. These were also to be rotated each month. According to Nikêforos, not even this sufficed, because they were after all Armenians and therefore unlikely to perform their duties well. This gloomy view of the Armenians as border guards must have resulted from personal experience. In other words, it is probable that the Armenian border guards performed their duties very poorly, so the Saracens had managed to surprise the Romans during Nikêforos' tenure as *stratêgos* of Anatolikon in 945–56. It was presumably as a result of this that the *De velitatione* (12) includes instructions for situations in which the enemy had launched a surprise attack. It was also because of this that Nikêforos required the use of spies (*kataskopoi*) to compensate for the incompetence of the Armenian border guards. Nikêforos gives the spies the name *trapezites*. These consisted of the robbers and raiders of the borderlands (*akritai*). Groups of these under competent commanders were to raid the Syrian countryside constantly to capture prisoners for interrogation. The *stratêgos* was also expected to use actual spies, which in the text consisted of traders dispatched to the Muslim lands in addition to which the *stratêgos* was also expected to befriend and bribe the emirs of the fortresses of the border regions so that he could obtain information from them directly.

According to Leôn's *Taktika* 18.119, the Saracens launched their main attack during warmer seasons to enable the Jihadists to join the inhabitants of Tarsus for a joint invasion. Nikêforos (DV 7) confirms this by noting that the Jihadists typically arrived in large numbers, from Egypt, Palestine, Phoenicia, and southern Syria to Cilicia, in the cities of Antioch and Aleppo in August, where they added Arabs to their numbers so that they began their invasions of Roman territory in September.

The assembly points given suggest that the Saracens typically launched a double invasion, with one force advancing from Antioch probably to Tarsus whence it launched an attack, while another force advanced from Aleppo, typically under the emir of Aleppo (during this era Sayf ad-Dawla) against another portion of the Roman border.

Nikêforos instructed the *stratêgos* to obtain information of these major invasions from his merchant spies and from the emirs he had bribed. These major raiding forces appear to have always included both infantry and cavalry. In addition to this, according to Leôn o Sofos, the Saracens of Tarsus, Adana and other cities of Cilicia raided Roman territory at other times of the year, which is also confirmed by Nikêforos. These raids could consist solely of a small group of select cavalry raiders without infantry and of larger invasions in which the infantry accompanied them. These types of activities appear to have been more typical than the larger invasions, because when there was peace between the Ikshidids of Egypt and Constantinople, the Jihadists obviously did not join the Cilician Arabs.

4. Facing the enemy at the border: DV 3, 5 (see also LT 9.28)

If the general (*stratêgos*) had learnt of the impending invasion in a timely manner, he was to collect his entire infantry force if possible and march towards the border. The purpose was to occupy the mountain heights and passes in advance of the enemy. If the enemy raided only with a small force of cavalry, then he was to engage and crush them with infantry and cavalry immediately. The infantry was to be placed on the higher ground (on both sides of the pass if possible) and even in gorges. The cavalry forces were to join the infantry wherever the terrain permitted this. In regions which did not allow the use of cavalry, the public road leading into Roman territory was to be blocked by a double phalanx of infantry, each of which consisted of *oplitai* (hoplites) equipped as *aspidoforoi* (shield-bearers) or as *akontistai* (javelineers) and behind them were 'the men who threw stones by hand' (i.e. *lithoboloi*), archers (*toxotai*), and slingers (*sfendonetai*). The composition of the phalanxes suggests that the heavy infantry portion of the phalanx was deployed so that the front rankers (ranks one to four) consisted of the shield-bearing and spear-armed hoplites, behind whom (ranks five-to-eight) were the men who threw javelins,[6] while the light infantry was deployed in such a manner that the stone-throwers formed the next rank, followed by a rank of archers, so that the *sfendonistai*-slingers formed the rear in irregular formation. It is probable that the light-infantry portion of the two phalanxes was shallower than the standard paper strength (half the number of heavy infantry), because a significant proportion of the light infantry was posted on both sides of the pass – probably not more than the equivalent of two or three ranks. On both sides of the road were placed *akontistai* (javelineers), *psiloi* (means here the archers and stone-throwers because these are not mentioned separately), and *sfendonistai* (slingers). In like manner, the *stratêgos* was to place infantry forces to

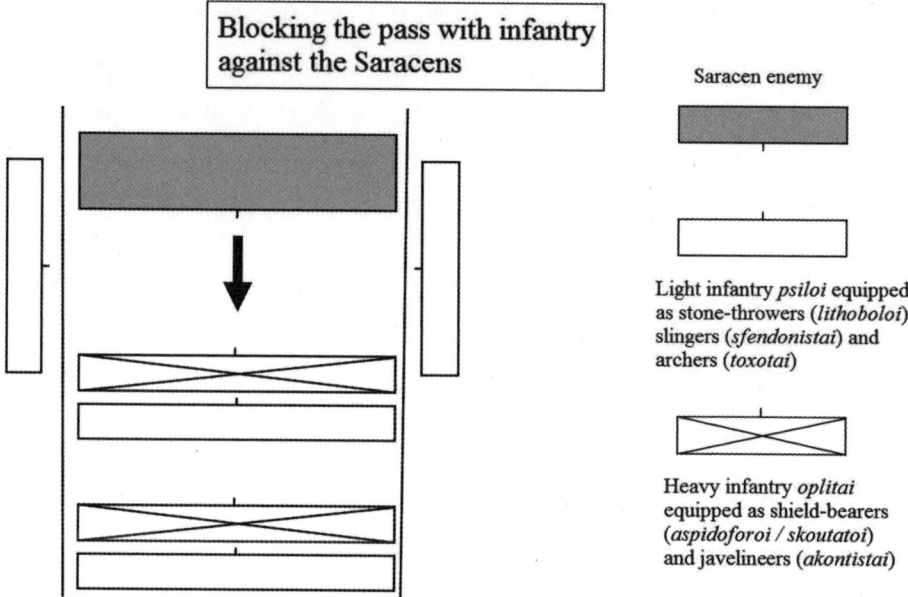

block any paths (*atrapoi*) off to the right and left of the public road so that the enemy could not bypass the larger concentration of Roman forces blocking the public road. Book 5 notes the importance of controlling the springs in the passes so that the Romans soldiers would not suffer from thirst. If there were none in the vicinity, then each *ekatontarchia* was to carry ten bags of water.

When the enemy then learnt that it was impossible to bypass the Roman force, they either attacked the well-prepared Romans on their own chosen battlefield, usually with poor results, or they would seek another road further away.[7] If the Saracens adopted the latter alternative the Saracen force typically became worn out as a result of being forced to march for several days in difficult terrain, with the result that they became demoralized while the Romans became emboldened. According to the DV, Sayf ad-Dawla was defeated twice during the reign of Kônstantinos VII and once during the reign of Rômanos II as a result of this. All of the *stratêgoi* along the Tarsus range cooperated and simultaneously blocked all of the defiles so that the Saracens of Tarsus and Cilicia were defeated in every place. This last piece of information means that the author did not refer to any of the well-known instances in which Sayf ad-Dawla was defeated in a pass when retreating away from enemy territory, but to such instances in which he was unable to even reach Roman territory.

5. Shadowing Warfare when the enemy entered Roman Territory

5.1. Romans aware of the enemy invasion. The beginning stages (DV 4–8, 12, 23–5)[8]

Nikêforos Fôkas considered it advantageous to allow the enemy to enter Roman territory, so that the invaders could then be engaged only when they were already returning to their own territory because at that time the enemy would be worn out as a result of the Roman guerrilla warfare and because they were also burdened by baggage, animals and captives. When the general learnt that the enemy was preparing to invade, the *stratêgos* assembled his whole army and dispatched an experienced *tourmarchês* with picked men into enemy territory to intercept the Saracen forces before they entered Roman territory, after which the *tourmarchês* shadowed them while keeping the *stratêgos* informed of the enemy's activities. The enemy was then allowed to enter Roman territory, while the general took his forces to a strong location and the *expilatores* (scouts) prepared the civilians for the impending invasion by taking the inhabitants with their animals to safe locations such as fortified towns or high up in the mountains.

After the above initial stages the actual shadowing warfare against the invader began, usually ending only when the enemy was leaving Roman territory, at which point the Romans blocked the passes leading out with infantry and cavalry forces. In fact, the *stratêgos* or *stratêgoi* were expected to start assembling their infantry forces when the enemy entered their territory (while the cavalry shadowed and harassed the foe) so that these were dispatched behind the advancing enemy to block their routes of retreat. This method had been one of the favourite defensive strategies ever since the fourth century.

5.2. Skirmishing tactics against single raiding parties (*monokoursa*)[9] (DV 6)

The Muslim enemies were in the habit of launching small raiding parties of swift cavalry (*koursa*) into Roman territory. The standard practice against this was to send ahead a *tourmarchês* or another officer with a select force of cavalry to shadow/tail the enemy raiding force whilst keeping in contact with the *stratêgos*.[10] When it was observed that the enemy force had scattered to plunder, the general was to bring his force to the scene of operations and engage the enemy. However, if the enemy became aware of the presence of the general's army that simply meant that the enemy would flee immediately.

5.3. Enemy using separate cavalry raiders (*koursa*) with the emir following (DV 7–9, 14–6)

The Romans knew from experience that the enemy usually began their major invasions in September.[11] This meant that the *stratêgos* could send his spies (businessmen) to observe the preparations while he himself cultivated his own contacts by pretending to be a friend of the emirs in control of the castles of the border regions. During this period, the general was also required to send his own raiding parties across the border more frequently. The purpose was to find out what the size of the enemy force was, what the proportion of cavalry to infantry was, who was in command, and the area which they intended to attack. The typical large invading force consisted of about 6–12,000 cavalry raiders (*koursa*) and of c.12–24,000 men (infantry, cavalry, servants, artisans, cooks etc.) belonging to the main force.[12] Another alternative appears to have been that the whole enemy force consisted of only cavalry raiders (*koursa*).[13]

When the *stratêgos* learned of the impending invasion, he sent a picked body of horsemen under a very experienced *tourmarchês* (or another officer) to intercept and shadow the enemy force before it reached Roman territory whilst the inhabitants were evacuated to safe locations. In the meanwhile, the general himself took the main force consisting of cavalry to a good and strong position to wait for the opportunity to launch an attack against the enemy. The shadowing troops carried only one day's rations (bread, cheese, dried meat and fodder) and were regularly rotated. The vanguard shadowing the enemy posted its own scouts in advance and in depth (see the diagram below) and during the night some of the scouts were required to dismount and move closer to the enemy camp.[14] The commander of the vanguard was instructed to be overly cautious lest the enemy ambush him. The general in his turn approached the scene unobserved (the men wore *epanoklibana*-surcoats over their armour) and used a *saka* (rearguard) whilst marching. If during the night march the army had to cross difficult terrain, then each *thema* and *tagma* was marched separately one after another. As a safety measure, the general was also required to change his camp once or twice during the night, and even during the day.

When the *stratêgos* was getting close to the enemy, he was instructed to send his baggage train far off to a fortified place or fortress. The army took provisions and fodder to last for two or three days, which were transported on fast mules or in saddlebags on the horses.[15] The baggage train was again united with the main force when this was required. When the general got really close to the enemy and his force consisted of 3,000 or more cavalrymen,[16] he was to send the grooms and

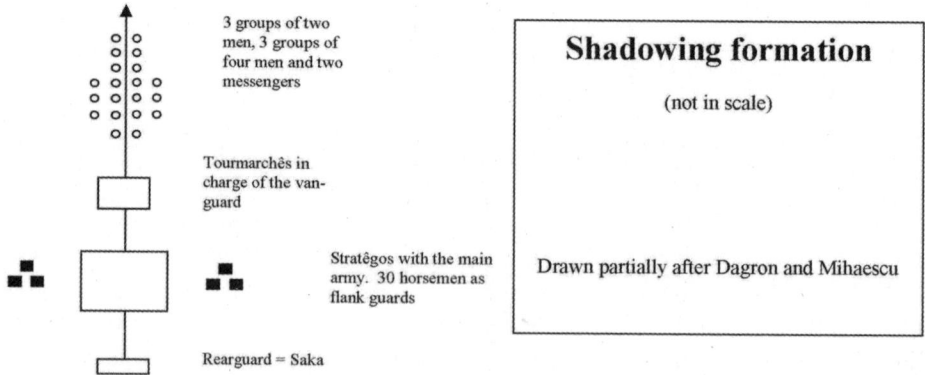

the men carrying the fodder away to a strong position, whilst he arrayed his army in battle formation.

If the Roman cavalry force was large and reached the figure of 3,000, the *stratêgos* divided it in two (*dichê*) so that behind the vanguard under the *tourmarchês* (*prokoursatôres*) marched the first line (a third of the army) under a capable leader, after which followed the second line, the large *parataxis* under the *stratêgos* himself. The general was also to post behind his own line a few horsemen (*to saka opisthen sou met' oligôn ippeôn*) to serve as a rear guard (*saka*).[17] The key problem for the interpretation is that the above information with its vanguard, first line, second line and *saka* fits both main types of cavalry formations in use at this time. However, in light of the fact that in this text Nikêforos divided the battle array only in two (*dichê*) while assigning only a few horsemen (*oligôn ippeôn*) to the *saka*, it is likelier that Nikêforos actually means the cavalry battle formation given in the *Strategikon* of Maurikios and *Taktika* of Leôn. This conclusion receives further support from the fact that Nikêforos does not mention the use of the *katafraktoi* wedge, even if he also noted that the cavalry force could include tagmatic forces alongside the thematic forces (D 16.21; GM 16.2). In other words, it is probable that the array in question usually consisted of: 1) the vanguard; 2) the first line consisting of three divisions, outflankers and flank guards (even if the latter are not mentioned); and 3) a second line of four divisions with possible fill-up *banda* between, or alternatively a second line with three divisions with no fill-up units in the intervals, with a third-line rear-guard called *saka* posted behind the second line on both flanks.[18] However, it is possible that at this time the second line no longer had the fill-up *banda* between the

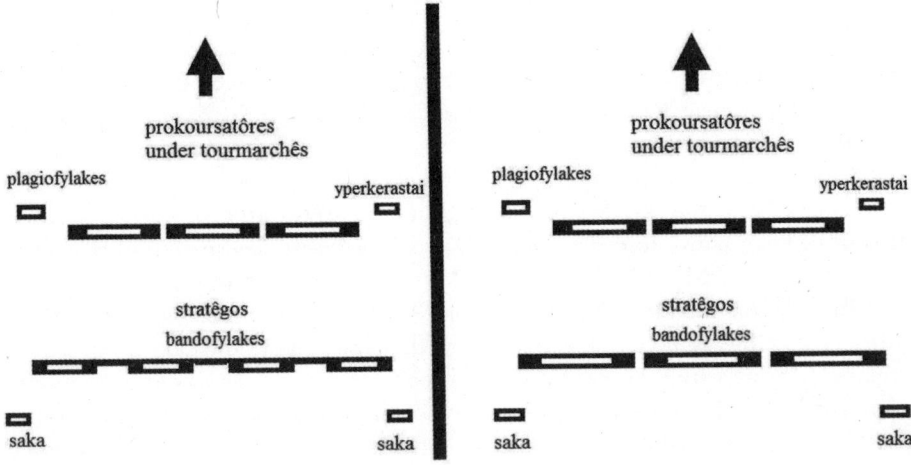

divisions because Nikêforos did not include those with the other cavalry formation that he presented in the PM. Similarly, it is uncertain if the divisions were separated into *koursôres* and *difensôres*.

If the enemy ambushed the *tourmarchês*, the first line engaged them. As a result of this, it was considered certain that the enemy would be so disordered that the second line under the general would certainly defeat them if it came to that.

If the enemy was unaware of the Romans following them and did not ambush them, then the *stratêgos* was to place his men in ambush before dawn and wait until the enemy raiders rode away from the emir's force so that the emir was left with only a few men. Then the general was to dispatch three divisions of equal size (*parataxeis = merê*) to attack while he remained behind with the other three or four divisions (*parataxeis*) and followed the first line. If the first line struggled, the general was to dispatch the flanking divisions (both of which existed in the three- and four-division versions) against the enemy's flanks. If this was not enough, then the general was to lead his remaining reserves into the combat. According to Nikêforos, if the *stratêgos* had 3,000 horsemen this was usually enough to crush the emir's battle line, because in this situation the emir had only a few men left.

If the *stratêgos* had access only to the cavalry forces of his own theme and the size of the force was small (i.e. less than 3,000 horsemen), then the general was not to engage the emir but was to shadow the raiding force and ambush only those of the enemy forces that charged into a village and spread out to pillage. The treatise also includes another only slightly different alternative version of the same.

When the *stratego*s had figured out the objective of the enemy raid, he was to outflank the enemy force during the night, conceal his forces, and then reconnoitre in person. He was to launch his attack against the emir's camp or his army when the raiding party of the enemy (*koursa/kourson*) had gone far enough. If he didn't feel confident enough because the enemy camp had natural defences complemented by strong fortifications, he was to leave behind a force of horsemen to observe the emir, which acted as a shielding force while he attacked the raiding party when they had dispersed.

If the raiders used a large *foulkon* (here the equivalent of cavalry *defensôres*) to protect the raiders who had spread out to pillage, the general was to divide his forces in two. When the first group had joined battle with the *foulkon*, the second half under the general was to charge into the enemy *foulkon* with great speed and much shouting.

If, after all this, the enemy still resisted, the general was to rest his men for three days while his infantry forces massed to protect the passes leading out of Byzantine territory. In the PM (6.3), Nikêforos Fôkas instructed that when the enemy was near the general was to distribute the battle plan to his officers, after which the entire army was assembled and purified with a fast (eating only once toward the evening), during which the men promised repentance for their sins after which the army partook in Holy Communion just before advancing against the enemy. It is possible that we are here dealing with a similar three-day rest as in the PM, but it is even likelier that in this case a real three-day rest was meant because the men had already fought against the enemy, so there was no longer any need for 'purification' whereas there was a need for a real rest. Most importantly, the DV does not refer to any fasting in this context – only to the need to rest the men before the battle. According to the DV, it was only after the three-day rest that the general was to get his forces in front of the enemy and engage the enemy with infantry and cavalry whilst they attempted to move through the passes.

5.4. Lightning strike with a cavalry vanguard while the emir remained close to the mountain pass to escort the invaders back home (DV 7–11)

It was also possible that the large mixed Saracen army sent most of its horsemen in a lighting strike to plunder in advance while the baggage train with the infantry (which also included small numbers of horsemen) followed behind. The enemy infantry force then pitched its camp close to the mountain passes so that it could escort the horsemen through the rough terrain and defiles after they had returned. In this case, the *stratêgos* was instructed to attack the raiding party when they had scattered to plunder. If this was not possible thanks to some blunder, the general was to fight against the encamped army under the emir and call the infantry to join him. He was also expected to dispatch 40 horsemen under an experienced officer to guard the road that the returning enemy raiders would have to take when returning to the main force.

If the *stratêgos* suspected on the basis of information provided by deserters and/ or prisoners that the encamped enemy force would change its campsite, he was to prepare two ambushes on either side of the road the enemy would take, separate still another force of 100 horsemen close to some villages near the enemy's expected

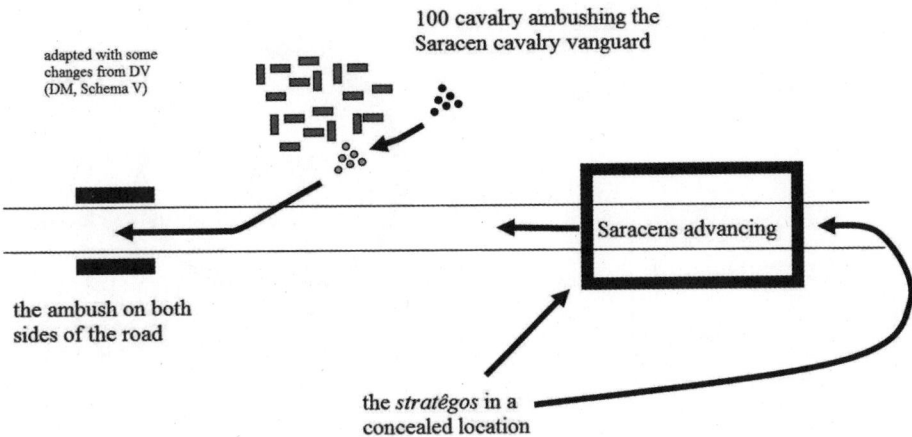

The ambush of the Saracen main army (infantry, baggage with some cavalry) when it seeks to change site of marching camp.

route, and conceal his main forces in a secure location close to the scene. When the enemy vanguard consisting of cavalry began to search the houses of villages and dismounted to pillage, the concealed 100-man ambushing force would charge out so that they cut off their route of retreat to the main enemy force. The pursuers guided the fugitives towards the ambushes placed on both sides of the main road. When the general observed this he launched most of his army against the main enemy force while some of his men attacked their rear.

If the morale of the enemy did not collapse, the Saracens unloaded their pack animals to form a defensive rampart in a circle formation.[19] In this case, the *stratêgos* was to continue the fight against them by arraying his force into a circle formation. The use of infantry was of paramount importance if they had arrived in time, and if not, then some of the horsemen were to dismount and fight with bows, slings, spears and shields. The general was also to bring his equipment and baggage train to the scene and set up a camp nearby to destroy the morale of the enemy.[20] Even if this attack did not destroy the enemy force completely, it was considered sufficiently scary to demoralize them. It was always considered safe to attack the enemy's baggage train included in the marching column of the main army under the emir because it did not contain adequate numbers of cavalry for the enemy to effectively pursue the Romans if the latter had failed in their attack.[21] If the general did not know in advance the marching route of the enemy, he simply arrayed his forces for attack against their marching column if he considered his chances of success good. Nikêforos noted that the attacks against the enemy's baggage train, especially when the Roman infantry had arrived in time, had always succeeded and led to the annihilation of both the enemy and the baggage train – he also noted that the same had happened to the Roman baggage trains if the enemy had attacked it.

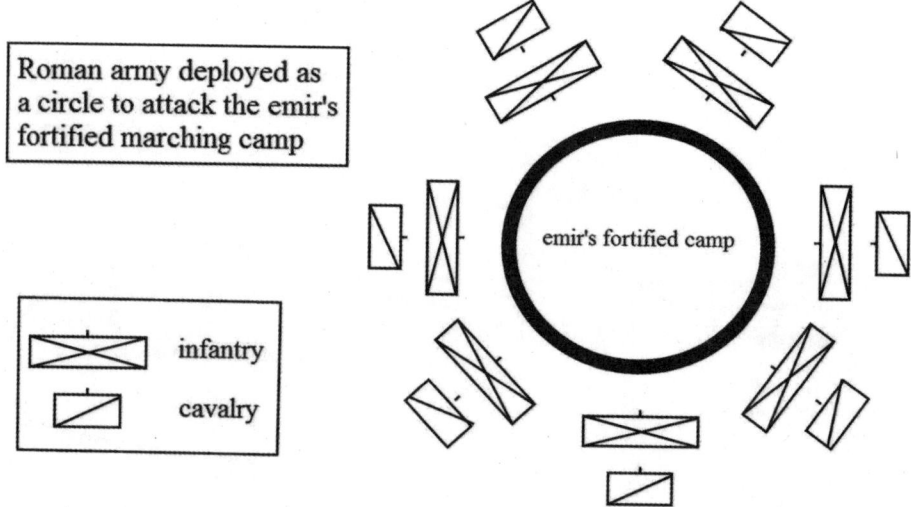

De velitatione of emperor Nikêforos Fôkas

The author (i.e. Nikêforos) stressed that attacking the enemy's baggage train was a sound tactic which had been used with great success by both the Romans and Saracens. He had witnessed this in person, read about it from the books of history, and had been taught so by his predecessors. This stands as clear evidence of the very high quality of the thematic forces, because they were always able to defeat numerically superior Saracen forces inside fortified marching camps protected by infantry forces. Similarly, this account suggests that Nikêforos had annihilated the emir's main army and baggage train several times during his tenure as *stratêgos* of the Anatolikon, with the implication that in these situations the enemy's cavalry vanguard had managed to penetrate into Roman territory thanks to the lightning tactics they used, which also means that Nikêforos had failed to catch the enemy's vanguard so that he had been forced to attack the emir's main army instead. It is no wonder that Nikêforos warned against attempts at pursuing the *Arabitai* Bedouin cavalry in his *Praecepta militaria*. The Bedouins with their Arabic horses moved really fast for short distances so that it required a serious and determined effort from the Romans to catch them.

If the emir's army remained in their original campsite close to the pass leading out of Roman territory and waited for the return of the cavalry raiders, the *stratêgos* had several different options to choose from depending on the reactions of the enemy. Firstly, he could still attack the emir's camp but if he chose to do this he was to delay this attack until such moment that the infantry forces were assembled and brought to him. Nikêforos still emphasized that the attack against the emir's camp was not to be delayed because there existed the danger that the Saracen cavalry raiders would return and make the attack impossible. If the enemy had pitched

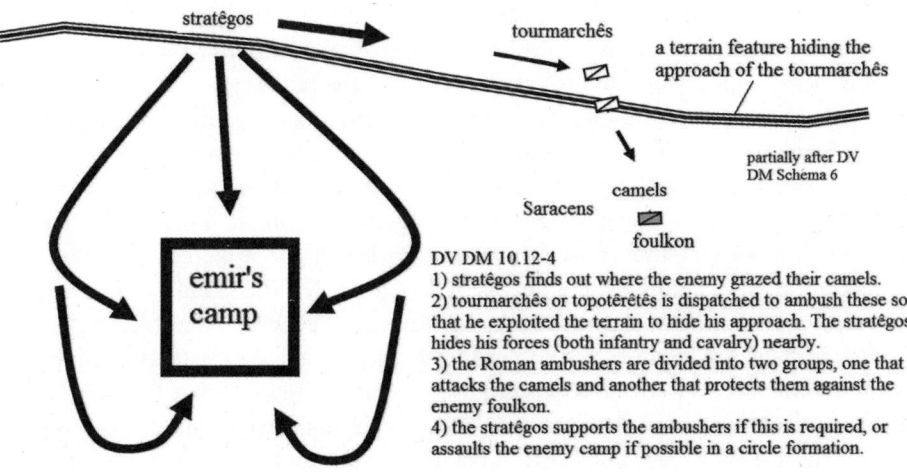

attack against the Saracen camels and emir's camp when the emir waited the return of the raiding party close to the mountain pass and did not send out foraging parties that could be ambushed

partially after DV DM Schema 6

DV DM 10.12-4
1) stratêgos finds out where the enemy grazed their camels.
2) tourmarchês or topotêrêtês is dispatched to ambush these so that he exploited the terrain to hide his approach. The stratêgos hides his forces (both infantry and cavalry) nearby.
3) the Roman ambushers are divided into two groups, one that attacks the camels and another that protects them against the enemy foulkon.
4) the stratêgos supports the ambushers if this is required, or assaults the enemy camp if possible in a circle formation.

their camp next to a river or a stream which protected one side of the camp, then the general was to pitch his camp opposite the ford to frighten the enemy by his presence.

In the meanwhile, the *stratêgos* was to launch his attacks against the foragers dispatched from the enemy's marching camp. He was to place some horsemen (two groups, one in ambush and another to protect them) in ambush against the foraging parties of the enemy. This type of attack was bound to succeed because the emir's camp had only a small number of cavalry left.

If the emir did not send out foragers and remained in position, the general was to find out from what side of the camp the enemy led the camels out to graze. Then he was to send a select force of cavalry under a *tourmarchês* or *topotêrêtês* to capture the camels, while another force remained behind to protect them against the enemy *foulkon* (defenders in close order, who in this case may have included infantry). The general was also to place his forces nearby in concealment in case the enemy engaged those sent ahead. The *stratêgos* would thus be able to engage the enemy forces in combat outside the marching camp if the situation required this, or alternatively he could launch his forces against the enemy's camp. This was to be done so that each unit of infantry and cavalry was assigned a sector to attack so that they attacked the enemy camp in a circle formation if this was possible.

Then, if the general was unable to defeat the enemy on the first day thanks to the fierce enemy resistance aided by their infantry and terrain, he was still to remain nearby and call in more infantry reinforcements. In the meanwhile, the *psiloi* and *sfendonêtai* were used to attack the camp during the night from different directions and large numbers of fires were lit around the enemy camp to give an impression of large numbers. The idea was to demoralize and tire the enemy, who would not even get the opportunity to rest. The general was also expected to encourage his light infantry to engage the enemy in hand-to-hand combat, and if as a result of this the light infantry on one sector made their way inside the enemy camp, this was expected to raise the morale of the rest of the units, with the result that these also rushed into the enemy encampment in the hopes of capturing valuable plunder. The author clearly understood the psychology of the masses based on animal instincts and what it meant for the morale of both the attackers and defenders. When the whole Roman army joined the assault as a mob and rushed impetuously to kill and plunder, this launched the survival instincts among the defenders, with the result that the defenders no longer fought in any organized manner. Their only thought now was how to save themselves through panicked flight, which in this case was almost impossible because the Romans had surrounded the camp on all sides. In this version of the attack against the enemy camp, the general did not leave the side leading into enemy territory open to induce flight, but sought the total annihilation of the enemy force. However, if this did not happen because of some blunder or bad luck, as Nikêforos put it, then the soldiers who got inside the enemy encampment during the night at least killed many enemies while capturing a huge amount of booty in the form of horses, mules and other things. In other words, even if the attack failed, it still caused major damage to the enemy.

If the scouts that had been dispatched to guard the route that the enemy raiders were likely to take informed that the enemy raiders were returning, the general was to abandon all attempts and be satisfied with the booty he had got. However, if the raiders had sent a *veredon* (after the Latin *veredus*, meaning the public post horses used by envoys and couriers)[22] to announce their arrival, it could be ambushed if it had advanced too far from the main group.

After this, the *stratêgos* was to send his foot and horse behind the emir's camp to occupy and block the passes leading out of Roman territory. Once the enemy had been forced to abandon the attempt to get through, the Romans were not to give the enemy any respite from attacks. If the *stratêgos* could not prevent the enemy from marching through because he did not possess enough infantry, he was still expected to be able to cause damage to the enemy with his blocking force while giving prisoners a chance to flee to safety.

If the *stratêgos* had too small numbers available to him to block the passes, he could still try to use ambushes. He was advised to seek a very secure place suitable for infantry, with a fortress nearby if possible. The infantry was concealed in ambushes on both sides of the road and the cavalry under the *stratêgos* just behind them. 100 horsemen were selected to act as baits. These were hidden near some village at night. When the enemy horsemen were observed to dismount to pillage, the officer in charge sent 60–70 horsemen to assault them and the remaining 30–40 horsemen in support if necessary. The officer was expected to provoke the enemy into following him, so at times he charged them while at other times he fled away from them. When the pursuing enemy reached the site of ambush, the infantry attacked. And if some of the enemy managed to get through the infantry then the cavalry engaged them.[23] The purpose was clearly to exploit the terrain, situation, and ambush to the fullest.

Ambush against Saracen vanguard in a situation in which the general had too few men to engage the main force.

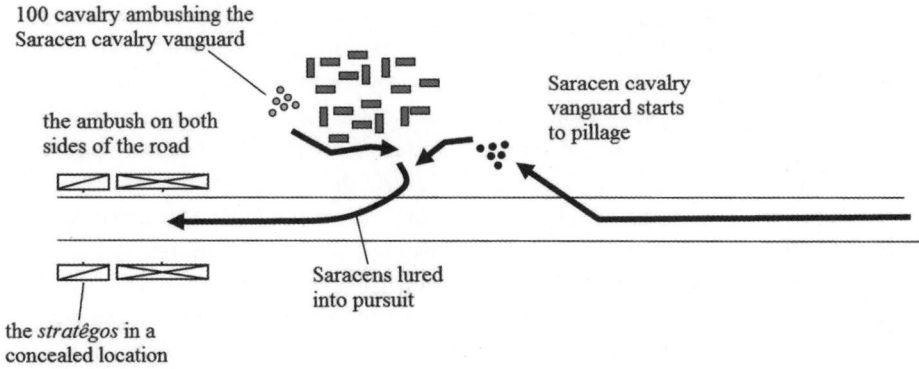

5.5. The cautious invading enemy did not divide their army: version 1 (DV 13)

When the Saracen invaders were particularly cautious and did not send their raiding parties to any great distance, the *stratêgos* had to alter his tactics. He had to guess where the enemy would encamp next. If the distance from the present camp to the new camp was very long (16 miles or more and so the enemy would be tired when they reached the new camp), then he was to figure out if the place was suitable for the placing of an ambush. If the answer was in the affirmative, then he placed 200–300 horsemen in an ambush with instructions to attack the advance party of the enemy troops – called *mensuratores* as they measured the camp in advance[24] – when they were in the process of arranging the camp, whilst he placed the rest of the troops under his own command in a second ambuscade in some suitable place protected by some fortifications. The presence of a fortress nearby was considered to be particularly useful in such situations as a place of refuge. If footmen were needed, these could also be taken from the garrison of the fortress to assist the force under the *stratêgos*. If the enemy managed to withstand the first ambush, then they were led to the second ambush. The presence of the infantry garrison at the fortress ensured that the enemy would be unable to defeat the Romans. The rest of the defensive campaign was undoubtedly carried out as prescribed elsewhere in the *De velitatione* according to circumstances.

5.6. The cautious invading enemy who did not divide their army: version 2 (DV 17–8)

When the enemy collected its entire army (cavalry and infantry) with the intention of penetrating deep into Roman territory while the Romans assembled their army in preparation for this, the enemy usually followed a set of precautions because they knew of the presence of the Romans nearby. In this case the *stratêgos* was to devise ambushes similar to the ones described above or below. However, if the enemy did not give any opportunities for this because they knew of the presence of the Roman army and were therefore very cautious, then the general could also make a diversionary invasion into enemy territory (see below).

The skirmishing tactics against a cautious large invasion force of Saracens relied on the use of feigned flight and ambushes. The only real difference with the tactics adopted in this case concerned the size of the Roman force, which was exceptionally large as the Romans had been aware of the impending enemy invasion so that they had been able to assemble 5–6,000 cavalrymen against the invaders. The *stratêgos* was once again expected to use ambushes and feigned flight to even out the odds.

In this larger version of the skirmishing tactics, the *stratêgos* concealed 200–300 horsemen in an ambush near such villages as the enemy was likely to enter in search of food and booty. The main cavalry force was divided into two ambuscades: 2,000 horsemen were to be placed in an ambuscade with a high observation post and behind them a further 3,000 horsemen. If possible the latter were placed near a fortified place which had infantry to support them. According to Nikêforos Fôkas, the *stratêgos* needed no more than 5–6,000 men and the assistance of God to achieve a victory over the enemy. When one remembers that the major Saracen invading force in the DV (D 14.40–8) could consist of 6–12,000 cavalry raiders (*foulka*) and the main force of 18–36,000 footmen, cavalry and servants under the emir himself, it is clear that Nikêforos expected the thematic forces to outclass the Saracen forces in every respect, which indeed appears to have been the case when he led them. The key factor here is the morale of the thematic forces, which was high if they were treated with respect and the generalship of the *stratêgos* was high. In sum, it is clear that the thematic forces fought well when they were led by an uncorrupted *stratêgos* who was also known to be a good commander.

The commander of the first ambushing group sent 100 or more horsemen to attack when the enemy forces dismounted to pillage, and kept the rest as defenders. The 300 cavalrymen were expected to force the enemy into flight with ease, so that they then pursued the enemy until they faced the enemy's supporting forces (*foulkon*) who then charged against the Romans. The 300 Romans responded to this with a feigned retreat. If the enemy pursuing the 300 men were not numerous, the Roman *archêgos* (commander) could try to defeat them on his own. Otherwise, his mission was to lure the enemy into pursuit by feigning flight. If a large enemy force conducted its pursuit in a disorderly manner, the commander could wheel about a part of his force so that, if there were wounded men, men needing spare horses etc., they got more time to flee. When the men feigning flight approached the second ambush, they turned left or right to make room for those in the second ambush of about 2,000 men to then charge the disordered Saracen pursuers with a wide front. Therefore, the location of the ambush was to be level and broad with nothing to obstruct the charge. It is possible that the 2,000 horsemen were divided into three divisions as if they were the first line of the standard cavalry battle formation, even if this is not specified.

It was obviously preferable for the men feigning flight to wheel left, as this gave them better changes of shooting backwards at their pursuers while exposing the enemy's shieldless side to the Roman second ambush, but the deciding factor in the wheel was obviously the lay of the land. When the ambushing force charged out with much shouting, the fleeing horsemen wheeled around against the enemy's flank.

If the enemy still managed to hold their ground by bringing up their reserves, then, at a prearranged signal, command or trumpet sound, the men retreated to the third ambuscade consisting of about 3,000 horsemen. Nikêforos fails to state how these were organized, but one would expect that they were deployed either as four divisions or three divisions as in the standard cavalry formation mentioned elsewhere in the DV, but that this time they did not need *saka*-rear guards because the rear was protected by the infantry, the terrain (as the ambuscade was located in a safe hidden place) and a fortress. Again, the men in flight were to wheel either left or right of the ambushing place so that the ambushers could charge right into the flank of the pursuers while the fleeing force then wheeled about to face and outflank their pursuers.[25]

396 Nikephoros II Phokas, 912–969

5-6,000 Roman horsemen performing a triple ambush with a feigned flight against a large cavalry force

1st ambush	2nd ambush	3rd ambush
300 horsemen	2,000 horsemen	3,000 horsemen with possible infantry support

not in scale

phase 1:
a) 300 Roman horsemen ambush the Saracens raiders in a village and pursue them up to their defenders after which they perform a feigned retreat.
b) if the pursuing enemy force was not large then the Romans could attempt to defeat them.
c) if the pursuing enemy force was large, then the ambushers led them to the second Roman ambush.

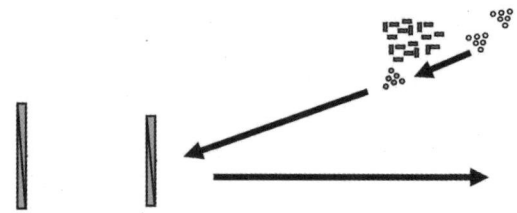

phase 2:
a) the 300 horsemen wheel either left or right to expose the enemy to the second ambush of 2,000 horsemen.
b) if the second ambush did not result in the defeat of the enemy because they had still reserves left, the Romans retreated to the third ambush.

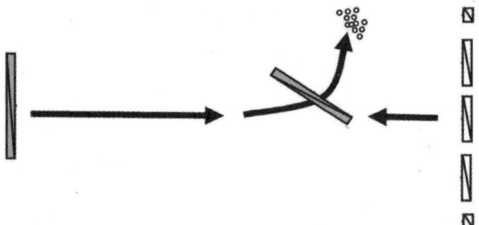

phase 3:
a) the retreating cavalry wheeled either left or right and exposed the pursuing cavalry to the third ambush of 3,000 horsemen.
b) if the enemy was not yet defeated because of some blunder, then the presence of Roman infantry forces ensured victory to the Romans.

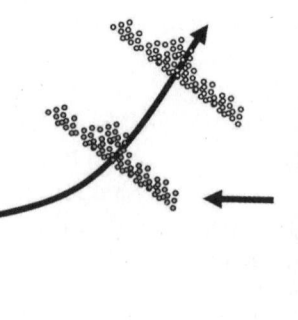

If the enemy still managed to withstand this shock because of some blunder or because the enemy fought with exceptional ferocity, then the general could use his infantry (if present) to defeat the enemy or at least to save his army. Even if the Romans could not defeat the enemy completely, Nikêforos still considered this effort worthwhile because many Muslims would be killed and even more captured as prisoners of war so that this would have instilled fear among the enemy so that the remaining enemy forces were likely to retreat into their own territory.

If after the previous defeat the enemy still continued to wander about pillaging (the following tactics were obviously relevant also in other, similar instances), then the general could send a detachment to ambush their foraging parties when they had gone three- to four-miles from their army. When, as a result, the food became scarce the enemy would retreat. If the enemy did not allow this to happen, then the general ambushed the *foulkon* that was the slowest in returning to their camp. Real farmers and herdsmen, grouped together with some horsemen dressed like farmers (all on horseback, not more than twenty in number), were sent with herds of animals from one village to another to lure this *foulkon* into following them. Again, the Roman army was divided in two. The enemy *foulkon* was lured into the first ambush, and if the site of the ambush was near other enemy forces they were bound to try to revenge the ambush by sending horsemen out. The second ambush under the *stratêgos* was placed two miles behind the first. As before, the purpose was to lure the enemy into successive ambushes and ultimately to either destroy them on the spot or to force them into retreat through the passes and further disasters.[26]

These other versions of feigned flight and ambush in the DV differed from the ones presented in the MS (3.14, 3.16, 4), LT (14.36–54) and ST (23, 46.12–3, 46.27, 46.30, 46.33) and can be considered as further elaborations of these schemes. The MS and LT and also the ST have the ambushers either attached to the main battle formation (ambushers behind the outflankers), or placed outside on both sides of it, or hidden in some terrain feature where those who feigned flight could lead the enemy. The DV also does not include the use of feigned flight across hidden trenches, pits or fields of caltrops that can be found in the older treatises. However, there were also similarities. In the MS and LT, when the larger force was visible to the enemy it retained its combat formation, while the smaller ambushing forces used the *drouggos*-order, but when the unit that feigned flight consisted of a small number of men, then the main force retained its combat formation while those who feigned flight used the *drouggos* order.

5.7. Use of a diversionary invasion when the Romans were heavily outnumbered: DV 20

If there did not exist a large enough army to confront the large enemy army ravaging Roman territory, Nikêforos recommended the use of a diversionary invasion. In this case, there existed the danger that while the Roman general could not ambush the enemy, the invaders could ambush the defending general. In these circumstances it was preferable to transfer the action to enemy lands. The author noted that this strategy had been successfully used in the past, which he clarified with three recent examples and with the referral to this tactic in the military handbook of the wisest emperor Leôn.

According to Nikêforos Fôkas and his editor, the diversionary operation against the enemy could be carried out in four different manners: 1) the general could invade enemy lands while his most trusted generals engaged the invading enemies in guerrilla warfare; 2) the general could stay behind while his most trusted general invaded enemy lands at the head of a significant army of cavalry and infantry; 3) the local commanders could act on their own by sending raiding bands when the enemy invaded; and 4) the order to follow emperor Leôn's instructions regarding diversionary invasions (LT 18.131–2) means that Nikêforos foresaw a situation in which the Kibyrraiôtai Fleet or some other Roman fleet could be used to attack the enemy's coasts when they were invading by land.

The man in charge of the diversionary invasion directed his attack against the enemy civilian population and local garrisons, ravaging (chopping down trees, vines and everything that bore fruit), pillaging and burning everything (fields, houses, fortresses, suburbs, cities), and besieging fortified towns. The luckiest Roman invaders were able to capture the relatives of the invading emir together with other illustrious people. The purpose was to force the enemy to leave Roman territory while the diversionary army returned without suffering any harm. It is possible that the diversionary campaign followed the tactical scheme described by Nikêforos in the PM when the army included infantry.

The man in charge of the defence against the enemy invaders protected the local evacuated civilians by staying close to the areas threatened by the enemy. If the enemy encamped near some high ground allowing the use of night attack against their camp, the man in charge was required to do just that (see below). If the enemy withstood the night attack and the enemy persisted in its search for the civilians, then the general in charge protected the roads leading there by placing javelin throwers (*akontistai*) and light-armed (*psiloi*) infantry in narrow and rugged places. If the enemy also used infantry, then the civilians were evacuated into more remote and defensible areas.

5.8. What to do when the enemy besieges a fortified *kastron* (town) (DV 21)

The defending general was also required to determine which fortified towns were open to a siege. The extreme ruggedness of the terrain in places prevented this. In those places, the general had to make sure that all those taking refuge in such a place had a minimum of four months' supplies with them and that the cisterns had enough water to last the siege. Notably, the author noted that he did not need to give a detailed account of the defensive procedures and siege engines because there were already detailed treatises that could be consulted. In other words, the author presupposed the use of these by the officers in charge. This means that the detailed descriptions of siege equipment and tactics, including the reproduction of the ancient treatises, were indeed still in use – as was also noted in the DRM and OT a little later. The author (Nikêforos) restricted himself to giving very basic instructions for the use of the relief army in defence. As the enemy usually encamped in a circle around the besieged town and did not fortify it due to the ruggedness of the terrain, the general was to attack the besiegers by using infantry against one sector of the enemy army at night while the men inside the fort made a sally. If the ruggedness of the terrain forced the besiegers to deploy their forces only on one or two sides, then the general concentrated on the use of a scorched-earth policy while the enemy foragers were ambushed. Eventually, this would force the enemy away as they would begin to suffer from hunger. On the other hand, if the besieged Romans began to suffer from hunger, relief could be brought by dividing the army in two. While one half threatened the enemy and forced them to concentrate their forces, the other half carried supplies into the fortress on horseback.

5.9. What to do when the enemy did not besiege a *kastron* (DV 22)

If the enemy did not besiege any towns but pillaged the countryside, the defending general sought to use ambushes against their foragers so that they would begin to suffer from hunger. If, as a result, the enemy was forced to divide their army into two or three sections to facilitate supply so that a half or a third of the enemy army became separated from the rest, the general was expected to destroy the separate divisions one at a time if possible. When one enemy division had been sent to gather provisions simultaneously from several villages, the general divided his army in two divisions and concealed his forces. The general then waited to see how the enemy acted. If the enemy *foulkon* defending the raiders returned to the enemy's main camp close to nightfall, the *stratêgos* attacked those enemy forces which were still scattered among the Roman villages. The first portion of the Roman army then charged on horseback against the scattered enemy while the general with the second portion of the army stayed close and protected them. If the enemy *foulkon* remained in position, the general engaged it close to sunset by using two cavalry lines. If things went badly, the Romans could still withdraw practically unscathed into the safety of the night. The aim of this exercise was to force the enemy out of the land through hunger.[27]

5.10. The Saracens make a surprise invasion (DV 12)

The methods described above were not possible when a large enemy force managed to surprise the Romans before their forces were assembled, and so the *stratêgos* had not even been able to assemble his own forces let alone be reinforced by the forces of the neighbouring *stratêgoi*. In such circumstances, the general was to dispatch a *tourmachês* or other officers immediately to the region the enemy had invaded with orders to evacuate inhabitants and their animals to places of refuge. In the meanwhile, the general was to approach the enemy and then make his presence known to them when he noted that the enemy was planning to attack the villages. When faced by this the enemy was likely to attack the force under the general, with the result that he conducted a retreat. The result was that the enemy did not pillage the villages that it had planned to. The other tactic was that the general posted the main force in some strong position and dispatched some selected horsemen against the enemy, and when the enemy then counterattacked these retreated to the strong position occupied by the general. With these measures and by shadowing the enemy force the *stratêgos* gave time for the civilians to evacuate to places of refuge. The remainder of the defensive campaign undoubtedly was carried out as prescribed elsewhere in the *De velitatione* according to the circumstances.

6. Retreat of the enemy, the occupation of the mountain passes in advance, and night attacks against the saracens: DV 4, 5, 23–5

The DV deals with the tactic of blocking the passes from the retreating enemy in Books 4 and 23–5 which were clearly written down originally at different times for separate treatises. Book 4 first notes the usefulness of surprise attacks and ambushes at all times, after which it notes that in many cases it was preferable to allow the enemy to invade and enter Roman territory and then engage their forces with only skirmishing tactics while blocking the passes through which the enemy could retreat. This gave the *stratêgos* time to assemble his infantry forces from a wider area while wearing out the invaders. When the enemy were returning home they were already worn out and burdened with baggage, captives, and animals, while the Roman forces were fresh and ready for combat. The general was to ensure that the soldiers dispatched to occupy the mountain passes in advance also took possession of the water springs, and if this was not possible then every group of 100 soldiers was to carry ten bags of water.

Books 23–5 provide a far more detailed treatment of this tactic. When the enemy was withdrawing from Roman territory, the infantry was dispatched beforehand to occupy the roads/passes in the mountains. Nikêforos listed the *themata* and *kleisourai* through which the enemy might choose to retreat from west to east as follows: Seleukeia and Anatolikon up to the Taurus Mountains bordering Cilicia; Kappadokia and Lykandos; Germanikeia and Adata (Hadath); Kaisun, Danoutha, Melitene and Kaloudia; and regions beyond the Euphrates River that bordered Chanzeti and the enemy territory as far as Romanoupolis.

When the Roman *stratêgos* who was shadowing the enemy was four stations/campsites (i.e. 4 days) away from the mountain passes, he was to get in front of the enemy and join with his infantry while one of the ablest commanders was left behind to shadow the enemy. When the enemy was two days away from the pass, the general assembled his whole army and called in as many additional infantry forces as possible.[28] Now that battle was inevitable, the general encouraged his troops with eloquent speeches. All of the high points of the mountains and roads were secured by infantry. The cavalry was distributed to those roads and places where they could fight alongside the infantry. The battle formations were the same as when the Romans defended the passes against the invaders. For the battle formation, see the beginning of the appendix. Nikêforos foresaw two possible outcomes: 1) The enemy would realize that it was impossible to pass through and seek another road; or 2) the enemy would accept the foolish risk, only to be beaten back – with the result that they still had to seek another road.

When, as a result, the enemy was retreating, the general was to send cavalry together with *psiloi* to act as a vanguard while he followed them with the rest of his forces. At this point the battered enemy was expected to seek to reach their homes safely and so would attempt to avoid fighting. The *stratêgos* could therefore expect that the enemy would try to reach the next pass by force-marching at night. It was because of this that the general was instructed to hurry after them immediately, because it was certain that the enemy would be tired at this stage. See the narrative of the events of the years 950 and 953! The infantry with cavalry support was to attack the enemy's *saka* while the *stratêgos* dispatched other *psiloi* with cavalry on both sides of the road ahead so that these could then attack the sides of the actual enemy marching column. According to Nikêforos, if the enemy was then put to flight and so tried to flee in the middle of the night they were doomed if the Romans pursued them relentlessly.

However, Nikêforos also listed other possible outcomes. If the enemy became aware of the presence of the Roman forces shadowing them, they could pitch their tents and set up a fortified camp. Now the general could use another standard

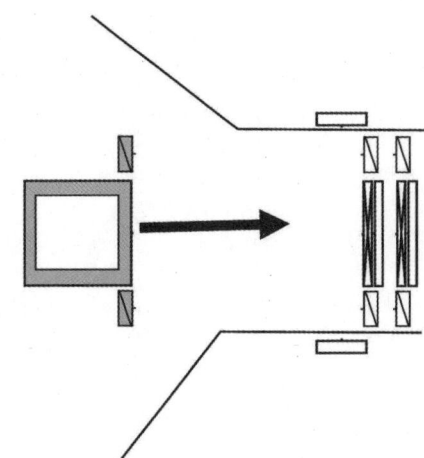

Blocking the pass against the Saracens returning home

1) the overall stratêgos joined the infantry when the enemy was at a distance of four days from the pass. He left the best of the other stratêgoi behind with some cavalry to prevent enemy's raids.
2) when the enemy was at a distance of two days from the pass, the cavalry left behind joined the stratêgos at the pass.
3) in this example the pass is suitable for the inclusion of the cavalry which in this example are placed on the flanks of the infantry phalanxes. If the terrain did not allow the inclusion of the cavalry in it, the Romans used only infantry as described in the earlier diagram.

Roman tactic – a night attack against the enemy camp. The main attack was to be conducted from the rear by infantry units under the general himself while the remaining infantry forces were divided into six divisions (*parataxeis*), three on each flank. Each of the infantry divisions had cavalry reserves and was placed under a single commander. The infantry divisions under the general undoubtedly had a similar frontage to the flanking ones, but I would not exclude the possibility that it might have had some additional infantry and cavalry reserves because it was still the main force under the general, who also had his own unit of bodyguards accompanying him. The side with the road leading out of Roman lands was to be left open to induce the enemy to flee rather than fight.

If the layout of the enemy camp was extended due to the terrain, the infantry divisions were to be spread about a bowshot apart from each other. On the other hand, if the layout of the camp was a circle, then the Roman infantry was also to be arrayed in a circle around it, but again with an opening on the side leading out of Roman lands. Note the difference between this type of night attack and the alternative offensive circle formation given earlier in the treatise in the context of shadowing warfare – the probable reason for leaving an opening for the enemy to flee through in this case is that when the armies were closer to the border the enemy was more likely to flee to its own territory when the opportunity for this was given.[29]

> **Night attack against retreating enemy**
>
> 1) the *stratêgos* attacked the rear while the rest of the forces were divided into six divisions each consisting of infantry and cavalry. The route of retreat was left open to induce the enemy into flight.
> 2) each of the Roman divisions was arrayed with light infantry in front, heavy infantry in the middle and cavalry behind.
> 3) the attack progressed so that the middle divisions started the assault followed up by the front divisions so that the *stratêgos* was the last to attack.

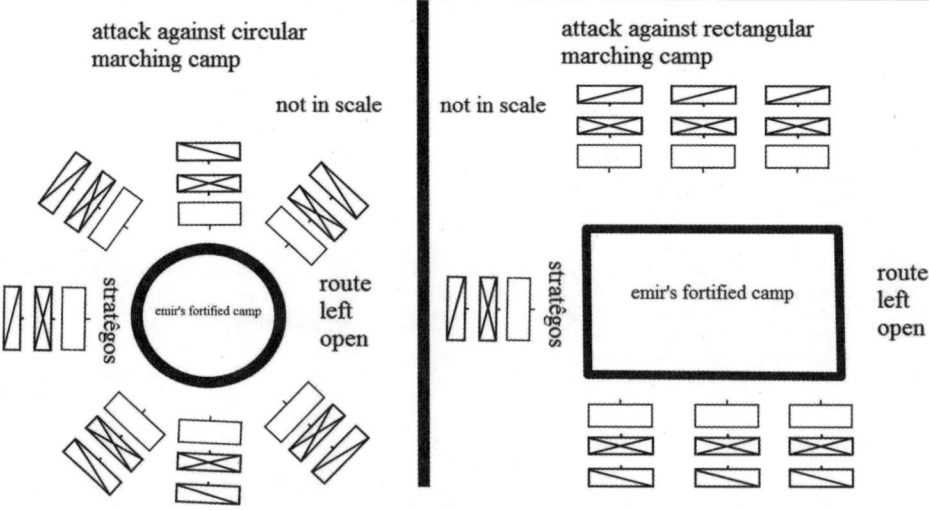

When the units of the Roman army had been arrayed around the enemy encampment in preparation for the attack, the Romans encamped close to the enemy and around it in the positions they had taken and lit a large number of fires to intimidate them. After the preliminary preparations had been made, the general sent light infantry *psiloi* (men who threw stones by hand, slingers and archers) ahead to attack the enemy camp. According to the treatise, those in the middle (the centre of the three divisions) began the attack and then those 'up in front' (= flanks closest to the enemy territory?). If the ground rose on one or both sides, then the infantry launched their attacks first with missiles from those sides, followed by an attack conducted by the rest of the infantry who did this with much shouting and battle cries. If the enemy cavalry charged out, it could do no harm to the light infantry because of the terrain. This attack was then followed by the general's forces.

If the enemy did not flee after the barrage of missiles, the *psiloi* and the ones who had been sent ahead were encouraged by their officers to rush into the tents of the enemy to take the enemy's horses, mules, and other possessions while capturing enemies as prisoners. When the rest of the Romans saw this, all of them would want to join the looting and butchery, with the result that they would overrun the enemy in an orgy of killing. In the words of Nikêforos, the soldiers would go through the enemy tents sparing nobody while cutting them down with swords. The defenders were bound to scatter in panic, and all who could would mount their horses and flee through the opening left for them. The idea was clearly to exploit the animal instincts of both the attackers and defenders. Nikêforos again demonstrated his great insight into the psyche of the period soldiery.

According to Nikêforos, it was typical that at the break of the following day the Saracens who survived this butchery often stopped at some level ground and halted

Attack against retreating enemy in a narrow sloping terrain
1) the general was to post four divisions of infantry in the narrows so that there were two divisions on both sides of the pass while leaving behind the enemy an ambuscade composed of infantry and cavalry under a brave veteran commander.
2) the narrows forced the enemy to halt and advance in column which made them vulnerable to the attacks from the flanking heights.
3) the ambushing force left behind was to attack the enemy *saka* if they were in high spirits while it was still on level ground, but if it was not they were to assault it when it hurried down the pass to join the main force.

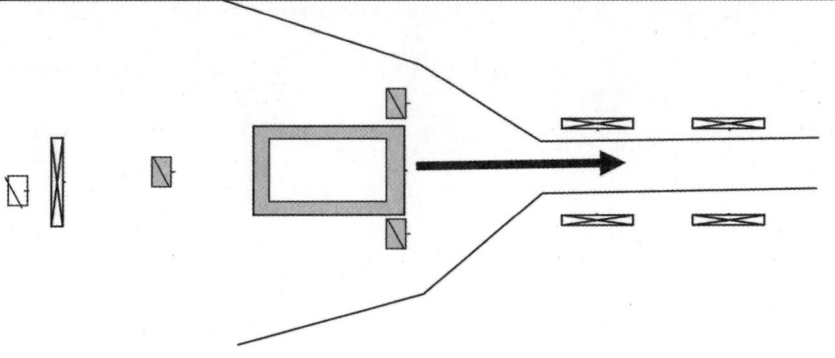

for a rest. The level terrain made this location unsuitable for night attacks, which meant that the *stratêgos* was to take all his forces, both infantry and cavalry, and get in front of the enemy so that he could occupy the heights and the pass before the enemy. According to Nikêforos, by the grace of Christ the enemy would now be ready to be annihilated. This tactic was to be used when the terrain was level without any difficult sections.

If the pass leading out of Roman territory sloped downward and became very narrow and rough, Nikêforos advised the use of a different tactic because such terrain forced the enemy forces to halt and proceed through the narrow section in column formation. When the Saracens were in the process of doing this, they were very vulnerable. The *stratêgos* was therefore instructed to exploit this by placing two infantry units on each side of the pass (i.e. four in total) and a separate ambuscade consisting of infantry and some cavalry in the rear against the enemy *saka* on level ground. When the enemy's marching column reached the site of the ambush in the pass, the ambuscade higher up could launch their attack against the *saka* rear guard, but if the men above were still unsure, they could wait until the enemy *saka* had to begin its descent and then launch their attack when the enemy was below them. The likely outcome was that the rear of the enemy column would hasten its march towards the now-blocked narrow passage, become very tightly pressed, and so annihilated to the last man (see pp.232–7).[30]

Appendix III

Nikêforos Fôkas' Military Reform and *Praecepta Militaria* in ca. 957

1. Background

Nikêforos Fôkas replaced his father as *domestikos tôn scholôn* with the task of reforming the Roman military system in 956/7, beginning with recruitment, equipment and training and ending in the reform of combat tactics. The results of this reform are visible in the *Praecepta militaria*. As noted by Eric McGeer (1995, 180), it is not impossible that the original form of the *Praecepta militaria* was circulated among the officers when Nikêforos Fôkas was *domestikos tôn scholôn*. Regardless, McGeer (1995, 180–1) still suggests that the treatise dates from the period when Nikêforos was already emperor on the basis of the demand that the leader of the light-cavalry skirmishers had to be a *stratêgos* or *topotêrêtês* appointed by the emperor. In his opinion such an appointment could be made only in the field. I disagree with this assessment. It was perfectly possible for such an appointment to be made in advance – after all the thematic and tagmatic *stratêgoi* were similarly appointed in advance.

Indeed, I would suggest that the original version of the *Praecepta militaria* was made available to the officers as one part of the military reform instigated by Nikêforos Fôkas as *domestikos tôn scholôn* in 957 and that the final version such as we have dates from the period after his reign, and that it was because of this that it required the explanation in the title *Nikêforou despotou* to explain who Nikêforos wrote the treatise for. The reason for this conclusion is that the equipment demanded from the impoverished infantry and cavalry *stratiôtai* reflected the circumstances prevailing in the 950s which Nikêforos set out to correct when he became emperor by ordering every category of soldier to fulfil greater demands than previously, with the implication that their equipment was also required to reflect their new status. This is clear from the fact that, after the second reform, which can be dated to the actual reign of Nikêforos, even the regular cavalry *stratiôtai* were required to be equipped like *katafraktoi*, which is not the case in the *Praecepta militaria*, where most of the cavalry consists of *kontaratoi* or *toxotai*. In other words, when Nikêforos reformed the recruitment pattern of the army as emperor, all major divisions of the cavalry were required to possess *katafraktoi* and not only the *katafraktoi* wedges as in the *Praecepta militaria*. In short, it is clear that the requirements in the *Praecepta militaria* reflect the situation prior to the second reform. The principal intention of the *Praecepta militaria* was to streamline and simplify the offensive battle tactics for use against the Hamdanids in Cilicia and Syria at the same time as Nikêforos recruited and drilled new soldiers.

The defensive strategy and tactics used against the Saracens had already achieved perfection, so there was no need to reform those, but it is still probable that Nikêforos Fôkas had already distributed his personal instructions for their use when he was the *domestikos tôn scholôn*, and which were then after his reign compiled and rearranged by an unknown author. The result of this work was the so-called *De velitatione* and it was done at the behest of Nikêforos Fôkas himself lest the defensive tactics be forgotten. See Appendix II. The same author was also given the task of writing a military treatise on how to conduct a military campaign in the Balkans (possibly the so-called *De re militari*), which suggests a likelihood that the author had been given these tasks in about 968–9 with the result that the treatises were completed only after the death of Nikêforos.

2. Cavalry Tactics (PM 3–4)

Nikêforos Fôkas (PM 3–4) divided the cavalry into the *prokoursatôres* (skirmishers/vanguard) and their *foulkon* (the *defensôres* in the ST), consisting of both *kontaratoi* (*kontos*-bearers) and *toxotai* (archers), *kaballarioi* (regular cavalry consisting of *kontaratoi* and *toxotai*) and *katafraktoi* (cataphracts). As noted by Eric McGeer (1995, 211), it is probable that the *katafraktoi* consisted mainly of the tagmatic forces while the rest consisted of the thematic forces (PM 1.16, 2.17, 3.10, 4.10). The *scholarioi* (e.g. PM 4.14) which were included in the theoretical model army of Nikêforos Fôkas are likely to have meant primarily the detachments that were dispatched to bolster the numbers of the thematic forces in the key areas facing the Arabs in the tenth century.

In the idealized theoretical scheme presented in the *Praecepta militaria*, the cavalry army consisted of the 300- (200 in the van and 100 as *foulkon*) or 500-horseman (350 in the van and 150 in the *foulkon*) *prokoursatôres*; a first line with three divisions (flank divisions consisting of 500 men and the centre division of a 504- or 384-horseman wedge), 100 outflankers on the right and 100 flankguards on the left; a second line of four 500-horseman divisions with the *stratêgos* in the middle; a third line with three divisions similar to the first line; a bowshot behind the third line the baggage train; and three divisions of unspecified size behind the baggage train as rear guards (presumably about 300 men in total, as in the corresponding formation in the ST). This gives us a theoretical total of about 5,568 – 6,008 horsemen plus the bodyguards (*foulkon, bandofylakes*) of the *stratêgos*. The same principles as Nikêforos (PM 4.4) presented in the text were to be followed whether the cavalry force was larger or smaller.

The equipment of the cavalry forces used as vanguard differed slightly from the typical *kontaratoi* and *toxotai*. In the model cavalry army of Nikêforos Fôkas the *prokoursatôres* consisted of 500 horsemen, of whom 110–20 consisted of archers (*toxotai*) and 380–90 lancers (*kontaratoi*). All of them wore *klibania* (sing. *klibanion*) or *lôrikia* (sing. *lôrikion*), together with helmets (sing. *kasidion*, pl. *kasidia*), swords (sing. *spathion*, pl. *spathia*) and maces (sing. *rabdion/rhabdion*, pl. *rabdia/rhabdia*). In addition they had modest-sized shields (PM 4.1.34–9). The *toxotai* were obviously equipped with bows and quivers while the *kontaratoi* were equipped with the *kontos*. All of them were required to possess a spare horse to enable them to move longer distances fast. The men assigned to the *foulkon* of the commander of the *prokoursatôres* consisted of similarly-equipped men and one may assume that they too had spare horses.[1]

The regular cavalry lancers (*kontaratoi* = *kontos*-armed; the *doryforoi* of the ST) were equipped with modest-sized shields (*skoutaria*) measuring four or five *spithamai* (93.6–117cm), *klibania* (sing. *klibanion*, lamellar armour) or *lôrikia* (sing. *lôrikion*, usually a mail shirt which was often used together with the *klibanion*), *kontaria* (sing. *kontarion*, lances 3.74m or 4.2m in the ST), *spathia* (sing. *spathion*, sword), *rabdia* (sing. *rabdion*, maces) and helmets (sing. *kasidion*, pl. *kasidia*). Their horses were not expected to be armoured. When deployed in the main battle formation, the regular cavalry *toxotai* were also expected to carry shields, *klibania* and swords similar to the *kontaratoi* (PM 4.1.34–9).[2] The equipment requirements for the lancers represent a change from the days of Leôn. Nikêforos did not expect his *kontaratoi* to carry bows when employed as lancers. This represents a return to the equipment requirements of Maurikios, who similarly did not require his lancers to be equipped with bows when they formed the front ranks, even if he required all of the horsemen to train to use the bow. It is possible that the omission of the bow from the equipment requirements of the *kontaratos* is just an overlook and that Nikêforos still expected them to carry them so that they could use them, or that this is a reflection of the diminishing numbers of men able to use the bow while mounted. I would suggest that the former is true, because elsewhere Nikêforos required the troopers to be able to chase the *Arabitai* cavalry away with bows (PM 4.17). In short, I would suggest that the equipment requirements mean only the equipment that the troopers usually used when in formation, in addition to which they carried other pieces of equipment in their saddles or belt.

Each *katafraktos* was to be equipped with: a *klibanion* with sleeves to the elbow (clearly chain-mail armour), with a hanging skirt of *zabai* covering the wearer to the knees; an *epilôrikion*-surcoat worn over the *klibanion* made of cotton and raw silk, with openings at the elbows so that sleeves were attached to the back of the shoulders with loops; *chalkotouba* (sing. *chalkotoubon*, leg-guards, greaves); *manikela* (sing. *manikelion*, arm-guards often made of cotton or coarse silk covering the area from elbow to the wrist and the back of the hand), which have '*zabai*' made of cotton or coarse silk (means presumably that pieces of mail were stitched into the thickly stitched cotton or silk); iron helmets (sing. *kasidion*, pl. *kasidia*) with *zabai* two- three layers thick (i.e. a triple layer of chain mail) so that only the eyes were visible; shields (*skoutaria*) of unspecified size (probably the same as the *kontaratoi* had, i.e. 93.6–117cm in height).[3]

The horses of the *katafraktoi* were protected by *katafraktos*-armour, consisting of pieces of felt or boiled leather reaching the knees of the horse (padded armour) which were fastened together so that only the lower portion of the horse's legs, eyes and nostrils were visible while the stomach remained open, or alternatively the horses were protected by *klibanion*-armour which covered the chest of the horse and was made of bison hides (pieces of hide stitched together like lamellar) so that it was split at the legs and underneath to allow the horse to move its legs freely. The requirement that the horse armour was split at the legs obviously means that there were also types of horse armour which was not split. One wonders if this instruction was also put into effect in such cases in which the *katafraktos* already had horse armour of the wrong type, because the changing of its structure would undoubtedly have cost money. Nikêforos therefore no longer expected that horse armour would also include armour made out of metal. This is once again a reform which saved money, both for the state when the *katafraktoi* consisted of the *scholarioi* of the *tagmata* and from the *stratiôtai* when the *katafraktoi* consisted of the thematic forces.

The second of the reforms concerns the equipment. Whereas Leôn had equipped all of his *katafraktoi* with spears, Nikêforos required that the first to the fourth ranks in the cavalry wedge were to be equipped with *spathia* (sing. *spathion*, double-edged swords), *sidêrorabdia* (iron maces with sharp corners or three, four or six-cornered), or with *parameria* (sing. *paramerion*, a waist-held sword which was often a sabre) and *sidêrorabdia*. They were to have either swords or maces in their hands and other maces hanging from their belts or saddles.[4]

The purpose of equipping the front ranks with maces, and not with spears that enabled the men to retain a distance from the enemy, was to force the men to charge into close contact where they could employ their maces in such instances in which the enemy formation did not collapse immediately. This change must have resulted from lessons learnt, namely from such an instance in which the *katafraktoi* did not charge through the enemy infantry formation but stopped in front in an attempt to create the opening with spears alone, which was unlikely to succeed. The outer edges of the wedge from the fifth down to the twelfth rank consisted of ranks in which every other rank had the spear or mace/sword (i.e. fifth rankers had spears, sixth rankers mace/sword and so forth).[5] It should also be noted that while Leôn required all of his *katafraktoi* to be equipped with bows, this was no longer required by Nikêforos. The likely reason for this is that whereas Leôn had required the *katafraktoi* to pursue the enemy, this mission was no longer given to them by Nikêforos, even if it is still very likely that the *katafraktoi* usually carried bows to enable them to vary their combat tactics. Another important change is that whereas Leôn had allowed the wedge to contain *doryforoi* among the heavy-armed, in Nikêforos' version all heavy-armed were expected to be cataphracted.

Nikêforos (PM 2.11, 4.13) also required his *katafraktoi* to conduct their attack at the trot/canter, unlike Leôn (ST 46.9) who had required them to use the gallop.[6] This change had a dual purpose: 1) the trot/canter forced the men to retain their

504 horseman wedge of katafraktoi (PM 3)

𝆑 mace or sword bearer
𝆑 kontos bearer
𝆑 mounted archer or javeliner

the wedge with 12 ranks:
- the first rank 20 horsemen
- each rank four horsemen more
- the last 12th rank has 64 horsemen

504 horsemen:
- 354 mace- and lance bearers
- 150 mounted archers or javeliners.

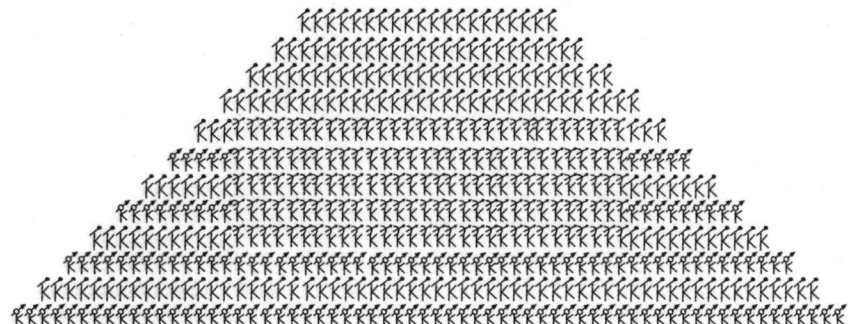

order and cohesion better, which in its turn meant that they retained the wedge/trapezium formation until contact; and 2) the fact that the men retained cohesion of formation forced all of the men to participate in the charge. This change in procedure must have resulted from the breakup of the cavalry wedge as a result of the use of the gallop in some of the battles before Nikêforos issued his instructions, which in its turn would have enabled the men on the front flanks to refrain from making their way into the enemy formation. As noted earlier by Eric McGeer (1995, 288–9), the wedge with the blunt face forced the *katafraktoi* forward because the men on the edges in the front could not easily leave their positions when each following rank had two more men outside and behind. The use of the gallop was frightening to the enemy but it also had the tendency of breaking up the formation when the bolder men and horses advanced faster than slower horses and timid men, which in its turn enabled the cowardly to avoid making contact.

The *toxotai* were deployed in the middle (PM 3.6: i.e. inside) of the wedge from the fifth rank to the 'rear'. They were equipped with only *klibania*, swords, bows, quivers and helmets. If possible the horses of the *toxotai* were to be cataphracted, but if not possible then the men were to wear at least *kabadia* (padded armour made of cotton or coarse silk) hanging from their belts so that these protected them from the waist down while also protecting parts of their horses. Nikêforos (PM 3.9) also noted that the cavalry wedge could also include javelineer (*akontistai*) cavalry, which were to be deployed inside the wedge if present. He fails to state how these were equipped, but it is probable that their equipment had remained the same as in the *Sylloge tacticorum* (39.8). In that text Leôn states that the light-armed (*psiloi*) cavalry also included the *akontistai* (javelineers) equipped with two or three javelins (2.8m in length), a 3.74m spear, a helmet and a shield (rectangular 93.6cm in height; round 70.2cm in width). One may assume that the *akontistai* cavalry belonged to the *tagmata* that had been dispatched to serve in the key areas facing the Arabs. Since the *akontistai* were unable to use bows and used unarmoured horses, it is probable that these consisted of the mercenaries probably of western, Nordic or Slavic origins, or of the Bedouins, because one would assume that the Saracens, Armenians, Georgians, Bulgarians, Pechenegs, Turks and other mercenaries of similar origins would know how to employ bows on horseback.

On the basis of the *Praecepta militaria* (4.3, 4.20), it would appear that the ideal cavalry army was always accompanied by an infantry hollow square and a baggage train, so the cavalry force was deployed in sixteen units, but fortunately on the basis of Ouranos' *Taktika* (61.3) we know that pure cavalry armies were also divided into sixteen units when separated from their infantry support. Ouranos had available to him a better version of the *Praecepta militaria*, so it is clear that the same was true under Nikêforos Fôkas. In the idealized army of Nikêforos the *prokoursatôres* consisted of 500 horsemen (380–90 *kontaratoi*, 110–20 *toxotai*) so the vanguard consisted of 350 horsemen and its reserve (the *foulkon*) of three *banda* (150 horsemen) under the *stratêgos* or *topotêrêtês* appointed by the emperor. If the army was not large enough to detail this many men to the vanguard, then the commander was to employ 300 *prokoursatôres* (240 *kontaratoi*, 60 *toxotai*), with 200 used in front and two *banda* (100 horsemen) as its reserve under the *stratêgos* or *topotêrêtês* appointed by the emperor.[7]

The first cavalry line consisted of: the left outer wing of 100 flank guards (*plagiofylakes* of *kontaratoi* and *toxotai* so most of them were archers); the left division (*parataxis*) of 500 horsemen (300 *kontaratoi*, 200 *toxotai*) deployed five deep, with each rank consisting of two *banda* of 50 men for a total of 100 horsemen per rank (two ranks of *kontaratoi* in front, two ranks of *toxotai* in the middle and one rank of *kontaratoi* behind); the centre of a twelve-deep cavalry wedge of 504 horsemen (384 *katafraktoi*, 150 *toxotai*), or 384 horsemen (304 *katafraktoi*, 80 *toxotai*) if there were inadequate numbers of *katafraktoi* available; the right division of 500 horsemen deployed five deep just like the left division; and the right outer wing of 100 outflankers (*yperkerastai* of *kontaratoi* and *toxotai* so most of them were archers). The key reform concerning the first line was that Nikêforos eliminated the ambushers, because their duties were already performed by the *prokoursatôres*. The purpose of posting the *katafraktoi* wedge in front of the wings was to enable it to crush the enemy formation before the other units would make contact with the enemy. This was basically a variation of the Late Roman tactic of sending the middle division in front of the flanks when the enemy outnumbered the Romans.[8]

The second line consisted of: four 500 strong divisions (*parataxeis*) each deployed five ranks deep like similar divisions of the first line, each rank consisting of two *banda* of 50 men for a total of 100 horsemen; the commander's bodyguards were with him in the middle of the second line.

The key reform concerning the second line was that Nikêforos eliminated the fill-up *banda* between the divisions. The intervals between the divisions of the second line were to be wide enough so that the divisions of the third line could pass through easily. In short, the probable reason for the reform was that the presence of the fill-up *banda* made it more difficult for the divisions of the third line to pass through its intervals. The depth of five ranks with the double-fronted disposition (two ranks of *kontaratoi*, two ranks of *toxotai*, one rank of *kontaratoi*) was to be retained even when the army was very small or much larger so that the width of the Roman battle line could be stretched out according to the size of the cavalry force. In other words, there were no longer to be ten-deep regular cavalry divisions as there had been in Leôn's *Taktika* and the *Sylloge tacticorum*. The third line, the *saka*, was like the first line except that it did not have the outer wings. If there were not enough *katafraktoi* available, the middle division of the *saka* was to be equipped like the other two flanking divisions (lacuna in the PM 4.5 emended from OT 61.5).

Eric McGeer (1995, 289) has observed quite correctly that the reason for the preference to also possess a second *katafraktoi* wedge in the third line resulted from the fact that the *katafraktoi* wedge was a weapon that could be used only once and if the attack failed it had to be regrouped and reformed in the rear. It was because of this that it was preferable to possess another *katafraktoi* wedge in readiness so that the general could make another try without having to wait for the first wedge to reform itself in the rear.

The baggage train (or the infantry hollow square with the baggage train) followed at a distance of a bowshot (ca. 330m), and behind it were posted three units of rear guards (*opisthofylakes*), which consisted of 100 horsemen each for a total of 300 men (ST 46.27, OT 61.6). When the infantry hollow square followed, the spare horses were posted inside the infantry hollow square between the infantry and baggage train or separately behind the cavalry force (PM 1.15, 4.7; OT 61.7). In both cases the horses of each *bandon* were to be distinguished from the others with their own pennant. When the cavalry was inside the hollow square, their spare horses were directly behind them so that the baggage train was in the middle. Neither Fôkas nor Ouranos specify the location where the spare/reserve horses were when the array consisted solely of cavalry, but one may make the educated guess that it was just behind the third line or baggage train because Ouranos states that the spare horses were at a distance of three to four *orguiai* behind something unnamed (the baggage train is likelier) and that the trooper who had injured his horse could head back to the place where the spare horses of his unit were, after which he returned back to his place in the line.[9] The army was to campaign without any superfluous baggage and spare horses.

Nikêforos Fôkas foresaw several different ways in which the cavalry battle could progress. The following diagrams and their captions present a summary of his views. However, since Nikêforos Fôkas was a professional well-read soldier, he also knew that it would be impossible to present all of the possible scenarios in a treatise. Therefore, he instructed (PM 4.16) the *stratêgos* to use his reserves as he saw fit and suitable for the situation.

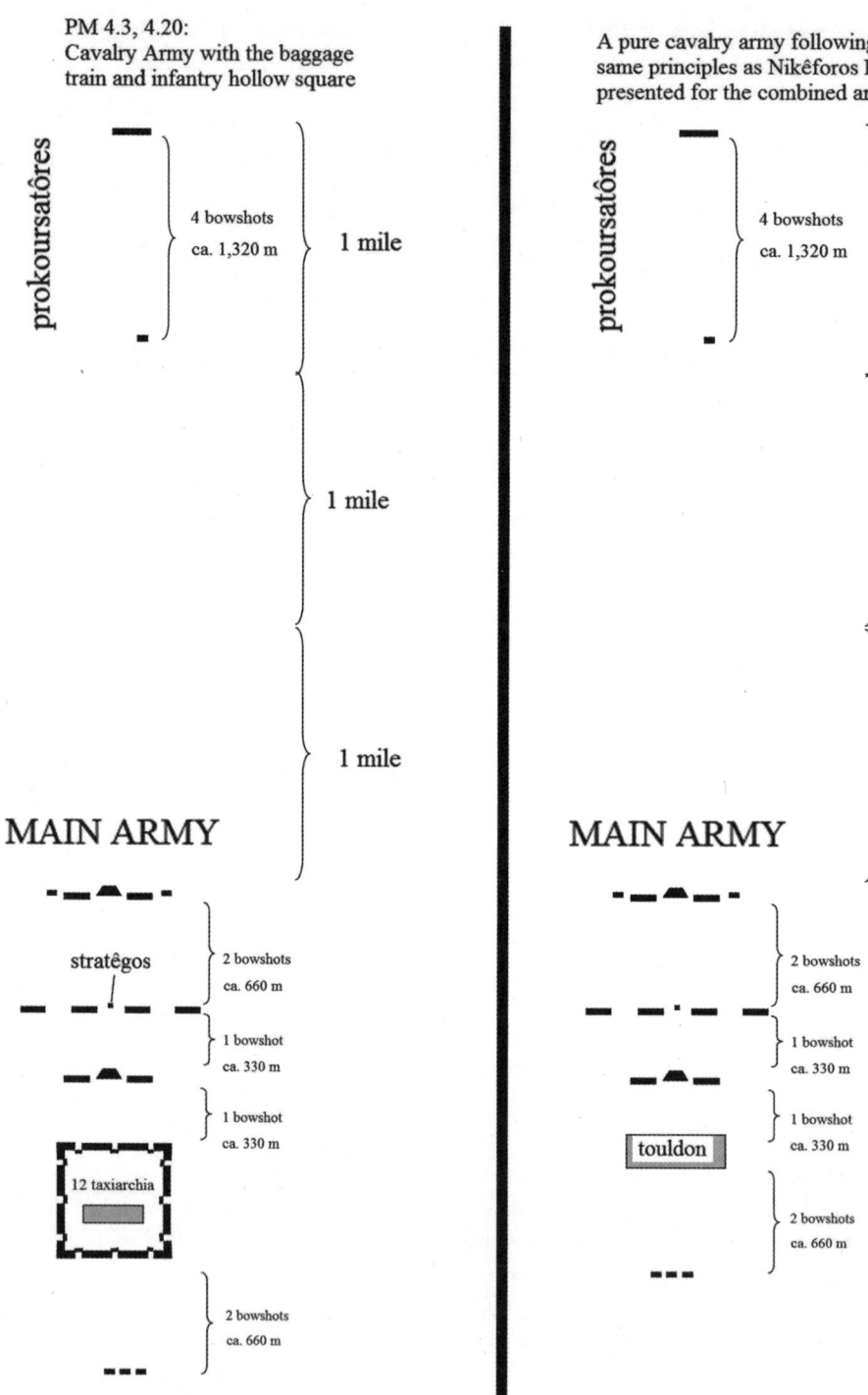

3. Combat procedure with cavalry formation:

1) The *stratêgos* was expected to find out first the size of the enemy army before engaging the foe in pitched battle. If the enemy force outnumbered the Romans both in infantry and cavalry, then the general was to use stratagems and ambushes. In such cases the correct time for a general engagement was only when the enemy had fled once, twice or three times and was suffering from poor morale while the Romans were in high spirits. By following this procedure it was possible to defeat an enemy force which was twice the size of the Roman force. The general was expected to follow the same procedure also when the two sides were equally strong, which means that a general engagement in the initial stages of combat was allowed only when the Romans outnumbered the enemy significantly. PM 4.19.

2) If the general had decided to engage the enemy and advanced towards the foe, then the procedure depended on how the enemy conducted itself. If the enemy advanced in a disorderly manner, then the *prokoursatôres* were to engage the enemy with ambushes and feigned flight. If the enemy advanced in good order, the *prokoursatôres* were still expected to skirmish with them, but in this case the expectation was that they then retreat between the intervals of the first line, after which they were arrayed behind the intervals so that they protected the flanks of the wedge and a battle proper began. PM 4.10. See also McGeer (1995, 292–3: 2.1).[10]

3) When the enemy drew near, the cavalry army started its advance with a prayer, after which they advanced silently until the trumpet signalled the time for the second prayer and the beginning of the attack. PM 4.11. See also McGeer (1995, 293: 2.2).

4) The *katafraktoi* wedge was to charge the location where the enemy commander was. The commander of the *prokoursatôres* dispatched 50 horsemen on both sides of the Roman wedge to protect its flanks against possible enemy diversionary attacks. This was a reform clearly resulting from lessons learnt. The Saracens must have attacked the flanks of the wedge successfully in the past. If the enemy attacked in strength, then the commander of the *prokoursatôres* sent more men to protect the wedge. PM 4.12. Ouranos (OT 61.12) states that the entire force of *prokoursatôres* was then sent to the flanks of the wedge if the enemy attacked the wedge in force. PM has a lacuna here, so it is probable that the same was meant. The posting of the *prokoursatôres* shows the principal weakness of the use of the protruding *katafraktoi* wedge in comparison with the use of the line formation in attack. It enabled the enemy to divert the centre with a small number of men directed at its sides, in particular in situations in which the flanking divisions were not close enough. The targeting of the enemy commander was seen as useful because the armies usually

lost morale if their commander either fled or died. See McGeer (1995, 293: 2.2; 303–5). In my opinion it is also probable that the elite status of the *katafraktoi* wedge formed out of the *tagmata* negatively influenced the morale of the thematic units posted on both sides of it because the expectation was that the elite *katafraktoi* would be the deciding division. This problem was not present in the original version of the Roman cavalry formation as presented in the sixth-century *Strategikon* and LT. Nikêforos sought to lessen this possibility with harsh discipline and drilling and in particular by showing respect to the thematic forces.

5) When the enemy arrows started hitting the front of the *katafraktoi* wedge, the Roman mounted archers were to start their archery against the foe. PM 4.13. See McGeer (1995, 293. 2.3–4; 305). The Roman archery aimed to disorder the enemy formation before the *katafraktoi* reached them because this increased the likelihood of the enemy formation breaking either before contact or immediately after contact had been made.

6) The wedge and its flanking divisions were to advance at the trot/canter together with a perfectly aligned formation against the enemy, while the outflankers (and possibly the flank guards?) tried to outflank the enemy. PM 4.13. See also McGeer (1995, 293: 2.3–4).

7) The extant text of the PM 4.13–4 regarding the pursuit of the routed enemy is unfortunately marred by a lacuna. The existing text states that the pursuit was conducted by the two flanking divisions of the first line, after which the *saka* advanced through the intervals of the second line to join the pursuit while the *katafraktoi* followed them at their own pace (canter/trot). This leaves out the *prokoursatôres* and outflankers, which must also have pursued as is actually stated immediately after the lacuna, and it also leaves out the exact role of the two *katafraktoi* wedges (when there were two) in pursuit because the text implies that the *katafraktoi* followed the pursuers as their 'defenders'. It is clear that the *prokoursatôres* and outflankers joined the two flanking divisions and the third line in pursuit, but what were the duties of the *katafraktoi* of the third and first lines and what were the flank guards doing? Fortunately, we can clarify the sequence from the text of Nikêforos Ouranos (OT 61.13–5) who had a better copy of the PM.

   a) According to Ouranos, if the enemy force fled only the *prokoursatôres* and outflankers began the pursuit, while the *katafraktoi* and the two divisions on both sides followed them in an orderly manner at the canter/trot. This was to ensure that the Roman battle formation was not broken prematurely, because when the first line retained its cohesion it could serve as *defensôres* for the pursuers. See also McGeer (1995, 293: 2.4–5).

b) It was only when the rout of the enemy was certain that the two flanking divisions of the first line broke their formation and joined the pursuit, after which the *saka* passed through the intervals of the second line and joined the pursuit and hereafter the second line advanced too so that it left the *katafraktoi* wedge of the first line behind to follow it at the canter/trot as a new third line. See also McGeer (1995, 293: 2.4–5).

c) The extant PM does not contain any similar referral to a cautious initial pursuit so it is indeed possible or even likely that the cautious approach was a later addition introduced after the reign of Nikêforos Fôkas either by Iôannês Tzimiskes or Nikêforos Ouranos or by some other general – this caution may have been a necessary addition to avoid the danger of being lured into an ambush by a feigned flight of the enemy. I would therefore suggest that in the PM the pursuit was always performed by the *prokoursatôres* (in irregular order), the two flank divisions of the first line (in irregular order), and the outflankers (in irregular order; it is possible that the flank guards did the same) as well as the three divisions of the *saka* (retaining their formation), while the second line and the *katafraktoi*-wedge of the first line (and flank guards in irregular array?) followed them as their defenders, and so the initial cautious pursuit was a later addition. The use of the flank divisions of the first line instead of the *katafraktoi* wedge was a reform, because in the *Sylloge tacticorum* Leôn had used the wedge as pursuers while the flank divisions followed up as their *defensôres*. The resulting interval between the two pursuing flank divisions was filled by the *prokoursatôres*, who also pursued the enemy. The likely reason for this change was that the unarmoured horses of the flanking divisions enabled faster pursuit for longer distances than was the case with the *katafraktoi*. The rest of the instructions concerning the pursuit are the same in both treatises.

d) If the routed enemy force was large, the rest of the cavalry units sent in pursuit (both the *saka* and the *katafraktoi*) were to follow the pursuing units in front of them using the irregular formation at the gallop so that they could support them immediately if this was necessary.

e) If the *prokoursatôres*, outflankers and the two flank divisions of the first line (and outflankers?) were deemed adequate for the pursuit, then only one of the units of the *saka* was sent in their support at the gallop, while the rest followed them while retaining their formation.

f) If the enemy was more numerous than the Roman host, then the *stratêgos* was to send the two flanking divisions of the second line in support of the pursuers (*prokoursatôres*, outflankers, two flank divisions of the first line, the *saka*) while he retained the two middle ones with him (with the *katafraktoi* wedge of the first line being behind him), and presumably also the flank guards on the left because these are not included among the pursuers in any of the versions. See also McGeer (1995, 293: 2.5).

g) Since none of the texts mention the flank guards among the pursuers, it is probable that these were usually retained behind for that duty unless the Romans had managed to outflank the enemy on both sides. However, it is clear (see alternative 8 below) that when the flank guards were included among the outflanking forces they joined the rest in pursuit of the enemy.

8) If the enemy had *katafraktoi* of its own and engaged the first line on equal terms, then the *stratêgos* was to send the three units of the *saka* through the intervals of the second line to outflank the enemy on both sides. Nikêforos fails to state where the middle unit of the third line was sent, but one may make the educated guess that this varied according to the situation, but that the preferred side would have been the Roman right flank if it was used for outflanking. However, even if this is not stated either by Nikêforos or Ouranos, I would still suggest that the *katafraktoi* wedge of the *saka* was usually dispatched forward to serve as a reserve line for the *katafraktoi* wedge of the first line, so it could repeat the attack against the enemy's centre if the *katafraktoi* of the first line were forced to retreat. If the enemy was even able to withstand the outflanking by the *saka*, then the commander was to dispatch the two flank divisions of the second line in support of the attackers while he still retained the two middle divisions of the second line as his last reserves. Nikêforos simply states that the *stratêgos* was to use his units as the situation required, which in my personal opinion also included the use of the *katafraktoi* wedge of the *saka* for repeating the attack in the manner I suggested above – this is the way it would have been used when the *saka* served as a reserve for the first line during the pursuit! If the enemy then fled, the *stratêgos* and his two remaining reserve units were also to join the pursuit, presumably as *defensôres*. PM 4.15–7. See also McGeer (1995, 293–4: 2.6–7).

9) If the enemy brought a large number of *Arabitai* (light Bedouin cavalry mounted on very swift Arab horses) and these attempted to encircle the Romans, the troopers were to ward them off with arrows and not pursue them because it was impossible to catch them. PM 4.17. See also McGeer (1995, 294: 2.8).

10) If the Romans had managed to encircle the entire enemy host, then even the units guarding the baggage train were also to join them if there was no longer any fear of the *Arabitai* attacking the baggage train. PM 4.17. See also McGeer (1995, 29: 2.8).

The *Praecepta militaria* has one very significant omission, which is that Nikêforos does not consider it probable that one, two or all three of the first line divisions could be forced to retreat by the enemy so that one, two or three of its divisions would then retreat to regroup themselves in the interval or intervals (or just behind the intervals) of the second line while the required divisions of the second line moved forward to face their pursuers. In the *Strategikon* of Maurikios, the *Taktika* of Leôn and even in the *Sylloge tacticorum* of Leôn, the main function of the second cavalry line was to act as a support line for the first when one, two or all three of its divisions were forced into flight. It is indeed possible that Nikêforos did not consider this likely, with the implication that he expected the frontline divisions to stay and fight even when the enemy had not fled, or that it was just too self-evident that the second line was there to protect the first that he did not even consider it worth noting. The other possibility is that Nikêforos simply did not state that the first line divisions retreated at the same time as the reserves, (whether the third line or the flanking divisions of the second line) moved forward. My suggestion is that in practise both versions could be true, namely that the first line divisions stayed in place and fought while the reserves were sent to their assistance, while it was also possible that some of the units did indeed retreat at the same time as the reserves came to their help.

As already noted the cavalry formation followed the same principles, regardless of whether the cavalry force was larger or smaller (PM 4.4), which represented a break with the principles laid out by Leôn in the *Sylloge tacticorum*. Nikêforos Ouranos (OT 61.4/61.92–8, 61.6, 61.18), who had a better copy of the *Praecepta militaria* available to him, clarifies the principle even better. He states that the model army had 6,000 horsemen, which was to be adapted to the size of the actual host, so that the same principles were retained regardless of whether the army was smaller or larger. If the army consisted of more men, the five-deep divisions were to be widened while the depth of five men (two ranks of *kontaratoi* in front followed by two ranks of archers, with the rear consisting of one rank of *kontaratoi*) was retained. The same was true of the *katafraktoi* wedge. It was to retain its depth of twelve ranks – only its width was adjusted according to the actual size of the host. The same was true for all units. Only the width and size of the units was altered according to the size of the cavalry force. The implication is that the only units in this array that were equipped as *katafraktoi* were the two wedges, which also represents a break with the past. The likely reason for this is that in Nikêforos Fôkas' scheme the flanking divisions of the first line were always intended to serve as pursuers if the situation so allowed. However, it should still be remembered that the reformed version of the cavalry formation of the *Sylloge tacticorum* was not the only one that Nikêforos Fôkas envisaged for his forces. The best evidence for this comes from the fact that he wrote instructions and memoranda for guerrilla warfare that were later compiled into the *De velitatione* by someone at his urging. This treatise includes the cavalry formations that had three divisions in front and either four or three (this is a new development) divisions behind as its reserve line.

418 Nikephoros II Phokas, 912–969

The same approach can also be found in the *Taktika* of Nikêforos Ouranos, who included the *Taktika* of Leôn in chapters 1–55. In short, the Romans continued to use the same tactics as we find in the sixth-century *Strategikon* as an alternative for the new tactics.

4. Infantry Tactics (PM 1–2)

According to the new Byzantine military doctrine as expounded by the *Praecepta militaria* of Nikêforos Fôkas, the *Romaioi/Rhomaioi* (Romans) and Armenians, large in stature and under forty, formed the preferred recruits for the Roman heavy infantry (*oplitai/aspidoforoi*). The men were to be organized into tent groups, with relatives staying with relatives and friends with friends so that the men cooperated better. The regulation equipment of the hoplites consisted of ersatz armour (short tunics/*kabadia konta*, reaching to the knees) made of cotton or coarse silk;

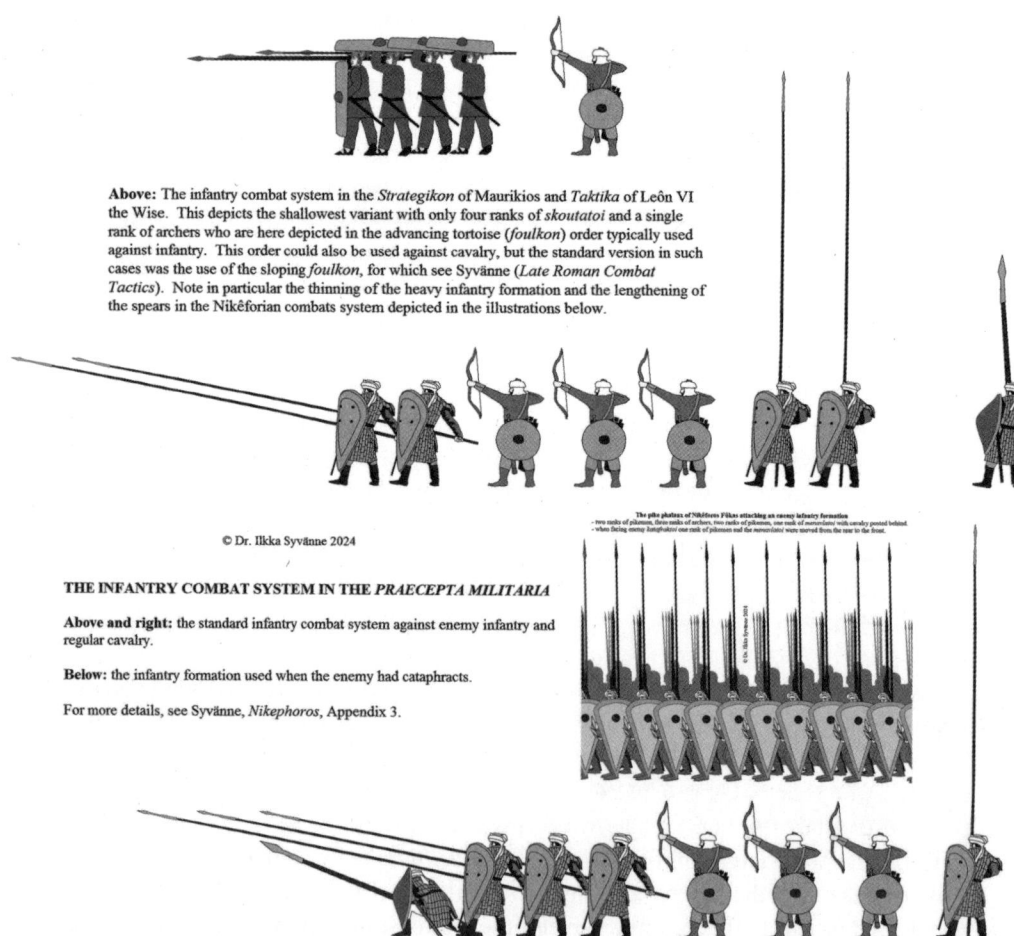

Above: The infantry combat system in the *Strategikon* of Maurikios and *Taktika* of Leôn VI the Wise. This depicts the shallowest variant with only four ranks of *skoutatoi* and a single rank of archers who are here depicted in the advancing tortoise (*foulkon*) order typically used against infantry. This order could also be used against cavalry, but the standard version in such cases was the use of the sloping *foulkon*, for which see Syvänne (*Late Roman Combat Tactics*). Note in particular the thinning of the heavy infantry formation and the lengthening of the spears in the Nikêforian combats system depicted in the illustrations below.

THE INFANTRY COMBAT SYSTEM IN THE *PRAECEPTA MILITARIA*

Above and right: the standard infantry combat system against enemy infantry and regular cavalry.

Below: the infantry formation used when the enemy had cataphracts.

For more details, see Syvänne, *Nikephoros*, Appendix 3.

ersatz helmet (felt cap with turban), shield (*skoutarion*) not less than six *spithamai* (140cm) in size, but preferably even larger (no shape given); boots folded to the knees or unfolded to the thighs; thick and sturdy spear (*kontarion*) 25–30 *spithamai* in length (5.85–7.02m); sword (*spathion zôstikia*); axe (*tzikourion*); and iron mace (*sidêrorabdion*).[11]

The acceptance of ersatz armour and helmet instead of proper gear is a reflection of the general poverty of the border region *stratiôtai* in the 950s, which Nikêforos Fôkas apparently sought to change later when he became emperor by placing greater demands on the equipment worn by the various classes of *stratiôtai*. However, one of the principal reforms of Nikêforos Fôkas in this context was the lengthening of the infantry spear from the *dorata*-spears of the *Sylloge tacticorum* which were only 3.74–4.7m in length (see Appendix 1) to 5.85–7.02m. The principal reasons for the change in length were: 1) the new pike (ca. 6–7m) gave the footmen longer reach than the Arabic cataphracts had with their lances; and 2) the new system for the use of the *menavlatoi* in combat required this. In the *Sylloge tacticorum* the *menavlatoi* had been posted 30–40 *orguiai* (ca. 56–75m) in front of the hoplites to break up the enemy's *katafraktoi* charge. Nikêforos Fôkas considered this a risky tactic and placed the *menavlatoi* with their 3–4 metre-long spears as the first rank of the heavy infantry formation so that the spears of the three ranks of hoplites behind them reached beyond the spear points of the first rank of *menavlatoi* (ST 1.10). In short, Nikêforos Fôkas lengthened the spears/pikes in a similar manner to the Hellenistic rulers when they faced enemies using pike phalanxes and cataphracted cavalry. The effectiveness of the reform is clear from the fact that the sources do not give us any instances in which the Roman infantry formation was broken with a frontal attack during the period when Nikêforos was either *domestikos* in 957–63 or emperor in 963–9.

Each of the light infantry archers (*toxotai*) were to be equipped with two quivers (one with 60 arrows and one with 40 arrows), two bows, four bowstrings, a small shield, a two-edged sword, an axe, and slings. The equipment of the slingers (*sfendobolistai*) was obviously the same, but without the archery equipment. When the army had lots of cavalry and it was necessary to increase the size of the hollow infantry square, the light infantry could also be equipped with spears, *menavlia*, and large shields (PM 2.14).[12]

The javelineers (*akontistai, riptaristai*) and *menavlatoi* were equipped like the hoplites, except that they had smaller shields and did not carry the spear (*kontarion*). Naturally, the javelineers were equipped with javelins and shorter throwing spears, while the *menavlatoi* were equipped with the very thick *menavlion* spears (shaft length 1.5–2 *orguiai*/2.7–3.6m plus spearpoint 1.5–2 *spithamai*/35–47cm = ca. 3–4m). The Russians (*Rôs, Rhôs*) and other foreigners were considered to belong to this class of soldiers.[13]

It should be noted that the size of the ideal campaign army given by Nikêforos Fôkas (11,200 *oplitai*, 4,800 *psiloi/toxotai*, and an unknown number of javelineers, Russians and slingers) does not tally with the figures that he gives for the twelve *taxiarchiai* and other units. See the discussion below. The twelve *taxiarchiai* had a total of 4,800 hoplites (4 ranks x 100 files x 12) proper so that there were an extra 6,400 hoplites not assigned to do anything. This means that we should include the *menavlatoi* (100 per *taxiarchia*) and javelineers (200 per *taxiarchia*) among the hoplites so that the twelve *taxiarchia* had a total of 8,400 hoplites (12 x 400 hoplites, plus 100 *menavlatoi* and 200 javelineers). The remaining 2,800 hoplites (hoplites proper, Russians, *menavlatoi*, javelineers and slingers) were presumably used as reserves for the protection of the intervals and for other duties. The twelve *taxiarchiai* had a total of 3,600 archers (12 x 300), which leaves 1,200 archers to the same sort of duties as the extra 'hoplites'.[14]

As noted, the ideal campaign army of Nikêforos Fôkas had 11,200 hoplites (spearmen) and 4,800 archers organized as a double-fronted hollow square formation consisting of twelve *taxiarchiai* (divisions) each consisting of a *chiliarchia* (1,000 men) plus the reserves. When the cavalry force was large and the enemy did not bring as many infantry as the Romans, there were to be twelve intervals between the divisions. When the cavalry force was not large and the enemy used infantry, then there were to be only eight intervals in order to make the array more secure. Nikêforos borrowed both of these instructions from the *Syntaxis armatorum quadrata* or from its source.[15] And when the commander wanted to make the square really secure he used only four intervals (PM 2.17). This is one of the reforms made by Nikêforos to the *Sylloge tacticorum*. Unfortunately, he does not explain when this variant was employed, but one may make the educated guess that it was employed in circumstances in which the enemy force was exceptionally powerful, requiring a diminishing of the numbers of intervals in the formation. The width of the intervals was set to be wide enough for 12-to-15 horsemen to pass through simultaneously. This is once again a change from the instructions of the *Sylloge tacticorum* (43.8, 47.4–7) which required intervals wide enough for eighteen horsemen to pass through, which the text appears to equate with the width of 13 *orguiai* (ca. 24m).[16] One may perhaps think that the slightly-narrowed interval was now about 16–20 metres wide, the latter being the likelier approximation.

Each of the 12 infantry divisions were led by one *taxiarchês/taxiarchos* and consisted of one division of 400 hoplites, 300 archers, 100 *menavlatoi*, and 200 javelineers. The javelineers and reserve slingers and archers were deployed behind the intervals. The divisions were organized into 100-file-wide units of hoplites and archers seven ranks deep (two ranks of hoplites, three ranks of archers, two ranks of hoplites), each of which was led by one *(h)ekatontarchos* and two *pentêkontarchoi*. The *ekantotarchos* stood in the middle of the line and the *pentêkontarchoi* on both flanks to direct the movements of the hoplite unit. The hoplites were trained to manoeuvre with their spears and shields, to defend themselves, and to fight against both infantry and cavalry. The *menavlatoi* were organized in similar manner behind the *taxiarchia*, or in front of it when required (PM 1.9, 1.12). The *taxiarchiai*-divisions were deployed in seven ranks of 100 men each, so there were two ranks of hoplites in front and two behind with three ranks of archers in between. The aim

TAXIARCHIA

E ekatontarchos	○ hoplite	✝ javeliner	⌐ slinger
⊓ pentēkontarchos	† menavlos	✝ archer	K kaballarios

When the enemy used katafraktoi, one of the ranks of hoplites in the rear and menavlatoi (if these were not already posted in front) advanced through the intervals to the front so that the menavlatoi became the first rank of the heavy infantry formation.

if the enemy employed katafraktoi the javeliners (and the menavlatoi of the neighbouring taxiarchiai) were to advance through the intervals on both sides (PM 1.12) to distract the enemy katafraktoi

if the enemy employed katafraktoi the javeliners (and the menavlatoi of the neighbouring taxiarchiai) were to advance through the intervals on both sides (PM 1.12) to distract the enemy katafraktoi

When the slingers were used as slingers they would have adopted more open formation for this purpose e.g. behind the hoplites, but when they advanced together with the javeliners, they employed their close quarters weapons.

was to enable each unit to withstand possible enemy breakthroughs, but it should be noted that this was not quite as secure as the system that had been advocated by Syrianos Magistros (PS 16.47ff.) in the sixth century (and whose text was still recommended reading according to Kônstantinos VII), which placed four ranks and four files of hoplites on the edges of the array.

Nikêforos Fôkas was well-read, so he felt it necessary to justify why he had made the infantry files only seven ranks deep (eight with the *menavlatoi*) when the ancient Hellenistic military theory required 10-, 12- or 16-deep formations. He noted that those deep arrays were outdated because the Romans did not face elephants and deep arrays were no longer used even by the Saracens.

When the enemy had *katafraktoi*, one of the last ranks of hoplites was also dispatched to the front, so the *pentêkontarchoi* on both sides led their men through the files just behind the hoplites posted in front so that there were three ranks of hoplites in the front. The *metôpaiôn oplitôn* used by Nikêforos for the hoplite front may mean either the first rank or the first two ranks, the latter being likelier so that these undoubtedly moved forward to make room for the new third rank behind them. The *menavlatoi*, which in normal circumstances appear to have been posted behind the last line of hoplites (there were 100 of them, so this is the likeliest place for them when they were behind the *taxiarchiai*: note also OT 56.9), were then sent forward through the intervals in like manner so that they became the first rank of the *taxiarchia*. The sequence in sending the files to the front is therefore clear. It is also possible that in the PM the *menavlatoi* formed the front rank all the time. The spears of the three ranks of hoplites reached beyond their *menavlia*. If the spears of these three ranks were smashed by the enemy *katafraktoi*, it was expected that the *menavlatoi* with their extra-thick *menavlia* would bravely withstand the enemy charge (PM 1.10). On the basis of the description of the *menavlon* in combat it is probable that the *menavlatoi* either knelt or crouched so that they could place the butts of their thick *menavlia* against the ground, but it is not known if the hoplites did the same because in the past and later the standard method for infantry facing cavalry was that when the front rank knelt, the second crouched and the following ranks stood upright.[17]

On the basis of Nikêforos Fôkas' instruction (PM 1.9–12) to send one of the last ranks through the intervals to the front as files, and Fôkas' statement that the front consisted of three ranks of hoplites and one rank of *menavlatoi*, it is clear that the *taxiarchiai* were organized in the *synaspismos/syskouton* order (file width 62.46cm) for combat because the spear points of the fourth rank had to project beyond the *menavla*.[18] The only way for the rear ranks to move to the front when the men were arrayed in the *syskouton* order was indeed to pass through the intervals as two 50-man files of soldiers.

Behind the intervals of the 12 divisions stood 30, 40, or 50 javelineers (*akontistai*) consisting of Russians or other foreigners, and behind them stood the foot archers and slingers. These were drawn from the ranks of the extra 'javelineers' who made up the twelve *taxiarchiai* and from the extra javelineers, archers and slingers not belonging to the *taxiarchiai*. See the attached diagram of a *taxiarchia*. Their mission was to block access to the interval when necessary, to protect the Roman cavalry in retreat, to attack the flanks of an approaching enemy cavalry formation when possible (this would have made the formation a unit level *epikampios emprosthia* or *menoiedes*), and to support Roman cavalry in an offense when needed. The most notable thing about this is the acknowledged bravery of the Russians and other foreigners in such combat.

If the enemy infantry formation was not a hollow square (i.e. it was a phalanx), the *menavlatoi*, *akontistai* and other *psiloi* advanced through the intervals from both sides of the Roman infantry square and attacked the flanks of the enemy infantry phalanx (PM 1.13). If the enemy employed a hollow infantry phalanx, then the *menavlatoi* and *akontistai* filled the intervals and fought together with the hoplites (PM 1.13).

The advantages of the hollow square formation both in combat and as a marching camp have been aptly summarized by Eric McGeer (1995, 263–4): 1) The hollow square formation forced the enemy to attack either one or two sides of the formation, because if they attacked three or four sides they dispersed and weakened their attack; 2) It was advantageous for morale and discipline because the men knew that their flanks and rear were secure; 3) It could not be outflanked; 4) It prevented easy flight; 5) It provided the cavalry forces with a secure base for attacks and retreats; and 6) It was easy to use as the men used it when encamping, marching and fighting.

The cavalry was arrayed separately behind the infantry at a distance of 3–4 *orguiai* (ca.5.6–7.5m) from the rear ranks of the infantry so that the *tagmata* and *themata* were deployed separately in their own *tourmai* (PM 1.16). There were to be clear intervals between each *tagma* and *thema* to enable the couriers to move through them without hindrance. The spare horses were posted behind the horsemen and the baggage in the middle of the hollow square. When the cavalry force was not large and the enemy used infantry, then there were to be only eight intervals in order to make the array more secure. This undoubtedly implies that in this case there was only enough cavalry to protect eight intervals. When needed, the troopers undoubtedly supported the infantry with missiles and cavalry sorties.

The spare horses and baggage train were deployed in the middle of the hollow square. Military doctrine still required that the greater part of the non-combatants and the bulk of the baggage animals would be left behind in a base camp in the 'Byzantine-Roman' territory when invading enemy territory. Each group of four foot soldiers was to possess one servant to take care of the animals, baggage and provisions. See also Chapter 2.8. In other words, the Romans would have left the best part of their baggage animals, baggage train, non-combatants and unneeded spare horses behind in a base camp from which the army would have advanced forward to do combat, and which was presumably used as a logistical base when the Romans besieged a city in enemy territory.

Behind the infantry (i.e. among the baggage train in the middle of the hollow square) followed the baggage animals carrying the spare 'imperial arrows' for each of the infantry divisions. There were 15,000 spare arrows per division, so each of the 300 archers had 50 additional arrows besides their own arrows (100 per archer). Eight-to-ten extra light infantrymen were detailed to carry these arrows to the archers so that the archers would not have to leave their position. The men who brought arrows were also used to fetch water for the soldiers, while some other men were also detached to carry stones and water for the slingers. The availability of water was of utmost importance, in particular during the summer.[19]

When the enemy cavalry charged the foot archers were likely to be able to release approximately four volleys before the enemy reached the Roman lines. If the enemy force consisted of *katafraktoi*, it was likely that they would be able to ride through these showers of arrows and so would then come face-to-face with the *menavlatoi* and hoplites. The best effect the archers could hope for was that their archery had disrupted the cohesion of the enemy formation before this happened. When the enemy cavalry reached the Roman lines the archers changed their weapons for swords. However, when facing less-well-armoured cavalry like the Bedouins, the archers were far more effective and could be expected to keep such unarmoured forces away from the Roman lines.[20]

If the Romans faced an enemy with equal strength employing a similar battle array, the commander was expected to employ field artillery to tip the scales in his favour. This artillery component consisted of unspecified numbers of small *cheiromaggana* (hand-machines; probably small traction trebuchets),[21] three *êlakatia* (probably cart-mounted arbalests/ballistae),[22] and a portable flamethrower (a swivel tube operated with a hand pump used to shoot liquid fire) which had apparently been invented by Leôn o Sofos (Leo VI the Wise).

5. Nikêforos Fokas envisaged the following potential stages for a combat involving both the cavalry and hollow infantry square:

1) If the enemy advanced towards the Roman army, then the commander was to dispatch either 500 or 300 lightly-equipped *prokoursatôres* to seek contact with the enemy. The aim was to ambush their *prokoursatôres*, if possible, so that their panicky flight would also panic the main enemy force. The *prokoursatôres* were also instructed to capture a prisoner from the enemy force for interrogation. PM 2.3. See also McGeer (1995, 290: 1.1).[23]

2) If the enemy cavalry pursued the Roman *prokoursatôres*, the general dispatched the first line (undoubtedly together with the flank guards and outflankers) in their support while he followed them in an orderly manner with the four divisions of the second line.[24] This obviously means that the third line was retained inside the hollow square as a reserve, while the rearguard cavalry protected the rear of the hollow infantry square probably by staying outside. PM 2.4. See also McGeer (1995, 290: 1.2), who interprets the material slightly differently.

3) If the enemy cavalry pursued the *prokoursatôres* hotly, it was preferable to allow the enemy to come close to the infantry formation and only then dispatch the three divisions of the first line through the intervals of the infantry formation in attack, while maintaining good order. This presumably means that the divisions of the first line advanced in column formation through the intervals and then turned to form the battle line, or that the infantry wheeled back and forth to make room for the cavalry. It is probable that this also included the flank guards and outflankers. If there were other cavalry units present these were to follow after them by using the same intervals. With the standard cavalry formation, this meant that the third line followed after the first so that it became the reserve line for the first line. After this, the *stratêgos* led out the four divisions accompanying him and acted as *defensôres* for the cavalry army in front of him. If the entire enemy force was routed and this was confirmed by prisoners and deserters, the general was to send the two flanking divisions into pursuit of the foe while he still retained the two middle divisions as his last reserve. The infantry and the remaining cavalry units followed the *stratêgos* in proper formation. PM 2.5. See also McGeer (1995, 290–1: 1.3).
4) If the enemy cavalry did not approach the Roman hollow square, then the commander was expected to send three cavalry divisions out from one side, one after another, and another three divisions from the other side, one after another. These were to halt close to the enemy so that they remained outside bow distance. If there were other cavalry units, they were to be dispatched close to the ones already sent. This presumably means that the outflankers formed the extreme right flank and the flank guards formed the extreme left flank while any other possible cavalry units (e.g. the rearguards) took positions close by. The commander with his four divisions followed them in proper order. PM 2.6. See also McGeer (1995, 291: 1.4).
   a) If the enemy then fled, the *prokoursatôres* pursued in irregular order at the gallop while the other the units which had been sent forward pursued while retaining their formation. It was only when the entire enemy force was in flight that all six divisions sent forward were allowed to break their formation for the pursuit. The troopers were not to capture prisoners or horses and they were also not allowed to capture booty – this was the duty of the attendants and *stratiôtai* with no combat duties. PM 2.7. See also McGeer (1995, 291: 1.5).
   b) If the enemy formation remained in place and did not flee, then the *prokoursatôres* charged to provoke battle, while the six divisions followed after them in good order and attacked the flanks of the enemy formation. The four divisions under the general followed up in proper formation and supported those in front while the infantry

hollow square followed them. PM 2.8. See also McGeer (1995, 291: 1.5).

c) If the enemy still did not flee thanks to a morale boost provided by their *katafraktoi* or by the size of their host, then the infantry javelineers, archers and slingers moved through the intervals of the hoplites and joined their cavalry force to tilt the balance in favour of the Romans. If the enemy still persisted in fighting, the Romans were to do the same and put their faith in God. PM 2.8–9. See also McGeer (1995, 291: 1.6).

5) If the enemy attacked in close order in proper formation with a large force of cavalry and infantry, and advanced against one flank of the Roman army while the *Arabitai* (the light Bedouin cavalry) encircled the Roman hollow infantry square, then *stratêgos* was to retain the cavalry inside the hollow square. The horsemen were also instructed not to chase or pursue the *Arabitai* because it was impossible to catch them thanks to the speed of their horses. The *katafraktoi* wedge and its flanking divisions were to be in readiness to engage the enemy wherever they appeared. When the enemy then approached, the *katafraktoi* and its flanking divisions moved through the intervals and engaged the enemy calmly in proper formation, even when the enemy force approaching consisted of infantry – the flank guards and outflankers are likely to have formed the outer wings, even if this is not specifically stated. The *prokoursatôres* may also have been included. The *katafraktoi* wedge was to be aimed at the spot where the enemy commander was. The attack was to proceed in an orderly, calm manner so that the *katafraktoi* received the enemy arrows with no emotion and then broke into pieces the enemy spears (*kontaria*) and *menavlia*. The enemy would then be defeated with the 'help of the God'. When this happened, the pursuit was to be performed by the two flanking divisions and not by the *katafraktoi*, while the remaining cavalry units moved through the intervals on both flanks to scatter the enemy *Arabitai* with arrows so that they would not bother the pursuers. The cavalry was forbidden to pursue the *Arabitai*. The commander of the army with his four divisions was to follow the pursuers, while the *katafraktoi* wedge of the first line retreated inside the hollow square to reform itself. According to PM 2.5, the commander was to keep his four divisions in proper formation until he saw that the entire enemy host, both infantry and cavalry, were in rout. It was only then that the general was to dispatch two units from his forces in pursuit while he still kept the other two with him. PM 2.5, 2.10–2. See also McGeer (1995, 292: 1.8–10).

6) If the enemy attacked the Roman infantry square so quickly that it was impossible to send the *katafraktoi* against them, then they were to head

out through one of the flanking intervals with the other two divisions following after them. PM 2.13. See also McGeer (1995, 292: 1.11).
7) If the Romans had so large a number of cavalry that it could not be fitted inside the hollow square, then the commander was to make the infantry divisions shallower so that the formation became roomier. PM 2.14.
8) If the terrain was flat and open, then the commander could widen the frontage by placing four or five divisions in front and back with one or two units on the flanks. In narrow terrain, the commander did the opposite. The hollow square could also be arrayed with four intervals (two in front and back) with the horsemen of the *themata* and *tagmata* were deployed behind these intervals, the baggage train and non-combatants in the corners, and all infantry javelineers and light infantry in front of the cavalry in the intervals. This array was used when the commander wanted to protect the cavalry more securely inside the hollow square. PM 2.15–7. See also McGeer (1995, 257–62).
9) Even if not specifically stated, the commander could obviously also decide to engage the enemy cavalry by using primarily his infantry hollow square instead of using his cavalry, in which case he used the above-mentioned system of using the hoplites, *menavlatoi*, javelineers and light-armed infantry against the enemy *katafraktoi* and cavalry (PM 1.1–12). The Roman cavalry undoubtedly pursued in the manner described above, with the flanking divisions of the first line and *prokoursatôres* leading the pursuit with the others following as required.
10) The Roman commander could decide to use his infantry force instead of the cavalry for breaking the enemy infantry formation (PM 1.13–5). If the enemy employed a regular infantry phalanx, then the *menavlatoi* and javelineers moved through the flank intervals to attack the enemy's flanks, but if the enemy also used the hollow square then the *menavlatoi* and javelineers advanced through the intervals to form a united front with the hoplites for the purpose of frontal combat. In situations like this, the commander could employ the small *maggana*, three *elakatia* and the flame-thrower as his final means of breaking the enemy formation.

6. Marching Camp (PM 5)

The instructions concerning the marching camp and security measures were traditional (PM 5). The marching camp was to be located on level ground with access to water. The shape of the camp was the same as the marching and fighting formation; in other words, a hollow square with the hoplites forming the outer edge, but in this case having only two ranks facing the enemy. There were to be eight gates, with the *menavlatoi* plus some archers and slingers protecting them, so the encampment had four roads. The hoplites formed the outer edge. The hoplites formed a bulwark for the camp by fixing their spears on the ground so that these leaned against shields. The foot archers were posted behind the hoplites. If there existed the danger of an enemy attack, then the soldiers were required to dig a trench called a *chandax*. The commander of the army had his quarters at the centre of the encampment, while the other officers were located where their forces were. The cavalry horses and baggage animals were quartered at a distance of a bowshot from the ditch for safety reasons. Patrols and pickets were to surround the camp. Any spies that had entered the camp could be found easily by ordering everyone to their quarters. See also the DRM, which has a slightly different camp structure by having three gates and roads per side, while its marching formation also differed from the one described by Nikêforos so that the depth of infantry formation on the edges in the hollow square consisted of two ranks (one rank of hoplites with light infantry forming the second rank), while each side was protected by six *parataxeis* of cavalry (with scouts, flank guards, vanguard and rear guard posted in addition to these), but so the front had an extra 1,000 horsemen under the emperor in the second line (the front therefore being the vanguard; a first line with three *parataxeis*, a second line of four *parataxeis* consisting of two regular *parataxeis* on the flanks and two imperial *parataxeis* forming the centre). Light infantry could also be posted in support of the cavalry.

When the Romans learnt that the enemy was near, the commander distributed the battle plan for the officers, after which the army purified itself and fasted for three days with the soldiers eating only once a day, in the evening. The soldiers were also required to show their repentance for their sins. Once these rituals had been performed, the priests performed the holy sacrifices the day before the battle and the men then took Holy Communion. The seeking of the help of God was particularly typical for Nikêforos Fôkas, who was a fanatically religious person. The help of God had to be sought and the soldiers had to be convinced that God was fighting on their side against the infidels. The fasting was obviously not good for the stamina, but the results of the regimen under Nikêforos' inspiring leadership suggest that the religious side of the rituals more than compensated for this. The soldiers were indoctrinated into Warriors of God and fought as such against the infidels.

Appendix IV

The Anonymous *De re militari* and Fighting in the Mountains

1. The date and authorship of the *De re militari*

The author of the *De re militari*, also known as *Peri katastaseôs aplektôu*, or *De castrametatione*, or *On Campaign Organization and Tactics*, is not known and neither is the exact date of its composition. Furthermore, the beginning and the end of the treatise is no longer extant. What is known is that the final version of the treatise was written for a young inexperienced emperor by an experienced military commander who had served both in the Balkans and East, and that the instructions concerned in particular campaigning in the mountainous terrain of the Balkans, without forgetting their applicability also to the mountainous terrain of the east.

The consensus opinion among previous research is that the treatise was probably written for the emperor Basileios B Boulgaroktonos (Basil II the Bulgarslayer), but this had already been challenged a hundred years previously by R. Vári, who suggested that the text was originally written earlier, during the reign of Nikêforos o Fôkas. I agree with this proposition. This is indeed likely if one identifies the author as Leôn Fôkas, whose advice Nikêforos would definitely have sought after 967 when he had just abandoned the campaign against the Bulgarians as a result of noting the difficulties presented by the terrain that he was unfamiliar with. Furthermore, the arguments presented against this are not conclusive, because it is entirely plausible that the contents of the original were later changed to meet the new reality. As already noted in Chapter 8.8 after Leo the Deacon (5.4, 6.2, 8.4), it is unlikely to be a coincidence that Nikêforos Fôkas had placed his brother Leôn in charge of the campaign against the Russians in December 969 and that the size and composition of the force subsequently led by Tzimiskês against the Russians in 971 closely resembled the recommendations of the author of the *De re militari*.

What is certain, however, is that the final form of the treatise dates from the reign of Basileios II, because the treatise includes the *tagma* of *athanatoi* which was created by Iôannês o Tzimiskês. R. Vári has proposed that Nikêforos Ouranos in addition to his *Taktika* also wrote the *De velitatione* and this treatise. This has not found acceptance among the scholars because the style of writing is so different, not to mention the fact that Ouranos has actually excerpted entire sections from the DRM into his *Taktika* (64) while not agreeing (OT 65) with the instructions that the DRM (21–7) presents for sieges. Eric McGeer has suggested that the author of the DRM is the same as the author of the *De velitatione* on the basis of the fact that its author promises to write a treatise dealing with warfare in the Balkans, but this is obviously not accepted by those who note the differences in language, style and terminology. Once again the arguments against this are not conclusive, because the *De velitatione* was originally written by Nikêforos o Fôkas so that its style reflected mainly his language and not that of the editor of the text. Regardless, for the reasons already given I am inclined to accept Eric McGeer's theory as the likeliest one, namely that in about 967/8 Nikêforos ordered a treatise from someone familiar with the Balkans, but the project was delayed when Nikêforos was murdered by Iôannês o Tzimiskês.[1] As noted, in my opinion the author was Leôn Fôkas.

It is also notable that the author of the DRM (28–9) paid particular attention to the need to protect the thematic soldiers from the abuse of the imperial tax collectors and from contemptuous treatment, as did the editor of the DV (19), while also noting the necessity of keeping the muster rolls in order so that the men who were not included in them would not be able to escape service. The author also noted that he had intended to write another treatise dealing with the offensive war against the Agarenes, but refrained from doing so because so many generals had personal experience of this and so the methods were well-known. This once again supports the authorship of Leôn who may have originally considered it as a complement to the DV and DRM. In sum, the likeliest editor of the DV and author of the DRM/PKA is therefore Leôn Fôkas. In the following discussion I will therefore occasionally use Leôn Fôkas when I name the author of this anonymous treatise.

One of the things that set apart the author of the DRM and also the DV from the PM of Nikêforos Fôkas is that it is entirely factual and analytical, while the PM (4.11, 6.2–3) is full of religious formulae, including even the three days of fasting before battle that Nikôforos ordered to be followed in order to achieve victory over the enemy. Leôn does include the standard formula of the Will of God as one of the elements involved in the fighting, but he does not stress the importance of the formulaic repetition of religious rituals prior to combat to the same extent as his brother. Nikêforos was clearly a broken man inside who sought consolation from God and religious rituals. Therefore, there is every reason to believe that Nikêforos really abstained from meat after the death of his son until the day of his marriage with Theofanô (Skylitzes 14.2), but obviously there still remains the possibility that Skylitzes is correct in his suspicions about that because religious persons are entirely capable of hypocrisy.

2. The size of the ideal model army (DRM 1, 3, 5–8, 10, 13, 15, 17, 21)

When campaigning in mountainous, wooded, devastated or waterless terrain, the unknown author (probably Leôn Fôkas) did not consider it advisable to lead a large army there, or an army with a large numbers of useless non-combatants, or more baggage than was needed, or a large number of beasts of burden because these only slowed down the army while consuming the scarce supplies available. Leôn Fôkas (7.29ff.) noted that the invading Romans had not only achieved successes with large armies, but at times with very small numbers of men. It is therefore clear that Leôn did not advise the emperor to use very large numbers of men in such terrain.

Leôn's model army consisted either of sixteen or twelve *taxiarchiai* of infantry (16,000 or 12,000 men), in addition to which there were to be four *taxiarchiai* of *psilôi* (4,000 men) and more than 8,200 cavalry,[2] plus the *tagmata* and imperial bodyguards that accompanied the emperor (cavalry minimum 1,000 horsemen, the number of infantry unknown). These figures, however, were the bare minimum size for the army when the emperor campaigned, which Leôn noted in the context of his figures for the cavalry arm (DRM 8). Leôn used the figure of 8,200 horsemen only as a convenient model suited to the numbers he had given for the infantry. This means that in the actual campaigning force there could also be more infantry and cavalry than in the model army, but the emperor was never to lead a large army into difficult territory that lacked sources of water. In short, Leôn used numbers in the same manner as the ancient military theorists when they had stated that the ideal army had 16,384 *(h)oplitai*, 8,198 *psilôi* and 4,096 *hippeis*. These represented just the idealized proportions of an ideal combined army which the commanders then altered according to circumstances and the availability of men, just as Leôn expected the emperor to do with the figures he had given.

This means that we do not know what the maximum envisaged size for the army was in the DRM, while we know the minimum number of men the emperor was expected to take on a campaign in waterless, wooded and mountainous terrain with narrow roads. This is a pity because we do not know how large an army the author expected the Romans to be able to provision during a long campaign in the Balkans. However, it is still absolutely clear that Leôn Fôkas did not envisage the use of any really large army in the Balkans because he stated that the emperor was never to take a large force with a mass of workmen and pack animals to a location which had wooded mountain passes with narrow and difficult roads, as there was in particular in the land of the Bulgarians (DRM 15, 20.81–5). Furthermore, he stressed the fact that small armies consisting of well-trained veterans could defeat enemies consisting of myriads of men (DRM 28). In this context he noted the need for yearly campaigning, and also repeated drilling for the thematic forces of the interior because without drill they became little better than merchants or farmers. In contrast to them, the men of the frontier *themata* were always combat ready thanks to the continuous warfare along the borders. Leôn also stressed the importance of showing proper respect towards these men. In short, in his opinion it was possible to defeat the enemy even with a small army if it consisted of well-drilled veterans motivated to fight.

The model infantry formation had sixteen *taxiarchiai* (16,000) of infantry, each of which consisted of 500 *oplitai* (hoplites; it is possible that 100 of these were actually *menavlatoi*), 200 *akontistai* (javelineers; it is possible that 100 of these were actually *menavlatoi*) and 300 *toxotai* (archers). In addition to these, the army could also possess four *taxiarchiai* of *psilôi* (presumably 4,000 men). These *psilôi* would have been used for blocking the intervals between the sixteen (or twelve, see below) *taxiarchia*. The sixteen *taxiarchiai* and the unattached *psilôi* presumably also included the *menavlatoi* amongst their ranks, because the army included the *menavlatoi* (DRM 20.130). Each *taxiarchia* was commanded by a *taxiarchês*. The commander of all infantry forces was the *oplitarchês* (also known as *archêtês*). Their use would have been explained in the lost beginning of the treatise which described the battle formations and their use in greater detail. In the model army the cavalry component consisted of 8,200 horsemen that were divided into twenty-four *parataxeis* (subunits), each consisting of 300 horsemen. Almost half of the cavalry force must have consisted of the elite *scholarioi* and *etaireiai* because the treatise states that the *tagma* of the *scholai* consisted of 30 *banda* (DRM 1.134–8). Since the minimum size for the cavalry *bandon* (ST 35.4) was 50 horsemen, it is clear that the *scholai* consisted of at least 1,500 horsemen, and since the *etaireiai* occupied an even greater proportion of the marching camp (see the drawings on pages 435–6) it is clear that they numbered at least the same number of *banda*.[3] The rest of the *tagmata* that were posted under the *drouggarios tês biglas* consisted at least of the *bigla* (DRM 1.158–68), but it is not known if these were included in the cavalry totals or were just considered to belong to the guards of the encampment and baggage train. Since the proportion of the imperial elite cavalry was so remarkable, one may even suspect that the infantry *tagmata* of the *teichistai* and *noumeroi* also dispatched detachments to accompany the emperor when he campaigned in the Balkans.

The 24 *parataxeis* of cavalry were divided so that each side of the hollow square had six *parataxeis*. If there were more than 8,200 horsemen, then the size of each *parataxeis* was proportionally increased. If the emperor campaigned in person, he was to have more than 8,200 horsemen. However, Leôn also includes smaller numbers as examples, presumably for situations in which the army was led by a general or for situations in which the cavalry had suffered casualties and had fewer men left. Consequently, if there were less than 8,200 horsemen, then there were to be only five *parataxeis* per side (presumably deployed three in front two behind) and if there were even fewer horsemen left then each side was to have only four *parataxeis* (presumably deployed three in front one behind).

The emperor's own *parataxis* consisted of at least of the members of the units that were assigned to his own portion of the encampment. These included the *tagmata* of the *athanatoi, megas etaireia*, other *etaireiai* (presumably the infantry *Ros/Rhos*, see below), and the imperial bodyguard units the *basilikoi* and *magklabitai*. In the model army presented by the DRM, the emperor's cavalry *parataxis* consisted of 1,000 horsemen,[4] while his infantry contingent consisted of an unspecified number of Russians (*Rhôs/Rôs*) and *malartioi*. These accompanied the emperor when he was outside the hollow infantry square. This would not have been the total strength of these units, because it is clear that some of the bodyguards of the emperor remained inside the hollow infantry square and still others in Constantinople or elsewhere on special missions. The exact meaning of the word *malartioi* is not known, but it is probable that they were *kontaratoi* (armed with the *kontos*, shield and sword) because a monk from Cos identifies them as such in a document dating from October 1079.[5] I would suggest that we should equate the Russians and *malartioi* with the *etaireiai* and *basilikoi* accompanying the emperor in the treatise of Kônstantinos VII, so that the *Rhôs-etaireiai* would have numbered 300 men and the *basilikoi-malartioi* 100 men.

The above discussion is also important from the point of view of methodology, because it is clear that Leôn did not consider the fighting strength of approximately 30,000 soldiers (16 *taxiarchiai*, 4 *taxiarchiai* of *psilôi*, 8,200 cavalry, 1,000 horsemen of the imperial *parataxis*, plus unspecified numbers of Russians, *malartioi, bigla* and others) as a large army. In short, the self-delusional historians who still follow the outdated and faulty methodology of Hans Delbrück should finally acknowledge the fact that they have been utterly wrong in dismissing the larger army sizes in the sources without any analysis whatsoever. The 'Late Romans and Byzantine Romans' were entirely capable of fielding much larger forces, as stated in the sources, and one of the reasons why such forces came to disaster was precisely the fact that these armies were too large for the difficult waterless terrain – as warned by Leôn Fôkas.

3. Things to consider before the campaign (DRM 16–9, 28–30)

Before embarking on campaign, Leôn Fökas stressed the importance of proper training and equipping of the men. The emperor was to make sure that the soldiers were not subjected to corruption and insults to that they would be in high spirits and well-motivated. He was also to ensure that the men were properly drilled as individuals and in units, and campaigned yearly. Additionally, the men were to be equipped properly without any useless luxurious gold- and silver-decorated panoply. All the men needed were the best horses, the finest sturdy armour, helmets made of iron, and strong iron swords. The lower-ranking officers were also not to take any tents with them. The army was also not to take with it any superfluous baggage, large numbers of beasts of burden, or useless non-combatants, because these only slowed down the army while consuming the scarce supplies available. The army was also to be assembled before the campaign so that the soldiers could encamp three or four times together to learn their proper place both in the marching camp and marching formation. All of the men were also to be enrolled into muster rolls at the beginning of the campaign so that there would not be men who would consider deserting the force. These very same muster rolls enabled the emperor also to assess the size and quality of his force and also the casualties suffered when the soldiers were again counted after the campaign.

Before embarking on a campaign the emperor was to ensure that he had experienced and knowledgeable guides (*doukatôroi*) to guide the army. These were expected to know all the routes across the mountains – even the ones the enemy did not know – the topography of the area where the campaign took place, the distances between suitable campsites, and the locations of the sources of water. It was also expected that there were to be large numbers of high-quality *chônsarioi* (hussars), also known as *trapezitai*, who raided enemy territory to obtain prisoners for interrogation. The most important source of intelligence was the spies proper (*kataskopoi*), who the *domestikos tôn scholôn* and the *stratêgoi* of the border were to have, not only among the Bulgarians, but also among the Pechenegs, Hungarians and Russians. The captured enemy prisoners could also be used as spies if the Romans had also captured their wives and children. Their liberty could be promised in return for the husband acting as a spy.

The emperor was expected to dispatch spies (*kataskopoi*), guides (*doukatôroi*), and hussars (*chônasarioi*) well in advance of the planned invasion to reconnoitre the roads and routes before embarking on a campaign so that he could formulate the campaign plan.

4. The Marching camp (DRM 1–7, 11, 18–9)

The placing of marching camps in enemy territory was done on the basis of the intelligence obtained by the spies, guides, and hussars, which the general/emperor then combined with his knowledge of the topography of the area. The measuring of the marching camp for the army was the duty of the head *minsuratôr* and by the *minsuratôres/mensuratôres* of the other officers. In hostile territory they were escorted by guards (*bigla*), which in this case undoubtedly means the guide or guides with the hussars. The marching camp was not to be situated close to a mountain, or a dense wood, or a hilly area.[6] Ideally the location had a river, a lake, a cliff, or a ravine to protect one or two sides of the marching camp. If the location had a small river or stream, then it was to pass through the camp, but the horses were to be watered downstream.

The model camp was rectangular in shape, but other forms were accepted if the terrain made this absolutely necessary. In the model given the marching camp was a square, each side of which was 2,000 (or 1,870) metres long.[7] The marching camp was first measured by the *minsuratôres*, after which it was built by the men assigned to the task while other units protected them. It was only after the camp was built that the men outside were allowed to enter. The camp was fortified so that it had a trench seven-to-eight feet deep and five-to-six feet wide. The dirt from the trench was used to build a wall on the inside. The outer edge of the camp was guarded by the *oplitai*, behind who were the *akontistai* and *toxotai*. This made the infantry formation behind the wall and trench two ranks deep (one rank of hoplites and another of javelineers and light infantry). The PM (5.3) gives the same depth for the soldiers posted on the outer edges, so it is clear that this practise was not new. The Romans also used a field of caltrops (each man had eight caltrops tied to a rope which were then tied to stakes) outside the encampment, which were placed

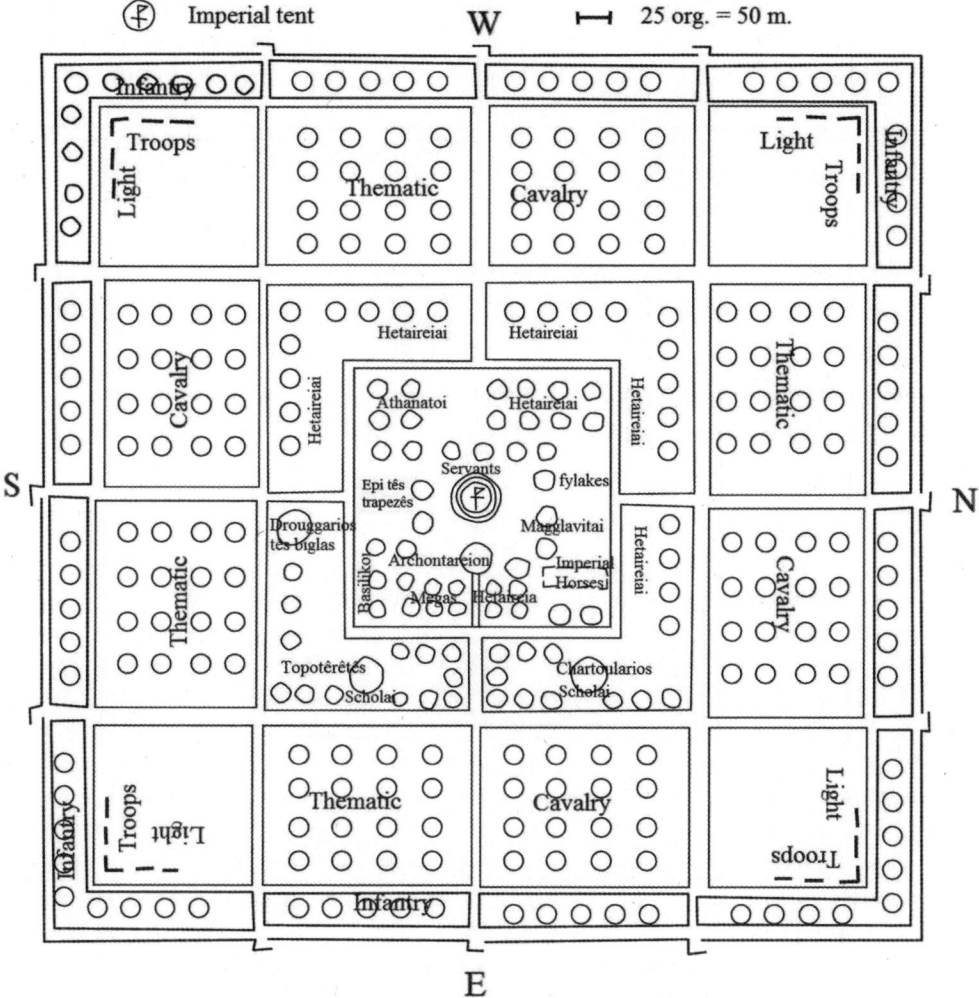

Imperial Marching Camp in the *De re militari*
(*De castrametatione / Peri katastaseôs aplêktou*)
(drawn after G.T. Dennis, *Campaign Organization and Tactics*)

at a distance of twenty metres from the ditch. The men also dug pits with wooden stakes which were marked on the ground so that the Romans would not run into those. As an additional security measure, the men also tied bells on strings that were tied to rods to alarm them of the approach of the enemy. The infantry along the wall was separated from the cavalry and imperial quarters with an empty space which had a dual purpose: it protected the cavalry from enemy arrows, while also allowing the thematic cavalry on the outer edges to assemble on foot as phalanxes to act as reserve forces for the men along the walls. The unattached *psiloi* were deployed

Imperial Quarters of the Marching Camp
according to *De re militari / De castrametatione / Peri katastaseôs aplêktou*
(drawn after G.T. Dennis, *Campaign Organization and Tactics*)

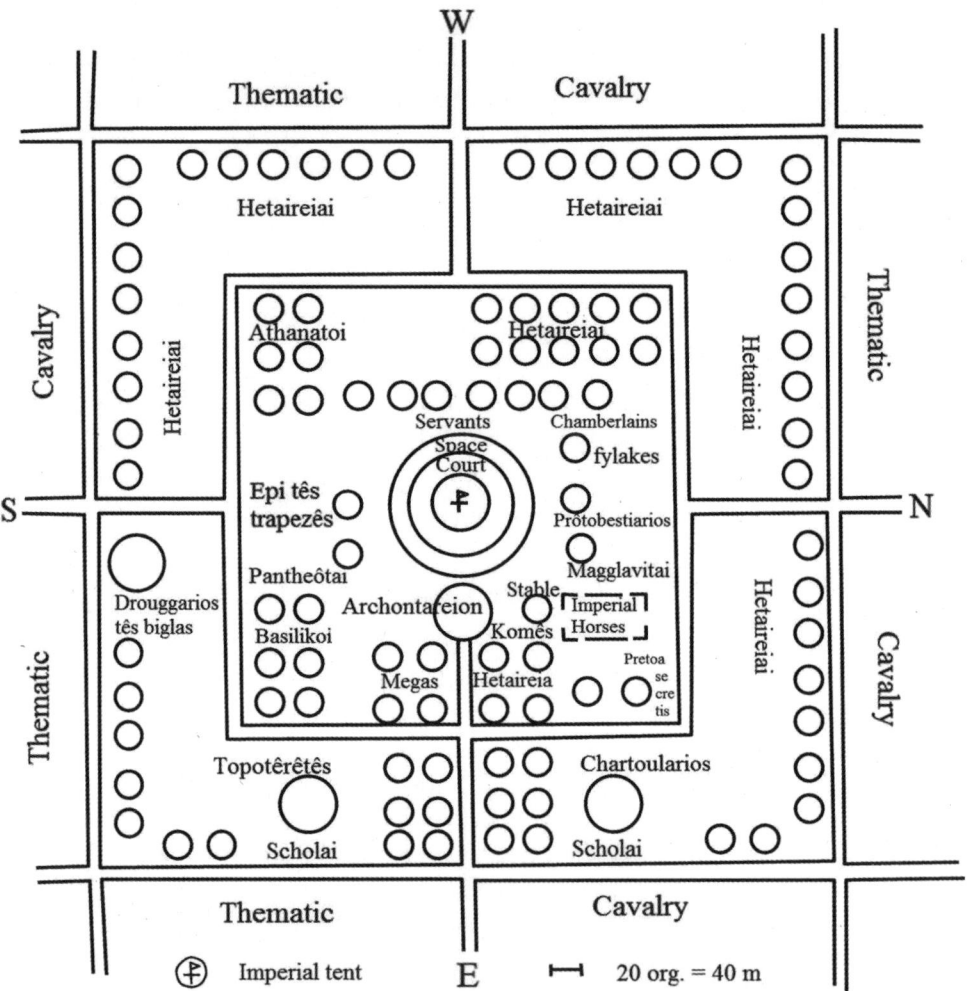

at the angles in L-shaped formations. The camp had four major roads and eight major L-shaped gates. The gates were protected by guards assigned to this duty. For the shape of the camp and locations of the troops and officers and emperor, see the diagrams above.

The marching camp was also protected by layers of sentinels, patrols and guards. Each *taxiarchês* was to post guards for the night, while the *oplitarchês* with 100 unattached *psiloi* ensured that the camp was properly guarded and that the patrols were changed regularly. The *oplitarchês* was expected to go around the empty space of the camp until daybreak to make sure that the camp was properly guarded. If he did this without breaks, it is clear that he was not in fighting condition during daytime, but I suspect that he had also deputies, or that there were two separate *oplitarchai*, one for the period up to midnight and another for the night. Whatever the truth, the first batch of 100 *psiloi* under the *oplitarchês* performed the duty until midnight after which they were replaced by another 100 *psiloi*.[8] It is probable that the *drouggarios tês biglas* performed a similar duty, even if this is not mentioned in the DRM, because we find him performing this in the treatise of Kônstantinos VII, or that the *drouggarios* was also an *oplitarchês* in the DRM.

The outside guards consisted of four layers, two of infantry and two of cavalry. The innermost two layers of guards consisted of infantry (*pezoi*), javelineers (*akontistai*), and archers (*toxotai*). These were deployed so that the innermost layer was placed at a distance of a bowshot from the ditch and the second layer a stone throw from it. Each of the inner watch posts consisted of eight men and the outer watch posts of four men known as *tetradia*. Each infantry *taxiarchia* was to place five inside and outside watch posts about 100 metres apart from each other. If the terrain was level and unobstructed then the cavalry posted beyond the infantry watch posted guards so that the inner layer consisted of groups of six horsemen and the outer layer of groups of four horsemen. If the terrain was not passable, the cavalry guarded only those portions that were vulnerable. During the day only the cavalry was used as guards at a long distance from the camp if the terrain was unobstructed and clear.

If the cavalry force accompanying the army was small, then the infantry along the edges was deployed in a tighter formation (three per one *orguia* of 1.87–2m = *synaspismos* order). If the cavalry force was too large for the regular encampment, then the commander was to enlarge the encampment by posting some javelineers alongside the *oplitai* on the edges of the camp. If the infantry force consisted only of twelve *taxiarchiai* (as it did in the PM), then each side of the marching camp was to consist only of 1,500 metres. In those cases in which the space was not sufficient for the building of a single large marching camp, it was deemed better to divide the army into two similarly-fortified marching camps which were spacious enough for this. If the camps were close enough it was possible for the men in each camp to support each other, but if this was not possible because this was prevented by distance or terrain (e.g. by a mountain), the author still considered the division of the marching camp preferable to the use of single a camp in an unsuitable location. If the soldiers followed the regulations, they were expected to prevail over any attacker.

If the intelligence operatives informed the emperor that the enemy was planning to attack the Roman marching camp at night, the expectation was that the emperor posted ambushes close to the camp. When the enemy then attacked the fortifications, the ambushers attacked them from behind. The defeated enemy was not hunted down because the night prevented effective pursuit.

5. The marching formation (DRM 9–10, 31)

a) Leaving the marching camp (DRM 9): When the expeditionary army marched out of the camp it was to be performed by the book following the regulations. Just before dawn the trumpets sounded the sign for everyone to be prepared for marching. The officers commanding the vanguard, flank guards and rear guard went to the courtyard and received commands from the emperor. When the trumpets sounded for a second time, the forces started preparing the things for the march while the commander of the vanguard, together with the *doukatôroi* and three *parataxeis* of horsemen, advanced one to two bowshots in front of the camp, after which the commanders of the flank guards and *saka* each dispatched one *parataxis* of cavalry to the same distance. Leôn noted that this precaution was not taken because there would have existed the danger of a major attack – which would have been detected well in advance – but because there existed the danger of small groups of enemy making their way into the camp when everyone was busy making their preparations for the march. When the trumpet sounded for the third time, the emperor mounted his horse and rode outside with the rest of the army following.

b) The regular marching formation (DRM 10): The actual marching formation was assumed only when the army had marched out of the encampment, so the vanguard consisted of six *parataxeis* of cavalry and the emperor's own *parataxis*. One of the cavalry *parataxeis* was dispatched as a vanguard (*prokoursatôres*) for the advance guard with orders to reconnoitre. The remaining five cavalry *parataxeis* were deployed three in front and two behind as a second line. The emperor's cavalry *parataxis*, consisting of 1,000 horsemen, was placed between the two cavalry *parataxeis*. The term *parataxis* implies a single unit, but this is not conclusive because it is quite possible that this term was used in the collective sense to denote all units, both infantry and cavalry, serving under the direct command of the emperor. Therefore, when one takes into account the fact that the other cavalry *parataxeis* consisted of 300-horseman units, it is quite possible or even probable that the emperor's 1,000 horsemen were actually divided into two 350–400 men units ('*tês basileias allagia*'in the ST 35.5), so the remaining 200–300 men were used as fill-up *banda* between all four units belonging to the second cavalry line.[9] I would suggest that it is probable that this is the deployment pattern rather than the use of one extra large division in the middle. I would also suggest that it is probable that the flanking *parataxeis* of the first line dispatched a *bandon* of 50 horsemen each to their flanks to serve as outflankers and flank guards. There was no need for rear guards, because the infantry protected the rear. It is probable that all of the units were deployed at the same distances as we find in the ST.

If the terrain was level and spacious the infantry followed behind the vanguard in the same array as it had used when encamping (DRM 10.11–8), with the baggage train with servants placed in the middle. If one takes this literally, then this would mean that the infantry was deployed only two deep with the unattached *psiloi* and

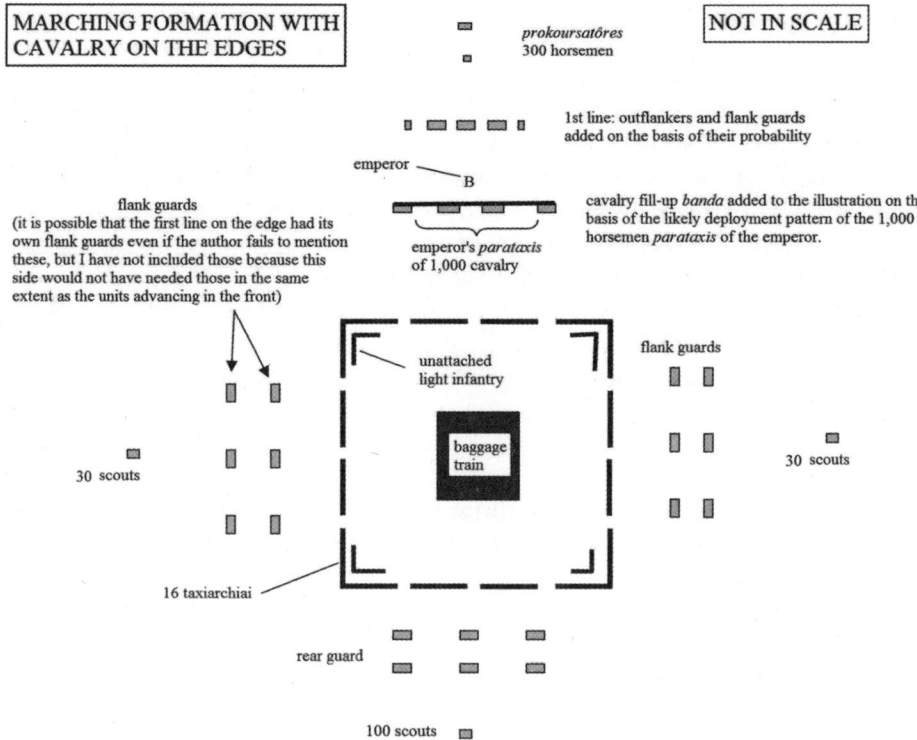

some other smaller units behind. This is actually confirmed by the details concerning the deployment pattern of the cavalry flank guards (see below) and possibly also by the *Syntaxis armatorum quadrata* (see Appendix I) which has only two ranks of heavy infantry on the edges with light infantry behind. The depth of the infantry array reflected its intended usage in wooded, rough, narrow and mountainous terrain, because we also find Maurikios (MS 12.B.20, esp. 12.B.20.12–7) recommending the use of two- or four-deep marching columns in such terrain. It is still clear that the quality of the infantry force was exceptionally high at this time, because Leôn expected that the two deep infantry formation would be able to counter any enemy attack that got through the cavalry outer edges. On the other hand, it is still safe to say that if the Romans learnt that the enemy was anywhere near and the terrain was not too forbidding that the array was deepened and tightened to meet the enemy attack because we find period Romans using deeper and tighter arrays in all other treatises. The flanking cavalry *parataxeis* on both sides were deployed so that three of those were deployed closer to the infantry and the three others further away. Both of these groups were to choose about 30 men (undoubtedly 'hussars') who were dispatched further away as scouts. The commander of the rear guard deployed his six units in like manner towards the rear. Additionally, he chose 100 men to serve under a qualified officer who were used as scouts in the rear. It is of note that this deployment for the flanks and rear (three divisions in front and three behind) can also be found in the DV, as can the likely deployment pattern of the vanguard (three divisions in front and four behind).

Leôn (DRM 31) instructed the emperor to relieve the troops performing rearguard duty (*saka*) periodically while keeping their commander in place if he performed his duties well. The reason for this was that the duty among the rearguard was particularly stressful and demanding. The former required the rotation of troops while the latter required an experienced good commander. When the army marched into enemy territory the military gear and siege equipment were carried by the *monoprosopa*. These were carried on horses, mules or wagons. If these were left behind or had been used in the course of the campaign, the *monoprosopa* were divided into three sections: the first carried whatever equipment was left; the second transported supplies for the *monoprosopa*; and the third joined the *saka* to transport the wounded, weak, sick and those troopers who had lost their mounts.

c) **Marching formation with light infantry added to the edges (DRM 10.31–8):** When the Romans faced Arabs and Hungarians who were known to make bold attacks, the twelve cavalry *taxiarchiai* posted on outside as first lines were given 150 foot archers each to support them. These 1,800 infantry archers were drawn from the *psiloi taxiarchiai*. The emperor was to take with him as many infantry archers as he saw necessary, in addition to which he was to be protected by the Russians (*Rôs*) and *malartioi*. The latter were undoubtedly used as a protective wall for both the foot archers and the emperor. The combination of light infantry with cavalry was obviously an age-old practice, but in this case it is clear that the combination of light infantry foot archers with cavalry had been copied from the Arabs who used it apparently to counter the Roman mounted archers (LT 18.109–10, 18.123, 18.129). We find Nikêforos Fôkas also employing light infantry archers and slingers in support of his *katafraktoi* at the Battle of Tarsus in 965 (Leo the Deacon 4.3; see the narrative), so it is clear that the use of the light infantry, javelineers, Russians and *malartioi* was always one of the possible methods that the commander could choose to oppose enemy cavalry.

If the emperor desired to plunder villages for provisions en route, he was to dispatch select men to do this. If the villages were off to the side, the emperor was expected to dispatch units from the flank guards to protect those while the trumpets sounded halt for the duration of the distraction.

d) **Forced marches (DRM 10.46ff.):** When there was a need for a forced march because the next camping site was located far away, this could result in the breaking of the infantry formation. Leôn advised that in such case the cavalry *parataxeis* of the flanks were to form up as columns of six to protect the infantry. The distance between the *parataxeis* was to be a bowshot or two. This suggests the use of the same formation by the infantry both in the camp and when marching because when the cavalry was deployed in this manner it covered a distance of 2,010 metres when

The Anonymous *De re militari* and Fighting in the Mountains   441

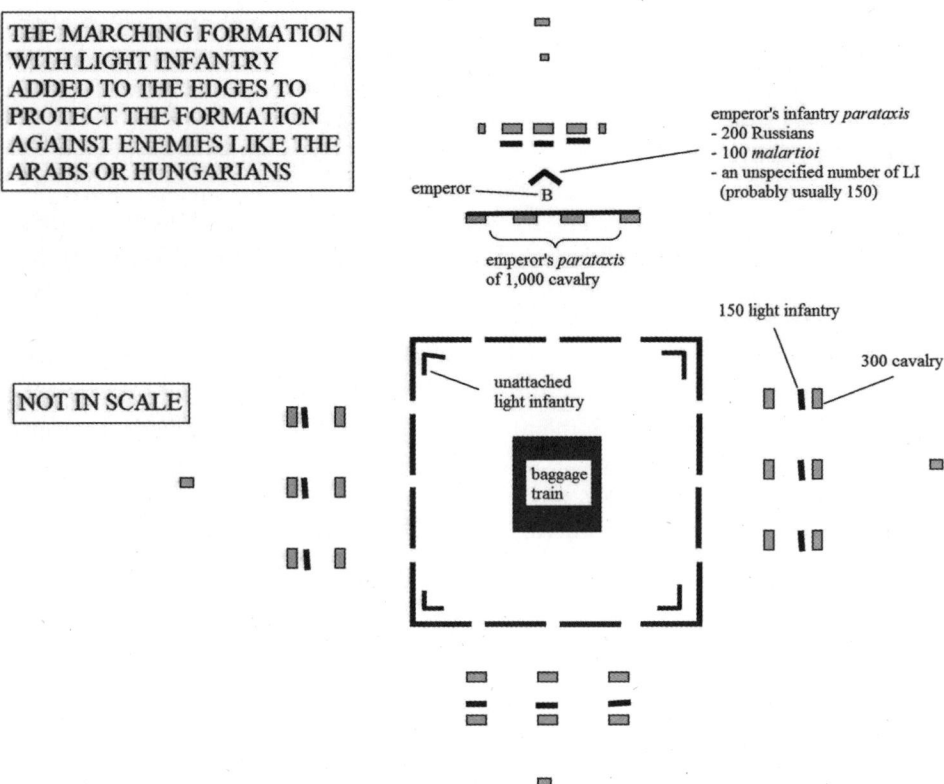

the *parataxeis* were deployed a bowshot apart.[10] The distances between the cavalry *parataxeis* was lengthened when the marching columns became extended as a result of the men becoming tired, so that new intervals appeared in the flanks of the formation while the formation started to lose its shape.[11] If even this was not enough because more and more men dropped behind and could not cope with the marching speed, then two *parataxeis* from the vanguard and two from the rear guard were to be added to the flanks so that both cavalry columns had eight *parataxeis*. If even this was not enough, then the emperor was to halt his advance so that the infantry was able to catch up. Otherwise there existed the danger that swift moving enemies such as the Hungarians and Arabs could exploit this. When the army then reached the camping site, some of the units were arrayed in a circle to form a protective ring around those who built the camp. The men were allowed to enter the camp only after the *saka* had reached the scene.

e) Fighting a pitched battle (DRM 12): When the emperor was informed that the enemy was about to attack them with a large force he was to order a halt after which the servants put down their baggage and the imperial tent. Immediately after this the emperor assembled his highest-ranking officers for a quick parley. Following this, the soldiers were armed and arrayed properly according to the battle plan, after which the emperor led them against the enemy while the baggage train remained in place under guard. Leôn does not specify what types of battle formations he envisaged, because he would have dealt with those at the beginning of the treatise – which is lost. This leaves us three likely possible battle formations that the Romans could have adopted, depending on the situation: 1) they could have employed the cavalry formation depicted in the *Strategikon* or Leôn's *Taktika*, while the infantry was left behind to protect the baggage; 2) they could have left the baggage inside a hollow infantry square while the cavalry advanced against the enemy in the formation depicted in Nikêforos Fôkas' *Praecepta militaria* (the arming of the men for combat can mean the adding of cataphract armour for the horses of those men designated to serve in the wedges); and 3) the entire force, both infantry and cavalry, could have marched forward in the manner depicted in the PM while the baggage train remained behind under guard. If the Romans won with 'God's help' and there was no water source in the place where the Romans had halted, then the officer left in charge of the baggage train was directed to a new campsite.

6. Fighting and marching in difficult terrain (DRM 13–4, 18–9, 32)

a) Obtaining intelligence (DRM 18–9): The invasion route into enemy territory and back was done on the basis of the intelligence obtained by the spies, guides, and hussars, which the guides leading the force then combined with their knowledge of the topography of the area. The emperor and his staff were expected to deliver orders in writing to the officers before their expected implementation on the following day, so that they would know what was expected of them.

b) The initial stages of the invasion when the enemy had not blocked the passes and narrows (DRM 19): Leôn's sound advice to the emperor was that he was to avoid both difficult and waterless terrain at all costs, and that it was always preferable to take the longer route if it was level and wide rather than march through waterless or difficult terrain. However, if this was not possible for some reason, Leôn still provided the emperor with a set of sound advice on how to do this as safely as possible. If the emperor intended to invade enemy territory, he was expected to dispatch the spies, guides, and hussars several days in advance of the invasion to learn which roads and passes the enemy occupied. If it was absolutely necessary to use a narrow road which was not occupied by the enemy (DRM 19), then the emperor was to dispatch an infantry army under an able officer one or two days before the invasion to secure all routes that the enemy might use in an effort to attack the Romans when they were marching through the narrows.[12] This force was to consist primarily of the archers and javelineers rather than of the hoplites. If the terrain allowed, a detachment of cavalry was sent with them because this served as a great boost for the morale of the footmen. This force was to be guided by the best guides and was to include men drawn from the western *taxiarchiai* because they knew the territory better than others. Their mission was to capture the highest place or a fort if such had been built to guard the intended route, and also the other possible routes that the enemy might use to attack the Romans when they were marching through the narrows.

When the infantry vanguard had secured the route they informed the emperor, who then launched the invasion proper by dispatching ahead of the cavalry two infantry *taxiarchiai* (presumably from the front half of the hollow infantry square, see below) equipped with axes and cutting tools for the purpose of clearing the road for the cavalry and main army. Whenever the vanguard of the two *taxiarchiai* encountered narrows or otherwise difficult terrain, they were to leave behind some infantry to guard these locations so that the army could march through these safely. The vanguard of the main force consisted of the cavalry usually preceding the emperor (are these the vanguard cavalry of six *parataxeis*?) followed by the infantry (Russians, *malartioi,* and archers) that usually accompanied the emperor. The emperor and his entourage marched next, followed by the cavalry units that usually rode behind him (are these the 1,000-horseman *parataxis* of the emperor?). After this followed the rest of the army in the same order of march as the author described earlier, but which he now modified a bit as noted above and below. He noted that the two *taxiarchiai* that had been sent in advance retained their order, as did the rest of the units in the marching formation, but two *taxiarchiai* (presumably from the rear of the infantry hollow square) were posted behind the *saka*. The 100 horsemen that had been detailed scouting duties in the rear were presumably further to the rear than these two *taxiarchiai* of infantry. The commander who had been dispatched in advance of the invading force held his position until the entire army had passed through the narrows and only then followed them.

c) Crossing bridges and fords not occupied by the enemy (DRM 14): If the guides informed the emperor (DRM 14) that on the following day they would have to cross a narrowing in the road (e.g. a bridge or a ford), the emperor was to dispatch *taxeis* (units) of infantry to occupy it in advance, after which he was to give orders as to the sequence in which the army were to pass through the narrows. The marching order for the units was such that an infantry *taxiarchia* posted in the front marched together with a cavalry *parataxis* (the vanguard of the advance guard) and once these were across and in position the other units followed, one after the other in a predetermined order. The first to cross were the emperor together with his own forces and the cavalry posted in front. Then followed the right wing cavalry flank guards, and after them the right flank infantry. The baggage train marched next, followed by the left flank infantry and after them the left flank cavalry. The rear of the formation was held by a *taxiarchia* of infantry. This implies that when the army marched through a narrows it adopted a narrower formation so that the front and rear of the hollow oblong consisted only of a single *taxiarchia* of infantry, which then marched in column formation through the narrows in the above-mentioned sequence.

d) Mountain passes blocked by the enemy (DRM 20): If the enemy occupied the pass or passes that the emperor intended to use, then he was advised to avoid that route and also any other routes occupied by the enemy, and seek another unoccupied pass at a distance of three or four days away. The reason for this was that it was always dangerous to attack the enemy when it held an advantageous position. The emperor was to dispatch an infantry force in advance in the same manner as in the previous example, but if that location had also been occupied by the enemy, then the guides were to lead a sizeable force of infantry through side roads and paths to attack the enemy force holding the pass either from behind or from the flanks. The expectation (DRM 18.1–15, 19.1–24, 20.19–57) was that the Roman guides knew the territory far better than the enemy, which then enabled them to exploit their better knowledge of the terrain to the Roman advantage. However, if the enemy force blocking the pass was in a securely-held fortress or on a high outcropping rock that could not be attacked, then Leôn advised the emperor to dispatch a force of light infantry ('*elaffroi ... pezoí*') against it along the public road with orders to provoke the enemy into leaving its advantageous position to fight, after which they were to flee to a place of ambush posted for this purpose. If this was not possible because the location was so rough that it could not even be approached, which the author noted to have witnessed in person many times, then it was possible to ignore it completely and continue the march because the same rough terrain prevented the enemy from exploiting their position.

    The author added that it was also possible to pass through the mountains by using side paths and routes unknown to the enemy but which were known to the experienced Roman guides. He added that he had used such roads many times without any trouble whatsoever. It was because of this that Leôn instructed the emperor to follow the guides' advice when they informed of the existence of such a road. The emperor was once again expected to dispatch an infantry force in advance to occupy the route in the manner described, after which the army marched through the road. The road and any side paths and roads were to be secured by this infantry force just in case there were any enemy fortresses or high secure locations nearby. If the emperor intended to return through this road or use it for the transport of supplies, the infantry guards were to remain in their places. However, if the emperor intended to return by using another road, the infantry forces left their stations and advanced there to guard it until the emperor marched through it.

    If the emperor did not leave an infantry army behind to guard the mountain pass, he was to observe the same precautions when leaving enemy territory as he had when entering it. In fact, Leôn stated that this was even more important when returning because the enemy usually occupied the passes leading away from their territory to block the route of retreat from the Romans who were by then tired and burdened by prisoners and herds. This is precisely what the DV instructed the Romans to do against the Saracens in Asia Minor. If the emperor then faced an enemy force blocking his route of retreat through the mountain pass, he was to rest his army, especially his infantry force, before proceeding to attack the enemy.

Similarly, as in the DV, there is no mention of any fasting in the context of the rest, which means that we should interpret the resting to mean real resting to recuperate strength before any engagement. This was definitely wiser than the instruction to fast for three days before the battle in the PM (6.3) and may be a purposeful change by the author who clearly did not place quite as much importance to religious matters as did Nikêforos Fôkas in the PM. The final editor of the DV and the author of the DRM were clearly more interested in the technical, practical side of warfare. The Roman marching camp was also to be placed close to the pass so that the soldiers would not have to march a long distance before combat. The men were rested for the rest of the day and also the following day while the emperor and officers exhorted them to bravery. The attack against the enemy was to begin on the third morning in the manner already described. In other words, the guides were to lead the men through secret paths against the enemy's rear and/or flanks.

When the Roman army was in a defile and the enemy was nearby behind and there were three roads not far from one another, the emperor was to post three infantry *chiliarchoi* (commanders of the *taxiarchiai*) from the rear of the hollow square to protect the rear while the three front *chiliarchoi* of the hollow square occupied the mouths of the three passes. After this the remaining six *chiliarchoi* from the flanks led their infantry through the flanking passes while the cavalry passed through the middle pass. The baggage train and other units were probably led through the middle pass as well. If there was reason to suspect that the enemy was at the opposite end of the passes, the three *chiliarchoi* of the front marched through the passes in advance of the rest of the army. They were to take position at the front to protect the army until all cavalry and infantry had made their way through the passes. The emperor was to follow a similar procedure even when there existed only one or two passes leading away from the defile.

If the Roman army was in a really bad predicament in that it had enemy forces blocking all roads leading out of the defile and there was no other way out, the emperor was to rest his army in a location that had access to water. If the enemy then approached from the rear, the emperor was to order his cavalry forces to charge them and if the Romans won with Divine Help then the pursuit was to be pressed home until the enemy's formation was completely broken and they were in flight. If the enemy force shadowing the Romans was large and ready to engage the Romans, the Roman infantry was ordered to follow the cavalry force when the cavalry charged into contact with the enemy. This straight desperate frontal cavalry charge in a defile with the infantry following was obviously the only option available in the circumstances. If the Romans were successful and then returned to their encampment with much shouting and joyous cheering, Leôn envisaged this would frighten the enemy forces in front sufficiently so that they would rather flee and leave their passes undefended. However, if the morale of the enemy forces in front still remained unchanged and steadfast, the emperor was to find out their numbers and quality and deployment pattern. After this, the emperor was to ready his infantry *parataxeis* and send them against the enemy three at a time. If the enemy occupied the heights in broken terrain on both sides of the pass, the emperor was to dispatch his *akontistai* (javelineers), *psiloi* (light infantry), *toxotai* (archers) and *sfendonistai* (slingers) against them. When possible, the *menavlatoi* were to assist them by joining the attack. Leôn expected that the prolonged harassment by the archers, javelineers and slingers would do the trick, but if this did not happen, then the emperor was to dispatch one or two *parataxeis* of *oplitai* through the level portion of the pass to assist the attack. With 'Divine Help' the Romans would then prevail and the enemy would be forced into flight. After this, the rest of the army would march through the pass.

The above set of instructions prove that Leôn also foresaw a situation in which the Roman emperor and his guides had been completely outmanoeuvred by the enemy so that they had been entrapped in a defile with no way out. In such circumstances the emperor had to resort to really desperate measures to extradite himself and his army from danger. It is these that Leôn described above.

7. Sieges (DRM 21–7)

a) **Preliminary preparations (DRM 21.1–17)**: Leôn had very sound advice concerning the preliminary stages of the siege. When the intention was to capture walled cities, the emperor or the Roman commander was to subject the countryside around to a prolonged period of raiding by fast raiders (*koursôres*) and hussars (*trapezitai/chôsarioi*). The raiders were to chop down the vines and fruit trees, burn their crops, take away their animals and capture or kill everyone they came across so that it would be very difficult for the defenders to stock their cities with supplies and fighters.

b) **Securing supplies (DR; 21.18–42)**: When besieging a city, the Romans also needed enough supplies for the length of the siege in a situation in which these could not be obtained locally. It was here that the problem lay. It was not realistic for the army to attempt to transport more than twenty-four days' supply of barley for the horses, which meant that the Romans had to organize convoys from their own territory to the army besieging the city. According to Leôn, this was even more necessary in the area belonging to Bulgaria because it lacked all forms of necessities and above all barley. The supply route was secured in the same manner as the marching route so that some troops occupied a mountain pass which the mules and other beasts of burden and wagons (when possible) were required to use when bringing supplies. Another force of infantry and cavalry were to escort the supply column when necessary.

c) **The advance to the city (DRM 21.43–65)**: When the emperor intended to march against the city, the first step to take was to send an advance party of cavalry under a courageous *stratêgos* (implies the use of the local *stratêgos* with a good knowledge of the area) three to four days before the intended date of the invasion. The *stratêgos* was to launch a lightning attack while capturing men and animals. This had a dual purpose: it frightened the enemy and at the same time the prisoners provided information. If the *stratêgos* feared that the enemy might launch a counter attack, he was to join the emperor's main force, but if he learnt that there were no enemies nearby he was to stay longer and continue his pillaging and ravaging. The emperor was to conduct his invasion in the already prescribed manner, and when he approached the city to be besieged he was to halt and make camp when he was at a distance of six miles from the city. After this, he dispatched a moderately-sized cavalry force against the city to test the morale and size of the garrison. The cavalry force was divided into two parts/lines, with the front half advancing closer to the city while the second half was placed in an ambush as *defensôres*. Those who advanced closer to the city were to destroy any parks, vineyards and trees by cutting them down, by uprooting them, or by setting them on fire. If the enemy on the walls rushed out to protect their property, the first cavalry line feigned flight and tried to draw the enemy into the ambush prepared for them. If this test then demonstrated to the Romans that the enemy lacked adequate manpower, they could then proceed with their siege operations. This piece of advice leaves open the question of what happened when the test demonstrated that the enemy still possessed sizeable forces inside the city. Perhaps, it was then up to the emperor if he wanted to take the risk, even if it is clear that Leôn implies that in such cases the siege was to be abandoned until such time that the enemy inside the city had clearly been weakened enough.

d) Putting the city under siege (DRM 21.66–107): After the preliminary test of the enemy strength had been done, the emperor was to choose a select elite force of well-equipped horsemen from all cavalry units (means undoubtedly cataphracted horsemen armed with bows and melee weapons) as his escort when he advanced to inspect the defences of the city by riding around it. It was then on the basis of this that he designated in writing the places where the commanders and units were to take their places in the siege lines around the city. After this the emperor returned to the camp. On the following morning the army advanced to begin the siege proper. The army was paraded before the enemy in perfect order to frighten the defenders, after which the emperor posted units opposite each of the gates for the purpose of protecting those who built the siege lines around the city. The Romans surrounded the city with a double rampart, which also served as their marching camp. The camp was to a have a ditch and rampart both in front and behind. If the siege was expected to be prolonged the Romans also constructed a wall. The inner rampart was placed two bowshots or more away from the city wall at a distance where the enemy's arrows, missiles and stone-throwers could not reach the Roman encampment. However, it was still to be close enough to the walls for the Romans to be able to send support for the siege engines and their crews if the enemy sortied out. The imperial tenting area was to be located in the strongest and highest location. If there was marshy terrain or a mountain, then the siege lines were to be located in the nearest safe location.

e) Siege operations (DRM 21.99ff., 27): The siege operations were to be started immediately so that supplies would not be wasted, and kept up night and day by attacking the city from all sides. The siege equipment and methods were the same as had been since antiquity, so that Leôn offered only a summary of these and it was for this reason that Leôn referred the emperor to consult the ancient authorities. Leôn did not name these, but it is clear that he meant treatises by Biton, Filon of Byzantion, Athenaios, Heron of Alexandria and Apollodoros of Alexandria, or the treatises known as *De constructione helepoleos*. One may assume that there were also other ancient treatises available at this time which are no longer extant today. Oddly, Leôn fails to mention the period author Heron of Byzantion among these sources. The siege tactics and methods that Leôn mentioned were the use of tunnelling, mounds of earth and wood, battering rams, tortoises, stone-throwing engines (the *petroboloi* encompassed many different kinds of devices: ballistae, catapults, *onagri* and various kinds of trebuchets), ropes, wooden towers (many different variants), ladders (many variants) and other devices and engines that could be found from the ancient treatises.

The stronger and more effective siege machines were to be posted along the more level portion of the terrain and used in particular against the weakest portion of the enemy wall. It was there that the best troops and commanders were also to take their place. Leôn envisaged that the relentless attack by night and day would eventually demoralize the enemy so that the city would either surrender on terms or be taken by force.

f) Protecting the foragers outside the camp (DRM 22–3): While the siege was still in progress the Romans continued to dispatch men either to collect provisions or to collect grass and pasturage for the horses. Since the enemy could be expected to target these, the emperor was to post guards for this in locations suited to this. It was also possible to exploit the enemy's willingness to attack the foragers. When the emperor learnt of the enemy harassment, he was to send two groups of cavalry ambushers at night into their places of ambush. When the enemy then attacked the foragers, the first group launched its ambush and charged straight at the enemy while the second ambushing force followed behind while maintaining its formation (note the use of two cavalry battle lines) to protect it. It was only when the Romans learnt from prisoners that there was no other enemy force posted behind as ambushers that the entire force, the second line included, pressed their pursuit to the hilt with the idea of destroying the enemy force in its entirety. It was also possible to lure the enemy into attacking the foragers by dressing even the guards in servants' garb so that it would appear as if there were no accompanying guards. If the enemy then attacked the foragers, they faced a double surprise: the disguised soldiers carried weapons while the two groups of cavalry ambushers attacked them in the same manner as above.

g) Facing a moderately-sized relief army (DRM 24): In those instances in which the intelligence operatives informed the emperor of the impending enemy attack against the Roman army or its foragers, the emperor was to collect a sizeable cavalry force which he was to lead in person while still leaving behind an adequate force for the defence of the marching camp and siege equipment. In such instances the siege operations could be slowed or halted. The emperor was to conceal this force in a suitable location and when he then learnt of the enemy attack either against the Roman camp or foragers, he was to dispatch help for them while he followed behind. Note once again the use of two cavalry lines. If the first line was successful, the emperor, or any military commander leading this force, was not to pursue the enemy far. The second line was also required to retain its cohesion and formation at all times except when the enemy force was very large and had defeated the first line. It was only then that the formation could be broken by charging against the approaching enemy.

h) A night attack against moderately sized relief army (DRM 25): If the Romans learnt from spies, prisoners or deserters the exact location of the enemy encampment and that the size of their force was smaller than the Roman army and it were within the reach of a night march, the emperor could attempt a night attack. In that case the emperor chose a cavalry force which was larger than the enemy force into which he added some infantry javelineers, archers, *oplitai* and mounted Russians. He left behind a sufficient force for the protection of the camp and siege equipment and then started his march in the evening under the guidance of capable guides. He was not to inform anyone except his closest advisors about the object of his actions.[13] The approach was to be orderly and fast, but still cautious. The cavalry together with the mounted Russians advanced in front and the infantry followed behind. The likely reason for the inclusion of the mounted Russians among the cavalry is that they could be dismounted to face any enemy *katafraktoi* with the expectation that they would prevail over these in the same manner as they had prevailed over the rebel *katafraktoi* when they had fought on behalf of Basileios II in the civil wars. If the cavalry forces managed to surprise the enemy in their encampment at dawn, it was likely that they would prevail and even if the enemy had been roused to action Leôn still expected the Romans to prevail because their cavalry outnumbered the enemy cavalry. The target of the Roman attack was the destruction of the enemy fighting force. The soldiers were not to be allowed to start pillaging the enemy's supply train or baggage, because the enemy had often used it as bait when ambushing the Romans. Furthermore, if the enemy fled, even if the pursuit was to be pressed home hard, the emperor was still not to pursue the fleeing foe without taking proper precautions because there always existed the danger of ambush. If the enemy cavalry force fled to some mountain or other strong and easily-defended place, then the emperor was to halt and wait for the arrival of the infantry force. After this, the infantry force was sent to the attack with the support of the cavalry. If the enemy force included their rulers, then the emperor was to prevent their flight by any means, and if the situation required he was even expected to order the rest of the army to the scene so that the enemy would not be able to escape. The attack against the enemy leaders was to be pressed home without mercy until the enemy was either completely defeated or they had abandoned their horses and fled through the mountains on foot.

i) Stratagem against the defenders of the city (DRM 26): Leôn includes also a stratagem against the defenders of the city which he had himself employed with success. The aim was to mislead the defenders into the false belief that the Roman cavalry had marched out of the camp against a relief army and so had left insufficient numbers of defenders behind. With this in mind the emperor was to hide a sizeable force of infantry inside the tents while the cavalry marched out of the camp. The cavalry was posted in ambuscades in such locations that were not visible from the city. The camp was made to look as if it was deserted. The enemy forces outside the city were also to be fooled into thinking that the foragers were left without protection. When the besieged then observed and so became emboldened to charge out of the gates against the siege works and engines, the men guarding these were instructed to flee inside the camp with the idea of inducing the enemy to follow them there. The soldiers hidden in the tents were to remain in hiding until the enemy started plundering the camp and it was only then that they charged out and the cavalry charged out of their hiding places. The cavalry was instructed to gallop as fast as possible to the gates leading back into the city so that the enemy forces that had entered the Roman camp would be entrapped. This was possible because the circular shape of the camp meant that the enemy was able to enter the Roman camp only in some sections while the Romans (those parts where the men were hidden in the tents) still held the other sections through which they could go behind the enemy. Leôn had witnessed the use of this ruse several times. It had always resulted in severe enemy casualties and sometimes also in the capture of the enemy fortress.

j) Facing a large enemy relief army (DRM 26.35–8): When the enemy had collected a large relief army, Leôn advised against the continuation of the siege. It was preferable to withdraw and pitch the marching camp in a suitable location which was far enough from the city and there wait for the enemy attack – which the Romans were to face with a standard battle formation.

Appendix V

The *Gotha Ms.* and the Muslim Art of War

1. The *Gotha ms*: The Background (before 1348)

In 1880, F. Wüstenfeld edited and translated into German the second half of *Gotha ms* 258, f.110–215. This edition, *Das Heereswesen der Muhammedaner nach dem Arabichen (Abhandlungen der Historisch-Philologischen Classe der Königlichen Gesellschaft der Wissenschaften zu Göttingen 26*, 1880) is basically the same, word for word, as *Nihayat al-Su'l*, excepting that some chapters are wanting in the previous. This means that the text in question has been extracted from Nihayat or from some common source.[1] The text of the *Gotha ms* itself has been compiled from some unknown earlier Muslim military manuals and from some Arabic translation of Aelian. The earlier Muslim military treatises in their turn appear to have been based on earlier Arabic translations and compilations of Sasanian military treatises which date from the Abbasid period. The treatise is full of direct references to former Sasanian kings and their military instructions. A part of the text has also been directly lifted from al-Kindi's treatise on Swords.[2] However, the author has picked his sources rather carelessly and sometimes mixes different military traditions in his military instructions, and the actual presentation is also poorly organized. In addition, the first few chapters deal mainly with the characteristics of horses, while some of the later chapters in the text of Wüstenfeld deal with single combat. The following discussion offers a summary of the main contents.

2. General information[3]

Following Persian practice, the author instructed the emir to hold military reviews/examinations of the troops before engaging the enemy in combat to assess their fighting capability and the quality of their equipment. The information concerning the types of troops and equipment is somewhat muddled, because the author mixes information derived from different sources. In military reviews the troops were apparently assessed primarily according to the quality and amount of equipment. In the first row were placed those who were fully equipped and wore armour reaching the ground; in the second and third rows were placed those who had shorter clothes and armour; and in the fourth and fifth rows were the similarly less-well equipped. The cavalry formation was therefore five deep. The equipment of a fully-equipped horseman evidently consisted of a good strong horse, strong armour, cap and helmet, greaves and shin guards, two strong composite bows, 30 arrows, arrow case, javelin, sword, dagger, mace, hatchet, and 30 stones for throwing in two saddlebags. This information represents the Sasanian system after the reign of Chosroes I.

The division of the soldiers into nine different types is somewhat muddled because the author has mixed the classification of troops in Aelian with those of the Sasanians and the Abbasids. However, the list is not wholly without value, because each of the troop types does find its match amongst the troops mentioned elsewhere in the treatise. In fact, the troop classifications are by and large representative of actual troop types in the Abbasid armies. The author classified the infantry (types 1–3) into three different classes: 1) the fully equipped infantry (= hoplites?); 2) the shield bearers that were used to make a palisade (i.e. a shieldwall/phalanx) in battle; and 3) the light-armed (= *psiloi*), i.e. the Khorasanis, bolt shooters (either crossbowmen or archers using arrow guides?), and naptha/nafta shooters/throwers. The three cavalry classes (types 4–6) were: 1) the riders who carried lances (i.e. lancers), a few of whom might be earthenware-pot-throwers (= throwers of hand grenades filled with inflammable material?); 2) the riders who threw short spears or javelins;[4] and 3) the mounted archers. Oddly, the author did not include the fully-equipped and -armed horseman (type 7), or the horseman/'armour bearer' (type 8) who rode with two horses (i.e. he had a spare horse for his 'knight') amongst the cavalry proper, while these were included in the review above. The rest of the forces (type 9) consisted of servants, baggage, and elephant handlers when elephants were used.

Notably, the treatise also mentions that these different classifications meant different battlefield functions for each of these different troop types, but then gives only two instances when both infantry and cavalry were present: cavalry was to be used only against cavalry, whilst infantry could be used against both cavalry and infantry. By mentioning this, the author has given us a really important piece of information regarding the battlefield efficiency of infantry. It was regarded capable of facing both cavalry and infantry.

3. Campaign: marching formation and camp[5]

The campaigns and battles were to begin on a 'favourable day' (Thursday or Saturday) if possible. Before campaign each of the officers and troops were assigned to their proper places. The recommended marching formation was the traditional *al-khamis* formation that had been used basically by all well-organized armies ever since antiquity. It consisted of the scouts, vanguard, rear guard, two wing units and centre. Following the age-old Persian custom, the troopers were not allowed to let their horses go pasture freely during the campaign. Instead, the servants collected the fodder by hand.

The treatise also includes instructions for the making of a marching camp which derive directly from the Sasanian period. The camp was to be placed on level terrain with a plentiful supply of water and fodder. The camp was to be fortified

The *Gotha Ms.* and the Muslim Art of War

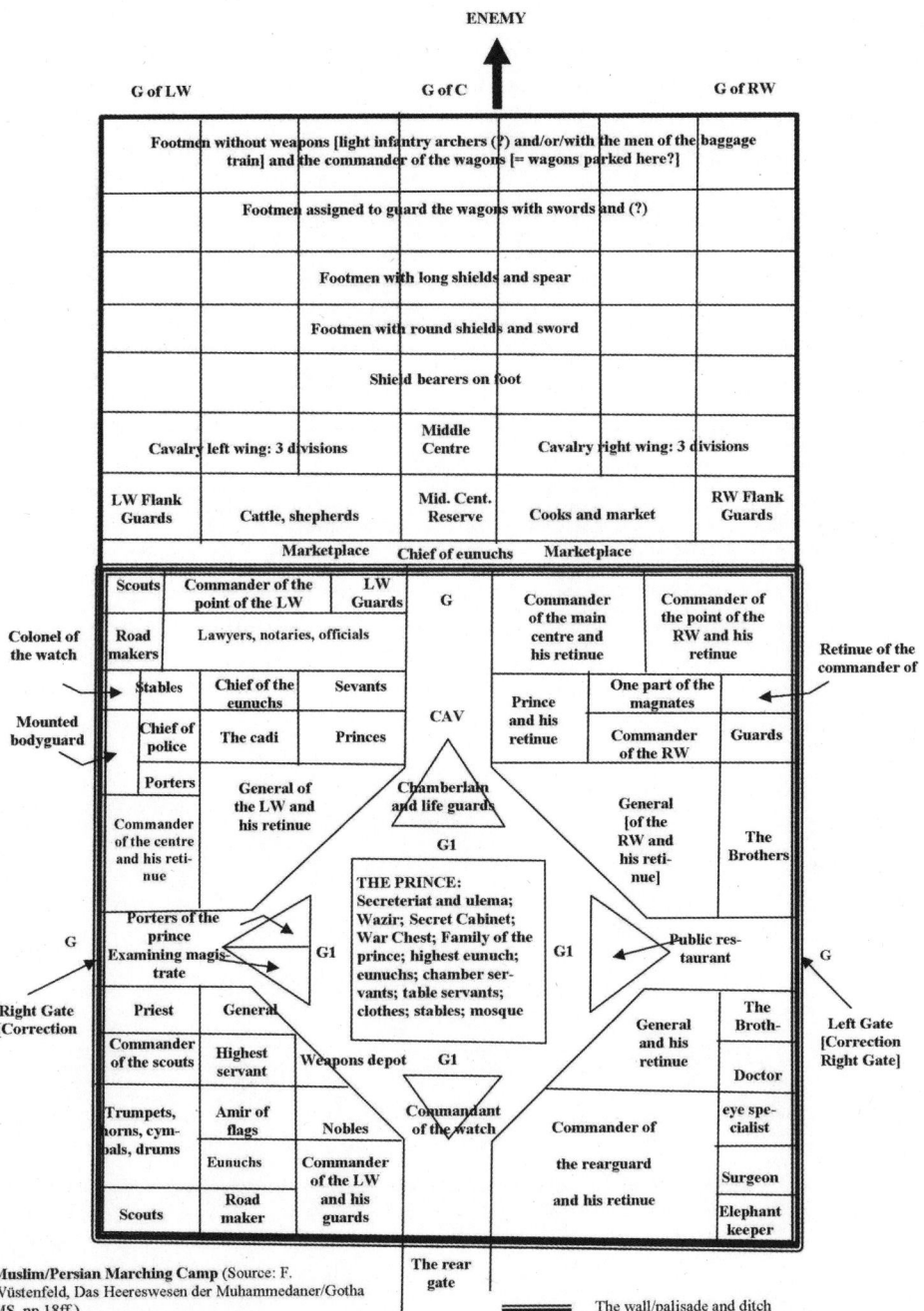

Muslim/Persian Marching Camp (Source: F. Wüstenfeld, Das Heereswesen der Muhammedaner/Gotha MS, pp.18ff.)

I have added emendations to the diagram in square brackets. In addition, one should note that despite the fact that the symbols in the diagram give a wall/palisade and ditch only to the main part of the camp, it is likely that some sort of fortification is also meant by the line surrounding the whole camp. In addition, the guards (LW; C; RW) outside the camp probably imply the use of cavalry patrols outside the camp noted for example in the text and also in the Tafrīj that were used as ambushers against approaching enemies.

▬▬▬ The wall/palisade and ditch
G of LW: Guard for the support of the LW and for creating disorder
G of C: Guard for the support of the centre and for creating disorder
G of RW: Guard for the support of the RW and for creating disorder
G: Guards
G1: Guards to horses and foot [lifeguards of the king]
CAV: Post of armed cavalry

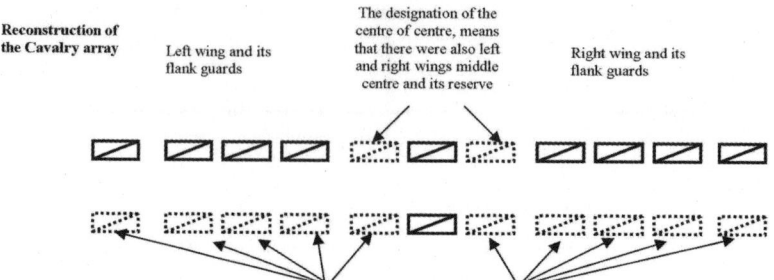

The fact that centre of centre had its own reserve implies that all of the units in the front line probably had their own reserves, too. My educated guess is that the generals and their retinues and commanders would have been used to form the second reserve lines for the wings and centre. I have also made the guess that the overall commanders for the wings would have been the generals. See below.

The reconstruction of the places of the commanders in the cavalry battle array is more problematic. The diagram lists the following: 1) Commander of the point of the left wing; 2) Commander of the left wing; 3) General of the left wing; 4) Commander of the point of the right wing; 5) Commander of the right wing; 6) Commander of the main centre; 7) Commander of the centre; 8-10) three generals without designations; 11) Commander of the scouts; 12) Commander of the rearguard; 13) Colonel of the Watch; 14) Chief of Police; 15) And the Prince. It is clear that of these we leave out the numbers 13 and 14, as these would have been used as security forces for the camp or baggage train duding combat. The rear guard would also have been used for the protection of the rear rather than for actual combat. The treatise tells us elsewhere (p.34) that the commander of the army/prince positioned himself in the middle of the centre. This leaves out the problems of three generals without designations and the relative hierarchy of the various officers. My educated guess in this respect is that the generals (emirs) were superior to the commanders. This means that we should assign amend the text with generals for the centre and right wings and also assign a general to the middle of each of the divisions. This still leaves out one general without assignment, but a good guess is that he would have been put in charge of infantry or baggage train/camp. The notable thing is that the reconstruction based on the diagram is in agreement with the other parts of the *Gotha manuscript* and even with the other information (esp. with the *Tafrij*) that we possess of the cavalry battle array.

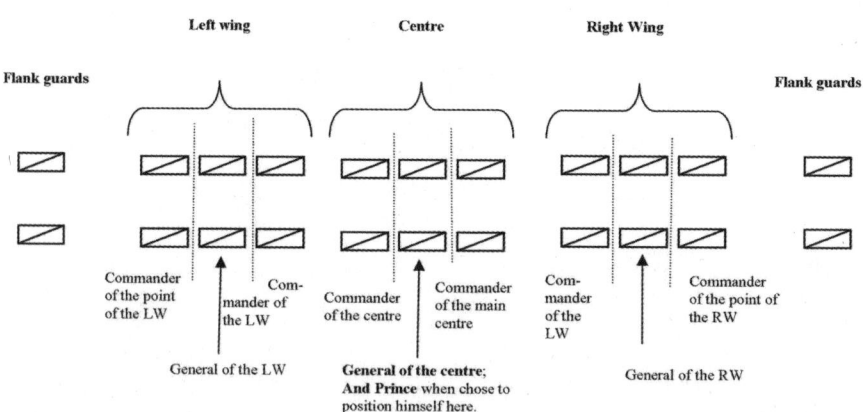

The *Gotha Ms.* and the Muslim Art of War 455

Reconstruction of a mixed battle formation as a phalanx based on the structure of the marching camp after the army had marched out of the camp.

Note that the use of the long shields in front and round shields behind made it possible to form a shield wall with a roof of shields (i.e. *testudo/foulkon*) against incoming missile attacks of the enemy. Note also that the placing of different types of footmen in the phalanx resembles the structure found in *Adab al-harb* / Fakhr-i Mudabbir. The place of the foot archers is not known, but was usually probably behind the phalanx.

INFANTRY

▬▬▬ Footmen with long shields and spear
■ ■ ■ Footmen with round shields and sword
● ● ● Shield bearers on foot and archers

CAVALRY

1. **Cavalry line**: LW Flank Guards in line with infantry; Left cavalry wing behind infantry, 3 divisions; Centre, retinue, middle centre, retinue; Right cavalry wing, 3 divisions; RW Flank Guards in line with infantry.
2. **Cavalry line**: Flank guard reserve/retinue; LW Reserve 3 divisions of retinue; Centre, retinue, middle centre reserve, retinue; RW reserve 3 divisions of retinue; RW flank guard retinue.

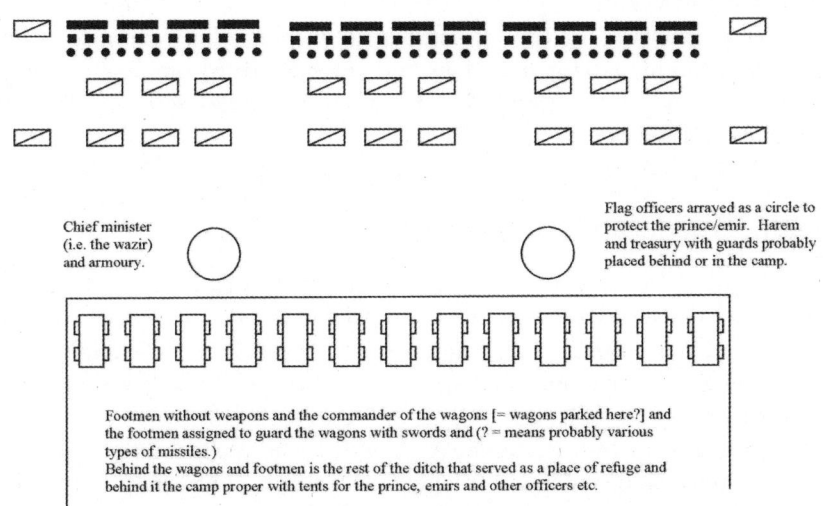

Chief minister (i.e. the wazir) and armoury.

Flag officers arrayed as a circle to protect the prince/emir. Harem and treasury with guards probably placed behind or in the camp.

Footmen without weapons and the commander of the wagons [= wagons parked here?] and the footmen assigned to guard the wagons with swords and (? = means probably various types of missiles.)
Behind the wagons and footmen is the rest of the ditch that served as a place of refuge and behind it the camp proper with tents for the prince, emirs and other officers etc.

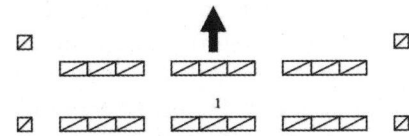

Persian and Muslim cavalry battle formation with camp (not in scale) Based on the *Strategikon*, *Tafrij*, *Gotha*, and Fakhr-i Mudabbir.

1. Two lines of cavalry in battle formation.
2. Wagons and infantry.
3. Place of refuge for cavalry.
4. The third cavalry line to protect the baggage train.
5. The fourth cavalry line to protect the rear of the baggage train
6. The cavalry rear guard
7. Spare horses
8. Prisoners and guards

The inner structure of the camp is given in greater detail above.

Wagons and infantry placed in front with ditch all around to serve as a place of refuge for the cavalry

Camp proper.

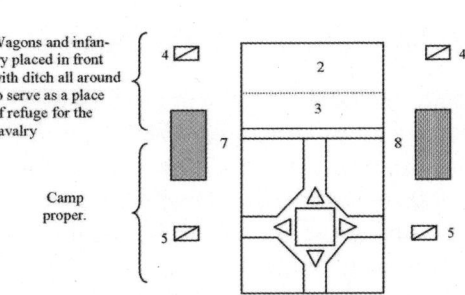

with a ditch to protect the army during the night. Two groups of soldiers were also assigned for guard duty for the night, so that whilst one group performed guard duty the other rested. In addition, it was recommended that the Muslims would use an ambushing force behind the camp which could then be used against enemies intending to attack their camp. The use of the wagons and ditch to protect the side opposite the enemy is the most peculiar feature of this Persian marching camp. The inner structure of this camp was not as safe as the Roman version with the empty space between the edges and centre of the camp and was therefore more vulnerable if the attacking enemy used bows and arrows. The solution of not having a gate on the side facing the enemy could also be a weakness if the army had to retreat through that particular side.

One can reconstruct the cavalry battle array from the diagram of the camp by making some simple educated guesses and emendation to the text. Notably, the resulting diagram agrees with all the other sources describing the cavalry array of the Persians and Abbasids.

4. Night Attacks and Ambushes[6]

The treatise does not concern itself greatly with the actual details of night attacks (the matters to be taken into account when placing an ambush occupy most of the attention), but states that such operations were entirely acceptable and could even be very profitable, even if such operations were directed at the wives and children of the unbelievers.

When the emir intended to ambush the enemy he was naturally instructed to choose a suitable commander and troopers for the task.[7] The horses were to be fast and well behaved, and the troopers lightly-equipped. The ambuscade was to be set up in covered terrain near a source of water so that both the men and horses could stay there for a while whilst they waited for the arrival of the enemy. Naturally, the men and horses were expected to lay low and maintain silence until the ambush would be launched. The actual ambush was to consist of at least two fighting groups and scouts, so if the first group suffered a defeat or feigned flight, the second could salvage the situation. See also the wedge battle formation (Section 5.6) below.

5. Battle Formations and Combat[8]

According to the *Gotha ms*, one of the former writers had written a description of battle orders with seven figures. These figures are the same as can be found from the *Nihayat al-Su'l*. The battle arrays in question are: 1) the simple crescent (two cavalry lines) to outflank the enemy; 2) the crescent (two cavalry lines) with flank guards to outflank the enemy; 3) the square formation (two cavalry battle lines); 4) the convex array to break through the enemy's centre (the counter manoeuvre against the covered convex array was to divide the front line into two parts to the right and left, and then advance the second line into the gap); 5) the rhombus when the enemy outnumbered the Muslims, used to counter the enemy crescent (there were actually different types of rhomboids for the armies and units, which should not be confused with each other; note the similarity to the Roman cavalry array in the ST, for which see Appendix 1); 6) the half-rhombus, either to widen the frontage or to break through the enemy in wedge formation (there were actually different types of wedges for entire armies and single units which should not be confused with each other); and 7) the circle (infantry and/or dismounted cavalry on the edges) as a defensive formation.

5.1. Crescent (*hilālī*) without flank guards

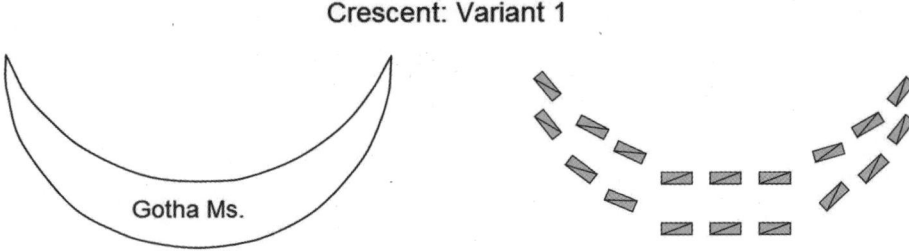

According to the *Gotha ms*, the former Persian kings considered the crescent to be the best of the fighting formations. It came in two variations – the crescent proper and the crescent with flank guards/ambushers – and it was used to encircle the enemy on both flanks. The *Gotha ms* leaves most of the actual directions as to its use and composition to the second version, and I have also chosen to follow the same course of action, with the exception that I have added on the right the reconstruction (diagram on the right) of the actual array behind the figure (diagram on the left).

5.2. Crescent with flank guards/ambushers (*mujannah*)

The second version of the crescent had flank guards attached to the wings in four parts (units). The diagram on the left is the original and the reconstructed battle array is on the right.

According to the *Gotha ms*, the distance between the tips of the flanks (under a very brave and skilled commander) and their flank guards/ambushers was a quarter mile (400m). The commanders of the points of the flanks were apparently placed in the second battle line. This position gave the wing commanders a chance to direct the reserves in support of the first line if deemed necessary. The distance between the front half of the flank guards/ambushers, consisting of mounted archers, and the rear half of the flank guards/ambushers was a half mile (c.800m). This use of mounted archers in front also suggests a similar practice for the main battle

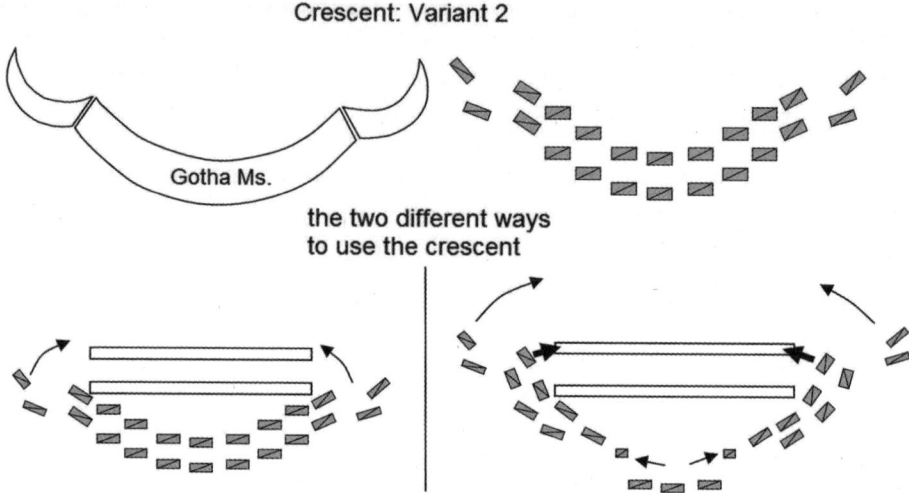

Crescent: Variant 2

Gotha Ms.

the two different ways to use the crescent

array. In other words, it is probable that the first main battle line also consisted of mounted archers. The distance to the enemy was a mile (c.1.6km). The length of the main battle line was one-and-a-half to two miles (c.2.4–3.2km). The distance between the first battle line and the second battle line was a quarter mile (400m) or more as the formation was widened to form the encircling crescent array. This was undoubtedly done in the same manner as the Roman crescent formation in which the flanks encircled the enemy by using the column formation. This description of the distances indisputably reflects the initial situation when the battle array was still arrayed in approximately straight lines. The first diagram shows a reconstruction of this initial battle formation. The space occupied by such an army also has implications as to the size of the envisaged army, which would have been smaller under the Hamdanids. Allowing 400 metres for the intervals and assuming the use of close order[9] (c.1m per horse in width) and an average of ten men per file, this gives a figure of 40,000–56,000 horsemen for the main formation, in addition to which came the flank guards/ambushers that were placed on the wings. With files of five horsemen, the same array would have had 20,000–28,000 horsemen plus the flank guards/ambushers.[10]

5.3. Square or oblong (*murabbaʿ*) cavalry formation

The oblong/square battle formation was the standard cavalry battle formation, consisting of two battle lines of cavalry. The overall commander/prince, baggage train and some additional reserves were posted behind the battle formation proper. We can find the same structure for the battle formation and marching camp also in the Tafrij. When necessary, the prince advanced forwards to get a better view of the events as well as to encourage the troops through exhortation. When necessary,

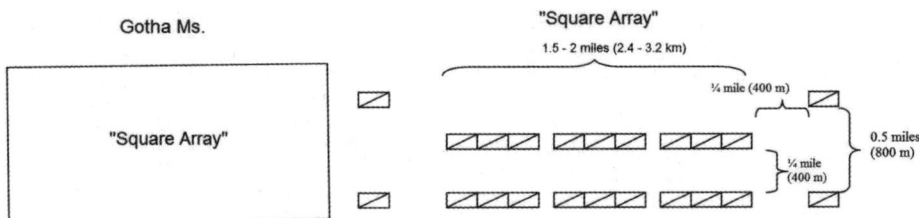

the prince also sent reinforcements to support the troops in distress and again new reinforcements to support those already sent. According to the text, the sending of reinforcements belonged to the modifications of 'modern times'. Unfortunately, it is not entirely certain to which period this refers. It may refer to the author's period or it may have been borrowed from an older treatise.

5.4. Convex or covered formation (*el-caff el-dabbabi*)

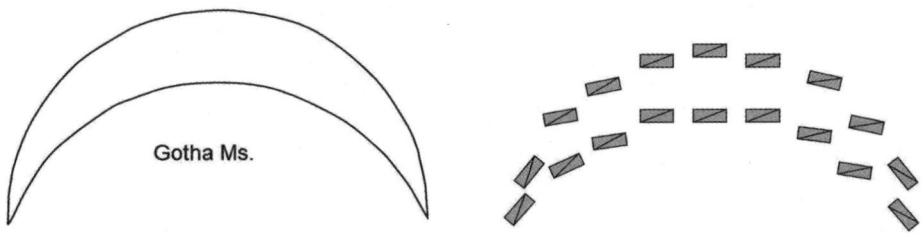

The convex (or covered) formation was the exact opposite of the crescent both in formation and purpose. The primary purpose of the convex was clearly to break through the enemy line in the middle while the flanks were held back in defensive refused posture. This formation would have been used when the commander had fewer men than the enemy. According to the *Gotha ms*, the counter manoeuvre against the covered convex array was to divide the front line into two parts to the right and left, and then advance the second line into the gap. And after that, the divided front line was to attack the enemy flanks. As noted before, everything again depended on the timing of the manoeuvres by each of the opposing sides.

5.5. Rhombus (*mu'ayyan*)

The fifth battle formation in the *Gotha ms* is called a rhombus. According to the text, it had a small depth with sufficient length. The treatise gives three different pictures of the rhombus formation, in addition to which we also have a different version of it in the *Nihayat al-Su'l*. According to the treatise, the rhombus was the easiest of the formations to form and use and was most frequently employed 'in his time'. The array was undoubtedly in frequent use in the fourteenth century,

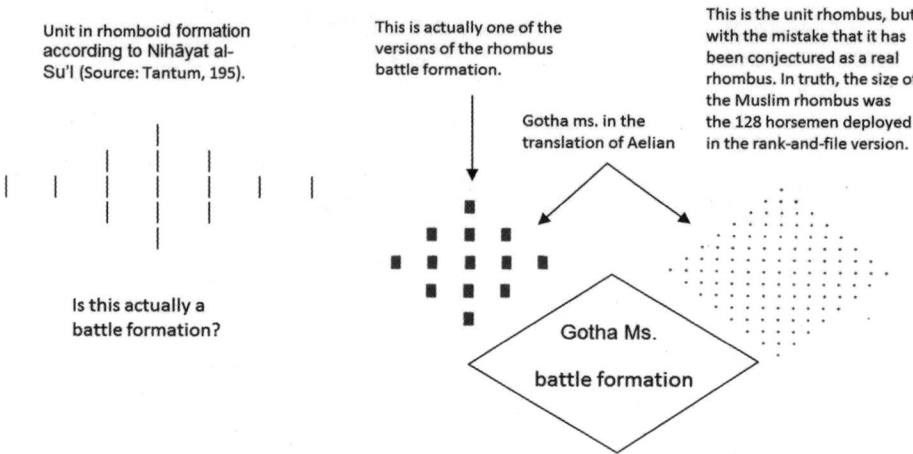

but it is equally clear that it would have been in use also in the tenth century, as it is basically the same in concept as the Roman cavalry formation of that era (see Appendix 1). The rhombus was considered to be the best battle array when one had inferior numbers of men and the enemy used a crescent. The width and depth of the formation allowed the sudden lengthening of the line when the enemy tried to outflank the formation. The ideal proportion of reserves/ambushers in this formation was one third of the whole army; one fourth of the whole was also acceptable but not less than this.

The diagrams and text in both the *Nihyat al-Su'l* and the *Gotha ms.* describe several different types of rhomboids, both for the armies and for units. The cavalry unit formation was actually a 128-man *kurdus* deployed as two wedges back-to-back in rank-and-file arrays which the author has misunderstood – as Aelian had. The text and diagrams in the *Gotha ms.* give two different versions for the battle formation proper, which are given in the accompanying reconstructions, the key difference in these being the number of divisions in the rear. It is possible that the Arabs had copied this concept of three cavalry lines with a vanguard and rear guard from the Chinese or Turks, both whom employed this type of battle formation. The Chinese gave a similar array the name 'well-formation' or 'eightfold formation', while in the text of Fakhr-i Mudabbir the Turkish formation consisted of nine divisions deployed three by three. The so-called Old Polish battle array of the sixteenth- to eighteenth-centuries is similar to the Turkish array. However, it is also possible that the Arabs invented this type of array themselves by using their contacts with the Chinese and Turks as sources of inspiration, because there are still differences between all of those while it is likely that the Romans copied the concept of *saka* from the Arabs. The key difference between the Muslim cavalry array and the Roman cavalry array as depicted in the ST (see Appendix I) is that the Muslims placed five divisions in the second actual battle line (the units on the edges protecting the flanks of the first line?) while the Romans placed their flank guards

The *Gotha Ms.* and the Muslim Art of War   461

and outflankers in the first line. However, it is possible to think that the treatise has simply omitted some of the details, so that in truth it was very similar to the one used by the Romans in the following manner: a) the vanguard would have consisted of the front line and their defenders; b) the first line would have had separate flank guards and outflankers; c) the centre of the second line could have consisted of the commander's flag-guard, but this could also be in actual combat formation as a *katafraktoi* wedge of *ghilman*; and d) the rear guard could have been similarly divided into three separate units. In short, it is quite possible that the Roman and Arab arrays were very similar to each other.

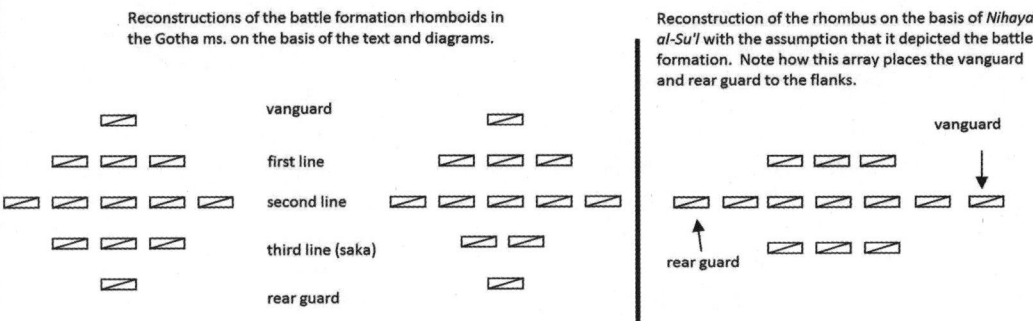

5.6. Half-Rhombus/wedge (*mustaṭīl*)[11]

The text includes a wedge/half-rhombus formation which was meant as an ambushing formation in the same manner as in the *De velitatione* (see Appendix II: 5.6), but so that it had even more ambushers than the Roman version. The battle

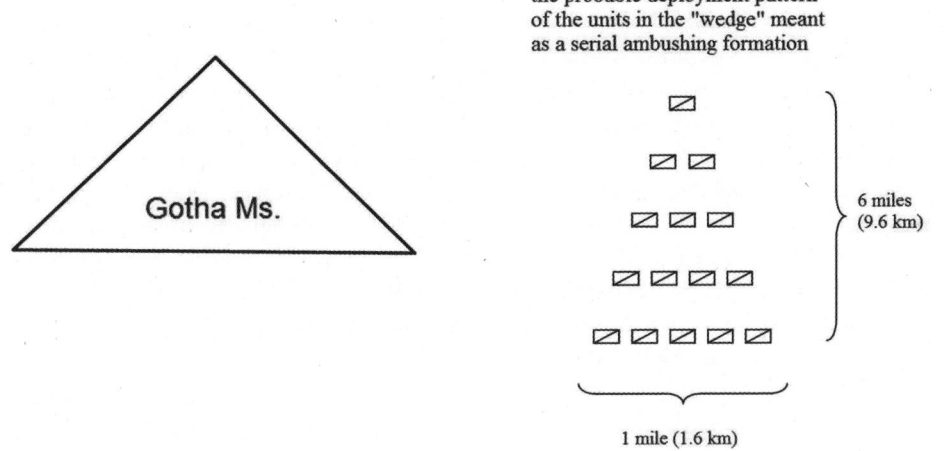

formation appears to have had a width of one mile and a depth of six miles or more, so that the units placed behind as ambushers were expected to outflank/ambush the enemy if these pursued those in front.

5.7. Circle (*kurah*)

The circle was a defensive formation that simply consisted of two consecutive lines that had been formed into an all-around defensive circle to protect both the army and the baggage train inside it.

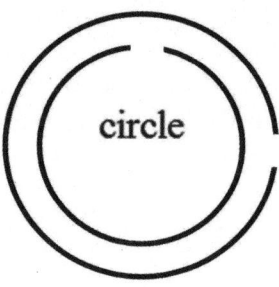

6. The Seven Formations in Combat

To begin with, the information provided by the *Gotha ms.* implies that the Muslim military theorists considered the crescent and rhombus formations as the best and most useful as battle formations. These two formations get most of the positive comments, and it was these two formations that the author recommended the commander to adopt if both sides initially used the crescent or circle formations. However, it is still equally clear that the other formations were still considered useful in the right circumstances. Furthermore, it is also clear that the crescent and convex formations would have been originally formed out of the basic oblong/square array in the course of combat.

In combat, the crescent formation was used to outflank the enemy on both flanks. This was done in two different ways. The first version was that whilst the centre stayed in place the flanks simply advanced simultaneously outwards and forward to encircle the enemy. The outermost tips of the wings advanced faster than the wings so that when the tip advanced two steps, the left and right wings advanced one step. By staying behind, the centre was able to act as a reserve force. However, if the flight of the enemy became evident it too started to advance slowly and methodologically forwards. After the front halves of the wings had made contact with the enemy flanks, the rear halves of the wings acted as their reserves. In the second version, the 'unbelievers' used a square/oblong formation and the Muslims the crescent. The author wisely noted that it was absolutely necessary for the commander to pay close attention to the relative strengths of the opposing forces when using the crescent. Regardless, the *Gotha ms.* still promised a victory even when the armies were evenly matched in numbers. Nevertheless, it was still recommended that in that case the first line of the centre would be ordered to follow the wings in their support. The first line of the centre was expanded outwards until it occupied half of the frontage of the battle line. This manoeuvre allowed the wings to advance so far outwards that it was possible to attack the flanks of tbe enemy's rear line. According to the text, the use of the crescent formation in these circumstances would bring success, even if the unbelievers were to use the rhombus formation. The author also considered the lengthening of the battle line by the enemy useless because it would simply result in a weakened line.

The weakest formation against the crescent was apparently the use of the defensive circle formation by the enemy, because it evidently allowed the Muslims to encircle the enemy without resistance. However, when describing the other formations and their combat manoeuvres (especially the oblong), the author inadvertently acknowledges the truth that the counter manoeuvres could also be successful when employed against the crescent. In truth, the success of each of the formations and manoeuvres depended solely upon the timing of the manoeuvres and counter-manoeuvres by each of the participants. Furthermore, even though the *Gotha ms.* does not mention it, the crescent was also vulnerable when attacked by close-order lancers. The tips of the wings of the lengthened line of mounted archers were particularly vulnerable when attacked by lancers in close order. This, however, was not the typical Roman response to the outflanking because the recommended method against the encircling Bedouins was the use of archery by cavalry and/or the addition of infantry archers and slingers to the Roman cavalry formation (PM 4.17; narrative of the years 954 and 965). On the other hand, even when the Romans could use archery as a counter tactic, the use of the crescent array with mounted archers still had the advantage of giving the mounted archers deployed a loose order a very good chance of fleeing to the safety of the reserves while constantly shooting showers of arrows backwards at the pursuers if the enemy chose to do so. Nikêforos Fôkas (PM 4.17) advised against the pursuit of such cavalry forces. When the mounted archers employed this tactic purposefully in the form of feigned flight, it also gave them a psychological advantage, because the pursuers would have been in a surprised state of mind and in disorder when they finally faced the heavy cavalry reserves of the centre. See the narrative of the year 954.

The oblong formation was accurately considered vulnerable if the enemy used the crescent formation to outflank its vulnerable wings. Notably, as in Greece and Rome, the extension of the battle line to oppose the crescent was not the recommended solution. Its use was considered a great folly, because the thin long line was simply too weak to offer resistance in those circumstances. Indeed, when the 'unbelievers' were using the crescent, the Muslims were instructed to direct their attacks against the flanks and rear of the tips of the crescent if at all possible. The commander of the front line flank guards/ambushers was instructed to proceed as far as was necessary to make the line equal in length to the enemy line. If the enemy visibly outflanked the Muslims, the commander of the ambushers on the flank [evidently the commander of the flank of the second line] was expected to divide the ambushers into three, four, or five sections as necessary to extend the line as far as necessary.

As already noted, the convex (or covered) formation was the exact opposite of the crescent both in formation and purpose. The main purpose of the convex was to break through the enemy line in the middle while the flanks were held back in a defensive, refused posture. This formation would have been used when the

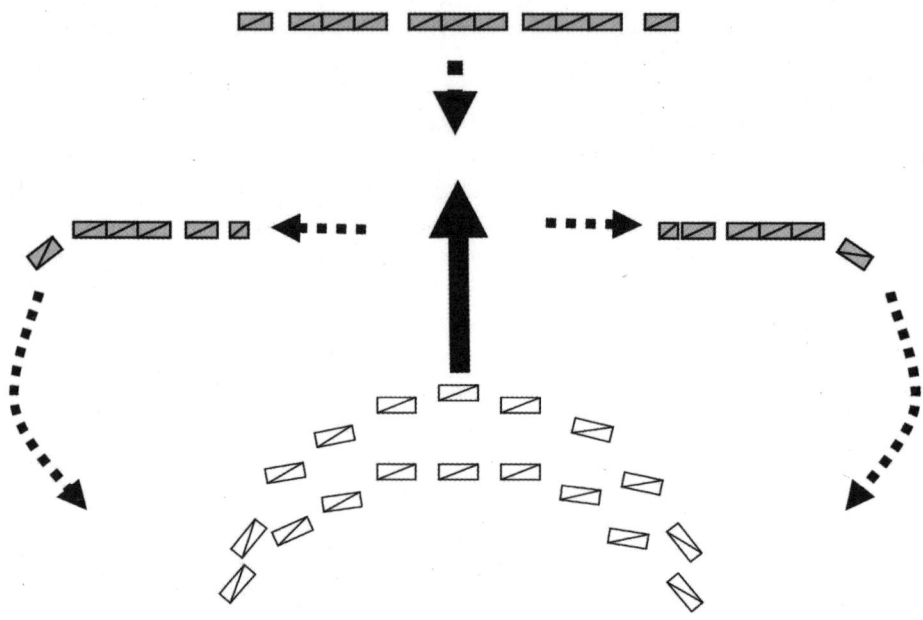

commander had fewer men than the enemy. According to the *Gotha ms.*, the counter manoeuvre against the covered convex array was to divide the front line into two parts to the right and left, and then advance the second line into the gap. And after that, the divided front line was to attack the enemy flanks. As noted before, everything again depended on the timing of the manoeuvres by each of the opposing sides.

Notably, the Rhombus formation was considered to be the best formation against the crescent formation because in it the wings were extended and refused, and because the presence of numerous reserves on the wings and rear made the centre of the formation very powerful.

In combat, the wedge formation was used to hide the presence of reserves behind the battle line from the eyes of the enemy. These reserves were in their turn used to outflank the enemy when the front had achieved contact with the enemy. It was a formation that had several ambushes deployed in depth.

The circle formation was rightly considered the weakest of the lot. It was to be used as a defensive formation only in extreme distress when the enemy outnumbered the Muslims and/or had managed to caught the Muslims unprepared.

If both of the opposing sides used the same formation, with the exception of circle or crescent formations, the *Gotha ms.* states the obvious, as in that case the result of the frontal combat primarily depended on the actions of the frontline. The use of the circle and crescent array by both sides simultaneously was considered extremely unlikely, but in the event of this unlikely occurrence, the Muslim commander was told to use the crescent against the circle and the rhombus against the crescent.

7. Aelian, Infantry Phalanx and the Past Masters of War

As already noted, the treatise contains large sections borrowed from some Arabic translation of Aelian. The author combines Aelian with instructions taken from some past masters of the art of war and also adds to this concoction his own comments – that are not always very sensible. For example, he mixes information concerning cavalry tactics of his day with the infantry sections of Aelian. However, these sections are still very valuable because these show what the author expected from the infantry in combat, and also precisely because he also mixed into the text comments taken from the earlier Persian and Muslim treatises.

The theoretical strength of the army was 16,384 heavy infantry, 8,192 light infantry, and 4,096 cavalry. The army was also divided into divisions and other smaller units to make it more readily manoeuvrable. As noted already above, these readily-divisible theoretical unit sizes in the treatise were as follows: 16, 32, 64, 128, 256, 512, 1,024, 2,048, 4,096, 8,192, 16,384 men. It is quite obvious that these numbers are taken from Aelian, and are therefore not representative of actual unit sizes. The only relevance of the above is that the army units had to be readily divisible if they were to operate on the field.

The *Gotha ms.* gives various figures for the number of men in an infantry and cavalry file. According to the *Gotha ms.*, one of the former kings [i.e. Sasanian kings], was of the opinion that the smallest number of men in a file was six men, which was therefore considered the perfect number. It is not known whether this referred to infantry or cavalry, but the subsequent details suggest that he meant here cavalry. After this piece of information, the treatise inserts a piece directly taken from Aelian. In other words, the treatise gives three different numbers (10, 12 or 16) for the file. Then, the author states that in his opinion the number should now be eight because in his time eagerness to fight had diminished.[12] Then the author makes a quite unjustified own emendation to the text of Aelian by stating that a 16-man file would then have 8 fully-equipped horsemen and 8 lightly-equipped horsemen. It should be noted that this implies the use of two cavalry lines rather than a single file of sixteen men.[13] In short, this implies that the author expected that the cavalry of his day should use 8-deep formations. The following pieces of information taken from Aelian regarding the file structure were undoubtedly accurate during all periods, namely: the use of file leaders and rear guards; and the division of files into first- or second-rank men to make it readily divisible. Later, the treatise naturally adds that the file leaders and rear guards were to be outstanding fighters.

The infantry phalanx of the *Gotha ms.* consisted of four divisions that were required to be approximately equally effective. As a result, the treatise includes a long and tedious theoretical mathematical discussion on how to make the units equally effective that is not included in any of the extant manuscripts of Aelian, but is still at least partially derived from him. After Aelian, the treatise also notes that the phalanx had an in-built reserve, i.e. the rear rank men were expected to advance to any place vacated by front rank men. However, he gives this instance in the context of cavalry, i.e. if a man fell from his horse, the man behind him advanced to the place vacated by the former.

After Aelian, the treatise mentions that there were three unit orders; the open order (each man occupied a frontage of 4 cubits, ca. 1.87m); the closed order (the *pyknosis*, in which each man occupied a frontage of 2 cubits, ca.94cm), and the very close order (i.e. the interlocked-shields order, the *synaspismos*, in which each man occupied a frontage of 1 cubit, ca 47cm.[14] The first was used when the army marched, the second when the army attacked, and the third when the army was attacked or fought during the night. The treatise states that in open order the [= theoretical] width of the phalanx was then 4,096 cubits or ten arrowshots. In other words, the treatise equates the length of a stadium with the length of an arrowshot, but this figure is slightly inaccurate because it gives c.122m for the length of both the stadium and the arrowshot. However, if one adds to the above theoretical figures the probably intervals left out, it is quite likely that one can equate the bowshot and 184m-stadium with each other. The bowshot was therefore shorter than was period Roman practice.

After Aelian, the treatise gives a long discussion about the structure of the Macedonian phalanx armed with long *sarissa* pikes, in which the pikes of the front five ranks projected in front of the array. However, unlike in the original Macedonian phalanx, the author specified that in his day the infantry phalanx consisted of only five ranks, which is consistent with the statement of Nikêforos who notes the shallower depth of period Muslim phalanx (see Appendix III). He also gave the variation in which the rear ranks had longer spears than the front rank to present an even line of pikes against the enemy. The lengths of the pikes are the same as in Aelian, namely according to the original design 16 cubits (7.488m), but in actuality 14 cubits (6.552m). However, the treatise also specifies that in his day the Maghribis (North Africans) still used 16-cubit pikes in combat. The text also specifies the way in which the pikes were to be projected in front of the array: the first rank held the points of the pikes two stretches over the ground, the second two stretches above (behind?) them, the third two stretches above the latter, the fourth two stretches above the third, and the fifth two stretches above the fourth. According to the author, in this way the points of the pikes protected the men behind them from thrown spears and stones or other missiles, and also presented to attacking cavalry and infantry an impenetrable obstacle.

After Aelian, the treatise also names a great number of unit manoeuvres which enabled the phalanx to perform a flexible number of tactical battlefield manoeuvres. The units could widen their frontage by having every other man in a file step forward and deepen the array by having every other rank step between the ranks. The units could also be wheeled, turned or countermarched (Macedonian, Laconian, Cretan, Persian) in different ways to change their frontage. The units could be marched in columns or in lines, or even in oblique order. The men in units could be ordered to face left, right, front and behind to present a new front towards the chosen direction. The light infantry could be placed between the files, on one or both wings of the phalanx, behind the phalanx, at an angle behind the wings of the phalanx, or in any of these combinations as necessary. If the heavy infantry had 16 men-per-file, the light infantry had eight or less men in a file, as deemed necessary. The use of the above standard phalanx unit manoeuvres would have enabled the Muslims to use a great variety of battlefield tactics including: the outflanking of enemy array on one or both flanks with a lengthened line; the crescent; the use of a deep formation to puncture the enemy line; the hollow square array; the facing of threats coming from the flank or behind; the wheeling of units into a defensive circle; and the use of wing divisions to project backwards or forwards.

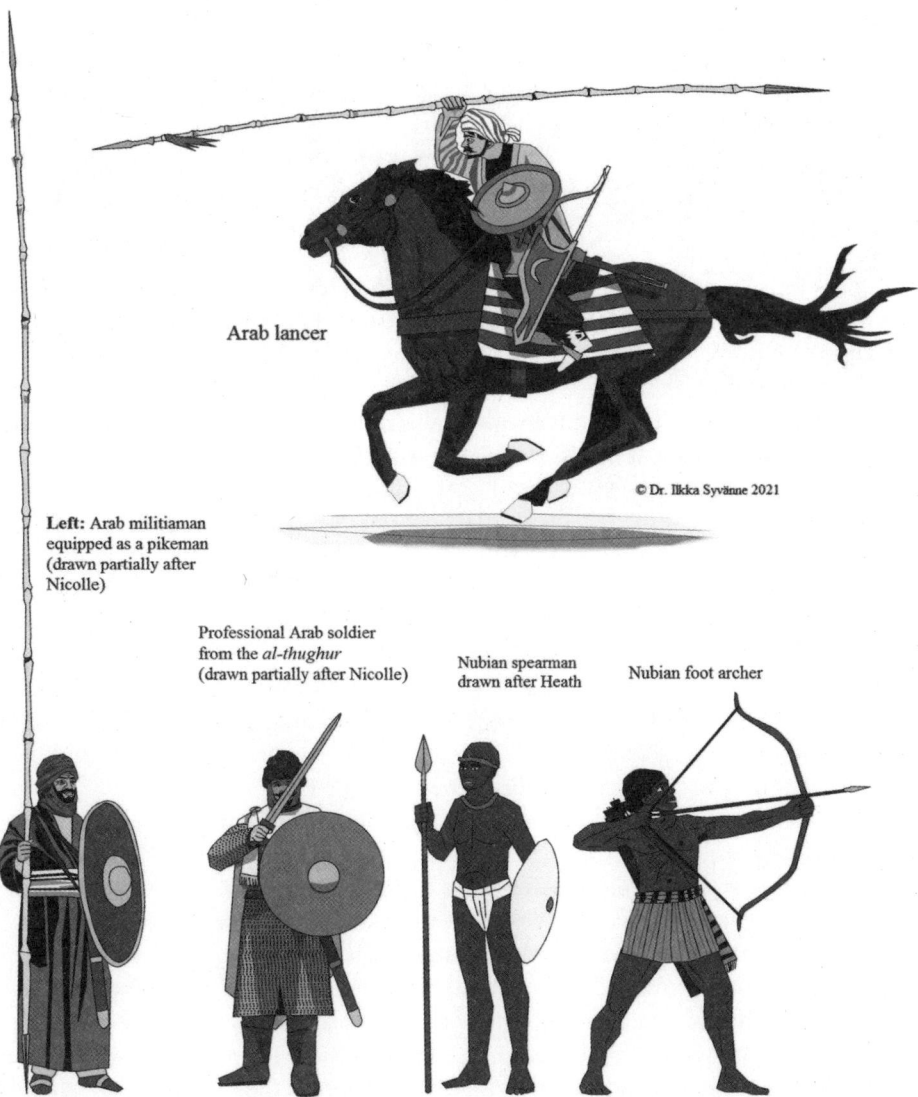

Arab lancer

Left: Arab militiaman equipped as a pikeman (drawn partially after Nicolle)

Professional Arab soldier from the *al-thughur* (drawn partially after Nicolle)

Nubian spearman drawn after Heath

Nubian foot archer

Unsurprisingly, in the translation of Aelian, the cavalry unit orders (square and rhombus) were also based on the text of Aelian. The square order in ranks and files was the basic unit order, while the rank-and-file rhombus (the 128-man *kurdus*[15]) was employed mainly by mounted archers for skirmishing, as it was when Khalid ibn al-Walid employed it at the battle of Yarmuk in 634 (see Syvänne, MHLR 8). The Romans also continued to employ the rhombus, but they employed the non-rank-and-file version of it as one of the forms of the *drouggos*-order (irregular order) – for which see Syvänne, *Late Roman Combat Tactics*.

Imperial Fleet fetching Nikêforos Fôkas to be crowned in 963. Note the ramp for loading and unloading at the stern of the ship. (*Skylitzes, public domain*)

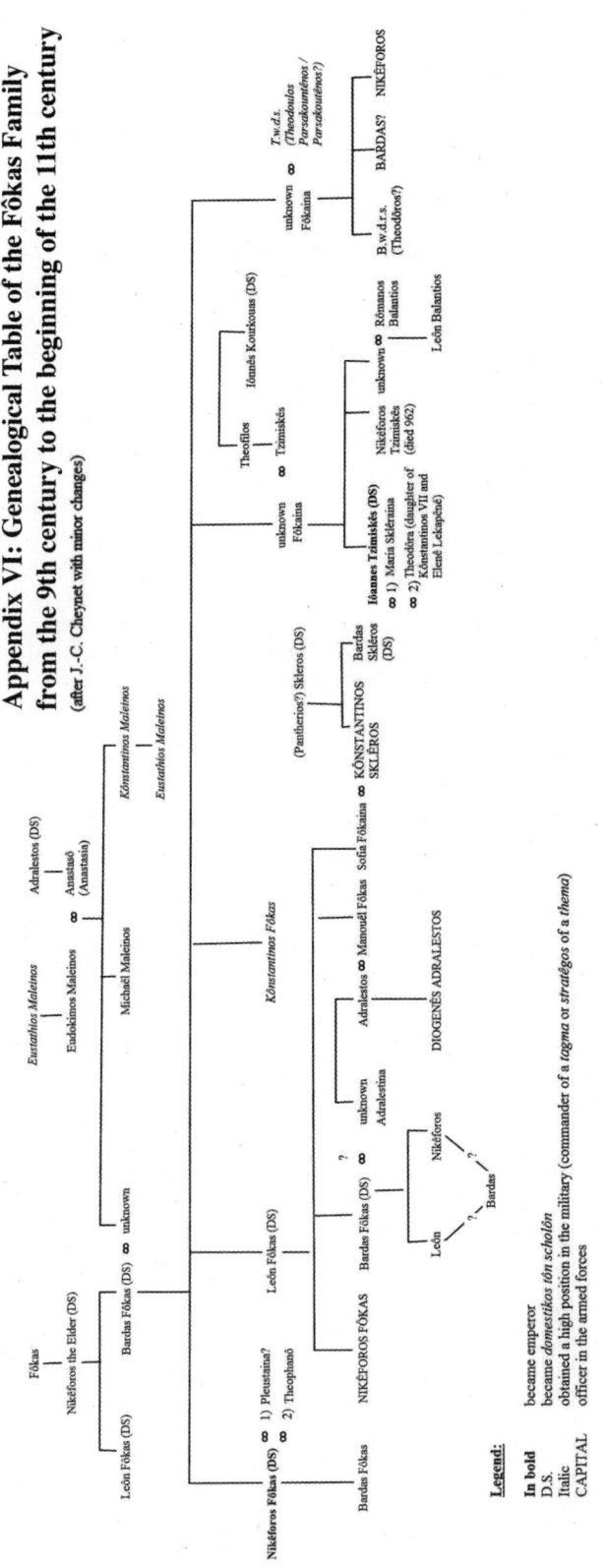

Notes

Chapter 1

1. I have classed Bar Hebraeus among the 'Arabic' sources in order to simplify my comments. In truth, he was a Jew who had converted to Christianity. Therefore, one should not expect that in this book all of the 'Arabic' sources would all be written by Muslim Arabs. Another good example of this is Yahya. He was an Arab born in Egypt, but he fled from there to Roman Antioch where he could be a Christian without the fear of persecution.
2. This is based on McGeer (2000, 1–31) and his translations of the land legislation of the Macedonian emperors, and on my analysis of the numbers (see Chapter 1.4).
3. Novels of Kônstantinos VII Prophyrogenitus (McGeer 2000, E.1, p.71).
4. Provincial fleets separate from the Imperial Fleet and thematic fleets, and the ships of the *archôntes* in Ahrweiler, 97–111).
5. A novel of Kônstantinos VII (1) in McGeer (2000, E.1, p. 71).
6. Ahrweiler, 109–111.
7. This is not new information. E.g. Kaldellis (2019, 11) notes that thematic troops consisted of both cavalry and infantry, but oddly enough the researchers have failed to take this into account when counting the size of the armed forces. The sources which they have used for this actually enumerate only the cavalry.
8. It should still be noted, however, as Kaldellis (2019, 16–7), that we do not know the exact extent of the problem because it was the perceived duty of the good emperors to protect the poor against the powerful. Therefore, it is possible that we get too grim a picture of the reality on the basis of the legislation.
9. I have here followed Dagron's (1986, 2011, 2014, 304–11) view that the principal aim of Nikêforos was to ensure availability of soldiers by militarizing the entire society. so there would also be thematic soldiers available and not only soldiers financed through the *themata*.
10. The following builds upon the analyses of the Arab geographers and their numbers in: Haldon (2000, 305–54); Treadgold (1995, 64–86); Brooks (1901). Their argumentation is re-analyzed here on the basis of what the sources actually stated, with the result that my reconstruction differs significantly from the previous estimates because I have accepted Leôn VI the Wise' figures as accurate. This is actually obvious on the basis of the fact that he wrote his treatise for practical use and not as a piece of propaganda to be spread among the enemy. It is a methodological folly to dismiss a reliable period source and replace it with one's own subjective 'must-have-been'.
11. John Haldon (2000, 316) notes, on the basis of al-Yaqubi's claim, that the Romans had 40,000 horsemen in total, which has then caused him to suggest that the infantry component consisted of 80,000 footmen. This is a mistake. The extant text of al-Yaqubi (Vol., p.159) states that an unspecified number of Roman *themata*, which included the *themata* of Charsianon (500 horsemen), Seleucia (500 horsemen), Thrakesion (5,000 horsemen), Macedonia (3,000 horsemen), and a total of 40,000 horsemen drawn from the *themata*, but thanks to the fact that the text is a fragment we lack further details. Furthermore, on the basis of Leo's *Taktika* it is clear that the estimation of 40,000 horsemen for the entire

Roman Empire is a serious mistake. It is clear that if we are to understand al-Yaqubi's text to mean the entire strength (which is uncertain), then his source has mistakenly understood the 40,000 horsemen that the Arabs typically faced when the Romans massed their forces to mean the entire cavalry force available to the Romans. This is the size of the force the Arabs faced for example when Michaêl III fought against them at the Battle of Poson in 863 (Theophanes Cont. 177.18–22, Genesios 4.14). According to Theophanes Continuatus (4.24, p.253) and Genesios (4.14), Michaêl III had 40,000 men especially from Thrace and Macedonia and also from the rest of the *themata* when he marched against the enemy. According to Theophanes Continuatus (4.39, p.289), Theoktistos also commanded over 40,000 men when he was defeated by the Muslims. On the basis of Leo's instructions it is clear that the figures provided by the Arab geographers refer only to the size of the combat-ready selected cavalry units of each *thema* and do not include infantry at all. This in turn means that the Romans fielded far greater armies than previously understood. The underestimation of the numbers results from the tendency to dismiss all the evidence that supports the use of large armies in the narrative sources, even when this is supported by statements such as Leôn's in his *Taktika*.

12. In my opinion Treadgold (1980, esp. 277; 1995, 64–75) is correct when he trusts the figures given by Qudama for the size of the Roman armed forces. I am merely going a little bit further in my arguments by taking into account also the soldiers which did not belong to the selected (*epilektoi*) soldiers. The *epilektoi* were the ones recorded by the Arab geographers.
13. De Goeje p.197 emends as *skoutarioi*, which would mean the *bigla/arithmos tagma*.
14. Haldon (1984, 248) suggests *foideratoi*, while Treadgold (1980, 272–3) suggests *ikanatoi*. It is impossible to be certain which of the interpretations is correct, but I am still inclined to accept Treadgold's spelling because the *foideratoi* are not known to have been a unit of bodyguards, while the *ikanatoi* are known to have been such. If Qudama included the *foideratoi* but not the *ikanatoi* his account would date from the era before the *ikanatoi* were formed in 809 (as suggested by Haldon, 1984, 248), or alternatively that Qudama just ignored the *ikanatoi* because these were initially not created as a combat unit. Haldon suggests that the *foideratoi tagma* was formed by Nikeforos I as a counterbalance against the other units existing in the capital and that it was formed from the units of *foideratoi* that had already existed during the Late-Roman era. Haldon (1984, 245–56) also suggests that the *foideratoi* consisted predominantly of the Lycaonians who are known to have supported Nikeforos. He also suggests that their stay in the capital was short-lived because their supposed commander in 820, Thomas the Slav, was *strategos* of Anatolikon and commander of the *exkoubitoi* at that time. This is not conclusive because the same commander could hold several titles simultaneously, which means that we do not know when the *foideratoi* stopped being a *tagma* based in Constantinople and Thrace, but we know, as Haldon notes, that Theophilus created at least two new units of bodyguards; the Persians and Ethiopians. It is possible that these replaced the *foideratoi* in the capital, or that these were included in the *foideratoi*, or that their recruitment meant the creation of the new unit called *etaireia/etaireiai* (companions) which included also foreigners just like the original *foideratoi*. The other possibility is that the *etaireia/etaireiai* were created by Basileios I the Great because the *etairia* consisted of Macedonians and Basileios I originated in Macedonia. Unlike Haldon (1984, 246) claims, the simultaneous existence of units of *foideratoi* and *etaireiai* does not prove that the *etaireiai* could not have included units that had previously belonged to the *tagma* of *foideratoi*. The reason for this is that there were also other *foideratoi* units in existence both in Thrace and Asia Minor that were remnants of the Late-Roman-era forces. Regardless of this, I am still inclined to agree with Haldon that the *tagma* of *etaireia* was not just a renamed *tagma* of *foideratoi*, but a new unit created by Basileios I, which served as his

personal retinue during the campaigns just like the *foideratoi* had served for Nikeforos. The reason for this is that the ethnic composition of the *etaireia* suggests that it was a new unit.
15. The *foideratoi* were a major combat unit commanded by the *archôn tôn foideratôn* (*phoideratoi* occurs five times in Theophanes Continuatus and clearly means the *komês tôn foideratôn*, *comes foederatorum*) under whom served *tourmarchai*.
16. Haldon (2000, 330–1) analyses the material differently and suggests that it was Qudama rather than Ibn Khurdadhbih who made the mistake of increasing the size of the garrison, while Treadgold (1980, 272–3) in my opinion correctly accepts Qudama's figures.
17. Treadgold (1980, 273, 277) suggests that we should accept Qudama's *optimatoi* to be the second of the infantry *tagmata* based in Constantinople, so that Qudama's word *noumera* would have been used like *numeri/arithmoi* were used during the Late-Roman period as a generic term for a unit, so it would have meant both the *noumera* proper and the *teichos*; which in its turn would have meant that both had 2,000 men for a total of 4,000 men, while the *optimatoi* would have had the remaining 4,000 men. However, I consider Qudama's *optimatoi* in this context as a mistake, because he also includes the *optimatoi* among the *themata*. Haldon (1984, 256–75, esp. 271ff.) does not accept an early date for the *noumera* and suggests that it was actually formed out of the members of the circus factions. He claims that Anastasius I had not given garrison forces to the two *vicarii* of Thrace (military and civilian in charge of supplying) and that when Justinian I united the two *vicarii* as *Praetor of Thrace* the same was still true. This claim is just silly. It is clear that the *vicarii* and *praetor* had subordinates serving under them so that they could perform their duties. The circus factions and regular forces were just used to bolster the numbers of the garrison of the *Makron Teichos* during major invasions when such were available. In other words, I accept the view held by earlier historians concerning the origins of the *teichistai*.
18. *LT* 6.15: every three or four cavalrymen were to possess a servant with pack-animal.
19. Kônstantinos' treatises in Haldon (1990): B text 58ff.; C text 312–5, 335–46, 377–9, 488–96, 525–7, 536ff., 599–684.
20. For the opposite conclusion, see Haldon (2000, 330ff.). He considers Oudama's figures inflated on the basis of the figures given for the units of *tagmata* during campaigns. I disagree with this conclusion because historically speaking the imperial bodyguard units rarely accompanied the emperor or commander-in-chief in their entirety. Haldon's conclusions (2000, 220, 332) regarding the sizes of the detachments sent from the *tagmata* to accompany the naval expedition to Crete in 949 is also based on a misunderstanding. Translation by Haldon (2000, 220): 'From the *thema* of Thrace the *topotêrêtês*, and officers from the 4 *tagmata*, 139 men; *scholarioi* from the 4 *tagmata*, 354 men; Altogether, officers and *scholarioi* from the 4 *tagmata*, 493 men. From the *thema* of Macedonia, the *topotêrêtês*, and officers from the 4 *tagmata*, 83 men; *scholarioi* from the 4 *tagmata*, 293 men; Altogether, officers and *scholarioi* from the 4 *tagmata*, 869 men'. Haldon interprets this so that the four *tagmata* would mean the *scholarioi, bigla, exkoubitoi and hikanatoi*. This is possible, but it could also be a misunderstanding. Kônstantinos' text can also be thought to mean the four *tagmata* (equivalents of the *banda*) were subunits of the *scholarioi* in each *thema*/province and not part of the imperial *tagmata*. In other words, the eight *tagmata* were subunits of the *tagma* of the *scholarioi*. The same concerns the next headings in the same text. The *tagmata* in these chapters are likely to mean the subunits of each larger *tagma* mentioned. In short, regardless of how one interprets the material, it is clear that the figures given by Kônstantinos mean the size of the detachment drawn from the units and not the entire units in question.
21. McGeer, 2000, 16–9, 71–6.

22. Haldon's estimate is based on the totals given in the DC 45.1–11 and should be an accurate estimate for the year 949.
23. This is based on Haldon's (2000, 354–9) estimates, but I have re-estimated the size of the thematic fleets, which follows below.
24. The earliest extant treatise that gives us recipes of the 'Greek Fire' is the treatise of Marcus Graecus. This treatise is very controversial and many of the commentators even deny his very existence (see e.g. Partington) and suggest that the treatise was actually a translation from an original written in Arabic and that it would consist of several different layers of composition so that its latest form would date from the thirteenth century. It has also been claimed that the treatise was a forgery written by a Jew in Muslim Spain. However, the arguments put against the authorship of Marcus Graecus and its dating to the ninth-tenth century (e.g. A. Dain, 1967, 375 dates it to the tenth cent.) are not valid. The inclusion of Arabic names does not mean that it would not have been originally written in Greek. Note for example the use of the Arabic word *saka* by the Romans in the tenth century. The Romans had always been ready to borrow foreign words. There were also direct contacts between Constantinople and al-Andalus which would have enabled the transmission of a Greek treatise at such a time when the Arabs already knew the secret of Greek Liquid Fire. Note e.g. BELA 1, 328–32: in 948–9 the Caliph asked the emperor to dispatch a copy of a Greek medical treatise and then a translator for it. As regards the statements that the information concerning the Roman candles and other bits and pieces in which there are referrals to saltpetre and gunpowder being evidence for the addition of material in the thirteenth century, these are similarly useless in the dating of the text. The reason for this is that there existed both direct contacts and indirect contacts via the Arabs between Constantinople and China. A good example of the Chinese borrowing a Roman invention is the introduction of liquid fire (i.e. Greek Fire) siphons (flame throwers) by about 900. For this, see SCC 2, pp.80ff. It is probable that they copied it from the Arabs. It is equally plausible that the Arabs (or Roman diplomats) copied Chinese fireworks based on the use of saltpetre roughly at the same time, because it is in this form that it is preserved in the treatise of Marcus Graecus; i.e., the gunpowder was used for entertainment, just as it was in China, and not for military purposes. In short, there is every reason to believe that the treatise of Marcus Graecus was based on material also known in tenth-century Constantinople.
25. My estimates are based on the following assumptions based on Kônstantinos' text. Peloponnesus sent 4 *chelandia* under the *tourmarchês* of the coast together with ca. 1,000 *Mardaites* (who acted as rowers). The calculation is an estimate based on the statement that the *themata* of the west, Nikopolis, Peloponnesus and Kephallenia dispatched 3,000 Mardaites for the protection of Constantinople, which I have divided between the three. The 1,000 *Mardaites* would equal roughly 9 *chelandia*. It is probable that there were at least two *tourmarchês* of the coast, so these would have had at least 8 *chelandia* in total. One may also assume that there would have been another 1,000 *Mardaites* left behind with 9 *chelandia* so that the total strength of the *thema* of Peloponnessus was 34 *chelandia* with 16 *ousiai* (ca. 1,760 rowers) of regular rowers and 18 *ousiai* of *Mardaites* (ca. 2,000 rowers). I have assumed that Nikopolis and Kephallenia had the same number of *Mardaites* as Peloponnesus but not any regular naval units under a *tourmarchês*, so both had 18 *ousiai* of *Mardaites* (ca. 2,000 rowers) for a total of 18 *chelandia*.
26. Ahrweiler, 109–111. Cosentino (2018, 326) notes that the galleys of the naval *themata* and the Imperial Fleet posted detachments of ships to serve under the officers of the army. This was definitely true.
27. Cosentino (2018, 327–8, 331–5).
28. Ahrweiler, 99–102.

29. After the conquests of the 960s the new ranking in the *taktikon Scurialense* for ca. 971/5 was as follows: *stratêgos tôn Kibyrrhaiôtôn, stratêgos tou Kyprou, stratêgos tou Krêtês, stratêgos tês Samou, stratêgos tou Aigaiou Pelagous; stratêgos tôn Kykladôn nêsôn*, and *drouggarios tôn ploimôn*. The commander of the Imperial Fleet, the *drouggarios tôn ploimôn*, still served as de facto overall commander also for the thematic fleets despite the fact that he ranked below them in the official hierarchy. Cosentino (2018, 325) does not consider Cyprus or Crete as actual naval *themata* despite their designation in the list because in his opinion it is clear that they had also detachments from the army serving under them. Cosentino also states that the even if all of the preserved *taktika* of the ninth- and tenth-centuries include *stratêgos tês Kefalônias/Kefhallênias*, it is clear that it was not considered as a naval *thema* proper because Kônstantinos VII Porfyrogennêtos does not list it as a naval *thema*. This is undoubtedly true and we do not know why this was so. It is also possible that it was just overlooked by Kônstantinos so that its omission should be considered a mistake. Cosentino suggests (2018, 325–6) that it is possible that the Kefalonian *thema* lost its islands when the Cyclades were created as a naval *thema* and that it fell under the jurisdiction of Samos. This is also possible.
30. Dagron (1986, 2011, 2014, 257–71).
31. After 602 the *protectores* were usually called *protiktores* in the Greek version and the *domestici* as *domestikoi* in Greek.
32. The exact date when these were created is contested. The extant sources state that they already existed under the Gordiani, but this is not accepted by all historians. Most modern historians date the creation of these units to the fourth century because they do not accept the existence of these units for the third century as these are mentioned by much later sources like Cedrenus / Kedrenos. My own theory is that the first unit of *scholarii* was probably created by Septimius Severus (he is known to have created the first *scholae*-schools for his soldiers and he had a unit of 600 personal bodyguards accompanying him) and that his successors added new units to it. These units were originally given the names *aulici, corporis in aula*, and *protectores*. However, one cannot entirely preclude the possibility that the units were already created during the reign of Commodus. For further information, see Syvänne (*Septimius Severus, Caracalla, Gordian III and Philip the Arab, Gallienus, Aurelian and Probus, MHLR 1*). For later developments during the Late-Roman period, see Syvänne, *MHLR* vols. 2–8 and the forthcoming Syvänne, *Military History of Byzantine Rome*.
33. Referral to the number of *kometes* and units of *scholai* in the mid-tenth century in Bury (1911, 49–50).
34. For details of the early *exkoubitoi*, see Syvänne, *MHLR* vols. 5–8.
35. Based on: Bury (1911, 60–2); Haldon (1984, 236–45); D'Amato (2012, 22–3); with my analysis of the numbers.
36. It is usually (e.g. by Bury, Haldon and D'Amato) assumed that the *tagma* included units drawn from the former Late Roman Army of Thrace (so that it included e.g. *comites Arcadiaci* (called *arithmoi* in period sources), but in my opinion the use of the word *scutarii* for the troopers suggest that other units must also have been used besides those created by Arcadius and other emperors of his era. These include e.g. the praesental units: *equites primi scutarii* (ND, Or. 5), *equites secundi scutarii* (ND, Or.6), and *equites scutarii* (ND, Or.6). The fact that each of the *tagmata* were 4,000-horsemen strong (Qudama pp.196–7) means that the *bigla* were built from several cavalry *arithmoi*.
37. The analysis is based on Haldon (1984, 245–56); D'Amato (2012, 23–4); and my analysis of the numbers.
38. Based on: Bury (1911, 106–7); Treadgold (1995, 110); D'Amato (2012, 30–1); ODB hetaireiia, hetaireiarches; Appendix 3. Haldon (1984, 252) suggests that the *etaireia* may

have been created from a detachment of foreigners belonging to the *bigla*, possibly under Michaêl II.
39. Discussion of the places which the *noumera* guarded in Constantinople can be found in Haldon (1984, 256ff.) and D'Amato (2012, 24–5). Haldon does not accept any role for the *noumera* in the defence of the Theodosian Walls, but D'Amato is surely correct that the *noumera* were not only expected to defend the walls of the Palace and the prison. My suggestion is that as marines they guarded the sea walls of the Theodosian Walls close to the Imperial Palace. D'Amato, however, accepts Haldon's suggestion regarding the origins of the *noumera* and *teichistai* (originally recruited from the circus factions for the defence of the capital) – which I do not accept.
40. Based on, with some significant changes: ODB *komes ton teicheon*; D'Amato (2012, 24–6).
41. Based on Treadgold (1995, 28–9); Bury (1911, 66–7); Haldon (1984, 206ff.).
42. Based on Syvänne, *MHLR* vols.1–8; Bury (1911, 108–111); Ahrweileir, 97–111; D'Amato (2012, 27–30); Kônstantinos, DAI 51.
43. The name *abydykoi* as an alternative term for the regional *komêtes-archôntoi* comes from the extension of the *archôn-komês* of the city of Abydos to cover the other regional *archontoi*, so that these could also be called *abydykoi* even when stationed elsewhere. The *komês* of Abydos controlled the sea traffic through the Hellespont.
44. Ahrweiler, 99–102.
45. Based on: ODB *basilikoi anthropoi*; Bury (1911, 111–3); D'Amato (2012, 36–8); Treadgold (1995, 109–10). The *spatharioi* (sword-bearers) were originally eunuchs who protected the imperial family, but the title was soon expanded to cover also non-eunuchs, after which it became an honorary title. In addition to this, there were also *spatharioi* of the *stratêgoi* who were simply personal adjutants of the commander. These are not to be confused with the *basilikoi anthrôpoi*.
46. Bury (1911, 112) and ODB consider the *domestikos tôn basilikôn* to have been a subordinate of the *prôtospatharios* while D'Amato (2012, 37) suggests the opposite by stating that from the reign of Leôn VI onwards the *prôtospatharios* served as vice commander of the *domestikos*. I have here followed Bury.
47. The usual educated guess is that all *spatharioi* were initially eunuchs who protected the imperial family, but that the title was soon expanded to cover non-eunuchs and personal sword-bearers (adjutants) of the generals and other officers, while it also started to be used as an honorary title. These *spatharioi* are not to be confused with the imperial non-eunuch *spatharioi* who were housed in the Imperial Palace and had a special hall for them called the *spatharikion*. The bearded non-eunuch imperial *spatharioi* may have been placed under the *prôtospatharios* at the same time as Kônstantinos V created the *tagmata* or at the latest in the ninth century. In the third century and during the Late-Roman period the *kandidatoi* (*candidati*) belonged to the *VI Schola* and *VII Schola*, and these detached 40 *candidati* to serve as an escort for the emperor. The title was soon granted as an honorary title to outsiders too. Kônstantinos V reformed the system so that there were two categories of honorary bearers and the actual *kandidatoi* (housed in the *V, VIII, IX scholai*) who fought. The *kandidatoi* appear to have been separated from the *scholai* in the ninth century and were placed to serve under the *prôtospatharios*. The *mandatôres* were simply adjutants of the higher-ranking *basilikoi* and spokesmen of the emperor.
48. ODB, Manglabites; *De re militari/Campaign Tactics*, 1.120 (p.250); D'Amaro (2012, 34–6).
49. ibid.
50. ibid.
51. Theophylact 8.4.13–5.1 with Syvänne, *MHLR 7*, 317.
52. D'Amato (2012, 38).

53. D'Amato (2012, 38–9).
54. Based on: ODB *komes tou staulou, stratores*; Bury (1911, 113–4). The inclusion of the *stratores* among the bodyguard units is mine. I follow in this my earlier inclusion of the *stratores* among the second- and third-century imperial bodyguards, for which see, Syvänne, *Septimius Severus* and *Caracalla*. In my opinion it is clear that the grooms/squires of the Imperial Household formed an integral part of the bodyguard units of the emperor and also accompanied him during military campaigns.
55. Based on: Kônstantinos VII Porfyrogennêtos DAI 51; ODB *protokarabos, protospatharios tes phiales*; D'Amato (2012, 32–3).
56. Based mainly on Bury (1911, 105–6), with Syvänne (*MHLR* vols.6–8).
57. Bury (1911, 105–6); Haldon (1984, 256ff.).
58. D'Amato, 2012, 25; Haldon 1984, 256ff.; Bury, 1911, 69–73.
59. Kônstantinos VII (Haldon, 1990, B text 58ff., C text 665ff.) appears to give this representative the titles *tribounos praisentalios* (praesental tribune) and *fylarchos parousias* (Chief in Presence).
60. *ST* 1.8 with McGeer's (1995, 203).
61. For the sixth-century use of separate infantry commanders, despite their omission from the *Strategikon*, see Syvänne, *Age of Hippotoxotai, MHLR 7* with *LRCT*. Separate commander for the infantry in the sixth century e.g. in Theophylact 2.12.7 (*taxiarchos*), 6.6.3, 7.3.8 (*tês pezikês dynameôs egemôn*).
62. Chatzelis and Harris (126, n.143).
63. For the *Strategikon*, see Syvänne (2004, *LRCT*).
64. Based mainly on: *LT* 6.1.-28, 7.1–36, 12.14–80, 18.136–50; Leôn, ST; DV esp. 16; Syvänne, 2008.
65. For the Family Kourkouas, see Andriollo. Note, however, that this study of mine changes the career pattern of Iôannês Kourkouas.
66. *LT* 18.136–50; DV DM 16.5–7 (with p.200), D 16.35ff.
67. *LT* 18.12–3, 18.136 /18.713–6.
68. See e.g.: Vegetius *Epitoma rei militaris* 3.23; Syvänne, 2004 Chapter 5.4 with the *LRCT* Chapter 6.7.
69. Based mainly on: *LT* 4.58–76, 6.20–34, 7.1–3, 7.37–70, 9, 14.58–101; *ST* 38.
70. Interpretation of the *zaba* and *lôrikion* based on Haldon, 2014 175–6, 185–6.
71. For further details, see Syvänne (2004 with *LRCT*).
72. See e.g. *LT* 9.56–74 (mainly after the *Strategikon*).
73. *Strategikon* 12.B.20.17–9.
74. McGeer (1995, 180–1) suggests that Nikêforos had a role in the writing of the DRM so that his death delayed the project. I accept this idea. See Appendix 4.
75. See Dain, 1967 with Sullivan (2000, 2003).
76. The following is based on Syrianos, *Naumachika* (also in *The Age of Dromon*, pp. 453–81); *LT* 19 (also in *The Age of Dromon*, Leo VI, *Naumachica*, pp 483–519); Anon. *Naumachika* (in *The Age of Dromon*, pp. 521–45); Kônstantinos DC (also in *The Age of Dromon*, 547–70); Pryor and Jeffreys; Pryor, 1995a-b; La Mantia; Hocker; Zuckerman (2015); Cosentino (2018, 327–8, 331–5); Agius, 334–8; Syvänne, 2004, *MHLR* series with the presentations at the McMullen Conferences. Note, however, that my current interpretation of the evidence differs from my earlier interpretation and that I am here presenting a new revised view which has taken into account the latest research by Zuckerman and Cosentino in such a manner that I have developed their views further on the basis of the extant evidence.
77. I have here accepted Zuckerman's (2015, 73ff., esp. 83ff.) argumentation concerning the *pamfyloi*, but not his argumentation about the composition of the Roman fleet before the

tenth century, nor his views concerning the development of the ship types in the tenth century. However, Zuckerman is quite clearly correct about the fact that the tenth-century *pamfyloi* did not carry the 70 soldiers on the deck (the *dromônia* had these), because the entire deck had been reserved for the rowers who also doubled as soldiers. Note, however, that when the cavalry was landed directly on the beach in combat formation that on those occasions the *pamfyloi* definitely also carried on board the cavalrymen riding these horses. In the Cretan campaign in 911 each *dromôn* carried 230 rowers/marines and 70 fighters, while each *pamfylos* had a crew of 130 or 160 rowers/marines (these doubled as marines) together with the horses placed in the hold. He is also correct to note that the period *pamfyloi* were used as horse transports and flag ships of the admirals/general. Zuckerman (2015, 87) also correctly points out that *pamfylos* was clearly a specific type of vessel and not a select crew. He also correctly notes (2015, 87ff.) that while the ship could be built originally as a *pamfylos*, the *dromôn* could also be converted into a *pamfylos*. The way in which a *dromôn* was converted into a *pamfylos* was simple: the bireme *dromôn* was converted into a monoreme by transferring the rowers away from the hold (the deck below) with the result that only the rowers on the deck remained – the surplus rowers were apparently transferred to other ships or left in the port so that the deck of the converted *pamfylos* would have only 130 or 160 rowers, depending on the size of the vessel – the flagships may have had more than this. The conversion enabled the *stratêgos* to convert the hold into living quarters, or use the hold for transporting horses or other necessary things. Zuckerman does not suggest with this that the Romans would have used the *alla sensile* oarage system (three oars grouped together) of the Western galleys of the Middle Ages. My educated guess is that the transformation meant that each oar was rowed by three rowers and that the three-rowers-per-oar system was also used in the actual *pamfylos*. In my opinion, Zuckerman's suggestions also explain why we find the West Europeans using two distinct types of *galea* later, a monoreme version and a bireme version. I would suggest that the monoreme version is the *pamfylos* proper and the bireme version the western adaptation of the bireme *dromôn*.
78. For a description of these types of ships, see Viereck (85–8). Zuckerman (2015, 86) and Pryor/Jeffreys (191–2): all note that the *pamfyloi* were probably originally intended to be transport ships rather than combat ships.
79. Zuckerman (2015, 90) also notes that the *dromônia* (i.e. *dromônes*) and *pamfyloi* could differ in size, which means that there could be larger *dromônia* and *pamfyloi* than indicated by the standardized numbers in Leôn's *Taktika* or Kônstantinos' DC.
80. For this, see Cosentino (2018, 327–8, 331–5).
81. Relevant referral in *The Age of Dromon* p. 560 (4.1).
82. Christides (1984, 45–6) notes the use of rudders by both Romans and Muslims in the tenth century.
83. The following is based on Syranos, *Naumachika* (also in *The Age of Dromon*, pp. 453–81); *LT* 19 (also in *The Age of Dromon*, Leo VI, *Naumachika*, pp 483–519); Anon. *Naumachika* (in *The Age of Dromon*, pp. 521–45); Kônstantinos DC (also in *The Age of Dromon*, 547–70); Syvänne (2004, *MHLR* series and imperial biographies) together with the presentations given at the McMullen Conferences in Annapolis.

Chapter 2
1. Based mostly on *LT* 18.74–92.
2. Prigent, 186–9; Nef, 211ff.; Loud, 627–9.
3. For the organization of the forces of East Francia proper, see David Bacrach 70–101, and for their training, see ibid. 102–68, and for their tactics, see ibid. 193–225. See also Nicolle, 2005.

4. David Bachrach, 192–208.
5. This description is largely based on *LT* 18.38–73 (based on the *Strategikon*), DAI 37–40. For further information about Hungarians, see Moravcsik, 1970.
6. For a Finn it is easy to see that the Hungarian clan/tribe names were based on the Fenno-Ugrian language, because for example the name of the eighth tribe, 'Kasi', means the number eight in Finnish (kasi is the colloquial form of kahdeksan in Finnish).
7. I see no reason to doubt Kônstantinos' information as it was based on the best information available to an emperor and it was also period information.
8. Based mostly on Leôn (*Taktika* 18.93–102) and Kônstantinos (DAI 29–36). For the information concerning the fighting methods of the Slavs in the sixth- and seventh-centuries, see Syvänne, *Age of Hippotoxotai*, *MHLR* vols.6–8 and *Late Roman Combat Tactics*.
9. Dates of the various extant manuscripts in Dain, 1967, 382–8.
10. I see no reason to doubt the veracity of the account. Stranger things have happened in history.
11. In general, for the Rus and Russians of this era, see Nicolle (1999) with Franklin and Shepard (esp. 112–80).
12. ibid. with Kônstantinos (DAI 1–13); Skylitzes 10.31.
13. Kônstantinos, DAI 1–13. For the Khazars in general, see Nicolle & Zhironov. For the Volga Bulgars in general, see Nicolle & Shapakovsky.
14. The following is based on Kônstantinos (DAI 9) with the comments in the DAI Vol. 2, 18–58.
15. I.e. the medieval Iberia was no longer the same as the ancient Iberia. In late antiquity the eastern portion of Georgia was called Iberia and its western portion either Lazica or Colchis.
16. In antiquity and late antiquity this area was known as Lazica or Colchis.
17. See Suny 20–33.
18. *LT* 18.21–37.
19. E.g. the military treatises *Ayin nameh*, *Gotha ms.* and *Tafrij*, and the archery texts borrowed from the original Persian texts in the '*Arab Archery*' and '*Saracen Archery*'. The Arabs also copied Roman practices, hence the inclusion of Aelian's text in the *Gotha ms.* and Leôn's *Taktika* (18.114) comment about the Saracen imitation of Romans. For the employment of old Roman and Greek tactics against the Romans by Muslim armies during the early conquest period, see Syvänne, *MHLR 8*.
20. It is possible that during the Sasanian era the 400 - 500 elite cavalrymen were sometimes deployed as a wedge/triangle so that these served as an inspiration for the Roman triangle in the centre. The Muslim military treatises allow the further elaboration of the original Persian array and that the Persians then deployed their centre division into three divisions (left wing, centre, right wing) while they gave their flank divisions the names of outer left and outer right flanks. The Romans considered the flanks (the outer flanks of the Perso-Arab military theory) vulnerable to outflanking and ambushes because in their opinion the Persians did not post adequate flank guards for their protection.
21. Christides (1984) quite correctly notes that Crete was not only a haven for the pirates, but an actual border region with the Muslim emirate fighting the war of Jihad against the infidels just as in Sicily or Tarsus. Regardless, it is still clear that it was also a haven of pirates, just as many other Muslim coastal cities. The Barbary coast was to become particularly famous for this until the nineteenth century.
22. Christides, 1984, 66–7, 164.
23. Arcifa, 490.

24. In general, for Sardinia see Spanu. However, it should be noted that on the basis of the presence of Sardinians in the imperial bodyguards I consider the relationship between East Rome and Sardinia to be closer in the tenth century than usually recognized. In the absence of literary sources, it is not known when the *archôn* of Sardinia, the ruler of Sardinia placed as supreme commander of the island in Caralis/Cagliari and his subordinate *lociservator* (appointed to defend the coastal areas; these became the three other kings) was replaced by the medieval four kingdoms of Sardinia. The *archôn* belonged to the family of Lacon-Gunale and all of the kings of the four kingdoms (Cagliari, Arborea, Gallura and Torres) came from the same family. The first time the four kingdoms are mentioned in the sources dates from the year 1073. The army of the period kingdoms consisted of the professional soldiers and free conscripted citizens. The elite consisted of *bujekasos* cavalry serving under *janna de majore*. They were armed with the sword, chain mail, shield, helmet and the *birrudu* (from the Latin *verutum*). The militia and infantry (*birrudos*) also used the *birrudu*. The Sardinians had a special sword called a *leppa* with a bone handle and curved blade 50 to 70cm long. The bow of choice was the longbow. On the basis of the armament it is probable that the equipment and organization of the armed forces reflected those that were in existence already during Roman rule and I would suggest that Sardinia still recognized Roman rule in the tenth century.
25. Christides (1984, 39).
26. Excellent summary of the methods used in Kaldellis (2019, 24).
27. See e.g. Syvänne, *Age of Hippotoxotai*, *LRCT*, and *MLHR* vols.1–8.
28. For the use of the *karadis*, see e.g. Syvänne, *MHLR 8*, Index Yarmuk.
29. See the narrative with e.g. *PM* 2.8.
30. The existence of Turkish baths, i.e. Hungarian bath, is curious because modern day Hungarians are not famous for their own bath while their language relatives the Finns are famous for their sauna. The Russians also have a sauna of their own which may result from the mixing of the Finnish and Slavic tribes in the region of Moscow.
31. This and the following comment is taken from my presentation held at the McMullen Symposium in 2015. It should be noted that it is possible that the oneirocrital book (sleep interpretation) and the book on occurrences were included in the list for rational reasons to explain things in the best possible way for those who were superstitious, but it is equally possible that Kônstantinos really believed in such treatises. There were always those who believed in superstitious things while there were also those who did not. The narrative histories of Psellos, Skylitzes and Nikêtas Choniates include several rulers and officers who believed in dreams, prophecies, talismans and astrology. Good examples of this are Manouêl I Komnenos (1143–80) and Andronikos I Komnenos (1183–85). It should also be noted that the study of the art of war did not make emperors competent commanders, as is shown by the career of Rômanos III (1028–1034). His officers knew better than the inexperienced ruler that it was not wise to start a campaign in Syrian summer heat when the soldiers would suffer from the double effect of heat and lack of water, but he was a firm believer in his own excellence and believed that his study of the military treatises and narrative histories had made him a conqueror equal to Trajan, Hadrian, Augustus, Caesar, and Alexander the Great. He was also a firm believer in all superstitious toys such as talismans and Icons without understanding the psychology behind their use. See Psellos' Book 3.
32. Kônstantinos' treatises in Haldon (1990): B text 58ff.; C text 312–5, 335–46, 377–9, 488–96, 525–7, 536ff., 599–684.
33. It is clear that the envisaged cavalry battle formation was the same as we find in the *Strategikon* and Leôn's *Taktika*, because there were no *tagmata* left for the third line. The

expectation with the new cavalry formation was that the third line was like the first one. This should not be a surprise as the cavalry formation of the *Strategikon* remained in use (note e.g. OT chapters 1–55 contain the *Taktika* of Leôn) even after the new cavalry array was introduced, on top of which it should be remembered that Kônstantinos was using Leôn Katakylas' treatise as his source.

34. Strictly speaking these should be called *skoutarioi* because the rank-and-file *scholarioi* who belonged to the *arithmoi/bigla/vigla* were given this name. The 100 *skoutarioi/scholarioi* which were accompanying the *drouggarios tês biglas* consisted probably of those who guarded the hippodrome so that during the imperial campaign these were probably replaced by an *ousia* (108 or 110 men) from the imperial *dromônion*. See Kônstantinos, DAI 51.40ff.
35. This chapter is based on McGeer (1995, 225–46), BELA 1 (268ff.) and other sources mentioned separately.
36. Mentioned by Dagron (DV, 1986, 243) on the basis of the list of *themata* in the *Taktikon of Escurial* (precise dates of formation unknown).
37. BELA 1, 270.
38. BELA 1, 270–2.
39. BELA 1, 273–8 with most of the sources translated in the BELA 2.
40. Runciman, 1929, 142–3; BELA 1, 278–84 with most of the sources (ibn Zafir, Dahabi, Abu Mahasin, Abu Firas) translated in the BELA 2 (120–1, 239, 271, 358).
41. According to Kônstaninos (DAI 45, esp. 45.95–175), at this time the city of Theodosioupolis (Karin) was in Iberian hands. He appears to have considered both branches of the Bagratuni to be Iberian. The city and its surrounding lands were traditionally considered to be Armenian, hence the name Karin.
42. Runciman, 1929, 143–4; BELA 1, 284–95 with most of the Arabic sources translated in the BELA 2 (122–3, 173–4, 238–40, 357–8); TC 6.42, p.428; Skyl. 10.32; DAI 45.95–175. The best account is provided by Ibn Zafir (BELA 2, pp.122–3).
43. The standard Roman tactic in such situations was that the commander brought to the scene a cavalry army while infantry forces would try to assemble at some suitable passes to block those. See Appendix 2. The ability of Sayf to continue his flight after the battle also suggests that he had a cavalry force.
44. BELA 1, 284–95 with most of the Arabic sources translated in the BELA 2 (122–3, 173–4, 238–40, 357–8); TC 6.42, p.428; Skyl. 10.32; DAI 45.95–175. The best account is provided by Ibn Zafir (BELA 2, pp.122–3).
45. TC p.429; Skyl. 11.9; Zonaras 16.23 (PG 135, pp.109–112) with the translation and commentary of McGeer, 1995, 179–80.
46. McGeer (1995, 230–2); Haldon and Kennedy; Bonner; Dagron (DV 1986, 149–53, 2014, 119–24).
47. McGeer (1995, 232–46).
48. The Daylami in the Late-Roman period: Agathias 3.17.6–9; Procopius *Wars* 8.14.5–13. The Daylami in the middle ages: Beshir, 42–43; McGeer (1995), 233–234; Bosworth, 1965–6/1977, ibid. 1960; The Daylami as royal bodyguards, Zakeri Mohsen, 116–8, 181–2. In general: McGeer (1995), 232–6; Syvänne (2004; *MHLR* vol.6).
49. See e.g. *Arab Archery* and *Saracen Archery* and other sources therein.
50. McGeer (1995, 236–7); Bosworth (Buyids, 153–9; Ghaznavids, 52–4).
51. McGeer (1995, 237–8); Bosworth (Ghaznavids, 56–7).
52. McGeer (1995, 238–42).
53. Based on my research of the Arabic military treatises noted above.
54. McGeer (1995, 242–6).

55. This chapter is based on Lev (1984, 1987) and Beshir. For the Fatimid forces after 969, see Hamblin. Anyone interested to learn more about the Muslim ships in general is advised to consult the outstanding study of Agius. Konstam's book gives also a good general overview of the naval capabilities of the respective navies.
56. BELA 1, 310–1; Runciman, 1929, 194.
57. Jawhar was a general of the Caliph al-Mu'izzli-Din Allah (19.3.953–21.12.975). He was better known as Jawhar al-Siqilli, al-Qaid al-Siqilli (The Sicilian General) or al-Saqlabi (The Slav) or al-Rumi. He is reputed to have been originally from the Roman Empire, and that his father was a slave while he was a freedman. He rose fast in the ranks thanks to his superior military talents.
58. For the *saqaliba* troops of the Aghlabids, see Mihsin.
59. Doubts about the figures in Beshir (esp. 37–8, 44–5) and confirmation of similar numbers in antiquity in Syvänne (*MHLR* series vols. 1–8).
60. Lev, (1985, 1987).
61. The following is based on Agius, 330–57. However, see also Konstam, who offers a slightly different view of the meaning of the ship names. The same is true of Vassilios Christides (1984, 42–56) who equates the *shalandī* and *shīnī* with each other unlike Agius. Christides also includes interesting details concerning the crews of the Roman and Muslim ships which I use for further elaboration on the question of ship sizes. Firstly, the Romans and Muslims recruited their crews differently. Both used drafting, but in different ways. In the Roman Empire most of the sailors, oarsmen and marines came from the ranks of the thematic soldiers who were given land in return for service. In Egypt and presumably in other places as well the Muslim authorities demanded a set number of sailors from administrative districts where registers of persons liable to do service were kept. It was possible to be exempted from this duty by a money payment, which was the method usually used, so the taxpayers paid professional sailors to perform their duty. During the early period the sailors and oarsmen had consisted of the Christians of Syria and Egypt while the fighting force on board consisted of Muslim soldiers. This division of labour became permanent, so the Muslims did not require their oarsman/rowers and sailors to fight unlike the Romans who always expected the rowers to be able to fight on the deck when asked to do so. In my opinion, it is probable that it was this that required the Muslims to use larger ships than the Romans because if their ships would have been of similar size (all dromons) then the Romans would have had superiority in the numbers of men available for combat. Therefore, the Muslims needed larger ships that were also taller than the Roman ships.

Chapter 3
1. The chapter on Fôkades is based on the Appendix Les Phocas by J.-C. Cheynet in the DV (1986 ed., pp.289–317; 2014 ed., pp. 319–61), but note that I have significantly altered the career pattern of Bardas Fôkas and his sons.
2. Cheynet (DV 1986 ed. 290, 2014 ed. 320).
3. Note e.g. that the Cappadocian emperor Maurikios (Maurice) was descendant of Italian settlers.
4. Based on Cheynet (DV 1986, 291–6, 2014, 322–30); Personnaz, 29–32.
5. One may in fact speculate that the usurper Fôkas also came from Cappadocia, the home of the emperor Maurikios, and that the reason for his appointment to the *excubitores* (the predecessors of the *exkoubitoi*) was that he originated from the same province as the ruling emperor. One may speculate further that the usurper Fôkas was also a distant relative of the Fôkades, which they wanted to forget and had also effectively buried from memory. If this line of speculation is correct, then one might speculate further that Fôkas I was encouraged

to pursue his career because the family legend stated that they descended from the Fabii and were therefore better justified to be emperors than Maurikios.
6. For the Argyroi in general, see Vannier.
7. For the Doukai in general, see Polemis. The family name Doukas appears to have come from the title *dux/doux* (duke). As a family name Doukas appears for the first time in the middle of the ninth century. According to Polemis, and despite the claims of some eleventh- and twelfth-century Roman writers to the contrary (they claimed that the name belonged to a single noble family), the name appears to have been adopted by several families so the name Doukas never signified a single family.
8. Based on Cheynet (DV 1986, 296–9; 2014, 330–5) and Pesonnaz (32–3) but with the account expanded on the basis of the following sources: Theophanes Cont. (*Basileia Kônstantinou tou Leontos*) pp.381ff.; Skyl. 9; SLw 135; LG pp.288–303; Nestor AM 6423. For a fuller analysis and narrative of the events, see the forthcoming Syvänne, *MHBR* Vol.3.
9. Cheynet in Wortley/Skyl. p.201, n.49.
10. See Skyl. 9.2.
11. E.g. Cheynet (DV 1986, 298; 2014, 332–3).
12. Based on Personnaz's excellent educated guesses (pp.37–40).

Chapter 4
1. Liutprand, *Retribution*, 5.13–20.
2. The following is based on: Nestor AM 6449; *The Life of St. Basil the Younger* (3.23–8); TC pp.423–9, GM pp. 914–6; Zonaras 3.476 (PG 113, p.96–7); Skyl. 10.31; LG pp.323–5; Liutprand, *Retribution*, 5.13–20; Runciman, 1929, 109–113; Zuckerman, 1995, 258–68; Cheynet (DV 1986, 296–9; 2014, 330–5); and the comments of Sullivan (2019) regarding TC plus the comments of Wortley in Skylitzes. Note, however, that my reconstruction differs considerably from the ones given by Runciman and Cheynet. For example, I accept larger figures for the Russian army, reconstruct the career of Bardas and his family differently, while I also reconstruct some of the details concerning the campaign differently because I interpret the unit composition and their sizes differently.
3. Zuckerman, 1995, 265.
4. TC Bonn p.436, Sullivan, Text 1 TC, pp.8–9; Skyl. 11.9; SLw 136.73, 137.2. For the modern historians, see the notes above.
5. The family name suggested by Wortley (Skyl., p.222) but originally suggested by Cheynet. Seibt's study of the family of the Sklêroi does not include this person.
6. The chosen men (*ekkritôn andrôn*) mistakenly translated as infantry in the Latin translation of TC in the Bonn edition (p.424) and also by Runciman (1929, 112).
7. TC Bonn, pp.423–6; Skyl.10.31; SLw 136.73; Nestor AM 6449.
8. None of the sources (Skylitzes; TC; al-Athir; Gregorios; Kônstantinos VII, *Narratio de Imagine Edessana* PG 113; Yahya) that previous researchers have claimed (Runciman 1929, 144–6; Vasiliev BELA 1 295–7) to mention Iôannês Kourkouas actually mention him after 941. In fact, both TC and Skylitzes mention the invasion of the Turks in 943 after they have described the dismissal of Iôannês Kourkouas from office which took place at the same time as a *domestikos* (who must be Pantherios) was besieging Edessa and ravaging Mesopotamia in 943–4. Zonaras (PG 113, p.96–7) also places the sacking of Iôannês and Theofilos Kourkouas between the Russian campaign and the siege of Edessa in 944.
9. As noted, earlier researchers falsely assume this man to have been Iôannes.
10. Rômanos I had urged Oleg to attack the Khazars and he had suffered a defeat at their hands.
11. Liutprand, *Retribution*, 5.13–20.
12. BELA 1, 295 with BELA 2 (156, 174, 240, 248, 266).

13. The Arabic sources merely state *domestikos*, who would now be Pantherios as discussed above. Modern historians have added the name Iôannês Kourkouas without good reason to these accounts.
14. BELA 2, 160; Skylitzes 14.6–7; Lev, 1985, 233–5; Arcifa, 490; Metcalfe, 53.
15. See the next endnote for the sources.
16. See the next endnote.
17. Skyl. 10.37; SLw 136.80–4; LG pp.322–6; GM pp.325–6; Gregorios the Refendarius; Kônstantinos, *Narratio de Imagine Edessena*, Nikon (914, pp.50–1); Yahya 32–5 in PO 18, pp.730–3; BELA 1, 295–306 with BELA 2 (Yahya, 91–3 with the other sources on pp.: 156–7, 174, 190, 195, 223, 226, 240, 248, 260, 271, 273).
18. BELA 1, 304–5; BELA 2, 41–2, 93–4, 157, 174, 180, 240, 249, 271; Miskawayh, Vol. 5, 43–81. One wonders if the leaders of the Turkish *ghilman* had already been corrupted by Roman money at this stage because we find them cooperating with the Romans a few years later when Nikêforos Fôkas was the *domestikos* and then later during the reign of Tzimiskês? The circumstantial evidence seems to suggest this, but it is of course possible that their actions against other Muslims that served Roman interests on multiple occasions were just coincidences excepting of course those cases in which there is firm evidence for collusion. The matter is discussed at greater length in the biography of Tzimiskês.
19. Skyl. 10.34; SLw 136.77; GM p.325; TC 6.45 (pp.430–1); LG p.325; Nestor AM 6451; Moravcsik, 1970,55–6.
20. The following is based on Nestor (AM 6452–5) and on the comments of Cross and Wetzor.
21. Skyl. 10.35; TC Rômanos 6.46 (p.423); DAI 26; SLw 136.78; LG p.325.
22. Sullivan (RFNF p.7) suggests that the meaning was that Stefanos shared the information with Kônstantinos Lakapênos and Michaêl son of his deceased brother Christoforos. I disagree with this interpretation.
23. This and the following is based on: Skyl. 10.39–11.3; TC Rômanos 6.52-Kônstantinos 6.6, pp.435–41 (RFNF p.6ff.); SLw 136.79, 136.84, 137.1–8; Liudprand, *Antapodosis* 5.21–5; LG 328–9; BELA 2, 93–4. For a different interpretation of the events, see Runciman (1929, 232–4) who does not believe the details concerning the cabal.
24. For the Taronites/Tornikioi in general, see Adontz (*Byzantion* 1934–6, 1939) with Wortley/ Cheynet (Skyl. p.128). The Tornikioi were an Armenian family from Taron. The father or grandfather of Nikolaos and Leôn was the Prince of Taron, Tornik the son Apoganem. Tornik had had a conflict with his cousin Bagrat, with the result that Tornik donated his country to the Roman emperor. Rômanos I Lakapênos in his turn brought Tornik's family to Constantinople.
25. BELA 1 (305–6) calls the *domestikos* Bardas Fôkas, which would date the invasion to the period after 16 December because Bardas was appointed only after the overthrow of Rômanos on 16 December 944. However, in the text Vasiliev then has the fighting to take place in the autumn before the onset of winter. If the combat took place during that period, the *domestikos* would have been Pantherios.
26. Dated to the year 333 (24 Aug. 944–12 Aug. 945) at winter time. See Dahabi (BELA 2, 240).
27. BELA 1, 304–6; BELA 2, 41–2, 93–4, 157, 174, 180, 240, 249, 271.

Chapter 5
1. The following is based on TC 440ff.; Skyl. 11.2ff.; LG 229ff.; PSs 752–5; GM (PG ed.) 874ff. (p.1182ff.); BELA 2, 93–4.
2. See the comments of Wortley (Sklyl. pp.227–8).
3. Staffan Wahlgren (SLw translation, 252) suggests 946 presumably because in the TC (442–3) the appointment is followed by the negotiations for the exchange of prisoners that took

place in October 946. However, I prefer the year 945 because TC states that it was after Kônstantinos VII had become sole emperor that he appointed his *prôtobestiarios* Basileios as *patrikios*, *parakoimômenos* and *paradynasteuôn* of the Senate. Denis Sullivan (RFNF, 19) uses the same phrase as evidence that the conspiracy took place in 948 after the death of Rômanos I. I find this dating unconvincing because the appointment of Basileios clearly took place before the negotiations for the exchange of prisoners in 946.
4. Based on Skyl. 11.3; TC 445ff.
5. TC 441–2 confirms that even if Kônstantinos had good intentions he failed to pay adequate attention to details, which gave corrupt men a chance to exploit the situation. According to TC, there was an earthquake in January 945 roughly at the same time as Stefanos and Kônstantinos were expelled from the palace. The earthquake destroyed the houses of Iôannês Kourkouas and *magistros* Rômanos Sarônites. Kônstantinos VII gave the order to *eparchos* Theofilos Erotikos to rebuild those. Theofilos then ordered his *prôtokankellarios* and a man called Zonaras to rebuild the houses. Zonaras, however, was corrupt to the bone so that he stole whatever he found in the houses and gave the owners only about one-tenth of the valuables recovered. According to TC, Kônstantinos was planning to remove him from office, but the man was so good with words and flattery that Kônstantinos actually ended up rewarding him. According to TC, it was thanks to this that Zonaras was able to continue his stealing in such a manner that he was stated to be a disease for the Roman Empire.
6. See the comments of Sullivan (RFNF, 23).
7. For a list of those, see Dain (1967) with Syvänne (2013b).
8. e.g. PM 1.7; DV (DM Preface; D Preface pp.146–8).
9. BELA 1, 313–4.
10. BELA 1, 314–6.
11. DV D Preface esp. 42ff./DM Preface esp. 7–8. See Appendix 2.
12. This assumption is based on DV 6–7, which notes that there were single raids with cavalry alone and large massive invasions with Jihadist reinforcements brought from Egypt, Palestine, Phoenicia and southern Syria that had been combined with the forces already present in Cilicia and/or Aleppo. Since it is known that the Jihadist reinforcements did not arrive every year (e.g. because there was peace between Ikshidid Egypt and Rome) and it was possible for the Cilician Arabs to launch more than one small raid with cavalry per year, it is clear that the figure of two-to-three raids per year gives us a good estimate for the number of raids faced by Nikêforos during his tenure.
13. For these, see BELA 1, 265–6.
14. Filotheos/Philotheos, *Klêtorologion* 712–4, 727–9, Bury ed. pp. 136, 146; Moffat ed. (in Kônstantinos, DC) pp.712–4, 727–9; Psellos (*Istoria syntomos*, *Historia Syntomos*, 103); Zonaras (16.23).
15. Mentioned by Dagron (DV, 1986, 243) on the basis of the list of *themata* in the *Taktikon* of Escurial (precise date of formation unknown).
16. BELA 1 (316) has not noted this campaign of Sayf, which is mentioned by al-Makin (BELA 2, 190).
17. BELA 1 (353) notes that one of the Arabic sources for the Battle of Adata in 954 states that the captured Roman officers included the patrician Tzamandos and Lykandos. If this is not a mistake (the sources offer conflicting evidence), it is possible that the man was the famous Mleh the Great and that he died in captivity or that the man was his son or grandson who then became *domestikos* under Iôannês Tzimiskês.
18. TC 442–3; Liudprand Antapodosis/Retribution Book 6; BELA 1, 314–6.

19. Nestor (AM 6456–63, 6464–72) with the comments of Cross and Sherbowitz-Wetzor (pp.239–40); Wortley/Cheyner in Skyl. pp.231–2.
20. ibid.
21. Skyl. 11.5; Kônstantinos (DAI 40, DC 46); Moravczik, 55–7.
22. The conspiracy was noted even by Muslim sources (e.g. BELA 2, 94).
23. It is probable that his name was inadvertly placed in the wrong place by Liudprand when he discussed the betrayal of the plan by the Lakapênoi brothers to kill Kônstantinos. It was this plot to kill Kônstantinos that Diabolinos betrayed and not the previous one.
24. BELA 1, 317–8; BELA 2, 95, 123, 240–1, 271.
25. It would be easy to think that later sources would hide an unsuccessful raid by Nikêforos Fôkas or by his brothers, but the fact that the emir of Tarsus remained inactive suggests that this was not the case, hence it is clear that the invader was none of the Fôkades.
26. BELA 1, 317–8; BELA 2 95, 123, 180, 240–1, 266–7.
27. Canard, 1961, 520–2.
28. Tim Greenwood is not the only one who has suggested that Theofilos Kourkouas would be the commander of the Roman army and that Iôannês Tzimiskês would have served under him. We can find the same suggestion also in PMBZ (Ioannes I. Tzimiskes, Theophilos Kurkuas).
29. In short, the possible leaders of the campaign are the *domestikos* Bardas Fôkas (likeliest candidate on the basis of Stephen of Taron), and the *stratêgoi* of Armeniakon, Mesopotamia, Chaldia, Sebasteia, and Koloneia. For the names of the possible *stratêgoi* of the *themata*, see DOS 4 (Armeniakoi 4.67ff.; Chaldia 4.98ff.; Koloneia 4.127ff.; Sebasteia only a seal of *taxiarchês* Elias 4.128; Mesopotamia 4.139ff.).
30. This and following discussion of the events on land is based on: Bar Hebraeus 164–5; Miskawayh 114; Stephen of Taron (pp.230–1); (BELA 2, 95, 180–1; Yahya 767–8. BELA 1 (318–9) also discusses this campaign, but interprets the evidence differently by suggesting that it was Leôn Fôkas who captured Tarsus after his victory at Marash (Germanikeia), but this fails to take into account the evidence in the DV regarding the activities of Nikêforos Fôkas. It would be very odd if Nikêforos would not have had any role in the capture of Tarsus as he was the *stratêgos* of the neighbouring province. It is far likelier that the Romans launched a double invasion by the brothers so that Nikêforos exploited the success of the previous year while Leôn exploited his previous success a Hadath which had opened up the route from the Pass of Hadath to Germanikeia while allowing him to block the supply route to the city of Germnikeia from south.
31. The DRM (24–5, 26.35–8) provides us with a three possible different schemes of how Leôn defeated Sayf which are particularly relevant if its author was Leôn, as McGeer has suggested. If the enemy force approaching the Roman siege lines was moderate in size, the commander had two options available to him: he could post most of his cavalry forces in a double ambush (two cavalry lines) close to the siege lines and then ambush the enemy when it attempted to attack the Roman marching camp (a circle with two walls), or he could launch a night attack against the enemy when it was close enough for this. If the enemy force was considered large, then the commander was to abandon the siege and build a new marching camp at a suitable location and there await the arrival of the enemy, after which he fought a pitched battle. It is probable that if this happened that Leôn used the tactics described in the *Sylloge tacticorum*. This is probably the likeliest alternative, because it would have been strange if Sayf had brought with him only a moderately-sized force when the object was to defend as large a city as Germanikeia. However, it is also possible that Leôn achieved his victory with the methods described in the *De velitatione* (see Appendix 2) which are not

really that different from the methods described in the DRM as both favoured the use of ambushes and surprise attacks.
32. Kamal al-Din (BELA 2, 180–1) places the capture of both Marash (Germanikeia) and Tarsus immediately after the defeat of Sayf ad-Dawla by Leôn.
33. This and the following is based on Makkari 6.5 (pp. 2.137–42), BELA 1 (320–33) with referrals to BELA 2 therein.
34. ibid. The account of the diplomatic missions contains interesting evidence about the state of scientific knowledge in al-Andalus and the Roman Empire. In about August-September 947 eunuch and chamberlain Salomon led another embassy to meet Abd ar-Rahman. The envoys brought as presents a medical text of Dioskouridês and a Latin historical text of Orosius. The caliph dispatched Hisham b. Hudayl al-Gataliq (Catholicos) as his envoy to the court. The Jewish medical doctor Hasday b. Shaprut, who held a high position in the court of Cordoba dispatched Isaac b. Nathan as his envoy with a letter to the Jewish *Khagan* of the Khazars. The emperor did not allow Isaac to travel to Khazaria and then after six months dispatced him back to Hasday with a letter which detailed his excuses. The real reason was obviously the prevention of contact between the Jewish co-religionists which could have resulted in an alliance between al-Andalus and Khazaria. The Arabs of al-Andalus did not possess researchers who could translate the Greek text of Dioskouridês, which meant that the medical knowledge in the text was incomprehensible to the Arabs before they could obtain a translator from Constantinople. Kônstantinos did not send such immediately, but waited for the reaction of the caliph to the military campaigns in Crete and elsewhere. Once he was satisfied that the Spanish Arabs would not resume their hostilities, he dispatched a professor of Greek and Latin to Spain in about 951. It is this that suggests some sort of agreement between the two powers.
35. This and the following list of ships and men are based on DC 2.44–5 (included in the DC, partially in Pryor and Jeffreys, and in full with commentary in Haldon 2000); Skylitzes 11.15; LD 1.2; BELA 1, 332–41 with referrals to BELA 2 therein. For discussion of the numbers and their discrepancies, see Haldon 2000 with BELA 1.
36. It is therefore clear that the Roman reinforcements for Italy and Sicily mentioned by al-Athir (BELA 2, 160) did not arrive yet, but in 950.
37. ibid. Totals calculated from BELA 1 (337) and Haldon (2000, 308).
38. The following account of Sayf's invasion and Roman response is based on BELA 1 (341–35); BELA 2 (70–1, 95–6, 111, 115–6, 124, 159–60, 174, 181, 190, 241–3, 267, 307–14, 320, 359); Skylitzes 11.9; Miskawayh 5.129 (2.125); Bar Hebraeus p.165; Elias of Nisibis Year 339. The studies of Canard (1961, 763–771), Vasiliev (BELA 1, 341–5) and al-Mallah (2009) provide the basis for the analysis (e.g. dates and identification of most of the locales) but my narrative of the campaign is still based primarily on the analysis of the texts of Mutanabbi (BELA 2, 307–14 with al-Mallah's translation) and Firas (BELA 2, 359–60) who participated in the campaign, and on Dahabi's (BELA 2, 241–2) and Zafir's accounts (BELA 2, 124) that supplement the information with details that Mutanabbi and Firas left out. The other sources mentioned in the BELA 2 or in my notes also provide some pieces of evidence that fill-in the blank spots, but are not as important as these four sources. This information is then compared with the topography and the information provided by the DV to fill out the blanks. This means that I either supplement or correct the information provided by Vasiliev in the BELA 1.
39. BELA 1, 341–2; BELA 2, 108–9, 111, 307–14, 359, 366.
40. Mutanabbi's poem (BELA 2, 307) dates the arrival of Sayf at Sanabus to 15 Nov.–13 Dec. 950, but if the entire campaign lasted for two months (60 days) as Firas (BELA 2, 359) states

and started in August–September 950, it is clear that this must have taken place already in September.
41. The list of Dahabi (BELA 2, 211–2) gives the order Kaisareia, al-Funduq, Tzamandos and Charsianon, but it is easy to correct the order on the basis of the map. Locations (including Sanabus) identified by Vasiliev.
42. Firas (BELA 2, 359) claims that the Muslims burned both Sariha and Charsianon, but since Mutanabbi was actually present in person and states that they burned only the suburbs, churches and surrounding areas, it is clear that the Muslims were unable to capture either of the cities. This is also confirmed by Ibn Zafir (BELA 2, 124) who also states that the Muslims burned only the suburbs of these cities.
43. It is unlikely that Kônstantinos, the *stratêgos* of the Seleukian theme, would have joined his father and brothers because his theme was located so far away from the action.
44. In their translation of Mutanabbi, Vasiliev, Grègoire and Canard (BELA 2, 311) emend the text of Mutanabbi which states that there were the sons of Fôkas present at the Battle of the Valley of Luqan (Lykos, Lycus) to read Bardas Fôkas. Firas (BELA 2, 359) also notes that the sons of the *domestikos* were present at the battle of Lykos.
45. Leôn the Wise (LT 18.147–9) expected that in the usual circumstances each theme was able to provide 4,000 horsemen so that the army sizes consisted of 4,000, 8,000, 12,000 and over 30,000-horseman armies. Notably the 12,000-horseman army consisted of the united forces of three *stratêgoi*, which would have been the minimum strength for the united forces of Bardas and his sons Nikêforos and Leôn if they followed the instructions of Leôn. Even with the figures provided by the DV (Appendix 2: 5.3), the minimum size for the united army of three *stratêgoi* would have been about 9,000 horsemen, because a single *stratêgos* was expected to able to assemble a cavalry force of 3,000 or less.
46. E.g. Vasiliev (BELA 1, 344) Personnaz (pp.54–5) and Canard (1961, 766–7, 769) suggest that it was Leôn who attacked the rear of the Muslim army while G.T. Dennis (DV, p.149) notes that the DV may refer to the campaign of 950, but with the caveat that there were so many campaigns taking place that this is uncertain. Vasiliev and Caanard both fail to distinguish between different parts of the text of Skylitzes (Cedrenus/Kedrenos) so they confused the beginning of Skylitzes' text (11.9.1–25: describes events that took place 953–6) with the latter portion of the text (11.9.25ff.) which describes the campaign of Sayf in 950, in the course of which Nikêtas Chalkoutzês relayed information to Bardas Fôkas.
47. It is quite probable that this pass was also blocked by Roman forces (under Kônstantinos Fôkas?), hence the need to use a guide, but the Arabic sources do not mention this.
48. According to Yahya (BELA 2, 96), the prisoners were killed at some point in time between 15 Nov. and 13 Dec. 950, but I have accepted here the earlier dating.
49. Both Vasiliev (BELA 1, 345) and Canard (1961, 368) accept this smaller figure, but this does not tally with the details given by the Muslim sources which state that Sayf lost control of his army, which refused to fight, so he was able to fight his way to safety accompanied by only a few followers.
50. BELA 1, 345–6; BELA 2, 160, 174, 242–3, 271, 314–5.
51. BELA 2, 71
52. Canard, 1961, 770; BELA 1, 345–6; BELA 2, 70–1, 174–5, 242–3, 271, 314–7.
53. Al-Athir 356 /353 (also in BELA 2, 160); Skylitzes 14.6–7; Lev, 1985, 233–4; Metcalfe, 53–4; BELA 2, 105, 160, 224.
54. The list is from Canard, 1961, 771–3.
55. The following account is based on: Canard 1961, 771–3; BELA 1, 347; BELA 2, 71, 109, 111–2, 160–1, 181, 197, 224, 243, 249, 268, 271, 317–9, 356–7; Miskawayh 341 (2.143,

p.150); Elias of Nisibis Year 341 (year began on Saturday 9 June May 952). Note that my reconstruction of the events differs from BELA 1 by Vasiliev while it is fairly close to the reconstruction of Canard, but that I add some new material and conclusions.

56. Skylitzes 14.7; al-Athir 356–73/353–6 (also in BELA 2, 160–1); Lev, 1985, 233–4; BELA 1, 368–70; BELA 2, 160–1, 224.
57. The following account is based on: Skylitzes 11.9; BELA 2, 96, 109, 112, 126–7, 175, 181–2, 195–6, 243, 260, 322–8, 361–3, 374; Elias of Nisibis Year 342 (year began on Wednesday 18 May 953). Specific locations mentioned where important for the argumentation and other sources (means mainly BELA 1, 347–51 and Canard, 1961, 773–7) added where relevant.
58. BELA 1, 347–8; Canard, 1961, 773–4.
59. My conclusion based on the time it would have required for the Romans to conduct their operations.
60. BELA 1, 349–50; Canard, 1961, 775.
61. A footnote in BELA 1 (349) includes the suggestions made by researchers which include Mûsher/Mishar Dagh (river left of Euphrates, north of Melitene) and fortress Masara south-east of Melitene.
62. Canard, 1961, 775; BELA 1, 349–50.
63. BELA 1, 350; Canard, 1961, 775.
64. If the Romans used a combined army against the enemy we can use the DRM (1, 3, 5–8, 13, 15, 21) and PM (see later) for the making of an estimation for the size of the combined army of infantry and cavalry. Note, however, that the LT, DV, PM and DC all include the raiding of enemy territory with a pure cavalry army in the manner described in the text, and given the distances and quickness of the raid this is the likelier alternative. The DRM (21) specifically noted that the land of the Agarenes (Muslim territory) lacked sources of food because it was so often raided by the Romans and advised against the use of large armies in such terrain. This was obviously true for the cavalry armies too, but not to the same extent as it was for the combined armies because the cavalry raid was meant to be shorter in duration which enabled the use of larger armies than was the case when infantry accompanied them. The model army in the DRM consisted either of sixteen or twelve *taxiarchiai* of infantry (16,000 or 12,000 men) plus four *taxiarchiai* of *psilôi* (4,000 men) and more than 8,200 cavalry (the meaning in the DRM 8.14–21 is that the emperor was to have more than 8,200 horsemen, even if the author then rounds this down to 8,000), plus the units that accompanied the emperor (cavalry minimum 1,000 horsemen, the number of infantry unknown). These figures are slightly greater than the figures given by Nikêforos Fôkas in his PM for the combined army to be used in invasions (see later) under a *stratêgos* of a theme, but is still consistent with those. I would suggest that in this case the *domestikos* took this slightly-stronger force of approximately 30,000 men with him when he invaded enemy territory that had suffered raids in the previous years.
65. The account of Skylitzes can be connected with this battle on the basis of the referral to the wounding of Bardas Fôkas.
66. The reaction of the Roman forces to the greed of their commander had clearly demoralized the Romans. This was not the only instance in which the soldiers abandoned their greedy commander to the enemy. A good early example of this same phenomenon is the betrayal of Solomon to the Moors by the Roman army at the Battle of Tebeste in 544 because Solomon had refused to distribute the booty to the soldiers. For this, see Syvänne, *MHLR 6*, 189.
67. If the Roman army would have been a combined army against all reason and not a cavalry army, we can use the DRM to fill in the blank spots. It is probable that the Romans had left

an infantry force at the Pass of al-Kankarun to protect the route of retreat so that there was now no need for the sending of infantry in advance to occupy it. When this was the case the marching order of the combined army (when it marched through a pass not occupied by the enemy in the DRM 19) would have been as follows. In a mixed combined army, the rear guard could consist of cavalry alone or of both infantry and cavalry, so it is impossible to say what type of solution was adopted in this case, but in light of the instructions in the DRM the latter option is likelier. It is probable that that when the Romans had invaded that they had left an infantry force to secure the Pass of al-Kankarun (DRM 20.46ff) so there was no need for the sending of infantry in advance to occupy it (e.g. LT 9.27, 9.44), which means that the marching sequence (DRM 14, 19; LT 9.37) was roughly as follows: an infantry *taxiarchia* or two *taxiarchiai* posted at the front marched together with a cavalry vanguard; the emperor (here the *domestikos*) together with his own forces and the cavalry posted in front; the right wing cavalry flank guards and the right flank infantry; the baggage train; the left flank of the infantry and after them the left flank cavalry; the *saka* cavalry rear guard; and last a *taxiarchia* or two *taxiarchiai* of infantry. In this case, however, it is possible that Bardas was actually further to the rear, because the above account suggests that the forces under Nikêforos and Leôn escaped the debacle relatively unscathed. If the forces under Nikêforos and Leôn included infantry forces, this is not surprising because these would have had an advantage over the cavalry forces of Sayf in difficult terrain. However, if we assume that Bardas was where the DRM expected him to be, just behind the vanguard, then it is clear that he would have turned around towards the rear with his men in an attempt to save his son Kônstantinos while the army around him melted away.
68. BELA 1, 351–2; Canard, 1961, 775–6.
69. Canard, 1961, 778–81; Theotokis, 276–8 (he fails to note that this battle was one of those in which the Roman forces just melted away thanks to their attitude towards Bardas' corruption); BELA 2.2, 331–2; Mutanabbi (French tr. BELA 2, 332–4; Latham, English tr. by al-Mallah, encyclopedia.com); Latham, 1979; al-Mallah's analysis of Mutanabbi's poem at encyclopedia.com. Mutanabbi gives us a poem on the appearance of the Roman iron-clad *katafraktoi* to extol the achievement of Sayf and his *ghilman*.
70. In my opinion the sending of the flank divisions of the second line to their assistance (as advised in the sixth century *Strategikon*; see Syvänne, 2004) would have been wiser because these were closer to the outflanking enemy than the units of the third line, but in the PM (4.15–6) the procedure was to send first the third line to outflank the enemy and only after that the flank divisions of the second line. The presence of the fill-up *banda* would certainly have made this procedure more difficult, hence their removal by Nikêforos. For further details, see Appendix 3.
71. In short, I have accepted the consensus view regarding the location of the city of al-Hadath which is shown also in the accompanying map which I have drawn after the Barrington Atlas and TIB. The location south of Lake al-Hadath/Inekli suggested by R. Hartmann (see S. Ory) does not make sense in the context of this battle because if al-Hadath would have been located in that location, Sayf would have abandoned his safe route of retreat and bypassed the enemy and so would have been behind them in the north.
72. Leo the Deacon (4.3.) states that Nikêforos employed similar tactic by deploying the infantry archers and slingers behind the front-line cavalry at the Battle of Tarsus in 965. See the narrative of the campaigns of the year 965 for further details.
73. See appendices 1 and 3.
74. The system of constructing the wedge means that the size of the wedge depended on the size of the force. The likeliest size for the wedge is 960-horseman strong (58, 62, 66, 70, 74,

78, 82, 86, 90, 94, 98, 102 = 960) because it is consistent with the size of the units beside it. The wedge of 1,152 cavalry (74, 78, 82, 86, 90, 94, 98, 102, 106, 110, 114, 118 = 1152) would give us a figure of 12,914, which is closest to the figure of 13,000 horsemen, but since this is far greater in size than the flanking divisions I would consider this less likely.
75. The 50 *bandofylakes* remained constant in all army sizes.
76. BELA 2, 127, 196, 334–7.
77. Personnaz, 59–61; Canard, 1961, 785–6; BELA 1, 355–6; BELA 2, 97, 125, 337–40.
78. ibid.
79. Skylitzes 14.7–8; Idris pp.112–4; BELA 2, 106, 124–5, 257; BELA 1, 371–3; Lev, 1985, 235–6. The *Cambridge Chronicle* (BELA 2, 106) claims that the commander of the Muslim fleet was Ammar, but then states that it was actually emir Hasan (i.e. al-Hasan b. Ali b. al-Husayn) who then encountered the enemy in the first battle in 955–6, while in the following year 957–8 Hasan joined his brother Ammar and engaged Marianos Argyros. *Kitab al-Uyun* (BELA 2, 224–5) claims that the commander in 345 (15 April 956–3 April 957) was Hasan while in the following year the commander was Ammar.
80. BELA 1, 312; Runciman, 1929, 197; DC p.691. For the Battle of Lechfeld, see Bowlus. Moravcsik (p.55) suggests that it was also in 955 that the Hungarians of Botand invaded Thrace, but this is clearly a mistake. It is clear that the next major Hungarian invasion took place in 958. Furthermore, it is quite possible that we should identify Botand with Boulosoudes (Boultzous *karchas* of DAI 40.66–8, the third in hierarchy) who was killed at Lechfeld in 955 so he would definitely not have been invading Thrace in 955.
81. This and the following is based on: BELA 2, 97, 127–8, 182–3, 340–7; Skylitzes 11.9; Bar Hebraeus 182–3, p.165; al-Makin (p.238) year 343; Yahya (pp.772–3, chapter 74 / 114 also in BELA 2, 97). The modern narratives by Vasiliev (BELA 1, 356ff.), Canard (1961, 788ff.) and Howard-Johnston (1983, 241–6, 254–5, 289–90) have also been found very useful, but I will still offer a far more detailed account on the basis of the sources while also departing from their conclusions due to the fact that I identify the HQ of the Patrician differently.
82. According to Michael the Syrian/Rabo 10.5, before becoming emperor the residences of Iôannês Tzimiskês were Melitene, Hanzit (Harput) and other well-known locations. The list suggests various places of residence for Iôannes when he was still the *stratêgos* of Melitene, so Arshkeni was not the only one of those. One may assume that the HQ was transferred from Arshkeni as a result of its destruction during this campaign season.
83. Canard, 1961, 247–8, 789; Howard-Johnston, 254–5, 289–90.
84. Canard (1961, 791–2) also speculates that Nikêforos may have been present at the battle, but in that case he would have been the *domestikos*. I disagree with this because it is clear that the *domestikos* at this time was still Bardas.
85. Yahya (pp.772–3, chapter 74 / 114 also in BELA 2, 97) year 345 (15 April 956–3 April 957); Kamal ad-Din, BELA 2, 182–3.
86. The following is based on: Bar Hebraeus (182–3, p.165.); BELA 2, 97, 109, 161–2, 175, 183. Modern sources mentioned separately where relevant.
87. BELA 1, 359–60.
88. This and the following is based on: TC 452–3; Bar Hebraeus 182–3, p.165; BELA 2, 109, 162, 175, 268, 272. The principal sources are the TC and Bar Hebraeus.
89. The title 'admiral' comes from Arabic. The Greco-Roman terms at this time, depending on the position in the hierarchy, were *drouggarios*, *stratêgos*, and *nauarchos*.
90. TC 452–3.
91. ibid.
92. It is also possible that this victory contributed to the Roman ability to assemble a sizeable fleet for the retaking of the island of Crete in 960 without any fear of a Tarsiote response,

or at least that is the view adopted by Canard (793), Pryor and Jeffreys (72) and presumably also by Sullivan because he includes these comments in his commentary to the translation of Theophanes Continuatus. It should be remembered, however, that the most immediate consequences of this victory were the ability to dispatch Basileios to Italy in 957 and then Marianos Argyros to Italy in 958. It is uncertain if the victory still contributed to the inactivity of the Tarsiote fleet in 960, because by then there had already been four years of time to rebuild it. It is actually likelier that the Tarsiotes did indeed rebuild their navy in the meanwhile, but in the absence of Egyptian support the fleet did not threaten the Romans in the same manner as before. The reason for the inactivity of the Egyptian fleet lay primarily with the results of the campaign of Marianos Argyros, whose success against the Fatimids convinced the emir of Egypt to seek peace with Rome.

93. Idris pp.112–4; BELA 1, 371–3; BELA 2, 106, 124–5, 162, 257; Lev, 1985, 235–6.

Chapter 6

1. TC p.479.
2. Canard, 776; Dennis after Canard in DV, p.149.
3. This and the following are based on: Yahya 76, p.774 also in BELA 2, 97–8; Kamal ad-Din in BELA 2, 183; Bar Hebraeus AD 957 pp.165–6; Appendices 2 and 3; and the other sources mentioned therein.
4. Kamal ad-Din in BELA 2, 183.
5. Miskawayh 168 year 347, vol. 5.180.
6. Miskawayh 168 year 347, vol. 5.180; Bar Hebraeus AD 957, 165–6.
7. Nestor (AM 6456–63, 6464–72) with the comments of Cross and Sherbowitz-Wetzor (pp.239–40); Wortley/Cheyner in Skyl. pp.231–2.
8. ibid.
9. Idris pp.112–4; BELA 1, 372–3.
10. Idris pp.112–4; BELA 2, 106, 124–5, 257.
11. TC 6.30–2, 453–6; Idris pp.112–4 (ignores Fatimid defeats). Sullivan (RFNF, 35) and Vasiliev (BELA 1, 371–8) date Marianos' arrival in Italy to the year 956, but Vasiliev further suggests that Marianos remained at the scene until 958. Wortley (Skylitzes, p.256) follows Falkenhauzen and places the arrival of Marianos even earlier in 955. I follow here a different dating scheme based on the Arabic sources which state that the first officer dispatched to Italy was Basileios. For an alternative reconstruction of these events, see BELA 1, 372–5.
12. The following analysis is based on: TC 6.30–2 (pp.453–6), 6.44, pp.461–2, 6.47 (pp.462–3); Bar Hebraeus 183, p.166; BELA 2, 98, 106, 112, 117, 175, 182–4, 224–5, 244, 257, 268, 368–40; Miskawayh year 347; Stephen of Taron 3.7 (p.231); Matthew of Edessa 1(anno 407 = AD 958; Bedrosian p.1, grabar ed. 1) provides a confused account of the campaign of Basileios *parakoimômenos*; Michael the Syrian (13.4 confuses Basileios *parakoimômenos* with Basileios II); Anon. notary, 42, 55–6 (Botond's adventures in Francia); Simone de Kéza, 42; *Illuminated Chronicle*, 62; DAI 40. There will be specific sources where the narrative needs additional argumentation and other sources are mentioned where relevant.
13. TC 6.30–2, 453–6; Skylitzes 14.8; *Cambridge Chroncile* 6466–7; BELA 1, 371, 375–6.
14. TC 6.30–2, 453–6; Skylitzes 14.8; BELA 2, 106, 224–5, 257. For an alternative reconstruction of the events, see BELA 1 (376–8), which ignores most of the evidence presented by TC.
15. ibid.
16. TC 6.30–2, 453–6; BELA 2, 106, 224–5; Lev, 1985, 235–6.
17. TC 6.30–2, 453–6; BELA 2, 106, 224–5.
18. ibid with Lev, 1985, 235–6.

19. Anon. notary, 42, 55–6 (Botond's adventures in Francia); Simone de Kéza, 42; *Illuminated Chronicle*, 62; DAI 40. Moravcsik's treatise (55–60) also analyses the invasion of 959, but fails to understand that the leader of the expedition was Taksony, the grandson of Arpad, who was actually the King (*megas archôn*) of Hungary. He suggests that the invader was the tribe of Botond. However, I agree with Moravcsik in that the story of the single combat is plausible and that this event could have taken place either in 934 or 959 when the Hungarians advanced as far as the gates of Constantinople. However, I prefer the date 959 on the ground that Simone de Kéza (40–1) and the *Illuminated Chronicle* (60–1) describe the defeat at Lechfeld in 955 before the campaign against Constantinople.
20. The original sources mentioned at the beginning of the chapter 958 with BELA 1 (362–3) and Canard (1961, 795).
21. This and the following are based for the most part on Miskawayh, 168–73 year 347, vol. 5.180–6, with additional material from Canard where noted.
22. The background is influenced by two facts. Nasir ad-Dawla thought that he held Jazira securely because North Syria was under his brother Ali while one portion of Diyar Modar and of Diyar Bekr were controlled by his sons. In contrast, Mu'izz faced constant trouble in lower Iraq due to the bandit leader Imran b. Chahin and the prince of Oman Yusuf b. Wajih, who controlled Basra and was allied with the Qarmates of Bahrain. For this, see Canard, 1961, 521. One can add to this also the fact that Nasir's brother Sayf controlled all the territory north and west of him.
23. Miskawayh 347–8, 172–5. In general, for the revolt and its outcome, see Canard (1961, 522–7). Note, however, that I date the events differently: e.g. I prefer to follow Miskwayh while Canard follows Yahya's dating without noting the discrepancy in the dating of the Battle of Ra'ban and the start of Mu'izz ad-Dawla's campaign.
24. The following account is based on: Yahya 79–81 (777–9); Bar Hebraeus 184, pp.166–7; BELA 2, 98, 112, 175–6, 244; Skylitzes 11.16–8; TC 6.48–54, 463–9; Manasses, 5547ff. Other sources are mentioned where relevant.
25. In other words, I reconstruct the events differently from what is found in the PMBZ (Lilie et all.), which connects the capture of Abu'l-Fawaris Muhammad with the campaign of Leôn Fôkas against Edessa (al-Ruha) and Harran (Carrhae). In my opinion this is a mistake, because it is clear that Leôn's spring/summer offensive was stopped at Kyros. The Roman offensives against the region of Edessa and Harran are therefore to be connected with the offensive launched by Tzimiskês further east, just as was done by Canard (1961, 799).
26. The original sources mentioned at the beginning of the chapter with Canard (1961, 789).
27. Skylitzes 11.16–8; TC 6.48–54, 463–9; PSs 756–7), Manasses, 5547ff.

Chapter 7

1. The following is based on: TC 469–72; Skylitzes 12.3; PSs 756–8.
2. The following account is based on: Yahya 79–81 (777–9); Bar Hebraeus 184, pp.166–7; BELA 2, 98, 112, 175–6, 244; Skylitzes 11.16–8; TC 6.48–54, 463–9; Manasses, The Reign of Constantine; PSr 97–8. Other sources are mentioned where relevant.
3. The location of al-Haruniyya (it was at a distance of ca. 72km/ca. 45 miles from the city of Kyros/Qurus as the crow flies) suggests a possibility that it was only now that Leôn advanced as far as Kyros/Qurus, meaning that both Dahabi and Yahya have misplaced their information concerning the timing of Muhammad b. Nasir's campaign against the Romans and the Roman campaign against Kyros/Qurus to the period before the death of the emperor. However, since both place these events to have taken place before the death of Kônstantinos, I am here making the assumption that Leôn now returned to Roman territory and did not advance to Kyros to be defeated there by Sayf.

4. Canard (1961, 799) suggests that it was after the capture of al-Haruniyya that Leôn continued his march east towards Diyar Bakr with Sayf ad-Dawla in pursuit, but with the result that Leôn inflicted a defeat on Sayf in which his nephew Muhammad b. Nasir was captured. As noted, I consider this version unlikely.
5. The following discussion expands my earlier analysis presented: 1) in the book chapter entitled East Roman Naval Warfare and the Military Treatises 641–1071 forthcoming as a book chapter in a book due to be published by Helion; 2) a research paper 'Training the Byzantine Officers for Naval Combat in 641–1071' presented at *PIASA Conference*, Gdansk 2019; 3) a research paper 'East Roman Naval Warfare and the Military Treatises 641–1071' presented at *McMullen Naval History Symposium*, Annapolis, MD, USA, 2015.
6. This is based mainly on TC 473–6, which offers most of the details we have of the initial discussions. See also SLs 98.
7. *anon. Naumachica* in Pryor & Jeffreys, (pp.521–45) Appendix 3 title and introduction to the treatise on pp.521–2.
8. Pryor & Jeffreys, 183–8: The anon. author had used as sources at least the following treatises: Leo VI's *Naumachica*, the *Onomasticon* of Julius Pollux (second century AD), the *Lexicon* of Hesychios of Alexandria (fifth-sixth centuries AD), Thucydides and Homer's Odyssey.
9. PMBZ with Sullivan's comment RFNF 71.
10. Christides, 1984, 186–91.
11. Yahya, 82–3, 780–1.
12. The following is based on Theodosius the Deacon, TC 475–81; Skylitzes 12.4; Attaleiates 28.1–8; LD 1.3–2.8; *Life of Athanasios Athonites*; PSs 758–9; SLs 98; Yahya 84, 782. Other sources mentioned where relevant.
13. TC 477; *Life of Athanasios Athonites* 11; Christides, 1984, 173–4.
14. ibid.
15. The following is based on the original sources mentioned and the presentations and book chapter of Syvänne and Christides, 1984, 176–8, 221–7. According to Christides (223), some local oral traditions on the island of Karpathos claim that Nikêforos stopped there, but he notes that this seems highly improbable because the best harbour of the island of Karpathos, Tristoma, cannot be used in the summer and autumn because of dangerous sea-breaking at its mouth. The anchorage at Palatia on the little island of Saria would have been equally dangerous. It would therefore have been strange if Nikêforos would have sailed his fleet there first when he could sail straight from Ios to the island of Dia via Therasia. I would suggest that the reason for the oral tradition may be twofold: 1) it is possible that the role of the Karpathian pilots became confused in the oral tradition; 2) or that Nikêforos visited the island during his return trip in 961 – of which we have no details at all.
16. The following is based on Theodosius the Deacon, TC 475–81; Skylitzes 12.4; Attaleiates 28.1–8; LD 1.3–2.8; *Life of Athanasios Athonites*; PSs 758–9; SLs 98; Yahya 84, 782. Other sources mentioned where relevant.
17. Roman naval combat doctrine preferred the avoidance of naval battles if other means like ambushes, stratagems and surprise attacks could be used instead of this: Leo *Taktika* 19.40.
18. The text used is the one in Sullivan (RFNF Text 4) so that I am also using the locating system adopted by Sullivan on the basis of the latest edition of the text by Panagiotes.
19. Sullivan in RFNF, Text 4, pp.124–32.
20. This type of landing craft was not a new invention. See Sidonius Apollinaris (5.440–446).
21. In the context of river crossings opposed by enemy forces, both Syrianos Magistros (*Peri Strategikes* 19) and Maurikios (*Strategikon* 12.21) state that the opposite shore was to be cleared of enemies with missiles and stones shot by naval artillery.

22. The speech was addressed to the *andres, stratêgoi, tekna, syndouloi, filoi Rômês ta neura* and *despotou pistoi filoi*, which Sullivan translates as 'soldiers, children, fellow servants, friends, sinews of Rome, faithful friends of the sovereign': i.e. he omits the men while he translates the word *stratêgoi* as soldiers. In this he follows Panagiotes who thinks that in this text the high-ranking officers *stratêgos, stratêgetês*, and *stratatarcês* should on occasion be translated simply as soldiers. There is no reason for this conjecture, because the speeches were undoubtedly also addressed to the *stratêgoi* of the themes and other generals accompanying the campaign. In short, there is no need to change the meaning. Note, however, that in the following discussion I will not state these differences in the translation between myself and Sullivan/Panagiotes.
23. For this, see Syvänne (2004, 319).
24. Theodosios, 269–70; LD 1.5.
25. This is my conjecture based on the statement of Attaleiates (28.3) that Nikêforos needed to build a temporary harbour for his fleet because Crete lacked a suitable harbour.
26. Theodosios, 269–70.
27. I connect Leo the Deacon's night attack against the enemy encampment (1.7) with the second Arab relief attempt because Leo places (1.3) the event to take place after the Pastilas incident and because its details differ from the accounts provided by Attaleiates and Theodosios.
28. It would be possible to think that the 50,000 represented 5,000 cavalry, but given the circumstances – the need to fight a decisive battle against the enemy's main army – it is probable that the 50,000 represented the total number of men that Nikêforos took with him.
29. Attaleiates 28.5–6; Theodosios 270–6, 278. Theodosios (276–8) connects the shooting of the heads over the city wall with the first assault stage of the siege
30. Theodosios 275–7.
31. The Roman invasion of Crete created turmoil in the Islamic world. As noted in the text, the Cretan Arabs sent an appeal for help to the Fatimid caliph al-Mu'izz and he acted as if he was willing to do so. Al-Mu'izz then wrote to Kafur, the Ikhshid ruler of Egypt, and proposed the uniting of the fleets of the Fatimids and Egypt in the Barqa region of Libya at the beginning of May–June 961. At the same time, he also dispatched a threatening letter to emperor Rômanos II in which he demanded the abandonment of the campaign. The Romans ignored the letter, while Kafur refused to cooperate with al-Mu'izz. The Ikhshids quite rightly suspected the motives of their enemy. It is very likely that al-Mu'izz's only purpose was the spreading of propaganda that stated that the Fatimids were the only true champions of *Jihad* against the infidels. Unsurprisingly, Crete fell without any help from any of the Muslim rulers, for which see Lev, 1985, 236. For an Ismaeli propaganda version of the events, see Idris (pp. 181–5).
32. Lev, 1985, 236.
33. I have here accepted the suggestion of Panagiotes (RFNF, p.157, n.100).
34. Theodosios 277–9; TC 477–8.
35. This and following is based mostly on Theodosios 279–92.
36. Sullivan (RFNF, p.129) suggests that this was actually Theodosios' unrevised attempt to prove the pre-eminence of the emperor over his general to his audience. It is possible that this was indeed the case, but it is also possible that this referred to an actual event. Belisarios had faced similar treatment at the hands of his jealous subordinates who repeatedly accused him of imperial ambitions in letters dispatched to Justinian.
37. Panagiotes and Sullivan both prefer to convert this word into common soldiers, but I see no reason for this.
38. Theodosios 279–92.

39. Theodosios 291–5; LD 1.9; TC 476–8, 480–1.
40. Theodosios 295–301; LD 1.3–7. I am here following the version of Theodosios and so unite it with Leo's version (wrongly placed at the beginning of the reconquest).
41. LD 2.6–8; TC 481; Theodosios 300–6; SLs 98; Skylitzes 12.4; Yahya 84, p.782. The conquest is also mentioned e.g. in the following sources: Makkari 2.4 (p.1.175) and Matthew of Edessa 1 (anno 408 = AD 959; Bedrosian p.1, grabar ed. 1–2). Matthew's version is extremely confused account of the Roman campaign against the Tachicks and against the Egyptians in Crete. The Armenians were also claimed to have defeated the forces of Hamdun, the military commander of the Tachicks, in the same year.
42. The translators of Leo the Deacon (p.79 n.45) Talbot and Sullivan note that the legal texts and the *Sylloge tacticorum* indicate that one-sixth was separated for the imperial treasury, while Leôn's *Taktika* suggests that one-fifth was to be sent to the treasury. It is not known which of these practices Nikêforos was following.
43. Yahya 84–5, pp.782–3; LD 1.5ff.; Theodosios 301ff.; Christides, 183–191.
44. This is not true of all of the slave troops. A significant number of them remained loyal to their masters, because the position also secured them a steady income and in some cases de facto power over their so-called masters thanks to the fact that the slave troops were armed. The Turkish emirs are the most obvious example of this phenomenon.
45. Zonaras 16.23; Skylitzes 12.10; Yahya 85–6, 783–4; Canard, 1961, 805; Schlumberger, 1890, 154.
46. The following is based on: LD 2.1–5; TC 479–80; LA 14; Skylitzes 12.4; SLs 98–9; Yahya 83–4, 781–2; Bar Hebraeus 184; Miskawayh 180–1, pp.195–6
47. LD 2.1–2.
48. The invasion is variously dated by modern historians to the years 959, 960 and 961. By far the likeliest of these is the year 960 for the following reasons: Lêon would not have had time to engage the Magyars in 959 because he was in the east; he became *dometikos tês dyseôs* in spring 960; the battle with the Hungarians took place before Leôn's campaign against Sayf in 960.
49. LD 2.1–5; TC 479–80; Skylitzes 12.4; SLs 98–9; Yahya 83–4, 781–2; Bar Hebraeus 184; Miskawayh 180–1, pp.195–6.
50. Canard, 1961 801; PMBZ Naga al-kasaki and Turniq; Schlumberger, 1890, 156 (confuses two different campaigns).
51. Schlumberger (1890, 139) claims on the basis of Bar Hebraeus that the entire force of 30,000 would have consisted only of cavalry, but it is clear that this is not the case. Bar Hebraeus does not state that the 30,000 would have consisted only of cavalry. He mentions only the number without any specifications to the type of forces.
52. The modern era opposition to this conclusion are just ill-founded and not based on period evidence. For example, it is ridiculous to claim that Sayf would not have wanted to lead his army through the theme of Seleukeia because it possessed garrisons or the fact that Sayf ended up in Miccica (Miççiça) would mean he could not have used the pass in the theme of Seleukeia but the Pass al-Kussuk/Kujuk along the river Jai'han north of Germanikeia/ Marash, as claimed by Canard (1961, 801). Personnaz (97–100) also thinks that Sayf marched straight towards Aleppo. As regards the bypassing of enemy strongholds, this is what Sayf had been doing all his career. He had always led his army past enemy headquarters and assembly points. In this case it was the easy pickings in the theme of Anatolikon that determined his route of retreat – the thematic forces of Seleukeia were just a nuisance to him, as had been the other themes before he reached the Anatolikon. As regards the place where Sayf ended up after his own flight, that does not indicate the route that he had taken with his army and neither does it tell us which route Sayf himself took. He might have

ended up at Miccica by using a route from the west, north-west or north. The key fact here is that we do not know the direction of Sayf's flight from his encircled army. After having left behind his pursuers, he would have hidden in the wilderness and he would have used the tracks and paths not often frequented by men with the idea of bypassing the Romans who were guarding the principal routes out of their territory.

53. List of those surrendered in Canard, 1961, 803.
54. Canard (1961, 803–4) suggests that Leôn departed from the east immediately after his victory and celebrated his triumph at Constantinople so that the defence of the east would have been left in the hands of the stratêgoi. This is clearly not the case, because the defence of the west against the Magyars was in the hands of Marianos Argyros and not in the hands of Leôn. The size of the army available for Leôn remained the same, so he preferred to remain on the defensive and not attempt any major invasions. It should be remembered that generals are always more aware of the defects of their own army than of the defects of the enemy force. Therefore, Leôn preferred to stay on the defensive. He did not know the exact state of the enemy forces after his victory, which was particularly important because, if anything, the events of the past had proved that the annihilation of Sayf's forces did not mean that he would not have possessed similar forces in the following year. Compare e.g. the events of the years 949–951.
55. TC 480.
56. Miskawayh 191; Bar Hebraeus, 185, p.167; Canard, 1961, 803–4.
57. Miskawayh 191; Canard, 1961, 804; PMBZ Naga.
58. The following is based on: Matthew of Edessa 1 (anno 410 = AD 961, and Bedrosian pp.1–2, grabar ed. 2–4). The Armenian sources are in disagreement about the name of the King of Armenia at this time. Smbat and Matthew of Edessa name Gagik I Bagratuni as the King of Armenia during the reigns of Kônstantinos VII, Rômanos II and Nikêforos, but Stephen of Taron claims that the ruler was Ashot son of Abas. Modern historians have usually adopted the latter view and therefore place the parade with 100,000 soldiers to take place only after the reign of Nikêforos, but in my opinion this requires additional research because it is clear that the accounts of both Smbat and Matthew of Edessa perfectly fit the period when Nikêforos served as *domestikos* and emperor. However, since the question still requires additional research, I have not named the king in the accompanying text.
59. In the same context Matthew of Edessa claims that the 'Arabs' captured Anazarba (Anawarza) and Aleppo from the Egyptians with much slaughter, most of the killed being Christians rather than Muslims. He clearly confuses the Arabs and Romans here, because it is very unlikely that the Egyptians would have captured both places in 960 so that Sayf would have needed to recapture those in 961.
60. Based on Miskawayh Year 350.
61. Skylitzes 13.7, 14.2.
62. Based on Miskawayh Year 951, 190; Yahya 85–6, 783–4; Bar Hebraeus 185–6, pp.167–8; LD 2.9; Skylitzes 12.10; PSs760; Stephen of Taron 3.8 (p.234); Michael the Syrian/Rabo 13.4. Other sources mentioned where relevant,
63. On the basis of the PM one could assume that this would be the total, but this is not the case for three reasons: Nikêforos was leading the same army with likely reinforcements as he had in Crete; he was the *domestikos*; and the figures in the PM were meant for the thematic armies. One could also think that the Arab sources confused the 16,000 infantry army (e.g. in the PM the *stratêgos* was expected to lead an infantry force of 11,200 hoplites and 4,800 archers) with the 160,000 soldiers/horsemen, but when one remembers that the figure of 16,000 represented only the infantry and not the combined army of ca. 22,000 men the likelihood diminishes even further.

64. We should remember that in the PM Nikêforos envisaged also larger cavalry forces (PM 2.14, 4.4, 4.18), even for the thematic *stratêgoi*, with the implication that the infantry force could also be enlarged in like manner by the *stratêgoi* so that the cavalry forces could fit inside the hollow square without stretching it too much.
65. Canard (1961, 807) and Schlumberger (1890, 197) place the end of the campaign to 30 March, presumably on the basis of the Catholic calendar (in truth the fasting would have started on Wednesday 31 March in 962), but Nikêforos would have followed the Eastern calendar which places the fasting to the Clean Monday which in 962 was on 29 March.
66. ibid. with as-Suyti: 354 Muslim era. Even if as-Suyti dates this to the year 354 (965), it had already taken place for the first time in 351.
67. I.e. I disagree with Canard (1961, 807–8) and the PMBZ Nikephoros II Phokas and Ibn az-Zayyat (by Lilie, Ludwig, Zielke and Pratsch) both of which put the figure at 4,000. The reasons are given in my narrative.
68. Canard (1961, 808) suggests that Rashiq an-Nasimi would have succeeded az-Zaayat.
69. Yahya 86, p.784; Canard, 1961, 808.
70. Canard, 1961, 810; Schlumberger, 1890, 219–20. As already noted, the date for the capture in both treatises, November 962, is unlikely to be correct. Both accept the dating of al-Athis, while I prefer the dating scheme of Yahya.
71. Adonz; Canard, 1936, 450–60; PMBZ Nikephoros II. Phokas and Theodoros Parasakoutenos.
72. Canard, 1961, 808. The PMBZ Naga does not include this campaign.
73. The following account is primarily based on the analysis of Canard (1961, 808–9).
74. The following account is primarily based on Yahya (86–9) and al-Shimsati (tr. in Forsyth, 107–9) and on the analysis of Canard (1961, 809–12), but I reinterpret it on the basis of military probability while also seeking to reconcile the different versions of the contradictory Arabic sources. Other sources are mentioned where relevant for my argumentation and re-evaluation of the evidence. The date of the battle comes from Canard (1961, 815, n.211). For a different reconstruction, see Schlumberger, 1890, 219–32. The campaign is obviously mentioned in multiple different sources, most of which do not give any details. A good example of this is the *Chronicle 1234* (230). I leave these unmentioned as these do not add any information.
75. The map of Canard has Jibrin just a few km south-east from Aleppo, so it is clear that his account and map do not match. What is certain, however, is that Nikêforos approached from the north because Sayf posted his army at the Gate of the Jews which is located on the northern wall of Aleppo.
76. Based mainly on Canard (1961, 813–7) and Schlumberger (1890, 238–51), but noting that I reconcile the different versions given by the Arab sources, because these can clearly be reconciled. Other sources include e.g. Yahya (89), Miskawayh (192–4) and Bar Hebraeus (186–7); Shimshati (tr in Forsyth, 109–10). The dating scheme is based on Canard (1961, 815–6, n.211). and Schlumberger.
77. Ibn al-Athir (p.403/p.362); Amari 2, 254–9; Metcalfe, 55; Eickhoff, 343–5.
78. The following account is based primarily on LD (2.10–3.8); Kônstantinos VII *De cer.* 1.96/pp.433–40 (as is clear this text was not written by Kônstantinos, but added later by an unknown person); Skylitzes (12.11–13.7); the Revised Chronicle of Symeon the Logothete (RFNF Text 2a, 23, p.102). The principal source for the usurpation is Leo the Deacon who was a period author and who also provides us with most of the details and evidence. He was also used as a source by Skylitzes. Other sources are mentioned where relevant. I have not included mere comments like e.g. that of Stephen of Taron (3.8, pp.234–5) or Smbat (pp.1–2, g.1–2), which do not add any information to the above.

79. See e.g. note 60 on page 83 in the translation of LD by Talbot & Sullivan together with Schlumberger (1890, 252–4). Personnaz (111–2) follows this consensus view.
80. I.e. I agree with Hupchick (228) who also accepts the information provided by Skylitzes.
81. I follow here the suggestion of Sullivan/Talbot (LD, English tr. p.247, n.12).
82. I have here accepted the suggestion of Sullivan/Talbot (LD p.95) that the Tornikioi meant these two persons.
83. *Die Byzantinische Kleinchroniken* CFHB 12.1, p.141. This is also noted by Wortley (Skylitzes, p.249) who refers to the comment of Schneider regarding this.

Chapter 8
1. The dates are also confirmed by the Byzantine Minor Chronicle 14.59–60 (*Die Byzantinische Kleinchroniken* CFHB 12.1, p.141) and 15.2–4 (ibid. p.158) and 16.5–8 (ibid.165).
2. The following is primarily based on LD 3.8–9; Skylitzes 14.1–2.
3. ODB Proedros.
4. Ibid, original sources with Personnaz (117–9). I have one disagreement with his assessment, however. He considers it probable that while Nikêforos wanted the marriage Theofanô did not thanks to the age difference and unattractive appearance of Nikêforos. This is possible, but I would still consider it likelier that Theofanô was initially very desirous of the marriage before she learnt of the religious lifestyle of Nikêforos the hard way. A man with Herculean strength could easily have made her desirous of him. The sources support this view rather than the opposite one.
5. Note also Manasses, 5700ff.
6. Sullivan and Talbot (LD p.100) note that Haldon suggests on the basis of this that the three-fingered Mediterranean release had done a comeback. This is probably taking the evidence a bit too far, because it is clear that the three fingered release had never been entirely abandoned, because it is equally clear that the archers were expected to be able to vary their releasing techniques according to the chosen archery technique.
7. In the commentary to Leo the Deacon (p.113) Sullivan and Talbot note that the palace complex was probably the Boukoleon Palace, for which see the maps section together with my academia.edu posting about the imperial palace.
8. The following is based on: Bar Hebraeus 187; Miskawayh 195–203; and Yahya 94, 792. Other sources mentioned where relevant. The dating of these events is imprecise and I have tried to reconcile the information and sources as far as possible.
9. Canard, 1961, 817–8.
10. The following is based on: Skylitzes 14.10; Zonaras 16.24; Yahya 95–6, 793–4; Bar Hebraeus 188; Dhahabi's account by Canard, 1961, 818; Miskawayh 202–8; al-Makin year 363 (p.233).
11. He claims that the emperor Nikêforos led the men, but this is a mistake.
12. The following is based on: Bar Hebraeus 188–9; Skylitzes 14.11–2; LD 3.10–4.3; Zonaras 16.25. Other sources mentioned where relevant. For an alternative reconstruction, see Canard, 1961, 818–21. Ibn al-Athir suggests that it was during this campaign and the siege of Tarsus that Iôannês Tzimiskês fell on the ground during pursuit just in front of the walls of Tarsus, but I agree with Schlumberger (1890, 424, 496) that this incident took place later in 965.
13. Personnaz, 142–5.
14. I.e. I agree with Personnaz (145–6) who prefers the account of Skylitzes and Yahya as do I.
15. Rametta/Rometta and Roman counter offensive: Ibn al-Athir (p.403, 411–3 / p.362–5); Idris pp.115–30, 170, 191; *Cambridge Chronicle* 6469–73; Nuwayri, Sicily 964–5, 423–9; Zonaras 16.24; Skylitzes 14.8; LD 4.7–8. Other sources mentioned where relevant.

16. The translators of LD (Sullivan and Talbot, p.115) note that the word *autanepsios* used by Leo could mean either nephew or cousin, while Skylitzes identifies Manuêl as the illegitimate son of Nikêforos' uncle Leôn Fôkas. Considering the referrals to the youth of Manuêl, I agree with Sullivan & Talbot that it is likelier that Manuêl would have been the illegitimate son of Nikêforos' brother Leôn.
17. For a different interpretation, see Eickhoff, 348.
18. The following is based primarily on Miskawayh 201–11; Smbat (2, g.2) I, 413 A.E. (AD 964). Other sources mentioned where relevant.
19. Inbreeding is still a quite common phenomenon among the Muslim countries, even if many Muslim countries have woken to its dangers. It should be noted that the marriages between cousins was also very common among the European nobility for the very same reason, the aim of keeping the property in the hands of the same family while ensuring alliances between the members of the same family.
20. Miskawayh 263–7; Canard, 1961, 527–31.
21. Miskawayh 208–9; al-Makin year 363 (p.233).
22. al-Athir 434–5 (pp.365–6); Idris pp.115–30, 170, 191; LD 4.7–8; al-Makin year 364 (p.233); Lev, 1985, 236; Eickhoff, 349–51; Metcalfe, 55–6; Personnaz, 158–9.
23. The following is based on: Bar Hebraeus 188–9; Skylitzes 14.11–4; LD 3.10–4.4; Zonaras 16.25; Yahya 97–8, 795–6; Idris, pp. 186–90; Matthew of Edessa 1 (412; Bedrosian p.2, grabar ed. 4–5). Other sources are mentioned where relevant.
24. I.e. in this case I agree with the interpretation of Sullivan & Talbot (LD p.107) and McGeer (1995, 315) that we should not take the word myriad literally, because it is probable that we are here dealing with the first cavalry line only, as was the case when the commander led forward the *katafraktoi*-wedge and its wing units from within the infantry square. See Appendix 3: 5.5. It would be possible to think that each of the cavalry divisions would have had 10,000 horsemen because this would have only just outflanked the enemy if it was deployed as a single phalanx, but as noted the standard practice was to employ only the first cavalry line against such an array. In short, I am assuming that the cavalry force that Nikêforos led forward consisted of 10,000 horsemen in total all under his command as emperor, which is consistent with the figure of 30,000 horsemen that he had led against the city of Aleppo.
25. Schlumberger, 1890, 496 suggests that the centre would have been under Leôn Fôkas, which is possible but this would result in the problem of who was in charge of the reserves. That man had to be experienced and reliable, hence my suggestion that it was Leôn.
26. It should be noted, though, that I do not agree with Theotokis' short reconstruction of the Battle of Tarsus on page 278–9, because he fails to note that the Arabs attacked the Roman marching camp from which Nikêforos led out the three cavalry divisions. In short, there would not have been an infantry battle formation just behind the cavalry, but the fortified marching camp.
27. Schlumberger, 1890, 488. Note that Schlumberger reconstructs the order of events differently.
28. Canard, 1961, 823.
29. Skylitzes 14.14; Yahya 96, 794.
30. Miskawayh 209, 210–5; Yahya 97–100 (795–8).
31. This version can be found in Manasses 5735ff. and after him in the *Nikonian Chronicle* (60–2).
32. Based on Skylitzes 14.19 (267–7); LD 4.5–6, 5.1; Zonaras 16.26. Other sources mentioned where relevant.

33. I.e. He places it to the year 966. Personnaz (167–8) also places the campaign to take place immediatel after the envoys had arrived. This is patently false in light of the texts of Yahya and Skylitzes, the latter of who dates Nikêforos' campaign to the year 967.
34. Conclusion of the treaty between Otto and Peter is from Runciman. In his study of the first Bulgarian Empire Runciman (1930, pp.167, 178–81; Browning, 70–1 also dates the death to 965) date the death of Maria-Irene to the year 965 so that the new bolder stance would have resulted from this and led to the sending of envoys in 966 (Stephenson 48, also dates the embassy to this year). When Nikêforos then campaigned against the Bulgarians, Peter became once again conciliatory and dispatched his sons as hostages in return for peace which Nikêforos was unwilling to give (same view also in Stephenson). Instead of this he decided to use the Russians as his proxies. This view is contradicted by the account of Skylitzes 12.5 who places the death of Maria-Irene to the year 963 and the renewal of the peace treaty with the sons sent as hostages also to take place under the caretaker government of Iôsêf Briggas. I follow his dating.
35. Zonaras 16.25, PG 135 BELA, pp. 119–22.
36. Also analyzed in Dagron (304–7) with English translation of the relevant portion of Zonaras' text in McGeer (1995, 196).
37. I follow here the interpretation of McGeer (2000, 97–9) and Personnaz (178), both after Lemerle.
38. Ibn Hawkal in Dagron (306) and Vasiliev-Canard (2.2., 417).
39. For further details of the policies of Septimius Severus and Caracalla, see my biographies of them.
40. Wortley in Skylitzes p.263; Personnaz 132–4.
41. Syvänne, 2020b.
42. Skylitzes 14.18, 15.1; Zonaras 16.25.
43. See my biographies of Septimius Severus, Caracalla, Gordian III and Philip the Arab, and Gallienus. The same trick had also been used by the emperor Heraclius when he ran out of money, for which see *MHLR* Vol.8.
44. Skylitzes 14.18; Zonaras 12.25 (Hendy translates the relevant part). For a fuller analysis of the coin and its impact, see Hendy (507–8).
45. Kühn, 158–242; McGeer, 1995, 201. Treadgold (1995, 114) mistakenly dates the reform to the reign of Tzimiskês.
46. Kühn, 184–7, 209–21.
47. Kühn, 170–84, 221–2 (katepanate of Mesopotamia).
48. Kühn (158–63).
49. Based on Personnez (121–39), Morris (100–11), PMBZ (Nikephoros II. Phokas) and sources therein (in particular LA and in it 14, 16, 19–20, 22–3, 30–1, 34, 36), but note that my account just like that of Skylitzes is more cynical towards the intentions of Nikêforos.
50. Note that I date the tenure as *stratêgos* of the Anatolikon differently than others – for which see the previous chapters.
51. Lev, 1984, 237; Metcalfe, 57; Brett, 75.
52. Yahya 105–6 (803–4); Canard, 1961, 824–5; al-Makin Year 354 (p.233).
53. The following is based on: Miskawayh 209, 213–5; al-Makin, year 354 p.233; Yahya 97–100 (795–8), 106–9 (804–7), Yahya has divided the account of the crushing of the revolt of Antioch and the killing of Naga into several different places so it requires diligence to connect the parts together in their right sequence.
54. Based mainly on Yahya 107–8 (805–6); Bar Hebraeus 189. Yahya is the only source to preserve some sort of cohesive chronology in his account. The texts of Skylitzes (14.15–7, 14.21) and Leo the Deacon (4.10–1) appear to unite two different campaigns of Nikêforos

Notes   501

into a single campaign. Their texts, however, are still used to shed light on some of the matters mentioned by Yahya. Other sources mentioned where relevant. For a different reconstruction, see Takirtakoglou, 100–3.
55. Schlumberger, 1890, 524.
56. Canard, 1961, 825.
57. Schlumberger (1890, 523), however, suggests that Nikêforos used the Resaina and Harran route.
58. It is clear that both Skylitzes and Leo the Deacon describe the second campaign against the city of Antioch and not the one in 966, because both claim that Nikêforos did not attempt to assault the city while Yahya clearly states that Nikêforos did that for seven days in succession without result. Schlumberger (1890, 526–8), however, accepts that Nikêforos merely made a demonstration before the city by parading and drilling his army for eight days in an effort to demoralize the defenders into surrender. I follow here Yahya, who states that Nikêforos assaulted the city during this campaign. The parading of the troops before the city would have taken place during the next campaign. Takirtakoglou (101) suggests on the basis of Dhahabi that Nikêforos did not besiege Antioch because the Antiochians paid him a ransom, handed over the hand of Saint John the Forerunner and allowed him to visit the Christian shrines of the city after which Nikêforos advanced against Manbij. The order of the progress of the campaign is clearly wrong. I therefore prefer the version provided by Yahya.
59. Yahya 108–15, 806–13; al-Makin, year 364 p.233; Miskawayh 231, 238–9, 254–6, 289–92.
60. Age 54 comes from Yahya. Sclumberger (1890, 526), while noting Yahya's information, on the basis of other sources puts the age of Sayf on his deathbed at 52 years, 2 months and 8 days.
61. There was actually a continuous string of Jihadists arriving from Khorasan, some of them even bringing elephants with them. However, instead of attacking the Romans, some of these groups ended up attacking their fellow Muslims. A good example of this is provided by Miskawayh (222ff.), who states that 20,000 Khorasani raiders with elephants (with reinforcements following) raided Rayy while he was living there.
62. Yahya 115, 813.
63. LD 5.1; Liudprand, *Legatione* 43.
64. According to Stephen of Taron (3.8), in 415 (30.3.966–29.3.967) the sun darkened (= eclipse of the sun on 22 July 966; see ODB Ashot III) and Ashot III died and the Romans annexed Taron. When one combines this with the information provided by Smbat (see later in this chapter) it is clear that Ashot III had definitely died before 29 March 967, after which the flight of his sons took place in early 967. (Nikêforos was preparing to launch a campaign against Armenia in the spring). Notably Stephen leaves out the year 416 (30.3.967–28.3.968) so that it is probable that the actual annexation took place in about April–May 967.
65. Smbat (2, g.2) I, 413 A.E. (AD 964); Stephen of Taron 3.8 anno 415 (p.235). The Armenian sources are in disagreement about the name of the King of Armenia at this time. Smbat and Matthew of Edessa state that the King of Armenia during the reigns of Kônstantinos VII, Rômanos II and Nikêforos was Gagik I Bagratuni, while Stephen of Taron claims that the ruler during the reign of Nikêforos was Ashot son of Abas. Modern historiography supports the latter view, but in my opinion this is not conclusively so because the details given by Smbat and Matthew fit perfectly what took place during the reign of Nikêforos, even if modern historiography has these take place only later during the supposed rule of Gagik I Bagratuni. I have therefore included Smbat's account here because its information fist perfectly, but I have not named the king because the name of the king for this period is contested. I will return to this question in greater detail in the book series *Military History*

of Byzantine Rome. However, at this stage of research I would tentatively accept the view of Smbat and Matthew rather than the view of Stephen, but this question still needs further research.

66. Stephen of Taron 3.8 (415–7), p.235; Skylitzes 14.21; ODB Taron, Taronites.
67. I consider the Pege incident to be separate from this one.
68. Based on Skylitzes 14.19 (267–7); LD 4.5–6, 5.1; Zonaras 16.27. Other sources mentioned where relevant.
69. Personnaz (167–8) mistakenly places the campaign immediately after the second Cilician campaign (took place in 965) while also making the mistake that the Great Fence would still have been the border between the Roman Empire and Bulgaria. After the conquests of the *tsar* Symeon the border lay further south, which is the reason why Nikêforos advanced as far as the 'Fence' while capturing fortresses held by the Bulgarians.
70. Moravcik, 59.
71. Nestor AM 6464–6472 to 6475 and Nikonian (pp.57–8, 62–5); Franklin and Shepard, 144–5; Vernadsky, 43; Vasiliev, *Goths*, 128–9. I do not accept Vernadsky's redating of the Khazar campaign to the year 963, because it is likely that the Russians were fighting in Crimean territory just before the Romans concluded peace with them, on top of which the reasons given for the alteration of the chronology from the text of Nestor results only in further problems.
72. McGeer (1995, 181).
73. Yahya 109 (807), 115 (813); Bar Hebraeus 190 (p.171–2).
74. ODB *epi tes trapezes*: an aulic courtier in charge of imperial banquets who introduced the guests, waited upon the emperor, and delivered dishes from the emperor's table to the guests. I.e. it would have been an *epi tês trapezes* who took food from the emperor's table to the Otto's envoy Liudprand – for which see the chapter dealing with his embassy.
75. See ODB stratopedarches.
76. The account of the Russian operations between 967 and 970 is based on LD 4.6, 5.1–4, 6.8–10; Skylitzes 14.20, 15.5; Nestor AM 6464/6472–6478; Nikonian (pp.58–69).
77. For some inexplicable reason Hupchick (230) does not accept the quite reasonable figure given by Leo the Deacon and replaces it with his own guess of 10–12,000 men. Schlumberger (1890, 568) also considers the figure an exaggeration, but this does not really tally with the evidence which we have of the period armies. The period armies ranged from small to large, as they always have.
78. Hupchick (230–1) claims that Peter was surprised by Sviatoslav because he had collected his forces against the Romans who had invaded in 966 (also the wrong year). This is not born out by the facts. Peter was aware of the impending invasion and shadowed the Russians along the Danube, not to mention the idiotic habit of Sviatoslav – of warning the enemy in advance.
79. On the basis of this Runciman (1930, 181) suggests that Nikêforos dispatched an additional batch of bribes in late 967, but suggests that this was just a continuation of the previous policy. He also suggests that the subsequent invasion of Russian territory by the Pechenegs was done at the instigation of the Bulgarian court and not at the instigation of the Roman court. I find the latter more likely in light of the timing of the new alliance between Bulgaria and Rome which took place in June 968 (see the chapter on the embassy of Liudprand).
80. Hupchick (231), Stokes (477–8) and Stephenson (49) have accepted the modern theory of Ivanov that Peter I stepped down after his stroke and had already been replaced by his son Boris II in 967. They do not accept the statement of Skylitzes that the sons were returned to Bulgaria only after the death of their father in January 969 and take it as a mistake made by Skylitzes. I prefer to follow Skylitzes (13.5).

81. The question of who asked the Pechenegs to invade Russia has divided modern historians so that some of them think that the Romans had sent the request (e.g. Franklin & Shepard, 146) while others think that the Bulgarians called them to their assistance (e.g. Runciman, 1930, 181; and Browning, 71) while others remain uncommitted (e.g. Personnaz, 170, who makes no suggestion – implying perhaps that the Pechenegs just exploited the situation).
82. For sometimes very different reconstructions of the events, see Runciman (1930, 180–5), Hupchick (230–4), Stephenson (48–51), Stokes, Personnaz (168–71), and Frankin & Shepard (146–7). The main difference between their reconstructions and mine is that I have put more trust in the dating of the events in Leo the Deacon, Skylitzes and Nestor/Nikonian. There is no reason to doubt that the Russians invaded Bulgaria again only in 970 and not in 969 as conjectured by modern historians. Nestor (6479) places the second invasion of Bulgaria to the year 971, but on the basis of the campaigns conducted during the reign of Tzimiskês it is clear that it must have taken place already in 970.
83. My analysis of the rivalry of Nikêforos II and Otto I in Italy during the reign of Nikêforos in 966–9 is primarily based on the outstandingly-good book chapter of Jules Gay: 'Rivalité de Nicèphore Phocas et d'Otton dans l'Italie mériodale. politique nouvelle de Jean Tzimiskes. Rapports des principautes Lombardes avec les deux empires (966–973)', pp.289–23. Gay bases his analysis on the following original sources: Leo the Deacon; Cedrenus (i.e. Skylitzes); *Codices Cryptenses*; *Chronicon Salernitatum*; *Privilegium* of Otto for the Catholic Church; *Diplomata* of Otto I; *Liber Pontificalis*; Liudprand (*Historia Ottonis, Legatio*); Widukind of Corvey (*Res gestae Saxonitae*); *Chronicon Vulturensis*; Amari (Arabic sources translated into Italian); Benedicti S. *Andrea monachi chronicon*; Continuator of Regino of Prûm (Regino Continuator); Thietmar of Merseburg (*Chronicon*); *Annales Lobienses; Benzonis episcope Albensis ad Heinricum*. Gay's list of original sources for this period does not include *Annales Lupi Protospatharii* (a.967–770), but this overlook is meaningless as it does not add anything important to the analysis. For the reconstruction of the events the principal sources are Liudprand (*Legatio*), Thietmar of Merseburg and *Chronicon Salernitatum*, so Gay's account is built around these. In the context of the relationship between Nikêforos II and Otto I, I will refer to the original sources only when my view is at variance with that of Gay, or when this is important for an understanding of the analysis. For the reign of Tzimiskês, Gay's account includes also *Vita Mathildis, Vita Deoderici, Annales ildesheim, Annales Corbiensis, Diplomata Ottonis II*, and *Codex diplomatico Cavensis*. All of the sources are available online. Most of the Latin texts can be found in the *Monumenta Germaniae historia* (MGH) or in the *Rerum Italicarum Scriptores* (RIS).
84. Gay (296–300) and sources therein (esp. SAC 169); Personnaz, 160.
85. Gay, 300–1 and sources therein.
86. Gay (302–3) with Personnaz 160–1; conclusions concerning the Armenian and Bulgarian campaigns are mine.
87. Personnaz (161) with Gay (304–5) and sources therein, and in particular Liudprand (*Legatio* 11) with SAC (169–70) and Lupus Protospatharius (a.966).
88. Gay (304) analyses the situation differently and considers Otto's policies naïve, but as the examples that I give demonstrate Otto had good reasons to think otherwise. The Romans had demonstrated weakness in the past which could perhaps be exploited.
89. On the contrary, Gay (305) believes that the invasion and siege were abandoned because of the advice given by Liudprand who knew the Romans better than Otto. However, as noted, Gay interpreted the material in the wrong light because he did not remember that the Bulgarians and Arabs had achieved success with similar means. Liudprand was just improving his own credentials as an ambassador while claiming that the failure of Otto's campaign did not result from the strength of the Roman defences but from his advice.

90. Skylitzes 14.18–20. LD 4.6–7, 4.9; Zonaras 16.27–8; Manasses 5713ff; see also the chapter dealing with the embassy of Liudprand.
91. Skylitzes claims that it was the emperor who sold the grain for profit, but contradicts himself immediately by noting that the emperor was unaware of it.
92. Skylitzes includes also an anecdote about this. He states that on one occasion when Nikêforos led the army onto the plains to drill it in combat manoeuvres, there he was met by a grey-haired man who wanted to become enlisted into his forces. Nikêforos asked why such an old person would want to do that, to which the man responded that he was now much stronger than in his youth because then he had needed two asses to carry grain worth one piece of gold while now he could carry on his shoulders grain worth two gold coins. Nikêforos understood the joke and did not react to it.
93. Liudprand, *Legatio* 34, 44.
94. This is based on Liudprand's *Legatio*, with specific locations mentioned where important for the argumentation.
95. PMBZ Eugenios.
96. Stephen of Taron 3.8 (415–8); Yahya 101–4 (799–802), 116–9 (814–7), 124–6 (822–4); Skylitzes 14.15–7, 14.21, 15.1, 15.3; LD 4.10–11, 5.1, 5.4–5; Bar Hebraeus 190–1; Ibn al-Dawadari (tr. in Forsyth, 116; Ibn Zafir (in Forsyth, 117–8); Ibn al-Qalanisi (in Forsyth, 117–8); Idris (p.134). Schlumberger (1890, 701ff.) has failed to note that Nikêforos advanced first against Martyropolis, just as he has failed to note the march to Damascus. For a different reconstruction, see Takirtakoglou (103–7).
97. The northern route had been pillaged in 966 so it was preferable to pillage a new area.
98. Bar Hebraeus presents the portion of the campaign after Nikêforos had reached the neighbourhood of Aleppo as follows: Nikêforos did not proceed to Antioch immediately, but placed a base camp in the territory between Emesa and Aleppo because there was no man who could resist him. It was because of this that he then pillaged the area for two months.
99. Michaêl Bourtzês was one of the murderers of Nikêforos because the latter had punished him for having disobeyed the orders.
100. Yahya claims that both Petros and Michaêl were attacking the mountain side of the wall together, but the Roman sources are to be preferred because Petros escaped punishment.
101. According to the version given by Bar Hebraeus, Michaêl dispatched some Christians inside the city as false deserters and captured the city with their help, but this is less likely than the version presented by the Roman sources because he also claims that it was Leôn Fôkas who two months later captured the citadel. However, this cannot entirely be ruled out either. It is possible that some of the Christian false refugees did indeed help Michaêl when he had got his men through the wall thanks to the information provided by Aulax. Takirtakoglou (107ff.) accepts this version. For a modern analysis of how effective the blockade of Antioch had been before its capture, see Lucas McMahon. He sheds further light on the effectiveness of the blockade through the use of view-sheds and a cost-distance algorithm (based on a GIS technique).
102. Based on SAC 171–4 and Gay (310–1). Other sources mentioned where relevant.
103. Gay, 313–4; Widuking 3.71; Thietmar 2.15.
104. Gay, 314 with SAC 172.
105. Gay (314) after SAC 171–2.
106. Gay (314–5) mainly after Widukind (3.72), Thietmar (2.15), and SAC 172–4.
107. Based on LD 5.5–9, 6.1–3; Skylitzes 14.22–3, 15.1–3; Manasses 5735ff. The other accounts of the murder by non-Roman sources e.g. Yahya, Bar Hebraeus and Matthew of Edessa, are not as reliable.

108. Note, however, as already discussed, that it is possible that the religious side of it was meant only as a show – or at least this was suspected by both Athanasios (LA 34) and Skylitzes 14.2.
109. The recent translators of Leo, Sullivan and Talbot (LD; p.139, n.76) note that there are two different interpretations for the *akoufion*, one in which it is considered as a hooked hammer (pickaxe, warhammer) and another by Parani who thinks that the word means a sabre. Considering the fact that the men entered the imperial chambers with swords drawn it is clear that Parani is correct.
110. There are also other versions of the event, e.g. that by Matthew of Edessa 1 (anno 418 = AD 969; Bedrosian p.2–3, grabar ed. 5–6), but it is clear that these are not quite as reliable as the Roman sources, hence it suffices to include only the versions of Matthew of Edessa, Yahya and Psellos. According to Matthew of Edessa, in 418 (AD 969) the impious and obscene empress secretly brought Iôannês Tzimiskês, a man who had been condemned to death and who was living in exile on an island, into Constantinople. She made a pact with him to assassinate Nikêforos and she promised to become the wife of Iôannês and to seat him on the imperial throne. Tzimiskês agreed to the plan. Consequently, when Nikêforos was seated on his throne reading the Bible by candlelight, the empress came and hugged him so that she was able to tie Nikêforos' sword-strap in such a manner that he would later be unable to defend himself. After this, she went to meet Iôannês and gave him the sword with which to kill her husband. Then Tzimiskês ran to the imperial chamber with the result that Nikêforos shouted to him 'What do you want here, you mad dog?' The emperor rose up, reached for his sword but found it securely bound. It was then that Tzimiskês attacked wildly, and stabbed and cut the emperor into three parts. The murderers then witnessed the humility of the emperor. He was wearing a goat's hair shirt against his skin hidden underneath the imperial purple. Nikêforos was then buried in a cemetery close to the other emperors. Tzimiskês then sat on the throne, but did not marry the wicked empress. The sons of Rômanos II, Basileios and Kônstantinos, were taken to the district of Handzit (Harput) under the great of Spramik, mother of Mxit'ar, so that the empress could not poison and kill them. Tzimiskês suffered from a bad conscience because of the murder of Nikêforos. According to the version given by Psellos (*Historia syntomos* 105) and Yahya (129–32, pp.827–30) in the autumn there was a rumour according to which Nikêforos intended to castrate Basileios II and Kônstantinos VIII and nominate his brother Leôn as emperor which then spurred their mother and wife of Nikêforos Theofanô into action in a situation in which Nikêforos did not sleep with her. Theofanô then convinced Tzimiskês to participate in the plot by promising herself to him. Psellos then goes on to claim that the intention was not to kill Nikêforos but to force him to abdicate. It is clear that this version is pure nonsense because we know from Leo the Deacon and Skylitzes that Nikêforos had carnal desires towards his wife and that he planned to marry the sons to the daughters of the tsar of Bulgaria. One may assume that this is a purposeful rumour spread after the murder of Nikêforos to justify the action taken by Tzimiskês and Theofanô. In short, I disagree with Morris (108–9, 111–5) who favours the account of Yahya.

Chapter 9

1. This sentence has some words from the translation of Sullivan and Talbot (LD p.140) because I was unable to come up with any better. According to the commonly accepted version Nikêforos Fôkas died without offspring of his own, but this is not necessarily so because the Cretan Kallergis/Kallergês (Kalergis, Calergis, Kallergi, Callergi, Calergi) family claims to be his descendants. We know that Nikêforos claimed to be without offspring in 963, but this does not preclude the possibility that he could have had illegitimate children

who were later recognized by his family or that his second wife Theôfano was pregnant at the time of his murder and that this would have played a role in the decision of Iôannês Tzimiskês to punish her to a monastery where she could have given birth secretly to a son who was later adopted into the family. It is a well-known fact among those who study family trees that most Finns can claim to be descendants of nobility if we just trace our ancestry far enough into the past (both bastards and legitimate ones) and the same is definitely case when the population of the location is even smaller as it is in Crete. According to the later tradition preserved in Crete and also by the Kallergis family in Venice, Alexios II Komnênos dispatched 12 nobles to the island of Crete to strengthen the Roman hold on the island. These families then became the leading noble houses of the island. One of the men dispatched to the island was Iôannês Fôkas who claimed to be a descendant of Nikêforos. It was then during the Venetian occupation of the island that the family changed its name into Kallergis which is derived from the Greek words *kalon* (beautiful) and *ergon* (from the verb *ergô* = task, work, accomplishment). When the Ottoman Turks conquered the island, several members of the family fled to the Ionian Islands, Euboea, Venice and other places so that descendants of the family are found in many other places besides Crete. Whatever the truth about these claims, it is usually assumed that the Fôkades in Crete actually descend from Lêon Fôkas and it is clear that the direct descendants of Nikêforos did not play any major role in Roman affairs outside the island of Crete.

Appendix I

1. The following analysis is based primarily on Syvänne (2008) and Dain's edition of the ST (1938), and secondarily on the translation of the ST by Chatzelis and Harris (2017) who suggest alternative readings.
2. McGeer, 1995, 210: *menavlion* = a short very thick spear constructed of a single sapling or wood cut into sections; length ca. 3.0–4m.
3. Ten men from each *tagma* were detailed to serve among the *bandofylakes* of the *stratêgos*, two were used as messengers, and ten as *kribantes* (medical corpsmen) mounted on horses for the purpose of carrying the wounded to the doctors.
4. The text calls this *antistomos difalaggia* (against facing double phalanx), which is actually an incorrect term because in that case the facing of both phalanxes would have been towards each other. The correct term would have been *amfistomos difalaggia* (double-fronted/opposite sides facing double phalanx) so that the front phalanx would have faced the front and the second phalanx the rear.
5. *ST* 10, 19, 32–3.
6. The translation and commentary by Chatzelis and Harris (p.66, 132) fail to note that the *bandofylakes* did not actually consist of 500 men but of 50 men.
7. Equipment in Dawson, 2002, 86.
8. The numbers (including the totals) in the *Sylloge* are only theoretical approximations.
9. For a different interpretation of the structure of the wedge, see Theotokis, 207–8.
10. The sixth-century *Strategikon* contains both this version and the other version in which the fill-up units were placed on a level with the frontline of the support line. In light of the fact that the *Strategikon* contains several *lacunae* and possible later emendations, it is possible that the illustration/diagram with the fill-up unit placed in the rear has resulted from a later interpolation. For an analysis of the *Strategikon*, see Syvanne, 2004 and *LRCT*.
11. As such, the fill-up units undoubtedly had many beneficial sides to recommend their usage, for example that their use eased the maintenance of correct distances between the units, made it easier to stop the flight of the front line units, and gave the *stratêgos* extra units to use as reserves, but the fact that they blocked the direct route for the third line made their presence more a hindrance than a bonus.

Notes 507

12. The shallower depth should usually be seen as a sign of better quality, but in this instance it reflects the greater need for widening the frontage in order to avoid being outflanked by the enemy. The fact that these men wore less armour than those belonging to the 18,770 men army shows that these men did not belong to the elite units.
13. I have accepted the emendation of Chatzelis and Harris as proven beyond doubt.
14. For the earlier Roman use of the hollow square with cavalry, see e.g. Syvänne (2004, 2009c, 2010–11, 2017a-b, 2019c, *MHLR* vols. 1–8, 2021a, 2023).

Appendix II
1. The following analysis is based on the editions of the DV by Dennis (1985) and Dagron and Mihaescu (1986).
2. DV Preface; Dennis in DV, 137–41; G. Dagron in the Dagron & Mihaescu edition (1986, 161–75; 2011, 137–58); McGeer, 1995, 180–1.
3. It is also possible that the beginning of the book (DV D 19.3-12; DM 19.1) belonged originally to book 18.
4. This Melias may have been either the famous Armenian prince Melias (Malih al-Armani, Mleh-mec = Mleh the Great) who became *stratêgos* of Lykandos and Tzamandos, but I would suggest that it was actually his son because the campaigns of Melias are dated to have taken place when Sayf ad-Dawla controlled Aleppo. See ODB Melias; DAI 50.133ff (pp.238–40); *De Thematibus* 12; DV 20.7. The ODB suggests that Melias the Great died in 934, but it is possible that this is a mistake because one Arabic source (BELA 1, 353, n.2) mentions that at the Battle of al-Hadath/Hadat/Adata in 954 Sayf ad-Dawla's forces captured the patrician of Tzamandos and Lykandos. I.e. it is possible that he survived until that battle. However, it is equally possible or even likelier in my opinion that the Melias who was captured at the Battle of Hadath was a similarly named son or grandson of Melias who later became *domestikos tôn scholôn* and participated during the campaigns of Iôannês Tzimiskês and died in 973.
5. See also the observations of Dagron (DV, 1986, 245–57, 2011, 253–71) concerning intelligence gathering along the frontiers.
6. The composition of the heavy infantry portion of the phalanx appears to have been traditional so that each consisted of eight ranks to enable them to withstand the enemy charge – this is an assumption based on the fact that the treatise does not contain instructions similar to the ones we find in the PM which specifically notes the use of the shallower formation.
7. Similarly, in LT 9.28.
8. For the Late-Roman version, see Syvänne (2004 with *MHLR* vols.1–8 and *Late Roman Combat Tactics*).
9. *koursa* is a plural form of *kourson* and it was because of this that Nikêforos used the term *monokoursa* (single-raiders) to denote the use of a single raiding force.
10. The size of the enemy force could be estimated through visual observation, or by observing the area trampled by hoofs (hoof prints) or by calculating the size of the enemy's camp. See DV 6, 14.27ff.
11. The following is based on DV 7–10, 14–16. The text has several chapters that are basically doublets of the earlier chapters.
12. DV 14.40-8: a third of the space of the camp consisted of 6,000–12,000 horsemen. On the basis of this one can make the conjecture that the total size of the large invading force consisted of about 18,000–36,000 men. This is a rough estimate since it is clear that infantry occupied less space than the cavalry. However, when one remembers that besides the infantry the encampment also included additional cavalry, baggage, and additional horses, mules and camels, it is fair to conjecture that the raiding force did indeed constitute about a

third of the whole force as well as of the space of the camp. One notable detail in this is the roughly-similar army sizes in use by all of the armies since antiquity.
13. DV 16 describes the *strategos* following a raiding party which was led by an emir. The treatment suggests that the whole force consisted of cavalry and did not include a separate encampment with infantry, although the use of the *parataxis* to describe the emir's detachment doesn't exclude the use of infantry.
14. It should be noted that the vanguard (= *prokoursatôres*) or the select ambushing forces near the villages (100–300 horsemen) had basically the same military purpose (ambushing, harassing, and/or luring the enemy into the chosen battleground or ambush).
15. Note the similarity with the Late-Roman practice of placing the baggage train out of harms way either in a base camp or fortress. See Syvänne 2004, 100–113.
16. The text has some contradictions. It considered a 3,000-horseman army strong, but at the same time suggested that the army could include forces from several themes and *tagmata*.
17. The basic concept was already in use during the Late-Roman period (vanguard, three battle lines and rear guards). This marching formation is given e.g. by the *Strategikon* of Maurikios: The cavalry marching formation consisted of: the scouts followed by the vanguard (*prokoursatôres*); the first battle line consisting of three divisions and wing units; the second battle line consisting of four divisions with fill-up *banda* between; the rear-guard of two divisions (the third line); the baggage train and spare horses; and the actual rear guard following the army at a distance of several miles. For this, see Syvänne (2004).
18. Dagron and Mihaescu (1986, 208; 2011, 200) have noted the similarity to the cavalry formations in the *Strategikon* of Maurikios and the *Taktika* of Leôn, but note that they have reconstructed the battle formation in the wrong manner by not including the third line (the rear guards) in the diagram while also making the unsubstantiated claim that this array would have had infantry outflankers and flank guards, which is simply untrue. It is indeed very probable that the cavalry formation which had four divisions in the second line is the same as described by Leôn the Wise in his *Taktika* with the possible exception of not having fill-up *banda* in the intervals. The second of the versions which had three divisions in front and behind is unlikely to have had any fill-up units because the slightly later *De re militari* (8.1–13) which had six units (three in front and three behind) on each side of the hollow infantry square certainly did not have these. It is actually very probable that the formation that had three units in front and behind was roughly similar to the ancient Persian battle formation, which the Romans sources claim to have consisted of three divisions both in the first and second line. The Muslim sources describe the same array to have consisted of five divisions (outer left, left, centre, right, outer right) deployed in two lines, which is actually quite similar to the Roman version when one remembers that the first line had flank guards and outflankers and the second line the rear guards on both sides.
19. The Muslim defensive formation was undoubtedly circular because their military manuals (*Gotha ms.* pp.38–9) recommended this formation, and the Roman attacking force also assumed the circle formation in attack (DV 10.59, 87).
20. Undoubtedly, one of the unmentioned purposes was also to use the marching camp as a last place of refuge if things went badly.
21. Nikêforos noted that the attacks against the enemy baggage, especially when the infantry had arrived in time, had always succeeded and led to the annihilation of both the enemy baggage trains as well as to the annihilation of Roman baggage trains when the enemy had attacked them. The author had witnessed such occurrences in person, read about them from history books, and had been passed such information also by his predecessors.
22. DV, Dennis, 1985, p.183, n.2.

23. The reconstruction of this ambushing tactic in the DV DM (Schèma VII) contains a mistake. The position of the *stratêgos* was immediately behind the infantry so that the infantry was posted closer to the enemy and the cavalry further away from the enemy (DV D, 11.37–9; DM 11.5).
24. For the term, see DV Dennis p.191, n.1 (*mensuratores, minsores, minsoratores*).
25. The reconstruction of the ambushes in the DV DM Schema 11 is incorrect as it places the ambushes on both sides of the pursuing enemy, whereas Nikêforos placed the ambushes with a wide front towards the front of the pursuers so that the Romans feigning flight wheeled either left or right to expose the flank of the pursuers to the Roman ambushers.
26. DV 18.
27. DV 22.
28. Dagron and Mihaescu (1986, 212) are undoubtedly correct in interpreting this sentence as an indication that the commander in charge of the shadowing force also joined the general in the pass.
29. Note also the difference between the standard Late-Roman and Persian/Muslim practise of making a night march and dawn attack against the enemy encampment rather than a true night attack. See Syvänne, 2004, 287–8.
30. DV 25.

Appendix III

1. See also McGeer (1995, 211–2) with the PM.
2. See also McGeer (1995, 212–4) with the PM.
3. See also McGeer (1995, 214–7) with the PM.
4. McGeer (ibid.) also notes the change from spears into close range melee weapons. Note, however, that I also include material which is not in McGeer.
5. My interpretation differs from that of Eric McGeer (1995, 37, 286–9). My analysis of the evidence has the benefit of having the exactly same numbers as we find in the PM. McGeer's reconstruction results in 147 archers while my reconstruction has 150 archers as Nikêforos demands. My reconstruction also places the archers inside the heavy-armed as expected by the treatise.
6. This has also been noted by McGeer (1995, 306–7).
7. In the ST 46.26 an army of this size would have had 334 *prokoursatôres* and 166 *defensôres* (*foulkon* of Nikêforos) for a total of 500 horsemen, so Nikêforos only added more flexibility by allowing smaller numbers for smaller forces.
8. For this see in particular Syvänne (2004, *MHLR 7, LRCT*). Note, however, that this same information can also be found in most of my other studies.
9. The spare horses cannot have been three to four *orguiai* behind each cavalry unit because this would have hindered the cavalry operations, not to mention the fact that the demand to have pennants marking the spare horses of each *bandon* would have been unnecessary in such a case.
10. The referrals here and below to McGeer mean that he includes basically the same information in his analysis, despite the fact that there might be minor differences in details and what we have included in the summary from the original text that he has edited and translated.
11. McGeer (1995, 203–6) with the PM.
12. McGeer (1995, 206–8) with the PM.
13. McGeer (1995, 208–11) with the PM.
14. See also McGeer (1995, 202–11) whose interpretation differs slightly.
15. McGeer (1995, 184).

16. There are discrepancies in the width of the intervals and number of horsemen passing through (horizontal intervals of 6 *orguiai* would not have been wide enough for 18 horsemen), for which see Appendix 1.
17. See also McGeer (1995, 268ff.) who suggests that all four ranks, the *menavlatoi* and three ranks of hoplites placed the butts of their spears against the ground and either knelt or crouched, which also helped the archers behind in their shooting. In light of the fact that the kneeling version of the *foulkon* against cavalry that is described by both Arrian and Maurikios I would suggest that it is likelier that ranks two-to-four remained upright, but that they did not place their shields rim-to-boss in depth as in the ancient *testudo/foulkon* because they had to use their long spears with two hands in the same manner as the Macedonians. It was this system that Ouranos then changed and deployed his men differently in the more open *pyknosis* order, which enabled the men to place their spears between the shields with greater ease as they did not have to tilt their shields towards the left as much as the men who were deployed in the *syskouton/synaspismos* order. For the *foulkon* and the testudo, see Syvänne, 2004, *Septimius Severus* with *LRCT*.
18. The system was changed by the time Nikêforos Ouranos wrote his *Taktika* (56. 9–10) because he stated that when the enemy *katafraktoi* were detected, the *menavlatoi* of the target unit advanced through the intervals so that they became the first rank, after which the files were interjected into files. The end result was the traditional 16-deep array in the *pyknosis*-order (93.69cm per file in width) consisting of two ranks of *menavlatoi*, four ranks of hoplites, six ranks of archers and four ranks of hoplites. Eric McGeer (1995, 275–7) speculates that the increasing of the depth would have resulted from the increased use of armour by the Fatimids, so it would have been this that required the deepening of the spear formation. I do not agree with this view because it is clear that the Saracens already used *katafraktoi* when the PM was written. It is likelier that the deepening of the formation was actually a reflection of the poorer quality of the infantry recruits after Nikêforos Fôkas reformed the recruiting process as emperor by demanding that the sailors would henceforth be ranked as infantry (English tr. of the relevant portion of Zonaras in McGeer, 1995, 196). The manoeuvre of interjecting file-into-file widened the file widths from the *syskouton*-order (62.46cm per file) into *pyknosis*-order (93.69cm) which was probably needed so that ranks four-to-six could present their spears forward between the files, because in this formation ranks four-to-six could grasp their spears with two hands while pointing those towards the enemy between the men to their front.
19. McGeer (1995, 270–2) with the PM.
20. McGeer (1995, 270–2) with the PM.
21. McGeer (1995, 65) suggests portable arrow launchers (i.e. crossbows/arbalests).
22. McGeer (1995, 65) suggests that the *êlakatia* meant windlass or tubes through which the arrows were discharged.
23. The referrals here and below to McGeer mean that he includes basically the same information in his analysis despite the fact that there might be minor differences.
24. The actual text in the PM contains a problem, because it states that if the enemy dispatched its forces to pursue the Roman *prokoursatôres*, the general was to send a second and a third cavalry *parataxeis* to protect them while he followed after them with his four divisions of the second cavalry line (PM 2.4) as was outlined in the cavalry section. This begs the question: what second and third units? On the surface it would appear as if this meant that the general sent two flank units from the front line or from the third line in support, or that the general dispatched the first and third lines against the enemy's flanks while he followed behind with the four divisions of the second line. However, Ouranos (OT 57.6) clarifies this by stating that the general dispatched the first, second and third *parataxeis* against the enemy while he

followed in good order with the four *parataxeis* accompanying him. The extant text of the PM clearly has a *lacuna* so that the first unit has dropped from the text.

Appendix IV
1. Dennis, 1985, 241–4; McGeer, 1995, 181.
2. The meaning in the text (DRM 8.14–21) is that the emperor was to have more than 8,200 horsemen, even if the author then rounds this down to 8,000 when stating this.
3. If the *etaireiai* had the same number of *banda* as the *scholai* (30 *banda*), then it is clear that they had a greater number of men allocated to each *banda/allagia*.
4. The cavalry *parataxis* accompanying the emperor should be identified to have included all of the cavalry units belonging to the imperial tenting area proper (DRM 1.99ff.).
5. Identification of the *malartioi* as *kontaratoi* in Dennis (1985, 283). G.T. Dennis (1985, 283) suggests that the Rhos and *malartioi* both formed a *tagma* of 300-to-500 men for a total of 600 to 1,000 footmen. However, I would suggest that it is likelier that on campaign the emperor was accompanied by 300 *etaireiai* (the Rhos/Russians) and 100 *basilikoi* (*malartioi*) which we find in Kônstantinos' treatise on imperial campaigns. See the introduction.
6. These very same instructions can also be found in practically every treatise dealing with marching camps, but all the same these very same ancient wisdoms seem worth repeating because during the modern era we find the French placing their military base in Dien Bien Phu and the Americans in the valleys of Afghanistan. It seems that the military men are always apt to commit the same plunders despite the ancient knowledge of the dangers of such.
7. I have here used the measurements and translation given by G.T. Dennis (DRM 1). The actual text states that there were to be two *oplitai* per *orguia* (usually 187cm, but could also be 2m) which Dennis transforms into one regular soldier per metre. Dennis also uses the metre measurements in other places instead of the *orguiai* given in the treatise, which I have here adopted for the sake of ease: i.e. it is easier for the modern reader to read metres instead of *orguiai*.
8. This definitely suggests the likelihood that there were either two *oplitarchai*, one for the day and another for the night, or that the *oplitarchês* and his second-in-command divided their duties when the army was encamped.
9. The other alternative, namely that the 1,000 horsemen were divided into two 400-man units so that 100 horsemen were placed between those under the emperor is less likely.
10. It is clear that the cavalry *parataxeis* were deployed in fighting order (five ranks deep, sixty files) to enable it to face enemy attacks. This gives us the following approximate measurements if one assumes that each cavalry file had the width of a metre: (5 x 330m) + 6 x 60m) = 2,010m. If the infantry columns became even more prolonged, the cavalry then enlarged the gaps up to two bowshots and/or added units from the front and back.
11. I.e. I do not interpret the material in the same way as McGeer (1995, 337), who thinks that the men who could not keep up with the formation dropped behind and marched as individuals behind the hollow square. In my opinion it is far likelier that when some of the individuals grew tired that initially this caused the entire marching column behind these individuals to slow down so that the formation started to break up, with the result that new intervals appeared between the men while the formation started to lose its square shape. It would have been only later that the individuals would have started to drop behind, while most of the men still marched in the hollow square that had become extended and seriously disordered.
12. This was an ancient military wisdom and can also be found e.g. in LT 9.28.
13. This is the very same procedure that the *stratêgos* Komentiolos/Comentiolus followed in 598 when he cleared the Shipka Pass of the Avars. He did not inform anyone besides his closest

advisors which the future usurper Phokas Fôkas I and others interpreted purposefully as a desertion of the army by Komentiolos. For this, see Syvänne, *MHLR 7*, 306–9. On the basis of Komentiolos' actions it is very likely that the operating procedure when attacking the enemy suddenly in the morning had remained the same ever since late antiquity, if not before. Secrecy was always important for the success of such operations because there always existed the danger of some deserter informing the enemy.

Appendix V
1. The text of Nihayat al-Su'l was a compilation using earlier Muslim military manuals, Arabic translation of Aelian's Taktika, and of Sasanian military treatises (either in Arabic translation or borrowed from later Muslim compilations). The author cites ninth-century writers such as al-Bukhārī, Muslim, Abū Dā'ūd, al-Tirmidhī, and Ibn Hanbal. Lesson One on archery was copied from 'various unnamed masters'. Lesson Two on lance play was copied from Najm al-Dīn Ayyūb al-Ahdab al-Rammāh. The section on swords and metallurgy is taken from al-Kindī's treatise (c.850), and the latter part of Lesson Nine is copied from Ibn 'Ishaq. Lessons Eight and Nine include material from Sasanian sources and an Arabic translation of Aelian. In addition, many of the other details have been borrowed from Sasanian or Abbasid military treatises. The *Gotha ms.* is similarly a compilation of these earlier treatises. For additional comments, see Scanlon, 2–4, 9–11; Syvänne, 2004.
2. See Kindi/ *Medieval Islamic Swords and Swordmaking*, p.7.n17.
3. For the following, see *Gotha ms.*, 8–13.
4. Note how the above ideal horseman also carried a javelin besides his other weapons. It is quite clear that this class of troopers results from the use of Aelian's list as a source and doesn't necessarily reflect the whole truth. However, the author also included the rider with complete equipment in his list. And it is also still quite certain that some of the ethnic units undoubtedly fought by using javelins (note for example the Berbers).
5. See, *Gotha ms*, 8–10, 16–24 (with the diagram of the marching camp).
6. *Gotha ms*, p.13.
7. The author also gave the reserves the name 'ambushers', but I have not included information regarding this in the text proper as these are not real ambushers. As far as the actual battle formations and tactics are concerned, the author stated that one of the former kings (i.e. probably a Sasanian *shahanshah*) said that half of the army was to consist of ambushers (i.e. of reserves and other support troops). Others were of the opinion that the ambushers were to form two thirds of the army. The smallest allowed number was a third of the army. The ambushers were divided into three divisions. The first and second were placed on the wings to attack the flanks of the enemy, whilst the third was placed behind the last of the battle lines of the Muslims as a reserve (i.e. as the *saka*). In the given example the width of the enemy battle line was 1 mile (c. 1.6km) which indicates that this array was meant for a major cavalry battle. Unfortunately, it is not entirely clear whether the main army in this also included the flank units.
8. See esp. *Gotha*, 24–39, 57–9.
9. The Abbasids (and their models the Sasanian Persians) appear to have favoured the use of close order in combat. See the pictures accompanying this article with Syvänne, 2004, Chapter 10.1.
10. See Syvänne, 2004, Chapter 10.1.
11. Nicolle (1993, 13) and Wüstenfeld in the translation (p.38) place the blunt end of the diagram as its frontage, but the diagram in the Arabic text (Wüstenfeld, 9) has the sharp end facing the upper half of the page (all other diagrams place the face of the array upwards with the implication that this is also the case in this instance). Therefore, the diagram should be interpreted as a wedge facing the enemy. In fact, Scanlon also translates the Arabic term as a wedge and I follow his example here.

Notes   513

12. This statement resembles Nikêforos Fôkas' opinion in *Praecepta*. It is quite possible that there was also in existence another Byzantine interpolated version of Aelian that is not extant today that had been translated into Arabic.
13. In this example, unlike in the battle arrays given above, the light cavalry, armed with short lances, missiles, and arrows, was placed behind the knights. In other words, in this case either Wüstenfeld has translated the text incorrectly or the author has simply confused the infantry section of Aelian with the heavy infantry front and the cavalry array of his day.
14. It is clear that the cubit here is 46.8cm rather than 31.23cm or 62.46cm.
15. The text (p.57) retains the mistake present in the original text of Aelian, namely that it omits one rank of riders so that the total is 113 horsemen instead of the 128-horseman *kardus*.

An old man mocks Nikêforos. (*Skylitzes, public domain*)

Select Bibliography

Select Primary Sources

Aelian, Ailianos, Byzantine Interpolation of Aelian,
  a) in Dain, *L'Histoire du texte d'Elien le Tacticien des origins a la fin du moyen age*, Thèse pour le Doctorat èt lettres, Université de Paris, Paris (1946), ed. Dain, 92–100, 102–106, 156–7;
  b) English tr. by Devine, A.M., 'Aelian's Manual of Hellenistic Military Tactics. A New Translation from the Greek with an Introduction', *Ancient World 19* (1989), 31–64, the Byzantine Interpolation of Aelian 59ff.
  c) Christopher Matthew, *The Tactics of Aelian or On the Military Arrangements of the Greeks. A New Translation of the Manual that Influenced Warfare for Fifteen Centuries.* Revised, translated and edited by Christopher Matthew. Barnsley 2012; This is now the definitive edition and translation of Aelian, but it assumes that the so-called *Byzantine Interpolation of Aelian* formed part of the original. The text includes modern diagrams. For the diagrams closer to the original, see Syvänne, Septimius Severus, Appendix on Arrian, which includes diagrams from the Barnsley manuscript of Aelian to illustrate Arrian's text and LRCT.

The Age of Dromôn, The Age of ΔPOMΩN. The Byzantine Navy ca 500–1204, J.H. Pryor and E.M. Jeffreys. Leiden and Boston 2006. Contains editions and translations of the naval treatises of Leo VI, anon. Naumachica, Syrianus Magister, Ouranos' *Naumachica*, Constantine VII Prophyrogenitus' *De Ceremoniis* 44–5, and Muhammed ibn Mankali's naval treatise.

Akolouthia for Nikephoros Phokas, in RFNF, 192ff.

al-Athir, ibn, *in Ibn el-Athir, Annales du Maghreb & de l'Espagne*, French tr. by E. Fagnan. Alger 1898; partial translations also in BELA 2 and Amari, Michele (1880), *Biblioteca arabo-sicula, versione italiana, vol.1*, Torino e Roma (Turin and Rome).

Anon. *Naumachica, Naumachika syntachtheta para Basileiou patrikiou kai parakoimoumenou, produced for parakoimômenos Basileios in The Age of Dromôn*, 521–45.

Anon. notary, in *Anonymi Bele Regis notarii Gesta Hungarorum. Anonymus, Notary of King Bela. The Deeds of the Hungarians.* ed. tr. M. Rady and L. Veszprémy, and *Magistri Rogerii Epistola in miserabile Carmen super destructione Regni Hungarie par tartaros facta, Master Roger's Epistle to the Sorrowful Lament upon the Destruction of the Kingdom of Hungary by the Tatars*, tr. J. Bak and M. Rady. Budapest 2010.

Apparatus bellicus (tenth century), partial edition and French tr. in, Zuckerman, Constantin, Chapitres peu connus de L'Apparatus bellicus, *TM 12* (1994), 359–389.

Arab Archery *An Arabic Manuscript of about A.D. 1500, 'A Book on the Excellence of the Bow & Arrow', and the Description thereof*, Translated and edited by Nabih Amin Faris and Robert Potter Elmer, Princeton UP, New Jersey (1945).

Attaleiatês, Michaêl, *The History*, ed. and tr. by A. Kaldellis and D. Krallis. Washington D.C. (2012).
Ayin Nameh, 'The Sasanian Military Theory from the Russian of Prof C.A. Inostrancev, translated by Mr. L. Bogdanov', *The K.R. Cama Oriental Institute*, 7–52. The treatise in 13–16.
BELA 1 and 2 = *Byzance et les Arabes*, A.A., Vasiliev, H. Grégoire, and M. Canard, Brussels/Bruxelles, Vol.1 (1935), Vol. 2.1 (1968), Vol.2.2. (1950).
Byzantine Minor Chronicles, Die Byzantinische Kleinchroniken, ed. P. Schneider, CFHB 12.1–3, Vienna 1975–7.
Cambridge Chronicle, in Amari, Michele (1880), *Biblioteca arabo-sicula, versione italiana, vol.1*, Torino e Roma (Turin and Rome), 277–93 and partial translation also in BELA 2.
Campaign Organization and Tactics, see *De re militari*.
Cedrenus (Kedrenos), see *Skylitzes*
Chronicle 1234, *Anonymi auctoris chronicon AD A.C. 1234 pertinenst vol.2*, tr. by A. Abouna. Louvain 1974.
Constantine Manasses, *Synopsis Chronike, Constantini Manassis Breviarum Chronicum*, ed. Odysseus Lampsidis, *CFHB XXXVI/1–2*, Athens (1996); *The Chronicle of Constantine Manasses*, English tr. by Linda Yuretich (Liverpool 2018/20)
Constantine VII Porphyrogenitus/Porphyrogennetos (Kônstantinos Porfyrogennêtos):
 - *De Administrando Imperio*, Vol.1, Greek text by Gy. Moravcsik, English tr. by H.J.H. Jenkins (Budapest 1949).
 - *De Administrando Imperio*, Vol.2. Commentary b F. Dvornik, R.J.H Jenkins, B. Lewis, Gy. Moravcsik, D. Obolensky, S. Runciman, edited by R.J.H. Jenkins (London 1962)
 - *De Ceremoniis, Constantine Porphyrogennetos: The Book of Ceremonies*. Translated by Ann Moffatt and Maxeme Tall. Leiden and Boston 2012/2017. The military portions also separately edited, translated and commented in: *Constantine Porphyrogenitus, Three Treatises on Imperial Military Expeditions*, Introduction, Edition, Translation and Commentary by John F. Haldon, *CFHB XXVIII*, Wien (1990); and in John Haldon, 'Theory and Practice in the Tenth-Century Military Administration. Chapters II, 44 and 45 of the Book of Ceremonies', in *TM 13* (2000), 201–392.
 - *De Thematibus*, ed. by A. Pertusi (Vatican 1952); *The De Thematibus ('on the themes') of Constantine VII Porphyrogenitus*, English tr. by John Haldon, Liverpool (2021).
 - *Narratio de Imagine Edessena*, in *PG 113*.
CS = Chronicon Salernitatum
De obsiditione toleranda, Anonymous, ed. Hilda van den Berg, Leyden (1947). 'A Byzantine Instructional Manual on Siege Defense: The De obsidione toleranda', Introduction, English Translation and Annotations by Denis F. Sullivan (with a reprint of the Greek text edited by Hilda van den Berg), in *Byzantine Authors: Literary Activities and Preoccupations, Text and Translations dedicated to the Memory of Nicolas Oikonomides*, ed John W. Nesbitt, Leiden/Boston (2003).
De re militari (c. 990's, *Anonymou Biblion taktikon/Peri katastaseōs aplēktou/De castrametatione*), ed. and tr. by G.T Dennis, *Three Byzantine Military Treatises*, CFBH 25, Washington D.C. (1985), 241ff, under the title *Campaign Organization and Tactics*.
De velitatione bellica, (Peri paradromês), ed. and tr. by G.T Dennis, *Three Byzantine Military Treatises*, CFBH 25, Washington D.C. (1985), 137–239 under the title 'Skirmishing'; ed. by G. Dagron and H. Mihăescu, French tr. and commentary by Gilbert Dagron, (Appendix by J.-C. Cheynet). *Le traité sur la guérilla (De velitatione) de*

l'empereur Nicéphore Phocas (963–969), Paris (1986), 29–135 (reprint of the French text as *Traité de la guérilla* in 2011, 2014).

Dumbarton Oaks Seals (DOS), *Catalogue of the Byzantine Seals at Dumbarton Oaks and in the Fogg Museum of Art*, vols.1–6, several eds. Washington DC (1991–2009).

Elias of Nisibis, *Chronographie de Mar Élie Bar Šinaya Métropolitain de Nisibe*, French tr. by L.-J. Laporte. Paris 1910.

Filon, *see Philon*

Genesios, *Iosephi Genesii Regum Libri Quattuor*, ed. A. Lesmueller-Werner and I. Thurn, *CFHB XIV*, Berlin and New York 1978.

Georgius Monachus (George the Monk) and its Continuation (the continuation is also known as Pseudo-Symeon); *Chronicle, Chronographia*,
- in *Theophanes Continuatus, Joaennes Cameniata, Symeon Magister, Georgius Monachus*, ed. Bekker (Bonn, 1838);
- in *Patrologia Graeca* (PG) 110, Georgius Monachus/Hamartolus (Paris 1863).
- and also in RFNF Text 3(here abbreviated as PSs), pp.110ff.
- in the text and notes both Georgius Monachus and its Continuation are here known as GM (Georgius Monachus) when I refer to the Bekker ed. or as PSs when I refer to the Sullivan ed

Gotha ms., 'Das Heereswesen der Muhammedaner nach dem Arabischen von F. Wüstenfeld, 1879 'Die Arabische Übersetzung der Taktik des Aelianus 1880'. *Abhandlungen der Hist. Phil. Classe der Königlichen Gesellschaft der Wissenschaften zu Göttingen 26.1*.

Gregorios the Refendarius, *Homily*, in A.-M. Dubarle, 'L'homélie de Grégoire le référdaire pour la **réception de l'image d'Edesse**', in *REB 55* (1997), 5–51; includes Greek edition and French translation.

Heron of Byzantium=*Anon, Parangelmata Poliorcetica and Geodesia* in *Siegecraft. Two Tenth-Century Instructional Manuals by 'Heron of Byzantium'*, ed. and tr. By Dennis F. Sullivan, Dumbarton Oaks Studies XXXVI, Washington D.C., (2000).

Ibn Khurdadhbih, in *Biblioteca Geographorum Arabicorum, Ibn Khordadbeh and Kodama ibn Djafar*, French tr. by M.J. de Goeje. Leiden (1889), 1–143.

Idris Imad al-Din, *Uyun al-akhbar, The Founder of Cairo. The Fatimid Imam-Caliph al-Mu'izz and his Era*, tr. by Shainool Jiwa. London (2013).

Illuminated Chronicle, in *Chronica de Gestis Hungarorum e Codice Pieto Saec. xiv., The Illuminated Chronicle. Chronicle of the Deeds of the Hungarians from the Fourteenth-Century Illuminated Codes*, ed. and tr. J.M. Bak and L. Veszprémy with a Preface by N. Kersken. Budapest (2018).

Kamal ad-Din, *The History of Aleppo*, in *Regnum Saahd-aldaulae in oppido Halebo, Regierung des Saahd-aldaula zu Aleppo*, German tr. by Dr. G.W. Freytag, Bonn (1820).

Keza, Simonis de, in *Simonis de Kéza, Gesta Hungarorum, Simon of Kéza, The Deeds of the Hungarians*, ed. tr. L. Veszprémy and F. Schaer with a study by J. Szucs. Budapest (1999).

Kônstantinos/Konstantinos, *see Constantine*

Leo the Deacon, *Leonis diaconi Caloensis Historiae libri decem*, ed. C.B. Hase (Bonn, 1828); *The History of Leo the Deacon. Byzantine Military expansion in the Tenth Century*, English tr. by Alice-Mary Talbot and Denis F. Sullivan, Washington D.C. (2005).

Leo VI the Wise, *Taktika, The Taktika of Leo VI*, text. tr. and commentary by George T. Dennis, revised edition, Washington D.C. (2014). Leo's *Naumachica* can also be found in *The Age of Dromôn. For a commentary, see Haldon*.

Leôn, *see Leo*
Life of Athanasios Athonites, in O. Lampsides, 'Ein unbekannter Kunstgriff des Nikephoros Phokas bei der Landung auf Chandax (Kreta) (960)', in *BZ 69* (1969), 9–12.
Life of Patriarch Ignatius, *Nicetae Davidis Vita Ignatii Patriarchae*, text and translation by A. Smithies with notes of J.M. Duffy, *CHFB 51*. Washington D.C. (2013).
LA = *Life of Athanasios of Athos, Version B*, in 'Holy Men of Mount Athos', eds. R.P.H. Greenfield and A-M. Talbot, (DOML), Dumbarton Oaks Medieval Library 40, Washington DC, *Life of Athanasios* translated by Talbot, pp. 127–367.
Liudprand/Liutprand of Cremona, *Liudprandi episcope Cemonensis, Opera Omnia*, in *Scriptores Rerum Germanocarum*. Hannover (1877); 'The Works of Liudprand of Cremona', tr. by F.A. Wright; *The Complete Works of Liudprand of Cremona*, ed. and tr. by Paolo Squarriti. Toronto 2007. Here the relevant works are: *Antapodosis; Liber de Rebus Gestis Ottonis (Historia Ottonis)*; and *Relatione de Legatione Constantinopolitana (Legatione)*.
Lupus Protospatharii, *Annales Lupus Protospatharii*, in MGH V.
al-Makin, *History of the Saracens, Historia Saracenica qua Res Gestae Muslimorum*, Latin tr. by Thomas Erpineus, Batavia 1625. *Histoire Mahometane*, French tr. Pierre Vattier. Paris 1657.
al-Makkari, Ahmed ibn Mohammed, *The Rise of the Mohammedan Dynasties in Spain*, 2 vols., tr. by Pascual de Gayangos. London and Paris (1843).
al-Maqrizi/Makrizi, *Takyoddini Ahmedis al-Makrizii Naratio de expeditionibus, a graecis francisque adversus Dimyatham, ab A.C. 708 AD 1221 susceptis*, Latin tr. by Henricus Arentius Hamaker. Amsterdam 1824; *Description topographique et historique de l'Egypte*, tr. by U. Bouriant in *Mémoires publiés par les membres de la mission archéologique Française du Caire*. Paris (1895).
Manasses, *Synopsis Chronike, Constantini Manassis Breviarum Chronicum*, ed. Odysseus Lampsidis, *CFHB 36.1–2*. Athens (1996); English tr. *The Chronicle of Constantine Manasses* by Linda Yuretich. Liverpool (2018/2020).
Marcus Graecus, *De ignium ad comburendos hostes*, in vol.1 (89ff., ed. and French tr. on pp.100–20) M. Bethelot, *Histoire des sciences. La chimie au moyen âge*. 2 vols. Paris 1893; partial translation with commentary in J.R. Partington, *A History of Greek Fire and Gunpowder*, Cambridge (1960).
Matthew of Edessa, *Chronicle*, tr. by Robert Bedrosian, *Sources of the Armenian Tradition Long Branch, N.J. 2017* (graciously released into the public domain Robert Bedrosian). References are to this edition unless otherwise stated. French tr. by M. Edouard Dulaurier, *Chronique de Matthieu d'Edesse (962–1136) avec la continuation de Grégoire le Prétre jusqu'en 1162*, Paris (1863).
Mémorandum inédit sur la defense des places, Anon., ed. A.Dain, *Revue des études grecques*, 123–136. English tr. in Sullivan, 2003, 145–9.
Mutanabbi al-, (Ahmad ibn al-Husayn)
- *Poems*, partial French translation in BELA 2;
- *Ode on the the Reconquest of al-Hadath*, partial French translation in BELA 2, 531–4; Complete English translation by M. Al-Mallah with commentary at *encyclopedia.com*; partial English translation with commentary in Latham (1979).
- Ode of the Campaign in 950: partial French translation (but with some additional material not in the al-Mallah tr.) in BELA 2, 307–14; Complete English tr. in al-Mallah, 2009, 110–3 (with full analysis and comments).

Naumachica of Syrianus Magister, in Pryor J.H. and Jeffreys E.M. (2006), *The Age of Dromôn.* Leiden and Boston.; and also *Syriani Magistri Naumachiae*, in Dain, *Alphonsus, Naumachica partim adhuc inedita in unum nunc primum congressit et indice auxit*, Paris (1943). See also the *Peri strategikes/strategias and Rhetorica militaris*.

Nestor, *Chronicle of Nestor*, English tr. *The Russian Primary Chronicle. Laurentian Text.*, tr. and ed. by S.H. Cross and O.P. Sherbowitzt-Wetzor, Cambridge 1953; Finnish tr. *Nestorin Kronikka*, tr. by Marja-Leena Jaakkola, Porvoo. Helsinki. Juva 1994.

Nikephoros Ouranos, *Taktika*, in Eric McGeer, *Sowing the Dragon's Teeth: Byzantine Warfare in the Tenth Century*, Dumbarton Oaks, Washington D.C. (1995), Dumbarton Oaks Studies; 33. 'Douce chapitres inédits de la Tactique de Nicéphore Ouranos', in Foucault *TM 5* (1973), 281–311; *Naumachica* in Dain, *Naumachica*, Paris (1943).

Nikonian, *The Nikonian Chronicle.* Vol.1, edition, introduction and annotation by S. A. Zenkovsky, tr. by S. A. and B. J. Zenkovsky. Princeton 1984.

al-Nuwayri, History of Africa, 'Histoire de la province d'Afrique et Maghreb, traduite de l'arabe d'En-Noweiri (Mac Guckin de Slane)', in *Journal Asiatique*: troisième série XI, 1841, 97–135, 557–83; XII 1841, 441–83 ; XIII, 1842, 49–64.

On Campaign Organization and Tactics, see *De re militari*

Peri katastaseōs aplēktou, see *De e militari*

Peri strategikes/strategias, G.T. Dennis, *Three Byzantine Military Treatises*, CFHB XXV, Washington 1985, The introduction, text and tr. of the *Anonymous Byzantine Treatise on Strategy*, 1–135. H. Köchly and W. Rüstow, *Byzantini anonymi Peri Strategikes* in *Griechische Kriegsschriftsteller II.2*, Leipzig 1855, 1–209, notes 311–355. See also *Naumachica* and *Rhetorica Militaris*.

Philon of Byzantium,
– *Mēchanikē syntaxis*, book V, Edition and French tr. by Y. Garlan, *Recherches de poliorcétiquegrecque*, Paris (1974), 291–404.
– *Belopoiika*, in Marsden 1971, 106–184.

Phokas, Nikephoros, see *De velitatione bellica, Praecepta militaria*

Polyaenus, Edition and translation in Polyaenus, *Stratagems of War*, Vols. I–II, ed. and tr. by Peter Krenz and Everett L. Wheeler, (Chicago, 1994).

Praecepta militaria, Nikêforos Fôkas in Eric McGeer, *Sowing the Dragon's Teeth: Byzantine Warfare in the Tenth Century*, Dumbarton Oaks, Washington D.C. (1995), Dumbarton Oaks Studies 33.

Psellos, *Istoria syntomos, Michaelis Pselli Historia Syntomos*, CFHB 30, English tr. by W.J. Aerts. Berlin and New York 1990. *Chronographia / Chronografia, Michel Psellos, Chronographie ou Histoire d'un Siècle de Byzance (976–1077)*, 2 vols., ed and French tr. by Émile Renaud, Paris 1928. *Michael Psellus, Fourteen Byzantine Rulers*, English tr. by E.R.A. Sewter, Penguin Press 1966.

Pseudo-Hyginus, *Pseudo-Hygin. des fortifications du camp*, ed. and French tr. M. Lenoir, Paris (2002); *Polybius and Pseudo-Hyginus: The Fortification of the Roman Camp*, ed. and tr. by M.C.J. Miller and J.G. DeVoto, Chicago 1994.

Qudama, Qudamah, Ibn Qudamah, in *Biblioteca Geographorum Arabicorum, Ibn Khordadbeh and Kodama ibn Djafar*, French tr. tr. by M.J. de Goeje. Leiden 1889, 144–208.

Rhetorica Militaris. Siriano, *Discorsi di Guerra a cura di Immacolata Eramo con una nota di Luciano Canfora, Ed. and Italian tr. Immacolata Eramo. Bari 2010; Byzantine Military Rhetoric in the Ninth Century. A Translation of the Anonymi Byzantini Rhetorica Militaris*,

English tr. and commentary by Georgios Theotokis and Dimitrios Sidiropoulos. London and New York 2021.
RFNF = *The Rise and Fall of Nikephoros II Phokas. Five Contemporary Texts in Annotated Translations, Byzantina Australiensia 23*, tr. by Denis Sullivan. Leiden/Boston (2019).
The Russian Primary Chronicle, see Nestor
SAC = *Salerno Chronicle*, *Chronicon Salernitatum*, ed. by U. Westerbergh. Stockholm 1956.
Saracen Archery. *An English Version and Exposition of a Mameluke Work on Archery (ca. A.D. 1368)* With Introduction, Glossary, and Illustrations by J. D. Latham and W. F. Paterson, London (1970).
Skylitzes, Skylitzês, Ioannes, Johannes, *Ioannis Scylitzae Synopsis historion*, ed. I. Thurn, Berlin and New York 1973; *John Skylitzes, A Synopsis of Byzantine History 811–1057*, English tr. by John Wortley with Introduction by Jean-Claude Cheynet and Bernard Flusin and Notes by Jean-Claude Cheynet, Cambridge (2010).
Smbat Sparapet, *Chronicle*, English tr. by Robert Bedrosian as *Smbat Sparapet's Chronicle*. New Jersey (2005).
Stephen of Taron, *The Universal History of Step'annos Tarōnec'i*, Introduction, Translation, and Commentary Tim Greenwood, Oxford (2017). German tr. by H. Gelzer and A. Burchard, *Stephanos von Taron. Armenische Geschichte*. Leipzig (1907); *Etienne Açoghig de Daron, Histoire universelle / Étienne Asolik de Tarôn, Histoire universelle*, Vol.1 (Books 1–2), French tr. by E. Dulaurier. Paris, (1883), Vol. 2 (Book 3), French tr. by Fréderic Macler, Paris, (1917). All references in the notes are to the latest translation by Tim Greenwood.
Strategikon, *The Strategicon, Das Strategikon des Maurikios*, CFHB XVII, Vienna (1981), edited by G.T. Dennis and German tr. by Ernst Gamillscheg; *Maurice's Strategicon. Handbook of Byzantine Military Strategy*, English tr. by G.T. Dennis, Philadelphia (1984).
Sylloge Tacticorum, *Sylloge tacticorum, quae olim Inedita Leonis Tactica dicebatur*, ed. A. Dain, Paris, 1938; *A Tenth-Century Byzantine Military Manual: The Sylloge Tacticorum*. English tr. by G. Chatzelis and J. Harris. London and New York 2017.
Symeon the Logothete, *Chronicle*
    SLs: In the RFNF Text 2: *The Revised Chronicle of Symeon the Logothete for the Years 948–963 from Vat.gr.163 and the Interpolations on Nikephoros the Elder from Vat.gr.153*
        RFNF a) The Revised Chronicle of Symeon the Logothete for the Years 948–963 from Vat.gr.163, 81ff.
        RFNF b) The Revised Chronicle of Symeon the Logothete: Interpolations on Nikephoros the Elder from Vat.gr.153 in RFNF 105ff.
    SLw: *Chronicle, Chronographia*, ed. S. Wahlgren, *Symeonis Magistri et Logothetae Chronicon (Berlin 2006)*; English tr. by S. Wahlgren, *The Chronicle of the Logothete* Liverpool (2019).
Pseudo-Symeon, *see Georgius Monachus (George the Monk)*.
as-Suyti, Jalalu'ddin, *History of the Caliphs*, tr. by Major H.S. Jarrett, Calcutta (1881).
Syntaxis armatorum quadrata, see McGeer (1992); Dain (1946, 156–7); Aelian (Devine ed. and Dain ed.).
Syrianus Magister, *see Peri strategikes, Naumachica, Rhetorica militaris*.
SC = *Synopsis Chronike*, *see Constantine Manasses*
Tafrij, *A Muslim Manual of War being Tafrij al-Kurub fi Tadbir al-Hurub by Umar ibn Ibrahim al-Awasi al-Ansari*, edited and translated by George T. Scanlon, Cairo (1961).
Theodosios the Deacon, *The Capture of Crete* in RFNF, 124ff.

Theophanes Continuatus, *Chronicle, Chronographia*,
- in *Theophanes Continuatus, Joaennes Cameniata, Symeon Magister, Georgius Monachus*, ed. Bekker (Bonn, 1838), 3–481; *Chronographiae quae Theophanis Continuati nomine fertur libri I–IV*, eds. Jeffrey Michael Featherstone and Juan Signes-Codoñer (Boston/Berlin 2015).
- in RFNF, Theophanes Continuatus Book 6, Years 944–961, 6ff.

Thietmar of Merseburg, *Chronicon* in MGH 1862; tr. by D.A. Warner, *Ottonian Germany*, Manchester and New York (2001).

Vaticanus graecus 163, in A. Markopoulos, 'Le témoignage du Vaticanus gr. 163 pour la période entre 945–963', in *Byzantina Symmeikta* 3, 83–119; and in RFNF Text 2 (SLs).

Widukind of Corvey, *Res gestae Saxoniae* in MGH 1866/1882; English tr. by B.S. Bachrach and D.S. Bachrach, *Deeds of the Saxons*. Washington D.C. (2014).

Yahya of Antioch, *Histoire de Yahya ibn-Said al-Antaki, Continuator de Said ibn-Bitriq*, ed. and tr. by I Kratchovsky and A. Vasiliev *PO 18* (1924), 700–833, *PO 23* (1923), 347–520. Partial French translation in BELA 2.

Zonaras, PG 13.

Select Secondary Sources

Adontz, Nicolas:
(1965), *Etudes Armeno-Byzantines*, Lisbon.
Byzantion (1939), 'La gènèalogie des Taronites', in *Etudes*, 339ff.
Byzantion (1934–6), 'Les Taronites en Arménie et à Byzance', in *Etudes*, 197ff.

Adontz, N. and Canard, M. (1936), 'Quelques noms de personages byzantins dans une pièce du poète arabe Abû Firâs', in *Byzantion 11* (1936), 450–60.

The Age of Dromôn (2006), Pryor J.H. and Jeffreys E.M., Leiden and Boston.

The Age of Galley, Mediterranean Oared Vessels since Pre-Classical Times (1995), eds. Robert Gardiner and John Morrison, *Conwey's History of the Ship*. London.

Agius, Dionisius A. (2008/2014), *Classic Ships of Islam Fom Mesopotamia to the Indian Ocean*. Leiden and Boston.

Alertz, Ulrich (1995), 'The Naval Architecture and Oars Systems of Medieval and Late Galleys', in *The Age of the Galley*, pp. 142–62.

Andriollo, Luisa (2012), 'Les Kourkouas (IXe-XIe siècle)', in eds. J.-C. Cheynet, C. Sode, *Studies in Byzantine Sigillography Vol.11*, available also at academia.edu.

Arcifa, Lucia, 'Byzantine Sicily', in *A Companion to Byzantine Italy*, pp. 472–95.

Barrington Atlas of the Greek and Roman World (2000), Ed. R.J.A. Talbert. Princeton.

Bachrach, David (2012, 2014), *Warfare in the Tenth-Century Germany*. Woodbridge and Rochester.

Ballan, Mohammad (2010), 'Fraxinetum: An Islamic Frontier State in Tenth Century Province', in *Comitatus: A Journal of Medieval and Renaissance Studies 41*, 23–76. An updated version of the article with maps and photos is available from his blog at ballandus. wordpress.com/2015/fraxinetum (complete link available from Wikipedia).

Barford, P.M. (2001), *The Early Slavs. Culture and Society in Early Medieval Eastern Europe*, London.

Beshir, B.J. (1978), 'Fatimid Military Organization', *Der Islam 55 (1978)*, 37–56.

Bonner, M.D. (1987), *The Emergence of the Thughur: The Arab-Byzantine frontier in the Early Abbasid Age*, PhD diss. Princeton University.

Bosworth, C.E.:

(1965–6), 'Military organization under the Buyids of Persia and Iraq', in *The Medieval History of Iran, Afganistan and Central Asia (Variorum Repr. London 1977) III, originally Oriens XVIII–XIX*, 1965–6, 143–167.

(1960), 'Ghaznevid Military Organization', *Der Islam 36*, 37–77.

Bowlus, Charles R. (2006), *The Battle of Lechfeld and its Aftermath, August 955. The End of the Age of Migrations in the Latin West*. Aldeshot and Burlington.

Brett. Michael (2017), *The Fatimid Empire. The Edinburgh History of the Islamic Empires*. Edinburgh.

Brooks E. W. (1901), 'Arabic Lists of the Byzantine Themes', in *JHS 21* (1901), 67–77.

Browning, Robert (1975), *Byzantium and Bulgaria. A Comparative syudy across the early medieval frontier*. London.

Bury J.B., (1911), *The Imperial Administrative System In the Ninth Century: With A Revised Text of Kletorologion of Philotheos*. London.

El Cheik-Saliba, Nadia Maria, Byzantium viewed by the Arabs, Ph.D. Harvard University 1992.

Christides V. (1984), *The Conquest of Crete by the Arabs (ca. 824). A Turning Point in the Struggle between Byzantium and Islam*. Athens.

A Companion to Byzantine Italy, *see Cosentino*.

Cosentino, Salvatore (2021), *A Companion to Byzantine Italy*, ed. Salvatore Cosentino, Brill Leiden and Boston.

(2018), 'Naval Warfare: Military, Institutional and Economic Aspects' in *Companion to the Byzantine Culture of War, ca.300–1204*, Vol.3, ed. Wolfram Brandes and Yannis Stouraitis. Leiden and Boston, pp. 308–55.

Dagron, Gilbert, *see De velitatione*.

Dain, Alphonse:

(1967), 'Les Stratégistes Byzantins', *TM 2 (1967)* , the text completed by J.-A. de Foucault, 317–392.

(1946), *L'Histoire du texte d'Elien le Tacticien des origins a la fin du moyen age*, Thèse pour le Doctorat èt lettres, Université de Paris. Paris.

D'Amato, Raffaele (2012), *Byzantine Imperial Guardsmen 925–1025. The Tághmata and Imperial Guard*. Oxford.

Dawson, Timothy:

(2007), *Byzantine Infantryman, Eastern Roman Empire c.900–1204*, Oxford.

(2002), 'Suntagma Hoplôn: The Equipment of Regular Byzantine Troops, c.950 to c.1204', in *Companion to Medieval Arms and Armour*, ed. by David Nicolle, Suffolk and Rochester, 2002, 81–90 with the illustrations VII.1–13.

Dennis, G.T.:

(2014), *The Taktika of Leo VI*, text. tr. and commentary by George T. Dennis, revised edition, Washington D.C.

(1985), *Three Byzantine Military Treatises*, CFHB XXV, Washington DC.

(1984), *Maurice's Strategicon. Handbook of Byzantine Military Strategy*, English tr. by G.T.Dennis, Philadelphia.

(1981), *Das Strategikon des Maurikios*, CFHB XVII, Vienna 1981, edited by G.T. Dennis and German tr. by Ernst Gamillscheg.

Eickhoff, Ekkehard, (1966), *Seekrieg und Seepolitik zwichen Islam und Abenland. Das Mittelmeer unter byzantinischer und arabischer Hegemonie (650–1040)*, Berlin 1966.

Forsythe, John Harper (1977), *The Byzantine-Arab Chronicle (938–1034) of Yahya b. Sa'I al-Antaki*, The University f Michigan, Ph.D. 1977, History, Medieval.

Franklin Simon and Shepard Jonathan (1995), *The Emergence of the Rus 750–1200.* London and New York.

Gay, Jules (1904), *L'Italie meriodale et l'empire byzantin depuis l'avenement de Basile Ier jusqu'à la prise de Bari par les normands (867–1071).* Paris.

Grosse, R. (1912), 'Das römisch-byzantinische Marschlager vom 4.-10. Jahrhundert', *BZ22*, 90–121.

Haldon, John F.:

(2021), *The De Thematibus ('on the themes') of Constantine VII Porphyrogenitus*, English tr. by John Haldon, Liverpool (2021).

(2014), *A Critical Commentary on the Taktika of Leo VI*, Washington D.C.

(2008), 'Structures and Administration', in *The Oxford Handbook of Byzantine Studies*, eds. E. Jeffreys, J. Haldon, and R. Cormack, 539–553.

(2000), 'Theory and Practice in the Tenth-Century Military Administration. Chapters II, 44 and 45 of the Book of Ceremonies'. in *TM 13* (2000), 201–392.

(1990), *Constantine Porphyrogenitus, Three Treatises on Imperial Military Expeditions, Introduction, Edition, Translation and Commentary by John F. Haldon*, CFHB XXVIII, Wien (Vienna).

(1984), *Byzantine Praetorians: an Administrative, Institutional and Social Survey of the Opsikion and Tagmata, c.580–900*, Poikila Byzantina 3. Bonn.

Haldon J. and Kennedy H. (1980), 'The Arab-Byzantine Frontier in the Eight and Ninth Centuries: Military Organization and Society in the Borderlands', in *ZRVI 19*, 79–116.

Hamblin, William James (1985), *The Fatimid Army During the Early Crusades*, Ph.D dissertation, University of Michigan.

Hendy M.F. (1985), *Studies in the Byzantine Monetary Economy c.300–1450.* Cambridge.

Hocker, Frederick M, 'Late Roman, Byzantine, and Islamic Galleys and Fleets', in *The Age of Galley*, 86–100.

Howard-Johnston, J.D. (1983), 'Byzantine Anzitene', in *Armies and Frontiers in Roman and Byzantine Anatolia*, ed. S. Mitchell, BAE International Series 156, Oxford (1983), 239–90.

Hupchick, Dennis P. (2017), *The Bulgarian-Byzantine Wars for Early Medieval Balkan Hegemony. Silver-Lined Skulls and Blinded Armies.* Springer Int. Publishing.

Kaldellis, Anthony (2017/2019), *Streams of Gold, Rivers of Blood.* Oxford.

Kindi, al-, *Medieval Islamic Swords and Swordmaking: Kindi's Treatise 'On Swords and their Kinds'*, tr. and commentary by R.G. Hoyland and B.J.J. Gilmour. Warminster 2006.

Konstam, Angus (2015), *Byzantine Warship vs Arab Warship 7th–[11]th [ce]nturies.* Oxford.

Kühn, Hans-Joachim (1991), *Die byzantinischen Armee im 10. und 11. Jahrhundert. Studien zur Organization der Tagmata.* Wien (Vienna).

Latham, J. Derek (1979), 'Towards a Better Understanding of al-Mutanabbi's Poem on the Battle of al-Hadath', in *Journal of Arabic Literature 10*, 1–22.

Lev, Yaacov:

(1984), 'The Fatimid Navy, Byzantium and the Mediterranean Sea 909–1036 C.E./297–427 A.H.', in *Byzantion 54.1*, 220–52.

(1987), 'Army, Regime, and Society in Fatimid Egypt, 358–487/968–1094', in *Middle Eastern Studies 19*, 337–66.

Lilie et al. = Lilie Ralph-Johannes, Claudia Ludwig, Beate Zielke and Thomas Pratsch, 'Abu l-Fawaris Muhammad b. Nasiraddawla', in the *PMBZ*.

Loud, G.A. (2008), 'Southern Italy in the tenth century', in *NCMH 3*, 624–45.

Al-Mallah, M.,

Ode on the the Reconquest of al-Hadath by al-Mutanabbi with commentary at *encyclopedia. com*.
(2009), 'A Victory Celebration after a Military Defeat? Al-Mutanabbi's Ayniyyah of 339/950', *Journal of Arabic Literature 40*, 107–28.
Mantia, Salvatore La (2008), *Il Dromone (VII–X secolo) Ipotesi Ricostruttiva*. (includes original sources).
McGeer, Eric:
(2000), *The Land Legislation of the Macedonian Emperors*, English translation, introduction and notes by E. McGeer, *Medieval Sources in Translation 38*. PIMS Toronto.
(1995), *Sowing the Dragon's Teeth: Byzantine Warfare in the Tenth Century*, Dumbarton Oaks, Washington D.C. (1995), *Dumbarton Oaks Studies 33*. Contains the tenth-century military manual *Praecepta militaria* of Nikêforos Fôkas and chapters 56–65 of the *Taktika* of Nikêforos Ouranos.
(1992), 'The Syntaxis armatorum quadrata: a Tenth-Century Tactical Blueprint', in *REB 50*, 219–29.
McMahon, Lucas (2025?), "Strangling Antioch: a spatial approach to conquest," in *"The Sword of the Faith" Nikephoros Phokas and His Time*, ed. Georgios Theotokis and Mamuka Tsurtsumia (Leiden: Brill, forthcoming). Draft version kindly provided for author by McMahon in advance of publication.
Metcalfe, Alex (2009), *The Muslims of Medieval Italy*. Edinburgh.
MHLR = see Syvänne, *Military History of Late Rome vols. 1–8*.
Mihsin, Dmitrij (1998), 'The Saqāliba in the Aghlabid State', in *The Annual of Medieval Studies at the Central European University 1996–7*, 236–44.
Mohsen, Zakeri (1995), *Sasanid Soldiers in Early Muslim Society. The Origins of Ayyaran and Futuwwa*, Wiesbaden.
Moravcsik, Gyula (1970), *Byzantium and the Magyars*. Budapest.
Morris, Rosemary, "The two faces of Nikephoros Phokas", in *BMGS 12* (1988) 83–115.
Nef, Annliese (2021), 'Byzantium and Islam in Southern Italy (7th-11th Century)', in Cosentino, pp.200–24.
Nicolle, David:
(2005), *Carolingian Cavalryman AD 768–987*. Oxford.
(1999), *Armies of Medieval Russia 750–1250*. Oxford.
Nicolle, David & Mikhail Zhironov (2019), *The Khazars*. Oxford.
Nicolle, David & Viacheslav Shapakovsky (2013), *The Armies of the Volga Bulgars & Khanate of Kazan*. Oxford.
ODB = *Oxford Dictionary of Byzantium* (1991), A. P. Kazhdan, A-M. Talbot, A. Cutler, T.E. Gregory, N.P. Ševčenko, 3 vols. Oxford.
Ory, S. (1986), 'al-Hadath', in *The Encyclopaedia of Islam. New Edition*. Vol.3, 19–20, Leiden and London.
Personnaz, Charles (2013), *L'empereur Nicéphore Phocas. Byzance face à l'Islam 912–969*. Paris.
PMBZ = *Prosopographie der mittelbyzantinischen Zeit Online*, Berlin, Boston: De Gruyter 2013 (www.degruyter.com).
Polemis, Demetrios I. (1968), *The Doukai. A Contribution to Byzantine Prosopography*. London.
Prigent, Vivien, 'Byzantine Administration and Army', in *A Companion to Byzantine Italy*, ed. Salvatore Cosentino, Brill Leiden and Boston 2021, pp. 140–68.

Pryor J.H. and Jeffreys E.M. (2006), *The Age of Dromôn*. Leiden and Boston.
Pryor, John H: *see also The Age of Dromon*
    (1982), 'Transportation of Horses by Sea during the Era of the Crusades: Eighth Century to 1285 A.D., Part I: to c.1225', *Mariner's Mirror 68.1 (1982)*, 9–27. 'Part II: 1228–1285', *Mariner's Mirror 68.2 (1982)*, 103–125.
    (1995a) 'From Dromōn to Galea: Mediterranean bireme galleys AD 500–1300', in *The Age of Galley*, 1995,101–116.
    (1995b), 'The Geographical Conditions of Galley Navigation in the Mediterranean', in *The Age of Galley*, 1995, 206–216.
RFNF = *The Rise and Fall of Nikephoros II Phokas. Five Contemporary Texts in Annotated Translations, Byzantina Australiensia 23*, tr. by Denis Sullivan. Leiden/Boston (2019).
Runciman, Steven
    (1930), *A History of the First Bulgarian Empire*. Cambridge.
    (1929), *The Emperor Romanus Lecapenus*, Cambridge.
SCC = *Science and Civilization in China*, 2 vols. Needham et al. Cambridge 1986.
Schlumberger, Gustave (1890), *Un empereur byzantine au dixième siècle Nicéphore Phocas*. Paris.
    (1896), *Le Epopée Byzantine. Vol. 1*. Paris.
Seibt, Werner (1976), *Die Skleroi. Eine prosopographisch-sigillographische Studie*. Wien (Vienna).
Sinclair T. (1983), 'Byzantine and Islamic Fortifications in the Middle East – Photographic Exhibition', in *Armies and Frontiers in Roman and Byzantine Anatolia*, ed. S. Mitchell, BAE International Series 156, Oxford (1983), 305–36.
Spanu, Pier, Giorgio, 'Byzantine Sardinia', in *A Companion to Byzantine Italy*, pp.496–521.
Stephenson, Paul (2002), *Byzantium's Balkan Frontier. A Political Study of the Northern Balkans, 900–1204*. Cambridge.
Stokes, A.D. (1962), 'The Balkan Campaigns of Svyatoslav Igorevich', in *The Slavonic and East European Review 40.95*, 466–96.
Sullivan, Denis, *see RFNF, Heron, De obsidione*
Suny, Ronald, Grigor (1994), *The Making of the Georgian Nation*. Bloomington and Indianapolis.
Syvänne, Ilkka:
    (2024), (LRCT), *Late Roman Combat Tactics*. Barnsley.
    (2023a), *Emperor Septimius Severus. The Roman Hannibal*. Barnsley.
    (2015–2022), *Military History of Late Rome, vols. 1–8*. Pen and Sword. Barnsley.
        (2022b) *MHLR* Vol.8 (602–641)
        (2022a) *MHLR* Vol.7 (565–602)
        (2021c) *MHLR* Vol.6 (518–565)
        (2020e) *MHLR* Vol.5 (457–518)
        (2020d) *MHLR* Vol.4 (425–457)
        (2020c) *MHLR* Vol.3 (395–425)
        (2018) *MHLR* Vol. 2 (361–395)
        (2015) *MHLR* Vol.1 (284–361)
    (2021b), 'The Three Hephthalite Wars of Peros 574/5–484', *Historia i Swiat 10*, 96–116.
    (2021a), *Gordian II and Philip the Arab*. Barnsley.

(2020b), 'Holy War and a Place in Paradise? Development of the East Roman Holy War from the 4th until the 11th Century', written with the generous support of the ASMEA Research Grant.
(2020a), *Aurelian and Probus. The Soldier Emperors Who Saved Rome*. Barnsley.
(2019c), *The Reign of Emperor Gallienus. The Apogee of Roman Cavalry*. Barnsley.
(2019b), *Britain in the Age of Arthur. A Military History*. Barnsley.
(2019a), 'The Capture of Jerusalem by the Muslims', *Historia i Swiat 8*, 37–58. Written with the generous support of the ASMEA Travel Grant.
(2017b), 'Parthian Cataphract vs. the Roman Army 53 BC–AD 224', in *Historia i Swiat 2017*.
(2017a), *Caracalla. A Military Biography*. Barnsley. Paperback ed. 2022 with some changes.
(2016), 'The Eyes and Ears: The Sasanian and Roman Spies AD 224–450', *Historia i Swiat 2016*, Based on research paper of *The 8th ASMEA Conference*, Washington DC, 2015. Written with the generous support of the ASMEA Research Grant.
(2015), A Research paper, 'East Roman Naval Warfare and the Military Treatises 641–1071', 2015 *McMullen Naval History Symposium, Annapolis*, MD, USA.
(2014), 'Persia, la caida de un imperio', in *Desperta Ferro 24*, Julio 2014.
(2013c), 'las campañas de Belisario contra los Sasánidas', in *Desperta Ferro 18*.
(2013b), 'Byzantine Military Doctrine', in *Philosophers of War*, 2vols. eds. D. Coetzee and L.W. Eysturlid, Praeger, 331–8.
(2013a), 'Arrian, Governor of Cappadocia, Lucius Flavius Arrianus (Arrianos) Xenophon', in *Philosophers of War*, 2 vols. eds. D. Coetzee and L.W. Eysturlid, Praeger, 259–63.
(2012), 'La batalla Liegnitz 1241', in *Desperta Ferro 12*.
(2011–2), 'East Roman Cavalry Warfare and Tactics 410–641', three parts (based on a lecture) in *Slingshot 279* (Nov. 2011), *280* (Jan. 2012), and *281* (March 2012).
(2011c), 'The Reign of Decius 249–251', in *Slingshot* May 2011, 2–8.
(2011a-b), An enlarged version of the research paper 'Campaigns of Germanicus, 13–16 AD', *Historicon 2011*. Available online at academia.edu. A research paper 'Campaigns of Germanicus, 14–16 AD', *6th International Fields of Conflict Conference, 15th–18th April 2011 in Osnabrück and Kalkriese*.
(2010), 'Macedonian Art of War. The Balkans 335 BC, Granicus River 334 BC, and Gaugamela 331 BC', in *Saga Newsletter 123*, 31–99.
(2009c), 'Teutoburg Forest 9 AD', in *Saga Newsletter 119* June 2009, 9–23.
(2009b), 'The Battle of Melitene in AD 576', in *Saga Newsletter 120* Aug./Sept. 2009, 32–64.
(2009a), 'The Campaign and Battle of Sambre in 57 BC', in *Saga Newsletter 117* March 2009, 5–16.
(2008), 'The New cavalry Formations in the Sylloge Tacticorum, AD 904', in *Saga Newsletter 112*, republished in *Slingshot 291*, 2014. Available online at academia.edu with additional comments.
(2004), *The Age of Hippotoxotai*. Tampere.
Tabula Imperii Byzantini (TIB), several writers, Vienna 1976.
Takirtakoglou, Kônstantinos (2015), "oi polemoi metaxu tou Nikêforou Fôka kai tôn Arabôn," in *Byzantina Symmeikta 25*, 57–114.

Theotokis, Georgios (2018), *Byzantine Military Tactics in Syria and Mesopotamia in the Tenth Century. A Comparative Study.* Edinburgh.
Treadgold, Warren:
  (1997), *History of the Byzantine State and Society*, Stanford.
  (1995), *Byzantium and Its Army 284–1081*, Stanford (1995).
  (1992), 'The Army in the Works of Constantine Porphyrogenitus', in *Rivista di Studi Bizantini e Neoellenici 29*, 77–162.
  (1980), 'Notes on the Numbers and Organization of the Ninth-Century Byzantine Army', in *GRBS 21*, 269–88.
Vannier, J.F. (1975), *Familles byzantines: Les Argyroi, IXe–XIIe siècles.* Paris.
Vasiliev A.A. (1936), *The Goths in the Crimea.* Cambridge, Mass.
Vernadsky, George (Third ed. 1959), *Kievan Russia*, New Haven.
Zuckerman Constantin (2015), 'On the Byzantine Dromon (With a Special Regard to De. Cerim. II, 44–45)', in *REB 73*, 57–98.

Nikêforos receiving envoys of Tarsus. (*Skylitzes, public domain*)

Index

Abdila, *patrikios, katepanô*, 342
Abu-l-Ma'li, *see* Hamdanids, Saad
Abydos, city of, 24–5, 266, 475
abydykos (pl. *abydykoi*), originally the title of the *archon-komês* of the city of Abydos who controlled the sea traffic through the Hellespont. The title *abydykoi* was later extended to cover other regional *komêtes-archontoi*, 4, 18, 25, 475
Adana, city in Cilicia, xii, xxviii, 73, 98, 174, 182–4, 212, 273, 275–6, 383
Adata, al-Hadath, Hadata, Hadat, xii–xiii, xxviii, 132, 149–55, 162, 164, 166–77, 182, 188–9, 199–200, 204, 212, 248, 282, 285–6, 300, 400, 507
Aelian, Ailianos, Aelianus Tacticus,
  Aelian's *Taktika* and its *Byzantine Interpolation* and *Syntaxis armatorum quadrata* (SAQ), xvi, 47, 64, 102, 366–9, 371, 373, 420, 439, 512, 514, 519, 523
  see also Polybios
  Arabic translation, Gotha, Nihayat, 451–2, 460, 465–8, 478, 512–13, 516
Aghlabids, emirate of, 72, 91–3, 481, 523
agrarion (pl. *agraria*), a barge, in this book often the imperial red and black barges, 27–8, 53
akolouthia, 'succession', a liturgical rite for a new saint, 346, 514
akolouthos (follower, *pl. akolouthoi*), a liaison officer of the *bigla/arithmoi* assigned to the entourage of the emperor, an officer in charge of the foreigners in the *tagma* of *arithmoi* who later became the commander of the Varangian Guard, 12, 28
akritai, *see* Hussars
Aleppo, city and emirate of, xiii, 83, 88–9, 114, 116, 120–1, 124, 126–7, 132–4, 136–7, 143–4, 156, 162–6, 174, 177, 181, 184, 189, 195, 198–200, 202, 205, 210–12, 239, 241–2, 247–8, 250, 252–8, 260–1, 263, 271–2, 290, 296, 300–304, 306, 313, 332, 336–9, 380, 382–3, 484, 495–7, 499, 504, 507, 516
  see also Hamdanids, Mosul
allagion (pl. *allagia*), a unit of ca. 50 to 400 men, the equivalent of *arithmos, bandon* and *tagma*, 33, 438, 511
Alptekin, Turkish *ghilman* commander, 189
Amalfi, duchy, 58, 118, 329
Ambush, ambuscade, ambushers, xiii, 13–14, 36–7, 40, 42, 55, 61, 63–4, 74, 77, 80, 87, 89–90, 93, 113, 120, 144–5, 148–50, 159–60, 163, 171, 200, 207, 226, 228, 234–5, 238–9, 275, 279, 287, 304, 341, 355, 358, 360, 365, 377, 386, 388–90, 392–400, 404, 410, 413, 415, 424, 437, 444, 447–50, 456–8, 460–4, 478, 485–6, 493, 508–509, 512
  enedroi (*tôn egkrymmatôn tagmata* = hidden *tagmata*), 37, 76–7, 81, 360–1, 364
  see also Drouggos, Guerrilla, *Prokoursatôres*, Stratagem, Surprise attacks
Amida, xii, xxxv, 115, 143, 155–6, 158–60, 163–4, 178, 181, 198–9, 202–206, 211, 302, 331–3
Anastasios, Anastasius,
  Anastasios I, emperor, 12, 23, 472
  Anastasios Goggylios, *see* Goggylês
Anazarbos/Anazarba, city of, xiii, 150, 239, 241–7, 250, 276, 284, 496
anthrôpoi, *see basilikoi anthrôpoi*
Antioch, city and emirate of, xii, xxviii, xxxvii, 88, 120, 124, 127, 131, 138, 142, 144, 185, 238, 252–4, 287–90, 296, 300–301, 303–304, 313–14, 317, 332–3, 336–40, 343, 380, 382–3, 470, 500–501, 504, 523
apelatai, *see* Hussars
aplêkton (pl. *aplekta*), a fortified camp; an assembly point for the armies and supplies in the *themata*; logistical depot/supply dumb; billeting of troops, 78–80, 144–5, 200, 276
Arabissos, 120, 143, 156, 248
arabitai, *see* Bedouin

archêgetês, overall commander of infantry, same as *oplitarchês*, 32
archêgos, admiral or commander, 24, 395
Archers, *toxotai*, xi, 37, 41, 43, 60–1, 63, 69–70, 74–5, 89–90, 93, 102, 137, 152, 170–1, 181, 216, 219, 223, 227, 229, 253, 270, 285–6, 331, 356–60, 366, 371, 383, 403, 405–407, 409–11, 414, 417, 419–20, 422, 424, 426–8, 432, 434, 437, 440, 442–3, 446, 449, 452, 457–8, 463, 468, 478, 480, 489, 496, 498, 509–10, 512, 514, 519
see also Javelineers, *psiloi*, Slingers
archôn, a commander holding a command (*archê*) who could be ruler of a foreign country or commander of a detachment of guardsmen in the Imperial Palace (*archon* of the Pantheon) or a commander in charge of the defence and commercial activity of a section of the coast or just a leader of some sort (e.g. of the *demes*, Cherson, *foideratoi*), 4, 19–21, 25, 27, 62, 67, 81, 107, 129, 166, 174, 184, 227, 229, 267, 311, 470, 472, 475, 479, 492
see also *abydykos*
archôntogennematai (the sons of the officers), imperial bodyguards, 21, 27, 107
Argyros Family, Argyroi, 97, 482, 526
   Leôn Argyros, 118
   Marianos Argyros, *patrikios*, *komes tou staulou*, *monostratêgos tês Macedonias* and *katepanô tês dyseôs*, usurper, 118–20, 122, 191–4, 196, 213, 238, 264–7, 310, 490–1, 496
   Pothos Argyros, *patrikios* and *domestikos* of the *exkoubitoi*, 197–8, 208, 310
   Rômanos Argyros, husband of Agatha Lakapêna, 118
arithmos 1 (pl. *arithmoi*), the Watch, an imperial *tagma* also called *bigla* and *arithmoi*, xiv, 11–12, 20–2, 24, 26, 28–9, 81–3, 101, 119, 122, 197, 212, 346, 432–4, 437, 471–2, 474, 480
arithmos 2 (pl. *arithmoi*), a unit of ca. 50 to 400 men, the equivalent of *allagion*, *bandon* and *tagma* or of unspecified infantry units, 23, 472, 474
Armenia, Armenians, Armenian soldiers, small Armenian *themata/kleisurai*, King of Armenia, xii, 1, 14, 19, 67–9, 73–4, 79, 83–4, 86, 88–9, 92, 96–8, 107, 119, 127, 130, 132–3, 138, 145, 147, 150, 163, 166–7, 229–30, 232–3, 239–40, 246, 248, 265, 271–3, 280–1, 288, 294, 297, 300, 308–10,
320, 322, 350, 382, 410, 418, 480, 483, 485, 495–6, 501, 503, 507, 517
   Armeniakon *thema*, 10, 78–9, 98, 107, 130, 145, 147, 150, 265, 271, 485
   see also Bagratuni, Georgia, Karin, Martyropolis, Manzikert, Melitene, Taron
Arsamosata, Simsat, Shimsat, 84–5, 163, 178, 232
Arqanin (mod. Ergani/Arghana, south of Arghana Maden), HQ of *thema*, 159, 161, 163, 178
Arzen, 86, 115, 332
aspidoforoi (*aspidoforos*), shield-bearer, 354–6, 366, 373–5, 383, 418
Assassinations, assassins, murder, poison, 26, 64, 75, 82, 143, 166, 207, 262, 294, 302, 319, 339, 343–7, 430, 504–506
Athanasios/Athanasius the Athonite, Saint, xi, xvi, 216, 218, 222, 232, 297–9, 493, 505, 517
Atzypotheodôros, a friend of Tzimiskês, 344, 346–7
Augoustos, Augustus, 'August', emperor, 1, 27, 319–20, 323, 326, 479
Augousta, Augusta, empress, 1, 27–8, 103
autokratôr, a person with complete control of all matters, i.e. the emperor, 215, 263, 292
axiomatikos, (pl. *axiomatikoi*), junior officers among the *scholai*, the equivalents of the earlier *centenarii* and *ducenarii*, 12
Azaz, 252–4

Bagras, Baghras, Bagrai, Pagrai, Black Mountain, fortress of, xii, xxxiv, 120, 337
Baghdad, capital of the Abbasid caliphs and of one branch of the Buyid sultans, 68, 71–2, 85–6, 90–1, 115–16, 124, 133, 190, 196, 199, 202, 238, 240, 261, 275, 280, 300–301, 306
Bagratuni, Bagratids, Bagrationi, (Ashot IV, Ashot V, Abas, Gagik I), 67–9, 86, 480, 496, 501
   see also Armenia, Georgia, Karin, Martyropolis, Manzikert, Melitene, Taron
Balis, 256–7, 303, 332
bandoforos (pl. *bandoforoi*), a flag-bearer carrying *bandon*-flag (rectangular or square in shape terminating in smaller pointed streamers called *flamoulae*), 12, 360
bandofylakes, flag-guards and *defensôres* (defenders/bodyguards) of the *stratêgos*,

77, 171, 354, 360, 363, 365–6, 373–4, 406, 490, 506
bandon (pl. *banda*), 'a flag', a unit of ca. 50 to 400 men, the equivalent of *allagion*, *arithmos*, and *tagma*, 26, 32–3, 35–7, 40, 77, 82, 168–9, 171, 174, 387, 410–11, 432, 438, 472, 489, 508–509, 511
Bardas, *see* Fôkades, Skleroi
Basileios, Basil,
  Basileios I–II, *see* Macedonian Dynasty
  Basileios *parakoimômemos*, *see* Lakapênos
  Basileios Examilitês, probably to be identified with Basileios *prôtokarabos*, xiv, 183–4, 192, 339
  Basileios *prôtokarabos*, 184–5, 192, 195, 491
  Basileios Peteinos, *prôtospatharios*, *patrikios*, *magistros*, *megas etaiarchês*, 118–20, 122, 214
  Basileios of Rhodes, 161–2
  Basil the Younger, Saint, 105, 107, 109–12, 116, 482
  Basil the Great, Saint, 295
basileus, 'King', the official title of the emperor since Heraclius, 1, 22, 28, 323, 331, 340–2
Basilissa, 'Queen', means empress, 1, 28
Basilika dromônia, basilikodromônion, basilikon dromônion, basilika agraria, the emperor's two *dromônia* (war galleys) and the two *agraria* (barges) of the empress, and their crews, 16, 21, 27–8, 53, 106, 477, 480
basilikê etaireia, *see* etaireia
Basilikoi anthrôpoi / basilikoi ('imperial men'), it is possible that some of these were bearded *spatharioi* protecting the emperor's bedroom, 13, 21, 25–7, 80–1, 83, 209, 432–3, 475, 511
Basilikou ploimou / Basilikoploimon, Imperial Fleet, 4–5, 13, 15–18, 20, 23–5, 28, 31, 97, 99–100, 104, 106, 113, 119, 122–3, 141, 183, 209, 213, 215, 282, 288, 346, 470, 473–4
Battle, battles, battle formation, battlefield, vii, xi, xiii, 14, 33, 36–7, 40–3, 55–6, 60–1, 63–4, 70, 74, 76–8, 81, 83, 85, 87, 90, 93, 99, 109, 127, 129, 136, 149, 153, 157, 159–60, 162, 186–7, 189, 191, 197, 223–4, 226, 238, 247, 290, 292, 301–302, 308–309, 312–13, 316, 319, 337, 350–1, 353–78, 384, 387–9, 395, 397, 401, 403, 405–28, 430, 432, 440–2, 445, 448, 450, 452, 456–68, 479–80, 485, 488–90, 492–4, 497, 508, 512–13, 521, 525

Some important Roman battles:
  Abdila vs Germans in 969, 342
  Acheloos/Achelaus in August 917, 99
  Adana in 964, 273–5
  Adata/Germanikeia, passes of in 950, xiii, 148–55
    see also al-Kankarun
  Adata/Hadath in 954, xiii, 127, 164, 166–76, 189, 285–6, 484, 489, 507, 522
  Adrassos, Adrassus in 960, xiii, 233–7
  Aleppo in 962, xiii, 250–7, 260
  Anazarbos in 961, 242–5
  Anazarbos in 962, 246–7
  Baqsaya or Darb al-Hayyatin (Pass of Tailors or Lady's Suit) in 956, 179–81
  Basileios Examilites vs Tarsus, Hamdanids and Jihadists in a naval battle on the coast of Lycia in autumn 956, 177, 181–4
  Basileios *parakoimômenos* vs Sayf ad-Dawla in 959, 201–204
  Chandax (A) in 960, 219–22
  Chandax (B) in 960, 223–4
  Chandax (C) in 960, 224
  Chandax (D) in 960, 225–6
  Crete (A) Karamountes vs Pastilas in 960–1, 228
  Crete (B) Nikêforos Fôkas vs Karamountes in 960–1, 228–9
  Charsianon 1 (950), 144–6, 149–50
  Charsianon 2 (952), 160
  Charsianon 3 (956), 182–4
  Charsianon 4 (960), 233
  Cyprus in 965, Egyptian fleet destroyed, 289
  Germanikeia in 949, 136, 138, 485–6
  Germanikeia/Adata, passes of in 950, *see* Adata
  Germanikeia in 952, 159–61
  Germanikeia on 25 July 953, 163–5
  Foinikia in Crete in 960, 222–3
  Iôannês Kourkouas vs Sayf ad-Dawla in 938, 85–6
  Iôannês Kourkouas vs Sayf ad-Dawla in 940, 86–7
  Iôannês Tzimiskês vs Naga al-Kasaki in 959, 198–200
  Katasyrtai in 917, 99
  al-Kankarun in 950 (formed a part of the battle of the passes of Adata/Germanikeia), xiii, 151–4
    see also Adata/Germanikeia
  Khorasanis vs Romans in 967, 313
  Lechfeld in 955, 129, 176, 490, 521

Leôn Fôkas vs Hungarians in 960, 232, 495
Lykos Valley/River (950), xiii, 145–9, 487
Petros vs Hungarians in ca. 967, 292
Poson in 863, 471
Rametta/Rometta in 964, 278–80
Reggio (naval battle) in 965, 282
Romans vs Fatimids in Sicily in 952, 161
Romans vs Fatimids in Sicily in 957, 191
Romans vs Fatimids (naval battles) in 958, 193–6
Romans vs Russians on land in September 941, 109, 111–12
Romans vs Russians at sea in 941 (at Hieron and then on the coast of the Black Sea), 109–110, 112
Tarsus in 965, xiii, 285–7, 296, 440, 489, 499
Tarsus (coast of Cilicia-Syria) in 965, Egyptian fleet destroyed, 288
Tebeste in 544, 488
see also Guerrilla
Bedouins, *arabitai*, Banu, xi, 84, 89–90, 92, 115, 162, 177–8, 199, 203–204, 207, 231, 252, 254, 257, 284–5, 290, 299, 301–302, 391, 407, 410, 416, 424, 426, 463
Beirut, garrisoned by Romans in 968(?), 333, 335
Berengar II of Ivrea, King of Italy, 59, 113, 125, 141, 201, 318–19, 323
bigla, see arithmos 1
Blacks, Black-African slave troops ('Negroes'), *Zanj*, Nubians, Sudanese, Ethiopians, Indian, slave troops in Muslim service, xv, 23, 71, 74–5, 92–3, 157, 181, 225, 231, 290, 299, 338, 466, 471
see also *ghilman*, *saqaliba*
Black Sea, 25, 67, 110–11, 113, 117, 266, 312, 314–15
Booty, spoils of war, 5, 62, 73, 85, 110, 121, 132, 156, 160–1, 163, 165, 181, 186, 188, 192, 197–8, 204, 211–12, 227, 230, 236–7, 246, 250, 257–8, 263, 272, 280, 288, 313–14, 335–9, 341, 393–4, 425, 488
see also Slaves
Bulgaria, Bulgarians, xii, xv, xxxix, 19, 40, 45, 61–5, 67, 71, 97–9, 103–105, 113, 116–17, 166–7, 175, 193–8, 200–201, 210, 215, 232, 238, 264, 292–3, 296, 300, 307, 310–18, 320–1, 326, 328–9, 344, 350, 410, 429, 431, 434, 446, 500, 502–503, 505, 521–2, 524
Boris II, son of Peter I, 264, 317, 502

Peter I, tsar of Bulgaria (927–69), 62, 103, 197, 264, 292–3, 310, 315, 317, 325, 500, 502
Rômanos, son of Peter I, 264, 317, 502
Symeon, Simeon, tsar of Bulgaria, 97–8, 103, 116, 292, 321, 326, 502
Volga Bulgars, 61, 65–6, 312, 478, 523
Burgundy, 59, 103
Buyids, Buwayhids, Buwaihids, emirs and sultans, 68, 71, 116, 124–5, 133, 189–90, 196, 198–9, 201–202, 238–40, 272, 280–1, 290, 304, 306, 480, 521
see also Aleppo, Baghdad, Daylami, Egypt, Fatimids, *Ghilman*, Hamdanids, Mosul

Cappadocia, Cappadocian, Kappadokia, xii, xxii, 9–10, 79, 88, 96–8, 100–102, 107–108, 114, 122, 127, 132, 136, 143–5, 147, 187, 233, 238, 264, 276, 284, 298, 379, 400, 481, 525
see also *Themata*/Kappadokia
cataphract, see *katafraktoi*
chartoularios (pl. *chartoularioi*), senior administrator in charge of entire administration of the imperial *tagma* including its enlistment and payments. When the commander of the imperial *tagma* was absent, he served as second-in-command for the *topotêrêtês*, 12, 27
chaganus, khagan, *chagan*, khan, prince/ruler of nomadic/semi-nomadic groupings like the Khazars and also of some settled peoples like Russians, 61–2, 66, 312, 486, 523
Chandax (Heraklion/Iraklion), x, 142, 216, 218–19, 221–4, 227, 229–30, 298, 517
chandax, trench, 428
chelandion, *ousiakon chelandion* (pl. *chelandia*), a galley with an *ousia* (108 or 110 men) of rowers; a small *dromôn*. The increased use of the flame-thrower *chelandia* instead of the larger vessels may have been a reform of Rômanos I Lakapênos, 16–18, 24, 28, 51, 94, 106, 110, 113, 141–2, 216, 218, 288, 327, 473
Cherson, see *Themata*/Kherson
Christianity, Church, Theotokos, Saints, Relic, Bible, vii, x–xi, 1, 3–4, 6, 61–4, 67–9, 73, 79–80, 84, 97, 102, 105, 107, 109–13, 115–16, 128–9, 145, 156, 161–2, 166, 181, 185, 191, 214, 222–3, 230–3, 236, 250, 258, 261, 263, 265–7, 269–70, 281, 288–9, 294, 296–300, 302, 304, 308–10, 316, 319, 322,

326–7, 332, 334–7, 342, 344, 348–9, 351–2, 404, 470, 481–2, 487, 496, 501, 503–505
  see also Athanasios, Monastery, Monophysite
Christoforos Lakapênos, see Lakapenoi
Christoforos, Patriarch of Antioch, 304
Christoforos *patrikios*, eunuch, 330–1
Cilicia, Kilikia, Cilicia-Syria, xiv, 9, 71, 73, 79, 88, 92–3, 116, 127, 133, 136, 142–5, 150, 174, 182, 212, 222, 242, 246, 273, 276, 281, 285, 290, 293, 312, 318, 337, 339, 350, 382–4, 400, 406, 484, 502
  see also Adana, Antioch, Mopsuestia, Tarsus
Comes, count, see *Komês*
Convex formation, 55, 183, 456, 459, 462–4
Crescent unit order and formation, 36, 55, 149, 159, 168, 170–1, 174, 456–60, 462–4, 467
Crete, Cretan, island and Arab emirate of, x, xii–xiv, xxxii, 11, 16–17, 53, 71–2, 132–4, 139–41, 186, 193–5, 204, 207, 212–32, 235, 237, 241–2, 252–3, 261, 263, 298, 339, 466, 472, 474, 477–8, 486, 490, 494–6, 505–506, 520–1
Croatia, Croats, 15, 60, 62, 64–5
Cyprus, island and province of, 25, 72, 139, 215, 282, 289–90, 339, 474

Damascus, city, 47, 116, 124, 127, 275, 300, 333, 336–7, 504
Dara, 87, 115, 206, 302
Daylami, Dailami, Dilemnites, tribesmen and mercenaries, 69, 71, 84, 89, 92, 116, 124, 163, 189–90, 198–9, 231, 255, 258–9, 280, 290, 480
  see also ghilman
Dazimon, *aplêkton*, 78, 82, 145–6
deêseos, secretary of the pleas, 28
defensôres/defensores, see *difensôres*
dekanos (pl. *dekanoi*), *dekarchos* (*dekarchoi*), *dekarchês* (*dekarchai*) commander of ten men, 26, 31–2
demokratês (pl. *demokratai*), title of the demarch of the factions or of the Domestics of the Schools and *Excubitores* when in command of the men of the demes probably in military capacity, 30
demarchos tôn Benetôn, Demarch of the Blue Circus Faction/Demes, 30
demarchos tôn Prasinôn, Demarch of the Blue Circus Faction/Demes, 30

Demes (Circus Factions): Blues with Whites and Greens with Reds, 13, 20, 24, 28, 30, 266–7, 270, 324–5, 472, 475
Deserters, 84, 223, 225–8, 230, 254, 389, 425, 449, 504, 512
  see also Spy, Stratagem
diatrechon (pl. *diatrechontes*), messengers and fighters of the *arithmoi/bigla*, 12
difensôres (sing. *difensôr*, spelling used in LT), (older spelling: *defensôres*), cavalry defenders, the centre of a division (*meros*, *tourma*) on both sides of which were *koursôres*. The *difensôres* retained the close order and the canter pace after the *koursôres* had begun the pursuit of the enemy and acted as their defenders if they were forced to retreat, 36, 40, 76–7, 149, 354, 356, 358–60, 363, 365, 374–5, 388, 406, 414–16, 425, 447, 509
  see also bandofylakes
Diogenês, *stratêgos*, 118
Diplomacy, foreign policy, embassy, ambassador, envoy, couriers, messengers, mandatôres, messages, letters, 15–16, 25–6, 46, 62, 66, 79, 82, 84, 86, 93, 99–101, 104, 111, 114–15, 117–18, 123–6, 128–9, 140–3, 150, 152–3, 155, 161–2, 165–6, 174–6, 188–90, 194–6, 200, 210, 225, 240, 245, 247, 264–6, 275, 281, 284, 288, 292–3, 300–301, 308–11, 314–23, 325–8, 330–1, 338–41, 343, 347, 354, 381–2, 393, 423, 473, 475, 486, 494, 500, 502–504, 506
  see also Liudprand
division, see meros, tourma
Diyar:
  Diyar Bekr/Bakr, 84, 177, 198, 202, 205, 210, 232, 261, 492–3
  Diyar Modar/Mudar, 84, 158–9, 206, 272, 333, 492
  Diyar Rabia, Ra'bia, Ra'biah, 84, 199, 206, 280, 333
  Diyarbekir, see Amida
Djabal, Jableh, Hisn-Djabalah, 335–6
domestikos (pl. *domestikoi*), a commander of a *tagma* (*scholai, excubitoi, ikanatoi, optimatoi, noumeroi*), 2, 11–12, 21–4, 28–31, 79, 83, 85, 87, 97–100, 103, 107, 109, 111, 114–15, 118–20, 122, 126–7, 132–4, 144–5, 147–50, 155, 159, 162–3, 166–7, 169, 171, 175, 180–4, 186–90, 192, 194, 196–7, 199, 201, 205, 207–12, 214, 221, 227, 232, 238, 247–8, 253, 263–6, 269, 276, 291, 313–14,

349, 380, 405–406, 419, 434, 482–5, 487–90, 496, 507

domestikos (pl. *domestikoi*), junior officers of the *scholai* (A), (successors of the *protectores domestici*) acting as commanders of ten cavalry *scholarioi*, but so that the unit of the *domestikoi* included also *domestikoi peditou* in command of the *scholarioi peditou* which presumably implies that these *domestikoi* were seconded as commanders (presumably as *bikarioi* or *kentarchai*) of infantry *tagmata* (*noumeroi, teichistai, optimatoi*); Junior officers of the *Basilikoi anthrôpoi* (B); Overall commander of the *stratôres tou stablou* (C), 25, 27, 29, 474–5

domestikos tôn scholôn (Domestic of the Schools), *domestikos tês dyseôs* (Domestic of the West)/*domestikos tôn scholôn tês duseôs*, *domestikos tês anatolês* (Domestic of the East)/*domestikos tôn scholôn tês anatolês: domestikos tôn scholôn* was the commander of the *scholai* and as such the supreme commander of all field armies. The office was divided during the reign of Rômanos II in ca. 959–60 into eastern and western halves, but so that the commander or the eastern *scholai* was the senior commander as *megas domestikos*, vii, 2, 11–12, 21, 28–31, 79, 83, 85, 87, 97–100, 103, 107, 109, 111, 114–15, 118–20, 122, 126–7, 132–4, 144–5, 147–50, 155, 159, 162–3, 166–7, 169, 171, 175, 180–4, 186–90, 192, 194, 196, 199, 201, 205, 207–12, 214, 221, 227, 232, 238, 247–8, 253, 263–6, 269, 276, 291, 313–14, 349, 380, 405–406, 419, 434, 482–5, 487–90, 496, 507

Doukas Family, Doukai, 97, 100, 482

Iôannes Doukas, 100

doux (pl. *doukes*, duke), first attested under Nikêforos II for a commander of a field army. After the reign of Johannes I Tzimiskes commander of several *themata* (alternative title *katepanô*). The title derived from the Latin *dux* (pl. *duces*). Not to be confused with the Doukas family (Doukai); Roman military duchy, duchies, ducates, 285, 295–6, 310–11, 331–2, 347, 482

Italian and Armenian feudal duchies, 58–60, 68, 340–2

see also Katepanô

dromôn (pl. *dromônes*), a war galley, the workhorse of the Roman navy. The *dromôn* was a general term for a war galley of several different sizes (e.g. *chelandia*, *pamfylia, dromon trieres*), or it meant only the largest class of galleys also called *dromôn trieres* (crews of at least 300 men), 16–18, 51–3, 55–6, 73, 94, 101, 106, 110, 141–2, 216, 221, 476–7, 481, 514, 516, 518, 520, 523–4, 526

dromônion (pl. *dromônia*), a diminutive term for the *dromôn,* which in this book designates the imperial *dromônion* with a crew of 300, 16, 27–8, 106, 480

drouggarios, (pl. *drouggarioi*), a commander of irregular sized unit, or a subordinate of a *tourmarchês*, or a commander of the Imperial Fleet or *bigla,* 11–13, 16–17, 19, 22, 24–5, 28, 31–3, 77, 82–3, 97, 99, 101, 119, 122–3, 209, 215, 346, 432, 437, 474, 480, 490

Drouggos:

drouggos 1, originally a subdivision/unit of the army which was irregular in size or which used irregular (*drouggos*) formation. In the seventh century the *drouggos* replaced the *moira* as a military term so that during this era it meant a subdivision of a *tourma* (*meros*) that could be 1,000 to 3,000 men strong, *drouggos* 2, irregular non rank-and-file unit order (could be e.g. sphere, ball, rhombus, *maza*-order, wedge, *drouggisti*), 13, 32–3, 35–6, 63, 75–7, 149, 355, 358, 363, 397, 468

Duluk (Doliche), Delouk, 156, 158, 162–4, 177, 180–1, 247–8, 248, 253

Dvin (Dwin, Duin, Dubios), emirate of Dabil, 68

dynatos (pl. *dynatoi*), the 'powerful' defined in legislation as: 1) those who could influence others by using their contacts or position in civil, military or ecclesiastical hierarchy; 2) *magistroi* and *patrikioi,* men with high office, *strategoi,* men with high civilian or military dignities, ex-officials, metropolitans, archbishops, bishops, members of the Senate, *(h)egoumenoi,* ecclesiastical officials, supervisors and heads of pious or imperial houses, 3–4, 6, 8–9, 15, 31, 87, 130, 186, 271, 293, 380–1

Edessa, city, tile and Mandylion of, xiii, 114–15, 117, 206, 271, 297, 300, 302–303, 482–3, 492, 515

Egypt, Ikhshidids, 71–3, 85, 88, 91–2, 116, 120–1, 124–7, 139, 143, 155, 160, 177, 181,

195–6, 199, 201, 214–15, 225, 231, 282, 284, 288–9, 299–300, 306–308, 331–3, 336, 338–9, 382–3, 470, 481, 484, 491, 494–6, 517, 522
see also Buyids, Fatimids
Emesa, Hims, Homs, city and emirate, 124, 306, 332–3, 339, 504
eparchos tês poleôs (Prefect of the City), *eparchos*, Prefect of Constantinople; controlled the markets (e.g. silk trade), supervised foreigners; in charge of the criminal and civil cases as a judge in Constantinople and its suburbs; governor of Constantinople when the emperor was not present, 13, 30–1, 80, 209, 310, 484
epilorikioi, epilorikoforoi (*lorika/lorica* – wearers; cuirass/corselet-wearer, 'armoured'), 294, 407
see also katafraktoi
epi tou magglabiou, commander of the *magklabitai*, 26
(h)etaireia, basilikê etaireia (Companions of the Basileus) imperial bodyguard unit with four subdivisions *megas/megalê etaireia, mese/mesaia etaireia, mikra etaireia, pezetairoi; megas etaireia* consisted of the Macedonians (possibly Slavs in this case), but the rest appear to have consisted mostly of foreigners, xiv, 11, 13, 20–3, 27, 80, 82–3, 97, 100, 109, 118–19, 266, 329, 432–3, 471–2, 474, 511
etaireiarchês (pl. *etaireiarchai*), a commander of one of the four units/divisions of the *etaireia*; the supreme commander of all units of *etaireia* was known as *megas etaireiarchês*, 23, 28, 82, 100, 107, 109, 118–19, 122, 209, 214
Eugenios, *patrikios, katepanô*, 327, 341–2, 504
exkoubitoi, exkoubites, excubitores, one of the *tagmata*, 11–12, 20–1, 24, 27, 29–31, 81–2, 197, 471–2, 474, 481

Farganoi, mercenaries from Fergana, 23
Fatimids, 71–2, 91–5, 104, 114, 140–2, 155, 157, 160–1, 175–7, 185, 188, 191–6, 200, 214–15, 225, 261, 278–80, 282, 284, 289, 299–300, 307–308, 320–1, 335, 338, 347, 350, 481, 491, 494, 510, 516, 520–2
see also Aghlabids, Egypt, Fleet, Italy, Manuêl Fôkas, Marianos Argyros, Sicily, Umayyads
Filippos, conspirator, 118
Filippos, King of Albania, 239

First line, *promachos taxis*, 13, 36–40, 70, 76–7, 81–2, 136, 149, 152, 168–9, 171, 174, 219, 273, 275, 285–6, 359–65, 372, 374–6, 387–8, 395, 405, 410–11, 413–17, 424–8, 438, 440, 449, 457, 460–2, 508
Flame-thrower, Greek Fire, liquid fire, naphta, 16, 48, 51, 53, 56–7, 66–7, 93–5, 106, 110, 112, 184, 194, 216–17, 221, 282, 327, 424, 427, 452, 473, 517
Fleets (navy, naval, navigation, ships, shipping, shipwright, shipment, galleys, on board, trireme, bireme, monoreme, rafts, landing craft, amphibious, embarkation, disembarkation, barges, boats, cutter, vessel, maritime, marines, rowers, sailors, seamen, navigate, *ousia*), x, xi, xiii, 1, 4–5, 8–9, 11, 13, 15–20, 23–5, 27–8, 31, 41, 50–8, 65–8, 71–4, 79–80, 91, 93–5, 97, 99–100, 102, 104–106, 109–14, 117, 120, 134, 139, 141–2, 156–7, 175–8, 182–5, 188, 191–5, 207, 213–19, 221–3, 225–7, 229–30, 252, 266–7, 271, 273, 278, 280, 282, 288–9, 293–4, 296, 309–10, 314–16, 318, 320–1, 323, 325, 327, 331–3, 335, 339, 345, 350, 398, 470, 472–7, 480–1, 486, 490–1, 493–4, 514, 520–2, 524–5
see also Basilika dromônia, Basilikou ploimou, chelandion, drômon, drômonia, flame-thrower, *galea, mardaitai, pamfyla,* trireme
foideratoi, foederati, Federate forces, units or a unit originally consisting of foreigners, which from the reign of Honorius I onwards included also natives; attested to have existed still in the 11th century; sometimes claimed to have been created as a unit of personal bodyguards by Nikephoros I so that it would have been recruited from the Anatolikon *thema* so that its forces were stationed in Lykaonia and Pisidia, but it is likelier that units of *foideratoi* had existed continuously from the late Roman era onwards, 4, 11, 19–20, 471–2
FÔKADES, Fôkades, Fôkas Family (Phokas, Phocas), vii, 86–8, 96–103, 119–20, 122, 133, 187, 207–208, 210, 214, 246, 266, 469, 481, 485, 506
Bardas Fôkas the Elder (son of Nikêforos the elder and father of Nikêforos II), vii, xi–xii, 86–8, 96, 98–103, 106–12, 114, 118–20, 122–3, 126–7, 129, 131–4, 137, 144–55, 157–61, 163–7, 169–77, 181–4, 186–7, 189,

234, 246, 265–7, 269–70, 279, 292, 316, 327, 337, 343, 348, 379–80, 481–3, 485, 487–90
see also Appendix 2
Bardas Fôkas the Younger (son of Leôn Fôkas Jr., nephew of Nikêforos II), doux of Chaldia, xi, 296, 330–2, 334, 347
Bardas, the son of Nikêforos the Younger, 201, 265
Iôannês Fôkas, 12th century, claimed to be descendant of Nikêforos II, 506
Kônstantinos Fôkas, brother of Nikeforos II, 88, 98, 107–108, 122, 132, 147, 153, 156, 158–9, 162–6, 487, 489
Leôn Fôkas the Elder (son of Nikêforos the elder), 98–101, 499
Lêon Fôkas the Younger (son of Bardas Fôkas Jr. and brother of Nikêforos II), xi, xiv, 47, 88, 98, 107–108, 114, 118–20, 122–3, 132–6, 138–9, 144, 146–7, 149–50, 152–3, 156, 159, 163–5, 175, 177, 180–1, 187–8, 198, 205–206, 210–12, 214, 222, 231–8, 241, 246, 265–7, 269, 282, 287, 291, 296, 310, 313, 317, 322–3, 325–6, 328–31, 346–8, 379–80, 429–50, 485–7, 489, 492–3, 495–6, 499, 504–506
DRM, *De re militari*, Appendix 4, vii, xvi, 1, 13, 20, 22, 32, 40, 46–7, 50, 134, 137–8, 170, 187–8, 211–12, 222–3, 226–7, 242, 285, 287, 312–13, 317, 366–7, 379, 399, 406, 428–50, 475–6, 485–6, 488–9, 508, 511, 515, 518
see also Appendix 2
Manuêl Fôkas, nephew or cousin of Nikêforos II Fôkas, 273, 278, 499
Nikêforos Fôkas the Elder (grandfather of Nikêforos II), 45, 96–9
Nikêfokas Fôkas the Younger, *Nikêforos o Fôkas*, Nikêforos II Fôkas, emperor (963–9), v, vii, x–xiv, 1, 8–9, 46, 62–3, 85, 87–8, 90, 96
Nikêforos in the appendices, 353, 357, 359–60, 362–3, 367, 371, 373, 377, 379–30, 440, 442, 445, 463, 466
Nikêforos in the endnotes and bibliography, 470, 476, 483–5, 487–90, 493–510, 513, 516, 518, 523–5
Youth in 912–45, 96, 98, 101–102, 107–108, 112, 114–15, 118–21
stratêgos of the Anatolikon in 945–56, 108, 122–6, 129, 131–4, 136–9, 143–65, 168–77, 180–5, 484–5, 487–90, Appendix 2

domestikos tôn scholôn under Kônstantinos VII in 956–9, 108, 181, 183, 186–94, 196–208
domestikos tôn scholon / megas domestikos under Rômanos II in 959–63, 108, 209–34, 237–68, 493–7
Cretan Campaign in 960–1, 212–31, 237, 241, 493–5
Emperor in 963–9: 269–47
(The Beginning of the reign from Aug. 963 until Spring 964), 108, 269–72, 498
(Campaign Year 964), 273–81
(Campaign Year 965), 282–96, 489, 499–500
(966 until early 967), 299–307, 500–501, 503
(Campaign Year 967), 307–15, 318–22, 500, 502–503
(Campaign Year 968), 315–16, 320–37, 340, 503–504
(Campaign Year 969), 212–13, 317–18, 338–47, 503–505
Assessment of the achievements of Nikêforos, 348–52
Military reforms, v, vii, xi, 9, 85–7, 131, 136, 159, 165, 168–9, 188–91, 204, 207, 211, 253, 268, 293–6, 318, 328–30, 332, 349–51, 466, 470, 500, 510, Appendices 1–4 (esp. 1 and 3)
Religious policy, 162, 296–9
Domestic policy, 162, 268–71, 289, 292–9, 309–10, 313, 321–5, 328–30
tetarteron, 295, 328
DV, *De velitatione*, Appendix 2, vii, xvi, 1, 19, 35–6, 40, 70, 73–4, 78, 85–8, 97, 107–108, 110, 124–7, 131–3, 136, 143–5, 147, 149–50, 152–3, 156–7, 160, 162–3, 171, 182, 187–8, 200, 215, 224, 233, 235, 248, 274, 294, 324, 349–50, 379–404, 406, 417, 429–30, 440, 444–5, 461, 476, 480–2, 484–8, 491, 507–509, 515, 518, 521
PM, *Praecepta militaria*, Appendix 3, vii, 1, 40, 78, 87, 90, 115, 124, 131, 136–7, 150, 159, 168–71, 174, 187–8, 200, 203–204, 206, 219, 242, 253, 257, 274–5, 287, 311, 349, 359–60, 362, 367, 371, 388, 391, 398, 405–28, 430, 434, 437, 442, 445, 463, 466, 474, 479, 484, 488–9, 496–7, 499, 507, 509–11, 513, 518, 523
see also Appendix VI, Maleinoi, Pleustai, Tzimiskês, Theofanô
foulkon, commander's escort and/or reserve (*defensôres*), originally shield-interlocking

(*syskouton*) formation that in infantry usage typically had a shield roof also known as *chêlône/testudo* (tortoise) and *synaspismos*, 149, 287, 388, 392, 395, 397, 399, 406–407, 410, 509–10
  see also difensôres
Franks, Francia, East and West, xi, 23, 41, 58–61, 70–2, 104, 113, 118, 128–9, 176, 191, 193, 200, 311, 323, 325, 328, 342, 477, 491–2
  see also Burgundy, German, Italy, Ottos
Fraxinetum, Muslim principality, xii, xlii, 91, 103–105, 113, 195, 319, 323, 520

galea, galeai, a single-banked galley, 17–18, 51, 53, 94, 104, 142, 216, 218, 224, 327, 477, 524
Garidas Family,
  Iôannês Garidas, *magistros*, 100
  Symeon Garidas, 100
genikon, the principal department in charge of the imperial revenues; determined the rate of taxation and collected the taxes under the direction of a *logothetês*, 209
Georgia, Iberia, Abkhazia, 67–9, 86, 96, 100, 240, 281, 410, 478, 480, 524
  see also Armenia, Bagratuni
Geôrgios, *prôtospatharios* and cupbearer, 122
German, Germans, 176, 319–20, 341–2, 350
  see also Franks, Italy, Liudprand, Otto I–II
Germanikeia, Marash, city of, xii–xiii, xxviii, 120, 132–9, 143, 149, 154, 158–61, 163–4, 177, 199, 204, 212, 233, 247–8, 282, 297, 300, 304, 400, 485–6, 495
ghilman (sing. *ghulam*, servant, slave), slave soldiers in Muslim countries which in Egypt were known as *mamluks*. The *ghilman* were usually of Turkic origin so that they formed the elite forces of the ruler. However, as elite military forces, the *ghilman* eventually became de facto rulers in many of the Muslim countries, xi, 70, 88–9, 92, 116, 124, 163–4, 166, 168, 174, 178, 182, 188–90, 193, 198–200, 202–204, 206, 231, 279, 301, 349, 362, 461, 483, 489
  see also Daylami, *Saqaliba/Saqāliba*, Turks
Goggylios/Goggylês:
  Anastasios Goggylios, 100
  Kônstantinos Goggylios/Goggylês, admiral, 100, 119, 122, 134, 142
Greek Fire, *see* flame-thrower
Gregorios:
  Gregorios of Macedonia, 129

Gregorios of Taron, 309
Guerrilla warfare, skirmishing, xiii, xvi, 36, 40, 42, 50, 73, 75, 86, 91–2, 107–108, 110, 112–13, 125, 132, 144, 150, 161–2, 167, 171–2, 182, 187–8, 205, 227, 238, 302–303, 309, 321, 342, 358–9, 379–406, 413, 417, 468, 515
  raiding, raids, raiders, chevauchëe, piracy, pirates, piratical, 16, 19, 25, 45, 51, 62, 65–6, 71–3, 83, 87, 91, 98, 110, 116, 125, 132, 139, 149, 156–7, 159–60, 164, 176–8, 180, 183–4, 200–201, 205–206, 211–14, 223–5, 230, 238, 248, 250, 282, 290, 292–3, 300, 304, 307, 310, 313, 321, 329–32, 340, 382–3, 385–6, 388–9, 391, 393–5, 398–9, 446, 478, 484–5, 488, 501, 507–508
  foulka, cavalry raiders, 395
  koursa, monokoursa, runners, raiders, 385–6, 388, 507
  see also Ambush, *Prokoursatôres*, Stratagem, Surprise attacks

Hamah (Hama), 332
Hamdanids, Hamdanid Family of emirs, xi, xiii, 71–2, 75, 83–4, 86, 88–91, 93, 114, 124–5, 133, 150, 157–8, 174, 185, 193, 195–201, 205, 207–208, 214, 225, 230, 237, 239–40, 250, 257, 279–81, 289, 304, 406, 458
  Abu'l Asha'ir Husayn b. Ali b. Husayn b. Hamdan, (Abou-l-Achair ibn-al-Hasan-ibn-al Housein-ibn-Hamdan), cousin of Sayf ad-Dawla, 177, 181
  Abu'l-Bakarat, son of Nasir, 306
  Abu'l-Fawaris Muhammad ibn Nasir ad-Dawla (Muhammad, the son of Nasir ad-Dawla), the nephew of Sayf ad-Dawla and governor of Aleppo, 205, 492, 522
  Abu'l-hayga (Abdallah b. Hamdan), emir of Mosul, father of Nasir and Sayf ad-Dawla, 84
  Abu Firas al-Harith ibn Sa'id ibn Hamdan, governor of Manbij, historian, cousin of Sayf, 86, 158, 162–3, 167, 169, 193, 198, 201–203, 205, 247–8, 250, 480, 520
  Abulmakarim, son of Sayf, 281
  Abu Taglib, Taghlib, son of Nasir, 280–1, 304, 306
  Abu Zuhair, brother of Nasir and Sayf, 199
  H'amdan/Hamdan, son of Nasir, 280, 306

Hibat Allah, son of Nasir, nephew of Sayf, 272
Muhammad/Mohammed b. Nasir ad-Dawla, 137–8, 205–206, 210–11, 301, 492–3
Nasir ad-Dawla ('Defender of the Dynasty'), al-Hasan ibn Hamdan, emir of Mosul, 84, 87, 116, 124–5, 133, 190, 198–9, 202, 205–206, 210–11, 240, 272, 280–1, 301, 306, 492–3, 522
Oumm-Abu-l-Ma'ali, the wife of Sayf ad-Dawla, 272
Saad ad-Dawla (Abu-l-Ma'li ibn Sayf ad-Dawla), Abulma'ali, Sayf's son, 281, 306, 332, 337–9
Sa'id b. Hamdan, uncle of Nasir and Sayf, 84
Sayf ad-Dawla/Daulah/Dawlah, Sayf al-Dawla/Daulah, ('Sword of the Dynasty'), Ali ibn Hamdan, Chambdan, emir of Aleppo, xii–xiii, 79, 84–9, 91, 114, 116, 120–1, 124–7, 131–3, 136–9, 142–50, 153, 155–75, 177–84, 187–90, 193, 196, 198–205, 207, 210–13, 225, 232–41, 245, 247–8, 250, 252–8, 260, 264–5, 271–3, 275, 280–2, 285, 289–91, 300–304, 306–307, 313, 349, 380, 383–4, 480, 484–7, 489, 492–3, 495–7, 501, 507
Harput, Harpoot, Hisn Ziyad, Handzit, Hartabird, Ziata, city, fortress and HQ of a *stratêgos*, 85, 127, 178, 206, 250, 271, 290, 332, 490, 505
see also *Themata*/Hanzit
Harran, Carrhae, city of, 115, 155–6, 162, 177, 206, 272, 302, 332, 492, 501
Her, emirate of Huy/Khoy, 68
Hilat, Khilat, Xiat, emirate of, 68, 86, 272
hollow square, oblong, 35, 37, 40, 42–3, 46, 70, 74–5, 90, 136, 160, 167, 190, 203–204, 219, 223, 229, 257, 266, 285, 353, 356, 366–78, 401, 403, 410–12, 418–21, 423–8, 432, 442–3, 445, 467, 497, 507–508, 511
Hugh of Provence, Hugues D'Arles or Hugues de Provence, King of Italy, 59, 103–104, 111, 113, 117–18, 125
Hungarians, Magyars, 23, 40, 60–6, 80, 83, 97, 99, 103, 116, 128–9, 170, 176–7, 193–8, 201, 207, 230, 232, 234, 237–8, 292, 296, 300, 310, 315, 319, 329–30, 343, 440–1, 478–9, 490, 492, 495–6, 514, 516, 523
Hussars, 19, 434, 439, 442, 446
  akritai (sing. *akritês*, from *akron/akra* extremity/summit), soldiers posted at the extremity of a combat formation, marching camp or territory, the usual meaning being a frontiersmen along the eastern frontier so that it meant either army units along the border, their commander or the civilians of the border region, 19, 82–3, 96–7, 102, 382
  chonsarioi, chôsarioi (sing. *chonsarios, chôsarios*, from Bulgarian thieves), fast lightly-equipped cavalry raiders in the west. The word Hussar derives from this, 19, 83, 434, 446
  apelatai (sing. *apelatês*, 'one who drives away'), irregular lightly-equipped cavalry who raided enemy territory and acted as scouts and guides for the expeditionary armies. These were recruited from the Armenian and Bulgarian bandits and from the *stratiôtai* of the *themata* who were unable to serve as line cavalry. The *apelatai* were included in the thematic muster lists, but it is not known if they possessed *stratiotika themata* or were paid to serve, 19, 83
  trapezites, trapezitai (sing. *trapezitês*), (tablemates), fast cavalry raiders known among the Armenians as *tasanaroi*. Same as *apelatai* and *chosarioi*, 19, 83, 382, 434, 446
see also *Prokoursatôres*, Spy

ikanatoi (*hikanatoi*), *tagma* of, 29
Ikhshidids, see Egypt
Imperial Fleet, see *Basilikou ploimou*, Fleets
Iôannês, John, Johannes,
  Iôannês Kourkouas, see Kourkouai
  Iôannês Tzimiskês, see Tzimiskês
  Iôannês Fôkas, see Fôkades
  Iôannês, son of Filateros, 26
  Iôannês, *asêkrêtis*, 141
  Iôannês Bogas, envoy, 99
  Iôannês Choirinas/Choinos, 209
  Iôannês Doukas, see Doukai
  Iôannês Garidas, see Garidas
  Iôannês, Patriarch of Jerusalem, 289
  Iôannês VIII of Sarug, Patriarch, 297
  Iôannês Pilatos, 161
  Iôannês, *praipositos*, 267
  Iôannês *raiktôr*, 129
Iôsêf Briggas, *sakellarios, drouggarios tou plôimou*, 123, 207, 209, 213–15, 230–1, 246, 261–7, 269, 278, 500

Italy, Italian, xii, xl–xli, 1, 58–62, 71–2, 91, 93–4, 96–7, 103, 113–14, 117, 125, 141, 155, 157, 160–1, 175–7, 184–5, 191–4, 196, 200–201, 213, 215, 282, 289, 293, 296, 299–300, 308, 311, 318–20, 326–8, 340, 342, 350, 481, 486, 491, 503, 520–1, 523–4
see also Fatimids, Franks, Germans, Liudprand, Ottos, Sicily

Javelineers, *riptaratoi, riptaristai, akontistai,* javelin-throwers, 32, 41–2, 69, 137, 152, 253, 356–7, 359, 371, 373, 383, 398, 409–10, 419–20, 422–3, 426–7, 431, 434, 437, 440, 442, 446, 449
see also Archers, *Menavlatoi, Psiloi,* Russians, Slingers
Jazira, Gazira, 84, 88, 116, 125, 156, 162, 205, 260, 280, 492

Kafartouta, Castra Maurorum, 87, 332
Kafur al-Ikhshidi, Kafur the Eunuch (died on 3 May 967), de facto ruler of Egypt, 121, 124–5, 127, 195, 199, 201, 215, 225, 299, 306, 331, 494
see also Egypt
Kaisareia, Caesarea, *aplêkton*, HQ of Kappadokia, 78–9, 82, 143–5, 200, 241–2, 246, 248, 265, 273, 276, 284, 332, 487
Kalokyros, usurper, 311–12, 314–16
kaminobiglatores (sing. *kaminobiglatôr*), road guards, 382
karabion (pl. *karabia*) (or karabos), a monoreme ship, ship in general or transport ship, Viking/Russian vessel, 141, 216
Karin (Erzerum, Theodosioupolis), city and emirate of Qaliqala, xii, 68, 86, 133–4, 137–9, 239, 271, 332, 480
see also Armenia, Georgia
Katakylas Family,
Anna Katakylas, 103
Leôn Katakylas, 78, 80, 206, 212, 480
katafraktoi (sing. *katafraktos*), a fully armoured horseman mounted on an armoured horse (could be fully covered in armour or only frontally). Also known as *cataphractarii, clibanarii, klibanoforoi, epilorikioi, epilorikoforoi* and *pansidêroi ippotai*, xi, 8, 34–5, 37, 40, 42, 66–7, 70, 75, 85, 89–90, 92, 101, 131, 136, 157, 164, 167–8, 189, 203–204, 219, 221, 227, 253, 257, 273, 279, 285–6, 293–4, 314, 316, 349–50, 353, 356–65, 373–6, 378, 387,

405–11, 413–17, 419, 422, 424, 426–7, 440, 442, 447, 449, 461, 489, 499, 510, 525
see also ghilman, wedge
katepanô, a senior commander of a military unit or field army; a commander of a detachment of soldiers sent into a *thema* whose command was separate from the command of the *stratêgos*; from the reign of Johannes I Tzimiskes onwards synonymous with *doux,* 238, 287, 295–6, 311, 327, 341–2, 500
katepanô tôn basilikôn, commander of the *basilikoi anthrôpoi/basilikoi* who could also be called *protospatharios tôn basilikôn,* 25
see also doux
kentarchês (pl. *kentarchoi, kentarchai*), centurion, commander of 100 men, the equivalent of *(h)ekatontarches,* 12, 31–3, 384, 420
Khazars, 23, 61–2, 65–6, 113, 166–7, 203, 312, 478, 482, 485, 502, 523
see also Turks
Khorasan, Khurasan, Khorasani Jihadists, 71, 133, 189, 261, 272, 275, 300–301, 304, 306, 309, 313, 452, 501
kleisoura, a fortified mountain pass and military district, 10, 19, 69, 227, 234, 382, 400
kleisourarchês, commander of the *kleisoura,* 10, 19
koitonitês, koitônitai (attendants of the bedchamber, some of these were probably eunuch *spatharioi*), 209, 214, 344
komês (pl. *komêtes*), 'a count', a commander or officer of a unit or region, or *komês tês kortês* in charge of the tents, postal horses and guard circuits in a marching camp for each *stratêgos*, but so that the commander/emperor had a separate *komês tês kortês* superior to the other *komêtes,* 4, 11–13, 18–21, 24–7, 31–3, 82–3, 119, 122, 342, 472, 474–6
see also abydykos, archôn
Kônstantinos = Constantinus, Constantine,
Kônstantinos I Megas (Constantine the Great), emperor, 346, 350
Kônstantinos V Kopronymos (the Dung-named), emperor (741–75), 21, 24, 270, 475
Kônstantinos VII-VIII, *see* Macedonian Dynasty

Kônstantinos the *parakoimômenos*, see Lakapênoi
Kônstantinos Barys, 101
Kônstantinos Lakapênos, see Lakapênoi
Kônstantinos Goggylios/Goggylês, see Goggylês
Kônstantinos Fôkas, see Fôkades
Kônstantinos Malelia, 100
Kônstantinos Maleinos, see Maleinoi
Kosmas, *magistros*, 115, 125
Kourkouai, Kourkouas Family,
   Eufrosynê, daughter of Iôannês Kourkouas, 111
   Iôannês Kourkouas, famous Roman *domestikos*, 35, 71, 83, 85, 87–8, 98, 101, 103–104, 106–107, 109, 111–12, 115, 125, 476, 482–4, 520
   Rômanos Kourkouas, son of Iôannês Kourkouas, 103, 265, 476, 520
   Theofilos Kourkouas, brother of Iôannês, *stratêgos*, 87–8, 98, 101, 103, 133, 476, 482, 485, 520
kouropalatês (*cura palatii, curopalates*), caretaker of the palace and honorific title; one of the highest positions usually occupied by a member of the imperial family; the ruler of Iberia was also usually given this title, 269, 322, 331
koursôres (sing. *koursôr*), (spelling in MS and LT) *koursatôres* (spelling in ST), cavalry runners, skirmishers and pursuers posted in the flanks of the division (*meros, tourma*). The *koursôres* could accompany their division on both flanks of the *difensôres* by using the close order (*pyknosis*) at canter after which they pursued the retreating enemy by using the gallop which disordered their formation so that the pursuit was performed in irregular (*drouggisti*) order. In some cases, the *koursatôres* could also be used as skirmishers before the main battle. Alternative names for them were *promachoi* and *proklastai*, 36, 75–7, 358–9, 388, 446
   see also Hussars, *prokoursatôres*
Kourtikios, 97, 118–19, 122
   Manuêl Kourtikios, 118–19, 122
Krinitês, *stratêgos* of Calabria, 114
Krinitês, Prokopios, 97
Kurd, Kurdish, 68–9, 75, 89, 92, 131–2, 255, 275, 304, 338

Lakapênoi, Lakapênos Family, Lakapêna, (Lakapene):
   Agatha Lakapêna, 118
   Basileios Lakapênos *prôtobestiarios, patrikios, parakoimômenos, paradynasteuon, proedros*, the Eunuch, son of Romanos I, xiv, 1, 122–3, 193, 198, 201–203, 207–209, 213, 215, 266–7, 269, 308, 325, 343–4, 346, 484, 491, 514
   Christoforos, eldest son of Rômanos I, 100, 103, 122, 483
   Elenê (Helen) Lakapêna, empress and wife of Kônstantinos VII, 100, 103, 119, 123, 209
   Kônstantinos Lakapênos, son of Rômanos I, 103, 115, 118–20, 122, 129, 483–5
   Maria/Maria-Irene Lakapêna, daughter of Christoforos Lakapêna, the wife of Tsar Peter I, 62, 103, 118, 264, 292–3, 500
   Michaêl, son of Christoforos Lakapênos, 122, 483
   Rômanos I Lakapênos, emperor (919–44), vii, 8, 28, 62, 84, 91, 99–101, 103–107, 109, 111–19, 122–3, 130, 141, 193, 209, 259, 264, 266, 482–4
   Rômanos, son of Stefanos, 111, 122
   Stefanos, son of Rômanos I, under Kônstantinos VII he was in charge of the defence of Rhodes, 103, 115, 118–20, 122, 129–30, 141–2, 264, 483–4
Land tax, *demosion*, 6
Latakia, al-Laziqiah, Laodicea ad Mare, Laodikeia, xii, xxxvi, 336
Leôn, Leo:
   Leo VII, see Pope
   Leôn III, emperor, 24
   Leôn VI, see Macedonian Dynasty
   Leôn Fôkas the Elder and Younger, see Fôkades
   Leôn Katakylas, see Katakylas
   Leôn Katakalon Abidelas, 97
   Leôn Agelastos, 130
   Leôn Argyros, see Argyroi
   Leôn Balantios, 182
   Leôn Balantês, Abalantês, 345, 347
   Leôn Kladon, 129
   Leôn Maleinos, see Maleinoi
   Leôn Pastilas, 228
   Leôn Pediasimos, 344
   Leôn Tornikios, see Tornikioi
logothetês tou dromou, the head of the Imperial Postal Services; responsible for the reception of foreign ambassadors and

envoys; in charge of internal and external security; the equivalent modern titles would be minister of foreign affairs and chief of espionage, 28, 269, 323
logothetês tou genikou, logothete of the *genikon*, a head of the state treasury, 209
Lucania, 58–9, 97, 340

Ma'arreh-Macrin (Maarat Misrin), 332
Ma'areh al-Nouman (Maarat al-Nouman), 332
Macedonia, Macedonians (including *megas etaireia*), Macedonian Dynasty, Macedonian phalanx, 8–10, 23, 78, 97, 107, 109, 111, 119–20, 129, 182, 193, 195–6, 213, 216, 221, 227, 238, 266–7, 320, 329, 466, 470–2, 510, 523, 525
see also etaireia, *Themata*/Macedonia
Macedonian Dynasty, members of,
Agatha, sister of Rômanos II, 209
Alexandros, emperor (912–13), 61
Anna, daughter of Rômanos II and Theofanô, 261
Anna, sister of Rômanos II, 209
Basileios I the Macedonian (867–86), emperor, xiv, 78, 96–7, 186, 212, 471
Basileios II (963–1025), emperor, x–xi, xiv, 20, 47, 209, 261–2, 267, 346, 350, 379–80, 429, 449, 491, 505
Kônstantinos VII Porfyrogennêtos, emperor (913–59/945–959), vii, x, xiv, xvi, 1, 4–5, 8, 12–13, 15–16, 22, 28, 40, 53, 58, 62, 64–7, 74, 78–80, 83, 99–101, 103–104, 108–109, 111, 114–20, 122–5, 128–31, 133–4, 140–1, 157, 174, 177, 184, 186, 188, 190, 192–3, 197, 200–201, 204–14, 323, 331, 380, 384, 422, 433, 437, 470, 472–80, 482–6, 492, 496–7, 501, 505, 511, 515–16
DAI, *De administrando imperio*, xvi, 1, 15, 28, 58, 62, 65–6, 116, 123, 129, 133, 196, 475–6, 478, 480, 483, 485, 490–2, 507, 515
DC, *De Ceremoniis, Three treatises on Imperial Expeditions*, xvi, 1, 4, 12, 16–17, 22, 33, 53, 78–83, 128–9, 141–2, 157, 186, 213, 266–7, 472, 476–7, 484–6, 488, 490, 497, 514–15, 522, 526
De Thematibus, On Themes, 1, 507, 515, 522
Kônstantinos VIII, emperor (960–1028), 209, 261–2, 267, 316, 346, 380, 505

Leôn VI the Wise, Leôn o Sofos, LT, emperor (886–912), xiv, 1, 9–11, 13–14, 16–17, 19, 28, 31–5, 37, 40–6, 48, 51, 53, 60–4, 69–70, 73–8, 85, 88, 92–4, 97, 102, 109, 131, 136, 149, 155, 157, 194, 214–15, 242, 274, 294, 314, 353–78, 380–3, 387, 397–8, 407–409, 411, 414–15, 417–18, 424, 431, 440, 442, 470–2, 475–80, 487–9, 493, 495, 507–508, 511, 514, 516, 521–2
LT, *Taktika*, 1, 9–10, 13, 17, 19, 31, 32–3, 35, 37, 40–2, 44–6, 48, 51, 53, 61–3, 70, 73, 75–7, 94, 97, 102, 136, 149, 155, 157, 194, 206, 215, 274, 294, 314, 353–4, 358, 360, 378, 380–3, 387, 397–8, 411, 414, 417–18, 440, 442, 470–2, 476–80, 487–9, 493, 495, 507–508, 511, 516, 521–2
ST, *Sylloge tacticorum*, Appendix 1, vii, xi, xvi, 1, 32–5, 37, 40–4, 46–8, 75, 77, 81, 131, 134, 136, 157, 159, 168–71, 187, 274, 353–78, 381, 397, 406, 407–409, 411, 415, 417, 419–20, 432, 438–9, 457, 460, 476, 485, 495, 506, 509–10, 519, 525
Rômanos II, son of Kônstantinos VII, emperor (959–63), vii, 11, 21, 103–104, 108, 111, 117–18, 122, 186, 188, 204, 207, 209–10, 213–14, 225–6, 231, 241, 246, 260–2, 266, 339, 380, 384, 494, 496, 501, 505
Theodôra, sister of Rômanos II, 209
Zôê, sister of Rômanos II, 209
Zôê, empress, mother of Kônstantinos VII, 99, 101
magistros, magister, a high-ranking dignity, 24, 99–100, 115, 119, 122, 125, 130, 210, 214, 269, 282, 484
magklabitai/magglabites/magglabitai (mace-bearers), a detachment of the imperial bodyguards who were armed with a *mag(g)labion* (cudgel) and sword, 13, 26, 432
Makroiannês, admiral, 157
Maleinoi, 98
Kônstantinos Maleinos, *stratêgos* and a maternal uncle of Nikêforos II, 108, 187–8, 233, 238, 272, 379
Leôn Maleinos, 165
Michaêl Maleinos (894–961), uncle of Nikêforos II, spiritual guide, 102, 298, 347
Mamluk, see ghilman

Manbij, Hierapolis, Membeze, city of, 247–8, 250, 302, 332, 501
Manuêl, see Fôkades, Kourtikios
Manzikert city of (Minasrjird, Manazkert), and Qaysid Emirate of Minasjird (Manzikert), 68–9, 86, 271–3, 281, 309, 330–2
  see also Naga
Maraqiyah, 335
mardaitai, Mardaites, a special group of sailors/rowers/marines, 17, 296, 473
Marianos Argyros, *see* Argyroi
Martyropolis/Mayyafariqin/Maiperkat, city and emirate of, xii, xxxvi, 86, 115, 137–8, 143, 159, 180, 182–4, 198–9, 202, 206, 211, 239, 250, 261, 272, 280–2, 289–91, 301–302, 304, 306, 332, 337–8, 504
Maurice, Maurikios, *see Strategikon*
Melias (Malih al-Armani, Mleh-mec = Mleh the Great) and similarly named son and grandson, 127, 132, 144, 159, 380, 484, 507
Melitene, city of, and emirate of Malatya, v, xii, xxviii, 71, 83–4, 101, 103, 127, 132, 159, 162–4, 202, 239, 271–2, 297, 332, 400, 488, 490, 525
  see also Themata/Melitene
menavlatos (pl. *menavlatoi*), footman armed with *menavlion*. The soldiers are named after *menavlion, menavlon* (pl. *menavlia*), a thick spear with long point, 32, 42, 366, 373–4, 378, 419–24, 427, 431–2, 446, 510
merarchês (pl. *merarchai*), a commander of a *meros*; synonym of *tourmarchês*, 24, 31–2, 77
meros (pl. *mere*), *see tourma*
Mesopotamia (not to be confused with the similarly named theme or later katepanate), xii, xxx, 71, 84, 87, 98, 115–17, 132, 158, 202, 214, 298, 300, 328, 330, 333, 482, 485, 500, 520, 526
Messengers, including military, *see* Diplomacy
Michaêl:
  Michaêl II, emperor, 474
  Michaêl III, emperor, 78–9, 471
  Michaêl Barys, 101
  Michaêl Bourtzês, 333, 337–40, 344, 347, 504
    a black servant of Bourtzês, 338
  Michaêl the Cleric, 101
  Michaêl, Servant of Nikêforos Fôkas, 262–3
  Michaêl Diabolinos, 120, 129
    see also Diavolinus, Basileios Peteinos
  Michaêl Maleinos, *see* Maleinoi
  Michaêl the Overseer, *koitônitês*, eunuch, 214, 344
  Michaêl, Melkite Church of Saint, 231
  Michaêl Tornikios, *see* Taron
  Michaêl, son of Christoforos Lakapênos, *see* Lakapênoi
military lands, *see stratiotika ktemata*
moira (pl. *moirai*), *see drouggos*
Monastery, monasteries, nunneries, 4, 6, 101–102, 110, 232, 264, 267, 270, 297–9, 349, 352, 506
  Abramitai, 267
  Mt Athos, xi, xvi, 222, 232, 297–9, 310, 352, 517
  Mt Kyminas, 232, 298
  Mt Olympos, 79, 206–207, 298
  Monks, 4, 115, 118, 222, 264, 269, 295, 297–8, 310, 343, 347, 352, 433, 516, 519
  Nuns, 4, 209
  see also Athanasios, Laura, Michaêl Maleinos
Monastêriotês, a military officer, 287
Monophysite, Miaphysite, Jacobite Church, 281, 297
Mopsuestia, city, xii, xxviii, 272–3, 275–6, 282, 287–8, 290, 293, 313, 336
Mosul, city and emirate of, 83–4, 89, 115, 124, 133, 156, 190, 198–9, 240, 261, 280, 304, 306
  see also Aleppo, Buyids, Egypt, Hamdanids
Mutanabbi, 1, 144–5, 147–8, 159, 161–4, 167–9, 174–5, 177–8, 180, 486–7, 489, 517, 522–3

Naga al-Kasaki, Turkish *ghulam*, emir, 198, 200, 232–3, 239–40, 250, 252–4, 260, 271–2, 280–1, 290, 301–302, 495–7, 500
Nikêforos,
  Nikêforos I, emperor, 22, 471–2
  Nikêforos Botaneiatês, 96
  Nikêforos Fôkas, *see* Fôkades
  Nikêforos Pastilas, *stratêgos*, 223, 228, 494
Nikêtas:
  Nikêtas the Butler, 207
  Nikêtas Chalkoutzês, admiral vs Hamdanids and Egyptians, 142, 150, 152, 282, 289, 487
  Nikêtas, *prôtospatharios*, 129
  Nikêtas, *patrikios*, 103
  Nikêtas the Eunuch, *patrikios*, brother of Michaêl, admiral vs Fatimids, 278, 282, 307
Nikolaos Tornikios, *see* Taron

Nikolaos, Patriarch, 99–100
Nisibis, 84, 86, 115, 133, 160–2, 199, 202, 206, 280, 302, 306, 332, 486, 488, 516
nomisma (pl. nomismata), a gold coin with 4.45g of 24 carat gold (solidus, pl. solidi), x, 8, 295
noumeroi, noumera, numeri, tagma of, 12, 16, 20, 22–3, 29–30, 79, 432, 472, 475
novel (novellus, novella) a formal legal document enacting new imperial legislation; roughly equivalent to the English statute, 5, 130–1, 270, 293–5, 470

oikos (pl. oikoi), a house, usually the palace and estates of the dynatos, 97
oplitai (oplitês), hoplites, means usually heavy infantry, but could also mean heavy cavalry, xiv, 32, 40–2, 134, 137–8, 150, 152, 253–4, 353–4, 356, 360, 363, 367, 373–4, 383, 418–20, 422–4, 426–8, 431, 434, 437, 442, 446, 449, 452, 496, 510–11
  heavy-armed, heavy infantry, xvi, 19, 41, 69, 74, 216, 253, 353, 366, 383, 408, 418–19, 439, 465, 467, 507, 509, 513
  see also aspidoforoi, psiloi, peltastai, skoutatoi
oplitarchês, overall commander of infantry, same as archêgetês, 32, 432, 436–7, 511
optimatoi/optimates, see Themata
Ottos, Ottonian, 60–1, 300, 321, 326, 340, 350, 520
  Otto I the Great, Kaiser of the German Reich, xi, 59, 118, 125, 128–9, 140–1, 176, 191, 200–201, 292, 296, 299, 318–21, 323–31, 340–2, 350, 500, 502–503
  Otto II, Kaiser of the German Reich, son of Otto I, 318, 320, 323–4, 341–2
  see also Berengar, Franks, German, Hugh, Italy, Liudprand, Theofanô
Ouranos, Nikêforos, general under Basileios II,
  Taktika, OT, xvi, 1, 35, 40, 46, 48, 50, 274, 357, 362, 399, 410–11, 413–18, 422, 429, 480, 510, 518, 523
  Naumachica, 514

pamfyla, pamfylos, pamfylon, ousiaka pamfyla (pl. pamfylia, pamfyloi), a galley with a crew of 120, 130, 150, or 160 men; drômon could be converted into a pamfylos; megas pamfylos was either a high ranking office, or a unit serving in the basilika dromônia, 16–18, 51–4, 141, 216, 476–7
Paphlagonia, 6–7, 9–10, 27, 79, 107, 110, 134, 265

paradynasteuôn, an unofficial imperial favourite and assistant, often a close colleague, 123, 209, 484
parakoimômenos, the highest position in the Imperial Court, in charge of the security of the Imperial Bedcamber; usually a eunuch, 1, 28, 99–100, 112, 122–3, 193, 201, 207–209, 213, 266, 269, 343–6, 484, 491, 514
Parsakoutênoi, Parsakountênos/ Parsakoutênos,
  Theodôros Parsakoutênos, 98, 248, 497
  Theodoulos Parsakountênos/ Parsakoutênos, 98, 174, 189
Paschalios, stratêgos, 157
Paschalios, patrikios, 266
Pass, Passes, Gates, Darb-
  Cilician Gates, 116, 136, 144–5, 174, 182, 212, 285
  Darb Baqasaya (Pass of Tailors), 180, 183, 206, 234, 332
  Darb al-Hadath (Adata), 132–4, 164, 182, 248, 485
  Darb al-Hayyatin (Pass of Lady's Suit), 180, 183, 206, 234, 332
  Darb al-Kankarun, xiii, 120, 143, 150–3, 156, 160, 163–4, 182, 233, 248, 252, 254, 489
  Darb al-Manzar, 162, 164
  Darb al-Qulla, 162, 164
  Darb al-Rahib, 116
  Darband al-Marri, 304
  Eyerbel, 182
  Illyris Pass, 332
  Kylindros, kleisoura, 234
  Shipka Pass, 511
  Syrian Gates, Syriai Pylai, 304, 337
  see also kleisoura, Valley
patrikios, patricius, patrician, a high dignity, 31, 78, 80, 82, 86, 97, 103, 105, 107, 109, 116, 119–20, 122–3, 126, 129–30, 134, 178, 181–3, 197, 201, 207–209, 213–14, 232, 266, 278, 282, 289, 309, 311, 330, 341–2, 484, 490, 507, 514
Pechenegs, Patzinakia, 40, 61–2, 64–7, 99, 105, 117, 312, 317–18, 350, 410, 434, 502–503
peltastai (peltastês), medium infantry (during Komnenian era light cavalry), xi, 40, 42, 354
Petros, eunuch and stratopedarchês, 292, 313–14, 337–9, 504
phalanx, double phalanx, phalangites, 40, 42–3, 55, 60–1, 66, 69, 74, 80, 89–90,

152–3, 219, 221, 223, 228–9, 257, 285, 311, 316, 354, 355, 373, 383, 419, 423, 427, 435, 452, 465–7, 499, 506–507
plagiofylakes, flank guards, usually only on the left side of the first cavalry line, 13, 36–7, 40, 70, 76–7, 82–3, 170, 285, 360, 363, 365, 375, 377, 387, 406, 410, 414–16, 424–6, 428, 438–40, 443, 456–8, 460–1, 463, 478, 489, 508
Pleustai, 107–108
  Pleustaina, 1st wife of Nikêforos II, 107–108, 240–1, 269, 469
Polybios, 47, 219, 367, 369, 373, 378, 518
  see also Aelian
Polyeuktos, Patriarch, 128, 206, 240, 263, 265–7, 269–70, 295, 321, 326
Poor, the poor meant in legislation basically everyone else except the *dynatoi* so it did not mean actual poverty but a weaker ability to defend one's rights against the powerful, 3, 6, 8, 130, 470
Pope, Papal State, 58–9, 318–20
  John XII, 59, 318–19
  Leo VIII, Pope, 319
  John XIII, 319, 321, 330–1, 341
primikerios, a member of any group of functionaries, 122
proedros, title/rank, 269, 308, 325, 498
proklastai, *see koursôres*
prokoursatôres (ST spelling)/*prokoursatores* (PM spelling), (sing. *prokoursatôr*) skirmishers (older spelling *prokoursôres*), those who ran (i.e. galloped) 2–3 miles ahead of the army to provoke the enemy by skirmishing in irregular order while their *difensôres* followed. The tenth century *prokoursatôres* performed a similar mission as the *koursôres*, vanguard and ambushers, but were deployed in a different manner so that when they were part of the cavalry array they were posted only on the flanks and behind of the centre division, which was usually arrayed as a wedge/triangle, 40, 87, 168, 174, 204, 285, 354–6, 358–65, 372, 374–5, 387, 406–407, 410, 413–15, 424–7, 438, 508–10
  guide, guides (*doukatôroi*), 19, 83, 153, 218, 229, 288, 433–4, 438, 442–6, 449, 487
  vanguard, advance guard, 40, 82–3, 87, 93, 143–5, 148–9, 163, 171, 178, 202–203, 223, 254, 287, 318, 356, 358, 386–7, 389–91, 401, 406, 410, 428, 438, 440–1, 443, 452, 460–1, 489, 508

skirmishers, skirmishing, xiii, xvi, 36, 75, 77, 108, 125, 167, 171–2, 187, 238, 303, 309, 342, 358–9, 379–80, 385, 394, 400, 405–406, 413, 468, 515
  see also Ambush, Guerrilla, *koursôres*, Spy
promachoi, *see* First line, *difensôres*, *koursôres*
Prokopios Krinitês, 97
prosopa, powerful 'persons', either land-owning individuals or institutions like monasteries, 6
protektôr/*protiktôr* (pl. *protektôres*, *protiktôres*), direct descendants of the late Roman *protectores domestici*, during this era bearers of the *skeuoi* (imperial emblems), 12, 474
prôtoasekretis, head of the *asekretis*; head of the Imperial Chancery, 100
prôtobestiarios, head of the Imperial Wardrobe, 28, 106, 122–3, 278, 347, 484
prôtokankellarios (pl. *prôtokankellarioi*), a secretary of any of the central departments, 484
prôtokarabos, a subordinate of a *stratêgos* of a naval theme; a ship's pilot or steersman, who served under *kentarchos*. The warships had two *prôtokaraboi*, the senior of whom was called *prôtos prôtokarabos*. The *prôtokarabos* of the *dromônion* of *basileus* was usually also the *prôtospatharios tês fialês*, 28, 184–5, 192, 476
prôtomagglabitai, commander of the *magklabitai*, 26
prôtomandator (pl. *prôtomandatores*), a liaison officer assigned to the entourage of the emperor, 12
prôtonotarios, the official in charge of the fiscal administration of a *thema*, 83, 123, 130
prôtospatharios (A), a dignity carried by the commanders of the *themata* and men of similar rank, the first to grant access to the Senate. (B) *prôtospatharios tôn basilikôn* commander of the *basilikoi anthrôpoi*/*basilikoi* who could also be called *katepanô tôn basilikôn*. (C) *prôtospatharios tês fialês*, Protospatharios of the Basin, originally commander of the barges (*agraria*) or *dromônia* of the *basileus*, but after the reign of Rômanos I Lakapênos the commander of the two imperial *dromônia* of the emperor and of the two barges of the empress; he also acted as a judge of their crews, 25, 118, 122, 129, 141, 209, 309, 475–6
prôtostratôr, the first of the imperial stable masters accompanying the emperor during

some ceremonies; later the supreme commander of the cavalry. Chief of the imperial *stratorês*, 25, 27, 83, 97
prôtobestiarios, head of the Imperial Wardrobe, 28, 106, 122–3, 278, 347, 484
proximos (pl. *proximoi*), a liaison officer of the *scholai* assigned to the entourage of the emperor, 17, 29
psiloi (sing. *psilos*), usually light infantry, but in the ST could also mean light cavalry, xi, 32, 40–2, 137–8, 150, 152, 212, 253–4, 284, 354–60, 362–3, 365–6, 371, 373–4, 383, 392, 398, 401, 403, 409, 419, 423, 427, 431–3, 435–8, 440, 446, 452, 488
see also Archers, Javelineers, Slingers
Pylai, city, 12, 79–80

Qarghoyah, Qarghuyah, Qarghonyah, Qarghuwayh, chamberlain, 290, 305–306, 332, 337–9
Qaysids, *see* Manzikert, Naga
Qinnasrin (Chalcis), 256, 258, 260, 302–303
quaestor, a high-ranking financial official, 2, 130

Ra'ban, Raban, fortress, 156, 158–9, 161, 175, 199, 202–204, 212, 247–8, 492
Ras al-Ain, Resaina, Ras Ain, Ra's Ayn, Funduq al-Ra's, 87, 115, 206, 302, 332, 501
Rhomboid, rhombus, unit order and battle formation, 74, 93, 314, 457, 459–60, 462, 464, 468
Rômanos,
  Rômanos I, *see* Lakapênoi
  Rômanos, son of Stefanos Lakapênos, *see* Lakapênoi
  Rômanos II, *see* Macedonian dynasty
  Rômanos III, emperor (1028–34), 479
  Rômanos Argyros, *see* Argyroi
  Rômanos Kourkouas, *see* Kourkouas
  Rômanos Balantios/Balantas, 181–2
  Rômanos Mouseles, 130
  Rômanos Sarônites, 130, 484
  Rômanos, son of Tsar Peter I, *see* Bulgaria
Romanoupolis (Bingöl), a small *thema*, 331–2, 400
Russia, *Ruscia*, Russians, Rus', Rhos, the Rhos consisted mainly of Scandinavians (mainly Swedes) and their subjects that ruled parts of the territory of modern Estonia, Belarus, Ukraine and Russia. In this book these are collectively called Russians, xii, xiv–xv, xxxviii, 1, 16, 23, 40, 61, 65–8, 71, 87, 103–13, 117, 122, 128–9, 137, 141, 166–7, 175, 188, 190–1, 193, 200, 212, 216, 227, 229, 253, 296, 307, 311–12, 314–18, 326–7, 347, 350, 419–20, 422–3, 429, 432–4, 440, 443, 449, 478–9, 482, 500, 502–503, 511, 515, 518–19, 522–3, 526

saka (from Arabic *saqah*), third line or rear guards. The terminology and meaning depended on the situation and individual using the term. When the *saka* meant the rear guards, the alternative terms were *nôtofylakes*, or *opisthofylakes*, 13–14, 37, 40, 61, 77, 82–3, 149–50, 152–3, 164–5, 169, 171, 174, 204, 206, 227, 275, 279, 354, 356, 360, 362–3, 365, 377–8, 386–7, 395, 401, 404, 406, 411, 414–16, 424–5, 428, 438–41, 443, 452, 460–1, 465, 473, 489, 508, 512
see also Third line
sakellarios, sacellarius, a financial official/treasurer in charge of a *sakellion/sakelle*. *Sakellion* was the Imperial Treasury or Treasury of the Great Church of Constantinople. The *sakelle* was also the jail of the Great Church for clerics. Its twin institution was the *bestiarion*, state warehouse and treasury and arsenal to store and supply the fleet and army with precious goods and money, 123
Saqaliba/Ṣaqāliba/saqaliba, 'Slavic' slave soldiers in Muslim countries that actually included all nationalities from the Balkans and East Europe, 92, 230, 481, 523
see also Blacks, Daylami, *ghilman*, Turks
Sardinia, 21, 25, 27, 60, 72, 479, 524
Sardoi (Sardinians), imperial bodyguards, 21, 27, 72
Saruq, Sarug, Saruj, Serugh, 115, 159, 162, 297 313
scholai (former *scholae*), a cavalry *tagma*, 11–12, 20–1, 24, 29–31, 81–2, 118, 197, 263, 432, 474–5, 511
see also *domestikos tôn scholôn*
scholarios (pl. *scholarioi*), rank-and-file soldiers of the *tagmata* in general and of the *tagma* of the *scholai*, 4, 11, 29, 82–3, 142, 166–7, 169, 174, 221–2, 406, 408, 432, 472, 480
scouts, scouting, patrols, guards, pickets, sentinels, reconnaissance, reconnoitre, 3, 19, 22–3, 25–6, 44, 55, 63, 73, 79, 82, 87, 89–90, 106–107, 109–10, 129, 141, 145, 156, 160, 163, 169, 171, 178, 221–3, 264, 266–7, 323, 325, 327, 330, 338, 382, 385–6,

388–9, 393, 428, 432, 434, 436–9, 442–4, 448, 452, 456, 475, 480, 508
ekspêlatôr (pl. ekspêlatores), from the Latin expilator (plunderer/robber), a scout, 382
Second line (taxis deutera, deuteros), support line (boêthos taxis), 13, 36–7, 40, 70, 77–8, 81–2, 149, 168–9, 171, 174, 203–204, 275, 359–60, 362–3, 365, 377, 387–8, 405–406, 410, 414–17, 424, 428, 438, 446, 449, 457, 459, 461, 463–4, 489, 506, 508, 510
Serbia, 62, 64–5, 197
Sergios the monk, 115
Shimsat, Simsat, see Arsamosata
Siege, sieges, besiege, 47–51, 57, 72–3, 80, 87, 102, 115–16, 132, 137–8, 144–5, 157, 159, 161, 175, 180, 182, 187, 189, 197–8, 202, 206, 212, 254, 273, 275, 278–9, 281, 287, 290, 296, 303, 306, 317–19, 335–8, 340–1, 380, 398–9, 423, 429, 440, 446–50, 485, 494, 498, 501, 503, 515–16
Some important Roman sieges:
Adana in 964, 276
Adata in 948, 132
Adata in 955, 175, 177
Adata in 957, 188–9
Agrigento in ca. 940–1, 91
Aleppo in 962, xiii, 250–61
Aleppo in 969–70, 339
Anazarbos/Anazarba in 961–2, xiii, 241–6
Anazarbos in 964, 276
Antioch in 966, 303–4
Antioch in 968–9, 336–9
Arka in 968, 335
Artah (Artach), 303
Bari in 968, 321
Bovino in 969, 340–1
Chandax in 960–1, 218–30
Charsianon in 950, 145–50
Constantinople in 958, 197
Edessa in 943–4, 115–16
Fraxinentum in 942, 113
Germanikeia in 944, 120
Germanikeia in 949, xii, 133–9, 485–6
Germanikeia in 959–62, 204, 212, 233, 247–8
Edessa in 944, 482
Karin in 949, xii, 133–4, 137–9
Koloneia in 940, 87
Kyros in 959, 205
Manbij in 966, 302–303
Manzikert in 968–9, 331–2
Mopsuestia in December 963, 275
Mopsuestia in early spring 964, 275–6

Mopsuestia in 965, 276, 287
Naples in 958, 194
Nisibis in 943, 115
Rametta in 963–5, 278–80
Sis in 962, xiii, 250–1
Taormina in 962, 261
Tarsus in 949, xii, 132–4, 136–9, 143, 276
Tarsus in 964, 276–8, 498
Tarsus in 965, 283–9, 498
Tizin in 966, 303
Sis, city and fortress, xiii, 150, 242, 250–1, 253, 273
Sicily, Sicilian, 11, 18, 58, 60, 71–2, 91, 93–4, 104, 113–14, 140–1, 157, 160–1, 175–6, 183, 185, 191–2, 196, 215, 261, 271, 273, 278, 284, 289, 308, 321, 350, 478, 481, 486, 498, 520
see also Fatimids, Franks, Italy
Sidon, 333
Sisinios, prôtospatharios, 209
Sisinnios, eparchos, 310
Sklêroi, Sklêros Family,
Bardas Sklêros, famous general and usurper, 343
Maria Sklêraina, first wife of Tzimiskês, sister of Bardas, 340
Pantherios Sklêros, domestikos, 109, 111–12, 114–15, 478–9
skoutarios (pl. skoutarioi), scutarii, rank-and-file soldiers of the arithmoi/bigla, 22, 29, 471, 480
skoutatoi (skoutatos), shield-bearer, 40–3, 353–4
see also aspidoforoi, oplitai
skribon (pl. skribones), officer of the tagma of the exkoubitoi, 12, 21, 29
Slaves, captives, prisoners, prisoner exchanges, slave troops, 22–3, 73, 84–5, 87–9, 92–3, 110, 112, 114–16, 121, 123, 125–8, 130, 132, 141–2, 147, 155–7, 159, 161–3, 165–6, 174, 180, 182–4, 189, 192, 198, 200, 203–205, 214, 218, 223, 228, 230–1, 233, 236–9, 246, 248, 250, 254, 258–9, 261, 266, 271, 280, 287, 289, 300–301, 303, 307, 313–14, 326–7, 329, 335–6, 339, 341–2, 382, 385, 389, 393, 397, 400, 403, 424–5, 434–4, 447–9, 481, 483–4, 487, 495
see also Booty
Slavs, 61–2, 64–5, 67, 89, 92, 105, 117, 166–7, 175, 216, 229–30, 478, 520
Slingers, sfendonistai, sfendobolistai, sfendonetai, 32, 74, 137, 152, 170–1, 253,

285–6, 383, 392, 403, 419–20, 422, 424, 426–7, 440, 446, 463, 489
spatharios (pl. *spatharioi*), a sword-bearer, a modest dignity, 25–6, 83, 209, 475
spatharokoubikoularioi, eunuch bodyguards of the empress, 25
Spy, spying, intelligence/information gathering, espionage, *kataskopoi* (spies), traitor, special operations, 15, 21, 26, 50–1, 141, 167, 189, 218, 222, 253, 269, 330–4, 326, 382, 434, 437, 442, 449, 507
  see also Assassination, Deserter, Diplomacy, *Prokoursatôres,* Scouts
Stefanos, *magistros,* 99–100
Stefanos Lakapênos, *see* Lakapênoi
Stratagem, ruse, fooling the enemy, betray, treachery, 36, 42, 45, 47, 60–1, 74, 80, 117, 120, 156, 159, 161–2, 169, 175, 189, 218–19, 223–6, 239, 254, 264–5, 271, 312, 315, 319, 323–4, 326–8, 341–4, 349–50, 450, 381, 413, 450, 485, 488, 493, 518
  see also Ambush, Deserters, Guerrilla, Spy, Surprise attacks
stratêgos (pl. *stratêgoi*), a general. The term *stratêgos* had four different meanings: 1) when the emperor was called *stratêgos* he was the overall commander of all armed forces and all other generals below him were called *ypostratêgoi;* 2) governor/general of a *thema*; 3) overall commander of an army (*stratêgos* or *monostratêgos*) that could have *stratêgoi* of the *themata* serving under him; 4) *stratêgos autokratôr* (a general with temporary imperial powers) 5, 8, 13–14, 17–20, 24, 32, 35, 45, 51–3, 56, 60–1, 70, 73, 76–7, 79, 82, 86–7, 97–8, 100, 102, 106–109, 114, 118, 122–3, 125–7, 130–4, 137, 141, 144, 147, 150, 152–3, 156–7, 159–61, 171, 174, 181–4, 186–7, 193, 197, 205, 210, 212–15, 223, 225–8, 233–4, 238, 248, 250, 263, 265, 276–7, 282, 292, 298, 313–14, 327, 336, 341, 347, 349, 353–4, 356, 358, 360, 362–3, 365, 373, 379–97, 399–401, 404–406, 410–11, 413, 415–16, 425–6, 434, 446–7, 471, 473–5, 477, 485, 487–8, 490, 494, 496–7, 500, 506–509, 511
monostratêgos (could also possess the powers of *stratêgos autokratôr*), 238, 327
stratêgos autokrator, 215, 263, 292
  see also Appendices 1–3. The instructions were meant primarily for the *stratêgoi* of the thematic forces. Appendix 4 was meant primarily for the emperor, but includes also instructions for the thematic *stratêgoi*
  see also Themata, *ypostratêgos*
stratêgetês, 227, 494
Strategikon of Maurikios (*Stratêgikon*), MS, xvi, 24, 26, 32–46, 48, 60, 64–5, 70, 74, 77–8, 85, 102, 206, 274, 294, 357–60, 375, 377–8, 381, 387, 397 407, 414, 417–18, 439, 442, 476, 479–82, 489, 493, 506, 508, 510, 519, 521
stratêia, military service of the *stratiôtês,* 5, 8, 14
stratêlatês, 'general' originally the same as *stratêgos* and *magister militum,* but which may have disappeared in the ninth century only to reappear under Johannes I Tzimiskes as a title of senior army officer probably placed in charge of the *tagma* of *stratelatai,* x, 97, 109
stratiôtês (pl. *stratiôtai*), a soldier, specifically a soldier belonging to the *themata,* 4–5, 14, 18–20, 31, 87, 123, 130–1, 136, 142, 186–8, 232, 253, 353, 405, 408, 419, 425
stratiôtika ktêmata, military lands used to support the *stratiôtai* from the *themata,* 5, 14, 18, 130
stratopedarchês, a general/commander of a field army (usually eunuch), could also possess the powers of a *stratêgos autokratôr,* 292, 295, 314, 337, 502
stratôres (grooms, squires), four meanings: grooms of the *schola* under *komês tou stablou*; imperial *stratôres* serving under *prôtostratôr* in the unit of the *magklabitai*; grooms of the important officials in the provinces; grooms in general, 21, 25–7, 81, 83, 476
Subuktin, Sabuktakin, Sabuktin, chamberlain, Turkish ghilman commander, 240, 280
Surprise, night attack, 36, 42, 50, 55, 61, 63–5, 73, 90, 120, 142, 146, 164–5, 183, 198, 205, 223, 228, 232, 282, 381–2, 398, 400, 402, 404, 449, 456, 485–6, 493–4, 509
  see also Ambush, *drouggos,* Guerrilla, *Prokoursatôres,* Stratagem
Syria, Cilicia-Syria, Coelo-Syria, xii, xxiv, 9, 71–3, 79–80, 83, 88, 92–3, 116, 131–2, 139, 156, 163, 177, 186, 204–206, 210–12, 214, 260, 276, 282, 288, 290, 302, 304, 306, 332–3, 337, 350, 382, 406, 479, 481, 484, 492, 526
Syrianos Magistros, Syrianus Magister, *Peri strategikes, Peri strategias, Naumachica,*

Rhetorica militaris, 1, 40, 48, 80, 194, 282, 422, 476, 493, 514, 518–19

tagma (pl. *tagmata*)
  tagma 1: units of professional soldiers posted originally near Constantinople, but which later dispatched detachments to serve among the *themata*
  tagma 2: a unit of ca. 50 to 400 men, the equivalent of *allagion, arithmos, bandon*
  tagma 3: a generic division, *see* Appendix 1 xii, 4–7, 10–13, 15, 18–24, 27–33, 35, 47, 53, 70, 77, 79–82, 97, 100, 118–19, 147, 164, 197, 222, 228–9, 263, 278, 286, 295–6, 329, 350, 354–6, 358–60, 362–3, 365–9, 371, 373, 374–5, 377, 386–7, 405–406, 408, 410, 414, 423, 427, 429, 431–2, 471–2, 474–5, 479, 506, 508, 511, 522

Taron, Taronites, Taronitai, Tornikioi, Turniq, Tornik, Tornikios, Tornikês, 1, 86, 133, 214, 281, 308–309, 331–2, 483, 485, 491, 496–7, 501–502, 504, 519–20
  Ashot III, Prince of Taron (ca.940–966/7), 308–309, 483
  Bagrat (Pankratios) of Taron, 309
  Bagrat of Taron, cousin of Tornik, 483
  Gregorios of Taron, 309
  Tornik the son Apoganem, Prince of Taron, 483
  Tornikios, Taronites, Taronitai, Tornikioi, Turniq, Tornik, 86, 119, 232–3, 266, 309, 483, 495, 498, 502, 520
  Leôn Tornikios, 119, 266, 483, 498
  Michaêl Tornikios, Michaêl of Hanzit, Patrikios Turniq, 232–3
  Nikolaos Tornikios, 119, 266, 483, 498
  see also Armenia, Bagratuni, Manzikert

Tarsus, Tarsos, Tarsiotes, city of, emir and emirate of Tarsos, xi–xiv, xxviii, 72–3, 79, 87, 96–7, 107–108, 114, 116, 125–6, 132–4, 136–7, 139, 143–4, 149, 155–6, 158, 170, 174, 177, 181–4, 187–8, 192, 210–13, 233–4, 238–42, 245–7, 261, 271–3, 275–6, 281–2, 284–5, 287–90, 292–3, 300, 313, 336, 338–9, 382–4, 440, 478, 485–6, 489–91, 498–9

Tartus, Tortosa, Artharthons, Antardos, xii, xxxvi, 335

tasanarioi, see Hussar

Taurus Mountains, 19, 73, 89, 132, 333, 382, 400

taxiarchia and *taxiarchos* (pl. *taxiarchoi*) or *taxiarchês* (pl. *taxiarchai*), in the *Strategikon* the *moirarchês* of the *optimatoi*, but in the 10th century an infantry commander of 1,000 infantrymen unit *taxis* called *taxiarchia* who was also known as *chilirarchos/chiliarchês* (commander of 1,000). However, the size of the *taxiarchia* varied in practice according to the size of the army, 32, 46–7, 212, 345, 367, 371, 420, 422–3, 431–2, 436–7, 440, 443, 445, 476, 485, 488–9

chiliarchos, chiliarchia, 32, 367, 420, 445

teichistai, teichos (the Walls), an infantry *tagma*, 12, 20, 23–4, 29–30, 79, 432, 472, 475

themata (themes) *thema*, (a theme), a military district/province with soldiers (*stratiôtai*) settled on military lands (*stratiôtai ktêmata*) under a *stratêgos*, xii, 1, 3–12, 14–22, 24, 31, 33, 35, 53, 58, 73–4, 76, 78–84, 86–8, 90, 97–8, 100, 102, 107–10, 114, 120, 122, 125–7, 130–2, 136–7, 141–5, 147, 150, 155–7, 164, 177, 182–4, 186–9, 192, 197, 214, 216–17, 227, 229–30, 233, 235, 238, 241, 248, 250, 263, 265, 271, 276–8, 285, 288–9, 293, 295–7, 309, 311, 313, 321, 326, 329–30, 340, 347, 350, 353, 358, 363, 365, 379–82, 386–8, 391, 395, 400, 405–406, 408, 414, 423, 427, 430–1, 435, 470–4, 480–1, 484–5, 487–8, 494–7, 507–508, 515, 521–2

Armenian *themata*, Armenian themes 1) (small border infantry themes usually categorized as *kleisourai* or as 'minor themes'), 73–4, 83, 382

Armenian *themata* 2 = Armeniakon, Chaldia, Kôloneia, Charsianon 'minor themes' centred on some individual city e.g. Tarsus, Edessa, Melitene, Mopsuestia, Romanoupolis, Adata, etc., which were subjected to serve under some larger regular *thema* (this biography does not attempt to list all of these)

Adata (minor theme created in 957), 189, 400

Aêgaios Pelagos, Aigaion Pelagos (Aegean Sea, naval), 4, 6–7, 10–11, 16–18, 25, 100, 141, 473–4

Anatolikon, xii, 6–7, 9–10, 79, 86, 88, 98, 100, 102, 107–108, 114, 122, 125–7, 130–3, 137, 147, 161, 187, 205, 212–14, 216, 227, 233–4, 237, 265, 277, 298, 313, 349, 379, 382, 391, 400, 471, 495, 500

Anazarbos in 964(?), 284

Apulia, *see* Loggobardia
Armeniakon, 6–7, 10, 78–9, 98, 107, 130, 145, 147, 150, 265, 271, 485
Arsamosata (created in 935–6 or after 970), 84
Boukellarion, Bucellarii, 6–7, 10, 24, 107, 197
Calabria, Kalabria, 58, 97
Chaldia, 6–7, 10, 79, 86, 182, 485
Charsianon, Kharsianon, theme and city of, xii, xxii, 6–7, 10, 33, 79, 97, 114, 132, 144–5, 147, 149–50, 156, 160, 182–4, 233, 248, 313, 470, 487
Crete (created in 961), 230, 473–4
Cyclades, Kykladôn nêsôn, 474
Cyprus (created in 965), 289, 473
Dalmatia, 6–7, 16, 62, 141
Danoutha (listed as a theme in DV), 400
Dyrrachion, 6–7, 11, 16, 141
Germanikeia (created in 962), 248, 304, 400
Hanzit (created in 935), 6–7, 84, 98, 127, 183, 202, 214, 232–3, 250, 490
see also Harput
Hellas, 4, 6–7, 11, 16–17
Kaisun (listed as a theme in DV), 400
Kaloudia (created in 935), 6–7, 400
Kappadokia, Cappadocia, xii, xxii, 6–7, 9–10, 79, 88, 97–8, 100–102, 107–108, 114, 122, 127, 132, 136, 143–5, 147, 187, 233, 238, 264, 379, 400
see also Cappadocia
Karabisian theme (abolished by Leôn III), 24
Kephallênia, Kefalônias, Kefhallênias, Kephalonia, Cephalonia, 4, 6–7, 11, 16–17, 473–4
Kharsianon, *see* Charsianon
Kherson, Cherson (Klimata, Climata), 6–7, 11, 25, 66, 105, 117, 311
Kibyrraiôtai Kibyraiôtai (Kibyrrhaiotai) (naval), xii, xxvi, 4, 6–7, 11, 16–18, 73, 141, 156, 182–4, 192, 213, 398, 473
Koloneia, 6–7, 78–9, 87, 332, 485
Laggobardia, Loggobardia, Langobardia (theme of 'Apulia'), 6–7, 58, 97, 340
Lukania, Lucania (it may have been created at the same time as the katepanate of Italy in 969, but this is uncertain), 58, 97, 340
Lykandos, xii, xxii, 6–7, 120, 127, 132, 134, 143–4, 147, 159, 174, 313, 380, 400, 484, 507
Macedonia, Makedonia, 6–7, 10, 182, 193, 195–6, 213, 216, 227, 238, 470–2

Melitene (minor theme created in 935), 6–7, 84, 400, 490
emir of Melitene in Roman service, 159, 239
see also Melitene
Mesopotamia, 6–7, 98, 132, 214, 485
see also Duchy
Mopsuestia (a katepanate/minor theme created in 965), 288, 313
Nikopolis, xii, xxviii, 4, 6–7, 16–17, 473
Opsikion, 6–7, 10, 24, 101, 130, 197, 216, 522
Optimaton, optimatoi (problematically simultaneously a *thema* and *tagma* under a *domestikos*, because its members served as baggage handlers for the *tagmata* while being stationed on land that was called a *thema*), 6–7, 10, 12, 20, 24, 29, 79–80, 472
Paphlagonia, 6–7, 9–10, 79, 107
Peloponnêsos, Peloponnesus, 4, 6–7, 11, 16–18, 473
Samos (naval), 4, 6–7, 16–18, 141, 156, 473–4
Sebasteia, 6–7, 79, 132, 145, 147, 271, 313, 485
Seleukeia, Seleucia, xii, xxvi, xxviii, 6–7, 10, 79, 98, 114, 127, 132, 156, 235, 400, 470, 495
Sikelia (Sicily/Calabria until 902), 11
Strymôn, 6–7
Taron (and Keltzene) (minor theme created in 967), 309
Tarsus (minor theme created in 965), 288, 313
Thessalonikê, Thessaloniki, 6–7, 11
Thrakê, Thrace, 6–7, 10
Thrakêsion, 6–7, 10, 33
see also Appendices 1–4, which describe warfare waged by thematic forces
see also kleisourai, stratêgos, stratiôtai
Theodoros:
Theodôros Zoulfinezer, 100
Theodoros the Bishop of Kyzikos, 206
Theodôros Dafnopatês, 209
Theodôros Dekapolitês, 130
Theodôros, 'nephew of emperor', 258–9
Theodôros the One-Eyed, 174, 189
Theodôros Parsakoutênos, *see* Parsakoutênoi
Theodôros Spoggarios, the *Stratêgos/ Stratêlatês*, 109, 111–12
Theodôros the Tutor, 99–101
Theodosios, head groom, 129

Theofanês, *prôtobestiarios*, admiral, *parakoimômenos*, 106, 109–10, 112, 116, 122
Theofanô:
    Theofanô, Anastasia/Anastasô, empress, wife of Rômanos II and second wife of Nikêforos II Fôkas, 188, 207, 209, 240–1, 261–4, 269–70, 276, 291, 294, 297–8, 343–4, 347–8, 430, 498, 505–506
    Theofanô, the future wife of Otto II, daughter of Kônstantinos Sklêros (brother of Bardas Sklêros) and Sofia Fôkaina (daughter of Leôn Fôkas the Younger), 342
Theofilos:
    Theofilos Kourkouas, see Kourkouai
    Theofilos, emperor, 78
    Theofilos Erotikos, 484
    Theofilos, the quaestor, 130
Theofylaktos, Patriarch, 115, 122–3, 128
Third line (*tritos*), could mean the rear guards or the *saka*, 13, 37, 40, 77–8, 82, 168–9, 203–4, 360, 362, 365, 387, 405, 410–11, 414–17, 424–5, 479–80, 489, 506, 508, 510
    see also saka
Thomas the *primikêrios*, 122
Thomas the Slav, rebel, 471
toparchês, toparchai, a lord of an independent territory which was still a client state or allied state, 228, 346
topotêrêtês (vice, substitute), second-in-command of the *scholai*. *Exkoubitoi, bigla, ikanatoi*, 392, 405, 410, 472
Tornikioi, Tornikios, Tornikês, see Taron
tourma, tourmai, turma (also known as *meros*), a military division consisting of 2,000–3,000 to 9,000 men, 13, 32, 35–7, 42, 76–7, 81–2, 356, 388, 423
    parataxis, parataxeis (division, subdivision, subunit), 22, 183, 212, 366–7, 371, 387–8, 402, 410, 428, 432–3, 438–41, 443, 445–6, 508, 510–11
tourmarchês (pl. *tourmarchoi/tourmarchai*), a commander of a *tourma* (formerly known as *merarchês*). The term could mean the *tourmarchoi* of the *themata*, or the divisional commanders of an army (i.e. the *stratêgoi* of the *themata* could be called *tourmarchoi* when they acted as commanders of divisions in a large army; in such cases the senior *tourmarchês* were called *upostratêgos*) when the overall commander was called with the generic term *stratêgos* (he could be e.g. *domestikos tôn scholôn* by office), 11, 13, 17–18, 20, 31–2, 46, 77, 97, 101, 142, 385–8, 392, 472–3

touldos, touldon, baggage train of the army under a separate commander. The *touldos* included the servants and other supporting personnel, pack-animals, spare horses, equipment, provisions and their guards. The *optimatoi* served as a special transport unit for the cavalry *tagmata*, 38–9, 43, 81, 355, 361–2, 364, 368–9, 372, 374–6, 412
    baggage train, 40, 42, 61, 63, 70, 80, 83, 90, 145, 149, 153, 155, 161, 200, 253, 354, 362–3, 386, 389–91, 406, 410–11, 416, 423, 427, 432, 438, 442–3, 445, 458, 462, 489, 508
o epi tês trapezês, domestikos tês basilikês trapezes (Master of the Table, a person in charge of the table), 28, 313, 502
trapezites, see Hussars
Tripoli, city and emirate of, xii, xxxv, 131, 212–13, 333, 335
Tripoli in Libya, 93
trireme, *trieres*, 18, 51, 53, 94, 99, 106, 110, 216, 218, 230, 266, 278
    see also Crete, *drômon, drômonion*, flame-thrower, fleet
Tur Abdin, 302, 332
Turks, Turkish, as words, xi, 23, 61–4, 66–7, 80, 89, 92, 116, 124–5, 163, 170, 182, 189–90, 193, 196, 198, 200, 203, 231, 280, 349, 362, 410, 460, 479, 482–3, 495, 505
    see also ghilman, Hungarians, Khazars
Tyre, city, 72
Tzimiskês, Iôannês, Iôannês o Tzimiskês, emperor (969–75), x, xiv, 8–9, 20, 46–7, 98, 123, 126–7, 133, 160, 177–8, 180–4, 188–9, 198–200, 202–207, 210–12, 214, 233, 236, 248, 252–4, 256–7, 262, 265, 269, 271–6, 279, 282, 285, 287, 290–2, 296–7, 301, 313, 317, 333, 335, 342–7, 349–52, 377, 379–80, 415, 429–30, 483–5, 490, 492, 498, 500, 503, 505–507

Umayyads, al-Andalus, Spain, 16, 71–2, 91, 103–104, 113, 139–41, 175–6, 183, 185, 188, 191–2, 195, 200, 214, 225, 473, 486, 517

Valleys, 226, 234, 511
    Adata Lake and Pass, 153, 155, 175
    Barada River, 153
    Bekaa, 333
    Demon, in Sicily, 114

Lykos, xiii, 145–8, 150, 487
Orontes, 131
Pyramos, 163–5
Sumnin, 180
see also Pass
Vegetius, 74, 476
Venice, Venetian, 58, 60, 320, 327, 329, 341, 506

wedge (*embolon, embolos*), *triangle* (*trigônos taxis*), *trapezium*, 34–5, 37, 40, 70, 75, 85, 90, 136, 157, 168, 171, 174, 204, 219, 221, 227, 257, 285, 287, 294, 342, 349, 354–5, 359, 362–3, 365, 373, 375, 378, 389, 405–406, 408–11, 413–17, 426, 442, 456–7, 460–1, 464, 478, 489–90, 499, 506, 512
see also *katafraktoi*

yperkerastai (*hyperkerastai*), outflankers, usually posted on the right flank of the first cavalry line, 13, 36–7, 40, 70, 76–7, 82, 171, 285, 360, 363, 365, 377, 387, 397, 405, 410, 414–15, 424–6, 438, 461, 508

ypostratêgos (pl. *ypostratêgoI*), lieutenant general/second-in-command. When the emperor was called *stratêgos* all other generals were called *ypostratêgoi*, but in a field army the *ypostratêgos* meant the second-in-command (the senior commander of the divisional commanders), 77, 160, 202, 238, 248, 511

zeugarion (pl. *zeugaria*), a plot of land that a team of oxen could plough in a season, 8

Dear Reader,

We hope you have enjoyed this book, but why not share your views on social media? You can also follow our pages to see more about our other products: facebook.com/penandswordbooks or follow us on X @penswordbooks

You can also view our products at www.pen-and-sword.co.uk (UK and ROW) or www.penandswordbooks.com (North America).

To keep up to date with our latest releases and online catalogues, please sign up to our newsletter at: www.pen-and-sword.co.uk/newsletter

If you would like a printed catalogue with our latest books, then please email: enquiries@pen-and-sword.co.uk or telephone: 01226 734555 (UK and ROW) or email: uspen-and-sword@casematepublishers.com or telephone: (610) 853-9131 (North America).

We respect your privacy and we will only use personal information to send you information about our products.

Thank you!